AIRLIFE'S WORLD AIRCRAFT

AIRLIFE'S WORLD AIRCRAFT

The Complete Reference to Civil, Military and Light Aircraft

Rod Simpson

First published in the UK in 2001
by Airlife Publishing Ltd

British Library Cataloguing-in-Publication Data
A catalogue record for this book
is available from the British Library

ISBN 1 84037 115 3

Typeset by Gray Publishing, Russell House, Grove Hill Road,
Tunbridge Wells, Kent TN1 1RZ, UK
Colour repro by Livesey Ltd, Shrewsbury
Printed in Italy

Airlife Publishing Ltd

101 Longden Road, Shrewsbury, SY3 9EB, England
E-mail: airlife@airlifebooks.com
Website: www.airlifebooks.com

CONTENTS

237
EXPERIMENTAL
N8284M
Beech MkII
Beechcraft

INTRODUCTION

The purpose of *Airlife's World Aircraft* is to fill an important aviation reference gap by providing a quick source of information on the majority of aircraft currently flying with military and civil users around the globe. There are, of course, several well-respected sources of information on aircraft in current production – and there are excellent books on military aircraft currently in service. However, there is no single publication which gathers together the historical background and specification data for all the aircraft which may be found currently in service whether they be new or old, military or civil.

It is only when one tries to create a list of the aircraft which need to be included that the range and variety of the world aviation scene comes into focus. Indeed, during the compilation of *Airlife's World Aircraft* we were continually adding new types which had been omitted from the original list. It is, perhaps, inevitable that some aircraft have been left out – and we apologise if any important types have been inadvertently overlooked. We have concentrated on powered aircraft, so *Airlife's World Aircraft* includes rotary wing types – but excludes balloons, hang gliders, gliders and sailplanes. The main qualification for the inclusion of a commercially produced aircraft type is that we have good reason to believe that at least one example remains currently active or is being restored to airworthiness. In the case of amateur-built aircraft, we have had to be selective and only include those types which have been offered in the form of plans or kits and built in appreciable quantities or are clearly significant and likely to be built in volume. For Ultralights (Microlights), the emergence of new regulations setting an upper weight limit of 450 kg has resulted in a huge growth in this category and we have included as many of these aircraft as possible, concentrating on those types which have been built in the greatest numbers and are in the higher weight classification.

One of the most obscure areas is the field of warbirds and antiques. Enthusiasm for restoration of military aircraft has grown rapidly over the past few years and many rare and unique aircraft have been brought back from extinction by the amazing efforts of restorers. We have included many warbird types, although some may have been omitted where their status is uncertain or where they fly only on rare occasions. In the case of antiques, the pages of *Airlife's World Aircraft* include the most important restored aircraft which are currently flying and which have made an appearance at recent air shows and meetings around the world.

It was decided at an early stage that *Airlife's World Aircraft* would be arranged in alphabetical order by manufacturer. This has its pitfalls – not least because of numerous changes of ownership of aircraft designs and alterations in the names of many aircraft manufacturers over the years. As an example, the Erco Ercoupe has been built, at various times, by Erco, Air Products, Forney, Alon and Mooney. For the purposes of this book we have used the original manufacturer's (or designer's) name where the aircraft type is no longer in production and the current manufacturer's name where aircraft are still being produced. Thus, the Ercoupe appears under Erco Ercoupe – but the F-16, formerly produced by General Dynamics, is shown under Lockheed Martin (its latest 'owner'). In some cases, we have taken the decision to list an aircraft under its best-known manufacturer name. For instance, the Ag-Cat is shown under Grumman (its designer) rather than Schweizer which was the principal manufacturer. Hopefully, any confusion will be resolved through the Index which aims to provide a detailed cross reference. In the case of engine manufacturers, we have generally used their current names (e.g. Teledyne Continental, Textron Lycoming) unless this creates a clear historical inconsistency.

For reasons of space, the Aircraft Specification tables are limited to the main dimensions, performance and weights. For some categories of aircraft the standard table of specifications is not suitable and has been modified. For instance, it is normal to quote take-off distance rather than rate of climb for air carrier aircraft and cruising speed is largely irrelevant in the case of high performance jet fighters. In any reference book, specifications are a headache for the compiler and a potential source of confusion. Therefore, so far as possible the information has been derived from original manufacturers' data or certification records on a consistent basis. Even this approach has its pitfalls when performance data is selected by manufacturers to show the best characteristics of a particular aircraft on the most favourable basis for each parameter. Nevertheless, every attempt has been made to ensure that a balanced and consistent presentation of information has been provided. For the guidance of readers, a Glossary of Terms and Abbreviations has been included and this gives a brief definition of the headings used in the Specification tables.

Unearthing photos of all these types has also been a considerable challenge. The majority have come from my own collection – gleaned from visits to innumerable air shows and airfields over the years. However, I am most grateful to many aircraft manufacturers and to Phil Dunnington, Mike Hooks, the late Peter Keating, John Mounce, M. Newall, Gordon Reid, Charles Trask and Dave Welch who have trawled their archives for illustrations of the more obscure types. Some photographs have been obtained without information on the original photographer and I apologise if we have been unable to give credit for these. And, once again, I am more than appreciative of the tolerance of my wife, Valerie, and my family during long sessions locked away with the word processor.

Rod Simpson
April, 2001

BY UNITED

AAI AA-2 Mamba — Australia

The high-wing Mamba light aircraft was originally designed by Aircraft Industries of Australia (AIA) and was later taken over by Australian Aircraft Industries Pty. Ltd. Although a civil model, the AA-2C, with a 116 h.p. Textron Lycoming O-235 engine, was to be available, the main role for the Mamba was military artillery spotting and Forward Air Control. The Mamba prototype first flew on 25th January 1989 and was later fitted with a 160 h.p. O-320-D1A. It was followed by the production standard version the following December. The Mamba is a braced high-wing tandem two-seater with a fixed tricycle undercarriage and a large cockpit with extensive transparencies giving excellent all-round vision. It is of steel tube construction with light alloy skinning. The proposed military AA-2M would have a 200 h.p. Textron Lycoming IO-360-A1B6 engine, but no orders have yet been obtained.

AA-2S Mamba, VH-FCX

Specification	AAI AA-2A Mamba	
Powerplant	One 160 h.p. (119 kW) Textron Lycoming O-320-D1A piston engine	
Dimensions		
Span	8.4 m	(27 ft 5 in)
Length	7.5 m	(24 ft 6 in)
Height	2.7 m	(9 ft 0 in)
Performance		
Max speed	230 km/h	(125 kt, 144 mph)
Cruising speed	212 km/h	(115 kt, 132 mph)
Initial climb	335 m/min	(1,100 fpm)
Range	1,259 km	(684 nm, 787 miles)
Weights		
Max takeoff	909 kg	(2,000 lbs)
Useful load	274 kg	(600 lbs)

AASI Jet Cruzer — USA

Design of the Jet Cruzer was initiated in 1983 by Advanced Aerodynamics and Structures Inc. (AASI) of Long Beach, California as a new technology business-aircraft. The Jet Cruzer 500 has a canard layout and is of mixed construction with a graphite carbon composite fuselage and aluminium flying surfaces. Power is provided by a Pratt & Whitney PT6A turboprop in a pusher installation driving a five-blade propeller and the cabin can accommodate six including crew. The Jet Cruzer is also expected to fulfil other roles including cargo carriage, military surveillance and medical evacuation. The proof of concept prototype Jet Cruzer 450 first flew on 11th January 1989 followed by the production prototype Model 500 in April 1991. A later derivative, the Stratocruzer 1250, will be a stretched 11-seat version with two rear fuselage-mounted Williams-Rolls FJ44-2 turbofans. 188 Jet Cruzers had been ordered by October 2000.

AASI Jet Cruzer 500, N200JC

Specification	AASI Jet Cruzer JC-500	
Powerplant	One 1,572 s.h.p. (1,172 kW) Pratt & Whitney PT6A-66A turboprop	
Dimensions		
Span	12.9 m	(42 ft 2 in)
Length	9.2 m	(30 ft 2 in)
Height	1.3 m	(4 ft 3 in)
Performance		
Max speed	589 km/h	(320 kt, 368 mph)
Cruising speed	515 km/h	(280 kt, 322 mph)
Initial climb	1,067 m/min	(3,500 fpm)
Range	2,995 km	(1,627 nm, 1,871 miles)
Weights		
Max takeoff	2,500 kg	(5,500 lbs)
Useful load	1,100 kg	(2,420 lbs)

Acro Sport Inc. Acro Sport — USA

The concept of the Acro Sport amateur-built biplane originated in the EAA Biplane, designed as an easily constructed sport aircraft under the auspices of the Experimental Aircraft Association and its founder, Paul Poberezny. The single-seat EAA Biplane first flew on 10th June 1960 and was of classic tube, wood and fabric construction with a fixed tailwheel undercarriage and an 85 h.p. Continental C85 engine. Over 7,000 sets of plans were sold and many examples are flying. While externally similar, the EAA Acro Sport I was virtually a new design with a substantially stronger airframe giving full aerobatic capability and a 180 h.p. Lycoming IO-360 engine providing much improved overall performance. The first Acro Sport flew on 11th January 1972 and was followed by the Super Acro Sport which flew on 28th March 1973 and was stressed for unlimited class aerobatics and fitted with a higher-powered 200 h.p. Lycoming IO-360-A2A engine. The Acro Sport I was further developed with a longer-span wing and a stretched fuselage accommodating two tandem open cockpits. This Acro Sport II first flew on 9th July 1978. These designs are marketed in kit form by Acro Sport Inc. and many hundreds are flying worldwide.

Acro Sport I, G-BTWI

Specification	Acro Sport Inc. Acro Sport I	
Powerplant	One 180 h.p. (135 kW) Textron Lycoming IO-360-A4B piston engine	
Dimensions		
Span	6.6 m	(21 ft 8 in)
Length	5.7 m	(18 ft 10 in)
Height	1.8 m	(6 ft 0 in)
Performance		
Max speed	228 km/h	(124 kt, 142 mph)
Cruising speed	197 km/h	(107 kt, 123 mph)
Initial climb	457 m/min	(1,500 fpm)
Range	481 km	(260 nm, 299 miles)
Weights		
Max takeoff	690 kg	(1,520 lbs)
Useful load	293 kg	(645 lbs))

Acro Sport Inc. Pober Pixie — USA

Paul Poberezny of the EAA designed the Pober Pixie in 1974, flying the prototype in July of that year. It was conceived as a simple and easy-to-build single-seater which would benefit from the economy of a 60 h.p. Limbach-converted Volkswagen engine. The Pixie is a parasol-wing monoplane with a fixed tailwheel undercarriage and an open cockpit. The fuselage is of welded steel tube construction, the wings are wooden and the whole structure is fabric-covered. The Pixie is marketed by Acro Sport Inc. and both plans and parts kits are available with many examples now flying in the USA and Europe.

Pober Pixie, N81JL

Specification	Acro Sport Inc. Pober Pixie	
Powerplant	One 60 h.p. (45 kW) Limbach SL.1700 piston engine	
Dimensions		
Span	9.1 m	(29 ft 10 in)
Length	5.3 m	(17 ft 3 in)
Height	1.88 m	(6 ft 2 in)
Performance		
Max speed	165 km/h	(90 kt, 104 mph)
Cruising speed	132 km/h	(72 kt, 83 mph)
Initial climb	152 m/min	(500 fpm)
Range	462 km	(250 nm, 289 miles)
Weights		
Max takeoff	409 kg	(900 lbs)
Useful load	161 kg	(355 lbs)

Adam M-309 — USA

The M-309 has been designed by Burt Rutan (Scaled Aircraft Composites) as a high performance business and personal aircraft. Constructed of carbon-composite materials it is a pressurised six-seater with a low wing, twin booms with a bridge tailplane and a retractable tricycle undercarriage. The two turbocharged Continental TSIO-550 engines, which are mounted in the nose and rear of the fuselage, counter rotate to neutralise propeller torque. They are fitted with FADEC control and the M-309 incorporates the latest developments in glass cockpit technology. The M-309 prototype made its first flight in March 2000 and the aircraft is expected to enter production in 2003.

Adam M-309

Specification	Adam M-309	
Powerplant	Two 350 h.p. (261 kW) Teledyne Continental TSIO-550 piston engines	
Dimensions		
Span	12.8 m	(42 ft 0 in)
Length	10.52 m	(34 ft 6 in)
Height	2.9 m	(9 ft 6 in)
Performance		
Max speed	463 km/h	(250 kt, 288 mph)
Cruising speed	408 km/h	(220 kt, 253 mph)
Initial climb	518 m/min	(1,700 fpm)
Range	2,760 km	(1,500 nm, 1,725 miles)
Weights		
Max takeoff (est.)	2,721 kg	(6,000 lbs)
Useful load	1,043 kg	(2,300 lbs)

Adam RA-14 Loisirs and RA-15 Major — France

The Adam RA-14 Loisirs ('Leisure') was designed by Ets. Roger Adam in 1945 as a tube, wood and fabric two-seater suitable for amateur construction. The company sold plans and manufactured parts and the aircraft could be fitted with a range of engines including the 65 h.p., 75 h.p., 80 h.p. Continental and several other indigenous engines such as the Regnier 4D. Approximately 40 examples were built and five are currently active in France. Adam also designed a higher-powered version, the RA-15 Major with plywood covering and an enlarged rudder. Rights to the Loisirs were sold to the Canadian Maranda Aircraft Company who sold plans for amateur construction of the Loisirs RA14BM1 and the later Maranda Super Loisirs with an enlarged wing and 90 h.p. Continental C90 engine.

Adam RA-14 Loisirs, F-PYVS

Specification	Adam RA-14 Loisirs	
Powerplant	One 65 h.p. (49 kW) Continental A65-8 piston engine	
Dimensions		
Span	10.9 m	(35 ft 9 in)
Length	7 m	(22 ft 11 in)
Height	2.2 m	(7 ft 3 in)
Performance		
Max speed	139 km/h	(76 kt, 87 mph)
Cruising speed	120 km/h	(65 kt, 75 mph)
Initial climb	122 m/min	(400 fpm)
Range	448 km	(243 nm, 280 miles)
Weights		
Max takeoff	480 kg	(1,056 lbs)
Useful load	200 kg	(440 lbs)

Adventure Air Adventurer — USA

The Adventurer was designed by Happy Miles of Berryville, Arkansas with assistance from Molt Taylor (designer of the Coot, Aerocar and other well-known amateur designs). The Adventurer, which originated in the Miles Happy Adventure homebuilt, is a kit-built amphibian with a retractable tricycle or tailwheel undercarriage and a high wing. It is a two-seater in standard form but can be fitted with a rear bench seat if the fuel capacity is reduced. The prototype had a pusher 150 h.p. Lycoming engine mounted on pylon struts above the wing centre section but most aircraft will have a 200 h.p. Lycoming and the Adventurer 333 has a converted Chevrolet car engine. The fuselage is made up of two fibreglass shells with internal tubular-steel structure and the wings and other control surfaces are of fibreglass-covered foam construction. The wings are strut-braced but are easily detachable for storage. The first aircraft flew in 1994 and over 120 kits have been sold, with approximately ten aircraft completed.

Adventurer 333, N58CM

Specification	Adventure Air Adventurer 333	
Powerplant	One 333 h.p. (248 kW) Chevrolet 350CI piston engine	
Dimensions		
Span	10.9 m	(35 ft 9 in)
Length	7.5 m	(24 ft 6 in)
Height	2.6 m	(8 ft 6 in)
Performance		
Max speed	253 km/h	(137 kt, 158 mph)
Cruising speed	224 km/h	(122 kt, 140 mph)
Initial climb	366 m/min	(1,200 fpm)
Range	960 km	(522 nm, 600 miles)
Weights		
Max takeoff	1,500 kg	(3,308 lbs)
Useful load	591 kg	(1,300 lbs)

Aeritalia-Alenia G.222 — Italy

Originally intended as a standard tactical transport for NATO forces, the G.222 was designed by Fiat in 1962 and became primarily an Italian Air Force project, being first flown at Turin on 18th July 1970. By this time Fiat was part of Aeritalia which then became part of Alenia. The G.222 was extensively redesigned, having been planned, initially, with lift jets in the lower engine nacelles and wingtips. The production aircraft was a conventional twin turboprop with 62-troop capacity and a rear loading ramp, and the first of 44 aircraft for the AMI was delivered in 1976. G.222s of the AMI have also been used for airways checking and for ECM work. Further sales were made to the air forces of Dubai, Argentina, Libya, Nigeria, Thailand, Venezuela and Somalia. Over 100 G.222s had been delivered when production closed in 1989. The C-27A Spartan was a special missions version, ten of which were ordered for the USAF in 1997 from a reopened production line, and the C-27J Spartan, which first flew on 25th September 1999, is a new Lockheed Martin–Alenia joint venture aircraft fitted with Rolls Royce AE2100 engines and upgraded avionics.

Aeritalia G.222, MM62130

Specification	Aeritalia-Alenia G.222	
Powerplant	Two 3,400 s.h.p. (2,535 kW) Fiat-General Electric T64-GE-P4D turboprops	
Dimensions		
Span	28.7 m	(94 ft 2 in)
Length	22.7 m	(74 ft 5.5 in)
Height	9.8 m	(32 ft 2 in)
Performance		
Max speed	540 km/h	(292 kt, 335 mph)
Cruising speed	440 km/h	(235 kt, 275 mph)
Initial climb	520 m/min	(1,700 fpm)
Range	2,500 km	(1,359 nm, 1,563 miles)
Weights		
Max takeoff	28,000 kg	(61,740 lbs)
Useful load	12,620 kg	(27,827 lbs)

Aermacchi MB.326 — Italy

The prototype MB.326, which flew on 10th December 1957, had been designed to provide the Italian Air Force (AMI) with a new jet basic trainer. With a low wing and tandem seating it was powered by a Rolls Royce Viper 11 turbojet with small air intakes in the wing roots and over 800 MB.326s were completed. The first of 135 AMI aircraft was delivered in early 1962 and further examples were sold to Alitalia, Tunisia and Ghana (as the armed MB.326F), Togo, Dubai, Paraguay, Zambia and Zaire. In Australia, the RAAF and RAN ordered 97 which were built under licence by CAC as the CA-30. For South Africa, Atlas

Aircraft Corp. of Johannesburg set up a production line, building 151 examples of the Atlas Impala Mk.1, initially from Aermacchi-supplied kits. The MB.326G was an upgraded version with a Viper 20 engine and additional wing hardpoints which was sold to Argentina and was adopted by the Brazilian Air Force as the T-26 Xavante. Some 182 examples were built by Embraer with ground attack capability for the FAB and the Xavante remains in service in Paraguay. Substantial numbers of MB.326s remain in service although the production line is now closed.

CAC-Aermacchi MB.326H, A7-023

Specification	Aermacchi MB.326G	
Powerplant	One 3,410 lb.s.t. (15.2 kN) Rolls Royce Viper 20 Mk.540 turbojet	
Dimensions		
Span	10.85 m	(35 ft 7 in)
Length	10.7 m	(36 ft 0 in)
Height	3.7 m	(12 ft 2 in)
Performance		
Max speed	866 km/h	(470 kt, 540 mph)
Cruising speed	798 km/h	(430 kt, 495 mph)
Initial climb	1,845 m/min	(6,050 fpm)
Range	1,850 km	(1,005 nm, 1,156 miles)
Weights		
Max takeoff	4,575 kg	(10,090 lbs)
Useful load	1,732 kg	(3,819 lbs)

Aermacchi/Atlas MB.326K — Italy

The two-seat MB.326 proved to be an excellent trainer and several versions were fitted with underwing weapons hardpoints to allow the aircraft to be used in a dual role as a ground attack aircraft. This led Aermacchi to develop the dedicated single-seat MB.326K Veltro tactical air support variant. The rear cockpit was eliminated and the MB.326K fitted with twin 30 mm nose-mounted cannon, additional fuel capacity and ammunition storage in the centre fuselage. Three underwing hardpoints were provided under each wing allowing carriage of miniguns, bombs, rockets and air-to-air missiles. The Italian Air Force did not order the MB.326K but 26 were sold to Ghana, Zaire, Dubai and Tunisia. Atlas Aircraft again produced this variant as the Impala Mk.2 for the South African Air Force and more than 90 were delivered between 1974 and 1980.

Aermacchi MB.326KD, 202 (Dubai AF)

Specification	Aermacchi MB.326K	
Powerplant	One 4,000 lb.s.t. (17.8 kN) Rolls Royce Viper 20 Mk.540 turbojet	
Dimensions		
Span	10.85 m	(35 ft 7 in)
Length	10.7 m	(36 ft 0 in)
Height	3.7 m	(12 ft 2 in)
Performance		
Max speed	890 km/h	(480 kt, 552 mph)
Cruising speed	798 km/h	(430 kt, 495 mph)
Initial climb	1,980 m/min	(6,500 fpm)
Range	1,035 km	(560 nm, 645 miles)
Weights		
Max takeoff	5,444 kg	(12,000 lbs)
Useful load	2,500 kg	(5,500 lbs)

Aermacchi MB.339 — Italy

The success of the MB.326 led Aermacchi to design the MB.339, with a pressurised cockpit, improved canopy, new ejection seats and modified systems. It was powered by an upgraded Piaggio-Rolls Royce Viper Mk.632-43 and the prototype flew on 12th August 1976. The Italian Air Force (AMI) ordered a batch of 101 MB.339As to replace MB.326s, first deliveries taking place in 1980, and further orders were received from Argentina, Ghana, Malaysia, UAE, Peru and Nigeria. The MB.339 was unsuccessfully entered in the American JPATS competition. The single-seat ground attack MB.339K, which has only flown as a development aircraft, has six underwing hardpoints and twin 30 mm DEFA 553 guns in the forward fuselage. The MB.339C is an improved version with a 520 lbs gross weight increase, larger Viper 680-3 engine, the MB.339K wing and a HOTAS cockpit management system, 18 of which have been sold to New Zealand. The MB.339CD has a full digital cockpit and the MB.339FD is a similar lead-in fighter trainer and light ground attack version with increased power.

Aermacchi MB.339 (Cont.)

Aermacchi MB.339CD, MM55063

Specification	Aermacchi MB.339FD	
Powerplant	One 4,340 lb.s.t. (19.3 kN) Rolls Royce-Piaggio Viper Mk.680-43 turbojet	
Dimensions		
Span	11.2 m	(36 ft 9 in)
Length	11.24 m	(36 ft 10 in)
Height	3.94 m	(12 ft 11 in)
Performance		
Max speed	902 km/h	(490 kt, 563 mph)
Cruising speed	818 km/h	(440 kt, 505 mph)
Initial climb	2,012 m/min	(6,600 fpm)
Range	1,932 km	(1,050 nm, 1,207 miles)
Weights		
Max takeoff	6,350 kg	(14,000 lbs)
Useful load	3,016 kg	(6,650 lbs)

Aermacchi/Lockheed LASA-60 — Italy/USA

The Lockheed Georgia Company designed the strut-braced high-wing LASA-60 single-engined utility aircraft, flying the prototype on 15th September 1959. They subsequently constructed 44 examples at their Lockheed-Azcarate factory in Mexico. The all-metal LASA-60 had a boxy fuselage with double rear port-side cargo doors and a fixed tricycle undercarriage. In 1959 the Italian company Aermacchi commenced building 101 examples under licence as the AL-60 Santa Maria, the majority with a Continental TSIO-470-B turbocharged engine. Their production included the strengthened AL-60-C5 Conestoga with a 400 h.p. Lycoming IO-720-A1A and tailwheel undercarriage. The AL-60 was widely exported to South Africa, Yugoslavia, France, Germany, the United Kingdom and Switzerland. Batches were also delivered to the Rhodesian Air Force (as the Trojan) and the Air Force of the Central African Republic, and the Conestoga formed the design basis for the Atlas Kudu military liaison aircraft. Approximately 40 of the LASA-60 series are still active.

Aermacchi AL-60B2, F-BRIE

Specification	Aermacchi AL-60B2 Santa Maria	
Powerplant	One 260 h.p. (194 kW) Teledyne Continental TSIO-470-B piston engine	
Dimensions		
Span	12.01 m	(39 ft 4 in)
Length	8.6 m	(28 ft 1 in)
Height	3.3 m	(10 ft 8 in)
Performance		
Max speed	245 km/h	(133 kt, 153 mph)
Cruising speed	189 km/h	(103 kt, 118 mph)
Initial climb	256 m/min	(840 fpm)
Range	880 km	(478 nm, 550 miles)
Weights		
Max takeoff	1,730 kg	(3,815 lbs)
Useful load	603 kg	(1,328 lbs)

Aermacchi AM-3C — Italy

The AM-3C was derived from the Aermacchi AL-60 Santa Maria and jointly designed by Aerfer and Aermacchi to meet an Italian Air Force (AMI) specification for an army liaison and forward air control aircraft. It used the AL-60 wing, strengthened to incorporate two hardpoints, combined with a new tail and a fuselage incorporating a 360-degree vision cockpit with a single pilot seat and two rear seats. The first of three prototypes flew on 12th May 1967 but, following evaluation, the SIAI SM.1019 was ordered in 1972 by the AMI in preference to the AM-3C. Aermacchi sold three AM-3Cs to Rwanda and 40 to the South African Air Force where they operated as light ground attack aircraft and for casualty evacuation. All but eight of the South African aircraft were assembled by Atlas Aircraft and most have now been declared surplus with several passing into private ownership.

Aermacchi AM-3C, N949CM

Specification	Aermacchi AM-3C	
Powerplant	One 340 h.p. (254 kW) Piaggio-Lycoming GSO-480-B1B6 piston engine	
Dimensions		
Span	12.65 m	(41 ft 6 in)
Length	8.94 m	(29 ft 4 in)
Height	2.72 m	(8 ft 11 in)
Performance		
Max speed	276 km/h	(150 kt, 172 mph)
Cruising speed	244 km/h	(133 kt, 153 mph)
Initial climb	420 m/min	(1,378 fpm)
Range	988 km	(537 nm, 618 miles)
Weights		
Max takeoff	1,700 kg	(3,748 lbs)
Useful load	620 kg	(1,367 lbs)

Specification	Aermacchi M-290TP RediGO	
Powerplant	One 500 s.h.p. (372.8 kW) Allison 250-B17F turboprop	
Dimensions		
Span	10.6 m	(34 ft 9 in)
Length	8.53 m	(28 ft 0 in)
Height	3.2 m	(10 ft 6 in)
Performance		
Max speed	415 km/h	(225 kt, 260 mph)
Cruising speed	325 km/h	(175 kt, 200 mph)
Initial climb	695 m/min	(2,275 fpm)
Range	1,400 km	(761 nm, 875 miles)
Weights		
Max takeoff	1,900 kg	(4,190 lbs)
Useful load	930 kg	(2,052 lbs)

Aermacchi M-290TP RediGO — Finland/Italy

The Finnish manufacturer, Finavitec (formerly Valmet), successfully delivered 30 examples of their L-70 Vinka piston-engined basic trainer in the 1980s and this was further developed with a stretched fuselage, modified wing and retractable undercarriage into the L-80TP (later L-90TP) RediGO training and liaison aircraft. The low-wing RediGO first flew on 1st July 1986 powered by a 500 s.h.p. Allison 250 turboprop engine which was the production standard powerplant even though the second aircraft was fitted with a Turboméca TP.319. It was intended as a multi-mission aircraft with underwing hardpoints for weapons training and a rear bench seat for two passengers for the liaison role. The Finnish Air Force acquired ten aircraft and Valmet then sold a further ten to the Mexican Navy and eight to Eritrea. After production ceased in 1995, rights to the RediGO were sold to Aermacchi who are marketing it as the M-290TP RediGO for training, coastal patrol, medevac and light attack with six underwing hardpoints, and for military communications.

Aermacchi-SIAI S.211A — Italy

First flown on 10th April 1981, the SIAI-Marchetti S.211 was a new-generation tandem two-seat jet trainer tailored to the needs of emergent air arms. It was intended to offer low-cost basic instruction capability with the flexibility of a hardened wing with four pylons to facilitate tactical weapons training. Alternatively it could be pressed into service as an effective light ground attack aircraft. SIAI-Marchetti selected the well-proved Pratt & Whitney JT15D turbofan to power the S.211. The aircraft was not adopted by the AMI but SIAI sold 32 to Singapore in kit form for local assembly and four to Haiti which quickly resold them. A further 24 were sold to the Philippines and 14 of these were locally assembled by PADC. In 1991 Agusta (who had acquired SIAI) teamed with Grumman to offer the S.211A in the USAF JPATS competition, but this was unsuccessful. All rights to the S.211 were acquired by Aermacchi in January 1997.

Valmet RediGO, RG-10 (Finnish AF)

Aermacchi/Agusta S.211A, I-PATS

Aermacchi-SIAI S.211A (Cont.)

Specification	Aermacchi S.211A	
Powerplant	One 3,190 lb.s.t. (14.19 kN) Pratt & Whitney JT15D-5C turbofan	
Dimensions		
Span	8.5 m	(27 ft 11 in)
Length	9.5 m	(31 ft 4 in)
Height	3.8 m	(12 ft 4 in)
Performance		
Max speed	736 km/h	(400 kt, 460 mph)
Cruising speed	699 km/h	(380 kt, 437 mph)
Initial climb	1,448 m/min	(4,750 fpm)
Range	1,454 km	(785 nm, 909 miles)
Weights		
Max takeoff	4,008 kg	(8,838 lbs)
Useful load	1,904 kg	(4,198 lbs)

Aermacchi-SIAI SF.260 — Italy

The well-known Italian designer Stelio Frati designed the F.250 three-seat high-performance light aircraft which was built by Aviamilano and first flown on 15th July 1964. It was followed by the SF.260 which had a larger 260 h.p. Lycoming O-540-E engine. The SF.260 was an all-metal aircraft, aimed primarily at military users, using F.8 Falco wings with a retractable tricycle undercarriage, wingtip fuel tanks and a cockpit with two crew seats and a rear optional passenger-seat enclosed by a sliding bubble canopy. It was built in quantity by SIAI-Marchetti in civil and military versions, major customers including the air forces of Italy, Belgium and Singapore, with recent sales to Venezuela, Uruguay and Zimbabwe. Main variants were the civil SF.260C and SF.260D, the latter with a strengthened airframe, the SF.260M military training variant, the SF.260W Warrior ground attack aircraft with underwing hardpoints and the SF.260SW Sea Warrior for maritime patrol. The civil variants were marketed in the USA as the Waco TS-250 Meteor. The SF.260TP was a development with a 350 s.h.p. Allison 250B-17 turboprop and several existing SF.260s were converted in addition to SIAI providing new-build aircraft. The current SF.260E/F which is marketed by Aermacchi, who took over the design from SIAI-Marchetti, is certificated to FAR Part 23 and has a modified fuel system and avionics. Total production exceeds 850 aircraft delivered to 39 countries with many of these currently in service.

Aermacchi-SIAI SF.260D, N71PA

Specification	Aermacchi-SIAI SF.260TP	
Powerplant	One 350 s.h.p. (260.9 kW) Allison 250-B17D turboprop	
Dimensions		
Span	8.4 m	(27 ft 5 in)
Length	7.4 m	(24 ft 4 in)
Height	2.4 m	(7 ft 11 in)
Performance		
Max speed	423 km/h	(230 kt, 264 mph)
Cruising speed	397 km/h	(216 kt, 248 mph)
Initial climb	661 m/min	(2,170 fpm)
Range	948 km	(515 nm, 593 miles)
Weights		
Max takeoff	1,350 kg	(2,974 lbs)
Useful load	500 kg	(1,100 lbs)

Aero 3 — Yugoslavia

Immediately after World War II, the Yugoslav Air Force re-equipped its basic training fleet with the two-seat Aero 2 which served until the mid-1950s, at which time it was replaced by the very similar Aero 3. The low-wing Aero 3 was slightly larger and had more power, using a Lycoming O-435 in place of the Aero 2's Walter Minor. It was of wood and fabric construction with a fixed tailwheel undercarriage and a large rearward-sliding blister canopy enclosing the tandem two-seat cockpit. First deliveries were made in 1957 and over 100 were eventually completed. These served with the JRV for about 20 years at which point the surviving Aero 3s were handed on to the State flying club network. Some of these are still airworthy in Croatia, France and elsewhere and several have been sold to private owners in the United States.

Aero 3, F-AZEC

Specification	Aero 3	
Powerplant	One 190 h.p. (141.6 kW) Textron Lycoming O-435-A piston engine	
Dimensions		
Span	10.5 m	(34 ft 5 in)
Length	8.6 m	(28 ft 2 in)
Height	2.7 m	(8 ft 10 in)
Performance		
Max speed	230 km/h	(125 kt, 143 mph)
Cruising speed	180 km/h	(98 kt, 112 mph)
Initial climb	228 m/min	(750 fpm)
Range	782 km	(425 nm, 488 miles)
Weights		
Max takeoff	1,200 kg	(2,646 lbs)
Useful load	255 kg	(560 lbs)

Aero L-29 Delfin
— Czech Republic

The L-29 basic jet trainer was designed in 1958 by the Aero factory to replace Czech Air Force Zlin Z-126 and C-11 (Yak-11) piston trainers. The prototype XL-29 was powered by a Bristol Siddeley Viper turbojet and flew on 5th April 1959 but production L-29s used the locally built Motorlet M.701 engine. The aircraft was fitted with a strongpoint under each wing to carry overload tanks or light armament. In 1961, the L-29A was chosen as the standard Warsaw Pact basic trainer and deliveries were made to Czechoslovakia, Hungary, Romania, Bulgaria and the USSR. Other Soviet-aligned nations such as Iraq, Syria, Uganda, Afghanistan, Nigeria and Guinea also received the aircraft and over 3,500 were completed. Some are still in use and the Delfin is a popular private jet warbird. Aero also built prototypes of the L-429 Akrobat single-seater and the L-29R two-seat ground attack variant but neither of these was built in quantity.

Aero L-29A, ES-YLH

Specification	Aero L-29 Delfin	
Powerplant	One 1,962 lb.s.t. (8.73 kN) Motorlet M.701C turbojet	
Dimensions		
Span	10.3 m	(33 ft 9 in)
Length	10.8 m	(35 ft 6 in)
Height	3.1 m	(10 ft 3 in)
Performance		
Max speed	655 km/h	(353 kt, 407 mph)
Cruising speed	543 km/h	(295 kt, 339 mph)
Initial climb	840 m/min	(2,755 fpm)
Range	640 km	(345 nm, 397 miles)
Weights		
Max takeoff	3,540 kg	(7,805 lbs)
Useful load	916 kg	(2,019 lbs)

Aero L-39 Albatros
— Czech Republic

The L-39 dates from the mid-1960s when Aero saw a need for a new jet trainer to replace the L-29 Delfin as the standard Warsaw Pact instructional aircraft. The design, which had significantly better performance than the L-29, had a tapered straight wing with tip tanks and a pressurised tandem cockpit with a raised rear instructor's seat and zero-level ejection seats. The prototype flew on 4th November 1968 and first deliveries took place in 1973. Variants included the L-39ZO weapons trainer and the single-seat L-39ZA with underwing hardpoints for ground attack work and additional fuel capacity in place of the rear seat. They also built the target-towing L-39VE. Over 2,800 L-39s have been delivered by Aero Vodochody to the Soviet Air Force and to most countries within the Soviet sphere of influence including Bulgaria, Romania, Algeria, Cuba, Libya and Syria. Many have been civilianised and sold in the USA as warbirds but the L-39 continues in widespread military service.

Aero L-39ZO

Specification	Aero Vodochody L-39ZO Albatros	
Powerplant	One 3,795 lb.s.t. (16.88 kN) ZMDB-Progress AI-25TL turbojet	
Dimensions		
Span	9.46 m	(31 ft 1 in)
Length	12.13 m	(39 ft 10 in)
Height	4.77 m	(15 ft 8 in)
Performance		
Max speed	846 km/h	(460 kt, 529 mph)
Cruising speed	736 km/h	(400 kt, 460 mph)
Initial climb	1,262 m/min	(4,140 fpm)
Range	1,086 km	(590 nm, 679 miles)
Weights		
Max takeoff	4,709 kg	(10,383 lbs)
Useful load	1,160 kg	(2,557 lbs)

Aero L-59 and L-159
— Czech Republic

The Aero L-39 was succeeded by the L-59 (formerly L-39MS) which first flew on 30th September 1986. This was a higher-performance aircraft with a new turbofan engine developed by ZVL and the Soviet Lotarev bureau and a strengthened airframe. The L-59 also has a modernised cockpit with a HUD and an improved tactical navigation system. The main production variant has been the L-59E weapons trainer with four underwing hardpoints and a belly-mounted gun pod and 48 have been sold to Egypt and 12 to Tunisia. The Czech Air Force has ordered 72 of the L-159 which is a single-seat close support version with an International Turbine Engines F-124 turbofan. Aero Vodochody, as the company is now titled, also entered the USAF JPATS competition with the L-139 Albatros 2000 which was equipped with a Garrett TFE731-4-1T turbofan but they were unsuccessful in the competition and no production aircraft have been built.

Aero L-59 and L-159 (Cont.)

Aero L-139 Albatros 2000, 5501 (Czech AF)

Specification	Aero Vodochody L-59 Albatros	
Powerplant	One 4,850 lb.s.t. (21.58 kN) ZMDB-Progress DV-2 turbofan	
Dimensions		
Span	9.55 m	(31 ft 4 in)
Length	12.2 m	(40 ft 1 in)
Height	4.77 m	(15 ft 8 in)
Performance		
Max speed	875 km/h	(473 kt, 545 mph)
Cruising speed	764 km/h	(415 kt, 477 mph)
Initial climb	1,560 m/min	(5,120 fpm)
Range	1,140 km	(620 nm, 713 miles)
Weights		
Max takeoff	5,700 kg	(12,565 lbs)
Useful load	1,552 kg	(3,422 lbs)

Aero Boero AB.95, AB.115 and AB.180 — Argentina

Aero Tallares Boero flew the prototype Aero Boero 95 three-seat trainer and club aircraft on 12th March 1959. The strut-braced high-wing Model 95 was built of steel tube and fabric and powered by a 95 h.p. Continental C90. The later Model 95A had a 100 h.p. Continental O-200A and was also used for glider towing and crop spraying. After building 36 of the AB.95/95A the company moved on to build the similar AB.115 with a 115 h.p. Lycoming O-235 and the AB.150 with a 150 h.p. Lycoming O-320. This was followed by the four-seat AB.180 with a 180 h.p. Lycoming O-360 which was also sold as the AB.180RV with a cut-down rear fuselage and rear cabin window and the AB.180RVR with glider-towing equipment. Out of total production of over 600 aircraft many are still active in South America including a large batch of AB.180RVRs and AB.115s built for Brazil in the early 1990s. Aero Boero is no longer an active aircraft manufacturer.

Aero Boero 115, PP-GLK

Specification	Aero Boero AB.180RV	
Powerplant	One 180 h.p. (134 kW) Textron Lycoming O-360-A1A piston engine	
Dimensions		
Span	10.9 m	(35 ft 9 in)
Length	7.27 m	(23 ft 10 in)
Height	2.1 m	(6 ft 10 in)
Performance		
Max speed	245 km/h	(132 kt, 152 mph)
Cruising speed	211 km/h	(114 kt, 131 mph)
Initial climb	360 m/min	(1,180 fpm)
Range	1,180 km	(641 nm, 738 miles)
Weights		
Max takeoff	844 kg	(1,860 lbs)
Useful load	294 kg	(648 lbs)

Aero Cad Cozy — USA

The Cozy was developed by Nat Puffer from the Rutan Varieze canard homebuilt and first flown on 19th July 1982. Compared with the Varieze, the Cozy has a wider fuselage allowing the cabin to accommodate two people in front and one behind. The wing area was also enlarged with an additional forward section. The Cozy has a tricycle undercarriage with a retractable nose-wheel and fixed main wheels and the cabin is entered by means of an upward-hinged canopy. Construction of the Cozy is composite and it has the same pusher engine installation as the Varieze. Plans for the Cozy were marketed by Aero Cad but rights to the aircraft, now known as the Cozy Classic, are owned by Cosy Europe based in Germany who sell plans and kits. The Cozy Mk.IV is a four-seat version launched in 1993 and sold as a kit or plans by Co-Z Development Corp. of Mesa, Arizona. Some 250 examples of the Cozy and 38 of the Cozy IV have flown and over 1,600 sets of plans have been sold.

Aero Cad Cozy, N397CZ

Specification	Co-Z Development Corp. Cozy Mk.IV	
Powerplant	One 180 h.p. (134.2 kW) Textron Lycoming O-360 piston engine	
Dimensions		
Span	8.76 m	(28 ft 9 in)
Length	5.16 m	(16 ft 11 in)
Height	2.29 m	(7 ft 6 in)
Performance		
Max speed	367 km/h	(198 kt, 228 mph)
Cruising speed	338 km/h	(183 kt, 210 mph)
Initial climb	610 m/min	(2,000 fpm)
Range	1,600 km	(870 nm, 1,000 miles)
Weights		
Max takeoff	930 kg	(2,050 lbs)
Useful load	454 kg	(1,000 lbs)

Aero Commander 520, 560, 500 and 680 — USA

Designed by Ted Smith and flown as the L.3805 prototype on 23rd April 1948 the high-wing Aero Commander twin was aimed at providing mini-airliner comfort in the four-to six-seat light twin business-aircraft category. The initial production version, of which 150 were built, was the Commander 520 with an unswept fin and 260 h.p. Lycoming GO-435-C engines. This was succeeded by the 500, 560 and 680, of which 1,368 were completed, with swept fins, slimmer engine nacelles and Lycoming engines of 250 h.p., 280 h.p. and 340 h.p. respectively. Aero Commander also built the pressurised Model 680FP and 720 Alti Cruiser. Rockwell, who acquired Aero Commander, rationalised the basic Commander range to one model, the 500S/500U Shrike Commander with 290 h.p. engines, a more pointed nose and other detailed refinements. Some 372 were built from 1964 to 1979. Piston Commanders remain in widespread civil use and are also flown by military users such as the Argentine Air Force.

Rockwell Shrike Commander 500S, N9116N

Specification	Aero Commander 500U Shrike Commander	
Powerplant	Two 290 h.p. (216.2 kW) Textron Lycoming IO-540-E1A5 piston engines	
Dimensions		
Span	14.95 m	(49 ft 0 in)
Length	10.7 m	(35 ft 1 in)
Height	4.51 m	(14 ft 9 in)
Performance		
Max speed	350 km/h	(190 kt, 219 mph)
Cruising speed	313 km/h	(170 kt, 195 mph)
Initial climb	442 m/min	(1,450 fpm)
Range	1,979 km	(1,076 nm, 1,236 miles)
Weights		
Max takeoff	3,062 kg	(6,750 lbs)
Useful load	1,091 kg	(2,402 lbs)

Aero Commander 680FL, 680FLP and 681 — USA

The standard Aero Commander twins were well regarded for their stability and comfort and Aero Commander decided to offer a higher-capacity model with a maximum 11-seat capacity. The prototype Model 680FL Grand Commander first flew on 24th April 1962 powered by two fuel-injected 340 h.p. Lycoming IGSO-540 engines. It was, essentially, a Model 680 with a 5 ft 10 in fuselage stretch and was normally delivered with a six-passenger main cabin layout. The prototype was later converted with a pressurised cabin as the 680FL(P) and 157 of the 680FL (later named Courser Commander) and 37 of the 680 FL(P) were sold between 1963 and 1970. Rockwell subsequently introduced the very similar Model 685, 66 of which were built in the mid-1970s. This was a version of the turboprop 690 with 435 h.p. Continental GTSIO-520-K piston engines. Some 120 of the stretched Commander piston twins were registered in the USA at the end of 1999.

Aero Commander 680FL Grand Commander, PT-CGU

Specification	Aero Commander 680FL Grand Commander	
Powerplant	Two 380 h.p. (283.3 kW) Textron Lycoming IGSO-540-B1A piston engines	
Dimensions		
Span	14.95 m	(49 ft 0 in)
Length	12.58 m	(41 ft 3 in)
Height	4.51 m	(14 ft 9 in)
Performance		
Max speed	435 km/h	(235 kt, 270 mph)
Cruising speed	393 km/h	(212 kt, 244 mph)
Initial climb	396 m/min	(1,300 fpm)
Range	2,315 km	(1,258 nm, 1,447 miles)
Weights		
Max takeoff	3,855 kg	(8,500 lbs)
Useful load	1,500 kg	(3,308 lbs)

Rockwell Turbo Commander 690A, N48AZ

Aero Commander (Rockwell, Gulfstream) Turbo Commander — USA

The Model 680T Turbo Commander was a natural development of the Aero Commander 680FL(P) Pressurised Grand Commander with two Garrett AiResearch TPE331-43 turboprops. The prototype flew on 31st December 1964 and 138 of the essentially similar 680T, 680V and 680W were built. Under North American Rockwell the Model 681/681B Hawk was introduced (72 built) with improved pressurisation and this was replaced by the Model 690 with higher power and a lengthened wing centre section. The popular 690 series went through several variants with changes to cabin windows, pressurisation, gross weight and performance. From 1981, under Gulfstream Aerospace, the line consisted of the Jetprop 840 (690C) based on the 690 with increased wingspan, wingtip winglets and 840 s.h.p. TPE331-5-524K engines, Jetprop 980 (695) with 735 s.h.p. TPE331-10-501K engines, the Jetprop 900 (690D) which was similar to the Jetprop 840 but with a longer cabin and the Jetprop 1000 (695A) which was a Jetprop 900 with the larger TPE331-10-501K engines. Total turboprop-powered Commander production was 1,121, built between 1965 and 1986.

Specification	Gulfstream Commander 695A Jetprop 1000	
Powerplant	Two 820 s.h.p. (611 kW) Honeywell (Garrett) TPE331-10-501K turboprops	
Dimensions		
Span	15.89 m	(52 ft 1 in)
Length	13.1 m	(42 ft 11 in)
Height	4.56 m	(14 ft 11 in)
Performance		
Max speed	571 km/h	(308 kt, 354 mph)
Cruising speed	560 km/h	(302 kt, 348 mph)
Initial climb	854 m/min	(2,802 fpm)
Range	3,855 km	(2,095 nm, 2,409 miles)
Weights		
Max takeoff	5,103 kg	(11,250 lbs)
Useful load	1,797 kg	(3,961 lbs)

Aero Commander 1121 Jet Commander and 1123 Westwind — USA/Israel

Under the ownership of Rockwell Standard, Aero Commander designed the Jet Commander to add to their range of piston-engined business aircraft. The Model 1121, which first flew on 27th January 1963, had a mid-set straight tapered wing positioned to the rear of the main cabin section of the fuselage and was fitted with CJ610 turbojets in rear fuselage pods. Over 130 were built before Aero Commander was forced by government ruling to sell the design to Israel Aircraft Industries (IAI) in 1967. IAI completed the remaining Aero Commander airframes as the Commodore Jet and then produced an improved version, the Model 1123 Westwind, with a longer fuselage, modified wings, higher gross weight, wingtip tanks and increased power. Some 36 were built, followed by 256 Model 1124 Westwinds with Garrett TFE731 turbofans and further gross weight increases and the IAI-1124A Westwind II which had small winglets attached to the wingtip tanks. The total includes three IAI-1124N Seascan military surveillance aircraft which were built for the Israeli Air Force and fitted with a large nose radome and two fuselage-mounted hardpoints for anti-submarine weapons. Around 220 of the various Jet Commander and Commodore fleet are still active.

IAI-1124 Westwind I, N92FE

IAI-1124N Seascan, 4X-JYR

Specification	Israel Aircraft Industries IAI-1124A Westwind II	
Powerplant	Two 3,700 lb.s.t. (16.46 kN) Honeywell TFE731-3-1G turbofans	
Dimensions		
Span	13.65 m	(44 ft 9 in)
Length	15.93 m	(52 ft 3 in)
Height	4.81 m	(15 ft 9 in)
Performance		
Max speed	872 km/h	(471 kt, 542 mph)
Cruising speed	741 km/h	(400 kt, 460 mph)
Initial climb	1,524 m/min	(5,000 fpm)
Range	4,815 km	(2,617 nm, 3,009 miles)
Weights		
Max takeoff	10,660 kg	(23,500 lbs)
Useful load	1,542 kg	(3,400 lbs)

Aero Kuhlmann Scub — France

The Scub is a production ultralight aircraft for sale to private owners and flying clubs. It made its debut at the Paris Air Show in 1997 following a first flight on 5th May 1996. A tandem two-seater, it has a high strut-braced wing and a fixed tailwheel undercarriage. The wings can be folded for ground transportation or storage and the cabin has large transparencies which give excellent all-round vision. Construction is of steel tube, wood and fabric. It is supplied as a factory-complete aircraft with JAR-VLA certification and is built by Aero Kuhlmann at La Ferté Alais near Paris. A total of 27 Scubs had been completed by the middle of 1999. The Scub is used in some numbers for crop spraying in Madagascar and several examples have been delivered with twin floats. The powerplant is a four-cylinder JPX engine of 85 h.p. driving a two-bladed ground-adjustable propeller.

Aero Kuhlmann Scub, 75-MH

Specification	Aero Kuhlmann Scub	
Powerplant	One 85 h.p. (63.4 kW) JPX-47X75A piston engine	
Dimensions		
Span	10.2 m	(33 ft 6 in)
Length	7.1 m	(23 ft 4 in)
Height	1.8 m	(6 ft 0 in)
Performance		
Max speed	165 km/h	(91 kt, 105 mph)
Cruising speed	128 km/h	(70 kt, 80 mph)
Initial climb	250 m/min	(820 fpm)
Range	999 km	(543 nm, 624 miles)
Weights		
Max takeoff	450 kg	(992 lbs)
Useful load	182 kg	(400 lbs)

Aero Spacelines 377-PG and 377-SGT Guppy — USA

The needs of the US space programme for transport of large components resulted in On-Mark Engineering of Van Nuys modifying a Boeing 377 Stratocruiser as the Model 377-PG 'Pregnant Guppy'. On-Mark removed the upper lobe of the fuselage and built a bulbous outsize upper fuselage. They also stretched the rear fuselage and made the whole tail section detachable for loading Saturn IV rocket sections. This aircraft, which first flew on 16th September 1962, was followed by the smaller Mini Guppy 377-MG and 377-SG Super Guppy with YT-34-P turboprop engines. Two further turboprop Mini Guppies were built and Airbus Industrie in France acquired four Model 201 Super Guppies with Allison 501 engines for transporting Airbus components around Europe. Two of these were built by UTA in France. The Airbus Super Guppies were replaced by Airbus A300-608STs in 1997 and one was sold for use by NASA and is currently airworthy.

UTA-Aero Spacelines Super Guppy 377-SGT-201, F-BPPA

Specification	Aero Spacelines 377-SGT Super Guppy 201	
Powerplant	Four 4,912 s.h.p. (3,662 kW) Allison 501-D22C turboprops	
Dimensions		
Span	47.75 m	(156 ft 8 in)
Length	43.84 m	(143 ft 10 in)
Height	14.71 m	(48 ft 3 in)
Performance		
Max speed	463 km/h	(250 kt, 288 mph)
Cruising speed	407 km/h	(220 kt, 253 mph)
Initial climb	457 m/min	(1,500 fpm)
Range	4,700 km	(2,554 nm, 2,938 miles)
Weights		
Max takeoff	77,110 kg	(170,028 lbs)
Useful load	24,494 kg	(54,010 lbs)

Aerocomp CompMonster — USA

The Aerocomp CompMonster was designed by Ron Leuck as a simply-assembled four-seat sport utility aircraft. It is a strut-braced high-wing all-composite kit machine, capable of operating on floats and with a design flexible enough to be expanded into a range of larger light aircraft. It first flew on 3rd April 1995. Operating on tricycle or tailwheel gear, the CompMonster can have engines ranging from a 110 h.p. Hirth to the 150 h.p. Lycoming O-320 (Model 150G) or the 180 h.p. O-360 (180G). The Model 180SF is a float-equipped version. By adding a fore-and-aft fuselage splice to widen the cabin, the aircraft can become the CompAir CA6G (CompAir Six) six-seater with a 220 h.p. engine and this is available as the CA6SF on floats, the CA6AF amphibious version, the CA6 Sportster aerobatic version and the CA6TW with a tapered wing. The eleven-seat CompAir 10 has a larger fuselage and wing and twin vertical fins. Powered by a 285 h.p. Continental engine or a Walter 601B turboprop it has a rear cabin for nine people and a belly-mounted cargo hold. Over 100 CompAir kits have been sold.

AeroComp CompAir Six, N61262

Specification	Aerocomp CompMonster 180G	
Powerplant	One 180 h.p. (134.2 kW) Lycoming O-360 piston engine	
Dimensions		
Span	10.7 m	(35 ft 0 in)
Length	7.9 m	(26 ft 0 in)
Height	2.4 m	(8 ft 0 in)
Performance		
Max speed	226 km/h	(123 kt, 142 mph)
Cruising speed	212 km/h	(115 kt, 132 mph)
Initial climb	366 m/min	(1,200 fpm)
Range	1,056 km	(574 nm, 660 miles)
Weights		
Max takeoff	1,250 kg	(2,756 lbs)
Useful load	636 kg	(1,400 lbs)

Aeromot AMT-100 Ximango and Fournier RF9 — France/Brazil

The RF9 motor glider was designed by René Fournier, making its first flight on 20th January 1977. This followed the general design of previous Fournier motor gliders with a 68 h.p. Limbach SL.1700E engine, a side-by-side two-seat cockpit with a blister canopy and a retractable tailwheel undercarriage. Including prototypes, 14 were built by Fournier at Nitray and the RF9 is now being built in Germany by ABS Aviation. The later RF10 was externally similar to the RF9 but was of all-composite construction and the first of three prototypes first flew on 6th March 1981. Ten production RF10s were built by Soc. Aérostructure at Marmande in France in the early 1980s, including four for the Portuguese Air Force, and these differed from the prototypes in having a T-tail. The design and tooling were then taken over by Aeromot of Porto Alegre in Brazil who started building the AMT-100 Ximango in 1986. In standard form the Ximango has an 80 h.p. Limbach L.2000-EO1 engine but the AMT-200 Super Ximango has an 80 h.p. Rotax 912A and this is the predominant version now in production. The turbocharged AMT-300 has also been developed and Aeromot has produced a military surveillance version with an external sensor pod. Approximately 100 Ximangos had been built by the end of 1998 and many had been exported to the USA and Europe. The AMT-600 Guri is a 115 hp trainer version with a fixed tricycle undercarriage.

Aeromot AMT-200 Super Ximango, PT-POQ

Specification	Aeromot AMT-200 Super Ximango	
Powerplant	One 80 h.p. (59.65 kW) Rotax 912A piston engine	
Dimensions		
Span	17.47 m	(57 ft 4 in)
Length	8.05 m	(26 ft 5 in)
Height	1.93 m	(6 ft 4 in)
Performance		
Max speed	205 km/h	(110 kt, 127 mph)
Cruising speed	180 km/h	(97 kt, 112 mph)
Initial climb	180 m/min	(590 fpm)
Range	1,250 km	(679 nm, 781 miles)
Weights		
Max takeoff	850 kg	(1,874 lbs)
Useful load	245 kg	(540 lbs)

Aeronca C-3 — USA

Known affectionately as the 'Flying Bathtub' the C-3 was a developed version of the C-2 which first flew on 20th October 1929. This single-seat ultralight monoplane had fabric-covered wings supported by a central mast with wire bracing. Its manufacturer, the Aeronautical Corporation of America (Aeronca), decided also to produce the enlarged C-3 Duplex with side-by-side seating for two and a 36 h.p. Aeronca E-113 engine. Over 400 were completed between 1931 and 1937 and 81 are currently registered in the United States. The C-3, despite its low power, was frequently operated on floats. In Britain, the Aeronautical Corporation of Great Britain built a series of C-3s under the title Aeronca 100 and these were fitted with a 40 h.p. Aeronca-JAP J-99 engine and had a fully enclosed cabin with side windows. Some 24 aircraft were built by the British company including four sold to Australia and seven are currently active or under restoration.

Aeronca C-3, G-ADYS

Aeronca C-3 (Cont.)

Specification	Aeronca C-3	
Powerplant	One 36 h.p. (26.8 kW) Aeronca E-113 piston engine	
Dimensions		
Span	11 m	(36 ft 0 in)
Length	6.1 m	(20 ft 0 in)
Height	2.3 m	(7 ft 6 in)
Performance		
Max speed	129 km/h	(70 kt, 80 mph)
Cruising speed	105 km/h	(57 kt, 65 mph)
Initial climb	152 m/min	(500 fpm)
Range	320 km	(174 nm, 200 miles)
Weights		
Max takeoff	398 kg	(875 lbs)
Useful load	186 kg	(409 lbs)

Aeronca K and L-3
— USA

Aeronca moved on, in 1937, from the rather basic C-3 to a larger and more conventional aircraft, the Model K. With a strut-braced high wing and fully enclosed two-seat cabin it was built of steel tube and fabric and could be operated on wheels, floats or skis. The 'K' was powered by a 40 h.p. two-cylinder Aeronca E-113-CB engine but later versions included the KC with a Continental A40, the KCA (Model 50-C) with a Continental A65, the KF (Model 50-F) with a Franklin 50, the Model 50-L Chief with a Lycoming O-145, the KM with a Menasco M-50 and the 65 h.p. Model 65. A tandem two-seat version, the Model 65TC Defender with extensive cockpit transparencies and a 65 h.p. Continental O-170-3 engine or, as the 65TL, with a Lycoming O-145, was designed for wartime spotting use and 1,447 were delivered as the O-58 and L-3. The majority of the surviving Aeronca Ks are in the USA where 440 are registered and 270 of the Model 65TC and TL also remain.

Specification	Aeronca 50-C KCA	
Powerplant	One 65 h.p. (48.46 kW) Continental A65 piston engine	
Dimensions		
Span	11 m	(36 ft 0 in)
Length	6.3 m	(20 ft 10 in)
Height	1.9 m	(6 ft 3 in)
Performance		
Max speed	167 km/h	(91 kt, 105 mph)
Cruising speed	153 km/h	(83 kt, 95 mph)
Initial climb	168 m/min	(550 fpm)
Range	416 km	(226 nm, 260 miles)
Weights		
Max takeoff	568 kg	(1,250 lbs)
Useful load	230 kg	(506 lbs)

Aeronca 7AC Champion
— USA

To meet the postwar demand for light aircraft, Aeronca produced a civil equivalent of the tandem two-seat L-3 military spotter. The most popular version of the Model 7 Champion, several thousand of which are still flying, was the 7AC with a standard 65 h.p. Continental engine or optional 85 h.p. or 90 h.p. Continental. In 1951, after 7,200 Champions and 735 of the 7BCM and 7CCM military version (L-16A and L-16B) had been built, the design was acquired by Champion Aircraft. They produced the 90 h.p. 7EC Traveler and the tricycle gear 7FC Tri-Traveler. The 7-series airframe was also strengthened to take a 140 h.p. Lycoming O-290 in the Champion 7GC Sky-Trac and a 150 h.p. O-320 in the 7GCA which was fitted with a hopper in place of the rear seat for crop spraying. Other Champion variants included the 7JC Tri-Con with a reverse tricycle undercarriage, the 7HC DX'er and the 7GCB Challenger. Champion Aircraft built 2,192 examples of these various models. The 7ACA Champ was a 7AC reintroduced in 1970 and a total of 71 were built with a 60 h.p. Franklin engine. It will be reintroduced in 2001 by American Champion, powered by a Jabiru engine. Later derivatives of the Champion design included the Citabria and Scout, referred to in the Champion entry.

Aeronca 65C, D-ETUI

Aeronca 7AC Champion, F-BFPX

Champion 7FC Tri-Traveler, N7695E

Specification	Aeronca 7AC Champion	
Powerplant	One 65 h.p. (48.46 kW) Continental A65-8 piston engine	
Dimensions		
Span	10.7 m	(35 ft 2 in)
Length	6.6 m	(21 ft 6 in)
Height	2.1 m	(7 ft 0 in)
Performance		
Max speed	160 km/h	(87 kt, 100 mph)
Cruising speed	136 km/h	(74 kt, 85 mph)
Initial climb	152 m/min	(500 fpm)
Range	399 km	(217 nm, 250 miles)
Weights		
Max takeoff	600 kg	(1,320 lbs)
Useful load	232 kg	(510 lbs)

Aeronca 11AC Chief — USA

Having started postwar production of the tandem-seat Model 7AC Champion, Aeronca realised that side-by-side seating was more popular for private owners and they modified the 7-series fuselage to produce the Model 11AC Chief. This was, effectively, a modernised version of the prewar Model 65 Chief with an updated cabin, and the facility for operation on floats. Introduced in 1946, 1,866 examples of the 11AC were built. The 11BC Super Chief (181 built) was a version with an enlarged fin and an 85 h.p. Continental C85-8F and the 11CC Super Chief (277 built) had a larger cabin interior, extra baggage space, luxury fitments and additional fuel capacity. The 11CC was built in India during the 1950s as the Hindustan HUL-26 Pushpak with a 90 h.p. Continental C90 engine and 154 were delivered to Indian flying clubs. Around 1,100 Chiefs are still active in North America and many are overseas including 22 in the United Kingdom.

Aeronca 11AC Chief, N3288E

Specification	Aeronca 11AC Chief	
Powerplant	One 65 h.p. (48.46 kW) Continental A65-8F piston engine	
Dimensions		
Span	11 m	(36 ft 0 in)
Length	6.3 m	(20 ft 10 in)
Height	2.1 m	(6 ft 11 in)
Performance		
Max speed	167 km/h	(91 kt, 105 mph)
Cruising speed	153 km/h	(83 kt, 95 mph)
Initial climb	152 m/min	(500 fpm)
Range	528 km	(287 nm, 330 miles)
Weights		
Max takeoff	591 kg	(1,300 lbs)
Useful load	250 kg	(550 lbs)

Aeronca 15AC Sedan — USA

The Sedan was a four-seat private aircraft which Aeronca added to their product line in 1947. Substantially larger than the Champion, it followed the well-tried Aeronca steel tube and fabric construction and the same strut-braced high-wing layout. It had a roomy cabin which was well sound-proofed and upholstered and was distinguished by a vertical tail which appeared to be swept forward. The normal powerplant was the 145 h.p. Continental C145 but some Aeronca 15AFs were built with a 165 h.p. Franklin 6A4-165-B3. Many Sedans were fitted with floats and were popular in Canada and Alaska for bush operations. Aeronca built 561 Sedans, half of which are still registered, before the company ceased aircraft manufacture in 1951. The 15AC was used as the basis of the Hindustan Krishak military AOP aircraft built in India in the early 1960s, although no Krishaks remain in service.

Aeronca 15AC Sedan, N1365H

Aeronca 15AC Sedan (Cont.)

Specification	Aeronca 15AC Sedan	
Powerplant	One 145 h.p. (108.1 kW) Continental C145-2 piston engine	
Dimensions		
Span	11.4 m	(37 ft 6 in)
Length	7.7 m	(25 ft 3 in)
Height	2.1 m	(6 ft 11 in)
Performance		
Max speed	191 km/h	(104 kt, 120 mph)
Cruising speed	167 km/h	(91 kt, 105 mph)
Initial climb	198 m/min	(650 fpm)
Range	640 km	(348 nm, 400 miles)
Weights		
Max takeoff	932 kg	(2,055 lbs)
Useful load	409 kg	(900 lbs)

Aeroplastika LAK-X — Lithuania

The Lithuanian company Aeroplastika designed and built the LAK-X light sport trainer and flew the prototype on 2nd August 1992. The LAK-X, which is built from composite materials has a side-by-side two-seat cockpit and a fixed tricycle undercarriage. It is powered by a Rotax 912 in standard LAK-XA form but can be fitted with a Limbach L.2400, Rotax 914 or even a 125 h.p. Teledyne Continental IO-240-A engine. A small number of examples of the LAK-X have been completed but it is not currently in large scale production.

Aeroplastika LAK-X, LY-XMH

Specification	Aeroplastika LAK-XA	
Powerplant	One 79 h.p. (59 kW) Rotax 912 piston engine	
Dimensions		
Span	10.68 m	(35 ft 1 in)
Length	7 m	(22 ft 9 in)
Height	2.2 m	(7 ft 2 in)
Performance		
Max speed	200 km/h	(108 kt, 124 mph)
Cruising speed	160 km/h	(86 kt, 99 mph)
Initial climb	235 m/min	(770 fpm)
Range	850 km	(462 nm, 531 miles)
Weights		
Max takeoff	650 kg	(1,433 lbs)
Useful load	250 kg	(551 lbs)

Aeropract A-21M Solo — Russia

The Solo is a small single-seat ultralight aircraft developed by Aeropract at Samara and sold as a kit to amateur builders. The Solo is built from composite materials and powered by a 50 h.p. Rotax or similar lightweight engine. It has a classic low-wing layout with a fixed tricycle undercarriage which uses spring-steel main legs and the cockpit is enclosed by a large bubble canopy. The Solo can be fitted with skis or twin floats and has a hardpoint in the belly to mount a baggage pod or additional fuel tank. The wings are removable for ground transport. Aeropract has built a small series of Solos but it is believed that the type is only operating in Russia and no export kits have been completed.

Aeropract A-21M Solo, FLARF-02177

Specification	Aeropract A-21M Solo	
Powerplant	One 50 h.p. (37.28 kW) Rotax 503 piston engine	
Dimensions		
Span	6.65 m	(21 ft 7 in)
Length	4.73 m	(15 ft 6 in)
Height	1.85 m	(6 ft 1 in)
Performance		
Max speed	190 km/h	(103 kt, 118 mph)
Cruising speed	150 km/h	(81 kt, 93 mph)
Initial climb	300 m/min	(985 fpm)
Range	215 km	(116 nm, 134 miles)
Weights		
Max takeoff	280 kg	(617 lbs)
Useful load	100 kg	(220 lbs)

Aeroprakt A-22 — Ukraine

While technically an ultralight, the A-22 Valor (originally named 'Shark' and now known as the Foxbat in the UK) is a substantial light aircraft designed by Yuri Yakovlev and first flown in 1996 with all-metal construction and the range and speed to allow good cross-country touring performance. Manufactured in the Ukraine as a kit by Aeroprakt Ltd., who also produce the tandem two-seat A-20 Vista and A-26 Vulcan, it has a strut-braced high wing which is fabric covered and can be folded for storage and ground transportation. The cabin has side-by-side seating for two with dual controls and the transparent rear cabin panels allow excellent all-round vision.Aeroprakt had manufactured over 25 of the A-22s by mid-2000 with exports going to several counries including the UAE, Germany, Lithuania, the UK and Poland.

Aeroprakt A-22 Foxbat, G-FBAT

Specification	Aeroprakt A-22	
Powerplant	One 100 h.p. (74.56 kW) Rotax 912S piston engine	
Dimensions		
Span	10 m	(32 ft 10 in)
Length	6.3 m	(20 ft 8 in)
Height	2.4 m	(7 ft 10 in)
Performance		
Max speed	170 km/h	(92 kt 106 mph)
Cruising speed	140 km/h	(75 kt 87 mph)
Initial climb	270 m/min	(886 fpm)
Range	900 km	(490 nm 563 miles)
Weights		
Max takeoff	450 kg	(992 lbs)
Useful load	188 kg	(414 lbs)

Aeroprogress T-101 Grach — Russia

Faced with the problem of an ageing fleet of Antonov An-2 utility biplanes, the Roks-Aero design bureau made a proposal for its new Grach high-wing aircraft with a square-section fuselage capable of accommodating passengers or freight in remote-area operations. To maintain simplicity the tailwheel undercarriage is fixed and the Grach can be fitted with amphibious floats or skis. The Grach is powered by an OMKB TVD-10B turboprop engine in view of the increasing scarcity of fuel for reciprocating engines in the distant locations where the type would operate. Later variants may use a Pratt & Whitney PT6 or Honeywell TPE331. The T-101 prototype first flew on 7th December 1994. Production will be handled by MAPO and marketing by the parent Aeroprogress company. Major orders had not been placed by the end of 1998 although eight aircraft had been completed by mid-1999. A military variant has also been proposed with underwing hardpoints and fuselage-mounted sponsons for further armament.

Aeroprogress T-101, FLARF-01466

Specification	Aeroprogress T-101 Grach	
Powerplant	One 1,010 s.h.p. (755 kW) OMKB TVD-10B turboprop	
Dimensions		
Span	18.18 m	(59 ft 8 in)
Length	15.04 m	(49 ft 4 in)
Height	6.67 m	(21 ft 11 in)
Performance		
Max speed	300 km/h	(162 kt, 186 mph)
Cruising speed	250 km/h	(135 kt, 155 mph)
Initial climb	285 m/min	(935 fpm)
Range	1,400 km	(761 nm, 875 miles)
Weights		
Max takeoff	5,250 kg	(11,574 lbs)
Useful load	1,924 kg	(4,243 lbs)

Aérospatiale SE.3130 Alouette II and Llama — France

Designed by Sud-Est, the five-seat general-utility Alouette II helicopter was first flown on 12th March 1955 and went into production in 1956. It was ordered in large numbers for the French military forces with some 420 of the total 1,679 production being delivered for use by the ALAT, Armée de l'Air, Aéronavale and Gendarmerie. Most Alouettes were fitted with skid landing gear but some naval examples were delivered with a four-wheel undercarriage. Alouettes were also frequently fitted with externally mounted armament including machine guns and rocket pods. Military export sales for the SE.3130 (later designated SE.313B) were received from many countries including Belgium, Germany, Switzerland, Sweden and Lebanon and civil examples were sold widely, particularly in the USA where Republic sold it as the Lark. The SA.318C Alouette Astazou was a higher-powered version with an Astazou IIA turbine. In 1958, the SE.3150 (later SA.315) Llama was introduced for hot and high operations with a 500 s.h.p. Artouste III engine and this was often fitted with a taller undercarriage. Licence production was undertaken by Helibras in Brazil as the Gaviao and by Hindustan in India as the SA.315B Cheetah.

Aérospatiale SE.3130 Alouette II, F-GLPV

Aérospatiale SE.3130 Alouette II and Llama (Cont.)

Specification	Aérospatiale SA.318C Alouette II Astazou	
Powerplant	One 360 s.h.p. (268.4 kW) Turboméca Astazou IIA turboshaft	
Dimensions		
Rotor diameter	10.2 m	(33 ft 6 in)
Length	12.1 m	(39 ft 8 in)
Height	2.75 m	(9 ft 0 in)
Performance		
Max speed	205 km/h	(110 kt, 127 mph)
Cruising speed	180 km/h	(97 kt, 112 mph)
Initial climb	306 m/min	(1,004 fpm)
Range	720 km	(388 nm, 447 miles)
Weights		
Max takeoff	1,650 kg	(3,638 lbs)
Useful load	760 kg	(1,676 lbs)

Aérospatiale SA.316A Alouette III — France

The Alouette III was a new aircraft, owing little to the Alouette II other than the use of certain dynamic components. It had an all-metal monocoque fuselage in place of the open tube structure of the SE.3130 and a tricycle undercarriage. The prototype SE.3160 first flew on 28th February 1959 and the production aircraft (later designated SA.316A) served with all the French forces. The later SA.316C was a more powerful variant with an Artouste IIID turboshaft and the SA.319 was upgraded to an Astazou XIV. The Alouette III was again built by Hindustan as the Chetak and by IAR in Romania as the IAR-316B. A proposed Romanian gunship version, the IAR-317 Skyfox, was only flown in prototype form. Most Alouette III sales were for military use and many of the 1,400 built remain in operation in France and in other countries including Austria, Ethiopia, Iraq, Ireland, Lebanon, Libya and Pakistan. One Alouette III has been converted to Cirstel configuration by Denel in South Africa with a directed thrust tail torque compensation system similar to the McDonnell Douglas NOTAR.

Aérospatiale SA.316B Alouette III, 9H-AAV

Specification	Aérospatiale SA.316B Alouette III	
Powerplant	One 570 s.h.p. (425 kW) Turboméca Artouste IIIB turboshaft	
Dimensions		
Rotor diameter	11.02 m	(36 ft 2 in)
Length	12.84 m	(42 ft 1 in)
Height	3 m	(9 ft 10 in)
Performance		
Max speed	210 km/h	(113 kt, 130 mph)
Cruising speed	185 km/h	(100 kt, 115 mph)
Initial climb	270 m/min	(885 fpm)
Range	480 km	(258 nm, 298 miles)
Weights		
Max takeoff	2,200 kg	(4,850 lbs)
Useful load	1,078 kg	(2,376 lbs)

Aérospatiale SA.321 Super Frelon — France

Sud Aviation responded to a French military requirement for a medium-capacity transport helicopter by designing the SE.3200 Frelon which flew in June 1959. This was enlarged with a long tail boom, a boat hull for water operations and twice the power to become the SE.3210 (later SA.321) Super Frelon which made its first flight on 7th December 1962. In this form it was ordered by the Armée de l'Air and Aéronavale who together received 25 aircraft most of which are still in use in general transport operations and as the SA.321G for ASW duties. Super Frelons were exported to South Africa (16), Iraq (10), Israel (12) and Libya (9) and a number of these are still operational. A batch was also sold to China and a modified version was built there as the Changhe Z-8. Production of the Super Frelon totalled 120 including prototypes. Aérospatiale also tried to sell the civil SA.321J version but this was not successful.

Aérospatiale SA.321G Super Frelon, No.162

Specification	Aérospatiale SA.321G Super Frelon	
Powerplant	Three 1,630 s.h.p. (1,215.3 kW) Turboméca Turmo IIIC6-70 turboshafts	
Dimensions		
Rotor diameter	18.9 m	(62 ft 0 in)
Length	23.03 m	(75 ft 7 in)
Height	4.94 m	(16 ft 2 in)
Performance		
Max speed	275 km/h	(148 kt, 171 mph)
Cruising speed	249 km/h	(135 kt, 155 mph)
Initial climb	400 m/min	(1,312 fpm)
Range	820 km	(442 nm, 509 miles)
Weights		
Max takeoff	13,000 kg	(28,665 lbs)
Useful load	6,388 kg	(14,086 lbs)

Aérospatiale SA.341 Gazelle — France

Sud Aviation's SA.340 light helicopter was required as a replacement for existing Alouette IIs and under Aérospatiale it was developed into the SA.341 Gazelle, the production standard prototype flying on 17th April 1968. The all-metal Gazelle was distinctive in having a shrouded 'fenestron' multi-blade tail rotor. Initial customers were the British forces who received 282 Astazou IIIN-powered Gazelle AH.1, HT.2, HT.3 and HCC.4, which were built by Westland, and the French ALAT who received 340 examples of the SA.341F with the Astazou IIIC engine and the later SA.342M which was a dedicated anti-tank model for the ALAT with the larger Astazou XIVH turboshaft. On this version, anti-tank weapons were mounted on the skids and on external weapons pylons. A civil version, the SA.342L, was exported to the UK, the USA and many other countries. Large overseas military users included Egypt (96), Libya (40), Kuwait (20) and Syria (55). Soko in Yugoslavia also built 132 of the SA.341H Partizan and several SA.342Ms. Production of the Gazelle totalled 1,234.

Aérospatiale SA.341G Gazelle, G-LOYD

Specification	Aérospatiale SA.342M Gazelle	
Powerplant	One 858 s.h.p. (640 kW) Turboméca Astazou XIVH turboshaft	
Dimensions		
Rotor diameter	10.5 m	(34 ft 5 in)
Length	11.97 m	(39 ft 3 in)
Height	3.18 m	(10 ft 5 in)
Performance		
Max speed	264 km/h	(142 kt, 164 mph)
Cruising speed	238 km/h	(128 kt, 148 mph)
Initial climb	510 m/min	(1,670 fpm)
Range	670 km	(361 nm, 416 miles)
Weights		
Max takeoff	1,900 kg	(4,188 lbs)
Useful load	925 kg	(2,039 lbs)

Aérospatiale TB-30 Epsilon — France

To meet an Armée de l'Air specification for a new basic trainer, Aérospatiale's SOCATA subsidiary designed the low-wing tandem two-seat Epsilon based on the TB-10 Tobago but with a slimmer fuselage and retractable tricycle undercarriage. The prototype, with a 300 h.p. Lycoming AEIO-540 fuel-injected piston engine, flew on 22nd December 1979 and French orders were placed for 150 production aircraft with a modified rear fuselage and tail unit and longer-span wings. First deliveries were in 1983 with the final aircraft being handed over late in 1989. Aérospatiale also built four Epsilons, equipped with four underwing armament hardpoints for the Force Aérienne Togolaise and in Portugal OGMA assembled 18 Epsilons for the Portuguese Air Force. Aérospatiale later developed the TB-31 Omega with a 488 s.h.p. Turboméca TP319 turboprop and this flew on 9th November 1989 but has not yet secured any production orders. A development Epsilon has been fitted with the new Morane-Renault MR.300 engine and the production line would be reopened if orders were received for this model.

Aérospatiale TB-30 Epsilon, No.45

Aérospatiale TB-30 Epsilon (Cont.)

Specification	Aérospatiale TB-30 Epsilon	
Powerplant	One 300 h.p. (224 kW) Textron Lycoming AEIO-540-L1B5D piston engine	
Dimensions		
Span	7.92 m	(26 ft 0 in)
Length	7.59 m	(24 ft 11 in)
Height	2.66 m	(8 ft 9 in)
Performance		
Max speed	380 km/h	(205 kt, 236 mph)
Cruising speed	358 km/h	(193 kt, 222 mph)
Initial climb	564 m/min	(1,850 fpm)
Range	1,341 km	(725 nm, 833 miles)
Weights		
Max takeoff	1,250 kg	(2,755 lbs)
Useful load	318 kg	(700 lbs)

Aérospatiale SN-601 Corvette — France

The SN-600 Diplomate small business jet project was initiated by Sud Aviation and Nord Aviation and the first prototype was flown under the Aérospatiale banner on 16th July 1970. The SN-600, which became the Corvette, was a low-wing monoplane with a tricycle undercarriage and twin Pratt & Whitney JT15D turbofans in rear fuselage pods. Some Corvettes were also fitted with optional wingtip fuel tanks. The definitive SN-601 Corvette 100 with a larger fin and longer fuselage flew on 20th December 1972 and the type went into production in 1973 but few orders were received. Aérospatiale was forced to lease early examples to Air France, Air Alpes and TAT as 14-seat commuter aircraft and completed production with the 40th aircraft. The production Corvettes were subsequently sold to various air taxi operators, a few executive users and the governments of Libya and the Central African Republic. By the end of 1998, 32 Corvettes remained in service, mostly in France.

Aérospatiale SN-601 Corvette, EC-DQG

Specification	Aérospatiale SN-601 Corvette	
Powerplant	Two 2,300 lb.s.t. (10.23 kN) Pratt & Whitney JT15D-4 turbofans	
Dimensions		
Span	12.87 m	(42 ft 2 in)
Length	13.83 m	(45 ft 4 in)
Height	4.23 m	(13 ft 10 in)
Performance		
Max speed	760 km/h	(410 kt, 472 mph))
Cruising speed	565 km/h	(305 kt, 351 mph)
Initial climb	914 m/min	(3,000 fpm)
Range	1,470 km	(795 nm, 915 miles)
Weights		
Max takeoff	6,300 kg	(13,890 lbs)
Useful load	2,816 kg	(6,209 lbs)

Aérospatiale GY-80 Horizon — France

The French designer Yves Gardan designed the GY-80 as a private venture and flew a prototype on 21st July 1960. It was an all-metal low-wing four-seat light touring aircraft with a retractable tricycle undercarriage with partially enclosed main units, a swept vertical tail and a choice of 150 h.p. Lycoming O-320-A, 160 h.p. O-320-B or 180 h.p. O-360-A3A engines. Sud Aviation adopted the design for production as the GY-80 Horizon and it was built at their factories at Rochefort and Nantes with the first production machine flying in 1963 and the last of the 267 production run being completed in 1968. The Horizon was successfully exported to more than 20 countries including most European territories and Canada, the United States, New Zealand and South Africa. Over 100 of these remain in service including 14 in the United Kingdom and 60 in France.

Aérospatiale GY-80 Horizon 160, F-BLVR

Specification	Aérospatiale GY-80 Horizon 160	
Powerplant	One 160 h.p. (119.3 kW) Textron Lycoming O-320-B piston engine	
Dimensions		
Span	9.7 m	(31 ft 10 in)
Length	6.64 m	(21 ft 9 in)
Height	2.6 m	(8 ft 6 in)
Performance		
Max speed	235 km/h	(127 kt, 146 mph)
Cruising speed	228 km/h	(123 kt, 142 mph)
Initial climb	201 m/min	(660 fpm)
Range	1,368 km	(743 nm, 855 miles)
Weights		
Max takeoff	1,100 kg	(2,425 lbs)
Useful load	492 kg	(1,085 lbs)

Aérospatiale ST-10 Diplomate
— France

With the GY-80 Horizon light aircraft in full production, Sud Aviation decided to build a new version with higher performance and load capacity. The ST-10 Super Horizon had virtually the same wing but used a much modified fuselage with a larger cabin area and a taller vertical tail with a small ventral fin. The undercarriage was redesigned with the main units retracting inwards with fully enclosing doors. The prototype was flown on 7th November 1967 and Aérospatiale/SOCATA built 54 between 1970 and 1972. Approximately half were exported and these included a batch of six sold to Brazil for the Varig Training School. The name of the production aircraft was changed to 'Provence' but this was later altered to 'Diplomate'. Some 14 aircraft still fly in France together with one example of the stretched ST.60 Rallye 7 which was a much modified version of the Diplomate built only in prototype form.

Aérospatiale ST-10 Diplomate, EI-BUG

Specification	Aérospatiale ST-10 Diplomate	
Powerplant	One 200 h.p. (149.1 kW) Textron Lycoming IO-360-C1B piston engine	
Dimensions		
Span	9.7 m	(31 ft 10 in)
Length	7.26 m	(23 ft 10 in)
Height	2.88 m	(9 ft 5 in)
Performance		
Max speed	280 km/h	(151 kt, 174 mph)
Cruising speed	265 km/h	(143 kt, 165 mph)
Initial climb	306 m/min	(1,003 fpm)
Range	1,385 km	(753 nm, 866 miles)
Weights		
Max takeoff	1,220 kg	(2,690 lbs)
Useful load	497 kg	(1,096 lbs)

Aérospatiale TB-9 Tampico and TB-10 Tobago
— France

In 1975, Aérospatiale's SOCATA division decided to produce a successor to the highly successful Rallye series of light aircraft. Their newly designed TB series of low-wing four-seaters was specified for ease of construction and had a large cabin making the aircraft into a comfortable touring machine. Following a first flight in April 1977 SOCATA put the TB into production in 1978 as the TB-9 Tampico and TB-10 Tobago with 160 h.p. Lycoming O-320-D2A and 180 h.p. Lycoming O-360-A1AD engines respectively. A reduced specification special version for flying clubs and schools was later marketed as the TB-9C Tampico Club and SOCATA subsequently also announced the TB-200 Tobago XL. This model, which first flew on 27th March 1991, was an improved TB-10 with a 200 h.p. Lycoming IO-360-A1B6 engine. In 1999 they altered the range with a number of modifications as the 'Nouvelle Génération', designated TB-9NG, TB-10NG etc. Changes included a higher cabin roof line, reshaped fin, larger baggage door and improved interior. Over 1,350 of the fixed-gear TB series had been built by the end of 2000.

Aérospatiale TB-200 Tobago XL, F-GNHG

Aérospatiale TB-9 Tampico and TB-10 Tobago (Cont.)

Specification	Aérospatiale SOCATA TB-10 Tobago	
Powerplant	One 180 h.p. (134 kW) Textron Lycoming O-360-A1AD piston engine	
Dimensions		
Span	9.76 m	(32 ft 0 in)
Length	7.71 m	(25 ft 3 in)
Height	3.02 m	(9 ft 11 in)
Performance		
Max speed	247 km/h	(133 kt, 153 mph)
Cruising speed	198 km/h	(107 kt, 123 mph)
Initial climb	240 m/min	(790 fpm)
Range	1,275 km	(693 nm, 797 miles)
Weights		
Max takeoff	1,150 kg	(2,535 lbs)
Useful load	450 kg	(992 lbs)

Aérospatiale TB-20 Trinidad NG, F-WWRG

Specification	Aérospatiale SOCATA TB-20 Trinidad	
Powerplant	One 250 h.p. (186 kW) Textron Lycoming IO-540-C4D5D piston engine	
Dimensions		
Span	9.76 m	(32 ft 0 in)
Length	7.71 m	(25 ft 3 in)
Height	2.85 m	(9 ft 4 in)
Performance		
Max speed	310 km/h	(167 kt, 192 mph)
Cruising speed	294 km/h	(160 kt, 184 mph)
Initial climb	385 m/min	(1,260 fpm)
Range	1,640 km	(891 nm, 1,025 miles)
Weights		
Max takeoff	1,400 kg	(3,085 lbs)
Useful load	600 kg	(1,323 lbs)

Aérospatiale TB-20 Trinidad — France

Aérospatiale's SOCATA Tobago four-seat light aircraft had been designed from the outset with growth in mind and an early modification was to fit a retractable undercarriage and a larger engine. The new TB-20 Trinidad had a fuel-injected 250 h.p. Lycoming IO-540-C4D5 piston engine with a variable pitch propeller and later versions could be supplied with de-icing equipment. The first Trinidad was flown on 14th November 1980 and the aircraft became popular as a crew trainer for airline training schools as well as being a capable small business aircraft. Large batches were sold to China for use by the State Aviation College and 22 were delivered to the Israeli Air Force. SOCATA subsequently added the TB-21 Trinidad TC which offered high-altitude cruise performance with a turbocharged Lycoming TIO-540-AB1AD engine. The TB-20 is also expected to be sold with the new Morane-Renault MR.250 powerplant and was upgraded in 1999 with the 'Nouvelle Génération' modifications referred to under the section on the Tampico and Tobago. Over 620 Trinidads have been sold to date.

Aérospatiale TB-20 Trinidad, N397TB

Aérospatiale TBM700 — France

Originally launched as a joint project between Aérospatiale and Mooney, the TBM700 single-turboprop business aircraft was first announced in 1987. It was a low-wing aircraft with a forward two-crew cockpit and a four-/five-seat main cabin with club seating and a rear airstair entry door. Equipped with a retractable tricycle undercarriage it was fitted with a 700 s.h.p. Pratt & Whitney PT6A-64 turbine engine. The first TBM700 was flown at SOCATA's Tarbes factory on 14th July 1988 and American FAA type certification was received in August 1990. Mooney subsequently withdrew from the programme and SOCATA now manufactures and markets the aircraft. A total of 155 had been built by the end of 2000 of which half have been sold in the United States and 16 are operating with the Armée de l'Air as liaison aircraft. Others are in service in Australia, Germany, Spain, Austria, Holland, Indonesia and Canada. The TBM700 is offered as a multi-role platform for photography, mapping, navaid calibration etc. and is also being offered as a convertible light freighter with an additional pilot door and a large port-side freight door and hardened interior.

Aérospatiale TBM.700, N724DM

Specification	Aérospatiale SOCATA TBM700	
Powerplant	One 700 s.h.p. (522 kW) (derated) Pratt & Whitney PT6A-64 turboprop	
Dimensions		
Span	12.68 m	(41 ft 7 in)
Length	10.64 m	(34 ft 11 in)
Height	4.35 m	(14 ft 3 in)
Performance		
Max speed	555 km/h	(300 kt, 345 mph)
Cruising speed	450 km/h	(245 kt, 280 mph)
Initial climb	725 m/min	(2,380 fpm)
Range	2,870 km	(1,560 nm, 1,795 miles)
Weights		
Max takeoff	2,985 kg	(6,578 lbs)
Useful load	1,125 kg	(2,478 lbs)

Aerosport Scamp — USA

The tiny Scamp has been a very popular semi-aerobatic single-seat homebuilt designed by Harris Woods and sold in the form of plans. First flown in 1973, it follows the Aerosport Quail and the Rail which have also flown in some numbers. The Scamp, which involves fairly simple construction techniques, is an all-metal biplane intended for the first-time homebuilder who has limited construction space. It has an open cockpit, fixed tricycle undercarriage and a T-tail. The upper wing is supported by a single pillar in front of the cockpit and normal power is a converted 1600 cc Volkswagen. The prototype Scamp flew on 21st August 1973. Over 1,000 sets of plans were sold and around 100 Scamps have been completed including three in Britain and a modified crop-spraying version, the Scamp-B, which was manufactured in Colombia.

Aerosport Scamp, G-BOOW

Specification	Aerosport Scamp A	
Powerplant	One 60 h.p. (44.5 kW) 1834 cc Volkswagen piston engine	
Dimensions		
Span	5.33 m	(17 ft 6 in)
Length	4.27 m	(14 ft 0 in)
Height	1.69 m	(5 ft 6 in)
Performance		
Max speed	169 km/h	(91 kt, 105 mph)
Cruising speed	145 km/h	(78 kt, 90 mph)
Initial climb	183 m/min	(600 fpm)
Range	200 km	(110 nm, 125 miles)
Weights		
Max takeoff	349 kg	(768 lbs)
Useful load	113 kg	(248 lbs)

Aerosport Woody's Pusher — USA

The Woody's Pusher was designed by the late Harris L. Woods and was inspired by many of the features of the pre-war Curtiss-Wright Junior. It is a parasol-wing monoplane with tandem seating for two, the front cockpit being positioned well ahead of the wing, and is fitted with a fixed tail-wheel undercarriage. The engine, normally a Continental of 65 h.p. to 85 h.p., is fitted in the pusher position on the wing centre section. The Pusher has been marketed as plans and partial kits from 1970 by Aerosport for home construction and the aircraft has a welded steel tube or wooden fuselage and wooden wings with fabric covering. Plans for the design are no longer available but around 100 examples have flown.

Aerosport Woody's Pusher, G-BSFV

Specification	Aerosport Woody's Pusher	
Powerplant	One 75 h.p. (55.9 kW) Teledyne Continental A75 piston engine	
Dimensions		
Span	8.84 m	(29 ft 0 in)
Length	6.22 m	(20 ft 5 in)
Height	2.13 m	(7 ft 0 in)
Performance		
Max speed	158 km/h	(85 kt, 98 mph)
Cruising speed	140 km/h	(76 kt, 87 mph)
Initial climb	183 m/min	(600 fpm)
Range	350 km	(190 nm, 220 miles)
Weights		
Max takeoff	522 kg	(1,150 lbs)
Useful load	237 kg	(523 lbs)

Aérostructure Pipistrelle — France/UK

The Pipistrelle ultralight monoplane was designed by Robert Jacquet in 1981. It is an all-fibreglass aircraft with a front fuselage pod containing the open single-seat cockpit and a pylon structure to mount the wings and a pusher JPX engine. The rear fuselage consists of a slim tailboom with a large V-tail and the Pipistrelle has a fixed tailwheel undercarriage. A small series of 20 Pipistrelles was built in France before the design was taken over by the English company Southdown Aerostructures. They modified three aircraft for British approval but did not build further examples.

Aérostructure Pipistrelle, G-MJTM

Specification	Southdown Aérostructure Pipistrelle 2C	
Powerplant	One 30 h.p. (22.4 kW) JPX PUL-505 piston engine	
Dimensions		
Span	11.2 m	(36 ft 9 in)
Length	5 m	(16 ft 5 in)
Height	1.8 m	(5 ft 11 in)
Performance		
Max speed	100 km/h	(54 kt, 62 mph)
Cruising speed	85 km/h	(46 kt, 53 mph)
Initial climb	113 m/min	(370 fpm)
Range	167 km	(90 nm, 103 miles)
Weights		
Max takeoff	250 kg	(550 lbs)
Useful load	118 kg	(260 lbs)

Aerotec T-23 Uirapuru — Brazil

The Brazilian-built A-122 Uirapuru was produced to fulfil a Brazilian Air Force (FAB) proposal for a primary trainer to replace existing Fokker S-11s and the first aircraft flew on 2nd June 1965. It was a conventional all-metal aircraft with a low wing and fixed tricycle undercarriage, initially powered by a 108 h.p. Lycoming O-235. The definitive T-23 Uirapuru for the FAB had a 160 h.p. Lycoming O-320-B2B and Aerotec, which was newly established to construct the aircraft, was awarded a contract to build 30 (later increased to 70) units. A further 26 Uirapurus were built for Bolivia and Paraguay. Aerotec also completed 24 civil A-122Bs which were delivered to Brazilian flying clubs and several of these are still flying together with a number of the Bolivian and Paraguayan machines. The A-122 was developed into the upgraded 160 h.p. A-132 (YT-17/T-23B) Tangara which flew in 1981 but production of this only amounted to six for the Bolivian Air Force.

Aerotec A-122B Uirapuru, PP-KBG

Specification	Aerotec A-122B Uirapuru	
Powerplant	One 160 h.p. (119.3 kW) Textron Lycoming O-320-B2B piston engine	
Dimensions		
Span	8.5 m	(27 ft 11 in)
Length	6.6 m	(21 ft 8 in)
Height	2.7 m	(8 ft 10 in)
Performance		
Max speed	225 km/h	(122 kt, 140 mph)
Cruising speed	185 km/h	(100 kt, 115 mph)
Initial climb	240 m/min	(787 fpm)
Range	800 km	(435 nm, 500 miles)
Weights		
Max takeoff	840 kg	(1,852 lbs)
Useful load	288 kg	(634 lbs)

Aerotechnik (Evektor) Vivat — Czech Republic

The L-13E Vivat is an all-metal motor glider derived by Aerotechnik (now owned by Evektor) from the successful L-13 Blanik sailplane. The Vivat uses the wing, rear fuselage and tail unit of the Blanik married to a new forward fuselage containing a side-by-side two-seat cockpit and the engine bay. The prototype L-13B had a shoulder-set wing but the XL-113, fitted with a tricycle undercarriage, and the definitive L-13SW had the wing lowered to a centre fuselage position. The L-13SW with a retractable monowheel undercarriage first flew in September, 1989 powered by a Rotax 503 engine. The later L-13SE used an Aerotechnik-built 65 h.p. Walter Mikron IIIAE in-line engine and was later offered as the L-13SDM with a conventional tailwheel undercarriage. A further version with a Limbach L-2000-EO1 engine is designated L-13SDL. Over 600 have been built most of which have been exported to the USA and European countries.

Aerotechnik Vivat L-13SDM, OK-3905

Specification	Aerotechnik Vivat L-13SDM	
Powerplant	One 65 h.p. (48.5 kW) Aerotechnik Mikron IIIAE piston engine	
Dimensions		
Span	16.8 m	(55 ft 1 in)
Length	8.3 m	(27 ft 2 in)
Height	2.3 m	(7 ft 6 in)
Performance		
Max speed	175 km/h	(94 kt, 109 mph)
Cruising speed	160 km/h	(86 kt, 100 mph)
Initial climb	150 m/min	(493 fpm)
Range	500 km	(270 nm, 310 miles)
Weights		
Max takeoff	720 kg	(1,587 lbs)
Useful load	210 kg	(463 lbs)

Agusta A.109 Hirundo and A.119 Koala
— Italy

The A.109 has proved to be not only a highly flexible executive helicopter able to compete commercially with Sikorsky and Bell but also a machine capable of fulfilling a wide range of military roles. First flown on 4th August 1971 the A.109 has capacity for seven passengers and a pilot and is fitted with a retractable tricycle undercarriage and twin coupled Allison 250 turboshafts driving a single main rotor. With deliveries commencing in 1975, the civil A.109A sold well in the United States and the A.109 has become well accepted in the aeromedical role. Some 24 of the A.109EOA armed version have been sold to the Italian Air Force and the Belgian Air Force acquired 46 A.109BAs for anti-tank and scout missions. The A.109C (military A.109CM) has a strengthened transmission and composite main rotor and the latest A.109E Power has a wider cabin, fixed undercarriage, modified tail and 640 s.h.p. PW206C or optional Turboméca Arrius 2K1 turboshafts. The A.119 Koala variant entered production in 1999 and it differs from the standard A.109 in having a single Pratt & Whitney PT6B-37 turboshaft, an open box main cabin to facilitate utility operations and a fixed tricycle undercarriage. Over 450 A.109s have been built to date.

Agusta A.109 Power, G-POWR

Agusta A.119 Koala, I-KOAL

Specification	Agusta A.109 Power	
Powerplant	Two 640 s.h.p. (477 kW) Pratt & Whitney PW206C turboshafts	
Dimensions		
Rotor diameter	11 m	(36 ft 1 in)
Length	11.45 m	(37 ft 7 in)
Height	3.5 m	(11 ft 6 in)
Performance		
Max speed	309 km/h	(168 kt, 193 mph)
Cruising speed	283 km/h	(154 kt, 177 mph)
Initial climb	588 m/min	(1,930 fpm)
Range	964 km	(524 nm, 603 miles)
Weights		
Max takeoff	2,850 kg	(6,284 lbs)
Useful load	1,280 kg	(2,822 lbs)

Agusta A.129 Mangusta and Scorpion
— Italy

To meet an Italian Army requirement issued in 1975, the Mangusta was designed as a state of the art all-weather scout attack helicopter with night operating capability and the ability to carry a wide range of offensive stores. Agusta came up with a tandem-seat layout with heavily stepped cockpits giving the rear-seat crew member excellent visibility. The A.129 has a fixed tailwheel undercarriage and two Piaggio-Rolls Royce Gem turboshafts mounted in pods on either side of the main pylon driving a single four-blade composite rotor through a combining gearbox. All stores are on two external pylons which have two hard points each to carry Hellfire, HOT or TOW-2A anti-tank missiles and a variety of AAMs and rocket pods. The Mangusta prototype flew on 11th September 1983 followed by five further test units and two production batches totalling 60 aircraft for the Italian Air Force. Agusta has launched the A.129 International with full all-weather capability and LHTEC CTS800-2 turboshafts but they have not yet sold any export aircraft. The A.129 Scorpion is an enhanced attack version equipped with Hellfire missiles, a three-barrel 20 mm cannon and enhanced avionics.

Agusta A.129 International, I-INTR

Specification	Agusta A.129 Mangusta	
Powerplant	Two 881 s.h.p. (657 kW) Rolls Royce Mk.1004 turboshafts	
Dimensions		
Rotor diameter	11.9 m	(39 ft 1 in)
Length	12.45 m	(40 ft 10 in)
Height	3.35 m	(11 ft 0 in)
Performance		
Max speed	275 km/h	(149 kt, 172 mph)
Cruising speed	250 km/h	(135 kt, 155 mph)
Initial climb	614 m/min	(2,010 fpm)
Range	565 km	(305 nm, 351 miles)
Weights		
Max takeoff	4,100 kg	(9,040 lbs)
Useful load	1,575 kg	(3,474 lbs)

AIDC AT-3 Tsu Chiang
— Taiwan

A key programme in the strategic development of the Taiwanese aircraft industry, the AT-3 Tsu Chiang was a replacement for the remaining Lockheed T-33s and the Northrop T-38s which were standard equipment in the mid-1970s. Employed on primary jet training, the Tsu Chiang has tandem seating and a pair of Honeywell (Garrett) TFE731-2 turbofans fitted on either side of the fuselage. The XAT-3 prototype was flown on 16th September 1980 and delivery of the first of 60 AT-3 (later redesignated AT-3A) aircraft for the Republic of China Air Force took place in 1984. AIDC completed the last of this order in the spring of 1990. A further ground attack version, the AT-3B, was devised with four wing hardpoints, a centreline stores pylon and a belly ordnance bay. Some 20 AT-3s were converted and AIDC also flew two prototypes of a proposed air superiority version, the A-3, but this was not built in quantity.

AIDC AT-3 Tsu Chiang, 0862 (RoCAF)

Specification	AIDC AT-3A Tsu Chiang	
Powerplant	Two 3,500 lb.s.t. (15.57 kN) Honeywell TFE731-2-2L turbofans	
Dimensions		
Span	10.46 m	(34 ft 4 in)
Length	12.9 m	(42 ft 4 in)
Height	4.36 m	(14 ft 4 in)
Performance		
Max speed	899 km/h	(485 kt, 558 mph)
Cruising speed	880 km/h	(475 kt, 546 mph)
Initial climb	3,080 m/min	(10,100 fpm)
Range	2,275 km	(1,236 nm, 1,422 miles)
Weights		
Max takeoff	7,940 kg	(17,508 lbs)
Useful load	4,085 kg	(9,007 lbs)

AIDC Ching Kuo, 77-8001

AIDC IDF Ching Kuo
— Taiwan

With a well-developed aircraft manufacturing industry in place, Taiwan launched a plan in 1982 to replace its existing F-104 fleet with a modern interceptor. With technical help from American companies including General Dynamics, AIDC designed the Ching Kuo. This advanced fighter has a highly tapered straight wing incorporating large inboard leading-edge extensions and is powered by two locally built Honeywell TFE1042 turbofans. It has been produced in single- and tandem two-seat versions and has a digital fly-by-wire control system. Armament consists of a single M61A Vulcan cannon fitted in the port wing root and wingtip-mounted Sky Sword AAMs. There are four underwing hardpoints and a fuselage centreline mounting all of which can carry a mixed load of up to 8,600 lbs of rockets bombs or fuel tanks. AIDC have built 102 single-seat and 28 two-seat Ching Kuos which are now in service.

Specification	AIDC IDF Ching Kuo	
Powerplant	Two 6,300 lb.s.t. (28 kN) Honeywell TFE1042-70 turbofans with reheat	
Dimensions		
Span	8.53 m	(28 ft 0 in)
Length	14.22 m	(46 ft 7 in)
Height	4.72 m	(15 ft 6 in)
Performance		
Max speed	1,298 km/h	(700 kt, 805 mph)
Cruising speed	1,012 km/h	(550 kt, 635 mph)
Range (est)	555 km	(300 nm, 345 miles)
Weights		
Max takeoff	12,250 kg	(27,011 lbs)
Useful load	5,773 kg	(12,729 lbs)

Air Light Wild Thing
— Romania/Germany

Air Light is marketing the Wild Thing light aircraft in Europe. The Wild Thing is based on the Murphy Rebel and is a strut-braced high-wing aircraft of all-metal construction and with a side-by-side two-seat cabin. The wings are foldable for storage and the Wild Thing has a fixed tailwheel undercarriage as standard, but can be fitted with tricycle gear. It is built by Aerostar in Romania and sold in Europe in the ultralight category. The standard engine is the 80 h.p. Jabiru but the Wild Thing can also be supplied with a Hirth F.30 engine. Over 50 aircraft had been built at the end of 1999.

Air Light Wild Thing

Specification	Air Light Wild Thing	
Powerplant	One 80 h.p. (59.7 kW) Jabiru piston engine	
Dimensions		
Span	9.2 m	(30 ft 2 in)
Length	6.9 m	(22 ft 8 in)
Height	1.98 m	(6 ft 6 in)
Performance		
Max speed	215 km/h	(116 kt, 134 mph)
Cruising speed	184 km/h	(100 kt, 115 mph)
Initial climb	500 m/min	(1,640 fpm)
Range	900 km	(489 nm, 563 miles)
Weights		
Max takeoff	450 kg	(992 lbs)
Useful load	177 kg	(391 lbs)

Air Tractor — USA

The Air Tractor was designed in 1972 by Leland Snow following his already successful Snow S-2 crop sprayers and it followed a similar low-wing configuration with a fixed tailwheel undercarriage. The initial AT-300 had a single-seat enclosed cockpit, fixed tailwheel undercarriage and a 320 USG hopper mounted between the cockpit and the engine firewall. It was fitted with a 450 h.p. Pratt & Whitney R-985 radial piston engine and first flew in September 1973 with first deliveries the following year. Later versions included the AT-301 (600 h.p. R-1340) and AT-302 (Lycoming LTP101 turboprop). Air Tractor then developed several variants with increasingly large airframes and with various combinations of hopper size and, generally, turboprop engines. These included the AT-400 with a 400 USG hopper, slimmer fuselage, larger wing and 680 s.h.p. PT6A-15AG turboprop, the AT-400A with a 320 USG hopper and 550 s.h.p. PT6A-20 and the AT-402 based on the AT-400 with a longer-span wing. The AT-501 is a larger two-seat variant with a 500 USG hopper and a 600 h.p. R-1340-S3H1-G piston engine and the equivalent turboprop version is the AT-502 with the PT6A-15AG. The largest Air Tractor is the AT-802 which has an 800 USG capacity tank for crop spraying or fire bombing and has two seats or, as the AT-802A, a single crew cockpit and is normally powered by a 1,350 s.h.p. PT6A-67AG turboprop. Over 1,800 Air Tractors had been built and were in worldwide operation by the end of 1999.

Specification	Air Tractor AT-502	
Powerplant	One 680 s.h.p. (507 kW) Pratt & Whitney PT6A-15AG turboprop	
Dimensions		
Span	15.24 m	(50 ft 0 in)
Length	9.9 m	(32 ft 6 in)
Height	2.99 m	(9 ft 9 in)
Performance		
Max speed	290 km/h	(156 kt, 180 mph)
Cruising speed	253 km/h	(136 kt, 157 mph)
Initial climb	232 m/min	(760 fpm)
Range	800 km	(435 nm, 500 miles)
Weights		
Max takeoff	4,175 kg	(9,206 lbs)
Useful load	2,305 kg	(5,083 lbs)

Air Tractor AT-301, VH-FAA

Air & Space 18A — USA

The precursor of the Air & Space 18A, the Umbaugh U-18 autogyro, was built by Fairchild and first flown in 1959. It was a tandem two-seat machine with a triple fin tail and a fixed tricycle undercarriage. It had a three-bladed main rotor and used a pusher 180 h.p. Lycoming O-360 engine for forward propulsion positioned behind the main rotor pylon. Production by Air & Space Manufacturing commenced in 1965 and 67 were completed before the company went out of business and over 40 of these are still in existence although many are not currently active. Further development of the 18A was taken over by Farrington Aircraft who have designed a modified kit-built version. The Farrington Twinstar has the same tandem seating, tricycle undercarriage and pusher engine as the 18A but the cockpit is open and the tailplane and twin fins are attached directly to the fuselage pod. The aircraft is fitted with dual controls. Construction is of steel tube with a moulded composite fuselage shell and the Twinstar has a two-bladed main rotor. The first Twinstar flew in 1991 and five were flying in the United States by early 1999.

Air Tractor AT-802A, VH-ODZ

Air & Space 18A, N6155S

Farrington Twinstar, N711FS

Specification	Air and Space 18A	
Powerplant	One 180 h.p. (134.2 kW) Textron Lycoming O-360 piston engine	
Dimensions		
Rotor diameter	10.67 m	(35 ft 0 in)
Length	6.04 m	(19 ft 10 in)
Height	2.82 m	(9 ft 3 in)
Performance		
Max speed	177 km/h	(96 kt, 110 mph)
Cruising speed	160 km/h	(87 kt, 100 mph)
Initial climb	216 m/min	(710 fpm)
Range	480 km	(261 nm, 300 miles)
Weights		
Max takeoff	816 kg	(1,800 lbs)
Useful load	182 kg	(400 lbs)

Airbus A300 — International

The A300 was the first product of Airbus Industrie – a consortium of Aérospatiale, Deutsche Airbus, British Aerospace and CASA. A wide-body airliner of conventional low-wing layout with twin turbofans in underwing pods, the prototype A300B1 was flown on 28th October 1972. The definitive short-haul A300B2 had a longer fuselage for 345 passengers. Manufactured in Hamburg, Hatfield and Madrid, the A300 is assembled at Toulouse and the first delivery was made to Air France in May 1974. A variety of General Electric CF6-50C and Pratt & Whitney JT9D-59A turbofan engines in the 49,000 to 59,000 lb.s.t. (218 kN to 262 kN) power range are customer-specified for the A300. The A300B4 is a medium haul variant with an additional centre section tank; the A300B4-600 has a 21-inch fuselage stretch raising capacity to 361 passengers. The A300B4-605R long-range high gross weight variant has extra tailplane tanks, a computerised trimming system and 61,500 lb.s.t. CF6-80C2A5 engines. Cargo variants are the A300C4 and long-range A300F4-605R together with the equivalent A300C4-605R and A300C4-203 Combi models. Over 490 A300s have been built.

Specification	Airbus A300B4-605R	
Powerplant	Two 61,500 lb.s.t. (273.5 kN) General Electric CF6-80C2A5 turbofans	
Dimensions		
Span	44.84 m	(147 ft 1 in)
Length	54.1 m	(177 ft 5 in)
Height	16.52 m	(54 ft 2 in)
Performance		
Max speed	890 km/h	(480 kt, 553 mph)
Cruising speed	865 km/h	(470 kt, 540 mph)
Takeoff field length	2,280 m	(7,480 ft)
Range	7,500 km	(4,076 nm, 4,688 miles)
Weights		
Max takeoff	170,500 kg	(375,953 lbs)
Useful load	80,327 kg	(177,121 lbs)

Airbus A300B4-622R, HS-TAK

Airbus A300 Beluga/Super Transport — International

An essential component of the multi-site production of the Airbus airliners is the transport of oversize airframe sections around Europe. With the Boeing/Aero Spacelines Super Guppies used for the task reaching the end of their useful lives, Airbus decided to build a replacement based on the airframe of the A300B4. The A300B4-608ST Super Transport, otherwise known as the Beluga, has the upper fuselage of the A300 removed and replaced by a bulbous upper lobe. To allow the fitment of a full-size hinged cargo door at the front of the load space, the crew cockpit is repositioned at the front of the lower fuselage section. The Beluga also has an enlarged vertical tail and additional finlets on the tailplane. Four Belugas have been built by SATIC (Super Airbus Transport International) for use by Airbus Industrie and it is intended that a further aircraft will be built for on-demand commercial oversize charter work.

Airbus A300B4-608ST Super Transport, F-GSTC

Specification	Airbus (SATIC) A300B4-608ST Super Transport	
Powerplant	Two 59,000 lb.s.t. (262.5 kN) General Electric CF6-80C2A8 turbofans	
Dimensions		
Span	44.84 m	(147 ft 1 in)
Length	56.16 m	(184 ft 3 in)
Height	17.25 m	(56 ft 7 in)
Performance		
Cruising speed	780 km/h	(420 kt, 485 mph)
Takeoff field length	2,280 m	(7,480 ft)
Range	1,665 km	(905 nm, 1,041 miles)
Weights		
Max takeoff	150,000 kg	(330,750 lbs)
Useful load	45,500 kg	(100,328 lbs)

Airbus A310 – International

After the successful launch of the Airbus A300, Airbus Industrie produced a new smaller-capacity short-haul version, the A310. The A300 fuselage was shortened by nearly 23 feet and the A310 had a smaller wing which was, essentially, a new design. This resulted in an aircraft with 280-passenger capacity, again powered by Pratt & Whitney JT9D-7 or General Electric CF6-80 engines of various thrust outputs. Airbus flew the A310 prototype on 3rd April 1982. The basic passenger version is the A310-200 and the first A310-203s with CF6-80A3 turbofans were delivered to Lufthansa and Swissair in March 1983. The A310-300 series is an extended range variant with extra tailplane fuel tanks and computerised fuel management. As the A300-324ET, these aircraft are approved for North Atlantic ETOPS operations. Over 250 A310s have been built for large operators including Federal Express with A310-203(F) freighters, Singapore Airlines and Emirates Airlines. The A310 is also in military service, particularly with the Canadian armed forces as the CC-150 Polaris.

Airbus A310-222, 9V-STE

Specification	Airbus A310-200	
Powerplant	Two 48,000 lb.s.t. (213.5 kN) Pratt & Whitney JT9D-7R4D1 turbofans	
Dimensions		
Span	43.89 m	(144 ft 0 in)
Length	46.66 m	(153 ft 1 in)
Height	15.8 m	(51 ft 10 in)
Performance		
Cruising speed	973 km/h	(529 kt, 608 mph)
Takeoff field length	1,860 m	(6,100 ft)
Range	6,759 km	(3,673 nm, 4,224 miles)
Weights		
Max takeoff	142,000 kg	(313,110 lbs)
Useful load	61,984 kg	(136,675 lbs)

Airbus A319, A320 and A321 — International

To compete with the Boeing 737 and DC-9 in the short-haul market, Airbus launched the A320 project in 1980. A brand-new design, the A320 was a conventional low-wing aircraft with up to 180 passenger seats and fly-by-wire control systems. The cockpit was designed from the outset with a six-screen EFIS and side sticks in place of the conventional control column. The first CFM56-powered A320-111 flew on 22nd February 1987 with the first delivery to Air France in March 1988. The A320-200 is a longer-range version with wingtip winglets and some A320s are powered by the IAE V2500 series turbofans. The A319, which flew on 28th August 1995, is a maximum 145-seat version with a 12 ft 3 in shorter fuselage and the A321 which made its maiden flight on 12th December 1996 is an A320 with a 22 ft 9 in fuselage stretch to carry 220 passengers. The A321-200 is a long-range version. Production of the A320, A319 and A321 had passed 1,300 by the end of 2000.

Airbus A320-231, LZ-ABB

Airbus A321-111, F-WWID (I-BIXU)

Specification	Airbus A320-200	
Powerplant	Two 26,500 lb.s.t. (117.9 kN) CFM International CFM56-5A3 turbofans	
Dimensions		
Span	33.9 m	(111 ft 3 in)
Length	37.57 m	(123 ft 3 in)
Height	11.8 m	(38 ft 8 in)
Performance		
Cruising speed	949 km/h	(516 kt, 593 mph)
Takeoff field length	2,336 m	(7,665 ft)
Range	5,000 km	(2,717 nm, 3,125 miles)
Weights		
Max takeoff	73,500 kg	(162,068 lbs)
Useful load	31,720 kg	(69,943 lbs)

Airbus A330 and A340 — International

The long-range market dominated by Boeing with the 747 and the 767-300 was addressed by Airbus with the A330/A340 design. Based on the A300 with a 32 ft 10 in fuselage stretch, FBW systems, an EFIS cockpit and a redesigned wing with wingtip winglets, the new aircraft was offered with either two engines (Rolls Royce Trent, Pratt & Whitney PW4000 or GE CF6) as the A330-300 or with four engines (normally CFM56) as the A340-200. Maximum A330-300 capacity is 440 passengers but a short-fuselage A330-200 carries 406 passengers. The A340-200, with 420 passenger capacity, has a 14 ft shorter fuselage but longer range than the A330, the A340-300 version has a small stretch to accommodate an extra 20 passengers and the A340-500/600 are new stretched versions with 440 passenger-loads. The A330 prototype flew on 2nd November 1992 followed by the A340 on 25th October 1996. Major airlines using the two types include Thai Airways International, Cathay Pacific, LTU, Malaysian, Garuda and Korean Air (A330); Virgin Atlantic, Gulf Air, Lufthansa, Air France, Air Canada and Sabena (A340). Approximately 340 of the two models had been built by the end of 2000.

Airbus A330-200, G-MLJL

Airbus A340-311, G-VBUS

Specification	Airbus A340-200	
Powerplant	Four 32,500 lb.s.t. (144.6 kN) CFM International CFM56-5C3 turbofans	
Dimensions		
Span	60.3 m	(197 ft 10 in)
Length	59.39 m	(194 ft 10 in)
Height	16.74 m	(54 ft 11 in)
Performance		
Cruising speed	999 km/h	(538 kt, 624 mph)
Range	13,800 km	(7,500 nm, 8,625 miles)
Weights		
Max takeoff	257,000 kg	(566,575 lbs)
Useful load	133,915 kg	(295,283 lbs)

Aircraft Designs Inc. Stallion — USA

Typical of the technically advanced designs available to kit builders is the Stallion, designed by Martin Hollman of Aircraft Designs Inc. of Monterey, California. The cantilever high-wing Stallion resembles the Cessna 210 and has a welded steel tube frame to give structural strength to the moulded-glass/carbon-fibre body shell. The wings are the same as those of the Lancair ES, as is the horizontal tail. The retractable undercarriage, again a Lancair IV component, has main units which rotate backwards into wells in the rear fuselage. The Stallion is a four-seater with removable rear seats for carriage of bulky loads and is fitted with a port-side split-entry door and a large double door giving full cabin access on the starboard side. The prototype first flew on 19th June 1994 powered by a 280 h.p. Teledyne Continental IO-550-G with a three-blade constant-speed propeller.

Aircraft Designs Stallion, N408S

Specification	Aircraft Designs Stallion	
Powerplant	One 280 h.p. (209 kW) Teledyne Continental IO-550-G piston engine	
Dimensions		
Span	10.66 m	(35 ft 0 in)
Length	7.47 m	(24 ft 6 in)
Height	2.74 m	(9 ft 0 in)
Performance		
Max speed	435 km/h	(234 kt, 270 mph)
Cruising speed	418 km/h	(226 kt, 260 mph)
Initial climb	457 m/min	(1,500 fpm)
Range	2,095 km	(1,139 nm, 1,309 miles)
Weights		
Max takeoff	1,451 kg	(3,200 lbs)
Useful load	612 kg	(1,350 lbs)

Aircraft Hydroforming Bushmaster 2000 — USA

The Bushmaster is a modernised version of the well-known prewar Ford 4-AT Tri-Motor. It was designed by the originator of the Ford, William B. Stout, and is substantially a new aircraft despite its external similarity to the Ford. First flown in 1966, the Bushmaster has a high wing and a square-section fuselage covered with corrugated aluminium panels. Two of the three fully cowled Pratt & Whitney R-985 radial engines are mounted on struts outboard of the wing root and the Bushmaster has a fixed tailwheel undercarriage. It is intended as either a general-utility freighter for which it is fitted with a strengthened floor and a port-side cargo door or as a 15-passenger transport. Two aircraft were completed and both are currently active on sightseeing work in the United States.

Bushmaster 2000, N750RW

Specification	Aircraft Hydroforming Bushmaster 2000	
Powerplant	Three 450 h.p. (335.5 kW) Pratt & Whitney R-985-AN-14B piston engines	
Dimensions		
Span	23.72 m	(77 ft 10 in)
Length	15.09 m	(49 ft 6 in)
Height	4.19 m	(13 ft 9 in)
Performance		
Max speed	209 km/h	(113 kt, 130 mph)
Cruising speed	185 km/h	(100 kt, 115 mph)
Initial climb	244 m/min	(800 fpm)
Range	1,125 km	(611 nm, 703 miles)
Weights		
Max takeoff	5,670 kg	(12,500 lbs)
Useful load	2,268 kg	(5,000 lbs)

Aircraft Spruce One Design — USA

The International Aerobatic Club (IAC), has established a 'one design' class aimed at making competition aerobatics accessible to the ordinary aerobatic enthusiast who would compete in one standard aircraft. This formula led to Dan Rihn designing the DR-107 One Design in 1992 and the prototype flew in August 1993. The very small single-seat One Design has a low wing which is straight and of equal taper with a symmetrical aerofoil. It has a fixed spring-steel undercarriage and is built of tube and fabric with some aluminium cladding. With almost full span ailerons and a 160 h.p. Lycoming AEI0-320 engine it provides performance to equal the Sukhoi Su-26 Extra and other modern production light aerobatic aircraft. The One Design will be built by amateur constructors from plans sold by Aircraft Spruce and Specialty and it is expected that future examples will use a variety of Powerplants of up to 200 horsepower.

Aircraft Spruce One Design, N107FP

Specification	Aircraft Spruce DR-107 One Design	
Powerplant	One 160 h.p. (119.3 kW) Textron Lycoming AEIO-320D piston engine	
Dimensions		
Span	5.9 m	(19 ft 6 in)
Length	5.2 m	(17 ft 0 in)
Height	1.4 m	(4 ft 6 in)
Performance		
Max speed	294 km/h	(160 kt, 184 mph)
Cruising speed	256 km/h	(139 kt, 160 mph)
Initial climb	609 m/min	(2,000 fpm)
Range	600 km	(326 nm, 375 miles)
Weights		
Max takeoff	523 kg	(1,150 lbs)
Useful load	186 kg	(410 lbs)

Airtech (CASA/IPTN) CN-235 and CN-295 — Spain/Indonesia

Airtech was a joint company formed in 1982 by CASA and IPTN to develop the CN-235 medium transport. It was larger than the earlier C-212 Aviocar with a circular section fuselage incorporating a rear loading ramp and external fairings to accommodate the fully retractable undercarriage. The majority of the 155 aircraft built on the Spanish and Indonesian production lines have been sold to military users as the CN-235M (known as the Tetuko in Indonesia). These include the air forces of Chile, France, Spain, Indonesia, Ireland and Saudi Arabia. Aircraft for the Turkish Air Force are being licence-built in Turkey. Civil aircraft, with 44 seats, have been sold to Austral and Binter Canarias. The Spanish prototype flew on 11th November 1983 and initial production CN-235-10 aircraft had General Electric CT7-7A engines. The later CN-235-100 has larger CT7-9C turboprops. The CN-235-200 has a strengthened airframe, modified wing and increased fuel load and the CN-235-300 has a glass cockpit, in-flight refuelling and improved pressurisation. A maritime patrol variant, designated CN-235MPA, has been sold to Brunei, Indonesia and Spain. CASA has also developed the CN-295 independently from Airtech. This aircraft, which first flew on 28th November 1997 and is on order for the Spanish Air Force, has a 9 ft 8 in fuselage stretch giving a 50% increase in freight capacity, Pratt & Whitney PW127G engines and six-blade propellers.

CASA CN-235M-100, CNA-MF

CASA CN-295, EC-296

Specification	Airtech CN-235-100	
Powerplant	Two 1,750 s.h.p. (1,305 kW) General Electric CT7-9C turboprops	
Dimensions		
Span	25.8 m	(84 ft 8 in)
Length	21.4 m	(70 ft 2 in)
Height	8.18 m	(26 ft 10 in)
Performance		
Max speed	445 km/h	(240 kt, 276 mph)
Cruising speed	423 km/h	(230 kt, 265 mph)
Initial climb	465 m/min	(1,525 fpm)
Range	835 km	(454 nm, 522 miles)
Weights		
Max takeoff	15,100 kg	(33,296 lbs)
Useful load	5,300 kg	(11,687 lbs)

AISA I-11B Peque — Spain

The attractive little I-11B Peque was produced in the 1950s by Aeronautica Industrial SA as a civilian club trainer and as a basic trainer for the Spanish Air Force. The prototype I-11, which flew in 1950, had a tricycle undercarriage but the definitive I-11B was fitted with fixed tailwheel gear. The low-wing Peque was of all-wood construction with ply skinning and had side-by-side seating for two under a blister canopy. AISA commenced deliveries in 1954 to fulfil a 125 aircraft military order and a further 81 aircraft were built for civil purchasers. In standard form, the I-11B was VFR-equipped but later examples had a full blind-flying panel for instrument training. In service with the Spanish Air Force, the I-11B was designated L.8C and many of these aircraft were sold to civil users during the 1970s. Many of the I-11Bs have now been withdrawn from use but around 20 are still active in Spain.

AISA I-11B Peque, EC-BUY

Specification	AISA I-11B Peque	
Powerplant	One 90 h.p. (67.1 kW) Teledyne Continental C90 piston engine	
Dimensions		
Span	9.34 m	(30 ft 7 in)
Length	6.47 m	(21 ft 3 in)
Height	1.9 m	(6 ft 3 in)
Performance		
Max speed	199 km/h	(108 kt, 124 mph)
Cruising speed	176 km/h	(96 kt, 110 mph)
Initial climb	220 m/min	(725 fpm)
Range	640 km	(347 nm, 398 miles)
Weights		
Max takeoff	670 kg	(1,475 lbs)
Useful load	250 kg	(550 lbs)

AISA I-115 — Spain

AISA designed the I-115 aerobatic primary trainer for the Spanish Air Force and this made its first flight on 20th June 1952. Externally similar to the DH Chipmunk, the I-115 was initially designated E.6 in military use but this was later changed to E.9. The tandem two-seat cockpit was equipped with dual controls, a full blind-flying panel and a sectional sliding canopy. The aircraft was fitted with a fixed tailwheel undercarriage and the tapered straight wing had slotted flaps. As with its sister aircraft, the I-11B, the I-115 was of all-wood monocoque construction and was powered by a 150 h.p. ENMA Tigre in-line piston engine although a few were fitted with a 145 h.p. de Havilland Gipsy Major and some aircraft have been fitted with a 190 h.p. Lycoming O-435-A. Some 450 examples of the I-115 were delivered and many were later civilianised. Nineteen are believed to be still active with flying clubs and private owners in Spain.

AISA I-115, EC-DEO

Specification	AISA I-115	
Powerplant	One 150 h.p. (111.8 kW) ENMA Tigre G-IV-B piston engine	
Dimensions		
Span	9.54 m	(31 ft 3 in)
Length	7.35 m	(24 ft 1 in)
Height	2.1 m	(6 ft 10 in)
Performance		
Max speed	240 km/h	(129 kt, 149 mph)
Cruising speed	204 km/h	(110 kt, 127 mph)
Initial climb	225 m/min	(738 fpm)
Range	880 km	(478 nm, 550 miles)
Weights		
Max takeoff	900 kg	(1,985 lbs)
Useful load	279 kg	(614 lbs)

Akrotech G-200, G-202 and CAP222 — USA/France

The G-200 is an unlimited single-seat aerobatic monoplane designed by Richard Giles to offer high performance while using a relatively small powerplant. First flown on 7th March 1994, it is constructed entirely from carbon fibre and is very light with a gross weight of 1,000 lbs and powered by a 200 h.p. Textron Lycoming AEIO-360 engine. The wing has a swept leading edge and is fitted with vortex generators to improve low-speed handling. The aircraft is sold as a kit by Akrotech and more than 18 were flying in the United States at the end of 1999. In December 1995, Akrotech flew the first G-202 which is a stretched two-seat version of the G-200, still powered by a 200 h.p. IO-360 engine and also sold in kit form. The G-202 has been adopted by CAP Aviation in France and is being sold as the CAP222 with a wing slightly modified to incorporate the wing section used on the CAP232 competition aerobatic aircraft.

Akrotech G-202, N101PZ

Specification	Akrotech G-202	
Powerplant	One 200 h.p. (149 kW) Textron Lycoming IO-360 piston engine	
Dimensions		
Span	6.71 m	(22 ft 0 in)
Length	6.05 m	(19 ft 10 in)
Height	1.6 m	(5 ft 2 in)
Performance		
Max speed	407 km/h	(220 kt, 253 mph)
Cruising speed	328 km/h	(175 kt, 203 mph)
Initial climb	760 m/min	(2,493 fpm)
Range	1,450 km	(788 nm, 906 miles)
Weights		
Max takeoff	725 kg	(1,600 lbs)
Useful load	295 kg	(650 lbs)

Alberta Aerospace Phoenix Fanjet — Canada

The Promavia Jet Squalus, a side-by-side two-seat jet trainer, was designed in Italy by Stelio Frati's General Avia company and flown on 30th April 1987 with a Garrett TFE76 turbofan engine. After much development and unsuccessful attempts to sell the design to various air forces and a failed bid for the USAF JPATS competition, the Jet Squalus project has been acquired by Alberta Aerospace who are developing it as a jet trainer for civilian airline flying schools (the SigmaJet) and as a four-seat business aircraft (the MagnaJet). The main modifications to convert the original Jet Squalus to a four-seater include fitting wing tanks in place of the fuselage fuel tank, extending the wings and extending the existing cabin rearwards to provide two passenger seats. At the end of 2000 the SigmaJet was being tested using the original Jet Squalus prototype powered by a Williams FJ44 engine.

Alberta Aerospace SigmaJet, N112SQ

Specification	Alberta Aerospace SigmaJet	
Powerplant	One 1,600 lb.s.t. (7.1 kN) Williams-Rolls FJ44-1A turbofan	
Dimensions		
Span	10.7 m	(35 ft 2 in)
Length	9.35 m	(30 ft 8 in)
Height	3.6 m	(11 ft 9 in)
Performance		
Max speed	585 km/h	(315 kt, 364 mph)
Cruising speed	485 km/h	(261 kt, 300 mph)
Initial climb	720 m/min	(2,360 fpm)
Range	1,325 km	(720 nm, 828 miles)
Weights		
Max takeoff	2,313 kg	(5,100 lbs)
Useful load	767 kg	(1,692 lbs)

Alexander (AMI) Eaglerock — USA

Designed by Alexander Aircraft Company, the Eaglerock biplane appeared in 1925. Built of tube and fabric with power from a Curtiss OX-5 engine, it had two tandem cockpits accommodating four people and long-span wings providing good stability. Several wing options were offered including the Short Wing, the Long Wing and the Combo Wing (with a long upper and short lower wing). The A-series Eaglerocks introduced in 1928 had a new upper wing centre section and were powered by various engines including the J-5 Whirlwind (Model A-1), OX-5 (A-2), 150 or 180 h.p. Hisso (A-4 and A-5) and the 140 h.p. Comet radial (A-12). Nearly 1,000 Eaglerocks had been built by 1931 when Alexander Aircraft ceased operation and transferred the business to Aircraft Mechanics Inc. (AMI). Some 18 Eaglerocks are currently registered in the USA including one active Model A-1 with a Wright J-5 engine.

Alexander Eaglerock A-1

Specification	Alexander Eaglerock A-1	
Powerplant	One 220 h.p. (164 kW) Wright J-5 Whirlwind piston engine	
Dimensions		
Span	11.2 m	(36 ft 8 in)
Length	7.3 m	(23 ft 11 in)
Height	3 m	(9 ft 10 in)
Performance		
Max speed	202 km/h	(110 kt, 126 mph)
Cruising speed	173 km/h	(94 kt, 108 mph)
Initial climb	329 m/min	(1,080 fpm)
Range	805 km	(435 nm, 500 miles)
Weights		
Max takeoff	1,130 kg	(2,491 lbs)
Useful load	357 kg	(786 lbs)

Alfa SL-A — Russia

The SL-A, marketed by the Russian company Alpha-M, is a two-/three-seat light aircraft designed by the Russian Interavia design organisation as the I-1L (also named SL-90 Leshii) in 1988 and first flown in February 1991. Alpha-M has been selling the SL-A and also introduced a version as the Alfa A-211 for the American market. The all-metal SL-A was sold as a factory-complete aircraft or as a kit and is built by LMZ factory (part of MiG-MAPO) and by the Bulgarian company Aviotechnica. It is a lightweight aircraft with a forward-swept strut-braced high wing and a spring-steel tailwheel undercarriage. The extensively glazed cabin has a rear upward-opening hatch for loading baggage or cargo. A choice of powerplants can be fitted including the three-cylinder 110 h.p. M-3 radial, the 140 h.p. LOM M332A or various American horizontally opposed engines including the 125 h.p. Teledyne Continental IO-240. It is believed that over 50 aircraft have been built to date although many remain unflown and unsold at the Moscow factory.

Alfa (Interavia) I-1L, N677A

Specification	LMZ Alpha-M SL-A	
Powerplant	One 140 h.p. (104.4 kW) LOM M332A piston engine	
Dimensions		
Span	10 m	(32 ft 10 in)
Length	6.4 m	(21 ft 0 in)
Height	2.8 m	(9 ft 2 in)
Performance		
Max speed	160 km/h	(86 kt, 99 mph)
Cruising speed	140 km/h	(75 kt, 87 mph)
Initial climb	192 m/min	(630 fpm)
Range	750 km	(405 nm, 466 miles)
Weights		
Max takeoff	750 kg	(1,652 lbs)
Useful load	250 kg	(550 lbs)

Alpla AVo.68V Samburo — Austria

The Samburo is a low-wing motor glider designed by Prof. Wernher Vogel and flown initially as the AVo.60 with a 60 h.p. Limbach SL.1700EA engine. Of wood and fabric construction, the Samburo has a side-by-side two seat cockpit enclosed by a bubble canopy and is fitted with a monowheel undercarriage with outrigger stabilising wheels. Production of the AVo.68V, which had foldable outer wings and a 68 h.p. Limbach SL.1700E1 engine was undertaken by Alpla-Werke in 1977 and 29 had been completed when production ceased in 1979. Variants of the basic design included the AVo.68S-2000 (Limbach L-2000EC) and AVo.68V-2000 (Limbach L.2000E-01) and some Samburos have been built with conventional tailwheel undercarriages. The Samburo was relaunched in 1999 by the German company, Nitsche Flugzeugbau with a wider cabin, conventional or monowheel undercarriage and other improvements as the AVo.68R-80 (80 h.p. Rotax 912A3), AVo.68R-100 (100 h.p. Rotax.912FS3) and AVo.68R-115 (115 h.p. Rotax 914F3).

AVo.68S Samburo, HB-2039

Specification	Nitsche AVo.68R-100 Samburo	
Powerplant	One 100 h.p. (73.5 kW) Rotax 912FS3 piston engine	
Dimensions		
Span	16.68 m	(54 ft 8 in)
Length	7.6 m	(24 ft 11 in)
Height	1.78 m	(5 ft 10 in)
Performance		
Max speed	215 km/h	(116 kt, 134 mph)
Cruising speed	180 km/h	(97 kt, 112 mph)
Initial climb	246 m/min	(807 fpm)
Range	1,000 km	(543 nm, 625 miles)
Weights		
Max takeoff	730 kg	(1,610 lbs)
Useful load	200 kg	(441 lbs)

Alvarez Polliwagen — USA

Designed by Joe Alvarez in California, the Polliwagen is a low-wing side-by-side two-seat sporting aircraft of all-GRP construction and fitted with a retractable tricycle undercarriage. It was first flown in July 1977 powered by a Revmaster 2100D engine. The Polliwagen has a complex flap system and a wing developed from sailplane technology. It is fitted with wingtip fuel tanks and has a very capacious cabin enclosed by a large clear-view canopy opened via a scissor-action mechanism. The Polliwagen is marketed in the form of plans accompanied by a number of major component kits. The PW.235 Supernova is a higher-powered version with a 115 h.p. Lycoming O-235 engine and other eligible powerplants include the 100 h.p. Continental O-200, and 150 h.p. Lycoming O-320. A number of Polliwagens are flying in the USA and examples have also been built in Switzerland and Austria.

Alvarez Polliwagen PW235 Supernova, OE-CHE

Specification	Alvarez Polliwagen	
Powerplant	One 75 h.p. (56 kW) Revmaster 2100D turbocharged piston engine	
Dimensions		
Span	7.92 m	(26 ft 0 in)
Length	4.88 m	(16 ft 0 in)
Height	1.7 m	(5 ft 7 in)
Performance		
Max speed	322 km/h	(174 kt, 200 mph)
Cruising speed	270 km/h	(146 kt, 168 mph)
Initial climb	229 m/min	(750 fpm)
Range	2,445 km	(1,329 nm, 1,528 miles)
Weights		
Max takeoff	567 kg	(1,250 lbs)
Useful load	273 kg	(600 lbs)

Ambrosini F.4 and F.7 Rondone — Italy

One of the earliest creations of the prominent Italian designer Stelio Frati, the F.4 Rondone was an elegant low-wing monoplane with side-by-side seating for two in an enclosed cabin. It was of all-wood construction with plywood skinning and was fitted with a retractable tricycle undercarriage. The first Rondone flew in 1951 powered by an 85 h.p. Continental engine and nine production GF.4 Rondones were built by Soc. S.A.I. Ambrosini, mostly with 90 h.p. Continental C.90 engines but one with a 65 h.p. Walter Mikron III. Two remain active in France and Italy. The later F.7 Rondone II had a longer fuselage with a bigger cabin and a third seat in the rear. The prototype flew on 10th February 1954. The standard Continental C.90 was replaced by a 100 h.p. O-200 or a 135 h.p. Lycoming O-290 in a number of these aircraft. Nine production Rondone IIs were built by Pasotti and two are currently active in Italy and one in Germany.

Ambrosini F.7 Rondone II, D-ECUN

Ambrosini F.4 and F.7 Rondone (Cont.)

Specification	Ambrosini/Pasotti F.7 Rondone II	
Powerplant	One 135 h.p. (100.6 kW) Textron Lycoming O-290-D2 piston engine	
Dimensions		
Span	9.3 m	(30 ft 6 in)
Length	6.8 m	(22 ft 4 in)
Height	2.3 m	(7 ft 5 in)
Performance		
Max speed	263 km/h	(143 kt, 165 mph)
Cruising speed	232 km/h	(126 kt, 145 mph)
Initial climb	259 m/min	(850 fpm)
Range	696 km	(378 nm, 435 miles)
Weights		
Max takeoff	900 kg	(1,980 lbs)
Useful load	370 kg	(816 lbs)

AMC Texas Bullet 205 — USA

The Johnson Rocket (see separate entry) was a high-performance two-seat personal aircraft of tube and fabric construction. In 1950, the Aircraft Manufacturing Company produced a refined version of the Rocket known as the AMC Texas Bullet 205. It was a full four-seater with a fully enclosed cabin with forward-opening doors on both sides and in addition to its higher-powered 205 h.p. Continental E185-1 engine it differed from the Rocket in having a redesigned square vertical tail, lower gross weight and all-metal construction with light alloy cladding. It also had a tailwheel undercarriage in place of the tricycle gear of the Rocket. One prototype and five production Bullets were completed. Gem Aircraft Co. also tried unsuccessfully to reopen the production line in the 1960s. Three Bullets are currently active in the United States.

AMC Texas Bullet 205, N78852

Specification	Aircraft Manufacturing Co. Texas Bullet 205	
Powerplant	One 205 h.p. (152.8 kW) Teledyne Continental E-185-1 piston engine	
Dimensions		
Span	8.5 m	(28 ft 0 in)
Length	7.1 m	(23 ft 2 in)
Height	2.2 m	(7 ft 3 in)
Performance		
Max speed	337 km/h	(183 kt, 210 mph)
Cruising speed	296 km/h	(161 kt, 185 mph)
Initial climb	274 m/min	(900 fpm)
Range	1,207 km	(652 nm, 750 miles)
Weights		
Max takeoff	1,043 kg	(2,300 lbs)
Useful load	386 kg	(850 lbs)

American Eagle 101 and 129 — USA

Amid the flurry of new light aircraft emerging in the 1920s, the American Eagle A-1, created by E.E. Porterfield, was one of the more successful. First flown on 9th April 1926 it was a three-seat biplane with two tandem open cockpits and a tightly cowled nose section housing a 90 h.p. Curtiss OX-5 engine with the radiator extending underneath. Several other engines such as the 150 h.p. Hispano Suiza and the 120 h.p. Anzani were also fitted to individual aircraft. The American Eagle A-129 of 1929 was fitted with a five-cylinder, 100 h.p. Kinner K5 radial engine in a narrower cowling with the cylinder heads exposed and this changed the appearance considerably. The 1930 Model 201 was a substantially redesigned version with a squarer tail and a larger Kinner K5 radial which made it less attractive than the earlier models. Some 15 American Eagle A-1/101s and 129s still exist and at least five are active.

American Eagle 101, NC7172

Specification	American Eagle A-1	
Powerplant	One 90 h.p. (67.1 kW) Curtiss OX-5 piston engine	
Dimensions		
Span	9.1 m	(30 ft 0 in)
Length	7.3 m	(24 ft 1 in)
Height	2.5 m	(8 ft 4 in)
Performance		
Max speed	158 km/h	(86 kt, 99 mph)
Cruising speed	136 km/h	(74 kt, 85 mph)
Initial climb	152 m/min	(500 fpm)
Range	620 km	(335 nm, 385 miles)
Weights		
Max takeoff	926 kg	(2,041 lbs)
Useful load	370 kg	(814 lbs)

Specification	American Eaglecraft Eaglet 230	
Powerplant	One 30 h.p. (22.4 kW) Szekely SR-3 piston engine	
Dimensions		
Span	10.5 m	(34 ft 4 in)
Length	6.6 m	(21 ft 9 in)
Height	2.4 m	(7 ft 9 in)
Performance		
Max speed	129 km/h	(70 kt, 80 mph)
Cruising speed	112 km/h	(61 kt, 70 mph)
Initial climb	198 m/min	(650 fpm)
Range	451 km	(243 nm, 280 miles)
Weights		
Max takeoff	394 kg	(867 lbs)
Useful load	182 kg	(400 lbs)

American Eaglecraft Eaglet — USA

American Eagle Aircraft responded to the prewar craze for ultralight aircraft by building the two-seat parasol-wing Eaglet. The prototype, which was built and flown in the summer of 1930, was an open cockpit aircraft with side-by-side seating and a fixed tailwheel undercarriage. The production Eaglet 230 had a 30 h.p. Szekely three-cylinder radial engine and the bulk of the production run was produced following American Eagle's merger with Lincoln Aircraft in 1931. The Model 231 was similar but had a 40 h.p. Salmson 9AD radial and the B-31 had a 45 h.p. Szekely SR-3-0. Total production of the Eaglet was just under 100 aircraft including a dozen of the B-31 version. About a dozen are still in existence and at least two are currently in flying condition.

Ameur Baljims – France

Now sold as a kit by Ameur Aviation, the Baljims has evolved from the Balbuzard L-235 amateur-built prototype. This was designed with the objective of transporting two people at minimum cost at a speed of 190 knots over a 1,400 km range and this was achieved by using very lightweight composite materials and by innovative aerodynamic design. The developed version, known as the Baljims, has the same pusher-engined layout as the prototype with the engine buried in the centre fuselage with a long drive shaft to the tail-mounted propeller. Continental, Lycoming, Limbach or JPX powerplants in the 100 to 120 h.p. range can be installed. The Baljims, which has a large side-by-side two-seat cockpit, is fitted with a retractable (Baljims RG) or fixed (Baljims FG) tricycle undercarriage and a V-tail and has split flaps. Two prototypes had flown by the end of 1998 and a number are under construction by amateurs.

American Eaglecraft Eaglet 230, NC548Y

Ameur Baljims, F-PTCD

Ameur Baljims (Cont.)

Specification	Ameur Baljims RG	
Powerplant	One 118 h.p. (88 kW) Textron Lycoming O-235 piston engine	
Dimensions		
Span	7.32 m	(24 ft 1 in)
Length	5.76 m	(18 ft 10 in)
Height	2 m	(6 ft 7 in)
Performance		
Max speed	350 km/h	(190 kt, 218 mph)
Cruising speed	331 km/h	(180 kt, 207 mph)
Initial climb	457 m/min	(1,500 fpm)
Range	1,400 km	(761 nm, 875 miles)
Weights		
Max takeoff	645 kg	(1,422 lbs)
Useful load	340 kg	(750 lbs)

Specification	Aviation Enterprises Chevvron 2-32C	
Powerplant	One 32 h.p. (24 kW) Koenig piston engine	
Dimensions		
Span	13.41 m	(44 ft 0 in)
Length	7 m	(23 ft 0 in)
Height	1.50 m	(4 ft 11 in)
Performance		
Max speed	120 km/h	(65 kt, 75 mph)
Cruising speed	96 km/h	(52 kt, 60 mph)
Initial climb	114 m/min	(375 fpm)
Range	320 km	(174 nm, 200 miles)
Weights		
Max takeoff	345 kg	(760 lbs)
Useful load	195 kg	(429 lbs)

AMF (Aviation Enterprises) Chevvron — UK

The Chevvron 2-32C is an advanced three-axis ultralight designed by Angus Fleming and first flown in its production configuration in October 1986. Of conventional mid-wing layout, the Chevvron has a fixed tricycle undercarriage. The high-aspect-ratio wing, which has split flaps and a glass-fibre main spar, is slightly forward swept and is detachable for storage and transport. The Chevvron has a side-by-side two-seat cockpit with a hinged upward-opening polycarbonate canopy. Construction is of Kevlar carbon fibre with composite glass-fibre sandwich panels and some polyester film surface covering. Because of its extremely light construction the Chevvron provides satisfactory performance using a 32 h.p. Koenig two-stroke engine. One Chevvron has been fitted with floats for water operation and the 2-40CS was a version tested with a 40 h.p. Koenig. In total, more than 40 aircraft have been completed.

AMF Chevvron 2-40CS, G-MYGN

AMX International AMX — Italy/Brazil

Aermacchi/Alenia conceived the AMX tactical reconnaissance/strike aircraft in 1979 to replace the Fiat G.91 and joined with Embraer in 1980 to produce the aircraft for the Italian and Brazilian air forces under the AMX International banner. The first Italian AMX flew on 15th May 1984 and the Brazilian prototype (designated YA-1) on 16th October 1985. The partners subsequently added the AMX-T (Brazilian TA-1/A-1B) tandem two-seat operational trainer which maintains the full tactical capability of the standard AMX. The AMX has four underwing hardpoints, a centreline weapons station and wingtip mountings for two AIM-9 Sidewinder or MAA-1 Piranha AAMs. The first aircraft entered service in both countries in 1989 and deliveries are in progress from the combined manufacturing organisation to meet Brazil's requirement for 79 aircraft (comprising 64 A-1s and 15 TA-1s) and Italy's for 187 AMXs and 51 AMX-Ts.

AMX International AMX (two-seat), MM55042

Specification	AMX International AMX (single-seat)	
Powerplant	One 11,030 lb.s.t. (49.1 kN) Rolls Royce Spey RB168-807 turbofan	
Dimensions		
Span	8.87 m	(29 ft 2 in)
Length	13.23 m	(43 ft 5 in)
Height	4.55 m	(14 ft 11 in)
Performance		
Max speed	1,047 km/h	(569 kt, 654 mph)
Cruising speed	960 km/h	(522 kt, 600 mph)
Initial climb	3,124 m/min	(10,250 fpm)
Range	925 km	(500 nm, 575 miles)
Weights		
Max takeoff	13,000 kg	(28,660 lbs)
Useful load	6,314 kg	(13,922 lbs)

Anahuac Tauro — Mexico

The Tauro is a single-seat agricultural aircraft designed by the Fabrica de Aviones Anahuac in 1967 to operate in Mexican conditions. The Tauro T300 is a strut-braced constant-chord low-wing aircraft with a fixed tailwheel undercarriage. Construction is of steel tube with removable aluminium panels and spray bars are fitted along the length of the wing trailing edge. The chemical hopper with a 210 USG capacity is positioned between the enclosed cockpit and the engine compartment. The prototype Tauro first flew on 3rd December 1968 powered by a 300 h.p. Jacobs R-755-A2M1 uncowled radial engine and this powerplant was used on the seven production Tauro T300s. A subsequent batch of four Tauro T350s was built and these featured improved systems and were fitted with the 350 h.p. Jacobs R-755-SM engine. Seven Tauros are believed to remain active in Mexico.

Anahuac Tauro T300, XB-AUL

Specification	Anahuac Tauro T300	
Powerplant	One 300 h.p. (223.7 kW) Jacobs R-755-A2M1 piston engine	
Dimensions		
Span	11.44 m	(35 ft 6 in)
Length	8.21 m	(26 ft 11 in)
Height	2.34 m	(7 ft 8 in)
Performance		
Max speed	193 km/h	(104 kt, 120 mph)
Cruising speed	145 km/h	(78 kt, 90 mph)
Initial climb	152 m/min	(500 fpm)
Range	375 km	(202 nm, 233 miles)
Weights		
Max takeoff	1,606 kg	(3,542 lbs)
Useful load	713 kg	(1,569 lbs)

Anderson Kingfisher — USA

The EA-1 Kingfisher homebuilt amphibian was conceived by Earl Anderson and is sold by way of plans to amateur builders. It first flew on 24th April 1969 and is a wooden aircraft with glass-fibre cladding using strut-braced Piper J3 or PA-18 wings on a new fuselage. Wire-braced fixed outrigger floats are positioned at the wingtips. The enclosed cabin has side-by-side seating for two and the tailwheel undercarriage has main units which retract forwards for cruising flight and for water landings and a tailwheel which twists sideways to clear the water rudder. Normally, engines in the 100–120 horsepower range are used but powerplants up to the 160 h.p. Lycoming O-320 have been used. The engine is mounted on a tubular frame above the wing centre section and well clear of water spray. Over 200 sets of plans have been sold and several dozen Kingfishers operate in the United States and elsewhere.

Anderson Kingfisher, N99887

Anderson Kingfisher (Cont.)

Specification	Anderson EA-1 Kingfisher	
Powerplant	One 100 h.p. (74.5 kW) Teledyne Continental O-200 piston engine	
Dimensions		
Span	11 m	(36 ft 1 in)
Length	7.16 m	(23 ft 6 in)
Height	2.44 m	(8 ft 0 in)
Performance		
Max speed	156 km/h	(85 kt, 98 mph)
Cruising speed	136 km/h	(74 kt, 85 mph)
Initial climb	153 m/min	(500 fpm)
Range	550 km	(300 nm, 345 miles)
Weights		
Max takeoff	680 kg	(1,500 lbs)
Useful load	213 kg	(468 lbs)

Andreasson BA-4B — Sweden

Björn Andreasson, one of the most prolific of light aircraft designers, designed the BA-4 light single-seat wood and fabric biplane, flying the prototype, powered by a 28 h.p. two-stroke Scott Squirrel engine, in 1944. The design was revived 20 years later as the BA-4B which was built by apprentices at the MFI training school in Malmö. Andreasson re-engineered it as an all-metal aircraft suitable for amateur construction. The BA-4B has an open cockpit and a spring-steel tailwheel undercarriage and can be powered by a variety of engines in the 90 to 120 h.p. category including the Continental O-200-A used on the prototype. Many sets of plans have been sold to homebuilders and an initial batch of four aircraft was built by members of the Swedish EAA. The prototype now flies in the UK and a further five are UK-registered, three of which are active.

Andreasson BA-4B, G-AWPZ

Specification	Andreasson BA-4B	
Powerplant	One 100 h.p. (74.5 kW) Rolls Royce Continental O-200-A piston engine	
Dimensions		
Span	5.34 m	(17 ft 7 in)
Length	4.6 m	(15 ft 0 in)
Height	1.9 m	(6 ft 1 in)
Performance		
Max speed	225 km/h	(122 kt, 140 mph)
Cruising speed	193 km/h	(104 kt, 120 mph)
Initial climb	610 m/min	(2,000 fpm)
Range	280 km	(155 nm, 175 miles)
Weights		
Max takeoff	375 kg	(827 lbs)
Useful load	109 kg	(240 lbs)

Angel Aircraft Angel — USA

Carl Mortensen, designer of the Evangel missionary support aircraft, has produced a prototype of the Angel light transport which is also intended for use in remote locations for operations off unprepared airstrips. The low-wing Angel, which has been developed by the King's Engineering Fellowship and is also known as the King's Angel, has a rugged retractable tricycle undercarriage and complex wing control surfaces including full-span flaps and a combination of small ailerons and spoilers for roll control. The eight-seat cabin can be quickly converted for freight carrying and is entered by a large port-side split airstair door. The most unusual feature of the Angel is the pair of Lycoming IO-540 engines which are mounted as pusher units on the rear of the wings and are fitted with large streamlined propeller spinners. Roles intended for the aircraft include mining and oil support flights, aerial survey and medevac work. Only one Angel has been completed to date. It made its first flight on 13th January 1984, receiving its type certificate on 20th October 1992 but no production aircraft have been built to date.

Angel Aircraft Angel, N44KE

Specification	Angel Aircraft Corp. Angel	
Powerplant	Two 300 h.p. (223.7 kW) Textron Lycoming IO-540-M1C5 piston engines	
Dimensions		
Span	12.2 m	(40 ft 0 in)
Length	10.2 m	(33 ft 4 in)
Height	3.5 m	(11 ft 6 in)
Performance		
Max speed	331 km/h	(180 kt, 207 mph)
Cruising speed	329 km/h	(176 kt, 202 mph)
Initial climb	410 m/min	(1,345 fpm)
Range	2,087 km	(1,134 nm, 1,304 miles)
Weights		
Max takeoff	2,630 kg	(5,800 lbs)
Useful load	870 kg	(1,920 lbs)

Specification	Anglin Karatoo J-6	
Powerplant	One 52 h.p. (39 kW) Rotax 503 piston engine	
Dimensions		
Span	9.9 m	(32 ft 6 in)
Length	6.1 m	(20 ft 0 in)
Height	1.68 m	(5 ft 5 in)
Performance		
Max speed	137 km/h	(74 kt, 85 mph)
Cruising speed	120 km/h	(65 kt, 75 mph)
Initial climb	228 m/min	(750 fpm)
Range	441 km	(240 nm, 276 miles)
Weights		
Max takeoff	409 kg	(900 lbs)
Useful load	236 kg	(520 lbs)

Anglin Karatoo — USA

One of the early aircraft from the American designer Jesse Anglin was the Karatoo J-6 which followed on from Anglin's previous J-3 Kitten and J-4 Sportster ultralights. The Karatoo is a high-wing side-by-side two-seater with a strut-braced high wing and a fixed tailwheel undercarriage. It has an enclosed cockpit with a rear baggage compartment and can be fitted with dual controls. The fuselage is steel tube and the wings are of wooden construction with fabric covering. It won the 'outstanding homebuilt design' award at the 1985 Oshkosh Fly-In and many kits have been sold by Skyway Aircraft and, in Australia, by Australian Aviation Works who also market a single-seat version named the KaraOne and a parasol-wing version called the Karasport.

Anglin Space Walker — USA

Jesse Anglin built the original Space Walker in 1986. This design for amateur builders was a low-wing single-seater with a fixed undercarriage and a 65 h.p. Continental engine. Construction was of tube and fabric and the Space Walker I was marketed by Anglin's company, Country Air Inc. (later Anglin Engineering), with many examples being completed by American homebuilders. The design rights were sold to Warner Aircraft in 1997 and the Space Walker has also been sold in Australia as a kit by Australian Aviation Works. Warner Aircraft now sell the aircraft as the Revolution I. The Revolution II is a tandem two-seat version of the Space Walker, first flown in 1990 and powered by engines in the 65 h.p. to 125 h.p. range. It is sold as a kit by Warner and also sold in Australia as the Space Walker II. A much modified version with a new wing and enlarged fuselage, the Sportster, was introduced by Warner in 1998.

Anglin Karatoo, N46SN

Anglin Warner Revolution II, N516HM

Anglin Space Walker (Cont.)

Specification	Anglin Warner Revolution II	
Powerplant	One 65 h.p. (48.4 kW) Teledyne Continental A.65 piston engine	
Dimensions		
Span	8.5 m	(28 ft 0 in)
Length	6 m	(19 ft 9 in)
Height	1.7 m	(5 ft 6 in)
Performance		
Max speed	239 km/h	(130 kt, 150 mph)
Cruising speed	184 km/h	(100 kt, 115 mph)
Initial climb	366 m/min	(1,200 fpm)
Range	480 km	(261 nm, 300 miles)
Weights		
Max takeoff	636 kg	(1,400 lbs)
Useful load	273 kg	(600 lbs)

Antonov An-3, 9801

Antonov An-2
— Poland/USSR/Ukraine

The An-2 (NATO name 'Colt') biplane has been the standard light utility transport for the Soviet Union since its introduction in 1947. Of all-metal construction it has a capacious fuselage and a fixed tailwheel undercarriage which may be fitted with floats or skis. The prototype flew on 31st August 1947. Roles include transport, crop spraying, parachuting, firefighting and geophysical survey. Antonov built 3,480 An-2s before production passed to PZL-Mielec in Poland who built 11,650. Variants include the An-2T general-utility version, the An-2P passenger model and the An-2R for agricultural operations. The An-2 was used widely by Aeroflot and large numbers went to the Soviet Air Force and to all other Warsaw Pact air arms. It was built in China as the Y-5. Antonov have also flown the prototype of the An-3 which is an An-2 with a fuselage stretch and a 940 s.h.p. Glushenkov TVD-10B turboprop. More than 5,000 An-2s are believed to be still in service and many have been sold in Europe and the USA.

Specification	Antonov-PZL An-2P	
Powerplant	One 1,000 h.p. (746 kW) PZL-Kalisz ASz-62IR piston engine	
Dimensions		
Span	18.18 m	(59 ft 7 in)
Length	12.74 m	(41 ft 9 in)
Height	4.01 m	(13 ft 2 in)
Performance		
Max speed	258 km/h	(139 kt, 160 mph)
Cruising speed	185 km/h	(100 kt, 115 mph)
Initial climb	210 m/min	(690 fpm)
Range	900 km	(489 nm, 563 miles)
Weights		
Max takeoff	5,500 kg	(12,125 lbs)
Useful load	2,054 kg	(4,520 lbs)

Antonov An-2P, HA-ANK

Antonov An-8
— USSR/Ukraine

In 1955, the Antonov design bureau produced a new twin turboprop transport for use by the Soviet Air Force as a larger-capacity replacement for the Li-2 (DC-3). This An-8 set a pattern for a range of Antonov freight and passenger transports with its high wing, ventral tail loading ramp and fuselage-mounted main undercarriage housings for the four-wheel main bogies. The An-8 had a large unpressurised hold and was fitted with a tail gun position and a glazed nose with a chin radar bulge for the navigator or for additional armament. Approximately 155 An-8s (NATO name 'Camp') were built, entering service with the Soviet Air Force in 1957 and a small number were used as freighters by Aeroflot. The majority are now out of service but up to 20 remain in use, some with Russian civil carriers and others with commercial freight operators in Liberia and Angola.

Antonov An-8, EL-RDK

Specification	Antonov An-8	
Powerplant	Two 5,100 s.h.p. (3,802 kW) Kuznetsov NK-2M turboprops	
Dimensions		
Span	30 m	(98 ft 5 in)
Length	26 m	(85 ft 3 in)
Height	9.7 m	(31 ft 10 in)
Performance		
Max speed	610 km/h	(329 kt, 379 mph)
Cruising speed	480 km/h	(259 kt, 298 mph)
Initial climb (est.)	427 m/min	(1,400 fpm)
Range	2,780 km	(1,511 nm, 1,738 miles)
Weights		
Max takeoff	40,000 kg	(88,200 lbs)
Useful load	19,000 kg	(41,895 lbs)

Antonov An-12, RA-11324

Antonov An-12
— USSR/Ukraine

Antonov followed the An-8 with the larger, four-engined An-10 pressurised passenger transport which served Aeroflot from 1959 to 1973 and was then withdrawn. A parallel development was the An-12 (NATO name 'Cub') freighter which had greater capacity than the An-8 and used the An-10 airframe with an upswept rear fuselage and double ventral loading doors. It retained the tail turret and glazed nose and was powered by four AI-20M turboprops. The majority of the 1,243 An-12s believed to have been built were delivered to the Soviet Air Force but commercial versions (An-12B) were used by Aeroflot, LOT, TABSO etc. and military aircraft were used by Bulgaria, Czechoslovakia, Poland and the Indian Air Force. A paratroop transport version was designated An-12BP and the type was built in China as the Shaanxi Y-8 with a longer pointed nose and other minor changes. Many An-12s are still in service.

Specification	Antonov An-12BP	
Powerplant	Four 3,945 s.h.p. (2,942 kW) Ivchenko AI-20K turboprops	
Dimensions		
Span	38 m	(124 ft 8 in)
Length	33.1 m	(108 ft 7 in)
Height	10.53 m	(34 ft 6 in)
Performance		
Max speed	777 km/h	(419 kt, 482 mph)
Cruising speed	670 km/h	(361 kt, 416 mph)
Initial climb	600 m/min	(1,970 fpm)
Range	5,700 km	(3,098 nm, 3,563 miles)
Weights		
Max takeoff	61,000 kg	(134,505 lbs)
Useful load	33,000 kg	(72,765 lbs)

Antonov An-22 Antheus — USSR/Ukraine

Despite considerable experience of designing large freighters Antonov made a major leap in 1962 with initiation of the An-22 Antei (Antheus). Fulfilling a requirement of the Soviet Air Force and Aeroflot, the An-22 was almost twice as long as the An-12 but had the same high-wing layout with ventral rear loading doors and externally podded main undercarriage units. Power was from four NK-12MA turboprops with contra-rotating propellers. The tail unit had dual fins which allowed the An-22 to carry cradled loads for the space programme and for other aerospace projects. The forward fuselage was pressurised but the main cargo hold was unpressurised. The first of three prototype An-22s (NATO name 'Cock') flew on 27th February 1965 and 68 production An-22Ms were completed between 1967 and 1975. A small number of these are believed to remain in service with the Russian Air Force.

Antonov An-22, CCCP-67691

Specification	Antonov An-22 Antheus	
Powerplant	Four 15,000 s.h.p. (11,185 kW) Kuznetsov NK-12MA turboprops	
Dimensions		
Span	64.4 m	(211 ft 4 in)
Length	57.92 m	(190 ft 0 in)
Height	12.53 m	(41 ft 1 in)
Performance		
Max speed	740 km/h	(399 kt, 460 mph)
Cruising speed	629 km/h	(340 kt, 391 mph)
Takeoff distance	1,295 m	(4,250 ft)
Range	10,950 km	(5,951 nm, 6,844 miles)
Weights		
Max takeoff	250,000 kg	(551,250 lbs)
Useful load	136,000 kg	(299,880 lbs)

Antonov An-24 — USSR/Ukraine

The An-24 is a 44-seat pressurised feederliner designed by the Antonov Bureau in 1957 as a replacement for the Il-14s then in operation with Aeroflot on its huge network of short-haul routes. With Antonov's established high-wing layout and Ivchenko AI-24VT turboprop engines it was similar to the Fokker F.27 but was structurally designed for remote airport operations. The first aircraft flew on 20th December 1959 and the An-24 entered passenger service with Aeroflot in late 1962 being followed by the An-24V with an extended 50-seat cabin and the An-24RV with a supplementary jet engine for extra takeoff power. A total of 1,360 aircraft was built with users spanning the Warsaw Pact military forces and a large number of airlines including Iraqi, Tarom, LOT, MIAT and Cubana. The An-24 has been built in China under licence by the X'ian factory (XAC) as the Y7-200A with Harbin WJ5A-1 engines, four-blade scimitar propellers and wing modifications. The latest version is the further improved 60-seat MA60 of which more than 70 are on order.

Antonov An-24B, EW-46404

Specification	Antonov An-24V	
Powerplant	Two 2,550 s.h.p. (1,902 kW) Ivchenko AI-24A turboprops	
Dimensions		
Span	29.2 m	(95 ft 9 in)
Length	23.53 m	(77 ft 2 in)
Height	8.32 m	(27 ft 3 in)
Performance		
Max speed	478 km/h	(260 kt, 299 mph)
Cruising speed	450 km/h	(243 kt, 280 mph)
Initial climb	204 m/min	(670 fpm)
Range	550 km	(299 nm, 344 miles)
Weights		
Max takeoff	21,000 kg	(46,305 lbs)
Useful load	6,302 kg	(13,896 lbs)

Antonov An-26, An-30 and An-32 — USSR/Ukraine

The An-24 provided an ideal basis for further development and the first major new version was the An-26 which appeared in 1969. It was a cargo-carrying aircraft with the basic An-24 structure but with an upswept rear fuselage incorporating a loading ramp and with two large ventral strakes. It had a hardened militarised freight fuselage without windows and was fitted with a floor freight handling system and loading hoist. The An-26 (NATO name 'Curl') is also used for electronic intelligence tasks and can carry bombs on external fuselage mountings. For passenger transport, up to 40 seats can be fitted. Total production is reported as 1,398. It was followed by the An-32 which is an An-26 for hot and high operations with AI-20D-5 engines in deep nacelles set above the chord line of the wing. Approximately 350 have been built (NATO name 'Cline'). The An-30 ('Clank') is a specialised An-26 for survey and mapping with a fully glazed nose and belly-mounted cameras.

Specification	Antonov An-32	
Powerplant	Two 5,112 s.h.p. (3,812 kW) Ivchenko AI-20D Srs.5 turboprops	
Dimensions		
Span	29.2 m	(95 ft 9 in)
Length	23.78 m	(78 ft 0 in)
Height	8.75 m	(28 ft 8 in)
Performance		
Max speed	530 km/h	(286 kt, 329 mph)
Cruising speed	470 km/h	(254 kt, 292 mph)
Takeoff distance	760 m	(2,495 ft)
Range	2,000 km	(1,087 nm, 1,250 miles)
Weights		
Max takeoff	27,000 kg	(59,535 lbs)
Useful load	10,200 kg	(22,491 lbs)

Antonov An-30, 1107 (Czech AF)

Antonov An-28 and An-38 — USSR/Ukraine

In the 1950s, Antonov designed a small piston twin-engined STOL transport designated An-14 Pchelka which was used for some years by the Soviet Air Force. In 1969, the first of three prototypes of a developed tuboprop version, the An-28 (NATO name 'Cash'), was flown. This was a light turboprop 17-passenger transport with a strut-braced high-aspect-ratio wing, twin tail fins and a fixed tricycle undercarriage. The production version was built by PZL-Mielec who flew their first aircraft on 22nd July 1984 and completed approximately 200 aircraft, primarily for Aeroflot, by the time the line closed in 1992. A batch of search & rescue aircraft designated An-28B1R was delivered to the Polish Navy. A new version with Pratt & Whitney PT6A engines, the M-28 Skytruck, has entered production with over 20 built to date. The latest version of this design is the An-38-100 which first flew on 23rd June 1994 and has an 8 ft fuselage stretch to give 24-passenger capacity. Powered by Allied Signal TPE331-14GR turboprops it will be built in the Ukraine rather than at PZL.

Antonov (PZL) An-28, 1008 (Polish Navy)

Antonov An-28 and An-38 (Cont.)

Antonov An-38-100, RA-41900

Specification	Antonov (PZL) An-28	
Powerplant	Two 960 s.h.p. (716 kW) WSK-PZL Rzeszow TWD-10B turboprops	
Dimensions		
Span	22.06 m	(72 ft 4 in)
Length	13.10 m	(42 ft 11 in)
Height	4.90 m	(16 ft 1 in)
Performance		
Max speed	350 km/h	(189 kt, 217 mph)
Cruising speed	335 km/h	(181 kt, 208 mph)
Initial climb	210 m/min	(690 fpm)
Range	1,365 km	(742 nm, 853 miles)
Weights		
Max takeoff	6,500 kg	(14,330 lbs)
Useful load	2,600 kg	(5,733 lbs)

Antonov An-70 — Ukraine

With an ageing fleet of An-12s in service, Antonov started design work in 1987 on a new turboprop freighter, designated An-70, for civil and military applications. This was a larger aircraft with more than double the gross weight of the An-12 but it followed the familiar Antonov high-wing layout with a ventral rear loading ramp and externally podded main undercarriage fairings. Unlike previous freighters, the An-70 has a fully pressurised cargo area and is fitted with a powered loading system including travelling cranes and rollamat floor. The D-27 turboprop engines are fitted with counter-rotating propellers with curved composite blades. The An-70 prototype flew on 16th December 1994 but was destroyed in February 1995 in a collision with an An-72 chase aircraft. The second prototype then took over the test programme. Production will be by Aviacor but no An-70 orders have been placed to date.

Antonov An-70, UR-NTK

Specification	Antonov An-70	
Powerplant	Four 14,000 s.h.p. (10,440 kW) Ivchenko-Progress/Zaporozhye D-27 propfan engines	
Dimensions		
Span	44.06 m	(144 ft 7 in)
Length	40.7 m	(133 ft 8 in)
Height	16.38 m	(53 ft 9 in)
Performance		
Max speed	797 km/h	(430 kt, 495 mph)
Cruising speed	741 km/h	(400 kt, 460 mph)
Takeoff distance	1,800 m	(5,900 ft)
Range	4,900 km	(2,663 nm, 3,063 miles)
Weights		
Max takeoff	130,000 kg	(286,650 lbs)
Useful load	47,090 kg	(103,833 lbs)

Antonov An-72 & 74 — Ukraine

Antonov's small turbofan freighter, the An-72, was first flown on 31st August 1977. It embodied a number of highly innovative features, the principal one being the mounting of the twin D-36 turbofans above and forward of the wing centre section. This resulted in STOL performance from the An-72 as a result of the jet exhaust blowing over the wing surface and giving improved lift coefficients. The An-72 (NATO name 'Coaler') has a rear loading ramp, T-tail and externally podded landing gear. The military An-71 is fitted with a fuselage-mounted tailplane and a forward-swept fin with a large rotodome on top for AEW&C tasks. The An-74 has increased fuel capacity and, in some versions, cabin windows and seating for up to 52 passengers. Over 100 An-72s and 160 An-74s have been built and most are operating in the CIS with military and civil users although some have been delivered to the air forces of Peru, Bangladesh and Angola.

Antonov An-74-200, UR-74055

Specification	Antonov An-72A	
Powerplant	Two 14,330 lb.s.t. (63.74 kN) Lotarev D-36 turbofans	
Dimensions		
Span	31.9 m	(104 ft 7 in)
Length	28.07 m	(92 ft 1 in)
Height	8.65 m	(28 ft 4 in)
Performance		
Max speed	705 km/h	(380 kt, 438 mph)
Cruising speed	598 km/h	(325 kt, 374 mph)
Takeoff distance	930 m	(3,050 ft)
Range	4,800 km	(2,609 nm, 3,000 miles)
Weights		
Max takeoff	34,500 kg	(76,073 lbs)
Useful load	15,450 kg	(34,067 lbs)

Antonov An-124 Ruslan — Ukraine

Originally designed for a Russian military requirement, the An-124 (NATO name 'Condor') is the largest commercial freighter in current world service and is in considerable demand due to its ability to carry very heavy outsize loads. First flown on 26th December 1982, the high-wing An-124 is powered by four Lotarev D-18T turbofans on underwing pylons. It has an upward-opening nose section and tail ramp to allow through-loading of freight and palletised cargo. An upper deck is incorporated with seating for up to 88 passengers. A total of 53 An-124s has been built of which nearly half are used commercially by Volga Dnepr, Polet and Antonov Design Bureau and the remainder are in Russian Air Force service. The latest An-124 models, introduced in 1999, include the An-124-100M with Progress D-18 Srs.3 turbofans and the An-124-210 powered by Rolls Royce RB211 engines. Antonov ASTC is also considering the An-124-200 with General Electric CF6-80C2 engines and Aviastar has also proposed a similar version with a modernised cockpit which they designate An-124-130.

Antonov An-124-100, UR-82027

Specification	Antonov An-124-100M Ruslan	
Powerplant	Four 51,590 lb.s.t. (229.5 kN) Lotarev D-18T turbofans	
Dimensions		
Span	73.3 m	(240 ft 6 in)
Length	69.1 m	(226 ft 8 in)
Height	20.78 m	(68 ft 2 in)
Performance		
Max speed	865 km/h	(467 kt, 537 mph)
Cruising speed	800 km/h	(432 kt, 497 mph)
Takeoff distance	2,520 m	(8,270 ft)
Range	16,500 km	(8,967 nm, 10,313 miles)
Weights		
Max takeoff	405,000 kg	(893,025 lbs)
Useful load	230,000 kg	(507,150 lbs)

Antonov An-140 — Ukraine

The An-140 has been developed as a replacement for the An-24 and An-26 for short-haul routes in the eastern bloc countries. Its design layout follows the familiar Antonov philosophy with a high wing and externally mounted undercarriage. Seating capacity is for 52 passengers in standard form and up to 80 in high density and the An-140 is powered by a pair of Ivchenko TV3 turboprops mounted on the inboard wing section. Plans are in hand for further versions with Western engines, particularly the Pratt & Whitney PW127A built by Klimov. The first of two prototype An-140s made its first flight on 17th September 1997. It is intended that the An-140 will be built at the HESA plant in Iran in addition to the main Aviakor production plant at Samara and at KhSAPO at Kharkov.

Antonov An-140, UR-NTP

Antonov An-140 (Cont.)

Specification	Antonov An-140	
Powerplant	Two 2,500 s.h.p. (1,864 kW) Ivchenko-Progress TV3-117VMA-SB2 turboprops	
Dimensions		
Span	24.25 m	(79 ft 7 in)
Length	22.46 m	(73 ft 8 in)
Height	8.04 m	(26 ft 4 in)
Performance		
Max speed (est.)	593 km/h	(320 kt, 368 mph)
Cruising speed (est.)	565 km/h	(305 kt, 351 mph)
Takeoff distance	1,341 m	(4,400 ft)
Range	2,100 km	(1,141 nm, 1,313 miles)
Weights		
Max takeoff	17,371 kg	(38,303 lbs)
Useful load (est.)	7,000 kg	(15,435 lbs)

Antonov An-225 Mriya
— Ukraine

The An-225 is the world's largest aircraft, built as a 'piggy-back' carrier for the Russian Buran space shuttle vehicle. It was based on the An-124 airframe with a 50 ft fuselage stretch and a larger wing mounting six underslung D-18T turbofans. The main undercarriage was enlarged with seven twin-wheel bogies on each side and the tail was redesigned with twin fins in order to give clearance for the longer loads which might be carried. A cradle was fitted to the upper fuselage in order to carry the Buran and other loads which would not fit inside the fuselage. Only one An-225 ('Cossack') has been built to date and it flew on 21st December 1988 at Kiev. It was eventually withdrawn from use in 1995 but is expected to be restored to flight condition and a second aircraft completed if finance and a suitable role is found.

Antonov An-225, UR-82060

Specification	Antonov An-225 Mriya	
Powerplant	Six 51,590 lb.s.t. (229.5 kN) Lotarev D-18T turbofans	
Dimensions		
Span	88.4 m	(290 ft 0 in)
Length	84 m	(275 ft 7 in)
Height	18.2 m	(59 ft 8 in)
Performance		
Max speed	850 km/h	(460 kt, 530 mph)
Cruising speed	800 km/h	(430 kt, 497 mph)
Takeoff distance	3,200 m	(10,500 ft)
Range	15,400 km	(8,370 nm, 9,625 miles)
Weights		
Max takeoff	600,000 kg	(1,323,000 lbs)
Payload	250,000 kg	(551,250 lbs)

APM-20 Lionceau
— France

Philippe Moniot, General Manager of Issoire Aviation and a specialist in composite construction, has designed the low-wing Lionceau monoplane and flew the prototype on 24th November 1995. It is constructed, principally, from carbon fibre and is aimed at the club training market. The Lionceau, which is JAR-VLA certified, has a side-by-side two-seat cockpit with a large sliding canopy and is fitted with a fixed tricycle undercarriage. The production standard aircraft, being built at Issoire by Avions Philippe Moniot (APM), has a larger tail unit than the prototypes and improved useful load. The Lionceau is fitted with an 80 h.p. Rotax 912 but can use engines of up to 120 h.p.

APM-20 Lionceau, F-WWXX

Specification	APM-20 Lionceau	
Powerplant	One 80 h.p. (59.6 kW) Rotax 912 piston engine	
Dimensions		
Span	8.4 m	(27 ft 7 in)
Length	6.5 m	(21 ft 4 in)
Height	2.4 m	(7 ft 11 in)
Performance		
Max speed	234 km/h	(126 kt, 145 mph)
Cruising speed	208 km/h	(112 kt, 130 mph)
Initial climb	150 m/min	(490 fpm)
Range	1,100 km	(600 nm, 690 miles)
Weights		
Max takeoff	620 kg	(1,367 lbs)
Useful load	260 kg	(573 lbs)

Aquila A-210 — Germany

One of the new group of all-composite light aircraft from Germany, the Aquila is a side-by-side two-seater designed by Aquila Technische of Schönhagen. It was introduced in 1999 and features a computer-designed wing with a curved outboard leading edge and straight trailing edge. The Aquila prototype, which flew in March 2000, is aimed at the low-cost training market, is fitted with a fixed tricycle undercarriage and offers high performance with a relatively low-powered Rotax 912 engine.

Aquila A-210, D-EQUI

Specification	Aquila A-210	
Powerplant	One 100 h.p. (74.5 kW) Rotax 912 piston engine	
Dimensions		
Span	10.3 m	(33 ft 9 in)
Length	7.3 m	(23 ft 11 in)
Height	2.3 m	(7 ft 7 in)
Performance		
Max speed	305 km/h	(165 kt, 190 mph)
Cruising speed	240 km/h	(130 kt, 149 mph)
Range	1,850 km	(1,005 nm, 1,156 miles)
Weights		
Max takeoff	750 kg	(1,654 lbs)
Useful load	260 kg	(573 lbs)

Arado Ar.79B — Germany

Originally designed in the mid-1930s, the Arado Ar.79 was a side-by-side two seat light trainer and communications aircraft built for the German sport flying movement and later the Luftwaffe. Construction consisted of a steel tube and fuselage with fabric and metal covering and wooden wings with ply covering. The Ar.79B had a tailwheel undercarriage with inward-retracting main units and was powered by a Hirth inline engine. Production of the Ar.79B was completed in 1941 but the design led to the Arado 396 trainer. One Ar.79B is currently active in Germany.

Arado Ar.79B, D-EMVT

Specification	Arado Ar.79B	
Powerplant	One 105 h.p. (78.3 kW) Hirth HM504A-2 piston engine	
Dimensions		
Span	10 m	(32 ft 9 in)
Length	7.6 m	(25 ft 0 in)
Height	2.1 m	(6 ft 10 in)
Performance		
Max speed at sea level	228 km/h	(124 kt, 143 mph)
Cruising speed	202 km/h	(110 kt, 127 mph)
Initial climb	311 m/min	(1,020 fpm)
Range	739 km	(400 nm, 460 miles)
Weights		
Max takeoff	761 kg	(1,675 lbs)
Useful load	300 kg	(660 lbs)

Arctic Tern and Interstate Cadet — USA

The Interstate S-1A was a high-wing tandem-seat light aircraft built from tube and fabric, 321 of which were built in the 1930s. It was followed by the wartime Interstate L-6 (Model S-1-B1) Cadet army liaison aircraft which had more extensive cabin glazing, 236 of which were built, powered by a 113 h.p. Franklin O-200-5 engine. A number of both models still fly in the USA. In 1977 Arctic Aircraft revived the S-1A Cadet as the S-1-B2 Arctic Tern. Built from modern materials, the Tern used a 150 h.p. Lycoming O-320 engine and could be fitted with floats or skis. It was widely used as a bush aircraft and was equipped with a removable rear seat to allow the loading of long and bulky items and is frequently fitted with large tundra tyres. Including the prototype, Arctic built 32 production Terns at its factory in Anchorage and the type is now built by Interstate Aircraft of Lebanon, New Hampshire together with a four-seat version – the Arctic Privateer.

Arctic Tern and Interstate Cadet (Cont.)

Arctic Tern, N46243

Specification	Arctic Tern S-1-B2	
Powerplant	One 150 h.p. (112 kW) Textron Lycoming O-320 piston engine	
Dimensions		
Span	10.97 m	(36 ft 0 in)
Length	7.32 m	(24 ft 0 in)
Height	2.13 m	(7 ft 0 in)
Performance		
Max speed	282 km/h	(152 kt, 175 mph)
Cruising speed	188 km/h	(102 kt, 117 mph)
Initial climb	389 m/min	(1,275 fpm)
Range	1,049 km	(570 nm, 656 miles)
Weights		
Max takeoff	862 kg	(1,900 lbs)
Useful load	827 kg	(1,823 lbs)

Arnet Pereyra Aventura II, N32913

Arnet Pereyra Aventura II
— USA

The Aventura ultralight kit-built seaplanes are the creation of Arnet Pereyra Aero Design of Rockledge, Florida. They combine the fabric-covered steel tube construction of normal ultralights with a fibreglass hull to give a good water performance. The Aventura is fitted with retracting main wheels and is sold in single-seat Aventura form, either as a Part 103 ultralight or as a standard experimental aircraft, and as the side-by-side two-seat Aventura II and Buccaneer II. The powerplant, which is fitted in pusher configuration behind the wing centre section, is normally a 65 h.p. Rotax 582, but various engines in the 65 to 80 horsepower range can be used. Over 350 Aventuras are currently flying. A landplane version of the Aventura II is sold as the Sabre II with a fixed tailwheel undercarriage.

Specification	Arnet Pereyra Aventura II	
Powerplant	One 65 h.p. (48.5 kW) Rotax 582 piston engine	
Dimensions		
Span	9.3 m	(30 ft 8 in)
Length	7 m	(23 ft 0 in)
Height	2.1 m	(7 ft 0 in)
Performance		
Max speed	143 km/h	(78 kt, 90 mph)
Cruising speed	112 km/h	(61 kt, 70 mph)
Initial climb	152 m/min	(500 fpm)
Range	232 km	(126 nm, 145 miles)
Weights		
Max takeoff	523 kg	(1,150 lbs)
Useful load	232 kg	(510 lbs)

Arno Chereau J300 Joker — France

The J300 Joker ultralight has become popular in France where it is marketed as a kit for homebuilders by Sauper Aviation. Designed by Jean-Claude Chereau, it is of classic steel tube and fabric construction with composite wing structure and is fitted with a triangulated steel tube undercarriage with elastic damping. The J300 has side-by-side seating for two in an enclosed cabin and can be powered either by the 79 h.p. Rotax 912 or various other Rotax, JPX, BMW or Limbach engines in the 70 to 120 h.p. range. The J300 can also be operated on skis or floats and has been offered as a light military liaison type. Several have been equipped with spraybars and chemical tanks for agricultural operations.

Arno Chereau J300

Specification	Arno Chereau J300 Joker	
Powerplant	One 79 h.p. (58.9 kW) Rotax 912 piston engine	
Dimensions		
Span	10.2 m	(33 ft 5 in)
Length	5.95 m	(19 ft 6 in)
Height	1.95 m	(6 ft 5 in)
Performance		
Max speed	190 km/h	(102 kt, 118 mph)
Cruising speed	120 km/h	(65 kt, 74 mph)
Initial climb	300 m/min	(984 fpm)
Range	800 km	(435 nm, 500 miles)
Weights		
Max takeoff	450 kg	(992 lbs)
Useful load	275 kg	(606 lbs)

Arrow Active II — UK

The original Arrow Active sporting biplane was built by Arrow Aircraft of Leeds in 1931. It was of all-metal tubular construction with steel main wing spars, metal covering for the forward fuselage and fabric covering on the wings, tail and rear fuselage. The Active I was powered by a 115 h.p. Cirrus Hermes IIB in-line piston engine. The aircraft had an open single-seat cockpit and a fixed tailwheel undercarriage and was fully aerobatic. The company built a second aircraft known as the Active II with modified wing centre section attachments and a 120 h.p. de Havilland Gipsy III engine. This machine was first flown in 1932. The first Active was destroyed in an accident in 1935 but the Active II was restored in 1957 following wartime storage and was used for many years with the Tiger Club. Now owned by Desmond Penrose it remains in operation with the Shuttleworth Trust.

Arrow Active II, G-ABVE

Specification	Arrow Active II	
Powerplant	One 120 h.p. (89.5 kW) de Havilland Gipsy III piston engine	
Dimensions		
Span	7.3 m	(24 ft 0 in)
Length	5.7 m	(18 ft 10 in)
Height	2.3 m	(7 ft 6 in)
Performance		
Max speed	230 km/h	(125 kt, 144 mph)
Cruising speed	206 km/h	(112 kt, 129 mph)
Initial climb	253 m/min	(830 fpm)
Range	640 km	(347 nm, 400 miles)
Weights		
Max takeoff	602 kg	(1,325 lbs)
Useful load	182 kg	(400 lbs)

Arrow Sport — USA

Around 100 examples of the Arrow Sport biplane were built in the late 1920s by Arrow Aircraft. The prototype had some very advanced features for its day and was built in 1926 to the design of Swen Swenson. It featured cantilever wings, but inter-wing bracing struts were incorporated for cosmetic reasons. The tapered wings were of wooden construction and the fuselage was built of welded steel tube, the whole airframe being covered in fabric. The Arrow Sport was a side-by-side two-seater with an open cockpit and it had a wide-track undercarriage with oleo bracing struts. On the prototype a 60 h.p. Le Blond engine was used but production A2-60s had a six-cylinder Anzani radial and the Sport Pursuit was fitted with a 100 h.p. Kinner. Only one Arrow Sport is currently active in the USA and it has been fitted with a 90 h.p. Ken Royce engine.

Arrow Sport (Cont.)

Arrow Sport, NC804M

Specification	Arrow Sport A2-90	
Powerplant	One 90 h.p. (67.1 kW) Ken Royce piston engine	
Dimensions		
Span	7.9 m	(25 ft 10 in)
Length	5.9 m	(19 ft 3 in)
Height	2.3 m	(7 ft 6 in)
Performance		
Max speed	177 km/h	(96 kt, 110 mph)
Cruising speed	153 km/h	(83 kt, 95 mph)
Initial climb	229 m/min	(750 fpm)
Range	449 km	(244 nm, 280 miles)
Weights		
Max takeoff	577 kg	(1,270 lbs)
Useful load	209 kg	(459 lbs)

ARV Super2 — UK

Designed in 1983 by Richard Noble's ARV Aviation Ltd. the prototype Super2 first flew on 11th March 1985. The Super2 is a shoulder-wing side-by-side two-seater with a fixed tricycle undercarriage. Built from Supral light alloy for ease of production the aircraft was powered by a 77 h.p. three-cylinder two-stroke Hewland AE.75 engine. Some aircraft were later converted with an 80 h.p. Rotax 912 flat-four engine and the Super2 has been tested with the Mid-West Aero Engines AE.100R. Some 28 aircraft were built before ARV ceased operation in June 1988 but a further eight aircraft were built by Island Aviation Ltd. The design was taken over by ASL Hagfors in Sweden who completed two aircraft to achieve JAR-VLA certification and renamed the Super2 as the Opus 280. They also went out of business in 1995. In 1999 rights to the Super2 were acquired by the American company Skycraft International who are selling kits for the aircraft. At the end of 1999 the majority of ARV Super2s were still active in the UK.

ARV Super2, G-DEXP

Specification	ARV Super2	
Powerplant	One 77 h.p. (57.4 kW) Hewland AE.75 piston engine	
Dimensions		
Span	8.69 m	(28 ft 6 in)
Length	5.49 m	(18 ft 0 in)
Height	2.31 m	(7 ft 7 in)
Performance		
Max speed	202 km/h	(109 kt, 126 mph)
Cruising speed	177 km/h	(96 kt, 110 mph)
Initial climb	244 m/min	(800 fpm)
Range	685 km	(370 nm, 426 miles)
Weights		
Max takeoff	499 kg	(1,100 lbs)
Useful load	211 kg	(465 lbs)

Atlas C4M Kudu — South Africa

Having assembled a batch of 32 Aermacchi AM-3C liaison aircraft, Atlas Aircraft developed a new general-utility aircraft for the South African Air Force using many of the features of the Italian type. The C4M Kudu was a strut-braced high-wing aircraft with a fixed tailwheel undercarriage. It used the wing design of the Aermacchi AL-60 and had a very similar square-section fuselage. Atlas selected the same Lycoming GSO-480 geared piston engine used on the Aermacchi AL60-C4 but the Kudu was fitted with a new swept vertical tail and a starboard-side parachute door. Internal accommodation was for up to six troops and two crew or equivalent freight. The prototype flew on 16th February 1974 and 40 are believed to have been delivered. Most of these are now out of service with the SAAF but some are now in private commercial operation.

Atlas C4M Kudu, 995

Specification	Atlas C4M Kudu	
Powerplant	One 340 h.p. (254 kW) Piaggio-Lycoming GSO-480-B1B3 piston engine	
Dimensions		
Span	13.1 m	(42 ft 11 in)
Length	9.3 m	(30 ft 6 in)
Height	3.66 m	(12 ft 0 in)
Performance		
Max speed	259 km/h	(140 kt, 161 mph)
Cruising speed	233 km/h	(126 kt, 145 mph)
Initial climb	244 m/min	(800 fpm)
Range	1,290 km	(700 nm, 806 miles)
Weights		
Max takeoff	2,040 kg	(4,497 lbs)
Useful load	810 kg	(1,786 lbs)

Auster (Taylorcraft) Plus D — UK

The Taylorcraft Plus C and Plus D were British-built versions of the American Taylor-Young Model A high-wing side-by-side two-seat light aircraft. Launched in 1938 the Plus C had a 55 h.p. Lycoming O-145 engine but the main production version, the Plus D, was fitted with a 90 h.p. Blackburn Cirrus Minor in-line engine. Many Plus Cs were re-engined with Cirrus Minors as the Plus C.2. The Plus D first flew in June 1939 and immediately became adopted for wartime army cooperation duties as the Auster I. Some 100 examples of the Auster I were built and more than half of these were civilianised after the war as Taylorcraft Plus Ds. The Auster III (Model F) followed the Auster I into production and it had a 180 h.p. DH Gipsy Major engine and split trailing edge flaps. Nine Taylorcraft Plus Ds and four Auster IIIs are active in the UK and others fly in Ireland and Australia.

Auster III, LB312 (G-AHXE)

Specification	Auster (Taylorcraft) Plus D	
Powerplant	One 90 h.p. (67.1 kW) Blackburn Cirrus Minor 1 piston engine	
Dimensions		
Span	11 m	(36 ft 0 in)
Length	7 m	(22 ft 10 in)
Height	2.4 m	(8 ft 0 in)
Performance		
Max speed	191 km/h	(104 kt, 120 mph)
Cruising speed	164 km/h	(89 kt, 102 mph)
Initial climb	305 m/min	(1,000 fpm)
Range	521 km	(283 nm, 325 miles)
Weights		
Max takeoff	659 kg	(1,450 lbs)
Useful load	255 kg	(560 lbs)

Auster 5 and J/1 — UK

The wartime Auster III was replaced by the Auster 4 (Model G) and Auster 5 (Model J) with a larger three-seat fuselage and all-round vision canopy and powered by a 130 h.p. Lycoming O-290. After the war further Mark 5s were built and surplus military aircraft sold to civil customers. The J airframe then became the J/1 Autocrat with a 100 h.p. Blackburn Cirrus Minor. The J/5 Adventurer was a J/1 with a 130 h.p. Gipsy Major 1 and the J/1B Aiglet (or J/1N Alpha-Autocrat conversion) was a J/5 with a larger tail. The D5 Husky was a J/1N with a 160 h.p. Lycoming O-320-A and a further variant, the D.5/180, had a 180 h.p. Lycoming O-360-A2A engine and an enlarged fin and was built by Beagle as the Beagle Husky and by OGMA in Portugal. The J/2 Arrow was a side-by-side two-seat variant of the J airframe fitted with a 75 h.p. Continental C75-12 engine, later developed into the D4 with a 108 h.p. Lycoming. The J/1U Workmaster was a strengthened Autocrat with a 180 h.p. Lycoming O-360, primarily intended for crop spraying, fitted with underwing Micronair atomiser units. A total of 1,740 standard J series was built together with 73 with the J/2 airframe and around 200 are still active.

Auster (Beagle) D5/180 Husky, G-ATCD

Auster 5 and J/1 (Cont.)

Auster J/1 Autocrat, D-EHUN

Specification	Auster J/1 Autocrat	
Powerplant	One 100 h.p. (74.56 kW) Blackburn Cirrus Minor 2 piston engine	
Dimensions		
Span	11 m	(36 ft 0 in)
Length	7.1 m	(23 ft 5 in)
Height	2 m	(6 ft 6 in)
Performance		
Max speed	191 km/h	(104 kt, 120 mph)
Cruising speed	160 km/h	(87 kt, 100 mph)
Initial climb	174 m/min	(570 fpm)
Range	515 km	(278 nm, 320 miles)
Weights		
Max takeoff	841 kg	(1,850 lbs)
Useful load	363 kg	(798 lbs)

Auster 6, T.7 and Beagle Terrier — UK

After the war, Auster produced the AOP.6 as a replacement for the wartime Auster 4 and Auster 5 army observation posts. This had more extensive cabin transparencies, a strengthened rear fuselage, 145 h.p. DH Gipsy Major 7 in-line engine and distinctive separated trailing edge flaps. Some 379 AOP.6s and 83 of the T.7 dual-control trainer version were supplied to the RAF and to the air forces of Belgium, Canada, New Zealand and South Africa. In 1961, Beagle launched the A.61 based on refurbished AOP.6 airframes; 82 were completed and sold as the three-seat A.61 Terrier for flying clubs and the A.61 Tugmaster for glider towing. The Terrier 2 had a larger tail and a modified undercarriage and flaps and the single Terrier 3 was fitted with a 180 h.p. Lycoming O-320 engine. Around 50 aircraft are in civil use in the UK and others are flying in Sweden, Finland and Ireland.

Auster AOP.6, TW641 G-ATDN

Specification	Auster (Beagle) A.61 Tugmaster	
Powerplant	One 145 h.p. (108.1 kW) de Havilland Gipsy Major 10 Mk.1-1 piston engine	
Dimensions		
Span	11 m	(36 ft 0 in)
Length	7.2 m	(23 ft 9 in)
Height	2.5 m	(8 ft 4 in)
Performance		
Max speed	197 km/h	(107 kt, 123 mph)
Cruising speed	177 km/h	(96 kt, 110 mph)
Initial climb	244 m/min	(800 fpm)
Range	512 km	(278 nm, 320 miles)
Weights		
Max takeoff	998 kg	(2,200 lbs)
Useful load	364 kg	(800 lbs)

Auster J/5 Autocar and J/5 F Aiglet Trainer — UK

The J/5B Autocar was based on the three-seat J/1 Autocrat but with a wider rear fuselage and raised rear cabin to accommodate four people. It was first flown in August 1949 with a 130 h.p. Gipsy Major 1 engine and was followed by the J/5E (155 h.p. Cirrus Minor 3) and J/5G (155 h.p. Cirrus Major 3). A number of J/5Gs were used as crop sprayers. One example of the J/5V with a 160 h.p. Lycoming O-320-B2B was also built. The two-seat J/5F Aiglet Trainer, despite its designation and 130 h.p. Gipsy Major 1 engine, owed more to the J/1 than to the Autocar. It was the first aerobatic Auster and other variants included the J/8L (145 h.p. Gipsy Major 10), J/5K (155 h.p. Cirrus Major 3) and the three-seat J/5R Alpine which was a J/8L with Autocar wings. Production of the Autocar totalled 202 and 132 of the Aiglet Trainer and related variants were built. Over 50 still exist in the UK, Australia, Argentina etc.

Auster J/5B Autocar, PH-NEH

Specification	Auster J/5G Autocar	
Powerplant	One 155 h.p. (115.6 kW) Blackburn Cirrus Major 3 piston engine	
Dimensions		
Span	11 m	(36 ft 0 in)
Length	7.1 m	(23 ft 2 in)
Height	2 m	(6 ft 6 in)
Performance		
Max speed	202 km/h	(110 kt, 127 mph)
Cruising speed	177 km/h	(96 kt, 110 mph)
Initial climb	216 m/min	(710 fpm)
Range	780 km	(422 nm, 485 miles)
Weights		
Max takeoff	1,110 kg	(2,450 lbs)
Useful load	491 kg	(1,083 lbs)

Auster AOP.9 — UK

The AOP.9 (Auster B.5) was a major departure from the traditional Auster tube and fabric construction and was a completely new design although it retained the familiar strut-braced high-wing Auster layout. Built as a replacement for the Auster AOP.6, it first flew on 19th March 1954 and was an all-metal aircraft with a slab-sided fuselage and a three-seat cabin with large window area for its forward air control role. It was powered by a 180 h.p. Blackburn Cirrus Bombardier 203 in-line piston engine. Deliveries were made to the British Army and to the South African Air Force and the Indian Army with total production of 182 aircraft. After the sale of Auster to Beagle, one AOP.9 was converted to become the Beagle E.3 (also A.115 or AOP.11) with a 260 h.p. Continental IO-470-D engine but Beagle did not build it in quantity. Some 16 AOP.9s together with the E.3 are currently in use with UK private owners.

Auster AOP.9, XK417 G-AVXY

Specification	Auster AOP.9	
Powerplant	One 180 h.p. (134.2 kW) Blackburn Cirrus Bombardier 203 piston engine	
Dimensions		
Span	11.1 m	(36 ft 5 in)
Length	7.2 m	(23 ft 8 in)
Height	2.6 m	(8 ft 5 in)
Performance		
Max speed	203 km/h	(110 kt, 127 mph)
Cruising speed	176 km/h	(96 kt, 110 mph)
Initial climb	283 m/min	(930 fpm)
Range	394 km	(214 nm, 246 miles)
Weights		
Max takeoff	968 kg	(2,130 lbs)
Useful load	305 kg	(670 lbs)

Avia FL.3 and Lombardi Meteor — Italy

The low-wing two-seat Lombardi FL.3 dates back to 1936 when AVIA started production of over 300 for the Regia Aeronautica and a further 53 FL.3s were built after the war by Francis Lombardi. The FL.3, of which there are three in Italy and one in the UK, was a wood and fabric aircraft with a fixed tailwheel undercarriage and a 60 h.p. CNA D.4 engine. Some used the 65 h.p. Continental A65. AVIA also built seven LM.5 Aviastars with a 90 h.p. Continental C90, a modified rear fuselage and a retractable undercarriage (one of which still exists in Italy). The FL.3 design was taken over by Meteor SpA who built 39 of a modernised version. Its Meteor FL.53 had a cut-down rear fuselage and a clear bubble canopy and was fitted with a 65 h.p. Continental A65 engine. The three-seat FL.54 with a longer cockpit had a 90 h.p. Continental C90 and the four-seat FL.55 had four seats and a 135 h.p. Lycoming O-290-3.

Avia FL.3 and Lombardi Meteor (Cont.)

AVIA Lombardi Meteor FL.3, I-PADA

Specification	Meteor FL.54	
Powerplant	One 90 h.p. (67.1 kW) Teledyne Continental C90 piston engine	
Dimensions		
Span	9.85 m	(32 ft 3 in)
Length	6.37 m	(20 ft 10 in)
Height	1.8 m	(5 ft 10 in)
Performance		
Max speed	195 km/h	(106 kt, 122 mph)
Cruising speed	180 km/h	(98 kt, 113 mph)
Initial climb	61 m/min	(200 fpm)
Range	416 km	(226 nm, 260 miles)
Weights		
Max takeoff	700 kg	(1,543 lbs)
Useful load	320 kg	(706 lbs)

AviaBellanca Skyrocket III — USA

Bellanca Development Co., formed by the aviation pioneer Guiseppe Bellanca and his son August T. Bellanca, designed the Bellanca Model 19-25 Skyrocket II in the late 1960s and flew a prototype in March 1975. The six-seat Skyrocket is a streamlined low-wing cabin monoplane with a retractable tricycle undercarriage and a laminar-flow wing. It is built from composite materials and powered by a 435 h.p. Continental GTSIO-520-F six-cylinder piston engine. The prototype is claimed to be the world's fastest six-seat piston-engined aircraft and has achieved five FAI closed-circuit speed records. AviaBellanca was formed in 1983 to develop the Skyrocket and certification testing is under way with both pressurised and unpressurised variants in view. The Skyrocket III is a kit-built version of the aircraft which is now being sold to amateur builders.

AviaBellanca Skyrocket III, N771AB

Specification	AviaBellanca Skyrocket III	
Powerplant	One 435 h.p. (324.3 kW) Teledyne Continental GTSIO-520F piston engine	
Dimensions		
Span	10.67 m	(35 ft 0 in)
Length	8.23 m	(27 ft 0 in)
Height	2.74 m	(9 ft 0 in)
Performance		
Max speed	547 km/h	(296 kt, 340 mph)
Cruising speed	505 km/h	(273 kt, 314 mph)
Initial climb	634 m/min	(2,080 fpm)
Range	2,880 km	(1,565 nm, 1,800 miles)
Weights		
Max takeoff	1,905 kg	(4,200 lbs)
Useful load	776 kg	(1,710 lbs)

Aviakit Hermès — France

The French company Aviakit (also known as Kitair) designed the Hermès as a practical ultralight two-seater which would be capable of assembly by inexperienced builders in a reasonable timescale. The Hermès, which has a side-by-side cabin and a cruciform tail, is constructed of wood and composite materials and has a relatively high useful load due to its lightweight construction. It can be fitted with various engines in the 60 to 80 horsepower range including the Rotax 582, Rotax 912 and the Jabiru. The latest version of the Hermès is the Véga which has been redesigned with all-composite construction.

Aviakit Véga

Specification	Aviakit Véga	
Powerplant	One 80 h.p. (59.6 kW) Jabiru 2200 piston engine	
Dimensions		
Span	13.4 m	(43 ft 10 in)
Length	7.2 m	(23 ft 7 in)
Height	1.4 m	(4 ft 6 in)
Performance		
Max speed	230 km/h	(124 kt, 143 mph)
Cruising speed	200 km/h	(108 kt, 124 mph)
Initial climb	360 m/min	(1,180 fpm)
Range	1,200 km	(652 nm, 750 miles)
Weights		
Max takeoff	450 kg	(992 lbs)
Useful load	181 kg	(399 lbs)

Aviamilano/Aeromere F.8L Falco — Italy

The Falco was designed by Stelio Frati for sale to discerning private owners and licensed to various companies for manufacture. It is a highly streamlined side-by-side two-seater with a bubble cockpit canopy and retractable tricycle undercarriage. Construction is of wood and plywood and the prototype first flew on 15th June 1955 powered by a 90 h.p. Continental engine. The initial production Aviamilano Falco I, ten of which were built, used a 135 h.p. Lycoming O-290-D2B and the second batch of ten Falco IIs had a 150 h.p. Lycoming O-320-A2A. Manufacture was taken over by Aeromere who completed 36 F.8L Falco III Americas and the final batch of 20 Falco IVs, known as the Falco Super, was built by Laverda and fitted with a 160 h.p. Lycoming O-320-B3 engine. The Falco design has been made available to amateur builders as the Sequoia Falco and over 30 have been completed.

Aviamilano F.8L Falco I, HB-UOK

Specification	Aviamilano F.8L Falco Srs.II	
Powerplant	One 150 h.p. (111.8 kW) Textron Lycoming O-320 piston engine	
Dimensions		
Span	8 m	(26 ft 3 in)
Length	6.5 m	(21 ft 4 in)
Height	2.27 m	(7 ft 6 in)
Performance		
Max speed	323 km/h	(175 kt, 202 mph)
Cruising speed	288 km/h	(156 kt, 180 mph)
Initial climb	300 m/min	(985 fpm)
Range	1,120 km	(609 nm, 700 miles)
Weights		
Max takeoff	780 kg	(1,720 lbs)
Useful load	260 kg	(573 lbs)

Aviamilano F.14 Nibbio — Italy

The F.8 Falco designed by Stelio Frati achieved considerable success in the 1950s and was followed by a four-seat version, the F.14 Nibbio. Using a scaled-up version of Falco's wood and plywood structure, the Nibbio had a fully enclosed cabin in place of the sliding bubble canopy of the earlier aircraft. The Nibbio has a retractable tricycle undercarriage and is powered by a 180 h.p. Lycoming engine. The prototype first flew on 16th January 1958 and ten production Nibbios were built by Aviamilano. Several of these are currently flying in Europe.

Aviamilano Nibbio, I-CHER

Specification	Aviamilano F.14 Nibbio	
Powerplant	One 180 h.p. (134.2 kW) Textron Lycoming O-360-A1A piston engine	
Dimensions		
Span	9.47 m	(31 ft 1 in)
Length	7.26 m	(23 ft 10 in)
Height	2.46 m	(8 ft 1 in)
Performance		
Max speed	336 km/h	(182 kt, 210 mph)
Cruising speed	312 km/h	(169 kt, 195 mph)
Initial climb	366 m/min	(1,200 fpm)
Range	990 km	(539 nm, 620 miles)
Weights		
Max takeoff	1,152 kg	(2,539 lbs)
Useful load	470 kg	(1,035 lbs)

Aviamilano P.19 Scricciolo
— Italy

In 1960, Aviamilano was declared winner of the Aero Club d'Italia competition for a new two-seat club trainer. Its low-wing two-seat design, the P.19 Scricciolo, was a conventional tailwheel aircraft with side-by-side seating and a large rearward-sliding bubble canopy. Construction was of steel tube, wood and fabric and the prototype first flew on 13th December 1959 powered by a 95 h.p. Continental C90-12F engine. The production model was fitted with a 100 h.p. Continental O-200-A and the P.19R glider-towing version, which was built from 1964 onwards, had a 150 h.p. Lycoming O-320-A1A engine. Two batches of 25 production aircraft were built, ten of which, designated P.19Tr, were fitted with tricycle undercarriages. One Scricciolo is currently active in Austria and six in Italy including two of the glider tug version.

Aviamilano Scricciolo I-GUID

Specification	Aviamilano P.19 Scricciolo	
Powerplant	One 100 h.p. (74.6 kW) Teledyne Continental O-200-A piston engine	
Dimensions		
Span	10.2 m	(33 ft 7 in)
Length	7 m	(23 ft 0 in)
Height	2.1 m	(6 ft 9 in)
Performance		
Max speed	208 km/h	(113 kt, 130 mph)
Cruising speed	184 km/h	(100 kt, 115 mph)
Initial climb	168 m/min	(550 fpm)
Range	656 km	(357 nm, 410 miles)
Weights		
Max takeoff	786 kg	(1,730 lbs)
Useful load	260 kg	(573 lbs)

Aviat-Pitts S-1 Special
— USA

The Pitts Special biplane was designed and built by Curtis Pitts in 1943 and has become one of the best known of all aerobatic aircraft. Constructed of tube and fabric, the single-seat Pitts S-1C was sold initially in the form of plans for amateur builders by Pitts Enterprises with various engines in the 55 h.p. to 150 h.p. range and the S-1D was a developed version with four ailerons. A factory-built Pitts Special, the S-1S with a 180 h.p. Lycoming IO-360 (or S-1T with a 200 h.p. engine) was produced by Aerotek and they also sold kits for the S-1E. In 1981, rights to the Pitts Specials passed to Christen Industries which became Aviat in 1991 and they have continued to sell the S-1T and plans for the S-1S. Curtis Pitts has developed the new S-1-11B Super Stinker which is marketed by Aviat in kit form. This has new wings, a deeper fuselage with a single rear-set cockpit and a 300 h.p. Lycoming O-540 engine.

Pitts Special S-1S, LX-POL

Specification	Aviat-Pitts S-1T Special	
Powerplant	One 200 h.p. (149 kW) Textron Lycoming AEIO-360-A1E piston engine	
Dimensions		
Span	5.28 m	(17 ft 4 in)
Length	4.72 m	(15 ft 6 in)
Height	1.91 m	(6 ft 3 in)
Performance		
Max speed	298 km/h	(161 kt, 185 mph)
Cruising speed	282 km/h	(152 kt, 175 mph)
Initial climb	853 m/min	(2,800 fpm)
Range	495 km	(268 nm, 308 miles)
Weights		
Max takeoff	521 kg	(1,150 lbs)
Useful load	145 kg	(320 lbs)

Aviat-Pitts S-2 — USA

First flown in 1967, the Pitts S-2 was a stretched two-seat version of the popular S-1 Pitts Special, powered by a 180 h.p. Lycoming IO-360. Aerotek put the S-2 into production as the the S-2A, generally fitted with a bubble canopy covering the tandem cockpits and powered by a 200 h.p. Lycoming AEIO-360-A1A engine. The later S-2B was an S-2A with a 260 h.p. AEIO-540 and the S-2S was an S-2B with a single rear cockpit. The S-2E and S-2SE are the S-2A and S-2S built by amateurs from a factory kit. Under Aviat, the S-2C was introduced in 1998 with a cleaned-up airframe, a flatter vertical tail, modified wings with squared-off rear tips, a redesigned cockpit canopy and new engine cowling. Aviat continue to build the S-2C and the S-2S. More than 675 Pitts S-2s had been completed by Aerotek, Christen and Aviat by the end of 1999.

Aviat-Pitts Special S-2C, N119PS

Specification	Aviat-Pitts S-2B	
Powerplant	One 260 h.p. (194 kW) Textron Lycoming AEIO-540-D4A5 piston engine	
Dimensions		
Span	6.1 m	(20 ft 0 in)
Length	5.71 m	(18 ft 9 in)
Height	2.02 m	(6 ft 8 in)
Performance		
Max speed	338 km/h	(182 kt, 210 mph)
Cruising speed	282 km/h	(152 kt, 175 mph)
Initial climb	823 m/min	(2,700 fpm)
Range	510 km	(277 nm, 319 miles)
Weights		
Max takeoff	737 kg	(1,625 lbs)
Useful load	361 kg	(796 lbs)

Aviat A-1 Husky — USA

In March 1991 Christen Industries changed hands and was renamed Aviat. Christen had designed the tandem two-seat A-1 Husky which closely resembled the Piper Super Cub and flew the first prototype in 1986. It is of tube and fabric construction with a strut-braced high wing and fixed tailwheel undercarriage and it is powered by a 180 h.p. Lycoming O-360-C1G engine with a Hartzell constant-speed propeller. The Husky went into production at Afton, Wyoming in the following year and total production to date exceeds 570 aircraft. The aircraft is widely used for bush operations and for glider towing and other utility work. The latest version is the Husky A-1A with a strengthened wing and undercarriage and a higher useful load. The A-1B is a further version aimed at government forestry and wildlife agencies with a further gross weight increase. The Husky has been exported to many countries, particularly Canada where its good takeoff performance and ability to operate on skis or floats is an important asset.

Aviat Husky A-1, N49364

Specification	Aviat A-1B Husky	
Powerplant	One 180 h.p. (134.2 kW) Textron Lycoming O-360-A1P piston engine	
Dimensions		
Span	10.82 m	(35 ft 6 in)
Length	6.9 m	(22 ft 7 in)
Height	2.01 m	(6 ft 7 in)
Performance		
Max speed	231 km/h	(126 kt, 145 mph)
Cruising speed	222 km/h	(121 kt, 140 mph)
Initial climb	457 m/min	(1,500 fpm)
Range	1,255 km	(687 nm, 791 miles)
Weights		
Max takeoff	907 kg	(2,000 lbs)
Useful load	367 kg	(810 lbs)

Aviatika 890 — Russia

Built by the Moscow Industrial Aviation Association, the Aviatika 890 is a single-seat ultralight biplane, first flown in 1990, which has been constructed in some numbers and is in operation with private owners in several European countries. It has a basic tubular frame structure on which is fitted a fibreglass cabin pod, a vertical pylon mounting the pusher engine and upper wing and the tail unit. The 890 has a fixed tricycle undercarriage and the cabin is fully enclosed. Mounting points for accessories are provided on the engine nacelle and these are used on some 890s for the spray tank for Micronair agricultural spraying equipment. The 890U is a side-by-side two-seat version with dual controls using the same airframe. Both variants are powered by either a 64 h.p. Rotax 582 or an 80 h.p. Rotax 912. Aviatika have also flown an autogyro version with a freewheeling rotor in place of the upper wing.

Aviatika 890 (Cont.)

Aviatika 890

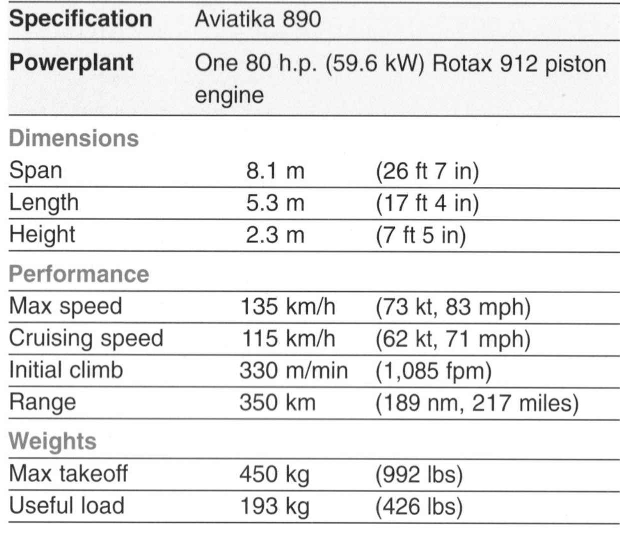

Specification	Aviatika 890	
Powerplant	One 80 h.p. (59.6 kW) Rotax 912 piston engine	
Dimensions		
Span	8.1 m	(26 ft 7 in)
Length	5.3 m	(17 ft 4 in)
Height	2.3 m	(7 ft 5 in)
Performance		
Max speed	135 km/h	(73 kt, 83 mph)
Cruising speed	115 km/h	(62 kt, 71 mph)
Initial climb	330 m/min	(1,085 fpm)
Range	350 km	(189 nm, 217 miles)
Weights		
Max takeoff	450 kg	(992 lbs)
Useful load	193 kg	(426 lbs)

Aviation Traders ATL.98 Carvair — UK

The Carvair was devised by Aviation Traders (Engineering) Ltd. of Southend as a replacement for the Bristol 170s which were operating on the vehicle ferry services across the English Channel. It was based on the Douglas DC-4 (C-54) airframe with a completely new nose section grafted on ahead of the wing and a new vertical tail similar to that of the DC-6. The new forward fuselage had a side-opening nose door to allow loading of the vehicles or freight pallets and the cockpit was moved to a new structure above the roof line. The ATL.98 could carry five cars and had a rear cabin for up to 26 passengers. The first Carvair was flown on 21st June 1961 and delivered to Channel Air Bridge in February 1962. It was followed by 20 further conversions, the last of which was completed in April 1969. The Carvairs later served various carriers as freighters and five are still extant.

ATL.98 Carvair, N89FA

Specification	Aviation Traders ATL.98 Carvair	
Powerplant	Four 1,450 h.p. (1,081.1 kW) Pratt & Whitney R-2000-7M2 Twin Wasp piston engines	
Dimensions		
Span	35.82 m	(117 ft 6 in)
Length	31.27 m	(102 ft 7 in)
Height	9.09 m	(29 ft 10 in)
Performance		
Max speed	402 km/h	(217 kt, 250 mph)
Cruising speed	342 km/h	(185 kt, 213 mph)
Initial climb	198 m/min	(650 fpm)
Range	5,560 km	(3,004 nm, 3,455 miles)
Weights		
Max takeoff	33,475 kg	(73,812 lbs)
Useful load	14,743 kg	(32,508 lbs)

Avid Flyer — USA

Designed by Dean Wilson, following his very successful Kitfox, the ultralight Avid Flyer was first flown in 1983 as a kit aircraft for amateur construction. A classic tube and fabric design with an enclosed side-by-side two-seat cabin, the Flyer could be fitted with either a tailwheel, tricycle or float under-carriage. The early models had a distinctive tail with a curved leading edge and straight trailing edge and foldable standard or 'Speed' wings. Power was a 45 h.p. Cayuna or 65 h.p. Rotax 532. The current Avid Mk.IV introduced by Avid Aircraft in 1992 has a new rounded rudder, rear baggage compartment and a Rotax 582 or 912, and the economy version, the Bandit, uses the 50 h.p. Rotax 503. The heavier Avid Magnum is powered by a 160 h.p. Lycoming O-320 or other engines in the 125 h.p. to 180 h.p. range and can be fully IFR-equipped. Over 2,000 kits for the Avid Flyer and Magnum have been sold.

Avid Mk.IV Aerobat, G-EFRY

Specification	Avid Flyer Mk.IV STOL	
Powerplant	One 65 h.p. (48.5 kW) Rotax 582 piston engine	
Dimensions		
Span	9.11 m	(29 ft 10 in)
Length	5.46 m	(17 ft 11 in)
Height	1.85 m	(6 ft 1 in)
Performance		
Max speed	169 km/h	(91 kt, 105 mph)
Cruising speed	148 km/h	(80 kt, 92 mph)
Initial climb	305 m/min	(1,000 fpm)
Range	547 km	(295 nm, 340 miles)
Weights		
Max takeoff	522 kg	(1,150 lbs)
Useful load	290 kg	(640 lbs)

Avid Amphibian/Catalina — USA

The Avid Amphibian was first flown on 12th July 1985 as a three-seat amphibian for construction by amateur builders and kits were sold by Light Aero (later Avid Aircraft) from 1986 onwards. The Amphibian uses many parts from the Avid Flyer and is a strut-braced high-wing machine with a planing hull and additional sponsons set on the fuselage sides which also contain the retractable main undercarriage units. The forward fuselage is a glass-fibre shell and the rear fuselage and wings, which are foldable, are fabric-covered. It is powered by a 65 h.p. Rotax 582 or a 100 h.p. AMW engine mounted as a pusher in a nacelle above the wing centre section. Avid subsequently updated the Amphibian to incorporate additional wing-mounted floats, the Avid Mk.IV tail unit and an improved windshield in which form it is known as the Catalina. Over 150 of the Amphibian/Catalina are flying.

Avid Catalina, N61HS

Specification	Avid Catalina	
Powerplant	One 65 h.p. (48.5 kW) Rotax 582 piston engine	
Dimensions		
Span	10.97 m	(36 ft 0 in)
Length	5.92 m	(19 ft 5 in)
Height	1.75 m	(5 ft 9 in)
Performance		
Max speed	144 km/h	(78 kt, 90 mph)
Cruising speed	120 km/h	(65 kt, 75 mph)
Initial climb	305 m/min	(1,000 fpm)
Range	525 km	(285 nm, 328 miles)
Weights		
Max takeoff	545 kg	(1,200 lbs)
Useful load	273 kg	(600 lbs)

Avions de Transport Regional ATR42 — Italy/France

ATR (Avions de Transport Regional) was formed in July 1980 by Aérospatiale and Aeritalia to produce a new regional airliner for world airlines. Targeting the 42/50-passenger market, the ATR42 was announced in 1981 and the first ATR42-200 was flown on 16th August 1984. The ATR42 has a high-wing layout with a T-tail and two 1,800 s.h.p. Pratt & Whitney PW120 turboprops. The retractable tricycle undercarriage incorporates lower fuselage fairings for the main units. The first customer ATR42-300 with a strengthened structure was delivered in December 1985. The later ATR42-320 had 1,900 s.h.p. PW121 engines and it was upgraded to ATR42-510 standard with 2,400 s.h.p. PW127E with 6-blade propellers, a higher gross weight, reduced cabin noise and an improved cockpit. The ATR42 Surveyor is a maritime patrol version which can be fitted with a range of internal and external sensors and radars. Most of the 370 ATR42s which had been built by the end of 2000 remain in operation worldwide, the largest fleet being American Eagle's with 45 aircraft.

ATR42-510, A4O-AS

Avions de Transport Regional ATR42 (Cont.)

Specification	Avions de Transport Regional ATR42-510	
Powerplant	Two 2,160 s.h.p. (1,611 kW) Pratt & Whitney Canada PW127E turboprops	
Dimensions		
Span	24.57 m	(80 ft 7 in)
Length	22.67 m	(74 ft 5 in)
Height	7.59 m	(24 ft 11 in)
Performance		
Max speed	561 km/h	(305 kt, 350 mph)
Cruising speed	515 km/h	(280 kt, 322 mph)
Takeoff distance	1,097 m	(3,600 ft)
Range	1,600 km	(870 nm, 1,000 miles)
Weights		
Max takeoff	18,636 kg	(41,092 lbs)
Useful load	7,364 kg	(16,238 lbs)

Avions de Transport Regional ATR72 — Italy/France

The success of the ATR42 programme led to a demand for a larger-capacity version of the aircraft. A fairly simple stretch was carried out which added 14 ft 9 in to the fuselage and provided an increase in passenger capacity from 50 passengers to 74. The wings of the new ATR72 were lengthened by 8 ft 1 in and the area of the tail fin was increased. The ATR72 was powered, initially, by 2,160 s.h.p. Pratt & Whitney PW124B turboprops but the later ATR72-210 had 2,480 s.h.p. PW127s with new four-bladed propellers. The ATR72-510 was equipped with six-bladed Ratier propellers giving it much improved cruise performance and also featured the noise reduction changes used on the ATR42-500. The ATR72 prototype made its maiden flight on 27th October 1988 and production aircraft started to enter service the following year with Finnair and Binter Canarias. American Eagle again built up a large fleet and nearly 250 ATR72s were in service by mid 2000.

ATR72-212A, 4X-AVZ

Specification	Avions de Transport Regional ATR72-210	
Powerplant	Two 2,160 s.h.p. (1,611 kW) Pratt & Whitney Canada PW124B turboprops	
Dimensions		
Span	27.05 m	(88 ft 9 in)
Length	27.17 m	(89 ft 2 in)
Height	7.65 m	(25 ft 1 in)
Performance		
Max speed	515 km/h	(280 kt, 322 mph)
Cruising speed	496 km/h	(270 kt, 310 mph)
Takeoff distance	1,122 m	(3,680 ft)
Range	2,200 km	(1,196 nm, 1,375 miles)
Weights		
Max takeoff	21,545 kg	(47,507 lbs)
Useful load	9,120 kg	(20,110 lbs)

Avro 616 Avian IVM — UK

Originally built as the Avro 581 which first flew in 1926, the production Avro 594 Avian and Avro 616 Avian IVM were successful club and training biplanes built in quantity for the prewar market. The early Avians, 195 of which were built and one of which is under restoration to flying condition, were of wood, ply and fabric but the Avian IVM had a welded steel fuselage frame. This was intended as an export version due to its greater structural strength and 381 were built including aircraft sold to Canada, China, Australia, Argentina and Singapore. Several engines were fitted including the 100 h.p. DH Gipsy I, the 115 h.p. Cirrus Hermes II and the 135 h.p. Armstrong Siddeley Genet Major. The only surviving airworthy Avian is owned by Lang Kidby in Australia and was used for the 1998 Bert Hinkler commemorative flight from England to Australia.

Avro Avian IVM, VH-UFZ

Specification	Avro 616 Avian IVM	
Powerplant	One 115 h.p. (85.7 kW) Cirrus Hermès II piston engine	
Dimensions		
Span	8.53 m	(28 ft 0 in)
Length	7.39 m	(24 ft 3 in)
Height	2.59 m	(8 ft 6 in)
Performance		
Max speed	161 km/h	(87 kt, 100 mph)
Cruising speed	145 km/h	(78 kt, 90 mph)
Initial climb	183 m/min	(600 fpm)
Range	579 km	(313 nm, 360 miles)
Weights		
Max takeoff	726 kg	(1,600 lbs)
Useful load	272 kg	(600 lbs)

Avro 643 Cadet Mk.II — UK

Derived from the Avro Tutor military trainer used by the RAF in the 1930s, the Cadet was an open-cockpit tandem two-seat biplane for use by civilian flying clubs. It was also widely used by the commercial training schools which sprang up in the prewar period. The Cadet differed from the Tutor in having a wooden wing structure but it retained the tubular steel fuselage frame and was covered in fabric. The initial Model 631 appeared in 1931 with a 135 h.p. Genet Major radial engine and it was succeeded by the Model 643 with a slightly larger fuselage and the Cadet Mk.II with a 150 h.p. Genet Major IA engine. A batch of 34 Cadets was delivered to the Royal Australian Air Force out of a total of 65 completed aircraft. Most of the surviving Cadets are Cadet IIs and two remain in Ireland, one in the USA and five in Australia, including one Jacobs-engined example, although not all of them are currently airworthy.

Avro 643 Tutor Mk.II, VH-AFX

Specification	Avro 643 Cadet II	
Powerplant	One 150 h.p. (111.8 kW) Armstrong Siddeley Genet Major IA piston engine	
Dimensions		
Span	9.19 m	(30 ft 2 in)
Length	7.54 m	(24 ft 9 in)
Height	2.69 m	(8 ft 10 in)
Performance		
Max speed	187 km/h	(100 kt, 116 mph)
Cruising speed	161 km/h	(87 kt, 100 mph)
Initial climb	213 m/min	(700 fpm)
Range	520 km	(283 nm, 325 miles)
Weights		
Max takeoff	907 kg	(2,000 lbs)
Useful load	324 kg	(714 lbs)

Avro Lancaster — UK

The Avro 683 Lancaster was, arguably, the most famous British World War II heavy bomber. Derived from the twin-engined Avro Manchester, the Lancaster had a mid-set wing, twin tailfins and four Rolls Royce Merlin engines. It could carry 7,000 lbs of bombs, was fitted with three gun turrets and had a range of over 2,500 miles which made it highly effective in the night raids on Germany. The Lancaster prototype first flew on 9th January 1941 and 7,374 production aircraft were completed. After the war, the Lancaster continued to operate as a maritime patrol aircraft with the RAF, French Aéronavale and the RCAF. At least 21 Lancasters are maintained as museum exhibits, one continues as a flying performer in Canada, another is under restoration and the RAF Battle of Britain Memorial Flight's Lancaster B Mk.1 remains a popular performer on the British airshow circuit.

Avro Lancaster B Mk.1, PA474

Avro Lancaster (Cont.)

Specification	Avro 683 Lancaster B Mk.1	
Powerplant	Four 1,280 h.p. (954.4 kW) Rolls Royce Merlin XX piston engines	
Dimensions		
Span	31.09 m	(102 ft 0 in)
Length	21.13 m	(69 ft 4 in)
Height	6.25 m	(20 ft 6 in)
Performance		
Max speed	462 km/h	(250 kt, 287 mph)
Cruising speed	322 km/h	(174 kt, 200 mph)
Initial climb	76 m/min	(250 fpm)
Range	4,048 km	(2,200 nm, 2,530 miles)
Weights		
Max takeoff	22,675 kg	(50,000 lbs)
Useful load	6,142 kg	(13,543 lbs)

Specification	Avro 696 Shackleton MR.2	
Powerplant	Four 2,450 h.p. (1,826.7 kW) Rolls Royce Griffon 57A piston engines	
Dimensions		
Span	36.57 m	(120 ft 0 in)
Length	28.19 m	(92 ft 6 in)
Height	5.11 m	(16 ft 9 in)
Performance		
Max speed	435 km/h	(235 kt, 270 mph)
Cruising speed	410 km/h	(222 kt, 255 mph)
Initial climb	280 m/min	(920 fpm)
Range	2,880 km	(1,565 nm, 1,800 miles)
Weights		
Max takeoff	44,444 kg	(98,000 lbs)
Useful load	18,685 kg	(41,200 lbs)

Avro 696 Shackleton — UK

Owing much to the design of the Avro Lancaster and Lincoln bombers, the Shackleton was designed from the outset as a maritime reconnaissance aircraft for use by RAF Coastal Command and it served from the early 1950s until retired in 1991. The initial Shackleton MR.1, which first flew on 9th March 1949, had a mid-set wing, twin-fin tail unit, a tailwheel undercarriage and a chin radome for the ASV antenna. Power came from four 2,450 h.p. Rolls Royce Griffon engines with counter-rotating propellers. Three prototypes and 77 production MR.1s were built followed by the MR.2, of which 69 were completed with a longer nose and the radar in a retractable ventral rear fuselage container. The MR.3 was an improved MR.2 with a tricycle undercarriage, modified cockpit canopy, redesigned wing with wingtip tanks and nose-mounted guns. Some 42 MR.3s were completed including eight for the South African Air Force. Shackletons have all been withdrawn from military service but an MR.2 flies in the USA, an MR.3 in South Africa and others are awaiting restoration in Cyprus and the UK.

Avro Shackleton MR.2, WL790

Avro Anson — UK

In 1935, Avro built the Avro 652 low-wing twin-engined civil light transport monoplane. This was of mixed construction and fitted with a retractable undercarriage and powered by a pair of 290 h.p. Armstrong Siddeley Cheetah engines. As the Model 652A Anson it was built in large quantities for wartime use and when the war ended the company continued to build the Anson 12 with its deeper fuselage and 425 h.p. Cheetah 15 engines. With oval windows and a nine-passenger cabin it became the Avro 19. The majority of Avro 19s were delivered to the RAF, but a number of civil aircraft were built and many of the military aircraft were subsequently civilianised. A handful of former RAF Ansons still survive including two airworthy examples in the UK.

Avro 19, G-AIWX (G-VROE)

Specification	Avro Anson 19	
Powerplant	Two 420 h.p. (313.2 kW) Armstrong Siddeley Cheetah 15 piston engines	
Dimensions		
Span	17.22 m	(56 ft 6 in)
Length	12.88 m	(42 ft 3 in)
Height	4.11 m	(13 ft 6 in)
Performance		
Max speed	293 km/h	(158 kt, 182 mph)
Cruising speed	270 km/h	(146 kt, 168 mph)
Initial climb	229 m/min	(750 fpm)
Range	1,312 km	(713 nm, 820 miles)
Weights		
Max takeoff	4,717 kg	(10,400 lbs)
Useful load	1,351 kg	(2,980 lbs)

Ayres Thrush — USA

The Thrush is a low-wing agricultural aircraft manufactured by Ayres Corporation at Albany, Georgia. It originated in the S-1 designed by Leland Snow which first flew on 17th August 1953. The production Snow S-2A had a Continental W-670 radial engine and the S-2B used a 450 h.p. Pratt & Whitney R-985. Some 95 were built in the 1950s followed by 1,466 of the S-2C and the Rockwell-built S-2R with a larger 400 USG hopper and higher power. A good number are still operational. The original S-2 had an open cockpit protected by a substantial rollover cage, a fixed tailwheel undercarriage and a forward chemical hopper, but an enclosed cockpit was installed on the S-2R Thrush Commander. Ayres acquired the design from Rockwell in 1977 and a wider range of Thrushes appeared. Although some of the S2R-1820 Bull Thrush with a Wright R-1820 piston engine and a 510 USG hopper were produced, the company largely moved to turboprop models some of which were fitted with two-seat cockpits. The Ayres Turbo Thrush variants currently on offer include the S2R-G1 with a Garrett TPE331-1 engine and a 400 USG hopper, the S2R-G6 with a TPE331-6 (400 or 510 USG hopper), the S2R-10 with a TPE331-10 (510 USG hopper), the S2R-T15 with a Pratt & Whitney PT6A-15AG (400 USG hopper) and the S2R-T34 with a PT6A-T34AG and 510 USG hopper. Ayres has also developed the Model 660 Turbo Thrush which has a 660 USG hopper and will be powered by a range of optional engines from the 940 s.h.p. Garrett TPE331-10 up to the 1,300 s.h.p. Pratt & Whitney PT6A-65AG. Total Thrush production by Ayres was more than 900 by mid 2000.

Ayres Turbo Thrush S2R-T34DC, J7-DAB

Specification	Ayres Turbo Thrush S2R-T34	
Powerplant	One 750 s.h.p. (559 kW) Pratt & Whitney PT6A-T34AG turboprop	
Dimensions		
Span	10.06 m	(33 ft 0 in)
Length	14.48 m	(47 ft 6 in)
Height	2.79 m	(9 ft 2 in)
Performance		
Max speed	256 km/h	(138 kt, 159 mph)
Working speed	161 km/h	(87 kt, 100 mph)
Initial climb	530 m/min	(1,740 fpm)
Range	1,231 km	(669 nm, 769 miles)
Weights		
Max takeoff	2,721 kg	(6,000 lbs)
Useful load	1,088 kg	(2,400 lbs)

Ayres Turbo Thrush 660, N29A

B

BA Swallow II — UK

The British Aircraft Manufacturing Co. ('BA') was the successor to the British Klemm Aeroplane Co. which manufactured the Klemm L.25C during the early 1930s. In May, 1935 they introduced the BA Swallow II which was a L.25C-1A with a more angular tail , squared-off wing planform and a simplified rear fuselage decking. The Swallow II had tandem open cockpits, folding wings and a fixed tailwheel undercarriage. Early Swallow IIs were powered by an 85 h.p. Pobjoy Cataract II or 90 h.p. Cataract III radial engine but later production aircraft used the 90 h.p. Cirrus Minor in-line engine and some were fitted with a Pobjoy Niagara II or III. At least one BA Swallow had a fully enclosed cabin canopy. A total of 105 Swallow IIs was built, many of which were exported to India, Australia and various European countries. Seven are currently registered in the UK, all with Cirrus Minor engines, and others exist in Ireland and Australia.

BA Swallow II, G-AEVZ

Specification	BA Swallow II	
Powerplant	One 90 h.p. (67.1 kW) Blackburn Cirrus Minor 1 piston engine	
Dimensions		
Span	13 m	(42 ft 8 in)
Length	8 m	(26 ft 3 in)
Height	2.1 m	(6 ft 11 in)
Performance		
Max speed	166 km/h	(90 kt, 104 mph)
Cruising speed	144 km/h	(78 kt, 90 mph)
Initial climb	244 m/min	(800 fpm)
Range	672 km	(365 nm, 420 miles)
Weights		
Max takeoff	680 kg	(1,500 lbs)
Useful load	232 kg	(510 lbs)

BA Eagle — UK

The BA Eagle was an attractive low-wing private-owner aircraft built by the British Aircraft Manufacturing Co. between 1934 and 1939. The low-wing Eagle 1 was of all-wood construction with a fully enclosed cabin accommodating the pilot together with two passengers on a rear bench seat. It had a tailwheel undercarriage with the main units retracting outwards into wing wells and was powered by a 130 h.p. de Havilland Gipsy Major in-line engine. Like the Swallow, it had foldable wings. The Eagle was flown in many prewar air races including the 1934 MacRobertson race to Australia. The BA Eagle 2 was an improved version with a deeper rear fuselage, larger forward-opening entry doors and a modified rudder. Six Eagle 1s and 37 Eagle 2s were built with export aircraft going to Australia, Spain and Malaya. One Eagle is currently airworthy in the UK and another is under restoration in Australia.

BA Eagle 2, G-AFAX

Specification	BA Eagle 2	
Powerplant	One 130 h.p. (96.9 kW) de Havilland Gipsy Major piston engine	
Dimensions		
Span	12 m	(39 ft 3 in)
Length	7.9 m	(26 ft 0 in)
Height	2.1 m	(6 ft 11 in)
Performance		
Max speed	237 km/h	(129 kt, 148 mph)
Cruising speed	208 km/h	(113 kt, 130 mph)
Initial climb	213 m/min	(700 fpm)
Range	1,040 km	(565 nm, 650 miles)
Weights		
Max takeoff	1,088 kg	(2,400 lbs)
Useful load	431 kg	(950 lbs)

BAC-Sud Concorde — UK/France

The Concorde supersonic transport was developed under a 1962 British/French agreement by British Aircraft Corporation, Sud Aviation, Rolls Royce and SNECMA. Almost every aspect of the aircraft was revolutionary and the design included a complex ogival delta wing, a drooping nose to give improved vision for take-off and landing and four Olympus 593 turbojets mounted in twin box-section fairings under the wings. The cabin was configured for 100 first-class passengers. The first of two prototype, two production prototype and three pre-production (Model 100) aircraft flew on 2nd March 1969. BAC and Aerospatiale built 13 production aircraft designated Model 101 (French-built for Air France) and Model 102 (British built for British Airways). Concorde went into service on the North Atlantic in January 1976 and 12 were in operation at the time of their grounding on 15th August 2000 following the Paris disaster.

BAC-Sud Concorde 101, F-BVFB

Specification	BAC-Sud Concorde 101	
Powerplant	Four 38,050 lb.s.t (169.27 kN) Rolls Royce/SNECMA Olympus 593 Mk.602 turbojets	
Dimensions		
Span	25.6 m	(83 ft 10 in)
Length	62.1 m	(203 ft 9 in)
Height	11.3 m	(37 ft 1 in)
Performance		
Max speed	2,180 km/h	(1,175 kt, 1,354 mph)
Cruising speed	1,930 km/h	(1,040 kt, 1,205 mph)
Initial climb	1,525 m/min	(5,000 fpm)
Range	6,300 km	(3,424 nm, 3,938 miles)
Weights		
Max takeoff	181,435 kg	(400,065 lbs)
Useful load	102,170 kg	(225,285 lbs)

BAC One-Eleven — UK

The BAC-111 medium-haul regional airliner was first flown on 20th August 1963 and was intended as replacement for the Vickers Viscount. It has a low wing, T-tail and rear fuselage-mounted engines and the initial model was the Series 200 with 89 passenger seats and fitted with two Rolls Royce Spey 506-14 turbojets. A longer-range version, the Series 300 was also built with Spey 511-14 engines and a higher gross weight. The BAC-111-400 was a restricted weight variant for the U.S. market. A total of 149 of the short-fuselage 111s was built including some sold for executive use and substantial fleets for Braniff, Mohawk Airlines, American and British United. The BAC-111-500 was a stretched version with capacity for 119 passengers which first flew on 30th June 1967. Some 86 were built by BAC and a further nine were assembled by Romaero in Romania. Approximately 100 BAC-111s remain in service.

BAC One-Eleven 412EB, AN-BBI

Specification	BAC One-Eleven Srs.500	
Powerplant	Two 12,550 lb.s.t. (55.8 kN) Rolls Royce Spey Mk.512DW turbofans	
Dimensions		
Span	28.50 m	(93 ft 6 in)
Length	32.60 m	(107 ft 0 in)
Height	7.47 m	(24 ft 6 in)
Performance		
Max speed	870 km/h	(470 kt, 541 mph)
Cruising speed	740 km/h	(400 kt, 460 mph)
Initial climb	695 m/min	(2,280 fpm)
Range	2,730 km	(1,484 nm, 1,705 miles)
Weights		
Max takeoff	47,400 kg	(104,500 lbs)
Useful load	22,640 kg	(49,920 lbs)

BAe-Hunting Jet Provost T.Mk.1 to T.Mk.4 — UK

Designed by Percival (later Hunting Percival), the P.84 Jet Provost ab initio trainer was derived from the piston-engined Provost. It was a low-wing aircraft with side-by-side seating for instructor and pupil and a single Viper ASV.5 turbojet. First flown on 26th June 1954, the Jet Provost T.Mk. 1, ten of which were built, was developed into the T.Mk.2 with a shorter undercarriage and clear cockpit canopy. The production Jet Provost T.Mk.3 had a higher-powered 1,735 lb.s.t. Viper ASV.8 engine, fixed wingtip tanks and ejection seats and delivery of the first of 201 aircraft was made to the RAF's 2FTS in 1958. Some were upgraded with new avionics as the Mk.3A. The subsequent Jet Provost T.Mk.4, 198 of which were built between 1960 and 1964, was fitted with the 2,500 lb.s.t. Viper Mk.202 engine. Some 65 Jet Provosts were exported to Iraq, Sudan, Kuwait, Sri Lanka and Venezuela. A number of Jet Provosts remain in service as warbirds with private owners.

BAe Jet Provost T.3, XM387

Specification	BAe Jet Provost T.4	
Powerplant	One 2,500 lb.s.t. (11.12 kN) Rolls Royce (Bristol Siddeley) Viper Mk.202 turbojet	
Dimensions		
Span	11.25 m	(36 ft 11 in)
Length	9.88 m	(32 ft 5 in)
Height	3.11 m	(10 ft 2 in)
Performance		
Max speed	656 km/h	(356 kt, 410 mph)
Cruising speed	624 km/h	(339 kt, 390 mph)
Initial climb	1,035 m/min	(3,400 fpm)
Range	1,120 km	(609 nm, 700 miles)
Weights		
Max takeoff	3,356 kg	(7,400 lbs)
Useful load	1,250 kg	(2,750 lbs)

BAe-Hunting Jet Provost T.Mk.5 and Strikemaster — UK

The Jet Provost T.Mk.5 (BAC.145) was a much developed version of the T.Mk.4 with a new forward fuselage incorporating a pressurised cabin with a new cockpit canopy and a longer nose. The wings were also redesigned and tip tanks were not fitted as standard. The prototype T.5 was first flown on 28th February 1967 and 110 examples of the T.Mk.5 were delivered to the RAF. Most of these were later modified to T.Mk.5A standard with new navaids. Five T.55 versions were sold to the Sudan. The BAC.167 Strikemaster was an armed version of the T.Mk.5 with four weapons hardpoints under each wing and a 3,410 lb.s.t. Viper Mk.535 engine and, generally, fixed tiptanks. The prototype flew in October 1967 and all the 144 aircraft built went for export as Strikemaster 80s to nine countries including Saudi Arabia, Kuwait, Kenya, Oman, Singapore and Ecuador.

BAe. Strikemaster, N167S

Specification	BAe Strikemaster Mk.89	
Powerplant	One 3,410 lb.s.t. (15.17 kN) Rolls Royce (Bristol Siddeley) Viper Mk.535 turbojet	
Dimensions		
Span	11.23 m	(36 ft 10 in)
Length	10.27 m	(33 ft 8 in)
Height	3.34 m	(10 ft 11 in)
Performance		
Max speed	835 km/h	(450 kt, 518 mph)
Cruising speed	725 km/h	(390 kt, 450 mph)
Initial climb	1,600 m/min	(5,250 fpm)
Range	2,210 km	(1,200 nm, 1,382 miles)
Weights		
Max takeoff	5,215 kg	(11,500 lbs)
Useful load	2,406 kg	(5,305 lbs)

BAE Systems (Handley Page) Jetstream — UK

The H.P.137 Jetstream was a low-wing light turboprop business and commuter aircraft designed by Handley Page and first flown on 18th August 1967. Forty were completed with Turboméca Astazou XIVC engines before Handley Page ceased operations in 1969 and two of these remain operational. The Jetstream was taken over by Scottish Aviation (later British Aerospace and, from 2000, BAE Systems) who built 26 Jetstream T Mk.1s for the RAF with 996 s.h.p. Astazou XVID engines. These were followed by the Jetstream 31 which first flew on 28th March 1980 and has Garrett TPE331 turboprops. It has been sold widely for use by commuter operations with a 19-seat, single-aisle configuration. Principal users include Northwest Airlink, TW Express/Trans States and United Express/Westair. Later versions included the Jetstream 32 (Super 31) with a modified wing, higher gross weight, longer range and increased power. The last of 384 Jetstreams was completed in 1994.

Specification	BAE Systems Jetstream 31	
Powerplant	Two 1,020 s.h.p. (760 kW) Honeywell (Garrett) TPE331-12UAR turboprops	
Dimensions		
Span	15.85 m	(52 ft 0 in)
Length	14.37 m	(47 ft 1 in)
Height	5.38 m	(17 ft 8 in)
Performance		
Max speed	489 km/h	(264 kt, 304 mph)
Cruising speed	452 km/h	(245 kt, 280 mph)
Initial climb	683 m/min	(2,240 fpm)
Range	1280 km	(696 nm, 800 miles)
Weights		
Max takeoff	7,349 kg	(16,204 lbs)
Useful load	2,772 kg	(6,112 lbs)

Scottish Aviation Jetstream T Mk.1, XX495

BAE Systems Jetstream 41 — UK

British Aerospace's Prestwick Division which was building the Jetstream 31 launched the 29-seat Jetstream 41 in 1989. This was based on the earlier aircraft but with a 16 ft fuselage stretch, an enlarged vertical tail, redesigned windshield, EFIS cockpit and structural modifications for the higher gross weight. The wing installation incorporated a much enlarged centre section fairing with additional baggage capacity. The Jetstream 41 also used new 1,500 s.h.p. Garrett TPE331-14 turboprops in enlarged nacelles. Accommodation was provided for 29 passengers in 2-1 single-aisle format and a new forward airstair door replaced the rear door of the Jetstream 31. BAe flew the prototype on 25th September 1991 and built 104 Jetstream 41s before production ceased in 1998. Most of these are current with operators such as TW Express, United Express and the South African SA Airlink.

BAE Systems Jetstream Super 31, N302PX

BAE Systems Jetstream 41, G-MAJF

BAE Systems Jetstream 41 (Cont.)

Specification	BAE Systems Jetstream 41	
Powerplant	Two 1,500 s.h.p. (1,118 kW) Honeywell (Garrett) TPE331-14HR turboprops	
Dimensions		
Span	18.29 m	(60 ft 0 in)
Length	19.25 m	(63 ft 2 in)
Height	5.74 m	(18 ft 10 in)
Performance		
Max speed	541 km/h	(292 kt, 336 mph)
Cruising speed	482 km/h	(260 kt, 300 mph)
Initial climb	670 m/min	(2,200 fpm)
Range	1,086 km	(590 nm, 679 miles)
Weights		
Max takeoff	10,148 kg	(22,377 lbs)
Useful load	4,006 kg	(8,833 lbs)

BAE Systems ATP/Jetstream 61 — UK

With many Hawker Siddeley HS.748s in worldwide operation, BAe (now BAE Systems) started to develop a larger-capacity version. This was launched in 1980 as the ATP and involved a major redesign using the Andover airframe with a 16 ft 6 in fuselage stretch giving 64 passenger seats in a four-abreast single-aisle layout, enlarged tail and wing and undercarriage modifications. The ATP (Advanced TurboProp) was powered by a pair of Pratt & Whitney PW126 engines in new nacelles driving specially designed six-blade Hamilton Standard propellers. The ATP prototype first flew on 6th August 1986 and first deliveries were made to British Midland in March 1988. Other customers included British Airways, Air Wisconsin, Bangladesh Biman, Merpati and the Portuguese airlines LAR and SATA-Air Acores. The ATP was renamed Jetstream 61 in 1996. A total of 65 aircraft was built including the prototype and the last Jetstream 61 was completed in July 1995.

Specification	BAE Systems ATP	
Powerplant	Two 2,653 s.h.p. (1,978 kW) Pratt & Whitney PW126 turboprops	
Dimensions		
Span	30.63 m	(100 ft 6 in)
Length	26 m	(85 ft 4 in)
Height	7.14 m	(23 ft 5 in)
Performance		
Max speed	552 km/h	(300 kt, 345 mph)
Cruising speed	496 km/h	(269 kt, 310 mph)
Initial climb	549 m/min	(1,800 fpm)
Range	3,424 km	(1,860 nm, 2,140 miles)
Weights		
Max takeoff	22,925 kg	(50,550 lbs)
Useful load	9,333 kg	(20,580 lbs)

BAE Systems BAe 146 and Avro RJ — UK

The BAe 146, originally a Hawker Siddeley project, was relaunched by British Aerospace in 1978 and the prototype flew on 3rd September 1981. It is a short-haul high-wing airliner with a T-tail and four underwing pylon-mounted Lycoming ALF502R-3 turbofans. The standard BAe 146-100 has 93 passenger seats and the 146-200, which has a 7 ft 10 in longer fuselage, has 109 seats. The 146-300, which first flew on 1st May 1987, has a further 15 ft 9 in fuselage stretch. All the models are also offered as 'QT' freighters which are converted off-line. Some 35 of the BAe 146-100 have been built together with 115 BAe 146-200s and 69 BAe 146-300s. In 1990, the line was relaunched as the 85-seat Avro RJ70 (formerly -100), 100-seat RJ85 (-200), 112-seat RJ100 and 116-seat RJ115 (-300) and over 150 of these versions have been sold. Principal operators include Crossair (RJ100), KLM-UK, Okada Air, Lufthansa CityLine (RJ85), Sabena (RJ85/100), United Express and Northwest Airlink (RJ85). The forthcoming redesigned RJX series will be powered by Honeywell AS977 engines.

BAE Systems ATP, G-OEDE

BAE Systems BAe.146-200, EI-JET

Specification	Avro RJ100	
Powerplant	Four 7,000 lb.s.t. (31.1 kN) Honeywell LF507 turbofans	
Dimensions		
Span	26.2 m	(86 ft 0 in)
Length	30.99 m	(101 ft 8 in)
Height	8.6 m	(28 ft 3 in)
Performance		
Max speed	763 km/h	(412 kt, 474 mph)
Cruising speed	720 km/h	(390 kt, 445 mph)
Takeoff distance	1,798 m	(5,900 ft)
Range	2,742 km	(1,490 nm, 1,714 miles)
Weights		
Max takeoff	46,030 kg	(101,500 lbs)
Useful load	21,088 kg	(46,500 lbs)

BAE Systems HS.801 Nimrod — UK

The Nimrod maritime reconnaissance aircraft was based on the de Havilland Comet 4C four-jet airliner from which it differed principally in having a shorter fuselage with a lower lobe added to house a large weapons bay, a redesigned vertical tail with a tip-mounted antenna, a MAD boom extending from the rear fuselage and a large nose radome to house the search radar. The prototype first flew on 23rd May 1967 and the first of 46 Nimrod MR.1s, powered by four Spey turbofans, entered service with the RAF in 1969. The surviving fleet of 35 aircraft was upgraded to MR.2 standard in the early 1980s with new radars and equipment and later as MR.2Ps with in-flight refuelling probes and tail finlets. The RAF also operates three Nimrod R.Mk.1 intelligence-gathering aircraft which lack the MAD tail boom and have wing-mounted electronics pods in place of the external wing tanks. It is intended that the Nimrod will be upgraded to Nimrod 2000 (MRA.4) standard with BMW Rolls BR710 turbofans and a new mission system, with 21 aircraft being converted by 2005.

BAE Systems Nimrod MR.2, XV236

Specification	BAE Systems Nimrod MR.2	
Powerplant	Four 12,140 lb.s.t (54 kN) Rolls Royce RB.168-20 Spey Mk.250 turbofans	
Dimensions		
Span	35 m	(114 ft 10 in)
Length	38.6 m	(126 ft 9 in)
Height	9.08 m	(29 ft 9 in)
Performance		
Max speed	925 km/h	(500 kt, 575 mph)
Cruising speed	880 km/h	(475 kt, 545 mph)
Takeoff distance	1,462 m	(4,800 ft)
Range	9,600 km	(5,217 nm, 6,000 miles)
Weights		
Max takeoff	87,075 kg	(192,000 lbs)
Useful load	48,073 kg	(106,000 lbs)

BAE Systems Hawk — UK

Hawker Siddeley (later British Aerospace) designed the HS.1182 Hawk to replace their Gnat T Mk.1 which was the standard RAF jet trainer in the 1960s. The Hawk followed the same general design layout as the Gnat with a tandem-seat cockpit, low wing and single Rolls Royce Turboméca Adour turbofan. However it was a larger aircraft which offered greater flexibility and weapons-carrying potential. The first Hawk T Mk.1 was flown on 21st August 1974 and RAF deliveries started in mid-1976. Hawks have been acquired by 13 overseas countries including Abu Dhabi (Mk.63A), Finland (Mk.51), Indonesia (Mk.53), South Korea (Mk.67), Saudi Arabia (Mk.65) and Switzerland (Mk.66). Local assembly has been carried out in Finland and Switzerland. In the United States, the Hawk was adopted by the US Navy as its standard advanced trainer as the T-45A Goshawk and 172 examples were delivered by McDonnell Douglas commencing in 1988. The Hawk 200 is a single-seat ground attack version which has been sold to Indonesia, Malaysia (Srs.208), Saudi Arabia (Srs.205) and Oman (Srs.203). The prototype flew on 19th May 1986. British Aerospace also offer the Hawk 100 which is an improved version of the Hawk T Mk.1 with modified wings incorporating wingtip Sidewinder rails to provide enhanced ground attack capability and a longer nose incorporating a FLIR sensor. Over 700 Hawks had been built at the end of 1999.

BAE Systems Hawk T Mk.1, XX235

BAE Systems Hawk (Cont.)

BAE Systems Hawk 200, ZJ201

Specification	BAE Systems Hawk T Mk.1	
Powerplant	One 5,200 lb.s.t. (23.1 kN) Rolls Royce Turboméca Adour 151-01 turbofan	
Dimensions		
Span	9.39 m	(30 ft 9 in)
Length	10.77 m	(35 ft 4 in)
Height	3.98 m	(13 ft 0 in)
Performance		
Max speed	990 km/h	(535 kt, 615 mph)
Cruising speed	928 km/h	(504 kt, 580 mph)
Initial climb	3,600 m/min	(11,800 fpm)
Range	2,895 km	(1,575 nm, 1,810 miles)
Weights		
Max takeoff	5,699 kg	(12,566 lbs)
Useful load	2,052 kg	(4,525 lbs)

BAE Systems Harrier
— UK

The Harrier continues to be unique as the world's only effective V/STOL fixed-wing combat aircraft and has been sold to several air arms. The Harrier originated in the Hawker P.1127 first flown on 21st October 1960. This used a vectored-thrust Rolls Royce Pegasus engine which has been the key to the Harrier's success. The production Harrier GR Mk.1 for the RAF first flew on 31st August 1966 and was primarily used as a ground attack aircraft fitted with a fuselage pylon and four underwing hardpoints. The GR3 was powered by a more powerful Pegasus 103 engine and two-seat versions of the single-seaters were also built as the T2 and T4. Most GR1s and GR3s have now been replaced by the GR Mk.5 which has been developed jointly by BAE Systems and McDonnell Douglas and has a Pegasus 105 engine, a larger wing, a redesigned forward fuselage with a larger cockpit canopy and eight underwing hardpoints. A dedicated night attack version is designated GR Mk.7 and existing GR5s have mostly been converted to this standard. The Harrier was built for the US Marine Corps as the McDonnell Douglas AV-8A and the AV-8B Harrier II is the equivalent of the Harrier GR5. Spain has acquired the AV-8A (as the AV-8S Matador and TAV-8A(S)) and the AV-8B (designated EAV-8B) and Italy has also acquired the AV-8B and TAV-8B.

BAE Systems TAV-8A Matador, VAE.1-2 (Spanish Navy)

BAE Systems Harrier GR7, ZD354

Specification	BAE Systems Harrier GR Mk.7	
Powerplant	One 21,750 lb.s.t. (96.75 kN) Rolls Royce Pegasus Mk.105 vectored thrust turbofan	
Dimensions		
Span	9.25 m	(30 ft 4 in)
Length	14.53 m	(47 ft 8 in)
Height	3.55 m	(11 ft 8 in)
Performance		
Max speed	1,082 km/h	(590 kt, 674 mph)
Cruising speed	975 km/h	(530 kt, 609 mph)
Range (typical)	1,095 km	(595 nm, 684 miles)
Weights		
Max takeoff	14,512 kg	(32,000 lbs)
Useful load	7,390 kg	(16,295 lbs)

BAE Systems Sea Harrier
— UK

The P.1184 Sea Harrier FRS Mk.1 was a dedicated carrier-based version of the RAF's Harrier GR Mk.3 developed for the Royal Navy and first flown on 20th August 1978. It differed from the GR3 in having a revised forward fuselage with a raised cockpit canopy and a pointed radome containing Blue Fox radar. The Sea Harrier also had a 21,490 lb.s.t. Pegasus Mk.104 engine and some structural modifications for the naval role. Some 57 Sea Harriers (and four two-seat trainers) were delivered to the Royal Navy and the Indian Navy acquired 23 single-seat FRS Mk.51s and four two-seat FRS Mk.60s. The Sea Harrier FRS Mk.2 (later designated FA Mk.2) is an upgraded version of the earlier Sea Harrier with Blue Vixen radar in a larger nose radome, improved systems with a modernised cockpit, a lengthened rear fuselage and a Pegasus Mk.106 engine. Some Harrier FRS Mk.1s have been modified to this standard and 30 new aircraft have also been built.

BAE Systems Sea Harrier FA2, ZE691

Specification	BAE Systems Sea Harrier FA Mk.2	
Powerplant	One 21,500 lb.s.t. (95.6 kN) Rolls Royce Pegasus Mk.106 vectored-thrust turbofan	
Dimensions		
Span	7.7 m	(25 ft 3 in)
Length	14.17 m	(46 ft 6 in)
Height	3.60 m	(11 ft 10 in)
Performance		
Max speed	1,185 km/h	(640 kt, 735 mph)
Cruising speed	972 km/h	(528 kt, 608 mph)
Range (typical)	1,932 km	(1,050 nm, 1,207 miles)
Weights		
Max takeoff	9,841 kg	(21,700 lbs)
Useful load	3,467 kg	(7,645 lbs)

Bakeng Duce — USA

The Duce light two-seat homebuilt was designed by Jerry Bakeng of Seattle and first flown in April 1970. It is a tandem-seat open-cockpit aircraft with a parasol wing and a spring-steel tailwheel undercarriage. Construction of the fuselage is steel tube and fabric and the constant-chord wing, which is wooden with fabric covering, is fitted with flaps and Frieze-type ailerons. It has a wide wing centre section allowing specially good forward visibility through the main supporting struts and the aircraft has very good short field performance. Power for the prototype was a 125 h.p. Lycoming O-290-G but other builders have fitted larger engines. A large number of Duces together with a few of the biplane Double Duce have been built from the available plans and over 50 are believed to be currently airworthy in the United States although the type has not appeared elsewhere in any numbers.

Bakeng Duce, N110AC

Specification	Bakeng Duce	
Powerplant	One 125 h.p. (93.2 kW) Textron Lycoming O-290-G piston engine	
Dimensions		
Span	9.2 m	(30 ft 4 in)
Length	6.3 m	(20 ft 9 in)
Height	1.9 m	(6 ft 1 in)
Performance		
Max speed	192 km/h	(104 kt, 120 mph)
Cruising speed	168 km/h	(91 kt, 105 mph)
Initial climb	457 m/min	(1,500 fpm)
Range	805 km	(435 nm, 500 miles)
Weights		
Max takeoff	623 kg	(1,374 lbs)
Useful load	145 kg	(320 lbs)

Bay Aviation Super V — USA

Oakland Airmotive (later Bay Aviation) of Oakland, California saw the V-tailed Beech Bonanza as an ideal prospect for twin-engined conversion. In 1956 they engineered a modification which replaced the existing Continental E-185 engine with a pair of wing-mounted 170 h.p. Lycoming O-360-A1As. This conversion, applicable to the Bonanza 35, A35 and B35, gave the Super V, as it was titled, a performance equivalent to the more powerful Piper Aztec. The Bonanza engine nacelle was replaced by a new nose containing a baggage hold, combustion heater and radio installation. Bay Aviation carried out nine conversions before transferring rights to Pine Air (later Fleet) of Fort Erie, Ontario, Canada who built a further eight Pine Air Super Vs. Externally, the Super V resembled the Beech 95 Travel Air, other than for its V-tail.

Bay Aviation Super V (Cont.)

Bay (Pine Air) Super V, N551B

Beagle A.109 Airedale, G-ASWB

Specification	Bay/Oakland Super V	
Powerplant	Two 170 h.p. (126.7 kW) Textron Lycoming O-360-A1A piston engines	
Dimensions		
Span	10 m	(32 ft 10 in)
Length	7.5 m	(24 ft 9 in)
Height	2 m	(6 ft 6 in)
Performance		
Max speed	314 km/h	(170 kt, 196 mph)
Cruising speed	256 km/h	(139 kt, 160 mph)
Initial climb	472 m/min	(1,550 fpm)
Range	2,080 km	(1,130 nm, 1,300 miles)
Weights		
Max takeoff	1,545 kg	(3,407 lbs)
Useful load	627 kg	(1,380 lbs)

Specification	Beagle A.109 Airedale	
Powerplant	One 180 h.p. (134.2 kW) Textron Lycoming O-360-A1A piston engine	
Dimensions		
Span	11.1 m	(36 ft 4 in)
Length	8.02 m	(26 ft 4 in)
Height	3.05 m	(10 ft 0 in)
Performance		
Max speed	226 km/h	(123 kt, 141 mph)
Cruising speed	212 km/h	(115 kt, 133 mph)
Initial climb	198 m/min	(650 fpm)
Range	1,328 km	(722 nm, 830 miles)
Weights		
Max takeoff	1,250 kg	(2,756 lbs)
Useful load	477 kg	(1,050 lbs)

Beagle A.109 Airedale — UK

The Airedale was a four-seat light aircraft introduced by Beagle following its acquisition of Auster in 1960. Derived from the Auster C.6 Atlantic project and owing much to the Autocar and other traditional Auster designs, the A.109 had a strut-braced high wing, swept tail and fixed tricycle undercarriage. It was of tube and fabric construction with a metal rear fuselage decking and belly panels. The four-seat cabin had front and rear entry doors and the powerplant was a 180 h.p. Lycoming O-360. The first Airedale flew on 16th April, 1961 and 43 production aircraft were completed but the A.109 could not compete with more modern American aircraft and the line was closed in 1963. Most Airedales were sold in the UK but exports were made to Australia, New Zealand, Holland, Portugal and Switzerland. Currently, at least 22 are active in the UK, Australia, Portugal and New Zealand.

Beagle B.121 Pup — UK

Smallest of the new range of Beagle light aircraft launched in the mid-1960s was the Pup, an all-metal low-wing single-engined aircraft for private or club flying. The fully aerobatic Pup had stylish lines, a fixed tricycle undercarriage and a fully enclosed cabin. The Pup 100 was a two-seater powered by a 100 h.p. Continental O-200-A and the Pup 150 had a four-seat cabin and a 150 h.p. Lycoming O-320-A2B. A small number of Pup 160s were also built with the 160 h.p. Lycoming O-360-A. The prototype first flew at Shoreham on 8th April 1967 and first deliveries were made a year later. In 1969 Beagle went into receivership and some Pups from the final production total of 176 were completed elsewhere. Pups were exported to many European countries and to Australia, Iran, New Zealand and the USA. Over half the production Pups are still operational including 67 in the UK.

Beagle Pup 150, G-AVLN

Specification	Beagle B.121 Pup 150	
Powerplant	One 150 h.p. (111.8 kW) Textron Lycoming O-320-A2B piston engine	
Dimensions		
Span	9.45 m	(31 ft 0 in)
Length	7.01 m	(23 ft 0 in)
Height	2.06 m	(6 ft 9 in)
Performance		
Max speed	222 km/h	(121 kt, 139 mph)
Cruising speed	206 km/h	(112 kt, 129 mph)
Initial climb	256 m/min	(840 fpm)
Range	968 km	(526 nm, 605 miles)
Weights		
Max takeoff	862 kg	(1,900 lbs)
Useful load	368 kg	(810 lbs)

Beagle Bassett CC.1, XS770 (G-HRHI)

Specification	Beagle B.206S	
Powerplant	Two 340 h.p. (253.5 kW) Rolls Royce Continental GTSIO-520-C piston engines	
Dimensions		
Span	13.96 m	(45 ft 9 in)
Length	10.26 m	(33 ft 8 in)
Height	3.43 m	(11 ft 3 in)
Performance		
Max speed	415 km/h	(224 kt, 258 mph)
Cruising speed	354 km/h	(191 kt, 220 mph)
Initial climb	485 m/min	(1,590 fpm)
Range	2,560 km	(1,391 nm, 1,600 miles)
Weights		
Max takeoff	3,401 kg	(7,499 lbs)
Useful load	1,309 kg	(2,886 lbs)

Beagle B.206 and Basset
— UK

The largest aircraft built by Beagle, the B.206 originated in the four-seat Bristol 220 design but during development it grew to seven-seat capacity, largely to meet an RAF requirement. The prototype B.206X first flew on 15th August 1961 and the larger production standard B.206Y with 310 h.p. GIO-470A engines flew almost one year later. The B.206 was an all-metal aircraft with a low wing, fully enclosed cabin with a port rear-entry door and a retractable tricycle undercarriage. The B.206C was the civil standard version and the B.206R, 20 of which were built, was the military Bassett CC.1 for the RAF. Beagle also built the B.206S with more powerful turbocharged Continental GTSIO-520-C engines. A larger ten-seat model, the B.206 Srs.3 with a deeper fuselage, was flown in prototype form and still exists in Brazil. Some 78 production B.206s were built and five are currently registered in the UK and 29 in the USA.

Bede BD-4 and BD-6
— USA

One of the most popular of Jim Bede's large range of kit-built amateur designs, the BD-4 is an all-metal aircraft constructed of flat aluminium sheets for maximum simplicity. It has a fixed tricycle or tailwheel undercarriage and a fully enclosed cabin which can accommodate two or four occupants depending on the powerplant fitted. Possible engines range from the 108 h.p. Lycoming O-235-C1 to the 150 h.p. Lycoming O-320 or 180 h.p. Lycoming O-360. The cantilever wings have a single-piece tubular mainspar, are fitted with split trailing-edge flaps and are foldable for ground transport. The BD-4 was first announced in 1968 and is flying in substantial numbers. The BD-6 is a scaled-down version of the BD-4 with a much narrower fuselage and a single seat. It is powered by a 55 h.p. or 70 h.p. Hirth engine and first flew in 1973.

Bede BD-4 and BD-6 (Cont.)

Bede BD-4, N400ED

Specification	Bede BD-4	
Powerplant	One 108 h.p. (80.5 kW) Textron Lycoming O-235-C1 piston engine	
Dimensions		
Span	7.77 m	(25 ft 6 in)
Length	6.67 m	(21 ft 10 in)
Height	1.89 m	(6 ft 2 in))
Performance		
Max speed	250 km/h	(135 kt, 156 mph)
Cruising speed	233 km/h	(126 kt, 145 mph)
Initial climb	274 m/min	(900 fpm)
Range	1,440 km	(783 nm, 900 miles)
Weights		
Max takeoff	703 kg	(1,550 lbs)
Useful load	268 kg	(590 lbs)

Bede BD-5 — USA

In its time, the BD-5 Micro was the most exciting kit-built aircraft to appear on the US market. Designed by Jim Bede, it was a tiny streamlined single-seater with a low-set straight tapered wing, retractable tricycle undercarriage and a tail-mounted pusher propeller driven by a 32 h.p or 70 h.p. Xenoah or a 55 h.p. Kiekhafer two-stroke engine which was buried in the fuselage behind the pilot's cabin. The prototype BD-5 had a butterfly tail but the standard BD-5B had a conventional fin and tailplane. Some BD-5s were built with a converted Honda Civic engine or a Rotax 912. The BD-5 prototype first flew on 12th September 1971 and two versions were sold: the BD-5A with a short-span wing and the longer-span BD-5B. Many BD-5 plans and kits were sold but Bede eventually went bankrupt with kits undelivered. A new company, BD-Micro Technologies, took over support of the aircraft and examples have been flown with a Solar T-62 turboprop and, as the BD-5J, with a 200 lb.s.t. Sermel TRS-18 turbojet. The BD-5 is now marketed by Alturair.

Bede BD-5A, N210LL

Specification	Bede BD-5B Micro	
Powerplant	One 70 h.p. (52.19 kW) Xenoah piston engine	
Dimensions		
Span	6.55 m	(21 ft 6 in)
Length	4.13 m	(13 ft 7 in)
Height	1.28 m	(4 ft 2 in)
Performance		
Max speed	373 km/h	(201 kt, 232 mph)
Cruising speed	369 km/h	(199 kt, 229 mph)
Initial climb	411 m/min	(1,350 fpm)
Range	1,495 km	(810 nm, 935 miles)
Weights		
Max takeoff	322 kg	(710 lbs)
Useful load	138 kg	(305 lbs)

Bede BD-17 Nugget — USA

Jim Bede's latest design is the BD-17 which is a single-seat, low-wing light aircraft designed for simple amateur construction using flat all-metal honeycomb panels from a kit marketed by BEDEAmerica Aerosport LLC. Externally, it closely resembles the original Bede BD-1 Yankee which was developed into the production Grumman American trainers and tourers but it has a high-aspect ratio wing and can be fitted with either tailwheel or tricycle gear. The wings can be folded for storage. The Nugget is designed to be powered by engines in the 45 h.p. to 80 h.p. range but the recommended powerplant is a Japanese-manufactured HKS-700 two-cylinder engine which results in good overall performance.

Bede BD-17 Nugget, N624BD

Specification	Bede BD-17 Nugget	
Powerplant	One 60 h.p. (44.7 kW) HKS-700 piston engine	
Dimensions		
Span	6.55 m	(21 ft 6 in)
Length	5.36 m	(17 ft 7 in)
Height	2.31 m	(7 ft 7 in)
Performance		
Max speed	266 km/h	(143 kt, 165 mph)
Cruising speed	241 km/h	(130 kt, 150 mph)
Initial climb	442 m/min	(1,450 fpm)
Range	1,120 km	(609 nm, 700 miles)
Weights		
Max takeoff	385 kg	(850 lbs)
Useful load	147 kg	(325 lbs)

Beech 17 — USA

Regarded as the 'Rolls Royce' of prewar personal light aircraft, the Beech 17 'Staggerwing' was the first product of the new Beech Aircraft and featured tube and fabric construction, a full four-seat cabin, retractable undercarriage and the distinctive back-staggered biplane wings. The initial Model 17R and A17F had fixed undercarriages and 420 h.p. Wright Whirlwind and 700 h.p. Wright Cyclone engines respectively and these were followed by the B17L (225 h.p. Jacobs L-4), the B17B, C17B, E17B and E17L with 285 h.p. Jacobs L-5 engines and the D17S with a 450 h.p. Pratt & Whitney R-985 which was built for wartime USAAF use as the UC-43 and the US Navy as the GB-1. The postwar G17S, built in 1946, was a D17S with a modified engine cowling and fin and a 450 h.p. R-985-AN-4 engine. A total of 781 Beech 17s was completed and over 250 are currently active in the USA and elsewhere.

Beech D17S, N17985

Specification	Beech G17S	
Powerplant	One 450 h.p. (335.5 kW) Pratt & Whitney R-985-AN-4 piston engine	
Dimensions		
Span	9.75 m	(32 ft 0 in)
Length	8.20 m	(26 ft 11 in)
Height	2.44 m	(8 ft 0 in))
Performance		
Max speed	339 km/h	(184 kt, 212 mph)
Cruising speed	321 km/h	(174 kt, 201 mph)
Initial climb	381 m/min	(1,250 fpm)
Range	800 km	(435 nm, 500 miles)
Weights		
Max takeoff	1,927 kg	(4,250 lbs)
Useful load	659 kg	(1,450 lbs)

Beech 18 and Super 18 — USA

Beech designed the twin-engined Model 18 to meet the needs of commercial operators for an economical six-/eight-seat transport and flew the prototype on 15th January 1937. It was an all-metal aircraft with a retractable tailwheel undercarriage. The C-45, built during the war, was a USAAF utility version and other variants were the AT-7 trainer and the RC-45H photo-reconnaisance aircraft and the SNB for the US Navy. In total 4,123 of these models were built. Beech also developed the B18S with a large glazed nose as the AT-11 Kansan, 1,582 of which were built for navigational training. Beech 18s served with many other air forces including the RCAF which named it the Expediter and many Model 18s were civilianised after the war for use by freight operators and local service airlines. Total production of the standard Beech 18 was 6,326. After the war, Beech redesigned the Model 18 (C-45 and C18/D18) with modified extended wings incorporating squared-off tips, a higher and wider cabin accommodating up to ten passengers and a modernised cockpit with larger windows. The initial E18S and G18S were further refined into the Super H18 which incorporated a fully enclosed Volpar tricycle undercarriage and extended nose. The 765th and last Super H18 was delivered to Japan in 1970. Many Super 18s have been converted to turboprop power, sometimes with stretched fuselages, as the Hamilton Turboliner, Volpar Turboliner, Dumod Infinité and Dumodliner. The Pacific Airmotive Tradewind, was a standard Super 18 with a single vertical fin sometimes fitted with PT6A turboprop engines. Around 1,000 Beech 18s and Super 18s are registered in the USA with many still operating in other countries.

Beech 18 SNB-5, N181MH

Beech 18 and Super 18 (Cont.)

Beech Super H18, N57PF

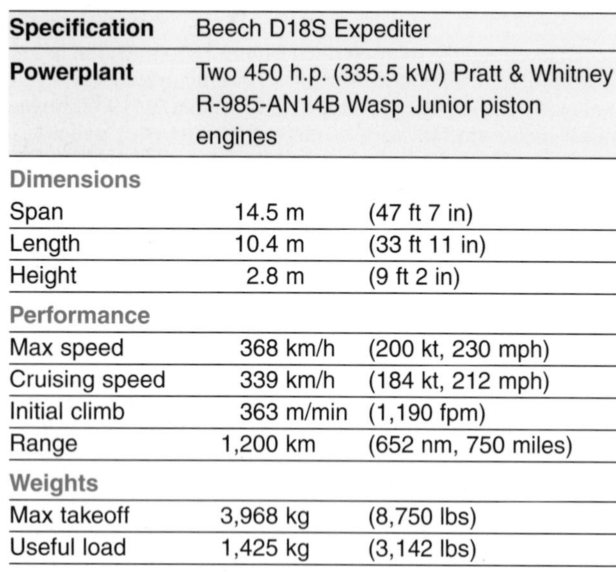

Specification	Beech D18S Expediter	
Powerplant	Two 450 h.p. (335.5 kW) Pratt & Whitney R-985-AN14B Wasp Junior piston engines	
Dimensions		
Span	14.5 m	(47 ft 7 in)
Length	10.4 m	(33 ft 11 in)
Height	2.8 m	(9 ft 2 in)
Performance		
Max speed	368 km/h	(200 kt, 230 mph)
Cruising speed	339 km/h	(184 kt, 212 mph)
Initial climb	363 m/min	(1,190 fpm)
Range	1,200 km	(652 nm, 750 miles)
Weights		
Max takeoff	3,968 kg	(8,750 lbs)
Useful load	1,425 kg	(3,142 lbs)

Beech 19 Sport, 23 Musketeer and 24 Sierra — USA

In order to compete with the Cessna 172 and Piper PA-28, Beech designed the Model 23 Musketeer low-wing four-seat light aircraft powered by a 160 h.p. Lycoming O-320-B. The prototype flew on 23rd October 1961 and 2,392 were built including 1,299 Sundowners with the 180 h.p. Lycoming O-360. Some 904 examples of a two-seat trainer version, the Model 19 Musketeer Sport, were built between 1966 and 1978 and the Model 24 Musketeer Super (369 built) was an improved Model 23 with higher gross weight, two optional extra seats and a 200 h.p. Lycoming IO-360-A2B. In 1974, the A24R Musketeer Super R was introduced, based on the Model 24, and this featured a retractable tricycle undercarriage and additional port-side rear entry door. It was later renamed the Sierra 200 and 793 were built between 1974 and 1982.

Beech B24R Sierra, N6978R

Specification	Beech C23 Sundowner 180	
Powerplant	One 180 h.p. (134.2 kW) Textron Lycoming O-360-A4K piston engine	
Dimensions		
Span	9.98 m	(32 ft 9 in)
Length	7.84 m	(25 ft 8 in)
Height	2.5 m	(8 ft 2 in)
Performance		
Max speed	221 km/h	(120 kt, 138 mph)
Cruising speed	214 km/h	(116 kt, 134 mph)
Initial climb	241 m/min	(790 fpm)
Range	936 km	(508 nm, 585 miles)
Weights		
Max takeoff	1,111 kg	(2,450 lbs)
Useful load	432 kg	(950 lbs)

Beech (Raytheon) 33, 35 and 36 Bonanza — USA

To compete in the postwar light aircraft boom, Beech designed the four-seat low-wing high-performance Model 35 Bonanza which featured a retractable undercarriage, a V-tail and a 165 h.p. Continental E-185 engine. It was of all-metal construction and a total of 10,403 of this deluxe private aircraft were built between 1947 and 1981. The design evolved over the 35 years of production and the final V35B had a 285 h.p. IO-520-B engine, six seats and a gross weight increase of almost 40% over the initial model. The Model 33 Debonair, built from 1960 to 1994, was substantially the same as the Model 35 but had a single vertical tail and was renamed Bonanza 33 in 1968. An aerobatic version was designated F33C and 3,137 of all variants of the Model 33 were built. These included a specialised military electronic surveillance version, the QU-22B, 33 of which were produced for USAF use in Vietnam. On 4th January 1968 the prototype Bonanza 36 was flown and this had a stretched fuselage with double rear doors and club seating. It remains in production in standard or turbocharged 300 h.p. TSIO-520 form with 4,270 built to date. A copy of the Model 33 is built in Iran as the Parastoo.

Beech P35 Bonanza, N8908M

Specification	Beech V35B Bonanza 35	
Powerplant	One 285 h.p. (212.49 kW) Teledyne Continental IO-520-BA piston engine	
Dimensions		
Span	10.2 m	(33 ft 5 in)
Length	8.04 m	(26 ft 4 in)
Height	2.3 m	(7 ft 7 in)
Performance		
Max speed	336 km/h	(183 kt, 210 mph)
Cruising speed	325 km/h	(176 kt, 203 mph)
Initial climb	346 m/min	(1,135 fpm)
Range	1,600 km	(870 nm, 1,000 miles)
Weights		
Max takeoff	1,542 kg	(3,400 lbs)
Useful load	614 kg	(1,350 lbs)

Beech A36 Bonanza, N3235D

Beech 45 Mentor T-34
— USA

Created to meet a USAF requirement for a new primary trainer, the Model 45 used the wings and retractable undercarriage of the Model 35 Bonanza married to a new fuselage with two tandem seats and a conventional fin and tailplane similar to that of the Beech 95. The prototype flew on 2nd December 1948 with a 205 h.p. Continental E-185 engine and the production T-34A Mentor, 350 of which went to the USAF, was powered by a 225 h.p. Continental O-470-13. Some 423 of the T-34B version were delivered to the US Navy together with the majority of the 272 production T-34C Turbo Mentors which had Pratt & Whitney PT6A-25 turboprops and enlarged tails. Export customers included Chile, Mexico and Colombia and the aircraft was built under licence in Argentina, by Fuji in Japan and by CCF in Canada. The Fuji version was further developed into the Fuji T3 (and KM-2 and TL-1) with a larger 340 h.p. Textron Lycoming IGSO-480-A1A6 engine. Many T-34s are currently flying with private owners in the USA and elsewhere and some remain in military service with the air forces of Colombia, Uruguay, etc.

Beech 45 Mentor T-34 (Cont.)

Beech T-34B Mentor, N4984

Specification	Beech T-34B Mentor	
Powerplant	One 225 h.p. (167 kW) Teledyne Continental O-470-13 piston engine	
Dimensions		
Span	10 m	(32 ft 10 in)
Length	7.8 m	(25 ft 10 in)
Height	2.92 m	(9 ft 7 in)
Performance		
Max speed	301 km/h	(163 kt, 188 mph)
Cruising speed	272 km/h	(148 kt, 170 mph)
Initial climb	354 m/min	(1,160 fpm)
Range	1,168 km	(635 nm, 730 miles)
Weights		
Max takeoff	1,331 kg	(2,935 lbs)
Useful load	320 kg	(704 lbs)

Beech D50E Twin Bonanza, N699V

Specification	Beech D50A Twin Bonanza	
Powerplant	Two 285 h.p. (212.49 kW) Textron Lycoming GO-480-G2D6 piston engines	
Dimensions		
Span	13.81 m	(45 ft 4 in)
Length	9.61 m	(31 ft 6 in)
Height	3.46 m	(11 ft 4 in)
Performance		
Max speed	342 km/h	(186 kt, 214 mph)
Cruising speed	325 km/h	(177 kt, 203 mph)
Initial climb	442 m/min	(1,450 fpm)
Range	2,640 km	(1,435 nm, 1,650 miles)
Weights		
Max takeoff	2,857 kg	(6,300 lbs)
Useful load	1,005 kg	(2,216 lbs)

Beech 50 Twin Bonanza and L-23/U-8 Seminole — USA

The Twin Bonanza was a six-seat light twin first flown by Beech on 11th November 1949. It used a modified version of the Model 35 wing and had a retractable tricycle undercarriage and 260 h.p. Lycoming GO-435 engines. Produced from 1952 to 1963 it was progressively improved with higher gross weights and increased fuel and range and a rear airstair entry door (D50C), 295 h.p. GO-480-G2F6 engines (D50E), 340 h.p. IGSO-480 engines (J50) and a longer cabin with extra windows (D50E). The US Army acquired a total of 211 L-23 Seminole (later designated U-8D to U-8G) army liaison aircraft including a number of aircraft rebuilt as SLAR-equipped RL-23Ds. In total, 1,021 examples of the Model 50 were built. Many Twin Bonanzas remain in service and several have been modified for increased performance with new windshields, improved undercarriage doors, longer noses etc. The popular Excalibur modification, engineered by Swearingen, includes replacement of the existing engines with 400 h.p. Textron Lycoming IO-720-A1A engines.

Beech (Raytheon) 95 Travel Air, 55, 56 and 58 Baron — USA

The Model 95 Travel Air was a twin-engined development of the Model 35 Bonanza with the tail unit of the Model 45 Mentor and 180 h.p. Lycoming O-360-A1A engines. It first flew on 6th August 1956 and was built as the 95, B95, B95A, C95A, D95A and E95 with progressive detail improvements from 1958 to 1968. The Model 55 Baron was a Travel Air with a swept tail, longer cabin and 260 h.p. Continental IO-470-L engines. This was also built as the Model 56TC with turbocharged TIO-541-E1B4 engines. Baron 55s were sold to the US Army as the T-42A Cochise and several other countries adopted the type for military use including Mexico, Chile, Spain, Venezuela and Pakistan. A total of 3,727 Model 55s was built between 1961 and 1985. The Model 58 is a stretched version with a rear double entry door and club seating. This is in current production and nearly 2,000 have been built. Beech also built 497 of the Model 58P pressurised version. In a joint venture with SFERMA in France, they also developed the SFERMA-60 (PD.146) Marquis, 18 of which were produced with 450 s.h.p. Turboméca Astazou IIJ turboprops in place of the standard Continentals.

Beech Travel Air E95, N6123V

Specification	Beech Model D55 Baron	
Powerplant	Two 285 h.p. (212.49 kW) Teledyne Continental IO-520-C piston engines	
Dimensions		
Span	11.52 m	(37 ft 10 in)
Length	8.84 m	(29 ft 0 in)
Height	2.82 m	(9 ft 3 in)
Performance		
Max speed	387 km/h	(210 kt, 242 mph)
Cruising speed	368 km/h	(200 kt, 230 mph)
Initial climb	509 m/min	(1,670 fpm)
Range	1,829 km	(994 nm, 1,143 miles)
Weights		
Max takeoff	2,404 kg	(5,300 lbs)
Useful load	1,011 kg	(2,229 lbs)

Beech Baron 58, N8124L

Beech 60 Duke — USA

The Duke was designed as a high-performance pressurised light twin with the comfort of a separate passenger cabin equipped with club seating. It was a completely new design with a streamlined fuselage although it used a version of the Baron wing and undercarriage. It was equipped with a port-side airstair entry door in the rear fuselage. The Duke prototype flew on 29th December 1966 and first deliveries to civil customers were made in 1968. The later A60 Duke had a higher gross weight and improved turbocharging and the B60 had an expanded passenger cabin, improved pressurisation from the Model 90 King Air and enlarged fuel capacity. A total of 596 Dukes had been built when production ceased in 1982. Many were exported and some 400 were registered in the United States at the end of 1999.

Beech 60 Duke (Cont.)

Beech B60 Duke, N9JL

Specification	Beech B60 Duke	
Powerplant	Two 380 h.p. (283.3 kW) Textron Lycoming TIO-541-E1C4 piston engines	
Dimensions		
Span	11.97 m	(39 ft 3 in)
Length	10.31 m	(33 ft 10 in)
Height	3.76 m	(12 ft 4 in)
Performance		
Max speed	432 km/h	(235 kt, 270 mph)
Cruising speed	416 km/h	(226 kt, 260 mph)
Initial climb	488 m/min	(1,600 fpm)
Range	2,256 km	(1,226 nm, 1,410 miles)
Weights		
Max takeoff	3,073 kg	(6,775 lbs)
Useful load	1,136 kg	(2,505 lbs)

Beech 65, 70 and 80 Queen Air — USA

The Model 65 Queen Air was an enlarged version of the Model 50 Twin Bonanza aimed at the commercial market and also at a US Army requirement for a general-utility aircraft. It used the Model 50 wing, tail and undercarriage with a new eight-seat fuselage and port-side airstair door and was fitted with two 340 h.p. Lycoming IGSO-480-A1A6 engines. The first flight was on 28th August 1958 and 315 were built (including 76 L-23Fs for the US Army). The Model 65 was followed by the Queen Air 80 which differed in having a swept tail and 380 h.p. IGSO-540 engines. The Model A65 was a Model 80 with the original 340 h.p. engines and the Model 70 was a commuter airline variant with 11 seats and longer wings which was introduced in 1969. Beech also built the Model 79 Queen Airliner with a higher gross weight. A number of Queen Airs were modified as the Swearingen Queen Air 800 with 400 h.p. Lycoming IO-720 engines in redesigned nacelles and low-drag wheel well fairings. In total, 957 Queen Airs were built between 1960 and 1976.

Beech Queen Air 65, N4203B

Specification	Beech Queen Air B80	
Powerplant	Two 380 h.p. (283.3 kW) Textron Lycoming IGSO-540-A1D piston engines	
Dimensions		
Span	15.32 m	(50 ft 3 in)
Length	10.74 m	(35 ft 3 in)
Height	4.47 m	(14 ft 8 in)
Performance		
Max speed	397 km/h	(216 kt, 248 mph)
Cruising speed	368 km/h	(200 kt, 230 mph)
Initial climb	453 m/min	(1,485 fpm)
Range	2,448 km	(1,330 nm, 1,530 miles)
Weights		
Max takeoff	3,991 kg	(8,800 lbs)
Useful load	1,645 kg	(3,627 lbs)

Beech 76 Duchess — USA

The Model 76 Duchess was first flown (as the Model PD.289) on 24th May 1977. It was a light four-seat piston twin aimed primarily at the twin-engined training market. In this respect it was intended to compete with the Piper Seminole and the Grumman Cougar but it was also to be sold to private owners. It was a completely new design with a T-tail and retractable tricycle undercarriage and was fitted with a pair of 180 h.p. Lycoming O-360 engines. The Duchess went into production at Wichita in 1978. Beech did develop a turbocharged version with Lycoming TO-360 engines but this did not reach production and the Duchess experienced only limited success, being discontinued in 1986 after 437 had been built.

Beech 76 Duchess, ZK-EZX

Specification	Beech 76 Duchess	
Powerplant	Two 180 h.p. (134.2 kW) Textron Lycoming O-360-A1G6D piston engines	
Dimensions		
Span	11.58 m	(38 ft 0 in)
Length	8.86 m	(29 ft 1 in)
Height	2.90 m	(9 ft 6 in)
Performance		
Max speed	315 km/h	(171 kt, 197 mph)
Cruising speed	278 km/h	(151 kt, 174 mph)
Initial climb	381 m/min	(1,250 fpm)
Range	1,152 km	(626 nm, 720 miles)
Weights		
Max takeoff	1,779 kg	(3,900 lbs)
Useful load	652 kg	(1,438 lbs)

Beech 77 Skipper — USA

Seeing the training market being dominated by the Cessna 150 and Piper PA-38, Beech launched the Model 77 Skipper two-seat trainer, flying the prototype (Model PD.285) on 6th February 1975. In external appearance, the Model 77 resembled the competing low-wing Piper Tomahawk with a high-aspect-ratio wing, a T-tail, a tricycle undercarriage and a bubble canopy enclosing the relatively wide cabin area. The Skipper was a key element in Beech's Aero Club concept and 312 were built from 1979 to 1983. However, the Skipper was unable to compete with the established competition despite its good-quality finish. Most of the Skippers built are still in operation with a substantial fleet flying in Australia.

Beech 77 Skipper, VH-PFV

Specification	Beech 77 Skipper	
Powerplant	One 115 h.p. (85.7 kW) Textron Lycoming O-235-L2C piston engine	
Dimensions		
Span	9.14 m	(30 ft 0 in)
Length	7.28 m	(23 ft 11 in)
Height	2.3 m	(7 ft 6 in)
Performance		
Max speed	195 km/h	(106 kt, 122 mph)
Cruising speed	184 km/h	(100 kt, 115 mph)
Initial climb	219 m/min	(720 fpm)
Range	600 km	(326 nm, 375 miles)
Weights		
Max takeoff	761 kg	(1,675 lbs)
Useful load	259 kg	(570 lbs)

Beech (Raytheon) 90 King Air — USA

In 1965 Beech flew the prototype Model 88. This was a development of the Queen Air A80 with a pressurised fuselage and circular windows and IGSO-540 piston engines. Only 47 were built because Beech was developing the aircraft by substituting 500 s.h.p. PT6A turboprop engines to create the Model 90 King Air. Several Model 88s were later converted to King Air standard. The King Air was a fast six-/eight-seat turboprop business aircraft and was an immediate success. The A90, B90 and E90 were progressively improved models with increased gross weights and higher-powered PT6A engines. The F90 was a high-performance C90 with a T-tail, larger wings, strengthened undercarriage and 750 s.h.p. engines. The current Raytheon production model is the C90B which uses the modernised cockpit of the Model 350 and improved pressurisation and electrical systems. The first King Air 90 was delivered in 1964 and over 2,200 of the civil Model 90 variants had been built by the end of 1999.

Beech E90 King Air, N77JX

Beech (Raytheon) 90 King Air (Cont.)

Specification	Beech E90 King Air	
Powerplant	Two 680 s.h.p. (507 kW) Pratt & Whitney PT6A-28 turboprops	
Dimensions		
Span	13.98 m	(45 ft 10 in)
Length	10.82 m	(35 ft 6 in)
Height	4.47 m	(14 ft 8 in)
Performance		
Max speed	459 km/h	(249 kt, 287 mph)
Cruising speed	432 km/h	(235 kt, 270 mph)
Initial climb	570 m/min	(1,870 fpm)
Range	2,072 km	(1,126 nm, 1,295 miles)
Weights		
Max takeoff	4,580 kg	(10,100 lbs)
Useful load	1,916 kg	(4,225 lbs)

Specification	Beech B200 Super King Air	
Powerplant	Two 850 s.h.p. (633.76 kW) Pratt & Whitney PT6A-41 turboprops	
Dimensions		
Span	16.6 m	(54 ft 6 in)
Length	13.36 m	(43 ft 10 in)
Height	4.53 m	(14 ft 10 in)
Performance		
Max speed	542 km/h	(295 kt, 339 mph)
Cruising speed	520 km/h	(283 kt, 325 mph)
Initial climb	747 m/min	(2,450 fpm)
Range	3,320 km	(1,804 nm, 2,075 miles)
Weights		
Max takeoff	5,669 kg	(12,500 lbs)
Useful load	2,255 kg	(4,972 lbs)

Beech (Raytheon) 100, 200 and 350 Super King Air — USA

The outstanding success of the Model 90 King Air led to Beech building the stretched Model 100 executive aircraft with a larger vertical tail, 15-seat maximum capacity and 680 s.h.p. PT6A-28 turboprops; 384 were built between 1969 and 1984. The Model 100 was followed by the Super King Air 200 which first flew on 27th October 1972 and this had a T-tail, larger wings, greater useful load and 850 s.h.p. PT6A-41 engines. While primarily for business users, the Model 200 was offered with an optional utility interior and rear cargo door or for aerial mapping. The Model 300 had a higher gross weight and 1,050 s.h.p. PT6A-60A engines with four-blade props and the Model 350 is a developed version of the 300 with a 17-passenger (max) stretched fuselage and modified wings with wingtip winglets. In total, Beech has built over 1, 800 civil Model 200s, 249 Model 300s and over 275 Model 350s.

Beech Super King Air 350, N1551T

Beech King Air 100, 331 (Chilean AF)

Beech (Raytheon) U-21, VC-6B and C-12 — USA

While Beech was developing the King Air they also produced a turboprop military version of the unpressurised Queen Air 80 which went into production in 1964 as the U-21A Ute (Model 65-A90-1). Used widely in Vietnam, the U-21 was modified for many roles including electronic surveillance (RU-21A, RU-21B, RU-21D, RU-21H etc.) frequently without cabin windows and with large wing-mounted blade antennae. Some standard pressurised King Air 90s were also acquired by the USAF as the VC-6B and 61 of a trainer version, the T-44A (Model H90), went to the US Navy. The Super King Air 200 was acquired by all four US services, over 350 having been delivered to date including the US Army C-12C and USN/Marines UC-12B with PT6A-41 engines. Many electronic monitoring and special missions variants (RC-12D, RC-12K) were delivered to the US Army fitted with different versions of the Guardrail COMINT/ELINT sensor systems. Twelve Raytheon Beech 1900s are in use with the USAF as the C-12J.

Beech RC-12N

Specification	Beech RC-12D Guardrail V	
Powerplant	Two 850 s.h.p. (633.76 kW) Pratt & Whitney PT6A-41 turboprops	
Dimensions		
Span	17.63 m	(57 ft 10 in)
Length	13.36 m	(43 ft 10 in)
Height	4.57 m	(15 ft 0 in)
Performance		
Max speed	480 km/h	(260 kt, 299 mph)
Cruising speed	438 km/h	(235 kt, 270 mph)
Initial climb	732 m/min	(2,400 fpm)
Range	2,915 km	(1,584 nm, 1,822 miles)
Weights		
Max takeoff	5,669 kg	(12,500 lbs)
Useful load	2,340 kg	(5,160 lbs)

Specification	Beech C99 Airliner	
Powerplant	Two 715 s.h.p. (533.1 kW) Pratt & Whitney PT6A-28 turboprops	
Dimensions		
Span	14 m	(45 ft 10 in)
Length	13.6 m	(44 ft 7 in)
Height	4.4 m	(14 ft 4 in)
Performance		
Max speed	493 km/h	(268 kt, 308 mph)
Cruising speed	456 km/h	(248 kt, 285 mph)
Initial climb	677 m/min	(2,220 fpm)
Range	1,680 km	(913 nm, 1,050 miles)
Weights		
Max takeoff	5,125 kg	(11,300 lbs)
Useful load	2,111 kg	(4,800 lbs)

Beech (Raytheon) 99 Airliner — USA

With the boom in commuter airline operations in the 1960s, Beech developed the Model 99 turboprop local service airliner. It was based on the unpressurised Queen Air 80 airframe with a stretched fuselage for 15 passengers and two crew and had a lengthened nose containing a baggage compartment. The airframe was developed with the modified PD.208 (LR-1) Queen Air followed by the definitive Model 99 prototype with two 550 s.h.p. PT6A-20 turboprops which first flew in July 1966. The first delivery was made to Commuter Airlines Inc. in May 1968 and the Model 99 stayed in production until 1987 by which time 239 aircraft had been built. The Model 99A was a later version with a higher gross weight and the B99, announced in 1972, had a further gross weight increase and 715 s.h.p. PT6A-28 engines. Over half those built are in service including a batch built for the Chilean Air Force.

Beech C99, N99CJ

Beech (Raytheon) 1900 — USA

In the early 1980s, with the Model 99 commuter airliner becoming obsolete, Beech designed a new turboprop which would offer significant improvements over the unpressurised Model 99. The Model 1900 was based on the pressurised Model 200 with a stretched 19-passenger fuselage, a T-tail with finlets and tail stabilising fins and a redesigned wing. Powered by two 1,100 s.h.p. PT6A-65B turboprops it first flew on 3rd September 1982 and was sold as the standard 1900 and as the 1900C with a port rear cargo door. The later 1900C-1 has a modified fuel system and a wet wing. The 1900C has been delivered to the USAF as the C-12J and to the air forces of Taiwan and Egypt. Some 250 1900Cs were built. The 1900D, which flew on 1st March 1990, had a new deeper fuselage giving a standup cabin, wingtip winglets and 1,279 s.h.p. PT6A-67D turboprops. The 1900D replaced the 1900C in production and first deliveries were made in November 1991. Over 400 Beech 1900Ds have been built and examples of the 1900 are flying with more than 80 airlines worldwide.

Beech 1900C, N198GA

Beech (Raytheon) 1900 (Cont.)

Beech 1900D, C-FCMV

Specification	Beech 1900D	
Powerplant	Two 1,279 s.h.p. (953.6 kW) Pratt & Whitney PT6A-67D turboprops	
Dimensions		
Span	17.6 m	(57 ft 9 in)
Length	17.6 m	(57 ft 9 in)
Height	4.54 m	(14 ft 11 in)
Performance		
Max speed	534 km/h	(290 kt, 334 mph)
Cruising speed	512 km/h	(278 kt, 320 mph)
Initial climb	800 m/min	(2,625 fpm)
Range	1,272 km	(691 nm, 795 miles)
Weights		
Max takeoff	7,687 kg	(16,950 lbs)
Useful load	2,970 kg	(6,550 lbs)

Beech (Raytheon) 2000 Starship I — USA

The Starship business turboprop represented a radical move by Beech from traditional construction methods to a totally composite structure. Designed by Burt Rutan of Scaled Aircraft Composites, the Starship resembled a scaled-up version of Rutan's successful Vari-eze canard homebuilt. It had a cabin for a maximum of eight passengers, a variable sweep forward control surface, complex swept wings with large winglets, a retractable tricycle undercarriage and two PT6A engines mounted as pushers on the inboard rear wings. An 85% proof-of-concept prototype flew initially, followed on 15th February 1986 by the first full-size prototype. During testing the weight and power were increased to meet certification requirements and the first production Starship 2000 was completed in 1990. The 2000A had improved useful load and fuel capacity and Beech completed 50 production aircraft before closing the line in 1996.

Beech 2000 Starship I, N3042S

Specification	Beech 2000 Starship I	
Powerplant	Two 1,200 s.h.p. (894.7 kW) Pratt & Whitney PT6A-67 turboprops	
Dimensions		
Span	16.6 m	(54 ft 5 in)
Length	14.05 m	(46 ft 1 in)
Height	3.68 m	(12 ft 1 in)
Performance		
Max speed	648 km/h	(352 kt, 405 mph)
Cruising speed	624 km/h	(339 kt, 390 mph)
Initial climb	1,030 m/min	(3,380 fpm)
Range	3,672 km	(1,996 nm, 2,295 miles)
Weights		
Max takeoff	6,349 kg	(14,000 lbs)
Useful load	2,306 kg	(5,085 lbs)

Beech (Raytheon) Beechjet 400 — USA

Raytheon acquired the Japanese Mitsubishi MU-300 Diamond business jet in 1985. Mitsubishi had flown the original Diamond prototype on 29th August 1978 and it was a conventional low-wing design with an eight-passenger cabin, a T-tail and two JT15D turbojets mounted on the rear fuselage. Mitsubishi had increased the power from 2,500 lb.s.t. JT15D-4s on the Diamond I to 2,900 lb.s.t. JT15D-5s on the Diamond II and had built 100 Diamonds before production was transferred to Beech at Wichita. The aircraft was renamed Beechjet and received minor cosmetic alterations. The Model 400A was an improved Beechjet with a larger internal cabin and a glass cockpit. The T-1A Jayhawk was a military Model 400A, 180 of which were delivered for the USAF's TTTS training programme, and nine Beech 400Ts are in service with the Japanese Air Self Defence Force. By mid 2000, Raytheon had completed 530 examples of the Beechjet series.

Beech T-1A Jayhawk, 93629 (USAF)

Specification	Beech (Raytheon) Beechjet 400A	
Powerplant	Two 2,965 lb.s.t. (13.19 kN) Pratt & Whitney JT15D-5 turbofans	
Dimensions		
Span	13.25 m	(43 ft 6 in)
Length	14.75 m	(48 ft 5 in)
Height	4.24 m	(13 ft 11 in)
Performance		
Max speed	867 km/h	(468 kt, 539 mph)
Cruising speed	834 km/h	(450 kt, 518 mph)
Initial climb	1,150 m/min	(3,770 fpm)
Range	3,115 km	(1,693 nm, 1,948 miles)
Weights		
Max takeoff	7,302 kg	(16,100 lbs)
Useful load	2,483 kg	(5,475 lbs)

Beech (Raytheon) PD.373 Texan II — USA

Raytheon has developed a new version of the Pilatus PC-9 turboprop trainer for use by the US Air Force and US Navy. This won the 1995 JPATS programme and over 700 are expected to be delivered as the T-6A Texan II. Initially named the Beech Mk.II, the first Beech-built production prototype (Model PD.373) first flew in December 1992. The aircraft has been extensively modified with a strengthened airframe and a 1,700 s.h.p. PT6A turboprop in place of the 1,150 s.h.p. version on the standard PC-9, and it has a three-piece canopy, modified tailplane and increased fuel capacity. The first production aircraft flew in July 1998 and the Texan went into USAF service in mid-1999. It has also been ordered by Greece and 24 for the Canadian Armed Forces are to be known as the Harvard II.

Specification	Beech (Raytheon) PD.373 Texan II	
Powerplant	One 1,700 s.h.p. (1,268 kW) Pratt & Whitney PT6A-68 turboprop	
Dimensions		
Span	10.19 m	(33 ft 5 in)
Length	10.17 m	(33 ft 4 in)
Height	3.26 m	(10 ft 8 in)
Performance		
Max speed	639 km/h	(345 kt, 397 mph)
Cruising speed	593 km/h	(320 kt, 368 mph)
Initial climb	958 m/min	(3,145 fpm)
Range	1,656 km	(900 nm, 1,036 miles)
Weights		
Max takeoff	2,857 kg	(6,300 lbs)
Useful load	857 kg	(1,885 lbs)

Beech Texan II, N8284M

Bell 47 — USA

The Bell 47 was the first truly practical mass-production helicopter and became instantly recognised with its open tubular rear fuselage framework and large plexiglass bubble canopy. First flown on 8th December 1945 and derived from the experimental Bell Model 30, it had a bench seat for two people and a two-blade main rotor and tail stabilising propeller. The Bell 47A had a 175 h.p. Franklin O-35-1 engine, the 47D had a 200 h.p. Franklin O-335-1 and engine power progressively increased up to the 280 h.p. Lycoming TVO-435 of the 47G-3B2. It was adopted by the US Army as the H-13 Sioux, often fitted with external stretcher mountings, and by the US Navy as the HTL. The Bell 47G was built under licence by Westland, Agusta and Kawasaki and was widely used for crop spraying and utility tasks. The 47H and 47J were models with fully enclosed fuselages. Some 6,391 Bell 47s were built together with 211 of the modified four-seat Kawasaki KH-4.

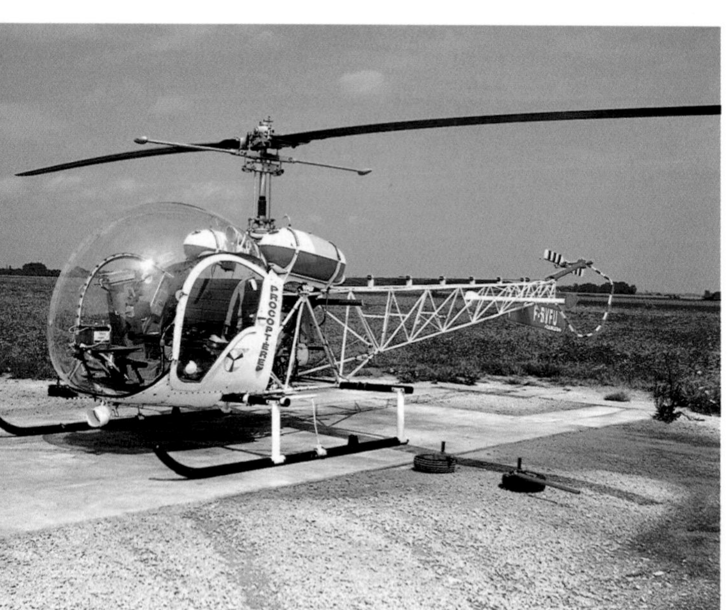

Bell 47G, F-BVFU

Specification	Bell 47G-4	
Powerplant	One 260 h.p. (193.8 kW) Textron Lycoming VO-540-B1B piston engine	
Dimensions		
Rotor diameter	11.32 m	(37 ft 1 in)
Length	9.62 m	(31 ft 7 in)
Height	2.83 m	(9 ft 4 in)
Performance		
Max speed	168 km/h	(91 kt, 105 mph)
Cruising speed	134 km/h	(73 kt, 84 mph)
Initial climb	183 m/min	(600 fpm)
Range	472 km	(257 nm, 295 miles)
Weights		
Max takeoff	1,341 kg	(2,950 lbs)
Useful load	533 kg	(1,173 lbs)

Bell 204 and 205 — USA

Responding to a US military requirement for a general-utility helicopter, Bell designed the Model 204 which first flew on 22nd October 1956. Of all-metal monocoque construction its main cabin was an open square box allowing the loading of stretchers and bulky loads or fitment of seats for up to eight troops. In its production UH-1 Iroquois form it was powered by an 860 s.h.p. Lycoming T53 turboshaft and became well-known as the 'Huey' with 11,730 being built, largely for the US military (360 were also built by Dornier in Germany). The Model 205 was a Model 204 with a longer fuselage and 12-troop capacity delivered to the US Army as the UH-1D and UH-1H Iroquois. It first flew on 16th August 1961 and 1,042 were built including licence production by Fuji, Agusta and AIDC. Both the 204 and 205 are still used by many military forces and civil operators. Civilianised UH-1s are widely operated by police and civil support organisations.

Bell UH-1H, N492DF

Specification	Bell 204B	
Powerplant	One 1,100 s.h.p. (820.16 kW) Textron Lycoming T5309A turboshaft	
Dimensions		
Rotor diameter	14.63 m	(48 ft 0 in)
Length	12.69 m	(41 ft 7 in)
Height	4.45 m	(14 ft 7 in)
Performance		
Max speed	221 km/h	(120 kt, 138 mph)
Cruising speed	216 km/h	(118 kt, 135 mph)
Initial climb	488 m/min	(1,600 fpm)
Range	368 km	(200 nm, 230 miles)
Weights		
Max takeoff	3,855 kg	(8,500 lbs)
Useful load	1,769 kg	(3,900 lbs)

Bell 206 Jet Ranger and Model 407 — USA

The Model 206 was Bell's unsuccessful entry in the 1960 US Army LOH competition which became very popular as a civil helicopter for corporate use and a wide range of utility tasks. It was later acquired by the US Army as the OH-58 Kiowa and by the US Navy as the TH-57A Sea Ranger and sold overseas as the military 406 Kiowa Warrior. An all-metal helicopter with two forward crew seats and a rear three-place bench seat, the Jet Ranger is powered by a 317 s.h.p. Allison 250-C18A turboshaft mounted above the cabin. It first flew on 10th January 1966 and nearly 8,000 have been built at Bell Helicopter Textron in Fort Worth and Canada and by Agusta. The 206L Long Ranger has a longer cabin with club seating for six passengers and was first flown on 11th September 1974. The current Model 407 has a four-bladed main rotor and a wider cabin. The Long Ranger III is powered by a 650 s.h.p. Allison 250-C30P and the Tridair Gemini is a conversion with twin Allison 250-C20R engines. Many surplus OH-58s have been civilianised for operation with law enforcement and other public agencies.

Bell TH-57C Sea Ranger, 162040

Bell 407, N407S

Specification	Bell 206B Jet Ranger III	
Powerplant	One 420 s.h.p. (313.15 kW) Allison 250-C20B turboshaft	
Dimensions		
Rotor diameter	10.16 m	(33 ft 4 in)
Length	11.91 m	(39 ft 1 in)
Height	2.91 m	(9 ft 6 in)
Performance		
Max speed	221 km/h	(120 kt, 138 mph)
Cruising speed	194 km/h	(105 kt, 121 mph)
Initial climb	604 m/min	(1,980 fpm)
Range	608 km	(330 nm, 380 miles)
Weights		
Max takeoff	1,361 kg	(3,000 lbs)
Useful load	722 kg	(1,593 lbs)

Bell 427 — USA

Having moved Jet Ranger production to the Canadian Mirabel factory, Bell developed an enhanced version of the Long Ranger, the Model 407 with a four-blade rotor and wider cabin. This in turn led to a major redesign of the airframe with a larger main cabin to accommodate six passengers and a higher gross weight and sufficient space to handle stretchers and other emergency service equipment. The 427 is powered by the Pratt & Whitney PW206D twin-turbine engine system mounted above the main cabin and driving a four-bladed main rotor. The first flight of the 427 was made on 15th December 1997 and it entered production at Mirabel in 1998.

Bell 427, C-GDSJ

Specification	Bell 427	
Powerplant	Two 640 s.h.p. (477 kW) Pratt & Whitney PW206D turboshafts	
Dimensions		
Rotor diameter	11.28 m	(37 ft 0 in)
Length	10.95 m	(35 ft 11 in)
Height	3.49 m	(11 ft 5 in)
Performance		
Max speed	250 km/h	(135 kt, 155 mph)
Cruising speed	241 km/h	(130 kt, 150 mph)
Range	663 km	(358 nm, 412 miles)
Weights		
Max takeoff	2,721 kg	(6,000 lbs)
Useful load	1,141 kg	(2,515 lbs)

Bell 209 HueyCobra and SuperCobra — USA

In 1962, success with the armed UH-1 'Huey' led Bell to design the Model 209 (AH-1) HueyCobra attack helicopter. This combined the Lycoming T53-L-13 engine and rotor system of the UH-1C and a new low-profile fuselage with a stepped tandem two-seat cockpit at the front, a fixed skid undercarriage and centre section stub wings each with two armament strongpoints. A chin-mounted turret was fitted containing a GAU-2B Minigun. The prototype flew on 7th September 1965 and first US Army AH-1G deliveries were made in June 1967. Later variants included the TH-1G trainer, the AH-1J SeaCobra for the Marine Corps with a PT6T-3 TwinPac powerplant and the AH-1S with a Lycoming T53-L-703. The AH-1W SuperCobra was a much developed version with two GE T700-GE-401 turboshafts, a three-barrel 20 mm cannon and provision for Hellfire or TOW missiles. The AH-1Z is an upgraded version for the Marine Corps capable of carrying AGM-114A laser-guided anti-tank missiles. Some 1,965 HueyCobras have been built including 24 constructed by Fuji.

Fuji-Bell AH-1S

Specification	Bell AH-1W SuperCobra	
Powerplant	Two 1,625 s.h.p. (1,212 kW) General Electric T700-GE-401 turboshafts	
Dimensions		
Rotor diameter	14.63 m	(48 ft 0 in)
Length	13.87 m	(45 ft 6 in)
Height	4.32 m	(14 ft 2 in)
Performance		
Max speed	280 km/h	(152 kt, 175 mph)
Cruising speed	264 km/h	(144 kt, 165 mph)
Initial climb	244 m/min	(800 fpm)
Range	632 km	(343 nm, 395 miles)
Weights		
Max takeoff	6,689 kg	(14,750 lbs)
Useful load	2,063 kg	(4,550 lbs)

Bell 212 and 412 — USA/Canada

The growth of the Model 205 Iroquois eventually required increased power and Bell produced the Model 212 with a 1,290 s.h.p. Pratt & Whitney PT6T-3 TwinPac twin turboshaft. The Model 212 prototype flew on 29th April 1965 and early orders were placed for the USAF, US Navy and Marine Corps as the UH-1N. Canada also acquired 50 CUH-1Ns (CH-135) and the 212 was sold to more than 30 overseas air arms. Agusta licence-built variants included the AB.212ASW anti-submarine version with an 1,875 s.h.p. PT6T-6 powerplant and search radar, sonar and provision for two Mk.44 torpedoes. The 14-seat Bell 212 was popular for offshore oil operations and civil utility work. The Bell 412, which replaced the 212, has a shorter rotor mast, four-bladed rotor and higher useful load and can be fitted with skids or a tricycle undercarriage. The 412 is operating with the UK armed forces as the Griffin HT Mk.1 and with the Canadian armed forces as the CH-146 Griffon. Other variants include the 412SP with increased fuel capacity, the 412HP with an improved transmission and the enhanced-performance 412EP with a PT6T-3D engine and EFIS and a digital flight control system. Some 1,052 Bell 212s and over 380 Bell 412s (including Indonesian production by Nurtanio) have been built.

Bell 412EP Griffin HT.1, G-BWZR (ZJ234)

Specification	Bell 412EP	
Powerplant	One 1,800 s.h.p. (1,342 kW) Pratt & Whitney Turbo TwinPac PT6T-3D turboshaft	
Dimensions		
Rotor diameter	14.02 m	(46 ft 0 in)
Length	12.7 m	(41 ft 8 in)
Height	3.48 m	(11 ft 5 in)
Performance		
Max speed	240 km/h	(130 kt, 150 mph)
Cruising speed	226 km/h	(122 kt, 140 mph)
Initial climb	411 m/min	(1,350 fpm)
Range	648 km	(352 nm, 405 miles)
Weights		
Max takeoff	5,397 kg	(11,900 lbs)
Useful load	2,317 kg	(5,110 lbs)

Bell 214 and 214ST
— USA

With a growing fleet of military and civil Bell 212s, it was inevitable that operators would want a larger and more powerful utility helicopter. The Model 214, named 'Huey-Plus', was a Model 205 with a more powerful 1,900 s.h.p. Lycoming T53-L-702 turboshaft. The main production Model 214A, which flew on 13th March 1974 and was delivered in quantity to the Iranian Air Force, had the even larger 2,930 s.h.p. T55-L-7C engine. The commercial version was the Model 214B, 73 of which were built. Bell next developed the eight-passenger 214ST Super Transport which was a 214B with an 8 ft fuselage stretch and two 2,930 s.h.p. Lycoming LTC4B-8D engines. This was first flown on 21st July 1979 and could be fitted with a skid or wheeled undercarriage. First production deliveries of over 100 aircraft started in 1982, mostly to civil users in the oil industry but also to the Peruvian, Venezuelan and Omani forces.

Bell 214ST Super Transport, HZ-RH1

Specification	Bell 214ST	
Powerplant	Two 2,930 s.h.p. (2,184.6 kW) Textron Lycoming LTC4B-8D turboshafts	
Dimensions		
Rotor diameter	15.85 m	(52 ft 0 in)
Length	15.02 m	(49 ft 3 in)
Height	4.84 m	(15 ft 10 in)
Performance		
Max speed	260 km/h	(140 kt, 160 mph)
Cruising speed	240 km/h	(130 kt, 150 mph)
Initial climb	543 m/min	(1,780 fpm)
Range	853 km	(463 nm, 533 miles)
Weights		
Max takeoff	7,937 kg	(17,500 lbs)
Useful load	3,653 kg	(8,055 lbs)

Bell 222 and 230
— USA

The developing executive helicopter market of the 1960s led Bell to design a new high-performance civil machine. The Model 222 was a streamlined helicopter with a forward two-crew cockpit and a main cabin with four executive or eight high-density seats, powered by two 592 s.h.p. Lycoming LTS101-650C-3 turboshafts. External fuselage-mounted sponsons were fitted to accommodate the retractable undercarriage and, when fitted, the pop-out emergency floats. The prototype first flew on 13th August 1976 and the 222 was certificated in August 1979. A total of 230 production 222s were built including 74 of the 222UT utility version with a fixed skid undercarriage.The later Model 230, 38 of which were built, has two 700 s.h.p. Allison 250-C30G2 turboshafts. Bell's development of advanced rotor systems led to the Model 430 which first flew on 25th October 1994 and has a four-bladed main rotor and an EFIS cockpit.

Bell 430, N430VR

Specification	Bell 222B	
Powerplant	Two 684 s.h.p. (510 kW) Textron Lycoming LTS 101-750C-1 turboshafts	
Dimensions		
Rotor Diameter	12.8 m	(42 ft 0 in)
Length	12.85 m	(42 ft 2 in)
Height	3.51 m	(11 ft 6 in)
Performance		
Max speed	275 km/h	(150 kt, 172 mph)
Cruising speed	256 km/h	(139 kt, 160 mph)
Initial climb	512 m/min	(1,680 fpm)
Range	528 km	(287 nm, 330 miles)
Weights		
Max takeoff	3,741 kg	(8,250 lbs)
Useful load	1,519 kg	(3,350 lbs)

Bell-Boeing V-22 Osprey — USA

Bell and Boeing established the joint Osprey project in 1982 in response to the military Joint Services Advanced Vertical Lift program which covered a wide performance envelope and multiple tasks. The resultant V-22 was based on the tilt-rotor concept tested earlier by Bell on its XV-15 which had flown in early 1977. The Osprey has a conventional transport aircraft fuselage largely built from composites with a ventral rear loading ramp and ability to carry 24 troops or 12 stretcher cases. The wing is mounted on top of the fuselage and has a complex flap/aileron system and two tip-mounted swivelling pods housing the Allison T406-AD-400 turbines which are fitted with large three-blade propeller/rotors. The XV-22A prototype flew on 19th March 1989 followed by nine prototype and development aircraft. A planned total of 523 Ospreys will be delivered to the USAF as the CV-22A, the Marines as the MV-22A and the US Navy as the HV-22A.

Specification	Bell-Boeing CV-22A Osprey	
Powerplant	Two 6,150 s.h.p. (4,586 kW) Allison T406-AD-400 turboshafts	
Dimensions		
Span	15.52 m	(50 ft 11 in)
Rotor diameter (each)	11.58 m	(38 ft 0 in)
Length	17.47 m	(57 ft 4 in)
Height	5.38 m	(17 ft 7 in)
Performance		
Max speed (est)	509 km/h	(275 kt, 316 mph)
Cruising speed (est)	469 km/h	(255 kt, 293 mph)
Initial climb (est)	700 m/min	(2,300 fpm)
Range	3,316 km	(1,800 nm, 2,073 miles)
Weights		
Max takeoff	27,437 kg	(60,500 lbs)
Useful load	12,639 kg	(27,870 lbs)

Bell-Boeing CV-22A Osprey

Bell XV-15A, N703NA

Bellanca 14 Cruisair, Cruisemaster and Model 260 — USA

The original Model 14 Junior was an all-wood low-wing two-/three-seater with a retractable tailwheel undercarriage, flown in 1937 by Bellanca Aircraft Corporation of New Castle, Delaware. It was distinctive for the small endplate fins attached to the tailplane. The early Models 14-7 and 14-9 had 90 h.p. Ken Royce engines but the 14-12F had a 120 h.p. Franklin 6AC. A few of the 59 built remain active. The post-war four-seat 14-13 Cruisair Senior was fitted with a 150 h.p. Franklin 6A4 and in 1949 the Model 14-19 Cruisemaster was introduced with a 190 h.p. Lycoming O-435A engine; 686 of these two variants were completed. Upgraded to a 230 h.p. Continental O-470K, the 14-19-2 was built by Northern Aircraft and the later 14-19-3 Bellanca 260, built by Downer, had a tricycle undercarriage, a redesigned vertical tail, fibreglass covering, and a 260 h.p. Continental IO-470F powerplant.

Bellanca 14-13-2, N74264

Specification	Bellanca 14-13-2 Cruisair Senior	
Powerplant	One 150 h.p. (111.8 kW) Franklin 6A4-150-B3 piston engine	
Dimensions		
Span	10.41 m	(34 ft 2 in)
Length	6.5 m	(21 ft 4 in)
Height	1.88 m	(6 ft 2 in)
Performance		
Max speed	270 km/h	(147 kt, 169 mph)
Cruising speed	245 km/h	(133 kt, 153 mph)
Initial climb	344 m/min	(1,130 fpm)
Range	880 km	(478 nm, 550 miles)
Weights		
Max takeoff	975 kg	(2,150 lbs)
Useful load	431 kg	(950 lbs)

Bellanca 17 Viking
— USA

In the mid-1960s, Bellanca was re-formed and the Model 14-19 Bellanca 260C was modified and returned to production as the Bellanca 17-30 Viking 300. The major change was a further power increase with the use of the 300 h.p. Continental IO-520-D engine but the aircraft retained the traditional tube and fabric construction. The subsequent Model 17-30A Super Viking introduced improvements to the nose cowling, undercarriage installation and cabin windows together with increased fuel capacity in new wing tanks. The Model 17-31 used a Lycoming IO-540 engine and the Model 17-31TC Turbo Viking was similar but was equipped with a Rayjay supercharger. The Model 17-30B Super Viking remains in small-scale production and over 1,370 of the Viking series have been built since 1967.

Bellanca 17-30 Viking 300, F-BRSV

Specification	Bellanca 17-31 Viking 300	
Powerplant	One 290 h.p. (216.2 kW) Textron Lycoming IO-540-G1B5 piston engine	
Dimensions		
Span	10.41 m	(34 ft 2 in)
Length	7.16 m	(23 ft 6 in)
Height	2.24 m	(7 ft 4 in)
Performance		
Max speed	363 km/h	(196 kt, 226 mph)
Cruising speed	312 km/h	(168 kt, 194 mph)
Initial climb	549 m/min	(1,800 fpm)
Range	1,600 km	(870 nm, 1,000 miles)
Weights		
Max takeoff	1,451 kg	(3,200 lbs)
Useful load	567 kg	(1,250 lbs)

Bensen B-7M and B-8M
— USA

Having produced a number of gyrogliders during the early 1950s, Igor Bensen produced his first powered gyrocopter, the B-7M, which made its first flight on 6th December 1955. The very basic B-7M has a tubular frame structure with a rear fin/rudder assembly and a fixed tricycle undercarriage. The pilot sits in the open with the 40 h.p. pusher Nelson air-cooled engine mounted behind him and operates the gyrocopter with a suspended control column connected to the rotor head. The later B-8M has a strengthened airframe, a larger square-shaped vertical tail and higher-powered 72 h.p. McCulloch 4318E engine. It first flew on 8th July 1957 and many examples of both models were constructed from Bensen plans by amateur builders. Most current models are fitted with a Rotax 582. The design formed the basis for numerous variations and commercially built versions including the Ken Brock KB-3 and RAF.2000 and, in the UK, those built by Wg Cdr Ken Wallace and the Campbell Cricket and Montgomery Merlin gyrocopters.

Bensen B-8MR, G-BOZW

Bensen B-7M and B-8M (Cont.)

Specification	Bensen B-8M Gyrocopter	
Powerplant	One 72 h.p. (53.68 kW) McCulloch 4318E piston engine	
Dimensions		
Rotor diameter	6.1 m	(20 ft 0 in)
Length	3.45 m	(11 ft 4 in)
Height	1.9 m	(6 ft 3 in)
Performance		
Max speed	136 km/h	(74 kt, 85 mph)
Cruising speed	96 km/h	(52 kt, 60 mph)
Initial climb	457 m/min	(1,500 fpm)
Range	160 km	(87 nm, 100 miles)
Weights		
Max takeoff	227 kg	(500 lbs)
Useful load	115 kg	(253 lbs)

Specification	Beriev Be-12 Chaika	
Powerplant	Two 4,190 s.h.p. (3,124 kW) Ivchenko AI-20M turboprops	
Dimensions		
Span	29.7 m	(97 ft 6 in)
Length	30.17 m	(99 ft 0 in)
Height	7 m	(22 ft 11 in)
Performance		
Max speed	608 km/h	(328 kt, 378 mph)
Cruising speed	320 km/h	(175 kt, 200 mph)
Initial climb	912 m/min	(2,990 fpm)
Range	7,500 km	(4,076 nm, 4,688 miles)
Weights		
Max takeoff	30,995 kg	(68,345 lbs)
Useful load	9,977 kg	(22,000 lbs)

Beriev Be-12 — Russia

The Be-12 'Chaika' is a large twin turboprop amphibian designed by the Beriev OKB for coastal patrol and other maritime duties and developed from the earlier piston-engined Be-6. Allocated the NATO name 'Mail', the Be-12 first flew in 1960. It has a deep flying boat hull and a retractable tailwheel undercarriage with the main units folding upwards into wells in the fuselage sides. The wing has heavily dihedralled inboard sections allowing the engines to be positioned out of the water spray line. The Be-12 normally has a prominent search radar housing in the nose and a tail-mounted MAD probe – although this does not appear on the Be-14 ASR version. With a crew of five, the aircraft has a large internal weapons bay with watertight doors in the lower hull. Over 200 are believed to have been built and at least 50 are thought to remain in service with the Russian Navy. It has been marketed as the Be-12M-300 for firebombing and other commercial roles.

Beriev Be-12M-300, RA00046

Beriev Be-30 and Be-32K — Russia

The Be-30 local service airliner was initiated in 1966 by the Beriev OKB as an An-2 replacement. It was a high-wing turboprop twin with a retractable undercarriage and the first of eight examples flew on 3rd March 1967. The Be-30 (NATO name 'Cuff') was not ordered by Aeroflot who decided on the larger-capacity Let-410 Turbolet. The Be-30 was revived in 1993 as the Be-32 with more powerful TVD-10B engines and a further version, the Be-32K, which flew on 15th August 1995, is fitted with two 1,100 s.h.p. Pratt & Whitney PT6A-65B turboprops which are to be manufactured by Klimov under licence as the PK6A-65B. The Be-32K, which is not pressurised, has internal accommodation for 16 passengers and two crew and is fitted with a galley and lavatory. An order for 50 for Moscow Airways was announced but production has not yet commenced.

Beriev Be-32K, RA67205

Specification	Beriev Be-32K	
Powerplant	Two 1,100 s.h.p. (820 kW) Klimov (P&W) PK6A-65B turboprops	
Dimensions		
Span	17 m	(55 ft 9 in)
Length	15.7 m	(51 ft 6 in)
Height	5.52 m	(18 ft 1 in)
Performance		
Max speed	480 km/h	(260 kt, 298 mph)
Cruising speed	363 km/h	(196 kt, 226 mph)
Initial climb	480 m/min	(1,575 fpm)
Range	800 km	(432 nm, 500 miles)
Weights		
Max takeoff	7,300 kg	(16,096 lbs)
Useful load	2,540 kg	(5,600 lbs)

Beriev A-40 Albatross — Russia

Currently the world's largest amphibian, the Albatross (NATO name 'Mermaid') was conceived as a long-range maritime patrol, surveillance, minelaying and anti-submarine warfare platform carrying eight crew in a pressurised fuselage. In its Be-42 version it can also carry out air-sea rescue missions and the Be-40P is a proposed passenger transport with up to 105 seats. The first of two A-40 prototypes was first flown in December 1986. It is a high-wing aircraft with a complex planing hull incorporating various strakes and contour variations. The main units of the retractable tricycle undercarriage have four-wheel bogies and retract into fairings on the rear wing beneath the housings for the two D-30KPV turbofans which are protected from spray by the large swept wing. The A-40 has a T-tail and small fixed wingtip floats. The A-40 still awaits a Russian Navy order.

Beriev A-40 Albatross

Specification	Beriev A-40 Albatross	
Powerplant	Two 26,455 lb.s.t. (117.7 kN) Aviadvigatel D-30KPV turbofans	
Dimensions		
Span	41.62 m	(136 ft 6 in)
Length	43.84 m	(143 ft 10 in)
Height	11.07 m	(36 ft 4 in)
Performance		
Max speed	760 km/h	(410 kt, 470 mph)
Cruising speed	720 km/h	(388 kt, 446 mph)
Initial climb	1,800 m/min	(5,900 fpm)
Range	5,500 km	(2,989 nm, 3,438 miles)
Weights		
Max takeoff	86,000 kg	(189,630 lbs)
Useful load	43,900 kg	(96,800 lbs)

Beriev Be-200 — Russia

Beriev has designed a large commercial utility amphibian, the Be-200, which is aimed at a range of civilian applications. First flown on 24th September 1998 it follows the general layout of the A-40 Albatross but has a much deeper and wider fuselage which can accommodate up to 66 passengers in a pressurised cabin or nine freight containers. The Be-200 has a T-tail, retractable tricycle undercarriage and twin D-436 turbofans mounted on rear fuselage pylons and has fly-by-wire systems and a modern technology cockpit. A principal role will be aerial firefighting for which it is equipped with a scoop system and capacity for 12 tonnes of water in underfloor tanks. The Be-200 will also be used for air sea rescue, ambulance and military patrol duties and has been ordered by the Russian Emergency Action Ministry and the Forestry Ministry.

Beriev Be-200, RA-21511

Specification	Beriev Be-200	
Powerplant	Two 16,550 lb.s.t. (73.6 kN) ZMKB-Progress D-436TP turbofans	
Dimensions		
Span	32.78 m	(107 ft 6 in)
Length	29.18 m	(95 ft 9 in)
Height	8.9 m	(29 ft 2 in)
Performance		
Max speed	700 km/h	(378 kt, 435 mph)
Cruising speed	550 km/h	(297 kt, 341 mph)
Initial climb	840 m/min	(2,755 fpm)
Range	2,000 km	(1,087 nm, 1,250 miles)
Weights		
Max takeoff	37,200 kg	(82,026 lbs)
Useful load	12,250 kg	(27,011 lbs)

Beriev Be-103 — Russia

The Be-103 amphibian was designed as a light passenger/cargo aircraft for operation in the remote areas of the CIS and was first flown on 15th July 1997. It has a low wing to give maximum air cushion effect and a six-seat cabin accessed through forward gull-wing doors. The two IO-360 piston engines are mounted on pylons on the rear fuselage and the Be-103 has a retractable tricycle undercarriage. The present status of the programme is unknown as both prototypes have been lost in accidents.

Beriev Be-103, RA-03002

Specification	Beriev Be-103	
Powerplant	Two 210 h.p. (156.6 kW) Teledyne Continental IO-360-ES4 piston engines	
Dimensions		
Span	12.72 m	(41 ft 9 in)
Length	10.65 m	(34 ft 11 in)
Height	3.72 m	(12 ft 3 in)
Performance		
Max speed	285 km/h	(154 kt, 177 mph)
Cruising speed	230 km/h	(124 kt, 143 mph)
Initial climb	390 m/min	(1,280 fpm)
Range	1,280 km	(696 nm, 800 miles)
Weights		
Max takeoff	2,050 kg	(4,520 lbs)
Useful load	510 kg	(1,125 lbs)

Blackburn B-2 — UK

The Blackburn B-2 two-seat trainer was first flown in 1932 and was unusual in being of all-metal construction with fabric-covered wings and tailplane and an aluminium-covered fuselage. It was also distinctive for its side-by-side seating at a time when most trainers had tandem cockpits and was fitted with a fixed tailwheel undercarriage. The B-2 was designed and built by Blackburn Aircraft Ltd. at Brough who completed a total of 42 examples for use by flying clubs and the Reserve Flying Schools. Its sturdy construction made it ideal for the hard training environment. A variety of powerplants were employed, the standard engine being the 120 h.p. de Havilland Gipsy III, but there were also examples with the 130 h.p. Gipsy Major, 135 h.p. Blackburn Cirrus Major I and 150 h.p. Cirrus Major III. Most B-2s did not survive the war but one example is currently active in the UK.

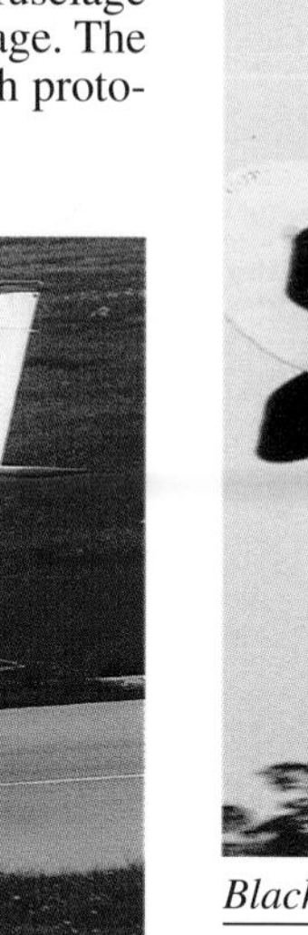

Blackburn B-2, G-AEBJ

Specification	Blackburn B-2	
Powerplant	One 130 h.p. (96.9 kW) de Havilland Gipsy Major I	
Dimensions		
Span	9.2 m	(30 ft 2 in)
Length	7.4 m	(24 ft 3 in)
Height	2.74 m	(9 ft 0 in)
Performance		
Max speed	179 km/h	(97 kt, 112 mph)
Cruising speed	152 km/h	(83 kt, 95 mph)
Initial climb	213 m/min	(700 fpm)
Range	512 km	(278 nm, 320 miles)
Weights		
Max takeoff	839 kg	(1,850 lbs)
Useful load	306 kg	(675 lbs)

Blanton Wichawk — USA

The Wichawk two-seater was designed by Dave Blanton of Wichita, Kansas and has been offered in the form of plans to homebuilders by Javelin Aircraft. The prototype Wichawk first flew on 24th May 1971 and over 30 had flown by the end of 1998. Construction is of classic wood, steel tube and fabric. The Wichawk is unusual in having side-by-side seating rather than the tandem seats more common in amateur-built biplanes. A three-seater version can be built and this has a larger powerplant. Various engines can be fitted in the 150 h.p. to 300 h.p. range and the aircraft is semi-aerobatic and has dual controls.

Blanton (Javelin) Wichawk, N78RW

Specification	Blanton Wichawk	
Powerplant	One 180 h.p. (134 kW) Textron Lycoming O-360 piston engine	
Dimensions		
Span	7.32 m	(24 ft 0 in)
Length	5.87 m	(19 ft 3 in)
Height	2.18 m	(7 ft 2 in)
Performance		
Max speed	225 km/h	(121 kt, 140 mph)
Cruising speed	204 km/h	(110 kt, 127 mph)
Initial climb	518 m/min	(1,700 fpm)
Range	640 km	(347 nm, 400 miles)
Weights		
Max takeoff	907 kg	(2,000 lbs)
Useful load	324 kg	(715 lbs)

Boeing 247 — USA

The Boeing 247 was the forerunner of the modern all-metal airline transport and first flew on 8th February 1933. A major advance on the commercial aircraft which had gone before, it had an all-metal monocoque structure, de-iced cantilever wings, a fully enclosed ten-passenger cabin and crew cockpit and a retractable tailwheel undercarriage. With its two Pratt & Whitney R-1340-S1D1 Wasp radial engines it offered high speed and 62 of the standard Model 247 were built. These were followed by 13 of the 247D with geared R-1340-S1H1-G engines. Several are currently registered in the USA with private owners and at least two are in active operation.

Boeing 247, CF-JRQ

Specification	Boeing 247D	
Powerplant	Two 500 h.p. (372.8 kW) Pratt & Whitney Wasp R-1340-S1H1-G piston engines	
Dimensions		
Span	22.6 m	(74 ft 0 in)
Length	15.7 m	(51 ft 7 in)
Height	3.7 m	(12 ft 2 in)
Performance		
Max speed	320 km/h	(174 kt, 200 mph)
Cruising speed	304 km/h	(165 kt, 190 mph)
Initial climb	350 m/min	(1,150 fpm)
Range	1,192 km	(648 nm, 745 miles)
Weights		
Max takeoff	6,190 kg	(13,650 lbs)
Useful load	2,043 kg	(4,505 lbs)

Boeing B-17 Fortress — USA

The Boeing B-17 was the leading long-range day heavy bomber employed in the European theatre in World War II, and it proved to be highly resilient and capable of carrying 4,000 lb bomb loads to the major German cities. The mid-wing Fortress first flew as the Boeing Model 299 on 28th July 1935 powered by four Wright R-1820 radial engines and early B-17A, B, C and D models had a narrow vertical tail and a slim fuselage. The B-17E had a redesigned rear fuselage and an enlarged fin with a prominent fillet. The Fortress was heavily armed with upper and lower turrets and guns in the nose and tail. The most numerous variant was the B-17G, 8,680 of which were built by Boeing, Vega and Douglas and this had improved controls, a chin nose turret and new engine turbochargers. B-17 production totalled 12,731. After the war, B-17s were used for civil freighting, aerial survey and fire bombing and at least six are currently airworthy as display warbirds.

Boeing B-17G, N5017N '2102516' (44-85740)

Boeing B-17 Fortress (Cont.)

Specification	Boeing B-17G	
Powerplant	Four 1,200 h.p. (894.7 kW) Wright R-1820-97 piston engines	
Dimensions		
Span	31.62 m	(103 ft 9 in)
Length	22.78 m	(74 ft 9 in)
Height	5.82 m	(19 ft 1 in)
Performance		
Max speed	486 km/h	(263 kt, 302 mph)
Cruising speed	290 km/h	(157 kt, 180 mph)
Initial climb	128 m/min	(420 fpm)
Range	3,200 km	(1,739 nm, 2,000 miles)
Weights		
Max takeoff	32,653 kg	(72,000 lbs)
Useful load	15,419 kg	(34,000 lbs)

Boeing 707 and 720 — USA

The Boeing 707, as the first of a new generation of US-designed jet transports, pioneered many new design concepts and set the pattern for Boeing's later airliners. First flown on 15th July 1954, the 367-80 'Dash-80' prototype had a swept wing and four engines mounted on underwing pylons to allow use of complex high-lift devices. The initial production model was the 707-100 with JT3C-6 engines and individual model numbers indicated the specification for each airline customer (e.g. 707-121 for Pan Am). The 707-138 for Qantas had a shorter fuselage, the 707-300 Intercontinental had a stretched fuselage with 189-passenger seating and the 707-400 was a Rolls Royce Conway-powered version for BOAC. The Model 720 was a 165-passenger 707 with a 9 ft shorter fuselage and JT3C-7 turbojets. Around 140 707s are still active, mostly for freighting, all having been fitted with hushkits or CFM56 turbofans.

Boeing 707-351C, N707DY

Specification	Boeing 707-300B	
Powerplant	Four 18,000 lb.s.t. (80.07 kN) Pratt & Whitney JT3D-3 turbofans	
Dimensions		
Span	44.4 m	(145 ft 9 in)
Length	46.6 m	(152 ft 11 in)
Height	12.7 m	(41 ft 7 in)
Performance		
Max speed	1,003 km/h	(545 kt, 627 mph)
Cruising speed	971 km/h	(528 kt, 607 mph)
Initial climb	719 m/min	(2,360 fpm)
Range	9,856 km	(5,356 nm, 6,160 miles)
Weights		
Max takeoff	151,927 kg	(335,000 lbs)
Useful load	88,435 kg	(195,000 lbs)

Boeing C-135 and KC-135 — USA

The KC-135A (Model 717-100A) is based on the Boeing 367-80 airframe and has served for many years as the standard USAF air refuelling tanker. It first flew on 31st August 1956 and 732 were built between 1956 and 1964. Most surviving KC-135s have been upgraded to KC-135R with CFM.56 turbofans and many have been converted for other roles such as airborne radio relay (EC-135A), nuclear test monitoring (NC-135A), weather reconnaissance (WC-135B), Looking Glass command post (EC-135C) and space vehicle tracking (EC-135N). These conversions often involve installation of extensive external antennae, radomes and fairings. The C-135A is a 707 standard transport version with 126-troop capacity and numerous variants include the RC-135A and RC-135B for photographic surveillance, the VC-137A, B and C presidential and VIP transports and several former civil 707s converted to C-18A/TC-18E crew trainers. The E-6B Mercury is a US Navy version for TACAMO airborne submarine communications missions.

Boeing RC-135W, 62-4132

Boeing KC-135R, 57-1499

Specification	Boeing KC-135A Stratotanker	
Powerplant	Four 11,200 lb.s.t. (49.83 kN) Pratt & Whitney J57-P-59W turbojets	
Dimensions		
Span	39.9 m	(130 ft 10 in)
Length	41.5 m	(136 ft 3 in)
Height	11.7 m	(38 ft 4 in)
Performance		
Max speed	936 km/h	(509 kt, 585 mph)
Cruising speed	848 km/h	(461 kt, 530 mph)
Initial climb	610 m/min	(2,000 fpm)
Range	1,840 km	(1,000 nm, 1,150 miles)
Weights		
Max takeoff	134,694 kg	(297,000 lbs)
Useful load	90,036 kg	(198,530 lbs)

Specification	Boeing E-3A Sentry	
Powerplant	Four 21,000 lb.s.t. (93.4 kN) Pratt & Whitney TF33-PW-100A turbofans	
Dimensions		
Span	44.4 m	(145 ft 9 in)
Length	46.6 m	(152 ft 11 in)
Height	12.7 m	(41 ft 9 in)
Performance		
Max speed	848 km/h	(461 kt, 530 mph)
Cruising speed	816 km/h	(443 kt, 510 mph)
Initial climb (est)	457 m/min	(1,500 fpm)
Range	4,800 km	(2,609 nm, 3,000 miles)
Weights		
Max takeoff	147,392 kg	(325,000 lbs)
Useful load (est)	70,295 kg	(155,000 lbs)

Boeing E-3 Sentry — USA

The success of the Boeing 707 as a military platform for a huge range of tasks made it the natural choice as the basis of an AWACS (Airborne Warning and Control System). The 707-320B airframe, powered by Pratt & Whitney TF33-PW-100 turbofans, has a large twin-pylon-mounted 30 ft diameter rotodome fitted to the upper rear fuselage for the large Westinghouse downlook radar. Internally, the aircraft accommodates 18 mission crew whose consoles and equipment are served by a powerful CC-2 computer. The E-3 (initially EC-137D) prototype first flew on 5th February 1972 and 34 have been delivered to the USAF, 20 serve with NATO and three E-3Fs have been sold to France. The USAF E-3As have been upgraded to E-3B and E-3C with improved radars. The RAF operates six E-3D Sentry AEW.Mk.1s and the Royal Saudi Air Force has five E-3As. Both of these models are being fitted with CFM56-2A-3 engines and the NATO E-3s are expected to be upgraded to this standard.

Boeing 727 — USA

Boeing's experience with the 707 and the airline relationships it created led to the design of a smaller medium-/short-range domestic airliner, the Model 727. Destined to become standard equipment for all the major US trunk carriers, the 727 had a shortened version of the 707 fuselage and three JT8D turbofans arranged in a tail cluster with the air intake for the centre engine in the base of the T-tailed fin. First flown on 9th February 1963, the 727 went into service less than a year later with Eastern Airlines. The 727-100 had a maximum of 131 passenger seats and 574 were built including export models for airlines as diverse as Lufthansa, South African Airways and Avianca. The 727-200 was a 189-passenger version with a 20 ft fuselage stretch and increased power which flew on 27th July 1967. Some 1,258 of the Boeing 727-200 were delivered between 1967 and 1983. Over 1,000 Boeing 727s remain in service, many flying with the main American carriers.

Boeing E-3A, ZH106 (RAF)

Boeing 727-287, LV-MIN

Boeing 727 (Cont.)

Specification	Boeing 727-200	
Powerplant	Three 16,000 lb.s.t. (71.18 kN) Pratt & Whitney JT8D-17 turbofans	
Dimensions		
Span	32.9 m	(108 ft 0 in)
Length	46.7 m	(153 ft 2 in)
Height	10.4 m	(34 ft 0 in)
Performance		
Max speed	1,008 km/h	(543 kt, 630 mph)
Cruising speed	964 km/h	(521 kt, 599 mph)
Initial climb	869 m/min	(2,850 fpm)
Range	4,480 km	(2,435 nm, 2,800 miles)
Weights		
Max takeoff	95,011 kg	(209,500 lbs)
Useful load	48,345 kg	(106,600 lbs)

Boeing 737-300, PT-TEF

Boeing 737-100, -200, -300, -400 — USA

Extending its jet airliner line, Boeing saw a place for an aircraft of smaller capacity than the 727 for short-range routes and this led to one of its most successful designs. The Model 737 bore a close family resemblance to the 707 and 727 but was a conventional low-wing aircraft with two JT8D turbojets fitted closely beneath its inboard wing section. The 124-seat aircraft first flew on 9th April 1967 and the first production model was the 737-100, 30 of which were delivered, mainly to Lufthansa. The 737-200, which flew on 8th August 1967, had a 6.5 ft fuselage stretch giving 12 more passenger seats and over 1,000 were sold including a number of freight 737-200C variants. The 737-300, introduced in 1981, had a further 104-inch fuselage stretch and was powered by CFM56 turbofans in oval section nacelles attached to lengthened underwing pylons. The 737-400, flown on 29th April 1988, had an additional 114-inch stretch raising capacity to 168 passengers. Total production of these models was 2,589 including 19 CT-43A transports for the US Air Force and many examples were sold to other air forces and to corporate operators.

Specification	Boeing 737-300	
Powerplant	Two 20,000 lb.s.t. (88.97 kN) CFM International CFM56-3B1 turbofans	
Dimensions		
Span	28.88 m	(94 ft 9 in)
Length	33.4 m	(109 ft 7 in)
Height	11.13 m	(36 ft 6 in)
Performance		
Max speed	855 km/h	(460 kt, 530 mph)
Cruising speed	816 km/h	(443 kt, 510 mph)
Takeoff distance	2,030 m	(6,650 ft)
Range	4,528 km	(2,461 nm, 2,830 miles)
Weights		
Max takeoff	62,812 kg	(138,500 lbs)
Useful load	31,338 kg	(69,100 lbs)

Boeing 737-200, LY-BSG

Boeing 737-500, -600, -700, -800 — USA

The Boeing 737-200 received a facelift in 1989 with the arrival of the improved 108-seat 737-500 which used the same fuselage but had extended wingtips, the -300 enlarged tail and CFM56 engine installation and an improved cockpit. The 737-600 which was a 'next-generation' development of the -500, first flew on 22nd January 1998 and had a 16.5 ft increase in wingspan, larger tail, more fuel, an EFIS cockpit and 132-passenger capacity. Similarly, the 737-300 was upgraded as the 737-700 with 149 seats and the same improvements as the -500 and the 737-400 became the 737-800 with similar treatment and 189 seats. The US Navy has purchased the 737-700C as the C-40A Clipper. The 737-700IGW Boeing Business Jet is an executive model based on the -700 with the -800 wing and it first flew on 4th September 1998. A proposed 737-900 will have an 8 ft 8 in fuselage stretch and 207-passenger capacity. Over 600 of the new generation 737s are in service.

Boeing 737-500, N914UA

Specification	Boeing 737-500	
Powerplant	Two 20,000 lb.s.t. (88.97 kN) CFM International CFM56-3C1 turbofans	
Dimensions		
Span	28.88 m	(94 ft 9 in)
Length	31 m	(101 ft 9 in)
Height	11.13 m	(36 ft 6 in)
Performance		
Max speed	1,004 km/h	(543 kt, 624 mph)
Cruising speed	912 km/h	(493 kt, 567 mph)
Takeoff distance	2,635 m	(8,650 ft)
Range	4,455 km	(2,420 nm, 2,784 miles)
Weights		
Max takeoff	60,544 kg	(133,500 lbs)
Useful load	28,567 kg	(62,990 lbs)

Boeing 747-100, -200
— USA

Still the world's largest passenger jet airliner, the Boeing 747 was first flown on 9th February 1969. Quickly nicknamed the 'Jumbo Jet' it has a similar layout to the 707 with a low-wing and four pylon-mounted underwing engines. The fuselage has a main deck accommodating up to 535 passengers, a large underfloor hold and a small upper deck housing the cockpit and up to 16 passenger seats. The first delivery of a 747-100 to Pan Am with JT9D turbofans took place in December 1969. The 747-200B had a strengthened airframe, higher gross weight, increased fuel capacity and range and a choice of 54,750 lb.s.t. Pratt & Whitney JT9D-7R4, 53,110 lb.s.t. Rolls Royce RB211-524 or 52,300 lb.s.t. General Electric CF6-50E turbofans. A 747-200B Combi version had a port-side rear freight door for combined cargo/passenger operations and the -200F is an all-freighter with an upward-opening nose door. A total of 564 747 'Classics' were built of which 475 are currently in service.

Boeing 747-200B Combi, I-DEMF

Specification	Boeing 747-200B	
Powerplant	Four 54,750 lb.s.t. (243.6 kN) Pratt & Whitney JT9D-74R4G2 turbofans (typical)	
Dimensions		
Span	59.6 m	(195 ft 8 in)
Length	70.7 m	(231 ft 10 in)
Height	19.33 m	(63 ft 5 in)
Performance		
Max speed	978 km/h	(525 kt, 610 mph)
Cruising speed	936 km/h	(509 kt, 585 mph)
Takeoff distance	3,322 m	(10,900 ft)
Range	9,840 km	(5,348 nm, 6,150 miles)
Weights		
Max takeoff	351,474 kg	(775,000 lbs)
Useful load	187,413 kg	(413,245 lbs)

Boeing 747-300, -400
— USA

Demand for even more seats than the maximum 551 capacity of the standard 747 led to Boeing modifying the 747-200B with a longer upper deck housing, normally, up to 56 economy seats and this took total passenger seating up to 630 although most airlines used mixed-class seating for around 370 passengers. The first -300 flew in 1982 and major users included Swissair, Cathay Pacific and Thai Airways International. The 747-400 was externally similar to the -300 but had wingtip winglets, a much revised and lighter structure, a completely redesigned EFIS cockpit and extra tailplane fuel tanks giving sufficient range to fly nonstop on all but the longest routes. The first -400 flew in August 1988 and the type is flown by the majority of the world's long-haul carriers. As with earlier Boeing 747 models, customers have a choice of powerplants including 54,750 lb.s.t. Pratt & Whitney PW4056, 58,000 lb.s.t. Rolls Royce RB211-524G or 56,750 lb.s.t. General Electric CF6-80C2B1F turbofans. Around 80 -300s and over 530 of the -400 have been built.

Specification	Boeing 747-400	
Powerplant	Four 54,750 lb.s.t. (243.57 kN) Pratt & Whitney PW4056 turbofans (typical)	
Dimensions		
Span	64.44 m	(211 ft 5 in)
Length	70.7 m	(231 ft 10 in)
Height	19.4 m	(63 ft 8 in)
Performance		
Max speed	979 km/h	(532 kt, 612 mph)
Cruising speed	944 km/h	(513 kt, 590 mph)
Takeoff distance	3,353 m	(11,000 ft)
Range	13,416 km	(7,291 nm, 8,385 miles)
Weights		
Max takeoff	396,825 kg	(875,000 lbs)
Useful load	215,374 kg	(474,900 lbs)

Boeing 747-400, JA8082

Boeing 747SP and 747SR
— USA

With the 747 successfully operating with many long-haul airlines, Boeing found a need for greater range on routes such as New York to Tehran or Tokyo and London to Johannesburg. The result was the 747SP (standing for Special Performance) which was a 747-100 with a 48 ft 4 in section of rear fuselage removed, additional fuel tanks and modification to the wings and tailplane. In normal mixed configuration the 747SP would carry 330 passengers. The SP first flew on 4th July 1975 and Pan Am was the first customer with others being delivered to Braniff, Iran Air, South African Airways and TWA. Customers had a choice of powerplants including 46,500 lb.s.t. Pratt & Whitney JT9D-7A, 50,100 lb.s.t. Rolls Royce RB211-524B2 or 46,500 lb.s.t. General Electric CF6-45A2 turbofans. A total of 52 were built, half of which are still operational. Another specialised version was the 747-100SR which was a special short-range version for use on domestic routes in Japan with 550 economy seats. It has a strengthened structure and a heavier undercarriage and 25 were delivered to Japan Air Lines and All Nippon.

Boeing 747SP, VH-EAA

Specification	Boeing 747SP	
Powerplant	Four 46,500 lb.s.t. (206.86 kN) Pratt & Whitney JT9D-7A turbofans (typical)	
Dimensions		
Span	59.6 m	(195 ft 8 in)
Length	56.3 m	(184 ft 9 in)
Height	19.9 m	(65 ft 5 in)
Performance		
Max speed	992 km/h	(539 kt, 620 mph)
Cruising speed	968 km/h	(526 kt, 605 mph)
Takeoff distance	2,667 m	(8,750 ft)
Range	10,776 km	(5,856 nm, 6,735 miles)
Weights		
Max takeoff	315,646 kg	(696,000 lbs)
Useful load	170,113 kg	(375,100 lbs)

Boeing 757 — USA

The gap in range and passenger capacity between the Boeing 727 and the 747 was filled by the short-/medium-range 757 and the medium-/long-range 767. The Boeing 757 first flew on 18th February 1982. It is a low-wing airliner with six-abreast single-aisle seating for up to 239 passengers, a large underfloor freight hold and two large turbofans in underwing pods. These may be 37,530 lb.s.t. Pratt & Whitney PW2037 or 38,200 lb.s.t. Rolls Royce RB211-535C engines according to customer choice. The first 757-200 delivery to British Airways took place in January 1983 and other early aircraft went to Eastern Airlines, Monarch Airlines and Delta. The 757-200CB is a combi version and the 757-200PF is a specialised small package freighter for United Parcel Service. The new 757-300 is a larger-capacity version with a 23 ft fuselage stretch and the prototype flew on 2nd August 1998.

Boeing 757-200, G-BYAT

Specification	Boeing 757-200	
Powerplant	Two 38,200 lb.s.t. (169.9 kN) Rolls Royce RB211-535C turbofans (typical)	
Dimensions		
Span	38.05 m	(124 ft 10 in)
Length	47.32 m	(155 ft 3 in)
Height	13.56 m	(44 ft 6 in)
Performance		
Max speed	1,046 km/h	(569 kt, 654 mph)
Cruising speed	980 km/h	(530 kt, 609 mph)
Takeoff distance	1,676 m	(5,500 ft)
Range	4,728 km	(2,570 nm, 2,955 miles)
Weights		
Max takeoff	108,843 kg	(240,000 lbs)
Useful load	51,011 kg	(112,480 lbs)

Boeing 767 — USA

The medium-/long-range Boeing 767 was developed alongside the 757 and while it follows a similar design layout it has a different wing and a wider fuselage with twin-aisle seven-abreast economy seating and 290-passenger maximum capacity. The prototype 767-200 first flew on 26th September 1981 and was certificated in July 1982. Powerplants include the 48,000 lb.s.t. P&W JT9D-7R4D, 57,900 lb.s.t. GE CF6-80C2 or 58,000 lb.s.t. Rolls Royce RB211-524G turbofans. First customers were United Airlines, American, Delta and TWA. The 767-300 is a larger-capacity model with a 21 ft fuselage stretch and up to 360 seats and both versions are also sold as extended-range models as the 767-200ER and 767-300ER. The 767-400ER is a -300 with a further 21 ft 2 in. fuselage extension, an upgraded flight deck and longer wings. It was first flown on 9th October 2000. Over 800 Boeing 767s had been built by the end of 2000.

Boeing 767-300ER, EI-CKE

Boeing 767 (Cont.)

Specification	Boeing 767-200	
Powerplant	Two 48,000 lb.s.t (213.54 kN) Pratt &Whitney JT9D-7R4D turbofans (typical)	
Dimensions		
Span	47.57 m	(156 ft 1 in)
Length	48.5 m	(159 ft 2 in)
Height	15.85 m	(52 ft 0 in)
Performance		
Max speed	992 km/h	(539 kt, 620 mph)
Cruising speed	960 km/h	(522 kt, 600 mph)
Takeoff distance	1,951 m	(6,400 ft)
Range	6,984 km	(3,796 nm, 4,365 miles)
Weights		
Max takeoff	142,857 kg	(315,000 lbs)
Useful load	61,950 kg	(136,600 lbs)

Boeing 777 — USA

Boeing's large twin airliner formula has been extended to fill the final capacity gap between the 767 and the 747 with the Boeing 777-200. Outwardly resembling a scaled-up 767 with two underwing large turbofans, the 777 has a main cabin twin-aisle layout with nine-/ten-abreast seating. In high-density configuration 440 passengers can be carried but normal multi-class layouts are for 304 seats. The prototype first flew on 12th June 1994. Boeing has also produced a 777-200IGW version with additional centre-section tankage and higher payload. The choice of engines includes the General Electric GE90-76B, Rolls Royce Trent 877 or the Pratt & Whitney PW4077. Uprated versions of these are used on the stretched Boeing 777-300 which flew on 16th October 1997 and offers a maximum capacity of 550 seats. More than 300 777s were in service by the end of 2000.

Specification	Boeing 777-200	
Powerplant	Two 78,700 lb.s.t (350.08 kN) General Electric GE90-76B turbofans (typical)	
Dimensions		
Span	60.93 m	(199 ft 11 in)
Length	63.73 m	(209 ft 1 in)
Height	18.52 m	(60 ft 9 in)
Performance		
Max speed	1,059 km/h	(576 kt, 662 mph)
Cruising speed	1,022 km/h	(556 kt, 639 mph)
Takeoff distance	2,530 m	(8,300 ft)
Range	9,480 km	(5,152 nm, 5,925 miles)
Weights		
Max takeoff	247,165 kg	(545,000 lbs)
Useful load	109,116 kg	(240,600 lbs)

Boeing B-52H Stratofortress — USA

As the key element of the USAF strategic nuclear bombing force for over 45 years, the B-52 has a commanding place in history. This large swept-wing bomber, now only operating in its later B-52H form, was designed by Boeing in 1949 and first flown on 2nd October 1952. Distinctive features are the eight Pratt & Whitney TF33 turbofans in four double pods slung below the wings and the complex four-unit undercarriage mounted in the lower fuselage. The B-52H was stressed for low-altitude operations and can carry up to eight AGM-86B cruise missiles internally and 12 on external pylons. Defensive armament includes a tail-mounted six-barrel Vulcan cannon. Between 1954 and 1962 a total of 744 B-52s was built. Approximately 85 remain in USAF service and the B-52 has given unparalleled service in Vietnam and other major combat situations.

Boeing 777-200, N790UA

Boeing B-52H, 60-0037

Specification	Boeing B-52H Stratofortress	
Powerplant	Eight 17,000 lb.s.t. (75.6 kN) Pratt & Whitney TF33-P-3 turbofans	
Dimensions		
Span	56.39 m	(185 ft 0 in)
Length	49.05 m	(160 ft 11 in)
Height	12.4 m	(40 ft 8 in)
Performance		
Max speed	952 km/h	(517 kt, 595 mph)
Cruising speed	816 km/h	(443 kt, 510 mph)
Takeoff distance	2,896 m	(9,500 ft)
Range	12,000 km	(6,522 nm, 7,500 miles)
Weights		
Max takeoff	229,025 kg	(505,000 lbs)

Specification	Boeing Stearman Model A75N1	
Powerplant	One 220 h.p. (164 kW) Continental R-670-5 piston engine	
Dimensions		
Span	9.8 m	(32 ft 2 in)
Length	7.5 m	(24 ft 9 in)
Height	2.9 m	(9 ft 8 in)
Performance		
Max speed	208 km/h	(113 kt, 130 mph)
Cruising speed	170 km/h	(92 kt, 106 mph)
Initial climb	256 m/min	(840 fpm)
Range	600 km	(326 nm, 375 miles)
Weights		
Max takeoff	1,195 kg	(2,635 lbs)
Useful load	317 kg	(700 lbs)

Boeing Stearman A75N1 — USA

The Stearman A75 was the principal two-seat primary trainer for the World War II American forces and, at the time of its introduction in 1936, was the latest in a long line of Stearman biplanes. Of steel tube, wood and fabric construction, the Kaydet, as it was known, had tandem open cockpits and a fixed tailwheel undercarriage. The initial PT-13 had a 215 or 220 h.p. Continental R-680 radial engine and the PT-13B had a 280 h.p. R-680-11. Some 1,391 PT-13s were built at the Wichita factory of Boeing Stearman together with 2,000 of the US Navy's N2S-2 and N2S-3. This was followed by the improved PT-17 (A75N1) with the 220 h.p. R-670, 3,064 of which were built for the USAAC and 1,649 (as the N2S-1, N2S-4 and N2S-5) for the USN. The PT-27 (D75N1) was a version for the RCAF with an enclosed cockpit. After the war many Stearmans were sold to private owners and used for crop spraying. Over 2,400 are registered in the USA and 40 are active in the UK.

Boeing Stearman A75N1

Boeing Vertol 107 and CH-46 — USA

Boeing Vertol followed the tandem-rotor concept which had been successful on the Vertol H-21 in their new turbine military and civil utility helicopter, the Model 107, which first flew on 22nd April 1958. It had a square-section fuselage with a large main cabin and introduced new low-vibration steel-sparred rotor blades and a simplified flight control system. It also had a sealed fuselage and outrigger floats allowing it to float on water. The V.107 was certificated as a civil model and was delivered as the V.107-II for airline shuttle applications with large airliner-style windows to New York Airways and others. It was also built in Japan by Kawasaki who completed 160 aircraft including 60 for the JGSDF and nine for the JMSDF. The military CH-46 assault transport variant was delivered in significant numbers to the Army and as the Sea Knight to the Navy and Marine Corps for SAR missions, medevac and general transport work. Boeing Vertol built 678 of the V.107 series and the last CH-46 was delivered in 1971. The V.107 was also delivered to the Canadian armed forces as the 'Labrador' and 'Voyageur' and to the Swedish Navy and Air Force.

Boeing Vertol CH-46F Sea Knight, Bu.154855

Boeing Vertol 107 and CH-46 (Cont.)

Specification	Boeing Vertol CH-46E Sea Knight	
Powerplant	Two 1,870 s.h.p. (1,394 kW) General Electric T58-GE-16 turboshafts	
Dimensions		
Rotor diameter (each)	15.24 m	(50 ft 0 in)
Length	13.66 m	(44 ft 10 in)
Height	5.08 m	(16 ft 8 in)
Performance		
Max speed	267 km/h	(144 kt, 166 mph)
Cruising speed	249 km/h	(135 kt, 155 mph)
Initial climb	439 m/min	(1,440 fpm)
Range	1,016 km	(552 nm, 635 miles)
Weights		
Max takeoff	11,020 kg	(24,300 lbs)
Useful load	5,766 kg	(12,715 lbs)

Boeing Vertol CH-47 Chinook — USA

The CH-47 Chinook is one of the most successful heavy tactical helicopters ever built. It was developed from the Vertol 107 as the V.117 (YCH-1B) which first flew on August 1959, and had a longer fuselage of squarer section, full-length external fairings containing fuel and equipment, a fixed four-leg undercarriage and twin T55 turboshaft engines mounted on the outside of the tail pylon. The first example of the definitive US Army CH-47A was handed over in August 1962 and the design was progressively improved as the CH-47B and CH-47C with higher-power turbines and modifications to the rotor and dynamic systems. The Chinook served widely in Vietnam and in the Persian Gulf. Early Chinooks have been upgraded to CH-47D standard involving complete refurbishment and installation of Honeywell T55-L-712 turbines and composite rotor blades. The MH-47E is a special forces version, first flown in June 1990 and fitted with a refuelling boom, improved radars and fixed armament. The Chinook has been sold to Spain, Singapore, Canada, the Netherlands, Australia and the RAF among others and has been built under licence by Meridionali in Italy and Kawasaki in Japan. A civil version, the Model 234, has also been built in small numbers for logging and offshore support. Over 750 Chinooks had been built by the end of 1999.

Boeing Chinook HC.2, ZH777 (RAF)

Specification	Boeing CH-47D International Chinook	
Powerplant	Two 3,000 s.h.p. (2,237 kW) Honeywell T55-L-712 turboshafts	
Dimensions		
Rotor diameter (each)	18.29 m	(60 ft 0 in)
Length	15.87 m	(52 ft 1 in)
Height	5.78 m	(18 ft 11 in)
Performance		
Max speed	289 km/h	(156 kt, 180 mph)
Cruising speed	239 km/h	(130 kt, 149 mph)
Initial climb	561 m/min	(1,840 fpm)
Range	585 km	(318 nm, 366 miles)
Weights		
Max takeoff	20,090 kg	(44,300 lbs)
Useful load	9,873 kg	(21,770 lbs)

Boeing RAH-66 Comanche — USA

Boeing has joined with Sikorsky to develop the RAH-66 Comanche two-seat armed reconnaissance helicopter to replace the US Army's OH-58, AH-1 and OH-6. The Comanche project was initiated in late 1990 and the consortium is to build six prototypes of the RAH-66. The YRAH-66 was first flown on 4th January 1996 but due to funding delays only the second had flown by mid-1999 and a third will fly in April 2004. Boeing has responsibility for all missions electronics integration, the rotor blades and the aft fuselage; Sikorsky handles the drive system, weapons integration and forward fuselage. The aircraft is largely built from composites and has fly-by-wire control systems. The twin LHTEC turboshaft engines are buried in the centre fuselage and are heavily shrouded for infrared protection. The tail rotor is a fenestron-type and the surrounding vertical fin is angled and topped by a horizontal tailplane. The two crew are in tandem stepped armoured cockpits and the tailwheel undercarriage is fully retractable.

Boeing-Sikorsky RAH-66 Comanche

Specification	Boeing-Sikorsky RAH-66 Comanche	
Powerplant	Two 1,432 s.h.p. (1,068 kW) LHTEC T800-LHT-801 turboshafts	
Dimensions		
Rotor diameter	11.9 m	(39 ft 0 in)
Length	13.2 m	(43 ft 4 in)
Height	3.37 m	(11 ft 1 in)
Performance		
Max speed (est)	322 km/h	(175 kt, 201 mph)
Cruising speed (est)	294 km/h	(160 kt, 184 mph)
Range	2,320 km	(1,260 nm, 1,450 miles)
Weights		
Max takeoff	5,818 kg	(12,828 lbs)
Useful load	2,296 kg	(5,063 lbs)

Boeing X-32 — USA

The X-32 is Boeing's contender in the Joint Strike Fighter (JSF) competition which is also being entered by Lockheed-Martin with the X-35A. Aimed at developing naval and air force aircraft with a common airframe to meet the requirements of the US and British forces, two demonstration prototypes have been built as the X-32A in conventional (CTOL) and carrier-based (CV) configuration and the X-32B STOVL version. The X-32B is required to replace the Harrier/AV-8B and Sea Harrier and the X-32A is an A-10, F/A-18 and F-16 replacement for the USAF and US Navy/Marines. The X-32, which first flew on 18th September 2000, is a single-seat aircraft with a high technology compound delta wing, twin tailfins and a large scoop nose air-intake. If selected, it is likely to be built by a consortium led by Boeing and including BAE Systems

Boeing X-32A

Specification	Boeing X-32A	
Powerplant	One Pratt & Whitney JSF119 turbofan	
Dimensions		
Span	10.21 m	(33 ft 6 in)
Length	13.7 m	(44 ft 11 in)
Height	11 m	(36 ft 1 in)
Performance		
Max speed	1,931 km/h	(1,043 kt, 1,200 mph)
Range	3,000 km	(1,630 nm, 1,875 miles)
Weights		
Max takeoff (est.)	22,680 kg	(50,010 lbs)
Useful load (est.)	12,000 kg	(26,460 lbs)

Boisavia B.601 Mercurey — France

The prototype Boisavia Mercurey first flew on 3rd April 1949 and was built in series by Société Boisavia for flying clubs and private owners. The basic B.60 (three built) was a strut-braced high-wing four-seat monoplane of attractive appearance powered by a 140 h.p. Renault 4Pei engine but the main production variant, the B.601/B.601L of which 30 were completed, used the 190 h.p. Lycoming O-435-A or O-360-C horizontally opposed engine. The remaining 13 production aircraft had various powerplants including the 170 h.p. Regnier 4L-O2 (B.605) and Argus AS.10 (Mercurey Special). Four Mercureys are flying in France.

Boisavia B.601L Mercurey, OO-KLO

Specification	Boisavia B.601L Mercurey	
Powerplant	One 190 h.p. (141.66 kW) Textron Lycoming O-360-C1A piston engine	
Dimensions		
Span	11.4 m	(37 ft 4 in)
Length	7.1 m	(23 ft 5 in)
Height	2.1 m	(6 ft 10 in)
Performance		
Max speed	234 km/h	(127 kt, 146 mph)
Cruising speed	195 km/h	(106 kt, 122 mph)
Initial climb	183 m/min	(600 fpm)
Range	1,088 km	(591 nm, 680 miles)
Weights		
Max takeoff	991 kg	(2,185 lbs)
Useful load	256 kg	(565 lbs)

Bölkow Kl.107 and F.207
— Germany

The Hans Klemm Flugzeugbau had designed the Kl.105 light aircraft before the war and developed and flew this as the Kl.107 low-wing two-seat light aircraft in 1955. The definitive Kl.107B was flown on 4th September 1956 and 25 production aircraft were built powered by a 150 h.p. Lycoming O-320. Klemm passed rights to the Ingenieurbau Bölkow who built a further 30 Kl.107Cs. The three-seat Bölkow Kl.107C incorporated numerous improvements including a redesigned tall fixed-tailwheel undercarriage. On 10th December 1960 Bölkow flew the improved Model F.207 which had a larger cabin with modified windows, four seats, wing fuel tanks and a 180 h.p. Lycoming O-360 engine; 91 examples were built between 1960 and 1962 and one aircraft was modified as the Bö.214 with a tricycle undercarriage. Several Kl.107s and F.207s are flying in Germany with further units registered in Luxembourg, the UK and Switzerland.

Bölkow F.207, D-EBLI

Specification	Bölkow F.207	
Powerplant	One 180 h.p. (134.2 kW) Textron Lycoming O-360-A1A piston engine	
Dimensions		
Span	10.81 m	(35 ft 6 in)
Length	8.30 m	(27 ft 3 in)
Height	2.25 m	(7 ft 4 in)
Performance		
Max speed	254 km/h	(138 kt, 159 mph)
Cruising speed	232 km/h	(126 kt, 145 mph)
Initial climb	216 m/min	(710 fpm)
Range	1,240 km	(674 nm, 775 miles)
Weights		
Max takeoff	1,200 kg	(2,645 lbs)
Useful load	485 kg	(1,070 lbs)

Bölkow/MFI Junior
— Sweden/Germany

In October 1958, Björn Andreasson flew his BA-7 side-by-side two-seat homebuilt prototype in California and this small mid-wing aircraft was subsequently developed by Malmö Flygindustri (MFI) into the MFI-9 Junior powered by a 100 h.p. Continental O-200 engine. It had a side-by-side two-seat cabin with a hinged single-piece transparent canopy and was fitted with a fixed tricycle undercarriage and forward-swept wings. MFI built 23 examples followed by 47 of the improved MFI-9B Trainer and military Mili-Trainer which had a larger tail and electric flaps. In Germany, Bölkow started building the substantially similar Bö.208 Junior under licence in 1962 and completed 186 aircraft. These principally differed from the MFI-9 in having a modified nose undercarriage. Juniors were exported widely and over 100 are currently active in Germany, Italy, the United Kingdom, USA etc.

Bölkow Bö.208 Junior, G-ATVX

Specification	Bölkow Bö.208 Junior	
Powerplant	One 100 h.p. (74.56 kW) Teledyne Continental O-200 piston engine	
Dimensions		
Span	7.42 m	(24 ft 4 in)
Length	5.79 m	(19 ft 0 in)
Height	1.98 m	(6 ft 6 in)
Performance		
Max speed	224 km/h	(122 kt, 140 mph)
Cruising speed	200 km/h	(109 kt, 125 mph)
Initial climb	210 m/min	(690 fpm)
Range	744 km	(404 nm, 465 miles)
Weights		
Max takeoff	600 kg	(1,323 lbs)
Useful load	240 kg	(529 lbs)

Bolkow Bö.209 Monsun — Germany

The design of the Bö.208 led to a new model conceived by Hermann Mylius with a foldable low wing and a modified wider cockpit with a full bubble canopy. This MHK-101 was developed by the Ingenieurbau Bölkow into the Bö.209 Monsun which was fitted with either the 150 h.p. Lycoming O-320-E1C or 160 h.p. Lycoming O-320-E1F engine. The prototype Bö.209 was first flown on 25th September 1970. Bölkow, which had become part of Messerschmitt-Bölkow-Blohm, built 102 production Bö.209s and some were equipped with a retractable nosewheel which improved the cruise performance of the aircraft. The Bö.209-160RV was a variant available with a variable pitch propeller. The majority of Bö.209s are still registered in Germany and other examples fly in Switzerland, the USA and the UK.

Bölkow Bö.209 Monsun 150F, D-EAAA

Specification	Bölkow Bö.209-160RV Monsun	
Powerplant	One 160 h.p. (119.29 kW) Textron Lycoming O-320-E1F piston engine	
Dimensions		
Span	8.4 m	(27 ft 7 in)
Length	6.6 m	(21 ft 8 in)
Height	2.2 m	(7 ft 2 in)
Performance		
Max speed	274 km/h	(148 kt, 170 mph)
Cruising speed	223 km/h	(121 kt, 139 mph)
Initial climb	360 m/min	(1,180 fpm)
Range	1,200 km	(652 nm, 750 miles)
Weights		
Max takeoff	820 kg	(1,808 lbs)
Useful load	336 kg	(741 lbs)

Bowers Fly Baby — USA

Pete Bowers, who designed the tiny single-seat Fly Baby, was the winner of the 1962 EAA contest for a simple aircraft for amateur construction. It first flew on 27th July, 1960 powered by a Continental A65 but the prototype and later versions were upgraded to a Continental C75 or other engines of up to 100 horsepower. The Fly Baby 1A, which has very docile handling characteristics, is an all-wood aircraft with fabric covering and has a wire-braced low wing with a folding mechanism. It has a fixed tailwheel undercarriage but can also be equipped with twin floats. It is sold in the form of plans and builders can also complete it as a biplane. In this form it can either have the original lower wings with a set of detachable upper wings positioned forward of the cockpit built with a swept-back profile or new shorter-span biplane wings. In this latter form it is known as the Model 1B Bi-Baby.

Bowers Bi-Fly Baby, G-BNPV

Specification	Bowers Fly Baby	
Powerplant	One 85 h.p. (63.4 kW) Teledyne Continental C75 piston engine	
Dimensions		
Span	8.5 m	(28 ft 0 in)
Length	5.6 m	(18 ft 6 in)
Height (monoplane)	2 m	(6 ft 6 in)
Performance		
Max speed	192 km/h	(104 kt, 120 mph)
Cruising speed	168 km/h	(91 kt, 105 mph)
Initial climb	274 m/min	(900 fpm)
Range	512 km	(278 nm, 320 miles)
Weights		
Max takeoff	419 kg	(925 lbs)
Useful load	145 kg	(320 lbs)

Brandli BX-2 Cherry — Switzerland

The Cherry is one of the more popular European-designed homebuilt light aircraft. It was designed by the Swiss amateur constructor Max Brandli who flew the prototype on 24th April 1982 and has subsequently sold plans and some components. The Cherry is an attractive low-wing machine with a side-by-side two-seat cockpit enclosed by a large transparent canopy. The structure of the BX-2 is mixed with a wooden internal frame and wing mainspar and expanded polystyrene foam cores with glass-fibre covering. The wings can be folded for easy transportation and the Cherry has a retractable tricycle undercarriage. Several powerplants have been fitted to completed aircraft including the 65 h.p. Teledyne Continental A65 used on the prototype and larger Continentals of up to 100 h.p. and the Rotax 912 or Limbach L.2400. Over 40 Cherries are flying and examples are operating in Holland, Switzerland, the UK and Austria with over 100 under construction.

Brandli BX-1 Cherry, F-PCHB

Specification	Brandli BX-2 Cherry	
Powerplant	One 90 h.p. (67.1 kW) Teledyne Continental C90 piston engine	
Dimensions		
Span	6.98 m	(22 ft 11 in)
Length	5.31 m	(17 ft 5 in)
Height	1.7 m	(5 ft 7 in)
Performance		
Max speed	260 km/h	(140 kt, 160 mph)
Cruising speed	200 km/h	(110 kt, 125 mph)
Initial climb	180 m/min	(590 fpm)
Range	800 km	(434 nm, 500 miles)
Weights		
Max takeoff	550 kg	(1,213 lbs)
Useful load	232 kg	(511 lbs)

Brantly B-2 — USA

The B-2 light helicopter was designed by N.O. Brantly to accommodate two people in the smallest practical fuselage. It was a tadpole-shaped all-metal machine with a large transparent nose containing the cockpit and individual perspex bubbles to give headroom for the two occupants. The production B-2 had a simple skid undercarriage and a single 180 h.p. Lycoming VO-360-A1A engine which was buried behind the cabin and drove a three-blade rotor. The first of three prototype B-2s flew on 21st February 1953 and production started in 1961 at Norman, Oklahoma using several variants of the VO-360 engine (A1A, A1B, B1A). Five B-2s were evaluated by the US Army in 1960 as the YHO-3BR. Eventually Brantly built 194 examples of the B-2, 18 B-2As with a larger canopy and 165 B-2Bs with increased power before ceasing production. The B-2B has now been revived by Brantly International of Vernon, Texas and 12 had been built by the middle of 1999.

Brantly B-2B, G-AXSR

Specification	Brantly International B-2B	
Powerplant	One 180 h.p. (134.2 kW) Textron Lycoming IVO-360-A1A piston engine	
Dimensions		
Rotor diameter	7.24 m	(23 ft 9 in)
Length	6.62 m	(21 ft 9 in)
Height	2.06 m	(6 ft 9 in)
Performance		
Max speed	161 km/h	(87 kt, 100 mph)
Cruising speed	143 km/h	(78 kt, 90 mph)
Initial climb	580 m/min	(1,900 fpm)
Range	399 km	(217 nm, 250 miles)
Weights		
Max takeoff	757 kg	(1,670 lbs)
Useful load	295 kg	(650 lbs)

Brditschka HB-23 — Austria

The designs of Heini Brditschka were highly innovative and followed the work of the glider designer, Fritz Raab. Brditschka's first powered aircraft was the single-seat HB-3, based on the Raab Krähe sailplane but with a pusher engine positioned behind the wing driving a propeller operating in a slot in the rear fuselage. Powered by a Rotax 642 this HB-3BR was built in small numbers from 1963 onwards. The HB-3 led to the larger HB-21 Hobbyliner tandem two-seater 30 of which were built, and then to the HB-23/2000 which had side-by-side seating, a T-tail and a 50 h.p. VW-Westermayer engine or 75 h.p. Porsche-VW-HB-2400-G engine. Some 35 were built and Brditschka (now named HB Flugzeugbau) also built nine of the Scanliner with a large fully glazed nose which was intended as an aerial surveillance platform for law enforcement roles. The last version to be built in limited quantity was the HB-202 with a 110 h.p. Volkswagen engine, modified tail and short-span wings.

Brditschka HB-23-2400 Hobbyliner, OE-9317

Specification	Brditschka HB-23-2400 Hobbyliner	
Powerplant	One 75 h.p. (55.92 kW) Porsche-VW-HB-2400-G piston engine	
Dimensions		
Span	16.4 m	(53 ft 10 in)
Length	8 m	(26 ft 3 in)
Height	2.45 m	(8 ft 1 in)
Performance		
Max speed	200 km/h	(108 kt, 124 mph)
Cruising speed	180 km/h	(97 kt, 112 mph)
Initial climb	230 m/min	(750 fpm)
Range	800 km	(435 nm, 500 miles)
Weights		
Max takeoff	760 kg	(1,676 lbs)
Useful load	200 kg	(442 lbs)

Breguet Br.1050 Alizé — France

Designed by Avions Louis Breguet, the Alizé carrier-borne long-range anti submarine aircraft was first flown in prototype form on 6th October 1956 and was required for operation from the aircraft carriers *Clemenceau* and *Foch* which were then being built. The Alizé has a crew of three – a pilot and two radar operators – and is an all-metal low-wing aircraft with a belly weapons bay to carry a torpedo or depth charges, wing-mounted pods to enclose the main undercarriage units and to house electronic equipment and a primary search radar in a retractable ventral rear fuselage housing. Two underwing hardpoints can carry Nord AS.12 missiles or depth charges. Some 78 Alizés, including three pre-production prototypes, were delivered to the French Navy and 12 were sold to the Indian Navy. A small number of Alizés remain in service.

Breguet Br.1050 Alizé, No.55

Specification	Breguet Br.1050 Alizé	
Powerplant	One 2,100 s.h.p. (1565.7 kW) Rolls Royce Dart R.Da.21 turboprop	
Dimensions		
Span	15.6 m	(51 ft 2 in)
Length	13.9 m	(45 ft 1 in)
Height	4.7 m	(15 ft 5 in)
Performance		
Max speed	456 km/h	(248 kt, 285 mph)
Cruising speed	416 km/h	(226 kt, 260 mph)
Initial climb	421 m/min	(1,380 fpm)
Range	2,500 km	(1,359 nm, 1,563 miles)
Weights		
Max takeoff	8,163 kg	(18,000 lbs)
Useful load	2,464 kg	(5,433 lbs)

Breguet (Dassault) Br.1150 Atlantic — France

Avions Louis Breguet designed the Atlantic as a replacement for the Lockheed Neptune which was the standard postwar NATO long-range maritime reconnaissance type. The Atlantic prototype flew on 21 October 1961. Production was a French, German, Dutch and Belgian project with final assembly handled by Breguet at Biarritz. The twelve-crew Atlantic was delivered to the French Aéronavale (40), Italy (18), the Netherlands (9) and the German Kriegsmarine (20) who have modified six for ELINT missions. The Br.1150 has a large belly weapons-bay capable of carrying bombs, depth charges and up to eight torpedoes and four underwing hardpoints. It is equipped with ASW avionics and a Thomson search radar. The Dassault Breguet Atlantique ATL2, 30 of which have been sold to the Aéronavale, is an upgraded version with completely new electronic equipment including wingtip-mounted ESM and a Tango FLIR in a nose housing and the proposed ATL3 would have Allison AE2100 turboprops and a new mission system.

Dassault Breguet Atlantic, MM40109 (Italian AF)

Specification	Dassault Breguet 1150 Atlantique ATL2	
Powerplant	Two 6,100 s.h.p. (4,549 kW) Rolls Royce Tyne RTy.20 Mk.21 turboprops	
Dimensions		
Span	37.46 m	(122 ft 11 in)
Length	31.72 m	(104 ft 1 in)
Height	11.3 m	(37 ft 1 in)
Performance		
Max speed	648 km/h	(350 kt, 403 mph)
Cruising speed	556 km/h	(300 kt, 345 mph)
Initial climb	610 m/min	(2,000 fpm)
Range	7,778 km	(4,227 nm, 4,861 miles)
Weights		
Max takeoff	46,192 kg	(101,853 lbs)
Useful load	20,494 kg	(45,190 lbs)

Bristol 170 Freighter 31 — UK

The Bristol 170 was developed from the prewar Bristol Bombay as a general-utility freighter. Its simple and rugged design included a fixed tailwheel undercarriage and a box-section fuselage with clamshell nose doors for easy freight loading. The aircraft has a high wing-mounted pair of Bristol Hercules radial engines. The prototype first flew on 2nd December 1945 and a number of versions were built including the Wayfarer which was an all-passenger model without the nose doors and fitted with up to 32 passenger seats. Sales were made to airlines around the world including Aer Lingus, Indian National and Aviaco. Pakistan, Canada and New Zealand bought Freighters for military use. In the UK Silver City Airways used the type for cross-Channel car ferry services and acquired 11 of the long-nosed Mk.32 Super Freighters. At least two Freighters remain active in Canada.

Bristol 170 Freighter Mk.31, C-FDFC

Specification	Bristol 170 Mk.31	
Powerplant	Two 1,980 h.p. (1,476.28 kW) Bristol Hercules 734 piston engines	
Dimensions		
Span	32.9 m	(108 ft 0 in)
Length	20.8 m	(68 ft 4 in)
Height	6.6 m	(21 ft 8 in)
Performance		
Max speed	360 km/h	(196 kt, 225 mph)
Cruising speed	261 km/h	(142 kt, 163 mph)
Initial climb	290 m/min	(950 fpm)
Range	1,312 km	(713 nm, 820 miles)
Weights		
Max takeoff	19,955 kg	(44,000 lbs)
Useful load	7,710 kg	(17,000 lbs)

Britten Norman BN-2 Islander — UK

The Islander light twin was designed by John Britten and Desmond Norman as a simple multi-purpose utility aircraft for use by air taxi, military and commuter operators and for light freighting, crop spraying, patrol and other tasks. It has a ten-seat cabin and, for simplicity, is fitted with a fixed tricycle undercarriage. The BN-2 prototype first flew on 20th August 1966 powered by 260 h.p. Lycoming O-540-E4B5 piston engines. Over 1,175 have been built at Bembridge and in Romania, some with 300 h.p. Lycoming IO-540-K1B5 engines as the BN-2A-2. The Defender is a military model and turbine variants include the BN-2A-41 Turbo Islander, which flew on 6th April 1977, with Lycoming LTP-101 turboprops and the BN-2T with 320 s.h.p. Allison 250-B17Cs. Britten Norman has also marketed the CASTOR BN2T with a large nose radome for maritime surveillance and the current production BN-2T-4 Defender 4000 which has a larger wing, stretched fuselage and 400 s.h.p. Allison 250-B17F turboprops.

Britten Norman BN-2B-26 Islander, G-BUBO

Britten Norman BN-2T-4R CASTOR Islander, G-RAPA

Specification	Britten Norman BN-2B Islander	
Powerplant	Two 260 h.p. (194 kW) Textron Lycoming O-540-E4C5 piston engines	
Dimensions		
Span	14.94 m	(49 ft 0 in)
Length	10.86 m	(35 ft 8 in)
Height	4.18 m	(13 ft 9 in)
Performance		
Max speed	274 km/h	(148 kt, 170 mph)
Cruising speed	258 km/h	(140 kt, 160 mph)
Initial climb	262 m/min	(860 fpm)
Range	1,175 km	(640 nm, 735 miles)
Weights		
Max takeoff	2,993 kg	(6,600 lbs)
Useful load	991 kg	(2,185 lbs)

Britten Norman BN-2A Mk.III Trislander — UK

Providing greater capacity for the BN-2 Islander was solved by Britten Norman through the relatively simple measure of stretching the existing fuselage by 7 ft 6 in to give an extra four rows of twin seats, each row having its own entry door, and by mounting a third Lycoming O-540 engine on the top of the vertical fin. Britten Norman also fitted the Trislander with an optional longer nose incorporating an extra baggage hold and raised the tailplane to the same level as the third engine. The Islander prototype was converted to this configuration and first flew on 11th September 1970. Some 72 BN-2s were built as Trislanders and have served with operators as varied as Air Tahiti, Aurigny Air Services, Air Martinique and Sierra Leone Airways. Approximately half of these are still in service. Rights to the Trislander were sold to International Aircraft Corporation of Miami in 1982, although no further production was undertaken by them, but a new series of Trislanders was launched by Britten Norman in 1999 to meet Chinese requirements.

Britten Norman BN2A Mk.III Trislander, G-JOEY

Specification	Britten Norman BN-2A Mk.III-3 Trislander	
Powerplant	Three 260 h.p. (194 kW) Textron Lycoming O-540-E4C5 piston engines	
Dimensions		
Span	16.15 m	(53 ft 0 in)
Length	15.01 m	(49 ft 3 in)
Height	4.32 m	(14 ft 2 in)
Performance		
Max speed	290 km/h	(156 kt, 180 mph)
Cruising speed	267 km/h	(144 kt, 166 mph)
Initial climb	298 m/min	(980 fpm)
Range	1,600 km	(868 nm, 1,000 miles)
Weights		
Max takeoff	4,535 kg	(10,000 lbs)
Useful load	1,885 kg	(4,157 lbs)

Brochet MB.50 Pipistrelle — France

Maurice Brochet was a prolific designer of light aircraft in the immediate postwar period and his first creation to be built in any numbers was the MB.50 Pipistrelle single-seater. It was intended as a simple aircraft for amateur construction and was constructed of wood and fabric with a strut-braced parasol wing and a fixed tailwheel undercarriage. The open

Brochet MB.50 Pipistrelle (Cont.)

cockpit was positioned just behind the wing and, due to the scarcity of engines, it was designed to have a variety of powerplants in the 25 h.p. to 90 h.p. range. The prototype, which flew in May 1947, had a 45 h.p. Salmson 9ADb radial engine but other MB.50s have used the 25 h.p. Sarolea Vautour, 27 h.p. Train, 45 h.p. Beaussier 4b, and the 45 h.p. in-line Persy II. Over 70 sets of plans were sold and at least ten MB.50s were flown but only one of these is known to be currently active in France.

Brochet MB.50 Pipistrelle, F-PEBZ

Specification	Brochet MB.50 Pipistrelle	
Powerplant	One 45 h.p. (33.55 kW) Salmson 9ADb piston engine	
Dimensions		
Span	8 m	(26 ft 3 in)
Length	4.8 m	(15 ft 9 in)
Height	1.6 m	(5 ft 2 in)
Performance		
Max speed	144 km/h	(78 kt, 90 mph)
Cruising speed	120 km/h	(65 kt, 75 mph)
Initial climb	152 m/min	(500 fpm)
Range	320 km	(174 nm, 200 miles)
Weights		
Max takeoff	350 kg	(772 lbs)
Useful load	109 kg	(240 lbs)

Brochet MB.70, MB.80
— France

The MB.70, derived by Maurice Brochet from the single-seat MB.50 Pipistrelle, was first flown on 28th January 1950. A conventional strut-braced wood and fabric high-wing tandem two-seater with a fixed tailwheel undercarriage, it was built by Constructions Aéronautique's Maurice Brochet in several versions including the MB.72 with a 65 h.p. Continental A65 engine, the MB.76 with a 90 h.p. Continental C90-14F and the MB.80 with a wider fuselage, spring-steel undercarriage and a 75 h.p. Minie 4DC. Twenty of the MB.70 and MB.80 series were built during the early 1950s. The larger three-seat MB.100 and MB.101 had a 100 h.p. Hirth HM.502 and the MB.110 was a utility version with a further power increase. Some 24 of the MB.100 series were completed and five are believed to be flying or in substantially complete condition in France.

Brochet MB.83D, F-PGLF

Specification	Brochet MB.72	
Powerplant	One 65 h.p. (48.46 kW) Teledyne Continental A65 piston engine	
Dimensions		
Span	10.5 m	(34 ft 6 in)
Length	6.5 m	(21 ft 4 in)
Height	2.5 m	(8 ft 2 in)
Performance		
Max speed	160 km/h	(87 kt, 100 mph)
Cruising speed	144 km/h	(78 kt, 90 mph)
Initial climb	235 m/min	(770 fpm)
Range	368 km	(200 nm, 230 miles)
Weights		
Max takeoff	570 kg	(1,257 lbs)
Useful load	198 kg	(437 lbs)

Brugger MB-2 Colibri
— Switzerland

The Colibri ('Hummingbird') is a classic low-wing aircraft and is one of the most popular European homebuilt single-seat designs. Conceived by Max Brugger as a prototype in 1965, the definitive version of the Colibri, the MB-2, made its first flight on 1st May 1970. Constructed from plans, the Colibri, which is powered by a Volkswagen engine of 1,500, 1,600 or 1,800 cc, is of all-wood construction with fabric covering. It features an all-moving vertical tail and a simple constant-chord cantilever wing to which the main units of the fixed tailwheel undercarriage are attached. The cockpit is fully enclosed with a clearview canopy. An all-metal development, the MB-3, which featured folding wings, was flown in March 1977 but this has not been built in quantity. Over 60 Colibris are currently flying, more than 30 of these in France and 12 in Sweden, and at least 100 are under construction.

Brugger MB-2 Colibri, HB-XVC

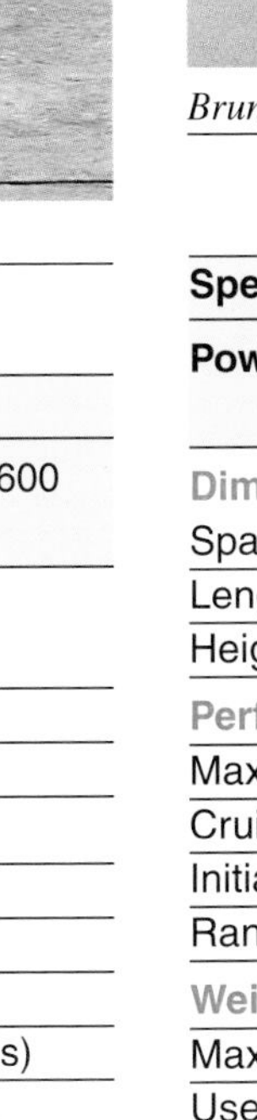

Specification	Brugger MB-2 Colibri	
Powerplant	One 40 h.p. (30 kW) Volkswagen 1600 piston engine	
Dimensions		
Span	6 m	(19 ft 8 in)
Length	4.8 m	(15 ft 9 in)
Height	1.6 m	(5 ft 3 in)
Performance		
Max speed	180 km/h	(96 kt, 110 mph)
Cruising speed	152 km/h	(83 kt, 95 mph)
Initial climb	180 m/min	(590 fpm)
Range	480 km	(261 nm, 300 miles)
Weights		
Max takeoff	570 kg	(1,257 lbs)
Useful load	198 kg	(437 lbs)

Brunner-Winkel Bird — USA

The Brunner-Winkel Aircraft Corporation (later renamed Bird Aircraft Corp.) produced the small Bird Model A and Bird BK in some numbers during the 1930s. The Bird biplane had a steel tube, fabric and metal fuselage and wooden fabric-covered wings. It accommodated two passengers in the forward open cockpit and the pilot in a separate rear cockpit. The Model A had a Curtiss OX-5 engine and the Model BK was powered by a 100 h.p. Kinner K5 radial. The Bird CK, 42 of which were built, had a modified fuselage to provide a three-seat forward cockpit and the powerplant was changed to the 125 h.p. Kinner B5. It was followed by the Bird CJ with an even larger Jacobs LA-1 engine of 170 h.p., six of which were completed. Rights to the aircraft passed to Perth-Amboy in 1933. Some 53 examples of the Bird series are registered in the United States of which 12 or so are currently airworthy.

Brunner-Winkel Bird BK, NC847W

Specification	Brunner-Winkel Bird BK	
Powerplant	One 100 h.p. (74.5 kW) Kinner K5 piston engine	
Dimensions		
Span	10.4 m	(34 ft 0 in)
Length	6.8 m	(22 ft 3 in)
Height	2.4 m	(8 ft 0 in)
Performance		
Max speed	176 km/h	(96 kt, 110 mph)
Cruising speed	144 km/h	(78 kt, 90 mph)
Initial climb	198 m/min	(650 fpm)
Range	800 km	(435 nm, 500 miles)
Weights		
Max takeoff	898 kg	(1,980 lbs)
Useful load	354 kg	(780 lbs)

Bücker Bü.131 Jungmann and Bü.133 Jungmeister — Germany

The Jungmann two-seat aerobatic trainer was originally designed for the prewar German sport flying movement and the prototype first flew on 27th April 1934. Distinguished by its sharply swept wings and forward-slanted undercarriage, the Bü.131A powered by an 80 h.p. Hirth HM.60R was widely used by the wartime Luftwaffe and 1,910 of this and the Bü.131B with a 105 h.p. Hirth HM.504 were built. Postwar production was carried out by CASA in Spain (as the CASA.I.131 of which over 200 were built), Dornier Werke in Switzerland (97 built) and Tatra in Czechoslovakia (the T-131). The Bü.133B Jungmeister single-seat competi-

Bücker Bü.131 Jungmann and Bü.133 Jungmeister (Cont.)

tion aerobatic biplane was based on the Bü.131 with a shortened fuselage and 160 h.p. Hirth HM.506 engine or, as the Bü.133C, with a 160 h.p. Siemens Sh.14A radial. In addition to the German production of Jungmeisters, 47 were built by Dornier Werke, 50 by CASA and 12 airframes were built by Joseph Bitz Flugzeubau in the 1960s. A new production line for the Jungmann has now been established by Historical Aircraft Services in Poland.

CASA.I.131 Jungmann, E3B-369 (G-BPDM)

Bücker Bü.133C Jungmeister, D-EKRE

Specification	Bücker Bü.131B Jungmann	
Powerplant	One 105 h.p. (78.3 kW) Hirth HM.504A piston engine	
Dimensions		
Span	7.4 m	(24 ft 3 in)
Length	6.6 m	(21 ft 8 in)
Height	2.3 m	(7 ft 5 in)
Performance		
Max speed	184 km/h	(100 kt, 115 mph)
Cruising speed	168 km/h	(91 kt, 105 mph)
Initial climb	366 m/min	(1,200 fpm)
Range	640 km	(348 nm, 400 miles)
Weights		
Max takeoff	668 kg	(1,474 lbs)
Useful load	289 kg	(638 lbs)

Bücker Bü.181D Bestmann — Germany

The side-by-side two-seat Bestmann was designed just before the war as a club touring and training aircraft but it became the Luftwaffe's primary trainer and 2,730 were built in Germany. A further 708 were completed by Fokker in Holland and 125 examples were also built in Sweden by AB Hagglund during the war years. The Bestmann was of all-wood construction with plywood covering and had a fixed tailwheel undercarriage and an enclosed cockpit. The powerplant was a 105 h.p. Hirth HM.504. The design was produced after the war by Zlin in Czechoslovakia as the Zlin 181 and they continued to build 79 Z-281s with a 105 h.p. Toma engine and then 314 of the Z-381 with a 105 h.p. Walter Minor 4-III. Another postwar producer was the Egyptian government who set up a line to build the Heliopolis Gomhouriya (see separate entry).

Bücker Bü.181 Bestmann, D-EDUB

Specification	Bücker Bü.181D Bestmann	
Powerplant	One 105 h.p. (78.3 kW) Hirth HM.504A piston engine	
Dimensions		
Span	10.6 m	(34 ft 9 in)
Length	7.7 m	(25 ft 5 in)
Height	2 m	(6 ft 5 in)
Performance		
Max speed	213 km/h	(116 kt, 133 mph)
Cruising speed	194 km/h	(105 kt, 121 mph)
Initial climb	213 m/min	(700 fpm)
Range	800 km	(435 nm, 500 miles)
Weights		
Max takeoff	748 kg	(1,650 lbs)
Useful load	270 kg	(595 lbs)

Bushby Midget Mustang and Mustang II — USA

Sold in kit form to homebuilders, the Midget Mustang was designed in 1948 by Dave Long and marketed in kit form by Bushby Aircraft. The MM-1-85 Midget Mustang is an all-metal low-wing single-seat racer with a wide-track fixed tailwheel undercarriage and enclosed cabin. The Super Midget, launched in 1962, is a version with a retractable tailwheel undercarriage. Powerplants range from the 85 h.p. Continental C85 to the 125 h.p. Lycoming O-290-D2. A side-by-side two-seat version, the Mustang II, first flew on 9th July 1966. This high-performance aircraft has a full bubble canopy and is powered by a 160 h.p. Lycoming O-320 or 180 h.p. O-360. It is aerobatic and can be fitted with folding wings and with either tailwheel or tricycle gear. Over 1,700 sets of parts or plans have been sold and nearly 300 Mustang IIs are now flying, mostly in the United States.

Bushby Midget Mustang and Mustang II (Cont.)

Bushby Mustang II, N8EJ

Specification	Bushby Midget Mustang	
Powerplant	One 85 h.p. (63.38 kW) Teledyne Continental C85 piston engine	
Dimensions		
Span	5.64 m	(18 ft 6 in)
Length	5 m	(16 ft 6 in)
Height	1.4 m	(4 ft 6 in)
Performance		
Max speed	304 km/h	(165 kt, 190 mph)
Cruising speed	240 km/h	(130 kt, 150 mph)
Initial climb	533 m/min	(1,750 fpm)
Range	368 km	(200 nm, 230 miles)
Weights		
Max takeoff	397 kg	(875 lbs)
Useful load	136 kg	(300 lbs)

C

CAB Minicab — France

The Constructions Aéronautique de Béarn (CAB) was the constructor of the GY-20 Minicab, a side-by-side two-seater designed by Yves Gardan. Gardan had already designed the similar SIPA 90, but the Minicab was considerably lighter and powered by a 65 h.p. Continental A65-8 engine. The prototype Minicab, built of wood and fabric, first flew on 1st February 1949. It had a fixed tailwheel undercarriage and a forward-hinged single-piece cockpit canopy. CAB built 22 Minicabs and sold plans to amateur builders who completed over 30 further aircraft. One version, fitted with a 90 h.p. Continental C90, was known as the Barritault JB-01. CAB also built seven examples of the GY-30 Supercab with a retractable tailwheel undercarriage. This was fitted with a 90 h.p. Continental C90 and the prototype flew on 5th February 1954. Over 40 GY-20s are now flying including eight in France, 11 in the UK and ten in Switzerland.

CAB Minicab, HB-SUM

Specification	CAB GY-20 Minicab	
Powerplant	One 65 h.p. (48.46 kW) Teledyne Continental A65-8 piston engine	
Dimensions		
Span	7.6 m	(24 ft 11 in)
Length	5.4 m	(17 ft 10 in)
Height	1.7 m	(5 ft 6 in)
Performance		
Max speed	200 km/h	(109 kt, 125 mph)
Cruising speed	176 km/h	(96 kt, 110 mph)
Initial climb	183 m/min	(600 fpm)
Range	560 km	(304 nm, 350 miles)
Weights		
Max takeoff	485 kg	(1,069 lbs)
Useful load	215 kg	(475 lbs)

CAC Ceres — Australia

The wartime Wirraway tandem two-seat trainer was, essentially, a development of the North American T-6 built by Commonwealth Aircraft Corporation (CAC). It had the same all-metal airframe and low-wing, tandem two-seat cockpit and retractable tailwheel undercarriage as the T-6 and four preserved examples are still flying in Australia. After the war, CAC developed the Wirraway into the CA-28 Ceres for agricultural operations. The Ceres used the basic Wirraway airframe but had a fixed undercarriage and had its fuselage lengthened by 2 ft 4 in to make space for a stainless-steel chemical hopper in front of the cockpit. The wing centre section was redesigned and the Ceres had modified ailerons and flaps. The prototype Ceres

CAC Ceres (Cont.)

flew on 18th February 1958 and CAC built a total of 20 aircraft. Two examples of the Ceres are still registered in Australia.

CAC Ceres, VH-SSY

Specification	CAC CA-28 Ceres	
Powerplant	One 600 h.p. (447.3 kW) Pratt & Whitney R-1340-S3H1-G piston engine	
Dimensions		
Span	14.3 m	(46 ft 11 in)
Length	9.4 m	(30 ft 9 in)
Height	2.74 m	(9 ft 0 in)
Performance		
Max speed	192 km/h	(104 kt, 120 mph)
Cruising speed	176 km/h	(96 kt, 110 mph)
Initial climb	221 m/min	(725 fpm)
Range	800 km	(435 nm, 500 miles)
Weights		
Max takeoff	3,360 kg	(7,410 lbs)
Useful load	1,329 kg	(2,930 lbs)

CAC Winjeel — Australia

Immediately after the war, CAC undertook design of a new basic trainer to replace the Wackett, Wirraway and Tiger Moth aircraft in service with the RAAF. The all-metal CA-25 Winjeel resembled the Hunting Provost which was being developed in Britain and had a fixed tailwheel undercarriage, low wing and Pratt & Whitney Wasp radial engine. The instructor and pupil were housed in side-by-side seating under a large framed canopy. The prototype Winjeel flew as the CA-22 on 3rd February 1951 and, as the CA-25 with a modified tail, went into production in 1954. Some 62 Winjeels were produced and the RAAF used them in its flying training schools and for forward air control tasks. They finally phased them out of service in 1994. At least 40 were sold as surplus and most were acquired by private owners in Australia, 33 of these being currently airworthy.

CAC Winjeel, A85-450 (VH-HOY)

Specification	CAC CA-25 Winjeel	
Powerplant	One 445 h.p. (332 kW) Pratt & Whitney R-985-AN-2 piston engine	
Dimensions		
Span	11.8 m	(38 ft 7 in)
Length	8.6 m	(28 ft 1 in)
Height	2.8 m	(9 ft 1 in)
Performance		
Max speed	296 km/h	(161 kt, 185 mph)
Cruising speed	264 km/h	(143 kt, 165 mph)
Initial climb	457 m/min	(1,500 fpm)
Range	1,360 km	(739 nm, 850 miles)
Weights		
Max takeoff	1,934 kg	(4,265 lbs)
Useful load	442 kg	(975 lbs)

Callair A-1 to A-4 — USA

Established at Afton, Wyoming just before the war, Callair designed a two-seat cabin light aircraft known as the Callair A. Constructed primarily of steel tube with fabric covering, the A had a wooden strut-braced low wing and a fixed tailwheel undercarriage. Only one Model A was built, powered by a Continental A 80 engine and the initial production models were the A-1, which had a similar structure but used the more powerful 100 h.p. Lycoming O-235 powerplant, the A-2 with a 125 h.p. Lycoming O-290 and the A-3 with a 125 h.p. Continental C-125-2. Callair built 35 of these models in the 1950s. In 1954, the A-4 was introduced and it had a slightly wider fuselage with a three-place bench seat and was powered by a 140 h.p. Lycoming O-290-D2. This was the most popular version and 66 were completed. Half of the Callairs are still registered in the USA although only around 20 are believed to be active.

Callair A-2, N2921V

Specification	Callair A-2	
Powerplant	One 125 h.p. (93.2 kW) Textron Lycoming O-290-A piston engine	
Dimensions		
Span	11 m	(36 ft 0 in)
Length	7.11 m	(23 ft 5 in)
Height	2.1 m	(7 ft 0 in)
Performance		
Max speed	192 km/h	(104 kt, 120 mph)
Cruising speed	163 km/h	(89 kt, 102 mph)
Initial climb	229 m/min	(750 fpm)
Range	592 km	(322 nm, 370 miles)
Weights		
Max takeoff	703 kg	(1,550 lbs)
Useful load	236 kg	(520 lbs)

Callair A-9 Sparrow and B-1 Snipe — USA

Using the basic structure of the A-4, Callair produced the A-5 and A-6 agricultural aircraft which had a cut-down fuselage decking and an offset open cockpit. These rather primitive machines led to the Callair A-9 crop sprayer which was developed by IMCO, who had acquired Callair, and it had a built-up and fully enclosed cabin and a hopper fitted between the 235 h.p. Lycoming O-540 engine and the cockpit. IMCO was sold to Rockwell in 1966 and they marketed the A-9 as the Sparrow Commander and the 260 h.p. A-9B as the Quail. Some 616 of the A-9 series were built by Rockwell/IMCO and 137 by AAMSA in Mexico who acquired rights to the design in 1971. The Rockwell B-1 Snipe Commander was a scaled-up version of the A-9 which flew on 15th January 1966 and had a 400 h.p. Lycoming IO-720-A1A engine and a larger 345 USG hopper. Only 36 of the B-1 were built and a few remain active.

Callair A-9A, VH-MPO

Specification	Callair A-9 Sparrow	
Powerplant	One 235 h.p. (175.2 kW) Textron Lycoming O-540-B2B5 piston engine	
Dimensions		
Span	10.67 m	(35 ft 0 in)
Length	7.32 m	(24 ft 0 in)
Height	2.3 m	(7 ft 7 in)
Performance		
Max speed	192 km/h	(104 kt, 120 mph)
Cruising speed	181 km/h	(98 kt, 113 mph)
Initial climb	198 m/min	(650 fpm)
Range	704 km	(382 nm, 440 miles)
Weights		
Max takeoff	1,497 kg	(3,300 lbs)
Useful load	771 kg	(1,700 lbs)

Canadair (Bombardier) CL-215 and CL-415 — Canada

The CL-215 is the only modern large civil utility amphibian to have been produced in quantity in the West. It is a high-wing all-metal aircraft intended for firefighting and general cargo carrying. The main units of the tricycle undercarriage retract into open recesses on the slab-sided fuselage and the planing hull has a large ventral hatch for dumping the water load of 1,176 Imperial gallons. The CL-215, powered by two 2,100 h.p. Pratt & Whitney CA-3 Double Wasp piston engines, first flew on 23rd October 1967 and the first of 125 production aircraft was delivered in June 1969. The CL-215B is for maritime patrol and the CL-215C is a 26-passenger version. The CL-215T was an upgrade to the CL-215 developed by Canadair (now Bombardier) with Pratt & Whitney PW123AF turboprops and large wingtip endplates and auxiliary fins mounted on the tailplane. As a new production aircraft, designated CL-415, and fitted with an EFIS cockpit and increased gross weight, this replaced the CL-215 in production. The CL-415M is a special missions version for governmental patrol and emergency work.

Canadair CL-215T, UD.13-29 (Spanish AF)

Canadair (Bombardier) CL-215 and CL-415 (Cont.)

Specification	Canadair (Bombardier) CL-415	
Powerplant	Two 2,380 s.h.p. (1,775 kW) Pratt & Whitney PW123AF turboprops	
Dimensions		
Span	28.6 m	(93 ft 11 in)
Length	19.82 m	(65 ft 0 in)
Height	8.98 m	(29 ft 6 in)
Performance		
Max speed	362 km/h	(197 kt, 227 mph)
Cruising speed	331 km/h	(180 kt, 207 mph)
Initial climb	419 m/min	(1,375 fpm)
Range	2,410 km	(1,310 nm, 1,506 miles)
Weights		
Max takeoff	19,887 kg	(43,850 lbs)
Useful load	7,176 kg	(15,825 lbs)

Canadair (Bombardier) CL600 Challenger — Canada

Originally conceived by Bill Lear as the Learstar 600, the Challenger first flew on 8th November 1978. Designated CL600-1A11, it is an intercontinental business jet with a wide-body interior normally accommodating 14 executive passengers, a T-tail and two rear fuselage-mounted Avco Lycoming ALF502L turbofans. First deliveries were made in 1980 and several military and special missions variants have been sold. The CL601 (CL600-2A12) has GE CF34-1A engines and wingtip winglets and has been produced in several variants including the long-range CL601-3A-ER and CL601-3R with CF34-3A1 engines, increased fuel load and redesigned air conditioning systems. The CL604 is a development of the CL601-3R with a new belly fairing, extra rear fuselage tanks, a larger cabin and CF34-3B engines. Over 500 of the Challenger series have been delivered.

Specification	Canadair (Bombardier) Challenger 604	
Powerplant	Two 9,220 lb.s.t. (41 kN) General Electric CF34-3B1 turbofans	
Dimensions		
Span	19.6 m	(64 ft 4 in)
Length	20.85 m	(68 ft 5 in)
Height	6.3 m	(20 ft 8 in)
Performance		
Max speed	880 km/h	(475 kt, 548 mph)
Cruising speed	850 km/h	(460 kt, 530 mph)
Initial Climb	549 m/min	(1,800 fpm)
Range	7,500 km	(4,078 nm, 4,690 miles)
Weights		
Max takeoff	21,859 kg	(48,200 lbs)
Useful load	9,864 kg	(21,750 lbs)

Canadair (Bombardier) Regional Jet — Canada

The Canadair Challenger as manufactured under the ownership of Bombardier has been the basis for development of the Canadair Regional Jet ('RJ') regional airliner and the Global Express long-range business jet. The RJ is based on the Challenger CL601-3A with a 20 ft longer fuselage and accommodation for up to 50 passengers. The prototype first flew on 10th May 1991 and the first delivery to Lufthansa Cityline was made in October 1992. Some have also been built as the Corporate Jetliner for high-density executive use. More than 300 RJs have been delivered, mostly the original Series 100 (CRJ-100) with CF34-3A1 engines. The current standard CRJ-200, which has improved CF34-3B1 engines with lower fuel consumption, has been supplemented by the CRJ700 which first flew on 27th May 1999. This has a stretched fuselage to accommodate 70 passengers and a deeper and wider interior cabin and is available in standard or extended-range versions. The first CRJ700 customer is Brit Air and other orders are in hand from American Eagle, Lufthansa Cityline and Horizon Air.

Canadair CL601-3R Challenger, N79AD

Canadair Corporate Jetliner, C-GATY

Specification	Canadair (Bombardier) CL600-2B19 Regional Jet 200	
Powerplant	Two 9,220 lb.s.t. (41 kN) General Electric CF34-3B1 turbofans	
Dimensions		
Span	21.21 m	(69 ft 7 in)
Length	26.77 m	(87 ft 10 in)
Height	6.22 m	(20 ft 5 in)
Performance		
Max speed	859 km/h	(464 kt, 534 mph)
Cruising speed	786 km/h	(424 kt 488 mph)
Initial climb	1,128 m/min	(3,700 fpm)
Range (max payload)	1,777 km	(965 nm, 1,110 miles)
Weights		
Max takeoff	21,519 kg	(47,450 lbs)
Useful load	7,791 kg	(17,180 lbs)

Canadair (Bombardier) Global Express — Canada

The BD700 Bombardier Global Express intercontinental business jet is externally similar to the Challenger but is 50% larger and is, essentially, a new design with a new wing and stretched fuselage. It has a wide-body cabin for between eight and 19 executive passengers and was first flown on 13th October 1996, powered by two BMW-Rolls Royce BR710 turbofans. The Global Express is aimed at business users requiring non-stop very long range capability at a high cruise speed over routes such as New York to Tokyo or Sydney to Los Angeles. It is also designed for good short-field performance. The first aircraft entered service in July 1999 at which time more than 20 aircraft had been delivered for completion.

Bombardier Global Express, C-FKGX

Canadair (Bombardier) Global Express (Cont.)

Specification	Canadair (Bombardier) BD700 Global Express	
Powerplant	Two 14,690 lb.s.t. (65.3 kN) BMW Rolls Royce BR710A2-20 turbofans	
Dimensions		
Span	28.65 m	(94 ft 0 in)
Length	30.3 m	(99 ft 5 in)
Height	7.57 m	(24 ft 10 in)
Performance		
Max speed	950 km/h	(513 kt, 590 mph)
Cruising speed	850 km/h	(460 kt, 530 mph)
Initial climb	1,097 m/min	(3,600 fpm)
Range	12,336 km	(6,700 nm, 7,710 miles)
Weights		
Max takeoff	42,404 kg	(93,500 lbs)
Useful load	20,272 kg	(44,700 lbs)

Canadair CL-41 Tutor — Canada

The Tutor is a side-by-side primary jet trainer designed by Canadair in the late 1950s to equip the RCAF (later Canadian Armed Forces) flying training schools. The first of two prototypes was flown on 13th January 1960. The Tutor has a low-set straight wing, tricycle undercarriage and a T-tail. The Orenda-built General Electric J85 turbojet, which is mounted in the rear fuselage, is fed by wing-root air intakes. Canadair started delivery of 190 CT-114 Tutors (CL-41A) to the RCAF in 1963, completing deliveries in 1966 and 120 of these remain in service. The only other operator of the Tutor was the Royal Malaysian Air Force which acquired 20, designated CL-41G. These were fitted with three hardpoints under each wing to hold stores for the secondary weapons training role. Named Tebuan in RMAF service, these aircraft have now been retired. Several Tutors now fly with private owners.

Specification	Canadair CL-41A Tutor	
Powerplant	One 2,633 lb.s.t. (11.7 kN) Orenda-GE J85/CJ610-1B turbojet	
Dimensions		
Span	11.13 m	(36 ft 6 in)
Length	9.75 m	(32 ft 0 in)
Height	2.84 m	(9 ft 4 in)
Performance		
Max speed	797 km/h	(433 kt, 498 mph)
Cruising speed	736 km/h	(400 kt, 460 mph)
Initial climb	1,280 m/min	(4,200 fpm)
Range	1,504 km	(817 nm, 940 miles)
Weights		
Max takeoff	3,332 kg	(7,348 lbs)
Useful load	1,134 kg	(2,500 lbs)

Canadair CL-44 — Canada

In March 1957 Canadair made the first flight of the CL-28 Argus piston-engined maritime reconnaissance aircraft based on the Bristol Britannia turboprop airliner. Having built 33 production CL-28s they developed the CL-44 which was a Britannia 300 with a 12 ft 4 in fuselage stretch and Rolls Royce Tyne Mk.515/10 turboprops and they flew the prototype on 15th November 1959. Twelve were built as the CC-106 Yukon for the RCAF with 134-seat interiors. The civil CL-44 was launched in 1960 as a commercial freighter and 27 of the production CL-44D4, which had a hinged tail unit, were built for Flying Tiger, Slick Airways, Loftleidir and Seaboard & Western Airlines. Four of these were converted to CL-44J standard with a 15 ft fuselage stretch, cabin windows and a 160-seat interior for use by Loftleidir. One CL-44 was converted as the Skymonster oversize freighter with a bulbous upper fuselage. At least four CL-44s are still operational as freighters.

Canadair CL-41, N401AG

Canadair CL-44, HC-AYS (Minus Props)

Specification	Canadair CL-44D4	
Powerplant	Four 5,730 s.h.p. (4,272 kW) Rolls Royce R.Ty.12 Tyne 515/10 turboprops	
Dimensions		
Span	43.4 m	(142 ft 4 in)
Length	41.7 m	(136 ft 11 in)
Height	11.2 m	(36 ft 8 in)
Performance		
Max speed	640 km/h	(348 kt, 400 mph)
Cruising speed	584 km/h	(317 kt, 365 mph)
Range	5,200 km	(2,826 nm, 3,250 miles)
Weights		
Max takeoff	95,238 kg	(210,000 lbs)
Useful load	55,093 kg	(121,480 lbs)

CAP Aviation CAP-10 — France

The CAP-10 two-seat aerobatic trainer originated in the CP.100 which was designed by Claude Piel as a development of the Super Emeraude and flown as a prototype in August 1966 by CAARP. With a broader chord rudder and various other modifications it was built as the CAP-10B from 1970 onwards by Avions Mudry and 51 were delivered to the French military forces. Other military users included Mexico (20) and South Korea (3) but the majority of the 280 aircraft built to date have been sold to civil owners and many of the military aircraft have been sold into the civil market. Avions Mudry ceased business in 1996 but was taken over by CAP Aviation (formerly Akrotech Europe) who are building the CAP-10C, which has a number of refinements.

Mudry CAP-10, F-GKKC

Specification	CAP Aviation CAP-10B	
Powerplant	One 180 h.p. (134 kW) Textron Lycoming AEIO-360-B2F piston engine	
Dimensions		
Span	8.06 m	(26 ft 5 in)
Length	7.16 m	(23 ft 6 in)
Height	2.55 m	(8 ft 4 in)
Performance		
Max speed	270 km/h	(146 kt, 168 mph)
Cruising speed	250 km/h	(135 kt, 155 mph)
Initial climb	480 m/min	(1,575 fpm)
Range	1,000 km	(543 nm, 625 miles)
Weights		
Max takeoff	830 kg	(1,830 lbs)
Useful load	280 kg	(617 lbs)

CAP Aviation CAP-20 and 231 — France

On 29th July 1969 Avions Mudry flew the prototype CAP-20, a single-seat wood and fabric aerobatic aircraft based on the CAP-10 powered by a 200 h.p. Lycoming AIO-360. Nine were built, mostly for the Armée de l'Air. Several improved versions followed, including the CAP-20B, the CAP-20L-180 and CAP-20LS-200 with 180 h.p. and 200 h.p. AEIO-360 engines and the CAP-21 which had a redesigned wing and a spring-steel undercarriage. The CAP-230 and CAP-231 were higher-powered versions of the CAP-21 with a more angular tail and a 300 h.p. AEIO-540-L1 engine. The CAP-231EX was another version, six of which were built with wings built by Walter Extra with carbon-fibre mainspars. The current version, which is now built by CAP Aviation is the CAP-232 with a new Mudry-designed carbon-fibre wing and modified ailerons. Production totalled 13 CAP-20Ls, 18 CAP-21s and 46 of the CAP-230, 231 and 232.

Mudry CAP-231, F-WZCI

CAP Aviation CAP-20 and 231 (Cont.)

Specification	CAP Aviation CAP-232	
Powerplant	One 300 h.p. (224 kW) Textron Lycoming AEIO-540-L1B5 piston engine	
Dimensions		
Span	7.39 m	(24 ft 3 in)
Length	6.76 m	(22 ft 2 in)
Height	1.9 m	(6 ft 2 in)
Performance		
Max speed	339 km/h	(183 kt, 211 mph)
Cruising speed	269 km/h	(145 kt, 167 mph)
Initial climb	914 m/min	(3,000 fpm)
Range	1,200 km	(652 nm, 750 miles)
Weights		
Max takeoff	816 kg	(1,800 lbs)
Useful load	227 kg	(500 lbs)

Caproni-Vizzola C.22J — Italy

The C.22J was developed by the Caproni subsidiary of Agusta as an inexpensive aircraft for flight screening of prospective military pilots and for ab initio training. Caproni had built several examples of the Calif jet-assisted sailplane and had experience with the Microturbo TRS-18 turbojets, two of which power the C.22J. The fuselage of the C.22J, which is of all-metal construction, has a main forward section housing the twin engines and a narrow rear boom which supports a T-tail. It has a side-by-side two-seat cockpit which is enclosed with a large clear canopy. The wings are unswept and of constant chord with wingtip fuel tanks and the aircraft has a retractable tricycle undercarriage. The first C.22J flew on 21st July 1980 followed by a production prototype in February 1983 which used higher-powered TRS-18-083 engines and is still airworthy. One aircraft was fitted with two underwing strongpoints for ground attack ordnance.

Caproni C.22J, I-GIAC

Specification	Caproni-Vizzola C.22J	
Powerplant	Two 326 lb.s.t. (1.45 kN) Microturbo TRS-18-083 turbojets	
Dimensions		
Span	9.2 m	(30 ft 2 in)
Length	6.26 m	(20 ft 6 in)
Height	1.88 m	(6 ft 2 in)
Performance		
Max speed	556 km/h	(300 kt, 345 mph)
Cruising speed	480 km/h	(260 kt, 300 mph)
Initial climb	600 m/min	(1,970 fpm)
Range	1,280 km	(700 nm, 800 miles)
Weights		
Max takeoff	1,255 kg	(2,767 lbs)
Useful load	517 kg	(1,140 lbs)

Carlson Sparrow — USA

Ernie Carlson has been one of the longest established producers of ultralight aircraft in the United States and Carlson Aircraft introduced the single-seat Sparrow in 1987. This is a simply constructed tube and fabric high-wing design with a fixed tricycle or tailwheel undercarriage and over 70 have been built by amateurs. The single-seat Sparrow has been replaced by the Sparrow Sport Special which has improved short-field performance and an aluminium wing structure and is powered by a 52 h.p. Rotax 503 engine. The Sparrow II is an enlarged version with side-by-side seating for two and a 66 h.p. Rotax 582 and a further development is the Sparrow II-XTC which has a higher useful load and increased power from an 85 h.p. Rotax or 100 h.p. Subaru engine. Around 30 of the Sparrow II variants have been built.

Carlson Sparrow II-XTC, N4CA

Specification	Carlson Sparrow II-XTC	
Powerplant	One 85 h.p. (63.4 kW) Rotax 912 piston engine	
Dimensions		
Span	9.5 m	(31 ft 2 in)
Length	5.5 m	(18 ft 0 in)
Height	2.1 m	(7 ft 9 in)
Performance		
Max speed	177 km/h	(96 kt, 110 mph)
Cruising speed	160 km/h	(87 kt, 100 mph)
Initial climb	335 m/min	(1,100 fpm)
Range	483 km	(262 nm, 300 miles)
Weights		
Max takeoff	567 kg	(1,250 lbs)
Useful load	295 kg	(650 lbs)

Specification	Carlson Skycycle	
Powerplant	One 55 h.p. (41 kW) Textron Lycoming O-145A piston engine	
Dimensions		
Span	6.1 m	(20 ft 0 in)
Length	4.8 m	(15 ft 10 in)
Height	1.4 m	(4 ft 7 in)
Performance		
Max speed	174 km/h	(95 kt, 109 mph)
Cruising speed	160 km/h	(87 kt, 100 mph)
Initial climb	267 m/min	(875 fpm)
Range	320 km	(174 nm, 200 miles)
Weights		
Max takeoff	204 kg	(450 lbs)
Useful load	70 kg	(155 lbs)

Carlson Skycycle — USA

Carlson Aircraft, the established producer of ultralight kit aircraft, has produced an amateur-built modern version of the Piper PA-8 Skycycle. Piper built two prototypes of the Skycycle in 1944 as a cheap postwar private-owner aircraft but did not put it into production. The PA-8 originally had a fuselage based on a war-surplus moulded drop tank which was fitted with a rear boom to carry the tail and short-span wings. The PA-8 had a fixed tailwheel undercarriage with the main units attached to the wing mainspar and a large bubble canopy covering the single-seat cockpit. The Carlson version, which was first flown on 8th December 1996, is sold in the form of plans with partial kits available for sections of the structure, has a tubular frame with moulded fibreglass covering, a metal tail boom and a 55 h.p. Continental O-145A engine.

CASA C-101 Aviojet — Spain

The C-101 was designed to meet a 1975 specification for a replacement for the Hispano HA200 jet trainers then in service with the Spanish Air Force. It is a conventional low-wing aircraft with a pressurised tandem two-seat cockpit, retractable tricycle undercarriage and a Garrett TFE731 turbofan in the rear fuselage with wing-root air intakes. The first of four prototypes flew on 27th June 1977. The Spanish Air Force received 92 C-101EB aircraft, designated E.25. The export C-101BB, four of which were sold to Honduras, is powered by a more powerful 3,700 lb.s.t. TFE731-3-1J engine and the C-101DD, which has flown in prototype form, has the TFE731-5-1J. Fourteen C-101BBs were delivered as weapons trainers, with six underwing hardpoints, to the Chilean Air Force, designated T-36. Eight of these were built by ENAER and they have also built 23 C-101CC (A-36 Halcón) ground attack variants for Chile and 16 for Jordan.

Carlson Skycycle, NX47Y

CASA C-101, E.25-27 (Spanish AF)

CASA C-101 Aviojet (Cont.)

Specification	CASA C-101BB Aviojet	
Powerplant	One 3,700 lb.s.t. (16.46 kN) Honeywell (Garrett) TFE731-3-1J turbofan	
Dimensions		
Span	10.6 m	(34 ft 10 in)
Length	12.5 m	(41 ft 0 in)
Height	4.25 m	(13 ft 11 in)
Performance		
Max speed	797 km/h	(430 kt, 495 mph)
Cruising speed	656 km/h	(355 kt, 406 mph)
Initial climb	1,152 m/min	(3,780 fpm)
Range	3,680 km	(2,000 nm, 2,300 miles)
Weights		
Max takeoff	5,599 kg	(12,345 lbs)
Useful load	2,122 kg	(4,679 lbs)

Specification	CASA C-212-300	
Powerplant	Two 900 s.h.p. (671 kW) Honeywell (Garrett) TPE331-10R-513C turboprops	
Dimensions		
Span	20.28 m	(66 ft 6 in)
Length	16.15 m	(53 ft 0 in)
Height	6.6 m	(21 ft 8 in)
Performance		
Max speed	370 km/h	(200 kt, 230 mph)
Cruising speed	354 km/h	(190 kt, 220 mph)
Initial climb	95 m/min	(312 fpm)
Range	1,422 km	(770 nm, 890 miles)
Weights		
Max takeoff	7,698 kg	(16,975 lbs)
Useful load	3,299 kg	(7,275 lbs)

CASA C-212 Aviocar — Spain

In 1969, CASA started work on the C-212 light utility STOL transport, primarily to meet a Spanish Air Force requirement. The high-wing Aviocar has a square-section fuselage, fixed tricycle undercarriage and an upswept rear fuselage incorporating a loading ramp. It is powered by two wing-mounted Garrett TPE331 turboprops and has 19 seats in passenger configuration. The first C-212-100 flew on 26th March 1971 and 79 were delivered to the Spanish Air Force designated T.12B (or TR.12A for survey work and TE.12B as dual control trainers). The C-212-200 is a higher-powered version with TPE331-5 engines, the C-212-300 has TPE331-10R-513C engines and winglets and a lengthened nose and the C-212-400 has TPE331-12 engines and a higher useful load. The C-212 has been built under licence by IPTN in Indonesia as the NC.212, and 327 had been built in Spain and 96 at IPTN by the end of 1998 for military and civil customers including the air forces of Mexico, Zimbabwe, Panama, Angola, Argentina and Bolivia and air carriers such as Pelita Air Services, Korean Air and Merpati Nusantara.

CASA C-212.100, N99TF

Cassutt Special — USA

The Cassutt Special is one of the most popular Formula One racers and is sold in plans form for construction by amateur builders. Designed by Thomas K. Cassutt, the Special prototype, known as the 'Jersey Skeeter', first flew in 1954 powered by an 85 h.p. Continental C85 engine. This was followed by many other plans-built aircraft with engines ranging up to 200 h.p. although most examples use the 100 h.p. Continental O-200. The Special is a small fully-aerobatic single-seater with an enclosed cockpit and fixed tailwheel undercarriage. The fuselage and tail have a tubular steel frame with fabric covering and the cantilever wings, which are centre-mounted on the fuselage, are of wooden construction. The current Cassutt IIIM, several hundred of which have been built, is available in plans or kit form from National Aeronautics and can be completed as the Sport or as the Racer, which has shorter-span wings.

Cassutt Racer IIIM, G-BOMB

Specification	National Aeronautics Cassutt IIIM Sport	
Powerplant	One 100 h.p. (74.56 kW) Teledyne Continental O-200 piston engine	
Dimensions		
Span	5.18 m	(17 ft 0 in)
Length	4.88 m	(16 ft 0 in)
Height	1.22 m	(4 ft 0 in)
Performance		
Max speed	322 km/h	(174 kt, 200 mph)
Cruising speed	290 km/h	(156 kt, 180 mph)
Initial climb	914 m/min	(3,000 fpm)
Range	788 km	(425 nm, 490 miles)
Weights		
Max takeoff	363 kg	(800 lbs)
Useful load	136 kg	(300 lbs)

Caudron C.601 Aiglon — France

The Aiglon was an open-cockpit tandem two-seat light monoplane designed for private owners and club use and was first sold in 1935. It was an all-wood design with a low wing and fixed tailwheel undercarriage and some examples were fitted with an enclosed cabin top. Avions Caudron built the C.600 with a 100 h.p. Renault 4Pgi Bengali four-cylinder inline engine and the more powerful Model 601 with the larger 140 h.p. Renault 4Pei. Approximately 180 Aiglons were built during the prewar years. Two examples of the C.601 are currently active in France.

Caudron C.600 Aiglon, F-BDXT

Specification	Caudron C.601 Aiglon	
Powerplant	One 140 h.p. (104.4 kW) Renault Bengali 4Pei piston engine	
Dimensions		
Span	11.4 m	(37 ft 4 in)
Length	7.6 m	(24 ft 11 in)
Height	2 m	(6 ft 7 in)
Performance		
Max speed	224 km/h	(122 kt, 140 mph)
Cruising speed	200 km/h	(109 kt, 125 mph)
Initial climb	213 m/min	(700 fpm)
Range	544 km	(296 nm, 340 miles)
Weights		
Max takeoff	878 kg	(1,936 lbs)
Useful load	299 kg	(660 lbs)

Caudron C.276 Luciole — France

In 1931 Avions Caudron flew the prototype of their Luciole two-seat biplane and production continued for eight years to meet the needs of French flying schools where it became one of the principal trainers in club use. The Luciole was of simple all-wood and fabric construction with a rugged tailwheel undercarriage and tandem cockpits with dual controls. Several variants were built using the same basic airframe but with various powerplants including the C.272/2 (140 h.p. Renault 4Pei), C.275 (100 h.p. Renault 4Pgi Bengali), and C.277 (120 h.p. Renault 4Pdi). In total, Caudron built 725 Lucioles, the most numerous variant being the C.275. Around ten Lucioles remain in existence, airworthy examples including the former British aircraft shown below, fitted with a Salmson 7AC radial engine and two in France with Renault engines.

Caudron C.270 Luciole, G-BDFM

Specification	Caudron C.272 Luciole	
Powerplant	One 140 h.p. (104.4 kW) Renault 4Pei Bengali piston engine	
Dimensions		
Span	9.9 m	(32 ft 5 in)
Length	7.67 m	(25 ft 2 in)
Height	2.76 m	(9 ft 0 in)
Performance		
Max speed	171 km/h	(93 kt, 107 mph)
Cruising speed	149 km/h	(81 kt, 93 mph)
Initial climb	335 m/min	(1,100 fpm)
Range	621 km	(337 nm, 388 miles)
Weights		
Max takeoff	840 kg	(1,852 lbs)
Useful load	355 kg	(783 lbs)

CERVA Guepard — France

Wassmer, based at Issoire in central France, designed and produced the Super IV touring aircraft during the 1960s (see separate entry). In 1972, Wassmer and Société Siren formed the CERVA partnership (the Consortium Européen de Réalisation et de Ventes d'Avions) which redesigned the Super 4/21 as the CE-43 Guepard. First flown on 18th May 1971, it was an all-metal aircraft with an integral four-/five-seat cabin, a retractable tricycle undercarriage and a 250 h.p. Lycoming engine. They also built one example of the CE-44 Cougar which had a 285 h.p. Continental Tiara 6-285P engine. The basic construction of the Guepard was carried out by Siren and final assembly and testing was Wassmer's responsibility. In total, 44 Guepards were built including a batch of 18 delivered to the Armée de l'Air for communications duties. The majority of the Guepards are still in active operation.

CERVA CE-43 Guepard, F-BSQJ

Specification	CERVA CE-43 Guepard	
Powerplant	One 250 h.p. (186.4 kW) Textron Lycoming IO-540-C4B5 piston engine	
Dimensions		
Span	10 m	(32 ft 9 in)
Length	8.4 m	(27 ft 6 in)
Height	2.8 m	(9 ft 2 in)
Performance		
Max speed	319 km/h	(172 kt, 198 mph)
Cruising speed	257 km/h	(139 kt, 160 mph)
Initial climb	329 m/min	(1,080 fpm)
Range	2,880 km	(1,565 nm, 1,800 miles)
Weights		
Max takeoff	1,600 kg	(3,528 lbs)
Useful load	755 kg	(1,665 lbs)

Cessna AW — USA

The 'A' series of three-seat cantilever high-wing monoplanes were the first production models built by the Cessna Aircraft Company in the late 1920s. The prototype, developed from the Cessna Comet, was built and flown in 1927 and the first customer delivery was made the following year. The 'A' Series, 71 of which were built, were of mixed construction with fabric covering and offered with a variety of engines to customer choice. The most popular was the AW, of which 48 were completed with a 110 h.p. Warner radial but other versions were the AA with a 120 h.p. Anzani, the AS with a 125 h.p. Siemens-Halske, the AC with a 130 h.p. Comet and the AF with a 150 h.p. Floco engine. The remaining 15 examples of the AW on the US register, four of which are believed to be active, have all been re-engined with either 160 h.p. Lycoming or 125 h.p. seven-cylinder Warner Scarab engines.

Cessna AW, NC4725

Specification	Cessna AW	
Powerplant	One 125 h.p. (93.2 kW) Warner Scarab piston engine	
Dimensions		
Span	12.3 m	(40 ft 6 in)
Length	7.2 m	(23 ft 8 in)
Height	2.2 m	(7 ft 4 in)
Performance		
Max speed	205 km/h	(111 kt, 128 mph)
Cruising speed	173 km/h	(94 kt, 108 mph)
Initial climb	213 m/min	(700 fpm)
Range	1,008 km	(548 nm, 630 miles)
Weights		
Max takeoff	1,043 kg	(2,300 lbs)
Useful load	476 kg	(1,050 lbs)

Cessna Airmaster C-37, C-38 and C-145 — USA

The Cessna A series of cantilever high-wing monoplanes formed the basis for the much improved Airmasters. The C-34 had a streamlined fuselage with a NACA engine cowling, flaps and a neat cantilever undercarriage without bracing struts. The prototype was flown in June 1935 and was built in substantial numbers together with the C-37 which had a wider cabin, improved undercarriage and electric flaps. It was powered by a 145 h.p. Warner Super Scarab engine. The C-38 had a taller vertical tail, curved undercarriage legs and a landing flap positioned under the fuselage. The C-145 and C-165, of which 80 were built, were improved versions of the C-38 with hydraulic brakes and electrically driven split flaps fitted at the wing mid-chord position. The C-145 had a 145 h.p. Warner SS646 and the C-165 had the 165 h.p.

SS2006. In total, 228 examples of the Airmaster were built before production ceased at the beginning of World War II and approximately 75 have survived.

Cessna C-165, NC19498

Specification	Cessna C-145 Airmaster	
Powerplant	One 145 h.p. (108.1 kW) Warner Super Scarab piston engine	
Dimensions		
Span	10.41 m	(34 ft 2 in)
Length	7.52 m	(24 ft 8 in)
Height	2.13 m	(7 ft 0 in)
Performance		
Max speed	259 km/h	(141 kt, 162 mph)
Cruising speed	229 km/h	(124 kt, 143 mph)
Initial climb	244 m/min	(800 fpm)
Range	1,256 km	(683 nm, 785 miles)
Weights		
Max takeoff	1,066 kg	(2,350 lbs)
Useful load	440 kg	(970 lbs)

Cessna T-50 Bobcat — USA

Immediately before the war, Cessna made a major leap from their high-wing single-engined Airmaster series into the twin-engined five-seat Model T-50 which first flew on 26th March 1939. Powered by two 245 h.p. Jacobs L4MB radials and fitted with a retractable tailwheel undercarriage, only 42 were built for civil sale before military orders commenced and the RCAF ordered 640 of the Crane I for use as a trainer for the Commonwealth Air Training Plan. This order was followed by the USAF's AT-8 (33 delivered) with 295 h.p. Lycoming R-680-9 engines and the AT-17 (1,330 delivered) which had 245 h.p. Jacobs R-775-9 engines. The USAF also acquired 3,356 UC-78 Bobcat communications transports. The T-50 was known as the 'Bamboo Bomber' due to its wooden construction and total production had reached 5,401 when the line closed in 1944. Some 155 Bobcats are currently registered with private owners in the United States.

Cessna T-50 Bobcat, N41759

Specification	Cessna T-50 (AT-17) Bobcat	
Powerplant	Two 245 h.p. (182.6 kW) Jacobs R-775-9 piston engines	
Dimensions		
Span	12.8 m	(41 ft 11 in)
Length	10 m	(32 ft 9 in)
Height	3 m	(9 ft 11 in)
Performance		
Max speed	312 km/h	(170 kt, 195 mph)
Cruising speed	300 km/h	(163 kt, 188 mph)
Initial climb	465 m/min	(1,525 fpm)
Range	1,200 km	(652 nm, 750 miles)
Weights		
Max takeoff	2,268 kg	(5,000 lbs)
Useful load	680 kg	(1,500 lbs)

Cessna 120 and 140 — USA

The Model 120 and 140 were Cessna's answer to the postwar demand for light aircraft by civilianised wartime fliers. They used the all-metal monocoque production techniques learned during the war combined with mass production systems to produce affordable modern light aircraft. The Cessna 140 was a high-wing side-by-side two-seater which first flew on 28th June 1945. It was equipped with metal and fabric wings with flaps and V-bracing struts and used an 85 h.p. Continental flat-four C 85-12 piston engine. The economy Cessna 120 was not fitted with flaps and had single bracing struts and no rear cabin windows. The fabric-covered wings of the Cessna 140 were later replaced on the 140A by all-metal wings and the engine was enlarged to 90 h.p. In total, Cessna built 5,432 Cessna 140s and 2,172 Cessna 120s between 1946 and 1952. The Model 120/140 series was replaced in 1959 by the Cessna 150.

Cessna 140, NC72570

Specification	Cessna 140	
Powerplant	One 85 h.p. (63.38 kW) Teledyne Continental C85-12 piston engine	
Dimensions		
Span	10.16 m	(33 ft 4 in)
Length	6.55 m	(21 ft 6 in)
Height	2.01 m	(6 ft 7 in)
Performance		
Max speed	192 km/h	(104 kt, 120 mph)
Cruising speed	168 km/h	(91 kt, 105 mph)
Initial climb	195 m/min	(640 fpm)
Range	720 km	(391 nm, 450 miles)
Weights		
Max takeoff	658 kg	(1,450 lbs)
Useful load	268 kg	(590 lbs)

Cessna 150 and 152 — USA

In the late 1950s it became clear that there was a need for a new two-seat trainer and Cessna designed the Model 150 which was broadly based on the Cessna 140 but with a tricycle undercarriage and a 100 h.p. Continental O-200A engine. The first Cessna 150 flew on 12th September 1957 and 648 were sold in the first full year of production. In successive years the design had annual improvements with, first, a rear-view cabin window structure and, in 1966, a swept vertical tail on the Model 150F. The Model 150F was the first version built at the French Reims Aviation factory and a total of 1,980 French Cessna 150/152s were eventually completed. Cessna also produced the FA.150 Aerobat for aerobatic training. In 1978, the Model 152 was introduced with many improvements including a 110 h.p. Lycoming O-235 engine. When Cessna 152 production ceased in 1985, 29,078 examples of the US-manufactured 150/152 series had been built.

Cessna 150M, N6482K

Specification	Cessna 152	
Powerplant	One 110 h.p. (82.02 kW) Textron Lycoming O-235-N2C piston engine	
Dimensions		
Span	10.16 m	(33 ft 4 in)
Length	7.34 m	(24 ft 1 in)
Height	2.59 m	(8 ft 6 in)
Performance		
Max speed	206 km/h	(109 kt, 125 mph)
Cruising speed	184 km/h	(100 kt, 115 mph)
Initial climb	218 m/min	(715 fpm)
Range	580 km	(315 nm, 362 miles)
Weights		
Max takeoff	760 kg	(1,675 lbs)
Useful load	257 kg	(566 lbs)

Cessna 170 — USA

With the Cessna 120 and 140 in full production, Cessna developed a four-seat version which was designated Cessna 170 and first flew in prototype form on 5th November 1947. The initial Model 170 was, essentially, an enlarged Model 140 with fabric-covered wings and a 145 h.p. Continental C-145 engine. With the Model 170A, the company introduced all-metal wings and a larger vertical tail and the Model 170B, sold from 1953 onwards, had the improved Continental O-300 engine in a longer cowling and larger slotted flaps. As with other Cessna aircraft there were minor detail improvements each year. By the time the Model 170 was introduced the postwar light aircraft boom was dying out and it was discontinued in 1956 after 5,173 had been built. It was replaced by the Model 172 which was similar in design but had a tricycle undercarriage and a re-shaped tail.

Cessna 170A, N5555C

Specification	Cessna 170B	
Powerplant	One 145 h.p. (108.1 kW) Teledyne Continental O-300 piston engine	
Dimensions		
Span	10.97 m	(36 ft 0 in)
Length	7.59 m	(24 ft 11 in)
Height	2.11 m	(6 ft 11 in)
Performance		
Max speed	217 km/h	(118 kt, 136 mph)
Cruising speed	200 km/h	(109 kt, 125 mph)
Initial climb	210 m/min	(690 fpm)
Range	816 km	(443 nm, 510 miles)
Weights		
Max takeoff	998 kg	(2,200 lbs)
Useful load	444 kg	(980 lbs)

Cessna 172 Skyhawk, P172, 175 and 172RG — USA

The Cessna 172 Skyhawk is probably the most popular four-seat light aircraft of all time with over 43,000 examples of the model range completed by mid-1999. Based on the Model 170 with a fixed tricycle undercarriage, 145 h.p. Continental O-300C engine and squared-off vertical tail, it first flew on 12th June 1955 with first deliveries in the following year. Progressive improvements included a swept vertical tail on the 1960 Model 172A, a rear-view 'omnivision' cabin window on the 1963 Model 172D and a larger 160 h.p. Lycoming O-320-H2AD engine on the Model 172N. Cessna expanded the range in 1958 with the higher-powered Model 175 and Skylark, fitted with a geared Continental GO-300-A engine, and with its successor, the P172D Skyhawk Powermatic, which was added in 1963. Higher-powered variants included the 210 h.p. Model R172 built for the USAF as the T-41 and the Reims-built FR172 Reims Rocket. Production of the standard 172 commenced at the French Reims factory with the F172D and 2,947 were completed. A retractable undercarriage was offered on the Model 172RG which was sold from 1980 to 1985. Many thousands of Cessna 172s are flying, in virtually every country in the world.

Cessna F172M, G-BBTG

Cessna 172, N8934B

Specification	Cessna 172M Skyhawk	
Powerplant	One 150 h.p. (111.84 kW) Textron Lycoming O-320-E2D piston engine	
Dimensions		
Span	10.97 m	(36 ft 0 in)
Length	8.2 m	(26 ft 11 in)
Height	2.61 m	(8 ft 9 in)
Performance		
Max speed	224 km/h	(121 kt, 140 mph)
Cruising speed	200 km/h	(109 kt, 125 mph)
Initial climb	197 m/min	(645 fpm)
Range	1,112 km	(604 nm, 695 miles)
Weights		
Max takeoff	1,043 kg	(2,300 lbs)
Useful load	454 kg	(1,000 lbs)

Cessna 177 Cardinal and 177RG Cardinal RG — USA

First conceived as the Model 172J replacement for the highly successful Cessna Skyhawk, the Model 177 Cardinal went into parallel production with the 172 in 1968 and was phased out ten years later after 2,751 had been produced. It was a streamlined four-seater with a cantilever wing and a 150 h.p. Lycoming O-320 engine. The first Model 177 prototype flew on 15th July 1966 and first deliveries took place in 1967. The 1969 model 177A was redesigned with a 180 h.p. engine and modified tailplane. As with the Model 172, an alternative Cardinal was offered with a retractable undercarriage, named the Cardinal RG. Introduced in 1971, the Cardinal RG was also built by Reims Aviation in France. A total of 1,366 Cardinal RGs were built in Wichita and 177 at Reims before production ceased in 1978.

Cessna 177B, N19103

Cessna 177 Cardinal and 177RG Cardinal RG (Cont.)

Specification	Cessna 177RG Cardinal RG	
Powerplant	One 200 h.p. (149.1 kW) Textron Lycoming IO-360-A1B6D piston engine	
Dimensions		
Span	10.82 m	(35 ft 6 in)
Length	8.31 m	(27 ft 3 in)
Height	2.62 m	(8 ft 7 in)
Performance		
Max speed	288 km/h	(157 kt, 180 mph)
Cruising speed	272 km/h	(148 kt, 170 mph)
Initial climb	282 m/min	(925 fpm)
Range	1,936 km	(1,052 nm, 1,210 miles)
Weights		
Max takeoff	1,270 kg	(2,800 lbs)
Useful load	515 kg	(1,135 lbs)

Cessna 180 and 185 Skywagon — USA

Expansion of the Cessna line in the early 1950s brought an upgraded version of the four-seat Model 170, designated Model 180. Essentially, this was a higher gross weight Model 170B fitted with a larger 225 h.p. Continental O-470-A engine and appropriately enlarged tail surfaces. With the Model 180A the power was further increased to 230 h.p. and the Cessna 180 became popular as a twin-float seaplane with bush operators. 1961 saw the arrival of the Model 185 Skywagon utility aircraft with its 260 h.p. Continental IO-470-F engine, strengthened structure, longer cabin and enlarged fin and this was regularly upgraded and built in parallel with the Model 180 Skywagon 180. A number of military U-17 versions of the Cessna A185E were delivered and an agricultural version of the 185 with spray bars was named the AgCarryall. Some 6,193 Model 180s were sold and the last of 3,978 Model 185s was delivered in 1985.

Cessna 180A, G-BTSM

Specification	Cessna A185F Skywagon	
Powerplant	One 285 h.p. (212.5 kW) Teledyne Continental IO-520-D piston engine	
Dimensions		
Span	10.97 m	(36 ft 0 in)
Length	7.8 m	(25 ft 7 in)
Height	2.36 m	(7 ft 9 in)
Performance		
Max speed	283 km/h	(154 kt, 177 mph)
Cruising speed	267 km/h	(145 kt, 166 mph)
Initial climb	328 m/min	(1,075 fpm)
Range	1,564 km	(850 nm, 977 miles)
Weights		
Max takeoff	1,519 kg	(3,350 lbs)
Useful load	751 kg	(1,655 lbs)

Cessna 182 Skylane and R182 Skylane RG — USA

The safety features of tricycle gear led to a similar upgrade for the Model 180 to that used to change the Model 170 into the 172. The Model 182, which first flew on 10th September 1955, was a Model 180 with a strengthened firewall mounting, the new nose leg and a more powerful 230 h.p. Continental O-470-R engine. First deliveries were made in 1956 and in 1958 the Skylane deluxe version was announced. The 1960 Model 182C was fitted with a swept tail and, from the 1962 Model 182E, the aircraft used various versions of the 'omnivision' rear windows. Later Skylanes had the optional turbocharged O-540 engine and Cessna also built the Model R182 with retractable gear from 1976 until 1985 when Cessna piston-engined aircraft production was suspended. A small number of the F182Q and R182 were built at the Reims factory. The 182S returned to production in 1997 and 20,623 Cessna 182s and 2,108 R182s had been built by the end of 1999. The Model 182T and turbocharged T182T are the current production models.

Reims-Cessna FR182 Skylane RG, G-GEAR

Specification	Cessna 182R Skylane	
Powerplant	One 230 h.p. (171.5 kW) Teledyne Continental O-470-U piston engine	
Dimensions		
Span	10.97 m	(36 ft 0 in)
Length	8.53 m	(28 ft 0 in)
Height	2.82 m	(9 ft 3 in)
Performance		
Max speed	269 km/h	(146 kt, 168 mph)
Cruising speed	258 km/h	(140 kt, 161 mph)
Initial climb	264 m/min	(865 fpm)
Range	1,885 km	(1,025 nm, 1,180 miles)
Weights		
Max takeoff	1,406 kg	(3,100 lbs)
Useful load	626 kg	(1,380 lbs)

Cessna 188 AgWagon, AgPickup, AgHusky and AgTruck — USA

The success of the Piper Pawnee in the mid-1960s led Cessna to design a low-wing strut-braced agricultural aircraft designated the Model 188. Using a derivative of the Cessna 180 wing, the AgWagon had a new single-seat fuselage with the chemical hopper located between the cockpit and the engine firewall and it could be fitted with either wing-mounted spraybars or an under-fuselage duster unit. The prototype 188 first flew on 19th February 1965 and the first deliveries took place in 1966. Two versions with a 230 h.p. or 300 h.p. engine (A 188) were offered and the 188 was later sold as the economy 188B AgPickup model and the higher-specification AgTruck. In 1982 Cessna added the T188C AgHusky with a turbocharged TSIO-520-T engine and a higher gross weight. The Model 188, which was also built in Argentina by DINFIA, was finally withdrawn from production in 1983 after 1,528 had been built.

Cessna A188B AgTruck, VH-SHM

Specification	Cessna A188B AgTruck	
Powerplant	One 285 h.p. (212.5 kW) Teledyne Continental IO-520-D piston engine	
Dimensions		
Span	12.7 m	(41 ft 8 in)
Length	7.9 m	(25 ft 11 in)
Height	2.49 m	(8 ft 2 in)
Performance		
Max speed	195 km/h	(105 kt, 121 mph)
Cruising speed	180 km/h	(97 kt, 112 mph)
Initial climb	168 m/min	(550 fpm)
Range	418 km	(226 nm, 260 miles)
Weights		
Max takeoff	1,814 kg	(4,000 lbs)
Useful load	833 kg	(1,836 lbs)

Cessna 190 and 195 — USA

In the immediate postwar years, Cessna used the design of the C-165 Airmaster as the basis for a four-/five-seat private-owner aircraft which could rapidly be placed in production. The first Cessna 190, which first flew on 7th December 1944, had a fabric-covered fuselage but the production 190 was an all-metal aircraft with a 240 h.p. Continental W670-23 radial engine and the spring-steel undercarriage legs which were to become a Cessna trademark. First sold in 1947, the Model 190 was joined by the 195 fitted with a 300 h.p. Jacobs engine. This was also delivered to the USAF as the LC-126A liaison aircraft and also became a popular utility aircraft, often equipped with twin floats. The Model 195 was also produced with 245 h.p. and 275 h.p. Jacobs engines and it was eventually phased out of production in 1954. Some 1,183 had been built and many of these are still in service.

Cessna 195A, N3026B

Cessna 190 and 195 (Cont.)

Specification	Cessna 195B	
Powerplant	One 275 h.p. (205 kW) Jacobs R-755B-2 piston engine	
Dimensions		
Span	11.02 m	(36 ft 2 in)
Length	8.33 m	(27 ft 4 in)
Height	2.16 m	(7 ft 1 in)
Performance		
Max speed	277 km/h	(150 kt, 173 mph)
Cruising speed	251 km/h	(136 kt, 157 mph)
Initial climb	346 m/min	(1,135 fpm)
Range	1,088 km	(591 nm, 680 miles)
Weights		
Max takeoff	1,519 kg	(3,350 lbs)
Useful load	599 kg	(1,320 lbs)

Cessna 210 Centurion — USA

The constant demand for improved performance resulted in Cessna developing the Model 210 high-performance single-engined aircraft. Based on the Model 182B, the 210 was unique in being a high-wing aircraft with a retractable undercarriage which involved complex retraction geometry. The 182 powerplant was also upgraded to the 260 h.p. Continental IO-470-E and a swept tail was fitted. Following first sale in 1960, successive models, named the Centurion, gained a lengthened cabin, omnivision windows and further power increases to 285 horsepower. An optional model, the T210, had the 285 h.p. TSIO-520-C or, later, the 310 h.p. TSIO-520-R turbocharged engine. A strutless cantilever wing was introduced on the 1967 Model 210G and the Model 210K was substantially redesigned with a new rear cabin structure. Cessna also produced 874 examples of a pressurised version, the P 210N, to add to the 8,462 standard Model 210s built between 1960 and 1986. The Cessna 210 has been a popular candidate for conversions to turboprop power, typically as provided by Basler on their 450 s.h.p. Pratt & Whitney PT6A-powered Turbo210.

Cessna 210M Centurion, N2533S

Cessna P210 Basler Turbo210, N210BT

Specification	Cessna 210R Centurion	
Powerplant	One 285 h.p. (212.5 kW) Teledyne Continental IO-520-L piston engine	
Dimensions		
Span	11.84 m	(38 ft 10 in)
Length	8.58 m	(28 ft 2 in)
Height	2.95 m	(9 ft 8 in)
Performance		
Max speed	322 km/h	(175 kt, 201 mph)
Cruising speed	304 km/h	(165 kt, 190 mph)
Initial climb	323 m/min	(1,060 fpm)
Range	1,417 km	(770 nm, 886 miles)
Weights		
Max takeoff	1,751 kg	(3,862 lbs)
Useful load	745 kg	(1,642 lbs)

Cessna 205 and 206 Stationair — USA

By 1962 Cessna had developed the Model 210 with an extended cabin and it formed the basis for a fixed-gear utility model which was launched in the 1963 model year as the 260 horsepower Cessna 205. Apart from the fixed undercarriage, this differed from the 210 primarily in having a large starboard-side rear loading door which was enlarged to a double door on the 1964 Model 206 Super Skywagon. This aircraft, and its deluxe version the P206 Super Skylane, also had a 285 h.p. Continental IO-520-A engine. Some cleaning up of the airframe took place in 1971 with introduction of the U206E Stationair. Optional versions with the turbocharged TSIO-520-C engine were also built and many Stationairs have been operated on floats or skis. Production continued till 1986 when production was suspended. It was reinstated in 1998 as the U206H and TU206H, and total production had reached 7,866 by the end of 1999.

Cessna U206F Stationair, PH-JBY

Specification	Cessna U206G Stationair 6	
Powerplant	One 285 h.p. (212.5 kW) Teledyne Continental IO-520-F piston engine	
Dimensions		
Span	10.97 m	(36 ft 0 in)
Length	8.61 m	(28 ft 3 in)
Height	2.82 m	(9 ft 3 in)
Performance		
Max speed	287 km/h	(156 kt, 179 mph)
Cruising speed	267 km/h	(145 kt, 168 mph)
Initial climb	280 m/min	(920 fpm)
Range	1,656 km	(900 nm, 1,035 miles)
Weights		
Max takeoff	1,633 kg	(3,600 lbs)
Useful load	755 kg	(1,665 lbs)

Specification	Cessna 207A Stationair 8	
Powerplant	One 285 h.p. (212.5 kW) Teledyne Continental IO-520-F piston engine	
Dimensions		
Span	10.97 m	(36 ft 0 in)
Length	9.80 m	(32 ft 2 in)
Height	2.92 m	(9 ft 7 in)
Performance		
Max speed	276 km/h	(150 kt, 172 mph)
Cruising speed	263 km/h	(143 kt, 164 mph)
Initial climb	247 m/min	(810 fpm)
Range	866 km	(470 nm, 541 miles)
Weights		
Max takeoff	1,723 kg	(3,800 lbs)
Useful load	765 kg	(1,688 lbs)

Cessna 207 Skywagon 207 — USA

The highly successful Cessna 206 utility aircraft led to the enlarged Cessna 207. This was a Model 206 with a 30-inch longer rear fuselage and an 18-inch additional section ahead of the engine firewall to house a nose baggage compartment. The Model 207, which was a seven-seater, used the same engine as the 206 but had a higher gross weight and strengthened wings and tail unit. In addition to the standard Continental IO-520-F engine the aircraft was supplied as the T207 with a 300 h.p. turbocharged TSIO-520-G. The prototype first flew on 11th May 1968 and 368 of the initial version were sold. The later Model 207A, 426 of which were built, had the optional 310 h.p. TSIO-520-M engine and from 1980 the aircraft was available with eight seats as the Stationair 8. Sales were largely to civil operators, particularly for parachuting, but military 207s were sold to the Argentine and some Soloy-Allison turboprop conversions have been carried out.

Cessna 207 Skywagon 207, F-BUIB

Cessna 208 Caravan I — USA

The Caravan is one of Cessna's most successful models and it was designed in 1982 as a multi-purpose civil and military utility aircraft. In its passenger form the standard 208 has seats for ten including the pilot. The high-wing Caravan has a fixed tricycle undercarriage and can operate on floats or skis. It is powered by a Pratt & Whitney PT6A turboprop and has large passenger/cargo doors on both sides of the fuselage. The prototype flew on 9th December 1982 and production of the Model 208A had exceeded 330 by the end of 2000. An all-freight version without cabin windows is named Cargomaster. The Model 208B has a 4 ft rear fuselage stretch and is available as the Super Cargomaster or Grand Caravan with a belly pannier. Cessna have also produced a military utility model designated U-27A which has been sold to the Malaysian Police and other governmental operators and is equipped with a roller-blind rear door and optional underwing hardpoints and centreline stores fittings. The first 208B flew on 3rd March 1986 and over 850 have been delivered. The major Caravan customer has been Federal Express which operates nearly 300 examples.

Cessna 208 Caravan I, N501P

Cessna 208 Caravan I (Cont.)

Cessna 208B Grand Caravan floatplane, N241KA

Specification	Cessna 208 Caravan I	
Powerplant	One 600 s.h.p (447 kW) Pratt & Whitney PT6A-114 turboprop	
Dimensions		
Span	15.88 m	(52 ft 1 in)
Length	11.46 m	(37 ft 7 in)
Height	4.27 m	(14 ft 0 in)
Performance		
Max speed	340 km/h	(184 kt, 212 mph)
Cruising speed	322 km/h	(175 kt, 201 mph)
Initial climb	320 m/min	(1,050 fpm)
Range	1,767 km	(960 nm, 1,104 miles)
Weights		
Max takeoff	3,629 kg	(8,000 lbs)
Useful load	1,876 kg	(4,138 lbs)

Cessna T303 Crusader, OE-FGT

Specification	Cessna T303 Crusader	
Powerplant	Two 250 h.p. (186 kW) Teledyne Continental TSIO-520-AE turbocharged piston engines	
Dimensions		
Span	11.9 m	(39 ft 0 in)
Length	9.27 m	(30 ft 5 in)
Height	4.06 m	(13 ft 4 in)
Performance		
Max speed	398 km/h	(215 kt, 247 mph)
Cruising speed	364 km/h	(195 kt, 227 mph)
Initial climb	427 m/min	(1,400 fpm)
Range	1,638 km	(890 nm, 1,024 miles)
Weights		
Max takeoff	2,336 kg	(5,150 lbs)
Useful load	1,040 kg	(2,293 lbs)

Cessna T303 Crusader — USA

Cessna's original Model 303 was a four-seat light twin intended to compete as a trainer with the Piper Seminole and Beech Duchess. First flown in 1978, this was replaced by the larger and completely redesigned T303 Clipper (later Crusader), the first of which flew on 17th October 1979. It was powered by two turbocharged flat six engines and had two forward crew seats and a rear four-seat main cabin with club seating and executive appointments. It had a sturdy retractable tricycle undercarriage incorporating trailing link main gear legs. The handling and performance of the Crusader were good but the aircraft market was in a downturn when it was launched. The first Crusaders were delivered in 1981 but the type only remained in production until 1986 at which time production totalled 315. Almost 200 of these were still operational in 2000.

Cessna 305, L-19 and O-1 Bird Dog — USA

In response to a US Army requirement Cessna developed the Model 305 high-wing military observation aircraft using the wing and undercarriage of the Cessna 170B, married to the Cessna 195 tail and a new fuselage with a 360-degree vision cabin. Large deflection flaps were fitted and a 190 h.p. (later 213 h.p.) Continental O-470 engine was used. The prototype flew in December 1949 and the first of an initial order for 418 L-19 (later O-1) Bird Dogs was delivered a year later, just in time for the Korean conflict. Bird Dog variants included the TL-19A and the TL-19D instrument trainer and many of the 3,265 aircraft built were delivered to the French, Italian and other overseas air arms. The L-19 served in Vietnam as a Forward Air Control aircraft and many still fly with military users and private owners. The Model 321 (OE-2), 25 of which were built for the US Navy, had a Cessna 185 vertical tail and 265 h.p. Continental O-470-E engine.

Cessna O-1 Bird Dog, N5247G

Specification	Cessna O-1 Bird Dog	
Powerplant	One 213 h.p. (159 kW) Teledyne Continental O-470-11 piston engine	
Dimensions		
Span	11.25 m	(36 ft 11 in)
Length	8.99 m	(29 ft 6 in)
Height	3.02 m	(9 ft 11 in)
Performance		
Max speed	381 km/h	(206 kt, 237 mph)
Cruising speed	352 km/h	(190 kt, 219 mph)
Initial climb	470 m/min	(1,540 fpm)
Range	1,248 km	(675 nm, 777 miles)
Weights		
Max takeoff	2,358 kg	(5,200 lbs)
Useful load	941 kg	(2,075 lbs)

Cessna 310 and L-27 Blue Canoe — USA

The Cessna 310 was designed as a fast light-executive aircraft to replace obsolete ex-wartime transports. The prototype 310, which flew on 3rd January 1953, was a stylish design with a square vertical tail, retractable tricycle undercarriage and large oval wingtip tanks. Production started in 1955. In progressive design changes, the 1960 Model 310D received a swept tail and new streamlined tip tanks were introduced on the Model 310G. The 310H had an enlarged cabin interior and the Model 310P of 1969 gained a cut down rear fuselage and rear view window and optional turbocharged engines. Some 196 examples of the Model 310A and 310E were delivered to the US Air Force as the L-27 (later U-3) Blue Canoe and Cessna also sold 577 of the Model 320 Skyknight with a lengthened six-seat cabin and TSIO-470 turbocharged engines. A total of 5,737 Cessna 310s was completed between 1955 and delivery of the final Model 310R was in 1981.

Cessna 310, N6708T

Cessna 310Q, G-REDB

Specification	Cessna 310R	
Powerplant	Two 285 h.p. (212.5 kW) Teledyne Continental IO-520-MB piston engines	
Dimensions		
Span	11.25 m	(36 ft 11 in)
Length	9.74 m	(31 ft 11 in)
Height	3.25 m	(10 ft 8 in)
Performance		
Max speed	383 km/h	(207 kt, 238 mph)
Cruising speed	360 km/h	(195 kt, 225 mph)
Initial climb	507 m/min	(1,662 fpm)
Range	2,087 km	(1,132 nm, 1,303 miles)
Weights		
Max takeoff	2,494 kg	(5,500 lbs)
Useful load	974 kg	(2,147 lbs)

Cessna 318, T-37 Tweety Bird — USA

The 1952 USAF competition for a primary jet trainer presented a new challenge for Cessna who entered a side-by-side two-seat design with a cruciform tail and two Continental-built Turboméca Marboré turbojets buried in the wing roots. The first of three prototypes was flown on 12th October 1954 and Cessna was eventually awarded contracts for 534 T-37As, the first being handed over in June 1956. The later T-37B (Model 318B) was fitted with higher-thrust J69-T 25 engines and improved avionics and fuel system. Some 552 T-37Bs were built and most T-37As were also upgraded to this standard. T-37s were sold to 15 countries including Portugal, Peru, Brazil and Chile. In 1961 the T-37C export ground attack variant was flown. It had wingtip tanks and underwing hardpoints and 273 were delivered.

Cessna 318, T-37 Tweety Bird (Cont.)

Cessna T-37B, 60-0112

Cessna A-37B, 603 (Chile AF)

Specification	Cessna T-37B	
Powerplant	Two 1,025 lb.s.t. (4.56 kN) Continental J69-T25 turbojets	
Dimensions		
Span	10.3 m	(33 ft 9 in)
Length	8.93 m	(29 ft 3 in)
Height	2.80 m	(9 ft 2 in)
Performance		
Max speed	680 km/h	(370 kt, 425 mph)
Cruising speed	576 km/h	(313 kt, 360 mph)
Initial climb	1,027 m/min	(3,370 fpm)
Range	1,392 km	(757 nm, 870 miles)
Weights		
Max takeoff	2,981 kg	(6,574 lbs)
Useful load	1,224 kg	(2,700 lbs)

Specification	Cessna A-37B Dragonfly	
Powerplant	Two 2,850 lb.s.t. (12.68 kN) General Electric J85-GE-17A turbojets	
Dimensions		
Span	10.93 m	(35 ft 11 in)
Length	8.93 m	(29 ft 4 in)
Height	2.7 m	(8 ft 11 in)
Performance		
Max speed	816 km/h	(440 kt, 507 mph)
Cruising speed	787 km/h	(425 kt, 489 mph)
Initial climb	2,134 m/min	(7,000 fpm)
Range	1,620 km	(878 nm, 1,012 miles)
Weights		
Max takeoff	6,349 kg	(14,000 lbs)
Useful load	3,696 kg	(8,150 lbs)

Cessna 318E, A-37B Dragonfly — USA

The Cessna T-37C jet trainer for export markets was built with light strike capability and this formed the basis for the YAT-37D close air support prototype flown by Cessna on 22nd October 1963. Compared with the standard T-37, the A-37 Dragonfly had a further strengthened wing with three hardpoints on each side, wingtip tanks as standard, cockpit armour plating, self-sealing fuel tanks, gross weight more than doubled to 14,000 lbs and new avionics including target acquisition. It was fitted with J85 turbojets providing nearly three times the power output of the standard J69s used on the T-37. The production A-37B was fitted with a flight-refuelling probe and a nose-mounted GAU-2B/A minigun and could carry a mixture of overload tanks, bombs and rockets underwing. It was pressed into service in Vietnam and many were delivered to other countries including Chile, Guatemala, Peru, Uruguay and Colombia which still operate the type. A total of 577 was built between 1968 and 1975.

Cessna 336 Skymaster and 337 Super Skymaster — USA

An emphasis on improved twin-engine safety led Cessna to design the unconventional Model 336 Skymaster which had a main fuselage pod with an engine at each end, a fixed undercarriage and a high wing with twin booms. It was powered by two 195 h.p. Continental IO-360-A engines. The six-seat 336 flew on 28th February 1961. Some 195 were built before it was replaced by the Model 337 with a retractable undercarriage similar to that on the Cessna 210, and 210 h.p. engines. Progressive improvements and gross weight increases were introduced and an optional turbocharged version was available. The French Reims Aviation factory built the Super Skymaster from the F337H onwards and a total of 1,948 Super Skymasters was built at Wichita and in France between 1965 and 1980. The two factories also built 379 of the T337G and P337H with a pressurised fuselage, horizontally split entry door and a 225 h.p. TSIO-360-C engine.

Cessna T337G Pressurised Skymaster, N364

Specification	Cessna 337D Super Skymaster	
Powerplant	Two 210 h.p. (156.58 kW) Teledyne Continental IO-360-C piston engines	
Dimensions		
Span	11.58 m	(38 ft 0 in)
Length	9.07 m	(29 ft 9 in)
Height	2.84 m	(9 ft 4 in)
Performance		
Max speed	370 km/h	(200 kt, 231 mph)
Cruising speed	304 km/h	(165 kt, 190 mph)
Initial climb	366 m/min	(1,200 fpm)
Range	2,152 km	(1,170 nm, 1,345 miles)
Weights		
Max takeoff	1,995 kg	(4,400 lbs)
Useful load	791 kg	(1,745 lbs)

Cessna O-2A, N5259W

Cessna O-2 and Reims Milirole — USA

The Model 337 was an ideal platform for the O-2 military observation and liaison aircraft which provided high speed and twin-engined redundancy for forward air controllers in Vietnam. Fitted with underwing hardpoints and enlarged cabin transparencies, 501 examples of the O-2A (M337) were delivered following the initial order in December 1966. In addition, 31 O-2Bs were produced by Cessna from civil Model 337s and these were fitted with propaganda loudspeakers in the lower fuselage and delivery chutes for dropping leaflets. The O-2A was also sold to the Imperial Iranian Air Force. Reims Aviation developed the FTB337G Milirole with a hardened wing and 225 h.p. TSIO-360-D turbocharged engines and delivered these to the Zimbabwean and other air arms. Many civilianised O-2s are now operated by private owners and more than 80 are registered in the USA.

Specification	Cessna O-2A	
Powerplant	Two 210 h.p. (156.58 kW) Teledyne Continental IO-360-C piston engines	
Dimensions		
Span	11.63 m	(38 ft 2 in)
Length	9.07 m	(29 ft 9 in)
Height	2.79 m	(9 ft 2 in)
Performance		
Max speed	370 km/h	(200 kt, 231 mph)
Cruising speed	304 km/h	(165 kt, 190 mph)
Initial climb	366 m/min	(1,200 fpm)
Range	1,248 km	(678 nm, 780 miles)
Weights		
Max takeoff	2,100 kg	(4,630 lbs)
Useful load	873 kg	(1,925 lbs)

Cessna 340 and 335 — USA

In 1970, Cessna had already found success with its Model 421 but saw a niche for a pressurised twin which would fit between the Model 310 and the 421. The Model 340 had the tail and wings of the Model 310 and 285 h.p. TSIO-520-K engines married to a new fuselage with a six-seat cabin and airstair entry door. It was first flown on 10th April 1970 and was first delivered in 1972. The 1976 340A was improved with 310 h.p. TSIO-520-N engines and better air conditioning and prop synchrophasers; 1,298 examples had been completed by 1985 when production was discontinued. In 1980, Cessna marketed the unpressurised Model 335 version but only 65 were sold and it was replaced by the larger Model T303. Just under 1,000 Cessna 335s and 340s are currently registered worldwide.

Cessna 340A, OE-FFP

Specification	Cessna 340A-II	
Powerplant	Two 310 h.p. (231 kW) Teledyne Continental TSIO-520-NB turbocharged piston engines	
Dimensions		
Span	11.62 m	(38 ft 1 in)
Length	10.46 m	(34 ft 4 in)
Height	3.84 m	(12 ft 7 in)
Performance		
Max speed	452 km/h	(244 kt, 281 mph)
Cruising speed	425 km/h	(229 kt, 264 mph)
Initial climb	503 m/min	(1,650 fpm)
Range	2,538 km	(1,377 nm, 1,586 miles)
Weights		
Max takeoff	2,717 kg	(5,990 lbs)
Useful load	838 kg	(1,847 lbs)

Cessna 401, 402, 414 and 421 — USA

With the Model 310 selling briskly, Cessna designed the larger Model 411 executive aircraft with wingtip fuel tanks and a passenger cabin with club seating for six separated from the flight deck. First sold in 1965 and powered by two 375 h.p. Continental GTSIO-520-M engines, it had a rear airstair entry door and oval windows. A lower-priced version was built as the Model 401 for corporate use and Model 402 for commuter airlines with 300 h.p. TSIO-520-E engines and a broader vertical tail. The Model 421 introduced in 1967 was, essentially, a pressurised Model 411 and Cessna also offered the Model 414 as a pressurised version of the Model 401. The later 421C Golden Eagle and 414A Chancellor had a new 'wet' wing which resulted in the elimination of the tip tanks which had been a trademark of the 400 series thus far. They were also fitted with a trailing link main undercarriage and narrower vertical tail. Cessna produced 2,190 Model 401/402s, 302 Model 411s, 1,070 Model 414s and 1,916 Model 421s before production ceased in 1986.

Cessna 402B, ZK-DSB

Cessna 421C Golden Eagle, N98998

Specification	Cessna 421C Golden Eagle	
Powerplant	Two 375 h.p. (280 kW) Teledyne Continental GTSIO-520-L turbocharged piston engines	
Dimensions		
Span	12.53 m	(41 ft 1 in)
Length	11.09 m	(36 ft 4 in)
Height	3.49 m	(11 ft 5 in)
Performance		
Max speed	478 km/h	(258 kt, 297 mph)
Cruising speed	360 km/h	(195 kt, 224 mph)
Initial climb	590 m/min	(1,940 fpm)
Range	2,740 km	(1,487 nm, 1,712 miles)
Weights		
Max takeoff	3,379 kg	(7,450 lbs)
Useful load	1,302 kg	(2,870 lbs)

Cessna 404 Titan and F406 Caravan II — USA/France

The success of the Cessna 402 in commuter airline service resulted in a stretched version, the Model 404 Titan. The ten-seat Model 402C had already been revised with a line of square cabin windows and the wing and undercarriage of the Model 414A and the new Model 404 was a 402C with a stretched fuselage and a maximum of 14 seats including crew. Some 396 Titans were built between 1977 and 1982. On 22nd September 1983 Reims Aviation flew the prototype F406 Caravan II which was a Titan with a pair of 500 s.h.p. Pratt & Whitney PT6A-112 turboprops and increased 9,850 lbs gross weight. The Caravan II is still in production and 80 had been built by mid-1998 for civil and military users. Customers include the French Gendarmerie and Customs, and the Greek Coast Guard who use the Polmar II version for surveillance with a belly-mounted search radar, and the French Armée de l'Air who use the Caravan II for target towing.

Reims Cessna F406 Caravan II, F-GPRA

Specification	Cessna (Reims) F406 Caravan II	
Powerplant	Two 500 s.h.p. (373 kW) Pratt & Whitney PT6A-112 turboprops	
Dimensions		
Span	15.08 m	(49 ft 5 in)
Length	11.89 m	(39 ft 0 in)
Height	4.01 m	(13 ft 2 in)
Performance		
Max speed	455 km/h	(246 kt, 283 mph)
Cruising speed	370 km/h	(200 kt, 230 mph)
Initial climb	564 m/min	(1,850 fpm)
Range	2,125 km	(1,153 nm, 1,326 miles)
Weights		
Max takeoff	4,467 kg	(9,850 lbs)
Useful load	2,008 kg	(4,427 lbs)

Cessna 441 Conquest and 425 Corsair — USA

The move towards turboprop business aircraft and the success of the Beech King Air and Piper Cheyenne in the early 1970s spurred Cessna to produce the Model 441. This was externally similar to the Model 421 Golden Eagle but had a scaled-up airframe with semi-square cabin windows and a standard interior for six passengers and two crew. The powerplants were Garrett TPE331-8-401S turboprops. First flight took place in August 1975 and the first delivery was in September 1977 with Cessna building 362 aircraft in the next ten years. To provide a more economical option with less range, speed and load capacity Cessna also sold a re-engined Model 421C titled the Model 425 Corsair (later named Conquest II). With 450 s.h.p. Pratt & Whitney PT6A-112 turboprops it could accommodate a maximum of five passengers and two crew and Cessna built 236 in its six years of production.

Cessna 441 Conquest I, N441KR

Specification	Cessna 441 Conquest I	
Powerplant	Two 635 s.h.p. (473.4 kW) Honeywell (Garrett) TPE331-8-401S/402S turboprops	
Dimensions		
Span	15.04 m	(49 ft 4 in)
Length	11.89 m	(39 ft 0 in)
Height	4.01 m	(13 ft 2 in)
Performance		
Max speed	548 km/h	(295 kt, 340 mph)
Cruising speed	515 km/h	(280 kt, 322 mph)
Initial climb	742 m/min	(2,435 fpm)
Range	4,072 km	(2,212 nm, 2,545 miles)
Weights		
Max takeoff	4,467 kg	(9,850 lbs)
Useful load	1,898 kg	(4,185 lbs)

Cessna 500 and 501 Citation and 525 CitationJet — USA

Cessna took a major financial gamble when it launched the Citation project in 1968. The low-wing eight-seat Citation 500 executive jet, powered by UACL JT15D-1 turbofans, first flew on 15th September 1969 and the first delivery took place in 1971. The later Citation I had JT15D-1A engines and a modified wing of higher aspect ratio. Cessna built 388 of the basic Citation and a further 303 Model 501 Citation I/SPs, certificated for single-pilot operation. In 1985, the Model 500/501 was discontinued in favour of the Model 550 but

Cessna 500 and 501 Citation and 525 CitationJet (Cont.)

there was a need for an entry-level business jet and Cessna designed the Model 525 CitationJet. This has a shortened Model 500 fuselage with a four-seat passenger cabin and a new T-tail and redesigned wings. The prototype, powered by two Williams-RR FJ44 turbofans, first flew on 29th April 1991 and 450 had been built by late 2000. The standard CitationJet has been improved with a higher gross weight and upgraded cockpit and is now known as the CJ-1. A second variant, the CJ-2, was introduced in 1998 and first flown on 26th April 1999. This has a lengthened fuselage providing a six-seat main cabin and 2,300 lb.s.t. FJ44-2C engines.

Cessna 500 Citation, VR-COM

Cessna 525A Citation CJ-2, N2CJ

Specification	Cessna CitationJet CJ-1	
Powerplant	Two 1,900 lb.s.t. (8.45 kN) Williams-Rolls Royce FJ44-1A turbofans	
Dimensions		
Span	14.26 m	(46 ft 9 in)
Length	12.98 m	(42 ft 7 in)
Height	4.19 m	(13 ft 9 in)
Performance		
Max speed	704 km/h	(380 kt, 437 mph)
Cruising speed	640 km/h	(348 kt, 400 mph)
Initial climb	1,010 m/min	(3,311 fpm)
Range	2,714 km	(1,475 nm, 1,696 miles)
Weights		
Max takeoff	4,807 kg	(10,600 lbs)
Useful load	1,950 kg	(4,300 lbs)

Cessna 550, 551, 552 and 560 Citation — USA

The Model 550 Citation II was a stretched development of the Model 500 with 12 seats and uprated JT15D-4 engines. The Model 551 Citation II/SP was an alternative version certificated for single-pilot operation. Cessna also built the improved S.550 Citation S/II with a modified wing section which allowed a 1,000 lbs gross weight increase and this was sold as a trainer to the US Navy as the T-47A. The current model is the 550B Citation Bravo with a seven-passenger cabin. In 1987, the Model 560 Citation V was introduced with a further stretched fuselage providing a larger main cabin and powered by JT15D-5A engines. This has been upgraded to become the Citation Ultra Encore with increased load and performance and improved avionics and EFIS. Many Citation IIs and Vs have been sold for military special missions including the USAF's UC-35A and the Spanish Air Force TR.20 which is fitted with an external SLAR pod. The OT-47B is a specialised tracker aircraft. By late 2000 over 1,025 of the Citation II series and 560 of the Citation V Ultra Encore had been built.

Cessna 560 Citation V, TR.20-01 (Spanish AF)

Specification	Cessna 560 Citation V Ultra Encore	
Powerplant	Two 3,360 lb.s.t. (14.95 kN) Pratt & Whitney PW535A turbofans	
Dimensions		
Span	15.91 m	(52 ft 2 in)
Length	14.90 m	(48 ft 10 in)
Height	4.57 m	(15 ft 0 in)
Performance		
Max speed	796 km/h	(430 kt, 495 mph)
Cruising speed	768 km/h	(417 kt, 480 mph)
Initial climb	1,289 m/min	(4,230 fpm)
Range	3,610 km	(1,960 nm, 2,255 miles)
Weights		
Max takeoff	7,392 kg	(16,300 lbs)
Useful load	3,197 kg	(7,050 lbs)

Cessna 560XL Citation Excel — USA

The Citation Excel business jet was introduced to provide an aircraft to fit between the Citation Ultra and the Citation VII with performance equivalent to the Ultra. The Excel uses a shorter version of the Citation X fuselage which gives capacity for seven passengers in a full stand-up cabin. This is combined with the wing of the Citation 560 Ultra and higher-thrust PW545A turbofans mounted on the rear fuselage. The prototype Excel first flew on 29th February 1996 and it is in current production with over 175 delivered by the end of 2000.

Cessna 560XL, N522XL

Specification	Cessna 560XL Citation Excel	
Powerplant	Two 3,804 lb.s.t. (16.92 kN) Pratt & Whitney PW545A turbofans	
Dimensions		
Span	16.98 m	(55 ft 8 in)
Length	15.79 m	(51 ft 9 in)
Height	5.24 m	(17 ft 2 in)
Performance		
Max speed	791 km/h	(430 kt, 494 mph)
Cruising speed	754 km/h	(410 kt, 471 mph)
Initial climb	940 m/min	(3,090 fpm)
Range	3,827 km	(2,080 nm, 2,392 miles)
Weights		
Max takeoff	8,707 kg	(19,200 lbs)
Useful load	3,487 kg	(7,690 lbs)

Cessna 650 Citation III, VI and VII — USA

With the Citation I and Citation II well established in the light business jet sector Cessna's next step was to the mid-sized Model 650 Citation III. This was a completely new design with a T-tail and a swept supercritical wing fitted below the lower fuselage line to give a flat cabin floor. It offered a 35% improvement in cruise speed over the Citation I with a stand-up cabin for six to eight passengers. The prototype was flown on 30th May 1979 and first deliveries were made in 1983. The Citation VI was a budget version of the Citation III with a completely standard avionics and systems package and the Citation VII, which was the final variant, had improved performance provided by higher thrust TFE731-4 engines and a number of systems improvements. By the end of 2000 when production ceased, 360 of the Cessna 650 series had been built.

Cessna 650 Citation III, 8P-KAM

Specification	Cessna 650 Citation VII	
Powerplant	Two 4,080 lb.s.t. (18.15 kN) Honeywell (Garrett) TFE731-4R-2S turbofans	
Dimensions		
Span	16.3 m	(53 ft 6 in)
Length	16.9 m	(55 ft 5 in)
Height	5.12 m	(16 ft 9 in)
Performance		
Max speed	876 km/h	(476 kt, 547 mph)
Cruising speed	800 km/h	(434 kt, 500 mph)
Initial climb	1,356 m/min	(4,450 fpm)
Range	4,011 km	(2,180 nm, 2,507 miles)
Weights		
Max takeoff	10,181 kg	(22,450 lbs)
Useful load	4,866 kg	(10,730 lbs)

Cessna 750 Citation X — USA

Cessna's flagship business jet, the Citation X, made its first flight on 21st December 1993. It was designed to give very-long-range high-speed performance with smaller capacity than the Gulfstream IV but equivalent comfort for passengers. It cruises at Mach 0.92 and at altitudes of up to 51,000 feet. The Cessna 750 was a completely new design with a swept wing and prominent T-tail. As with the Model 650, the wing is set below the fuselage line and the internal cabin height of 5 ft 8 in allows passengers to walk around in comfort. The Citation X is normally fitted with eight main cabin seats together with a galley and lavatory. Citation X production passed the 150 mark in early 2000.

Cessna 750 Citation X (Cont.)

Cessna Citation X, N750CX

Specification	Cessna 750 Citation X	
Powerplant	Two 6,400 lb.s.t. (28.47 kN) Allison AE3007C turbofans	
Dimensions		
Span	19.48 m	(63 ft 11 in)
Length	22 m	(72 ft 2 in)
Height	5.77 m	(18 ft 11 in)
Performance		
Max speed	1,120 km/h	(608 kt, 700 mph)
Cruising speed	1,094 km/h	(595 kt, 684 mph)
Initial climb	1,341 m/min	(4,400 fpm)
Range	6,072 km	(3,300 nm, 3,795 miles)
Weights		
Max takeoff	14,059 kg	(31,000 lbs)
Useful load	5,442 kg	(12,000 lbs)

CFM Shadow — UK

Designed by David Cook, the Shadow ultralight first flew in 1983 and has been built in considerable numbers as a kit for home construction by CFM Metalfax (now CFM Aircraft). It is of tube and composite construction with a tandem two-seat pod fuselage and a tubular aluminium tail boom which mounts an inverted tailfin and tailplane. The Shadow has a fixed tricycle undercarriage and a fully enclosed cabin. In standard microlight form it is powered by a 30 h.p. Rotax 447 engine which is fitted as a pusher immediately behind the rear fuselage bulkhead. The Streak Shadow, which falls outside the microlight category, has a new wing design and is fitted with a 65 h.p. Rotax 582 and the Star Streak uses a Rotax 618. Over 250 Shadows are active, the majority in the UK.

CFM Shadow, G-MTSG

Specification	CFM Streak Shadow	
Powerplant	One 65 h.p. (48 kW) Rotax 582 piston engine	
Dimensions		
Span	8.53 m	(28 ft 0 in)
Length	6.4 m	(21 ft 0 in)
Height	1.75 m	(5 ft 9 in)
Performance		
Max speed	195 km/h	(105 kt, 121 mph)
Cruising speed	160 km/h	(88 kt, 100 mph)
Initial climb	290 m/min	(950 fpm)
Range	480 km	(261 nm, 300 miles)
Weights		
Max takeoff	408 kg	(900 lbs)
Useful load	208 kg	(460 lbs)

Champion 7ECA Citabria and 8KCAB Decathlon — USA

After acquiring Aeronca's 7AC designs in 1954, Champion Aircraft produced the two-seat 7ECA Citabria aerobatic trainer. This is a high-wing tandem two-seat light aircraft of tube and fabric construction, based on the Model 7EC Traveler and powered by a 100 h.p. Continental O-200A engine. A total of 1,353 were built between 1964 and 1980, some by Bellanca which acquired Champion in 1970. It was followed by the 7GCBC Citabria of which 1,215 were built with a 160 h.p. O-320-D2A engine. The 7KCAB Citabria (624 built) had a new wing, spring-steel undercarriage and 150 h.p. Lycoming IO-320-E2A engine, and the 8KCAB Decathlon (736 built) was similar to the 7KCAB but with a strengthened airframe. The 8KCAB-180 Super Decathlon has a 180 h.p. AEIO-360-H1A engine. American Champion, which currently builds the Champion range and has produced around 380 aircraft, is in production with the 8GCBC Scout, which is a utility version of the 8KCAB-180, the 7ECA Aurora, the 7GCAA Adventure, the 7GCBC Explorer and the 8KCAB Super Decathlon.

Champion Super Decathlon 8KCAB-180, N79AC

Champion Scout 8GCBC, N186AC

Specification	American Champion 7GCBC Explorer	
Powerplant	One 160 h.p. (119 kW) Textron Lycoming O-320-B2B piston engine	
Dimensions		
Span	10.49 m	(34 ft 5 in)
Length	6.92 m	(22 ft 8 in)
Height	2.35 m	(7 ft 8 in)
Performance		
Max speed	259 km/h	(140 kt, 162 mph)
Cruising speed	232 km/h	(126 kt, 145 mph)
Initial climb	410 m/min	(1,345 fpm)
Range	960 km	(520 nm, 600 miles)
Weights		
Max takeoff	816 kg	(1,800 lbs)
Useful load	272 kg	(600 lbs)

Champion 402 Lancer — USA

The Lancer was conceived by Champion Aircraft as a low-cost aircraft for twin-engined training. It was based on a standard tandem two-seat 7GCBC Citabria airframe which was modified with a nose cone in place of the existing engine and two new 100 h.p. Continental O-200 engines mounted on the wings. The Citabria undercarriage was replaced by a new fixed tricycle gear with the main units attached to the engine nacelles and braced with struts to the fuselage. The cockpit contained a dummy lever to simulate retraction of the undercarriage. The Lancer prototype first flew in October 1961 and the first aircraft was delivered in 1963. The Lancer was not a commercial success, only 25 being completed. Most were sold in the United States but exports were made to Canada and Peru. At least four remain in flying condition in the USA.

Champion 402 Lancer, N9957Y

Specification	Champion 402 Lancer	
Powerplant	Two 100 h.p. (74.56 kW) Teledyne Continental O-200-A piston engines	
Dimensions		
Span	10.52 m	(34 ft 6 in)
Length	6.78 m	(22 ft 3 in)
Height	2.46 m	(8 ft 1 in)
Performance		
Max speed	208 km/h	(113 kt, 130 mph)
Cruising speed	192 km/h	(104 kt, 120 mph)
Initial climb	195 m/min	(640 fpm)
Range	1,136 km	(617 nm, 710miles)
Weights		
Max takeoff	1,111 kg	(2,450 lbs)
Useful load	299 kg	(660 lbs)

Chichester-Miles Leopard — UK

The Leopard is a lightweight business jet conceived by Ian Chichester-Miles. The design concept was for a four-seat aircraft with a cabin similar to that of conventional piston-engined light aircraft but offering the performance of contemporary business jets. The Leopard, which has a pressurised cabin with an EFIS panel, is of all-composite construction and has full wing and tail de-icing. The wings are tapered and have moderate sweep and the tricycle undercarrriage is fully retractable. The prototype was first flown on 12th December 1988, powered by two Noel Penny Turbines NPT301-3A turbojets. The second aircraft which flew on 9th April 1997 has a modified undercarriage, a longer nose and two Williams International FJX-1 light turbofan engines mounted on the rear fuselage. It was planned that the production Leopard would have more powerful FJX-2 engines, but the type may undergo a complete redesign.

CMC Leopard, G-BRNM

Chichester-Miles Leopard (Cont.)

Specification	CMC Leopard	
Powerplant	Two 700 lb.s.t. (3.11 kN) Williams International FJX-1 turbofans	
Dimensions		
Span	7.16 m	(23 ft 6 in)
Length	7.57 m	(24 ft 10 in)
Height	2.06 m	(6 ft 9 in)
Performance		
Max speed	974 km/h	(529 kt, 609 mph)
Cruising speed	925 km/h	(502 kt, 578 mph)
Initial climb	1,960 m/min	(6,430 fpm)
Range	2,760 km	(1,500 nm, 1,725 miles)
Weights		
Max takeoff	1,814 kg	(4,000 lbs)
Useful load	816 kg	(1,800 lbs)

Chilton DW.1A — UK

Designed by A. Dalrymple and A.R. Ward, the Chilton DW.1 was a very small single-seat sporting monoplane which first flew in April 1937. Constructed of wood with plywood covering, the Chilton had an open cockpit and was fitted with flaps and a fixed tailwheel undercarriage, the main units of which were enclosed in streamlined fairings. The powerplant of the prototype was a 32 h.p. Carden-Ford converted car engine. Three further Chiltons were built, one of them as the DW.1A with a 44 h.p. Train 4T engine. The performance of the Chilton was impressive and these aircraft were regular entrants in national air races for which various modifications were made to further streamline the airframe. All four prewar Chiltons exist although only one is airworthy. Construction of a further three examples has been undertaken by amateur builders and the first of these flew in 1987 powered by a Lycoming O-145 engine.

Chilton DW.1A, G-AFGI

Specification	Chilton DW.1	
Powerplant	One 32 h.p. (23.86 kW) Carden-Ford piston engine	
Dimensions		
Span	7.31 m	(24 ft 0 in)
Length	5.49 m	(18 ft 0 in)
Height	1.47 m	(4 ft 10 in)
Performance		
Max speed	179 km/h	(97 kt, 112 mph)
Cruising speed	160 km/h	(87 kt, 100 mph)
Initial climb	198 m/min	(650 fpm)
Range	800 km	(435 nm, 500 miles)
Weights		
Max takeoff	290 kg	(640 lbs)
Useful load	109 kg	(240 lbs)

Chrislea CH-3 Super Ace — UK

The Super Ace was one of the earliest post war light aircraft, designed by Richard Christopherides and first flown in September 1946. The Super Ace is a strut-braced high-wing aircraft of tube and fabric construction with a fixed tricycle undercarriage and an all-round vision cabin enclosure. It has a twin-fin tail unit and in production form as the Super Ace Srs.2 was fitted with a 145 h.p. de Havilland Gipsy Major 10 in-line engine. It was unusual in having an integrated control system with all controls being operated through a single steering wheel. Several Super Aces were later converted with a normal control column and rudder pedals and one example in South Africa was fitted with a single fin and rudder. A later version was the CH-3 Srs.4 Skyjeep which had a tailwheel undercarriage and a 155 h.p. Blackburn Cirrus Major 3 engine. A total of 15 Super Aces and six Skyjeeps were completed and two Super Aces and a Skyjeep are still flying in the UK.

Chrislea Super Ace, G-AKUW

Specification	Chrislea CH-3 Super Ace	
Powerplant	One 145 h.p. (108 kW) de Havilland Gipsy Major 10 piston engine	
Dimensions		
Span	10.97 m	(36 ft 0 in)
Length	6.55 m	(21 ft 6 in)
Height	2.31 m	(7 ft 7 in)
Performance		
Max speed	202 km/h	(110 kt, 126 mph)
Cruising speed	176 km/h	(96 kt, 110 mph)
Initial climb	229 m/min	(750 fpm)
Range	640 km	(348 nm, 400 miles)
Weights		
Max takeoff	1,066 kg	(2,350 lbs)
Useful load	454 kg	(1,000 lbs)

Chris-Tena Mini Coupe — USA

The Mini-Coupe light aircraft was designed by Bill Johnson of Laurelwood, Oregon as an easily built machine for home construction. Its design was loosely modelled on the Erco Ercoupe with a low-set constant-chord wing, tricycle undercarriage and twin fins. The single-seat cockpit can be open but is normally enclosed with a bubble canopy. The Mini-Coupe, which is of all-metal construction and assembled with pop-rivets, is sold as a kit by Chris-Tena Aircraft of Forest Grove, Oregon. Various engines have been used by builders to power the aircraft including several Volkswagen conversions and the 1,834 cc Revmaster. The aircraft will accommodate engines up to the 100 h.p. Continental O-200 but most examples are fitted with a Volkswagen or a Continental A65. Over 150 kits have been sold and at least 60 Mini Coupes have been completed with examples flying in the UK and South Africa.

Chris-Tena Mini Coupe, G-BPDJ

Specification	Chris-Tena Mini Coupe	
Powerplant	One 65 h.p. (48.5 kW) Volkswagen 1600 piston engine	
Dimensions		
Span	7.32 m	(24 ft 0 in)
Length	4.98 m	(16 ft 4 in)
Height	1.8 m	(5 ft 11 in)
Performance		
Max speed	169 km/h	(91 kt, 105 mph)
Cruising speed	145 km/h	(78 kt, 90 mph)
Initial climb	230 m/min	(750 fpm)
Range	480 km	(260 nm, 300 miles)
Weights		
Max takeoff	385 kg	(850 lbs)
Useful load	159 kg	(350 lbs)

Christen Eagle — USA

The Eagle two-seat biplane was designed by Frank Christensen as a direct competitor for the Pitts S-2 high-performance aerobatic aircraft and first flew in February 1977. It is a tandem two-seat biplane, which is known as the Eagle II in production form, with a fixed tailwheel undercarriage and a large bubble canopy to enclose the cockpit. This model is designed for general sporting purposes and for advanced aerobatic training and is fitted with a 200 h.p. Lycoming AEIO-360-A1D engine with a constant-speed propeller. The Eagle I is outwardly identical but is a single-seat version for competition aerobatics with a 260 h.p. Lycoming AEIO-540-E4B5 engine and a stronger airframe.The Eagles are constructed of tube and fabric and have been sold in kit form to amateur constructors. Over 600 Eagle kits, latterly marketed by Aviat, have been sold and more than 250 have flown.

Christen Eagle II, N44DD

Christen Eagle (Cont.)

Specification	Christen Eagle II	
Powerplant	One 200 h.p. (149 kW) Textron Lycoming AEIO-360-A1D piston engine	
Dimensions		
Span	6.1 m	(19 ft 11 in)
Length	5.64 m	(18 ft 6 in)
Height	1.98 m	(6 ft 6 in)
Performance		
Max speed	296 km/h	(160 kt, 184 mph)
Cruising speed	265 km/h	(143 kt, 165 mph)
Initial climb	640 m/min	(2,100 fpm)
Range	611 km	(330 nm, 380 miles)
Weights		
Max takeoff	725 kg	(1,600 lbs)
Useful load	260 kg	(575 lbs)

Cirrus VK30 — USA

The brainchild of Jeff Viken and Alan Klapmeier, the VK30 is an advanced amateur-built touring aircraft sold to homebuilders in kit form. The VK30 has a highly streamlined fuselage with a four-seat cabin and is fitted with a fully retractable tricycle undercarriage. Its fuselage is constructed from composite half shells and the wings are made of Kevlar and foam. Air intakes for the engine are situated on the fuselage sides behind the cabin. The standard recommended powerplant is a six-cylinder 290 h.p. Lycoming IO-540-G1A5 which is positioned in the centre fuselage behind the cabin and drives a tail-mounted variable-pitch propeller via a long drive shaft. The VK30 has also been fitted with an Allison 250-B17 turboprop and the Chevrolet V8 converted car engine. The first VK30 made its maiden flight on 11th February 1988 and more than 20 have been completed.

Cirrus VK30, N30VK

Specification	Cirrus VK30	
Powerplant	One 290 h.p. (216 kW) Textron Lycoming IO-540-G1A5 piston engine	
Dimensions		
Span	11.79 m	(38 ft 8 in)
Length	7.92 m	(26 ft 0 in)
Height	3.25 m	(10 ft 8 in)
Performance		
Max speed	417 km/h	(225 kt, 259 mph)
Cruising speed	402 km/h	(217 kt, 250 mph)
Initial climb	457 m/min	(1,500 fpm)
Range	2,080 km	(1,129 nm, 1,300 miles)
Weights		
Max takeoff	1,610 kg	(3,550 lbs)
Useful load	567 kg	(1,250 lbs)

Cirrus Design SR.20 — USA

Cirrus Design is one of the first American companies to have applied composite technology to a high-volume production light aircraft design. Its SR.20 is a low-wing four-seater with a 200 h.p. Continental IO-360-ES engine and a fixed tricycle undercarriage. The design is intended as the first in a family of aircraft which will include versions with larger cabins and retractable gear. It has a modern cockpit with a central navigation display and side sticks instead of the more conventional control columns. The most radical feature is a Ballistic Recovery System consisting of an emergency parachute housed behind the cockpit which can be activated to save the aircraft in the case of a power failure. The SR.20 prototype made its first flight on 31st March 1995 and went into series production in 1999 with 600 on order by mid-2000. The SR.22 is a higher powered version with a 310 h.p. IO-550N engine.

Cirrus SR.20, N203FT

Specification	Cirrus SR.20	
Powerplant	One 200 h.p. (149 kW) Teledyne Continental IO-360-ES piston engine	
Dimensions		
Span	10.85 m	(35 ft 7 in)
Length	8 m	(26 ft 3 in)
Height	2.82 m	(9 ft 3 in)
Performance		
Max speed	370 km/h	(200 kt, 230 mph)
Cruising speed	296 km/h	(160 kt, 185 mph)
Initial climb	275 m/min	(900 fpm)
Range	1,472 km	(800 nm, 920 miles)
Weights		
Max takeoff	1,315 kg	(2,900 lbs)
Useful load	526 kg	(1,160 lbs)

Civilian Coupé — UK

Designed in 1928 by the Civilian Aircraft Co., the Coupé was a neat little strut-braced monoplane for sale to private owners. It had an all-round vision cabin which accommodated two people and was fitted with a fixed tailwheel undercarriage. Construction was mixed with external plywood covering. The wings were foldable for hangar storage and the prototype Coupé, which flew in July 1929, was powered by a 75 h.p. ABC Hornet engine. Subsequent aircraft generally had the 100 h.p. Genet Major I radial engine. In total six Coupés were built and one of these remains airworthy in England at Biggin Hill.

Civilian Coupé Mk.II, G-ABNT

Specification	Civilian Coupé	
Powerplant	One 100 h.p. (74.56 kW) Armstrong Siddeley Genet Major I piston engine	
Dimensions		
Span	10.85 m	(35 ft 7 in)
Length	5.89 m	(19 ft 4 in)
Height	1.9 m	(6 ft 3 in)
Performance		
Max speed	177 km/h	(96 kt, 110 mph)
Cruising speed	154 km/h	(83 kt, 96 mph)
Initial climb	247 m/min	(810 fpm)
Range	480 km	(261 nm, 300 miles)
Weights		
Max takeoff	680 kg	(1,500 lbs)
Useful load	264 kg	(582 lbs)

Clutton-Tabenor FRED — UK

The FRED was designed by Eric Clutton as a simple amateur-built single-seater which would fly on a low-powered engine and be transportable behind a car from the owner's home to the flying field. The name FRED stood for Flying Runabout Experimental Design and the first Series I aircraft was flown on 3rd November 1963. This was powered by a 27 h.p. Triumph 5T engine but other engines including the 66 h.p. Volkswagen 1600 cc have been used. The FRED, which is said to be unstallable, is of wood and fabric construction with a strut-braced constant-chord parasol wing which can be folded for transportation. It has an open cockpit and fixed tailwheel undercarriage. The FRED Series II has a modified vertical tail and the FRED Srs.III is the current version modified for operation with a Continental A65 engine. Plans were made available for the FRED and over 30 are registered in the UK, 20 of which are active.

Clutton FRED Srs.2, G-BBBW

Specification	Clutton-Tabenor FRED Srs.III	
Powerplant	One 65 h.p. (48.46 kW) Teledyne Continental A65 piston engine	
Dimensions		
Span	6.86 m	(22 ft 6 in)
Length	5.2 m	(17 ft 0 in)
Height	1.8 m	(6 ft 0 in)
Performance		
Max speed	130 km/h	(70 kt, 81 mph)
Cruising speed	101 km/h	(55 kt, 63 mph)
Initial climb	122 m/min	(400 fpm)
Range	320 km	(173 nm, 200 miles)
Weights		
Max takeoff	350 kg	(773 lbs)
Useful load	108 kg	(240 lbs)

Colomban MC-15 Cri-Cri — France

One of the smallest aircraft ever built, and certainly the smallest twin, the Cri-Cri was designed by Michel Colomban and is marketed in the form of plans for amateur builders. The low-wing Cri-Cri is of all-metal construction with a slim square-section fuselage containing the single-seat cockpit which is enclosed with a large three-section clear canopy. It has a T-tail and a fixed tricycle undercarriage and the wings, which fold for ground transport, are fitted with full span flap/ailerons. The first MC-10 Cri-Cri flew at Guyancourt on 19th July 1973 powered by a pair of 9 h.p. Rowena 6507J chainsaw engines mounted on posts either side of the nose. The later MC-12 had Valmet SM.160J engines and the more common MC-15 has JPX PUL-212s. Over 500 sets of plans were sold subsequently, mainly to French homebuilders, and over 70 Cri-Cris are now flying in France.

Colomban MC-15 Cri Cri, F-PZTI

Specification	Colomban MC-15 Cri-Cri	
Powerplant	Two 9 h.p. (6.7 kW) Stihl or Rowena piston engines	
Dimensions		
Span	4.9 m	(16 ft 1 in)
Length	3.9 m	(12 ft 10 in)
Height	1.24 m	(4 ft 1 in)
Performance		
Max speed	295 km/h	(160 kt, 184 mph)
Cruising speed	256 km/h	(139 kt, 160 mph)
Initial climb	180 m/min	(590 fpm)
Range	704 km	(382 nm, 440 miles)
Weights		
Max takeoff	170 kg	(374 lbs)
Useful load	107 kg	(236 lbs)

Command-Aire 3C3 — USA

Designed by Albert Voellmecke, the Command-Aire three-seat biplane was built by Command-Aire Inc. of Little Rock, Arkansas in the late 1920s and early 1930s. It was used for general pleasure flying and training and had open cockpits with two passengers in front and the pilot behind. The initial 3C3 was powered by a 90 h.p. Curtiss OX-5 engine but other variants were the 3C3-A with a 110 h.p. Warner Scarab, the 3C3-B with a 113 h.p. Siemens-Halske SH-14, the 5C3 with a 185 h.p. Curtiss Challenger, the 5C3-A with a 150 h.p. Hisso-A and the 5C3-B with a 115 h.p. Axelson. The 3C3-T was a tandem two-seat trainer version with an OX-5 engine and a later version was the 3C3-BT with the Siemens-Halske SH-14. Over 200 Command-Aires were built and ten are registered in the United States including three of the trainer model although several have been re-engined.

Command-Aire 5C3, NC997E

Specification	Command-Aire 3C3	
Powerplant	One 90 h.p. (67.1 kW) Curtiss OX-5 piston engine	
Dimensions		
Span	9.6 m	(31 ft 6 in)
Length	7.47 m	(24 ft 6 in)
Height	2.54 m	(8 ft 4 in)
Performance		
Max speed	160 km/h	(87 kt, 100 mph)
Cruising speed	136 km/h	(74 kt, 85 mph)
Initial climb	155 m/min	(510 fpm)
Range	704 km	(383 nm, 440 miles)
Weights		
Max takeoff	998 kg	(2,200 lbs)
Useful load	358 kg	(790 lbs)

Commander 112 and 114 — USA

As part of its development of a comprehensive aircraft line, the Aero Commander Division of Rockwell International designed the Model 111, 112 and 114. With a common four-seat airframe and enclosed cabin, the Model 111 had a fixed tricycle undercarriage and a 180 h.p. engine and the 112 and 114 had retractable undercarriages and, respectively, a 200 h.p. Lycoming O-360-A1G6 and a 260 h.p. Lycoming IO-540-T4A5D. No production 111s were built but the prototype Commander 112 first flew on 4th December 1970 followed by 800 production aircraft including 269 of the turbocharged 112TC with a TO-360-C1A6D engine. The 114 and 114A (also named the Grand Turismo) had much improved performance and 429 were built by Rockwell. The Model 114B and 114TC (with a TIO-540-AG1A) were introduced in 1992 by Commander Aircraft, over 165 have been built to date. The Commander 115 and 115TC, announced in 2000, have a modified wing.

Commander 114TC, N595TC

Specification	Commander Aircraft Commander 114B	
Powerplant	One 260 h.p. (194 kW) Textron Lycoming IO-540-T4B5 piston engine	
Dimensions		
Span	10 m	(32 ft 9 in)
Length	7.59 m	(24 ft 11 in)
Height	2.57 m	(8 ft 5 in)
Performance		
Max speed	303 km/h	(164 kt, 189 mph)
Cruising speed	285 km/h	(155 kt, 180 mph)
Initial climb	326 m/min	(1,070 fpm)
Range	1,334 km	(725 nm, 834 miles)
Weights		
Max takeoff	1,474 kg	(3,250 lbs)
Useful load	544 kg	(1,200 lbs)

Rearwin 175 Skyranger, G-RWIN

Commonwealth Rearwin Skyranger — USA

In the 1930s, Rearwin Aircraft and Engines Inc. built a series of high-wing light aircraft including the two-seat Model 8090 Cloudster with a 120 h.p. Ken Royce 7F radial engine and the Model 8135 three-seater powered by a 135 h.p. Ken Royce 7G. These were constructed of tube and fabric with tailwheel undercarriages and formed the basis for the post-war Skyranger. The Model 175 Skyranger, based on the two-seat Model 165 Ranger prototype which first flew on 9th April 1940, was powered by a 75 h.p. Continental engine and 55 were built together with nine Model 180 Skyrangers with an 80 h.p. Continental, 17 Model 180Fs with an 80 h.p. Franklin engine and a single 90 h.p. Model 190F. Commonwealth Aircraft Corporation took over the designs in 1945 and put the Skyranger 185, powered by an 85 h.p. Continental C85-12 engine, into production. Some 296 examples were built before manufacture ceased in October 1946.

Commonwealth Rearwin 8135, NC34826

Commonwealth Rearwin Skyranger (Cont.)

Specification	Commonwealth Rearwin Skyranger 185	
Powerplant	One 85 h.p. (63.4 kW) Teledyne Continental C85 piston engine	
Dimensions		
Span	10.36 m	(34 ft 0 in)
Length	6.63 m	(21 ft 9 in)
Height	2.01 m	(6 ft 7 in)
Performance		
Max speed	182 km/h	(99 kt, 114 mph)
Cruising speed	165 km/h	(90 kt, 103 mph)
Initial climb	198 m/min	(650 fpm)
Range	800 km	(435 nm, 500 miles)
Weights		
Max takeoff	658 kg	(1,450 lbs)
Useful load	245 kg	(540 lbs)

Comper CLA.7 Swift — UK

Built by the Comper Aircraft Co. Ltd, the CLA.7 Swift was a sporty small single-seater which first flew in 1930. It had an open cockpit positioned so that the pilot could see over or under the strut-braced wing, a streamlined fuselage of wood and fabric and a fixed undercarriage with a tailskid. The first Swift was powered by a 35 h.p. ABC Scorpion horizontally opposed engine but production aircraft had the 50 h.p. Salmson AD.9 radial or 75 h.p. Pobjoy R. Swifts were popular for air racing. Three were built with the larger 120 h.p. Gipsy III or 130 h.p. Gipsy Major in-line engines. Some 41 production Swifts were completed and examples were exported to several countries including New Zealand, Australia, Egypt, Argentina and India. Five Swifts are registered in the UK and three are airworthy including an amateur-built replica Swift powered by a Pobjoy Niagara 1A.

Specification	Comper CLA.7 Swift	
Powerplant	One 75 h.p. (55.9 kW) Pobjoy R piston engine	
Dimensions		
Span	7.03 m	(24 ft 0 in)
Length	5.38 m	(17 ft 8 in)
Height	1.06 m	(5 ft 3 in)
Performance		
Max speed	224 km/h	(122 kt, 140 mph)
Cruising speed	192 km/h	(104 kt, 120 mph)
Initial climb	427 m/min	(1,400 fpm)
Range	608 km	(330 nm, 380 miles)
Weights		
Max takeoff	447 kg	(985 lbs)
Useful load	202 kg	(445 lbs)

Comper Swift, G-ABUU

Comte AC.4 Gentleman — Switzerland

The high-wing Gentleman was the first of a series of light aircraft for private owners designed and built in Zurich by Alfred Comte. The prototype AC.4 flew in 1928 and an initial series of six were completed with a 90 h.p. Cirrus III engine followed by five with a 140 h.p. Genet Major or 110 h.p. Cirrus Hermes. The Gentleman was a side-by-side two-seater with a strut-braced wing and fixed tailwheel undercarriage and was built of wood, tube and fabric. The later AC.8, three of which were completed, was a larger development with a six-seat cabin, and the AC.12 Moskito, of which ten were built, was a three-seater with a 100 h.p. Armstrong Siddeley Genet Major engine. Two AC.4s remain active in Switzerland powered respectively by Genet Major and Cirrus Hermes engines.

Comte Gentleman, HB-IKO

Specification	Comte AC.4 Gentleman	
Powerplant	One 140 h.p. (104.4 kW) Armstrong Siddeley Genet Major piston engine	
Dimensions		
Span	12.14 m	(39 ft 10 in)
Length	8.05 m	(26 ft 5 in)
Height	2.9 m	(9 ft 6 in)
Performance		
Max speed	176 km/h	(96 kt, 110 mph)
Cruising speed	136 km/h	(74 kt, 85 mph)
Initial climb	152 m/min	(500 fpm)
Range	720 km	(391 nm, 450 miles)
Weights		
Max takeoff	800 kg	(1,764 lbs)
Useful load	300 kg	(662 lbs)

Convair (Vultee) BT-13 Valiant — USA

First flown on 28th July 1939, the Vultee Model 54A Valiant was designed to meet a USAAC specification for a basic trainer. It was an all-metal low-wing machine with a tandem two-seat cockpit enclosed by a framed canopy and had a fixed tailwheel undercarriage. Built as the Model 54D BT-13 with a 450 h.p. Pratt & Whitney R-985-25 radial engine it entered service in June 1940 and 300 were built. The subsequent BT-13A, 6,407 of which were completed, had an R-985-AN-1 engine and it was succeeded by 1,125 of the later BT-13B, with a 24-volt electrical system. Consolidated Vultee also delivered 1,693 examples of the BT-15 and its US Navy version, the SNV, which was similar to the BT-13 but had the improved R-975-11 engine. Many of the BT-13s and BT-15s were sold as surplus after the war and placed in service with foreign air forces and flown by private owners. Some 174 BT-13s and 25 BT-15s appear on the US register although many are inactive.

Convair BT-13A, N59842

Specification	Convair BT-13 Valiant	
Powerplant	One 450 h.p. (335.5 kW) Pratt & Whitney Wasp Junior R-985-AN-1 piston engine	
Dimensions		
Span	12.8 m	(42 ft 0 in)
Length	8.79 m	(28 ft 10 in)
Height	3.51 m	(11 ft 6 in)
Performance		
Max speed	288 km/h	(156 kt, 180 mph)
Cruising speed	272 km/h	(148 kt, 170 mph)
Initial climb	488 m/min	(1,600 fpm)
Range	1,160 km	(630 nm, 725 miles)
Weights		
Max takeoff	2,039 kg	(4,496 lbs)
Useful load	508 kg	(1,120 lbs)

Convair (Stinson) L-13 — USA

The Stinson division of Convair produced the Model 105 (L-13) all-metal STOL liaison aircraft as a replacement for the Stinson L-5 Sentinel and flew the first of two prototypes in 1945. It had strut-braced folding high wings and a cruciform tail and was designed to carry a maximum of six people or a stretcher for ambulance duties. A total of 300 L-13As was built together with 28 L-13Bs with special heaters for operations in Alaska and other Arctic locations and they were powered by a 245 h.p. Franklin O-425 flat-six piston engine. Many L-13s were sold as surplus in the mid-1950s and some were converted as ACME Centaur 101s with a 300 h.p. Lycoming R-680 or Jacobs R-755 radial engine. Others were rebuilt as the six-seat Caribbean Traders Husky with a 450 h.p. Pratt & Whitney R-975-7 radial and modified vertical tail. Most L-13s have now been retired, but of the 26 currently registered a few are flying as warbirds in original military markings.

Convair L-13, N6615C

Convair (Stinson) L-13 (Cont.)

Specification	Convair L-13A	
Powerplant	One 245 h.p. (182.7 kW) Franklin O-425-9 piston engine	
Dimensions		
Span	12.3 m	(40 ft 5 in)
Length	9.68 m	(31 ft 9 in)
Height	2.57 m	(8 ft 5 in)
Performance		
Max speed	184 km/h	(100 kt, 115 mph)
Cruising speed	152 km/h	(83 kt, 95 mph)
Initial climb	320 m/min	(1,050 fpm)
Range	592 km	(322 nm, 370 miles)
Weights		
Max takeoff	1,315 kg	(2,900 lbs)
Useful load	379 kg	(835 lbs)

Convair PB4Y-2 Privateer, N3739G

Convair B-24 and PB4Y — USA

In total, 18,188 examples of the Liberator and its variants were built, making it the leading production World War II bomber produced by the USA. The B-24 had a deep fuselage with the wing in a high position to allow the largest possible bomb bay in the belly. Unlike its contemporaries, it had a tricycle undercarriage and was distinctive for its large twin-fin tail unit. Liberators were not only produced for heavy bombing but were also built for maritime patrol, as passenger aircraft and for photographic reconnaissance. First flown by Consolidated (later Consolidated-Vultee or Convair) on 29th December, 1939, variants included the LB-30A (RAF Liberator I with four 1,200 h.p. Pratt & Whitney R-1830-33 engines), Liberator II (RAF coastal reconnaissance), B-24D (USAAF with R-1830-43 engines and RAF Liberator III) and B-24J (R-1830-65 engines). The U.S. Navy received the B-24J as the PB4Y-1 and this was developed into the PB4Y-2 Privateer which had a longer fuselage, larger engines, additional gun turrets and a single vertical tail unit. Two B-24s are currently flying in the USA and several Privateers are still airworthy as fire bombers.

Specification	Convair PB4Y-2 Privateer	
Powerplant	Four 1,350 h.p. (1,007 kW) Pratt & Whitney R-1830-94 piston engines	
Dimensions		
Span	33.53 m	(110 ft 0 in)
Length	22.73 m	(74 ft 7 in)
Height	9.17 m	(30 ft 1 in)
Performance		
Max speed	381 km/h	(206 kt, 237mph)
Cruising speed	225 km/h	(122 kt, 140 mph)
Initial Climb	332 m/min	(1,090 fpm)
Range	4,480 km	(2,435 nm, 2,800 miles)
Weights		
Max takeoff	29,478 kg	(65,000 lbs)
Useful Load	12,478 kg	(27,515 lbs)

Convair LB-30A Liberator, N24927

Convair 28 – PBY Catalina and Canso — USA

Possibly the most famous flying boat ever built, the prototype XP3Y-1 first flew on 21st March 1935 having been designed to a US Navy requirement. As the production PBY-1, -2, -3, -4 and -5 it had a high wing mounted on a centre fuselage pylon and a cruciform tail. Several were also built for civil customers as the Model 28-1. The PBY-5A was an amphibian version with a retractable tricycle undercarriage and 1,428 of the 3,281 PBYs built were amphibious, some being PBY-6As with a taller tail. A total of 731 examples of the PBY were built in Canada as the Canso. PBYs served with the USN, USAAF, Soviet, Canadian and Australian air forces and the RAF, where it was named Catalina. After the war, many Catalinas were civilianised, being used for fire bombing, survey, search & rescue and general transport. Around 100 Catalinas remain in existence worldwide, and approximately 23 are active.

Convair PBY-5A Catalina, ZK-PBY

Specification	Convair PBY-5A Catalina	
Powerplant	Two 1,200 h.p. (895 kW) Pratt & Whitney R-1830-92 Wasp radial piston engines	
Dimensions		
Span	31.7 m	(104 ft 0 in)
Length	19.46 m	(63 ft 10 in)
Height	6.15 m	(20 ft 2 in)
Performance		
Max speed	286 km/h	(156 kt, 179 mph)
Cruising speed	192 km/h	(104 kt, 120 mph)
Initial climb	158 m/min	(520 fpm)
Range	4,072 km	(2,213 nm, 2,545 miles)
Weights		
Max takeoff	16,009 kg	(35,300 lbs)
Useful load	6,526 kg	(14,390 lbs)

Convair 240, 340 and 440 Convairliner — USA

Convair's answer to the postwar DC-3 replacement problem was the Model 240 which was based on the Model 110 prototype of 1946. The 240 was a low-wing pressurised airliner with a tricycle undercarriage and a 40-passenger interior. It was powered by two 2,400 h.p. Pratt & Whitney R-2800-CA3 radial engines and first flew on 16th March 1947. Some 176 Convair 240s were sold to a variety of airlines including American, KLM and Swissair. The T-29A was an unpressurised crew trainer for the USAF who also bought the pressurised T-29B, T-29C and C-131. The 240 was followed by the 340 with a 4 ft 6 in fuselage stretch and the 440 Metropolitan 52-seater with a lengthened radar nose and modified engine nacelles with rectangular exhaust shrouds. Other military versions included the R4Y-1 (340) for the US Navy and Marines and the C-131D with 2,500 h.p. R-2800-52W engines. A total of 1,086 Convairliners were built.

Convair C-131D, N131CW (54-2809)

Specification	Convair 440 Metropolitan	
Powerplant	Two 2,500 h.p. (1,864 kW) Pratt & Whitney R-2800-CB17 piston engines	
Dimensions		
Span	32.1 m	(105 ft 4 in)
Length	24.13 m	(79 ft 2 in)
Height	8.58 m	(28 ft 2 in)
Performance		
Max speed	539 km/h	(293 kt, 337 mph)
Cruising speed	480 km/h	(260 kt, 300 mph)
Initial climb	385 m/min	(1,260 fpm)
Range	2,080 km	(1,130 nm, 1,300 miles)
Weights		
Max takeoff	22,540 kg	(49,700 lbs)
Useful load	8,342 kg	(18,395 lbs)

Convair 540, 580, 600 and 640 — USA

Many Convairliners were given a new lease of life by conversion to turboprop power. After conversion of a Convair 340 with Napier Eland 504s in 1956 a batch of ten aircraft was rebuilt as CL-66B Cosmopolitans for the Canadian armed forces. The Convair 600 was a CV.240 fitted with two 2,559 s.h.p. Rolls Royce Dart R.Da.10/1 engines and the CV.340 and 440 when similarly converted were designated Convair 640. Some 55 of these Dart conversions were carried out. The main turboprop variant was the Convair 580, based on the larger 340/440 airframe and fitted with two 3,750 s.h.p Allison 501-D13D engines which improved the cruising speed of the CV.440 by 25% and allowed an 11,000 lbs increase in gross weight. A total of 159 Convairliners were modified and over 80 are still in air carrier service with further examples in corporate or private hands in the United States.

Convair 580, N39

Convair 540, 580, 600 and 640 (Cont.)

Specification	Convair 580	
Powerplant	Two 3,800 h.p. (2,833 kW) Allison 501-D13D turboprops	
Dimensions		
Span	32.1 m	(105 ft 4 in)
Length	24.13 m	(79 ft 2 in)
Height	8.58 m	(28 ft 2 in)
Performance		
Max speed	576 km/h	(313 kt, 360 mph)
Cruising speed	520 km/h	(283 kt, 325 mph)
Initial climb	1,036 m/min	(3,400 fpm)
Range	2,592 km	(1,409 nm, 1,620 miles)
Weights		
Max takeoff	26,374 kg	(58,156 lbs)
Useful load	11,678 kg	(25,750 lbs)

Corben Baby Ace and Junior Ace — USA

Corben Aircraft designed the Baby Ace single-seat amateur-built light aircraft in 1931. Postwar, it became popular through an article in *Mechanix Illustrated* magazine and parts and plans are still sold by Ace Aircraft Co. The Ace is a parasol-wing monoplane with an open cockpit and a fixed tailwheel undercarriage. It has a fabric-covered steel tube fuselage and wooden wings and can be powered by engines in the 50 h.p. to 85 h.p. range, although most have a 65 h.p. Continental. The current model is the Baby Ace D with a more angular tail which was first flown on 15th November 1956. The Junior Ace Model E is a side-by-side two-seat version with a wider fuselage structure, enlarged fuel tank and a full electrical system. The Junior Ace is normally powered by an 85 h.p. Continental C85-12F engine. Many hundreds of plan sets have been sold and over 230 Aces are recorded in the US civil register.

Specification	Ace Baby Ace D	
Powerplant	One 65 h.p. (48.46 kW) Continental A65 four-cylinder piston engine	
Dimensions		
Span	8.05 m	(26 ft 5 in)
Length	5.4 m	(17 ft 9 in)
Height	2.03 m	(6 ft 8 in)
Performance		
Max speed	176 km/h	(96 kt, 110 mph)
Cruising speed	160 km/h	(87 kt, 100 mph)
Initial climb	366 m/min	(1,200 fpm)
Range	560 km	(304 nm, 350 miles)
Weights		
Max takeoff	431 kg	(950 lbs)
Useful load	170 kg	(375 lbs)

Corby Starlet — Australia

John Corby flew the prototype of his single-seat Starlet on 9th August 1967 having designed it for a British light aircraft design competition. The Starlet is an ultralight aircraft intended to use a low-powered engine and most Starlets are fitted with a 50 h.p. Volkswagen 1500 conversion although larger powerplants can be used. This gives it excellent speed performance but quite docile landing characteristics. Construction of the Starlet is of wood with plywood and fabric covering and the tailwheel undercarriage uses spring-steel main legs. It is semi-aerobatic and its small cockpit is normally enclosed with a bubble canopy although some Starlets have an open cockpit. Early Starlets were built in Australia and New Zealand where more than 20 have been registered, but the design, which is sold in the form of plans, is popular in the United States and in the UK.

Corben (Ace) Baby D, G-BUAA

Corby Starlet

Specification	Corby Starlet	
Powerplant	One 50 h.p. (37.2 kW) Volkswagen 1500 piston engine	
Dimensions		
Span	5.64 m	(18 ft 6 in)
Length	4.5 m	(14 ft 9 in)
Height	1.5 m	(4 ft 10 in)
Performance		
Max speed	216 km/h	(117 kt, 135 mph)
Cruising speed	197 km/h	(107 kt, 123 mph)
Initial climb	213 m/min	(700 fpm)
Range	426 km	(231 nm, 266 miles)
Weights		
Max takeoff	340 kg	(750 lbs)
Useful load	136 kg	(300 lbs)

Specification	Jacques Coupé JC.2	
Powerplant	One 90 h.p. (67 kW) Continental C90 piston engine	
Dimensions		
Span	8.35 m	(27 ft 5 in)
Length	6.4 m	(21 ft 0 in)
Height	1.88 m	(6 ft 2 in)
Performance		
Max speed	200 km/h	(108 kt, 124 mph)
Cruising speed	160 km/h	(85 kt, 99 mph)
Initial climb	152 m/min	(500 fpm)
Range (est)	800 km	(435 nm, 500 miles)
Weights		
Max takeoff	750 kg	(1,655 lbs)
Useful load	250 kg	(551 lbs)

Coupé JC.01, JC.3 and JC.423G — France

An increasingly popular amateur-built type in France, the Jacques Coupé JC.01 made its first flight on 16th March 1976. It is a classic side-by-side two-seat low-wing light aircraft of wood and fabric construction with docile handling characteristics. Externally, it owes much to general Jodel design layout although it has an original design wing without the Jodel's outer wing dihedral. Powered by a 65 h.p. Continental A65 engine and fitted with either a tailwheel or tricycle undercarriage, more than a dozen have been constructed from plans sold by Coupé Aviation of Azay-sur-Cher. The JC.2, flown in 1981, is a later development following similar lines but with a swept tail, fixed tricycle undercarriage and powered by a 90 h.p. Continental, and the JC.3 of 1992 is a lighter weight version with an 80 h.p. Limbach engine. The latest design by Jacques Coupé is the JC.423G which flew in 1995 and is a little larger than the earlier designs and powered by a 100 h.p. Continental engine.

Jacques Coupé JC.01, F-PXKV

Creelman Seawind 2000 — Canada

Roger J. Creelman, a Canadian homebuilder, developed the advanced Seawind amphibian as a design for amateur kitbuilders. The prototype first flew on 23rd August 1982 powered by a 200 h.p. Lycoming IO-360 which is mounted on an extension to the cruciform tailplane. The Seawind is a high-performance four-seater constructed entirely from fibreglass and vinylester resin with PVC foam filling of the main surfaces. The kit, sold by SNA Inc., consists of ten major moulded sections. It has a mid-set wing with tip-mounted floats and the main units of the retractable undercarriage retract into wells behind the forward step of the planing hull. The large cabin is fully enclosed with a forward-opening clamshell canopy. Most Seawinds are now built with a 250 h.p. or 300 h.p. Lycoming engine driving a three-blade constant-speed propeller although one Allison turboprop-powered example has been flown. Over 140 kits have been sold and more than 35 Seawinds are flying in North America.

SNA Seawind, N46SW

Creelman Seawind 2000 (Cont.)

Specification	SNA Seawind 3000	
Powerplant	One 300 h.p. (224 kW) Textron Lycoming IO-540 piston engine	
Dimensions		
Span	10.67 m	(35 ft 0 in)
Length	8.28 m	(27 ft 2 in)
Height	2.34 m	(7 ft 8 in)
Performance		
Max speed	320 km/h	(174 kt, 200 mph)
Cruising speed	306 km/h	(166 kt, 191 mph)
Initial climb	381 m/min	(1,250 fpm)
Range	2,336 km	(1,270 nm, 1,460 miles)
Weights		
Max takeoff	1,542 kg	(3,400 lbs)
Useful load	499 kg	(1,100 lbs)

Croses EC-6 Criquet
— France

Emilien Croses has been one of the most assiduous followers of the Henri Mignet 'Pou du Ciel' tandem-wing concept and built his first two-seat EC-1-01 in 1948. This led to a range of improved Mignet designs including the EC-3 Pouplume ultralight, several of which have been built, the three-seat Boujon-Croses B-EC-7 Tous Terrains and the light cargo-carrying B-EC-9 Paras-Cargo. The most popular Croses type, which is sold in the form of plans to home-builders, is the EC-6 Criquet which first flew on 6th July 1965. Built of wood and fabric, the EC-6 has a side-by-side two-seat enclosed cabin, a large rudder incorporating the tail-wheel and a pair of streamlined main wing support struts. The tandem wings are of similar span and the Criquet has fibre-glass main undercarriage legs. More than 120 sets of plans have been sold and 40 Criquets are active in France, most of which are the LC-6 which is an improved variant modified by Gilbert Landray. The Criquet Léger is an ultralight version of the aircraft, first flown in 1989, powered by a Rotax 503, and more than 140 are under construction with 58 in operation.

Croses LC-6 Criquet, F-PYYR

Specification	Croses EC-6 Criquet	
Powerplant	One 90 h.p. (67 kW) Teledyne Continental C90-14F piston engine	
Dimensions		
Span	7.8 m	(25 ft 7 in)
Length	4.65 m	(15 ft 3 in)
Height	1.88 m	(6 ft 2 in)
Performance		
Max speed	213 km/h	(115 kt, 132 mph)
Cruising speed	192 km/h	(104 kt, 120 mph)
Initial climb	304 m/min	(1,000 fpm)
Range	480 km	(261 nm, 300 miles)
Weights		
Max takeoff	550 kg	(1,213 lbs)
Useful load	260 kg	(573 lbs)

Culver Cadet and NR-D
— USA

The Culver Cadet was designed by Al Mooney and production by the Culver Aircraft Co. started in 1939. The Cadet, which was built as the LCA with a 75 h.p. Continental A75-8 or the LFA with a Franklin 4AC-176-F3 engine, was a low-wing two-seat light aircraft with side-by-side seating in an enclosed cabin. It was of all-wood construction with a retractable tailwheel undercarriage and a distinctive curved wing outline. A total of 357 were built before Culver switched to wartime production of the similar LAR (PQ-8) target drone, 201 of which were completed. The later NR-D was a single-seater drone based on the Cadet but with a tricycle undercarriage. Culver built 2,571 of these as the military PQ-14A, PQ-14B and TD2C-1, powered by a 150 h.p. Franklin O-300-11 engine, and five were rebuilt as Jamieson Js. Many NR-Ds were sold to private owners after the war, and five are believed to be airworthy. The Cadet was relaunched in 1998 as the Aero Systems Cadet STF with a 90 h.p. Continental engine.

Aero Systems Cadet STF, N37828

Specification	Culver LCA Cadet	
Powerplant	One 75 h.p. (55.9 kW) Teledyne Continental A-75-8 piston engine	
Dimensions		
Span	8.23 m	(27 ft 0 in)
Length	5.38 m	(17 ft 8 in)
Height	1.68 m	(5 ft 6 in)
Performance		
Max speed	224 km/h	(122 kt, 140 mph)
Cruising speed	192 km/h	(104 kt, 120 mph)
Initial climb	244 m/min	(800 fpm)
Range	800 km	(435 nm, 500 miles)
Weights		
Max takeoff	592 kg	(1,305 lbs)
Useful load	252 kg	(555 lbs)

Culver V, N3038K

Culver V and Helton Lark — USA

After the war, the Culver Aircraft Co. launched a substantially modified version of the two-seat Culver Cadet. This was known as the Culver V (or, in celebration of peace, 'Victory V') and it had a more streamlined fuselage with a larger cabin and a retractable tricycle undercarriage. The most significant change was to the wing which was of longer span and incorporated upturned outer panels and large flaps which ran across the inner wings and centre section. The V was powered by an 85 h.p. Continental C85 engine and 393 of the basic model and the improved V-2 were built together with six of the later Superior Satellite; 37 are currently registered in the United States. The Helton Lark 95 was a new version of the LFA/LAR Cadet, 17 of which were built in the mid-1960s by Helton Aircraft with a tricycle undercarriage and a Continental C90-16F engine. Nine Larks still exist, one of which is active in the UK.

Specification	Culver V	
Powerplant	One 85 h.p. (63.4 kW) Teledyne Continental C85-12J piston engine	
Dimensions		
Span	8.84 m	(29 ft 0 in)
Length	6.25 m	(20 ft 6 in)
Height	2.06 m	(6 ft 9 in)
Performance		
Max speed	216 km/h	(117 kt, 135 mph)
Cruising speed	200 km/h	(109 kt, 125 mph)
Initial climb	201 m/min	(660 fpm)
Range	1,000 km	(543 nm, 625 miles)
Weights		
Max takeoff	726 kg	(1,600 lbs)
Useful load	257 kg	(567 lbs)

Helton Lark 95, G-LARK

Currie Wot — UK

The Wot amateur-built light aircraft dates back to 1937 when it was designed by R.J. Currie as a simple aerobatic single-seater powered by a 40 h.p. Aeronca-J.A.P. engine. Two pre-war Wots were built and in the mid-1950s plans were made available and the first new aircraft flew in September 1958 powered by a 60 h.p. Walter Mikron II. The Wot is an all-wood biplane with a fixed tailwheel undercarriage and an open single-seat cockpit. It can be powered by a variety of engines in the 50 h.p. to 120 h.p. range and examples have been flown with a Rover TP.60 light turboprop and a 115 h.p. Lycoming O-235. The Wot has also been flown off water on floats and has been used as the basis for six Slingsby-built SE5A film replicas. Most Wots have been built in the UK where 17 currently appear on the register together with one Turner TSW modified version with a 150 h.p. Lycoming O-320-A. One has been built in New Zealand.

Currie Wot, G-BDFB

Specification	Currie Wot	
Powerplant	One 85 h.p. (63.4 kW) Continental C90-8F piston engine	
Dimensions		
Span	6.73 m	(22 ft 1 in)
Length	5.56 m	(18 ft 3 in)
Height	2.06 m	(6 ft 9 in)
Performance		
Max speed	160 km/h	(87 kt, 100 mph)
Cruising speed	144 km/h	(78 kt, 90 mph)
Initial climb	213 m/min	(700 fpm)
Range	400 km	(217 nm, 250 miles)
Weights		
Max takeoff	408 kg	(900 lbs)
Useful load	159 kg	(350 lbs)

Curtiss 48 Fledgling — USA

The Curtiss-Wright company produced the Fledgling as a primary trainer for the US Navy in the mid-1920s. The Model 48 (and civil/export Model 51), designated N2C-1 by the Navy, was a large two-seat biplane of mixed construction with tandem open cockpits and a 220 h.p. Wright J5 radial engine. It had very long-span wings and a distinctive overhanging rudder. The tailwheel undercarriage had substantial faired shock absorbers but the Fledgling could also be fitted with a single float and outriggers for water operations. The N2C-2 used the 240 h.p. Wright J-6-7 engine and the civil models includes the lower powered J-1 and the Model 51 had a 170 h.p. Curtiss Challenger. Some 109 Fledglings were built, including examples sold to China and Canada. Seven are currently registered in the United States and one of these, now powered by a 220 h.p. Continental radial, is an active air show performer with the Old Rhinebeck flying circus.

Curtiss Fledgling, N271Y

Specification	Curtiss Fledgling J-1	
Powerplant	One 165 h.p. (123 kW) Wright J6 piston engine	
Dimensions		
Span	12.01 m	(39 ft 5 in)
Length	8.48 m	(27 ft 10 in)
Height	3.15 m	(10 ft 4 in)
Performance		
Max speed	163 km/h	(89 kt, 102 mph)
Cruising speed	139 km/h	(76 kt, 87 mph)
Initial climb	189 m/min	(620 fpm)
Range	624 km	(339 nm, 390 miles)
Weights		
Max takeoff	1,224 kg	(2,700 lbs)
Useful load	313 kg	(690 lbs)

Curtiss Robin — USA

The Robin high-wing cabin light transport and civil trainer was developed by the Curtiss-Robertson division of Curtiss-Wright and built in quantity from 1928 onwards. Built of steel tube, wood and fabric, the prototype Robin first flew on 7th August 1928. It had a fully enclosed cabin with the pilot in front and a two-place bench seat behind and the wing bracing struts had an aerofoil section to enhance lift. It was fitted with a strut-braced fixed tailwheel undercarriage. Most Robins were powered by the 90 h.p. Curtiss OX-5 engine but the Robin C-1 had a 185 h.p. Curtiss Challenger two-row radial, the J-1 had a 165 h.p. Wright J-6-5 and some other engines were fitted including the Warner Scarab and 150 h.p. Hispano. The Robin 4C-1A was a four-seat version with a wider cabin and extra entry door. A total of 769 Robins were built and 42 appear on the US register, many of which have been restored and are active.

Curtiss Robin, NC8303

Specification	Curtiss Robin J-1	
Powerplant	One 165 h.p. (123 kW) Wright J-6-5 piston engine	
Dimensions		
Span	12.49 m	(41 ft 0 in)
Length	7.64 m	(25 ft 1 in)
Height	2.43 m	(8 ft 0 in)
Performance		
Max speed	189 km/h	(103 kt, 118 mph)
Cruising speed	160 km/h	(87 kt, 100 mph)
Initial climb	229 m/min	(750 fpm)
Range	541 km	(294 nm, 338 miles)
Weights		
Max takeoff	1,071 kg	(2,361 lbs)
Useful load	327 kg	(720 lbs)

Curtiss JN-4 'Jenny' — USA

Undoubtedly the most famous World War I basic trainer, the Curtiss JN-4 was a tandem open-cockpit two-seat biplane with long-span wings and a conventional tailwheel undercarriage. Over 7,000 aircraft were built in the United States and Canada (as the 'Canuck') and after the war hundreds of Jennies were sold off as surplus. They served as civilian trainers and the barnstormers used them for joyriding, wing walking and aerial circus exhibitions during the 1920s and 1930s. The standard JN-4D, which was built in the largest numbers, was built of wood and fabric and had a 90 h.p. OX-5 engine. The later JN-4H and JN-6H used the 150 h.p. Hispano Suiza ('Hisso'). Several restored JN-4s, including a Canuck and a JN-4H, are still airworthy and several amateur builders have also produced full size and scale replicas of the Jenny.

Curtiss JN-4D

Specification	Curtiss JN-4D	
Powerplant	One 90 h.p. (67.1 kW) Curtiss OX-5 piston engine	
Dimensions		
Span	13.29 m	(43 ft 8 in)
Length	8.33 m	(27 ft 4 in)
Height	3.01 m	(9 ft 11 in)
Performance		
Max speed	120 km/h	(65 kt, 75 mph)
Cruising speed	96 km/h	(52 kt, 60 mph)
Initial climb	107 m/min	(350 fpm)
Range	480 km	(260 nm, 300 miles)
Weights		
Max takeoff	871 kg	(1,920 lbs)
Useful load	240 kg	(530 lbs)

Curtiss-Wright CW-1 Junior — USA

The two-seat Junior was designed in 1930 by Karl H. White of Curtiss-Wright based on an existing glider design which was fitted with a pusher engine mounted on the wing centre section. The distinctive CW-1 had a tube and fabric fuselage and parasol wooden wings which were positioned on supporting struts. The aircraft had tandem open cockpits in the nose and under the wing and it was fitted with a fixed tailwheel undercarriage. Curtiss flew the prototype CW-1, initially named 'Skeeter', on 5th October 1930 and built 261 examples before production ceased in 1932, many of which survived the war. The standard engine was the 45 h.p. Szekely SR-3-031 but several Juniors have been re-engined with the 65 h.p. Continental A65 or Lycoming O-145. Some 31 aircraft remain on the US civil register and one is registered in France. Most are in museum preservation but five are believed to be currently active.

Curtiss-Wright CW-1 Junior (Cont.)

Curtiss-Wright Junior, NC10967

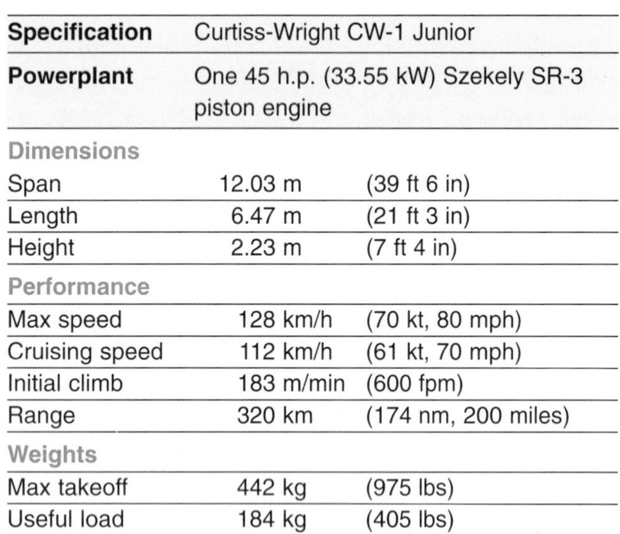

Specification	Curtiss-Wright CW-1 Junior	
Powerplant	One 45 h.p. (33.55 kW) Szekely SR-3 piston engine	
Dimensions		
Span	12.03 m	(39 ft 6 in)
Length	6.47 m	(21 ft 3 in)
Height	2.23 m	(7 ft 4 in)
Performance		
Max speed	128 km/h	(70 kt, 80 mph)
Cruising speed	112 km/h	(61 kt, 70 mph)
Initial climb	183 m/min	(600 fpm)
Range	320 km	(174 nm, 200 miles)
Weights		
Max takeoff	442 kg	(975 lbs)
Useful load	184 kg	(405 lbs)

Curtiss-Wright Travel Air 12, 14 and 16 — USA

After its merger with Curtiss-Wright in August 1929, Travel Air developed a new range of sporting two-seat biplanes (see also Travel Air entry for earlier models). The Model 12 was an attractive aircraft of mixed construction with tandem open cockpits. The Model 12Q had a 90 h.p. Wright-built Gipsy L320 engine, the Model 12K a 125 h.p. Kinner B5 and the Model 12W a 125 h.p. Warner Scarab 40. Some 41 Model 12s were built and 11 still exist, some of which have been re-engined with Warner Super Scarab radials. The Model 14 was a three-seat version with a wider front cockpit, 21 of which were built as the Model 16E with a 165 h.p. Wright R-540 and the 16K with a 125 h.p. Kinner B5 engine. Four of these are still flying, one on floats. The final Model 14 was a heavier model for civil and military use (named 'Osprey') built as the A-14D with a 240 h.p. Wright R-760-E or B-14B with a Wright R-975-E. Four Model 14s are still operational with private owners in the United States.

Curtiss-Wright Travel Air 16E, N12380

Specification	Curtiss-Wright Model 12Q	
Powerplant	One 90 h.p. (67.1 kW) Wright-Gipsy L320 in-line piston engine	
Dimensions		
Span	8.78 m	(28 ft 10 in)
Length	6.52 m	(21 ft 5 in)
Height	2.69 m	(8 ft 10 in)
Performance		
Max speed	168 km/h	(91 kt, 105 mph)
Cruising speed	152 km/h	(83 kt, 95 mph)
Initial climb	183 m/min	(600 fpm)
Range	624 km	(339 nm, 390 miles)
Weights		
Max takeoff	782 kg	(1,725 lbs)
Useful load	297 kg	(654 lbs)

Curtiss-Wright 6B Sedan — USA

The Model 6B Sedan was developed from the Travel Air 6000 following the takeover of Travel Air by Curtiss-Wright in 1930. It was a six-seat light transport and bush aircraft with a strut-braced high wing and fixed tailwheel undercarriage and had a 300 h.p. Wright R-975 engine in place of the 220 h.p. Whirlwind of the earlier aircraft. The airframe was fabric covered with a steel tube fuselage and wooden wing structure. It is thought that 80 examples of the Model 6000 were built during 1929/30 but production of the Model 6B totalled less than 10 aircraft. Several examples of the Model 6000 exist, although none appears to be currently airworthy, but a Model 6B Sedan has been restored and is flying with Delta Airlines based at Atlanta, Georgia painted in the colours of the airline's first Model 6000 introduced in June, 1929.

Curtiss-Wright 6B Sedan, NC8878

Curtiss C-46A, N7768B

Specification	Curtiss-Wright 6B Sedan	
Powerplant	One 300 h.p. (223.7kW) Wright R-975 piston engine	
Dimensions		
Span	14.23 m	(48 ft 7 in)
Length	9.58 m	(31 ft 5 in)
Height	2.82 m	(9 ft 3 in)
Performance		
Max speed	217 km/h	(117 kt 135 mph)
Cruising speed	185 km/h	(100 kt 115 mph)
Initial climb	229 m/min	(750 fpm)
Range	920 km	(500 nm 575 miles)
Weights		
Max takeoff	2,004 kg	(4,420 lbs)
Useful load	777 kg	(1,713 lbs)

Specification	Curtiss C-46A	
Powerplant	Two 2,000 h.p. (1,491.2 kW) Pratt & Whitney R-2800-51 piston engines	
Dimensions		
Span	32.9 m	(108 ft 0 in)
Length	23.26 m	(76 ft 4 in)
Height	6.62 m	(21 ft 9 in)
Performance		
Max speed	432 km/h	(235 kt, 270 mph)
Cruising speed	277 km/h	(150 kt, 173 mph)
Initial climb	183 m/min	(600 fpm)
Range	5,040 km	(2,739 nm, 3,150 miles)
Weights		
Max takeoff	20,408 kg	(45,000 lbs)
Useful load	6,803 kg	(15,000 lbs)

Curtiss C-46 Commando
— USA

Originally designed as the CW.20 commercial transport, the C-46 became a companion of the Douglas C-47 as the backbone of the Allied World War II medium transport fleet. The prototype CW.20 first flew on 26th March 1940 and 3,182 of the military C-46 had been built by the time production ceased in 1945. It was an all-metal low-wing aircraft with a distinctive streamlined twin-lobe fuselage incorporating an extensively glazed cockpit faired into the nose. The principal variant was the C-46A freighter with 2,000 h.p. Pratt & Whitney R-2800-51 engines and a rear cargo door and the C-46D was a passenger version capable of carrying 50 equipped troops. The C-46E, 17 of which were built, had a stepped windshield. After the war, the C-46 became popular with foreign air forces and with cargo operators in South America and Canada and many still serve as commercial freighters.

Cvjetkovic CA-65 Skyfly
— USA

The first of five CA-51 Volkswagen-powered single-seat ultralight aircraft, designed by Anton Cvjetkovic, was built and flown by the Zagreb Aero Club in Yugoslavia in 1951. Cvjetkovic subsequently emigrated to the United States where he developed the similar CA-61 Mini Ace. The CA-61 is a low-wing aircraft for amateur construction built of wood with plywood covering. It can be completed as a single-seater or with a wider two-seat fuselage and has a fixed tailwheel undercarriage or retractable gear (CA-61R). The normal powerplant is a 65 h.p. Continental A65 but some aircraft use a 1500 cc Volkswagen. The CA-65 Skyfly is a developed version with an inward-retracting undercarriage which first flew in July 1965. It has a larger tail unit and optional folding wings and is powered by a 125 h.p. Lycoming O-290-G or similar powerplant. A metal version, the CA-65A, has also been built.

Cvjetkovic CA-65 Skyfly (Cont.)

Cvjetkovic CA-65 Skyfly, N3353

Specification	Cvjetkovic CA-65 Skyfly	
Powerplant	One 125 h.p. (93.2 kW) Textron-Lycoming O-290-G piston engine	
Dimensions		
Span	7.63 m	(25 ft 0 in)
Length	5.8 m	(19 ft 0 in)
Height	2.25 m	(7 ft 4 in)
Performance		
Max speed	256 km/h	(139 kt, 160 mph)
Cruising speed	216 km/h	(117 kt, 135 mph)
Initial climb	305 m/min	(1,000 fpm)
Range	680 km	(370 nm, 425 miles)
Weights		
Max takeoff	680 kg	(1,500 lbs)
Useful load	272 kg	(600 lbs)

D

Daewoo KTX-1
— South Korea

The KTX-1 Woong Bee military primary trainer is the first aircraft to be designed and manufactured in South Korea. The KTX project was launched by Daewoo Heavy Industries in early 1988 as a replacement for the Korean Air Force's T-37 trainers and the prototype first flew on 12th December 1991 at Sachon. A further four flying prototypes have been employed on the flight test programme. The KTX-1 is very similar in layout to the Pilatus PC-9 with a low wing, stepped cockpit and retractable tricycle undercarriage and the first two aircraft were powered by 550 s.h.p. Pratt & Whitney PT6A-25A turboprops. The third and subsequent aircraft have the substantially higher-powered PT6A-62 and are fitted with a four-bladed propeller in place of the earlier three-blade Hartzell. It is expected that the South Korean Air Force will have a requirement for 85 KT-1 trainers and a further 20 KO-X versions equipped for forward air control.

Specification	Daewoo KT-1	
Powerplant	One 950 s.h.p. (708.3 kW) Pratt & Whitney PT6A-26A turboprop	
Dimensions		
Span	10.04 m	(32 ft 11 in)
Length	8.44 m	(27 ft 8 in)
Height	2.96 m	(9 ft 8 in)
Performance		
Max speed	518 km/h	(280 kt, 323 mph)
Cruising speed	512 km/h	(278 kt, 320 mph)
Initial Climb	1,067 m/min	(3,500 fpm)
Range	1,658 km	(900 nm, 1,036 miles)
Weights		
Max takeoff	2,481 kg	(5,470 lbs)
Useful Load	1,050 kg	(2,320 lbs)

Daewoo, KTX-1-01

Dallach Sunrise IIA
— Germany

Designed by Wolfgang Dallach, the Sunrise is a very small low-wing ultralight, normally flown as a single seater but capable of being constructed with tandem open cockpits. The Sunrise IIA is of wood and fabric construction with a fixed tailwheel undercarriage and various engines in the 35 h.p. to 50 h.p. range can be fitted. Some 39 examples of the Sunrise are believed to have been completed, all of which have flown in Germany.

Dallach Sunrise, D-MDBB

Specification	Dallach Sunrise IIA	
Powerplant	One 40 h.p. (30 kW) KKHD piston engine	
Dimensions		
Span	13.08 m	(42 ft 11 in)
Length	5.31 m	(17 ft 5 in)
Height	1.42 m	(4 ft 8 in)
Performance		
Max speed	149 km/h	(81 kt, 93 mph)
Cruising speed	120 km/h	(65 kt, 75 mph)
Range	255 km	(140 nm, 160 miles)
Weights		
Max takeoff (est)	250 kg	(550 lbs)
Useful load	100 kg	(220 lbs)

Dallach D3 Sunwheel
— Germany

The Sunwheel is a further design from Wolfgang Dallach who markets kits of this ultralight category biplane through WD Flugzeug Leichtbau. The Sunwheel, over 45 of which have been built, is a tube and fabric aircraft with tandem open cockpits for two and a fixed tailwheel undercarriage. Various engines in the 50 h.p. to 80 h.p. category can be fitted but the normal powerplant is a 65 h.p. Sauer ULM.2000 or 80 h.p. Rotax 912.

Dallach Sunwheel, D-MRSA

Specification	Dallach D3 Sunwheel	
Powerplant	One 80 h.p. (59.6 kW) Rotax 912UL piston engine	
Dimensions		
Span	7 m	(23 ft 1 in)
Length	5.7 m	(18 ft 8 in)
Height	2.2 m	(7 ft 3 in)
Performance		
Max speed	145 km/h	(78 kt, 90 mph)
Cruising speed	130 km/h	(70 kt, 81 mph)
Initial climb	37 m/min	(120 fpm)
Range	350 km	(191 nm, 220 miles)
Weights		
Max takeoff	450 kg	(992 lbs)
Useful load	230 kg	(507 lbs)

Dallach D4 Fascination
— Germany

The Fascination is a highly streamlined low-wing aircraft sold as a standard or quick kit by WD Flugzeug Leichtbau. In standard form it has a steel tube and fabric fuselage and composite wings but the latest Fascination GFK has a composite fuselage. The high-performance Fascination has a side-by-side two-seat cockpit enclosed by a large transparent bubble canopy and is fitted with a retractable tricycle undercarriage and equipped with flaps. The standard powerplant is the Rotax 912 fitted with a variable pitch propeller but it can also be fitted with the 100 h.p. DZ.100 engine. Around 30 Fascinations are now flying with at least 30 more under construction.

Dallach Fascination, D-MUXX

Specification	Dallach D4 Fascination	
Powerplant	One 100 h.p. (74.56 kW) Rotax 912UL piston engine	
Dimensions		
Span	9 m	(29 ft 6 in)
Length	6.98 m	(22 ft 11 in)
Height	1.85 m	(6 ft 1 in)
Performance		
Max speed	280 km/h	(155 kt, 174 mph)
Cruising speed	256 km/h	(139 kt, 160 mph)
Initial climb	503 m/min	(1,650 fpm)
Range	1,090 km	(590 nm, 680 miles)
Weights		
Max takeoff	450 kg	(992 lbs)
Useful load	160 kg	(353 lbs)

Dart Model G — USA

The little Dart Model G was designed by Al Mooney and initially built by Lambert Aircraft as the Monoprep G. Mooney later set up the Dart Aircraft Co. (later Culver) which put the aircraft into production as the Dart GK with a 90 h.p. Ken Royce radial engine and the Dart GW with a 90 h.p. Warner Scarab. The Dart is a low-wing light aircraft of steel tube, wood and fabric construction with a wide-track tailwheel undercarriage. It has an enclosed cabin with side-by-side seating for two and the wing has a distinctive shape with a straight leading edge and curved trailing edge. Fifty Darts were built by Culver before production ceased in 1940. After the war the Dart was built by Applegate & Weyant as the Dart GC with a 100 h.p. Continental A-100 engine but only 12 were completed. Some 21 Dart GKs, GWs and GCs are currently registered in the United States although only a handful are airworthy.

Dart GW, NC20941

Specification	Dart GW	
Powerplant	One 90 h.p. (67.1 kW) Warner Scarab Junior piston engine	
Dimensions		
Span	8.99 m	(29 ft 6 in)
Length	5.69 m	(18 ft 8 in)
Height	1.85 m	(6 ft 1 in)
Performance		
Max speed	210 km/h	(114 kt, 131 mph)
Cruising speed	189 km/h	(103 kt, 118 mph)
Initial climb	247 m/min	(810 fpm)
Range	792 km	(430 nm, 495 miles)
Weights		
Max takeoff	698 kg	(1,540 lbs)
Useful load	272 kg	(600 lbs)

Dassault MD.312 Flamant — France

Dassault designed the MD.303 to meet postwar French domestic and colonial military transport requirements and flew the prototype, powered by Béarn 6D engines, on 26th February 1947. The production versions for the French Armée de l'Air and Aéronavale were the MD.311 navigation trainer with a transparent bomb-aimer's nose and the MD.312 and MD.315 transport with a solid nose and fitted with six and ten seats respectively. These were all powered by 580 h.p. SNECMA 12S in-line piston engines. They entered service in 1950 and were finally phased out in 1985. Some 39 of the MD.311 were built together with 279 of the MD.312/315. Sixteen Flamants are registered in France with private owners, most of which are active.

Dassault MD.312 Flamant

Specification	Dassault MD.312 Flamant	
Powerplant	Two 580 h.p. (432.4 kW) SNECMA-Renault 12S piston engines	
Dimensions		
Span	20.67 m	(67 ft 10 in)
Length	12.5 m	(41 ft 0 in)
Height	4.5 m	(14 ft 9 in)
Performance		
Max speed	380 km/h	(205 kt, 236 mph)
Cruising speed	300 km/h	(162 kt, 186 mph)
Initial climb	300 m/min	(984 fpm)
Range	1,208 km	(658 nm, 755 miles)
Weights		
Max takeoff	5,787 kg	(12,760 lbs)
Useful load	1,546 kg	(3,410 lbs)

Dassault Falcon 20 and 200 — France

One of the earliest business jets, the Mystere 20 (later Falcon 20 or Fan Jet Falcon) operates worldwide with civil and military users. First flown on 4th May 1963, it is a low-wing mid-size business jet with twin rear fuselage-mounted General Electric CF700 turbofans and normal accommodation for nine passengers and two crew. In addition to its executive transport role, the Falcon 20 is widely used for carrying light cargo as well as being used for military electronics training, target towing, mapping and other special missions. A batch of 30 Falcons was bought as the initial equipment of Federal Express for small package freighting and these were the first Falcons to be fitted with a large port-side freight door and hardened interior. The Falcon 20D has CF700-2D engines and the 20F has increased range and modified wing slats. The 20G Gardian is a maritime patrol version operated by the US Coast Guard as the HU-25 and fitted with Garrett (Honeywell) ATF3-6-2C turbofans, as are the similar commercial Falcon 20H and Falcon 200. A total of 515 Falcon 20s were built and over 450 are operational.

Dassault Falcon 20, F-RAEE (French AF)

Specification	Dassault Falcon 200	
Powerplant	Two 5,200 lb.s.t. (23.1 kN) Honeywell ATF3-6A-4C turbofans	
Dimensions		
Span	16.31 m	(53 ft 6 in)
Length	17.14 m	(56 ft 3 in)
Height	5.33 m	(17 ft 6 in)
Performance		
Max speed	863 km/h	(469 kt, 539 mph)
Cruising speed	791 km/h	(430 kt, 494 mph)
Takeoff distance	1,234 m	(4,050 ft)
Range	4,784 km	(2,600 nm, 2,990 miles)
Weights		
Max takeoff	14,512 kg	(32,000 lbs)
Useful load	5,986 kg	(13,200 lbs)

Dassault Falcon 10 and 100
— France

Dassault designed the Falcon 10 (originally known as the MiniFalcon) as a complementary model to the successful Falcon 20. It is smaller than the Falcon 20 but otherwise generally similar in layout. The prototype Falcon 10 first flew on 1st December 1970 powered by two rear-mounted Garrett (Honeywell) TFE731-2 turbofans. The interior of the aircraft is equipped to carry a maximum of seven passengers but a four-seat interior is more normal and allows for a larger baggage compartment. The improved Falcon 100 has an extra cabin window and higher gross weight. The majority of Falcon 10s have been sold to corporate customers in the USA but the French Aéronavale has taken seven Falcon 10MER for radar training, liaison and target towing. A total of 229 Falcon 10s and 100s were built, including three prototypes, and production ceased in 1989. Some 207 aircraft are currently in service worldwide.

Dassault Falcon 100, VR-BCH

Specification	Dassault Falcon 100	
Powerplant	Two 3,230 lb.s.t. (14.37 kN) Honeywell (Garrett) TFE731-2-1C turbofans	
Dimensions		
Span	13.05 m	(42 ft 10 in)
Length	13.87 m	(45 ft 6 in)
Height	4.62 m	(15 ft 2 in)
Performance		
Max speed	902 km/h	(490 kt, 563 mph)
Cruising speed	767 km/h	(417 kt, 480 mph)
Takeoff distance	960 m	(3,150 ft)
Range	3,588 km	(1,950 nm, 2,242 miles)
Weights		
Max takeoff	8,499 kg	(18,740 lbs)
Useful load	3,420 kg	(7,540 lbs)

Dassault Falcon 50
— France

Having achieved considerable success with the short/medium-range Falcon 20 business jet, Dassault needed to offer a variant with transcontinental range. The Falcon 50, which first flew on 7th November 1976, used the basic forward fuselage structure of the Falcon 20 married to a new compound-sweep wing and a rear fuselage mounting three Garrett (Honeywell) TFE731-3 turbofans. The cabin is slightly larger, accommodating eight to 12 passengers, and there is a pressurised luggage hold. The Falcon 50, which has double the range of the Falcon 20, was certificated in February 1979 and nearly 300 have been built to date. The latest version is the Falcon 50EX with an EFIS cockpit and TFE731-40 engines giving improved climb performance, range and fuel consumption. The Falcon 50 has also been produced for military users including the French Aéronavale who operate the Gardian 50 maritime patrol version.

Dassault Falcon 50, T-783 (Swiss AF)

Dassault Falcon 50 (Cont.)

Specification	Dassault Falcon 50EX	
Powerplant	Three 3,700 lb.s.t. (16.46 kN) Honeywell (Garrett) TFE731-40 turbofans	
Dimensions		
Span	18.85 m	(61 ft 10 in)
Length	18.52 m	(60 ft 9 in)
Height	6.98 m	(22 ft 11 in)
Performance		
Max speed	896 km/h	(487 kt, 560 mph)
Cruising speed	791 km/h	(430 kt, 494 mph)
Initial climb	1,490 m/min	(4,890 fpm)
Range	6,044 km	(3,285 nm, 3,778 miles)
Weights		
Max takeoff	18,494 kg	(40,780 lbs)
Useful load	8,608 kg	(18,980 lbs)

Specification	Dassault Falcon 900EX	
Powerplant	Three 5,000 lb.s.t. (22.24 kN) Honeywell (Garrett) TFE731-60 turbofans	
Dimensions		
Span	19.33 m	(63 ft 5 in)
Length	20.21 m	(66 ft 4 in)
Height	7.55 m	(24 ft 9 in)
Performance		
Max speed	885 km/h	(481 kt, 553 mph)
Cruising speed	791 km/h	(430 kt, 494 mph)
Takeoff distance	1,535 m	(5,040 ft)
Range	8,280 km	(4,500 nm, 5,175 miles)
Weights		
Max takeoff	22,222 kg	(49,000 lbs)
Useful load	11,020 kg	(24,300 lbs)

Dassault Falcon 900
— France

Dassault's entrant in the large intercontinental business jet market is the Falcon 900. Following the Falcon 50's three-engined layout, the Falcon 900 has a similar wing design but a larger wide-body fuselage with a normal 12-passenger interior or high-density 19-seat cabin. The Falcon 900 prototype first flew on 21st September 1984 followed by first deliveries in 1986. The range of the 900 is 30% greater than the Falcon 50 and higher-thrust TFE731-5AR turbofans are used. The Falcon 900B, introduced in 1991, has TFE731-5BR engines giving improved speed and range. The Falcon 900EX is a 4,500 nm long-range model based on the 900B which is also upgraded with a Honeywell Primus EFIS cockpit and headup display. The Falcon 900C is the latest variant with the avionics suite of the 900EX. Over 240 Falcon 900s had been built by the end of 1999.

Dassault Falcon 2000
— France

The Falcon 2000 was designed to offer a similar range and speed performance to that of the Falcon 50 with a wider passenger cabin, similar to that of the Falcon 900. Operating economics are also improved by using two GE/Garrett (Honeywell) CFE738 turbofan engines rather than three TFE 731 turbofans, providing an equivalent power output. The passenger cabin is the same width and height as the 900 but is two-thirds of the length and can accommodate eight passengers in normal configuration. The cockpit is equipped with Dassault's new-generation EFIS and HUD equipment. The wing design is based on that of the Falcon 50 and Falcon 900 as is the tail unit, although the third engine installation is eliminated. Dassault flew the first Falcon 2000 on 4th March 1993 and delivered the first customer aircraft in 1995. By early 2000, over 100 aircraft had been delivered to customers in 14 countries.

Dassault Falcon 900EX, F-WREX

Dassault Falcon 2000, F-WNEW

Specification	Dassault Falcon 2000	
Powerplant	Two 5,918 lb.s.t. (26.33 kN) General Electric-Honeywell CFE738-1-1B turbofans	
Dimensions		
Span	19.33 m	(63 ft 5 in)
Length	20.22 m	(66 ft 4 in)
Height	7.06 m	(23 ft 2 in)
Performance		
Max speed	885 km/h	(481 kt, 553 mph)
Cruising speed	791 km/h	(430 kt, 494 mph)
Initial climb	1,658 m/min	(5,440 fpm)
Range	5,741 km	(3,120 nm, 3,588 miles)
Weights		
Max takeoff	16,553 kg	(36,500 lbs)
Useful load	6,825 kg	(15,050 lbs)

Specification	Dassault-Breguet-Dornier Alpha Jet	
Powerplant	Two 2,976 lb.s.t. (13.24 kN) Turboméca-SNECMA Larzac 04-C6 turbojets	
Dimensions		
Span	9.11 m	(29 ft 11 in)
Length	11.75 m	(38 ft 7 in)
Height	4.19 m	(13 ft 9 in)
Performance		
Max speed	1,000 km/h	(540 kt, 621 mph)
Cruising speed	960 km/h	(517 kt, 597 mph)
Initial climb	3,657 m/min	(12,000 fpm)
Range	2,880 km	(1,565 nm, 1,800 miles)
Weights		
Max takeoff	8,000 kg	(17,640 lbs)
Useful load	4,655 kg	(10,264 lbs)

Dassault-Breguet-Dornier Alpha Jet — France

The Alpha Jet was the result of one of the earliest European cooperative defence aircraft projects to create an advanced jet trainer for the French and German air forces. It is a tandem two-seat aircraft with a shoulder-mounted swept wing and two lower fuselage-mounted SNECMA Larzac turbofans. The prototype flew on 26th October 1973 and variants were the Alpha Jet E trainer and Alpha Jet A light attack variant with a belly-mounted cannon pod and four underwing hardpoints which was ordered by the Luftwaffe. Some 447 Alpha Jets were delivered including aircraft for Belgium and the Ivory Coast. Egypt received 45, designated MS1 and MS2, of which 37 were built by the Helwan factory, and Cameroon had seven tactical support variants similar to the Egyptian MS2. The Alpha Jet 2-NGEA is a new weapon-training version with Larzac 04-C20 engines but none have been ordered to date.

Dassault Super Etendard — France

The Dassault Etendard IVM single-seat naval strike fighter entered service with the Aéronavale in 1962. The low-wing Etendard was designed for French Navy carrier-borne strike operations and 90 were delivered. On 29th October 1974 Dassault flew the prototype of the follow-on Super Etendard, modified from an Etendard IVM, with a higher thrust SNECMA Atar 8K-50 engine and a new radar and attack system. Aéronavale received 71 Super Etendards with first deliveries taking place in 1978. Fourteen aircraft were also delivered to the Argentine Navy and were flown in the Falklands war. The Super Etendard is equipped with two installed DEFA.553 30 mm guns and can carry a variety of offensive stores including two Exocet or Matra Magic missiles on its four underwing hardpoints and centreline stores station. Production was completed in 1983.

Dassault-Breguet-Dornier Alpha Jet

Dassault Super Etendard, 0764 (Argentine Navy)

Dassault Super Etendard (Cont.)

Specification	Dassault Super Etendard	
Powerplant	One 11,025 lb.s.t. (49 kN) SNECMA Atar 8K-50 turbojet	
Dimensions		
Span	9.6 m	(31 ft 6 in)
Length	14.31 m	(46 ft 11 in)
Height	3.86 m	(12 ft 8 in)
Performance		
Max speed	1,200 km/h	(650 kt, 750 mph)
Cruising speed	1,088 km/h	(590 kt, 680 mph)
Initial climb	6,096 m/min	(20,000 fpm)
Range	1,656 km	(900 nm, 1,035 miles)
Weights		
Max takeoff	12,000 kg	(26,460 lbs)
Useful load	5,500 kg	(12,127 lbs)

Dassault Mirage IIIRS, R-2108 (Swiss AF)

Dassault/ENAER 50CN Pantera, 503 (Chile AF)

Dassault Mirage III, 5 and 50, Pantera and Kfir
— France

The Dassault Mirage has been one of the most successful fighter designs of modern times and has been sold to many air forces and built by other manufacturers. Between 1961 and 1992 Dassault delivered 1,422 examples of the Mirage III series. The Mirage I prototype of the delta-wing fighter first flew on 25th June 1955 followed by the Mirage III prototype on 17th November 1956. A total of 95 of the initial single-seat Mirage IIIC and 63 tandem two-seat Mirage IIIB trainers were delivered to the Armée de l'Air followed by 180 of the Mirage IIIE with improved strike capability including a centreline bomb-carrying hardpoint. The Mirage IIIR was a reconnaissance version with a multi-camera nose. Mirages were exported to 19 countries including South Africa (IIICJ), Argentina (IIIEA), Spain (IIIEE) and Switzerland (IIIS and IIIRS) and has been operated with numerous variations depending on customer requirements. The Mirage 5 is a simplified Mirage III with a slimmer nose, extra fuel and two fuselage hardpoints. The Mirage 50 is the Mirage III or 5 upgraded with the SNECMA Atar 9K-50 engine. Several local modifications have been made including the ENAER upgrade of Chilean Mirage 50Cs to 50CN Pantera standard with forward canard surfaces etc. In Israel, the Mirage III was copied as the IAI Nesher, 50 of which were built and later sold to Argentina. The Nesher was developed into the IAI Kfir C2 (and the C7 with upgraded avionics) which has the basic Mirage III airframe with a wider rear fuselage to house a 17,900 lb.s.t. General Electric J79 turbojet, a longer nose section, canard surfaces aft of the engine air intakes and a modified saw-tooth wing leading edge. The Kfir, in single- and two-seat form, was also sold to South Africa, Colombia and Ecuador and 212 examples were built.

Specification	Dassault Mirage 50	
Powerplant	One 11,023 lb.s.t. (49 kN) SNECMA Atar 9K-50 turbojet	
Dimensions		
Span	8.22 m	(26 ft 11 in)
Length	15.56 m	(51 ft 1 in)
Height	4.5 m	(14 ft 9 in)
Performance		
Max speed	2,318 km/h	(1,255 kt, 1,449 mph)
Cruising speed	957 km/h	(520 kt, 600 mph)
Initial climb	3,400 m/min	(11,150 fpm)
Range	2,576 km	(1,400 nm, 1,610 miles)
Weights		
Max takeoff	14,700 kg	(32,413 lbs)
Useful load	7,550 kg	(16,648 lbs)

Dassault Mirage F1
— France

Despite its name, the Mirage F1 was virtually a new design, owing little to the Mirage III/5 which had preceded it although it used the same Atar powerplant fitted to the Mirage 50. The fuselage is similar to that of the Mirage 5 with a long slim nose. The vertical tail is reshaped and the standard Mirage delta wing is replaced on the F1 with a completely new shoulder-set swept wing and rear fuselage-mounted tailplane. The main trailing link undercarriage is relocated to the lower fuselage. The Mirage F1 prototype first flew on 23rd December 1966 and first deliveries of the French Armée de l'Air F1C all-weather interceptor version were made in 1973 followed by the F1CR reconnaissance variant and the F1CT ground attack aircraft. The F1B and F1D are two-seat trainer variants and the F1AZ is a day fighter for the South African Air Force. The F1E is a multi-role export attack variant delivered to several countries including Iraq (F1EQ), Morocco (F1EH) and Spain (F1EE). Some 708 F1s were delivered by the time production ceased in 1989.

Dassault Mirage F1CT, No.267 (French AF)

Specification	Dassault Mirage F1C	
Powerplant	One 11,023 lb.s.t. (49 kN) SNECMA Atar 9K-50 turbofan	
Dimensions		
Span	8.4 m	(27 ft 7 in)
Length	15.3 m	(50 ft 3 in)
Height	4.5 m	(14 ft 9 in)
Performance		
Max speed	2,318 km/h	(1,255 kt, 1,449 mph)
Cruising speed	1,473 km/h	(800 kt, 920 mph)
Initial climb	10,668 m/min	(35,000 fpm)
Range	1,564 km	(850 nm, 977 miles)
Weights		
Max takeoff	16,197 kg	(35,715 lbs)
Useful load	8,844 kg	(19,500 lbs)

Dassault Mirage 2000
— France

For the third variant of the Mirage family, Dassault restored the delta wing layout and wing-mounted undercarriage of the Mirage III which was combined with a slightly larger area-ruled fuselage and a 14,462 lb.s.t. M53 turbofan. Armament consists of two DEFA544 belly-mounted cannon and external weapons on four wing hardpoints and a centreline pylon. The Mirage 2000 prototype flew on 10th March 1978. Variants are the 2000C all-weather interceptor, 2000B two-seat trainer, 2000E (and two-seat 2000ED) export version, 2000N nuclear strike aircraft and the similar 2000D conventional ground attack variant. The Mirage 2000-5 is a specialised export model with upgraded electronics and weapons integration and provision for four belly-mounted MICA missiles, and the Mirage 200-5 Mk.2 and 2000-9 are variants with further improvements to the datalink system, a new ECM system, Damocles laser designator, increased gross weight and a redesigned modular cockpit. Over 550 Mirage 2000s are in service with eight air forces.

Dassault Mirage 2000, No.43 (French AF)

Dassault Mirage 2000D, No. D01 (French AF)

Specification	Mirage 2000C	
Powerplant	One 14,460 lb.s.t. (64.3 kN) SNECMA M53-P2 turbojet	
Dimensions		
Span	9.13 m	(29 ft 11 in)
Length	14.36 m	(47 ft 1 in)
Height	5.2 m	(17 ft 1 in)
Performance		
Max speed	2,300 km/h	(1,245 kt, 1,437 mph)
Cruising speed	1,400 km/h	(760 kt, 875 mph)
Initial climb	16,765 m/min	(55,000 fpm)
Range	1,840 km	(1,000 nm, 1,150 miles)
Weights		
Max takeoff	17,000 kg	(37,485 lbs)
Useful load	9,500 kg	(20,948 lbs)

Dassault Mirage IV — France

Dassault built 62 examples of the Mirage IVA nuclear bomber in the mid-1960s and five remain operational with the Armée de l'Air. The Mirage IVA, which has a crew of two in a fully enclosed tandem cabin, is a scaled-up Mirage III with a slim delta wing and powered by two 11,023 lb.s.t. Atar 9K-50 turbojets with reheat. It is also equipped with rocket-assisted takeoff bottles and has two underwing hardpoints for fuel tanks or external weapons load. The main offensive nuclear load of one 60-kiloton bomb is carried semi-externally under the centre fuselage and the aircraft is fitted with two four-wheel bogie main undercarriage units. The prototype first flew on 17th June 1959 and the Mirage IVAs in service in the early 1990s were upgraded to Mirage IVP standard with revised avionics and a belly pylon to carry an Aérospatiale ASMP standoff nuclear weapon.

Dassault Mirage IVP, No.55 (French AF)

Specification	Dassault Mirage IVP	
Powerplant	Two 11,023 lb.s.t. (49.04 kN) SNECMA Atar 9K-50 turbojets	
Dimensions		
Span	11.85 m	(38 ft 10 in)
Length	23.5 m	(77 ft 1 in)
Height	5.65 m	(18 ft 6 in)
Performance		
Max speed	2,338 km/h	(1,262 kt, 1,461 mph)
Cruising speed	1,915 km/h	(1,036 kt, 1,196 mph)
Initial climb	2,591 m/min	(8,500 fpm)
Range	4,000 km	(2,174 nm, 2,500 miles)
Weights		
Max takeoff	31,600 kg	(69,616 lbs)
Useful load	17,097 kg	(37,700 lbs)

Dassault Rafale — France

In 1984 Dassault started development work on a new twin-engined multi-role fighter to meet the needs of the French Air Force and Navy, and the proof-of-concept Rafale A first flew on 4th July 1986. The definitive production Rafale, which flew in May 1991, is slightly smaller. It is a delta-wing aircraft, built with advanced material powered by twin SNECMA M88 turbofans in the lower fuselage and fitted with small foreplanes positioned beside the cockpit. Variants for the Armée de l'Air are the Rafale C single-seater and Rafale B two-seater. The Aéronavale is to receive the Rafale M which is a navalised carrier-borne version with modified twin-wheel nose gear, long-stroke main undercarriage legs and an arrester hook. The aircraft has six underwing hardpoints, two wingtip missile stations and a fuselage centreline pylon together with a 30 mm installed cannon. Four prototypes were used for flight testing and the first of 61 initial production aircraft flew in December 1998. The anticipated French military requirement is for 294 Rafales.

Dassault Rafale M, No.01 and 02 (French Navy)

Specification	Dassault Rafale C	
Powerplant	Two 19,555 lb.s.t. (86.98 kN) SNECMA M88-3 turbofans	
Dimensions		
Span	10.8 m	(35 ft 5 in)
Length	15.27 m	(50 ft 1 in)
Height	5.34 m	(17 ft 5 in)
Performance		
Max speed	2,125 km/h	(1,147 kt, 1,321 mph)
Cruising speed	1,012 km/h	(550 kt, 633 mph)
Initial climb	18,288 m/min	(60,000 fpm)
Range	3,680 km	(2,000 nm, 2,300 miles)
Weights		
Max takeoff	24,500 kg	(54,023 lbs)
Useful load	14,000 kg	(30,870 lbs)

Davis V-3 and D-1 — USA

The Davis V-3 was a pre-war two-seat light aircraft derived from the Vulcan American Moth which had been successful in many air races in 1928. The design was acquired by the Davis Aircraft Corporation who built 23 of a modified version known as the Davis V-3. The V-3 was a parasol high-wing machine of mixed construction with tandem open cockpits, a tailwheel undercarriage and a 65 h.p. Le Blond radial engine. This was succeeded by the Davis D-1 which had a larger vertical tail and an improved cockpit and by several further variants with different engines including the D-1K (100 h.p. Kinner K5), D-1-85 (85 h.p. le Blond 5DF), D-1L (Lambert 90) and the D-1W (125 h.p. Warner

Scarab). It is thought that 27 of the D-1 series were built and 14 of the Davis aircraft still exist in various states of airworthiness including one in Argentina.

Davis D-1W, NC13576

Specification	Davis D-1W	
Powerplant	One 125 h.p. (93.2 kW) Warner Scarab piston engine	
Dimensions		
Span	9.19 m	(30 ft 2 in)
Length	6.2 m	(20 ft 4 in)
Height	2.21 m	(7 ft 3 in)
Performance		
Max speed	224 km/h	(122 kt, 140 mph)
Cruising speed	192 km/h	(104 kt, 120 mph)
Initial climb	411 m/min	(1,350 fpm)
Range	560 km	(304 nm, 350 miles)
Weights		
Max takeoff	662 kg	(1,460 lbs)
Useful load	243 kg	(535 lbs)

Davis DA-2A — USA

The DA-2A has become one of the more popular amateur-built aircraft in the United States. It was designed by Leeon D. Davis and first flown on 21st May 1966. The DA-2A is an all-metal aircraft with the emphasis on simple construction which is sold in the form of plans and as a partial kit. It is distinctive in having an all-moving butterfly tail. The fuselage is streamlined to give a semi-aerofoil effect and has a fully enclosed cabin with side-by-side seating for two. The aircraft is fitted with a fixed tricycle undercarriage and powered by a flat-four engine in the 65 h.p. to 100 h.p. range. Over 60 DA-2As have been completed and others are under construction from plans supplied by D2 Inc. One DA-2A is flying in the UK, powered by a Continental O-200-A engine.

Davis DA-2A, G-BPFL

Specification	Davis DA-2A	
Powerplant	One 90 h.p. (67.1 kW) Teledyne Continental O-200-A piston engine	
Dimensions		
Span	5.86 m	(19 ft 3 in)
Length	5.44 m	(17 ft 10 in)
Height	1.14 m	(3 ft 9 in)
Performance		
Max speed	225 km/h	(121 kt, 140 mph)
Cruising speed	200 km/h	(110 kt, 125 mph)
Initial climb	152 m/min	(500 fpm)
Range	720 km	(390 nm, 450 miles)
Weights		
Max takeoff	567 kg	(1,250 lbs)
Useful load	227 kg	(500 lbs)

De Havilland DH.60 Moth — UK

The Moth two-seat biplane, designed by de Havilland in 1924, became the most popular and famous British club and training light aircraft because of its rugged design and 2,047 were produced in the UK, Canada, USA and Australia. Built of wood, ply and fabric it had wings of equal span and tandem open cockpits. It first flew on 22nd February 1925 and was powered by a 60 h.p. Cirrus I engine. The Cirrus II Moth had an 85 h.p. Cirrus II engine and a few Genet Moths were built with a 75 h.p. Armstrong Siddeley Genet radial. The DH.60G Gipsy Moth with a 100 h.p. Gipsy I or 120 h.p. Gipsy II was one of the most popular of the Moths with 595 completed. De Havilland also built 86 DH.60GIII Moth Majors with a 120 h.p. inverted Gipsy Major. The DH.60M Metal Moth, and military DH.60T, were versions with a steel tube fuselage in place of wooden frames.

De Havilland DH.60 Moth (Cont.)

De Havilland DH.60GM Moth, G-AADR

Specification	De Havilland DH.60G Gipsy Moth	
Powerplant	One 100 h.p. (74.6 kW) de Havilland Gipsy I piston engine	
Dimensions		
Span	9.14 m	(30 ft 0 in)
Length	7.29 m	(23 ft 11 in)
Height	2.69 m	(8 ft 10 in)
Performance		
Max speed	163 km/h	(89 kt, 102 mph)
Cruising speed	136 km/h	(74 kt, 85 mph)
Initial climb	152 m/min	(500 fpm)
Range	512 km	(278 nm, 320 miles)
Weights		
Max takeoff	748 kg	(1,650 lbs)
Useful load	331 kg	(730 lbs)

De Havilland DH.82 Tiger Moth — UK

De Havilland's DH.60T military Moth Trainer formed the basis for the DH.82 Tiger Moth designed to Royal Air Force requirements and equipped with the inverted 120 h.p. Gipsy III engine. To improve cockpit access the upper wing was moved forward and both sets of wings were slightly swept to compensate. The Tiger Moth first flew on 26th October 1931 and the pressures of war resulted in an eventual total of 8,811 aircraft being built by the time production ceased in 1945. Tiger Moths were also built in Australia, New Zealand, Canada, Sweden, Norway and Portugal and many pre-war aircraft were built for civil or domestic export sale. The main DH.82A version had a 130 h.p. Gipsy Major 1 engine but some Tiger Moths were fitted with a 145 h.p. Gipsy Major 1C. Some 420 DH.82B Queen Bee radio-controlled targets were also completed and some were fitted with full controls and joined ex-RAF Tiger Moths after the war with private owners. Over 200 DH.82s are still active in the UK with many others flying in the USA and Australia.

De Havilland DH.82A Tiger Moth, N4797

Specification	De Havilland DH.82A Tiger Moth	
Powerplant	One 130 h.p. (96.9 kW) de Havilland Gipsy Major 1F piston engine	
Dimensions		
Span	8.94 m	(29 ft 4 in)
Length	7.29 m	(23 ft 11 in)
Height	2.67 m	(8 ft 9 in)
Performance		
Max speed	166 km/h	(90 kt, 104 mph)
Cruising speed	144 km/h	(78 kt, 90 mph)
Initial climb	194 m/min	(635 fpm)
Range	480 km	(261 nm, 300 miles)
Weights		
Max takeoff	828 kg	(1,825 lbs)
Useful load	322 kg	(710 lbs)

De Havilland DH.80 Puss Moth and DH.85 Leopard Moth — UK

The private flying boom of the 1920s brought a demand for enclosed touring aircraft which led to de Havilland building the strut-braced high-wing DH.80 Puss Moth monoplane. The prototype first flew on 9th September 1929 and was followed by the production DH.80A which was of mixed construction with a tubular fuselage incorporating a three-seat cabin and a fixed strutted tailwheel undercarriage with fairings which could be turned to act as speed brakes. The Puss Moth was powered by a 120 h.p. Gipsy III or 130 h.p. Gipsy Major. A total of 284 were built including 25 in Canada and Puss Moths were used for many pioneering flights in the 1930s. The Leopard Moth which succeeded it had a lighter wooden fuselage, a 130 h.p. Gipsy Major engine and folding wings of more tapered planform, and 132 were built. Eleven DH.80s and DH.85s remain active on the British register.

De Havilland DH.85 Leopard Moth, G-ACMN

Specification	De Havilland DH.80A Puss Moth	
Powerplant	One 130 h.p. (96.9 kW) de Havilland Gipsy Major piston engine	
Dimensions		
Span	11.2 m	(36 ft 9 in)
Length	7.62 m	(25 ft 0 in)
Height	2.13 m	(7 ft 0 in)
Performance		
Max speed	205 km/h	(111 kt, 128 mph)
Cruising speed	173 km/h	(94 kt, 108 mph)
Initial climb	186 m/min	(610 fpm)
Range	480 km	(261 nm, 300 miles)
Weights		
Max takeoff	930 kg	(2,050 lbs)
Useful load	356 kg	(785 lbs)

De Havilland DH.83 Fox Moth — UK

De Havilland developed the Fox Moth as a light air taxi aircraft based on the Tiger Moth wings, tail unit and undercarriage married to a new fuselage. First flown on 29th January 1932, it was built of spruce and plywood and had an enclosed cabin positioned just behind the firewall of the Gipsy III engine with two facing bench seats to accommodate four passengers. The pilot was seated in a cockpit above and behind the main cabin. This was normally enclosed with a sliding bubble canopy although some Fox Moths had an open cockpit. The DH.83 was exported widely and was also built in Australia and in Canada where it was regularly operated on skis or floats. The DH.83 was used by many small airlines in the 1930s and was popular for pleasure flying. Some 98 were built in Britain, six in Australia and 54 in Canada. Three Fox Moths are currently active in the UK and one in Australia.

De Havilland DH.83 Fox Moth, G-ACEJ

Specification	De Havilland DH.83 Fox Moth	
Powerplant	One 130 h.p. (96.9 kW) de Havilland Gipsy Major piston engine	
Dimensions		
Span	9.42 m	(30 ft 11 in)
Length	7.85 m	(25 ft 9 in)
Height	2.67 m	(8 ft 9 in)
Performance		
Max speed	197 km/h	(107 kt, 123 mph)
Cruising speed	168 km/h	(91 kt, 105 mph)
Initial climb	184 m/min	(605 fpm)
Range	664 km	(361 nm, 415 miles)
Weights		
Max takeoff	939 kg	(2,070 lbs)
Useful load	440 kg	(970 lbs)

De Havilland DH.87 Hornet Moth — UK

The Hornet Moth biplane was a variation on the cabin light-aircraft design established by the Puss Moth and Fox Moth and was aimed at the club training market. The side-by-side seating and enclosed cabin offered a more civilised environment than the tandem open cockpits of the Moth, and the Hornet Moth quickly achieved popularity. Initially, the DH.87 had long-span tapered wings but most aircraft were the DH.87B with square-cut wingtips. Powered by a 130 h.p. Gipsy Major 1 in-line engine, the Hornet Moth had rotating fairings on the undercarriage struts to act as speed brakes. The prototype flew on 9th May 1934 and 164 production examples were built before production ceased in 1939. Hornet Moths were widely used for communications during the war and many survived to fly with private owners when peace arrived. Sixteen are currently active in the UK, three fly in Australia and one is current in the USA.

De Havilland DH.87B Hornet Moth, G-ADKC

De Havilland DH.87 Hornet Moth (Cont.)

Specification	De Havilland DH.87B Hornet Moth	
Powerplant	One 130 h.p. (96.9 kW) de Havilland Gipsy Major 1 piston engine	
Dimensions		
Span	9.73 m	(31 ft 11 in)
Length	7.59 m	(24 ft 11 in)
Height	2.01 m	(6 ft 7 in)
Performance		
Max speed	198 km/h	(108 kt, 124 mph)
Cruising speed	168 km/h	(91 kt, 105 mph)
Initial climb	210 m/min	(690 fpm)
Range	992 km	(539 nm, 620 miles)
Weights		
Max takeoff	907 kg	(2,000 lbs)
Useful load	345 kg	(760 lbs)

De Havilland DH.88 Comet — UK

The Comet was one of the most beautiful aircraft designed by de Havilland and was conceived to participate in the 1934 MacRobertson race to Australia. Five Comets were built, including one delivered as a high-speed mail plane to the French government, the first flying on 8th September 1934. The DH.88 was of all-wood stressed skin construction with a low wing, a graceful streamlined fuselage incorporating an enclosed tandem-seat cockpit and twin Gipsy Six in-line engines. It was fitted with a retractable tailwheel undercarriage. The red Comet G-ACSS *Grosvenor House* was the winner of the MacRobertson race. It is the only original survivor of the five Comets, based with the Shuttleworth Trust, but a replica, which was built in the United States by Repeat Aviation and first flown on 28th November 1993, flies regularly from FlaBob Airport in California.

DH.88 Comet replica, G-ACSS (N88XP)

Specification	De Havilland DH.88 Comet	
Powerplant	Two 230 h.p. (171.5 kW) de Havilland Gipsy Six R piston engines	
Dimensions		
Span	13.4 m	(44 ft 0 in)
Length	8.84 m	(29 ft 0 in)
Height	3.05 m	(10 ft 0 in)
Performance		
Max speed	381 km/h	(206 kt, 237 mph)
Cruising speed	354 km/h	(191 kt, 220 mph)
Initial climb	274 m/min	(900 fpm)
Range	4,680 km	(2,543 nm, 2,925 miles)
Weights		
Max takeoff	2,517 kg	(5,550 lbs)
Useful load	1,188 kg	(2,620 lbs)

De Havilland DH.84 Dragon and DH.89 Dragon Rapide — UK

The expansion of passenger services in the early 1930s led to de Havilland designing the DH.84 Dragon which first flew on 24th November 1932. Constructed of wood and ply the Dragon biplane had a fixed tailwheel undercarriage and two Gipsy Major engines mounted on the inboard lower wings. The Dragon, 202 of which were built, had a six-seat passenger cabin with the pilot seated in the nose of the aircraft. On 17th April 1934 the prototype DH.89 Dragon Rapide was flown and this improved version of the Dragon had tapered wings, a more elegant fuselage, streamlined 'trousered' undercarriage fairings and an eight-passenger interior. In total 206 commercial DH.89s were built. These were followed by 522 DH.89B Dominie wartime military trainer and communications aircraft. DH.89s were used widely after the war by commercial operators, some becoming eight-passenger Rapide Mk.3s and many being re-engined with Gipsy Queen 2 engines as the Mk.4. Over 30 DH.89s are currently airworthy together with Dragons in Ireland and New Zealand.

De Havilland DH.84 Dragon, EI-ABI

De Havilland DH.89A Dragon Rapide 6

De Havilland DH.90 Dragonfly, G-AEDU

Specification	De Havilland DH.89A Dragon Rapide	
Powerplant	Two 200 h.p. (149.1 kW) de Havilland Gipsy Queen 3 piston engines	
Dimensions		
Span	14.63 m	(48 ft 0 in)
Length	10.52 m	(34 ft 6 in)
Height	3.12 m	(10 ft 3 in)
Performance		
Max speed	251 km/h	(137 kt, 157 mph)
Cruising speed	211 km/h	(115 kt, 132 mph)
Initial climb	264 m/min	(867 fpm)
Range	925 km	(503 nm, 578 miles)
Weights		
Max takeoff	2,494 kg	(5,500 lbs)
Useful load	1,353 kg	(2,984 lbs)

Specification	De Havilland 90A Dragonfly	
Powerplant	Two 130 h.p. (96.9 kW) de Havilland Gipsy Major 10 Mk.1-3 piston engines	
Dimensions		
Span	13.11 m	(43 ft 0 in)
Length	9.65 m	(31 ft 8 in)
Height	2.79 m	(9 ft 2 in)
Performance		
Max speed	230 km/h	(125 kt, 144 mph)
Cruising speed	200 km/h	(109 kt, 125 mph)
Initial climb	223 m/min	(730 fpm)
Range	1,440 km	(783 nm, 900 miles)
Weights		
Max takeoff	1,814 kg	(4,000 lbs)
Useful load	686 kg	(1,513 lbs)

De Havilland DH.90 Dragonfly — UK

Externally resembling the Dragon Rapide, the five-seat Dragonfly was a smaller aircraft aimed at private owners requiring a luxury touring aircraft. It was of plywood monocoque construction and was highly streamlined with the minimum of interplane bracing wires and struts and swept tapered wings. Unlike the Rapide it had two forward seats for the pilot and co-pilot with dual controls. The first Dragonfly flew on 12th August 1935 followed by 66 production aircraft many of which were exported to customers in more than 20 countries including France, Australia, Iraq and South Africa. Several Dragonflys were operated on floats by commercial operators in Canada and many Dragonflys were impressed during the war although only a handful survived. Two DH.90s are currently active and another is believed to be under restoration in Australia.

De Havilland DH.94 Moth Minor — UK

Departing from their biplane tradition, de Havilland designed the Moth Minor low-wing trainer to compete with the Miles Hawk which was achieving success in the early 1930s. The Moth Minor was built of plywood and spruce in traditional de Havilland style and had a fixed tailwheel undercarriage and tandem open cockpits with dual controls. The wing was a new design with high aspect ratio and it could be folded back against the fuselage sides for storage. The aircraft was also fitted with a perforated flap which extended below the centre section. The first Moth Minor was flown on 22nd June 1937 powered by a 90 h.p. Gipsy Minor in-line engine. A total of 114 Moth Minors were built, nearly half of which were completed in Australia. Some were modified as Moth Minor Coupés with an enclosed cabin. Six Moth Minors are operational in the UK and others are flyable in the United States, Australia and New Zealand.

De Havilland DH.94 Moth Minor (Cont.)

De Havilland DH.94 Moth Minor, N9403

Specification	De Havilland DH.94 Moth Minor	
Powerplant	One 80 h.p. (59.65 kW) de Havilland Gipsy Minor piston engine	
Dimensions		
Span	11.15 m	(36 ft 7 in)
Length	7.44 m	(24 ft 5 in)
Height	1.93 m	(6 ft 4 in)
Performance		
Max speed	189 km/h	(103 kt, 118 mph)
Cruising speed	160 km/h	(87 kt, 100 mph)
Initial climb	180 m/min	(590 fpm)
Range	480 km	(261 nm, 300 miles)
Weights		
Max takeoff	703 kg	(1,550 lbs)
Useful load	268 kg	(590 lbs)

De Havilland DH.115 Vampire T.11, ZK-RVM

Specification	De Havilland DH.115 Vampire Trainer T Mk.11	
Powerplant	One 3,500 lb.s.t. (15.57 kN) de Havilland Goblin 35 turbojet	
Dimensions		
Span	11.58 m	(38 ft 0 in)
Length	10.52 m	(34 ft 6 in)
Height	1.88 m	(6 ft 2 in)
Performance		
Max speed	861 km/h	(468 kt, 538 mph)
Cruising speed	768 km/h	(417 kt, 480 mph)
Initial climb	1,372 m/min	(4,500 fpm)
Range	1,344 km	(730 nm, 840 miles)
Weights		
Max takeoff	5,057 kg	(11,150 lbs)
Useful load	1,710 kg	(3,770 lbs)

De Havilland DH.100 Vampire and DH.115 Vampire Trainer — UK

The Vampire was the first British single-seat jet fighter and was of unusual layout with a small pod fuselage built of plywood, containing the cockpit section and the de Havilland Goblin engine and twin booms carrying the fins and tailplane. Air intakes were buried in the wing roots and the Vampire had a retractable tricycle undercarriage. The first flight was on 20th September 1943 and 244 Vampire F.1s were built followed by the Vampire F.3 with redesigned tailfins and the FB.5 (exported as the FB.52 etc.) and FB.6 fighter bomber version with underwing strongpoints. It was also built in France by Sud Est as the Mistral and in India, Italy and Switzerland. The Vampire T.11 was a side-by-side two-seat trainer 921 of which were built. Exports were made to Australia, Austria, Venezuela, Sweden, Canada and Mexico. Total Vampire production was 4,342 aircraft and a number of single-and two-seat aircraft are flying with private owners in Britain and Europe.

De Havilland DH.104 Dove — UK

One of the products of the postwar development of passenger airliners was the DH.104 Dove which was designed as a light feeder liner and first flew on 25th September 1945. It was an all-metal aircraft with a retractable undercarriage and a separate flight deck and a main cabin capable of carrying up to ten passengers. De Havilland were very successful in selling the Dove 1 for airline use and the Dove 2 for executive operations and the Dove was exported widely including a number delivered to the United States. The RAF bought 95 as the Devon C.1 and 33 went to the Royal Navy as the Sea Devon C.20 fitted with larger 380 h.p. Gipsy Queen 70-2 engines. The Dove 6 was an executive version with the larger engines and the Dove 7 and Dove 8 had a deeper cockpit with a domed roof. A number of Doves were converted by Riley Aeronautics and McAlpine Aviation with Lycoming IO-540 engines. In total, 542 Doves were built between 1946 and 1957 and over 50 remain although only half are airworthy.

De Havilland DH.104 Dove 7, JY-RJU

Specification	De Havilland DH.104 Dove 8	
Powerplant	Two 400 h.p. (298 kW) de Havilland Gipsy Queen 70 Mk.3 piston engines	
Dimensions		
Span	17.4 m	(57 ft 0 in)
Length	11.96 m	(39 ft 3 in)
Height	4.06 m	(13 ft 4 in)
Performance		
Max speed	368 km/h	(200 kt, 230 mph)
Cruising speed	336 km/h	(183 kt, 210 mph)
Initial climb	433 m/min	(1,420 fpm)
Range	1,408 km	(765 nm, 880 miles)
Weights		
Max takeoff	4,059 kg	(8,950 lbs)
Useful load	1,393 kg	(3,072 lbs)

De Havilland DH.114 Heron 2, G-AORG

De Havilland DH.114 Heron — UK

The DH.114 Heron was, essentially, an enlarged version of the successful Dove light feeder liner. De Havilland stretched the fuselage, lengthened the wings and fitted four engines and marketed the Heron to commercial operators with up to 17 passenger seats. The early Heron 1 had a fixed tricycle undercarriage but the majority were Heron 2s with retractable gear as used on the Dove. Some 149 Herons were delivered between 1952 and 1964 and used by airlines such as Braathens, Garuda and Jersey Airlines and in military service by Jordan, Malaysia and the RAF Queens Flight (Heron 3). Among Herons sold to the United States, many were re-engined with 290 h.p. Lycoming IO-540 engines by Riley Aeronautics Corporation. Other more radical conversions included the stretched twin turboprop Saunders ST-27 and Carstedt CJ600A. Few Herons remain in service although one flies in the UK and two in Australia.

Specification	De Havilland DH.114 Heron 2C	
Powerplant	Four 250 h.p. (186 kW) de Havilland Gipsy Queen 30 Mk.2 piston engines	
Dimensions		
Span	21.8 m	(71 ft 6 in)
Length	14.8 m	(48 ft 6 in)
Height	4.75 m	(15 ft 7 in)
Performance		
Max speed	320 km/h	(174 kt, 200 mph)
Cruising speed	288 km/h	(157 kt, 180 mph)
Initial climb	328 m/min	(1,075 fpm)
Range	2,480 km	(1,348 nm, 1,550 miles)
Weights		
Max takeoff	6,122 kg	(13,500 lbs)
Useful load	2,267 kg	(5,000 lbs)

De Havilland DH.112 Venom — UK

De Havilland developed the Venom as a logical upgrade of the single-seat Vampire with a redesigned wing of thinner section and a swept leading edge and straight trailing edge. It was fitted with the larger DH Ghost turbojet engine and had jettisonable wingtip fuel tanks in addition to long-range tanks which could be mounted on the underwing pylons. The Venom first flew on 2nd September 1949 and the initial production FB.1 was replaced by the FB.4 which had redesigned vertical tail surfaces. A total of 250 Venom FB.50s were built by FFA in Switzerland and other export countries included Iraq, Venezuela, Sweden and France. Many of the Swiss Venoms were sold to private owners in the 1980s and 11 appear on the British register. The Sea Venom FAW.22 and Venom NF.3 were side-by-side two-seat all-weather fighter variants for the Royal Navy and RAF and one is airworthy in the USA. A total of 1,143 Venoms were built including 479 two-seaters.

De Havilland (FFA) Venom FB.50, G-GONE

Specification	De Havilland DH.112 Venom FB.50	
Powerplant	One 4,850 lb.s.t. (21.58 kN) de Havilland Ghost 103 turbojet	
Dimensions		
Span	12.7 m	(41 ft 8 in)
Length	9.7 m	(31 ft 10 in)
Height	1.88 m	(6 ft 2 in)
Performance		
Max speed	1,024 km/h	(557 kt, 640 mph)
Cruising speed	832 km/h	(452 kt, 520 mph)
Initial climb	2,743 m/min	(9,000 fpm)
Range	1,720 km	(935 nm, 1,075 miles)
Weights		
Max takeoff	6,943 kg	(15,310 lbs)
Useful load	2,770 kg	(6,108 lbs)

De Havilland DHA-3 Drover — Australia

The Australian company de Havilland Aircraft Pty. Ltd. ('DHA') designed the DHA-3 Drover utility aircraft for use by the Royal Flying Doctor Service and the prototype Drover made its first flight on 23rd January 1948. It was a six-/eight-seat low-wing aircraft which embodied much of the design philosophy of the DH.104 Dove. The Drover 1 had a fixed tailwheel undercarriage and three 145 h.p. Gipsy Major 10/2 piston engines with variable-pitch metal propellers while the Drover 1F had fixed-pitch propellers. Between 1950 and 1954 a total of 20 Drovers were built including five Drover 2s with double-slotted flaps. In the 1960s a number of Drovers, notably those used by the RFDS, were re-engined with 180 h.p. Lycoming O-360-A1A flat-four piston engines and redesignated Drover Mk.3. Several Drovers remain in existence in Australia.

De Havilland DHA-3 Drover 3, VH-FBC

Specification	De Havilland Australia DHA-3 Drover Mk.3	
Powerplant	Three 180 h.p. (134.2 kW) Textron Lycoming O-360-A1A piston engines	
Dimensions		
Span	17.37 m	(57 ft 0 in)
Length	11.12 m	(36 ft 6 in)
Height	3.28 m	(10 ft 9 in)
Performance		
Max speed	253 km/h	(137 kt, 158 mph)
Cruising speed	224 km/h	(122 kt, 140 mph)
Initial climb	317 m/min	(1,040 fpm)
Range	1,440 km	(782 nm, 900 miles)
Weights		
Max takeoff	2,948 kg	(6,500 lbs)
Useful load	862 kg	(1,900 lbs)

De Havilland DHC-1 Chipmunk — Canada/UK

The DHC-1 Chipmunk trainer was designed by the de Havilland Aircraft of Canada and first flown on 22nd May 1946. Intended as a modern primary trainer for the Royal Canadian Air Force it had a low-wing, fixed tailwheel undercarriage and tandem two-seat cockpit enclosed with a bubble canopy. While 217 were completed in Canada the main production was carried out in Britain where the parent de Havilland company built 1,000, mainly T.Mk.10 and T.Mk.20 for the RAF. These had a framed cockpit instead of the bubble of the Canadian version. Some 66 further aircraft were built in Portugal by OGMA. Chipmunks were exported to the air forces of Egypt, Syria, Eire, Ceylon and Burma among others. Many civilianised Chipmunks are currently flying together with some civil Mk.21s and 22s and a few of the Mk.23 crop-spraying single-seat version. Over 140 are operational in the UK and both British- and Canadian-built examples fly in North America.

De Havilland Canada DHC-1 Chipmunk, N950CK

Specification	De Havilland DHC-1 Chipmunk Mk.22	
Powerplant	One 145 h.p. (108.1 kW) de Havilland Gipsy Major 10 Mk.2 piston engine	
Dimensions		
Span	10.46 m	(34 ft 4 in)
Length	7.82 m	(25 ft 8 in)
Height	2.16 m	(7 ft 1 in)
Performance		
Max speed	221 km/h	(120 kt, 138 mph)
Cruising speed	190 km/h	(103 kt, 119 mph)
Initial climb	256 m/min	(840 fpm)
Range	448 km	(243 nm, 280 miles)
Weights		
Max takeoff	913 kg	(2,014 lbs)
Useful load	268 kg	(590 lbs)

De Havilland DHC-2 Beaver — Canada

The Beaver is one of the most respected bush aircraft and it is still the standard workhorse in Canada and Alaska with many further examples flying elsewhere around the world. It was designed by the de Havilland Aircraft of Canada and first flew on 16th August 1947. An all-metal aircraft, it has a square-section fuselage with large main cabin doors, a strut-braced high wing and fixed tailwheel undercarriage. The standard powerplant is the 450 h.p. Pratt & Whitney Wasp radial but 60 were completed as Turbo Beavers with the 578 s.h.p. Pratt & Whitney PT6A-6 turboprop. Some 970 Beavers were delivered to the US Army and USAF as the L-20 out of a production total of 1,692, and many of these have been civilianised. The Beaver can be operated on wheels, floats or skis and has been used for crop spraying, parachute dropping, forestry patrol and as a transport for up to seven passengers.

De Havilland DHC-2 Beaver floatplane, N67672

Specification	De Havilland Canada DHC-2 Mk.1 Beaver	
Powerplant	One 450 h.p. (335.5 kW) Pratt & Whitney Wasp R-985-AN-1 piston engine	
Dimensions		
Span	14.63 m	(48 ft 0 in)
Length	9.22 m	(30 ft 3 in)
Height	2.74 m	(9 ft 0 in)
Performance		
Max speed	262 km/h	(143 kt, 164 mph)
Cruising speed	224 km/h	(122 kt, 140 mph)
Initial climb	312 m/min	(1,025 fpm)
Range	720 km	(391 nm, 450 miles)
Weights		
Max takeoff	2,313 kg	(5,100 lbs)
Useful load	1,020 kg	(2,250 lbs)

De Havilland DHC-3 Otter — Canada

The success of the Beaver led de Havilland Canada to produce a larger scaled-up 14-passenger variant designated DHC-3 Otter. Once again, this proved to be attractive to the United States Army who acquired 190 as the U-1 and to the US Navy who purchased 16 UC-1s. The Otter first flew, powered by a 600 h.p. Pratt & Whitney R-1340 radial, on 21st December 1951 and 465 were completed. As with the Beaver, these were often operated on floats and were widely used by small airlines operating into remote locations carrying mixed loads of passengers and cargo. The Otter was also a good candidate for conversion to turboprop power and the DHC-3T conversion with a PT6A-27 has been carried out on a number of airframes. Other Otters have been converted to the Polish PZL.3S radial piston engine. Over 200 Otters remain in service worldwide.

De Havilland DHC-3 Otter, C-FSOR

De Havilland DHC-3 Otter (Cont.)

Specification	De Havilland Canada DHC-3 Otter	
Powerplant	One 600 h.p. (447.4 kW) Pratt & Whitney R-1340-S1H1-G piston engine	
Dimensions		
Span	17.69 m	(58 ft 0 in)
Length	12.75 m	(41 ft 10 in)
Height	3.83 m	(12 ft 7 in)
Performance		
Max speed	256 km/h	(139 kt, 160 mph)
Cruising speed	220 km/h	(120 kt, 138 mph)
Initial climb	260 m/min	(850 fpm)
Range	1,400 km	(761 nm, 875 miles)
Weights		
Max takeoff	3,628 kg	(8,000 lbs)
Useful load	1,619 kg	(3,570 lbs)

De Havilland DHC-5 Buffalo, 322 (Peruvian AF)

De Havilland DHC-4 Caribou and DHC-5 Buffalo — Canada

A United States Army requirement for a tactical transport with rear-loading capability resulted in de Havilland Canada producing the DHC-4 Caribou STOL transport. This had a high wing with an anhedralled centre section allowing unobstructed space in the square-section fuselage, a retractable tricycle undercarriage, an upswept rear fuselage incorporating a ventral loading ramp and a cruciform tail. It was powered by a pair of Pratt & Whitney R-2000 radial piston engines and the first flight was on 30th July 1958. Of the 253 built, 165 were built for the US Army as the CV-2A and others sold to Australia, Malaysia, India etc. The DHC-5 Buffalo which flew on 9th April 1964, was a developed Caribou with General Electric T64 turboprops and a T-tail. Only 126 Buffalos were built and the type was evaluated (as the CV-7A) but not adopted by the US Army although military sales were made to Canada, Brazil, Kenya and Peru.

De Havilland DHC-4 Caribou, N1017H

Specification	De Havilland DHC-4 Caribou	
Powerplant	Two 1,450 h.p. (1,081.1 kW) Pratt & Whitney R-2000-7M2 piston engines	
Dimensions		
Span	29.15 m	(95 ft 7 in)
Length	22.13 m	(72 ft 7 in)
Height	9.7 m	(31 ft 9 in)
Performance		
Max speed	346 km/h	(188 kt, 216 mph)
Cruising speed	288 km/h	(156 kt, 180 mph)
Initial climb	413 m/min	(1,355 fpm)
Range	2,080 km	(1,130 nm, 1,300 miles)
Weights		
Max takeoff	12,925 kg	(28,500 lbs)
Useful load	4,644 kg	(10,240 lbs)

De Havilland DHC-6 Twin Otter — Canada

The Twin Otter was designed by de Havilland Canada in response to the expansion of commuter airline operations in the mid-1960s. It was based on the strut-braced high-wing Otter but with a longer 19-passenger fuselage and a fixed tricycle undercarriage. The DHC-6 was powered by a pair of Pratt & Whitney PT6A-6 turboprops mounted on the inboard sections of the wing. The prototype flew on 20th May 1965 with production of the Series 100 starting shortly after. The Series 200 had a longer nose, increased baggage capacity and larger PT6A-20A engines. A number were sold to military users including Argentina, Norway and Paraguay. The Series 300 was further improved with PT6A-27 engines. DHC built a total of 844 Twin Otters and production ceased in 1988. More than half of these are in current operation around the world and some are operated on floats.

De Havilland DHC-6 Twin Otter 300, YV-526C

Specification	De Havilland Canada DHC-6 Srs.300 Twin Otter	
Powerplant	Two 652 s.h.p. (486.1 kW) Pratt & Whitney PT6A-27 turboprops	
Dimensions		
Span	19.81 m	(65 ft 0 in)
Length	15.77 m	(51 ft 9 in)
Height	5.66 m	(18 ft 7 in)
Performance		
Max speed	336 km/h	(183 kt, 210 mph)
Cruising speed	320 km/h	(174 kt, 200 mph)
Initial climb	488 m/min	(1,600 fpm)
Range	1,512 km	(822 nm, 945 miles)
Weights		
Max takeoff	5,669 kg	(12,500 lbs)
Useful load	2,494 kg	(5,500 lbs)

De Havilland DHC-7 Dash-Seven — Canada

The Dash-seven is a high-wing STOL commuter airliner developed to give increased capacity to existing Twin Otter operators. First flown on 27th March 1975 it was powered by four of the reliable PT6A turboprops and had accommodation for 48 passengers. It was primarily produced as the Series 100 passenger model but a few Series 101 freighters were also built. Total production was 113 aircraft and over 90 are currently active. Production was completed in 1988. Early deliveries were made to Rocky Mountain Airways and Golden West Airlines in California and the DHC-7 was also notable for being the only aircraft initially authorised to operate into the new London City Airport. Other large Dash-Seven users have included Arkia in Israel and Petroleum Air Services. Several are operating with military users including the Venezuelan Navy and the United States Army, who have a fleet of seven RC-7 reconnaissance aircraft.

De Havilland DHC-7 Dash Seven, 4X-AHD

Specification	De Havilland Canada DHC-7 Dash Seven	
Powerplant	Four 1,120 s.h.p. (835 kW) Pratt & Whitney PT6A-50 turboprops	
Dimensions		
Span	28.35 m	(93 ft 0 in)
Length	24.58 m	(80 ft 8 in)
Height	7.98 m	(26 ft 2 in)
Performance		
Max speed	448 km/h	(243 kt, 280 mph)
Cruising speed	424 km/h	(230 kt, 265 mph)
Initial climb	400 m/min	(1,310 fpm)
Range	2,280 km	(1,239 nm, 1,425 miles)
Weights		
Max takeoff	19,500 kg	(43,000 lbs)
Useful load	7,773 kg	(17,140 lbs)

De Havilland DHC-8 Dash-Eight — Canada

The established reputation of de Havilland Canada led to a completely new turboprop commuter design which could be developed into a family of local service airliners. The DHC-8 followed earlier DHC design philosophy with its high wing and T-tail and the first 40-passenger DHC-8-100 first flew on 20th June 1983. It was immediately successful with the Canadian regional operators and the feeder airlines for the American trunk operators. The DHC-8-200 had a higher gross weight and 2,150 s.h.p. PW123C engines and the DHC-8-300, which first flew on 15th May 1987, had a 56-passenger stretched fuselage and increased power. The DHC-8-400 is a further stretched variant first flown on 31st January 1998 which has a maximum 78-seat capacity. The Dash-Eight variants, now built by Bombardier Regional Aircraft, are all sold in Dash-Eight Q configuration fitted with an active noise suppression system. Over 550 DHC-8s are in current service.

De Havilland DHC-8 Srs.100, V2-LCX

De Havilland DHC-8 Dash-Eight (Cont.)

De Havilland DHC-8 Srs.400

Specification	De Havilland DHC-8-300A Dash-Eight	
Powerplant	Two 2,380 s.h.p. (1,775 kW) Pratt & Whitney PW123 turboprops	
Dimensions		
Span	27.43 m	(90 ft 0 in)
Length	25.68 m	(84 ft 3 in)
Height	7.49 m	(24 ft 7 in)
Performance		
Max speed	528 km/h	(287 kt, 330 mph)
Cruising speed	480 km/h	(260 kt, 300 mph)
Initial climb	549 m/min	(1,800 fpm)
Range	1,520 km	(826 nm, 950 miles)
Weights		
Max takeoff	18,639 kg	(41,100 lbs)
Useful load	6,975 kg	(15,380 lbs)

Specification	Denel AH-2A Rooivalk (Red Hawk)	
Powerplant	Two 1,845 s.h.p. (1,376 kW) Turboméca Makila 1K2 turboshafts	
Dimensions		
Rotor diameter	15.58 m	(51 ft 1 in)
Length	16.39 m	(53 ft 9 in)
Height	5.18 m	(17 ft 0 in)
Performance		
Max speed	272 km/h	(148 kt, 170 mph)
Cruising speed	256 km/h	(139 kt, 160 mph)
Initial climb	610 m/min	(2,000 fpm)
Range	760 km	(413 nm, 475 miles)
Weights		
Max takeoff	8,748 kg	(19,290 lbs)
Useful load	3,020 kg	(6,660 lbs)

Denel Rooivalk (Red Hawk) — South Africa

Atlas Aircraft flew the first prototype XH-2 (later CSH-2) Rooivalk on 11th February 1990. It is a tandem two-seater gunship and anti-tank helicopter with a tailwheel undercarriage and a four-blade main rotor and conventional five-blade tail rotor. It is powered by two Denel-built Topaz turboshafts derived from the Turboméca Makila 1K2 and rated at 1,845 s.h.p. with dynamic systems from the Eurocopter/Aérospatiale Puma. The definitive AH-2A Rooivalk is equipped with an advanced cockpit with a helmet-mounted night vision system and is fitted with a variety of infrared suppression shrouds. It has stub wings each with two hardpoints to carry Matra-BAe Mistral infrared guided missiles and a chin-mounted gun. An initial batch of 12 production machines for the SAAF was commenced in 1998.

Denel Rooivalk, ZU-AHC

Dewoitine (EKW) D-26 — Switzerland

Emile Dewoitine was a noted pre-war designer of fighter monoplanes commencing with the Dewoitine D-1 of 1922 and progressing to the D-37 series produced in the mid-1930s. The D-26 was a single seat fighter trainer developed in 1931. It had a parasol wing, fixed tailwheel undercarriage and an open single-seat cockpit and closely resembled the D-27 fighter which was built in Switzerland by EKW for the Swiss Air Force. Eleven D-26s were built and these served with the Swiss Air Force from 1931 to 1948 at which time the survivors were handed over to Swiss gliding clubs as tugs. Most of these were powered by a 250 h.p. Wright 9Qa radial engine but the last two aircraft had an improved 300 h.p. Wright 9Qc. Four airworthy aircraft remain in Switzerland, France, the UK and in the USA, the American example using a Jacobs engine.

Dewoitine D-26, N282DW

Specification	Dewoitine D.26	
Powerplant	One 250 h.p. (186.4 kW) Wright 9Qa piston engine	
Dimensions		
Span	10.29 m	(33 ft 9 in)
Length	6.55 m	(21 ft 6 in)
Height	2.77 m	(9 ft 1 in)
Performance		
Max speed	240 km/h	(130 kt 149 mph)
Cruising speed	169 km/h	(96 kt 105 mph)
Initial climb	320 m/min	(1,050 fpm)
Range	300 km	(162 nm 186 miles)
Weights		
Max takeoff	1,070 kg	(2,359 lbs)
Useful load	760 kg	(1,675 lbs)

Diamond Aircraft Dimona — Austria

The Hoffman H-36 Dimona is one of the most successful developments in the motor glider field. The prototype Dimona was built by Hoffman Flugzeugbau (later HOAC) and first flown on 9th October 1980 with production following in 1981. It is a glass-fibre aircraft with side-by-side dual seating, a T-tail and a fixed glass-fibre tailwheel undercarriage. It was powered by an 80 h.p. Limbach SL2000-EB1 engine. HOAC (now Diamond Aircraft) replaced the standard Dimona by the redesigned HK36R Super Dimona certificated to JAR-22 which had an 80 h.p. Rotax 912A3 engine, a new cowling, strengthened undercarriage, single-piece cockpit canopy etc. The later Super Dimona HK36-TTS has a turbocharged Rotax 914F3 engine and is fitted with glider-towing equipment. Equivalent versions with tricycle gear are the Super Dimona HK36-TC and Super Dimona HK36-TTC. Under Diamond Aircraft the standard and turbocharged models are named Katana Xtreme (HK36TS) and Turbo Xtreme (HK36TC). Over 690 of the H-36 series have been built.

HOAC H-36 Dimona, OY-XNO

Specification	Diamond Katana Xtreme HK36TTS	
Powerplant	One 115 h.p. (85.74 kW) Bombardier Rotax 914F piston engine	
Dimensions		
Span	16.61 m	(54 ft 6 in)
Length	7.16 m	(23 ft 6 in)
Height	1.75 m	(5 ft 9 in)
Performance		
Max speed	239 km/h	(130 kt, 149 mph)
Cruising speed	221 km/h	(120 kt, 138 mph)
Initial climb	366 m/min	(1,200 fpm)
Range	928 km	(504 nm, 580 miles)
Weights		
Max takeoff	770 kg	(1,698 lbs)
Useful load	231 kg	(510 lbs)

Diamond Aircraft Katana — Canada

On 16th March 1991, HOAC (now Diamond Aircraft) flew the prototype LF.2000 Turbo which was a lightweight short-wing derivative of the Super Dimona. Certificated under JAR-VLA rules, it was redesignated DV20 Katana. It had a lower gross weight than the Dimona, a tricycle undercarriage and a broader vertical tail. It retained the 80 h.p. Rotax 912A3 engine with a hydraulic constant-speed propeller and production commenced in March 1993. Production was transferred to Canada in 1994 where Diamond Aircraft built the DA20-A1 Katana which featured a new instrument panel, revised seating, landing lights and upturned wingtips. It was replaced by the DA20-C1 which has a Teledyne Continental IO-240B and slotted flaps and Diamond also sell the DV20 Katana 100 which has a 100 h.p. Rotax 912S. A further development was the high-performance DV22 Speed Katana Turbo which was first flown in 1996 powered by a 115 h.p. turbocharged Rotax 914F engine but this was not built in quantity. Over 580 Katanas had been completed by mid-2000.

Diamond DV20 Katana, G-BWFI

Diamond Aircraft Katana (Cont.)

Specification	Diamond Aircraft Katana DA20-C1	
Powerplant	One 125 h.p. (93.2 kW) Teledyne Continental IO-240B piston engine	
Dimensions		
Span	10.87 m	(35 ft 8 in)
Length	7.16 m	(23 ft 6 in)
Height	2.18 m	(7 ft 2 in)
Performance		
Max speed	276 km/h	(150 kt, 172 mph)
Cruising speed	243 km/h	(132 kt, 152 mph)
Initial climb	337 m/min	(1,105 fpm)
Range	962 km	(523 nm, 601 miles)
Weights		
Max takeoff	750 kg	(1,653 lbs)
Useful load	451 kg	(996 lbs)

Diamond Aircraft DA40 Diamond Star — Austria

Following on from its successful DA20 Katana, Diamond Aircraft has developed a larger four-seat aircraft designated DA40-180 Diamond Star. The DA40, which first flew in 1998, is constructed from the same composite materials as the Katana and has the same general low-wing layout with a T-tail and a fixed tricycle undercarriage. It is intended as a private-owner and club-touring aircraft with good cruise performance and fuel economy and is powered by a 180 h.p. Textron Lycoming engine. First deliveries are scheduled for early 2001 following JAR23/FAR23 certification.

Diamond DA40-180 Diamond Star, OE-VPC

Specification	Diamond Diamond Star DA40-180	
Powerplant	One 180 h.p. (134.2 kW) Textron Lycoming IO-360-M1A piston engine	
Dimensions		
Span	12 m	(39 ft 5 in)
Length	8.01 m	(26 ft 4 in)
Height	2 m	(6 ft 7 in)
Performance		
Max speed	285 km/h	(155 kt, 178 mph)
Cruising speed	270 km/h	(147 kt, 169 mph)
Initial climb	168 m/min	(550 fpm)
Range	1,288 km	(700 nm, 805 miles)
Weights		
Max takeoff	1,150 kg	(2,535 lbs)
Useful load	450 kg	(992 lbs)

Dinfia Ranquel — Argentina

On 23rd December 1957, the state-owned Argentine company Dinfia flew the prototype IA.46 Ranquel light aircraft. This was a fairly conventional strut-braced high-wing tube and fabric aircraft with a forward pilot's seat and a rear bench seat for two passengers. It was built for use by national flying clubs and intended for general club flying and glider towing and also for crop spraying. The Ranquel went into production in 1958 at Cordoba, powered by a 150 h.p. Lycoming O-320-A2B engine. For crop spraying it used an external 107 USG spray tank. The Super Ranquel was similar, but had a more powerful 180 h.p. Lycoming O-360-A1A engine. A subsequent development was the IA.51 Tehuelche which was a developed Super Ranquel with metal covering to the wings, larger flaps and agricultural load capacity raised to 110 imperial gallons. The prototype of this variant first flew on 16th March 1963. Over 220 of the Ranquel series were built and a number served in the Fuerza Aerea Argentina as glider tugs.

Dinfia IA.46 Super Ranquel

Specification	Dinfia IA.46 Super Ranquel	
Powerplant	One 180 h.p. (134.2 kW) Textron Lycoming O-360-A1A piston engine	
Dimensions		
Span	11.58 m	(38 ft 0 in)
Length	7.44 m	(24 ft 5 in)
Height	2.13 m	(7 ft 0 in)
Performance		
Max speed	184 km/h	(100 kt, 115 mph)
Cruising speed	168 km/h	(91 kt, 105 mph)
Initial climb	204 m/min	(670 fpm)
Range	640 km	(348 nm, 400 miles)
Weights		
Max takeoff	1,260 kg	(2,778 lbs)
Useful load	626 kg	(1,380 lbs)

Dinfia Guarani II — Argentina

In the early 1960s, the Argentine state company Dinfia produced a batch of IA-35-II Huanquero low-wing military piston-engined transport and crew trainer aircraft. This was further developed with a new ten-seat fuselage and fitted with a pair of 858 s.h.p. Turboméca Bastan III-A turboprops to create the Guarani I. The prototype first flew on 6th February, 1962 followed on 23rd April 1963 by the IA.50 Guarani II which had a shorter rear fuselage, swept single fin/rudder assembly in place of the earlier twin fins, 930 s.h.p. Bastan VI-A turboprops and accommodation for up to 15 passengers. The Guarani G-II could be fitted with supplementary wingtip fuel tanks. The majority of the 41 aircraft built were delivered to the Argentine military establishment, but they have now been retired. Several military aircraft have been transferred to the civil register.

Dinfia Guarani II, T-118 (Argentine AF)

Specification	Dinfia IA.50 Guarani II	
Powerplant	Two 930 s.h.p. (693.41 kW) Turboméca Bastan VI-A turboprops	
Dimensions		
Span	19.53 m	(64 ft 1 in)
Length	14.86 m	(48 ft 9 in)
Height	5.81 m	(19 ft 1 in)
Performance		
Max speed	496 km/h	(270 kt, 310 mph)
Cruising speed	480 km/h	(261 kt, 300 mph)
Initial climb	805 m/min	(2,640 fpm)
Range	2,560 km	(1,391 nm, 1,600 miles)
Weights		
Max takeoff	7,120 kg	(15,700 lbs)
Useful load	3,197 kg	(7,050 lbs)

Dornier Do.27 — Germany

Originally designed in Spain as the Do.25 by Prof. Claudius Dornier, the Do.27 is a light military utility aircraft designed for light transport and army cooperation tasks. It is a high-wing all-metal monoplane with a cantilever wing and a tailwheel undercarriage. In standard form it has a four-seat main cabin and two forward crew-seats. The Spanish prototype first flew at the CASA plant on 25th June 1954 and CASA built 50 Do.27s for military use. However, the main production line was in Germany where 428 examples of the Do.27A and Do.27B were built for the West German Air Force. The civil version, 65 of which were built, was the Do.27Q and export military versions were the Do.27H, Do.27J and Do.27K. Foreign military sales were made to Belgium, Switzerland and Portugal. Most of the military aircraft have now been retired but many are operating with private owners around the world and are popular with parachute clubs.

Dornier Do.27A-1, N21KM

Specification	Dornier Do.27Q-5	
Powerplant	One 270 h.p. (201.3 kW) Textron Lycoming GO-480-B piston engine	
Dimensions		
Span	11.99 m	(39 ft 4 in)
Length	9.6 m	(31 ft 6 in)
Height	2.8 m	(9 ft 2 in)
Performance		
Max speed	208 km/h	(113 kt, 130 mph)
Cruising speed	176 km/h	(96 kt, 110 mph)
Initial climb	198 m/min	(650 fpm)
Range	1,096 km	(596 nm, 685 miles)
Weights		
Max takeoff	1,846 kg	(4,070 lbs)
Useful load	717 kg	(1,580 lbs)

Dornier Do.28 and Do.28D Skyservant — Germany

On 29th April 1959 Dornier flew the prototype Do.28 which used the fuselage and wings of the Do.27 with the single engine replaced by two 180 h.p. Lycoming O-360 engines mounted on a beam in the nose. The Do.28 had a new fully faired fixed undercarriage attached to the engine nacelles. The production Do.28, 121 of which were built, was fitted with 250 h.p. Lycoming O-540 (Do.28A) or 290 h.p. Lycoming IO-540 engines (Do.28B). Most were sold to civil users but a large batch of around 40 aircraft went to the Israeli Air Force. Dornier subsequently did a major redesign to create the Do.28D Skyservant which was larger and had a completely new box-section fuselage with large freight doors, an enlarged tail and two 380 h.p. Lycoming IGSO-540 engines. This first flew on 23rd February 1966 and was built in quantity for the West German Air Force as the Do.28D and stretched Do.28D-2. A total of 233 Do.28Ds were completed and many have been civilianised and continue in operation.

Dornier Do.28 and Do.28D Skyservant (Cont.)

Dornier Do.28, ZS-JCI

Dornier Do.28D Skyservant, HA-ACP

Specification	Dornier Do.28D-2 Skyservant	
Powerplant	Two 380 h.p. (283.3 kW) Textron Lycoming IGSO-540 piston engines	
Dimensions		
Span	15.5 m	(50 ft 10 in)
Length	11.4 m	(37 ft 5 in)
Height	3.9 m	(12 ft 10 in)
Performance		
Max speed	320 km/h	(174 kt, 200 mph)
Cruising speed	286 km/h	(156 kt, 179 mph)
Initial climb	360 m/min	(1,180 fpm)
Range	1,824 km	(991 nm, 1,140 miles)
Weights		
Max takeoff	3,651 kg	(8,050 lbs)
Useful load	1,485 kg	(3,275 lbs)

Douglas DC-3, C-47 and Super DC-3 — USA

Without any doubt, the DC-3 is the most famous air transport ever built. First flown on 22nd December 1935, the DC-3 was developed from the DC-2, two of which remain active in the USA, and was an all-metal low-wing aircraft of very rugged construction with a retractable tailwheel undercarriage, a large freight door and accommodation for up to 28 passengers. Initially, it was produced as the DST (Douglas Sleeper Transport) for civil airline use but the bulk of production was military. It was built for wartime USAAF service named Skytrain and Dakota with designations from C-47 to C-53, and as the US Navy R4D. The DC-3A had 1,050 h.p. Pratt & Whitney R-1830-SC-G engines, the DC-3B had 1,100 h.p. GR-1820-G102A engines and the DC-3C, which was equivalent to the C-47, had 1,200 h.p. R-1830-92s. Over 13,000 were built including Russian Lisunov LI-2s and Japanese Mitsubishi 'Tabbys'. The DC-3/C-47 served with practically every major postwar airline and air force around the world and is famed for its strength and durability. Large numbers remain in service with civil and military operators and some have been converted to Pratt & Whitney PT6A turboprop power by Basler Turbo Conversions Inc. The Super DC-3 was a postwar variant with a 39-inch fuselage stretch, an enlarged square vertical tail and 1,450 h.p. Pratt & Whitney R-2000-D7 engines. Existing aircraft were converted to this standard as R4D-8 (C-117A) for the US Navy.

Douglas C-47A Dakota 4, G-DAKK

Douglas R4D-8 Super Dakota, FAC-1632 (Colombian AF)

Specification	Douglas DC-3A	
Powerplant	Two 1,000 h.p. (745.6 kW) Pratt & Whitney R-1830-S1CG piston engines	
Dimensions		
Span	28.95 m	(95 ft 0 in)
Length	19.66 m	(64 ft 6 in)
Height	5.16 m	(16 ft 11 in)
Performance		
Max speed	368 km/h	(200 kt, 230 mph)
Cruising speed	317 km/h	(172 kt, 198 mph)
Initial climb	344 m/min	(1,130 fpm)
Range	3,200 km	(1,739 nm, 2,000 miles)
Weights		
Max takeoff	11,428 kg	(25,200 lbs)
Useful load	3,780 kg	(8,335 lbs)

Douglas DC-4 and C-54 Skymaster — USA

Although conceived as a civil transport, the DC-4, which first flew on 14th February 1942, first entered production as the medium-/long-range military C-54 (US Navy R5D) freight and passenger transport. It was a low-wing all-metal aircraft, notable for its retractable tricycle undercarriage, and was powered by four 1,100 h.p. Pratt & Whitney R-2000-7 radial engines. As the C-54A for passenger operations it could accommodate up to 50 troops and in freight configuration it could carry 32,000 lbs of cargo which made it ideal for the Berlin Airlift. The postwar DC-4 was built in small numbers for commercial airlines with 44 seats. A total of 1,242 examples of the C-54/DC-4 were completed together with 70 of the Canadair-built C-54M/C-4 North Star with Rolls Royce Merlin 620 engines. DC-4s, most of which are civilianised C-54s, still operate in small numbers with freight companies in the Americas and the Far East and preserved examples fly in South Africa and Holland.

Douglas DC-4-1009, ZS-BMH

Specification	Douglas C-54A Skymaster	
Powerplant	Four 1,100 h.p. (820.16 kW) Pratt & Whitney Twin Wasp R-2000-7 piston engines	
Dimensions		
Span	35.81 m	(117 ft 6 in)
Length	28.6 m	(93 ft 10 in)
Height	8.38 m	(27 ft 6 in)
Performance		
Max speed	424 km/h	(230 kt, 265 mph)
Cruising speed	307 km/h	(167 kt, 192 mph)
Initial climb	206 m/min	(675 fpm)
Range	3,200 km	(1,739 nm, 2,000 miles)
Weights		
Max takeoff	33,107 kg	(73,000 lbs)
Useful load	16,327 kg	(36,000 lbs)

Douglas DC-6 and DC-7 — USA

In the early postwar years US trunk airlines required a larger and faster DC-4 and Douglas produced the improved DC-6. This had a 7 ft 9 in fuselage stretch, a pressurised cabin with square rather than round windows and up to 84 passenger seats. The prototype flew on 29th June 1946 and 702 were built including 167 of the USAF C-118A and US Navy R6D variants. The DC-6B was a DC-6A with a 5 ft fuselage stretch, many of which were used as freighters. The DC-7, flown on 18th May 1953, was a DC-6B with a further 40-inch fuselage stretch and high-density seating for 95 passengers and the DC-7B was a long-range version. The final model was the DC-7C Seven Seas for transatlantic operations with an additional 40-inch fuselage plug, longer-span wings and 3,400 h.p. Wright Turbo Compound R-3350 engines. Some 338 DC-7s were built. A number of DC-6s and DC-7s still serve with cargo airlines and for fire fighting.

Douglas DC-6A, G-APSA

Douglas DC-6 and DC-7 (Cont.)

Specification	Douglas DC-6B	
Powerplant	Four 2,400 h.p. (1,789.4 kW) Pratt & Whitney Double Wasp R-2800-CB16 piston engines	
Dimensions		
Span	35.81 m	(117 ft 6 in)
Length	30.66 m	(100 ft 7 in)
Height	8.86 m	(29 ft 1 in)
Performance		
Max speed	512 km/h	(278 kt, 320 mph)
Cruising speed	480 km/h	(261 kt, 300 mph)
Initial climb	341 m/min	(1,120 fpm)
Range	7,552 km	(4,104 nm, 4,720 miles)
Weights		
Max takeoff	48,526 kg	(107,000 lbs)
Useful load	23,420 kg	(51,643 lbs)

Douglas (McDonnell Douglas) DC-8 — USA

The DC-8 was built to compete with the four-jet Boeing 707 and the prototype was flown on 30th May 1958, entering service with United and Pan Am in 1960. A total of 289 of the basic DC-8 were built covering variants from the DC-8-11 to the DC-8-55 all with the standard fuselage and accommodation for 176 to 189 passengers. Early aircraft had four Pratt & Whitney JT3C-6 turbojets but JT3D-1 turbofans were introduced from the DC-8-51 and gross weights were progressively increased. With the DC-8-61 and later –60 and –70 variants, Douglas (later McDonnell Douglas) stretched the fuselage by 36 ft 8 in to give 259 passenger seats. The DC-8-62 was further stretched by 6 ft 8 in. Many DC-8 variants were built as freighters (e.g. DC-8-61F) or convertible passenger/freighters (e.g. DC-8-54CF) and others converted to freighters after retirement from passenger service. The DC-8-71, –72 and –73 are conversions with four 22,000 lb.s.t. CFM56-2-C1 turbofans. Production of the stretched DC-8s totalled 261. Over 250 DC-8s remain in service.

Douglas DC-8-54F, 3D-AFR

Douglas DC-8-61, CC-CAX

Specification	Douglas DC-8-61	
Powerplant	Four 18,000 lb.s.t. (80.08 kN) Pratt & Whitney JT3D-3B turbofans	
Dimensions		
Span	43.41 m	(142 ft 5 in)
Length	57.1 m	(187 ft 4 in)
Height	13.11 m	(43 ft 0 in)
Performance		
Max speed	928 km/h	(504 kt, 580 mph)
Cruising speed	848 km/h	(461 kt, 530 mph)
Initial climb	692 m/min	(2,270 fpm)
Range	9,160 km	(4,978 nm, 5,725 miles)
Weights		
Max takeoff	147,392 kg	(325,000 lbs)
Useful load	79,864 kg	(176,100 lbs)

Douglas (McDonnell Douglas) DC-9 — USA

The prototype DC-9 was first flown on 25th February 1965 at a time when the Sud Caravelle and the BAC-111 were attracting orders from United States regional and trunk carriers. The DC-9, which flew two years before its eventual arch rival the Boeing 737, was a classic design with a low swept wing, T-tail and twin Pratt & Whitney JT8D-5 turbofans mounted on the rear fuselage. The initial DC-9-11, DC-9-14 and DC-9-15 had high-density seating for 90 passengers but the DC-9-31 had a 15 ft fuselage stretch and 115-passenger capacity. Later -30 series aircraft had increased gross weights and higher-thrust engines and a number were delivered as the C-9 Nightingale to the USAF. Freighter versions were also available (e.g. DC-9-34F) and convertible passenger/freight variants (e.g. DC-9-32CF). The DC-9-41 had an additional 6 ft 2 in fuselage stretch and the DC-9-51 was further lengthened by 8 ft to give 139-seat passenger capacity. In total 975 of the early series DC-9s were built and many remain in service with major trunk carriers.

Douglas DC-9-32, N12508

Specification	Douglas DC-9-32	
Powerplant	Two 15,000 lb.s.t. (66.73 kN) Pratt & Whitney JT8D-11 turbofans	
Dimensions		
Span	28.47 m	(93 ft 5 in)
Length	31.82 m	(104 ft 5 in)
Height	8.38 m	(27 ft 6 in)
Performance		
Max speed	930 km/h	(505 kt, 581 mph)
Cruising speed	904 km/h	(491 kt, 565 mph)
Initial climb	838 m/min	(2,750 fpm)
Range	2,672 km	(1,452 nm, 1,670 miles)
Weights		
Max takeoff	45,351 kg	(100,000 lbs)
Useful load	21,478 kg	(47,360 lbs)

Douglas/McDonnell Douglas MD-80 and Boeing 717 — USA

On 18th October 1979, McDonnell Douglas flew the first DC-9-81 (MD-81) which was a major upgrade of the successful DC-9 airliner. Once again, the fuselage was stretched by 14 ft 3 in to give 172-passenger capacity and other changes included a modified fin with a bulged tip, modified flaps, increased fuel capacity and 18,500 lb.s.t. JT8D-209 turbofans. Further MD-80 variants followed including the shorter 139-seat MD-87 and 158-seat MD-90-30. Some 28 MD-82s were built in China by Shanghai Aviation Industrial Corp. The MD-90 series was an improved MD-80 with two 25,000 lb.s.t. IAE V2528-D5 turbofans. Following the Boeing takeover of McDonnell Douglas in 1997, the 100-seat MD-95 was relaunched as the Boeing 717-200 with the 80-seat Boeing 717-100 and 120-seat Boeing 717-300 also being offered. The Boeing 717-200 differs from earlier variants primarily in having BMW-Rolls Royce BR715 turbofans. Over 1,280 of the MD-80 and MD-90 series had been built by the end of 2000.

Boeing 717, N717XE

McDonnell Douglas MD-81, HB-IUG

Specification	McDonnell Douglas DC-9-83 (MD-83)	
Powerplant	Two 21,000 lb.s.t. (93.42 kN) Pratt & Whitney JT8D-219 turbofans	
Dimensions		
Span	32.87 m	(107 ft 10 in)
Length	45.07 m	(147 ft 10 in)
Height	9.04 m	(29 ft 8 in)
Performance		
Max speed	918 km/h	(500 kt, 574 mph)
Cruising speed	880 km/h	(478 kt, 550 mph)
Takeoff distance	2,553 m	(8,375 ft)
Range	4,608 km	(2,504 nm, 2,880 miles)
Weights		
Max takeoff	72,562 kg	(160,000 lbs)
Useful load	36,009 kg	(79,400 lbs)

Douglas DC-10 and McDonnell Douglas MD-11 — USA

The DC-10 wide-body long-range airliner was designed as a lower-density competitor to the Boeing 747. First flown on 29th August 1970, the 380-seat DC-10 had three General Electric CF6 turbofans mounted on the rear fuselage and lower fin. A total of 138 of the DC-10-10 and DC-10-15 were built for customers such as United and American Airlines. The DC-10-30 and DC-10-40 were long-range versions with higher-thrust CF6-50 series engines, 309 of which were completed. This total included 60 aircraft, based on the convertible DC-10-30CF, sold as the KC-10A Extender tanker to the USAF, and an extended-range DC-10-30ER was also marketed. McDonnell Douglas re-engineered the DC-10 as the MD-11 which flew on 10th January 1990. The MD-11 had an 18 ft 6 in fuselage stretch, modernised flight deck, modified wing with winglets and a 405-passenger interior. It could be powered by Pratt & Whitney PW4460, Rolls Royce Trent or General Electric CF6-80 engines. MD-11 production ceased in 2001 after 200 had been built including some MD-11F freighters.

Douglas DC-10-30CF, T-264 (Netherlands AF)

McDonnell Douglas MD-11, B-2175

Douglas DC-10 and McDonnell Douglas MD-11 (Cont.)

Specification	Douglas DC-10-30ER	
Powerplant	Three 53,200 lb.s.t. (236.67 kN) General Electric CF6-50C2B turbofans	
Dimensions		
Span	50.39 m	(165 ft 4 in)
Length	55.35 m	(181 ft 7 in)
Height	17.7 m	(58 ft 1 in)
Performance		
Max speed	950 km/h	(516 kt, 594 mph)
Cruising speed	918 km/h	(500 kt, 574 mph)
Takeoff distance	3,170 m	(10,400 ft)
Range	9,760 km	(5,304 nm, 6,100 miles)
Weights		
Max takeoff	263,039 kg	(580,000 lbs)
Useful load	141,859 kg	(312,800 lbs)

Douglas SBD Dauntless — USA

The Dauntless was one of the most potent of the World War II naval dive bombers. It had a wide-chord tapered wing with large perforated dive brakes running along the whole wing centre section and a retractable tailwheel undercarriage. Two crew were accommodated under a long framed canopy and the aircraft was fitted with belly and underwing hardpoints for a variety of bombs. It was also equipped with an arrester hook for carrier operations. The SBD prototype first flew on 22nd April 1938 and 5,938 of the SBD-1 to SBD-6 were built during the course of the war, mostly for the US Marine Corps. The different Dauntless variants had progressive improvements but the main production versions were the SBD-3 with a 1,000 h.p. Wright R-1820-52 engine and the SBD-5 with a 1,200 h.p. R-1820-60. Production also included batches of the A-24 for the US Army Air Corps. Today, six examples of the Dauntless, four of which are A-24s, are flying with warbird enthusiasts in the United States. One of these has been recovered from Mexico and the others have been reconstructed from several different airframes.

Douglas SBD-5 Dauntless, NL82GA

Specification	Douglas SBD-5 Dauntless	
Powerplant	One 1,200 h.p. (894.7 kW) Wright R-1820-60 piston engine	
Dimensions		
Span	12.65 m	(41 ft 6 in)
Length	10.09 m	(33 ft 1 in)
Height	3.91 m	(12 ft 10 in)
Performance		
Max speed	408 km/h	(222 kt, 255 mph)
Cruising speed	296 km/h	(161 kt, 185 mph)
Initial climb	518 m/min	(1,700 fpm)
Range	1,784 km	(970 nm, 1,115 miles)
Weights		
Max takeoff	4,244 kg	(9,359 lbs)
Useful load	1,338 kg	(2,950 lbs)

Douglas B-26 Invader — USA

Douglas designed the A-26 attack bomber during the mid-war period as a replacement for the B-25 Mitchell and A-20 Havoc. The A-26, designed by Ed Heinemann, was an elegant mid-wing aircraft with a conventional tail unit, wing-mounted Pratt & Whitney R-2800 radial engines and a generous lower fuselage providing a large bomb bay. The A-26 prototype flew on 10th July 1942 and the production B-26 Invader only just managed to take part in World War II. However, it did distinguish itself in Korea, Indochina, Algeria and in more clandestine theatres of war where its forgiving and adaptable airframe fitted it for conventional bombing, ground attack, night fighting and day and night reconnaissance. Apart from the USAF, users of the B-26 included the French Armée de l'Air and various air forces including those of Cuba, Indonesia, El Salvador and Colombia. Invaders were a popular choice for conversion to executive transports as the On-Mark Marketeer and pressurised On-Mark Marksman, and the On-Mark company also refurbished Invaders for the USAF and other air forces as A-26A Counter Invaders. More than 100 Invaders still exist as warbirds.

Douglas B-26B Invader, N34538

Specification	Douglas A-26B-60-DL (B-26B) Invader	
Powerplant	Two 2,000 h.p. (1,491.2 kW) Pratt & Whitney R-2800-27 piston engines	
Dimensions		
Span	21.34 m	(70 ft 0 in)
Length	15.44 m	(50 ft 8 in)
Height	5.64 m	(18 ft 6 in)
Performance		
Max speed	515 km/h	(280 kt, 322 mph)
Cruising speed	440 km/h	(239 kt, 275 mph)
Initial climb	326 m/min	(1,070 fpm)
Range	2,688 km	(1,461 nm, 1,680 miles)
Weights		
Max takeoff	11,790 kg	(26,000 lbs)
Useful load	1,650 kg	(3,640 lbs)

Douglas A-1 Skyraider — USA

First flown on 18th March 1945 as World War II was coming to a close, the AD-1 Skyraider was a large single-seat carrier-based torpedo-carrying dive bomber for the US Navy. All offensive ordnance was carried on 14 underwing pylons and a belly-mounted hardpoint. The basic AD-1 was a single-seater with a bubble canopy but later Skyraiders accommodated additional crew members. The AD-3W and AD-4W versions were carrier-borne radar pickets with a large ventral radome and a fuselage large enough to house two radar operators in rear fuselage compartments and the aircraft could carry up to 12 passengers if required. The AD-5 (A-1E) had a wider fuselage and a side-by-side two-seat cockpit and Skyraiders were used for other roles including electronics countermeasures. Examples of the single-seat A-1H and two-seat A-1G were widely used by the USAF for ground attack in Vietnam where they were able to carry large mission loads and absorb considerable battle damage. The Skyraider, 3,180 of which were built, was also used by the Royal Navy and the air forces of France, Cambodia, Vietnam and Chad and in civilianised form for target towing in Sweden. Skyraiders are popular with warbird collectors and at least 17 are currently airworthy.

Douglas EA-1E Skyraider, N65164

Specification	Douglas AD-6 Skyraider	
Powerplant	One 2,700 h.p. (2,013 kW) Wright R-3350-26WA piston engine	
Dimensions		
Span	15.47 m	(50 ft 9 in)
Length	11.89 m	(39 ft 0 in)
Height	4.75 m	(15 ft 7 in)
Performance		
Max speed	584 km/h	(317 kt, 365 mph)
Cruising speed	512 km/h	(278 kt, 320 mph)
Initial climb	869 m/min	(2,850 fpm)
Range	4,000 km	(2,174 nm, 2,500 miles)
Weights		
Max takeoff	8,617 kg	(19,000 lbs)
Useful load	3,832 kg	(8,450 lbs)

Douglas C-133A Cargomaster — USA

The Cargomaster was the first turboprop transport used by the US Air Force and it brought significant military load-carrying capacity during the 1960s. It had a high-aspect-ratio high wing mounting four Pratt & Whitney T34 engines and the circular-section fuselage had a relatively unobstructed interior and external fairings to house the main undercarriage units. It also had a large loading door in the underside of the rear fuselage to allow loading of Atlas and Thor intercontinental ballistic missiles. The C-133 prototype flew on 23rd April 1956 and first deliveries were made in mid-1957. The C-133A was the main variant but the final version was the C-133B with an increased useful load. In total, the USAF acquired 50 Cargomasters and they were eventually retired in 1971. A number of C-133s have been acquired by commercial users and at least two remain in restricted cargo use in Alaska.

Douglas C-133A, 56-2008

Douglas C-133A Cargomaster (Cont.)

Specification	Douglas C-133A Cargomaster	
Powerplant	Four 7,100 s.h.p. (5,293 kW) Pratt & Whitney T34-P-7W turboprops	
Dimensions		
Span	54.78 m	(179 ft 8 in)
Length	48 m	(157 ft 6 in)
Height	14.7 m	(48 ft 3 in)
Performance		
Max speed	578 km/h	(312 kt, 359 mph)
Cruising speed	520 km/h	(281 kt, 323 mph)
Initial climb	390 m/min	(1,280 fpm)
Range	6,400 km	(3,478 nm, 4,000 miles)
Weights		
Max takeoff	129,705 kg	(286,000 lbs)
Useful load	75,164 kg	(165,737 lbs)

Douglas EA-3B Skywarrior — USA

At its time, the Skywarrior was the largest and most advanced carrier-borne aircraft ever built and could carry a 12,000 lbs bomb load in its belly bomb-bay. Designed by Ed Heinemann's design group at El Segundo, the XA3D-1 attack bomber prototype first flew on 28th October, 1952 and 283 were completed as the A3D-1 (later A-3) for the U.S. Navy with a further 294 examples of the generally similar B-66 being built for the USAF. The Skywarrior had a swept shoulder wing with folding outer panels and with two Pratt & Whitney J57 engines in underslung pods. The three crew were accommodated in a glasshouse cockpit in the nose. Variants included the A-3A with 9,700 lb.s.t. J57-P-6 engines, the A-3B with 10,500 lb.s.t. J57-P-10 engines, the photo-reconnaissance RA-3B with belly cameras, the TA-3B radar trainer, the VA-3B on-board transport, the KA-3B flight-refuelling tanker, the EA-3B ECM aircraft with an internal cabin for countermeasures operators and the ERA-3B electronic aggressor trainer. The Skywarrior was retired in the early 1990s but twelve are used for test purposes by civilian operators.

Specification	Douglas A-3B Skywarrior	
Powerplant	Two 10,500 lb.s.t. (46.7 kN) Pratt & Whitney J57-P-10 turbojets	
Dimensions		
Span	22.10 m	(72 ft 6 in)
Length	23.27 m	(76 ft 4 in)
Height	6.95 m	(22 ft 9 in)
Performance		
Max speed	982 km/h	(530 kt, 610 mph)
Initial Climb	915 m/min	(3,000 fpm)
Range	1,680 km	(913 nm, 1,050 miles)
Weights		
Max takeoff	37,188 kg	(82,000 lbs)
Useful Load	19,478 kg	(42,590 lbs)

Douglas ERA-3B Skywarrior

Douglas A-4 Skyhawk
— USA

The compact A-4 Skyhawk carrier-borne attack aircraft was first flown by Douglas (later McDonnell Douglas) on 22nd June 1954. A relatively small single-seater it has a delta wing and conventional tail unit. Early US Navy A-4A, A-4B and A-4C versions used the Wright J65 turbojet but later variants starting with the A-4E had the Pratt & Whitney J52. The Skyhawk has four underwing hardpoints and a central belly pylon and some versions, particularly the A-4F, have a large dorsal fairing containing avionics. The TA-4 is a tandem two-seater for training and limited combat missions. Total production was 2,960 including export variants for Israel (the two-seat A-4H), New Zealand (A-4K), Australia (A-4G), Argentina (upgraded A-4AR and TA-4AR) and Malaysia (A-4PTM). The Singapore Air Force A-4Ss have been upgraded to A-4SU Super Skyhawk standard with larger J65-W-20 turbojets and a new weapons aiming system. The final version was the A-4M Skyhawk II with a larger cockpit canopy and a prominent hump on the upper fuselage containing improved electronics. Over 250 Skyhawks remain in active service.

Specification	McDonnell Douglas A-4M Skyhawk	
Powerplant	One 11,200 lb.s.t. (50 kN) Pratt & Whitney J52-P-408 turbojet	
Dimensions		
Span	8.38 m	(27 ft 6 in)
Length	12.29 m	(40 ft 4 in)
Height	4.57 m	(15 ft 0 in)
Performance		
Max speed	1,046 km/h	(569 kt, 654 mph)
Cruising speed	928 km/h	(504 kt, 580 mph)
Initial climb	2,438 m/min	(8,000 fpm)
Range	3,200 km	(1,739 nm, 2,000 miles)
Weights		
Max takeoff	11,111 kg	(24,500 lbs)
Useful load	6,213 kg	(13,700 lbs)

McDonnell Douglas A-4PTM Skyhawks (Malaysian AF)

Dragon Fly — Italy

The Dragon Fly was originally built as a small side-by-side two-seat helicopter which would be easily transportable for use in archaeological exploration. Two single-seat prototypes were flown in 1989 but the Dragon Fly 333 is the two-seat standard production model. It is designed to the Italian VLR (Very Light Rotorcraft) standard. The all-metal Dragon Fly has an enclosed pod fuselage with a fixed skid undercarriage and a tubular tail boom carrying a T-tail with a two-blade tail rotor. The main two-blade rotor is mounted above and behind the cabin and is driven by a 105 h.p. or 110 h.p. Dragon Fly/Hirth F30A two-stroke engine. The Dragon Fly can also be delivered as an unmanned drone for military use. The first production aircraft was delivered to a private owner in late 1993 and over 70 had been built by the end of 1999.

Dragon Fly 333

Specification	Dragon Fly 333	
Powerplant	One 110 h.p. (82 kW) DragonFly/Hirth F30A26AK piston engine	
Dimensions		
Rotor diameter	6.7 m	(22 ft 0 in)
Length	5.56 m	(18 ft 3 in)
Height	2.1 m	(6 ft 11 in)
Performance		
Max speed	133 km/h	(72 kt, 83 mph)
Cruising speed	129 km/h	(70 kt, 80 mph)
Initial climb	380 m/min	(1,250 fpm)
Range	307 km	(167 nm, 192 miles)
Weights		
Max takeoff	500 kg	(1,102 lbs)
Useful load	240 kg	(529 lbs)

Druine D.31 Turbulent and D.5 Turbi — France

The tiny single-seat Turbulent is one of the most successful French homebuilt light aircraft. Designed by Roger Druine and first flown in September 1950 it is a wood and fabric aircraft with a low-wing, fixed tailwheel undercarriage and an open cockpit. Most Turbulents have been the D.31 powered by converted Volkswagen engines of various power ratings but other variants include the D.30 (AVA 4-00), D.32 (Sarolea Epervier) and D.35 (Porsche). Rollason Aircraft in England built 29 production Turbulents with 45 h.p. Rollason-Ardem engines and in Germany, Stark Flugzeugbau produced 35 Stark Turbulent Ds with a tailwheel, full braking system, enclosed cockpit and 45 h.p. Stark Stamo engine. A tandem two-seat version, the D.5 Turbi, first flew in 1951 and is powered by a variety of 65 h.p. engines. Many Turbulents and Turbis have been built by amateurs from plans and more than 150 are believed to be active.

Druine (Stark) Turbulent D, D-EINU

Specification	Druine (Rollason) D.31 Turbulent	
Powerplant	One 45 h.p. (33.55 kW) Rollason-Ardem 4CO2 piston engine	
Dimensions		
Span	6.58 m	(21 ft 7 in)
Length	5.33 m	(17 ft 6 in)
Height	1.52 m	(5 ft 0 in)
Performance		
Max speed	174 km/h	(95 kt, 109 mph)
Cruising speed	160 km/h	(87 kt, 100 mph)
Initial climb	137 m/min	(450 fpm)
Range	400 km	(217 nm, 250 miles)
Weights		
Max takeoff	281 kg	(620 lbs)
Useful load	102 kg	(225 lbs)

Druine D.62 Condor — France

The Condor was a larger side-by-side two-seat light aircraft following on from Roger Druine's successful Turbulent and Turbi. The prototype made its maiden flight in November 1954 and, while some Condors were amateur-built, the majority have been produced commercially, particularly by Rollason Aircraft and Engines at Croydon. The prototype D.60 was powered by a 60 h.p. CNA D4 engine but later aircraft were the D.61 with a 65 h.p. Continental A65 and the D.62 with the Continental C90-14F. Rollason built two of the D.62A with a 100 h.p. Continental O-200-A engine together with four examples of the D.62C with the 130 h.p. Continental O-240-A. However, the main version, of which 42 were completed, was the Rollason D.62B based on the D.62A but with a shorter fuselage and flaps. Most of the Rollason aircraft and around ten amateur-built Condors are in current service in the UK and France.

Rollason D.62B Condor, G-AVOH

Specification	Druine (Rollason) D.62B Condor	
Powerplant	One 100 h.p. (74.56 kW) Rolls-Royce Continental O-200-A piston engine	
Dimensions		
Span	8.38 m	(27 ft 6 in)
Length	6.86 m	(22 ft 6 in)
Height	2.36 m	(7 ft 9 in)
Performance		
Max speed	203 km/h	(110 kt, 127 mph)
Cruising speed	184 km/h	(100 kt, 115 mph)
Initial climb	186 m/min	(610 fpm)
Range	560 km	(304 nm, 350 miles)
Weights		
Max takeoff	669 kg	(1,475 lbs)
Useful load	252 kg	(555 lbs)

Duruble RD.02 and RD.03 Edelweiss — France

Roland Duruble of Rouen designed the all-wood Edelweiss in association with Guy Chanut in 1961. The first aircraft flew on 7th July 1962 powered by a 65 h.p. Walter Mikron in-line engine. The Edelweiss was an attractive low-wing tourer with side-by-side seating for two in an enclosed cabin, a low wing and a retractable tricycle undercarriage. The RD.02 was followed by the RD.03 which was externally similar but of all-metal construction. This flew on 27th March 1982 powered by a 150 h.p. Lycoming O-320-A2B and was subsequently offered in the form of plans to amateur builders. Several are currently under construction in France.

Duruble RD.03 Edelweiss, F-PYIT

Specification	Duruble RD.03 Edelweiss 150	
Powerplant	One 150 h.p. (112 kW) Textron Lycoming O-320-A piston engine	
Dimensions		
Span	8.82 m	(28 ft 11 in)
Length	6.88 m	(22 ft 7 in)
Height	2.35 m	(7 ft 8 in)
Performance		
Max speed	272 km/h	(148 kt, 170 mph)
Cruising speed	248 km/h	(135 kt, 155 mph)
Initial climb	300 m/min	(985 fpm)
Range	1,096 km	(596 nm, 685 miles)
Weights		
Max takeoff	1,010 kg	(2,227 lbs)
Useful load	500 kg	(1,103 lbs)

Dyke Delta JD-1 — USA

The Dyke Delta is one of the more unconventional amateur-built light aircraft but it has gained considerable popularity and is an excellent performer. Designed by John W. Dyke, it first flew on 22nd July 1962 and has subsequently been offered to homebuilders in the form of plans. Around 400 are believed to be flying or under construction, mainly in the United States. The JD-1 has a large delta wing with the leading edge reaching as far as the front of the engine cowling. The fuselage, which fairs smoothly into the wing, has a fully enclosed cabin with a single front seat for the pilot and a three-passenger rear bench seat and is made of steel tubing and fibreglass. The Delta is fitted with a retractable tricycle undercarriage and has foldable outer wing sections for ease of transport and storage. The prototype flew with a 125 h.p. Lycoming O-290-D engine but the JD-2 has a 180 h.p. Lycoming O-360-A1A engine and other powerplants have been fitted.

Dyke Delta JD-2, N1261B

Dyke Delta JD-1 (Cont.)

Specification	Dyke JD-2 Delta	
Powerplant	One 180 h.p. (134 kW) Textron Lycoming O-360 piston engine	
Dimensions		
Span	6.76 m	(22 ft 2 in)
Length	5.79 m	(19 ft 0 in)
Height	1.68 m	(5 ft 6 in)
Performance		
Max speed	304 km/h	(165 kt, 190 mph)
Cruising speed	288 km/h	(156 kt, 180 mph)
Initial climb	610 m/min	(2,000 fpm)
Range	1,392 km	(756 nm, 870 miles)
Weights		
Max takeoff	884 kg	(1,950 lbs)
Useful load	404 kg	(890 lbs)

Dyn'Aero Ban-Bi — France

The MC.100 Ban-Bi was designed by Michel Colomban and first flown on 15th July 1994. It is an all-metal low-wing aircraft with a fixed tricycle undercarriage and side-by-side seating for two. Powered by an 80 h.p. Rotax 912, it is available in the form of plans for amateur construction. The Dyn'Aero MCR01 is a developed version with a composite fuselage and PVC foam-filled metal wings. It is sold as a kit by Dyn'Aero in four versions with different wings and different gross weights. These versions are the MCR01 VLA-912 and VLA-914 (with a 100 h.p. Rotax 914) to JAR-VLA standards with full span flaperons, the MCR01 Club two-seat trainer with separate flaps and ailerons and the MCR01 ULM with a long-span wing and double-slotted flaperons which allows it to fulfil European ultralight regulations. Over 100 kits were under construction at the end of 1998 and it is also intended that a certificated factory-complete model will be available in future.

Dyn'Aero MC.100 Ban-Bi, F-PCJD

Specification	Dyn'Aero MCR01 Ban-Bi VLA-Club 912	
Powerplant	One 80 h.p. (59.65 kW) Rotax 912 piston engine	
Dimensions		
Span	6.92 m	(22 ft 9 in)
Length	5.66 m	(18 ft 7 in)
Height	1.57 m	(5 ft 2 in)
Performance		
Max speed	300 km/h	(162 kt, 186 mph)
Cruising speed	260 km/h	(141 kt, 162 mph)
Initial climb	475 m/min	(1,558 fpm)
Range	480 km	(260 nm, 300 miles)
Weights		
Max takeoff	490 kg	(1,080 lbs)
Useful load	255 kg	(562 lbs)

Dyn'Aero MCR4S — France

Christophe Robin at Dyn'Aero has developed a four-seat version of its successful MCR01 light aircraft and the prototype flew at Dijon-Darois on 14th June 2000. The MCR4S has a longer and slightly wider fuselage than the MCR01 but shares many common components with the earlier aircraft. It retains the T-tail and has high aspect ratio wings with large slotted flaps and a fixed tricycle undercarriage. The cabin is accessed through a large forward-hinged canopy. It is of all carbon-composite construction and will initially be sold as a kit although a certificated factory-complete version may be available in future.

Dyn'Aero MCR4S, F-WWUZ

Specification	Dyn'Aero MCR4S	
Powerplant	One 114 h.p. (85 kW) Rotax 914F piston engine	
Dimensions		
Span	8.72 m	(28 ft 7 in)
Length	5.5 m	(18 ft 1 in)
Height	1.8 m	(5 ft 11 in)
Performance		
Max speed	320 km/h	(172 kt, 199 mph)
Cruising speed	287 km/h	(155 kt, 178 mph)
Initial climb (est.)	380 m/min	(1,247 fpm)
Range (est.)	1,290 km	(702 nm, 807 miles)
Weights		
Max takeoff	750 kg	(1,654 lbs)
Useful load	390 kg	(860 lbs)

Dyn'Aero CR.100 — France

Christophe Robin designed the CR.100 light aircraft and flew the prototype on 27th August 1992. The CR.100 is a low-wing aircraft with a fixed tailwheel undercarriage and conventional tail unit. It is intended for home assembly using a kit sold by Dyn'Aero and is of wood and fabric construction. The CR.100 is intended as a trainer and aerobatic aircraft. The standard powerplant is the 180 h.p. Textron Lycoming AEIO-360 but larger powerplants of up to 200 h.p. can be used. The two occupants are housed side-by-side in a cockpit enclosed by a large rearward-sliding canopy and full dual controls are provided. Over 35 are under construction with a dozen flying at the end of 1998 including two with the Armée de l'Air.

Dyn'Aero CR.100, F-PLEA

Specification	Dyn'Aero CR.100	
Powerplant	One 180 h.p. (134 kW) Textron Lycoming AEIO-360-B2F piston engine	
Dimensions		
Span	8.5 m	(27 ft 11 in)
Length	7.1 m	(23 ft 4 in)
Height	1.8 m	(5 ft 11 in)
Performance		
Max speed	376 km/h	(204 kt, 235 mph)
Cruising speed	304 km/h	(165 kt, 190 mph)
Initial climb	480 m/min	(1,575 fpm)
Range	480 km	(261 nm, 300 miles)
Weights		
Max takeoff	850 kg	(1,875 lbs)
Useful load	300 kg	(660 lbs)

EAC Explorer 350R — Australia

The Explorer is a nine-seat single-engined utility aircraft with a fuselage built from composite materials and a strut-braced high metal-wing with a parallel-chord centre section and tapered outer panels. It was first flown as a proof-of-concept (POC) prototype on 23rd January 1998. Designed by Graham Swannell and John Roncz for Explorer Aircraft Corp. Pty. Ltd., it has a capacious square-section interior which can be used for carrying cargo by loading through a large port-side rear double door or in passenger configuration can be fitted with eight quickly removable seats. The retractable tricycle undercarriage has fibreglass main units which are hinged from lower fuselage sponsons and retract inwards into belly recesses. The POC aircraft is the basic Explorer 350R with a 350 h.p. Continental TSIO-550-E3B piston engine but further versions include the Explorer 500R with a 500 h.p. Orenda V8 engine, the 500T with a Pratt & Whitney PT6A-135B turboprop and the stretched 17-seat 750T with a PT6A-60A turboprop.

EAC Explorer 350R, VH-ONA

EAC Explorer 350R (Cont.)

Specification	EAC Explorer 350R	
Powerplant	One 350 h.p. (261 kW) Teledyne Continental TSIO-550-E3B piston engine	
Dimensions		
Span	14.41 m	(47 ft 4 in)
Length	9.69 m	(31 ft 9 in)
Height	4.72 m	(15 ft 6 in)
Performance		
Max speed	278 km/h	(150 kt, 173 mph)
Cruising speed	259 km/h	(140 kt, 161 mph)
Initial Climb	244 m/min	(800 fpm)
Range	2,039 km	(1,108 nm, 1,274 miles)
Weights		
Max takeoff	2,177 kg	(4,800 lbs)
Useful Load	816 kg	(1,800 lbs)

Eagle DW-1 — USA

Designed by Dean Wilson of Eagle Aircraft Company of Boise, Idaho, the prototype Eagle DW-1 first flew in 1977. The Eagle was a single-seat agricultural biplane with tapered long-span wings, an enclosed cockpit and tailwheel undercarriage. The prototype was powered by a Jacobs R-755-B2 radial engine but the production Eagle 220 was fitted with either a 220 h.p. Continental W670-6N radial engine or, as the Eagle 300, with a 300 h.p. Lycoming IO-540-M1B5D flat-six engine which gave improved performance and reduced the visibility problems of the radial. The Eagle DW-1 was built by Bellanca Aircraft of Alexandria, Minnesota and production of 95 aircraft took place between 1975 and 1983. Over 40 of these remain flying with crop sprayers in the United States.

Specification	Eagle DW-1 Eagle 220	
Powerplant	One 220 h.p. (164 kW) Gulf Coast Continental W670-6N piston engine	
Dimensions		
Span	16.76 m	(55 ft 0 in)
Length	7.92 m	(26 ft 0 in)
Height	3.23 m	(10 ft 7 in)
Performance		
Max speed	176 km/h	(96 kt, 110 mph)
Cruising speed	144 km/h	(78 kt, 90 mph)
Range	288 km	(156 nm, 180 miles)
Weights		
Max takeoff	2,449 kg	(5,400 lbs)
Useful load	1,247 kg	(2,750 lbs)

Eagle XT-S — Australia/Malaysia

The Eagle XT-S is an all-composite light aircraft featuring two staggered main wing surfaces and a conventional tail unit. A single-seat proof-of-concept aircraft was built initially and the prototype side-by-side two-seat version first flew in 1988 powered by a 75 h.p. Aeropower engine. The Eagle XT-S has an enclosed cockpit with a forward-opening canopy and is fitted with dual controls for primary training. It has a fixed tricycle undercarriage and various engines have been fitted including the 100 h.p. Continental O-200, but the production version is the Eagle XT-S 150 with a 125 h.p. Continental IO-240. Certificated under JAR-VLA rules in September 1993 it went into production at Fremantle, Western Australia and a Malaysian factory produces components for the aircraft. FAA certification was gained in early 1999 and 21 aircraft had been completed by that time. HGP Aero, who import the Eagle into the USA, announced plans in early 2000 to build the Eagle at Augusta, Kansas.

Eagle 300, N8809U

Eagle XT-S 150, 9M-BCO

Specification	Eagle Aircraft Eagle 150	
Powerplant	One 125 h.p. (93.2 kW) Teledyne Continental IO-240-A piston engine	
Dimensions		
Span	7.16 m	(23 ft 6 in)
Length	6.45 m	(21 ft 2 in)
Height	2.31 m	(7 ft 7 in)
Performance		
Max speed	240 km/h	(130 kt, 150 mph)
Cruising speed	213 km/h	(115 kt, 132 mph)
Initial climb	317 m/min	(1,038 fpm)
Range	1,000 km	(543 nm, 625 miles)
Weights		
Max takeoff	639 kg	(1,410 lbs)
Useful load	213 kg	(470 lbs)

Edgar Percival EP.9 — UK

Edgar W. Percival, who had been reponsible for the line of prewar Percival light aircraft, designed the EP.9 which first flew at Stapleford on 21st December 1955. It was a multi-purpose light utility aircraft intended for use in Australia and remote locations. Constructed of steel tube, light alloy and fabric, the EP.9 had a pod and boom fuselage with rear-loading clamshell doors. It was designed with a strut-braced high wing and fixed tailwheel undercarriage and was powered by a 270 h.p. Lycoming GO-480 engine. Many of the 21 production aircraft were sold to Australia where they were used for crop spraying and to carry up to five passengers. Design rights were sold to Lancashire Aircraft Corporation who built five further LAC Prospectors with 295 h.p. Lycoming GO-480-G1A6 engines and one Prospector 2 with a 375 h.p. Armstrong Siddeley Cheetah radial. Several EP.9s still exist although only two are believed to be airworthy.

Edgar Percival EP.9, VH-SSV

Specification	Edgar Percival EP.9	
Powerplant	One 270 h.p. (201.3 kW) Textron Lycoming GO-480-B1B piston engine	
Dimensions		
Span	13.26 m	(43 ft 6 in)
Length	8.99 m	(29 ft 6 in)
Height	2.67 m	(8 ft 9 in)
Performance		
Max speed	234 km/h	(127 kt, 146 mph)
Cruising speed	205 km/h	(111 kt, 128 mph)
Initial climb	341 m/min	(1,120 fpm)
Range	928 km	(504 nm, 580 miles)
Weights		
Max takeoff	1,610 kg	(3,550 lbs)
Useful load	698 kg	(1,540 lbs)

Edgley Optica — UK

The Optica was developed by Edgley Aircraft Co. Ltd. as an observation platform combining the visibility of a helicopter and the economy of a fixed-wing aircraft. First flown on 14th December 1979, the Optica was built around a ducted fan nacelle which mounted a pusher 160 h.p. Lycoming O-320-B2B engine (later upgraded to a 180 h.p. Lycoming IO-360). It had constant-chord high-aspect-ratio wings, twin booms mounting the fins, with the tailplane set on top, a fixed tricycle undercarriage and a three-seat bubble cabin module. In a chequered ownership history the successor company to Edgley, Optica Industries, built 15 production aircraft, Brooklands Aerospace completed a further five as the Scoutmaster with a 260 h.p. IO-540 and Lovaux (FLS Aerospace) built two improved Optica OA7-300s. Further production in Malaysia was planned in 1996 but no additional Opticas were completed.

FLS Optica, N130DP

Specification	Edgley (FLS) Optica OA7-300	
Powerplant	One 260 h.p. (194 kW) Textron Lycoming IO-540-V4A5D piston engine	
Dimensions		
Span	12 m	(39 ft 4 in)
Length	8.15 m	(26 ft 9 in)
Height	1.98 m	(6 ft 6 in)
Performance		
Max speed	213 km/h	(115 kt, 132 mph)
Cruising speed	191 km/h	(103 kt, 119 mph)
Initial climb	247 m/min	(810 fpm)
Range	1,050 km	(570 nm, 656 miles)
Weights		
Max takeoff	1,315 kg	(2,900 lbs)
Useful load	367 kg	(810 lbs)

EDI Express — USA

This four-seat kit-built light aircraft was originally designed by Ken Wheeler as the Wheeler Express and was first flown on 28th July 1987. It is a highly streamlined low-wing aircraft with a fully enclosed cabin. In standard form it has a fixed tricycle undercarriage but this can be retractable if the builder wishes. The whole structure is composite and it achieves high performance either as the Express CT with a

EDI Express (Cont.)

250 h.p. Lycoming IO-540-C4B5 engine or as the Express S-90 with a 300 h.p. IO-540-K1G5. Around 300 kits had been delivered when Wheeler ceased operations, but the aircraft is now sold by Express Design Inc. and 50 were flying by the end of 1998. The latest version of the Express, designated Express 90, has a lowered tailplane in place of the standard cruciform tail and the aircraft can also be fitted with a belly pannier for additional baggage space and the Express 200RG will have a retractable undercarriage.

EDI (Wheeler) Express, N89MT

Specification	EDI Express S-90	
Powerplant	One 300 h.p. (223.68 kW) Textron Lycoming IO-540-K1G5 piston engine	
Dimensions		
Span	7.62 m	(25 ft 0 in)
Length	9.45 m	(31 ft 0 in)
Height	2.44 m	(8 ft 0 in)
Performance		
Max speed	423 km/h	(230 kt, 264 mph)
Cruising speed	350 km/h	(190 kt, 218 mph)
Initial climb	366 m/min	(1,200 fpm)
Range	2,153 km	(1,170 nm, 1,345 miles)
Weights		
Max takeoff	1,451 kg	(3,200 lbs)
Useful load	624 kg	(1,375 lbs)

EH Industries EH-101 — International

The medium term need for a replacement for the Sea King in British and Italian military service resulted in the European Helicopter Industries partnership between Westland and Agusta which was formed in 1980 to develop the EH-101. The EH-101 is a medium-lift helicopter with a central 30-seat cabin, a retractable tricycle undercarriage with main units retracting into external sponsons and an advanced technology five-blade main rotor. The three 1,275 s.h.p. General Electric CT.7-2A turbines are mounted above the fuselage and the EH-101 has a conventional tail unit with a four-blade anti-torque rotor. The first EH-101 was flown on 9th October, 1987 and nine prototype and pre-production aircraft were built including two of the civil version. Variants of the EH-101 include the Rolls Royce RTM 322 powered Merlin HM.Mk.1 (Royal Navy ASW version with folding tail unit), Merlin HC.Mk.3 (RAF 26-seat utility version with ventral rear loading ramp) and the Cormorant (SAR version with tail ramp for Canadian Armed Forces). Three Italian variants are on order comprising eight ASW aircraft, four surveillance radar pickets and four maritime utility transports (folding tail and rear loading ramp). The first Royal Navy Merlin entered service in December 1998 and 98 EH-101s had been sold by the end of 1999 to the Royal Navy (44), RAF (22), Italian Navy (16), Canadian Armed Forces (15) and to the Tokyo Police who have received the first civil Heliliner variant with full cabin windows and a 30-passenger interior.

EHI Merlin HM Mk.1, Royal Navy ZH827

EHI EH-101 Heliliner, G-OIOI

Specification	EH Industries EH-101 Merlin HM.Mk.1	
Powerplant	Three 2,101 s.h.p. (1566 kW) Rolls Royce Turboméca RTM322-01/8 turboshafts	
Dimensions		
Rotor Diameter	18.59 m	(61 ft 0 in)
Length	19.53 m	(64 ft 1 in)
Height	6.65 m	(21 ft 10 in)
Performance		
Max speed	278 km/h	(150 kt, 173 mph)
Cruising speed	259 km/h	(140 kt, 161 mph)
Range	778 km	(423 nm, 486 miles)
Weights		
Max takeoff	14,600 kg	(32,193 lbs)
Useful Load	5,520 kg	(12,172 lbs)

EKW C-3605 — Switzerland

The Eidg. Konstruktions Werkstatte (EKW) developed the C-3603 ground attack aircraft during the early 1940s based on the earlier C-3601 prototype. The C-3603 was a low-wing design with a retractable tailwheel undercarriage, twin-fin tail unit and an enclosed tandem cockpit with a rear-facing gunner's position. Powered by a 1,000 h.p. Hispano Suiza engine, it had underwing hardpoints and a forward-firing 20 mm Oerlikon cannon. Some 144 were built in the 1942–44 period. Subsequently, 26 were converted by Farner Werke to C-3605 target tugs, the prototype flying on 19th August 1968. The conversion involved fitting a 1,100 s.h.p. Lycoming T53-L-7 turboprop engine in a lengthened forward fuselage, adding an additional central fin and installation of a target-towing winch in the rear cockpit. The C-3605 Schlepp has now been withdrawn from service but three are operated privately in France and Germany.

EKW C-3605, F-AZGD

Specification	EKW C-3605	
Powerplant	One 1,100 s.h.p. (820 kW) Textron Lycoming T53-L-7 turboprop	
Dimensions		
Span	13.73 m	(45 ft 1 in)
Length	12.1 m	(39 ft 7 in)
Height	4.05 m	(13 ft 3 in)
Performance		
Max speed	429 km/h	(233 kt, 268 mph)
Cruising speed	416 km/h	(226 kt, 260 mph)
Initial climb	753 m/min	(2,470 fpm)
Range	968 km	(526 nm, 605 miles)
Weights		
Max takeoff	3,715 kg	(8,192 lbs)
Useful load	1,082 kg	(2,386 lbs)

El Gavilan 358 — Colombia

The Gavilan is a simple all-metal utility aircraft intended for use in Latin American countries where limited maintenance facilities are available. It has a slab-sided fuselage with a large unobstructed square-section cabin which can carry six passengers or four stretcher cases plus two crew. Two crew doors and a large double rear port-side cargo door are provided and the aircraft has a strut-braced high wing and fixed tricycle undercarriage. The prototype, which was developed in the United States, first flew on 27th April 1990 and the first deliveries were made in 1998 from the Bogotá factory to the Colombian Air Force who have ordered 12. The powerplant is a turbocharged Lycoming TIO-540 piston engine with a three-blade Hartzell constant-speed propeller.

El Gavilan 358, N358EL

Specification	El Gavilan 358	
Powerplant	One 350 h.p. (261 kW) Textron Lycoming TIO-540W2A turbocharged piston engine	
Dimensions		
Span	12.8 m	(42 ft 0 in)
Length	9.14 m	(30 ft 0 in)
Height	3.41 m	(11 ft 3 in)
Performance		
Max speed	267 km/h	(145 kt, 167 mph)
Cruising speed	248 km/h	(135 kt, 155 mph)
Initial climb	270 m/min	(880 fpm)
Range	1,760 km	(956 nm, 1,100 miles)
Weights		
Max takeoff	2,040 kg	(4,500 lbs)
Useful load	770 kg	(1,700 lbs)

Emair MA-1 Diablo — USA

The Murrayair (Emair) MA-1 is an extensively modified version of the Boeing Stearman NA75 Kaydet biplane for agricultural work. The MA-1 prototype first flew on 27th July 1969. It has a larger wing than the Stearman, a 380 USG chemical hopper fitted as an integral part of the forward fuselage and a 600 h.p. Pratt & Whitney R-1340-AN1 Wasp radial piston engine. The cockpit is fully enclosed and is fitted with a second jump seat for transport of a ground operative. The MA-1, named the Paymaster, was built at Harlingen, Texas and 28 were built. The design was later sold to Emroth Co. and the MA-1 was redesigned as the MA-1B Diablo 1200 with a re-shaped vertical tail, a larger hopper and a 1,200 h.p. Wright R-1820 engine. Emroth built 23 aircraft and several of the production MA-1s were converted to MA-1B standard. Production was completed in 1980.

Emair MA-1 Diablo (Cont.)

Emair Diablo, N9919M

Specification	Emroth MA-1B Diablo 1200	
Powerplant	One 1,200 h.p. (895 kW) Wright R-1820 piston engine	
Dimensions		
Span	12.7 m	(41 ft 8 in)
Length	9.14 m	(30 ft 0 in)
Height	3.58 m	(11 ft 9 in)
Performance		
Max speed	238 km/h	(128 kt, 148 mph)
Cruising speed	188 km/h	(102 kt, 117 mph)
Initial climb	520 m/min	(1,700 fpm)
Range	800 km	(435 nm, 500 miles)
Weights		
Max takeoff	3,810 kg	(8,400 lbs)
Useful load	1,882 kg	(4,150 lbs)

Embraer EMB-110 Bandeirante — Brazil

The successful Bandeirante twin-turboprop airliner has its origins in the ten-passenger IPD-6504 project from the Brazilian CTA which flew as a prototype on 22nd October 1968. Embraer was formed to build the production EMB-110, which was ordered by the Brazilian Air Force as the C-95 and had a longer 12-seat cabin and many detailed changes. The Bandeirante has a low wing with the PT6 turboprops mounted on the inboard sections and a retractable tricycle undercarriage. Many Bandeirantes were sold to American commuter airlines and variants included the 15-seat EMB-110C and executive EMB-110E. The EMB-110K had a 2 ft 9 in fuselage stretch and this was sold to commercial customers as the EMB-110P1 and military EMB-110P1K. The EMB-110P2 was a high-density 21-passenger version and the EMB-111A was a maritime patrol version for the Brazilian Navy. A total of 500 production Bandeirantes had been completed when the line closed in 1991.

Embraer EMB-110P1 Bandeirante, N404AS

Specification	Embraer EMP-110P2 Bandeirante	
Powerplant	Two 750 s.h.p. (559 kW) Pratt & Whitney PT6A-34 turboprops	
Dimensions		
Span	15.33 m	(50 ft 3 in)
Length	14.59 m	(47 ft 10 in)
Height	4.92 m	(16 ft 2 in)
Performance		
Max speed	460 km/h	(248 kt, 286 mph)
Cruising speed	335 km/h	(181 kt, 208 mph)
Initial climb	545 m/min	(1,788 fpm)
Range	1,990 km	(1,080 nm, 1,244 miles)
Weights		
Max takeoff	5,669 kg	(12,500 lbs)
Useful load	2,154 kg	(4,750 lbs)

Embraer EMB-120 Brasilia — Brazil

As a larger companion to the EMB-110 Bandeirante, Embraer produced the Brasilia which not only carried 30 passengers but also had a pressurised cabin and improved performance. Following the same low-wing layout of its predecessor, the Brasilia had a T-tail, circular section fuselage and twin 1,500 s.h.p. Pratt & Whitney PW115 turboprop engines. While a few Brasilias were sold to the Brazilian Air Force the majority of the production EMB-120RT with 1,800 s.h.p. PW118 engines were ordered by major US commuter operators, many of which also flew the Bandeirante. These included United Express, Continental Express and Comair. European customers included Air Littoral, Delta Air Transport and Luxair. The EMB-120ER was a longer-range variant with additional fuel tanks and a higher gross weight. More than 350 aircraft had been built by the end of 2000.

Embraer EMB-120 Brasilia, N216SW

Specification	Embraer EMB-120 Brasilia	
Powerplant	Two 1,800 s.h.p. (1,342 kW) Pratt & Whitney PW118 turboprops	
Dimensions		
Span	19.78 m	(64 ft 11 in)
Length	20 m	(65 ft 7 in)
Height	6.35 m	(20 ft 10 in)
Performance		
Max speed	608 km/h	(328 kt, 378 mph)
Cruising speed	482 km/h	(260 kt, 300 mph)
Initial climb	646 m/min	(2,120 fpm)
Range	2,966 km	(1,610 nm, 1,854 miles)
Weights		
Max takeoff	11,500 kg	(25,357 lbs)
Useful load	4,429 kg	(9,767 lbs)

Embraer ERJ-145 and ERJ-135 — Brazil

The expansion of the market for regional jets prompted Embraer to develop the Brasilia airframe into a twin-turbofan commuter aircraft. The EMB-145 (later named ERJ-145) was based on a stretched Brasilia fuselage married to a modified tail unit and a new supercritical wing. The two Allison AE3007A turbofans were positioned on the rear fuselage. The prototype first flew on 11th August 1995 and the type was certificated in December 1996. The ERJ-145 has accommodation for 50 passengers. Embraer has also launched the ERJ-145ER (extended range) and ERJ-145LR (long range) models with additional fuel capacity. The ERJ-135 is a 37-seat version of the ERJ-145 with a shortened fuselage which is also sold as the Legacy business jet. The prototype, converted from the ERJ-145 prototype, first flew on 4th July 1998. Over 300 ERJ-145s and -135s had been ordered by the end of 1998 including 99 for Continental Express and 117 for American Eagle. Embraer has also launched the EMB-145 AEW&C military surveillance version with a roof-mounted Ericsson Erieye antenna and the EMB-145RS special missions remote-sensing variant which is likely to be armed for Mexican service. The ERJ-145XR is a higher weight variant for longer routes with AE3007A1E engines, winglets and increased fuel. By spring 2000 over 250 of the ERJ-135 and -145 had been built.

Embraer ERJ-135, PT-ZJC

Embraer EMB-145 AEW&C, PP-XSA

Specification	Embraer ERJ-145	
Powerplant	Two 7,040 lb.s.t. (31.32 kN) Allison AE3007A turbofans	
Dimensions		
Span	20.04 m	(65 ft 9 in)
Length	29.87 m	(98 ft 0 in)
Height	6.75 m	(22 ft 2 in)
Performance		
Max speed	832 km/h	(452 kt, 520 mph)
Cruising speed	792 km/h	(430 kt, 495 mph)
Initial climb	777 m/min	(2,550 fpm)
Range	2,632 km	(1,430 nm, 1,645 miles)
Weights		
Max takeoff	19,196 kg	(42,328 lbs)
Useful load	12,544 kg	(27,660 lbs)

Embraer EMB-121 Xingu — Brazil

On 10th October 1976, Embraer flew the prototype Xingu executive aircraft. This had some features of the successful Bandeirante but was largely a new design with accommodation for five passengers and two crew in a shorter pressurised circular section fuselage, with a large T-tail and a fairly low-aspect-ratio low wing. Two 680 s.h.p. Pratt & Whitney PT6A-28 turboprops were mounted on the inboard wing sections. Production commenced in 1979 and was completed in 1987. Early production aircraft were designated EMB-121E Xingu I and 29 were delivered including a batch for the Brazilian Air Force as the VU-9. The later EMB-121A Xingu II had 750 s.h.p. PT6A-135 engines with four-bladed propellers, rear fuselage ventral strakes and a modified interior. A total of 82 of this model were built, including 41 delivered to the French Armée de l'Air and Aéronavale.

Embraer EMB-121 Xingu, No.67 (French Navy)

Embraer EMB-121 Xingu (Cont.)

Specification	Embraer EMB-121A Xingu II	
Powerplant	Two 750 s.h.p. (559.2 kW) Pratt & Whitney PT6A-135 turboprops	
Dimensions		
Span	14.45 m	(47 ft 5 in)
Length	12.25 m	(40 ft 2 in)
Height	4.74 m	(15 ft 6 in)
Performance		
Max speed	474 km/h	(256 kt, 295 mph)
Cruising speed	380 km/h	(205 kt, 236 mph)
Initial climb	548 m/min	(1,800 fpm)
Range	2,335 km	(1,268 nm, 1,460 miles)
Weights		
Max takeoff	5,669 kg	(12,500 lbs)
Useful load	1,960 kg	(4,321 lbs)

Embraer EMB-200 Ipanema
— Brazil

Built for the Brazilian agricultural industry, the Ipanema crop sprayer followed the lines of the competing Piper Pawnee and Cessna AgWagon with a low-wing 260 h.p. Lycoming O-540 engine and fixed tailwheel undercarriage. Construction is of tube and fabric and the aircraft has a fully enclosed single-seat cockpit and a 180 USG hopper. Designed by the Brazilian CTA, the Ipanema first flew on 30th July 1970 and went into production at Embraer in 1972. The EMB-200A was an improved model with a variable-pitch propeller and larger wheels. From the 74th aircraft the EMB-201 was introduced with a higher useful load and a 300 h.p. Lycoming IO-540-K1J5D engine; 203 were built before a change to the EMB-201A with a modified wing design. The latest version is the EMB-202 which has increased wingspan and a 251 USG hopper. The Ipanema is now built by Industria Aeronautica Neiva and total production to date exceeds 800 with most aircraft being sold for use in Brazil.

Embraer EMB-201 Ipanema, PT-GZZ

Specification	Embraer (Neiva) EMB-202 Ipanema	
Powerplant	One 300 h.p. (224 kW) Textron Lycoming IO-540-K1J5D piston engine	
Dimensions		
Span	11.7 m	(38 ft 4 in)
Length	7.43 m	(24 ft 4 in)
Height	2.2 m	(7 ft 2 in)
Performance		
Max speed	230 km/h	(124 kt, 143 mph)
Cruising speed	213 km/h	(115 kt, 132 mph)
Initial climb	283 m/min	(930 fpm)
Range	933 km	(506 nm, 583 miles)
Weights		
Max takeoff	1,800 kg	(3,968 lbs)
Useful load	780 kg	(1,719 lbs)

Embraer EMB-312 Tucano
— Brazil

Brazilian Air Force needs for a new advanced trainer resulted in Embraer developing the turboprop Tucano which first flew on 16th August 1980. The Tucano is of all-metal construction with a low wing and tandem two-seat cockpit and powered by a 750 s.h.p. Pratt & Whitney PT6A-25C. In Brazilian Air Force service it is designated T-27 and sales have also been made to Argentina, Honduras and Venezuela and to France as the EMB-312F with additional airbrakes. The Tucano has been licence-built in Egypt for Egypt and Iraq and 131 were built for the Royal Air Force by Shorts at Belfast as the S-312 Tucano T.Mk.1 with a 1,100 s.h.p. Garrett TPE331-12B turboprop and a modified cockpit canopy. The EMB-312H (later EMB-314) Super Tucano has a 4 ft 6 in fuselage stretch, a 1,600 s.h.p. PT6A-68 engine, and enlarged cockpit canopy and upgraded systems, and the AL-X armed version with five hardpoints is being built as the AT-29 and single-seat A-29 for the Brazilian Air Force.

Embraer EMB-312H Super Tucano, PP-ZTV

Specification	Embraer EMB-312H Super Tucano	
Powerplant	One 1,600 s.h.p. (1,193 kW) Pratt & Whitney PT6A-68-1 turboprop	
Dimensions		
Span	11.14 m	(36 ft 6 in)
Length	11.43 m	(37 ft 6 in)
Height	3.9 m	(12 ft 9 in)
Performance		
Max speed	556 km/h	(300 kt, 346 mph)
Cruising speed	530 km/h	(285 kt, 330 mph)
Initial climb	895 m/min	(2,935 fpm)
Range	1,557 km	(847 nm, 974 miles)
Weights		
Max takeoff	3,190 kg	(7,033 lbs)
Useful load	770 kg	(1,698 lbs)

Specification	Emigh A-2 Trojan	
Powerplant	One 85 h.p. (63.4 kW) Continental C82-12F piston engine	
Dimensions		
Span	9.63 m	(31 ft 7 in)
Length	6.22 m	(20 ft 5 in)
Height	1.96 m	(6 ft 5 in)
Performance		
Max speed	202 km/h	(110 kt, 126 mph)
Cruising speed	184 km/h	(100 kt, 115 mph)
Initial climb	244 m/min	(800 fpm)
Range	880 km	(478 nm, 550 miles)
Weights		
Max takeoff	658 kg	(1,450 lbs)
Useful load	261 kg	(576 lbs)

Emigh Trojan — USA

Built during the postwar light aircraft boom, the Emigh A-2 Trojan was designed by Harold Emigh and manufactured by the Emigh Aircraft Company at Douglas, Arizona. The all-metal low-wing Trojan had a side-by-side two-seat enclosed cabin and a fixed tricycle undercarriage. It was powered by a 85 h.p. Continental flat-four engine and was designed for ease of construction with interchangeable tail surfaces, control surfaces and wings. The wings incorporated external channel-section stiffeners to take the place of conventional internal ribs. The first Trojan was flown on 20th December 1946 and the type certificate was issued in December 1948. A total of 58 production Trojans was built before the production line was terminated in 1950; 20 are currently flying in North America.

ENAER Pillan — Chile

The Pillan is the result of a cooperative venture between ENAER and Piper Aircraft in order to produce a basic trainer for the Chilean Air Force. Piper's XBT prototype which flew on 6th March 1981 combined a PA-28 Warrior wing with a cut-down version of the PA-32R Saratoga fuselage incorporating a tandem two-seat cockpit with a large bubble canopy. It was powered by a 300 h.p. Lycoming IO-540-K1K5 piston engine and designated PA-28R-300. Piper provided kits for assembly by ENAER who delivered 105 T-35 Pillans, including 80 for the Chilean Air Force, ten for Panama (T-35D) and 15 for Paraguay. Another 41 have been built by CASA for the Spanish Air Force as the E.26 Tamiz. Other versions built as prototypes have included the T-35TX Aucan and the T-35DT both with a 420 h.p. Allison 250B-17D turboprop, and the T-35S single-seater, which has the rear cockpit deleted, but none of these has gone into production.

Emigh Trojan, N8345H

ENAER T-35 Pillan, 119 (Chile AF)

ENAER Pillan (Cont.)

Specification	ENAER T-35 Pillan	
Powerplant	One 300 h.p. (224 kW) Textron Lycoming IO-540-K1K5 piston engine	
Dimensions		
Span	8.84 m	(29 ft 0 in)
Length	8 m	(26 ft 3 in)
Height	2.64 m	(8 ft 8 in)
Performance		
Max speed	311 km/h	(168 kt, 194 mph)
Cruising speed	266 km/h	(144 kt, 166 mph)
Initial climb	465 m/min	(1,525 fpm)
Range	1,354 km	(735 nm, 846 miles)
Weights		
Max takeoff	1,338 kg	(2,950 lbs)
Useful load	408 kg	(900 lbs)

ENAER Namcu and EuroENAER Eaglet — Chile

ENAER initiated their light aircraft project in 1986 and designed a small side-by-side two-seater which would be suitable for general civilian club training and for military aircrew screening. The Namcu, which first flew in April 1989, was a classic low-wing design of all-composite construction (glass fibre, carbon fibre and foam) with a fixed tricycle undercarriage and an enclosed cabin fitted with gull-wing doors. It was powered by a 115 h.p. Lycoming O-235-N2C piston engine. Production commenced in 1999 with all basic components manufactured in Chile and final assembly being carried out in Holland by EuroENAER. The production aircraft is known as the EuroENAER Eaglet and compared with the prototypes it has a higher-powered 160 h.p. Lycoming O-320-D2A engine, modified cockpit and changes to the flaps and other control surfaces.

ENAER Eaglet, CC-PZI

Specification	EuroENAER Eaglet 160	
Powerplant	One 160 h.p. (119.3 kW) Textron Lycoming O-320-D2A piston engine	
Dimensions		
Span	8.7 m	(28 ft 7 in)
Length	7.05 m	(23 ft 2 in)
Height	2.42 m	(7 ft 11 in)
Performance		
Max speed	248 km/h	(135 kt, 155 mph)
Cruising speed	230 km/h	(125 kt, 144 mph)
Initial climb	171 m/min	(560 fpm)
Range	1,159 km	(630 nm, 724 miles)
Weights		
Max takeoff	850 kg	(1,874 lbs)
Useful load	310 kg	(684 lbs)

English Electric Canberra — UK

The Canberra was the first British jet-engined bomber, designed by English Electric in 1945 and first flown on 13th May 1949. It is a mid-wing aircraft with two Rolls Royce Avon turbojets mounted at mid-span and a three-seat cockpit with a small bubble canopy. The initial versions were the B.2, PR.3 and T.4 with 6,500 lb.s.t. Avon RA.3 Mk.101 engines and these were followed by the B.6 and PR.7 with 7,500 lb.s.t. Avon RA.7 Mk.109 engines. The B(I)8 interdictor version had a new nose section with an enlarged offset tandem two-seat blister canopy and the PR.9 high-altitude photo-reconnaissance model had larger wings and 11,000 lb.s.t. RA.24 Mk.206 engines. The Canberra was built by Martin in the USA as the B-57 with a tandem two-seat cockpit and it was exported widely to countries such as Australia, Venezuela and Peru. A small number of PR.9s remain in RAF service for strategic reconnaissance, Germany uses two for target towing, a few B(I)58s remain with the Indian Air Force, and at least three are flying in private hands.

English Electric Canberra PR.9, XH131

Specification	English Electric (BAe) Canberra PR Mk.9	
Powerplant	Two 11,000 lb.s.t. (48.94 kN) Rolls Royce Avon RA.24 Mk. 206 turbojets	
Dimensions		
Span	20.67 m	(67 ft 10 in)
Length	20.3 m	(66 ft 8 in)
Height	4.77 m	(15 ft 8 in)
Performance		
Max speed	832 km/h	(452 kt, 520 mph)
Cruising speed	784 km/h	(426 kt, 490 mph)
Initial climb	1,036 m/min	(3,400 fpm)
Range	5,808 km	(3,156 nm, 3,630 miles)
Weights		
Max takeoff	24,920 kg	(54,950 lbs)
Useful load	12,245 kg	(27,000 lbs)

Specification	English Electric (BAe) Lightning F.6	
Powerplant	Two 15,680 lb.s.t. (69.76 kN) Rolls Royce Avon 302 turbojets	
Dimensions		
Span	10.62 m	(34 ft 10 in)
Length	16.84 m	(55 ft 3 in)
Height	5.97 m	(19 ft 7 in)
Performance		
Max speed	2,400 km/h	(1,300 kt, 1,500 mph)
Cruising speed	1,840 km/h	(1,000 kt, 1,150 mph)
Initial climb	15,240 m/min	(50,000 fpm)
Range	1,280 km	(695 nm, 800 miles)
Weights		
Max takeoff	22,675 kg	(50,000 lbs)
Useful load	9,977 kg	(22,000 lbs)

English Electric Lightning — UK

The Lightning single-seat supersonic jet fighter originated in the English Electric P.1A prototype which flew on 4th August 1954. The P.1 had a parallel-chord fuselage and swept wings with square-cut tips containing the ailerons. The two Sapphire turbojets were in staggered mountings in the fuselage one above the other. The production P.1B Lightning had a modified bubble cockpit canopy and circular air intake with a central radome for the Ferranti Airpass radar. It flew on 4th April 1957. Between 1958 and 1972, 241 Lightnings were built as the F.1, F.3 and F.6 with Avon 200R and 301R engines, and 44 of the side-by-side two-seat version T4 and T5 were also completed. In addition to RAF deliveries, 54 went to Saudi Arabia (F52, F53, T54, T55) and Kuwait (F53K/T55K). The last Lightning was withdrawn from RAF service in 1987. A number of Lightnings have been sold to private owners and are flying or being restored for air displays particularly in South Africa.

English Electric Lightning F.2, XN768

Enstrom F-28 — USA

The F-28 light helicopter first flew on 12th November 1960. In production form it was a three-seater with a metal and fibreglass structure and a 195 h.p. Lycoming HIO-360-C1A piston engine driving a three-blade rotor. Production started in 1966 and 461 of the F28 and similar F28A and F28F Falcon were built. The F28F-P is a specialised police variant. The F28C, of which 177 were completed, had a higher-powered turbocharged engine and, on the F28C-1, a new moulded windscreen. The F280 Shark was an improved F-28 with a more streamlined fuselage, new tail fins and a Lycoming HIO-360-C1B engine. Enstrom have also built the turbocharged 280C and the current 280FX Shark which has a 225 h.p. Lycoming HIO-360-F1AD engine and numerous detailed changes to the undercarriage, tailplane and cockpit systems. Over 130 of the F280 series have been built.

Enstrom F-28C, G-BURI

Enstrom F-28 (Cont.)

Specification	Enstrom F28F Falcon	
Powerplant	One 225 h.p. (167.7 kW) Textron Lycoming HIO-360-F1AD turbocharged piston engine	
Dimensions		
Rotor diameter	9.75 m	(32 ft 0 in)
Length	8.56 m	(28 ft 1 in)
Height	2.74 m	(9 ft 0 in)
Performance		
Max speed	179 km/h	(97 kt, 112 mph)
Cruising speed	163 km/h	(89 kt, 102 mph)
Initial climb	442 m/min	(1,450 fpm)
Range	421 km	(229 nm, 263 miles)
Weights		
Max takeoff	1,179 kg	(2,600 lbs)
Useful load	467 kg	(1,030 lbs)

Enstrom TH-28 and 480 — USA

Enstrom Helicopters moved outside their traditional three-seat personal helicopter sector with the design of the TH-28 which was a contender in the United States Army SCAT basic trainer competition. Based on the Enstrom 280FX, the four-seat TH-28 had a wider fuselage to accommodate two rows of seats and a 420 s.h.p. Allison 250-C20W turboshaft engine driving a three-blade rotor. Fitted with a fixed skid undercarriage, it first flew on 7th October 1989. While it was unsuccessful in the competition it is still available to order but the commercial version is the Enstrom 480. This has a rearranged cabin with five seats in a staggered two-row arrangement and differs from the TH-28 in having a wider windshield and modified cabin structure. Over 60 of the Model 480 have been sold including eight sold in the United Kingdom and others to Thailand, Switzerland and South Africa.

Enstrom 480, G-OZAR

Specification	Enstrom 480	
Powerplant	One 420 s.h.p. (313 kW) Allison 250-C20W turboshaft	
Dimensions		
Rotor diameter	9.75 m	(32 ft 0 in)
Length	9.09 m	(29 ft 10 in)
Height	2.57 m	(8 ft 5 in)
Performance		
Max speed	210 km/h	(114 kt, 131 mph)
Cruising speed	192 km/h	(104 kt, 120 mph)
Initial climb	482 m/min	(1,580 fpm)
Range	760 km	(413 nm, 475 miles)
Weights		
Max takeoff	1,293 kg	(2,850 lbs)
Useful load	533 kg	(1,175 lbs)

Epervier Aviation Epervier — Belgium

The Epervier is one of the more substantial ultralight aircraft to be manufactured in Europe. It is produced as a factory-complete aircraft by Epervier Aviation of Gosselies in ultralight category and JAR-VLA certificated form with 450 kg and 750 kg gross weights respectively. The prototype first flew in September 1990 and it has been in production since 1992, principally for customers in Belgium and France. Construction is of composites with a fibreglass fuselage housing two side-by-side seats and a foam and GRP structure for the strut-braced wings. The Epervier has a spring-steel undercarriage and is fitted with full dual controls.

Epervier, F-67FG

Specification	Epervier Aviation Epervier	
Powerplant	One 75 h.p. (56 kW) Limbach L2000 piston engine	
Dimensions		
Span	11.15 m	(36 ft 7 in)
Length	6.82 m	(22 ft 4 in)
Height	2.55 m	(8 ft 4 in)
Performance		
Max speed	193 km/h	(104 kt, 120 mph)
Cruising speed	177 km/h	(96 kt, 110 mph)
Initial climb	149 m/min	(490 fpm)
Range	480 km	(261 nm, 300 miles)
Weights		
Max takeoff	750 kg	(1,654 lbs)
Useful load	350 kg	(772 lbs)

Erco Ercoupe 415
— USA

The little Ercoupe side-by-side two-seater was designed by Fred Weick to use a novel single-wheel control system which would make the aircraft especially safe and easy to fly. The prototype flew on 1st October 1937. It was an all-metal low-wing aircraft which, in its production 415C form, had twin tail fins, fixed tricycle undercarriage and a 65 h.p. Continental A65 engine. Some 112 were built before the war and 4,969 post-war including a number of 415D and 415CDs with higher gross weights. After Erco ceased production, 473 further examples were built as the Forney F-1 with a 90 h.p. Continental C90 and the Alon A-2 with a sliding bubble canopy and spring-steel undercarriage legs. The Mooney M-10 Cadet was a much modified version with a single vertical tail and a redesigned integral cabin, 61 of which were built between 1969 and 1970. Many Ercoupes are active worldwide with private owners.

Erco Ercoupe 415CD, N94860

Mooney M-10, G-BTOJ

Specification	Erco Ercoupe 415C	
Powerplant	One 75 h.p. (55.9 kW) Continental C75-12 piston engine	
Dimensions		
Span	9.14 m	(30 ft 0 in)
Length	6.15 m	(20 ft 2 in)
Height	1.9 m	(6 ft 3 in)
Performance		
Max speed	187 km/h	(102 kt, 117 mph)
Cruising speed	161 km/h	(87 kt, 100 mph)
Initial climb	229 m/min	(750 fpm)
Range	640 km	(348 nm, 400 miles)
Weights		
Max takeoff	571 kg	(1,260 lbs)
Useful load	209 kg	(460 lbs)

Euravial Fournier RF.47
— France

With a successful record of light aircraft design René Fournier produced the RF.47 to meet the needs of French flying clubs for an economical two-seat trainer. Whilst not being a normal motor glider, the RF.47 has the high-aspect-ratio wings which have characterised other Fournier designs. It has a side-by-side two-seat cockpit with dual controls and a rear-ward-opening canopy and is fitted with a fixed tricycle undercarriage powered by an 87 h.p. Limbach engine. Construction is of wood, carbon fibre and other composite materials. The prototype first flew on 9th April 1993 and the aircraft was certificated under JAR-VLA and placed in production at Epinal. It was either delivered as a factory-complete aircraft or as a kit for amateur construction. Five had been completed by the end of 1998 for purchase by French flying clubs but production was abandoned in 1999.

Euravial Fournier RF.47, F-GRTA

Specification	Euravial Fournier RF.47	
Powerplant	One 87 h.p. (64.87 kW) Limbach 2400 EB1-AA piston engine	
Dimensions		
Span	10 m	(32 ft 9 in)
Length	6.44 m	(21 ft 2 in)
Height	2.22 m	(7 ft 3 in)
Performance		
Max speed	200 km/h	(108 kt, 124 mph)
Cruising speed	178 km/h	(97 kt, 112 mph)
Initial climb	244 m/min	(800 fpm)
Range	1,030 km	(560 nm, 644 miles)
Weights		
Max takeoff	620 kg	(1,367 lbs)
Useful load	225 kg	(497 lbs)

Euro-ALA Jet Fox 97 — Italy

The Jet Fox was first flown in 1991 and is a popular modern ultralight aircraft which combines a traditional ultralight strut-braced high-wing layout with composite construction. It is built with a tube structure clad in a lightweight carbon-fibre pod-and-boom fuselage shell. The Rotax 912 is mounted above the fuselage centre section and the Jet Fox has a fully enclosed side-by-side two-seat cabin. It is fitted with a fixed tricycle undercarriage and the fabric-covered wings are foldable for transportation. Either a 64 h.p. Rotax 582 or an 80 h.p. Rotax 912 can be fitted. The initial model was the Jet Fox 91 and this was followed by the Jet Fox 97 with a fully enclosed engine pod. The latest Jet Fox JF.91S incorporates additional soundproofing. Over 200 examples of the Jet Fox have been built.

Euro-ALA Jet Fox 97

Specification	Euro-ALA Jet Fox 97	
Powerplant	One 80 h.p. (59.65 kW) Rotax 912 piston engine	
Dimensions		
Span	9.78 m	(32 ft 1 in)
Length	5.78 m	(18 ft 11 in)
Height	2.8 m	(9 ft 2 in)
Performance		
Max speed	175 km/h	(95 kt, 109 mph)
Cruising speed	150 km/h	(81 kt, 93 mph)
Initial climb	360 m/min	(1,180 fpm)
Range	320 km	(174 nm, 200 miles)
Weights		
Max takeoff	450 kg	(992 lbs)
Useful load	160 kg	(353 lbs)

Eurocopter SA330 Puma and AS332 Super Puma — France

The SA330 Puma was designed as a 20-troop tactical transport helicopter by Sud Aviation and first flown on 14th April 1965. It has a large main fuselage section with a forward two-seat cockpit and a central box-section cabin with large sliding doors. The twin 1,320 s.h.p. Turboméca Turmo turboshafts are above the cabin driving a four-blade main rotor. Built by Aérospatiale, Westland and by IAR in Romania and IPTN in Indonesia, over 700 were completed and sold widely to the French military (SA330B and H), the RAF (SA330E Puma HC.1) and many overseas countries. A few of the civil SA330G have been sold, largely for offshore oil operations. The AS332 Super Puma has a longer forward fuselage, ventral tail fin, a new rotor head and 1,775 s.h.p. Turboméca Makila engines and in military form is named Cougar. The AS332L is a further stretched version with 2,110 s.h.p. Makila turboshafts. Over 450 Super Pumas, now designated AS532, have been built, many in armed attack configuration.

Eurocopter AS332L2 Super Puma

Eurocopter AS532UL Cougar, S-419 (Netherlands AF)

Specification	Eurocopter AS332L2 Super Puma Mk.II	
Powerplant	Two 2,110 s.h.p. (1,573 kW) Turboméca Makila 1A2 turboshafts	
Dimensions		
Rotor diameter	16.2 m	(53 ft 1 in)
Length	16.79 m	(55 ft 0 in)
Height	4.6 m	(15 ft 1 in)
Performance		
Max speed	278 km/h	(150 kt, 170 mph)
Cruising speed	253 km/h	(136 kt, 158 mph)
Initial climb	441 m/min	(1,447 fpm)
Range	1,483 km	(806 nm, 927 miles)
Weights		
Max takeoff	9,297 kg	(20,500 lbs)
Useful load	4,612 kg	(10,170 lbs)

Eurocopter SA360 and AS365N Dauphin — France

The eight-/ten-passenger Dauphin helicopter was designed by Sud Aviation to fit between the Puma and the Gazelle. The initial SA360 which flew on 2nd June 1972 had a blunt nose, fixed tailwheel undercarriage, fenestron tail rotor and a single Turboméca Astazou XVI turboshaft. Some 36 were built. The SA365 Dauphin 2, flown on 24th January 1975, was a twin-engined development with a pair of 650 s.h.p. Turboméca Arriel 1A engines and the SA365N was a stretched version with a pointed radar nose, a separate 11-passenger cabin and retractable tricycle undercarriage. This was popular in the USA as an executive transport and the armed military SA365F and SA365M have been sold to France, Saudi Arabia and elsewhere. The AS366G1 HH-65A Dolphin is a search & rescue version for the US Coast Guard. Other military variants are all named Panther and include the AS565UB (formerly AS565UA) and AS565AB (formerly AS565AA) which are utility and attack versions with external stores mountings and ten-troop capacity, and the naval AS565MB and AS565SB for search & rescue and ASW duties respectively. The new EC-155 (formerly AS365N4) for offshore and executive use has a wider fuselage and five-blade rotor. Over 600 of the Dauphin 2 variants have been built.

Specification	Eurocopter AS365N2 Dauphin 2	
Powerplant	Two 739 s.h.p. (551 kW) Turboméca Arriel 1C2 turboshafts	
Dimensions		
Rotor diameter	11.94 m	(39 ft 2 in)
Length	11.63 m	(38 ft 2 in)
Height	3.98 m	(13 ft 1 in)
Performance		
Max speed	279 km/h	(150 kt, 174 mph)
Cruising speed	256 km/h	(139 kt, 160 mph)
Initial climb	408 m/min	(1,340 fpm)
Range	860 km	(465 nm, 535 miles)
Weights		
Max takeoff	4,250 kg	(9,371 lbs)
Useful load	1,970 kg	(4,344 lbs)

Eurocopter EC-155, D-HLTH

Eurocopter AS565SB, No.355 (French Navy)

Eurocopter AS350 and AS355 Ecureuil — France

The Ecureuil (Squirrel) is Aérospatiale's light general-purpose helicopter for the civil market although many have been sold to military customers. Designed for ease and speed of construction, the Ecureuil is fitted with the Starflex composite rotor head and has a fixed skid undercarriage. The prototype first flew on 26th June 1974. The production AS350B has a 641 s.h.p. Turboméca Arriel turboshaft engine but the AS350C A-Star, which has sold in large numbers in North America, has the 592 s.h.p. Lycoming LTS101. On 28th September 1979, Aérospatiale flew the first AS355E Ecureuil 2 (Twin Star in the USA) which has two 425 s.h.p. Allison 250-C20F turboshafts. The two models have also been manufactured in Brazil by Helibras as the Esquilo and on an unlicensed basis in China as the Changhe Z-11. The AS355M is an armed version for the French Army and other military customers and the AS350 and AS355 in military configuration are now designated AS550 Fennec and AS555 Fennec. The AS555 can be configured as the AS555MN for maritime surveillance and OTH targeting or the AS555SN armed with torpedoes for anti-submarine warfare. Production of all Ecureuil variants totalled approximately 3,000 by the end of 2000.

Eurocopter AS350D A-Star, N213EH

Eurocopter AS350 and AS355 Ecureuil (Cont.)

Eurocopter AS555MN, 3-H-302 (Argentine Navy)

Specification	Eurocopter AS355N Ecureuil 2	
Powerplant	Two 479 s.h.p. (357 kW) Turboméca TM319 Arrius 1A turboshafts	
Dimensions		
Rotor diameter	10.69 m	(35 ft 1 in)
Length	10.9 m	(35 ft 10 in)
Height	3.34 m	(10 ft 11 in)
Performance		
Max speed	222 km/h	(120 kt, 138 mph)
Cruising speed	217 km/h	(117 kt, 135 mph)
Initial climb	410 m/min	(1,340 fpm)
Range	720 km	(390 nm, 450 miles)
Weights		
Max takeoff	2,600 kg	(5,733 lbs)
Useful load	1,180 kg	(2,602 lbs)

Eurocopter EC-120B, N122TH

Specification	Eurocopter EC-120B Colibri	
Powerplant	One 504 s.h.p. (376 kW) Turboméca TM319 Arrius 2F turboshaft	
Dimensions		
Rotor diameter	10 m	(32 ft 10 in)
Length	9.6 m	(31 ft 6 in)
Height	3.4 m	(11 ft 2 in)
Performance		
Max speed	237 km/h	(128 kt, 147 mph)
Cruising speed	201 km/h	(109 kt, 125 mph)
Initial climb	435 m/min	(1,425 fpm)
Range	770 km	(416 nm, 479 miles)
Weights		
Max takeoff	1,680 kg	(3,704 lbs)
Useful load	785 kg	(1,730 lbs)

Eurocopter EC-120 Colibri
— France/Germany

Eurocopter, which was formed by Aérospatiale and Messerschmitt-Bölkow-Blohm in 1992, inherited the EC-120 Colibri light business helicopter which had been initiated by Aérospatiale in 1990. This high-performance helicopter is constructed of metal and composites and has five seats and a large rear baggage hold. The three-blade rotor is composite with a Spheriflex lubrication-free rotor head and the EC-120 has an eight-blade Fenestron shrouded tail rotor. It is fitted with a tubular-framed skid undercarriage. The prototype EC-120 was first flown on 9th June 1995. The production standard EC-120B has a 504 s.h.p. Turboméca Arrius 2F turboshaft engine and is built by an international consortium including Eurocopter, SAT and CATIC. Over 120 had been built by the end of 2000 with most aircraft going to business customers but several being used for aeromedical and police work.

Eurocopter EC-135
— France/Germany

The EC-135 is a larger companion to the EC-120 with a larger cabin and five to seven seats. Its design originated with the Bö.108 created by Messerschmitt-Bölkow-Blohm and first flown as a prototype on 15th October 1988. The EC-135, which first flew on 15th February 1994, has a larger cabin than the Bo.108, a ten-blade fenestron shrouded tail rotor and a bearingless main rotor head with a four-blade composite rotor. The cabin runs for the full length of the main fuselage and has a rear loading hatch. When the main cabin seats are removed stretchers or long items of cargo can be loaded directly into the cabin. Power is provided by either two Pratt & Whitney PWC206B (EC-135P) or Turboméca Arrius 2B turboshafts (EC-135T). The military version is designated EC-635. Sales of the EC-135 have been made to corporate operators, law enforcement and EMS users and to governmental organisations and over 160 had been delivered by the end of 2000.

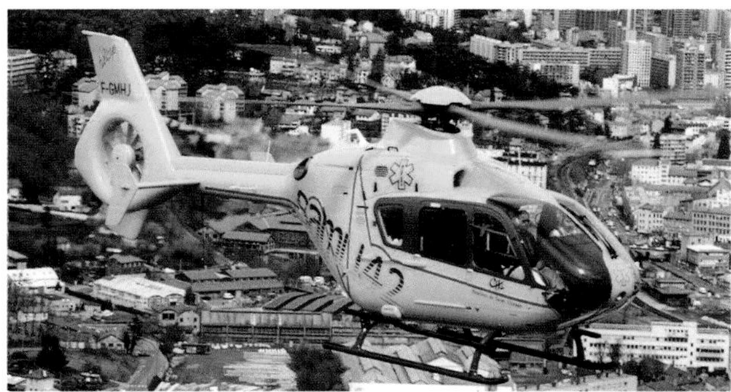

Eurocopter EC-135T1, F-GMHJ

Specification	Eurocopter EC-135T	
Powerplant	Two 559 s.h.p. (416.8 kW) Turboméca Arrius 2B turboshafts	
Dimensions		
Rotor diameter	10.2 m	(33 ft 5 in)
Length	10.16 m	(33 ft 4 in)
Height	3.62 m	(11 ft 10 in)
Performance		
Max speed	261 km/h	(141 kt, 162 mph)
Cruising speed	248 km/h	(135 kt, 155 mph)
Initial climb	533 m/min	(1,750 fpm)
Range	664 km	(360 nm, 415 miles)
Weights		
Max takeoff	2,630 kg	(5,800 lbs)
Useful load	1,202 kg	(2,650 lbs)

Eurocopter Tiger
— France/Germany

The Tiger (originally designated PAH-1) was the second of the jointly developed helicopters produced by Aérospatiale and MBB following the formation of Eurocopter. The Tiger is a tandem two-seat all-weather combat helicopter which will be produced in UHT combat/support and HAP escort/support versions. Built largely of composites, it is an all-weather aircraft with advanced avionics and weapons systems and stealth characteristics. It is designed to be able to fire Stinger air-to-air missiles and the Euromissile HOT-2 and TRIGAT anti-tank missiles. The first Tiger was flown at Marignane on 27th April 1991 followed by four further prototypes. Some 160 Tigers are on order for delivery from 2001 with an expected eventual total requirement of 427 for the French and German forces.

Eurocopter Tiger HAP, F-ZWWU

Specification	Eurocopter Tiger	
Powerplant	Two 1,285 s.h.p. (958 kW) MTU-Turboméca-Rolls Royce MTR390 turboshafts	
Dimensions		
Rotor diameter	13 m	(42 ft 8 in)
Length	15 m	(49 ft 3 in)
Height	3.8 m	(12 ft 6 in)
Performance		
Max speed	280 km/h	(150 kt, 174 mph)
Cruising speed	264 km/h	(144 kt, 165 mph)
Initial climb	690 m/min	(2,265 fpm)
Range	795 km	(432 nm, 497 miles)
Weights		
Max takeoff	5,925 kg	(13,065 lbs)
Useful load	2,625 kg	(5,788 lbs)

Eurofighter Typhoon
— UK/Germany/Italy/Spain

The high-technology Eurofighter is under development by BAE Systems, Daimler Chrysler Aerospace, Alenia and CASA and seven development prototypes, including two two-seaters, have flown, the first on 27th March 1994. Eurofighter is a twin-turbofan multi-role combat aircraft for close-in combat, ground attack, air interdiction and air defence beyond visual range and has good stealth characteristics. It is delta-winged with a forward canard surface and conventional vertical fin and is built in single-seat and tandem two-seat versions both of which are fully combat capable and fitted with 13 external stores stations and a 27 mm Mauser gun. Initial orders are for 620 aircraft for the four partner countries with service entry in 2002. The Eurofighter is equipped with fly-by-wire systems, advanced pilot management including a head-up display, helmet-mounted display and voice-activated instruments. It is named Eurofighter for use by the participating nations and Typhoon for export sale.

Eurofighter (single-seat), 9830

Eurofighter Typhoon (Cont.)

Eurofighter (two-seat), XCE.16-01

Specification	Eurofighter Typhoon	
Powerplant	Two 20,000 lb.s.t. (89 kN wet) Eurojet Turbo EJ200 turbofans	
Dimensions		
Span	10.95 m	(35 ft 11 in)
Length	15.96 m	(52 ft 5 in)
Height	5.28 m	(17 ft 4 in)
Performance		
Max speed	2,435 km/h	(1,323 kt, 1,522 mph)
Takeoff distance	300 m	(985 ft)
Range	3,680 km	(2,000 nm, 2,300 miles)
Weights		
Max takeoff	21,000 kg	(46,305 lbs)
Useful load	11,000 kg	(24,255 lbs)

Europa Aircraft Europa
— UK

The Europa light aircraft was designed by Ivan Shaw as a high-performance two-seater which could be sold as a kit and be easily assembled by inexperienced amateur builders. It is of all-composite construction with the kit being composed of half shells for the fuselage and wings. The Europa, which first flew in September 1992, has removable wings for storage and transport. It has a retractable monowheel undercarriage or an optional fixed tricycle gear and the side-by-side cockpit is fitted with dual controls. The latest Europa XS, powered by either an 80 h.p. Rotax 912, a 100 h.p. Rotax 912S or a 115 h.p. turbocharged Rotax 914 engine, uses a modified longer-span wing which is simpler to construct and has a larger baggage area. Alternative high-aspect-ratio wings can be fitted to turn the aircraft into a motor glider. Over 630 kits had been sold in 31 countries by mid-1999 and more than 130 were flying in the UK, USA, Austria, Germany and elsewhere. The Liberty XL-2 is a redesigned version launched in 2000, intended for certificated production with a metal wing and a 100 h.p. Rotax 912S engine.

Europa Turbo XS, G-GBXS

Specification	Europa Turbo XS	
Powerplant	One 115 h.p. (85.7 kW) turbocharged Rotax 914 piston engine	
Dimensions		
Span	8.28 m	(27 ft 2 in)
Length	5.84 m	(19 ft 2 in)
Height	1.32 m	(4 ft 4 in)
Performance		
Max speed	320 km/h	(174 kt, 200 mph)
Cruising speed	285 km/h	(155 kt, 178 mph)
Initial climb	396 m/min	(1,300 fpm)
Range (std)	1,345 km	(732 nm, 841 miles)
Weights		
Max takeoff	623 kg	(1,370 lbs)
Useful load	281 kg	(620 lbs)

Evangel Air Evangel II — USA

Evangel Aircraft Corporation was established at Orange City, Iowa to produce the Evangel 4500-300 twin-engined utility aircraft, designed by Carl Mortensen. The Evangel was intended as a rugged utility aircraft for use on missionary operations in South America and the prototype first flew in 1965. The original Evangel was an all-metal high-wing twin with a fixed undercarriage but it was totally redesigned with a low wing as the Evangel II and in this form flew in August 1968. It was fitted with a pair of 300 h.p. Lycoming IO-540-K1B5 engines and had a retractable tailwheel undercarriage, a slab-sided fuselage with large cargo doors on both sides and large wings incorporating dihedralled outer panels and drooping wingtips. The first Evangel was delivered in November 1972 and eight aircraft (including the prototype) were eventually completed. Few of these were actually used for missionary work and the survivors are flying commercially in Peru.

Evangel 4500-300, OB-T-1021

Specification	Evangel Air Evangel 4500-300	
Powerplant	Two 300 h.p. (223.7 kW) Textron Lycoming IO-540-K1B5 piston engines	
Dimensions		
Span	12.57 m	(41 ft 3 in)
Length	9.6 m	(31 ft 6 in)
Height	2.9 m	(9 ft 6 in)
Performance		
Max speed	370 km/h	(200 kt, 230 mph)
Cruising speed	293 km/h	(158 kt, 182 mph)
Initial climb	456 m/min	(1,500 fpm)
Range	1,200 km	(650 nm, 750 miles)
Weights		
Max takeoff	2,494 kg	(5,500 lbs)
Useful load	893 kg	(1,970 lbs)

Evans VP-1 and VP-2 — USA

Originally named the Evans Volksplane, the VP-1 was one of the most popular ultralight homebuilts of the 1970s. First flown in 1969, it is of wood and fabric construction with a strut-braced low wing and fixed tailwheel undercarriage. It has an all-moving fin and tailplane. The fuselage is just large enough to contain the engine and the single-seat cockpit, which is normally open but may be enclosed with a bubble canopy. Some VP-1s have a built-up rear fuselage and faired-in cockpit. The powerplant for the VP-1 is normally a converted Volkswagen of 1500 cc to 1800 cc but a number of other engines of around 60 h.p. can be fitted. Over 5,000 sets of plans have been sold and many hundreds of VP-1s are flying. The VP-2 is a development with a wider fuselage providing two seats side-by-side and is powered by a larger Continental C90 or other engine of up to 100 h.p.

Evans VP-1, EI-AYY

Specification	Evans VP-1	
Powerplant	One 40 h.p. (29.8 kW) Volkswagen 1500 piston engine	
Dimensions		
Span	7.32 m	(24 ft 0 in)
Length	5.49 m	(18 ft 0 in)
Height	1.56 m	(5 ft 1 in)
Performance		
Max speed	136 km/h	(74 kt, 85 mph)
Cruising speed	120 km/h	(65 kt, 75 mph)
Initial climb	122 m/min	(400 fpm)
Range	320 km	(174 nm, 200 miles)
Weights		
Max takeoff	336 kg	(740 lbs)
Useful load	132 kg	(290 lbs)

Evektor Eurostar EV-97 — Czech Republic

The Eurostar EV-97 is one of a number of modern light aircraft derived from the Pottier P.220 Koala, others being the SG Storm, the Aerotechnica-CZ and the Aero AT-3. Evektor acquired Aerotechnik which started production of the P.220UL ultralight version of the Koala and then developed the modified Eurostar which is also marketed as a kit by Ikarus in Germany. The Eurostar is an all-metal factory-built aircraft with side-by-side seating for two, a conventional low wing and a fixed tricycle undercarriage. By comparison with the Koala, the Eurostar embodies several changes, particularly to the tail unit and the fuel system. Over 30 Eurostars have been built with several being exported, particularly to Germany.

Evektor Eurostar EV-97, D-MPEV

Specification	Evektor Eurostar EV-97	
Powerplant	One 80 h.p. (59.65 kW) Rotax 912 piston engine	
Dimensions		
Span	7.9 m	(25 ft 11 in)
Length	5.98 m	(19 ft 7 in)
Height	2.34 m	(7 ft 8 in)
Performance		
Max speed	200 km/h	(108 kt, 124 mph)
Cruising speed	178 km/h	(97 kt, 112 mph)
Initial climb	270 m/min	(886 fpm)
Range	800 km	(435 nm, 500 miles)
Weights		
Max takeoff	450 kg	(992 lbs)
Useful load	175 kg	(386 lbs)

Extra EA230, EA220 and EA300 — Germany

In the early 1980s Walter Extra designed the single-seat Extra 230 to compete in the competition aerobatics field with the new Zlin and Sukhoi monoplanes. The EA230 was based on the American-designed mid-wing Stephens Akro but with a raised rear fuselage, faired-in canopy and modified wooden wing. The first EA230 flew on 14th July 1983 and 15 production aircraft were subsequently completed with the 200 h.p. Lycoming AEIO-360-A1E engine. The EA230 was developed into the EA300 which has a composite wing, tandem two-seat cockpit and 300 h.p. Lycoming AEIO-540 engine. The EA300S is a shorter single-seat version of the EA300 with a lower-set wing and the EA300L is the two-seater with the low wing. The latest variant is the lower-cost EA200 two-seater, based on the EA300L with a 200 h.p. Lycoming AEIO-360A1E engine, a lighter-weight airframe and lower gross weight. Over 220 Extras have been built.

Extra EA300, 024 (Chile AF)

Specification	Extra EA300L	
Powerplant	One 300 h.p. (223.68 kW) Textron Lycoming AEIO-540-L1B5 piston engine	
Dimensions		
Span	7.7 m	(25 ft 3 in)
Length	6.96 m	(22 ft 10 in)
Height	2.62 m	(8 ft 7 in)
Performance		
Max speed	386 km/h	(210 kt, 242 mph)
Cruising speed	331 km/h	(180 kt, 207 mph)
Initial climb	975 m/min	(3,200 fpm)
Range	764 km	(415 nm, 477 miles)
Weights		
Max takeoff	950 kg	(2,095 lbs)
Useful load	297 kg	(655 lbs)

Extra EA400 — Germany

On 4th April 1996 Extra flew the prototype of its EA400 six-seat pressurised touring aircraft. The EA400 is an all-composite cabin aircraft with a 350 h.p. Continental Voyager TSIOL-550A piston engine and a tricycle undercarriage which retracts into fully enclosed fuselage wells. It has a cantilever high wing and a highly streamlined circular-section fuselage which is fitted with a split airstair entry door giving access to the main air-conditioned cabin. Passenger accommodation is for four people in facing seats with a two-seat crew cockpit. The EA400 has a T-tail and is fitted with large Fowler flaps for approach control. The engine is a 350 h.p. six-cylinder Teledyne Continental TSIOL-550-A driving a three-bladed constant-speed propeller. Ten EA400s had flown by the end of 2000 and first customer deliveries were made in early 1999.

Extra EA400, D-EWCO

Specification	Extra EA400	
Powerplant	One 350 h.p. (261 kW) Teledyne Continental TSIOL-550-A piston engine	
Dimensions		
Span	11.5 m	(37 ft 9 in)
Length	9.5 m	(31 ft 2 in)
Height	3.09 m	(10 ft 2 in)
Performance		
Max speed	480 km/h	(259 kt, 300 mph)
Cruising speed	450 km/h	(244 kt, 280 mph)
Initial climb	427 m/min	(1,400 fpm)
Range	1,700 km	(924 nm, 1,063 miles)
Weights		
Max takeoff	1,950 kg	(4,300 lbs)
Useful load	744 kg	(1,640 lbs)

Fairchild KR-21 — USA

In April 1929, Fairchild Aircraft acquired Kreider-Reisner who had been building the OX-5-powered three-seat KR-31 (C-2) Challenger light biplane. Over 250 were completed including the KR-34A (C-4A) with a Challenger engine and the KR-34C (C-4C) with a Wright J6. The smaller KR-21 (C-6) was generally similar but was a tandem two-seat sport trainer with dual controls, tapered wings and a fixed tailwheel undercarriage. It was built from steel tube with fabric covering. In production KR-21A (C-6B) form it was powered by a 100 h.p. Kinner K5 five-cylinder radial engine and was also known as the Sportster when fitted with deluxe equipment such as brakes, navigation lights and a metal propeller. Some 43 KR-21As were built followed by three KR-21Bs with a 125 h.p. Kinner B5 engine. A total of 26 KR-31/34s and 12 KR-21s remain active in the USA.

Fairchild KR21, N107M

Specification	Fairchild KR-21B	
Powerplant	One 125 h.p. (93.2 kW) Kinner B5 piston engine	
Dimensions		
Span	8.23 m	(27 ft 0 in)
Length	6.58 m	(21 ft 7 in)
Height	2.59 m	(8 ft 6 in)
Performance		
Max speed	184 km/h	(100 kt, 115 mph)
Cruising speed	157 km/h	(85 kt, 98 mph)
Initial climb	244 m/min	(800 fpm)
Range	592 km	(322 nm, 370 miles)
Weights		
Max takeoff	785 kg	(1,730 lbs)
Useful load	277 kg	(610 lbs)

Fairchild 22 — USA

Having successfully sold several hundred KR-31 and KR-21 biplanes, Fairchild's Kreider-Reisner subsidiary produced the new Model 22 (C-7) tandem two-seat trainer. This aircraft was a parasol-wing monoplane with a new and distinctive rounded fin which was to become a Fairchild trademark and a fixed tailwheel undercarriage. Initially powered by an 80 h.p. Genet engine the production 22-C7 had a 75 h.p. Rover L-267 in-line engine and 12 were built. This was followed by further Model 22 variants including the 22-

Fairchild 22 (Cont.)

C7A with a 95 h.p. Cirrus Hi-Drive engine, the 22-C7B with a 125 h.p. Menasco C4, the 22-C7D with a 90 h.p. Wright Gipsy, the 22-C7E with a 125 h.p. Warner Scarab radial and the 22-C7F and -C7G with the 145 h.p. Warner Super Scarab. In total 118 Fairchild 22s were built and more than 25 are current survivors although several have been re-engined.

Fairchild 22-C7D, NC14302

Specification	Fairchild 22-C7B	
Powerplant	One 125 h.p. (93.2 kW) Menasco C4 piston engine	
Dimensions		
Span	9.7 m	(31 ft 10 in)
Length	6.68 m	(21 ft 11 in)
Height	2.44 m	(8 ft 0 in)
Performance		
Max speed	200 km/h	(109 kt, 125 mph)
Cruising speed	170 km/h	(92 kt, 106 mph)
Initial climb	320 m/min	(1,050 fpm)
Range	640 km	(348 nm, 400 miles)
Weights		
Max takeoff	794 kg	(1,750 lbs)
Useful load	336 kg	(740 lbs)

Fairchild 24 Argus — USA

Probably the most famous of the high-wing Fairchild light aircraft, and certainly the model produced in the largest numbers, the Model 24 started as an enclosed cabin version of the C-22 with a wider fuselage and two seats side-by-side. The 24-C8 had a 95 h.p. Cirrus and the C8A a 125 h.p. Scarab and 38 were built in total. The 24-C8C was given a longer cabin with a rear third seat and the -C8C to -C8F were fitted with various engines including the 145 h.p. Warner Super Scarab and 150 h.p. Ranger 390-D3 (-C8F and -C8H). Some 261 of the three-seaters were completed before the 24-C8G was introduced with a larger full four-seat cabin, hump-back fuselage and a larger pointed tail. The 24K and 24R9 were powered by a 165 h.p. Ranger 6-410B in-line engine and the 24W9 had a 165 h.p. Warner 50 radial. A total of 670 of the 24W were built as the wartime UC-61A Argus and 306 of the 24R were built as the UC-61K Forwarder and many of these remain in private operation.

Fairchild 24-C8C, NC15921

Fairchild 24R, G-AJPI

Specification	Fairchild F-24W-46	
Powerplant	One 165 h.p. (123 kW) Warner 165D radial piston engine	
Dimensions		
Span	11.1 m	(36 ft 4 in)
Length	7.3 m	(23 ft 10 in)
Height	2.3 m	(7 ft 7 in)
Performance		
Max speed	219 km/h	(119 kt, 137 mph)
Cruising speed	187 km/h	(102 kt, 117 mph)
Initial climb	250 m/min	(820 fpm)
Range	1,024 km	(557 nm, 640 miles)
Weights		
Max takeoff	1,165 kg	(2,569 lbs)
Useful load	414 kg	(911 lbs)

Fairchild F-45 — USA

The F-45, designed by Fairchild as a fast private and business aircraft, first flew on 31st May 1935 and was powered by a 225 h.p. Jacobs L-4 radial engine. The Model 45 was a low-wing aircraft with a retractable tailwheel undercarriage and was built of steel tube with wooden stringers and fabric covering. The fully enclosed cabin had seating for five and was fitted with entry doors on both sides. The production Model 45A had a larger 320 h.p. Wright R-760 engine and 16 were built, four of which are still flying with private owners in the United States. One was used by the US Navy as the JK-1 and two were sold to the Argentine Navy. Some of the survivors have been re-engined, one with a 475 h.p. Wright Whirlwind.

Fairchild F-45, NC1687

Specification	Fairchild F-45A	
Powerplant	One 320 h.p. (238.6 kW) Wright R-760-E2 piston engine	
Dimensions		
Span	12.04 m	(39 ft 6 in)
Length	9.17 m	(30 ft 1 in)
Height	2.44 m	(8 ft 0 in)
Performance		
Max speed	272 km/h	(148 kt, 170 mph)
Cruising speed	240 km/h	(130 kt, 150 mph)
Initial climb	305 m/min	(1,000 fpm)
Range	1,840 km	(1,000 nm, 1,150 miles)
Weights		
Max takeoff	1,814 kg	(4,000 lbs)
Useful load	675 kg	(1,488 lbs)

Fairchild FC-2 and 71 — USA

In the 1920s, Fairchild became known as a leader in the field of reliable light transports for operation in the outback. The FC-2 was a high-wing strut-braced monoplane with a fixed tailwheel undercarriage and an enclosed cabin housing a pilot and up to six passengers. Construction was of steel tube, wood and fabric. It was powered by a big 200 h.p. Wright J4B radial engine and the aircraft was popular as a small airliner with Pan Am and American Airlines. It flew with the Byrd Antarctic expedition and also flew in Canada where it was operated in remote bush locations on floats and skis and also built under licence by Canadian Vickers as the Model 71-C and the Model 7-CM with metal fuselage covering. It was later refined into the Fairchild 71 which had greater load-carrying ability, a plush passenger interior and a 420 h.p. Pratt & Whitney Wasp engine. At least four FC-2s still exist and five Fairchild 71s are airworthy in the USA and Canada, and a Fairchild 82 is under restoration in Argentina.

Fairchild 71, N2K

Specification	Fairchild 71	
Powerplant	One 420 h.p. (313.2 kW) Pratt & Whitney Wasp piston engine	
Dimensions		
Span	15.29 m	(50 ft 2 in)
Length	10.06 m	(33 ft 0 in)
Height	2.84 m	(9 ft 4 in)
Performance		
Max speed	220 km/h	(120 kt, 138 mph)
Cruising speed	176 km/h	(96 kt, 110 mph)
Initial climb	299 m/min	(980 fpm)
Range	1,040 km	(565 nm, 650 miles)
Weights		
Max takeoff	2,358 kg	(5,200 lbs)
Useful load	1,134 kg	(2,500 lbs)

Fairchild F-11 Husky — Canada

Fairchild Aircraft Ltd. of Canada gained a reputation for producing the Model 71 bush aircraft which was ideal for Canadian conditions. An all-metal version of this aircraft, the Super 71P, was developed after World War II into the F-11 Husky. The Husky was primarily intended as a seaplane, although wheels or skis could be fitted. It was a strut-braced high-wing machine with a waisted rear fuselage, a freight-loading door on each side and a high-set tail unit. It could carry six to eight passengers and a crew of two. The prototype made its first flight in June 1946 and was powered by a 450 h.p. Pratt & Whitney Wasp R-985-SB3 radial engine. Fairchild delivered a total of 12 Huskies between 1947 and 1949 and several attempts have been made since to revive the design. Two Huskies are operational in Canada, one of which has been fitted with an Alvis Leonides engine.

Fairchild F-11 Husky (Cont.)

Fairchild F-11 Husky, C-GCYV

Specification	Fairchild F-11 Husky	
Powerplant	One 450 h.p. (335.5 kW) Pratt & Whitney R-985-SB3 Wasp Junior piston engine	
Dimensions		
Span	16.69 m	(54 ft 9 in)
Length	11.4 m	(37 ft 5 in)
Height	5.41 m	(17 ft 9 in)
Performance		
Max speed	224 km/h	(122 kt, 140 mph)
Cruising speed	192 km/h	(104 kt, 120 mph)
Initial climb	235 m/min	(770 fpm)
Range	1,312 km	(713 nm, 820 miles)
Weights		
Max takeoff	2,902 kg	(6,400 lbs)
Useful load	998 kg	(2,200 lbs)

Fairchild M-62 Cornell
— USA

In March 1939, Fairchild flew the prototype of their M-62 primary trainer, designed to teach wartime pilots. By the time production was completed in April 1944 a total of 5,048 had been built. The Cornell was a low-wing aircraft with a fixed tailwheel undercarriage and tandem cockpits which were normally open but sometimes had a glazed canopy. The initial model, the PT-19 ((M-62A), had a 175 h.p. Ranger L-440-1 in-line engine or 200 h.p. L-440-3 (PT-19A) and an instrument training version was designated PT-19B. The PT-23 was a later version with a Continental R-670-5 radial engine which was left uncowled. A winterised version of the PT-19A for Canada with a cockpit canopy was designated PT-26 and over 1,000 were built in Canada by Fleet Aircraft. Many Cornells were civilianised after the war, some being converted to Funk F-23 crop sprayers. Over 300 M-62s are still active worldwide.

Fairchild (Fleet) PT-26B, N53366

Specification	Fairchild M-62A, PT-19A Cornell	
Powerplant	One 200 h.p. (149.12 kW) Ranger L-440-3 piston engine	
Dimensions		
Span	10.97 m	(36 ft 0 in)
Length	8.44 m	(27 ft 8 in)
Height	2.29 m	(7 ft 6 in)
Performance		
Max speed	208 km/h	(113 kt, 130 mph)
Cruising speed	176 km/h	(96 kt, 110 mph)
Initial climb	244 m/min	(800 fpm)
Range	720 km	(391 nm, 450 miles)
Weights		
Max takeoff	1,225 kg	(2,700 lbs)
Useful load	317 kg	(700 lbs)

Fairchild C-82 and C-119
— USA

In response to a USAF requirement for a specialised military freighter, Fairchild designed the C-82 which first flew on 10th September 1944. Because of its high-wing twin-boomed layout it could achieve rapid cargo loading through the rear clamshell doors in the fuselage pod and had a virtually unobstructed square-section cargo hold. Some 220 of the C-82A Packet, powered by two 2,100 h.p. Pratt & Whitney R-2800-85 engines, were built for the USAF. These were followed by 1,028 of the C-119 Flying Boxcar which had a wider fuselage, lower-set flight deck and a modified tail without ventral fins. The C-119B had 2,650 h.p. R-4360 engines and the C-119C 3,500 h.p. R-4360-20WA engines. Overseas air forces using the C-119 included Italy, Canada, India and Belgium. In Vietnam a gunship version, the AC-119K, was operated. A few C-119s continue in service for cargo operations in Alaska and for aerial firefighting with an auxiliary roof-mounted turbojet and internal chemical tanks and at least one C-82 operates in private hands.

Fairchild C-82 Packet, N9701

Specification	Fairchild C-119G Packet	
Powerplant	Two 3,400 h.p. (2,535 kW) Wright R-3350-89W piston engines	
Dimensions		
Span	33.3 m	(109 ft 3 in)
Length	25.96 m	(85 ft 2 in)
Height	8 m	(26 ft 3 in)
Performance		
Max speed	475 km/h	(258 kt, 297 mph)
Cruising speed	320 km/h	(174 kt, 200 mph)
Initial climb	229 m/min	(750 fpm)
Range	3,640 km	(1,978 nm, 2,275 miles)
Weights		
Max takeoff	33,741 kg	(74,400 lbs)
Useful load	15,600 kg	(34,400 lbs)

Fairchild C-123 Provider
— USA

A growing emphasis on tactical air operations in the late 1940s led to development of the Chase XC-123 Avitruck based on the Chase CG-20 cargo-carrying glider fitted with two Pratt & Whitney R-2800 radial engines. The improved XC-123A first flew on 21st April 1951 and the C-123B went into production with Fairchild in 1954. The C-123 was a medium-lift transport with a high wing, tail loading ramp and retractable tricycle undercarriage. The USAF acquired 308 aircraft in total and 183 were converted to C-123K configuration with a pair of supplementary General Electric CJ610 turbojets in underwing pods. The UC-123K was used in Vietnam with underwing spray bars for defoliation and was supplied to the air forces of Venezuela, Saudi Arabia, the Philippines, Taiwan and Thailand. Eight were used by the US Coast Guard. A number of Providers remain in service, mainly with civil freight operators or governmental agencies.

Fairchild C-123B, N87DT

Specification	Fairchild C-123B Provider	
Powerplant	Two 2,500 h.p. (1,864 kW) Pratt & Whitney R-2800-99W piston engines	
Dimensions		
Span	33.53 m	(110 ft 0 in)
Length	23.24 m	(76 ft 3 in)
Height	10.39 m	(34 ft 1 in)
Performance		
Max speed	400 km/h	(217 kt, 250 mph)
Cruising speed	296 km/h	(160 kt, 185 mph)
Initial climb	350 m/min	(1,150 fpm)
Range	3,904 km	(2,122 nm, 2,440 miles)
Weights		
Max takeoff	27,211 kg	(60,000 lbs)
Useful load	12,970 kg	(28,600 lbs)

Fairchild Dornier Do.228
— Germany

On 28th March 1981 Dornier flew the prototype of its Do.228-100 which was a 16-seat commuter aircraft developed from the smaller Do.28D Skyservant. It had a square-section unpressurised fuselage with external sponsons to accommodate the retracting main undercarriage units and was powered by a pair of Garrett TPE331 turboprops mounted on the high-mounted new-technology wing which had been developed by Dornier on its TNT development aircraft. Some 45 of the 228-100 and -101 were built, ten of which were completed by Hindustan in India. The Do.228-200 was a 20-seat version with a 5 ft fuselage stretch and more powerful engines. This was built as the Do.228-201, Do.228-202 and Do.228-212 with airframe strengthening and progressively increased gross weights and useful loads. Again, 12 were built by Hindustan and 192 by the parent Dornier company which was acquired by Fairchild in June 1996. Production ceased in Germany in 1998 and further output will come from the Indian factory. Over 120 Dornier 228s remain in service with airlines and military operators.

Dornier Do.228-212, D-CDIV

Fairchild Dornier Do.228 (Cont.)

HAL-Dornier Do.228-101, CG760 (Indian Coastguard)

Specification	Fairchild Dornier Do.228-212	
Powerplant	Two 776 s.h.p. (578.7 kW) Honeywell (Garrett) TPE331-5-252D turboprops	
Dimensions		
Span	16.97 m	(55 ft 8 in)
Length	16.56 m	(54 ft 4 in)
Height	4.85 m	(15 ft 11 in)
Performance		
Max speed	370 km/h	(200 kt, 230 mph)
Cruising speed	331 km/h	(180 kt, 207 mph)
Initial climb	570 m/min	(1,870 fpm)
Range	1,160 km	(630 nm, 725 miles)
Weights		
Max takeoff	6,400 kg	(14,110 lbs)
Useful load	2,660 kg	(5,865 lbs)

Fairchild Dornier Do.328 — Germany

The Do.328 is a 33-passenger high-wing pressurised commuter aircraft developed by Dornier using much of the design background of the Do.228. The wing follows the lines of the multi-tapered TNT wing used on the 228 but the fuselage is of circular section with three-abreast passenger seating. The aircraft has a T-tail and fuselage fairings to house the undercarriage. The prototype Do.328-100 first flew on 6th December 1991 and 35 had flown by 1998. The Do.328-110 has a larger tail and a higher gross weight and the Do.328-120 is a higher-performance version with PW119C engines. More than 110 Do.328s had been completed by the end of 2000 and had been delivered to a range of commuter airlines including Air Engiadina and Suckling Airways and the American operators Mountain Air Express and Horizon Airlines. Several examples of the corporate shuttle version have been sold to business aircraft users in the USA.

Fairchild Dornier Do.328-120, N329MX

Specification	Fairchild Dornier Do.328-110	
Powerplant	Two 2,180 s.h.p. (1,625 kW) Pratt & Whitney PW119B turboprops	
Dimensions		
Span	20.98 m	(68 ft 10 in)
Length	21.28 m	(69 ft 10 in)
Height	7.24 m	(23 ft 9 in)
Performance		
Max speed	620 km/h	(335 kt, 388 mph)
Cruising speed	592 km/h	(322 kt, 370 mph)
Takeoff distance	1,088 m	(3,570 ft)
Range	1,840 km	(1,000 nm, 1,150 miles)
Weights		
Max takeoff	13,990 kg	(30,848 lbs)
Useful load	5,070 kg	(11,179 lbs)

Fairchild 328JET — Germany

Fairchild Aerospace found that the Do.328 was an ideal platform for development of a regional jet to compete with aircraft such as the Embraer EMB-135. The prototype 328JET was converted from an existing 328 airframe with the turboprop engines removed and two 6,050 lb.s.t. PW306/9 turbofans fitted in underwing pylon-mounted pods. A pair of ventral fins was also fitted on the rear fuselage and the aircraft has a strengthened wing, some aerodynamic wing modifications and larger flaps. It first flew on 20th January 1998 and has been certificated as a derivative of the Do.328. It is being sold with a 34-passenger commuter interior or as an executive jet named the Envoy 3. A stretched version, the Do.428JET, has a longer fuselage, larger wing, 44 seats and PW308 engines.

Fairchild 328JET, D-BALL

Specification	Fairchild Dornier 328JET	
Powerplant	Two 6,050 lb.s.t. (26.9 kN) Pratt & Whitney PW306/9 turbofans	
Dimensions		
Span	20.98 m	(68 ft 10 in)
Length	21.28 m	(69 ft 10 in)
Height	7.24 m	(23 ft 9 in)
Performance		
Max speed	740 km/h	(400 kt, 460 mph)
Cruising speed	712 km/h	(387 kt, 445 mph)
Initial climb	686 m/min	(2,250 fpm)
Range	1,656 km	(900 nm, 1,035 miles)
Weights		
Max takeoff	15,200 kg	(33,516 lbs)
Useful load	6,000 kg	(13,230 lbs)

Fairchild-Hiller FH.1100 — USA

In May 1961 Fairchild Stratos acquired Hiller Helicopters and inherited the Hiller 1100 four-seat helicopter. It was of conventional layout with a skid undercarriage and the engine mounted above and behind the cabin and had been designed as the OH-5A to compete in the US Army Light Observation Helicopter competition of 1961. It first flew on 26th January 1963. It was unsuccessful in the military assessment but Fairchild-Hiller put it into production as the FH.1100 for civil customers. In commercial form it had five seats, a new rotor system and an Allison 250 engine. Some 245 were built by Fairchild-Hiller and a number of these still fly with civil users in the USA and South America. A further four aircraft were built by Rogerson Hiller who relaunched the type as the RH-1100B Pegasus in 1983 and also offered the RH-1100M Hornet for military customers. This programme was abandoned in 1990.

Fairchild-Hiller FH.1100, CC-CHI

Specification	Fairchild Hiller FH.1100	
Powerplant	One 317 s.h.p. (236.4 kW) Allison 250-C18 turboshaft	
Dimensions		
Rotor diameter	10.8 m	(35 ft 5 in)
Length	8.47 m	(27 ft 10 in)
Height	2.83 m	(9 ft 3 in)
Performance		
Max speed	203 km/h	(110 kt, 127 mph)
Cruising speed	192 km/h	(104 kt, 120 mph)
Initial climb	488 m/min	(1,600 fpm)
Range	557 km	(303 nm, 348 miles)
Weights		
Max takeoff	1,247 kg	(2,750 lbs)
Useful load	626 kg	(1,380 lbs)

Fairchild-Swearingen Merlin II and III — USA

The SA26-T Merlin II eight-seat executive turboprop aircraft was designed by Ed Swearingen based on experience with modification of Beech Queen Airs and Twin Bonanzas. The Merlin, which flew on 13th April 1965, had a circular-section pressurised fuselage, a low wing with two Pratt & Whitney PT6A-20 engines and a retractable tricycle undercarriage. The later eight-/ten-seat SA26-AT Merlin IIB had a higher useful load and AiResearch TPE331-1-151G engines. Some 180 Merlin IIs were built. The SA226-T Merlin III which followed was substantially redesigned with a deeper fuselage, larger cruciform tail and a new undercarriage with a forward-retracting nosewheel; 205 were built and variants included the Merlin IIIA with extra cabin windows, the SA226-T(B) Merlin IIIB with improved performance, the SA227-TT Merlin IIIC certificated to SFAR-41 standard and the Fairchild 300 with wingtip winglets and modified controls. A total of 66 Merlin IIs and 168 Merlin IIIs are active including five with the Belgian Air Force.

Swearingen Merlin II, A2-KAM

Fairchild-Swearingen Merlin III, YV-710CP

Specification	Fairchild-Swearingen Merlin IIIA	
Powerplant	Two 904 s.h.p. (674 kW) Honeywell (Garrett) TPE331-3U-303G turboprops	
Dimensions		
Span	14.1 m	(46 ft 3 in)
Length	12.85 m	(42 ft 2 in)
Height	5.12 m	(16 ft 9 in)
Performance		
Max speed	523 km/h	(282 kt, 325 mph)
Cruising speed	463 km/h	(250 kt, 288 mph)
Initial climb	770 m/min	(2,530 fpm)
Range	4,576 km	(2,487 nm, 2,860 miles)
Weights		
Max takeoff	5,669 kg	(12,500 lbs)
Useful load	2,313 kg	(5,100 lbs)

Fairchild-Swearingen Merlin IV and Metro — USA

By inserting a 17 ft 2 in centre section into the fuselage of the Swearingen Merlin III the company produced a 20-passenger commuter airliner which was designated SA226-TC Metro. It also became the SA226-AT Merlin IV as a 12-passenger executive aircraft. The power was increased to 940 s.h.p. Garrett AiResearch TPE331-3UW-303G turboprops and a forward airstair door and rear cargo door were fitted. The Metro II had rectangular windows instead of portholes and the SA227-AC Metro III was further improved with longer-span wings and 1,000 s.h.p. TPE331-11U-612G engines. It was also sold as the all-cargo Expediter and the executive SA227-AT Merlin IVC. The SA227-DC Metro 23 had a larger 25-seat cabin and optional belly pannier. Military users included the Swedish Air Force who acquired the Metro III with a roof-mounted Ericsson radar antenna and the US military forces who bought 14 C-26A (SA227-AC) utility transports and more than 37 C-26Bs (SA227-DC). In total, 760 had been delivered when production ceased in 1997.

Fairchild-Swearingen SA226-TC Metro II, LQ-MLV

Specification	Fairchild SA227-DC Metro 23	
Powerplant	Two 1,100 s.h.p. (820 kW) Honeywell (Garrett) TPE331-12UHR turboprops	
Dimensions		
Span	17.37 m	(57 ft 0 in)
Length	18.09 m	(59 ft 4 in)
Height	5.08 m	(16 ft 8 in)
Performance		
Max speed	542 km/h	(293 kt, 337 mph)
Cruising speed	520 km/h	(283 kt, 325 mph)
Initial climb	823 m/min	(2,700 fpm)
Range	2,056 km	(1,117 nm, 1,285 miles)
Weights		
Max takeoff	7,483 kg	(16,500 lbs)
Useful load	3,184 kg	(7,020 lbs)

Fairchild A-10 Thunderbolt II — USA

The A-10 is a specialised ground attack and close support aircraft designed by Fairchild Republic to the requirements of the US Air Force. The single-seat A-10 has a distinctive layout with twin fins and two General Electric TF34 turbofans mounted side-by-side in pods on the rear fuselage. The straight wing has fairings to house the retracted main undercarriage units and is fitted with ten hardpoints to carry a variety of ordnance including Maverick and Sidewinder missiles or up to 16,000 lbs of bombs. The A-10 has a nose-mounted multi-barrel 30 mm GAU-8A Avenger cannon in the nose. A two-seat version, the YA-10B, was tested in 1979 but was not produced in quantity. Nicknamed the 'Warthog' the first of two A-10 prototypes was first flown on 10th May 1972 and six pre-production and 648 production aircraft were built between 1976 and 1984. Over 350 remain in active service.

Fairchild OA-10A, 80-0204 (USAF)

Specification	Fairchild A-10	
Powerplant	Two 9,065 lb.s.t. (40.33 kN) General Electric TF34-GE-100 turbofans	
Dimensions		
Span	17.53 m	(57 ft 6 in)
Length	16.26 m	(53 ft 4 in)
Height	4.47 m	(14 ft 8 in)
Performance		
Max speed	702 km/h	(382 kt, 439 mph)
Cruising speed	619 km/h	(336 kt, 387 mph)
Initial climb	1,829 m/min	(6,000 fpm)
Range	1,984 km	(1,078 nm, 1,240 miles)
Weights		
Max takeoff	22,676 kg	(50,000 lbs)
Useful load	11,066 kg	(24,400 lbs)

Fairey Swordfish — UK

Fairey's Swordfish biplane was a rugged carrier-borne aircraft which distinguished itself during World War II as an effective torpedo attack aircraft, despite its modest performance and old-fashioned appearance. Originally designated TSR.II it first flew on 17th April 1934. It was a large aircraft with two open cockpits accommodating the pilot in front and two crew in the machine-gun-equipped rear cockpit. It had a fixed tailwheel undercarriage and could carry an 18-inch torpedo under its belly or rockets under the wings. Some Swordfish were fitted with a belly-mounted ASV radar and many were fitted with twin floats. In all 2,393 were built by Fairey and Blackburn before production ceased in June 1944. Two Swordfish are active with the British Royal Navy Historical Flight.

Fairey Swordfish II, W5856

Specification	Fairey Swordfish II	
Powerplant	One 690 h.p. (514.5 kW) Bristol Pegasus IIIM3 piston engine	
Dimensions		
Span	13.87 m	(45 ft 6 in)
Length	10.87 m	(35 ft 8 in)
Height	3.76 m	(12 ft 4 in)
Performance		
Max speed	222 km/h	(120 kt, 138 mph)
Cruising speed	193 km/h	(104 kt, 120 mph)
Initial climb	372 m/min	(1,220 fpm)
Range	872 km	(474 nm, 545 miles)
Weights		
Max takeoff	3,946 kg	(8,700 lbs)
Useful load	1,814 kg	(4,000 lbs)

Fairey Firefly — UK

Fairey designed the low-wing single-engined Firefly shipboard reconnaissance/fighter in the early years of World War II and flew the prototype Firefly I on 22nd December 1941. The first Firefly entered service in late 1943 and by the time production was completed in September 1951, 1,503 aircraft had been built including a number for export to India, Denmark, Sweden and Ethiopia. The initial Firefly F.1 and NF.2 were powered by a 1,735 h.p. Rolls Royce Griffon IIB engine but later versions were produced with the 2,250 h.p, Griffon 74 (FR.4, AS.5 and AS.6) and 1,965 h.p. Griffon 59 (AS.7 and T.7). Early Fireflys had two crew, a pilot in the forward cockpit and observer/system operator in the rear cabin, but the anti-submarine AS.7 had two radar operators in the rear compartment. A two-seat trainer version was built (T.3 and T.7) with a raised rear cockpit and civil Fireflys were used postwar for target towing. At least eight Fireflys are under restoration to flying condition including ex-Ethiopian aircraft and one AS.5 is flying with the FAA Historic Flight.

Fairey Firefly (Cont.)

Fairey Firefly AS.5, WB271

Specification	Fairey Firefly AS.5	
Powerplant	One 2,250 h.p. (1,678 kW) Rolls Royce Griffon 74 piston engine	
Dimensions		
Span	12.55 m	(41 ft 2 in)
Length	11.56 m	(37 ft 11 in)
Height	4.37 m	(14 ft 4 in)
Performance		
Max speed	597 km/h	(324 kt, 373 mph)
Cruising speed	352 km/h	(191 kt, 220 mph)
Initial climb	424 m/min	(1,390 fpm)
Range	1,056 km	(574 nm, 660 miles)
Weights		
Max takeoff	6,259 kg	(13,800 lbs)
Useful load	1,973 kg	(4,350 lbs)

Fairey Gannet — UK

The distinctive Gannet was the standard carrier-borne anti-submarine aircraft for the Royal Navy during the 1950s, replacing Douglas Skyraiders in RN service. It had a mid-set folding wing with cranked outer sections and a deep fuselage providing a capacious belly weapons-bay and space under the rear fuselage for a retractable radar 'dustbin'. The Gannet AS.1 had a counter-rotating 2,950 s.h.p. Double Mamba 100 twin turboprop engine and carried three crew in separate cockpits. A conversion trainer version, the T.2, was also built with a second set of controls in the observer's cockpit. At a later stage these variants were replaced by the AS.4 and T.5 with a 3,035 s.h.p. Double Mamba 101 and five AS.4s were converted to COD.4 on-board delivery aircraft. Other customers included Indonesia and West Germany. The Gannet was also built as the higher-powered AEW.3 airborne radar picket with a large belly-mounted external radome and radar operators' stations inside the fuselage. Some 304 standard Gannets and 44 AEW.3s were built and one T.5 and two AEW.3s survive with private owners.

Fairey Gannet AEW.3, XL502 (G-BMYP)

Specification	Fairey Gannet AEW.3	
Powerplant	One 3,875 s.h.p. (2,889 kW) Bristol Siddeley Double Mamba 102 twin turboprop engine	
Dimensions		
Span	16.61 m	(54 ft 6 in)
Length	13.41 m	(44 ft 0 in)
Height	5.13 m	(16 ft 10 in)
Performance		
Max speed	400 km/h	(217 kt, 250 mph)
Cruising speed	288 km/h	(157 kt, 180 mph)
Range	1,120 km	(609 nm, 700 miles)
Weights		
Max takeoff	11,338 kg	(25,000 kg)
Useful load	3,537 kg	(7,800 lbs)

Fantasy Air Allegro — Czech Republic

The Allegro is one of the popular ultralight-category aircraft which have appeared in large numbers in the past five years. It is an all-composite strut-braced high-wing aircraft manufactured in the Czech Republic and it has side-by-side seating for two, a T-tail and a fixed tricycle undercarriage. It can be equipped with either long- or short-span wings which provide different performance profiles. Initially known as the Cora, the Allegro was designed by Oldrych Olsansky and is sold as a factory-complete aircraft. It is fitted as standard with a Verner 1400 engine but can also be powered by a Rotax 582. Over 100 Allegros are flying, mainly in Germany, France and the Czech Republic.

Fantasy Air Allegro ST

Specification	Fantasy Air Allegro ST	
Powerplant	One 80 h.p. (59.65 kW) Verner 1400 piston engine	
Dimensions		
Span	10.6 m	(34 ft 10 in)
Length	7.49 m	(24 ft 7 in)
Height	1.83 m	(6 ft 0 in)
Performance		
Max speed	165 km/h	(90 kt, 103 mph)
Cruising speed	147 km/h	(80 kt, 92 mph)
Initial climb	180 m/min	(590 fpm)
Range	397 km	(216 nm, 248 miles)
Weights		
Max takeoff	420 kg	(926 lbs)
Useful load	220 kg	(485 lbs)

FFA Bravo — Switzerland

The Bravo was originally a joint development between SIAI Marchetti (who designated it S-202) and Flug und Fahrzeugwerke A.G. (FFA) and the first prototype was flown on 7th March 1969. Subsequently, FFA (later FFT) took exclusive control and built several versions of the AS.202. The AS.202 is an all-metal side-by-side two-seat trainer with a fixed tricycle undercarriage, intended for military and civil customers. It has been produced as the AS.202/15 with a 150 h.p. Lycoming O-320-E2A engine for civil flying clubs, the mainly military AS.202/18A with a 180 h.p. Lycoming AEIO-360-B1F and the AS.202/26A with a 260 h.p. AEIO-540-D4B5. The AS.202/18A was used by the British Aerospace Flying College as the Wren and batches were also sold to the air forces of Indonesia, Iraq, Oman and Morocco. Some 177 aircraft had been built when production ceased in the early 1990s and a substantial number of these are still flying. A four-seat development, the FFT.2000 Eurotrainer, was also flown in 1991. This had a retractable undercarriage and was of largely composite construction but only the prototype, which still exists, was completed.

FFA Bravo AS.202/18A-1, HB-HGA

Specification	FFA AS.202/18A Bravo	
Powerplant	One 180 h.p. (134.2 kW) Textron Lycoming AEIO-360-B1F piston engine	
Dimensions		
Span	9.75 m	(32 ft 0 in)
Length	7.5 m	(24 ft 7 in)
Height	2.81 m	(9 ft 3 in)
Performance		
Max speed	240 km/h	(130 kt, 150 mph)
Cruising speed	227 km/h	(122 kt, 140 mph)
Initial climb	280 m/min	(920 fpm)
Range	930 km	(504 nm, 581 miles)
Weights		
Max takeoff	1,050 kg	(2,315 lbs)
Useful load	385 kg	(849 lbs)

Fiat G.46 — Italy

The G.46 basic trainer formed the backbone of the postwar Italian Air Force training fleet and was produced in single-seat (G.46A) and tandem two-seat (G.46B) form between 1948 and 1952. The prototype flew in February 1948 and more than 220 were built for the air forces of Italy, Argentina, Syria and Austria. The Italian Air Force G.46-1B had a 205 h.p. Alfa 115bis in-line engine but the export G.46-2B was fitted with the 250 h.p. D.H. Gipsy Queen 30. The later G.46-3A, -4A, -3B and -4B had improved 225 h.p. Alfa 115ter engines. The all-metal G.46 had a low wing and retractable tailwheel undercarriage and many were transferred to Italian aero clubs under the state aviation support scheme. Several G.46s remain active in Italy, Argentina and the United States. One American-owned aircraft has been refitted with a Vedeneyev radial engine.

Fiat G.46B, Ea-441 (Argentine AF)

Fiat G.46 (Cont.)

Specification	Fiat G.46-4B	
Powerplant	One 225 h.p. (167.7 kW) Alfa Romeo 115ter piston engine	
Dimensions		
Span	10.39 m	(34 ft 1 in)
Length	8.48 m	(27 ft 10 in)
Height	2.39 m	(7 ft 10 in)
Performance		
Max speed	315 km/h	(170 kt, 196 mph)
Cruising speed	257 km/h	(139 kt, 160 mph)
Initial climb	305 m/min	(1,000 fpm)
Range	992 km	(539 nm, 620 miles)
Weights		
Max takeoff	1,405 kg	(3,100 lbs)
Useful load	300 kg	(660 lbs)

Fieseler Fi.156 Storch and MS.500 — Germany/France

The angular Fi.156 was aptly named Storch ('Stork') with its strut-braced high wing, slim fuselage and multi-strutted undercarriage but it was highly effective as an army cooperation aircraft for the wartime German forces and set the pattern for later STOL designs. First flown in May 1936 it was powered by a 240 h.p. Argus As.10c eight-cylinder inverted-V engine. A few were built as the civil Fi.156B but the bulk of the 2,800 built by Fieseler were the Fi.156C-1 army liaison model, the Fi.56C-2 and Fi.156D ambulance versions and the Fi.156C-3 light transport. The Storch was also built in Czechoslovakia as the K-65 Mraz Cap and in France where production was transferred to Morane Saulnier who built the Argus-powered MS.500, the MS.501 with a Renault 6Q and the MS.502 with a Salmson 9AB uncowled radial engine. Morane built 784 of the MS.500 series and some were converted to MS.505 standard with a 300 h.p. Jacobs R-915A radial. A number of examples of the Storch and MS.500 continue to fly with private owners.

Morane Saulnier MS.505 Cricquet, F-BAVB

Specification	Fieseler Fi.156C-1 Storch	
Powerplant	One 240 h.p. (178.9 kW) Argus As.10c piston engine	
Dimensions		
Span	14.25 m	(46 ft 9 in)
Length	9.91 m	(32 ft 6 in)
Height	3 m	(9 ft 10 in)
Performance		
Max speed	176 km/h	(96 kt, 110 mph)
Cruising speed	144 km/h	(78 kt, 90 mph)
Initial climb	274 m/min	(900 fpm)
Range	384 km	(209 nm, 240 miles)
Weights		
Max takeoff	1,320 kg	(2,910 lbs)
Useful load	390 kg	(860 lbs)

Fisher Aero Avenger and Mariah — USA

The Avenger, designed by Fisher Aero, is a low-wing amateur aircraft of conventional wood and fabric construction. It is sold in the form of kits or plans and is relatively simple to build. It has a large single-seat cockpit which can be either open or enclosed by a bubble canopy and is powered by a 48 h.p. Rotax 503 engine. The Avenger V is essentially the same aircraft but with improved performance from a 65 h.p. Volkswagen engine. Around 80 of the Avenger series are flying in the USA. The Mariah, which first flew in 1993, is a development of the airframe powered by a 65 h.p. Continental with tandem seating for two and foldable wings.

Fisher Aero Avenger, N40482

Specification	Fisher Avenger	
Powerplant	One 48 h.p. (35.8 kW) Rotax 503 piston engine	
Dimensions		
Span	8.23 m	(27 ft 0 in)
Length	4.98 m	(16 ft 4 in)
Height	1.52 m	(5 ft 0 in)
Performance		
Max speed	152 km/h	(83 kt, 95 mph)
Cruising speed	128 km/h	(70 kt, 80 mph)
Initial climb	274 m/min	(900 fpm)
Range	240 km	(130 nm, 150 miles)
Weights		
Max takeoff	272 kg	(600 lbs)
Useful load	150 kg	(330 lbs)

Fisher Aero FP.404, Celebrity and Youngster — USA

The Fisher FP.404 is a very small ultralight biplane designed by Fisher Flying Products and sold by Fisher Aero Inc. for home construction and sold as a kit to amateur builders. It is an open cockpit single-seater of wood and fabric construction powered by a 50 h.p. Rotax 503 or Volkswagen engine and it was first marketed in 1985. Around 150 are currently flying. The FP.404 has been replaced by the Youngster which has wooden external covering and larger wings. Fisher has also used the basic design to develop the Celebrity which is a tandem two-seat aircraft with a longer fuselage, increased wing area and a 100 h.p. Continental O-200 engine. This is also sold by Fisher Flying Products as the Fisher Classic with a 64 h.p. Rotax 582.

Fisher FP.404

Specification	Fisher Celebrity	
Powerplant	One 100 h.p. (74.5 kW) Continental O-200 piston engine	
Dimensions		
Span	6.71 m	(22 ft 0 in)
Length	5.18 m	(17 ft 0 in)
Height	1.83 m	(6 ft 0 in)
Performance		
Max speed	184 km/h	(100 kt, 115 mph)
Cruising speed	160 km/h	(87 kt, 100 mph)
Initial climb	366 m/min	(1,200 fpm)
Range	320 km	(174 nm, 200 miles)
Weights		
Max takeoff	567 kg	(1,250 lbs)
Useful load	295 kg	(650 lbs)

Fisher Aero Horizon 1 and 2 — USA

Fisher Aero has produced the plans for kit-built two-seat Horizons for amateur builders and over 40 are currently flying in the USA. The Horizon is a classic strut-braced high-wing monoplane with a fixed tailwheel undercarriage and a fully enclosed cabin with tandem seating. The Horizon 1 has a distinctive swept vertical tail and is constructed of wood and fabric. The alternative Horizon 2 has a cut-down rear fuselage and a modified cockpit area with a rear vision window. The tail unit is also redesigned with a more rounded shape.

Fisher Horizon 1, N116JL

Specification	Fisher Horizon 1	
Powerplant	One 80 h.p. (59.65 kW) Limbach piston engine	
Dimensions		
Span	7.92 m	(26 ft 0 in)
Length	5.69 m	(18 ft 8 in)
Height	1.83 m	(6 ft 0 in)
Performance		
Max speed	152 km/h	(83 kt, 95 mph)
Cruising speed	136 km/h	(74 kt, 85 mph)
Initial climb	274 m/min	(900 fpm)
Range	400 km	(217 nm, 250 miles)
Weights		
Max takeoff	476 kg	(1,050 lbs)
Useful load	240 kg	(530 lbs)

Fisher Koala, Super Koala and Dakota Hawk — USA

The prolific designer Michael Fisher developed a range of ultralight aircraft, the first of which was the wood and fabric FP.101 which first flew in 1982. It was a high-wing single-seater powered by a 27 h.p. Rotax 277 engine and was succeeded by the FP.202 Koala which resembled a scaled-down Piper Cub and incorporated a number of refinements including an optional steel tube fuselage structure. Over 300

Fisher Koala, Super Koala and Dakota Hawk (Cont.)

Koalas have been built. The Super Koala is very similar but has tandem two-place seating and is powered by a 64 h.p. Rotax 582. The latest high-wing model is the Dakota Hawk which has a wider fuselage with side-by-side seating and is powered by a 65 h.p. Continental or 85 h.p. Rotax 912. Like the other models it is sold by Fisher Aero Inc. as a kit for amateur construction.

Fisher Koala

Specification	Fisher Super Koala	
Powerplant	One 64 h.p. (47.7 kW) Rotax 582 piston engine	
Dimensions		
Span	9.45 m	(31 ft 0 in)
Length	5.51 m	(18 ft 1 in)
Height	1.7 m	(5 ft 7 in)
Performance		
Max speed	128 km/h	(70 kt, 80 mph)
Cruising speed	112 km/h	(61 kt, 70 mph)
Initial climb	244 m/min	(800 fpm)
Range	360 km	(196 nm, 225 miles)
Weights		
Max takeoff	376 kg	(830 lbs)
Useful load	195 kg	(430 lbs)

Fleet 2, 10 and 16B Finch
— USA/Canada

The Fleet biplanes had their origin in the World War I Consolidated PT3 trainers which were developed into the Fleet 1 and Fleet 2. They were chunky single-bay tube and fabric biplanes with tandem open cockpits and a fixed tailwheel undercarriage. They served as reliable civilian trainers in the 1920s and 1930s. The Fleet 2, of which a good number remain active, had the partially enclosed 100 h.p. Kinner K5 radial engine and could be operated on skis or floats, and the Fleet 7 and 10 were fitted with a larger rudder and a larger 125 h.p. Kinner B5 powerplant. The Fleet 8, introduced in 1931, was a three-seat version of the Fleet 7 with a side-by-side forward cockpit and a larger squared-off rudder and the Fleet 11 was a two-seater designed for military training and powered by a 160 h.p. Kinner R5. Production was taken over by the Canadian Fleet Aircraft Ltd. in the mid-1930s where over 600 of the Fleet 16B Finch Trainer were built for the RCAF. These were based on the Fleet 10 but frequently had an enclosed cockpit canopy. Over 90 of the early models and 40 Finches are registered in North America and others fly in Argentina, some being used as glider tugs.

Fleet 2, NC8689

Specification	Fleet 2	
Powerplant	One 100 h.p. (74.6 kW) Kinner K5 piston engine	
Dimensions		
Span	8.53 m	(28 ft 0 in)
Length	6.32 m	(20 ft 9 in)
Height	2.39 m	(7 ft 10 in)
Performance		
Max speed	181 km/h	(98 kt, 113 mph)
Cruising speed	152 km/h	(83 kt, 95 mph)
Initial climb	238 m/min	(780 fpm)
Range	576 km	(313 nm, 360 miles)
Weights		
Max takeoff	714 kg	(1,575 lbs)
Useful load	256 kg	(565 lbs)

Fleet 80 Canuck
— Canada

Well-known for their wartime production of Fleet 16B Finch biplanes, Fleet Aircraft of Canada Ltd. moved into commercial light aircraft with the Model 80 Canuck which was based on the existing Noury N-75. This was a high-wing side-by-side two-seater powered by an 85 h.p. Continental C85-

12J engine and it had a distinctive waisted rear fuselage and a fixed tailwheel undercarriage. The Canuck prototype was flown on 26th September 1945 and was designed to operate on floats and skis. Fleet went into production and built 208 aircraft before the rights were transferred to Leavens Brothers of Toronto, who completed a further 26 Canucks before the line was closed in 1949. Some 40 Canucks are still flying in Canada and the United States.

Fleet 80 Canuck, C-FDZA

Specification	Fleet 80 Canuck	
Powerplant	One 85 h.p. (63.4 kW) Teledyne Continental C85-12J piston engine	
Dimensions		
Span	10.36 m	(34 ft 0 in)
Length	7.77 m	(25 ft 6 in)
Height	2.36 m	(7 ft 9 in)
Performance		
Max speed	235 km/h	(127 kt, 147 mph)
Cruising speed	224 km/h	(122 kt, 140 mph)
Initial climb	335 m/min	(1,100 fpm)
Range	960 km	(522 nm, 600 miles)
Weights		
Max takeoff	1,338 kg	(2,950 lbs)
Useful load	635 kg	(1,400 lbs)

Fleetwings Seabird F-5
— USA

Fleetwings Inc. of Bristol, Pennsylvania designed the Seabird amphibian in the 1930s as a prestigious five-seat air yacht. It was remarkable for its welded stainless-steel construction which made it strong and corrosion free. The Seabird had a shoulder-mounted wing with wire bracing and was powered by a 285 h.p. Jacobs L-5 radial engine mounted on struts above the wing centre section. It had a retractable undercarriage with fixed fairings which folded up into wells in the fuselage sides and was equipped with a throwover control column to allow it to be flown from either front seat. Six Seabirds were built and one is currently flying in the USA.

Fleetwings Seabird, NC16793

Specification	Fleetwings Seabird F-5	
Powerplant	One 285 h.p. (212.5 kW) Jacobs L-5 piston engine	
Dimensions		
Span	12.34 m	(40 ft 6 in)
Length	9.75 m	(32 ft 0 in)
Height	3.81 m	(12 ft 6 in)
Performance		
Max speed	240 km/h	(130 kt, 150 mph)
Cruising speed	224 km/h	(122 kt, 140 mph)
Initial climb	274 m/min	(900 fpm)
Range	832 km	(452 nm, 520 miles)
Weights		
Max takeoff	1,723 kg	(3,800 lbs)
Useful load	590 kg	(1,300 lbs)

Flight Design CT-180
— Germany

Among modern composite light aircraft, the Flight Design CT is one of the more efficient types with a large side-by-side two-seat cabin, docile handling and a maximum speed of 134 kt using an 80 h.p. Rotax 912 engine. The CT has a cantilever high wing and fixed tricycle undercarriage and is sold in kit form as an ultralight at 450 kg gross weight or in standard category at 540 kg. It has a large baggage compartment and a substantial useful load in its standard category form. The CT was introduced in 1997 and over 70 had been completed by the middle of 1999.

Flight Design CT-180 (Cont.)

Flight Design CT-180, D-MPCT

Specification	Flight Design CT-180	
Powerplant	One 80 h.p. (59.6 kW) Rotax 912-UL2 piston engine	
Dimensions		
Span	9.3 m	(30 ft 6 in)
Length	6.22 m	(20 ft 5 in)
Height	2.16 m	(7 ft 1 in)
Performance		
Max speed	250 km/h	(135 kt, 155 mph)
Cruising speed	235 km/h	(127 kt, 146 mph)
Initial climb	228 m/min	(750 fpm)
Range	1,500 km	(816 nm, 938 miles)
Weights		
Max takeoff	540 kg	(1,191 lbs)
Useful load	255 kg	(562 lbs)

FLS Sprint 160, G-SCLX

FLS Sprint — UK

The Sprint light trainer was originally designed by Sydney Holloway as the SAH-1 and the prototype was built by Trago Mills Ltd. It is a low-wing all-metal trainer with a side-by-side cockpit enclosed by a blister canopy and a fixed tricycle undercarriage. The engine used on the prototype was the 118 h.p. Lycoming O-235-L2A. The design was later acquired by Brooklands Aerospace, who named it the Venture, and then, in 1991, by Lovaux/FLS Aerospace. FLS renamed it Sprint 160 and fitted it with a 160 h.p. Lycoming AEIO-320-D1B engine. The first production Sprint 160 flew on 16th December 1993 and FLS Aerospace built four further airframes, one of which was titled the Sprint Club with a 118 h.p. Textron Lycoming O-235-L2A engine. Further development of the Sprint has been suspended pending a sale of the design to new owners.

Specification	FLS Sprint 160	
Powerplant	One 160 h.p. (119 kW) Textron Lycoming AEIO-320-D1B piston engine	
Dimensions		
Span	9.35 m	(30 ft 8 in)
Length	6.68 m	(21 ft 11 in)
Height	2.31 m	(7 ft 7 in)
Performance		
Max speed	233 km/h	(126 kt, 145 mph)
Cruising speed	172 km/h	(93 kt, 107 mph)
Initial climb	393 m/min	(1,290 fpm)
Range	920 km	(500 nm, 575 miles)
Weights		
Max takeoff	871 kg	(1,920 lbs)
Useful load	278 kg	(614 lbs)

Fly Synthesis Storch
— Italy

The Fly Synthesis Storch manufactured by Alphatech in Italy is a popular ultralight aircraft with a side-by-side two-seat cabin equipped with twin stick controls and a braced high wing. The rear fuselage consists of a slim tail boom carrying the tail surfaces and the Storch is fitted with a fixed tricycle undercarriage. Construction is of composites. Several versions are sold including the Pulcino with a 46 h.p. Rotax 503, the Classic with an 80 h.p. Jabiru 2200 or 64 h.p. Rotax 582 and the Storch HS which is the Classic with lower empty weight and improved performance. Over 300 examples of the Storch are flying in Europe and around the world.

Fly Synthesis Storch, 9M-EAG

Specification	Fly Synthesis Storch HS	
Powerplant	One 64 h.p. (47.7 kW) Rotax 582 piston engine	
Dimensions		
Span	8.71 m	(28 ft 7 in)
Length	5.75 m	(18 ft 10 in)
Height	2.45 m	(8 ft 1 in)
Performance		
Max speed	150 km/h	(81 kt, 93 mph)
Cruising speed	120 km/h	(65 kt, 75 mph)
Initial climb	270 m/min	(890 fpm)
Range	480 km	(259 nm, 298 miles)
Weights		
Max takeoff	450 kg	(992 lbs)
Useful load	210 kg	(463 lbs)

FMA IA-58 Pucara
— Argentina

The Pucara ground attack aircraft was designed specifically to the requirements of the Argentine Air Force by the Fabrica Militar de Aviones (FMA). Equipped with tandem twin seating the Pucara was intended for operation off rough fields carrying a load of bombs or rockets on underwing hardpoints. It has an unswept low wing with dihedralled outer panels, a T-tail and retractable tricycle undercarriage. The first of six prototypes, which flew on 20th August 1969, was powered by two 904 s.h.p. Garrett TPE331-U-303 turboprops but the production IA-58A Pucara had 1,022 s.h.p. Turboméca Astazou XVIGs. In total 110 Pucaras were built including six for Uruguay, three for Colombia and four for Sri Lanka. Some Argentine Air Force aircraft have been fitted with additional fuel tankage in place of the rear seat and the IA-66 was a prototype variant with 1,000 s.h.p. Garrett TPE331-11-601W engines. Approximately 65 Pucaras remain in service.

FMA Pucara, A-584 (Argentine AF)

Specification	FMA IA-58A Pucara	
Powerplant	Two 1,022 s.h.p. (762 kW) Turboméca Astazou XVIG turboprops	
Dimensions		
Span	14.5 m	(47 ft 7 in)
Length	14.25 m	(46 ft 9 in)
Height	5.36 m	(17 ft 7 in)
Performance		
Max speed	500 km/h	(270 kt, 311 mph)
Cruising speed	478 km/h	(258 kt, 297 mph)
Initial climb	1,079 m/min	(3,540 fpm)
Range	1,300 km	(707 nm, 813 miles)
Weights		
Max takeoff	6,798 kg	(14,990 lbs)
Useful load	2,780 kg	(6,130 lbs)

FMA IA-63 Pampa
— Argentina

The Pampa was designed by the Argentine state military aircraft factory FMA in cooperation with Dornier, to give primary and advanced jet training as a replacement for the Argentinian Air Force MS.760s. The Pampa design followed the lines of the Alpha Jet and other jet trainers with a tandem-seat layout and retractable tricycle undercarriage. The shoulder wing is of low aspect ratio with no sweep and equal taper and the Pampa is powered by a 3,500 lb.s.t. Garrett TFE731 turbofan. The Pampa prototype made its first flight on 6th October 1984. The production Pampa which entered service in 1988 was fitted with five weapons hardpoints and standard equipment includes a centreline DEFA podded cannon to allow the aircraft also to be used for ground attack. Only 19 Pampas were delivered to the Argentinian Air Force but FMA, now owned by Lockheed Martin, delivered one further aircraft in 1999 and production of a further batch of 12 has been initiated.

FMA Pampa, E-811 (Argentine AF)

Specification	FMA IA-63 Pampa	
Powerplant	One 3,500 lb.s.t. (15.57 kN) Honeywell (Garrett) TFE731-2-2N turbofan	
Dimensions		
Span	9.69 m	(31 ft 9 in)
Length	10.93 m	(35 ft 10 in)
Height	4.29 m	(14 ft 1 in)
Performance		
Max speed	821 km/h	(443 kt, 510 mph)
Cruising speed	748 km/h	(404 kt, 465 mph)
Initial climb	1,561 m/min	(5,120 fpm)
Range	1,487 km	(809 nm, 930 miles)
Weights		
Max takeoff	5,000 kg	(11,025 lbs)
Useful load	2,180 kg	(4,807 lbs)

Focke Wulf Fw.44 Stieglitz
— Germany

In 1932, Focke Wulf Flugzeugbau GmbH flew the prototype of its highly successful Fw.44 Stieglitz. This tandem two-seat open cockpit training biplane was constructed of tube and fabric and became widely used by German flying clubs in the prewar period and with the Luftwaffe during the war. The initial Fw.44B and similar Fw.44D had a 150 h.p. Siemens Sh.14a uncowled radial engine and other variants included the Fw.44C with a 135 h.p. in-line Argus As.8 engine and the Fw.44E with an Argus As.8B. The main production variant was the Fw.44J which was similar to the Fw.44D and this was also built under licence by ASJA in Sweden and in Brazil, Austria, Bulgaria, and Argentina. Over 900 examples of the Stieglitz were completed and many remain with civil owners in Europe and in Argentina.

Focke Wulf Fw.44J Stieglitz, D-EMIG

Specification	Focke Wulf Fw.44B Stieglitz	
Powerplant	One 150 h.p. (111.84 kW) Siemens Sh.14a piston engine	
Dimensions		
Span	8.99 m	(29 ft 6 in)
Length	7.29 m	(23 ft 11 in)
Height	2.69 m	(8 ft 10 in)
Performance		
Max speed	185 km/h	(100 kt, 115 mph)
Cruising speed	172 km/h	(93 kt, 107 mph)
Initial climb	213 m/min	(700 fpm)
Range	672 km	(365 nm, 420 miles)
Weights		
Max takeoff	900 kg	(1,985 lbs)
Useful load	374 kg	(825 lbs)

Fokker S.11 Instructor — Netherlands

The S.11 was Fokker's first postwar production aircraft, designed to the requirements of the Royal Netherlands Air Force as a primary trainer. Constructed from steel tube and fabric, the Instructor had a broad-chord low wing with dihedralled outer panels, a wide cockpit with two seats side-by-side and a large sliding canopy. The tailwheel undercarriage had distinctive main legs which were attached to the wing leading edges and designed with trailing link shock absorption. Some 39 were built for the RNAF and 41 went to the Israeli Air Force. The S.11 was built under licence in Italy by Macchi as the M.416 and in Brazil by the Fabrica do Galeão. Fokker also re-engineered the S.11 as the S.12 with a tricycle undercarriage and this was built in Brazil as the T-22 for the Brazilian Air Force. A total of 360 S.11s and 50 S.12s were completed by the parent factory and the licensees. A number remain in Brazil, one is British-owned and at least six are flying privately in Holland.

Fokker S.11 Instructor, PH-HOL

Specification	Fokker S.11 Instructor	
Powerplant	One 190 h.p. (141.66 kW) Textron Lycoming O-435-A piston engine	
Dimensions		
Span	11 m	(36 ft 1 in)
Length	8.13 m	(26 ft 8 in)
Height	2.26 m	(7 ft 5 in)
Performance		
Max speed	209 km/h	(113 kt, 130 mph)
Cruising speed	164 km/h	(89 kt, 102 mph)
Initial climb	244 m/min	(800 fpm)
Range	640 km	(348 nm, 400 miles)
Weights		
Max takeoff	1,098 kg	(2,422 lbs)
Useful load	280 kg	(616 lbs)

Fokker F.27 Friendship and F.50 — Netherlands

Intended as a replacement for Douglas DC-3s used in post-war short-haul service, the F.27 was first flown on 24th November 1955. The high-set wing gave an unobstructed interior for 40 passengers in the pressurised fuselage and the 1,670 s.h.p. Rolls Royce Dart Da.6 Mk.514-7 turboprops which were fitted were to prove highly reliable and efficient. Initial F.27-100 deliveries were made in 1958. The later F.27-200 had 48-passenger capacity and 1,870 s.h.p. Dart Da.7 Mk.528 engines and the F.27-400 had 2,140 s.h.p. Dart Da.7 Mk.536-7R engines. Fokker also built the F.27-200MAR Maritime coastal patrol variant and the passenger/freight F.27-300 Combiplane. The F.27-300M and -400M Troopship were higher weight military variants. In total 586 of the F.27 were built by Fokker. The Fairchild F-27 was licence-built by Fairchild for North American sale with heavier external skinning, a radar nose and other detailed changes. The FH-227 was a Fairchild version with a stretched fuselage and a 56-passenger interior. Some 128 of the Fairchild F-27 were built and 79 of the FH-227. Fokker also stretched the fuselage of the basic F.27 by 5 ft to produce the F.27-500. This was developed into the Fokker 50-100 which first flew on 28th December 1985 and incorporated many changes including square cabin windows, an upgraded cockpit and 2,500 s.h.p. Pratt & Whitney PW125B turboprops with six-bladed propellers. The Fokker 50-300 was a hot-and-high variant with PW127A engines and the Fokker 60 is a military variant with an 8 ft 3 in forward fuselage stretch and a cargo door, four of which were built. Total production of the Fokker 50/60 was 226 aircraft. Many Fokker turboprops remain in airline service with over 300 of the F.27 and Fairchild F-27 and 190 of the Fokker 50 being active.

Fokker 50, D-AFKD

Fokker F.27 C-31A, 85-1608 (US Army)

Fokker F.27 Friendship and F.50 (Cont.)

Specification	Fokker 50	
Powerplant	Two 2,500 s.h.p. (1,864 kW) Pratt & Whitney PW125B turboprops	
Dimensions		
Span	29 m	(95 ft 2 in)
Length	25.25 m	(82 ft 10 in)
Height	8.32 m	(27 ft 3 in)
Performance		
Max speed	531 km/h	(287 kt, 330 mph)
Cruising speed	507 km/h	(274 kt, 315 mph)
Takeoff distance	850 m	(2,800 ft)
Range	3,010 km	(1,634 nm, 1,880 miles)
Weights		
Max takeoff	19,945 kg	(43,980 lbs)
Useful load	8,188 kg	(18,054 lbs)

Fokker 100, PT-MRA

Fokker F.28 Fellowship and F.100 — Netherlands

Fokker flew the prototype F.28 on 9th May 1967. It was a 65-passenger regional airliner with a classic layout of T-tail, low wing and rear fuselage-mounted twin turbofans and provided a step-up for airlines using the successful F.27 Friendship. The F.28-1000 was equipped with 9,750 lb.s.t. Rolls Royce Spey Mk.555-15 turbofans and it entered service with LTU in 1969. The F.28-2000 had a 7 ft 3 in fuselage stretch giving 79-passenger capacity and the F.28-4000 was an upgrade of this model with a longer-span wing and 9,900 lb.s.t. Spey Mk.555-15H engines. Fokker also built a few of the F.28-3000 with the shorter -1000 fuselage and the engines and other improvements of the -4000 and two F.28-6000s with full-span leading edge slats. In total, 243 F.28s were built. The F.28 was followed by the Fokker 100 which had a further fuselage stretch of 18 ft 10 in giving 122-passenger capacity, a longer wing, upgraded flight deck and 13,850 lb.s.t. Rolls Royce Tay Mk.620-15 engines. Some 280 Fokker 100s were built together with 45 of the 80-passenger Fokker 70 which had a 15 ft 2 in shorter fuselage. Fokker was declared insolvent in 1996 and Fokker 100 production ceased shortly thereafter. Over 300 Fokker 100s and 70s are flying together with over 170 F.28s.

Specification	Fokker 100	
Powerplant	Two 13,850 lb.s.t. (61.6 kN) Rolls Royce Tay Mk.620-15 turbofans	
Dimensions		
Span	28.07 m	(92 ft 1 in)
Length	35.53 m	(116 ft 7 in)
Height	8.48 m	(27 ft 10 in)
Performance		
Max speed	853 km/h	(461 kt, 530 mph)
Cruising speed	805 km/h	(435 kt, 500 mph)
Initial climb	1,855 m/min	(6,085 fpm)
Range	2,376 km	(1,292 nm, 1,485 miles)
Weights		
Max takeoff	43,084 kg	(95,000 lbs)
Useful load	18,494 kg	(40,780 lbs)

Fokker F.28, S-T-20 (Argentine Navy)

Ford 4-AT-E and 5-AT-B — USA

The famous Ford Trimotor was designed and built by the Stout Metal Airplane Co. which was owned by Ford Motor Company. Also nicknamed 'Tin Goose' the high-wing Model 4-AT-B was announced in June 1926 and was powered by three 22 h.p. Wright J4 or J5 Whirlwind radial engines. One 4-AT-B was converted to 9-AT-A specification with 300 h.p. Wasp Junior engines. The Ford had a slab-sided fuselage with 12 passenger seats and the external skinning of wings and fuselage was made of corrugated aluminium. Used by many leading airlines in the 1930s, it had a fixed tailwheel undercarriage and the two-seat cockpit was fully enclosed and positioned at the wing leading edge. The 4-AT-E had 300 h.p. Wright J6 engines and the 5-AT-B had the same airframe but 15 passenger seats and 450 h.p. Pratt & Whitney Wasp engines. The 5-AT-C had a lengthened fuselage and in 5-AT-CS form could be operated on floats. Ford also built the 5-AT-D which had a deeper fuselage. Production of the Ford Trimotor totalled 196 aircraft built between 1926 and 1932. The remaining active fleet in the USA includes four 4-AT-Es, four 5-AT-Bs and a single 5-AT-C.

Ford 4-AT-E, NC8407

Specification	Ford 5-AT-B	
Powerplant	Three 450 h.p. (335.5 kW) Pratt & Whitney Wasp piston engines	
Dimensions		
Span	23.72 m	(77 ft 10 in)
Length	15.19 m	(49 ft 10 in)
Height	3.86 m	(12 ft 8 in)
Performance		
Max speed	229 km/h	(123 kt, 142 mph)
Cruising speed	196 km/h	(106 kt, 122 mph)
Initial climb	366 m/min	(1,200 fpm)
Range	976 km	(530 nm, 610 miles)
Weights		
Max takeoff	6,009 kg	(13,250 lbs)
Useful load	2,573 kg	(5,674 lbs)

Fouga (Potez/Aérospatiale) CM.170 Magister — France

The Magister design originated in the series of sailplanes and the Sylphe and other jet-powered light aircraft developed by Castel Mauboussin in the 1950s. The prototype CM.170-1 first flew on 23rd July 1952 and was an all-metal military primary jet trainer with a tapered straight wing, a V-tail and two Turboméca Marboré IIA turbojets fitted to the fuselage sides. The Magister had a tandem two-seat cockpit with a double-framed canopy and a retractable tricycle undercarriage. The French Air Force acquired 400 Magisters and 32 went to the French Navy as the CM.175 Zephyr equipped with deck-landing equipment. The later CM.170-2 had improved Marboré VIC engines. Other air forces using the aircraft included those of Israel, Germany, Lebanon, Eire, Cambodia and Finland. A total of 920 Magisters were completed including licence production of 188 in Germany, 36 in Israel and 62 in Finland. A number of Magisters remain in military service and many have been sold to private owners as civil warbirds including eight in France and 80 in the United States.

Fouga Magister, No.526 (French AF)

Specification	Aérospatiale Fouga CM.170 Magister	
Powerplant	Two 882 lb.s.t. (3.92 kN) Turboméca Marboré IIA turbojets	
Dimensions		
Span	12.14 m	(39 ft 10 in)
Length	10.06 m	(33 ft 0 in)
Height	2.79 m	(9 ft 2 in)
Performance		
Max speed	714 km/h	(386 kt, 444 mph)
Cruising speed	692 km/h	(374 kt, 430 mph)
Initial climb	1,020 m/min	(3,345 fpm)
Range	920 km	(500 nm, 575 miles)
Weights		
Max takeoff	3,200 kg	(7,055 lbs)
Useful load	1,050 kg	(2,315 lbs)

Found Centenniel 100
— Canada

Captain S.R. Found designed the four-seat FBA-1A high-wing tube and fabric light utility aircraft and flew the prototype on 13th July 1949. It led to the improved FBA-2A which was a larger all-metal machine with a five-seat slab-sided fuselage. It had large cargo doors on each side and was powered by a 250 h.p. Lycoming O-540-A1D six-cylinder engine. The production version, 25 of which were built, was the FBA-2C with a lengthened cabin, a large dorsal fin and a tailwheel undercarriage which could be fitted with skis or floats. This was succeeded by the Centenniel 100 which was slightly larger with six seats and was first flown on 7th April 1967. It had a 290 h.p. Lycoming IO-540-G engine and five were completed before production ceased in 1968. The aircraft has been relaunched as the FBA-2C1 Bush Hawk and a new prototype was flown in October 1998. The Bush Hawk is powered by a 260 h.p. Lycoming IO-540 and has an enlarged cargo compartment.

Found Centenniel 100, CF-WFO

Specification	Found Centenniel 100	
Powerplant	One 290 h.p. (216.22 kW) Textron Lycoming IO-540-G piston engine	
Dimensions		
Span	11.89 m	(39 ft 0 in)
Length	8.07 m	(26 ft 6 in)
Height	2.54 m	(8 ft 4 in)
Performance		
Max speed	261 km/h	(141 kt, 162 mph)
Cruising speed	241 km/h	(130 kt, 150 mph)
Initial climb	381 m/min	(1,250 fpm)
Range	1,120 km	(609 nm, 700 miles)
Weights		
Max takeoff	1,587 kg	(3,500 lbs)
Useful load	680 kg	(1,500 lbs)

Fournier RF3 and RF4
— France

The amateur builder René Fournier conceived the idea of a combined glider and powered aircraft in the mid-1950s. His single-seat RF1 Avion-Planeur set the formula for many future motor glider designs and it first flew on 6th July 1960. Having built two further RF2 prototypes, Fournier formed Alpavia to build the RF3 which was an all-wood machine with a high-aspect-ratio wing, a retractable monowheel undercarriage and a small single-seat cockpit with a blister canopy. The 40 h.p. Rectimo-converted Volkswagen 1200 engine was mounted in the nose and could be shut down for soaring flight. A total of 89 RF3s were completed. The RF4 was a strengthened aerobatic version with the same engine. Three prototypes were built followed by 155 production RF4Ds produced by Sportavia-Putzer GmbH in Germany. They also built one RF7 which was a proposed kit version of the RF4 with shorter wings but this was not produced in quantity. Sportavia also built 12 examples of the SFS-31 Milan which consisted of an RF4D fuselage and engine married to the wing of a Scheibe SF-27M. This first flew on 1st August 1969. Examples of the RF3 and RF4D are still to be found in the USA and most European countries.

Fournier (Alpavia) RF.3, G-BNHT

Specification	Fournier (Sportavia) RF4D	
Powerplant	One 40 h.p. (29.8 kW) Volkswagen 1200 piston engine	
Dimensions		
Span	11.25 m	(36 ft 11 in)
Length	6 m	(19 ft 8 in)
Height	1.93 m	(6 ft 4 in)
Performance		
Max speed	180 km/h	(97 kt, 112 mph)
Cruising speed	161 km/h	(87 kt, 100 mph)
Initial climb	210 m/min	(690 fpm)
Range	656 km	(356 nm, 410 miles)
Weights		
Max takeoff	380 kg	(838 lbs)
Useful load	125 kg	(276 lbs)

Fournier RF5 and Sportavia RF5B Sperber
— France/Germany

Following success with the RF3 and RF4 single-seat motor gliders, René Fournier produced an enlarged two-seat version designated RF5. This aircraft, which first flew in January 1968, was, again, of all-wood construction with a larger wing and a lengthened version of the RF4D fuselage with a tandem two-seat cockpit and side-opening clear-view canopy. The retractable monowheel undercarriage was retained, the aircraft being fitted with small tubular wheeled outriggers on the outer wings and the RF5 had a 68 h.p. Limbach-Volkswagen SL.1700E engine. Some 127 RF5s were built by Sportavia, and Aero Jéan in Spain also built ten powered by the 80 h.p. Limbach L.2000-E01 engine. Sportavia developed the RF5 into the high-performance RF5B Sperber which flew on 15th May 1971 and had a cut-down rear fuselage and blister canopy and new long-span wings. In total 79 were built by Sportavia and 20 by the Egyptian Helwan factory.

Fournier (Sportavia) RF5, D-KLIK

Specification	Fournier (Sportavia) RF5	
Powerplant	One 68 h.p. (50.7 kW) Limbach SL.1700E piston engine	
Dimensions		
Span	13.72 m	(45 ft 0 in)
Length	7.8 m	(25 ft 7 in)
Height	1.96 m	(6 ft 5 in)
Performance		
Max speed	190 km/h	(103 kt, 118 mph)
Cruising speed	177 km/h	(96 kt, 110 mph)
Initial climb	180 m/min	(590 fpm)
Range	696 km	(378 nm, 435 miles)
Weights		
Max takeoff	650 kg	(1,433 lbs)
Useful load	230 kg	(507 lbs)

Fournier RF-6B
— France/Germany

René Fournier, who had designed the successful RF4 and RF5 motor gliders, developed the RF-6 light club trainer. This bore a similarity to the RF5 but was an all-wood aircraft with a fixed tricycle undercarriage and a side-by-side two-seat cockpit enclosed by a fully transparent scissor-opening canopy. Powered by a 100 h.p. Continental O-200-A engine, the first RF-6B was flown on 12th March 1974 and production was established at the Fournier factory at Nitray. Some 43 aircraft were completed. Fournier granted licences for the RF-6 to Slingsby, who developed it into the Slingsby T67 and Firefly, and to Sportavia who produced the RF-6C Sportsman and RS-180 (described separately).

Fournier RF-6B, F-GANB

Specification	Fournier RF-6B	
Powerplant	One 100 h.p. (74.5 kW) Rolls Royce Continental O-200-A piston engine	
Dimensions		
Span	10.5 m	(34 ft 5 in)
Length	7 m	(23 ft 0 in)
Height	2.52 m	(8 ft 3 in)
Performance		
Max speed	209 km/h	(113 kt, 130 mph)
Cruising speed	190 km/h	(103 kt, 118 mph)
Initial climb	210 m/min	(690 fpm)
Range	640 km	(348 nm, 400 miles)
Weights		
Max takeoff	740 kg	(1,632 lbs)
Useful load	265 kg	(584 lbs)

Fuji LM-1 Nikko and KM-2 — Japan

Having built a large number of Beech T-34 Mentors for the Japanese Air Self Defence Force, Fuji produced a redesigned version as a four-/five-seat military communications aircraft. Using the wings, engine and tail of the Mentor they produced a wider fuselage with a fully enclosed cabin to create the LM-1 Nikko. Some 27 were built for the JGSDF together with two higher-powered KM-1s with a 340 h.p. Lycoming GSO-480 engine. This was not built in quantity but Fuji did construct 61 examples of the KM-2 which was a side-by-side two-seat training version for the JMSDF. The KM-2s and LM-1s have all been retired but nine are owned by private individuals in the USA.

Fuji LM-1, N2121J

Specification	Fuji KM-2	
Powerplant	One 340 h.p. (253.5 kW) Textron Lycoming IGSO-480-A1B6 piston engine	
Dimensions		
Span	9.98 m	(32 ft 9 in)
Length	7.95 m	(26 ft 1 in)
Height	2.92 m	(9 ft 7 in)
Performance		
Max speed	378 km/h	(204 kt, 235 mph)
Cruising speed	298 km/h	(161 kt, 185 mph)
Initial climb	463 m/min	(1,520 fpm)
Range	960 km	(521 nm, 600 miles)
Weights		
Max takeoff	1,750 kg	(3,860 lbs)
Useful load	617 kg	(1,360 lbs)

Fuji T-1A — Japan

The T1F2 (later T-1A) was designed by Fuji as an ab initio jet trainer to replace the North American T-6 in JASDF service. First flown on 19th January 1958 the T-1 closely resembled the North American F-86 with a low swept wing, swept tail and with a nose intake. The cockpit has tandem seating with a hinged clamshell canopy. Two versions of the T-1 have been built: the T-1A (T1F2) with a 4,000 lb.s.t. Bristol (Rolls Royce) Orpheus 805 turbojet and the T-1B (T1F1) with a 2,645 lb.s.t. Ishikawajima-Harima J3-IHI-3 engine. Some of these were later converted to T-1C standard with a 3,085 lb.s.t. J3-IHI-7 turbojet. In total, 46 T-1As and 20 T-1Bs were built and a dwindling number still serve with the JASDF and are now being replaced by the Kawasaki T-4.

Fuji T-1A, 15-5815 (JASDF)

Specification	Fuji T-1A	
Powerplant	One 4,000 lb.s.t. (17.79 kN) Rolls Royce Orpheus Mk.805 turbojet	
Dimensions		
Span	10.5 m	(34 ft 5 in)
Length	12.12 m	(39 ft 9 in)
Height	4.09 m	(13 ft 5 in)
Performance		
Max speed	925 km/h	(500 kt, 575 mph)
Cruising speed	620 km/h	(335 kt, 385 mph)
Initial climb	1,981 m/min	(6,500 fpm)
Range	1,280 km	(695 nm, 800 miles)
Weights		
Max takeoff	5,000 kg	(11,025 lbs)
Useful load	2,580 kg	(5,689 lbs)

Fuji T-5 — Japan

Fuji, who had been building both the Beech T-34 Mentor and its four-/five-seat LM-1 and KM-2 variants, developed the T-5 for the JASDF following tests of a turboprop version of a KM-2 derivative (designated KM-2D). This was seen as a replacement for the KM-2 trainers of the JMSDF and Fuji refined the Mentor airframe as the KM-2Kai with a modified fuselage incorporating a new cockpit with side-by-side seating and an optional two-place rear bench, a sliding single-piece canopy and a swept tail. This conversion was powered by an Allison 250-B17D turboprop engine and first flew on 27th April 1988. Some 29 T-5s are in service with the JMSDF.

Fuji T-5, 6327 (JMSDF)

Specification	Fuji T-5	
Powerplant	One 350 s.h.p. (261.1 kW) Allison 250-B17D turboprop	
Dimensions		
Span	10.03 m	(32 ft 11 in)
Length	8.43 m	(27 ft 8 in)
Height	2.95 m	(9 ft 8 in)
Performance		
Max speed	357 km/h	(193 kt, 222 mph)
Cruising speed	258 km/h	(139 kt, 160 mph)
Initial climb	518 m/min	(1,700 fpm)
Range	944 km	(513 nm, 590 miles)
Weights		
Max takeoff	1,805 kg	(3,980 lbs)
Useful load	723 kg	(1,595 lbs)

Fuji FA-200 — Japan

The FA-200 is the only successful production light aircraft to have been built in Japan and was initiated by Fuji Heavy Industries in 1964. In layout it is a low-wing all-metal four-seat tourer with a fixed tricycle undercarriage and in service it proved to be a strong and resilient aircraft, many still remaining in active service. The prototype F.200-II was first flown on 21st August 1965 powered by a 160 h.p. Lycoming O-320-B2B engine. It went into production in 1967 as the FA-200-160 Aero Subaru and Fuji also built the FA-200-180 with a fuel-injected 180 h.p. Lycoming IO-360-B1B engine with a constant-speed propeller and a 200 lbs higher gross weight. A reduced specification was also offered on the FA-200-180AO which had a fixed-pitch propeller and a standard non-injected O-360 engine. Total production of the FA-200 series was 274 aircraft, most of which were exported to Europe and Australia.

Fuji FA-200-160, G-BBZO

Specification	Fuji FA-200-180	
Powerplant	One 180 h.p. (134.2 kW) Textron Lycoming IO-360-B1B piston engine	
Dimensions		
Span	9.42 m	(30 ft 11 in)
Length	7.96 m	(26 ft 1 in)
Height	2.63 m	(8 ft 7 in)
Performance		
Max speed	233 km/h	(126 kt, 145 mph)
Cruising speed	204 km/h	(110 kt, 127 mph)
Initial climb	232 m/min	(760 fpm)
Range	984 km	(535 nm, 615 miles)
Weights		
Max takeoff	1,150 kg	(2,535 lbs)
Useful load	510 kg	(1,125 lbs)

Funk (Akron) B.85 — USA

The Funk Model B prototype, powered by a three-cylinder 45 h.p. Szekley engine, was designed and built by the Funk Brothers at the end of 1933. The Funk was a high-wing side-by-side two-seater with a rather rotund fuselage and a fixed tailwheel undercarriage. The initial production Funk B was powered by a 63 h.p. Akron Model E-200-E4L engine modified from a Ford Model "B" car engine and it went into production at Akron Aircraft Inc. of Akron, Ohio. The later Model B.75L was upgraded to a 75 h.p. Lycoming GO-145-C2 or -C3 engine and two other aircraft were re-engined with a Continental A-75-8 engine as the Funk

Funk (Akron) B.85 (Cont.)

Model C (otherwise known as the Akron V). Production ceased in 1941 with the 151st aircraft but was resumed by Funk Aircraft who built 229 examples of the B.75L and the B.85C, which was powered by an 85 h.p. Continental C85-12F engine. Funk finally ceased production in 1948. A total of 168 Funks are still registered and active in the United States.

Funk B.85C, N24152

Specification	Funk B.85C	
Powerplant	One 85 h.p. (63.38 kW) Teledyne Continental C85-12F piston engine	
Dimensions		
Span	10.67 m	(35 ft 0 in)
Length	6.12 m	(20 ft 1 in)
Height	1.85 m	(6 ft 1 in)
Performance		
Max speed	185 km/h	(100 kt, 115 mph)
Cruising speed	161 km/h	(87 kt, 100 mph)
Initial climb	244 m/min	(800 fpm)
Range	576 km	(313 nm, 360 miles)
Weights		
Max takeoff	612 kg	(1,350 lbs)
Useful load	209 kg	(460 lbs)

Funk F-23A — USA

The F-23 was developed by the Donald D. Funk Company of Broken Arrow, Oklahoma and first flown in November 1962. It was a single-seat low-wing crop-spraying aircraft of largely original tube and fabric construction but using the fuselage frame of the Fairchild M-62 Cornell. Powered by a 240 h.p. Continental W-670-M radial engine, it had a 200 USG chemical hopper located between the cockpit and the firewall. Eleven production F-23A aircraft were built between 1964 and 1967 of which one was exported to Guatemala. The final three aircraft were designated F-23B and fitted with a 275 h.p. Jacobs R-755 engine. The design was taken over by Cosmic Aircraft of Norman, Oklahoma in May 1970 but no further aircraft were completed. All the F-23As remain registered in the USA although only five are thought to be active.

Funk F-23A, N1131Z

Specification	Funk F-23A	
Powerplant	One 240 h.p. (178.9 kW) Continental W-670-M piston engine	
Dimensions		
Span	12.5 m	(41 ft 0 in)
Length	8.13 m	(26 ft 8 in)
Height	2.29 m	(7 ft 6 in)
Performance		
Max speed	185 km/h	(100 kt, 115 mph)
Cruising speed	161 km/h	(87 kt, 100 mph)
Initial climb	137 m/min	(450 fpm)
Range	480 km	(261 nm, 300 miles)
Weights		
Max takeoff	1,950 kg	(4,300 lbs)
Useful load	930 kg	(2,050 lbs)

Funk (B&F Technik) FK.9 — Germany/Poland

The FK.9 was designed by Otto and Peter Funk (acting as B&F Technik) as an affordable ultralight aircraft and was based on the earlier FK.3 motor glider which achieved its performance through a complex aileron and flap system. The production FK.9 Mk.2 is a strut-braced high-wing tube and fabric aircraft with a fixed tailwheel undercarriage and a 35 h.p. Rotax 447, Jabiru or 50 h.p. Rotax 503 engine. The FK.9TG is similar but with a tricycle undercarriage. It is built at Krosno in Poland and marketed through F&K Technik in Germany and over 100 had been built by the end of 1998. The FK.9 Mk.3 is a redesigned version with a composite fuselage and tail unit and is powered by an 80 h.p. Rotax 912.

Funk FK.9, D-MYAK

Funk (B&F Technik) FK-12 Comet — Germany/Poland

The FK-12 Comet is a two-seat sporting biplane created by Otto and Peter Funk of the B&F Technik Vertriebs GmbH. It falls into the German ultralight weight category and is available as a kit which is manufactured at Krosno in Poland. The FK-12 has tandem open cockpits and slightly swept wings which can be folded for storage of the aircraft. It is fitted with a composite cantilever tailwheel undercarriage and powered by an 80 h.p. Rotax 912 although the turbocharged Rotax 914 engine may be fitted. The prototype first flew in 1997.

Funk FK.9 Mk.3, D-MUFK

Funk FK-12 Comet, D-MPLI

Specification	Funk FK.9 Mk.3	
Powerplant	One 80 h.p. (59.6 kW) Rotax 912 piston engine	
Dimensions		
Span	9.85 m	(32 ft 4 in)
Length	5.85 m	(19 ft 3 in)
Height	1.9 m	(6 ft 3 in)
Performance		
Max speed	240 km/h	(129 kt, 149 mph)
Cruising speed	190 km/h	(102 kt, 118 mph)
Initial climb	427 m/min	(1,400 fpm)
Range	640 km	(348 nm, 400 miles)
Weights		
Max takeoff	450 kg	(992 lbs)
Useful load	175 kg	(386 lbs)

Specification	Funk FK-12 Comet	
Powerplant	One 80 h.p. (59.6 kW) Rotax 912 piston engine	
Dimensions		
Span	6.71 m	(22 ft 0 in)
Length	5.31 m	(17 ft 5 in)
Height	2.11 m	(6 ft 11 in)
Performance		
Max speed	220 km/h	(119 kt, 137 mph)
Cruising speed	185 km/h	(100 kt, 115 mph)
Initial climb	427 m/min	(1,400 fpm)
Range	640 km	(348 nm, 400 miles)
Weights		
Max takeoff	450 kg	(992 lbs)
Useful load	210 kg	(463 lbs)

Funk (B&F Technik) FK-14 Polaris — Germany/Poland

Following their success with the FK.9 high-wing ultralight, B&F Technik have designed the FK-14 Polaris low-wing light aircraft which is to be available as a kit for amateur construction under German ultralight category rules. The Polaris is of all-composite construction and has an advanced-technology wing with upturned wingtips, a fixed tricycle undercarriage and a side-by-side two-seat cockpit enclosed by a bubble canopy. It can be powered by either an 80 h.p. Rotax 912 or a 100 h.p. Rotax 912S engine.

Specification	Funk FK-14 Polaris	
Powerplant	One 80 h.p. (59.6 kW) Rotax 912 piston engine	
Dimensions		
Span	8.9 m	(29 ft 3 in)
Length	5.35 m	(17 ft 7 in)
Height (est)	1.73 m	(5 ft 8 in)
Performance		
Max speed	290 km/h	(156 kt, 180 mph)
Cruising speed (est)	260 km/h	(140 kt, 162 mph)
Initial climb (est)	274 m/min	(900 fpm)
Range (est)	640 km	(348 nm, 400 miles)
Weights		
Max takeoff	450 kg	(992 lbs)
Useful load	190 kg	(419 lbs)

Funk FK-14 Polaris, D-MVFK

G

GAF Nomad — Australia

The Government Aircraft Factory (GAF) developed the Nomad twin turboprop utility aircraft for the needs of the Australian Army and for commercial operators. The N2 Nomad was a strut-braced high-wing monoplane with twin 400 s.h.p. Allison 250-B17 turboprops, a boxy 12-passenger fuselage with an upswept rear section and a cruciform tail. It had a retractable tricycle undercarriage, the main units of which were housed in external sponsons attached to the lower fuselage. The prototype was first flown on 23rd July 1971 and the initial production models were the N.22 for the Australian Army and the N.22B for civil customers and export military users such as the Indonesian Navy. Civil customers for the N.22B included the Royal Flying Doctor Service. GAF further developed the Nomad into the N.24A which had a 5 ft 9 in fuselage stretch and could accommodate up to 17 passengers. Some 170 Nomads were built between 1975 and 1984 and a number remain in service with the US Customs service, the RAAF, the Thai Navy and Air Force, the Philippines Air Force and commercial users in the South Pacific and Chile.

GAF N.22B Nomad, CC-CBV

Specification	GAF Nomad N.24A	
Powerplant	Two 400 s.h.p. (298 kW) Allison 250-B17B turboprops	
Dimensions		
Span	16.52 m	(54 ft 2 in)
Length	14.36 m	(47 ft 1 in)
Height	5.52 m	(18 ft 1 in)
Performance		
Max speed	310 km/h	(168 kt, 193 mph)
Cruising speed	290 km/h	(156 kt, 180 mph)
Initial climb	390 m/min	(1,280 fpm)
Range	1,344 km	(730 nm, 840 miles)
Weights		
Max takeoff	3,764 kg	(8,300 lbs)
Useful load	1,388 kg	(3,060 lbs)

Galaxy Aerospace Galaxy — Israel

The Galaxy super-midsize business jet was designed by Israel Aircraft Industries (IAI) and is built in Israel and marketed in North America by Galaxy Aerospace. Externally, it follows similar lines to the IAI-1124 Astra with a cruciform tail unit and a forward airstair entry door for passengers and crew. It uses a developed version of the Astra's advanced-technology wing but it is a larger aircraft and seats eight passengers for long-range executive use or can also be used as a corporate shuttle with up to 18 seats. The Galaxy, which is powered by two PW306A turbofans mounted on the upper rear fuselage, has full transatlantic range and is fitted with an advanced cockpit and systems. The prototype first flew on 25th December 1997, being certificated a year later, and first customer deliveries were made in 1999.

Galaxy, N505GA

Specification	Galaxy Aerospace Galaxy	
Powerplant	Two 5,700 lb.s.t. (25.36 kN) Pratt & Whitney PW306A turbofans	
Dimensions		
Span	17.73 m	(58 ft 2 in)
Length	18.97 m	(62 ft 3 in)
Height	6.53 m	(21 ft 5 in)
Performance		
Max speed	870 km/h	(470 kt, 540 mph)
Cruising speed	820 km/h	(443 kt, 510 mph)
Takeoff distance	1,841 m	(6,040 ft)
Range	6,672 km	(3,626 nm, 4,170 miles)
Weights		
Max takeoff	15,170 kg	(33,450 lbs)
Useful load	6,961 kg	(15,350 lbs)

Gardan GY-100 Bagheera — France

Yves Gardan is a talented light aircraft designer who has been responsible for several successful aircraft including the Minicab, Supercab, Coccinelle and the GY-80 Horizon. The GY-100 is an all-metal low-wing light aircraft with a fixed tricycle undercarriage and four-seat fully enclosed cabin which closely resembles a Piper Cherokee. The prototype, which first flew on 21st December 1967 powered by a 135 h.p. Lycoming O-320 engine, was lost during flight testing in 1969. However, the type was certificated and one higher-powered production example was built by Gardan's company, SITAR. This is currently operated by a flying club at Lognes in France.

Gardan GY-100 Bagheera, F-BRGN

Gardan GY-100 Bagheera (Cont.)

Specification	Gardan GY-100 Bagheera	
Powerplant	One 150 h.p. (111.84 kW) Textron Lycoming O-235-C piston engine	
Dimensions		
Span	8.2 m	(26 ft 11 in)
Length	6.1 m	(20 ft 0 in)
Height	2.01 m	(6 ft 7 in)
Performance		
Max speed	249 km/h	(135 kt, 155 mph)
Cruising speed	225 km/h	(122 kt, 140 mph)
Initial climb	244 m/min	(800 fpm)
Range	960 km	(522 nm, 600 miles)
Weights		
Max takeoff	917 kg	(2,023 lbs)
Useful load	417 kg	(920 lbs)

Gatard AG.02 Statoplan Poussin — France

André Gatard was an amateur designer who produced several prototypes including the AG.1 Alouette, the AG.04 Pigéon and the most successful of his designs, the Volkswagen-powered AG.02 Statoplan Poussin. All of his Statoplan designs incorporated a special control system which used a variable-incidence tailplane with large endplates and full span flaperons. The AG.02 was an all-wood low-wing monoplane with a fixed tailwheel undercarriage and an enclosed single-seat cockpit. The first aircraft flew in 1957 followed by a second prototype and over 40 sets of plans were sold to other homebuilders. Five Poussins, including one with a tricycle undercarriage, are currently active in France.

Gatard Statoplan AG.02, F-PXKB

Specification	Gatard AG.02 Statoplan Poussin	
Powerplant	One 40 h.p. (29.8 kW) Volkswagen 4AR-1200 piston engine	
Dimensions		
Span	6.4 m	(21 ft 0 in)
Length	4.4 m	(14 ft 5 in)
Height	1.5 m	(4 ft 11 in)
Performance		
Max speed	150 km/h	(81 kt, 93 mph)
Cruising speed	135 km/h	(73 kt, 84 mph)
Initial climb	162 m/min	(530 fpm)
Range	375 km	(203 nm, 233 miles)
Weights		
Max takeoff	280 kg	(617 lbs)
Useful load	105 kg	(231 lbs)

General Avia F.22 Pinguino — Italy

Showing the unmistakable features of a Stelio Frati design, the F.22 Pinguino made its first flight on 13th June 1989. The F.22 is an all-metal low-wing aircraft with a side-by-side two-seat cockpit in production by General Avia for flying schools and private owners. The airframe has been designed for either fixed or retractable undercarriages and to take a variety of engines offering different levels of performance. Variants include the F.22A Pinguino (116 h.p. Textron Lycoming O-235-N2C engine), F.22B Pinguino (160 h.p. O-320-D2A) and F.22C (180 h.p. IO-360-A1A) with either fixed or retractable gear, the F.22 Bupp (160 h.p.) with a fixed undercarriage and the F.22R Pinguino Sprint with a 160 h.p. O-320-D1A engine, constant-speed propeller and retractable gear. Over 25 F.22s had been delivered by early 2000 and were flying in the USA, UK, Germany and Italy. General Avia has also developed and built a prototype of a four-seat cabin version of the F.22 designated F.220 Airone.

General Avia F.22B Pinguino, D-EDMJ

Specification	General Avia F.22R Pinguino Sprint	
Powerplant	One 160 h.p. (119.3 kW) Textron Lycoming O-320-D1A piston engine	
Dimensions		
Span	8.51 m	(27 ft 11 in)
Length	7.42 m	(24 ft 4 in)
Height	2.84 m	(9 ft 4 in)
Performance		
Max speed	306 km/h	(165 kt, 190 mph)
Cruising speed	269 km/h	(145 kt, 167 mph)
Initial climb	451 m/min	(1,480 fpm)
Range	1,290 km	(700 nm, 806 miles)
Weights		
Max takeoff	900 kg	(1,984 lbs)
Useful load	260 kg	(573 lbs)

General Avia F.20 Pegaso — Italy

Ing. Stelio Frati initiated the design of the F.20 Pegaso in 1970. It was a low-wing six-seat business aircraft with twin Continental IO-520 piston engines, an integral cabin with two entry doors, a retractable tricycle undercarriage and wingtip fuel tanks. The prototype Pegaso was built by General Avia and flown on 21st October 1971. This was followed by a second prototype and one production aircraft. No further production was undertaken and one of the three Pegasos remains in service in Italy. General Avia also built a prototype of the F.20TP Condor general-purpose military attack aircraft and this had a modified cabin with a sliding canopy and two Allison 250-B17B turboprop engines. The prototype first flew on 7th May 1983 but did not reach production status.

Specification	General Avia F.20 Pegaso	
Powerplant	Two 300 h.p. (233.7 kW) Continental IO-520-K piston engines	
Dimensions		
Span	10.35 m	(33 ft 11 in)
Length	8.22 m	(26 ft 11 in)
Height	3.5 m	(11 ft 6 in)
Performance		
Max speed	400 km/h	(216 kt, 249 mph)
Cruising speed	377 km/h	(203 kt, 234 mph)
Initial climb	550 m/min	(1,805 fpm)
Range	1,760 km	(955 nm, 1,100 miles)
Weights		
Max takeoff	2,250 kg	(4,960 lbs)
Useful load	514 kg	(1,134 lbs)

General Avia F.20 Pegaso, I-CBIE

General Dynamics F-111 — USA

The F-111 was the first successful production swing-wing combat aircraft. Originally planned in the early 1960s as a joint USAF and US Navy strike aircraft, the F-111 experienced early political and development delays and was eventually only built for the USAF and RAAF. The first F-111A flew on 21st December 1964 and went into service in 1967. It is a twin-turbofan aircraft with variable-sweep shoulder-mounted wings and a side-by-side two-seat cockpit. The wings have six hardpoints for tanks or ordnance and a belly weapons bay. The F-111A, powered by 18,500 lb.s.t. Pratt & Whitney TF30-P-3 afterburning turbofans, was widely used in Vietnam (and known as the Aardvark) and 24 were sold to Australia as the F-111C with longer-span wings and a strengthened undercarriage. Other variants were the F-111E with modified air inlets, the F-111D with improved avionics and higher engine power and the F-111F with 25,100 lb.s.t. TF30-P-100 turbofans. The FB-111A was a version equipped with a Boeing SRAM nuclear strike weapon. The EF-111A Raven is a variant developed by General Dynamics and Grumman for electronic countermeasures and fitted with a fin-mounted antenna for the ALQ-99E tactical jamming system. Except for a few test aircraft, all of the 563 USAF F-111s have been withdrawn from US service but the type remains in operation with the RAAF.

Specification	General Dynamics F-111C	
Powerplant	Two 18,500 lb.s.t.(82.3 kN) (dry) Pratt & Whitney TF30-P-3 turbofans	
Dimensions		
Span	21.34 m	(70 ft 0 in)
Length	22.4 m	(73 ft 6 in)
Height	5.22 m	(17 ft 1 in)
Performance		
Max speed	2,333 km/h	(1,260 kt, 1,450 mph)
Initial climb	7,136 m/min	(23,420 fpm)
Range	7,656 km	(4,161 nm, 4,785 miles)
Weights		
Max takeoff	50,180 kg	(110,646 lbs)
Useful load	28,646 kg	(63,165 lbs)

General Dynamics F-111C, A11-145

Gippsland GA-200 Fatman — Australia

The Melbourne-based Gippsland Aeronautics has developed the GA-200 Fatman agricultural aircraft. This is based on the Piper PA-25 Pawnee airframe with a wider fuselage to accommodate two people side-by-side, a much modified wing with upturned square wingtips, a new elevator and rudder and an enlarged 205 USG hopper. Seven Pawnees were converted as development aircraft and the type was certificated in March 1991. Powered by a 300 h.p. Lycoming O-540-K1A5 engine, the production GA-200C is fitted with a number of Gippsland's other agricultural improvements and complete airframes are now in production with 42 built by the end of 2000. In addition to crop spraying, the Fatman is being sold for agricultural pilot training with dual controls, fire bombing and aerial seeding roles.

Gippsland GA-200 Fatman, VH-MJC

Specification	Gippsland GA-200C Fatman	
Powerplant	One 300 h.p. (223.68 kW) Textron Lycoming O-540-K1A5 piston engine	
Dimensions		
Span	11.99 m	(39 ft 4 in)
Length	7.48 m	(24 ft 6 in)
Height	2.31 m	(7 ft 7 in)
Performance		
Max speed	177 km/h	(96 kt, 110 mph)
Cruising speed	161 km/h	(87 kt, 100 mph)
Initial climb	296 m/min	(970 fpm)
Range	885 km	(478 nm, 550 miles)
Weights		
Max takeoff	1,995 kg	(4,400 lbs)
Useful load	1,128 kg	(2,487 lbs)

Gippsland GA-8 Airvan — Australia

On 3rd March 1995 Gippsland Aeronautics of Latrobe Airport near Melbourne flew the prototype of the GA-8 Airvan strut-braced high-wing single-engined utility aircraft. The Airvan uses wings based on those of the GA-200, which are fitted with additional fuel tanks and married to a square-section six-seat fuselage. It has a fixed tricycle undercarriage and the prototype was powered by a 280 h.p. Lycoming O-540 piston engine with a constant-speed propeller although this is replaced by a 300 h.p. IO-540-K in the production version. Roles intended for the aircraft include cargo carrying, skydiving, survey and photography and transport of up to eight passengers and it is fitted with a large sliding cargo and passenger entrance door on the rear port side. The Airvan went into production in 1998.

Gippsland GA-8 Airvan

Specification	Gippsland GA-8 Airvan	
Powerplant	One 300 h.p. (233.7 kW) Textron Lycoming IO-540-K piston engine	
Dimensions		
Span	12.3 m	(40 ft 5 in)
Length	8.76 m	(28 ft 9 in)
Height	3.66 m	(12 ft 0 in)
Performance		
Max speed	259 km/h	(140 kt, 161 mph)
Cruising speed	240 km/h	(130 kt, 150 mph)
Takeoff distance	457 m	(1,500 ft)
Range	1,326 km	(720 nm, 829 miles)
Weights		
Max takeoff	1,814 kg	(4,000 lbs)
Useful load	907 kg	(2,000 lbs)

Globe GC-1 Swift — USA

The Globe Swift originated in the GC-1 low-wing two-seater which flew in 1941 and was built from moulded plywood. After the war the aircraft was redesigned with all-metal construction and the prototype GC-1A Swift first flew in January 1945. The high-performance GC-1A had a fully enclosed side-by-side two-seat cabin and a retractable tailwheel undercarriage. It was powered by an 85 h.p. Continental C85 and built by the Texas Engineering and Manufacturing Co. ('Temco'). The later GC-1B Swift was fitted with a 125 h.p. Continental C125 engine in a modified engine cowling. Swift production was completed in 1951 after 1,502 production Swifts and three prototypes had been built. An updated Swift has been developed by LoPresti as the Fury with a new wing and a 200 h.p. Lycoming IO-360 engine and the Swift is also being returned to production by Aviat Aircraft in modified form with a 180 h.p. engine. Many Swifts have been altered with sliding canopies and performance modifications including, in one case, a tricycle undercarriage, and with different powerplants, including an Allison 250 turboprop.

Globe GC-1B Swift, N3888K

LoPresti Fury, N217LP

Globe GC-1 Swift (Cont.)

Specification	Globe (Temco) GC-1B Swift	
Powerplant	One 125 h.p. (93.2 kW) Teledyne Continental C125 piston engine	
Dimensions		
Span	8.94 m	(29 ft 4 in)
Length	6.35 m	(20 ft 10 in)
Height	1.88 m	(6 ft 2 in)
Performance		
Max speed	241 km/h	(130 kt, 150 mph)
Cruising speed	225 km/h	(122 kt, 140 mph)
Initial climb	305 m/min	(1,000 fpm)
Range	672 km	(365 nm, 420 miles)
Weights		
Max takeoff	776 kg	(1,710 lbs)
Useful load	265 kg	(585 lbs)

Gloster Meteor T.7/8, WL419

Gloster Meteor — UK

The Meteor was the only British jet fighter to see active service in World War II and it formed the backbone of the postwar front line and RAuxAF squadrons in the late 1940s and 1950s. A total of 3,181 of all marks were manufactured. It was an all-metal low-wing aircraft with a cruciform tail and single-seat cockpit enclosed by a clear-view canopy. The Meteor was produced in single-seat (Mk.3, 4, 5, 6 and 8), tandem two-seat trainer (Mk.7), single-seat reconnaissance (FR.9 and PR.10) and two-seat night fighter (NF.11, 12, 13 and 14) versions. The main production model, of which 1,079 were built, was the F.8 air defence fighter, some of which were converted to U-16 target drones. The NF.11 was based on the T.7 airframe with an extended radar nose and a radar operator's position in the rear cockpit and some of these later became TT.20 target tugs. The last Meteors were withdrawn from front-line service in 1957 but several have continued as target drones, for ejection seat and other testing and with private warbird owners.

Specification	Gloster Meteor F.8	
Powerplant	Two 3,500 lb.s.t. (15.57 kN) Rolls Royce Derwent 8 turbojets	
Dimensions		
Span	11.3 m	(37 ft 2 in)
Length	13.59 m	(44 ft 7 in)
Height	3.9 m	(13 ft 0 in)
Performance		
Max speed	962 km/h	(520 kt, 598 mph)
Cruising speed	676 km/h	(365 kt, 420 mph)
Initial climb	1,433 m/min	(4,700 fpm)
Range	1,104 km	(600 nm, 690 miles)
Weights		
Max takeoff	7,120 kg	(15,700 lbs)
Useful load	2,275 kg	(5,016 lbs)

Gloster Meteor NF.11, WM167

Granville Bros. Gee Bee Racer — USA

In the 1930s, Granville Brothers Aircraft became involved in developing a series of unlimited class racers to participate in the air races which were becoming hugely popular. They built a series of 16 low-wing single-seat aircraft which used small streamlined airframes with large spatted fixed undercarriages, frequently powered by huge radial engines of high horsepower. The later versions (Z and R) had distinctive tubby fuselages and enclosed cockpits and the Y was a tandem two-seater. Variants included the Model D Sportster (125 h.p. Menasco), Model E Sportster (110 h.p. Warner Scarab), Model Y Senior Sportster (215 h.p. Lycoming R-680), Model Z (535 h.p. P&W Wasp Jr or 750 h.p.Wasp), Model R-1 Super Sportster (800 h.p. P&W R-1340) and R-2 Super Sportster (530 h.p. P&W R-985). None of the original Gee Bees has survived but two replicas of the Model E have been built together with single examples of the Models Y, Z and R-2.

Gee Bee R-2 Super Sportster replica, NR2101 (N117GB)

Specification	Granville Bros. Gee Bee Model Z	
Powerplant	One 535 h.p. (399 kW) Pratt & Whitney Wasp Junior radial piston engine	
Dimensions		
Span	7.77 m	(25 ft 6 in)
Length	4.6 m	(15 ft 1 in)
Height	1.73 m	(5 ft 8 in)
Performance		
Max speed	435 km/h	(235 kt, 270 mph)
Cruising speed	370 km/h	(200 kt, 230 mph)
Initial climb	457 m/min	(1,500 fpm)
Range	1,600 km	(870 nm, 1,000 miles)
Weights		
Max takeoff	1,034 kg	(2,280 lbs)
Useful load	399 kg	(880 lbs)

Great Lakes 2T — USA

The Great Lakes aerobatic biplane trainer, designed by Charles W. Meyers, was built by Great Lakes Aircraft Company between 1929 and 1932, 264 examples being completed. It was a tandem two-seat open-cockpit biplane with a swept upper wing and straight lower wing surfaces. The initial Model 2T-1 was powered by an 85 h.p. Cirrus Mk.3 in-line engine and the Model 2T-1A had a 90 h.p. Cirrus although several were fitted with Warner radial engines of up to 200 horsepower. The Great Lakes designs were revived in 1972 by a new Great Lakes Aircraft Inc. who built the Model 2T-1A-1 with a 150 h.p. Lycoming O-320-E2A and the 2T-1A-2 with a fuel-injected 180 h.p. Lycoming IO-360-B1F6. They built 138 of the Model 2T-1A-2 together with one example of the turboprop Model X2T-1T 'Turbine Lakes' powered by an Allison 250 turboprop. The Great Lakes was again revived in the mid-1980s but only 12 aircraft were completed, but further examples of the Great Lakes Sport Trainer have been built from plans which are available to homebuilders from Great Airplanes Inc. More than 250 Great Lakes are flying.

Great Lakes 2T-1A, N847K

Specification	Great Lakes 2T-1A-2	
Powerplant	One 180 h.p. (134.2 kW) Textron-Lycoming IO-360-B1F6 piston engine	
Dimensions		
Span	8.13 m	(26 ft 8 in)
Length	6.2 m	(20 ft 4 in)
Height	2.54 m	(8 ft 4 in)
Performance		
Max speed	209 km/h	(113 kt, 130 mph)
Cruising speed	177 km/h	(96 kt, 110 mph)
Initial climb	457 m/min	(1,500 fpm)
Range	480 km	(261 nm, 300 miles)
Weights		
Max takeoff	734 kg	(1,618 lbs)
Useful load	269 kg	(593 lbs)

Griffon Lionheart — USA

The amateur builder Larry French designed the Lionheart using modern materials but based on the design of the Beech 17 Staggerwing. The Lionheart is a four-seat cabin aircraft with reverse-stagger cantilever biplane wings and a retractable tailwheel undercarriage. It is of all-composite construction and is powered by a 450 h.p. Pratt & Whitney R-985 radial engine. Despite its external appearance, the shape, area and section of its wing and tail surfaces are completely different to those of the Staggerwing. The Lionheart first flew in 1997 and is now marketed as a kit to homebuilders.

Griffon Lionheart, N985L

Griffon Lionheart (Cont.)

Specification	Griffon Aerospace Lionheart	
Powerplant	One 450 h.p. (335.5 kW) Pratt & Whitney R-985 radial piston engine	
Dimensions		
Span	9.45 m	(31 ft 0 in)
Length	8.15 m	(26 ft 9 in)
Height	2.44 m	(8 ft 0 in)
Performance		
Max speed	370 km/h	(200 kt, 230 mph)
Cruising speed	338 km/h	(183 kt, 210 mph)
Initial climb	914 m/min	(3,000 fpm)
Range	2,400 km	(1,304 nm, 1,500 miles)
Weights		
Max takeoff	1,905 kg	(4,200 lbs)
Useful load	862 kg	(1,900 lbs)

Grinvalds (Aerodis) Orion — France

The Orion, designed by Jean Grinvalds, was one of the earliest composite-kit light aircraft to be produced in France. Its radical but effective layout resulted in a large four-seat cabin, entered through two gullwing doors, a low-set straight wing and a pusher engine buried in the centre fuselage. The T-tailed Orion has complex systems including an electrically-operated retractable tricycle undercarriage and flaps, and special engine indicator and control systems. It is constructed from glass-fibre shells reinforced with Kevlar and with foam filling in the wings. The G-801 prototype first flew on 2nd June 1981. The G-802, which has a wider cabin and slightly longer fuselage has been marketed in France and the USA by Aerodis. A revised version, the DG-87 Goeland, has also been built by amateurs in France. The kits are no longer in production but five Orions are flying in France and one in the USA with others under construction.

Grinvalds G-801 Orion, F-PYNA

Specification	Grinvalds G-801 Orion	
Powerplant	One 180 h.p. (134.2 kW) Textron Lycoming O-360 piston engine	
Dimensions		
Span	8.99 m	(29 ft 6 in)
Length	6.71 m	(22 ft 0 in)
Height	1.50 m	(4 ft 11 in)
Performance		
Max speed	330 km/h	(178 kt, 205 mph)
Cruising speed	249 km/h	(135 kt, 155 mph)
Initial climb	239 m/min	(785 fpm)
Range	1,491 km	(810 nm, 932 miles)
Weights		
Max takeoff	1,055 kg	(2,326 lbs)
Useful load	415 kg	(915 lbs)

Grob G 109 — Germany

After many years of successful production of the Astir series of glass-fibre sailplanes, Grob-Werke added the G 109 motor glider to their range. This was a side-by-side two-seater built of GRP with a fixed tailwheel undercarriage, a T-tail and an 80 h.p. Limbach L.2000-E1 engine. The G 109, which first flew on 14th March 1980, was fully capable of soaring with the engine stopped but had respectable speed and range for training and touring. Production of the G 109 reached 151 aircraft when the G 109B was introduced. This had the increased power of a 90 h.p. GVW.2500 engine, redesigned longer-span wings, a variable-pitch propeller and a larger sliding canopy with a fixed windshield. It was also built as the Ranger with additional fuel capacity. Some 377 examples of the G 109B had been built when production was completed including a batch of 54 delivered to the RAF as the Vigilant T.1.

Grob G 109B, G-BMMP

Specification	Grob G 109B	
Powerplant	One 90 h.p. (67.1 kW) Grob GVW.2500 piston engine	
Dimensions		
Span	17.4 m	(57 ft 1 in)
Length	8.1 m	(26 ft 7 in)
Height	1.8 m	(5 ft 11 in)
Performance		
Max speed	240 km/h	(130 kt, 149 mph)
Cruising speed	209 km/h	(113 kt, 130 mph)
Initial climb	198 m/min	(650 fpm)
Range	1,488 km	(809 nm, 930 miles)
Weights		
Max takeoff	850 kg	(1,874 lbs)
Useful load	230 kg	(507 lbs)

Grob G 115 and G 115T — Germany

In the early 1980s, Grob-Werke had built prototypes of the G 110 and G 112 two-seat trainers. These led to the G 115 which was a side-by-side two-seater bearing a family resemblance to the earlier G 109 motor glider but with a larger and heavier airframe with a wider fuselage, a large sliding cockpit canopy and a fixed tricycle undercarriage. It was powered by a 116 h.p. Textron Lycoming O-235-H2C engine. It first flew on 15th November 1985 and subsequently went into production at Mindelheim. The G 115B and G 115C were improved versions with 160 h.p. Lycoming O-320-D2A engines, additional baggage capacity and a redesigned cockpit canopy and the G 115D, marketed in the USA as the Bavarian, was fully aerobatic and was powered by a 180 h.p. AEIO-360-B engine. The G 115D 'Heron' has been used under contract for British naval officer training but the G 115E is a new version 99 of which were ordered for the RAF as a Bulldog replacement. A total of 260 Grob 115s had been built by the end of 2000. The Grob G 115T is an aerobatic model with a retractable undercarriage and powered by a 260 h.p. AEIO-540-D4A5 engine and 13 have been delivered to the United Arab Emirates Air Force as an ab initio trainer.

Grob G 115D-2 Heron, G-BVHC

Specification	Grob G 115E	
Powerplant	One 180 h.p. (134.2 kW) Textron Lycoming AEIO-360-B1F piston engine	
Dimensions		
Span	10 m	(32 ft 10 in)
Length	7.79 m	(25 ft 7 in)
Height	2.82 m	(9 ft 3 in)
Performance		
Max speed	250 km/h	(135 kt, 155 mph)
Cruising speed	230 km/h	(124 kt, 143 mph)
Initial climb	320 m/min	(1,050 fpm)
Range	1,260 km	(685 nm, 788 miles)
Weights		
Max takeoff	990 kg	(2,183 lbs)
Useful load	300 kg	(661 lbs)

Grob GF 200 — Germany

Burkhart Grob of Mindelheim has produced the prototype of the advanced GF 200 business and personal light aircraft. Among its many revolutionary features are a low-set wing with a straight trailing edge and compound leading-edge sweep, and a pusher engine installation consisting of a Continental TSIOL-550 piston engine buried in the rear fuselage driving a tail-mounted three-blade Muhlbauer constant-speed propeller via a patented composite drive shaft. The GF 200 has a retractable tricycle undercarriage and a four-seat cabin which is unpressurised in the prototype but would be pressurised for production aircraft. Cabin entry is via a split door in the forward port fuselage. The GF 200 is of all-composite construction and has a T-tail and ventral fin. The prototype was first flown on 26th November 1991 but development was halted in 1998 in favour of the larger GF 350 which will be an enlarged eight-seat version. The prototype GF 200 continues to be active.

Grob GF 200, D-EFKH

Specification	Grob GF 200	
Powerplant	One 310 h.p. (231.14 kW) Teledyne Continental TSIOL-550 piston engine	
Dimensions		
Span	11 m	(36 ft 0 in)
Length	8.7 m	(28 ft 6 in)
Height	3.42 m	(11 ft 2 in)
Performance		
Max speed	418 km/h	(226 kt, 260 mph)
Cruising speed	373 km/h	(202 kt, 232 mph)
Initial climb	372 m/min	(1,220 fpm)
Range	2,288 km	(1,243 nm, 1,430 miles)
Weights		
Max takeoff	1,700 kg	(3,748 lbs)
Useful load	900 kg	(1,984 lbs)

Grob 500 Egrett — Germany

Burkhart Grob, Garrett and E-Systems of Greenville, Texas have cooperated to build a series of five high-altitude surveillance aircraft the first of which was the Egrett I. Roles for the aircraft include military surveillance, police border patrol, mapping and geophysical survey. The prototype Egrett I, built by Grob with a single-seat cockpit, high-aspect-ratio wings and a fixed tricycle undercarriage, first flew on 24th June 1987. The Egrett has a large removable belly compartment to house a wide range of surveillance modules and sensors and is constructed of GRP and Kevlar. The D-500, which flew in 1989, has a pressurised cockpit, larger wings and a retractable undercarriage, and the single-seat G-520 Egrett II and two-seat G-520T are fitted with belly-mounted external equipment pods. The final variant is the Strato 1 with a larger equipment bay, wingtip winglets and other refinements. All these aircraft continue to operate on commercial contracts except for the Egrett I which has been retired. Grob has also built one example of the Strato 2C which is a completely new design built for the German BDLI for high-altitude research and powered by two pusher Teledyne Continental TSIOL-550 engines mounted above the wing. This first flew on 31st March 1995 but was grounded in 1996 due to official funding conflicts.

rob G-500 Egrett II, D-FGEE

Specification	Grob G-520T Egrett	
Powerplant	One 750 s.h.p. (559.2 kW) Honeywell (Garrett) TPE331-14F-801L turboprop	
Dimensions		
Span	33 m	(108 ft 3 in)
Length	13.67 m	(44 ft 10 in)
Height	5.66 m	(18 ft 7 in)
Performance		
Max speed	445 km/h	(240 kt, 276 mph)
Cruising speed	332 km/h	(179 kt, 206 mph)
Initial climb	427 m/min	(1,400 fpm)
Range	1,600 km	(870 nm, 1,000 miles)
Weights		
Max takeoff	4,700 kg	(10,363 lbs)
Useful load	1,000 kg	(2,205 lbs)

Groen Hawk 4 — USA

Groen Brothers Aviation (GBA) has developed the Hawk as a modern gyroplane capable of carrying out a wide range of tasks. Variants of the current Hawk 4 include the AgHawk which is fitted with a 65 USG chemical tank and spraybars for agricultural spraying, the military Hawk Defender with two machine guns in the stub wings and a dedicated police model for highway and border patrol. The original two-seat H.2X Hawk prototype first flew on 5th February 1997 powered by a Geschwender V-8 engine and it was followed on 29th September 1999 by the prototype Hawk 4 which has a four-seat interior. The Hawk is of largely metal construction and has twin booms, a fixed tricycle undercarriage and a pusher engine installation. Future versions include the Hawk 4T which will be powered by a 420 s.h.p. Allison 250-B17C turboshaft engine and the turbine powered six-seat Hawk 6 and eight-seat Hawk 8.

Groen Hawk 4, N402GB

Specification	Groen Hawk 4	
Powerplant	One 350 h.p. (261 kW) Teledyne Continental TSIO-550 piston engine	
Dimensions		
Rotor diameter	12.8 m	(42 ft 0 in)
Length	6.71 m	(22 ft 0 in)
Height	3.35 m	(11 ft 0 in)
Performance		
Max speed	241 km/h	(130 kt, 150 mph)
Cruising speed	209 km/h	(113 kt, 130 mph)
Initial climb	457 m/min	(1,500 fpm)
Range	672 km	(365 nm, 420 miles)
Weights		
Max takeoff	1,270 kg	(2,800 lbs)
Useful load	435 kg	(960 lbs)

Grumman G-21 Goose
— USA

First of a great tradition of Grumman amphibians, the Goose was designed for use by wealthy private owners and business users and the prototype made its first flight at Grumman's Bethpage, New York factory on 29th May 1937. It was an all-metal cantilever high-wing aircraft with a braced cruciform tailplane, fixed outrigger floats and a retractable undercarriage with main wheels folding into open wells on the fuselage sides. It was powered by a pair of 450 h.p. Pratt & Whitney Wasp Junior radial engines mounted on the wing and could accommodate a crew of two with up to six passengers in an enclosed cabin in the centre fuselage. The initial G-21 was followed by the G-21A with a modified hull and higher gross weight and the G-21B without the land undercarriage. The Goose was also built in large numbers for the US Navy as the JRF, the US Coast Guard (JRF-2) and the USAAC as the OA-9 and OA-13. In total 345 aircraft were built between 1937 and 1945. Several G-21s were converted with four Lycoming GSO-480 engines and retractable floats as the McKinnon G-21C or as the G-21G with two Pratt & Whitney PT6A-27 turboprops. Over 60 G-21s are flying worldwide.

Grumman G-21 Goose, N121GL

Specification	Grumman G-21 Goose	
Powerplant	Two 450 h.p. (335.5 kW) Pratt & Whitney Wasp Junior SB piston engines	
Dimensions		
Span	14.94 m	(49 ft 0 in)
Length	11.66 m	(38 ft 3 in)
Height	3.71 m	(12 ft 2 in)
Performance		
Max speed	314 km/h	(170 kt, 195 mph)
Cruising speed	282 km/h	(152 kt, 175 mph)
Initial climb	454 m/min	(1,490 fpm)
Range	1,840 km	(1,000 nm, 1,150 miles)
Weights		
Max takeoff	3,401 kg	(7,500 lbs)
Useful load	1,177 kg	(2,595 lbs)

Grumman F4F Wildcat
— USA

Grumman flew the prototype G-36 (XF4F-3) single-seat naval carrier fighter on 12th February 1939. Owing much to the design of Grumman's earlier military biplanes, the Wildcat had a mid-set wing and a tailwheel undercarriage with the main wheels retracting via a complex leg structure into wells in the belly. The F4F-3 was powered by a 1,200 h.p. Pratt & Whitney R-1830-76 radial engine and the F4F-4 and later variants were similar but fitted with manually folding wings and different versions of the R-1830 engine. The Wildcat was also built by Eastern Aircraft as the FM-1 and FM-2 (which had a larger tail, split flaps and a Wright R-1820 engine) and 1,123 were delivered to the Royal Navy as the Martlet. Production of all variants totalled 7,825. After the war, a number of Wildcats were restored by warbird enthusiasts and at least twelve are currently flying.

Grumman FM-2 Wildcat, N222FM

Specification	Grumman (Eastern) FM-2 Wildcat	
Powerplant	One 1,350 h.p. (1,007 kW) Wright R-1820-56 piston engine	
Dimensions		
Span	11.58 m	(38 ft 0 in)
Length	8.81 m	(28 ft 11 in)
Height	3.02 m	(9 ft 11 in)
Performance		
Max speed	534 km/h	(289 kt, 332 mph)
Cruising speed	264 km/h	(143 kt, 164 mph)
Initial climb	1,113 m/min	(3,650 fpm)
Range	2,096 km	(1,139 nm, 1,310 miles)
Weights		
Max takeoff	3,751 kg	(8,271 lbs)
Useful load	2,457 kg	(5,418 lbs)

Grumman TBM Avenger — USA

The TBM Avenger was the US Navy's standard carrier-based torpedo bomber in World War II and 9,839 were built. Designed by Grumman as the TBF most were manufactured by Eastern Aircraft as the TBM and the prototype flew on 7th August 1941. It was a mid-wing aircraft with a belly torpedo bay and a long three-man cockpit with a framed canopy incorporating a rear bubble gun turret. The Avenger had a retractable tailwheel undercarriage and a rear fuselage crew compartment with a ventral gun position. The TBF-1 and TBM-1 had a 1,700 h.p. Wright R-2600-8 radial engine. Many variants of the Avenger were built including the TBM-3 with a 1,900 h.p. R-2600-20 engine and versions with a variety of radar equipment including the TBM3W which had a large belly-mounted radome. Avengers served with the Royal Navy and the naval forces of Canada, Japan, France etc. until the late 1950s and many were then used as fire-fighting water bombers. Over 140 still exist in museums and elsewhere with around 50 airworthy with firefighting and warbird operators.

Grumman TBM-3R, 53319 (G-BTDP)

Specification	Grumman (Eastern) TBM-3E Avenger	
Powerplant	One 1,900 h.p. (1,416.64 kW) Wright R-2600-20 piston engine	
Dimensions		
Span	16.51 m	(54 ft 2 in)
Length	12.48 m	(40 ft 11 in)
Height	5 m	(16 ft 5 in)
Performance		
Max speed	444 km/h	(240 kt, 276 mph)
Cruising speed	237 km/h	(128 kt, 147 mph)
Initial climb	628 m/min	(2,060 fpm)
Range	3,072 km	(1,670 nm, 1,920 miles)
Weights		
Max takeoff	8,116 kg	(17,895 lbs)
Useful load	3,333 kg	(7,350 lbs)

Grumman G-44 Widgeon — USA

The Widgeon was a smaller and less expensive companion for the Goose amphibian and it first flew on 28th June 1940 at Bethpage. Of broadly similar high-wing layout to the Goose, the Widgeon had a retractable tailwheel undercarriage, fixed floats and a cruciform tail. It was powered by two 200 h.p. Ranger 6-440C-5 in-line engines and had accommodation for a pilot and four passengers. During the war the US Navy acquired Widgeons designated J4F-1 and they were also used by the US Coast Guard and by the Royal Navy as the Gosling. Postwar, the Widgeon was built for private owners and a production line was established by SCAN in France where 40 SCAN-30 airframes were built. Including these, 317 Widgeons were built and most of the 125-odd survivors have been re-fitted for better performance with various powerplants including horizontally opposed 260 h.p. Lycoming GO-435-C2B or Continental IO-470-D engines.

Grumman G-44A Widgeon, N86609

Specification	Grumman G-44 Widgeon	
Powerplant	Two 200 h.p. (149.1 kW) Ranger 6-440C-5 piston engines	
Dimensions		
Span	12.19 m	(40 ft 0 in)
Length	9.47 m	(31 ft 1 in)
Height	3.48 m	(11 ft 5 in)
Performance		
Max speed	246 km/h	(133 kt, 153 mph)
Cruising speed	222 km/h	(120 kt, 138 mph)
Initial climb	213 m/min	(700 fpm)
Range	1,472 km	(800 nm, 920 miles)
Weights		
Max takeoff	2,052 kg	(4,525 lbs)
Useful load	583 kg	(1,285 lbs)

Grumman G-51 (F7F) Tigercat — USA

The twin-engined Tigercat was one of the fastest piston-engined combat aircraft of World War II. Originally designed as a carrier-borne fighter it served mainly with the US Marines and was deployed extensively in Korea as a night fighter, the F7F-3N having an extended nose with an SCR-70 radar. The Tigercat, which first flew on 3rd November 1943, was a mid-wing single-seat design with a retractable tricycle undercarriage and was fitted with two 2,100 h.p. Pratt & Whitney R-2800-22W radial engines. The F7F-2 was a two-seat development with a tandem two-seat cockpit for pilot and radar operator and the F7F-3 had R-2800-34W engines, a larger tail and six wing strongpoints for rockets. Production of Tigercats was completed in late 1946 with 364 having been built. A number of Tigercats were civilianised as firebombers with a belly-mounted borate tank and eight remain as warbirds with civil owners.

Grumman F7F-3 Tigercat, N6178C

Specification	Grumman F7F-3 Tigercat	
Powerplant	Two 2,100 h.p. (1,565.76 kW) Pratt & Whitney R-2800-34W piston engines	
Dimensions		
Span	15.7 m	(51 ft 6 in)
Length	13.83 m	(45 ft 4 in)
Height	4.98 m	(16 ft 4 in)
Performance		
Max speed	724 km/h	(391 kt, 450 mph)
Cruising speed	357 km/h	(193 kt, 222 mph)
Initial climb	1,841 m/min	(6,040 fpm)
Range	3,040 km	(1,652 nm, 1,900 miles)
Weights		
Max takeoff	11,664 kg	(25,720 lbs)
Useful load	4,868 kg	(10,735 lbs)

Grumman G-58 (F8F) Bearcat — USA

The Bearcat arrived on the scene just as piston-engined fighters were facing obsolescence from jet aircraft. The G-58, which first flew on 31st August 1944, was a compact carrier-borne single-seat fighter with a low wing, retractable tailwheel undercarriage and a bubble-enclosed cockpit. As the F8F-1, it had the reliable 2,100 h.p. Pratt & Whitney R-2800 radial engine and was armed with four 0.50-inch guns. It also had upward-folding wings for carrier storage and four underwing hardpoints and a belly fuel tank pylon. The later F8F-2 had a 2,250 h.p. R-2800-34W engine. The F8F-1 Bearcat entered service in May 1945 and its main combat experience was with the French Air Force in Indo-China in the early 1950s. Bearcats also served with the Royal Thai Air Force. Many of the 1,265 production Bearcats were sold to private owners and have been used extensively in unlimited racing, frequently in a highly modified state. Thirteen Bearcats are currently flying and others are under restoration.

Grumman F8F-2P Bearcat, Bu.122674 (N7825C)

Specification	Grumman F8F-2 Bearcat	
Powerplant	One 2,250 h.p. (1,677.6 kW) Pratt & Whitney R-2800-34W piston engine	
Dimensions		
Span	10.82 m	(35 ft 6 in)
Length	8.43 m	(27 ft 8 in)
Height	4.17 m	(13 ft 8 in)
Performance		
Max speed	719 km/h	(389 kt, 447 mph)
Cruising speed	293 km/h	(158 kt, 182 mph)
Initial climb	1,347 m/min	(4,420 fpm)
Range	1,384 km	(752 nm, 865 miles)
Weights		
Max takeoff	6,120 kg	(13,494 lbs)
Useful load	2,632 kg	(5,804 lbs)

Grumman G-73 Mallard — USA

After the war Grumman continued its flying boat tradition with a new aircraft intended as a feeder airliner or 'air yacht' for wealthy private owners. The Mallard was an elegant amphibian, larger than the pre-war Goose with a ten-passenger main cabin. It had a high wing mounting two 600 h.p. Pratt & Whitney Wasp radial engines but, unlike the Goose, it had a retractable tricycle undercarriage and the fixed outrigger floats were fully faired. Some 59 Mallards were built, 41 of which still exist. Almost all of these were delivered to corporate users and two were sold to King Farouk of Egypt. Some Mallards have been converted to Frakes Turbo Mallard standard with 578 s.h.p. Pratt & Whitney PT6A-6 turboprops.

Grumman G-73 Mallard, N98BS

Specification	Grumman G-73 Mallard	
Powerplant	Two 600 h.p. (448 kW) Pratt & Whitney Wasp R-1340-S3H1 piston engines	
Dimensions		
Span	20.32 m	(66 ft 8 in)
Length	14.73 m	(48 ft 4 in)
Height	5.72 m	(18 ft 9 in)
Performance		
Max speed	346 km/h	(187 kt, 215 mph)
Cruising speed	290 km/h	(156 kt, 180 mph)
Initial climb	393 m/min	(1,290 fpm)
Range	2,210 km	(1,200 nm, 1,380 miles)
Weights		
Max takeoff	5,782 kg	(12,750 lbs)
Useful load	1,542 kg	(3,400 lbs)

Grumman G-64 Albatross — USA

At the end of World War II, Grumman was firmly established as the leading manufacturer of flying boats and amphibians and they drew up the G-64 design for a replacement for the Grumman Goose as an air-sea rescue aircraft. The G-64 was substantially larger than the Goose with an all-metal structure, a retractable tricycle undercarriage and a high wing mounting two Wright R-1820 radial piston engines. The prototype XJR2F-1 flew on 1st October 1947 and the production USAF version was the SA-16A Albatross (later HU-16A) which entered service in 1949, and the UF-1 (SA-16C) for the US Navy and UF-1G for the US Coast Guard. The G-111 (USAF SA-16B/HU-16B and US Navy UF-2) had improved performance and was fitted with longer-span wings, a larger tailplane and a taller and wider vertical tail. In total, 466 examples of the Albatross were built and deliveries were also made to 22 other countries including Argentina, Brazil, Germany, Indonesia, Japan and Norway. Virtually all Albatrosses have been retired from military service but nearly 100 are still active with commercial operators and private owners and some have been converted with Garrett TPE331, Pratt & Whitney PT6A or Rolls Royce Dart turboprop engines.

Grumman HU-16C Albatross, N7025J

Specification	Grumman G-111 Albatross HU-16B	
Powerplant	Two 1,425 h.p. (1,062.48 kW) Wright R-1820-76B radial engines	
Dimensions		
Span	29.46 m	(96 ft 8 in)
Length	19.15 m	(62 ft 10 in)
Height	7.87 m	(25 ft 10 in)
Performance		
Max speed	380 km/h	(205 kt, 236 mph)
Cruising speed	275 km/h	(149 kt, 171 mph)
Initial climb	357 m/min	(1,170 fpm)
Range	5,544 km	(3,013 nm, 3,465 miles)
Weights		
Max takeoff	17,007 kg	(37,500 lbs)
Useful load	6,629 kg	(14,617 lbs)

Grumman F9F Panther — USA

Grumman's F9F Panther (G-79) was designed for the US Navy as a carrier-borne single-seat fighter and was first flown on 21st November 1947. It had a distinctive straight wing which folded for carrier storage and had wingtip fuel tanks. The Panther, which was a versatile aircraft with night fighter capabilities and six underwing hardpoints for external stores, served in Korea and was also used by the Argentine Navy. A total of 1,385 Panthers were built and five are active as warbirds in the United States.

Grumman F9F-2B Panther, Bu.123078 (NX9525A)

Specification	Grumman G-79 Panther F9F-5	
Powerplant	One 7,000 lb.s.t. (31.14 kN) Pratt & Whitney J48-P-6 turbojet	
Dimensions		
Span	11.58 m	(38 ft 0 in)
Length	11.85 m	(38 ft 10 in)
Height	3.76 m	(12 ft 4 in)
Performance		
Max speed	972 km/h	(525 kt, 604 mph)
Cruising speed	772 km/h	(417 kt, 480 mph)
Initial climb	1,829 m/min	(6,000 fpm)
Range	2,080 km	(1,130 nm, 1,300 miles)
Weights		
Max takeoff	8,490 kg	(18,721 lbs)
Useful load	3,888 kg	(8,574 lbs)

Grumman G-134 (OV-1) Mohawk — USA

Grumman designed the Mohawk to meet the US Army's requirement for a dedicated battlefield surveillance aircraft and 380 were built between 1959 and 1970. The prototype OV-1 (later designated AO-1) flew on 14th April 1959. The OV-1A Mohawk was a mid-wing aircraft with a large bulged cockpit positioned well ahead of the wing so as to give excellent all-round visibility. It was fitted with a retractable tricycle undercarriage and had a triple-fin tail unit and two Lycoming T53 turboprop engines. The outer wing sections were fitted with up to three hardpoints each side which were used to carry a variety of long-range tanks, resupply containers, SLAR and ELINT pods and attack ordnance. The Mohawk, which was used widely in Vietnam, also routinely carried cameras in a belly installation and a SLAR pod on a centreline fitting. The OV-1D was fitted with long-span wings and higher-powered engines. Most Mohawks have now been retired although examples still serve with the Argentine Air Force, the US Customs Service, with private owners and as fire spotters with the US Forestry Service.

Grumman Mohawk OV-1D, AE-025 (Argentine Army)

Specification	Grumman G-134 Mohawk OV-1D	
Powerplant	Two 1,400 s.h.p. (1,043.84 kW) Lycoming T53-L-701 turboprops	
Dimensions		
Span	14.63 m	(48 ft 0 in)
Length	13.69 m	(44 ft 11 in)
Height	3.96 m	(13 ft 0 in)
Performance		
Max speed	491 km/h	(265 kt, 305 mph)
Cruising speed	330 km/h	(178 kt, 205 mph)
Initial climb	1,103 m/min	(3,618 fpm)
Range	1,616 km	(878 nm, 1,010 miles)
Weights		
Max takeoff	8,213 kg	(18,109 lbs)
Useful load	2,881 kg	(6,352 lbs)

Grumman G-164 Ag-Cat — USA

The Ag-Cat single-seat agricultural biplane was designed by Grumman in the mid 1950s and first flew on 22nd May 1957. The G-164 is a steel tube aircraft covered by largely removable aluminium panels and powered, initially, by a Continental W-670 radial piston engine. Early Ag-Cats were fitted with 250 USG hoppers and had an open cockpit although this was later supplanted by an enclosed cabin. The G-164B Super Ag-Cat has an increased load and a 600 h.p. R-1340 engine

Grumman G-164 Ag-Cat (Cont.)

but can also be powered by PT6A turboprops of various power ratings. The G-164C has a longer fuselage and a larger hopper and the G-164D Ag-Cat D Turbo uses the G-164C airframe with the Pratt & Whitney PT6A-15, -34 or -41 turboprop. Ag-Cats have also been converted with other engines including the Alvis Leonides and Lycoming LTP-101. The Ag-Cat was initially built by Schweizer Aircraft under licence but they acquired all rights from Grumman in 1981. It has also been licence-built by Admas Air Service in Ethiopia as the 'Eshet'. In 1995 production rights were sold to Ag-Cat Corporation who have built a small number of aircraft and have launched the turboprop Ag-Cat T500. Over 2,600 Ag-Cats have been built.

Grumman G-164D Ag-Cat Turbo, ZS-KPT

Grumman G-164 Ag-Cat, VH-JBB

Specification	Grumman (Schweizer) G-164D Ag-Cat Turbo	
Powerplant	One 750 s.h.p. (559.2 kW) Pratt & Whitney PT6A-34 turboprop	
Dimensions		
Span	12.88 m	(42 ft 3 in)
Length	10.46 m	(34 ft 4 in)
Height	3.48 m	(11 ft 5 in)
Performance		
Max speed	249 km/h	(135 kt, 155 mph)
Cruising speed	153 km/h	(83 kt, 95 mph)
Initial climb	427 m/min	(1,400 fpm)
Range	400 km	(217 nm, 250 miles)
Weights		
Max takeoff	3,855 kg	(8,500 lbs)
Useful load	2,290 kg	(5,050 lbs)

Grumman G-159 Gulfstream I — USA

The Gulfstream executive aircraft first flew on 14th August 1958 and was an up-market turboprop twin with accommodation for up to 21 passengers. It had a low wing and a retractable tricycle undercarriage and was powered by two Rolls Royce Darts. Backed by Grumman's reputation and a need for replacement of DC-3s and other older business aircraft the Gulfstream (later referred to as the Gulfstream I to avoid confusion with the Gulfstream business jets) entered production in 1959. Sales to non-executive operators included nine TC-4C Academe attack systems trainers for the US Navy. In total, 200 Gulfstreams had been completed when production ceased in 1969. Half of these remain in service, many with local service airlines and as small package freighters. In 1979, the GAC-159-C (later known as the G-159C) was introduced as a conversion for commuter airline use. This had a stretched fuselage giving accommodation for 38 passengers and the first of six G-159Cs flew on 25th October 1979.

Grumman G-159 Gulfstream I, VH-JPJ

Grumman F-14A Tomcat, Bu.158620

Specification	Grumman G-159 Gulfstream I	
Powerplant	Two 2,210 s.h.p. (1,647.78 kW) Rolls Royce R.Da.7/2 Dart 529-8E turboprops	
Dimensions		
Span	23.88 m	(78 ft 4 in)
Length	19.43 m	(63 ft 9 in)
Height	6.93 m	(22 ft 9 in)
Performance		
Max speed	575 km/h	(310 kt, 357 mph)
Cruising speed	538 km/h	(290 kt, 334 mph)
Initial climb	917 m/min	(3,010 fpm)
Range	4,000 km	(2,174 nm, 2,500 miles)
Weights		
Max takeoff	15,918 kg	(35,100 lbs)
Useful load	6,398 kg	(14,107 lbs)

Specification	Grumman F-14A Tomcat	
Powerplant	Two 12,350 lb.s.t (dry) (54.94 kN) Pratt & Whitney TF30-P-414A turbofans	
Dimensions		
Span	19.55 m	(64 ft 1 in)
Length	19.1 m	(62 ft 8 in)
Height	4.88 m	(16 ft 0 in)
Performance		
Max speed	2,485 km/h	(1,342 kt, 1,544 mph)
Cruising speed	982 km/h	(530 kt, 610 mph)
Initial climb	9,906 m/min	(32,500 fpm)
Range	3,840 km	(2,087 nm, 2,400 miles)
Weights		
Max takeoff	33,718 kg	(74,349 lbs)
Useful load	15,531 kg	(34,245 lbs)

Grumman G-303 F-14 Tomcat — USA

The design of the Tomcat resulted from the failure in the mid-1960s of the General Dynamics F-111 to meet the US Navy's carrier-borne multi-role specification. Grumman's G-303 was primarily an air superiority fighter with the ability to carry substantial ordnance for the ground attack role. First flown on 21st December 1970 the F-14 had a tandem two-seat cockpit, twin Pratt & Whitney TF30 reheated turbofans and variable-sweep wings. The tail unit consisted of twin fins and all-moving elevators and the Tomcat was fitted with a fully carrier-capable tricycle undercarriage and deck-landing gear. Hardpoints were fitted under the wings but the main load of Sparrow or Phoenix missiles was carried on fuselage-mounted pylons and these could also carry long-range tanks, a Tactical Air Reconnaissance (TARPS) pod or a range of countermeasures and sensor stores. Some 656 F-14A Tomcats were delivered between 1970 and 1988 including 80 for the Imperial Iranian Air Force. More than half of the US Navy aircraft remain in service as the standard carrier-based combat force.

Grumman G-89 (S-2) Tracker — USA

The Grumman S2F (later S-2) Tracker originated as a replacement for the US Navy's carrier-borne AF-2 Guardian anti-submarine aircraft. Larger than the Guardian, the G-89 Tracker was a high-wing aircraft with a two-crew flight deck and space for two systems operators in the main fuselage. It had a retractable tricycle undercarriage, folding wings, full carrier deck arrestor gear and comprehensive search equipment including an AN/APS-20 radar in a retractable radome and a tail mounted retractable MAD boom. Powered by two Wright R-1820 radial piston engines the XS2F-1 first flew on 4th December 1952. Some 1,169 examples of the S2F (later S-2A) Tracker were built together with 100 CS2F-1s completed in Canada by de Havilland Canada. They served with the U.S. Navy and the Japanese, Italian, Canadian, Dutch, Australian and Brazilian navies. Later variants were the S2F-2 (S-2C) with a larger bomb bay, the S2F-3 (S-2D) with a longer fuselage, larger wings and improved radars, the S-2E with automated tactical systems and the TF-1 Trader, 87 of which were built as a 9-seat COD transport for

Grumman G-89 (S-2) Tracker (Cont.)

carrier supply operations. Once declared surplus, many Trackers were used as fire bombers in the USA and France and some were re-engined as the S-2 Turbo with Garrett TPE331-14 turboprop engines. Later Grumman carrier-borne developments replacing the Tracker were the E-2 Hawkeye and C-2 Greyhound (see Northrop-Grumman).

Grumman S-2 Tracker, N405DF

Specification	Grumman G-89 Tracker S-2E	
Powerplant	Two 1,525 h.p. (1,137 kW) Wright R-1820-82A piston engines	
Dimensions		
Span	22.12 m	(72 ft 7 in)
Length	13.26 m	(43 ft 6 in)
Height	5.07 m	(16 ft 7 in)
Performance		
Max speed	402 km/h	(217 kt, 250 mph)
Cruising speed	241 km/h	(130 kt, 150 mph)
Initial climb	558 m/min	(1,830 fpm)
Range	2,080 km	(1,130 nm, 1,300 miles)
Weights		
Max takeoff	13,498 kg	(29,764 lbs)
Useful load	4,963 kg	(10,944 lbs)

Grumman/Gulfstream G-1159 G-II, G-III and G-IV — USA

The success of the G-159 Gulfstream business turboprop led to Grumman designing a new large intercontinental business jet. The resultant G-1159 Gulfstream II was powered by a pair of Rolls Royce Spey 511-8 turbofans, the first aircraft making its maiden flight on 2nd October 1966. The "G-II" was a low-wing aircraft with twin jets fitted to the rear fuselage, a T-tail and large oval cabin windows which were similar to those on the turboprop Gulfstream. The first G-1159 was delivered in December 1967. The Gulfstream IIER is a modified version with additional long-range tanks and the G-1159B Gulfstream IIB is a conversion of the Gulfstream II with a Gulfstream III wing. Under Gulfstream Aerospace the G-1159A Gulfstream III, which first flew on 2nd December 1979 had a 24-inch fuselage stretch, a revised nose and cockpit area and a modified wing with leading edge extensions and wingtip winglets. The "G-III" was replaced by the Gulfstream G-IV with a further 54-inch fuselage stretch, an upgraded cockpit and larger Tay 611-8 turbofans. The Gulfstream IVSP is an optional version with a higher gross weight and useful load. Military versions of the Gulfstream III and Gulfstream IV have been delivered to the USAF and US Navy as the C-20 and special missions versions have been delivered to Sweden as the Tp.102 ELINT aircraft, to Japan as the U-4 and to a number of other users. In total, 258 Gulfstream IIs, 200 Gulfstream IIIs and over 375 Gulfstream IVs have been built.

Gulfstream G-III, JY-HZH

Gulfstream G-IV (Tp-102) Korpen, 102002 (Swedish AF)

Specification	Gulfstream G.1159 Gulfstream IVSP	
Powerplant	Two 13,850 lb.s.t. (61.6 kN) Rolls Royce Tay Mk.611-8 turbofans	
Dimensions		
Span	23.72 m	(77 ft 10 in)
Length	26.92 m	(88 ft 4 in)
Height	7.45 m	(24 ft 5 in)
Performance		
Max speed	937 km/h	(506 kt, 582 mph)
Cruising speed	850 km/h	(459 kt, 528 mph)
Initial climb	1,256 m/min	(4,122 fpm)
Range	7,765 km	(4,220 nm, 4,853 miles)
Weights		
Max takeoff	33,832 kg	(74,600 lbs)
Useful load	19,521 kg	(43,044 lbs)

Gulfstream G-V — USA

Externally similar to the Gulfstream G-IV, the Gulfstream G-V is a developed version with full intercontinental range amounting to almost twice that of the G-IV. It has a 7 ft increase in fuselage length which allows a standard cabin layout for up to 19 passengers, optional sleeping compartments and a full galley and restroom. The cockpit has been enlarged and upgraded and is provided with a crew rest area. The wing is based on that of the G-IV but is larger in area and the vertical tail is taller with a pronounced tip fairing. The G-V is powered by a pair of 14,750 lb.s.t. BMW-Rolls Royce BR710-48 turbofans giving improved thrust and efficiency compared with the Speys and Tays of previous models. The first G-V was flown on 28th November 1995 and more than 90 had been delivered to customers by the end of 1999. The C-37A is a VIP version for the USAF.

Gulfstream G-V, N501GV

Gulfstream G-V C-37A, 97-0400 (USAF)

Specification	Gulfstream G-V	
Powerplant	Two 14,750 lb.s.t. (65.6 kN) BMW-Rolls Royce BR710-48 turbofans	
Dimensions		
Span	28.5 m	(93 ft 6 in)
Length	29.39 m	(96 ft 5 in)
Height	7.87 m	(25 ft 10 in)
Performance		
Max speed	1,065 km/h	(576 kt, 662 mph)
Cruising speed	980 km/h	(530 kt, 609 mph)
Initial climb	1,277 m/min	(4,188 fpm)
Range	11,976 km	(6,509 nm, 7,485 miles)
Weights		
Max takeoff	40,363 kg	(89,000 lbs)
Useful load	19,138 kg	(42,200 lbs)

Guizhou FT-7 and JJ-7 — People's Republic of China

The FT-7 is the export version of the JJ-7 advanced jet trainer built by Guizhou Aviation Industry (GAI) for China, Bangladesh and Pakistan. It is a tandem two-seat derivative of the J-7 single-seater which itself is a developed licence-built version of the delta-winged Russian MiG-21 fighter. The JJ-7 first flew on 5th July 1985 and the aircraft is fitted with two underwing rocket hardpoints and a fuselage centreline pylon to accommodate a fuel tank or cannon pod. The JJ-7/FT-7, which can also be fitted with an upper fuselage saddle fuel tank, has large twin ventral fins on the rear fuselage. The cockpit has a retractable periscope for the rear canopy. Several hundred JJ-7/FT-7 aircraft are in service.

Guizhou FT-7

Specification	Guizhou JJ-7	
Powerplant	One 9,690 lb.s.t. (dry) (43 kN) Liyang WP7B turbojet	
Dimensions		
Span	7.15 m	(23 ft 6 in)
Length	13.95 m	(45 ft 9 in)
Height	4.10 m	(13 ft 6 in)
Performance		
Max speed	2,510 km/h	(1,356 kt, 1,560 mph)
Initial climb	9,296 m/min	(30,500 fpm)
Range	1,280 km	(696 nm, 800 miles)
Weights		
Max takeoff	8,555 kg	(18,865 lbs)
Useful load	3,036 kg	(6,694 lbs)

Gulfstream American AA-1 Yankee, Trainer and Lynx — USA

The BD-1 civil light aircraft was the brainchild of the prolific designer Jim Bede and was flown as an amateur prototype on 11th July 1963. The production AA-1 Yankee was built by American Aviation and, whilst it had the same low-wing, side-by-side two-seat layout as the BD-1, it had a longer fuselage and wings, a slimmer fin, bonded metal honeycomb construction and a fixed tricycle undercarriage with fibreglass main legs. The powerplant was a 115 h.p. Lycoming O-235 piston engine. The basic AA-1 was a private-owner and club aircraft but the AA-1 Trainer had dual controls and a modified wing. A total of 1,150 AA-1s and AA-1As were completed. The AA-1B (and Tr-2 touring version) had an increased useful load and the AA-1C, which was also built by the successor companies Grumman American and Gulfstream American, was built as the T-Cat trainer and the Lynx tourer with single controls. In total 1,822 examples of the AA-1 series were built and many of these remain in service round the world.

Grumman American AA-1C Lynx, G-BTLP

Specification	Gulfstream American AA-1C Lynx	
Powerplant	One 115 h.p. (85.75 kW) Textron Lycoming O-235-L2C piston engine	
Dimensions		
Span	7.46 m	(24 ft 5 in)
Length	5.86 m	(19 ft 3 in)
Height	2.29 m	(7 ft 6 in)
Performance		
Max speed	233 km/h	(126 kt, 145 mph)
Cruising speed	208 km/h	(112 kt, 129 mph)
Initial climb	213 m/min	(700 fpm)
Range	707 km	(384 nm, 442 miles)
Weights		
Max takeoff	726 kg	(1,600 lbs)
Useful load	242 kg	(534 lbs)

Gulfstream American AA-5 Traveler, Cheetah and Tiger — USA

The AA-5 was a four-seat development of the American AA-1 Yankee first flown on 21st August 1970 and placed in production by Grumman American in 1972 as the AA-5 Traveler. In most respects it was virtually the same as the AA-1 but it had a 7 ft increase in wingspan and a 2 ft increase in internal cabin length. The powerplant was a 150 h.p. Lycoming O-320. The later AA-5A Cheetah was an improved version with a cleaned-up airframe, increased cabin window area, a redesigned engine cowling and an enlarged fin. The AA-5B Tiger was introduced in 1974 as a high-performance version with a 180 h.p. Lycoming O-360 and this was built by Gulfstream American and by American General Aircraft as the AG-5B with a 24-volt electrical system and other minor refinements. Production ceased in 1994. In total 3,230 AA-5s were completed.

Gulfstream American AA-5B Tiger

Specification	Gulfstream American AA-5B Tiger	
Powerplant	One 180 h.p. (134.2 kW) Textron Lycoming O-360-A4K piston engine	
Dimensions		
Span	9.6 m	(31 ft 6 in)
Length	6.71 m	(22 ft 0 in)
Height	2.44 m	(8 ft 0 in)
Performance		
Max speed	274 km/h	(148 kt, 170 mph)
Cruising speed	257 km/h	(139 kt, 160 mph)
Initial climb	259 m/min	(850 fpm)
Range	1,227 km	(667 nm, 767 miles)
Weights		
Max takeoff	1,088 kg	(2,400 lbs)
Useful load	494 kg	(1,089 lbs)

Gulfstream American GA-7 Cougar — USA

On 20th December 1974, Grumman American flew the prototype Cougar light twin. This used the outer wings of the single-engined AA-5 and had a fully enclosed four-seat cabin, initially with a sliding canopy but later with a normal cabin door. It was powered by twin 160 h.p. Lycoming O-320 engines and was of all-metal construction using the bonding system adopted on the single-engine models. A small number of Cougars were built by Grumman American and further batches were completed by Gulfstream American. However, a total of only 115 aircraft had been completed when the type was discontinued in 1979. In 1995 all rights were acquired by Aérospatiale (SOCATA) and the aircraft was launched as the TB.320 Tangara twin-engined trainer, but SOCATA suspended further development in 1999 without completing any production aircraft.

Gulfstream American GA-7 Cougar, G-FPCL

Specification	Gulfstream American GA-7 Cougar	
Powerplant	Two 160 h.p. (119.3 kW) Textron Lycoming O-320-D1D piston engines	
Dimensions		
Span	11.23 m	(36 ft 10 in)
Length	9.09 m	(29 ft 10 in)
Height	3.16 m	(10 ft 4 in)
Performance		
Max speed	311 km/h	(168 kt, 193 mph)
Cruising speed	296 km/h	(160 kt, 184 mph)
Initial climb	354 m/min	(1,160 fpm)
Range	2,155 km	(1,171 nm, 1,347 miles)
Weights		
Max takeoff	1,723 kg	(3,800 lbs)
Useful load	550 kg	(1,212 lbs)

Gyroflug SC-01B Speed Canard — Germany

The Speed Canard is a substantially modified derivative of the Rutan Varieze amateur-built light aircraft developed by Gyroflug as a factory-complete production type. Like the Varieze, it has a canard layout with a swept main wing to the rear and a forward control surface in the nose. The main wing, which has a new wing section, has large wingtip winglets and the Speed Canard is of all-composite construction. The fuselage has a tandem two-seat cabin of much wider dimensions than that of the Varieze and the tricycle undercarriage has fixed main legs and a retractable nosewheel. The 116 h.p. Lycoming O-235 engine is fitted in pusher mode behind the cabin driving a three-blade constant-speed propeller, and the later SC-01B-160 has a 160 h.p. Lycoming O-320 and larger winglets. The prototype Speed Canard flew on 2nd December 1980 and 62 aircraft were built by Gyroflug (and successor company FFT) between 1984 and 1992 with many being exported to the USA, Indonesia and various European countries.

Gyroflug SC-01B Speed Canard, D-EBKR

Specification	Gyroflug SC-01B-160 Speed Canard	
Powerplant	One 160 h.p. (119.3 kW) Textron Lycoming O-320-D1A piston engine	
Dimensions		
Span	7.77 m	(25 ft 6 in)
Length	4.7 m	(15 ft 5 in)
Height	1.81 m	(5 ft 11 in)
Performance		
Max speed	294 km/h	(159 kt, 183 mph)
Cruising speed	275 km/h	(149 kt, 171 mph)
Initial climb	396 m/min	(1,300 fpm)
Range	1,500 km	(816 nm, 938 miles)
Weights		
Max takeoff	715 kg	(1,576 lbs)
Useful load	275 kg	(606 lbs)

H

HAPI Cygnet — USA

Now marketed through home construction plans, the Cygnet light aircraft was originally designed by Bert Sisler and flown in 1973 as the SF-2 Whistler. In definitive SF-2A Cygnet form, its shoulder-wing layout is intended to give maximum all-round visibility over and under the wing for the two occupants who are housed in a side-by-side cockpit with a transparent canopy. The strut-braced wing has a complex internal latticework structure in place of multiple ribs. Otherwise the aircraft is conventional with a tailwheel undercarriage and mixed wood/tube/fabric construction. It is powered by a HAPI-Engines 1835 cc Volkswagen conversion and has particularly good short-field performance. Rights to the Cygnet were owned by Viking Aircraft but the type is now marketed by HAPI Engines Inc.

HAPI Cygnet SF-2A, G-BXCA

Specification	HAPI Cygnet SF-2A	
Powerplant	One 62 h.p. (46 kW) HAPI-Volkswagen 1800 piston engine	
Dimensions		
Span	9.14 m	(30 ft 0 in)
Length	5.79 m	(19 ft 0 in)
Height	1.78 m	(5 ft 10 in)
Performance		
Max speed	174 km/h	(94 kt, 108 mph)
Cruising speed	161 km/h	(87 kt, 100 mph)
Initial climb	177 m/min	(580 fpm)
Range	560 km	(304 nm, 350 miles)
Weights		
Max takeoff	499 kg	(1,100 lbs)
Useful load	234 kg	(515 lbs)

Harbin Y-12 — People's Republic of China

In the early 1970s many of the Y-5 (Antonov An-2) utility aircraft in China required replacement and the Harbin aircraft factory designed the high-wing Y-11. The eight-passenger Y-11 was powered by two 285 h.p. Quzhou-Huosai 6A radial engines and had a fixed tricycle undercarriage braced on fuselage sponsons and a square-section fuselage. The prototype flew in 1975 and went into production two years later with a total of 40 having been completed including some Y-11Bs with 350 h.p. Continental TSIO-550-B engines. The Y-11 was developed into the substantially redesigned Y-12 Turbo Panda which retained the strut-braced wing and undercarriage sponsons but had a longer and wider 17/19-passenger fuselage and used a pair of 500 s.h.p. Pratt & Whitney PT6A turboprop engines. This not only improved performance but made the aircraft more attractive to export customers and the Y-12, first flown on 14th July 1982, has been sold to civil operators in Mongolia, Malaysia, Laos and Nepal and the air forces of Sri Lanka, Eritrea, Peru, Zambia, Tanzania, Mauretania and Iran. Over 100 have been built and the latest Y-12-II has 680 s.h.p. PT6A-27 engines.

Harbin Y-12-II, T3-ATI

Specification	Harbin Y-12-II	
Powerplant	Two 680 s.h.p. (507 kW) Pratt & Whitney PT6A-27 turboprops	
Dimensions		
Span	17.22 m	(56 ft 6 in)
Length	14.86 m	(48 ft 9 in)
Height	5.69 m	(18 ft 8 in)
Performance		
Max speed	328 km/h	(177 kt, 204 mph)
Cruising speed	249 km/h	(135 kt, 155 mph)
Initial climb	486 m/min	(1,595 fpm)
Range	1,331 km	(723 nm, 832 miles)
Weights		
Max takeoff	5,299 kg	(11,684 lbs)
Useful load	1,700 kg	(3,750 lbs)

Harlow PJC-2 — USA

Only a handful of the four-seat Harlow PJC-2 were built but six remain active in the United States. The PJC-2 was built by Harlow Aircraft Co. of Alhambra, California and designed by Max B. Harlow. The prototype PJC-1 first flew on 14th September 1947 followed by eleven production examples produced between 1940 and 1941 and four of these were impressed by the USAAC as the UC-80. It was an all-metal light aircraft with a fully enclosed four-seat cabin, a low wing and a retractable tailwheel undercarriage. Power was provided by a 145 h.p. Warner Super Scarab radial engine but one Harlow has been fitted with a 185 h.p. Warner R-550.

Harlow PJC-2, NC54KC

Specification	Harlow PJC-2	
Powerplant	One 145 h.p. (108.1 kW) Warner Super Scarab Srs.50 piston engine	
Dimensions		
Span	10.92 m	(35 ft 10 in)
Length	7.11 m	(23 ft 4 in)
Height	2.21 m	(7 ft 3 in)
Performance		
Max speed	257 km/h	(139 kt, 160 mph)
Cruising speed	225 km/h	(122 kt, 140 mph)
Initial climb	229 m/min	(750 fpm)
Range	784 km	(426 nm, 490 miles)
Weights		
Max takeoff	1,179 kg	(2,600 lbs)
Useful load	426 kg	(939 lbs)

Hatz CB-1 — USA

The little Hatz biplane first flew on 19th April 1968 and has proved to be a popular plans-built aircraft for amateur construction. It is marketed by Dudley Kelly and has classic construction consisting of a welded steel tube fuselage and wooden wings covered in fabric. The fixed tailwheel undercarriage is a standard cross-braced triangulated structure with rubber chord shock absorbers. The upper wing is slightly longer than the lower and the Hatz has tandem open cockpits for two. The standard engine is a 100 h.p. Continental but the Hatz Classic, developed by Makelan Corp. and sold as a kit, uses a larger 150 h.p. Lycoming. Over 100 Hatz biplanes are flying, mainly in the USA.

Hatz CB-1, N560V

Specification	Hatz CB-1	
Powerplant	One 100 h.p. (74.6 kW) Teledyne Continental O-200 piston engine	
Dimensions		
Span	7.72 m	(25 ft 4 in)
Length	5.79 m	(19 ft 0 in)
Height	2.36 m	(7 ft 9 in)
Performance		
Max speed	169 km/h	(91 kt, 105 mph)
Cruising speed	137 km/h	(74 kt, 85 mph)
Initial climb	229 m/min	(750 fpm)
Range	400 km	(217 nm, 250 miles)
Weights		
Max takeoff	635 kg	(1,400 lbs)
Useful load	249 kg	(550 lbs)

Hawker Hurricane — UK

Famed for its part in the Battle of Britain, the Hurricane was designed by Sydney Camm and was first flown on 6th November 1935 and entered service with the RAF in November 1937. Like its contemporary, the Spitfire, it was powered by a Rolls Royce Merlin engine but, unlike its opposite number, its construction was of tube, fabric and light alloy rather than the all-metal monocoque structure which was to become standard for World War II fighters. Nevertheless, it was able to survive much battle damage and was particularly successful on anti-tank missions and for carrier-borne operations. The Hurricane Mk.1 had a 1,030 h.p. Merlin II but the main production Hurricane II had the 1,280 h.p. Merlin XX. The Hurricane IV had the 1,620 h.p. Merlin 24. In total 12,711 Hurricanes were delivered to the RAF and at least ten are airworthy, including one in New Zealand and two with the RAF Battle of Britain Memorial Flight, and at least a further ten are under restoration.

Hawker Hurricane (Cont.)

Hawker Hurricane IIB, BE417 (G-HURR)

Specification	Hawker Hurricane Mk.IIA	
Powerplant	One 1,280 h.p. (954.4 kW) Rolls Royce Merlin XX piston engine	
Dimensions		
Span	12.19 m	(40 ft 0 in)
Length	9.75 m	(32 ft 0 in)
Height	3.99 m	(13 ft 1 in)
Performance		
Max speed	550 km/h	(297 kt, 342 mph)
Cruising speed	515 km/h	(278 kt, 320 mph)
Initial climb	747 m/min	(2,450 fpm)
Range	752 km	(409 nm, 470 miles)
Weights		
Max takeoff	3,651 kg	(8,050 lbs)
Useful load	1,315 kg	(2,900 lbs)

Hawker Sea Fury — UK

Hawker was a major World War II producer of combat aircraft, in particular the single-seat Typhoon and Tempest. The Fury and naval Sea Fury were based on the low-wing Tempest but had a shorter-span wing. While the RAF Fury was not built due to the ending of the war, the Sea Fury was developed and the prototype first flew on 21st February 1945. The production Sea Fury FB.10 had folding wings for carrier storage and an arrester hook and was powered by a Bristol Centaurus 18 radial engine driving a five-bladed propeller. Some 725 Sea Furies were built, mostly as the FB.11 with underwing hardpoints but also as the T.20 tandem two-seat trainer. Sea Furies were used in Korea and were exported to Canada, the Netherlands, Iraq, Egypt and Pakistan. They were retired from Royal Navy service in 1954 but some 45 Sea Furies, of which 27 are thought to be active, are still in the hands of private owners, mostly in the United States where several have been modified as unlimited racers.

Hawker Sea Fury FB.10, N56SF

Specification	Hawker Sea Fury FB.11	
Powerplant	One 2,480 h.p. (1,849.1 kW) Bristol Centaurus 18 piston engine	
Dimensions		
Span	11.71 m	(38 ft 5 in)
Length	10.44 m	(34 ft 3 in)
Height	4.5 m	(14 ft 9 in)
Performance		
Max speed	740 km/h	(400 kt, 460 mph)
Cruising speed	644 km/h	(348 kt, 400 mph)
Initial climb	853 m/min	(2,800 fpm)
Range	1,120 km	(609 nm, 700 miles)
Weights		
Max takeoff	5,669 kg	(12,500 lbs)
Useful load	1,478 kg	(3,260 lbs)

Hawker Hunter — UK

The Hawker Hunter, developed as the P.1067, was probably the most elegant jet fighter ever built and it served with the RAF and many other air forces from 1954 till the mid-1990s. The prototype flew on 20th July 1950 and production single-seat variants included the Hunter F Mk.1 with the Avon 113 turbojet, F.2 with a Sapphire 101, F.4 with an Avon 115 and increased range, F.6 with the Avon 203 and shark's-tooth wing leading edges, FGA.9 ground attack version with the Avon 207 and tailpipe fairing and the FR.10 reconnaissance variant. The T.7 was a side-by-side two-seat trainer based on the F.4 which was produced both as a new-build aircraft and as a conversion and the T.8 was a naval version with an arrester hook. Hunters were delivered to many overseas customers including Switzerland, Singapore, India, Sweden, Lebanon, Denmark, Jordan and Iraq and each had its own designation (e.g. T.53 for Denmark and T.67 for Kuwait). Hunters were built in Holland and Belgium under licence by Aviolanda and Fairey. In total 1,841 Hunters were built and more than 50 are flying or in course of restoration for jet warbird enthusiasts.

Hawker Hunter F.4, XE677 (G-HHUN)

Specification	Hawker Hunter F.6	
Powerplant	One 10,000 lb.s.t. (44.49 kN) Rolls Royce Avon Mk.203 turbojet	
Dimensions		
Span	10.26 m	(33 ft 8 in)
Length	13.97 m	(45 ft 10 in)
Height	4.01 m	(13 ft 2 in)
Performance		
Max speed	1,151 km/h	(621 kt, 715 mph)
Cruising speed	966 km/h	(521 kt, 600 mph)
Initial climb	1,829 m/min	(6,000 fpm)
Range	2,941 km	(1,600 nm, 1,840 miles)
Weights		
Max takeoff	8,050 kg	(17,750 lbs)
Useful load	2,263 kg	(4,990 lbs)

Hawker Siddeley Gnat Trainer — UK

The Gnat T.Mk.1 was based on the earlier Midge lightweight fighter developed by Folland and the single-seat Fo.140 Gnat F.1 which was evaluated by the RAF in the mid-1950s. The Gnat F.1 was operated by the Finnish Air Force and was built in India as the Ajeet. The Gnat Trainer used the same basic airframe with a shoulder-mounted swept wing and a single Orpheus 101 turbojet but it had a larger wing with modified control surfaces, a taller fin and a lengthened forward fuselage containing a tandem two-seat cockpit with a clear clamshell canopy. In 1962 the first of 105 Gnat Trainers was delivered to the RAF to replace the Vampire Trainer and they were replaced by the Hawk in 1976. Eight civil Gnats are operational in Britain and several Ajeets and Gnat T.1s are flying in the USA.

Hawker Siddeley Gnat Trainer, G-FRCE

Hawker Siddeley Gnat Trainer (Cont.)

Specification	Hawker Siddeley Gnat T.Mk.1	
Powerplant	One 4,230 lb.s.t. (18.82 kN) Bristol Siddeley Orpheus 101 turbojet	
Dimensions		
Span	7.31 m	(24 ft 0 in)
Length	9.68 m	(31 ft 9 in)
Height	2.92 m	(9 ft 7 in)
Performance		
Max speed	1,024 km/h	(553 kt, 636 mph)
Cruising speed	950 km/h	(513 kt, 590 mph)
Initial climb	2,323 m/min	(7,620 fpm)
Range	1,104 km	(600 nm, 690 miles)
Weights		
Max takeoff	4,132 kg	(9,112 lbs)
Useful load	1,573 kg	(3,468 lbs)

Hawker Siddeley HS.748 and Andover — UK

The Hawker Siddeley 748 was originally designed by Avro as a short-haul Dakota replacement. The 44-seat Avro 748 was a low-wing aircraft of conventional layout with a pair of Rolls Royce Dart turboprops mounted in an over-centre position on the wings and with the main units of the retractable tricycle undercarriage in the lower part of the engine nacelles. The prototype flew on 24th June 1960 and first deliveries were made in 1962. The HS.748 was sold to a variety of airlines including Dan-Air, Indian Airlines, LIAT and Philippine Airlines. Total HS.748 production was 326 aircraft. Hawker Siddeley (which had taken over Avro) also entered into a licence agreement with Hindustan Aeronautics in India under which 89 of the military HS.748 Srs.2M was built for the Indian Air Force. Other military users included the Brazilian, Colombian, Belgian and Australian air forces and this led to Avro developing the specialised Avro 780 Andover military freighter for the Royal Air Force. The Andover used the forward fuselage and wing structure of the 748 with an upswept rear fuselage containing a ventral cargo loading ramp. Some 31 Andovers were delivered to the RAF, and later the RNZAF, and many of these were subsequently released onto the civil market and operate as freighters around the world.

Hawker Siddeley HS.748-2B, V2-LCQ

Hawker Siddeley Andover C.1, NZ7623

Specification	Hawker Siddeley HS.748 Srs.2	
Powerplant	Two 2,105 s.h.p. (1569.5 kW) Rolls Royce Dart RDa.7 Mk.531 turboprops	
Dimensions		
Span	30.02 m	(98 ft 6 in)
Length	20.42 m	(67 ft 0 in)
Height	7.57 m	(24 ft 10 in)
Performance		
Max speed	462 km/h	(250 kt, 287 mph)
Cruising speed	402 km/h	(217 kt, 250 mph)
Takeoff distance	838 m	(2,750 ft)
Range	3,056 km	(1,661 nm, 1,910 miles)
Weights		
Max takeoff	20,451 kg	(45,095 lbs)
Useful load	8,665 kg	(19,107 lbs)

HB Flug Alfa HB.207 — Austria

Designed and manufactured by the former Brditschka Aircraft, the two-seat Alfa HB.207 is a very refined high-performance kit-built light aircraft which first flew in March 1995. It is of all-metal construction and can be fitted with either a retractable or fixed tricycle undercarriage and has wings which are detachable for storage. The side-by-side cockpit, which is enclosed by a rear-sliding canopy, is very roomy and has a rear baggage area. The powerplant is a 110 h.p. Porsche Austria engine driving a five-bladed propeller but the HB.207 can also be powered by a Lycoming or Rotax engine. By mid-1999, 50 kits had been sold and 15 aircraft were flying, mainly in Austria and Germany.

HB Flug Alfa HB.207, OE-ALG

Specification	HB Flug Alfa HB.207	
Powerplant	One 110 h.p. (82 kW) Porsche Austria piston engine	
Dimensions		
Span	8.99 m	(29 ft 6 in)
Length	5.94 m	(19 ft 6 in)
Height	1.88 m	(6 ft 2 in)
Performance		
Max speed	306 km/h	(165 kt, 190 mph)
Cruising speed	241 km/h	(130 kt, 150 mph)
Initial climb	329 m/min	(1,080 fpm)
Range	896 km	(487 nm, 560 miles)
Weights		
Max takeoff	640 kg	(1,411 lbs)
Useful load	210 kg	(463 lbs)

Heath Parasol — USA

The original Parasol ultralight aircraft was designed and built by Ed Heath in 1926 and became one of the earliest kit-built light aircraft for amateur builders. It was an open cockpit single-seater with a strut-braced wing mounted on vertical triangulated frame mounts. The Heath had a conventional tail unit and a fixed tailwheel undercarriage and was constructed of steel tube, wood and fabric. As the LNB-4 the Parasol was also built as a factory-finished aircraft by Heath Aircraft Corp. with a 27 h.p. Heath B-4 in-line engine. Several hundred Parasols were built during the 1930s and four are known to have survived including a British example with a 32 h.p. Bristol Cherub III engine and an American LNA-40 aircraft with a 40 h.p. Continental A-40.

Heath Parasol, N7123

Specification	Heath Parasol LNA-40	
Powerplant	One 40 h.p. (29.8 kW) Continental A-40 piston engine	
Dimensions		
Span	9.52 m	(31 ft 3 in)
Length	5.26 m	(17 ft 3 in)
Height	1.88 m	(6 ft 2 in)
Performance		
Max speed	129 km/h	(70 kt, 80 mph)
Cruising speed	109 km/h	(59 kt, 68 mph)
Initial climb	152 m/min	(500 fpm)
Range	320 km	(174 nm, 200 miles)
Weights		
Max takeoff	317 kg	(700 lbs)
Useful load	107 kg	(235 lbs)

Helio Courier — USA

The Courier was the end result of experiments by Dr. Otto Koppen and Dr. Lyn Bollinger into very short takeoff and landing technology using the tube and fabric Helioplane which was evaluated by the US Army as the YL-24. The production H-391B Courier was a four-seat all-metal cantilever high-wing machine with a fixed tailwheel undercarriage and complex wing slats and flaps to provide STOL performance. It was powered by a 260 h.p. Lycoming GO-435-C2B piston engine and further variants were the H-392 Strato Courier with a 340 h.p. GO-480-C1D6 and the H-395 with a 295 h.p. GO-480-G1D6. The Courier was used by the USAF in Vietnam as the U-10 and remains in service with the Peruvian and Thai air forces. The H-250 and H-295, introduced in 1965, had a longer fuselage and the HT-295 was a tricycle-gear variant. The H-700 and H-800, introduced in the early 1980s, were updated models with a new undercarriage, modified wingspar, a new engine cowling and, respectively, 350 h.p. and 400 h.p. Lycoming engines. Helio ceased production in 1984 after 248 of the H-392/395, 215 of the H-250/295 and 18 of the H-700/800 had been built.

Helio H-295 (U-10D), N2706J

Helio HT-295 Super Courier, N5399G

Helio Courier (Cont.)

Specification	Helio H-295 Super Courier	
Powerplant	One 295 h.p. (220 kW) Textron Lycoming GO-480-G1D6 piston engine	
Dimensions		
Span	11.89 m	(39 ft 0 in)
Length	9.45 m	(31 ft 0 in)
Height	2.69 m	(8 ft 10 in)
Performance		
Max speed	269 km/h	(145 kt, 167 mph)
Cruising speed	257 km/h	(139 kt, 160 mph)
Initial climb	351 m/min	(1,150 fpm)
Range	1,056 km	(574 nm, 660 miles)
Weights		
Max takeoff	1,542 kg	(3,400 lbs)
Useful load	599 kg	(1,320 lbs)

Helio H-550A Stallion — USA

The successful Helio H-295 Courier was extensively redesigned by Helio Aircraft as a high performance STOL aircraft for military applications. Powered by a Pratt & Whitney PT6A-27 turboprop engine, the HST-550A had an enlarged swept tail, rearward-canted undercarriage legs, a modified wing, sometimes fitted with tip tanks, and underwing hardpoints for equipment pods or offensive stores. The production H-550A Stallion could accommodate two crew and eight passengers and had a large port-side double freight door and twin forward crew entry doors. The prototype first flew on 5th June 1964. A total of 18 production Stallions was built, the majority being delivered to the USAF as the AU-24A for service in Vietnam and being used by the Colombian police. Some of these remain in service with civilian owners.

Specification	Helio H-550A Stallion	
Powerplant	One 680 s.h.p. (507 kW) Pratt & Whitney PT6A-27 turboprop	
Dimensions		
Span	12.5 m	(41 ft 0 in)
Length	12.07 m	(39 ft 7 in)
Height	2.81 m	(9 ft 3 in)
Performance		
Max speed	348 km/h	(188 kt, 216 mph)
Cruising speed	332 km/h	(179 kt, 206 mph)
Initial climb	671 m/min	(2,200 fpm)
Range	712 km	(387 nm, 445 miles)
Weights		
Max takeoff	2,313 kg	(5,100 lbs)
Useful load	1,016 kg	(2,240 lbs)

Heliopolis Gomhouriya — Egypt

The Gomhouriya is an Egyptian-built version of the wartime Bucker 181D Bestmann military basic trainer. Built at the Egyptian government factory at Helwan in the early 1950s, it is an all-wood aircraft with a low wing, fixed tailwheel undercarriage and side-by-side seating for two in the enclosed cockpit. Some were fitted with a clear sliding canopy and a version with a tricycle undercarriage was also tested. A total of 300 were built including the basic Mk.1 (and fully aerobatic Mk.5) powered by a 105 h.p. Walter Minor 4-III and the Mk.2 (and aerobatic Mk.6) with a 145 h.p. Continental O-300A engine. Gomhouriyas were used by the Egyptian Air Force and by flying clubs. A number of military examples have been sold to private owners in Germany. The Gomhouriya was briefly relaunched in 1995 for sale in the USA as the Shadin G.10 Aeropony powered by a 145 h.p. Continental O-300D engine but is now being sold as a Helwan-manufactured kit for homebuilders as the KNR Bestmann Mk.6.

Helio Stallion, N9550A

Heliopolis Gomhouriya, D-EEXE

Specification	KNR Bestmann Mk.6	
Powerplant	One 145 h.p. (108.1 kW) Teledyne Continental O-300A piston engine	
Dimensions		
Span	10.59 m	(34 ft 9 in)
Length	7.9 m	(25 ft 11 in)
Height	2.06 m	(6 ft 9 in)
Performance		
Max speed	217 km/h	(117 kt, 135 mph)
Cruising speed	195 km/h	(105 kt, 121 mph)
Initial climb	210 m/min	(688 fpm)
Range	832 km	(453 nm, 520 miles)
Weights		
Max takeoff	828 kg	(1,825 lbs)
Useful load	229 kg	(505 lbs)

Specification	Heli-Sport CH-7 Kompress	
Powerplant	One 115 h.p. (85.7 kW) Rotax 914 piston engine	
Dimensions		
Rotor diameter	6.27 m	(20 ft 7 in)
Length	4.66 m	(15 ft 3 in)
Height	2.24 m	(7 ft 4 in)
Performance		
Max speed	208 km/h	(112 kt, 129 mph)
Cruising speed	161 km/h	(87 kt, 100 mph)
Initial climb	450 m/min	(1,475 fpm)
Range	720 km	(391 nm, 450 miles)
Weights		
Max takeoff	450 kg	(992 lbs)
Useful load	205 kg	(452 lbs)

Heli-Sport CH-7 Angel and Kompress — Italy

The CH-7 Angel ultralight helicopter has been designed by Heli-Sport of Turin and is sold as a kit to amateur builders. It was launched in 1992 and is a single-seat machine with a cabin fully enclosed by a large forward-opening transparent canopy in a tiny streamlined fuselage pod. It has a 64 h.p. Rotax 582 engine mounted in the centre section and a strut-braced tubular tail boom carrying a small fin and two-bladed tail rotor. The Angel has a two-bladed semi-rigid composite main rotor and a skid undercarriage which can be fitted with floats. The CH-7 Kompress is a tandem two-seat development with a slightly longer cockpit and a larger turbocharged 115 h.p. Rotax 914. Over 140 examples of the CH-7 have been completed.

Heli-Sport CH-7 Kompress

Hiller UH-12 — USA

Stanley Hiller's UH-12 light helicopter was a contemporary of the Bell 47 and first flew as the Hiller 360 in 1948. It was of all-metal construction with a basic fuselage pod containing a side-by-side two-seat cabin which was, initially, fitted with only a windshield but later was fully enclosed. It had a corrugated tail boom which carried a two-bladed anti-torque rotor. It was powered by a 175 h.p. Franklin 6V4-178-B32 piston engine (later upgraded to 200 h.p.) and 646 examples of the 360 were built including the US Army H-23A and the Royal Navy HT.Mk.1. The UH-12C was an improved version with a three-person bench seat and a moulded bubble canopy and this was built in large numbers as the military H-23D and H-23G Raven. The UH-12E was a higher-powered model with a 323 h.p. Lycoming VO-540-A1B engine and the UH-12E-4 had a stretched four-seat cabin. A total of 1,929 of the UH-12C, UH-12D and UH-12E were built, latterly by Rogerson Hiller. Several UH-12Ds have been refitted with a 400 s.h.p. Allison 250-C20B turboshaft engine by Soloy Conversions Inc.

Hiller 360, N212W

Hiller UH-12 (Cont.)

Specification	Hiller UH-12E	
Powerplant	One 323 h.p. (240.8 kW) Lycoming VO-540-A1B piston engine	
Dimensions		
Rotor diameter	10.77 m	(35 ft 5 in)
Length	8.53 m	(28 ft 0 in)
Height	2.98 m	(9 ft 9 in)
Performance		
Max speed	155 km/h	(83 kt, 96 mph)
Cruising speed	132 km/h	(71 kt, 82 mph)
Initial climb	408 m/min	(1,340 fpm)
Range	360 km	(196 nm, 225 miles)
Weights		
Max takeoff	1,247 kg	(2,750 lbs)
Useful load	476 kg	(1,050 lbs)

Hindustan HT-2 — India

Closely resembling the DHC Chipmunk, of which it was a close contemporary, the HT-2 was an ab initio military light trainer produced by Hindustan Aircraft Ltd. and first flown on 13th August 1951. It was of all-metal construction with a fixed tailwheel undercarriage and a tandem two-seat cockpit enclosed by a framed sliding canopy. In production form it had a 155 h.p. Blackburn Cirrus Major in-line piston engine. In total 153 HT-2s were completed, the majority going to the Indian Air Force (IAF) and Indian flying clubs but a handful also serving with the air forces of Indonesia, Singapore and Ghana. A few are believed to be still in the IAF inventory, mostly now powered by 160 h.p. Lycoming O-320 engines, and the Ghanaian examples are still extant and are thought to be under restoration for civil owners.

Hindustan HT-2, IX737 (Indian AF)

Specification	Hindustan HT-2	
Powerplant	One 155 h.p. (115.57 kW) Blackburn Cirrus Major piston engine	
Dimensions		
Span	10.72 m	(35 ft 2 in)
Length	7.52 m	(24 ft 8 in)
Height	2.72 m	(8 ft 11 in)
Performance		
Max speed	209 km/h	(113 kt, 130 mph)
Cruising speed	185 km/h	(100 kt, 115 mph)
Initial climb	244 m/min	(800 fpm)
Range	560 km	(304 nm, 350 miles)
Weights		
Max takeoff	989 kg	(2,180 lbs)
Useful load	281 kg	(620 lbs)

Hindustan Basant — India

In the early 1970s Hindustan Aircraft designed the HA-31 single-seat agricultural aircraft to meet Indian requirements. The definitive HA-31 Mk. II Basant made its maiden flight on 30th March 1972 and was certificated in March 1974. The Basant closely resembled the Piper PA-36 Pawnee Brave and had a 2,000 lbs capacity fibreglass hopper situated ahead of the fully enclosed pilot's cockpit and a low strut-braced wing and fixed tailwheel undercarriage. Construction was of tube and fabric. It was powered by a 400 h.p. Lycoming IO-720-C1B engine. Production commenced in 1976 and 39 examples were built and operated exclusively by India's Food & Agriculture Ministry. A small number of these survive and are currently active.

HAL HA-31 Basant Mk.II, VT-XAN

Specification	HAL HA-31 Basant Mk.II	
Powerplant	One 400 h.p. (298 kW) Textron Lycoming IO-720-C1B piston engine	
Dimensions		
Span	12 m	(39 ft 4 in)
Length	9 m	(29 ft 6 in)
Height	2.55 m	(8 ft 4 in)
Performance		
Max speed	225 km/h	(122 kt, 140 mph)
Cruising speed	185 km/h	(100 kt, 115 mph)
Initial climb	229 m/min	(750 fpm)
Range	640 km	(348 nm, 400 miles)
Weights		
Max takeoff	2,268 kg	(5,000 lbs)
Useful load	1,068 kg	(2,355 lbs)

Hindustan HJT-16 Kiran — India

Hindustan Aeronautics designed the HJT-16 Kiran as a replacement for the Indian Air Force fleet of DH.115 Vampire two-seat jet trainers. The Kiran, which first flew on 4th September 1964, was a conventional low-wing aircraft with side-by-side ejector seats, a retractable tricycle undercarriage and a 2,500 lb.s.t. Hindustan-built Bristol Siddeley Viper 11 turbojet installed in the rear fuselage. This engine was fed by two external air intakes positioned behind the cockpit. The

Indian Air Force and Navy took delivery of 118 Kiran Mk.I basic trainers and 72 Mk.IAs which were equipped with two wing hardpoints for weapons training. The Kiran Mk.II, which flew on 30th July 1976, was an improved version with an uprated 3,400 lb.s.t. Orpheus 701 engine, four wing hardpoints, two nose-mounted machine guns and improved avionics. A total of 61 were built for the Indian Air Force but no examples of the Kiran were exported. Over 150 Kirans remain in active service but the type is expected to be be replaced by the new Hindustan HJT-36 jet trainer from 2005 onwards.

Hindustan HJT-16 Kiran Mk.II, U851 (Indian AF)

Specification	Hindustan HJT-16 Kiran Mk.II	
Powerplant	One 3,400 lb.s.t. (15.13 kN) Rolls Royce (Bristol Siddeley) Orpheus 701-01 turbojet	
Dimensions		
Span	10.7 m	(35 ft 1 in)
Length	10.6 m	(33 ft 7 in)
Height	3.64 m	(11 ft 11 in)
Performance		
Max speed	703 km/h	(380 kt, 437 mph)
Cruising speed	621 km/h	(336 kt, 386 mph)
Initial climb	1,600 m/min	(5,250 fpm)
Range	608 km	(330 nm, 380 miles)
Weights		
Max takeoff	4,691 kg	(10,344 lbs)
Useful load	1,696 kg	(3,740 lbs)

Hindustan HPT-32 Deepak and HTT-34 — India

The Deepak is the Indian Air Force's standard basic trainer and was designed by Hindustan Aeronautics and first flown on 6th January 1977. An all-metal aircraft with a low wing and fixed tricycle undercarriage, the Deepak has a side-by-side two-seat cockpit with space behind for a third observer seat. The Deepak fulfils a wide range of roles including ab initio flying training, target towing, army liaison and aerobatic training. First deliveries were made in 1985 and 130 aircraft are in service with the Indian Air Force and Navy. The HTT-34 is a version developed by Hindustan using the HPT-32 airframe married to a 420 s.h.p. Allison 250-B17D turboprop engine. This was flown on 17th June 1984 but only the prototypes were flown and no Air Force orders have been placed.

Hindustan HTT-34, X2335

Specification	Hindustan HPT-32	
Powerplant	One 260 h.p. (193.86 kW) Textron Lycoming AEIO-540-D4B5 piston engine	
Dimensions		
Span	9.5 m	(31 ft 2 in)
Length	7.7 m	(25 ft 4 in)
Height	2.88 m	(9 ft 5 in)
Performance		
Max speed	266 km/h	(143 kt, 165 mph)
Cruising speed	193 km/h	(104 kt, 120 mph)
Initial climb	337 m/min	(1,105 fpm)
Range	736 km	(400 nm, 460 miles)
Weights		
Max takeoff	1,250 kg	(2,756 lbs)
Useful load	360 kg	(794 lbs)

Hindustan ALH — India

The 12-seat ALH (Advanced Light Helicopter) has been designed by Hindustan Aeronautics with assistance from MBB in Germany. It bears a similarity to the MBB Bö.105 although it is a substantially larger aircraft and is powered by twin 1,000 s.h.p. Turboméca TM333-2B turboshafts which are mounted above the cabin and drive a four-blade composite main rotor. The ALH makes use of an advanced Integrated Dynamic System which combines several rotor control features into an integrated module. The civil prototype ALH first flew on 23rd August 1992 at Bangalore followed by further civil and military prototypes. The naval version has the optional twin 1,656 s.h.p. Allied Signal LHTEC CTS800-4N engines, a folding tail boom, folding rotor blades, external stores-capable sponsons, a retractable tricycle undercarriage and a 1,000 kg increase in gross weight. Development is continuing with the prospect of Indian government orders for up to 200 examples.

Hindustan ALH (Cont.)

Hindustan ALH, Z3268

Specification	Hindustan ALH (Army/Air Force)	
Powerplant	One 1,000 s.h.p. (745.6 kW) Turboméca TM333-2B twin turboshaft	
Dimensions		
Rotor diameter	13.2 m	(43 ft 4 in)
Length	15.87 m	(52 ft 1 in)
Height	4.98 m	(16 ft 4 in)
Performance		
Max speed	270 km/h	(145 kt, 168 mph)
Cruising speed	245 km/h	(132 kt, 152 mph)
Initial climb	540 m/min	(1,775 fpm)
Range	816 km	(442 nm, 510 miles)
Weights		
Max takeoff	4,000 kg	(8,820 lbs)
Useful load	1,784 kg	(3,933 lbs)

Hipps Superbirds J-3 Kitten — USA

The series of ultralight aircraft from Hipps Superbirds has become very popular, particularly the J-3 Kitten and J-5 Super Kitten of which over 100 have flown. The Kitten is a wood, fabric and tube single-seater with a strut-braced high wing and an enclosed cockpit. It has a fixed tailwheel undercarriage and achieves good performance on only a 28 h.p. Rotax 277 engine. The Super Kitten is similar but has a 40 h.p. Rotax 447. The Reliant and Reliant SX are equivalent versions with a built-up rear fuselage. Hipps also offer the J-4 Sportster and Super Sportster which are equivalent to the J-3 and J-4 but with a parasol-wing configuration and an open cockpit.

Hipps Superbirds J-3 Kitten, D-MPFK

Specification	Hipps Superbirds Reliant SX	
Powerplant	One 40 h.p. (29.8 kW) Rotax 447 piston engine	
Dimensions		
Span	9.14 m	(30 ft 0 in)
Length	4.98 m	(16 ft 4 in)
Height	1.63 m	(5 ft 4 in)
Performance		
Max speed	161 km/h	(87 kt, 100 mph)
Cruising speed	121 km/h	(65 kt, 75 mph)
Initial climb	335 m/min	(1,100 fpm)
Range	192 km	(104 nm, 120 miles)
Weights		
Max takeoff	272 kg	(600 lbs)
Useful load	143 kg	(315 lbs)

Hirth Hi.27 Acrostar Mk.II
— Germany

Wolf Hirth GmbH designed the Acrostar Mk.II competition aerobatic aircraft to the requirements of aerobatic champion Arnold Wagner and flew the prototype on 16th April 1970. It was a streamlined low-wing aircraft with a fixed tailwheel undercarriage and single-seat cockpit with a full bubble canopy. Construction was largely of wood with ply covering and the mainspar was made of fibreglass. Nine Acrostars were completed by Wolf Hirth and sold in Germany, Switzerland and Spain and produced championship performances in international competitions in the 1970s. A single Acrostar Mk.III was also built with lighter airframe and detailed performance-improving modifications.

Hirth Acrostar MkII, HB-MSA

Specification	Hirth Acrostar Mk.II	
Powerplant	One 220 h.p. (164 kW) Franklin 6A-350-C1 piston engine	
Dimensions		
Span	8.28 m	(27 ft 2 in)
Length	6.11 m	(20 ft 1 in)
Height	1.78 m	(5 ft 10 in)
Performance		
Max speed	305 km/h	(164 kt, 190 mph)
Cruising speed	273 km/h	(147 kt, 170 mph)
Initial climb	870 m/min	(2,855 fpm)
Range	620 km	(337 nm, 387 miles)
Weights		
Max takeoff	700 kg	(1,543 lbs)
Useful load	180 kg	(397 lbs)

Hispano HA-200A Saeta
— Spain

Requirements of the Spanish Air Force led to Hispano Aviacion, under Prof. Willi Messerschmitt, developing the HA-200 basic jet trainer which first flew as a prototype on 16th August 1955. The Saeta, designated E-14A in air force service, used the wing, rear fuselage and tail unit of the piston-engined Hispano Triana. The new forward fuselage had a nose air intake and a tandem two-seat cockpit with a blister canopy and was equipped with a pair of Turboméca Marboré turbojets with jet pipes positioned in the rear wing roots. In total 112 examples of the Saeta were delivered including the basic HA-200A (E-14A), HA-200B (E-14B) with upgraded Marboré II engines, HA-220A Super Saeta (C-10A) and HA-220D (C-10B and C-10C) single-seat light attack versions with Marboré VI engines and underwing strongpoints. The HA-200B was also built in Egypt as the Helwan Al Kahira. On retirement from military service, many Saetas were acquired by private warbird operators in the USA.

Hispano HA-200A Saeta

Specification	Hispano HA-200A Saeta	
Powerplant	Two 880 lb.s.t. (3.91 kN) Turboméca Marboré turbojets	
Dimensions		
Span	10.42 m	(34 ft 2 in)
Length	8.88 m	(29 ft 1 in)
Height	3.26 m	(10 ft 8 in)
Performance		
Max speed	700 km/h	(378 kt, 435 mph)
Cruising speed	644 km/h	(348 kt, 400 mph)
Initial climb	1,020 m/min	(3,345 fpm)
Range	1,688 km	(917 nm, 1,055 miles)
Weights		
Max takeoff	3,173 kg	(6,996 lbs)
Useful load	1,496 kg	(3,299 lbs)

HK Aircraft Technology Wega — Germany

The Wega is an attractive two-seat aircraft designed in Germany and sold in kit form. It is certificated under JAR/VLA rules and first kit deliveries were made following its first flight on 9th April 1998. The Wega is an all-composite aircraft, very similar in appearance to the Aero Designs Pulsar, with a low wing, tricycle undercarriage and an efficient streamlined airframe. It has a side-by-side two-seat cockpit enclosed by a blister canopy.

HK Wega, D-ETHK

Specification	HK Wega	
Powerplant	One 115 h.p. (85.7 kW) Rotax 914 piston engine	
Dimensions		
Span	7.62 m	(25 ft 0 in)
Length	6.20 m	(20 ft 4 in)
Height	2 m	(6 ft 7 in)
Performance		
Max speed	314 km/h	(170 kt, 195 mph)
Cruising speed	290 km/h	(157 kt, 180 mph)
Initial climb	762 m/min	(2,500 fpm)
Range	1,487 km	(809 nm, 930 miles)
Weights		
Max takeoff	640 kg	(1,411 lbs)
Useful load	320 kg	(706 lbs)

Holste MH.1521 Broussard — France

The Broussard was an enlarged version of the MH.152 prototype built by Avions Max Holste and first flown in June 1951. Intended as a military general-purpose light transport, the Broussard had a strut-braced high wing, fixed tailwheel undercarriage and a slab-sided fuselage with six seats. Powered by a 450 h.p. Pratt & Whitney Wasp R-985 radial engine, the first prototype was flown on 17th November 1952. Holste built 318 of the military MH.1521M for the French Army and 52 examples of the civil MH.1521C with minor refinements and civilian interior trim. The company also experimented with the MH.1522 which was a conversion of an existing MH.1521M with full span leading edge slots and double slotted wing flaps to give enhanced short-field performance. Broussards were exported to most French colonial territories and were also widely used by the Argentine government. Over 50 military-surplus Broussards are flying with private owners in France, Luxembourg, the UK and elsewhere.

Holste MH.1521M Broussard, F-GGKI

Specification	Holste MH.1521M Broussard	
Powerplant	One 450 h.p. (335.5 kW) Pratt & Whitney R-985 Wasp piston engine	
Dimensions		
Span	13.75 m	(45 ft 1 in)
Length	8.65 m	(28 ft 4 in)
Height	3.67 m	(12 ft 1 in)
Performance		
Max speed	257 km/h	(139 kt, 160 mph)
Cruising speed	229 km/h	(123 kt, 142 mph)
Initial climb	239 m/min	(785 fpm)
Range	1,192 km	(648 nm, 745 miles)
Weights		
Max takeoff	2,700 kg	(5,954 lbs)
Useful load	1,050 kg	(2,315 lbs)

Howard DGA-15P Nightingale — USA

The great prewar racing ace, Benny Howard developed the DGA ('Damned Good Airplane') high-wing cabin monoplanes from his famous *Mr Mulligan* racer. The initial model was the DGA-8 which was a tube and fabric strut-braced high-wing aircraft with a cantilever tailwheel undercarriage and a large four-seat cabin. This was powered by a 320 h.p. Wright R-760 radial piston engine and later variants included the DGA-9 with a 285 h.p. Jacobs L-5, DGA-11 with a 400 h.p. Pratt & Whitney Wasp Junior and the DGA-12 with a 300 h.p. Jacobs L-6. The DGA-15 had a deeper and wider fuselage and a strut-braced undercarriage and was powered by a 330 h.p. Jacobs L-6MB (DGA-15J) or 450 h.p. R-985 Wasp Junior (DGA-15P). In the latter form it became the wartime GH-1 Nightingale for training and communications work, the GH-2 ambulance aircraft for the US Navy and the C-70 for the USAAF. Some 480 military DGAs and over 100 civil examples were built. More than 150 are currently registered in the USA.

Howard DGA-15P Nightingale, N35RH

Specification	Howard DGA-15P	
Powerplant	One 450 h.p. (335.5 kW) Pratt & Whitney R-985 Wasp Junior piston engine	
Dimensions		
Span	11.58 m	(38 ft 0 in)
Length	7.57 m	(24 ft 10 in)
Height	2.57 m	(8 ft 5 in)
Performance		
Max speed	323 km/h	(175 kt, 201 mph)
Cruising speed	306 km/h	(165 kt, 190 mph)
Initial climb	475 m/min	(1,560 fpm)
Range	1,528 km	(830 nm, 955 miles)
Weights		
Max takeoff	1,973 kg	(4,350 lbs)
Useful Load	748 kg	(1,650 lbs)

Howard 500 — USA

The Dee Howard Co. of San Antonio, Texas was one of the leading specialists in conversion of wartime bombers and transports to postwar executive configuration. They produced a number of Lockheed 18-based Howard 250s but concentrated primarily on civil versions of the Lockheed PV-1 Ventura naval patrol bomber, initially known as the Howard 350. This led to the Howard 500 which used modified wings and the tail from the Ventura married to a new longer and deeper pressurised fuselage with a full stand-up cabin. This could accommodate twelve passengers and the aircraft was powered by a pair of 2,500 h.p. Pratt & Whitney R-2800-CB17 radial engines. Dee Howard built 16 examples of the Model 500 before the design was overtaken by turboprop types such as the Gulfstream. Six Howard 500s remain of which two are in service with private owners including one in the UK.

Howard 500, N500HP

Specification	Howard 500	
Powerplant	Two 2,500 h.p. (1,864 kW) Pratt & Whitney R-2800-CB17 piston engines	
Dimensions		
Span	21.69 m	(71 ft 2 in)
Length	17.62 m	(57 ft 10 in)
Height	4.18 m	(13 ft 8 in)
Performance		
Max speed	563 km/h	(304 kt, 350 mph)
Cruising speed	451 km/h	(243 kt, 280 mph)
Initial climb	777 m/min	(2,550 fpm)
Range	4,480 km	(2,435 nm, 2,800 miles)
Weights		
Max takeoff	15,419 kg	(34,000 lbs)
Useful load	5,578 kg	(12,300 lbs)

Humbert Tetras — France

The little Tetras light monoplane is produced in kit form by Ets. Humbert of Ramonchamp near Mulhouse in eastern France and over 60 had been flown by mid-1999. Construction consists of a steel tube fuselage with ceconite covering and the strut-braced high wings have an aluminium structure with some Styroform filling and fabric covering. The Tetras has a fully enclosed two-place cabin with side-by-side seating and dual controls. It has a fixed tailwheel undercarriage and meets the ultralight weight category rules. Several different versions are available including the standard Tetras with an 80 h.p. Rotax 912, the Tetras B with flaps and the alternative HW.2000 engine and the Tetras BS with a 100 h.p. Rotax 912S.

Humbert Tetras (Cont.)

Humbert Tetras, 51-FY

Specification	Humbert Tetras BS	
Powerplant	One 100 h.p. (74.6 kW) Rotax 912S piston engine	
Dimensions		
Span	10.1 m	(33 ft 2 in)
Length	6.5 m	(21 ft 4 in)
Height	2.06 m	(6 ft 9 in)
Performance		
Max speed	200 km/h	(108 kt, 124 mph)
Cruising speed	160 km/h	(86 kt, 99 mph)
Initial climb	450 m/min	(1,476 fpm)
Range	750 km	(408 nm, 469 miles)
Weights		
Max takeoff	450 kg	(992 lbs)
Useful load	194 kg	(428 lbs)

Hummel Bird — USA

Designed by Morry Hummel, the Hummel Bird is one of the smallest amateur-built light aircraft and is intended for construction by first-time builders from plans with some prefabricated parts being available from the factory. It is an all-metal design with a streamlined fuselage made of single curvature panels and with a large blister canopy enclosing the single-seat cockpit. The low wing and tail are conventional and the main legs of the fixed tailwheel undercarriage are attached to the inboard wing sections. It is powered by a modified half-Volkswagen engine and the performance is outstanding due to its high power-to-weight ratio. The Hummel Bird first flew in June 1981 and around 120 have been built.

Hummel Bird, N56Q

Specification	Hummel Bird	
Powerplant	One 37 h.p. (27.6 kW) half-Volkswagen piston engine	
Dimensions		
Span	6.4 m	(21 ft 0 in)
Length	4.06 m	(13 ft 4 in)
Height	1.22 m	(4 ft 0 in)
Performance		
Max speed	217 km/h	(117 kt, 135 mph)
Cruising speed	185 km/h	(100 kt, 115 mph)
Initial climb	305 m/min	(1,000 fpm)
Range	400 km	(217 nm, 250 miles)
Weights		
Max takeoff	249 kg	(550 lbs)
Useful load	127 kg	(280 lbs)

Hunting Prince and Pembroke — UK

The Percival P.50 Prince originated in the P.48 Merganser light twin-engined transport which first flew on 9th May 1947. This was a high-wing all-metal aircraft with a six-seat main cabin and a forward crew compartment and in production form was powered by two wing-mounted Alvis Leonides 501/4 radial piston engines. Some 23 civil Princes were built by Hunting Percival for executive transport and survey and 54 were built for the Royal Navy as the P.57 Sea Prince. The main variant was the larger military P.66 Pembroke which first flew on 20th November 1952 and 128 were built as the Pembroke C.Mk.1 for the RAF and for the air forces of Belgium (C.51), Sweden (C.52), Denmark (C.52/2), Finland (C.53), West Germany (C.54) and Sudan (C.55). Many of these military Pembrokes were subsequently civilianised and five of the civil equivalent, the P.66 President,were also built. Over a dozen airframes remain of which one Prince and at least four Pembrokes are active in the UK and the USA.

Hunting Pembroke, WV740

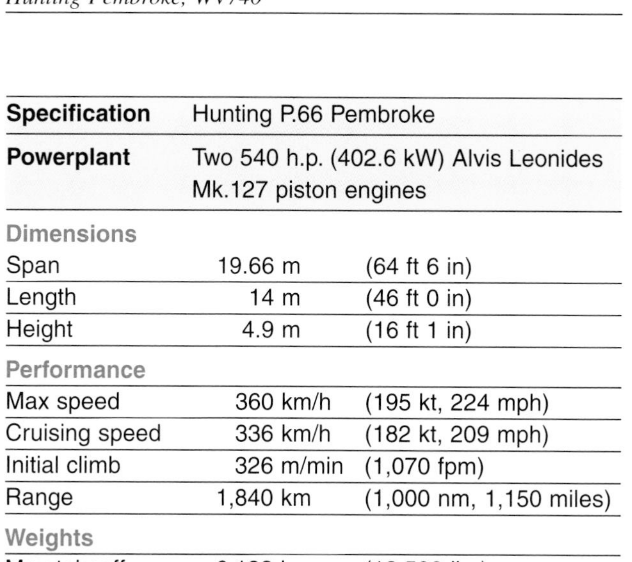

Specification	Hunting P.66 Pembroke	
Powerplant	Two 540 h.p. (402.6 kW) Alvis Leonides Mk.127 piston engines	
Dimensions		
Span	19.66 m	(64 ft 6 in)
Length	14 m	(46 ft 0 in)
Height	4.9 m	(16 ft 1 in)
Performance		
Max speed	360 km/h	(195 kt, 224 mph)
Cruising speed	336 km/h	(182 kt, 209 mph)
Initial climb	326 m/min	(1,070 fpm)
Range	1,840 km	(1,000 nm, 1,150 miles)
Weights		
Max takeoff	6,122 kg	(13,500 lbs)
Useful load	1,960 kg	(4,322 lbs)

Hunting Provost, WW397

Specification	Hunting P.56 Provost	
Powerplant	One 550 h.p. (410 kW) Alvis Leonides 126 piston engine	
Dimensions		
Span	10.72 m	(35 ft 2 in)
Length	8.85 m	(29 ft 0 in)
Height	3.66 m	(12 ft 0 in)
Performance		
Max speed	322 km/h	(174 kt, 200 mph)
Cruising speed	285 km/h	(154 kt, 177 mph)
Initial climb	671 m/min	(2,200 fpm)
Range	1,120 km	(609 nm, 700 miles)
Weights		
Max takeoff	1,995 kg	(4,400 lbs)
Useful load	476 kg	(1,050 lbs)

Hunting Percival P.56 Provost — UK

Percival's Provost became the standard basic trainer for the RAF during the 1950s and 1960s having flown on 24th February 1950 and subsequently having won an Air Ministry trial for a Percival Prentice replacement. The side-by-side two-seat Provost had an all-metal structure with a low wing and a fixed tailwheel undercarriage. As the Provost T.Mk.1 it was powered by a 550 h.p. Alvis Leonides radial piston engine and joined the RAF in 1953. Its sturdy structure made it an ideal partner for the Vampire T.11 in the RAF's training sequence and the Provost was finally phased out in 1969. Several Provosts were sold abroad to the Irish Air Corps (T.51), Ceylon, Malaysia and Oman. Several were fitted with underwing hardpoints for ground attack work and delivered to the Royal Rhodesian Air Force (T.52) and to Burma, Iraq and Sudan (T.53). Some 461 Provosts were built by Hunting Aircraft Ltd. including 397 delivered to the RAF and 12 remain in the hands of UK private owners.

Hurel Dubois HD.34 — France

Hurel Dubois carried out extensive research in the 1950s into very-high-aspect-ratio wings for modern transport aircraft which culminated in the testing of the prototype HD.31. A development of this aircraft, the HD.34, was built as a mapping and aerial survey machine for use by the Institut Geographique National (IGN). The HD.34 had a square-section fuselage to house the mapping cameras and their operating crew. Its long narrow wings allowed it to cruise at low speeds for long periods and the IGN found it to be an ideal photo platform. It was powered by two 1,525 h.p. Wright 982-C9 radial piston engines and fitted with a fixed tricycle undercarriage. The prototype HD.34 first flew on 26th February 1957 and was followed by a further seven aircraft. These served with the IGN until the mid-1970s and one aircraft remains in flying condition in France.

Hurel Dubois HD.34 (Cont.)

Hurel Dubois HD.34, F-BHOO

Specification	Hurel Dubois HD.34	
Powerplant	Two 1,525 h.p. (1,137 kW) Wright 982-C9 piston engines	
Dimensions		
Span	45.3 m	(148 ft 7 in)
Length	23.57 m	(77 ft 4 in)
Height	8.71 m	(28 ft 7 in)
Performance		
Max speed	349 km/h	(189 kt, 217 mph)
Cruising speed	274 km/h	(148 kt, 170 mph)
Initial climb	287 m/min	(940 fpm)
Range	3,600 km	(1,956 nm, 2,250 miles)
Weights		
Max takeoff	19,250 kg	(42,446 lbs)
Useful load	6,725 kg	(14,830 lbs)

I

IAI (Galaxy) 1125 Astra — Israel

The Astra design was based on that of the IAI-1124 Westwind (see Aero Commander 1121 entry). However, it is virtually a new aircraft and it offers a substantial improvement in operating economies and high-speed/long-range performance. The fuselage is deeper than that of the Westwind and the Astra has a high-technology swept wing which is mounted beneath the fuselage rather than centrally to give much improved cabin volume. The tail unit is similar to that of the Westwind and the two Garrett TFE731 engines are mounted in rear fuselage pods. The Astra SP was an improved version with greater range and speed and a new autopilot and EFIS. The Model 1125 Astra SPX is the current model with further improved performance, uprated Honeywell TFE731-40R-200G turbofans, a new interior and small wingtip winglets. The Astra entered production in 1985 and 110 had been built by the end of 1998 including two C-38As for the USAF. It is now marketed by Galaxy Aerospace.

Specification	IAI-1125 Astra SPX	
Powerplant	Two 4,250 lb.s.t. (18.9 kN) Honeywell (Garrett) TFE731-40R-200G turbofans	
Dimensions		
Span	16.64 m	(54 ft 7 in)
Length	16.96 m	(55 ft 7 in)
Height	5.54 m	(18 ft 2 in)
Performance		
Max cruise speed	867 km/h	(467 kt, 539 mph)
Initial climb	1,128 m/min	(3,700 fpm)
Range	5,987 km	(3,254 nm, 3,742 miles)
Weights		
Max takeoff	11,179 kg	(24,650 lbs)
Useful load	4,966 kg	(10,950 lbs)

IAI Astra, YV-785CP

IAI Arava — Israel

The IAI-101 Arava light utility transport was developed by Israel Aircraft Industries in the mid-1960s and first flown on 27th November 1969. The Arava has a strut-braced high wing with twin-booms carrying the tail section and a circular section fuselage with a hinged rear door for cargo loading. It can accommodate 20 passengers and a crew of two but has more commonly been sold as a military freighter and for ELINT and other special missions. The Arava is fitted with a fixed tricycle undercarriage and was powered initially by two 715 s.h.p. Pratt & Whitney PT6A-27 turboprops although these were upgraded to the 750 s.h.p. PT6A-34 in the production IAI-102. The IAI-101B, which had an improved interior and better hot-and-high performance, had PT6A-36 engines. Most aircraft have been the IAI-201 military version but IAI also built the IAI-202 which was longer and fitted with a wet wing and large dual wingtip winglets. Over 120 Aravas have been built, mainly for military users including Thailand, Colombia, Venezuela, Ecuador, Guatemala, Mexico, Honduras and Salvador.

IAI-201 Arava, P2-022 (Papua New Guinea Defence Force)

Specification	IAI Arava 201	
Powerplant	Two 750 s.h.p. (559 kW) Pratt & Whitney PT6A-34 turboprops	
Dimensions		
Span	20.96 m	(68 ft 9 in)
Length	13.03 m	(42 ft 9 in)
Height	5.22 m	(17 ft 1 in)
Performance		
Max speed	327 km/h	(177 kt, 203 mph)
Cruising speed	319 km/h	(172 kt, 198 mph)
Initial climb	393 m/min	(1,290 fpm)
Range	995 km	(541 nm, 622 miles)
Weights		
Max takeoff	6,803 kg	(15,000 lbs)
Useful load	2,805 kg	(6,184 lbs)

IAR-823 — Romania

The state-owned ICA-Brasov aircraft design and manufacturing company designed the IAR-823 four-seat light aircraft to meet the needs of the Romanian Air Force and flying clubs. It first flew in July 1973 and 80 were completed, including 12 sold to Angola, and has been used for general communications duties and primary training. The IAR-823 is an all-metal low-wing aircraft with a fully enclosed cabin and a retractable tricycle undercarriage. It is powered by a 290 h.p. Lycoming engine driving a constant-speed propeller. Most of the military IAR-823s have now been retired but a batch of these is up for sale in the USA and several examples remain in operation with Romanian flying clubs.

IAR-823, No.54 (Romanian AF)

Specification	ICA-Brasov IAR-823	
Powerplant	One 290 h.p. (216.2 kW) Textron Lycoming IO-540-G1D5 piston engine	
Dimensions		
Span	10 m	(32 ft 10 in)
Length	8.24 m	(27 ft 0 in)
Height	2.52 m	(8 ft 3 in)
Performance		
Max speed	310 km/h	(168 kt, 193 mph)
Cruising speed	290 km/h	(156 kt, 180 mph)
Initial climb	420 m/min	(1,378 fpm)
Range	1,280 km	(695 nm, 800 miles)
Weights		
Max takeoff	1,380 kg	(3,043 lbs)
Useful load	470 kg	(1,036 lbs)

IAR IS-28M2 — Romania

ICA-Brasov has a long history of producing high-performance sailplanes including the T-tailed IS-28B2 tandem two-seater. This all-metal glider was used as the basis of the IS-28M1 motor glider (later IAR-34) which had the wing position lowered and a 68 h.p. Limbach engine installed in the modified nose. The main production version was the higher-powered IS-28M2 which first flew on 26th June 1976. This had a wider fuselage to give side-by-side seating and a semi-retractable tailwheel undercarriage with the main units attached to the inboard wing section. The later IS-28M2A had strengthened wings. The current model is the IS-28M2/GR which is equipped with a 90 h.p. Rotax 912 engine and 77 aircraft had been delivered to 16 countries by mid-1999 although the aircraft is now only built to customer order. The IAR-46 is a new version under JAR-VLA rules with a shorter and broader wing, two prototypes of which have been built.

IAR IS-28M2 (Cont.)

IAR IS-28M2, F-CBBA

Specification	ICA Brasov IS-28M2A	
Powerplant	One 80 h.p. (59.7 kW) Limbach L.2000 EO1 piston engine	
Dimensions		
Span	17 m	(55 ft 9 in)
Length	7 m	(22 ft 11 in)
Height	2.15 m	(7 ft 1 in)
Performance		
Max speed	185 km/h	(100 kt, 115 mph)
Cruising speed	161 km/h	(87 kt, 100 mph)
Initial climb	138 m/min	(453 fpm)
Range	448 km	(243 nm, 280 miles)
Weights		
Max takeoff	760 kg	(1,675 lbs)
Useful load	200 kg	(441 lbs)

IAR IAR-93 (J-22 Orao) — Romania/Yugoslavia

The IAR-93/Orao fighter is a joint-venture project carried out by the Romanian company IAv.Craiova (now SC Avioane SA) and the Yugoslavian SOKO organisation. It was developed to meet the needs of the Romanian and Yugoslav air forces and was a single-seat ground attack fighter and photo reconnaissance aircraft. It had a conventional layout with a swept shoulder wing, tricycle undercarriage with the main units stowing in belly wells and one fuselage strongpoint and four wing weapons pylons. It was also equipped with a 23 mm cannon positioned in the forward fuselage. The prototypes from each manufacturer first flew on 31st October 1974 followed in January 1977 by a two-seat trainer version. The early IAR-93A and J-22 models were fitted with two Yugoslav-built Rolls Royce Viper 632-41R turbojets but later IAR-93B variants had the Viper 633-41 with reheat. The Orao 2 was also built with various modifications including a HUD and additional fuel capacity. Production was carried out in both countries with around 170 being built in Romania and fewer in Yugoslavia. It is thought that most Yugoslav aircraft are now out of service and that few of Romania's 80 aircraft are active.

Avioane IAR-93B, 002 (Romanian AF)

Specification	Avioane IAR-93B	
Powerplant	Two 4,000 lb.s.t. (17.8 kN) (dry) Rolls Royce Viper Mk.633-41 turbojets	
Dimensions		
Span	9.3 m	(30 ft 6 in)
Length	14.9 m	(48 ft 11 in)
Height	4.52 m	(14 ft 10 in)
Performance		
Max speed	1,020 km/h	(550 kt, 635 mph)
Cruising speed	740 km/h	(400 kt, 460 mph)
Initial climb	5,340 m/min	(17,500 fpm)
Range	515 km	(280 nm, 320 miles)
Weights		
Max takeoff	11,080 kg	(24,431 lbs)
Useful load	5,580 kg	(12,300 lbs)

IAR (Avioane) IAR-99 Soim — Romania

The IAR-99 Soim is a low-wing advanced jet trainer and ground attack aircraft developed by the Craiova factory of SC Avioane SA. Of conventional tandem-seat layout, the Soim first flew on 21st December 1985 and was aimed at a Romanian Air Force requirement to replace L-29 Delfin and L-39 trainers. The Soim, which uses a Romanian-built Rolls Royce Viper engine, is equipped with four underwing strongpoints capable of carrying a variety of bombs and rocket packs and a centreline hardpoint for a gunpack. It has an advanced cockpit compatible with that of the MiG-21 with a HUD and twin multifunctional display panels. It is believed that 24 aircraft (including prototypes) had been completed by the end of 1998 with a further order for 30 in hand for the Romanian Air Force.

Avioane IAR-99 Soim, 718 (Romanian AF)

Specification	IAR (Avioane) IAR-99 Soim	
Powerplant	One 4,000 lb.s.t. (17.79 kN) Turbomecanica Bucuresti Rolls Royce Viper Mk.632-41M turbojet	
Dimensions		
Span	9.85 m	(32 ft 4 in)
Length	11 m	(36 ft 2 in)
Height	3.9 m	(12 ft 10 in)
Performance		
Max speed	866 km/h	(468 kt, 538 mph)
Cruising speed	789 km/h	(426 kt, 490 mph)
Initial climb	2,103 m/min	(6,900 fpm)
Range	800 km	(435 nm, 500 miles)
Weights		
Max takeoff	5,560 kg	(12,260 lbs)
Useful load	2,360 kg	(5,204 lbs)

Ibis Ae 270 — Czech Republic/Taiwan

Ibis Aerospace, which is a joint venture between Aero Vodochody in the Czech Republic and AIDC in Taiwan, has designed the Ae 270 multi-purpose utility aircraft and flew the first of three flying prototypes, an Ae 270 P, in Prague on 25th July 2000. Of conventional all-metal construction, the Ae 270 is intended for various civil and military roles including 10-seat passenger transport, cargo carrying for which it has a large port-side loading door, air ambulance, maritime patrol and photo mapping. Two initial versions are proposed - the Ae 270 P with a pressurised cabin, retractable tricycle undercarriage and an 850 s.h.p Pratt & Whitney PT6A-42A engine and the simpler unpressurised Ae 270 W with a fixed undercarriage and a 777 s.h.p Walter M601F, but a later model will have a higher powered PT6 engine. Certification of the Ae 270 is expected at the end of 2001.

Ibis Ae 270 P, OK-EMA

Specification	Ibis Ae 270 P	
Powerplant	One 850 s.h.p (633.7 kW) Pratt & Whitney PT6A-42A turboprop	
Dimensions		
Span	13.82 m	(45 ft 4 in)
Length	12.23 m	(40 ft 1 in)
Height	4.78 m	(15 ft 8 in)
Performance		
Max speed	408 km/h	(220 kt, 254 mph)
Cruising speed	390 km/h	(210 kt, 242 mph)
Initial climb	588 m/min	(1,929 fpm)
Range	2,916 km	(1,585 nm, 1,823 miles)
Weights		
Max takeoff	3,300 kg	(7,277 lbs)
Useful load	1,512 kg	(3,334 lbs)

Ikarus-Comco C42 — Germany

The Ikarus C42, also known as the Cyclone, is a high-wing ultralight aircraft designed and built as a kit or factory-finished aircraft by Ikarus-Comco in Germany. It is also manufactured and marketed in the United States as the Flightstar C42. The aircraft has a conventional strut-braced wing which can be folded for storage and an enclosed cabin with side-by-side seating for two. It has a composite fuselage and steel tube, aluminium and fabric wing construction. It is fitted with a fixed tricycle undercarriage and can be equipped with an emergency parachute recovery system. Over 150 have been sold to date, the majority in Germany.

Ikarus (Flightstar) C42 Cyclone, N1186W

Ikarus-Comco C42 (Cont.)

Specification	Ikarus C42 Cyclone	
Powerplant	One 80 h.p. (58 kW) Rotax 912UL piston engine	
Dimensions		
Span	9.88 m	(32 ft 5 in)
Length	6.1 m	(20 ft 0 in)
Height	1.83 m	(6 ft 0 in)
Performance		
Max speed	177 km/h	(96 kt, 110 mph)
Cruising speed	169 km/h	(91 kt, 105 mph)
Initial climb	262 m/min	(860 fpm)
Range	560 km	(304 nm, 350 miles)
Weights		
Max takeoff	450 kg	(992 lbs)
Useful load	218 kg	(480 lbs)

Ilyushin Il-14 — Russia

Immediately after the war the Il-12 general-purpose transport was designed as a replacement for the Li-2/DC-3 and some 600 were built for the Soviet forces and Aeroflot. The Il-12 was a low-wing all-metal aircraft with up to 32 seats and it had a retractable tricycle undercarriage and two 1,775 h.p. Shvetsov radial engines. It was modified as the Il-14 with a more efficient wing, improved flaps and a larger square vertical tail. The Il-14 also had 1,900 h.p. ASh-82T engines. The later Il-14M had a 40-inch longer fuselage and the Il-14T was a military cargo version. The Il-14 (NATO name 'Crate') entered production in 1953 for Soviet users and was exported to the airlines and air forces of the Warsaw Pact and to China. It was also built by Avia in Czechoslovakia as the Avia-14 and by VEB in East Germany. Avia also produced the Avia 14 Super which was pressurised. In total 839 Il-14s were built in Russia and 203 in Czechoslovakia and a handful remain in operation in Russia and Poland with a few under restoration in the USA.

Specification	Ilyushin Il-14M	
Powerplant	Two 1,900 h.p. (1,416.6 kW) Shvetsov ASh-82T piston engines	
Dimensions		
Span	31.7 m	(104 ft 0 in)
Length	22.3 m	(73 ft 2 in)
Height	7.9 m	(25 ft 11 in)
Performance		
Max speed	426 km/h	(230 kt, 265 mph)
Cruising speed	322 km/h	(174 kt, 200 mph)
Initial climb	320 m/min	(1,050 fpm)
Range	1,488 km	(809 nm, 930 miles)
Weights		
Max takeoff	17,250 kg	(38,036 lbs)
Useful load	5,170 kg	(11,400 lbs)

Ilyushin Il-18 — Russia

The Il-18, which first flew on 4th July 1957, was the workhorse of Soviet domestic Aeroflot operations for more than 30 years. It was designed to serve short-haul routes and secondary airfields which were unsuitable for the Tu-104 and first entered service in 1959. The Il-18 (NATO name 'Coot') is a low-wing pressurised aircraft with a retractable tricycle undercarriage and capacity for 75 standard or 111 high-density passengers. It was initially powered by four Kuznetsov NK-4 turboprop engines but these were supplanted by the Ivchenko AI-20 at an early stage. A total of 569 Il-18s was completed for passenger operations and as freighters and the type was widely used by Aeroflot, the military forces and Soviet-influence airlines such as Tarom, TABSO, CSA, Interflug and LOT. While many Il-18s have been retired a significant number still serve with Aeroflot and CIS carriers such as Atlant-Soyuz, Domodedovo, Ramair and Gosnii and with Russian and other government and military units and test establishments. Most of these are the Il-18D with additional fuel capacity and 4,250 s.h.p. AI-20M engines. A military airborne command post variant is designated Il-22.

Ilyushin Il-14M, RA-01301

Ilyushin Il-18V, YR-IMG

Specification	Ilyushin Il-18D	
Powerplant	Four 4,250 s.h.p. (3,168.8 kW) Ivchenko AI-20M turboprops	
Dimensions		
Span	37.39 m	(122 ft 8 in)
Length	35.89 m	(117 ft 9 in)
Height	10.16 m	(33 ft 4 in)
Performance		
Max speed	674 km/h	(364 kt, 419 mph)
Cruising speed	624 km/h	(337 kt, 388 mph)
Takeoff distance	1,300 m	(4,265 ft)
Range	6,464 km	(3,513 nm, 4,040 miles)
Weights		
Max takeoff	63,945 kg	(141,000 lbs)
Useful load	28,998 kg	(63,940 lbs)

Specification	Ilyushin Il-38	
Powerplant	Four 4,250 s.h.p. (3,168.8 kW) Ivchenko AI-20M turboprops	
Dimensions		
Span	37.39 m	(122 ft 8 in)
Length	39.6 m	(129 ft 10 in)
Height	10.16 m	(33 ft 4 in)
Performance		
Max speed	708 km/h	(382 kt, 440 mph)
Cruising speed	624 km/h	(337 kt, 388 mph)
Takeoff distance	1,300 m	(4,265 ft)
Range	7,200 km	(3,913 nm, 4,500 miles)
Weights		
Max takeoff	63,945 kg	(141,000 lbs)
Useful load	27,500 kg	(60,637 lbs)

Ilyushin Il-38 — Russia

The versatile Ilyushin Il-18 transport served in many roles with the Soviet military forces and it formed an ideal platform for a dedicated maritime patrol aircraft for Soviet Naval Aviation. The Il-38 was first flown on 27th September 1961. The position of the wing was moved forward and the fuselage, which has only a few porthole windows, was lengthened by around 13 ft. The interior is equipped with surveillance monitoring stations for eight crew. In standard form, the Il-38 (NATO name 'May') has a MAD stinger tail boom and a large radome on the forward under fuselage. The Il-38 is equipped with a forward belly weapons bay but alternative variants are fitted with a SLAR pod on the forward under-fuselage or with various countermeasures antennae and fairings. These include the Il-20, the Il-22 airborne command post and the Il-24 ELINT/Sigint version. Over 100 of these special versions of the Il-18 are believed to have been built including five delivered to the Indian Navy, and a substantial number remain in service.

Ilyushin Il-38, '22' red (Russian Naval Aviation)

Ilyushin Il-28 — Russia

First flown on 8th July 1948, the Ilyushin Il-28 was the Soviet Union's standard tactical bomber throughout the 1950s and 1960s. It was equivalent to the British Canberra and had a high wing mounting two underslung Klimov turbojets, a circular-section fuselage with an enclosed belly weapons bay and a retractable tricycle undercarriage. The Il-28 (NATO name 'Beagle') was crewed by a pilot in the main cockpit enclosed by a blister canopy, a bomb aimer in the glazed nose and a tail gunner in the rear. Some examples are fitted with optional wingtip tanks. For training purposes a few Il-28U variants were built with a second cockpit in place of the standard nose. Around 2,000 Il-28s were built and the type was also produced in China as the Harbin H-5. A small number of Il-28s and H-5s still operate in Romania and Albania and the H-5 is still in service in the People's Republic of China.

Ilyushin Il-28, 708 (Romanian AF)

Ilyushin Il-28 (Cont.)

Specification	Ilyushin Il-28	
Powerplant	Two 5,952 lb.s.t. (26.48 kN) Klimov VK-1A turbojets	
Dimensions		
Span	21.46 m	(70 ft 5 in)
Length	17.65 m	(57 ft 11 in)
Height	6.71 m	(22 ft 0 in)
Performance		
Max speed	901 km/h	(487 kt, 560 mph)
Cruising speed	869 km/h	(470 kt, 540 mph)
Initial climb	899 m/min	(2,950 fpm)
Range	2,400 km	(1,304 nm, 1,500 miles)
Weights		
Max takeoff	21,200 kg	(46,746 lbs)
Useful Load	9,310 kg	(20,530 lbs)

Ilyushin Il-62 — Russia

With its established position in design of transport aircraft, Ilyushin developed the long-range Il-62 to operate Aeroflot routes to North America and the eastern Soviet Union. The Il-62 is a low-wing aircraft similar in layout to the Vickers VC-10 with a circular-section pressurised fuselage accommodating 186 passengers, a T-tail and four 23,150 lb.s.t. Kuznetsov NK-8-4 turbofans in two rear fuselage pods. The first aircraft flew on 3rd January 1963 and went into Aeroflot service in 1967. Production was completed in 1993 after 292 aircraft had been built. The improved Il-62M was a 198-passenger aircraft with upgraded avionics, additional fuel capacity and 25,350 lb.s.t. Soloviev D-30KU turbofans. A number of Il-62s were operated by the Soviet Air Force (NATO name 'Classic') and the Il-62 was exported to Soviet-friendly nations, serving with airlines such as Cubana, CSA, CAAC, Egypt Air and LOT. The Il-62 continues to be an important type in service with CIS airlines including Domodedovo Airlines, Trans-Asia, Uzbekistan Airways, Kras-Air and Dalavia and over 120 are believed to be operational.

Ilyushin Il-62M, RA-86518

Specification	Ilyushin Il-62M	
Powerplant	Four 25,350 lb.s.t. (112.77 kN) Soloviev D-30KU turbofans	
Dimensions		
Span	43.2 m	(141 ft 9 in)
Length	53.12 m	(174 ft 3 in)
Height	12.35 m	(40 ft 6 in)
Performance		
Max speed	901 km/h	(487 kt, 560 mph)
Cruising speed	853 km/h	(461 kt, 530 mph)
Initial climb	1,079 m/min	(3,540 fpm)
Range	10,240 km	(5,565 nm, 6,400 miles)
Weights		
Max takeoff	165,000 kg	(363,825 lbs)
Useful load	95,600 kg	(210,798 lbs)

Ilyushin Il-76 — Russia

The Il-76 freighter, which made its first flight on 26th March 1971, is the standard CIS medium/heavy cargo carrier for civil and military applications. Complementing or replacing the An-12 in service, the Il-76 is a pressurised aircraft with an anhedralled high-set wing mounting four podded 26,455 lb.s.t. Soloviev D-30KP turbofans. The wing is mounted on top of the fuselage to give an unobstructed internal load compartment with clamshell rear loading doors below the rear fuselage. The Il-76 has a glazed nose housing a navigator's station and many aircraft have a tail turret. Production of the Il-76 exceeds 920 aircraft and variants include the Il-76T with increased fuel capacity and the Il-76TD with Soloviev D-30KP-1 engines. Many Il-76s have been delivered for military use as the Il-76M (NATO name 'Candid') and have been widely modified as airborne command posts (Il-80), inflight refuelling tankers etc. The type is in use with the air forces of India and Iraq. More than 40 have been converted by Beriev as the A-50 (NATO name "Midas") for the AEW role with a pylon-mounted rear fuselage rotodome and associated radars and sensors. Civilian applications include firefighting. Large civil users include Ilavia, Tyumen Airlines, Atlant-Soyuz Airlines, Aviaenergo and Ukraine Cargo. One example of the Il-76MF has also been built with a 21 ft 8 in fuselage stretch, increased range and four 35,300 lb.s.t. Soloviev PS-90A76 turbofans.

Ilyushin (Beriev) A-50, RA-76453

Ilyushin Il-76MF, RA-76900

Specification	Ilyushin Il-76TD	
Powerplant	Four 26,455 lb.s.t. (117.69 kN) Aviadvigatel (Soloviev) D-30KP-1 turbofans	
Dimensions		
Span	50.49 m	(165 ft 8 in)
Length	46.58 m	(152 ft 10 in)
Height	14.76 m	(48 ft 5 in)
Performance		
Max speed	850 km/h	(459 kt, 528 mph)
Cruising speed	756 km/h	(409 kt, 470 mph)
Takeoff distance	1,700 m	(5,580 ft)
Range	6,660 km	(3,620 nm, 4,163 miles)
Weights		
Max takeoff	190,000 kg	(418,950 lbs)
Useful load	95,000 kg	(209,475 lbs)

Ilyushin Il-86 — Russia

With the Il-62 becoming obsolescent the Ilyushin OKB started design work in 1971 on a new large widebody transport aircraft with 350 seats and a range of over 2,000 miles. The resulting Il-86 has a low wing with four podded Kuznetsov NK-86 turbofans on underwing pylons. The Il-86 has an upper passenger deck and a substantial lower cargo hold which is partly allocated to carried-on passenger baggage on Aeroflot's domestic passenger routes. The Il-86 has passenger entrances at lower deck level with storage areas for luggage and internal stairs giving access to the seating section. The Il-86-300 (NATO name 'Camber') first flew on 22nd December 1976 and went into production in 1979 being delivered initially to Aeroflot. Some 106 were built but the Il-86 suffered from engine unreliability, poor fuel economy and problems in meeting international noise standards and it is proposed that some aircraft should be re-engined with CFM-56-5C2 or Aviadvigatel PS-90A turbofans. Main users of the Il-86 are Aeroflot, East Line Express, Pulkovo, Vnukovo Airlines and Air Kazakhstan. Four military airborne command post versions are designated IL-82 (NATO name 'Maxdome').

Ilyushin Il-86-300, RA-86145

Ilyushin Il-86 (Cont.)

Specification	Ilyushin Il-86-300	
Powerplant	Four 28,660 lb.s.t. (127.5 kN) Samara (Kuznetsov) NK-86 turbofans	
Dimensions		
Span	48.05 m	(157 ft 8 in)
Length	59.53 m	(195 ft 4 in)
Height	15.8 m	(51 ft 10 in)
Performance		
Max speed	950 km/h	(513 kt, 590 mph)
Cruising speed	901 km/h	(487 kt, 560 mph)
Takeoff distance	2,301 m	(7,550 ft)
Range	4,600 km	(2,500 nm, 2,875 miles)
Weights		
Max takeoff	208,000 kg	(458,640 lbs)
Useful load	92,000 kg	(202,860 lbs)

Ilyushin Il-96 — Russia

Problems with engine reliability and fuel economy resulted in a major redesign of the Il-86. The Il-96 was, in many respects, a completely new aircraft with a new supercritical wing with wingtip winglets and redesigned flaps and leading edge slats. In initial form it was fitted with four Aviadvigatel PS-90A turbofans. The lower-deck passenger boarding system was abandoned and the aircraft had fly-by-wire control systems and a modified tail and undercarriage. The prototype Il-96 flew on 28th September 1988 and was offered in standard (Il-96-300) form or as the stretched Il-96M with Pratt & Whitney PW2337 turbofans. The first Il-96-300s started to be delivered in 1992 to Aeroflot Russian International Airlines and Domodedovo Airlines and approximately 17 had been built by mid-2000. The Il-96T freighter with a large forward port-side cargo door has also been produced, first flying on 16th May 1997.

Ilyushin Il-96T, RA-96101

Specification	Ilyushin Il-96-300	
Powerplant	Four 35,274 lb.s.t. (156.92 kN) Aviadvigatel PS-90A turbofans	
Dimensions		
Span	60.09 m	(197 ft 2 in)
Length	55.34 m	(181 ft 7 in)
Height	17.58 m	(57 ft 8 in)
Performance		
Max speed	901 km/h	(487 kt, 560 mph)
Cruising speed	850 km/h	(460 kt, 530 mph)
Takeoff distance	3,000 m	(9,843 ft)
Range	13,920 km	(7,565 nm, 8,700 miles)
Weights		
Max takeoff	240,000 kg	(529,200 lbs)
Useful load	121,000 kg	(266,805 lbs)

Ilyushin Il-103 — Russia

The Il-103 has been designed by the Ilyushin Design Bureau as a competitor for American-built four-seat touring light aircraft. It is of all-metal construction with a low wing, fixed tricycle undercarriage and fully enclosed cabin entered through gullwing doors on both sides. The engine is a 210 h.p. Continental IO-360 but later versions are expected to be offered with a 180 h.p. powerplant and a higher-powered version with a retractable undercarriage is also proposed. The prototype Il-103 was first flown on 17th May 1994 and approximately 30 had been completed by mid 1999 with an order in hand for five for the Peruvian Air Force. The Il-103 is manufactured by the Lukhovitze factory of MiG-MAPO.

Ilyushin Il-103

Specification	Ilyushin Il-103	
Powerplant	One 210 h.p. (156.58 kW) Teledyne Continental IO-360-ES piston engine	
Dimensions		
Span	10.57 m	(34 ft 8 in)
Length	8 m	(26 ft 3 in)
Height	3.12 m	(10 ft 3 in)
Performance		
Max speed	250 km/h	(135 kt, 155 mph)
Cruising speed	225 km/h	(122 kt, 140 mph)
Initial climb	300 m/min	(984 fpm)
Range	1,064 km	(578 nm, 665 miles)
Weights		
Max takeoff	1,310 kg	(2,888 lbs)
Useful load	540 kg	(1,190 lbs)

Ilyushin Il-114 — Russia

The Ilyushin Il-114 is a 64-seat twin-turboprop aircraft of very similar appearance to the British Aerospace ATP with a low wing and retractable tricycle undercarriage. It first flew on 29th March 1990 powered by Klimov TV7 engines driving six-blade composite propellers and is intended as a replacement for many of the large fleet of An-24s in current service. First deliveries were made to Uzbekistan Airways in July 1998. Ilyushin has also designed and flown a cargo version of the Il-114. Also under development is the Il-114-100 with Pratt & Whitney PW127F engines for American and European airline customers. Approximately 12 prototypes and production aircraft had been completed by mid-1999 although few sales had been achieved.

Ilyushin Il-114-100, UK-91009

Specification	Ilyushin Il-114	
Powerplant	Two 2,500 s.h.p. (1,864 kW) Klimov TV7-117-3 turboprops	
Dimensions		
Span	30 m	(98 ft 5in)
Length	26.19 m	(85 ft 11 in)
Height	9.32 m	(30 ft 7in)
Performance		
Max speed	507 km/h	(274 kt, 315 mph)
Cruising speed	483 km/h	(261 kt, 300 mph)
Take off distance	1,554 m	(5,100 ft)
Range	4,768 km	(2,591 nm, 2,980 miles)
Weights		
Max takeoff	23,500 kg	(51,818 lbs)
Useful load	8,500 kg	(18,742 lbs)

Indraero Aero 101 — France

Developed by Jean Chapeau and J. Blanchet of the Société Indraero primarily for club training, the Aero 101 tandem two-seat light biplane was flown for the first time in 1950. Eleven aircraft of this type were built between 1952 and 1953 with both the Minié 4.DC-32 and (Aero 101C) Continental A65 engine. Three Minié-powered Aero 101s and two Continental-powered Aero 101Cs are currently registered in France. The Aero 101 is of wooden construction with fabric-covered monospar wings and I-type interplane struts. Dual controls are provided and the aircraft is fitted with wheel brakes and a tailwheel. The company also built one example of the Aero 110 which was of steel tube and fabric construction and powered by a 45 h.p. Salmson radial.

Indraero Aero 101, F-PGIC

Specification	Indraero Aero 101	
Powerplant	One 75 h.p. (55.92 kW) Minié 4.DC-32 piston engine	
Dimensions		
Span	7.59 m	(24 ft 11 in)
Length	5.59 m	(18 ft 4 in)
Height	2.36 m	(7 ft 9 in)
Performance		
Max speed	177 km/h	(96 kt, 110 mph)
Cruising speed	153 km/h	(83 kt, 95 mph)
Initial climb	192 m/min	(630 fpm)
Range	512 km	(278 nm, 320 miles)
Weights		
Max takeoff	454 kg	(1,000 lbs)
Useful load	181 kg	(400 lbs)

Interavia I-3 — Russia

The I-3 is a high-performance aerobatic aircraft designed and manufactured in Russia to compete with the Sukhoi Su-29 and Yak-54 in international competition. The I-3, which first flew on 10th August 1993, is an all-metal low-wing monoplane with a fixed tailwheel undercarriage and a Voronezh M-14P radial engine. It is constructed as a tandem two-seater but can be converted to single-seat configuration by replacement of the fuselage top decking and canopy with an alternative section. It is believed that over 30 have been built, largely for operation in Russia but also for sale in the United States where six have been delivered.

Interavia I-3 (Cont.)

Interavia I-3, RA-44496

Interplane Skyboy

Specification	Interavia I-3	
Powerplant	One 360 h.p. (268.5 kW) Voronezh M-14P piston engine	
Dimensions		
Span	8.1 m	(26 ft 7 in)
Length	6.71 m	(22 ft 0 in)
Height	2.21 m	(7 ft 3 in)
Performance		
Max speed	349 km/h	(189 kt, 217 mph)
Cruising speed	306 km/h	(165 kt, 190 mph)
Initial climb	900 m/min	(2,953 fpm)
Range	700 km	(378 nm, 435 miles)
Weights		
Max takeoff	1,059 kg	(2,335 lbs)
Useful load	290 kg	(640 lbs)

Specification	Interplane Skyboy	
Powerplant	One 50 h.p. (37.3 kW) Rotax 503 piston engine	
Dimensions		
Span	10.49 m	(34 ft 5 in)
Length	6.38 m	(20 ft 11 in)
Height	1.78 m	(5 ft 10 in)
Performance		
Max speed	140 km/h	(75 kt, 87 mph)
Cruising speed	120 km/h	(65 kt, 75 mph)
Initial climb	137 m/min	(450 fpm)
Range	338 km	(183 nm, 210 miles)
Weights		
Max takeoff	450 kg	(992 lbs)
Useful load	295 kg	(650 lbs)

Interplane Skyboy — Czech Republic

The Skyboy, which is manufactured at Zbraslavice in the Czech Republic, has proved to be a popular ultralight delivered either as a factory-complete aircraft or as a kit. It has a moulded forward fuselage pod with a slim boom carrying the tail unit and a strut-braced fabric-covered high wing. The Skyboy has a side-by-side two-seat cockpit and a fixed tricycle undercarriage with large fairings on the main units. The standard powerplant is a 50 h.p. Rotax 503 which is mounted as a pusher on the wing centre section but the Skyboy can also be fitted with a 64 h.p. Rotax 582 or a 76 h.p. Verner SVS140 engine. Two different wings are available to give standard or high-speed performance. A growing number of Skyboys are in service and the type has been exported to Germany and to France where seven are in operation.

IPTN N-250 — Indonesia

With a solid history of production of the CASA Aviocar and CN.235, IPTN (Nusantara Aircraft Industries Ltd.) launched the N.250 50-seat local-service airliner project in 1989. The N.250 had a similar general layout to that of the CN.235 but had a more conventional fuselage without the CN.235's sharply upswept rear fuselage. It had a high wing mounting two 3,271 s.h.p. Allison AE2100C turboprops with six-blade Dowty propellers, main undercarriage units retracting into external fuselage fairings and a high T-tail. The prototype N.250-50 was first flown on 10th August 1995. The second aircraft, which flew in December 1996, was built as the N.250-100 with a 5 ft fuselage stretch and maximum seating for 68 passengers. Progress with the N.250 programme has slowed and the future of the N.250 and the planned 70-seat N.270 is uncertain.

IPTN N-250-100, PK-XNG

Specification	IPTN N-250-100	
Powerplant	Two 3,271 s.h.p. (2,438.86 kW) Allison AE2100C turboprops	
Dimensions		
Span	27.99 m	(91 ft 10 in)
Length	28.14 m	(92 ft 4 in)
Height	8.79 m	(28 ft 10 in)
Performance		
Max speed	612 km/h	(330 kt, 380 mph)
Cruising speed	555 km/h	(300 kt, 345 mph)
Initial climb	564 m/min	(1,850 fpm)
Range	2,025 km	(1,100 nm, 1,266 miles)
Weights		
Max takeoff	24,800 kg	(54,684 lbs)
Useful load	9,100 kg	(20,065 lbs)

Isaacs Fury — UK

The Fury was designed by John O. Isaacs based on the general structure of the Currie Wot biplane but with changes to make the aircraft a 70% scale copy of the prewar Hawker Fury biplane fighter. The Fury, which is an open-cockpit single-seater, is of wood and fabric construction and the prototype, powered by a 65 h.p. Walter Mikron engine, first flew on 30th August 1963. The Fury Mk.2 was a revised version with the higher-powered 125 h.p. Lycoming O-290-D engine and plans were subsequently sold to amateur builders who have produced a number of further examples both in the UK and overseas, including New Zealand and the USA. Various powerplants have been fitted including the 90 h.p. Continental C90-12F, 105 h.p. Lycoming O-235 and 150 h.p. Lycoming O-320. Fifteen were registered in the UK at the end of 1999.

Isaacs Fury 2, G-AYJY

Specification	Isaacs Fury 2	
Powerplant	One 125 h.p. (93.2 kW) Textron Lycoming O-290-D piston engine	
Dimensions		
Span	6.4 m	(21 ft 0 in)
Length	5.87 m	(19 ft 3 in)
Height	2.16 m	(7 ft 1 in)
Performance		
Max speed	185 km/h	(100 kt, 115 mph)
Cruising speed	129 km/h	(70 kt, 80 mph)
Initial climb	488 m/min	(1,600 fpm)
Range	161 km	(87 nm, 100 miles)
Weights		
Max takeoff	450 kg	(992 lbs)
Useful load	200 kg	(441 lbs)

Israviation ST-50 — Israel

The ST-50 is a five-seat turboprop business aircraft which has been developed to prototype stage by Israviation in association with Cirrus Design Corp. in the USA based on the earlier Cirrus VK-30. The proof-of-concept prototype ST-50 first flew in the USA on 7th December 1994 with development testing transferred subsequently to Kiryat Shmona in Israel. The aircraft is an all-composite design with a highly streamlined pressurised fuselage, low-set wings and a cruciform tail. The PT6A turboprop engine is buried in the rear fuselage aft of the cabin and drives a three-bladed pusher propeller, and the ST-50 has a retractable tricycle undercarriage. The design concept is that the ST-50 will combine high-speed cruise performance with docile landing characteristics and cabin comfort.

Israviation ST-50, 4X-COD

Specification	Israviation ST-50	
Powerplant	One 600 s.h.p. (447 kW) Pratt & Whitney PT6A-135 turboprop	
Dimensions		
Span	11.89 m	(39 ft 0 in)
Length	7.92 m	(26 ft 0 in)
Height	3.56 m	(11 ft 8 in)
Performance		
Max speed	518 km/h	(280 kt, 322 mph)
Cruising speed	483 km/h	(260 kt, 300 mph)
Initial climb	549 m/min	(1,800 fpm)
Range	2,024 km	(1,100 nm, 1,265 miles)
Weights		
Max takeoff	2,381 kg	(5,250 lbs)
Useful load	884 kg	(1,950 lbs)

J

Jabiru Aircraft Jabiru — Australia

The Jabiru two-seat kit-built light aircraft was designed by Rodney Stiff and Phil Ainsworth of Bundaberg, Queensland and first flew in 1989. It is an all-composite side-by-side two-seater with a large, fully enclosed cabin and a strut-braced high wing and has a fixed tricycle undercarriage. The initial model was the Jabiru LSA, over 60 of which have been sold as factory-complete aircraft with the 60 h.p. Jabiru-designed Jabiru 1600 flat-four piston engine. The aircraft has also been built as the Jabiru ST with the 80 h.p. Jabiru 2200 engine. Kit versions include the Jabiru SK and an ultralight version, the Jabiru UL, which has a longer-span wing and stretched fuselage and a 450 kg gross weight. Both of these use the 80 h.p. powerplant.

Jabiru UL, G-MGCA

Specification	Jabiru SK	
Powerplant	One 80 h.p. (59.65 kW) Jabiru 2,200 piston engine	
Dimensions		
Span	8.1 m	(26 ft 4 in)
Length	5.1 m	(16 ft 6 in)
Height	2 m	(6 ft 7 in)
Performance		
Max speed	216 km/h	(116 kt, 134 mph)
Cruising speed	193 km/h	(104 kt, 120 mph)
Initial climb	305 m/min	(1,000 fpm)
Range	920 km	(500 nm, 575 miles)
Weights		
Max takeoff	450 kg	(990 lbs)
Useful load	215 kg	(473 lbs)

Jamieson J-1 — USA

After the war, the Jamieson Corporation of DeLand, Florida developed a modified version of the two-seat Culver Cadet, named the Jamieson J-1 with a tricycle undercarriage, enlarged vertical tail and a 140 h.p. Lycoming O-290-B engine and appear to have completed five conversions. They also built one Jamieson J-2-L1 Jupiter which had an extended three-seat cabin, a 115 h.p. Lycoming O-235-C1 engine and a butterfly tail. The prototype first flew in 1951 and the design was progressively refined, with the V-tail being replaced by a conventional fin and rudder. The prototype of the higher-powered production four-seat 'Jamieson J' (otherwise known as the J-2L-1B) first flew on 13th December 1962 and was followed by two additional aircraft before further development was abandoned. At least two Jamieson Js are still in private ownership in Florida.

Jamieson J-2L-1B, N2801Q

Specification	Jamieson J-2L-1B	
Powerplant	One 150 h.p. (111.8 kW) Textron Lycoming O-320-A3C piston engine	
Dimensions		
Span	8.84 m	(29 ft 0 in)
Length	6.55 m	(21 ft 6 in)
Height	2.21 m	(7 ft 3 in)
Performance		
Max speed	254 km/h	(137 kt, 158 mph)
Cruising speed	241 km/h	(130 kt, 150 mph)
Initial climb	305 m/min	(1,000 fpm)
Range	960 km	(522 nm, 600 miles)
Weights		
Max takeoff	853 kg	(1,880 lbs)
Useful load	451 kg	(995 lbs)

Jeffair Barracuda — USA

The Barracuda is a high-performance amateur-built aircraft designed by Geoffrey Siers and marketed in the form of plans by Buethe Enterprises of Cathedral City, California. The type first flew on 29th June 1975 and gained the Outstanding New Design award at Oshkosh that year. It is a side-by-side two-seater of all-wood construction and the wing has mild dihedral on the outer sections. The Barracuda is fitted with a retractable tricycle undercarriage based on that of the Piper PA-28R and various engines can be fitted in the 180 h.p. to 300 h.p. range. Typically, builders fit the 250 h.p. Lycoming IO-540 which gives a top speed of 210 mph and a stall speed of 60 mph and the aircraft is popular as a comfortable, fast cross-country tourer. Over 600 sets of plans have been sold and more than 30 Barracudas are flying in the United States.

Jeffair Barracuda, N159JB

Specification	Jeffair (Buethe) Barracuda	
Powerplant	One 250 h.p. (186.4 kW) Textron Lycoming IO-540 piston engine	
Dimensions		
Span	7.57 m	(24 ft 10 in)
Length	6.58 m	(21 ft 7 in)
Height	1.83 m	(6 ft 0 in)
Performance		
Max speed	338 km/h	(183 kt, 210 mph)
Cruising speed	322 km/h	(174 kt, 200 mph)
Initial climb	610 m/min	(2,000 fpm)
Range	1,280 km	(696 nm, 800 miles)
Weights		
Max takeoff	1,043 kg	(2,300 lbs)
Useful load	363 kg	(800 lbs)

Jodel D.9 Bébé — France

The Jodel D.9 is one of the most famous European amateur-built single-seat designs and was the creation of Edouard Joly and Jean Délémontez who flew the prototype on 21st January 1948. A wood and fabric aircraft of simple layout and construction, the D.9 Bébé has the distinctive wing design created by Délémontez comprising a parallel chord, undihedralled centre section and tapered, dihedralled outer panels. The D.9 normally has an open cockpit but can be fitted with a transparent canopy and is equipped with a fixed tailwheel undercarriage. Variants include the D.91 (ABC Scorpion engine), D.92 (1,200 or 1,500 cc Volkswagen), D.93 (35 h.p. Poinsard), D.97 (32 h.p. Sarolea Vautour) and the D.98 with a 25 h.p. AVA-40. Small-scale production was undertaken by Wassmer (D.96) and Survol (D.99). The Bébé Jodel has been built from plans by amateurs in many countries and at least 600 have been completed, mostly as D.92s with the 45 h.p. converted Volkswagen.

Jodel D.9 Bébé, G-AXKI

Specification	Jodel D.92	
Powerplant	One 45 h.p. (33.5 kW) Volkswagen 1600 piston engine	
Dimensions		
Span	6.2 m	(20 ft 4 in)
Length	5.6 m	(18 ft 4 in)
Height	1.52 m	(5 ft 0 in)
Performance		
Max speed	175 km/h	(94 kt, 109 mph)
Cruising speed	170 km/h	(91 kt, 105 mph)
Initial climb	240 m/min	(785 fpm)
Range	402 km	(217 nm, 250 miles)
Weights		
Max takeoff	384 kg	(847 lbs)
Useful load	150 kg	(331 lbs)

Jodel D.11 series — France

The Jodel D.11 was developed by Jean Délémontez following the success of the single-seat D.9 Bébé amateur-built single seater. The D.11, which first flew on 5th May 1950, had an enlarged version of the D.9's wing, a fixed tailwheel undercarriage and a larger and wider fuselage than the D.9 with side-by-side seating for two in an enclosed cabin. As with the Bébé, the D.11 could be fitted with various powerplants and, while the D.112 with a 65 h.p. Continental A65 was the most popular, other versions included the D.111 (75 h.p. Minié 4DC), D.113 (100 h.p. Continental O-200A), D.115 (75 h.p. Mathis 4-GF-60), D.118 (60 h.p. Walter Mikron) and various models with the Salmson 5A radial engine. The D.11 was, again, sold in the form of plans but was also built commercially in large numbers by SAN and Alpavia as the D.117 (90 h.p. Continental C90), by Wassmer as the D.112 and the improved D.120 Paris-Nice (equivalent to the D.117), and in Spain as the D.1190S by Aerodifusion. Most D.11s had a rear parcel shelf and extended rear cabin transparencies. At least 2,000 Jodel D.11 variants have been built and large numbers continue in operation.

SAN Jodel D.117, G-BIOU

Specification	Wassmer Jodel D.120	
Powerplant	One 90 h.p. (67.1 kW) Continental C90-12F piston engine	
Dimensions		
Span	8.22 m	(27 ft 0 in)
Length	6.36 m	(20 ft 10 in)
Height	1.73 m	(5 ft 8 in)
Performance		
Max speed	205 km/h	(110 kt, 127 mph)
Cruising speed	187 km/h	(100 kt, 116 mph)
Initial climb	210 m/min	(690 fpm)
Range	1,144 km	(622 nm, 715 miles)
Weights		
Max takeoff	650 kg	(1,433 lbs)
Useful load	275 kg	(606 lbs)

Jodel DR.100 Ambassadeur and derivatives — France

The DR.100 was an enlarged development of the popular all-wood Jodel D.11 designed by Pierre Robin and flown in 1957 as the Jodel Robin. It had a longer fuselage to accommodate an extended cabin with a two-place rear seat and also had a modified tail, streamlined engine cowling and spatted main undercarriage. The production DR.100A Ambassadeur first flew on 14th July 1958. It had a 2+2-seat cabin and, powered by a 90 h.p. Continental C90-14F engine, was built from 1961 onwards by Société Aéronautique Normande (SAN) and by Centre Est Aéronautique (CEA). Later examples (designated DR.105A) were fitted with a 100 h.p. Continental O-200-A. The subsequent DR.1050 Ambassadeur, which offered excellent performance on low power, had an improved fuel system and electrics and the DR.1051 had a 105 h.p. Potez 4E-20 engine. CEA built a deluxe version as the Sicile. The later DR.1050M and DR.1051M versions had a swept tail, all-moving tailplane and a revised engine cowling and these were built as the SAN Excellence and CEA Sicile Record. In total 295 of the DR.100 series were built by SAN and 334 by CEA and many of these continue in service throughout Europe. CEA later developed the DR.200 and DR.250 Capitaine which had a full four-seat cabin, extended inboard wing leading edges and a 160 h.p. Lycoming O-320-E engine. The prototype DR.200 flew on 17th November 1964. A simplified 2+2-seat variant for club training, designated DR.220, was built with the 105 h.p. Potez 105E engine and a full four-seat version, the DR.221 Dauphin, had a 115 h.p. Lycoming O-235-C engine. CEA (later Avions Robin) built 100 DR.250s and 145 of the DR.220/221 series. Later versions of these designs are described under Robin.

CEA Jodel DR.221 Dauphin, G-GOSS

CEA Jodel DR.1050 Sicile, F-BKIJ

Specification	Centre Est Jodel DR.1050M Sicile Record	
Powerplant	One 100 h.p. (74.56 kW) Teledyne Continental O-200-A piston engine	
Dimensions		
Span	8.72 m	(28 ft 7 in)
Length	6.35 m	(20 ft 10 in)
Height	1.83 m	(6 ft 0 in)
Performance		
Max speed	230 km/h	(124 kt, 143 mph)
Cruising speed	205 km/h	(110 kt, 127 mph)
Initial climb	180 m/min	(590 fpm)
Range	896 km	(487 nm, 560 miles)
Weights		
Max takeoff	780 kg	(1,720 lbs)
Useful load	380 kg	(838 lbs)

Jodel D.150 Mascaret — France

The Mascaret was designed by Jean Délémontez as a modernised version of the popular side-by-side two-seat Jodel D.112 with good performance and long range. It had a wider fuselage, the familiar Jodel cranked wing with a modified centre section, a separate swept fin and rudder, an all-moving tailplane, the undercarriage of the Ambassadeur, an improved engine installation and a 100 h.p. Continental O-200-A engine. First flown on 2nd June 1962, the D.150 Mascaret was built in series by SAN at Bernay, 44 being manufactured. In addition, 17 examples of the D.150A were built with the 105 h.p. Potez 105E engine. Plans for the D.150 have been sold to homebuilders and several amateur-built examples have been completed.

SAN D.150 Mascaret, G-BLAT

Specification	SAN Jodel D.150 Mascaret	
Powerplant	One 100 h.p. (74.56 kW) Teledyne Continental O-200-A piston engine	
Dimensions		
Span	8.15 m	(26 ft 9 in)
Length	6.3 m	(20 ft 8 in)
Height	1.76 m	(5 ft 8 in)
Performance		
Max speed	240 km/h	(130 kt, 150 mph)
Cruising speed	217 km/h	(117 kt, 135 mph)
Initial climb	244 m/min	(800 fpm)
Range	1,600 km	(870 nm, 1,000 miles)
Weights		
Max takeoff	720 kg	(1,588 lbs)
Useful load	306 kg	(675 lbs)

Jodel D.140 Mousquetaire — France

Such was the success of the two-seat Jodel D.11 series of light aircraft, designed by Jean Délémontez, that a larger four-/five-seat touring aircraft with good performance was initiated in 1957. It was a completely new model using the low-set cranked Jodel wing design and having an enlarged fuselage with a wide cabin accommodating two in the front seats and up to three passengers on a rear bench seat. It had a fixed tailwheel undercarriage and a large baggage compartment behind the cabin which could be opened up to house a stretcher case if necessary. The D.140 first flew on 4th July 1958 and Société Aéronautique Normande (SAN) built 101 production D.140As and D.140Bs. The later D.140C Mousquetaire III and D.140E Mousquetaire IV, 113 of which were built, had a swept vertical tail and the D.140R Abeille was a glider tug version with a cut-back bubble cockpit canopy, 28 of which were completed, mainly for the French Air Force. The D.140 is available for amateur construction and at least two have been built privately.

SAN Jodel D.140E Mousquetaire IV, French Air Force, 201

Jodel D.140 Mousquetaire (Cont.)

Specification	SAN Jodel D.140C Mousquetaire III	
Powerplant	One 180 h.p. (134.2 kW) Textron Lycoming O-360-A2A piston engine	
Dimensions		
Span	10.27 m	(33 ft 8 in)
Length	7.82 m	(25 ft 8 in)
Height	2.05 m	(6 ft 9 in)
Performance		
Max speed	254 km/h	(137 kt, 158 mph)
Cruising speed	240 km/h	(130 kt, 149 mph)
Initial climb	300 m/min	(985 fpm)
Range	1,392 km	(757 nm, 870 miles)
Weights		
Max takeoff	1,200 kg	(2,646 lbs)
Useful load	580 kg	(1,279 lbs)

SAB Jodel D.20 Jubilé, F-PSAB

Jodel D.18, D.19 and D.20
— France

The D.18 side-by-side two-seat light aircraft is based on the DC.1 developed by Jean Délémontez and Alain Cauchy as a modernised and more efficient successor to the Jodel D.11. Smaller and lighter than the D.11, it is powered by a 1,600 cc Volkswagen and is of wood and fabric construction with a fixed tailwheel undercarriage and a rearward-opening bubble canopy. It retains the familiar Jodel cranked wing but has a new wing section and is fitted with flaps. The prototype D.18 flew on 21st May 1984 and over 400 sets of plans have been sold with a large number of D.18s now flying. The D.19 is an alternative version with a tricycle undercarriage. The D.20 Jubilé is a further refinement of the D.19 with a revised undercarriage and a deeper fuselage with a wider cabin and tail resembling that of the Robin DR.300. It is powered by an 85 h.p. JPX-4T-X75/A engine and is being sold as plans by the Société Aéronautique Bourguignonne.

Specification	Jodel D.18	
Powerplant	One 58 h.p. (43 kW) Volkswagen 1600 piston engine	
Dimensions		
Span	7.5 m	(24 ft 7 in)
Length	5.7 m	(18 ft 8 in)
Height	1.63 m	(5 ft 4 in)
Performance		
Max speed	249 km/h	(135 kt, 155 mph)
Cruising speed	185 km/h	(100 kt, 115 mph)
Initial climb	180 m/min	(590 fpm)
Range	800 km	(435 nm, 500 miles)
Weights		
Max takeoff	460 kg	(1,014 lbs)
Useful load	230 kg	(507 lbs)

Jodel D.19, F-PEGY

Johnson Rocket
— USA

The Rocket 185 high-performance light aircraft was built by Johnson Aircraft Inc. and made its first flight in mid-1945. It was a streamlined side-by-side low-wing two-seater with a fabric-covered tube fuselage, enclosed cabin and wooden wings. It was fitted with a retractable tailwheel undercarriage and a 185 h.p. Lycoming O-435-A engine. In production form the Rocket was equipped with a tricycle undercarriage and first deliveries were made in late-1946. In total, 19 Rockets were completed before the company was taken over and renamed Rocket Aircraft Inc. However, no further Rockets were built. At least three Rockets (also known as the Pirtle Johnson Rocket after the subsequent type certificate holder) are active in the USA including the tailwheel prototype. A developed all-metal version was built by AMC as the Texas Bullet (see AMC Texas Bullet 205).

Specification	Johnson Rocket 185	
Powerplant	One 185 h.p. (137.9 kW) Textron Lycoming O-435-A piston engine	
Dimensions		
Span	9.40 m	(30 ft 10 in)
Length	6.65 m	(21 ft 10 in)
Height	2.13 m	(7 ft 0 in)
Performance		
Max speed	290 km/h	(156 kt, 180 mph)
Cruising speed	257 km/h	(139 kt, 160 mph)
Initial climb	290 m/min	(950 fpm)
Range	1,104 km	(600 nm, 690 miles)
Weights		
Max takeoff	1,156 kg	(2,550 lbs)
Useful load	351 kg	(775 lbs)

Johnson Rocket 185, NC90204

Jones White Lightning
— USA

The White Lightning is a very-high-performance amateur kit-built aircraft designed by Nick Jones and first flown on 9th March 1986. It is a four-seater of all-composite construction with a highly streamlined fuselage and mid-set short-span tapered straight wings. The White Lightning has a retractable tricycle undercarriage with the main units fitting into wells in the lower fuselage. Its fully enclosed cabin is entered by an upward-opening section of the port windshield and a port side hatch for the backward-facing rear seats. The aircraft can cruise at over 200 mph over distances of up to 2,000 miles and the prototype established several FAI Class C1 world speed records in 1986 and was the winner of the 1987 CAFE-400 aircraft efficiency contest. Over 40 kits have been sold and 15 aircraft are believed to be flying.

Jones White Lightning, N444WL

Specification	Jones White Lightning	
Powerplant	One 210 h.p. (156.6 kW) Teledyne Continental IO-360-CB piston engine	
Dimensions		
Span	8.43 m	(27 ft 8 in)
Length	7.11 m	(23 ft 4 in)
Height	2.18 m	(7 ft 2 in)
Performance		
Max speed	450 km/h	(243 kt, 280 mph)
Cruising speed	426 km/h	(230 kt, 265 mph)
Initial climb	442 m/min	(1,450 fpm)
Range	3,200 km	(1,739 nm, 2,000 miles)
Weights		
Max takeoff	1,224 kg	(2,700 lbs)
Useful load	544 kg	(1,200 lbs)

Junkers Ju.52/3M
— Germany

The Junkers Ju.52/3M, developed from the single-engined Ju.52ba which first flew on 13th October 1930, was the backbone of the wartime Luftwaffe transport fleet and, by the time the war commenced, had already established itself as a reliable commercial transport on European routes and had been used in the Spanish Civil War. It is an all-metal aircraft incorporating the distinctive corrugated skinning developed by Junkers and fitted with a low wing equipped with full-span external flaps. It has a fixed tailwheel undercarriage and in its original form used three 830 h.p. BMW-132A radial engines but was frequently fitted with Pratt & Whitney SH31-G Wasp engines. Accommodation is provided for up to 17 passengers but in wartime use it would carry up to 19 paratroops. German production totalled 3,234 aircraft, 430 of which were prewar commercial aircraft, and 415 were built by Amiot in France after the war as the AAC-1 Toucan and 170 in Spain as the CASA 352-L (T2B) with ENMA Beta B-4 engines. At least ten aircraft are active including four based at Dubendorf in Switzerland, one in South Africa, one in Germany and several in the USA.

CASA 352L (Ju.52/3M), HB-HOY

Specification	Junkers Ju.52/3M	
Powerplant	Three 830 h.p. (618.8 kW) BMW-132A piston engines	
Dimensions		
Span	29.2 m	(95 ft 10 in)
Length	18.9 m	(62 ft 0 in)
Height	4.52 m	(14 ft 10 in)
Performance		
Max speed	280 km/h	(151 kt, 175 mph)
Cruising speed	255 km/h	(137 kt, 158 mph)
Initial climb	207 m/min	(680 fpm)
Range	880 km	(478 nm, 550 miles)
Weights		
Max takeoff	10,500 kg	(23,152 lbs)
Useful load	4,800 kg	(10,584 lbs)

Jurca MJ.2 Tempête
— France

The Hawker Tempest fighter was the inspiration for Marcel Jurca's Tempête amateur-built single-seater. The Tempête is a wood and fabric low-wing design with a single-seat cockpit enclosed by a sliding bubble canopy. It has a fixed tailwheel undercarriage. The prototype first flew on 27th June 1956 and many further examples have been built by amateurs from Jurca plans. Most Tempêtes are MJ.2As powered by a Continental A65 engine but other variants have included the MJ.2B (Continental A75), MJ.2C (Continental A85), MJ.2D (Continental C90-14F), MJ.2E (Continental O-200-A), MJ.2F (Potez 4E-20), MJ.2H (Lycoming O-235) and MJ.2I (Lycoming O-290-G). Other variants include the MJ.22 which has a 150 h.p. engine and a strengthened airframe and the MJ.4 Shadow which has enlarged swept tail surfaces. Some Tempêtes have also been fitted with a rear second seat. More than 100 sets of Tempête plans have been sold and over 50 are flying including several in the USA.

Jurca MJ.2 Tempête, F-PXKU

Specification	Jurca MJ.2A Tempête	
Powerplant	One 65 h.p. (48.5 kW) Teledyne Continental A65-8 piston engine	
Dimensions		
Span	6 m	(19 ft 8 in)
Length	5.85 m	(19 ft 2 in)
Height	2.45 m	(7 ft 10 in)
Performance		
Max speed	193 km/h	(104 kt, 120 mph)
Cruising speed	164 km/h	(89 kt, 102 mph)
Initial climb	168 m/min	(550 fpm)
Range	531 km	(287 nm, 330 miles)
Weights		
Max takeoff	430 kg	(948 lbs)
Useful load	140 kg	(309 lbs)

Jurca MJ.5 Sirocco
— France

Marcel Jurca designed the MJ.5 as a two-seat development of his successful MJ.2 Tempête amateur-built single-seater. Like the MJ.2, the Sirocco is a low-wing aircraft with a wood and fabric structure but it has a longer fuselage to accommodate the tandem cockpit, a modified wing with extended inboard leading edges and squared-off tips and a taller swept vertical tail. The Sirocco has a tailwheel undercarriage which can be fixed or retractable. Over 500 sets of plans have been sold and at least 50 Siroccos are flying. As with the Tempête, several engines can be fitted including the Continental C90-8 (MJ.5A), Continental O-200-A (MJ.5B), Potez 4E-20 (MJ.5C), Potez 4E-30 (MJ.5D), Hirth (MJ.5E), Lycoming O-235 (MJ.5F) and Lycoming IO-360 (MJ.5L). The MJ.53 Autan is a modified version with a wider fuselage providing side-by-side seating and powered by a 200 h.p. Lycoming IO-360 engine.

Jurca MJ.5 Sirocco, F-PZZQ

Specification	Jurca MJ.5F Sirocco	
Powerplant	One 115 h.p. (86 kW) Textron Lycoming O-235-C2B piston engine	
Dimensions		
Span	7 m	(23 ft 0 in)
Length	6.15 m	(20 ft 2 in)
Height	2.6 m	(8 ft 6 in)
Performance		
Max speed	233 km/h	(126 kt, 145 mph)
Cruising speed	217 km/h	(117 kt, 135 mph)
Initial climb	250 m/min	(820 fpm)
Range	920 km	(500 nm, 575 miles)
Weights		
Max takeoff	680 kg	(1,500 lbs)
Useful load	250 kg	(551 lbs)

Jurca MJ.7 Gnatsum — France

Marcel Jurca has become well known for his range of plans-built amateur-built designs based on classic piston-engined fighters and the most popular has been the single-seat MJ.7 Gnatsum which is a 66% scale representation of the North American P-51D Mustang. Other fighter-inspired Jurca designs include the MJ.8 (a 75% scale Focke Wulf 190), the MJ.9 (a full scale Me.109), the MJ.10 (a 75% scale Supermarine Spitfire) and the MJ.12 (a 75% scale Curtiss P-40). The MJ.7 prototype first flew in Canada on 31st July 1969 and at least ten of this model and the 75% scale MJ.77 are flying. The Gnatsum can be built in several forms including steel tube and fabric, all-wood or wood and composites and has a fully retractable tailwheel undercarriage. Various engines in the 160 h.p. to 260 h.p. range have been fitted and one aircraft has been equipped with a 400 h.p. Chevrolet. The most common powerplant is the 260 h.p. Potez 4D-34 which powers the majority of French-registered examples, but several Gnatsums have been fitted with a 175 h.p. or 200 h.p. Ranger in-line engine.

Specification	Jurca MJ.7 Gnatsum	
Powerplant	One 175 h.p. (130.5 kW) Ranger 6-440-C2 piston engine	
Dimensions		
Span	7.52 m	(24 ft 8 in)
Length	6.55 m	(21 ft 6 in)
Height	1.98 m	(6 ft 6 in)
Performance		
Max speed	351 km/h	(190 kt, 218 mph)
Cruising speed	322 km/h	(174 kt, 200 mph)
Initial climb	305 m/min	(1,000 fpm)
Range	800 km	(435 nm, 500 miles)
Weights		
Max takeoff	850 kg	(1,874 lbs)
Useful load	175 kg	(386 lbs)

Jurca MJ.7 Gnatsum, F-PANG

Kaman HH-43 Husky
— USA

The American aviation pioneer Charles Kaman found a unique method of eliminating the instability inherent in helicopters by devising a system of closely coupled twin rotors which intermeshed and, by turning in opposing directions, eliminated torque. Kaman built a range of helicopters for the US Navy and USAF but the major production model, and the only version still flying, was the K-600-3, produced for the USAF as the HH-43B Husky. This unusual design had a square-section fuselage, twin booms mounting four fins and twin rotor masts above the cabin. It was powered by a T53 turboshaft with a large exhaust pipe extending rearwards. The Husky was mainly used for search & rescue duties and carried up to 12 crew and passengers or up to four stretcher cases. In total, 245 were delivered after the type was retired from USAF service and a number were civilianised and used for civil firefighting and utility work. Several remain active in the United States.

Kaman HH-43B Husky, USAF, 24533

Specification	Kaman K-600-3 Huskie HH-43B	
Powerplant	One 860 s.h.p. (641.2 kW) Textron Lycoming T53-L-1B turboshaft	
Dimensions		
Rotor diameter (each)	15.7 m	(51 ft 6 in)
Length	7.62 m	(25 ft 0 in)
Height	4.72 m	(15 ft 6 in)
Performance		
Max speed	193 km/h	(104 kt, 120 mph)
Cruising speed	156 km/h	(84 kt, 97 mph)
Initial climb	610 m/min	(2,000 fpm)
Range	376 km	(204 nm, 235 miles)
Weights		
Max takeoff	3,991 kg	(8,800 lbs)
Useful load	1,964 kg	(4,330 lbs)

Kaman H-2 Seasprite
— USA

In 1956, Kaman, which had provided many of its HTK, HOK, HUK and HH-43B helicopters to the US forces, designed a new long-range search & rescue helicopter for the US Navy and, unusually, it did not have the traditional Kaman intermeshing twin-rotor system. The H-2 (K-20) Seasprite was quite conventional with a single four-blade main rotor and a tapered fuselage with a vertical tail pylon mounting a stabilising propeller and a retractable undercarriage. It first flew on 2nd July 1959. A maximum of two crew and 12 passengers can be carried but an anti-submarine operations crew of three is normal. The UH-2A (originally HU2K-1) Seasprite was initially powered by a single 875 s.h.p. General Electric T58-GE-6 turboshaft but most aircraft were subsequently modified to UH-2C twin-turbine configuration with a pair of T58-GE-8B engines. Some 244 Seasprites were manufactured and several modification and life-extension programmes have been implemented including the anti-submarine LAMPS-1 conversion to SH-2D standard and the upgrade to SH-2F with new rotor blades, a modified undercarriage and 1,350 s.h.p. T58-GE-8F engines. The SH-2G Super Seasprite is a refurbished SH-2F with composite rotor blades and twin 1,723 s.h.p. General Electric T700 turboshafts in an enlarged installation. Many Seasprites have been retired by the U.S. Navy but surplus SH-2F airframes are being rebuilt to SH-2G standard and new airframes manufactured for export customers including Egypt, New Zealand and Australia.

Kaman SH-2G(E) Super Seasprite, Egyptian AF, 3051

Kaman H-2 Seasprite (Cont.)

Specification	Kaman SH-2G Super Seasprite	
Powerplant	Two 1,723 s.h.p. (1284.7 kW) General Electric T700-401 turboshafts	
Dimensions		
Rotor diameter	13.51 m	(44 ft 4 in)
Length	12.19 m	(40 ft 0 in)
Height	4.58 m	(15 ft 0 in)
Performance		
Max speed	270 km/h	(146 kt, 168 mph)
Cruising speed	222 km/h	(120 kt, 138 mph)
Initial climb	716 m/min	(2,350 fpm)
Range	1,032 km	(561 nm, 645 miles)
Weights		
Max takeoff	6,304 kg	(13,900 lbs)
Useful load	2,821 kg	(6,220 lbs)

Kaman K-1200 K-Max — USA

Having been out of helicopter manufacturing for several years, Kaman produced the innovative Model K-1200 'K-Max' which was specifically designed for logging, powerline construction, resupply of naval vessels and other external vertical lift applications. The K-Max is an unconventional large single-seat helicopter fitted with Kaman's intermeshing twin-rotor system with composite rotors incorporating servo tabs for pitch control. It has a fixed tricycle undercarriage which can be fitted with skis and has a large vertical fin and secondary fins on a small tailplane. The K-Max is powered by a Honeywell T53 turboshaft. For its heavy-lift role it has powerful underslung lifting gear and two passengers can be carried on external seats on the fuselage sides. The prototype K-Max first flew on 23rd December 1991 and 28 had been built by mid-2000 for customers in six countries.

Kaman K-Max, N21MX

Specification	Kaman K-1200 K-Max	
Powerplant	One 1,500 s.h.p. (1,118 kW) Honeywell T53-17A-1 turboshaft	
Dimensions		
Rotor diameter (each)	14.73 m	(48 ft 4 in)
Length	15.85 m	(52 ft 0 in)
Height	5.69 m	(18 ft 8 in)
Performance		
Max speed	185 km/h	(100 kt, 115 mph)
Cruising speed	130 km/h	(70 kt, 81 mph)
Initial climb	914 m/min	(3,000 fpm)
Range	278 km	(150 nm, 173 miles)
Weights		
Max takeoff	5,215 kg	(11,500 lbs)
Useful load	3,084 kg	(6,800 lbs)

Kaminskas Jungster — USA

The little Jungster biplane was designed by Rim Kaminskas of Monrovia, California and it was inspired by the Bucker Jungmann, although it is considerably smaller in overall dimensions and is only a single-seater. The Jungster I first flew in October 1962 and was marketed in the form of plans. Construction is of wood and fabric and the Jungster has a fixed tailwheel undercarriage and an open cockpit. The prototype had a 100 h.p. Lycoming O-235-C engine, but later aircraft used engines of up to 135 h.p. Over 1,500 sets of plans have been sold. The Jungster II was a monoplane development of the Jungster I, powered by a 180 h.p. Lycoming O-360-A1A engine and having a swept strut-braced parasol wing and a redesigned undercarriage with cantilevered legs. This first flew in March 1966 and was intended to give higher speeds and improved cross-country flying characteristics. Marketed by K&S Aircraft and later by MacFam, the Jungster II has also been built by amateurs in some numbers with around 800 sets of plans having been sold.

Kaminskas Jungster II, N376

Specification	Kaminskas Jungster I	
Powerplant	One 100 h.p. (74.6 kW) Textron Lycoming O-235-C piston engine	
Dimensions		
Span	5.08 m	(16 ft 8 in)
Length	4.88 m	(16 ft 0 in)
Height	1.83 m	(6 ft 0 in)
Performance		
Max speed	185 km/h	(100 kt, 115 mph)
Cruising speed	161 km/h	(87 kt, 100 mph)
Initial climb	457 m/min	(1,500 fpm)
Range	320 km	(174 nm, 200 miles)
Weights		
Max takeoff	385 kg	(850 lbs)
Useful load	111 kg	(245 lbs)

Specification	Kamov Ka-25BSh Hormone-A	
Powerplant	Two 900 s.h.p. (671 kW) Glushenkov (OMKB) GTD-3F turboshafts	
Dimensions		
Rotor diameter (each)	15.74 m	(51 ft 8 in)
Length	9.75 m	(32 ft 0 in)
Height	5.38 m	(17 ft 8 in)
Performance		
Max speed	209 km/h	(113 kt, 130 mph)
Cruising speed	193 km/h	(104 kt, 120 mph)
Range	640 km	(348 nm, 400 miles)
Weights		
Max takeoff	7,500 kg	(16,537 lbs)
Useful load	2,735 kg	(6,031 lbs)

Kamov Ka-25 — Russia

The Russian helicopter designer Nikolai Kamov developed a system of twin main rotors counter-rotating on a common rotor mast as a method of providing stability without the need for a stabilising tail rotor. In 1958, following on from his production Ka-15 and Ka-18 light helicopters, he designed the Ka-20 (later Ka-25) shipboard anti-submarine helicopter (NATO name 'Hormone'). This first flew in 1960 and it had a rectangular fuselage with the twin GTD-3F tuboshafts mounted on top and a small tailplane with three fins at the rear. It had a four-leg wheeled undercarriage. Over 450 were built including the Ka-25PL ASW version with a nose-mounted radome, a belly weapons bay and dipping sonar, the Ka-25BSh Hormone-A for minesweeping, the Ka-25K Hormone-B for airborne missile control with a larger radar nose and a retracting undercarriage and the Ka-25PS Hormone-C search & rescue and COD version with 12-passenger capacity and an external rescue hoist. In addition to Soviet/Russian Navy use the Ka-25 has also served with the military forces of Yugoslavia, Syria, Vietnam and India.

Kamov Ka-25

Kamov Ka-26 — Russia

Kamov designed the Ka-26 as a light multi-purpose utility helicopter, equipped with the Kamov twin-rotor coaxial rotor system. The Ka-26 (NATO name 'Hoodlum') is built around a central fuselage spine on which is mounted the rotor head, stub wings holding the two Vedeneyev M-14V-26 piston engine pods, a twin-boomed tail unit with twin fins and a forward two-seat crew pod. The empty space remaining can be fitted with a six-passenger or freight module, firefighting equipment, a geophysical sensor ring, agricultural chemical hoppers or heavy-lift gear. Around 1,200 Ka-26s have been built and are widely used in CIS countries, largely for crop spraying. The Ka-126 (Hoodlum-B) is a modified version with the twin piston engines replaced by a Mars Kobcyenko TVO-100 turboshaft mounted on the top of the fuselage. This first flew on 19th October 1987 and a further variant, the Ka-128 with Turboméca Arriel engines, is under development. The Ka-226, flown on 4th September 1997, is a more powerful version with twin Allison 250-C20B turboshafts, a modified cabin with a pointed nose, a larger seven-passenger transport module and a taller undercarriage.

Kamov Ka-26, HA-MPN

Kamov Ka-26 (Cont.)

Kamov Ka-226A, RA-00199

Kamov Ka-29RLD

Specification	Kamov Ka-226	
Powerplant	Two 450 s.h.p. (335.6 kW) Allison 250-C20B turboshafts	
Dimensions		
Rotor diameter (each)	13 m	(42 ft 8 in)
Length	8.1 m	(26 ft 7 in)
Height	1.4 m	(4 ft 7 in)
Performance		
Max speed	193 km/h	(104 kt, 120 mph)
Cruising speed	177 km/h	(96 kt, 110 mph)
Initial climb	539 m/min	(1,770 fpm)
Range	600 km	(326 nm, 375 miles)
Weights		
Max takeoff	3,400 kg	(7,497 lbs)
Useful load	1,450 kg	(3,197 lbs)

Kamov Ka-27, Ka-29 and Ka-32 — Russia

The successful Ka-25 coaxial twin-rotor naval helicopter provided the basis for the larger Ka-27 (NATO name 'Helix'). Following the same layout, but in reality a new design, the Ka-27 is almost twice the weight of the Ka-25 and has a longer and wider fuselage, twin tailfins and a much larger engine housing for its twin 2,170 s.h.p. Isotov/Klimov TV3-117BK turboshafts. The Ka-27 prototype flew on 8th August 1973 and deliveries of the production Ka-27PL Helix-A to the Soviet Naval Aviation for anti-submarine missions started in late 1977. Export versions are designated Ka-28. The search & rescue version is designated Ka-27PS Helix-D and it lacks the weapons bay of the Helix-A and has additional external fuel tanks and SAR equipment. A civil model is the Ka-32A which has no weapons bay, is fitted with 16 passenger seats and has two 2,190 s.h.p. Isotov/Klimov TV3-117V engines. This has been delivered also as the Ka-32A-1 for firefighting, the Ka-32A-2 for police operations, the Ka-32C for civil SAR and EMS operations, the stripped-down utility Ka-32T and the Ka-32K heavy-lift version. Military variants include the Ka-32A-7 (Ka-327) maritime patrol variant with large external weapons pylons capable of carrying a pair of Kh-35 anti-shipping missiles. Kamov has also developed the Ka-29 army assault helicopter, first flown on 28th July 1976, which has a wider forward fuselage and external armament racks for up to four rocket launchers. The Ka-29RLD Helix-B (Ka-31) is a specialised airborne radar picket with large external forward fuselage housings containing an extendable E-801 flat sensor array. Several overseas air arms use this series of Kamov helicopters including Serbia (Ka-27PL) and a small batch of Ka-29s is being built under licence by KAPA in India.

Kamov Ka-32A, RA-31065

Specification	Kamov Ka-32A	
Powerplant	Two 2,190 s.h.p. (1,633 kW) Isotov/Klimov TV3-117V turboshafts	
Dimensions		
Rotor diameter (each)	15.9 m	(52 ft 2 in)
Length	12.25 m	(40 ft 2 in)
Height	5.4 m	(17 ft 8 in)
Performance		
Max speed	249 km/h	(135 kt, 155 mph)
Cruising speed	230 km/h	(124 kt, 143 mph)
Initial climb	1,204 m/min	(3,950 fpm)
Range	640 km	(348 nm, 400 miles)
Weights		
Max takeoff	12,700 kg	(28,003 lbs)
Useful load	5,900 kg	(13,009 lbs)

Kamov Ka-50 and Ka-52
— Russia

The Ka-50 Black Shark (also named Werewolf) was designed to meet a Soviet requirement for a dedicated single-seat anti-armour combat strike helicopter. It is highly manoeuvrable and has a conventional fuselage with a retractable tricycle undercarriage, stub wings which are primarily used as a mounting for four stores pylons to carry Vikhr anti-tank missiles, a tall fin/rudder and a tailplane with elevators set on the rear fuselage. Two Klimov TV3-117VMA turboshafts are mounted either side of the rotor mast housing. Kamov's coaxial rotor system is used, driving two sets of three composite rotors. The Ka-50 (NATO name 'Hokum-A') is heavily armoured and the pilot is housed in a cockpit in the nose which is fitted with an ejection seat. It is fully equipped with detection and jamming equipment and has a Shipunov 30 mm cannon mounted on the starboard fuselage side. The Ka-50 prototype first flew on 17th June 1982 and low-level production started in 1991 for the Russian Army but only a handful are in service. The Ka-50N, which first flew on 5th March 1997, is a night-attack variant with a nose-mounted Samshit-50 FLIR ball and cockpit TV display and NVG provision. The Ka-50-2 is a joint-venture development with Israel Aircraft Industries incorporating an advanced avionics suite. The Ka-52 Alligator (Hokum-B) is a side-by-side two-seat all-weather version, first flown on 25th June 1997 and currently under development.

Kamov Ka-50, 024

Specification	Kamov Ka-50	
Powerplant	Two 2,200 s.h.p. (1,640 kW) Klimov TV3-117VMA turboshafts	
Dimensions		
Rotor diameter (each)	14.43 m	(47 ft 4 in)
Length	15.98 m	(52 ft 5 in)
Height	4.93 m	(16 ft 2 in)
Performance		
Max speed	314 km/h	(170 kt, 195 mph)
Cruising speed	274 km/h	(148 kt, 170 mph)
Initial climb	864 m/min	(2,835 fpm)
Range	467 km	(252 nm, 290 miles)
Weights		
Max takeoff	10,800 kg	(23,814 lbs)
Useful load	3,110 kg	(6,858 lbs)

Kamov Ka-60 and Ka-62
— Russia

The Kamov OKB initiated the design of the Ka-60 general-purpose helicopter in 1990. It is externally similar to the Eurocopter SA.365N Dauphin with a conventional fuselage incorporating a tail fenestron stabilising rotor. It is powered by two RKRM Rybinsk RD-600V turboshafts mounted above the main cabin driving a normal single four-blade main rotor and it has a retractable tailwheel undercarriage. The main cabin can accommodate up to 14 passengers or ten troops with full equipment. The Ka-60 Kasatka, which first flew on 10th December 1998, is a military model and the Ka-62 is the civil version. The Ka-64 Sky Horse is a proposed variant with General Electric CT7 engines under development by Kamov and Agusta.

Kamov Ka-60, 601

Specification	Kamov Ka-62	
Powerplant	Two 1,300 s.h.p. (969 kW) RKRM Rybinsk RD-600V turboshafts	
Dimensions		
Rotor diameter	13.51 m	(44 ft 4 in)
Length	13.46 m	(44 ft 2 in)
Height	4.62 m	(15 ft 2 in)
Performance		
Max speed	298 km/h	(161 kt, 185 mph)
Cruising speed	274 km/h	(148 kt, 170 mph)
Initial climb	625 m/min	(2,050 fpm)
Range	1,160 km	(630 nm, 725 miles)
Weights		
Max takeoff	6,500 kg	(14,332 lbs)
Useful load	3,020 kg	(6,659 lbs)

Kappa Sova — Czech Republic

The KP-2U Sova, manufactured by the Czech company Kappa 77, is a two-seat all-metal light aircraft designed to fit within the ultralight category weight limit of 450 kg. It has a side-by-side fully enclosed cabin with dual controls and a rear baggage compartment with a forward-hinged blister canopy. The Sova is fitted with an electrically driven retracting tricycle undercarriage, the main units retracting rearwards into partially recessed wells. The aircraft has a maximum speed of 150 mph but a stall speed of 30 mph, thanks to large retractable slotted flaps and its new-technology wing with GAW-1 and GAW-2 aerofoil sections. Several engines can be fitted including the 75 h.p. Rotax 618UL or 80 h.p. Rotax 912UL. Over 20 KP-2Us had been built by mid-1999.

Kappa Sova

Specification	Kappa KP-2U Sova (Owl)	
Powerplant	One 80 h.p. (59.65 kW) Rotax 912UL piston engine	
Dimensions		
Span	9.9 m	(32 ft 6 in)
Length	7.2 m	(23 ft 7 in)
Height	2.6 m	(8 ft 6 in)
Performance		
Max speed	240 km/h	(129 kt, 149 mph)
Cruising speed	185 km/h	(100 kt, 115 mph)
Initial climb	390 m/min	(1,280 fpm)
Range	1,000 km	(539 nm, 621 miles)
Weights		
Max takeoff	450 kg	(992 lbs)
Useful load	190 kg	(419 lbs)

Kawasaki C-1 — Japan

Kawasaki's twin-turbofan C-1 is the standard medium transport aircraft for Japan's JASDF. Its design layout is broadly similar to many other aircraft with an upswept rear fuselage incorporating a ventral loading hatch and ramp, a high-set T-tail and a high wing which allows minimum incursion of the wingspar into the internal load space. Internal capacity is for up to 60 troops or 36 stretcher cases. The wing, which has anhedral, carries two underslung Pratt & Whitney JT8D turbofans. The retractable tricycle undercarriage of the C-1 utilises external fuselage fairings to contain the main units. Mitsubishi flew the prototype XC-1 on 12th November 1970 and by 1981 all 31 production C-1s had been delivered, most of which remain in service with two JASDF squadrons. The total includes two C-1SKE variants with station-keeping equipment and one C-1Kai (EC-1) with a large nose radome which is used as an ECM trainer. One C-1 has been converted as the NAL Asuka experimental STOL transport with blown flaps and four overwing turbofans. No C-1s have been sold to export customers.

Kawasaki C-1, JASDF, 58-1011

Specification	Kawasaki C-1	
Powerplant	Two 14,500 lb.s.t. (64.5 kN) Mitsubishi-Pratt & Whitney JT8D-M-9 turbofans	
Dimensions		
Span	30.6 m	(100 ft 5 in)
Length	29 m	(95 ft 2 in)
Height	10 m	(32 ft 9 in)
Performance		
Max speed	805 km/h	(435 kt, 500 mph)
Cruising speed	703 km/h	(380 kt, 437 mph)
Initial climb	1,065 m/min	(3,495 fpm)
Range	3,336 km	(1,813 nm, 2,085 miles)
Weights		
Max takeoff	45,000 kg	(99,225 lbs)
Useful load	20,700 kg	(45,643 lbs)

Kawasaki T-4 — Japan

The T-4 was designed by Kawasaki as a replacement for the JASDF jet training fleet of Lockheed T-33s and Fuji T-1s. In total 180 examples have been delivered since production started in 1988. The T-4 has a swept shoulder-set wing, a tricycle undercarriage retracting into the fuselage and a pair of I-H F3-IHI-30 turbofans attached to the lower centre fuselage. Two pylons are fitted under each wing to carry long-range tanks and a fuselage centreline hardpoint can be used for target-towing equipment. The student and instructor are housed in a tandem-seat pressurised and air-conditioned cockpit with a large blister canopy. Fuji flew the first prototype XT-4 on 29th July 1985 followed by a further three test aircraft. The T-4 is now the JASDF's principal trainer and is also used for general communications by operational squadrons and equips the Blue Impulse demonstration aerobatic team.

Kawasaki T-4, JASDF, 06-5640

Specification	Kawasaki T-4	
Powerplant	Two 3,680 lb.s.t. (16.37 kN) Ishikawajima-Harima F3-IHI-30 turbofans	
Dimensions		
Span	9.94 m	(32 ft 7 in)
Length	13 m	(42 ft 8 in)
Height	4.6 m	(15 ft 1 in)
Performance		
Max speed	1,038 km/h	(561 kt, 645 mph)
Cruising speed	917 km/h	(496 kt, 570 mph)
Initial climb	3,048 m/min	(10,000 fpm)
Range	1,280 km	(696 nm, 800 miles)
Weights		
Max takeoff	7,500 kg	(16,537 lbs)
Useful load	3,800 kg	(8,379 lbs)

Kawasaki OH-1 — Japan

The OH-1 is a light observation helicopter designed as an OH-6D replacement by a joint Kawasaki, Mitsubishi and Fuji team for the JGSDF. It is constructed of metal and composites and features include a stepped tandem two-seat cockpit, a fixed tailwheel undercarriage and a tail fenestron shrouded anti-torque rotor. The OH-1 has a small tailplane and small stub wings for carriage of sensors and light stores. Twin Mitsubishi TSI-10 turboshafts are mounted on either side of the main rotor pylon and the aircraft is fitted with a hingeless four-blade composite main rotor. The OH-1 is fitted with a FLIR pod above and behind the cockpit. The first of six planned XOH-1 prototypes was first flown on 6th August 1996 and testing is continuing at Gifu. The OH-1 airframe may also provide the basis for a new combat helicopter for the JGSDF.

Kawasaki OH-1, 2001

Specification	Kawasaki OH-1	
Powerplant	Two 884 s.h.p. (659 kW) Mitsubishi TSI-10 turboshafts	
Dimensions		
Rotor diameter	11.5 m	(37 ft 9 in)
Length	12 m	(39 ft 4 in)
Height	3.8 m	(12 ft 5 in)
Performance		
Max speed (est)	249 km/h	(135 kt, 155 mph)
Cruising speed (est)	225 km/h	(122 kt, 140 mph)
Initial climb (est)	366 m/min	(1,200 fpm)
Range	402 km	(217 nm, 250 miles)
Weights		
Max takeoff	3,500 kg	(7,717 lbs)
Useful load (est)	1,800 kg	(3,969 lbs)

Kazan Ansat — Tatarstan

The Ansat is a medium-sized general-purpose helicopter and development was initiated by Kazan in 1994. It is of conventional layout with a fuselage accommodation module, a tail boom carrying a stabilising rotor and a housing for the twin Pratt & Whitney PW206C turboshafts above the cabin. The Ansat has a fixed skid undercarriage and is fitted with a composite mast and four-blade main rotor. It is of metal and composite construction and has a fly-by-wire control system. Internal capacity is for up to nine passengers and two crew. The first of two prototypes made its first flight on 17th August 1999 and Kazan is working on FAR Part-29 certification.

Kazan Ansat (Cont.)

Kazan Ansat

Specification	Kazan Ansat	
Powerplant	Two 630 s.h.p. (470 kW) Klimov-Pratt & Whitney PW206C turboshafts	
Dimensions		
Rotor diameter	11.5 m	(37 ft 9 in)
Length	10.85 m	(35 ft 7 in)
Height	3.27 m	(10 ft 9 in)
Performance		
Max speed (est)	274 km/h	(148 kt, 170 mph)
Cruising speed (est)	249 km/h	(135 kt, 155 mph)
Initial climb (est)	427 m/min	(1,400 fpm)
Range (est)	563 km	(304 nm, 350 miles)
Weights		
Max takeoff	3,300 kg	(7,276 lbs)
Useful load (est)	1,900 kg	(4,189 lbs)

Kestrel K-250 — USA

Kestrel Aircraft Company of Norman, Oklahoma has designed a four-seat high-wing light aircraft which resembles the Cessna 182 Skylane and made its first flight on 19th November 1995. The KL-1A proof-of-concept prototype is of all-composite construction with a cantilever wing and a fixed tricycle undercarriage with spring-steel main legs. It is powered by a 160 h.p. Textron Lycoming O-320-D2G engine and will be produced as the Model K-160 but other variants will include the K-180 with a 180 h.p. O-360-A4M engine, the K-250 and military K-250M with a 250 h.p. IO-520-P and the six-seat K-325 with a 325 h.p. TSIO-550-B. Additionally, Kestrel plan the K-200RG with a retractable undercarriage and a 200 h.p. IO-360-ES engine. Development is continuing.

Kestrel KL-1A, N960KA

Specification	Kestrel KL-1A	
Powerplant	One 160 h.p. (119.3 kW) Textron Lycoming O-320-D2G piston engine	
Dimensions		
Span	11.2 m	(36 ft 9 in)
Length	8.16 m	(26 ft 9 in)
Height	2.73 m	(8 ft 11 in)
Performance		
Max speed	230 km/h	(124 kt, 143 mph)
Cruising speed	200 km/h	(108 kt, 124 mph)
Initial climb	213 m/min	(700 fpm)
Range	1,743 km	(946 nm, 1,089 miles)
Weights		
Max takeoff	1,134 kg	(2,500 lbs)
Useful load	510 kg	(1,125 lbs)

Klemm Kl.35 — Germany

The Kl.35 was the successor to the successful Klemm Kl.25 low-wing two-seat light aircraft which was produced in large numbers by several manufacturers (see also entry on BA Swallow). The Kl.35, which is of mixed construction, is a low-wing aircraft with two tandem open cockpits and a fixed tailwheel undercarriage. The wing is unusual in having anhedral on the centre section and dihedral on the tapered outer sections. The initial Kl.35A, introduced in 1935, was powered by an 80 h.p. Hirth HM.60R engine but the later Kl.35B had the larger 100 h.p. HM.504A-2. Many Kl.35s were produced with a built-up rear fuselage and enclosed cockpit and the type was also operated on skis and floats. The Kl.35D, which was a strengthened trainer version, was built in Sweden in the early 1940s for the Royal Swedish Air Force and several of the surviving Kl.35s are from this source.

Specification	Klemm Kl.35D	
Powerplant	One 100 h.p. (74.6 kW) Hirth HM.504A-2 piston engine	
Dimensions		
Span	10.39 m	(34 ft 1 in)
Length	7.49 m	(24 ft 7 in)
Height	2.03 m	(6 ft 8 in)
Performance		
Max speed	201 km/h	(109 kt, 125 mph)
Cruising speed	177 km/h	(96 kt, 110 mph)
Initial climb	183 m/min	(600 fpm)
Range	768 km	(417 nm, 480 miles)
Weights		
Max takeoff	703 kg	(1,550 lbs)
Useful load	304 kg	(670 lbs)

Klemm Kl.35D, D-ECCI

Krunichev T-411 Aist — Russia

The T-411 utility aircraft originated in a design initiated by Aeroprogress in September 1992 but it was developed by the Krunichev Design Bureau. The first T-411 flew on 10th November 1993 and the production prototype was first flown on 15th August 1997. Another T-411 was produced in 1994 and has been completed from a kit by a private owner in the USA. The T-411 is a strut-braced high-wing aircraft with a fixed spring-steel tailwheel undercarriage and a large five-seat cabin with a rear baggage compartment and external hatch which facilitates use of the aircraft for air ambulance operations. The structure is steel tube with fabric and light alloy covering and the T-411 is powered by a Voronezh M-14P radial engine although equivalent Continental or Lycoming engines may be fitted to production aircraft. Krunichev expects certification in 2001.

Krunichev T-411 Aist, RA-01585

Krunichev T-411 Aist (Cont.)

Specification	Krunichev T-411 Aist	
Powerplant	One 360 h.p. (268 kW) Voronezh M-14P piston engine	
Dimensions		
Span	13.02 m	(42 ft 9 in)
Length	9.45 m	(31 ft 0 in)
Height	2.53 m	(8 ft 4 in)
Performance		
Max speed	200 km/h	(108 kt, 124 mph)
Cruising speed	180 km/h	(97 kt, 112 mph)
Initial climb	244 m/min	(800 fpm)
Range	1,200 km	(652 nm, 750 miles)
Weights		
Max takeoff	1,600 kg	(3,528 lbs)
Useful load	560 kg	(1,235 lbs)

K&S Cavalier SA.102.5, G-BCRK

K & S Cavalier SA.102.3 — Canada

The Cavalier is a much-modified version of the CAB (Béarn) Minicab low-wing two-seat light aircraft (see also section on CAB Minicab). It is a plans-built wood and fabric amateur aircraft with a two-seat cabin which is longer than that of the Minicab and it has a swept tail unit, a spring-steel undercarriage and a much more streamlined appearance than the earlier aircraft. Two versions of the Cavalier have been designed: the SA.102.3 with either a tailwheel or tricycle undercarriage and a fuselage fuel tank and the SA.102.5 with wingtip tanks. The prototype Cavalier flew in 1964 and over 4,000 sets of plans have been sold by K & S Aircraft and its successors, Squaircraft, McAsco Aircraft and MacFam of Great Falls, Montana. A wide variety of engines can be fitted to the Cavalier ranging from the 85 h.p. Continental C85 to a 135 h.p. Lycoming O-290. A further version is the SA.105 Super Cavalier which is substantially redesigned and is larger with a roomier cabin and extra baggage space. It is powered by a 160 h.p. Lycoming IO-320 and has a retractable undercarriage. The SA.103 is a simplified version with a fixed tailwheel undercarriage and the SA.104 has tricycle gear.

Specification	K & S Cavalier SA.102.5	
Powerplant	One 125 h.p. (93.2 kW) Textron Lycoming O-290 piston engine	
Dimensions		
Span	8.33 m	(27 ft 4 in)
Length	6.71 m	(22 ft 0 in)
Height	2.23 m	(7 ft 4 in)
Performance		
Max speed	298 km/h	(161 kt, 185 mph)
Cruising speed	249 km/h	(135 kt, 155 mph)
Initial climb	518 m/min	(1,700 fpm)
Range	1,328 km	(722 nm, 830 miles)
Weights		
Max takeoff	680 kg	(1,500 lbs)
Useful load	272 kg	(600 lbs)

L

Laird LC-B Commercial — USA

The LC-B was the successor to the Swallow biplane, designed by E.M. 'Matty' Laird and built in some numbers in the 1920s. The prototype LC-B, which first flew in 1924, was a streamlined two-seat light biplane designed for private owners with tandem open cockpits and fixed tailwheel gear. The wings were straight and had virtually no stagger and the nine-cylinder Wright Whirlwind engine was uncowled but faired into the nose and equipped with a streamlined spinner to minimise drag. Total production of the LC-B, some of which were powered by Curtiss OX-5 or C-6 engines, was over 36 aircraft and at least two are currently airworthy in the USA.

Laird LC-B Commercial, C-110

Specification	Laird LC-B Commercial	
Powerplant	One 220 h.p. (164 kW) Wright J.5 Whirlwind piston engine	
Dimensions		
Span	10.36 m	(34 ft 0 in)
Length	7.24 m	(23 ft 9 in)
Height	2.82 m	(9 ft 3 in)
Performance		
Max speed	209 km/h	(113 kt, 130 mph)
Cruising speed	177 km/h	(96 kt, 110 mph)
Initial climb	305 m/min	(1,000 fpm)
Range	1,040 km	(565 nm, 650 miles)
Weights		
Max takeoff	1,293 kg	(2,850 lbs)
Useful load	476 kg	(1,050 lbs)

Lake LA-4 and LA-250 Renegade — USA

The Lake LA-4 has been the world's leading mass-production light amphibian for many years. Originally designed as the Colonial C-1 Skimmer, the Lake is an all-metal aircraft with a cantilever shoulder wing, a cruciform tail and a Lycoming engine mounted on a pylon above the wing centre section. It has an enclosed three-seat cabin and a tricycle undercarriage with the main units retracting into the wing. The C-1, first flown on 17th July 1948, had a 150 h.p. O-320-A2A engine but the four-seat C-2 had a 180 h.p. O-360-A1A. Colonial built 42 aircraft before Lake Aircraft introduced the LA-4A with longer wings, a stronger airframe and other improvements. The LA-4-200 Buccaneer is a more powerful version with a 200 h.p. Lycoming IO-360, the LA-4-200EP has an extended propeller shaft and the LA-4-200EPR has a reversible propeller to assist manoeuvring. In total, 874 LA-4s were built before production ceased in 1986. The LA-4 was followed by the LA-250 Renegade which has a 38-inch longer fuselage, a larger five-/six-seat cabin and many modifications, including a restyled vertical tail and a 250 h.p. Lycoming IO-540 engine. It has also been built as the LA-250 Turbo with a turbocharged TIO-540-AA1AD engine and as the Turbo Renegade 270 with a 270 h.p. TIO-540. Lake's principal current production model is the LA-250 Seawolf military patrol aircraft with strengthened wings incorporating four hardpoints, a radar mounted on the engine nacelle and a 290 h.p. engine. More than 150 of the LA-250 series have been built.

Lake LA-4-200EP, N41EP

Lake LA-270, TG-WET

Specification	Lake LA-270 Turbo Renegade	
Powerplant	One 270 h.p. (201.3 kW) Textron Lycoming TIO-540-AA1AD piston engine	
Dimensions		
Span	11.7 m	(38 ft 4 in)
Length	8.64 m	(28 ft 4 in)
Height	3.04 m	(10 ft 0 in)
Performance		
Max speed	287 km/h	(155 kt, 178 mph)
Cruising speed	268 km/h	(145 kt, 167 mph)
Initial climb	274 m/min	(900 fpm)
Range	2,066 km	(1,120 nm, 1,290 miles)
Weights		
Max takeoff	1,424 kg	(3,140 lbs)
Useful load	483 kg	(1,065 lbs)

Lancair 320/360 — USA

Designed by Lance Neibauer, the Lancair is a high-performance two-seat kit-built aircraft which has been constructed by amateurs in many countries and is sold by Lancair International Inc. (formerly Neico). First flown in June 1984 as the Lancer 200, the aircraft is constructed from pre-moulded fibreglass shells and it has a retractable tricycle undercarriage and a fully enclosed side-by-side two-seat cabin. Early Lancairs had a 100 h.p. Continental O-200 engine but the main versions are the Lancair 235, introduced in 1985 with a 160 h.p. Lycoming O-320, and the similar Lancair 320. The Lancair 360 was a higher-powered version with a 180 h.p. Lycoming and constant speed propeller. These have become the Lancair 320/360 Mk.II with a larger fuselage and modified landing gear. In July 1999 Lancair introduced the new Legacy 2000 which has a larger cabin and greater baggage capacity and is powered by a 200 h.p. turbocharged Lycoming IO-360. Over 1,000 of the Lancair 320 series kits have been sold and approximately 200 two-seat Lancairs are flying.

Lancair 360, N594CL

Specification	Lancair 360	
Powerplant	One 180 h.p. (134 kW) Textron Lycoming O-360-A1A piston engine	
Dimensions		
Span	7.16 m	(23 ft 6 in)
Length	6.4 m	(21 ft 0 in)
Height	2.13 m	(7 ft 0 in)
Performance		
Max speed	418 km/h	(226 kt, 260 mph)
Cruising speed	386 km/h	(209 kt, 240 mph)
Initial climb	823 m/min	(2,700 fpm)
Range	2,320 km	(1,261 nm, 1,450 miles)
Weights		
Max takeoff	764 kg	(1,685 lbs)
Useful load	270 kg	(595 lbs)

Lancair IV — USA

Following on from the success of the composite kit-built Lancair 320, Lance Neibauer designed a completely new aircraft: the Lancair IV. While retaining the same general layout and wing design of the earlier aircraft, the Lancair IV, announced in June 1990, has a completely new carbon-fibre composite fuselage with a four-seat cabin and a new undercarriage with rearward-retracting main legs. It is powered by a 350 h.p. Continental TSIO-550 engine which makes it one of the fastest single-piston-engined aircraft and gives it a cruise speed in excess of 350 mph. The Lancair IV has gained several performance records. A pressurised version, the Lancair IVP, is also sold by Lancair, some of which have been fitted with substantially larger engines and they have built a prototype of the two-seat Tigress, based on the Lancair IV with a 650 h.p., Orenda V-8 engine, although this was not put into production.

Lancair IV, N409L

Specification	Lancair IV	
Powerplant	One 350 h.p. (261 kW) Teledyne Continental TSIO-550-B1B piston engine	
Dimensions		
Span	9.19 m	(30 ft 2 in)
Length	7.62 m	(25 ft 0 in)
Height	2.44 m	(8 ft 0 in)
Performance		
Max speed	587 km/h	(317 kt, 365 mph)
Cruising speed	531 km/h	(287 kt, 330 mph)
Initial climb	762 m/min	(2,500 fpm)
Range	2,320 km	(1,261 nm, 1,450 miles)
Weights		
Max takeoff	1,542 kg	(3,400 lbs)
Useful load	635 kg	(1,400 lbs)

Lancair Columbia 300 — USA

The Columbia is a factory-complete production aircraft based on the earlier Lancair kit-built two- and four-seat light aircraft. In July 1992, Lancair flew the prototype Lancair ES which was a simplified version of the earlier four-seat Lancair IV with a larger wing and built from epoxy/glass composites. Powered by a 210 h.p. Continental IO-360-ES engine, over 130 kits have been sold and the optional Super ES is also available with a 300 h.p. IO-550G engine. Lancair developed this design into the LC-40 Columbia 300 which is a fully certificated model and first flew in early 1996. The Columbia 300 has the same fixed undercarriage as the ES but is powered by a 300 h.p. Continental IO-550 which allows it to outperform equivalent retractable gear types. It has a modern cockpit with sidestick controls and modern avionics. The first customer delivery of a Columbia was made in 1999. Lancair is also developing the Columbia 400 which is powered by a 310 h.p. turbocharged Continental TS10-550-G engine.

Lancair Columbia 300, N142LC

Specification	Lancair Columbia 300	
Powerplant	One 300 h.p. (223.68 kW) Teledyne Continental IO-550-N1B piston engine	
Dimensions		
Span	11 m	(36 ft 1 in)
Length	7.67 m	(25 ft 2 in)
Height	2.44 m	(8 ft 0 in)
Performance		
Max speed	378 km/h	(204 kt, 235 mph)
Cruising speed	354 km/h	(191 kt, 220 mph)
Initial climb	408 m/min	(1,340 fpm)
Range	2,028 km	(1,100 nm, 1,267 miles)
Weights		
Max takeoff	1,542 kg	(3,400 lbs)
Useful load	884 kg	(1,950 lbs)

Learjet 23 to 36 — USA

The Learjet 23 was the first of the light business jets and it has carved itself an important place in aviation history. The brainchild of the inventor Bill Lear, it is a highly streamlined design with a straight low wing derived from the Swiss FFA P-16 fighter, a T-tail with a prominent "bullet" fairing, wingtip fuel tanks and twin General Electric CJ610-4 turbines mounted side-by-side on the rear fuselage. Accommodation is for two crew and up to six passengers. The prototype first flew on 7th October 1963 and first production deliveries took place the following year. Some 105 Learjet 23s were built before it was replaced by the higher-weight Learjet 24 with CJ610-6 engines. The Learjet 24C and 24D had a modified fin without the bullet fairing and square windows in place of the earlier semi-oval cabin windows. Gates Learjet, as the company became in 1968, introduced the Learjet 25 which first flew on 12th August 1966 and was a Model 24 with a stretched fuselage with up to eight cabin seats. In total, 626 Learjet 24s and 25s were built. A handful of Learjet 28s and 29s were produced with a modified wing with winglets but the replacement for the Model 24/25 was the Model 35 (and long-range six-passenger Model 36) which was based on the Learjet 25 with a further fuselage stretch, longer wings and two Garrett-AiResearch (now Honeywell) TFE731-2 turbofans. Some 735 of the Model 35/36 were built including 83 C-21As delivered to the USAF. The current model, which replaced the 35/36 in 1991, is the Learjet 31A which is a Model 35 with Model 55 wings with winglets (and no tip tanks), ventral rear delta fins, additional cabin windows and an upgraded EFIS cockpit. A total of 200 Learjet 31s had been delivered by the spring of 2000.

Learjet 23, N77VJ

Specification	Learjet 31A	
Powerplant	Two 3,500 lb.s.t. (15.56 kN) Honeywell (Garrett) TFE731-2 turbofans	
Dimensions		
Span	13.4 m	(43 ft 10 in)
Length	14.8 m	(48 ft 8 in)
Height	3.75 m	(12 ft 4 in)
Performance		
Max speed	858 km/h	(463 kt, 533 mph)
Cruising speed	849 km/h	(458 kt, 527 mph)
Takeoff distance	1,000 m	(3,280 ft)
Range	2,690 km	(1,460 nm, 1,681 miles)
Weights		
Max takeoff	7,484 kg	(16,500 lbs)
Useful load	2,431 kg	(5,360 lbs)

Learjet 35A, N85645

Learjet 55 and 60 — USA

The Learjet 55, which first flew on 19th April 1979, was a mid-sized business jet with the same general layout as the smaller Learjet 24 and 25 but with a larger and longer fuselage providing an eight-/ten-passenger cabin. The 'longhorn' wing was a new design and the wingtip tanks used on earlier models were replaced with prominent winglets with all fuel being situated in fuselage tanks. The Model 55, which was powered by two 3,700 lb.s.t. Garrett AiResearch TFE731-3A turbofans, retained the familiar Learjet T-tail. First deliveries took place in 1981 and the later Model 55B had a modernised cockpit, higher weights and thrust reversers, and the 55C was further developed with rear ventral delta fins and modified engine mountings. As the 55XLR, it had additional long-range fuel tanks. The Model 60, which flew on 13th June 1991, replaced the Learjet 55 from January 1993 and had a longer fuselage with two extra seats, modernised avionics and two Pratt & Whitney PW305 turbofans. The Model 60 remains in production at Learjet (now part of the Bombardier Group). In total, 147 Model 55s and 185 Learjet 60s had been built by early 2000.

Specification	Learjet Model 60	
Powerplant	Two 4,600 lb.s.t. (20.46 kN) Pratt & Whitney PW305A turbofans	
Dimensions		
Span	13.33 m	(43 ft 9 in)
Length	17.9 m	(58 ft 8 in)
Height	4.44 m	(14 ft 8 in)
Performance		
Max speed	859 km/h	(464 kt, 534 mph)
Cruising speed	839 km/h	(453 kt, 522 mph)
Takeoff distance	1,661 m	(5,450 ft)
Range	4,605 km	(2,503 nm, 2,878 miles)
Weights		
Max takeoff	10,657 kg	(23,500 lbs)
Useful load	4,019 kg	(8,860 lbs)

Learjet 60, N6100

Learjet 45 — USA

While the Learjet 45 is externally similar to the earlier Learjet series it is a completely new model which fits between the entry-level Model 31A and the larger Model 60. It has a redesigned wing with tip winglets, a deeper nine-place cabin than that of the Model 31A and substantially improved payload/range performance and handling characteristics. The Model 45 is equipped with an integrated avionics and flight instrumentation system. The prototype was first flown on 7th October 1995 and certificated in May 1998 with first deliveries taking place in that month. More than 80 were in service by the end of 2000.

Learjet 45, N456LJ

Specification	Learjet Model 45	
Powerplant	Two 3,500 lb.s.t. (15.56 kN) Honeywell (Garrett) TFE731-20 turbofans	
Dimensions		
Span	14.6 m	(47 ft 10 in)
Length	17.8 m	(58 ft 5 in)
Height	4.4 m	(14 ft 4 in)
Performance		
Max speed	867 km/h	(468 kt, 539 mph)
Cruising speed	846 km/h	(457 kt, 526 mph)
Takeoff distance	1,326 m	(4,350 ft)
Range	3,906 km	(2,120 nm, 2,440 miles)
Weights		
Max takeoff	9,299 kg	(20,500 lbs)
Useful load	3,265 kg	(7,200 lbs)

Legrand-Simon LS.60 — France

The LS.50 Dauphin was designed by P. Legrand and M. Simon who flew the prototype on 13th January 1957. It was an attractive strut-braced high-wing aircraft with a tailwheel undercarriage and a fully enclosed cabin with side-by-side seating for two. The Dauphin was constructed from wood, steel tube, fabric and fibreglass and powered by a 90 h.p. Continental C90 engine. With a view to a production model for use as a club trainer and glider tug, Legrand and Simon produced the improved LS.60 which flew on 27th April 1961 and this had a more angular tail unit, a wider cabin with bulged door panels, a cantilever undercarriage and a modified wing with flaps and leading-edge slats which gave the LS.60 excellent short-field performance. The LS.60 did not reach production but the prototype remains active in France.

Legrand-Simon LS.60, F-PJSA

Specification	Legrand-Simon LS.60	
Powerplant	One 90 h.p. (67.1 kW) Teledyne Continental C90-14F piston engine	
Dimensions		
Span	9.68 m	(31 ft 9 in)
Length	6.02 m	(19 ft 9 in)
Height	2.03 m	(6 ft 8 in)
Performance		
Max speed	185 km/h	(100 kt, 115 mph)
Cruising speed	169 km/h	(91 kt, 105 mph)
Initial climb	239 m/min	(785 fpm)
Range	696 km	(378 nm, 435 miles)
Weights		
Max takeoff	710 kg	(1,565 lbs)
Useful load	245 kg	(540 lbs)

Leopoldoff Colibri — France

The little Leopoldoff L.3 biplane was originally designed in 1932 by M.L. Leopoldoff. It is a tandem two-seater intended for use as an economical club trainer and sporting aircraft, and the prototype first flew at Toussus le Noble on 27th September 1933. The production Colibri was built by Aucouturier-Dugoua & Cie. and, later, by the Société des Avions Leopoldoff and 33 were completed, equipped with the 45 h.p. Salmson 9Adb radial engine. The L.31 was an L.3 retrospectively fitted with a 50 h.p. Boitel 5Ao engine, and the L.32 had a Walter Mikron III. Postwar production was carried out by the Société des Constructions Aéronautiques du Maroc who built six aircraft (as the CAM-1). The L.53 and L.55 were variants with 75 h.p. Minié and Continental C90 engines respectively. Three Colibris are currently active in France and one L.7, powered by a Continental A65-8S engine, flies in the UK.

Leopoldoff L.7 Colibri, G-AYKS

Specification	Leopoldoff L.55 Colibri	
Powerplant	One 90 h.p. (67.1 kW) Teledyne Continental C90-12F piston engine	
Dimensions		
Span	8.94 m	(29 ft 4 in)
Length	5.92 m	(19 ft 5 in)
Height	2.11 m	(6 ft 11 in)
Performance		
Max speed	174 km/h	(94 kt, 108 mph)
Cruising speed	153 km/h	(83 kt, 95 mph)
Initial climb	152 m/min	(500 fpm)
Range	448 km	(243 nm, 280 miles)
Weights		
Max takeoff	519 kg	(1,144 lbs)
Useful load	492 kg	(1,085 lbs)

LET Aero 45

— Czechoslovakia

The first postwar aircraft produced by the Aero factory in Prague was the Aero 45 light transport and utility model. It was a low-wing light twin of all-metal construction with a streamlined forward fuselage incorporating a four-/five-seat cabin and a retractable tailwheel undercarriage. The first flight took place on 21st July 1947 and by 1951 200 had been sold, mainly to Soviet bloc users but including a few to western European customers. It was powered by two 105 h.p. Walter Minor 4-III engines. LET took over the design from Aero and introduced the Aero 45S Super with higher weights and improved equipment. The later Super Aero 145 had improved performance due to its 140 h.p. Walter M-332 engines. A total of 228 Ae-45S and approximately 142 Ae-145s were built and a number of these continue in service with private owners in Europe and the USA.

LET Super Aero 145, OM-NHS

Specification	LET Super Aero 145	
Powerplant	Two 140 h.p. (104.38 kW) Walter M-332 piston engines	
Dimensions		
Span	12.24 m	(40 ft 2 in)
Length	7.77 m	(25 ft 6 in)
Height	2.29 m	(7 ft 6 in)
Performance		
Max speed	282 km/h	(152 kt, 175 mph)
Cruising speed	249 km/h	(135 kt, 155 mph)
Initial climb	300 m/min	(985 fpm)
Range	1,680 km	(913 nm, 1,050 miles)
Weights		
Max takeoff	1,499 kg	(3,305 lbs)
Useful load	540 kg	(1,190 lbs)

LET L-60 Brigadyr — Czechoslovakia

LET flew the prototype L-60 Brigadyr on 24th December 1953 and subsequently built 273 aircraft before production ceased in 1968. The Brigadyr was designed as a multi-purpose light aircraft for Soviet bloc countries for use as a light transport, air taxi and air ambulance aircraft. A substantial number were used for crop spraying and the Czech Air Force received a batch for army liaison use. The Brigadyr is of all-metal construction with a strut-braced high wing and strutted tailwheel undercarriage. The four-seat cabin has all-round transparencies and the Brigadyr is powered by a 220 h.p. Praga Doris B engine. In most cases, surviving Brigadyrs have been converted to L-60S standard with a 260 h.p. Ivchenko AI-14RA radial engine or to the L-60SF with an M-462-RF engine. Several dozen Brigadyrs remain in service, mainly in the Czech Republic and Slovakia where the type is used as a glider tug.

L-60SF Brigadyr, OK-KJA

Specification	LET Brigadyr L-60S	
Powerplant	One 260 h.p. (193.86 kW) Ivchenko AI-14RA piston engine	
Dimensions		
Span	13.94 m	(45 ft 9 in)
Length	8.46 m	(27 ft 9 in)
Height	2.72 m	(8 ft 11 in)
Performance		
Max speed	209 km/h	(113 kt, 130 mph)
Cruising speed	185 km/h	(100 kt, 115 mph)
Initial climb	259 m/min	(850 fpm)
Range	704 km	(383 nm, 440 miles)
Weights		
Max takeoff	1,560 kg	(3,440 lbs)
Useful load	590 kg	(1,300 lbs)

LET L-200 Morava — Czechoslovakia

The Morava was designed in 1956 by LET as a replacement for the ageing Aero 45 light twin. It was an elegant all-metal low-wing aircraft with a retractable tricycle undercarriage, twin tailfins and a straight wing with wingtip tanks. The five-seat cabin had a domed roof allowing all-round vision and the initial L-200 was powered by two 160 h.p. Walter Minor 6-III in-line engines. The prototype flew on 9th April 1957 and ten L-200s were built followed by 151 L-200As with 210 h.p. M-337 supercharged engines. LET (later named SPP) then built 196 L-200D Moravas which had increased useful load and electrically driven constant-speed propellers. Five Moravas were also built in Yugoslavia by LIBIS. A number of Moravas were used for military purposes, although all have now been withdrawn, but a significant number of civil Moravas are still active in the Czech Republic and in Sweden, Russia, Hungary and Poland.

LET L-200 Morava, SE-LAG

Specification	LET L-200D Morava	
Powerplant	Two 210 h.p. (156.58 kW) Walter M-337 piston engines	
Dimensions		
Span	12.31 m	(40 ft 4 in)
Length	8.61 m	(28 ft 3 in)
Height	2.25 m	(7 ft 4 in)
Performance		
Max speed	311 km/h	(168 kt, 193 mph)
Cruising speed	294 km/h	(159 kt, 183 mph)
Initial climb	480 m/min	(1,575 fpm)
Range	1,888 km	(1,026 nm, 1,180 miles)
Weights		
Max takeoff	1,950 kg	(4,300 lbs)
Useful load	676 kg	(1,490 lbs)

LET Z-37 Cmelak — Czechoslovakia

Agricultural aircraft were widely used in the Soviet bloc countries during the 1950s and 1960s and the Cmelak (Bumble Bee) was designed by LET (SPP) to replace existing types such as the Brigadyr and to provide higher hopper load capacity. The Cmelak is a low-wing aircraft of simple tube, fabric and light alloy construction with a fixed tailwheel undercarriage and a 700-litre hopper mounted directly behind the enclosed cabin. It could be fitted with either spray bars for liquid chemicals or a dry material spreader unit under the centre fuselage. The prototype XZ-37 flew, powered by a 310 h.p. Ivchenko AI-14VF radial engine, on 29th June 1963 but the production Z-37 was fitted with a 315 h.p. Walter M-462RF radial engine. LET built a total of 713 Cmelaks, the majority being the Z-37A with a strengthened airframe, and they were delivered to most eastern bloc countries and are still in widespread service. A number of Z-37A-2 trainers were also completed with a longer cabin with tandem seating for two. On 3rd September 1981, LET flew the first XZ-37T which had a longer fuselage, higher weights and a 690 s.h.p. Walter M-601B turboprop engine. The production Z-37T (later Z-137T) Agro-Turbo had the lower-powered 485 s.h.p. Motorlet M-601Z, a larger fin and wingtip winglets. Around 50 Z-37Ts have been built.

Specification	LET Z-37 Cmelak	
Powerplant	One 315 h.p. (234.86 kW) Walter M-462RF piston engine	
Dimensions		
Span	12.22 m	(40 ft 1 in)
Length	8.55 m	(28 ft 1 in)
Height	2.89 m	(9 ft 6 in)
Performance		
Max speed	193 km/h	(104 kt, 120 mph)
Cruising speed	180 km/h	(97 kt, 112 mph)
Initial climb	282 m/min	(925 fpm)
Range	640 km	(348 nm, 400 miles)
Weights		
Max takeoff	1,725 kg	(3,804 lbs)
Useful load	755 kg	(1,665 lbs)

LET Z-37 Cmelak, OM-OJN

LET Z-137T Agro-Turbo, OK-XJA

LET L-410 and L-420 — Czech Republic

LET designed the L-410 Turbolet as a replacement for the large fleet of Ilyushin Il-12s which operated in the Soviet bloc countries, and flew the prototype XL-410 on 16th April 1969. The production L-410A is a high-wing light transport with a circular-section fuselage providing a 19-passenger unpressurised main cabin. It has a cruciform tail and a retractable tricycle undercarriage with the main units retracting into external fuselage fairings. It is powered by two wing-mounted Pratt & Whitney PT6A-27 engines. Early deliveries were to Aeroflot as the L-410AS and large numbers of the various Turbolet models were exported to the Soviet Union. Only 30 PT6A-powered aircraft were built before the L-410M was introduced with 550 s.h.p. Motorlet M601A turboprops. Variants included the military L-410FG, the L-410MA with 730 s.h.p. M601B engines and the L-410MU equipped for Aeroflot, and the Turbolet is in large-scale use for local passenger services, parachute dropping and freighting. The L-410UVP, which is the largest production version, has a longer fuselage, larger wing and fin, a dihedralled tailplane and improved cockpit systems. It first flew on 1st November 1977. The later L-410UVP-E has wingtip tanks and 750 s.h.p. M601E engines, and the current L-420 is a westernised version with 778 s.h.p. M601F engines which has been marketed in the USA by LET's new owners, Ayres Corporation. Total Turbolet production to date exceeds 1,100 aircraft.

LET-410FG Turbolet, Czech AF, 0928

Specification	LET L-420	
Powerplant	Two 778 s.h.p. (580 kW) Motorlet M601F turboprops	
Dimensions		
Span	19.98 m	(65 ft 7 in)
Length	14.42 m	(47 ft 4 in)
Height	5.83 m	(19 ft 2 in)
Performance		
Max speed	384 km/h	(207 kt, 239 mph)
Cruising speed	370 km/h	(199 kt, 230 mph)
Initial climb	420 m/min	(1,378 fpm)
Range	1,350 km	(732 nm, 844 miles)
Weights		
Max takeoff	6,600 kg	(14,553 lbs)
Useful load	2,535 kg	(5,590 lbs)

Specification	LET L-610G	
Powerplant	Two 1,750 s.h.p. (1,305 kW) General Electric CT7-9D turboprops	
Dimensions		
Span	25.6 m	(83 ft 11 in)
Length	21.72 m	(71 ft 3 in)
Height	8.19 m	(26 ft 10 in)
Performance		
Max speed	450 km/h	(242 kt, 280 mph)
Cruising speed	438 km/h	(236 kt, 272 mph)
Initial climb	510 m/min	(1,673 fpm)
Range	2,420 km	(1,315 nm, 1,513 miles)
Weights		
Max takeoff	15,000 kg	(33,075 lbs)
Useful load	5,400 kg	(11,907 lbs)

LET L-610G — Czech Republic

The L-610 was designed by LET to the requirements of Aeroflot to provide greater capacity than was available with the L-410 Turbolet. The L-610 has a similar layout to that of the L-410 and is a high-wing aircraft with a T-tail and a retractable undercarriage using fuselage-mounted pods for the main gear. It has a pressurised 44-seat main cabin but can be equipped for mixed passenger/cargo operations. The prototype was flown on 30th December 1988 powered by two Motorlet M602 turboprops which are fitted to the L-610M variant, six of which are being delivered to the Czech Air Force. The commercial L-610G is powered by General Electric CT7-9D engines with four-blade Hamilton Standard propellers and is fitted with modern western Rockwell Collins Proline avionics. LET, through its owner, Ayres Corporation, announced plans to market this for commuter airlines as the Ayres 7000 and the first commercial sale, to Burundi, was made in late 1999 at which time 11 L-610s had been built.

LET-MONT Tulák and Piper UL — Czech Republic

The Tulák and Piper UL are ultralight aircraft modelled on the Piper Cub and designed by LET-MONT. They are sold either as kits or in factory-complete form. The Tulák is a side-by-side two-seater with a fully enclosed cabin and strut-braced high wing. The Piper UL is a tandem two-seat version with a narrower fuselage. Both aircraft have a steel tube and fabric fuselage and a fixed tailwheel undercarriage, and the wings, which are wood and fabric, are foldable on the Tulák. They are designed to fly with a Rotax 503 or 912 engine, although other powerplants of under 90 h.p. can be fitted. Examples of both versions are flying in the Czech Republic and in France.

LET L-610G, OK-CZD

LET-MONT Tulák, 57-NX

LET-MONT Tulák and Piper UL (Cont.)

Specification	LET-MONT Tulák	
Powerplant	One 80 h.p. (59.65 kW) Rotax 912 piston engine	
Dimensions		
Span	9.6 m	(31 ft 6 in)
Length	5.6 m	(18 ft 4 in)
Height	2 m	(6 ft 7 in)
Performance		
Max speed	160 km/h	(86 kt, 99 mph)
Cruising speed	135 km/h	(73 kt, 84 mph)
Initial climb	300 m/min	(984 fpm)
Range	600 km	(323 nm, 373 miles)
Weights		
Max takeoff	450 kg	(992 lbs)
Useful load	220 kg	(485 lbs)

Le Vier Cosmic Wind — USA

The tiny Cosmic Wind midget racer was designed and built by Tony Le Vier and a group of Lockheed engineers. Three aircraft named *Minnow*, *Little Toni* and *Ballerina* were built by the group in 1947/48 with a fourth (*Miss Cosmic Wind*) being completed later and a fifth being built by an amateur constructor. Another example was constructed in the UK in 1972 and two of the US-built aircraft were imported into the UK and raced during the 1960s with *Ballerina* winning the 1964 King's Cup. The Cosmic Wind is an all-metal low-wing monoplane with a fixed cantilever tailwheel undercarriage and a single-seat cockpit with a transparent blister canopy. The aircraft were initially powered by an 85 h.p. Continental C85 engine but the two active UK examples have the 100 h.p. Continental O-200-A engine.

Le Vier Cosmic Wind, G-ARUL

Specification	Le Vier Cosmic Wind	
Powerplant	One 85 h.p. (63.3 kW) Teledyne Continental C85 piston engine	
Dimensions		
Span	5.77 m	(18 ft 11 in)
Length	5.08 m	(16 ft 8 in)
Height	1.3 m	(4 ft 3 in)
Performance		
Max speed	298 km/h	(161 kt, 185 mph)
Cruising speed	257 km/h	(139 kt, 160 mph)
Initial climb	762 m/min	(2,500 fpm)
Range	512 km	(278 nm, 320 miles)
Weights		
Max takeoff	385 kg	(850 lbs)
Useful load	141 kg	(310 lbs)

Light Wing GA-55 — Australia

The Light Wing (also known as the Australian Light Wing and the Hughes Light Wing) was designed by C.W. Whitney and first flown in June 1986. It is a side-by-side two-seat ultralight with a conventional strut-braced high-wing layout and a fixed tailwheel undercarriage. The basic model, sold as a kit or in factory-finished form, was the Light Wing GR-582 powered by a 63 h.p. Rotax 582 engine, but the aircraft is also available as the Light Wing GR-912 with an 80 h.p. Rotax 912 engine. The GA-55 is a further version first flown in March 1987 at a 450 kg gross weight permitted under revised Australian regulations and it is powered by a 78 h.p. Aeropower engine. Over 150 Light Wings had been built by the end of 1998.

Light Wing GA-55, 25-374

Specification	Hughes Light Wing GA-55	
Powerplant	One 78 h.p. (58.2 kW) Aeropower piston engine	
Dimensions		
Span	9.09 m	(29 ft 10 in)
Length	5.69 m	(18 ft 8 in)
Height	1.9 m	(6 ft 3 in)
Performance		
Max speed	148 km/h	(80 kt, 92 mph)
Cruising speed	137 km/h	(74 kt, 85 mph)
Initial climb	122 m/min	(400 fpm)
Range	400 km	(217 nm, 250 miles)
Weights		
Max takeoff	500 kg	(1,102 lbs)
Useful load	220 kg	(485 lbs)

Lincoln PT-K — USA

In the period between the wars a considerable number of biplane trainers appeared on the American market, one of these being the Lincoln-Page PT which was a successor to the Lincoln-Page LP-3 and was certificated in 1929. It was a wood, tube and fabric design with a long narrow fuselage and the main undercarriage legs were set well forward of the lower wing. It had straight unstaggered wings and two tandem cockpits positioned under the wing centre section, and was fitted with a 90 h.p. Curtiss OX-5 engine. Around 32 were built and these were followed by 17 examples of the Lincoln PT-K with a 100 h.p. Kinner K5 radial engine and two-blade wooden propeller, and a few PT-Ws with a 110 h.p. Warner Scarab. They also produced a small batch of the PT-T with a Brownback Tiger engine. In total, around 62 PTs and 156 LP-3s were completed and four of the PT series are registered in the USA.

Lincoln PT-W, NC20731

Specification	Lincoln-Page PT-K	
Powerplant	One 100 h.p. (74.6 kW) Kinner K5 piston engine	
Dimensions		
Span	9.83 m	(32 ft 3 in)
Length	7.8 m	(25 ft 7 in)
Height	2.74 m	(9 ft 0 in)
Performance		
Max speed	167 km/h	(90 kt, 104 mph)
Cruising speed	137 km/h	(74 kt, 85 mph)
Initial climb	244 m/min	(800 fpm)
Range	528 km	(287 nm, 330 miles)
Weights		
Max takeoff	801 kg	(1,767 lbs)
Useful load	268 kg	(591 lbs)

Lockheed 10A and 12A
— USA

The Lockheed 10 Electra was one of the first of the modern all-metal monocoque twin-engined transport aircraft launched in the 1930s and used to develop modern, reliable public air transport. Designed by Lockheed's Hall Hibbard, the Electra was an elegant and efficient low-wing monoplane with a straight tapered wing, a twin-fin tail unit and a retractable tailwheel undercarriage. Its cabin could accommodate ten passengers and it was powered by two 450 h.p. Pratt & Whitney Wasp Junior radial engines which allowed it to cruise at nearly 200 mph. The prototype Lockheed 10A first flew on 23rd February 1934 with first deliveries shortly thereafter, and later variants included the 10B with 440 h.p. Wright R-975-E3 engines, the 10C with 450 h.p. Wasp SC.1s and the 10E with 600 h.p. Wasp S3H1s. In US military service impressed Electras were designated C-36. A total of 148 production Model 10s were delivered to airlines such as Northwest Airways, Pan American, Braniff and Eastern Air Lines. The Model 12 Electra Junior was a scaled-down version of the Model 10 with a six-seat main cabin, intended for air taxi, executive use and feeder services. First flown on 27th June 1936, the Model 12 was faster than the Model 10. Of the 130 aircraft built, 57 were exported, the majority for military use by the Netherlands East Indies government and most of the remainder went to companies and private individuals although seven JO-2s went to the US Navy and three C-40s were sold to the USAAC. Most were Model 12As with two 450 h.p. Wasp SB engines, but a handful of 12Bs with 440 h.p. Wright R-975-E3D engines and Model 12-25s with Wasp SB.3 engines were also sold. Some 22 Model 12As are registered in the USA and at least four Model 10s are airworthy including one in Australia.

Lockheed 10A Electra, VH-UZO

Lockheed 12A, N112LN

Lockheed 10A and 12A (Cont.)

Specification	Lockheed 12A	
Powerplant	Two 450 h.p. (335.5 kW) Pratt & Whitney Wasp Junior SB piston engines	
Dimensions		
Span	15.09 m	(49 ft 6 in)
Length	11.07 m	(36 ft 4 in)
Height	2.97 m	(9 ft 9 in)
Performance		
Max speed	362 km/h	(196 kt, 225 mph)
Cruising speed	346 km/h	(187 kt, 215 mph)
Initial climb	427 m/min	(1,400 fpm)
Range	1,280 km	(696 nm, 800 miles)
Weights		
Max takeoff	3,923 kg	(8,650 lbs)
Useful load	1,308 kg	(2,885 lbs)

Lockheed 14, 18 Lodestar and Ventura — USA

Having seen success with the Model 10 Electra, Lockheed's Hall Hibbard and Kelly Johnson designed the larger Model 14 Super Electra with a 14-passenger cabin, a deeper fuselage, a more tapered wing and half-span Fowler flaps with large external flap guides. The Model 14 prototype flew on 29th July 1937 powered by two 875 h.p. Pratt & Whitney S1E-G Hornet radial engines. More than half of the 231 completed were built in Japan by Tachikawa and Kawasaki and it led to the wartime Lockheed Hudson patrol bomber variant. However, the Model 14 was not a great commercial success and Lockheed developed the Model 18 Lodestar which had a 5.5 ft fuselage stretch and a raised tailplane. This increased capacity to a more economic 18 passengers. The Lodestar, which first flew on 21st September 1939, was much more successful than the Super Electra and 625 were eventually built by Lockheed of which 486 were military transports for the USAAF, USN and USCG, designated C-56, C-59, C-60 and C-66. A variety of engines were fitted ranging from the 875 h.p. Pratt & Whitney S1E2-G Hornet fitted to the Model 18-07 to the 1,200 h.p. Wright Cyclone R-1820-87 of the Model 218-56. After the war, Lodestars were widely used as executive aircraft and many were converted to Learstar or Howard 250 standard with various speed modifications, picture windows and interior improvements, and four received tricycle undercarriages. The Model 18 was developed into the wartime Model 37 Vega Ventura (and Harpoon) with an internal bomb bay, a ventral fuselage observation panel, mid-upper gun turret and a glazed nose. A total of 3,028 were built, mostly for the US Navy as the PV-1 and PV-2 (USAAF B-34 and B-37). Many were civilianised postwar and used for firebombing, crop spraying and freighting. Executive conversions included the Howard Super Ventura and the Howard 500 with a much enlarged wing. Over 160 Lodestars and Venturas have survived, mostly with private owners in the USA.

Lockheed 18 Lodestar

Lockheed PV-2 Ventura, N7265C

Specification	Lockheed 18-07 Lodestar	
Powerplant	Two 875 h.p. (652.4 kW) Pratt & Whitney S1E2-G Hornet piston engines	
Dimensions		
Span	19.96 m	(65 ft 6 in)
Length	15.19 m	(49 ft 10 in)
Height	3.61 m	(11 ft 10 in)
Performance		
Max speed	351 km/h	(190 kt, 218 mph)
Cruising speed	314 km/h	(170 kt, 195 mph)
Initial climb	290 m/min	(950 fpm)
Range	5,120 km	(2,783 nm, 3,200 miles)
Weights		
Max takeoff	8,707 kg	(19,200 lbs)
Useful load	3,605 kg	(7,950 lbs)

Lockheed 749 and 1049 Constellation — USA

On 9th January 1943, Lockheed flew the prototype of their pressurised heavy transport Model L.049. Originally conceived as a civil aircraft, the first 18 production Constellations went to the wartime USAAF as the C-69 powered by four 2,200 h.p. Wright R-3350-35 Double Cyclone engines. They were followed by 215 commercial aircraft for the world's intercontinental airlines with seating for 44 to 81 passengers. The Constellation had an elegant circular-section fuselage with a curving contour, a low wing mounting the four radial engines, a three-finned tail unit and a tall tricycle undercarriage. Variants included the L.649 with an improved undercarriage and higher weights, the L.749 long-range version (also military C-121A and C-121B) and the L.749A with 2,500 h.p. Wright 749-C18BD-1 engines. The PO-1W was an airborne radar picket version with dorsal and ventral radomes and an extended radar nose. The Model L.1049A Super Constellation was a lengthened Model 749 with capacity for up to 92 passengers and powered by four 2,700 h.p. Wright 956-C18CA-1 engines. It was sold to many airlines, including variants with a range of Wright engines such as the transatlantic L.1049G with wingtip tanks and the L.1049D and L.1049H which were dedicated freighters. Lockheed also sold almost 400 Super Constellations to the United States military forces as the C-121 and R7V and as the airborne early warning WV-2 (RC-121D). Some 183 commercial L.1049s were completed by close of production in 1958. One Constellation and four Super Constellations are still airworthy, mostly with preservation groups.

Lockheed 749A (C-121A) Constellation, N494TW

Specification	Lockheed L.1049G Super Constellation	
Powerplant	Four 3,250 h.p. (2,423 kW) Wright 972-TC18DA-3 piston engines	
Dimensions		
Span	37.62 m	(123 ft 5 in)
Length	34.62 m	(113 ft 7 in)
Height	7.54 m	(24 ft 9 in)
Performance		
Max speed	595 km/h	(322 kt, 370 mph)
Cruising speed	491 km/h	(265 kt, 305 mph)
Initial climb	335 m/min	(1,100 fpm)
Range	6,624 km	(3,600 nm, 4,140 miles)
Weights		
Max takeoff	62,358 kg	(137,500 lbs)
Useful load	29,243 kg	(64,480 lbs)

Lockheed Model 426, P2V (P-2) Neptune — USA

Completed too late to see service in World War II, the Neptune was the standard NATO maritime patrol aircraft in the immediate postwar years and served with the US Navy and the air forces of many other countries including the UK, Holland, France, Australia, Portugal, Canada, Chile and Brazil. It was an all-metal mid-wing monoplane with a retractable tricycle undercarriage, twin 2,300 h.p. Wright Turbo Compound R-3350-A8 radial engines, a mid-upper gun turret and nose and tail gun barbettes, underwing hardpoints, a belly weapons bay and radome and, from the P2V-4 onwards, wingtip fuel tanks. First flown on 17th May 1945 the P2V-1 entered service in 1947 and variants included the P2V-2 with 2,800 h.p. R3350-24W engines, P2V-3 with 3,200 h.p. R-3350-26Ws, P2V-5 with 3,250 h.p. R-3350-30WAs and larger tip tanks and the P2V-7 (P-2H) with 3,500 h.p. R-3350-32W engines. The P2V-7 had a clear-view glazed nose, a MAD tail probe, a larger cockpit canopy, no mid-upper turret and extra underwing J34 turbojets. In total 1,051 Neptunes were built, together with 82 P-2Js built by Kawasaki. Neptunes are no longer in military service but over 40 are retained for firefighting in the USA and flying examples are preserved as warbirds in the USA and Australia.

Lockheed P-2H Neptune, N299MA

Specification	Lockheed P-2H Neptune	
Powerplant	Two 3,500 h.p. (2609.6 kW) Wright R-3350-32W piston engines and two 3,250 lb.s.t. (14.46 kN) Westinghouse J34-WE-34 turbojets	
Dimensions		
Span	31.65 m	(103 ft 10 in)
Length	27.94 m	(91 ft 8 in)
Height	8.94 m	(29 ft 4 in)
Performance		
Max speed	649 km/h	(350 kt, 403 mph)
Cruising speed	306 km/h	(165 kt, 190 mph)
Initial climb	536 m/min	(1,760 fpm)
Range	5,896 km	(3,204 nm, 3,685 miles)
Weights		
Max takeoff	36,234 kg	(79,895 lbs)
Useful load	13,587 kg	(29,960 lbs)

Lockheed L-188 Electra — USA

With the replacement of piston-engined airliners by turbine models in the 1950s, Lockheed designed the L-188 Electra as a short-/medium-haul turboprop design for the domestic routes of American Airlines and Eastern Airlines. The low-wing L-188, with 96-passenger capacity, was larger than the Vickers Viscount and had almost twice the range. It was powered by four Allison 501-D13 engines and first flew on 6th December 1957. The L-188C had higher weights and increased fuel capacity. Between 1958 and 1961, 171 Electras were delivered; apart from American and Eastern they were sold to Qantas, Pacific Southwest, KLM and Braniff. Many Electras were converted as L-188CF freighters with fore and aft port-side freight doors following airline service. Over 50 Electras are still in service, mainly for cargo work with operators such as Channel Express and Atlantic Airlines but they are also used as fire bombers in northern California.

Lockheed L-188 Electra (Cont.)

Lockheed L-188C Electra, G-FIJV

Specification	Lockheed L-188A Electra	
Powerplant	Four 3,750 s.h.p. (2,796 kW) Allison 501-D13 turboprops	
Dimensions		
Span	30.17 m	(99 ft 0 in)
Length	31.85 m	(104 ft 6 in)
Height	10.01 m	(32 ft 10 in)
Performance		
Max speed	721 km/h	(390 kt, 448 mph)
Cruising speed	600 km/h	(324 kt, 373 mph)
Initial climb	600 m/min	(1,970 fpm)
Range	4,432 km	(2,409 nm, 2,770 miles)
Weights		
Max takeoff	51,247 kg	(113,000 lbs)
Useful load	25,215 kg	(55,600 lbs)

Lockheed P-3A Orion — USA

While it may have had a fairly short airline service life, the Lockheed L-188 Electra provided an ideal platform for development of a new maritime patrol aircraft to replace the ageing Lockheed Neptune. The P3V-1 (later YP-3A) Orion, which flew on 25th November 1959, had virtually the same airframe as the Electra but the cabin windows were deleted and it was fitted with an extended MAD tail boom, a large nose radar, three stores hardpoints on each outer wing panel and a large belly weapons bay to carry torpedoes, mines, bombs and rockets. Engines were 4,500 s.h.p. Allison T56-A-10W turboprops. The fuselage was packed with operator consoles for the various detection systems and the rear fuselage housed the aircraft's store of sonobuoys and droppable equipment. The P-3A entered service in 1962 with the US Navy and other users included Canada (CP-140 Aurora), Chile, Holland, Norway, Japan and Pakistan. The P-3B has uprated Allison T56-A-14 engines, the P-3C has an improved suite of ASW equipment and has undergone several subsequent updates, and export models include the P-3F (Iran), P-3K (New Zealand), P-3N (Norway) P-3P (Spain) and P-3W (Australia). The P-3A(CS) is an airborne surveillance version for the US Customs with a rotating dish antenna mounted above the fuselage. Many other Orion variants have appeared including hurricane hunters for the NOAA. Orion production ceased in 1995 with a total of 649 aircraft.

Lockheed P-3C Orion, JMSDF, 5022

Lockheed P-3A(CS), US Customs

Specification	Lockheed P-3C Orion	
Powerplant	Four 4,910 s.h.p. (3,660 kW) Allison T56-A-14 turboprops	
Dimensions		
Span	30.38 m	(99 ft 8 in)
Length	35.61 m	(116 ft 10 in)
Height	10.29 m	(33 ft 9 in)
Performance		
Max speed	764 km/h	(413 kt, 475 mph)
Cruising speed	612 km/h	(330 kt, 380 mph)
Initial climb	594 m/min	(1,950 fpm)
Range	7,625 km	(4,142 nm, 4,766 miles)
Weights		
Max takeoff	64,399 kg	(142,000 lbs)
Useful load	36,508 kg	(80,500 lbs)

Lockheed T-33A — USA

More than 50 years after its first flight, the T-33A is still in service with many air forces for training and communications. It is used by the air forces of Canada, Bolivia, Mexico, Greece and Pakistan and is a popular warbird with private owners. The T-33 is an advanced trainer with a low wing with large tip tanks, retractable tricycle undercarriage and a tandem two-seat cockpit with an upward-opening clear-view canopy. It was derived from the F-80 Shooting Star interceptor from which it differed in having a stretched fuselage to accommodate the longer cockpit, a lengthened nose and additional wing fuel capacity. Initially it was powered by a 4,600 lb.s.t. Allison J33-A-23 turbojet but later aircraft had the 5,200 lb.s.t. J33-A-25 and the CT-133 had a 5,100 lb.s.t. Rolls Royce Nene. The prototype first flew on 22nd March 1948 and 5,691 were built by Lockheed, 210 by Kawasaki in Japan and 656 by Canadair as the CL-30 (RCAF CT-133) Silver Star. Several variants have been produced including the RT-33A reconnaissance aircraft with a camera nose, a close-support AT-33A with underwing rocket pylons, the QT-33 target drone and the TV-2 (T-33B) trainer for the US Navy. A later derivative was the T2V-1 (T-1A) SeaStar which had a raised cockpit canopy and a modified tail, and 150 were used as deck-landing trainers by the US Navy.

Lockheed T-33A, Bolivian AF, 612

Specification	Lockheed T-33A	
Powerplant	One 5,200 lb.s.t. (23.13 kN) Allison J33-A-25 turbojet	
Dimensions		
Span	11.84 m	(38 ft 10 in)
Length	11.51 m	(37 ft 9 in)
Height	3.56 m	(11 ft 8 in)
Performance		
Max speed	966 km/h	(522 kt, 600 mph)
Cruising speed	732 km/h	(396 kt, 455 mph)
Initial climb	1,484 m/min	(4,870 fpm)
Range	2,040 km	(1,109 nm, 1,275 miles)
Weights		
Max takeoff	6,830 kg	(15,060 lbs)
Useful load	3,036 kg	(6,695 lbs)

Lockheed L-1329 Jetstar — USA

The Jetstar was developed by the Lockheed Georgia Company to a USAF requirement for a high-speed 10-/12-seat communications aircraft. It was a low-wing aircraft with most of the cabin section positioned forward of the wing and it had a cruciform tail and two Wright-built Bristol Orpheus engines mounted on the rear fuselage. The first of two prototypes was first flown on 4th September 1957 and testing resulted in the production L-1329-23A Jetstar-6 having a slightly longer fuselage and being fitted with four Pratt & Whitney JT12A turbojets in paired nacelles together with large slipper fuel tanks on the wings at mid-span. First deliveries to corporate customers took place in 1961. Military users included the USAF who received 18 as the C-140A navaid checking aircraft and C-140B VIP transport, the West German Luftwaffe (3) and Saudi Arabian Air Force (2). The Jetstar-8 had higher-powered JT12A-8 engines and the L-1329-25 Jetstar II, which first flew on 18th August 1976, had the JT12A turbojets replaced by four TFE731-3 turbofans. A number of older aircraft were upgraded to turbofan power by AiResearch and are known as Jetstar 731s. Jetstar production closed in 1980 with 204 examples having been built. Approximately 110 remain in service with corporate users.

Lockheed L-1328 Jetstar-8, Mexican AF, JS-10201

Specification	Lockheed L-1329-25 Jetstar II	
Powerplant	Four 3,700 lb.s.t. (16.5 kN) Honeywell (Garrett) TFE731-3 turbofans	
Dimensions		
Span	16.59 m	(54 ft 5 in)
Length	18.41 m	(60 ft 5 in)
Height	6.22 m	(20 ft 5 in)
Performance		
Max speed	880 km/h	(476 kt, 547 mph)
Cruising speed	818 km/h	(442 kt, 508 mph)
Initial climb	1,280 m/min	(4,200 fpm)
Range	5,104 km	(2,774 nm, 3,190 miles)
Weights		
Max takeoff	19,841 kg	(43,750 lbs)
Useful load	8,876 kg	(19,572 lbs)

Lockheed C-141 Starlifter — USA

In the early 1960s, Lockheed won a contract to develop a new heavy jet cargo transport for the USAF to replace the turboprop Douglas C-133 Cargomaster. Lockheed Georgia's Model 300 (C-141) Starlifter had slightly higher payload/range than the C-133 and first flew on 17th December 1963. It had a high wing to provide unobstructed fuselage cargo space and a ventral tail loading ramp. There were four wing-held underslung Pratt & Whitney TF33-P-7 turbofans and the C-141 had a high T-tail and externally podded main undercarriage units. The C-141A entered service in April 1965 and 284 were delivered to the USAF. Lockheed also built a civil L-300-50A demonstrator but failed to sell the Starlifter to either civil or export military customers. In its basic form, the C-141A was an excellent workhorse but a major upgrade resulted in 271 aircraft being modified as C-141Bs with a 23.3 ft fuselage extension and new air refuelling equipment. The first modified aircraft, which can carry up to 205 passengers, entered service in 1980. The C-141B remains in wide-scale use with USAF and ANG and AFRes squadrons but will eventually be replaced by the Boeing C-17.

Lockheed C-141B, USAF, 65-0245

Specification	Lockheed C-141B Starlifter	
Powerplant	Four 21,000 lb.s.t. (93.4 kN) Pratt & Whitney TF33-P-7 turbofans	
Dimensions		
Span	48.74 m	(159 ft 11 in)
Length	51.31 m	(168 ft 4 in)
Height	11.96 m	(39 ft 3 in)
Performance		
Max speed	911 km/h	(492 kt, 566 mph)
Cruising speed	797 km/h	(430 kt, 495 mph)
Initial climb	890 m/min	(2,920 fpm)
Range	10,224 km	(5,556 nm, 6,390 miles)
Weights		
Max takeoff	155,556 kg	(343,000 lbs)
Useful load	88,381 kg	(194,880 lbs)

Lockheed YO-3A — USA

The YO-3A was devised by Lockheed to provide stealthy surveillance of enemy movements in Vietnam. It was based on the earlier Q-Star which was itself a modified Schweizer SGS 2-32 tandem two-seat glider. The YO-3A had the low-set Schweizer high-aspect-ratio wing, a retractable tailwheel undercarriage and an enlarged cockpit with an upward-opening blister canopy. A 210 h.p. Continental IO-360 engine was fitted in the nose and surveillance sensor pods were fitted under the nose and rear fuselage. Some 14 YO-3As were built and, following Vietnam service, six were civilianised and now fly with private owners and government agencies.

Lockheed YO-3A, N123LT

Specification	Lockheed YO-3A	
Powerplant	One 210 h.p. (156.58 kW) Teledyne Continental IO-360-D piston engine	
Dimensions		
Span	17.37 m	(57 ft 0 in)
Length	8.94 m	(29 ft 4 in)
Height	2.77 m	(9 ft 1 in)
Performance		
Max speed	222 km/h	(120 kt, 138 mph)
Cruising speed	177 km/h	(96 kt, 110 mph)
Initial climb	187 m/min	(615 fpm)
Range	720 km	(391 nm, 450 miles)
Weights		
Max takeoff	1,723 kg	(3,800 lbs)
Useful load	304 kg	(670 lbs)

Lockheed U-2 and TR-1A
— USA

The U-2, designed at the Lockheed 'Skunk Works' at Palmdale, California by Kelly Johnson's team, became the world's best-known 'spyplane' and was notable for the incident when Francis Gary Powers was shot down over Russia in May 1960. An all-metal aircraft with high-aspect-ratio wings, a single-seat cockpit and a retractable monowheel undercarriage, the U-2A was powered by a single 10,500 lb.s.t. Pratt & Whitney J57-P-37 turbojet and it could operate at altitudes of over 60,000 feet. Cameras and sensors were fitted in the nose and in a centre-fuselage bay. The prototype first flew on 4th August 1955 and the U-2A entered service with the CIA and USAF the following year. The U-2B and U-2C were upgraded U-2As with, respectively, 15,800 lb.s.t Pratt & Whitney J75-P-13 and 17,000 lb.s.t. J75-P-13B engines and the U-2D was a tandem two-seat high-altitude research version. The U-2R was a completely redesigned, and 30% larger, development of the U-2C first flown in 1967 with wing-mounted sensor pods and increased internal provision for almost two tons of cameras and sensors. The related TR-1A (later U-2S) is a tactical reconnaissance version with different radars, a SIGINT suite and a Precision Location Strike System for enemy radar identification. A small number of TR-1B and U-2RT trainers have been delivered and other versions include an ER-2 for NASA research. Production of the U-2 and TR-1 is believed to total 102 aircraft, the last of which was delivered in October 1989.

Specification	Lockheed U-2R	
Powerplant	One 17,000 lb.s.t. (75.6 kN) Pratt & Whitney J75-P-13B turbojet	
Dimensions		
Span	31.4 m	(103 ft 0 in)
Length	19.13 m	(62 ft 9 in)
Height	5.18 m	(17 ft 0 in)
Performance		
Max speed	692 km/h	(374 kt, 430 mph)
Cruising speed	644 km/h	(348 kt, 400 mph)
Initial climb (est)	1,067 m/min	(3,500 fpm)
Range	4,800 km	(2,609 nm, 3,000 miles)
Weights		
Max takeoff	8,617 kg	(19,000 lbs)
Useful load	2,857 kg	(6,300 lbs)

Lockheed U-2S, 80-1081

Lockheed U-2R

Lockheed L-1011 TriStar — USA

The TriStar was Lockheed's contender in the medium-haul wide-body jet airliner market in competition with the Douglas DC-10. Like the DC-10 it had two wing pylon-mounted turbofans and a third engine in the tail and was designed around 42,000 lb.s.t. Rolls Royce RB211-22B turbofan powerplants. It had capacity for 400 passengers and the prototype flew on 16th November 1970. First deliveries of the L-1011-1 were made to Eastern Airlines in 1972 and other large TriStar operators included TWA, Delta Airlines, Air Canada and Cathay Pacific. The L-1011-50 was a version with higher weights, the L-1011-100 was a longer-range model and the L-1011-200 had higher-thrust 50,000 lb.s.t. RB211-525B4 engines. The L-1011-500 TriStar 500 was a 315-passenger long-range version with a shortened fuselage, longer wings and increased fuel capacity, and this was acquired by several major carriers including British Airways, Delta, Pan American and TAP. The Palmdale, California line was finally closed in 1983 with delivery of the 250th L-1011 but over 150 examples remain in service.

Lockheed L-1011-500 TriStar, N762DA

Specification	Lockheed L-1011-500 TriStar	
Powerplant	Three 50,000 lb.s.t. (222.4 kN) Rolls Royce RB211-524B turbofans	
Dimensions		
Span	50.09 m	(164 ft 4 in)
Length	50.04 m	(164 ft 2 in)
Height	17.02 m	(55 ft 10 in)
Performance		
Max speed	877 km/h	(474 kt, 545 mph)
Cruising speed	781 km/h	(422 kt, 485 mph)
Initial climb	930 m/min	(3,050 fpm)
Range	6,896 km	(3,748 nm, 4,310 miles)
Weights		
Max takeoff	224,943 kg	(496,000 lbs)
Useful load	114,739 kg	(253,000 lbs)

Lockheed F-104 Starfighter — USA

The F-104 (Lockheed 083) started out as a high-performance lightweight air superiority fighter which would replace the F-100 Super Sabre in USAF operations. In the event, its service with the USAF was less significant than its use by other NATO countries. The elegant F-104 had a slim, pointed fuselage, very short-span straight wings with anhedral and a T-tail, and the prototype made its maiden flight on 4th March 1954. The production F-104A (Lockheed 183) was powered by a 9,600 lb.s.t. General Electric J79-GE-3B engine with reheat and it was armed with a Vulcan cannon and Sidewinder missiles. Lockheed built 296 aircraft for the USAF including 47 examples of the F-104B and F-104D tandem two-seat conversion trainer. The F-104C was a strike version with underwing and fuselage centreline pylons. The main production model, however, was the F-104G (Lockheed 683) and reconnaissance RF-104G, which was designed for NATO air forces in Europe and built by Lockheed and under licence by Fiat, Fokker, MBB, and Sabca. In total 1,316 were completed together with 220 TF-104Gs. The F-104G had a 10,000 lb.s.t. J79-GE-11A engine which was made in Europe by MAN-Turbo and Fiat for the licence-built aircraft, a larger tail, improved combat electronics and increased weapons load. User air forces included Germany, Italy, Holland, Norway, Belgium, Turkey, Greece, Spain and Denmark. The F-104G was also built by Canadair as the CF-104 and CF-104D and by Mitsubishi as the F-104J with a Japanese-built IHI-J79-11A engine. The F.104S was a Fiat-built dual-purpose ground-attack/air superiority variant for the Italian Air Force with increased weapons load and powered by an 11,800 lb.s.t. J79-GE-19 turbojet. In total 2,578 Starfighters were built and the type remains in service with the Italian Air Force.

Fiat-Lockheed F.104S Starfighter, Italian AF, MM6879

Lockheed F-104B Starfighter, N104PB

Specification	Lockheed F-104S	
Powerplant	One 11,800 lb.s.t. (52.49 kN) Fiat General Electric J79-GE-19 turbojet	
Dimensions		
Span	6.68 m	(21 ft 11 in)
Length	16.69 m	(54 ft 9 in)
Height	4.11 m	(13 ft 6 in)
Performance		
Max speed	2,333 km/h	(1,261 kt, 1,450 mph)
Cruising speed	966 km/h	(522 kt, 600 mph)
Initial climb	16,764 m/min	(55,000 fpm)
Range	2,904 km	(1,578 nm, 1,815 miles)
Weights		
Max takeoff	14,059 kg	(31,000 lbs)
Useful load	7,302 kg	(16,100 lbs)

Lockheed Martin C-130 (L-382) Hercules — USA

The L-382 Hercules is another classic Lockheed-Georgia aircraft which has become standard equipment with many of the world's air forces and could prove to be in production for over 50 years. Designed to meet a USAF requirement, the C-130 is a high-wing four-turboprop freighter with a loading ramp under the rear fuselage and retractable tricycle gear with the main units housed in external fuselage fairings. The prototype flew on 23rd August 1954 and the initial C-130As, powered by 3,750 s.h.p. Allison T56-A-1A engines, were delivered to the USAF in 1956. Later variants included the C-130B (and US Navy C-130F) with increased fuel and 4,050 s.h.p. T56-A-7 engines, the C-130E long-range model with increased fuel and larger overload tanks, the C-130H with 4,508 s.h.p. T56-A-15s and the similar C-130K for the RAF. Most of these variants spawned dedicated special sub-types such as the AC-130A Spectre gunship, DC-130A target drone director, JC-130A missile-tracking aircraft, RC-130A for photo-reconnaissance, HC-130B search & rescue aircraft, WC-130B for weather reconnaissance, MC-130E for special operations, KC-130F aerial refuelling tanker, the NC-130H equipped with nose scissors for space capsule recovery and a range of EC-130E and EC-130H electronic surveillance and airborne communications aircraft, frequently fitted with complex external antennae and sensors. The VC-130H was a VIP transport variant for Saudi Arabia with a luxury interior and square cabin windows. Lockheed also produced the L-382-20 commercial freighter which was similar to the C-130B, and the L-100-30 with an extra 6.6 ft fuselage stretch and 4,508 s.h.p. Allison 501-D22A engines. A batch of 30 RAF C-130Ks was upgraded to this standard. The new-generation L-382U C-130J Hercules was launched in 1991 in standard and stretched C-130J-30 versions. First flown on 5th April 1996, the C-130J has higher powered Allison AE2100D3 engines with six-bladed propellers, greater range, higher speeds, an advanced two-crew cockpit with new mission computers and avionics and updated electrical, fuel and APU systems. Hercules production exceeds 2,200 aircraft and 62 countries operate it as a military airlifter.

Lockheed C-130J-30, RAF, ZH869

Lockheed C-130H, Israeli AF, 102

Lockheed Martin C-130 (L-382) Hercules (Cont.)

Specification	Lockheed-Martin C-130J-30 Hercules	
Powerplant	Four 4,591 s.h.p. (3,424 kW) Allison AE2100D3 turboprops	
Dimensions		
Span	40.41 m	(132 ft 7 in)
Length	34.36 m	(112 ft 9 in)
Height	11.81 m	(38 ft 9 in)
Performance		
Max speed	644 km/h	(348 kt, 400 mph)
Cruising speed	620 km/h	(335 kt, 385 mph)
Initial climb	640 m/min	(2,100 fpm)
Range	5,216 km	(2,835 nm, 3,260 miles)
Weights		
Max takeoff	79,365 kg	(175,000 lbs)
Useful load	43,406 kg	(95,710 lbs)

Lockheed S-3 Viking — USA

The Viking is the standard US Navy carrier-based anti-submarine patrol and attack aircraft. It is a high-wing aircraft with folding wing and vertical tail surfaces, twin TF34 turbofans in pylon-mounted underwing pods and a retractable tricycle undercarriage, the main units of which retract into fuselage bays. It has two belly weapons bays to carry up to four Mk.50 torpedoes and two wing hardpoints for fuel tanks or ordnance. The S-3 has a crew of four and is equipped with extensive search and attack avionics including a retractable tail MAD boom. The prototype first flew on 21st January 1972 and first S-3A operational deliveries took place in 1974. Lockheed has also produced a few of the US-3A COD transport. Most Vikings have now been upgraded to S-3B standard with enhanced offensive electronics and provision for carrying Harpoon cruise missiles, or as ES-3As for ECM missions. In total 187 Vikings have been built.

Lockheed ES-3A Viking, US Navy, Bu.159391

Specification	Lockheed S-3B Viking	
Powerplant	Two 9,275 lb.s.t. (41.26 kN) General Electric TF34-GE-2 turbofans	
Dimensions		
Span	20.93 m	(68 ft 8 in)
Length	16.26 m	(53 ft 4 in)
Height	6.93 m	(22 ft 9 in)
Performance		
Max speed	813 km/h	(439 kt, 505 mph)
Cruising speed	298 km/h	(161 kt, 185 mph)
Initial climb	1,310 m/min	(4,300 fpm)
Range	3,440 km	(1,870 nm, 2,150 miles)
Weights		
Max takeoff	23,828 kg	(52,540 lbs)
Useful load	11,742 kg	(25,890 lbs)

Lockheed C-5 Galaxy — USA

The Galaxy is the largest aircraft in the USAF inventory and is used as a strategic airlifter capable of carrying major equipment such as the CH-47 Chinook helicopter and M-60 battlefield tanks or up to 363 passengers in high-density seating. In general layout, the Galaxy is similar to the C-141 Starlifter but it is 50% larger and can carry more than two-and-a-half times the payload. It has through-loading with a ventral rear ramp and an upward-opening nose section and a 24-wheel main undercarriage composed of four separate six-wheel bogies with (on the C-5A) a crosswind landing compensation system. Standard accommodation for five flight crew is provided on an upper deck which can carry 73 passengers. The Galaxy first flew on 30th June 1968 and, between 1969 and 1989, 131 were delivered including 50 C-5Bs with improved systems. The surviving 126 Galaxies are to be re-engined with 60,000 lb.s.t. General Electric CF6-80C2L1F turbofans.

Lockheed C-5B Galaxy, USAF, 85-0005

Specification	Lockheed C-5B Galaxy	
Powerplant	Four 43,000 lb.s.t. (191.26 kN) General Electric TF39-GE-1C turbofans	
Dimensions		
Span	67.89 m	(222 ft 9 in)
Length	75.54 m	(247 ft 10 in)
Height	19.86 m	(65 ft 2 in)
Performance		
Max speed	917 km/h	(496 kt, 570 mph)
Cruising speed	837 km/h	(452 kt, 520 mph)
Initial climb	526 m/min	(1,725 fpm)
Range	10,352 km	(5,626 nm, 6,470 miles)
Weights		
Max takeoff	379,592 kg	(837,000 lbs)
Useful load	209,977 kg	(463,000 lbs)

Lockheed Martin F-117A Nighthawk — USA

The F-117A 'stealth fighter' is a product of the Lockheed 'Skunk Works' at Palmdale, California. Its very low radar signature is achieved by a multi-faceted airframe design and specialised surface coatings together with careful heat emission shrouding of the jet exhausts. Development started in 1976 and the resultant aircraft has fly-by-wire controls, a highly swept wing integrated with the fuselage to give a continuous dart shape, swept twin ruddervators and a variety of broken edge surfaces to disrupt radar energy reflections. It has two belly weapons bays to carry GBU-27 Paveway III laser-guided bombs or Texas Instruments AGM-88 HARM or Hughes/Raytheon AGM-65 Maverick air-launched missiles. The definitive F-117A prototype first flew on 18th June 1981 with initial operational deliveries being made in 1982. Six YF-117A prototypes and 58 production F-117As have been delivered and the type has been operationally deployed, with great effect, by the 49th Fighter Wing in 'Desert Storm' and in the 1999 Kosovo campaign.

Specification	Lockheed Martin F-117A	
Powerplant	Two 10,800 lb.s.t. (48.04 kN) General Electric F404-GE-F1D2 turbofans	
Dimensions		
Span	13.2 m	(43 ft 4 in)
Length	20.09 m	(65 ft 11 in)
Height	3.78 m	(12 ft 5 in)
Performance		
Max speed (est)	1,215 km/h	(656 kt, 755 mph)
Cruising speed (est)	1,102 km/h	(596 kt, 685 mph)
Range	2,096 km	(1,139 nm, 1,310 miles)
Weights		
Max takeoff	23,810 kg	(52,500 lbs)
Useful load (est)	10,430 kg	(23,000 lbs)

Lockheed Martin F-117A, USAF, 81-10796

Lockheed Martin F-16 Fighting Falcon — USA

The F-16 is the current standard NATO single-seat all-weather multi-role combat fighter and is in service with 20 air forces around the globe. It was developed by General Dynamics as a lightweight aircraft to complement the McDonnell Douglas F-15 air superiority fighter and the prototype first flew on 21st January 1974. The F-16 has a slim delta wing with a large fairing into the forward fuselage and a conventional all-moving tailplane. A distinctive feature is the large engine air intake on the underside servicing the single reheated Pratt & Whitney F100 turbofan. The F-16 has an internal 20 mm Vulcan cannon and carries four AIM-9 Sidewinders on wingtip and underwing pylons and an ECM pod on a fuselage centreline pylon. First F-16A deliveries were made in 1979 together with batches of F-16B tandem two-seat conversion trainers. The F-16 has also been built in Belgium by SABCA and in Holland by Fokker. Variants include the F-16A-ADF air defence fighter upgraded with three underwing hardpoints and radars to use AIM-7 Sparrow missiles and the F-16C (and two-seat F-16D), with improved all-weather radar, a HUD and LANTIRN infra-red night targeting. Early F-16Cs have a General Electric F110-GE-100 turbofan but later aircraft (Block 32 upwards) have a 23,840 lb.s.t. Pratt & Whitney F100-PW-220. The F-16N is an aggressor training version of the F-16C for the US Navy. The F-16 has been continually upgraded during its production life and existing aircraft are frequently reworked to higher block specifications. Over 4,000 F-16s have been built to date.

Lockheed Martin F-16B, Royal Netherlands AF, J-265

Lockheed Martin F-16A, USAF Thunderbirds

Specification	Lockheed Martin F-16C Block 50	
Powerplant	One 29,100 lb.s.t. (129.4 kN) Pratt & Whitney F100-PW-229 turbofan	
Dimensions		
Span	9.45 m	(31 ft 0 in)
Length	15.04 m	(49 ft 4 in)
Height	5.08 m	(16 ft 8 in)
Performance		
Max speed	2,446 km/h	(1,322 kt, 1,520 mph)
Initial climb (est)	15,240 m/min	(50,000 fpm)
Range	3,872 km	(2,104 nm, 2,420 miles)
Weights		
Max takeoff	12,136 kg	(26,760 lbs)
Useful load	3,705 kg	(8,170 lbs)

Specification	Lockheed Martin F-22A Raptor	
Powerplant	Two 35,000 lb.s.t. (155.7 kN) Pratt & Whitney F119-PW-100 turbofans	
Dimensions		
Span	13.56 m	(44 ft 6 in)
Length	18.92 m	(62 ft 1 in)
Height	5 m	(16 ft 5 in)
Performance (est)		
Max speed	2,446+ km/h	(1,321+ kt, 1,520+ mph)
Initial climb	15,240 m/min	(60,000 fpm)
Range	3,200 km	(1,739 nm, 2,000 miles)
Weights		
Max takeoff	24,943 kg	(55,000 lbs)
Useful load	10,431 kg	(23,000 lbs)

Lockheed Martin F-22A Raptor — USA

The F-22A advanced single-seat tactical fighter is under development by Lockheed Martin and Boeing for 2005 service introduction as an F-15 replacement for the USAF and the first of two prototypes was flown on 29th September 1990. The aircraft has an unusual layout to provide significant stealth characteristics with triangular-shaped wings, twin vertical fins and an all-moving tailplane set well back on the fuselage and is designed for highly agile performance. The prototypes are powered by two 35,000 lb.s.t. Pratt & Whitney F119-PW-100 afterburning turbofans serviced by large angled air intakes. The Raptor has a belly weapons bay to accommodate AIM-120 AMRAAM and AIM-7 Sparrow missiles and carries AIM-9 Sidewinders for interception and an internal M61A2 Vulcan 20 mm cannon. It will also be equipped with a GBU-32 JDAM 1,000 lbs guided bomb for precision all-weather attack missions. At the end of 2000 the 339-aircraft procurement programme for the USAF was still subject to achievement of development programme targets before production approval would be granted by the U.S. Congress.

Lockheed Martin X-35A — USA

The X-35A is Lockheed Martin's entry for the US/UK Joint Strike Fighter (JSF) competition where it is in competition with the Boeing X-32. The prototype first flew on 24th October 2000. The USAF has a requirement for 2,036 of the standard X-35A as an F-16 replacement and in this form it lands and takes off conventionally but the X-35B is a short takeoff and vertical landing (STOVL) version with an additional lift fan, vectoring exhausts and lateral roll nozzles. 642 STOVL variants are required for the U.S. Marine Corps and 150 for the RAF/RN. A naval variant, the X-35C, which meets the USN requirement for 300 F/A-18E/F replacements, is based on the X-35A but has a larger tail and wing with tip folding for improved carrier-based operation. The X-35 is highly agile and has excellent stealth characteristics assisted by similar wing and tailplane sweep angles and by reverse-angled engine inlets. Internal weapons bays can contain two 2,000 lbs class AGMs and two AAMs.

Lockheed Martin F-22A Raptor

Lockheed Martin X-35A

Lockheed Martin X-35A (Cont.)

Specification	Lockheed Martin X-35A	
Powerplant	One Pratt & Whitney F119 turbofan	
Dimensions		
Span (est.)	10.67 m	(35 ft 0 in)
Length (est.)	15.54 m	(51 ft 0 in)
Height (est.)	5.18 m	(17 ft 0 in)
Performance		
Max speed (est.)	1,931 km/h	(1,043 kt, 1,200 mph)
Range (est.)	3.040 km	(1,652 nm, 1,900 miles)
Weights		
Max takeoff (est.)	22,675 kg	(50,000 lbs)
Useful load (est.)	11,791 kg	(26,000 lbs)

Loehle P-40, N414L

Specification	Loehle P-40	
Powerplant	One 65 h.p. (48.5 kW) Rotax 582 piston engine	
Dimensions		
Span	8.74 m	(28 ft 8 in)
Length	6.98 m	(22 ft 11 in)
Height	1.83 m	(6 ft 0 in)
Performance		
Max speed	161 km/h	(87 kt, 100 mph)
Cruising speed	137 km/h	(74 kt, 85 mph)
Initial climb	366 m/min	(1,200 fpm)
Range	520 km	(283 nm, 325 miles)
Weights		
Max takeoff	401 kg	(885 lbs)
Useful load	129 kg	(285 lbs)

Loehle 5151 and P-40 — USA

The 5151 and P-40 are typical of a range of ultralight-category amateur-built aircraft which have been designed by Loehle Aircraft Corp., modelled on World War II fighters. The series started with the 5151 Mustang which was a 75% scale copy of the North American P-51, initially built with a fixed undercarriage but later sold as the 5151RG with retractable gear. Sold in the form of kits and plans, the Loehle 5151 first flew on 30th January 1986 and it is constructed of wood with some expanded foam sections and an overall fabric covering. The P-40, which is modelled on the Curtiss P-40, has substantially the same structure as the 5151RG with appropriate changes to the external shape including a turtleback fuselage and the familiar P-40 engine nose intake scoop. As with the Mustang copies, the P-40 is powered by a Rotax 582 engine. Loehle also sells replica kits for the Spad XIII, SE-5A and Fokker D-VII, and has launched the Spitfire Elite kit. This is a 75% scale Supermarine Spitfire which is somewhat heavier than the previous types and has fibreglass nose cowlings and an improved undercarriage.

Loving-Wayne Love — USA

Designed by Neal Loving, the little Love single-seater is a midget racer which has been built by a number of amateurs from plans. First flown on 7th August 1950, the Love is of wood, plywood and fabric construction and has a fixed tailwheel undercarriage and an enclosed cockpit. The wing is cranked downward and the main undercarriage units are positioned at the point where the inner and outer wing panels join. Most examples of the Love are fitted with an 85 h.p. Continental engine but at least one has flown with a 100 h.p. Continental.

Loehle 5151RG, N37JG

Loving-Wayne Love, N12LG

Specification	Loving-Wayne Love	
Powerplant	One 85 h.p. (63.3 kW) Teledyne Continental C85-8F piston engine	
Dimensions		
Span	6.1 m	(20 ft 0 in)
Length	5.23 m	(17 ft 2 in)
Height	1.35 m	(4 ft 5 in)
Performance		
Max speed	346 km/h	(187 kt, 215 mph)
Cruising speed	241 km/h	(130 kt, 150 mph)
Initial climb	640 m/min	(2,100 fpm)
Range	720 km	(391 nm, 450 miles)
Weights		
Max takeoff	380 kg	(839 lbs)
Useful load	91 kg	(200 lbs)

Lucas L-5 — France

Emile Lucas is a French amateur constructor whose first design, the Lucas L-4, was a low-wing two-seater which flew in 1962, powered by a small Salmson radial engine. In 1976, Lucas built his L-5 prototype which was, again, a low-wing aircraft with a fully enclosed side-by-side two-seat cabin and fitted with a fixed tricycle undercarriage. Of all-metal construction, it made its first flight on 13th August 1976 powered by a 115 h.p. Lycoming O-235 engine. The prototype was subsequently modified with retractable gear and later examples of the L-5 were also equipped with fixed or retractable tailwheel undercarriages. The aircraft is sold in the form of plans and at least 11 have flown. The L-5-320 is a three-seat version with a 100 h.p. Lycoming O-320 and the four-seat L-5-360 has a 180 h.p. O-320. Lucas has also produced the L-8 side-by-side two-seater which uses a 180 h.p. IO-360 engine and has a 190 mph maximum speed.

Lucas L-5, F-PYTD

Specification	Lucas L-5	
Powerplant	One 115 h.p. (85.7 kW) Textron Lycoming O-235 piston engine	
Dimensions		
Span	9.19 m	(30 ft 2 in)
Length	6.3 m	(20 ft 8 in)
Height	2.11 m	(6 ft 11 in)
Performance		
Max speed	274 km/h	(148 kt, 170 mph)
Cruising speed	217 km/h	(117 kt, 135 mph)
Initial climb	305 m/min	(1,000 fpm)
Range	992 km	(539 nm, 620 miles)
Weights		
Max takeoff	746 kg	(1,645 lbs)
Useful load	245 kg	(540 lbs)

Lucas-Pennec Dieselis — France

The Dieselis is a composite two-seat light aircraft built by Paul Lucas and Serge Pennec of the Brest Aero Club as a testbed for a 68 h.p. Opel (Isuzu) diesel engine. It has a side-by-side cockpit, a fixed tricycle undercarriage and wings from a Robin ATL. The Dieselis first flew in September 1998 and had accumulated 250 hours of test flying by mid-1999. The designers have plans to sell kits or drawings to amateur constructors once the diesel engine system has completed its testing.

Lucas-Pennec Dieselis, F-PTDI

Specification	Lucas-Pennec Dieselis	
Powerplant	One 68 h.p. (50.7 kW) Opel diesel engine	
Dimensions		
Span	9.34 m	(30 ft 7 in)
Length	5.90 m	(19 ft 4 in)
Height	1.78 m	(5 ft 10 in)
Performance		
Max speed	220 km/h	(119 kt, 137 mph)
Cruising speed	180 km/h	(97 kt, 112 mph)
Initial climb	300 m/min	(984 fpm)
Range	1,600 km	(870 nm, 1000 miles)
Weights		
Max takeoff	580 kg	(1,279 lbs)
Useful load	225 kg	(496 lbs)

Luscombe Phantom — USA

The Phantom was designed by Ivan Driggs and was one of the earliest all-metal production light aircraft. Owing much to the Monocoupe D-145 design, the Phantom had a strut-braced high wing fitted with electric flaps, a cantilever tailwheel undercarriage with 'oildraulic' compression strut legs and a fully enclosed side-by-side two-seat cabin. The fuselage was circular in section and the aircraft was powered by a cowled Warner Super Scarab radial engine. The prototype first flew on 1st May 1934 and production deliveries started at the end of that year. Phantoms were powered by either the 145 h.p. Warner Super Scarab, the 125 h.p. Scarab or the 90 h.p. Warner Junior engine. In total, 25 Phantoms were built and the prototype and one other aircraft remain.

Luscombe Phantom, N272Y

Specification	Luscombe Phantom	
Powerplant	One 145 h.p. (108.1 kW) Warner Super Scarab piston engine	
Dimensions		
Span	9.45 m	(31 ft 0 in)
Length	6.55 m	(21 ft 6 in)
Height	2.06 m	(6 ft 9 in)
Performance		
Max speed	270 km/h	(146 kt, 168 mph)
Cruising speed	230 km/h	(124 kt, 143 mph)
Initial climb	427 m/min	(1,400 fpm)
Range	776 km	(422 nm, 485 miles)
Weights		
Max takeoff	884 kg	(1,950 lbs)
Useful load	286 kg	(630 lbs)

Luscombe 8 Silvaire — USA

The Luscombe Model 50 (Luscombe 8) was developed by Luscombe as a mass-production light aircraft which would be cheaper to build than the high-quality Phantom. The Model 8 was an all-metal monocoque design with a fixed tailwheel undercarriage and a strut-braced high wing. The prototype, powered by a Continental A-50 engine, first flew on 18th December 1937 and the first production aircraft was completed in early 1938. The Model 8A, which followed in 1939, had a 65 h.p. Continental A-65 engine, the Model 8B Luscombe Trainer was a dual-control version with a 65 h.p. Lycoming O-145-B engine and the Model 8C Silvaire Deluxe (and Model 8D Deluxe Trainer) had a 75 h.p. Continental A-75. Luscombe built 1,112 aircraft before the war halted production and 4,778 between 1945 and 1951. A further 80 Model 8Fs were built by Silvaire Aircraft. Postwar models included the Model 8E with an 85 h.p. Continental C-85, the Model 8F with a 90 h.p. Continental C-90 and the T8F Observer which was a tandem-seat air observation variant. In 1998, an updated 8F was returned to production as the Luscombe Renaissance, powered by a 150 h.p. Lycoming O-320 (or LOM M332/A) with an optional tricycle undercarriage and manufactured in the Czech Republic for assembly in the USA.

Luscombe Silvaire 8E, G-BSSA

Specification	Luscombe 8F Renaissance	
Powerplant	One 150 h.p. (111.8 kW) Textron Lycoming O-320 piston engine	
Dimensions		
Span	10.67 m	(35 ft 0 in)
Length	6.71 m	(22 ft 0 in)
Height	2.13 m	(7 ft 0 in)
Performance		
Max speed	241 km/h	(130 kt, 150 mph)
Cruising speed	225 km/h	(122 kt, 140 mph)
Initial climb	488 m/min	(1,600 fpm)
Range	960 km	(522 nm, 600 miles)
Weights		
Max takeoff	635 kg	(1,400 lbs)
Useful load	204 kg	(450 lbs)

Luscombe 11A Sedan and Spartan — USA

During the postwar light aircraft boom, Luscombe Aircraft designed a four-seat aircraft to be a companion model to their popular Model 8 Silvaire. The Model 11A Sedan, which had a strut-braced high wing, was of all-metal construction with a fixed tailwheel undercarriage and the cabin had a rear window giving all-round vision. The prototype first flew on 11th September 1946 powered by a 165 h.p. Continental E-165 engine. Luscombe only built 198 aircraft before production was terminated in 1949. The Model 11 has been revived by Luscombe Aircraft Corporation as the Model 11E Spartan which has a tricycle undercarriage, a modernised cabin with a larger rear window and a 185 h.p. Continental IO-360-ES engine. To date one prototype has flown and certification is under way.

Specification	Luscombe 11A Sedan	
Powerplant	One 165 h.p. (123 kW) Teledyne Continental E-165 piston engine	
Dimensions		
Span	11.58 m	(38 ft 0 in)
Length	7.16 m	(23 ft 6 in)
Height	2.08 m	(6 ft 10 in)
Performance		
Max speed	225 km/h	(122 kt, 140 mph)
Cruising speed	209 km/h	(113 kt, 130 mph)
Initial climb	274 m/min	(900 fpm)
Range	800 km	(435 nm, 500 miles)
Weights		
Max takeoff	1,034 kg	(2,280 lbs)
Useful load	454 kg	(1,000 lbs)

Luscombe 11E Spartan, N747BM

Luscombe 11A Sedan, N1625B

Luton LA-4 Minor — UK

The ultralight single-seat Luton Minor monoplane is a pre-war design produced by C.H. Latimer-Needham and flown as the LA.3 prototype in 1936. It was built of wood and fabric and had a strut-braced parasol wing covering the open cockpit and a fixed tailwheel undercarriage. The LA.4 Minor was sold in the form of plans for amateur construction and early examples were powered by a 40 h.p. ABC Scorpion, 40 h.p. Aeronca J.A.P. J-99 or 35 h.p. Anzani. Six Minors were built before the war and at least 40 postwar examples have flown, mostly powered by the 34 h.p. Ardem 4CO2-1 converted Volkswagen, but in some cases with engines as large as the 65 h.p. Continental C65-8F. The majority are the LA.4A with a separate fin and rudder and improved undercarriage. One aircraft has been built as the two-seat Phoenix PM-3 Duet with a side-by-side cockpit and a Continental C90 engine.

Luton LA-4A Minor, G-ASXJ

Specification	Luton LA-4A Minor	
Powerplant	One 34 h.p. (25.35 kW) Rollason Ardem 4CO2-1 piston engine	
Dimensions		
Span	7.62 m	(25 ft 0 in)
Length	6.1 m	(20 ft 0 in)
Height	1.9 m	(6 ft 3 in)
Performance		
Max speed	137 km/h	(74 kt, 85 mph)
Cruising speed	121 km/h	(65 kt, 75 mph)
Initial climb	137 m/min	(450 fpm)
Range	288 km	(157 nm, 180 miles)
Weights		
Max takeoff	340 kg	(750 lbs)
Useful load	136 kg	(300 lbs)

Luton LA-5 Major — UK

Following on from the little LA-4 Luton Minor, C.H. Latimer-Needham designed the larger two-seat LA-5 Major. This was a conventional high-wing monoplane powered by a 62 h.p. Walter Mikron II engine and it had a fully enclosed tandem-seat cockpit. It was first flown on 12th March 1939 but due to the loss of the prototype in a fire it was only made available as amateur-built plans by Phoenix Aircraft in 1958. It is thought that only ten Majors have been completed, including examples in Australia and Switzerland, and four are currently registered in the UK. Various engines have been installed in these aircraft including the Walter Minor, Continental A65, Continental C90 and 100 h.p. Continental O-200-A.

Luton LA5-Major, VH-EVI

Specification	Luton LA-5 Major	
Powerplant	One 65 h.p. (48.5 kW) Continental A65 piston engine	
Dimensions		
Span	10.72 m	(35 ft 2 in)
Length	7.24 m	(23 ft 9 in)
Height	1.93 m	(6 ft 4 in)
Performance		
Max speed	169 km/h	(91 kt, 105 mph)
Cruising speed	153 km/h	(83 kt, 95 mph)
Initial climb	213 m/min	(700 fpm)
Range	480 km	(261 nm, 300 miles)
Weights		
Max takeoff	499 kg	(1,100 lbs)
Useful load	227 kg	(500 lbs)

Macchi MB.308 — Italy

In 1947, Aeronautica Macchi S.p.A. moved into light aircraft production with the MB.308 two-seat high-wing monoplane. Built of wood and fabric, it was a modern design with a cantilever wing, a fixed tricycle undercarriage and an enclosed side-by-side cabin. The basic MB.308 was powered by an 85 h.p. Continental C85 or 90 h.p. Continental C90 engine but the MB.308G had either a C90 or the larger 100 h.p. Continental O-200-A and had a longer cabin with a third rear seat and additional side windows. A number of MB.308s were operated on floats. The MB.308 served as a basic trainer to rebuild the Italian state flying clubs but it was also used widely in Argentina where Macchi came to a licence production arrangement with German Bianco SA who completed 46 MB.308Gs. In total 137 MB.308s were built and a small number remain in Italy, Spain and Argentina.

Macchi MB.308, I-DASA

Specification	Macchi MB.308G	
Powerplant	One 90 h.p. (67.1 kW) Teledyne Continental C90-12F piston engine	
Dimensions		
Span	9.98 m	(32 ft 9 in)
Length	6.53 m	(21 ft 5 in)
Height	2.16 m	(7 ft 1 in)
Performance		
Max speed	201 km/h	(109 kt, 125 mph)
Cruising speed	169 km/h	(91 kt, 105 mph)
Initial climb	213 m/min	(700 fpm)
Range	712 km	(387 nm, 445 miles)
Weights		
Max takeoff	730 kg	(1,610 lbs)
Useful load	299 kg	(660 lbs)

Magni M-19 — Italy

Vittorio Magni of Milan has developed a range of autogyros following his initial Bensen B-8 built in 1967. Their design follows classic lines with the forward welded tube structure mounting the engine, rotor pylon, tricycle undercarriage and cockpit and a substantial tubular boom carrying the three-fin tail unit. The range includes the M-5 single seater which is powered by a 64 h.p. Rotax 582 and has an enclosed composite structure and blister canopy, the M-14 Scout which is similar but has a tandem 1+1 cockpit and a 75 hp Rotax 618 engine, the M-18 Spartan which is a smaller single-seat machine (Rotax 582) and the M-16 Tandem Trainer which has an open tandem two-seat cockpit and exposed 75 hp Rotax 618 engine. A number of M-16 Tandem Trainers are fitted with the Arrow GT1000R engine. The most recent variants are the M-19 Shark which is a higher-powered tandem two-seater and the M-20 Talon which is an equivalent single seater - both of which have a fully moulded fuselage enclosing the engine, cabin and rotor pylon. More than 150 Magni autogyros are currently flying worldwide.

Magni M-19 Shark, W16JE

Specification	Magni M-19 Shark	
Powerplant	One 115 h.p. (85.7 kW) Rotax 912I piston engine	
Dimensions		
Rotor diameter	1.7 m	(5 ft 7 in)
Length	2.98 m	(9 ft 9 in)
Height	2.2 m	(7 ft 3 in)
Performance		
Max speed	185 km/h	(100 kt, 115 mph)
Cruising speed	145 km/h	(78 kt, 90 mph)
Takeoff distance	60 m	(197 ft)
Range	288 km	(157 nm, 180 miles)
Weights		
Max takeoff	450 kg	(992 lbs)
Useful load	170 kg	(375 lbs)

Maher Velocity — USA

Designed by Dan Maher, the Velocity is a composite kit-built light aircraft with a tail-first design similar to that of the Rutan VariEze. It has a swept wing with large tip winglets, a forward canard and a pusher engine positioned behind the cabin. The cabin, which is entered through a hinged roof hatch, can accommodate four people and is equipped to provide comfortable long-distance flying at speeds of up to 230 mph.The standard Velocity, fitted with a 200 h.p. Lycoming IO-360 engine, has a fixed tricycle undercarriage but retractable gear can be fitted to the Velocity RG. The Velocity 173 and 173RG have a larger wing and longer forward canard surface which gives more docile slow-speed performance, and the Elite XL and Elite XL-RG are deluxe models with two gull-wing doors, an improved interior and a 260 h.p. Lycoming IO-540 engine. The Velocity first flew in 1985 and more than 70 are now flying.

Maher Velocity, N193JD

Specification	Maher Velocity 173RG	
Powerplant	One 200 h.p. (149.1 kW) Textron Lycoming IO-360 piston engine	
Dimensions		
Span	9.45 m	(31 ft 0 in)
Length	5.84 m	(19 ft 2 in)
Height	2.36 m	(7 ft 9 in)
Performance		
Max speed	341 km/h	(184 kt, 212 mph)
Cruising speed	322 km/h	(174 kt, 200 mph)
Initial climb	366 m/min	(1,200 fpm)
Range	2,283 km	(1,240 nm, 1,427 miles)
Weights		
Max takeoff	1,088 kg	(2,400 lbs)
Useful load	476 kg	(1,050 lbs)

Marie JPM.01 Medoc — France

The Medoc, designed by Jean-Pierre Marie, is a wood and fabric amateur-built light aircraft with a fixed tricycle undercarriage and an enclosed side-by-side two-seat cabin fitted with a forward-opening canopy. It is built from plans supplied by the designer and over 50 are under construction with seven currently flying. The first aircraft flew on 8th September 1987 and was powered by a 65 h.p. JPX-4T-60A engine. However, most of the aircraft flown to date have a Volkswagen VW.1700 or Limbach L-2000-E engine.

Marie JPM.01 Medoc, F-PDLQ

Specification	Marie JPM.01 Medoc	
Powerplant	One 80 h.p. (59.65 kW) Limbach L-2000-E piston engine	
Dimensions		
Span	7.5 m	(24 ft 7 in)
Length	6.2 m	(20 ft 4 in)
Height	1.9 m	(6 ft 3 in)
Performance		
Max speed	210 km/h	(113 kt, 130 mph)
Cruising speed	190 km/h	(102 kt, 118 mph)
Initial climb	240 m/min	(787 fpm)
Range	665 km	(361 nm, 416 miles)
Weights		
Max takeoff	520 kg	(1,147 lbs)
Useful load	220 kg	(485 lbs)

Marco J-5 — Poland

Originally designed by Jaroslaw Janowski, the Marco J-5 is a single-seat recreational aircraft of unconventional appearance which is marketed by Andrzej Bienarz of Aviation Farm Ltd. in Poland and was first flown on 30th October 1983. The J-5 can be fitted with a retractable monowheel undercarriage with wingtip outriggers or a two-leg fixed tailwheel gear. The structure, which is of glass-fibre composites, consists of a main fuselage module containing the enclosed cockpit and a pusher Rotax 447UL engine, a slim tail-boom carrying the V-tail and relatively high-aspect-ratio wings with tapered inverted tips. An improved version, the J-6 Fregata, has also been built with a 52 h.p. J&AS 3PZ-800 liquid-cooled three-cylinder engine, but this remains under development.

Marco J-5, F-WZUE

Specification	Marco J-5	
Powerplant	One 42 h.p. (31 kW) Rotax 447UL piston engine	
Dimensions		
Span	8.1 m	(26 ft 7 in)
Length	4.65 m	(15 ft 3 in)
Height	1.4 m	(4 ft 7 in)
Performance		
Max speed	201 km/h	(109 kt, 125 mph)
Cruising speed	169 km/h	(91 kt, 105 mph)
Initial climb	183 m/min	(600 fpm)
Range	448 km	(243 nm, 280 miles)
Weights		
Max takeoff	282 kg	(622 lbs)
Useful load	104 kg	(229 lbs)

Marquart MA-5 Charger — USA

Ed Marquart's little two-seat Charger biplane was flown in prototype form in 1971, powered by a 125 h.p. Lycoming engine, and it has since become popular with amateur constructors based on plans marketed by the designer. The Charger is built from steel tube and fabric and has swept wings and tandem open cockpits. The undercarriage is a fixed tailwheel design with cantilever main legs. A range of powerplants can be fitted up to the 180 h.p. Lycoming O-360 although most Chargers use a 150 h.p. or 160 h.p. Lycoming O-320. Over 400 sets of plans have been sold and more than 80 are now flying including two in the UK.

Marquart MA-5 Charger, G-BVJX

Specification	Marquart MA-5 Charger	
Powerplant	One 180 h.p. (134 kW) Textron Lycoming O-360 piston engine	
Dimensions		
Span	7.31 m	(24 ft 0 in)
Length	6.71 m	(22 ft 0 in)
Height	2.18 m	(7 ft 2 in)
Performance		
Max speed	233 km/h	(126 kt, 145 mph)
Cruising speed	217 km/h	(117 kt, 135 mph)
Initial climb	366 m/min	(1,200 fpm)
Range	456 km	(248 nm, 285 miles)
Weights		
Max takeoff	816 kg	(1,800 lbs)
Useful load	258 kg	(570 lbs)

Martin B-26 Marauder — USA

The Marauder was designed by the Glenn L. Martin Company as a World War II high-speed medium bomber. It was an all-metal aircraft with a circular section 'cigar shaped' fuselage and a shoulder-mounted wing with constant taper. The two Pratt & Whitney Double Wasp engines were

Martin B-26 Marauder (Cont.)

enclosed in streamlined nacelles which mounted the main units of the retractable tricycle undercarriage. The B-26 had a glazed nose fitted with a 0.5-inch machine gun, a twin gun tail turret and a further mid-upper twin-gun turret and a 5,200 lb bomb load was carried in the large double-belly bomb bay. From the B-26B onwards, the aircraft was also fitted with four forward-firing guns in fairings under the forward fuselage. The first B-26 flew on 25th November 1940 and 5,157 aircraft were built, variants include the B-26A (1,850 h.p. Pratt & Whitney R-2800-39), B-26B (1,920 h.p. R-2800-41) and the B-26F and B-26G with altered wing incidence. Many detail changes were made during production and the gross weight rose from 26,625 lbs to 38,200 lbs as successive variants were introduced. A few Marauders were converted as executive aircraft after the war. At least one B-26 is currently airworthy in the USA.

Martin B-26 Marauder, N4297J

Specification	Martin B-26G Marauder	
Powerplant	Two 1,920 h.p. (1431.5 kW) Pratt & Whitney R-2800-43 piston engines	
Dimensions		
Span	21.64 m	(71 ft 0 in)
Length	17.09 m	(56 ft 1 in)
Height	6.2 m	(20 ft 4 in)
Performance		
Max speed	455 km/h	(246 kt, 283 mph)
Cruising speed	410 km/h	(222 kt, 265 mph)
Initial Climb	305 m/min	(1,000 fpm)
Range	1,760 km	(956 nm, 1,100 miles)
Weights		
Max takeoff	17,324 kg	(38,200 lbs)
Useful Load	5,850 kg	(12,900 lbs)

Martin 170 (JRM-3) Mars — USA

The Mars is probably the largest aircraft in current use for forest fire control in North America. This very large transport flying boat, powered by four Wright Duplex-Cyclone radial engines, was developed during World War II and was first flown as the XPB2M-1 on 3rd July 1942. It could carry over 35,000 lbs of cargo or could be used as a 132-passenger troop transport. Five JRM-1s (later JRM-3) were built, together with one JRM-2 with a higher gross weight, and they were operated by the US Naval Air Transport Service in the Pacific for a number of years before being withdrawn in 1956. The four surviving aircraft were sold in 1959 and converted to fire bombers and based at Sproat Lake in British Columbia, Canada. The Mars can carry 6,000 gallons of water which can be picked up by lake skimming. Two aircraft remain in service, named *Hawaii Mars* and *Philippine Mars*.

Martin JRM-3 Mars, CF-LYK

Specification	Martin JRM-3 Mars	
Powerplant	Four 2,300 h.p. (1714.9 kW) Wright R-3350-8 piston engines	
Dimensions		
Span	60.96 m	(200 ft 0 in)
Length	36.65 m	(120 ft 3 in)
Height	13.59 m	(44 ft 7 in)
Performance		
Max speed	383 km/h	(207 kt, 238 mph)
Cruising speed	257 km/h	(139 kt, 160 mph)
Range	3,200 km	(1,739 nm, 2,000 miles)
Weights		
Max takeoff	74,830 kg	(165,000 lbs)
Useful load	38,549 kg	(85,000 lbs)

Martin 2-0-2 and 4-0-4
— USA

The Martin 2-0-2 was one of the first postwar modern passenger airliners and closely resembled its main competitor, the Convair 240. It was an unpressurised 40-passenger low-wing aircraft with a retractable tricycle undercarriage and innovative features such as a retractable passenger entry stair under the rear fuselage. Power was provided by two 2,400 h.p. Pratt & Whitney R-2800-CA18 Double Wasp engines mounted on the inboard wing sections. The prototype was first flown on 21st November 1946 and the first delivery was to Northwest Airlines with other fleet sales being made to Eastern Airlines, TWA, Delta and Braniff. Some 47 Martin 2-0-2s were built including 13 Model 2-0-2-As which had R-2800-CB16 engines and increased fuel capacity. Lack of pressurisation was a major shortcoming and Martin developed the pressurised Model 4-0-4 which had a 39-inch fuselage stretch and 2,400 h.p. R-2800-34 Double Wasp engines. In total, 101 Martin 404s were delivered to Eastern and TWA and a further two were sold to the United States Coastguard as the RM-1Z (VC-3A). Production finally ceased in 1952. Five Martin 2-0-2s and 36 Martin 4-0-4s are registered in the USA but only seven are thought to be active.

Martin 4-0-4, N404CG

Specification	Martin 4-0-4	
Powerplant	Two 2,400 h.p. (1,789.4 kW) Pratt & Whitney R-2800-34 Double Wasp engines	
Dimensions		
Span	28.42 m	(93 ft 3 in)
Length	22.73 m	(74 ft 7 in)
Height	8.66 m	(28 ft 5 in)
Performance		
Max speed	502 km/h	(271 kt, 312 mph)
Cruising speed	451 km/h	(243 kt, 280 mph)
Initial climb	581 m/min	(1,905 fpm)
Range	1,729 km	(939 nm, 1,080 miles)
Weights		
Max takeoff	19,796 kg	(43,650 lbs)
Useful load	6,585 kg	(14,520 lbs)

Mauboussin 123 Corsaire
— France

The prewar aircraft designer Pierre Mauboussin developed the two-seat M.120 Corsaire trainer/tourer in the early 1930s from his earlier PM.XII which was first flown in September 1931. It was a wood and fabric aircraft with a low wing, two tandem open cockpits and a fixed tailwheel undercarriage. Production of the Corsaire was undertaken by Ets. Fouga who built 13 M.120s with a 60 h.p. Salmson 9Adr radial engine and five of the Corsaire Major M.121 and M.122 with, respectively, the 75 h.p. Cataract and 75 h.p. Salmson 9Aers. The main production variant was the M.123, also with a Salmson 9Adr, which was built as a trainer for the French Air Force. When the war was over, the Corsaire returned to production as the M.129-48 with a 75 h.p. Minié in-line engine and this was used by many flying clubs. Other engines fitted to the Corsaire included the Aster 4A (M.124), Regnier 4JO (M.125), Salmson 5AP-1 (M.126), Regnier 4EO (M.127) and Mathis G4-G (M.128). Several postwar conversions were carried out including the Mauboussin Beaujard, Metalair 1 and the Bison PG, and several Corsaires were fitted with Continental A65 or Hirth HM.504A engines. In total, 116 Corsaires were built and three are currently active in France with others under restoration.

Mauboussin M.127 Corsaire, F-PCIO

Specification	Mauboussin M.129 Corsaire	
Powerplant	One 75 h.p. (55.9 kW) Minié 4 DA-28 piston engine	
Dimensions		
Span	11.73 m	(38 ft 6 in)
Length	6.88 m	(22 ft 7 in)
Height	2.59 m	(8 ft 6 in)
Performance		
Max speed	177 km/h	(96 kt, 110 mph)
Cruising speed	153 km/h	(83 kt, 95 mph)
Initial climb	183 m/min	(600 fpm)
Range	640 km	(348 nm, 400 miles)
Weights		
Max takeoff	621 kg	(1,370 lbs)
Useful load	231 kg	(510 lbs)

Maule M-4 — USA

The Maule M-4 is a classic strut-braced high-wing light aircraft with a fixed tailwheel undercarriage, a wooden wing (later replaced by a metal structure) and a tubular steel fuselage which was covered in glass-fibre fabric. The prototype four-seat M-4 Bee Dee was designed by Belford D. Maule and first flown in February 1957. Powered by a 145 h.p. Continental O-300-A engine, it went into production at Jackson, Michigan in 1961 and several variants appeared with a variety of powerplants and airframe modifications. These included the M-4C Jetasen with a cargo door, the two-seat M-4T dual-control trainer, the M-4-180C Astro Rocket powered by a 180 h.p. Franklin 6A-335-B1A engine and the M-4-220C with a 220 h.p. Franklin 6A-350-C1. The M-4 was certificated for operation on floats and skis and was popular as a bush aircraft. The M-1 Cuauhtemoc, three of which were built, was a standard M-4 built in Mexico and powered by a 180 h.p. Lycoming O-360 engine. Maule built 474 aircraft before the M-4 was replaced in production at the Moultrie, Georgia factory by the M-5 in 1974.

Maule M-4, 9Q-CAP

Specification	Maule M-4C Jetasen	
Powerplant	One 145 h.p. (108.1 kW) Teledyne Continental O-300-A piston engine	
Dimensions		
Span	9.04 m	(29 ft 8 in)
Length	6.71 m	(22 ft 0 in)
Height	1.88 m	(6 ft 2 in)
Performance		
Max speed	253 km/h	(137 kt, 157 mph)
Cruising speed	238 km/h	(129 kt, 148 mph)
Initial climb	213 m/min	(700 fpm)
Range	1,200 km	(652 nm, 750 miles)
Weights		
Max takeoff	952 kg	(2,100 lbs)
Useful load	454 kg	(1,000 lbs)

Maule M-5, M-6 and M-7 — USA

Maule Aircraft had successfully built over 400 examples of the four-seat M-4 light aircraft, but in 1975 the aircraft was substantially redesigned with an enlarged and slightly swept vertical tail, extended flaps and numerous other improvements. The basic model was the M-5-180C with a 180 h.p. Lycoming O-360-C1F engine but other variants included the M-5-210C Strata Rocket with a 210 h.p. Continental IO-360-D, the turbocharged M-5-210TC Lunar Rocket with a TIO-360, the M-5-220C with a 220 h.p. Franklin 6A-350-C1 and the M-5-235C Lunar Rocket with a 235 h.p. Lycoming O-540-J1A5D. Over 640 examples of the M-5 were completed. The M-6-235 was further improved with a longer wing with larger flaps and an optional third row of child seats served by extra windows. The M-7, which is currently in production, had further alterations to make the cabin more capacious and it is available with the standard braced undercarriage (e.g. MX-7-180B), with spring aluminium main undercarriage legs (e.g. MX-7-180C) and with a fixed tricycle undercarriage (e.g. MXT-180). Three wing options are available and engine options include the 160 h.p. Lycoming O-320-B2D, 180 h.p. O-360-C4F, 235 h.p. O-540-B4B5 and the 260 h.p. IO-540-V4A5. The most powerful Maule is the M7-420 and MX7-420 with a 420 s.h.p. Allison 250-B17C turboprop, and this and other Maules can be fitted with skis or amphibious floats. By the end of 2000 production of the M-5, M-6 and M-7 series exceeded 1,700 aircraft.

Maule M-6-235, N524TR

Maule M-7-420, N420TP

Specification	Maule MX-7-180A Sportplane	
Powerplant	One 180 h.p. (134.2 kW) Textron Lycoming O-360-C4F piston engine	
Dimensions		
Span	10.03 m	(32 ft 11 in)
Length	7.16 m	(23 ft 6 in)
Height	1.93 m	(6 ft 4 in)
Performance		
Max speed	241 km/h	(130 kt, 150 mph)
Cruising speed	225 km/h	(122 kt, 140 mph)
Initial climb	280 m/min	(920 fpm)
Range	800 km	(435 nm, 500 miles)
Weights		
Max takeoff	1,088 kg	(2,400 lbs)
Useful load	476 kg	(1,050 lbs)

Specification	Maverick TwinJet 1200	
Powerplant	Two 560 lb.s.t. (2.49 kN) General Electric CT-58 turbojets	
Dimensions		
Span	9.75 m	(32 ft 0 in)
Length	8.69 m	(28 ft 6 in)
Height	2.74 m	(9 ft 0 in)
Performance		
Max speed	708 km/h	(382 kt, 440 mph)
Cruising speed	644 km/h	(348 kt, 400 mph)
Initial climb	1,066 m/min	(3,500 fpm)
Range	1,760 km	(957 nm, 1,100 miles)
Weights		
Max takeoff	2,358 kg	(5,200 lbs)
Useful load	1,134 kg	(2,500 lbs)

Maverick TwinJet 1200
— USA

The TwinJet 1200 has been designed by Robert Bornhofen and has been developed by Maverick Air of Pueblo, Colorado. Sold as a home assembly kit, the TwinJet 1200 is of all-composite construction and is a high performance personal jet with docile handling characteristics. It has a 4/5 seat fully enclosed pressurised cabin which is entered through an upward-opening door on the port side. The production version has provision for a radar antenna in the nose. The TwinJet 1200 has a mid-set straight wing with tip fuel-tanks and a retractable tricycle undercarriage. The engines are two General Electric CT-58 turbojets derated from 885 to 650 lb.s.t. and mounted on rear fuselage pylons. The prototype TwinJet 1200 made its first flight on 4th August 1999 and seven kits had been delivered by mid-2000.

Maverick TwinJet 1200, N750TJ

MBB HFB-320 Hansa
— Germany

In 1961, Hamburger Flugzeugbau (later to become a part of Messerschmitt-Bölkow-Blohm (MBB)) initiated design of the HFB-320 Hansa business jet. The 7-/12-seat Hansa had forward-swept wings with tip fuel tanks which allowed the cabin to be positioned forward of the wing mainspar giving an unobstructed interior. The aircraft had a T-tail and a pair of rear fuselage-mounted engines and the tricycle undercarriage retracted into fuselage wells. The prototype was flown on 21st April 1964 and the first production Hansa, powered by two 2,950 lb.s.t. General Electric CJ610-5 turbojets, was delivered in September 1967. Despite attempts to sell the aircraft to executive users in the USA only 45 aircraft were completed in addition to the two prototypes, including 14 for Luftwaffe use as VIP transports and as ECM aircraft. Production was completed in 1969 and 13 Hansas remain in service, mainly as small package freighters in the USA.

MBB HFB-320 Hansa, N92045

MBB HFB-320 Hansa (Cont.)

Specification	MBB HFB-320 Hansa	
Powerplant	Two 2,950 lb.s.t. (13.12 kN) General Electric CJ610-5 turbojets	
Dimensions		
Span	14.48 m	(47 ft 6 in)
Length	16.61 m	(54 ft 6 in)
Height	4.93 m	(16 ft 2 in)
Performance		
Max speed	795 km/h	(430 kt, 494 mph)
Cruising speed	676 km/h	(365 kt, 420 mph)
Initial climb	1,295 m/min	(4,250 fpm)
Range	2,304 km	(1,252 nm, 1,440 miles)
Weights		
Max takeoff	8,798 kg	(19,400 lbs)
Useful load	3,299 kg	(7,275 lbs)

MBB (Eurocopter) Bö.105 — Germany

The Bölkow (MBB/Eurocopter) Bö.105 has proved to be one of the most successful light-/medium-category helicopters and is in widespread use with civil and military operators. It is particularly popular as an emergency medical helicopter due to its through-loading fuselage module which allows easy loading of stretchers. Design was started in 1962 and the prototype flew on 16th February 1967. The four-/five-seat Bö.105 is of conventional layout with a main fuselage equipped with rear loading doors and fitted with a skid undercarriage, a tail boom with a two-blade anti-torque rotor and twin Allison 250 turboshaft engines mounted on top of the fuselage. Special features include a hingeless rigid-rotor system driving four composite main rotor blades. Variants include the Bö.105A with 317 s.h.p. Allison 250-C18 engines, the Bö.105C with higher weights and 400 s.h.p. Allison 250-C20s, the Bö.105CB with 420 s.h.p. Allison 250-C20Bs, the Bö.105CBS with a stretched fuselage and extra side windows, the Bö.105L (and stretched Bö.105LS) with 500 s.h.p. Allison 250-C28Cs, the military Bö.105M and the German Army's Bö.105P anti-tank helicopter. The aircraft has been built in Indonesia by PT Nurtanio, in the Philippines by PADC, and in Spain by CASA. The Bö.105LS is built in Canada by Eurocopter Canada. Current production models by Eurocopter are the Bö.105CBS-5 Super Five and Bö.105LSA-3 Super Lifter. Over 1,370 Bö.105s have been built to date including 212 for the German Army.

MBB Bö.105C, Mexican Navy, HMR-151

Specification	MBB (Eurocopter) Bö.105LSA-3	
Powerplant	Two 500 s.h.p. (373 kW) Allison 250-C28C turboshafts	
Dimensions		
Rotor diameter	9.91 m	(32 ft 6 in)
Length	11.86 m	(38 ft 11 in)
Height	3 m	(9 ft 10 in)
Performance		
Max speed	240 km/h	(130 kt, 149 mph)
Cruising speed	225 km/h	(122 kt, 140 mph)
Initial climb	552 m/min	(1,810 fpm)
Range	512 km	(278 nm, 320 miles)
Weights		
Max takeoff	2,600 kg	(5,733 lbs)
Useful load	1,170 kg	(2,580 lbs)

MBB (Eurocopter)/Kawasaki BK 117 — Germany/Japan

In 1977, under a cooperation agreement, Messerschmitt-Bölkow-Blohm (MBB) and Kawasaki Heavy Industries (KHI) started development of the 11-seat BK 117 helicopter. In general layout, it was a larger version of MBB's Bö.105 and, in particular, retained the rear loading clamshell doors which allowed through-loading of stretchers and oversize items. The BK 117, which first flew on 13th June 1979, was powered by a pair of Lycoming LTS101 turboshafts set above the cabin driving a four-blade main rotor. The rotor head was virtually identical to that of the Bö.105 and the tail boom was also based on the structure used in the earlier helicopter. First deliveries were made to customers following certification in December 1982. The production BK 117A-1 with 550 s.h.p. LTS101-650-B-1 engines has been sold exclusively to civil customers, particularly as an EMS helicopter and for executive use. Variants include the BK 117A-3 with increased weights and a larger tail rotor and the BK 117A-4 with increased range and a new flight control system. Current versions are the BK 117B-2 with 592 s.h.p. LTS101-750B-1 engines and a higher gross weight and the BK 117C-1 with two 708 s.h.p. Turboméca Arriel 1E engines. German BK 117 production totals more than 270 aircraft and over 110 have been built in Japan.

MBB BK 117C, N9127G

Specification	Eurocopter/Kawasaki BK 117C-1	
Powerplant	Two 708 s.h.p. (528 kW) Turboméca Arriel 1E turboshafts	
Dimensions		
Rotor diameter	11 m	(36 ft 1 in)
Length	9.91 m	(32 ft 6 in)
Height	3.36 m	(11 ft 1 in)
Performance		
Max speed	278 km/h	(150 kt, 173 mph)
Cruising speed	247 km/h	(133 kt, 153 mph)
Initial climb	540 m/min	(1,772 fpm)
Range	540 km	(291 nm, 336 miles)
Weights		
Max takeoff	3,350 kg	(7,387 lbs)
Useful load	1,618 kg	(3,568 lbs)

Specification	McCulloch (Aero Resources) J-2	
Powerplant	One 180 h.p. (134.2 kW) Textron Lycoming O-360-A2D piston engine	
Dimensions		
Rotor diameter	7.92 m	(26 ft 0 in)
Length	4.88 m	(16 ft 0 in)
Height	2.51 m	(8 ft 3 in)
Performance		
Max speed	177 km/h	(96 kt, 110 mph)
Cruising speed	161 km/h	(87 kt, 100 mph)
Initial climb	244 m/min	(800 fpm)
Range	400 km	(217 nm, 250 miles)
Weights		
Max takeoff	680 kg	(1,500 lbs)
Useful load	249 kg	(550 lbs)

McCulloch J-2 — USA

The McCulloch J-2 was a two-seat light autogyro designed by D.K. Jovanovich as a private owner aircraft. It was an all-metal machine with side-by-side seating in an enclosed cabin, a fixed tricycle undercarriage and a stub wing to support twin booms with a conventional tailplane and tailfins. The autogyro rotor was mounted above the cabin and the J-2 was powered by a 180 h.p. Lycoming O-360 engine driving a propeller mounted behind the cabin. The J-2 was first flown in June 1962 and was produced in series by McCulloch Aircraft, commencing in 1970. In total 96 examples of the J-2 were built, including five exported to Australia, and rights were eventually sold to Aero Resources who named it the Aero Resources J-2 but built no further aircraft. Two J-2s remain registered in Australia and 43 in the USA, although no more than 20 are thought to be active.

McCulloch J-2, F-BRGD

McDonnell Douglas F-4 Phantom II — USA

The Phantom II multi-role fighter, which was initiated in 1953, was intended for the US Navy as the F4H-1 but, in the event, the USAF used it in much larger numbers. In total, 1,264 F-4s operated with the USN and USMC, and the prototype, which first flew on 27th May 1958, had the USN designation YF4H-1. The F-4 has a low nearly-delta wing with upturned folding outer panels, a heavily anhedralled tailplane and a long nose section containing the tandem two-seat cockpit and a variety of radars, cameras etc. depending on the particular role and variant. Normally, the F-4 is fitted with four underwing and one centreline hardpoint capable of carrying a range of fuel tanks, air-to-air and ground attack missiles, mission avionics and countermeasures pods. Initially, the Phantom was fitted with two 14,800 lb.s.t. (reheated) General Electric J79-GE-3A turbojets but, progressively, higher-powered J79 variants were fitted, culminating in the 20,515 lb.s.t. Rolls Royce Spey engines on the F-4K. Phantom variants included the F-4A (USN with J79-GE-2A engines), F-4B (USN with J79-GE-8 engines), F-4C (USAF dual-control air superiority fighter with J79-GE-15 engines), F-4E (USAF version with 20 mm six-barrel nose cannon), F-4F (German Air Force version with J79-MTU-17A engines), F-4G Wild Weasel (USAF defence suppression version with AGM-45, AGM-78 or AGM-88 air to ground missiles), F-4J (USN/USMC ground attack variant with J79-GE-10 engines), F-4K (Royal Navy FG Mk.1 with Rolls Royce Spey turbofans) and F-4M (RAF version of F-4K). The RF-4B and RF-4C were reconnaissance aircraft with nose cameras and the QF-4S was a target duties aircraft converted for US Navy use. First deliveries of the F-4A took place in 1960 and a total of 5,195 Phantoms was built including a batch produced by Mitsubishi for the JASDF. F-4s were used by eleven air forces other than the USAF/USN/USMC and substantial numbers remain in service in Egypt, Germany, Greece, Iran, Israel, Japan, South Korea, Spain and Turkey.

McDonnell Douglas F-4 Phantom II (Cont.)

McDonnell Douglas F-4F Phantom, German AF, 3730

McDonnell Douglas QF-4S Phantom, US Navy, 155580

Specification	McDonnell Douglas F-4E Phantom II	
Powerplant	Two 17,900 lb.s.t. (79.6 kN) General Electric J79-GE-17A turbojets	
Dimensions		
Span	11.71 m	(38 ft 5 in)
Length	19.2 m	(63 ft 0 in)
Height	5.03 m	(16 ft 6 in)
Performance		
Max speed	2,390 km/h	(1,291 kt, 1,485 mph)
Initial climb	15,240 m/min	(50,000 fpm)
Range	3,160 km	(1,717 nm, 1,975 miles)
Weights		
Max takeoff	28,025 kg	(61,795 lbs)
Useful load	13,578 kg	(29,940 lbs)

McDonnell Douglas (Boeing) F-15 Eagle — USA

Now in front-line operation for more than 20 years, the F-15 long-range air superiority fighter has given excellent service with the USAF and other air forces and is only now reaching the end of its production life with 1,500 aircraft having been built. First flown on 27th July 1972, the F-15A has a shoulder-set semi-delta wing, twin fins and tailplane/elevators and a pair of 14,670 lb.s.t. Pratt & Whitney F100-PW-100 turbofans with large angled air intakes. The cockpit is enclosed by a streamlined bubble canopy and a large extendable air brake is fitted on the fuselage just behind the cockpit. Four wing weapons pylons can carry a combination of AIM-9M Sidewinders and overload tanks and the F-15A has additional fuselage hardpoints for up to four AIM-7M Sparrow missiles. It is also equipped with a 20 mm M61A Vulcan cannon, and electronic systems include a Hughes APG-63 pulse-Doppler radar. The F-15B is a fully combat-capable tandem two-seat version of the F-15A. The F-15C (and two-seat F-15D), which first flew in February 1979, has improved radars and F100-PW-220 engines and can be fitted with belly-mounted conformal fuel tanks (CFTs). The F-15E (originally named Strike Eagle) is a two-seat ground attack version with a weapons systems officer in the back seat and powered by two F100-PW-220 (later 229) engines. It has 12 fuselage ordnance stations fitted outboard of the CFTs in addition to its wing pylons and also carries external Lockheed Martin LANTIRN navigation and targeting pods. Variants for Israel and Saudi Arabia are referred to as the F-15I and F-15S, and the F-15J used by the Japanese Air Self Defence Force is built by Mitsubishi.

McDonnell Douglas F-15B, USAF, 76-0140

McDonnell Douglas F-15E, USAF, 85-0231

Specification	McDonnell Douglas (Boeing) F-15E Eagle	
Powerplant	Two 14,670 lb.s.t. (65.3 kN) Pratt & Whitney F100-P-220 turbofans	
Dimensions		
Span	13.05 m	(42 ft 10 in)
Length	19.43 m	(63 ft 9 in)
Height	5.61 m	(18 ft 5 in)
Performance		
Max speed	3,058 km/h	(1,652 kt, 1,900 mph)
Initial climb (est)	18,593 m/min	(61,000 fpm)
Range	4,416 km	(2,400 nm, 2,760 miles)
Weights		
Max takeoff	36,735 kg	(81,000 lbs)
Useful load	22,222 kg	(49,000 lbs)

McDonnell Douglas (Boeing) F/A-18A Hornet — USA

Originally derived from the Northrop YF-17 light fighter design, the F/A-18A Hornet has been built for the US Navy as a carrier-based combat fighter and attack aircraft. The prototype first flew on 18th November 1978 with first deliveries of the F/A-18A (and tandem two-seat F/A-18B) taking place in 1979. The Hornet is a semi-delta design with twin vertical fins and nine external weapons stations and it is powered by two 16,000 lb.s.t. General Electric F404-GE-400 (later GE-402) afterburning turbofans fitted in the rear fuselage with large air intakes under the wing centre section. It is fitted with wing folding and arrester gear for carrier operations. The F/A-18C (and two-seat F/A-18D), which commenced deliveries in 1994, is an upgraded F/A-18A with new AN/APG-73 radar and systems to allow operation of the AIM-120 AMRAAM air-to-air missile. It also has enhanced night operational capability through use of the externally carried Nite Hawk targeting system. The F/A-18E (and two-seat F/A-18F) Super Hornet is a substantially improved version, now in production, which has increased wingspan and fuselage length, a higher useful load providing increased fuel capacity and greater range, and improved combat damage resilience. It is powered by 22,000 lb.s.t. F414-GE-400 engines. The F/A-18G Growler is a radar and communications jamming variant intended as a replacement for the EA-6B Prowler. Total Hornet production now exceeds 1,400 of all variants, including Australian aircraft assembled by ASTA. In addition to the US Navy and US Marine Corps, users include Australia (AF-18A and ATF-18A), Canada (CF-18A/B or CF-188A/B), Finland, Kuwait, Malaysia, Spain (EF-18A/B designated C.15 and CE.15) and Switzerland.

McDonnell Douglas F/A-18B (EF-18B) Hornet, Spanish AF, CE15-1

McDonnell Douglas F/A-18E Super Hornet, US Navy, Bu.165167

Specification	McDonnell Douglas (Boeing) F/A-18E Super Hornet	
Powerplant	Two 22,000 lb.s.t. (97.87 kN) General Electric F414-GE-400 turbofans	
Dimensions		
Span	13.61 m	(44 ft 8 in)
Length	18.31 m	(60 ft 1 in)
Height	4.88 m	(16 ft 0 in)
Performance		
Max speed	2,221 km/h	(1,200 kt, 1,380 mph)
Cruising speed	1,287 km/h	(696 kt, 800 mph)
Range	3,312 km	(1,800 nm, 2,070 miles)
Weights		
Max takeoff (est)	29,478 kg	(65,000 lbs)
Useful load (est)	15,600 kg	(34,400 lbs)

McDonnell Douglas (Boeing) C-17A Globemaster III — USA

The C-17A strategic airlifter, now in service with the USAF, was designed to the 1980 C-X specification and its fuselage and tail design owes much to the smaller YC-15 transport built by McDonnell Douglas in 1975. The C-17A has a classic cargo transport layout with a ventral rear fuselage loading ramp, shoulder wing with a blown flap system, T-tail and externally podded main undercarriage bogies. It is designed for operation by three crew and is powered by four Pratt & Whitney PW2040 (F117-PW-100) turbofans in wing-mounted pods. The Globemaster III, which flew in prototype form on 15th September 1991, can carry complex loads including the M1 Abrams tank or three Bradley infantry vehicles and RAH-66 or AH-64 helicopters. In transport mode it can carry up to 102 troops or 48 stretcher cases. It not only has good STOL characteristics for tactical delivery but also has transcontinental range for strategic supply missons. The first USAF squadron became operational in January 1995 and 70 of the initial procurement of 120 C-17As had been delivered by mid-2000.

McDonnell Douglas (Boeing) C-17A Globemaster III (Cont.)

McDonnell Douglas C-17A, USAF, 96-0007

Specification	McDonnell Douglas (Boeing) C-17A Globemaster III	
Powerplant	Four 40,400 lb.s.t. (179.7 kN) Pratt & Whitney PW2040 turbofans	
Dimensions		
Span	51.76 m	(169 ft 10 in)
Length	53.03 m	(174 ft 0 in)
Height	16.79 m	(55 ft 1 in)
Performance		
Max speed	941 km/h	(509 kt, 585 mph)
Cruising speed	901 km/h	(487 kt, 560 mph)
Takeoff distance	2,359 m	(7,740 ft)
Range	10,000 km	(5,435 nm, 6,250 miles)
Weights		
Max takeoff	265,306 kg	(585,000 lbs)
Useful load	137,642 kg	(303,500 lbs)

MD Helicopters (McDonnell Douglas) MD500 series — USA

The MD500 light helicopter was originally designed by Hughes Helicopters as the Model 369 to compete in the US Army's light observation helicopter (LOH) competition of 1960. The Model 369 had an egg-shaped fuselage containing a four-seat cabin and a 316 s.h.p Allison 250 (T63-A-5A) turboshaft engine, a tapered tail boom and four-blade semi-rigid rotor. As the YOH-6A it first flew on 27th February 1963 and the US Army eventually acquired 1,445 of the OH-6A Cayuses which were delivered between 1966 and 1970 and were widely used in the Vietnam War. The OH-6A, often known as the 'Loach', was used for artillery observation, light transport and as an attack helicopter fitted with external weapons, most commonly including a 7.62 mm XM-27E gun pod mounted under the left-hand cabin door. Variants included the OH-6B with a 420 s.h.p. T63A-720 engine, the AH-6C attack helicopter with an external Hydra rocket pod and the special forces MH-6B and MH-6C. The OH-6A was supplied to many overseas air arms who continue to use them. Hughes also produced the five-seat civil Model 500 which flew on 13th September 1966 powered by an Allison 250-C18A engine and over 1,400 were built for business and commercial users. It was developed as the Model 500D (and military 500MD Defender) with a modified T-tail and 400 s.h.p. Allison 250-C20B engine, the 500E with a reshaped fuselage pod with a pointed nose and the 530F (and 530MG Defender) with a 650 s.h.p. Allison 250-C30 engine. The 500D was also built under licence by BredaNardi as the NH500D and NH500MD. On 17th December 1981, McDonnell Douglas Helicopters (which had taken over Hughes) flew the prototype NOTAR version of the Model 500. This has a large tubular ducted air tail boom with anti-torque control nozzles. As the Model 520N it went into production in 1991 and was subsequently joined by the MD600N which has an enlarged seven-/eight-seat fuselage with three rows of seats and is powered by an 808 s.h.p. Allison 250-C47M. In 1999 the MD500/600 series was sold to MD Helicopters who continue in production with the MD500E, MD530F, MD520N and MD600N. Total production exceeds 4,900 aircraft including batches of Model 500Cs built by Kawasaki in Japan.

MD Helicopters MD530MG Defender

MD Helicopters MD500E (top) and MD520N (bottom)

MD Helicopters (McDonnell Douglas) MD500 series (Cont.)

Specification	MD Helicopters MD520N	
Powerplant	One 425 s.h.p. (317 kW) Allison 250-C20R turboshaft	
Dimensions		
Rotor diameter	8.3 m	(27 ft 3 in)
Length	7.8 m	(25 ft 7 in)
Height	2.9 m	(9 ft 6 in)
Performance		
Max speed	245 km/h	(132 kt, 152 mph)
Cruising speed	233 km/h	(126 kt, 145 mph)
Initial climb	583 m/min	(1,913 fpm)
Range	410 km	(223 nm, 256 miles)
Weights		
Max takeoff	1,746 kg	(3,850 lbs)
Useful load	1,072 kg	(2,364 lbs)

MD Helicopters (McDonnell Douglas) MD900 Explorer — USA

The MD900 was designed to supplement the existing McDonnell Douglas MD500 and MD600 range and to provide increased internal capacity and greater passenger comfort. The MD900 Explorer has a forward two-crew cockpit and a main cabin with club seating for up to six passengers and a large rear baggage compartment. It has a skid undercarriage and a NOTAR tail boom and is powered by twin Pratt & Whitney PW206B turboshafts mounted above the cabin driving a five-blade bearingless all-composite main rotor. The MD901 is an alternative version with twin Turboméca Arrius 2C turboshafts and the MD902 was a version with PW206E engines. An armed military version has also been proposed. The prototype first flew on 18th December 1992 and 75 had been delivered by the end of 2000, many of which are for use by police and emergency services.

MD Helicopters MD900 Explorer, N9015P.

Specification	MD Helicopters MD900 Explorer	
Powerplant	Two 630 s.h.p. (469.7 kW) Pratt & Whitney PW206B turboshafts	
Dimensions		
Rotor diameter	10.31 m	(33 ft 10 in)
Length	9.85 m	(32 ft 4 in)
Height	3.66 m	(12 ft 0 in)
Performance		
Max speed	269 km/h	(145 kt, 167 mph)
Cruising speed	249 km/h	(135 kt, 155 mph)
Initial climb	853 m/min	(2,800 fpm)
Range	581 km	(316 nm, 363 miles)
Weights		
Max takeoff	3,057 kg	(6,740 lbs)
Useful load	1,576 kg	(3,475 lbs)

McDonnell Douglas (Boeing) AH-64A Apache — USA

The Apache is the standard US Army battlefield attack helicopter and it has been in service since February 1984. Originally designed as the Hughes Model 77, the YAH-64A first flew on 30th September 1975. It is a two-seat aircraft with stepped tandem cockpits with flat-plate glass screens, a slim fuselage, a prominent fin with a low-mounted elevator and stub wings with four hardpoints. Twin 1,696 s.h.p. General Electric T700-GE-701 turboshafts are fitted on either side of the central rotor mast housing. The production AH-64A has a nose-mounted M230 Chain Gun 30 mm automatic cannon and can carry up to 16 AGM-114A Hellfire anti-tank missiles or a combination of Hydra 70 rockets and other ordnance or AIM-9L Sidewinder air-to-air missiles. The Apache is fully night and all-weather capable. In total 937 Apaches have been delivered. The AH-64D Longbow Apache, which first flew on 15th April 1992 and is now built by Boeing (formerly McDonnell Douglas Helicopters), is an upgraded version fitted with mast-mounted Westinghouse Longbow radar, increased power, enlarged fuselage side fairings and more sophisticated avionics. It is also re-engined with 1,890 s.h.p. T700-GE-701C engines. A total of 227 existing US Army AH-64As are to be rebuilt with the Longbow radar and all other AH-64As will be upgraded with the AH-64D improvements. The AH-64D is also in production for the Netherlands and the AH-64A is in service with six other air forces including those of Egypt, Saudi Arabia and Israel. It is being built by Westland as the WAH-64D, powered by RTM.322 engines, to meet a 67-aircraft order for the British Army.

McDonnell Douglas AH-64A Apache, US Army, 82-23360

McDonnell Douglas AH-64D Longbow Apache

Specification	Boeing AH-64D Longbow Apache	
Powerplant	Two 1,890 s.h.p. (1,409 kW) General Electric T700-GE-701C turboshafts	
Dimensions		
Rotor diameter	14.63 m	(48 ft 0 in)
Length	15.47 m	(50 ft 9 in)
Height	4.95 m	(16 ft 3 in)
Performance		
Max speed	261 km/h	(141 kt, 162 mph)
Cruising speed	249 km/h	(135 kt, 155 mph)
Initial climb	450 m/min	(1,475 fpm)
Range	432 km	(235 nm, 270 miles)
Weights		
Max takeoff	10,106 kg	(22,283 lbs)
Useful load	2,177 kg	(4,800 lbs)

Merlin GT and Explorer
— Canada

The little Merlin GT is a very popular kit-built light aircraft and over 300 have been completed from kits sold by Merlin Aircraft (and latterly Aerocomp). It is a strut-braced high-wing ultralight with side-by-side seating for two and it has full-span flaperons mounted externally on its foldable constant-chord wing. In standard form it has a fixed tailwheel undercarriage but it can be operated on floats. A range of engines can be fitted including the Continental A65 and Continental O-200 but most aircraft are built as Merlin GT582s with a Rotax 582, Merlin GT-618s with a 74 h.p Rotax 618 or Merlin GT-912s with an 80 h.p. Rotax 912. The Formula Merlin is fitted with a 110 h.p. Subaru engine. Construction is of steel tube and fabric and the Merlin Explorer is a strengthened and developed model which is popular as a light bush aircraft for which it can be fitted with tundra tyres.

Merlin GT and Explorer (Cont.)

Merlin GT, N2100S

Merlin Explorer, N7156Y

Specification	Merlin GT-912	
Powerplant	One 80 h.p. (59.6 kW) Rotax 912 piston engine	
Dimensions		
Span	9.14 m	(30 ft 0 in)
Length	6.1 m	(20 ft 0 in)
Height	1.85 m	(6 ft 1 in)
Performance		
Max speed	193 km/h	(104 kt, 120 mph)
Cruising speed	153 km/h	(83 kt, 95 mph)
Initial climb	457 m/min	(1,500 fpm)
Range	560 km	(304 nm, 350 miles)
Weights		
Max takeoff	590 kg	(1,300 lbs)
Useful load	332 kg	(733 lbs)

Messerschmitt Bf.108 — Germany

The Bayerische Flugzeugwerke under Prof. Willi Messerschmitt designed the Bf.108 Taifun in 1934. It is a low-wing all-metal communications and touring aircraft with a fully enclosed three-seat cabin, a braced cruciform tail and a retractable tailwheel undercarriage. The initial Bf.108A was powered by a 160 h.p. Siemens Sh.14A engine but the main production version was the Bf.108B with a 240 h.p. Argus As.10c in-line engine. Some 885 were built including aircraft for prewar private owners and a large number for the wartime Luftwaffe which deployed the type for general communication duties. In 1942, production was passed to SNCAN in France who manufactured the last 170 Bf.108s and then produced 285 examples of the Nord Pingouin. The initial Nord N.1000 and the slightly modified N.1001 Pingouin I had the Argus As.10b engine but the N.1002 Pingouin II, which was largely built for the French Armée de l'Air, had a 233 h.p. Renault 6Q engine and a full four-seat cabin. Current flying examples include one Bf.108 in Germany and three Nord 1002s in France and the UK.

Messerschmitt Bf.108, D-EBEI

Specification	Nord 1002 Pingouin II	
Powerplant	One 233 h.p. (173.7 kW) Renault 6Q piston engine	
Dimensions		
Span	10.49 m	(34 ft 5 in)
Length	8.56 m	(28 ft 1 in)
Height	2.29 m	(7 ft 6 in)
Performance		
Max speed	298 km/h	(161 kt, 185 mph)
Cruising speed	266 km/h	(143 kt, 165 mph)
Initial climb	274 m/min	(900 fpm)
Range	848 km	(461 nm, 530 miles)
Weights		
Max takeoff	1,483 kg	(3,270 lbs)
Useful load	585 kg	(1,290 lbs)

Messerschmitt Bf.109 and Hispano HA-1112 — Germany/Spain

Over 30,000 examples of the Messerschmitt Bf.109 fighter were built during World War II and production continued in Czechoslovakia (as the Avia S-199) until 1948 and with Hispano in Spain as the Buchón until 1958. The Bf.109 was derived from the Bf.108 light aircraft and was designed by Willi Messerschmitt of the Bayerische Flugzeugwerke. The prototype Bf.109-V1 first flew in September 1935 and Bf.109Bs, powered by a 700 h.p. Junkers Jumo 210 engine, went into service in the Spanish Civil War in 1937. Numerous wartime variants followed including the Bf.109D (with a Daimler-Benz DB.601 engine), Bf.109E (1,100 h.p. DB601A), Bf.109F (with improved engine cowling, round wingtips and a 1,300 h.p. DB.601E-1 engine), Bf.109G (1,475 h.p. DB.605A engine and increased armament) and Bf.109H (high-altitude version with longer wingspan, larger tail etc.). After the war, Hispano developed the HA-1109-J1L which first flew on 2nd March 1945 and was powered by a Hispano Suiza HS-12Z-17 engine which required a prominent radiator air intake below the nose. Later variants were the HA-1109-K1L (and rocket-armed K2L) with a 1,300 h.p. HS-12Z-17 engine and HA-1110-K1L tandem two-seater. Hispano then re-engined existing aircraft with a 1,400 h.p. Rolls Royce Merlin 500-45 engine and the subsequent production HA-1109-M1L and M2L and the HA-1112-M1L (with modified flaps) all had this engine. Six Spanish-built HA-1112s are currently active together with one Bf.109E and 13 aircraft are under restoration.

Hispano HA-1112-M1L, NX109GU

Specification	Hispano HA-1112-M1L Buchón	
Powerplant	One 1,400 h.p. (1,043.8 kW) Rolls Royce Merlin 500-45 piston engine	
Dimensions		
Span	9.91 m	(32 ft 6 in)
Length	9.02 m	(29 ft 7 in)
Height	2.59 m	(8 ft 6 in)
Performance		
Max speed	665 km/h	(359 kt, 413 mph)
Cruising speed	603 km/h	(326 kt, 375 mph)
Initial climb	720 m/min	(2,362 fpm)
Range	760 km	(413 nm, 475 miles)
Weights		
Max takeoff	3,180 kg	(7,011 lbs)
Useful load	524 kg	(1,155 lbs)

Meyers OTW — USA

The Meyers Aircraft Company of Tecumseh, Michigan, led by Alan H. Meyers, designed the OTW biplane trainer, flying the prototype on 10th May 1936. Intended for the prewar Civil Pilot Training program the OTW was a simple but strong design with tandem open cockpits and a fixed tailwheel undercarriage, but it was unusual in having an all-metal fuselage and slightly staggered straight wooden wings. The basic model was powered by the 145 h.p. Warner Super Scarab radial engine (OTW-145) but it was also produced in 125 h.p. (OTW-125) and Kinner R-56 engine (OTW-160) versions. A total of 102 OTWs was built between 1936 and 1943 at which time the CPT program was cancelled and OTW production ceased. Many OTWs survived the war and more than half those produced are still registered in the USA with private owners.

Meyers OTW-145, NC343H

Specification	Meyers OTW-145	
Powerplant	One 145 h.p. (108.1 kW) Warner Super Scarab piston engine	
Dimensions		
Span	9.14 m	(30 ft 0 in)
Length	6.88 m	(22 ft 7 in)
Height	2.59 m	(8 ft 6 in)
Performance		
Max speed	193 km/h	(104 kt, 120 mph)
Cruising speed	169 km/h	(91 kt, 105 mph)
Initial climb	244 m/min	(800 fpm)
Range	496 km	(270 nm, 310 miles)
Weights		
Max takeoff	844 kg	(1,860 lbs)
Useful load	287 kg	(633 lbs)

Meyers MAC-145 — USA

After the war, Meyers Aircraft developed the small all-metal MAC-125 light aircraft which had a low wing, a retractable tailwheel undercarriage and a 125 h.p. Continental engine. This prototype was followed by the production Meyers MAC-145C which mainly differed in having a modified vertical tail and a 145 h.p. Continental O-300 engine in a modified engine cowling. The first aircraft was delivered in 1949 and production continued until 1956, by which time 20 MAC-145s had been built. The MAC-145 was later modified by Meyers Aircraft Company of Fayetteville, North Carolina as the Meyers 145 Spark and this was further developed into the SP-20 with a 200 h.p. Lycoming IO-360, enlarged bubble cockpit canopy and modified vertical tail. The design was acquired by Micco Aircraft, owned by the Florida Seminole Indian tribe, whose production SP20 has a modified sliding canopy, a redesigned wing centre section, retractable tailwheel and a modified vertical tail as used on the Aero Commander 200. It is being built at Fort Pierce, Florida for sale to private owners together with the SP.26 which has a 260 h.p. I0-540-T4B5 engine.

Micco SP-20, N820SP

Specification	Micco SP20	
Powerplant	One 200 h.p. (149.12 kW) Textron Lycoming IO-360-C1E6 piston engine	
Dimensions		
Span	9.25 m	(30 ft 4 in)
Length	7.16 m	(23 ft 6 in)
Height	1.83 m	(6 ft 0 in)
Performance		
Max speed	259 km/h	(140 kt, 161 mph)
Cruising speed	241 km/h	(130 kt, 150 mph)
Initial climb	335 m/min	(1,100 fpm)
Range	2,064 km	(1,120 nm, 1,290 miles)
Weights		
Max takeoff	1,179 kg	(2,600 lbs)
Useful load	363 kg	(800 lbs)

Meyer Little Toot — USA

The Little Toot single-seat sporting biplane was designed by George W. Meyer as a practical aerobatic aircraft for amateur construction. The prototype Little Toot was first flown on 5th February 1957 and more than 100 are believed to have flown based on plans sold by Meyer Aircraft. The Little Toot has wood and fabric wings with swept upper surfaces and a tubular steel fuselage with all-metal cladding. It has a spring-steel tailwheel undercarriage and can be powered by a range of engines between 85 h.p. and 180 h.p. Typically, the Little Toot is fitted with a 90 h.p. Continental C90 engine which fits into a tightly cowled nose section. Several examples have been built and painted to resemble the prewar Curtiss P-6E Hawk pursuit biplane.

Meyer Little Toot, N925BT

Specification	Meyer Little Toot	
Powerplant	One 90 h.p. (67.1 kW) Teledyne Continental C90 piston engine	
Dimensions		
Span	5.79 m	(19 ft 0 in)
Length	4.88 m	(16 ft 0 in)
Height	2.13 m	(7 ft 0 in)
Performance		
Max speed	204 km/h	(110 kt, 127 mph)
Cruising speed	177 km/h	(96 kt, 110 mph)
Initial climb	305 m/min	(1,000 fpm)
Range	560 km	(304 nm, 350 miles)
Weights		
Max takeoff	558 kg	(1,230 lbs)
Useful load	143 kg	(316 lbs)

Mignet HM.293 — France

Henri Mignet's 'Flying Flea' concept for an unstallable light aircraft produced much prewar scandal and, once the problems of stability were resolved, a plethora of postwar variants constructed by amateurs in France and elsewhere. The original HM.14, which flew on 10th September 1933, was a very simple wood and fabric aircraft with tandem wings and a 17 h.p. Aubier-Dunne engine mounted on a triangulated tube frame in the nose. Hundreds of Flying Fleas were built in France and the UK before the war but several fatal crashes resulted in the type being banned. The HM.290 series, launched in 1946, was a much developed single-seat version of wood and fabric construction, most of which were built as the HM.293, powered by a 25 h.p. to 40 h.p. engine such as one of the 1300 or 1600 cc Volkswagen conversions, and marketed by the Canadian company Falconar. The tube and fabric two-seat HM.350 first flew on 5th March 1957 and this and the single-seat HM.320 were redesigned models for commercial production. Equivalent amateur-built versions are the HM.380 and HM.360, both of which have been completed in some numbers. The HM.390 Auto Ciel is a three-seat development of the HM.380 with a 90 h.p. Continental engine. Many variants of the Mignet designs have been built including the Croses Criquet (separately described), Romibutter, LaFarge Pulga, Frebel F.5, Lederlin Ladybug, Briffaud GB-10 and Gilbert Landray's GL-1, GL-3 Pouss-Pou and GL.06. Most of the new Mignet single-seaters are now categorised as ultralights.

Mignet HM.293, 67-HT

Specification	Mignet HM.293	
Powerplant	One 36 h.p. (26.8 kW) Volkswagen VW1200 piston engine	
Dimensions		
Span	6.53 m	(21 ft 5 in)
Length	3.96 m	(13 ft 0 in)
Height	1.88 m	(6 ft 2 in)
Performance		
Max speed	153 km/h	(83 kt, 95 mph)
Cruising speed	137 km/h	(74 kt, 85 mph)
Initial climb	101 m/min	(330 fpm)
Range	400 km	(217 nm, 250 miles)
Weights		
Max takeoff	317 kg	(700 lbs)
Useful load	141 kg	(310 lbs)

Mignet HM.1000 Balerit and HM.1100 Cordouan — France

Mignet Aviation, successor to the business created by Henri Mignet, developed the HM.1000 as a two-seater embodying the Mignet tandem wing formula and fitting into the ultra-light weight category. The Balerit, which first flew on 9th April 1984, is an open-frame tubular steel aircraft with a rudimentary glass-fibre cockpit and side-by-side seating. Both wings, which are metal and of constant chord, are foldable for ease of transport and the Balerit is powered by a pusher Rotax 582 engine. It is a factory-built aircraft, more than 100 of which have been sold, including a batch for the French Army which are used as easily transportable artillery spotters. Mignet Aviation also markets the HM.1100 Cordouan as a kit-built aircraft. Following the same tandem wing formula but fitted with ailerons on the rear wing, the Cordouan is a side-by-side two-seater with foldable metal and fabric wings and a composite fuselage with an enclosed cabin. It has a fixed tricycle undercarriage and is powered by an 80 h.p. Rotax 912 or Jabiru 2200 engine.

Specification	Mignet HM.1000 Balerit	
Powerplant	One 64 h.p. (47.7 kW) Rotax 582 piston engine	
Dimensions		
Span	7.3 m	(23 ft 11 in)
Length	5 m	(16 ft 5 in)
Height	1.96 m	(6 ft 5 in)
Performance		
Max speed	150 km/h	(81 kt, 93 mph)
Cruising speed	110 km/h	(59 kt, 68 mph)
Initial climb	360 m/min	(1,181 fpm)
Range	398 km	(216 nm, 249 miles)
Weights		
Max takeoff	374 kg	(825 lbs)
Useful load	200 kg	(441 lbs)

Mignet HM.1000 Ballerit

Mignet Cordouan

Mikoyan MiG-15 and MiG-17 — Russia

The MiG-15 (NATO name 'Fagot') was the first successful jet fighter operated by the Soviet Union and it became standard equipment with all Warsaw Pact countries between its introduction in 1948 and the end of the 1960s. It is a swept-wing aircraft with a retractable tricycle undercarriage, swept cruciform tail and a single-seat cockpit with a clear-view bubble canopy. The 5,000 lb.s.t. Klimov RD-45F turbojet engine is positioned in the centre fuselage and serviced by a nose air intake. The prototype flew on 30th December 1947 and around 12,000 aircraft were built including the improved MiG-15bis with a Klimov VK-1 engine and strengthened structure. Variants included the tandem two-seat MiG-15UTI (NATO name 'Midget') and many single-seat MiG-15s were converted to this standard. Licence-built MiG-15s included the Polish Lim-1 (standard MiG-15), Lim-2 (MiG-15bis) and SBLim-1 and SBLim-2 trainer conversions and the Czech S-102 (MiG-15bis). The MiG-17 (NATO name 'Fresco') is an extensively upgraded MiG-15 with a redesigned wing and longer fuselage which flew on 13th January 1950 and almost 9,000 were built including the Polish Lim-5P (MiG-17PF) and Lim-6bis (MiG-17F) and Czech S-105. The MiG-17F has a VK-1F engine with an afterburner and the MiG-17P and MiG-17PF were night fighter variants. MiG-15s and 17s remain in service with a small number of countries including Albania, Guinea, Mali, Cuba and Syria and around 100, mainly Polish, aircraft have been sold for use as warbirds with private owners.

MiG-15UTI, (SBLim-2), VH-XIG

Specification	Mikoyan MiG-15UTI	
Powerplant	One 5,950 lb.s.t. (26.47 kN) Klimov RD-45FA turbojet	
Dimensions		
Span	10.16 m	(33 ft 4 in)
Length	10.11 m	(33 ft 2 in)
Height	3.76 m	(12 ft 4 in)
Performance		
Max speed	1,014 km/h	(548 kt, 630 mph)
Cruising speed	885 km/h	(478 kt, 550 mph)
Initial climb	2,012 m/min	(6,600 fpm)
Range	1,040 km	(565 nm, 650 miles)
Weights		
Max takeoff	5,400 kg	(11,907 lbs)
Useful load	1,650 kg	(3,638 lbs)

Specification	Mikoyan MiG-19S	
Powerplant	Two 7,275 lb.s.t. (32.36 kN) (wet) Tumanski RD-9BM turbojets	
Dimensions		
Span	9.63 m	(31 ft 7 in)
Length	11.23 m	(36 ft 10 in)
Height	3.81 m	(12 ft 6 in)
Performance		
Max speed	1,102 km/h	(596 kt, 685 mph)
Cruising speed	805 km/h	(435 kt, 500 mph)
Initial climb	3,901 m/min	(12,800 fpm)
Range	2,008 km	(1,091 nm, 1,255 miles)
Weights		
Max takeoff	6,068 kg	(13,380 lbs)
Useful load	2,131 kg	(4,700 lbs)

Mikoyan MiG-19 — Russia

Codenamed 'Farmer' by NATO, the MiG-19 was a supersonic interceptor flown by the Soviet Union and its Warsaw Pact neighbours during the 1950s and early 1960s. It replaced the MiG-15 and MiG-17 and was itself replaced by the MiG-21. It had highly swept tapered wings and retained the MiG-15's nose intake/tail efflux power configuration but had a lower-set tailplane and a distinctive broad-chord vertical tail unit. The prototype first flew on 5th January 1954 and around 2,500 examples were built and operated by various Soviet bloc countries including East Germany, Czechoslovakia and Poland, and by Indonesia, North Korea and Cuba. Variants included the night fighter MiG-19P, the MiG-19S with increased power and armament and the MiG-19PM with all-missile weaponry. It was also built in China at the Nanchang factory as the Shenyang J-6 (MiG-19M and MiG-19P), first flying in 1958 and entering service in 1963. The JJ-6 (and export FT-6) is a tandem two-seat trainer version, the J-6.III is an improved model with the WP6A engine, shorter wingspan and nose centre shock cone and the J-6A is an all-weather fighter with new radar, a new missile system and tail aggressor sensors. The MiG-19 is no longer in military service, although a few are active as warbirds in the USA, but the J-6 and JJ-6 still fly with ten countries including Albania, China, Pakistan and Zambia. A later development, the Nanchang A-5, is described separately.

Shenyang FT-6, Bangladesh AF, 10332

Mikoyan MiG-21 — Russia

The MiG-21 (NATO name 'Fishbed') has proved to be one of the most flexible and widely used of all modern-world jet fighter aircraft and over 10,900 have been built together with 2,500 of the Chinese Chengdu J-7/F-7. Designed to Mikoyan's familiar and straightforward through-flow layout with a nose radar cone, the MiG-21 has a highly swept delta wing, a conventional fin and tailplane and a retractable tricycle undercarriage with the main wing-mounted units folding inwards. The single-seat cockpit is faired into the fuselage with a spine which runs back to the fin leading edge and the MiG-21 has four underwing weapons pylons and a centreline hardpoint. The prototype first flew on 16th June 1955 and the first large-scale production aircraft was the MiG-21F-13 Fishbed-C powered by a Tumanski R-11F-300 reheated turbofan. Later variants included the MiG-21P with improved radars and avionics and an enlarged spine fairing behind the cockpit, MiG-21PF (and export MiG-21FL) with a broader vertical tail, ventral gun pack and modified radar, and the MiG-21PFS and MiG-21PFM with a separate cockpit windshield and canopy and the higher-powered R-11F2S-300 engine. The MiG-21PFM was employed in several versions including the MiG-21R tactical reconnaissance model with externally carried pods, and the related MiG-21S and MiG-21SM (export MiG-21M) were air superiority fighters with a GP-9 cannon and new radars. The final MiG-21 derivative was the MiG-21bis, externally identified by the much-enlarged dorsal spine containing additional fuel. This was designed to carry the AA-8 Aphid air-to-air missile and is powered by the 15,653 lb.s.t. Tumanski R-25-300 engine. In addition to the single-seat MiG-21s, tandem two-seat combat-capable trainers have also been built including the MiG-21U and MiG-21UM (Mongol). The MiG-21 has been built under licence in India by Hindustan and in Czechoslovakia. Major upgrades to the MiG-21 are being carried out by Hindustan in conjunction with MiG-MAPO (MiG-21-93 with electronics upgrades) and by Aerostar in Romania who are currently producing, with Elbit, the enhanced Lancer with a modernised cockpit and new offensive and defensive electronics. The Chinese Chengdu F-7 (later J-7), which first flew on 17th January 1966, is similar to the MiG-21F-13 and the F-7M Airguard is an air defence variant with improved radars. The JJ-7 (export FT-7) is a two-seat combat-capable trainer model and the J-7.III is equivalent to the MiG-21M. The MiG-21 continues in large-scale service with nearly 40 countries.

Mikoyan MiG-21 (Cont.)

MiG-21MF, Hungarian AF, 9602

MiG-21U Lancer B, Romanian AF, 9511

Specification	Mikoyan MiG-21MF Fishbed J	
Powerplant	One 9,340 lb.s.t. (41.55 kN) (dry) Tumanski R-13-300 turbojet	
Dimensions		
Span	7.14 m	(23 ft 5 in)
Length	12.29 m	(40 ft 4 in)
Height	4.50 m	(14 ft 9 in)
Performance		
Max speed	2,180 km/h	(1,178 kt, 1,355 mph)
Cruising speed	1,931 km/h	(1,043 kt, 1,200 mph)
Initial climb	9,144 m/min	(30,000 fpm)
Range	1,792 km	(974 nm, 1,120 miles)
Weights		
Max takeoff	9,800 kg	(21,609 lbs)
Useful load	3,950 kg	(8,710 lbs)

Mikoyan MiG-23 — Russia

Designed by the Mikoyan Bureau, the MiG-23 became the Soviet Union's principal new-generation single-engined interceptor in the 1970s to replace the MiG-21. It was intended to provide improved STOL and short-field performance and it departs from the traditional MiG fighter design layout in having variable-geometry flank air intakes and a variable-sweep shoulder wing with the main undercarriage units retracting into fuselage wells. It first flew on 10th June 1967 with first deliveries being made to Soviet forces in 1973, and output by MiG-MAPO had reached approximately 2,000 aircraft when production ceased in 1985. The MiG-23 (NATO name 'Flogger') has one under-fuselage-mounted 23 mm GSh-23L twin barrel gun, two centre fuselage pylons to carry AA-8 Aphid or AA-7 Apex air-to-air missiles and two pylons on the non-moving inner wing sections for air-to-surface rockets, bombs and other stores. Variants include the initial MiG-23S with a 22,050 lb.s.t. Tumanski R-27F2M-300 engine; the main-production MiG-23M with a 27,550 lb.s.t. R-29-300 engine, a modified wing, rear-mounted tailplane, ventral fin and additional fuel capacity; the Mig-23ML and MiG-23P with increased power and lighter gross weight; the MiG-23MLD with agile aerodynamic modifications; and the MiG-23B (and BK, BM and BN) fighter-bomber powered by a 25,350 lb.s.t. Lyulka AL-21F-300 engine with a slim pointed nose which does not carry the radar used on other variants. The MiG-27 is similar to the MiG-23BM but has fixed air intakes and modified afterburner. A tandem two-seat MiG-23UB was also built. The MiG-23 was being withdrawn from front-line operation by mid-1998 but its export MiG-23MF and MiG-23MS versions have been in service in 21 countries including Poland, the Czech Republic, Hungary, Romania, Cuba, India, Bulgaria and Iraq.

MiG-23MF, Romanian AF, 205

Specification	Mikoyan MiG-23ML	
Powerplant	One 28,660 lb.s.t. (127.5 kN) (wet) Tumanski R-35-300 turbojet	
Dimensions		
Span	13.94 m	(45 ft 9 in)
Length	16 m	(52 ft 6 in)
Height	4.83 m	(15 ft 10 in)
Performance		
Max speed	2,881 km/h	(1,556 kt, 1,790 mph)
Cruising speed	1,094 km/h	(591 kt, 680 mph)
Initial climb (est)	13,106 m/min	(43,000 fpm)
Range	2,240 km	(1,217 nm, 1,400 miles)
Weights		
Max takeoff	18,900 kg	(41,675 lbs)
Useful load	8,700 kg	(19,184 lbs)

Mikoyan MiG-25 and MiG-31 — Russia

The MiG-25 (NATO name 'Foxbat') was developed in the late 1950s as a high-altitude fighter to intercept new-generation American high-performance reconnaissance aircraft and strategic bombers such as the B-70 Valkyrie. First flown on 6th March 1964 as the Ye-155R, it is a very large Mach 3 fighter built around two 24,690 s.h.p. Tumanski reheated turbofans which are fed by sharply angled air intakes. It has a shoulder wing, twin vertical fins and a low-set tailplane. The retractable tricycle undercarriage has large single main wheels and the MiG-25 is fitted with four underwing pylons to carry AA-6 missiles. Variants included the initial MiG-25P which went into service in 1973, the MiG-25PU operational trainer with an additional cockpit in an extended nose, the MiG-25PD with improved engines and modified LD/SD radar and MiG-25PDS with an extended nose, the MiG-25R reconnaissance aircraft and the MiG-25RB bomber with additional fuselage strongpoints. The MiG-31 (NATO name 'Foxhound'), which first flew as the MiG-25MP on 16th September 1975, was a substantially redesigned MiG-25 with a larger fuselage, wing leading edge extensions, a tandem two-seat cockpit and twin-wheel main undercarriage units. Offensive weapons were carried on four wing pylons and six under-fuselage hardpoints supported by a 'Flashdance' radar, and the MiG-31 and improved MiG-31M are powered by two 34,170 lb.s.t. Soloviev D-30F6 reheated turbofans. Nearly 1,200 MiG-25s were built and used by India, Syria, Algeria, Iraq and Libya in addition to the Soviet forces. Around 400 MiG-31s are believed to have been completed but none has been exported.

Specification	Mikoyan MiG-25RB	
Powerplant	Two 24,690 lb.s.t. (109.8 kN) Tumanski R-15BD-300 turbofans	
Dimensions		
Span	13.39 m	(43 ft 11 in)
Length	21.56 m	(70 ft 9 in)
Height	5.99 m	(19 ft 8 in)
Performance		
Max speed	3,001 km/h	(1,622 kt, 1,865 mph)
Initial climb	13,533 m/min	(44,400 fpm)
Range	2,088 km	(1,135 nm, 1,305 miles)
Weights		
Max takeoff	66,000 kg	(145,530 lbs)
Useful load	32,000 kg	(70,560 lbs)

Mikoyan MiG-25PU, Russian AF, 91 (red)

Mikoyan MiG-31M, Russian AF, 057 (blue)

Mikoyan MiG-29 — Russia

The MiG-29 (NATO name 'Fulcrum') is a lightweight air defence fighter developed in the mid-1970s and the first prototype flew on 6th October 1977. Production MiG-29s entered service in 1983. The aircraft has a virtual-delta wing with large forward fairings, twin fins and prominent belly air intakes for the twin 18,300 lb.s.t (wet) Klimov RD-33 reheated turbofans. It has an all-moving tailplane and, in early models, additional ventral fins. Offensive armament, contained on six underwing pylons, normally consists of R-27R Alamo or R-73-RM2D Archer AAMs or B-8 rocket pods for ground attack missions, but the MiG-29 is nuclear capable and can carry the RN-40 nuclear bomb. Variants include the MiG-29A and B exports model for many countries including Bulgaria, Czechoslovakia, Cuba, India, Iran, Iraq, Poland and North Korea, the MiG-29 (9-13) Fulcrum-C and improved MiG-29S with a raised fuselage line containing additional fuel and ECM equipment, the MiG-29M with a lightened airframe and additional fuel, the MiG-29K naval variant with folding outer wings and eight wing pylons, and the MiG-29SMT which is an upgraded version with a large conformal fuel tank on the upper fuselage and RD-43 engines. Tandem two-seat combat-capable trainers include the MiG-29UB and the MiG-29UBT with the conformal fuel tanks. Around 1,500 MiG-29s have been built by MiG-MAPO and production is now largely for export customers with 22 non-Russian countries currently operating the aircraft.

MiG-29UB, Romanian AF, 15

Mikoyan MiG-29 (Cont.)

MiG-29A, Slovak AF, 6930

Specification	Mikoyan MiG-29S	
Powerplant	Two 18,300 lb.s.t. (81.4 kN) (wet) Klimov RD-33 turbofans	
Dimensions		
Span	11.35 m	(37 ft 3 in)
Length	16.28 m	(53 ft 5 in)
Height	4.72 m	(15 ft 6 in)
Performance		
Max speed	1,497 km/h	(809 kt, 930 mph)
Initial climb	11,582 m/min	(38,000 fpm)
Range	2,080 km	(1,130 nm, 1,300 miles)
Weights		
Max takeoff	19,700 kg	(43,939 lbs)
Useful load	8,800 kg	(19,404 lbs)

Mikoyan MiG-AT — Russia

The MiG-AT is a private-venture advanced jet trainer with combat capability developed by MiG-MAPO to a Russian Air Force requirement. It is in competition with the Yak-130. The MiG-AT is a low-wing tandem two-seater with two SNECMA Larzac turbofans fitted above the inner wing sections and it has fly-by-wire systems and French Sextant avionics. During development these nacelles have been lengthened with the air intakes moved to a point ahead of the wing. The prototype first flew on 16th March 1996 and two aircraft have been built, the second having underwing pylons. Up to wing hardpoints, two wingtip positions and one fuselage pylon are available. MiG-MAPO also plan a single-seater designated MiG-AC and a naval version with arrester gear and folding wings. By late 1999 only a small evaluation batch had been ordered by the Russian Air Force.

MiG-AT

Specification	MiG-MAPO MiG-AT	
Powerplant	Two 3,175 lb.s.t. (14.2 kN) SNECMA Larzac 04-R20 turbofans	
Dimensions		
Span	10.16 m	(33 ft 4 in)
Length	12.01 m	(39 ft 5 in)
Height	4.62 m	(15 ft 2 in)
Performance		
Max speed	853 km/h	(461 kt, 530 mph)
Cruising speed	772 km/h	(417 kt, 480 mph)
Initial climb	3,962 m/min	(13,000 fpm)
Range	2,576 km	(1,400 nm, 1,610 miles)
Weights		
Max takeoff	7,000 kg	(15,435 lbs)
Useful load	2,830 kg	(6,240 lbs)

Mil Mi-2 — Russia/Poland

The Mil Mi-1 (NATO name 'Hare') which first flew in September 1948, was designed by Mikhail L. Mil as a light utility helicopter for military and civil use and several thousand were built between 1950 and 1965. The Mi-1, which is now retired from service, was very modern for its time, having a four-seat cabin, an AI-26V piston engine in the centre fuselage and three-blade main and tail rotors. In 1955 production was taken over by PZL-Swidnik in Poland who built it as the SM-1 and modified SM-2 and they developed a modernised version, the Mi-2, which first flew in September 1961. This was virtually a new design with a modified fuselage with an increase to nine-seats, made possible by positioning the twin Isotov GTD-350 turboshafts above the cabin. A large port-side door allowed carriage of four stretchers for ambulance work and the Mi-2 could be used for heavy lifting or for agricultural work with two external spray tanks on the rear fuselage sides. Variants included the Mi-2R for search & rescue, Mi-2T military trainer and the Mi-2URN and Mi-2URP gunship and anti-tank models. The PZL Kania is a modified civil version, eight of which were built, with a longer nose, composite rotors and twin 420 s.h.p. Allison 250-C20B turboshafts. In total, 5,080 Mi-2s were built and the type remains in widespread use with 17 air arms in the former Warsaw Pact and with civil agencies.

Mil Mi-2, Slovak Police, B-2406

Specification	Mil (PZL) Mi-2	
Powerplant	Two 437 s.h.p. (325.8 kW) Isotov GTD-350 turboshafts	
Dimensions		
Rotor diameter	14.5 m	(47 ft 7 in)
Length	11.4 m	(37 ft 5 in)
Height	3.73 m	(12 ft 3 in)
Performance		
Max speed	209 km/h	(113 kt, 130 mph)
Cruising speed	201 km/h	(109 kt, 125 mph)
Initial climb	270 m/min	(885 fpm)
Range	576 km	(313 nm, 360 miles)
Weights		
Max takeoff	3,700 kg	(8,158 lbs)
Useful load	1,350 kg	(2,977 lbs)

Mil Mi-4 — Russia

Mikhail Mil established himself as a successful helicopter designer with the Mi-2 and this was followed by the Mi-4 built for the Soviet Army as a larger capacity 14-troop general-purpose helicopter. The Mi-4 (NATO name 'Hound'), which flew in May 1952, was very similar to the contemporary Sikorsky S-55, having a nose-mounted piston engine in an angled installation with an articulated drive to a four-blade rotor. The two-crew cockpit was in the nose above the engine with the main passenger compartment below and behind. The Mi-4 had rear clamshell doors to load military equipment and a fixed four-leg undercarriage. Over 3,000 military and civil Mi-4s were built and 545 were produced in China as the Harbin Z-5 and the enlarged Harbin Z-6. The Mi-4 was used in various roles including Aeroflot's civil passenger operations, for which it was fitted with square cabin windows (Mi-4P), and was employed for agricultural spraying (Mi-4Skh), army general-purpose transport, sometimes fitted with a belly gun pack (Mi-4T), and as a naval anti-submarine helicopter (Mi-4PLO). Mi-4s were exported to over 30 countries and, while most have been retired, a few still serve with the Albanian Air Force and Harbin Z-5s are active in China.

Mil Mi-4, CCCP-35277

Specification	Mil Mi-4	
Powerplant	One 1,700 h.p. (1,267.5 kW) ASh-82V piston engine	
Dimensions		
Rotor diameter	17.22 m	(56 ft 6 in)
Length	13.82 m	(45 ft 4 in)
Height	4.67 m	(15 ft 4 in)
Performance		
Max speed	209 km/h	(113 kt, 130 mph)
Cruising speed	195 km/h	(105 kt, 121 mph)
Initial climb	244 m/min	(800 fpm)
Range	256 km	(139 nm, 160 miles)
Weights		
Max takeoff	6,349 kg	(14,000 lbs)
Useful load	998 kg	(2,200 lbs)

Mil Mi-6 — Russia

In the mid-1950s, the Mil design bureau produced the world's largest helicopter, designated Mi-6 (NATO name 'Hook'). In many ways, the Soviet Union saw more potential for the helicopter during the 1950s than was accepted in the West. This huge helicopter, which first flew in September 1957, was conventional in general layout except for having optional short wings mounted on the centre fuselage, and was capable of carrying up to 90 troops. It used a pair of Soloviev D-25V turbines fitted on top of the fuselage to drive a large five-bladed main rotor. Around 800 examples were built between 1959 and 1980 and they were delivered to most Warsaw Pact air forces and were used extensively for civil passenger and cargo carrying, firefighting, aeromedical work and heavy lift tasks. The Mi-22 was a specialised military command post version. The Mi-6 design led to the Mi-10 aerial crane, which is no longer in service. The Mi-6 has largely been replaced by the Mi-26 but a number still serve with the Russian forces and with several other military arms including those of Egypt, Iraq, Laos, Syria and Vietnam.

Mil Mi-6 (Cont.)

Mil Mi-6, CCCP-21003

Specification	Mil Mi-6	
Powerplant	Two 5,500 s.h.p. (4,100 kW) Soloviev D-25V turboshafts	
Dimensions		
Rotor diameter	35 m	(114 ft 10 in)
Length	33.17 m	(108 ft 10 in)
Height	9.85 m	(32 ft 4 in)
Performance		
Max speed	298 km/h	(161 kt, 185 mph)
Cruising speed	249 km/h	(135 kt, 155 mph)
Initial climb	244 m/min	(800 fpm)
Range	1,440 km	(783 nm, 900 miles)
Weights		
Max takeoff	37,500 kg	(82,687 lbs)
Useful load	10,260 kg	(22,623 lbs)

Mil Mi-8 and Mi-17 — Russia

The Mil Mi-8 was a larger-capacity replacement for the Mi-4 utility helicopter and the prototype, designated V-8, was flown in 1961. The Mi-8 (NATO name 'Hip') has an almost circular-section fuselage with external tanks, a flight deck in the extreme nose, a conventional tail boom with a port-side stabilising rotor and two 1,700 s.h.p. Isotov TV2-117A turboshafts mounted on top of the fuselage so as to give a fully usable interior space. Civil Mi-8P (and VIP Mi-8S and Mi-8PS) versions have large rectangular cabin windows but the 24-seat military Mi-8T has porthole windows and rear clamshell doors for equipment loading. The Mi-8TB is fitted with a 12.7 mm Afanasayev machine gun and larger outriggers for six rocket pods and four anti-tank missiles and the standard Mi-8T is frequently fitted with outriggers to carry twin rocket launchers. The many Mi-8 variants include the export Mi-8TB, Mi-8MA for Antarctic support, Mi-8MB aeromedical version, the Mi-9 airborne command post and the Mi-8AMT hot-and-high version with TV3-117VM engines. The Mi-17 is an improved Mi-8 which first flew in 1976 and has the dynamic systems of the Mi-14, 1,950 s.h.p. TV3-117MT engines and a starboard tail rotor. Now built by Kazan Helicopters, the main versions are the civil Mi-17-1, the military Mi-17MT (often referred to as Mi-8M), the Mi-17P for communications jamming with a large rear fuselage antenna array, the export Mi-17M, the Mi-17MD high-capacity 40-troop transport with a rear ramp in place of the clamshell doors and an enlarged radar nose, and the Mi-173 (formerly Mi-18) with a 3 ft fuselage stretch and retractable undercarriage. Over 10,000 Mi-8s and Mi-17s have been built and exports have been made to more than 60 countries for both military and civil use.

Mil Mi-8, D-HOZH

Mil Mi-17MD

Specification	Mil Mi-17MT	
Powerplant	Two 1,950 s.h.p. (1,454 kW) Isotov/Klimov TV3-117MT turboshafts	
Dimensions		
Rotor diameter	21.28 m	(69 ft 10 in)
Length	18.21 m	(59 ft 9 in)
Height	5.54 m	(18 ft 2 in)
Performance		
Max speed	249 km/h	(135 kt, 155 mph)
Cruising speed	225 km/h	(122 kt, 140 mph)
Initial climb (est)	579 m/min	(1,900 fpm)
Range	1,600 km	(870 nm, 1,000 miles)
Weights		
Max takeoff	13,000 kg	(28,665 lbs)
Useful load	5,800 kg	(12,789 lbs)

Mil Mi-14 — Russia

The Mil Mi-14 (NATO name 'Haze') is a substantially redesigned version of the Mil Mi-8 transport helicopter, intended for naval shipboard anti-submarine operations and maritime patrol. The fuselage is deeper and has a boat hull for water landings and there is an additional tail-mounted float and external fuselage sponsons into which the main undercarriage units retract. The standard Mi-14PL does not have the rear clamshell doors of the Mi-8, this position being used to house the trailing magnetic anomaly detector equipment, and a prominent retractable radome is fitted under the forward fuselage for the Type 12-M radar antenna. The helicopter is powered by two 1,950 s.h.p. Isotov TV3-117MT turboshafts driving a five-blade main rotor, although some early examples have the TV2-117. Other versions include the Mi-14BT fitted for mine clearing and the Mi-14PS with a larger entry door and a winch for search & rescue. A civil passenger version, the Mi-14P has been produced with up to 24 seats. In addition to Russian Naval Aviation (whose aircraft are now largely in reserve), users include Cuba, Ethiopia, Libya, Bulgaria, North Korea, Poland and Romania. Two are in evaluative service with the USAF and production ceased in 1986 with a total of 273 aircraft.

Mil Mi-14PS, S9-TAJ

Mil Mi-14 (Cont.)

Specification	Mil Mi-14PL	
Powerplant	Two 1,950 s.h.p. (1,454 kW) Isotov/Klimov TV3-117MT turboshafts	
Dimensions		
Rotor diameter	21.28 m	(69 ft 10 in)
Length	18.36 m	(60 ft 3 in)
Height	6.93 m	(22 ft 9 in)
Performance		
Max speed	230 km/h	(124 kt, 143 mph)
Cruising speed	209 km/h	(113 kt, 130 mph)
Range	800 km	(435 nm, 500 miles)
Weights		
Max takeoff	14,000 kg	(30,870 lbs)
Useful load	5,100 kg	(11,245 lbs)

Mil Mi-24 — Russia

The Mil Mi-24 is unique in combining full anti-tank gunship capability with the capacity to carry eight ground troops. The engines and dynamic systems were largely taken from the Mi-8, and the Mi-24 (NATO name 'Hind') has a main central cabin for troops or equipment, a conventional tail boom with an anti-torque rotor on the port side (although early models had it on the starboard), a retractable tricycle undercarriage and large anhedralled stub wings, each with three hardpoints for rocket pods and anti-tank AT-2 Swatter missiles. Early Mi-24s had a large 'glasshouse' cockpit with a 12.7 mm machine gun in the nose but the later Mi-24D had echeloned tandem bubble cockpits with the pilot in the rear and the gunner in the front and a large chin-mounted gun turret. The Mi-24V was an upgraded version with improved systems including a HUD and fittings for AT-6 missiles. Alternative weapons are used in the Mi-24VP and the Mi-24K is an army reconnaissance model, while the Mi-24PS is for civilian police support operations. The Mi-25 and Mi-35 are export versions, often with downgraded equipment. Production exceeds 2,500 and the helicopter has been widely exported with Mi-24s operating with 35 countries.

Mil Mi-24V, Czech AF, 0710

Specification	Mil Mi-24V	
Powerplant	Two 2,225 s.h.p. (1,659 kW) Isotov/Klimov TV3-117VMA turboshafts	
Dimensions		
Rotor diameter	17.3 m	(56 ft 9 in)
Length	17.5 m	(57 ft 5 in)
Height	5.46 m	(17 ft 11 in)
Performance		
Max speed	338 km/h	(183 kt, 210 mph)
Cruising speed	281 km/h	(152 kt, 175 mph)
Range	1,120 km	(609 nm, 700 miles)
Weights		
Max takeoff	11,500 kg	(25,358 lbs)
Useful load	3,160 kg	(6,968 lbs)

Mil Mi-26 — Russia

The Mil Mi-26 was the replacement for the earlier Mi-6 heavy transport helicopter. It was first flown on 14th December 1977 and went into military service in 1985. Compared with its predecessor, the Mi-26 (NATO name 'Halo') has a lighter airframe and more powerful engines which results in much improved overall performance. The helicopter, which is in military and (as the Mi-26T) civil service, has a fixed tricycle undercarriage and a rear loading ramp for handling freight and military equipment. In passenger configuration it can carry 80 troops or up to 60 stretcher cases. The Mi-26 is also used for heavy lift work with large underslung loads and the Mi-26TM is fitted with an external crane operator's station on the port side. Other versions include the Mi-26P for firefighting, Mi-26TZ fuel supply tanker and Mi-26TM1 with improved avionics. The Mi-26 continues in production with Rostvertol and more than 270 have been built including military examples for India, Peru and North Korea.

Mil Mi-26, RA-29109

Specification	Mil Mi-26	
Powerplant	Two 11,400 s.h.p. (8,500 kW) Ivchenko-Progress D-136 turboshafts	
Dimensions		
Rotor diameter	32 m	(105 ft 0 in)
Length	33.73 m	(110 ft 8 in)
Height	3.17 m	(10 ft 5 in)
Performance		
Max speed	290 km/h	(157 kt, 180 mph)
Cruising speed	257 km/h	(139 kt, 160 mph)
Range	664 km	(361 nm, 415 miles)
Weights		
Max takeoff	56,000 kg	(123,480 lbs)
Useful load	27,700 kg	(61,078 lbs)

Specification	Mil Mi-28	
Powerplant	Two 2,225 s.h.p. (1,659 kW) Isotov/Klimov TV3-117VMA turboshafts	
Dimensions		
Rotor diameter	17.19 m	(56 ft 5 in)
Length	17.02 m	(55 ft 10 in)
Height	3.86 m	(12 ft 8 in)
Performance		
Max speed	298 km/h	(161 kt, 185 mph)
Cruising speed	266 km/h	(143 kt, 165 mph)
Initial climb	814 m/min	(2,670 fpm)
Range	1,104 km	(600 nm, 690 miles)
Weights		
Max takeoff	11,660 kg	(25,710 lbs)
Useful load	3,560 kg	(7,850 lbs)

Mil Mi-28 — Russia

The Mi-28 two-seat helicopter gunship (NATO name 'Havoc') was designed to meet a Russian Army requirement but was not ordered in quantity, the winner of the competition being the Kamov Ka-50. Nevertheless, the Mi-28 is still being offered for sale to overseas air forces. It is conventional in external layout with stepped tandem cockpits in the nose, a tailwheel undercarriage and twin Isotov TV3-117 turboshafts in separate pods either side of the main rotor pylon. The Mi-28 has stub wings with two weapons pylons and tip mountings for countermeasures pods, and typical offensive loads include 80 S-8 rockets in four pods or 16 Ataka missiles with 10 S-13 rockets. A turret beneath the nose houses a 30 mm 2A42 cannon with a 180-degree horizontal and 53-degree vertical field of fire. The prototype Mi-28A first flew on 10th November 1982 followed by three further prototypes, and Rostvertol have also built one Mi-28N night attack version, which flew on 14th November 1996 with an Almaz-28 radar ball on the top of the rotor mast.

Mil Mi-34 — Russia

The Mi-34 light helicopter is unusual in current circumstances in being powered by a piston engine. It was originally intended as a training helicopter for the DOSAAF civil flying organisation but production aircraft have been largely sold as the Mi-34P for police and civil agency work. The prototype first flew on 17th November 1986 and approximately 20 had been built by the end of 1999. The production Mi-34C (NATO name 'Hermit') is a four-seat machine with a fixed skid undercarriage, a four-blade main rotor and a conventional tail boom carrying a two-bladed composite anti-torque rotor. The engine is buried in the fuselage behind the cabin. For police work, external skyshouting amplifiers can be carried on fuselage outriggers and a searchlight and FLIR pod are fitted beneath the nose. A military version, designated Mi-34VAZ (or Mi-34M), which first flew in 1993, is being developed, powered by two VAZ-430 rotary piston engines, but no orders had been placed by the end of 1999.

Mi-28N, 014

Mil Mi-34

Mil Mi-34 (Cont.)

Specification	Mil Mi-34C	
Powerplant	One 325 h.p. (242 kW) Vedeneyev/ OKBM-Voronezh M-14V26 piston engine	
Dimensions		
Rotor diameter	10.01 m	(32 ft 10 in)
Length	8.71 m	(28 ft 7 in)
Height	3.05 m	(10 ft 0 in)
Performance		
Max speed	225 km/h	(122 kt, 140 mph)
Cruising speed	185 km/h	(100 kt, 115 mph)
Initial climb	317 m/min	(1,040 fpm)
Range	600 km	(326 nm, 375 miles)
Weights		
Max takeoff	1,450 kg	(3,197 lbs)
Useful load	500 kg	(1,102 lbs)

Miles M.2F and M.14 Hawk Trainer — UK

Miles Aircraft, as one of the largest prewar British producers of light aircraft, built a large number of tandem two-seat trainers during the 1930s. First flown on 29th March 1933 and introduced in 1934, the M.2F Hawk Major was a low-wing wood and fabric aircraft with a fixed tailwheel undercarriage and open cockpits and was powered by a 130 h.p. de Havilland Gipsy Major in-line engine. Minor variations gave rise to several alternative designations including M.2G (three-seat cabin model), M.2H (with split flaps), M.2R (with larger wings) and the M.2W and M.2X Hawk Trainers which had enlarged cockpits, blind flying equipment and dual controls. The M.2X formed the basis for the M.14 Hawk Trainer III which was built for wartime RAF training as the Magister. The Magister had a larger rudder than the M.2X, extra tail anti-spin strakes and modified main undercarriage spats. The M.14A had the 130 h.p. Gipsy Major engine but the M.14B was fitted with a 135 h.p. Blackburn Cirrus Major 2. In total, 53 M.2 Hawk Majors/Trainers and 1,293 Magisters were built together with 100 M.14 Ugurs completed in Turkey. At least two Hawk Majors and ten Hawk Trainer IIIs remain although only a handful are active.

Miles M.14 Hawk Trainer III, P6382 (G-AJRS)

Specification	Miles M.14A Hawk Trainer III	
Powerplant	One 130 h.p. (96.9 kW) de Havilland Gipsy Major piston engine	
Dimensions		
Span	10.31 m	(33 ft 10 in)
Length	7.49 m	(24 ft 7 in)
Height	2.03 m	(6 ft 8 in)
Performance		
Max speed	225 km/h	(122 kt, 140 mph)
Cruising speed	201 km/h	(109 kt, 125 mph)
Initial climb	229 m/min	(750 fpm)
Range	584 km	(317 nm, 365 miles)
Weights		
Max takeoff	862 kg	(1,900 lbs)
Useful load	278 kg	(614 lbs)

Miles M.3A Falcon Six — UK

With the open two-seat M.2 Hawk series well established in production, F.G. Miles designed a larger version with a fully enclosed cabin. The prototype M.3A Falcon Major first flew on 12th October 1934 powered by a Gipsy Major engine. It was very similar to the Hawk Major except for its wider fuselage and integral cabin which could accommodate a pilot and three passengers. The undercarriage had large streamlined fairings and the windscreen was raked forward. Several variants followed including the M.3B Falcon Six, which had improved performance as a result of being fitted with a 200 h.p. de Havilland Gipsy Six engine, and the M.3D, which was similar but had a strengthened airframe and higher gross weight and was fitted with a rounded windscreen. Two M.3As are active in the UK and Australia and an M.3C Falcon Six flies in Spain. Two examples of the similar two-seat M.11A Whitney Straight and three three-seat M.17 Monarchs are also extant, but currently inactive.

Miles M.3A Falcon Major, G-AEEG

Specification	Miles M.3A Falcon Major	
Powerplant	One 130 h.p. (96.9 kW) de Havilland Gipsy Major piston engine	
Dimensions		
Span	10.67 m	(35 ft 0 in)
Length	7.62 m	(25 ft 0 in)
Height	1.98 m	(6 ft 6 in)
Performance		
Max speed	233 km/h	(126 kt, 145 mph)
Cruising speed	201 km/h	(109 kt, 125 mph)
Initial climb	228 m/min	(750 fpm)
Range	984 km	(535 nm, 615 miles)
Weights		
Max takeoff	998 kg	(2,200 lbs)
Useful load	408 kg	(900 lbs)

Miles M.38 Messenger 4B, G-AKVZ

Miles M.38 Messenger — UK

In 1941, Miles Aircraft designed a new light military communications aircraft designated M.28 and flew the prototype on 11th July 1941. Of largely wooden construction, the M.28 had a low wing, a fully enclosed four-seat cabin, a retractable tailwheel undercarriage and a twin-finned tail unit. The six M.28s which were built had a variety of engines but most used the 150 h.p. Blackburn Cirrus Major III. The design was then developed into the M.38 Messenger army cooperation aircraft, powered by a 140 h.p. de Havilland Gipsy Major engine. The Messenger had a larger wing with external trailing edge flaps, a triple-fin tail unit and a fixed trailing-link undercarriage. It first flew on 12th September 1942 and 21 were built as four-seat AOP and liaison aircraft. After the war, the Messenger was built for civil sale as the Messenger 2A (Cirrus Major III), Messenger 3 (with electrical split flaps) and Messenger 4 (with a 145 h.p. Gipsy Major 10). Miles built 93 Messengers including 21 military aircraft and at least six are currently airworthy together with one M.28.

Specification	Miles M.38 Messenger 2A	
Powerplant	One 150 h.p. (111.8 kW) Blackburn Cirrus Major III piston engine	
Dimensions		
Span	11.02 m	(36 ft 2 in)
Length	7.31 m	(24 ft 0 in)
Height	2.9 m	(9 ft 6 in)
Performance		
Max speed	216 km/h	(117 kt, 134 mph)
Cruising speed	188 km/h	(102 kt, 117 mph)
Initial climb	227 m/min	(745 fpm)
Range	800 km	(435 nm, 500 miles)
Weights		
Max takeoff	1,088 kg	(2,400 lbs)
Useful load	390 kg	(860 lbs)

Miles M.28, OY-ALW

Miles M.65 Gemini — UK

The Gemini was designed by George Miles at the end of World War II for sale to postwar private owners. It was a straightforward adaptation of the Miles M.38 Messenger with the nose engine replaced by two wing-mounted 100 h.p. Blackburn Cirrus Minor in-line engines. The tail unit had two rather than three fins, extra fuel tanks were fitted and the Gemini had an electrically operated retractable tailwheel undercarriage. The prototype flew on 26th October 1945 and it went into production as the Gemini 1A shortly afterwards. Several variants followed including the Gemini 3 which was a higher-powered version with 145 h.p. Gipsy Major 1C engines. A total of 149 Geminis had been built when Miles collapsed in 1947. In addition, two examples of the M.75 Aries were built by F.G. Miles Ltd. and these had larger fins and 155 h.p. Blackburn Cirrus Major III engines. Two Geminis are airworthy although at least another five are under restoration.

Miles M.65 Gemini (Cont.)

Miles M.65 Gemini 1A, G-AKKB

Specification	Miles M.65 Gemini 1A	
Powerplant	Two 100 h.p. (74.6 kW) Blackburn Cirrus Minor II piston engines	
Dimensions		
Span	11.02 m	(36 ft 2 in)
Length	6.76 m	(22 ft 2 in)
Height	2.29 m	(7 ft 6 in)
Performance		
Max speed	235 km/h	(127 kt, 146 mph)
Cruising speed	211 km/h	(114 kt, 131 mph)
Initial climb	183 m/min	(600 fpm)
Range	1,584 km	(861 nm, 990 miles)
Weights		
Max takeoff	1,361 kg	(3,000 lbs)
Useful load	485 kg	(1,070 lbs)

Mitchell-Procter Kittiwake and Petrel — UK

The Kittiwake I was designed by Dr. C. Mitchell and built as a prototype by Mitchell-Procter Aircraft, making its first flight on 23rd May 1967. It is an all-metal low-wing single-seat light aircraft intended for glider towing or private recreational use and it has a fixed tricycle undercarriage, a large cockpit enclosed by a bubble canopy and a 100 h.p. Continental O-200-A engine. A second Kittiwake was built by Royal Navy apprentices in 1971 and used as a glider tug. Both Kittiwakes are currently active. A side-by-side two-seat version, the Kittiwake II, was also built and flown on 19th March 1972. Of similar layout to the Kittiwake I, it had a 130 h.p. Continental O-240 engine and was intended for production by Procter Aircraft Associates. A second aircraft, called the Procter Petrel, was also built but neither of the two-seaters is now airworthy.

Mitchell-Procter Kittiwake I, XW784 (G-BBRN)

Specification	Mitchell-Procter Kittiwake I	
Powerplant	One 100 h.p. (74.6 kW) Teledyne Continental O-200-A piston engine	
Dimensions		
Span	7.31 m	(24 ft 0 in)
Length	5.97 m	(19 ft 7 in)
Height	2.29 m	(7 ft 6 in)
Performance		
Max speed	211 km/h	(114 kt, 131 mph)
Cruising speed	196 km/h	(106 kt, 122 mph)
Initial climb	320 m/min	(1,050 fpm)
Range	864 km	(470 nm, 540 miles)
Weights		
Max takeoff	612 kg	(1,350 lbs)
Useful load	200 kg	(440 lbs)

Mitsubishi T-2 and F-1 — Japan

The Mitsubishi T-2 advanced trainer was the first indigenous supersonic military aircraft produced by the Japanese aircraft industry. Design was initiated in September 1967 and the aircraft was first flown as the XT-2 on 20th July 1971. After testing four prototypes the first production T-2 was delivered to the JASDF in March 1975. The T-2 is a tandem two-seat aircraft with a shoulder-set swept wing and conventional fin and anhedralled tailplane. The tricycle undercarriage retracts into fuselage wells. It is powered by two Rolls Royce Turboméca Adour reheated turbofans licence-built as the Ishikawajima-Harima TF40-IHI-801A and these are mounted side-by-side on the lower fuselage. When equipped for combat training the T-2A has six underwing hardpoints, a centreline fuel tank station and a Vulcan M61A-1 20 mm multi-barrel cannon in the lower port-side nose. Some 92 production T-2s were built for the JASDF. Such was the success of the T-2 that the JASDF ordered a single-seat version, designated F-1, as a close air support fighter and the first of two T-2s converted as prototypes flew on 3rd June 1975. The principal modifications were the enclosure of the rear cockpit to make an avionics bay for a bombing computer, navigation equipment, a Mitsubishi ASG-1 fire control system and radar warning together with fitment of wingtip AIM-9 Sidewinder hardpoints. A total of 77 T-2s had been built by March 1987 when production ceased.

Mitsubishi F-1, JASDF, 70-8201

Mitsubishi F-2 — Japan

The Mitsubishi F-2 is a substantially modified version of the F-16C Fighting Falcon developed by Mitsubishi in conjunction with Lockheed Martin and in joint production with Kawasaki and Fuji. The prototype single-seat XF-2A flew on 7th October 1995 and a further XF-2A and two XF-2B two-seaters have been used in the development programme. Changes from the F-16C include an enlarged composite wing with forward sweep on the rear edge, a new cockpit canopy with a separate windshield, modified wing leading edge root extensions and a revised under-fuselage profile to accommodate the General Electric F110-GE-129 reheated turbofan. The F-2 is fitted with a Vulcan M61A-1 20 mm multi-barrel cannon and has 13 external hardpoints which permit carriage of normal air-to-air and ground attack stores and ASM-1 and ASM-2 anti-ship missiles. Production deliveries were initiated in late 1999 to meet a JASDF requirement for 83 F-2As and 47 F-2Bs.

Mitsubishi T-2, JASDF, 19-5168

Mitsubishi F-2, 63-0001

Specification	Mitsubishi T-2	
Powerplant	Two 5,115 lb.s.t. (22.75 kN) (wet) Ishikawajima-Harima TF40-IHI-801A turbofans	
Dimensions		
Span	7.87 m	(25 ft 10 in)
Length	17.86 m	(58 ft 7 in)
Height	4.39 m	(14 ft 5 in)
Performance		
Max speed	1,963 km/h	(1,061 kt, 1,220 mph)
Initial climb	10,668 m/min	(35,000 fpm)
Range	2,576 km	(1,400 nm, 1,610 miles)
Weights		
Max takeoff	12,800 kg	(28,224 lbs)
Useful load	2,490 kg	(5,490 lbs)

Specification	Mitsubishi F-2	
Powerplant	One 29,600 lb.s.t. (131.7 kN) (wet) General Electric F110-GE-129 turbofan	
Dimensions		
Span	11.12 m	(36 ft 6 in)
Length	15.52 m	(50 ft 11 in)
Height	4.95 m	(16 ft 3 in)
Performance		
Max speed	2,446 km/h	(1,322 kt, 1,520 mph)
Initial climb (est)	15,240 m/min	(50,000 fpm)
Range (est)	1,600 km	(870 nm, 1,000 miles)
Weights		
Max takeoff	22,100 kg	(48,730 lbs)
Useful load	10,100 kg	(22,270 lbs)

Mitsubishi MU-2 — Japan

The MU-2 was one of the first business turboprop aircraft and the prototype, which first flew on 13th September 1963, embodied a number of unusual design features. The MU-2A, which had a circular-section seven-/nine-seat pressurised fuselage, had a high wing with full-span flaps and retractable spoilers in place of ailerons, two Turboméca Astazou engines on underwing pylons, large wingtip tanks and a tricycle undercarriage retracting into fuselage wells. The production MU-2B was fitted with Garrett TPE331-25A or TPE331-1-151A turboprops mounted directly on the wings. The majority of MU-2Bs were assembled and sold in the USA and several versions were built (i.e. MU-2D, MU-2F, MU-2K, MU-2M, MU-2P and Solitaire) with various changes to engines and weights. The MU-2C, MU-2E and MU-2S were unpressurised military SAR and communications versions built as the LR-1 for the JASDF and JGSDF. The MU-2B was joined by the stretched 11-seat MU-2G which featured external main undercarriage housings giving greater internal cabin volume, and subsequent long-fuselage versions included the MU-2J with 724 s.h.p. TPE331-6-251M engines, MU-2L with increased weights, MU-2N with 776 s.h.p. TPE331-5-252M engines and the Marquise (MU-2B-60) with 778 s.h.p. TPE331-10 engines and increased range. The last of 831 MU-2s (including 53 military aircraft) was completed at the end of 1983. Around 43 military and 470 civil aircraft remain, many of these having been converted as high-speed small-package freighters.

Specification	Mitsubishi MU-2G (MU-2B-30)	
Powerplant	Two 705 s.h.p. (525.6 kW) Honeywell (Garrett) TPE331-1-151A turboprops	
Dimensions		
Span	11.94 m	(39 ft 2 in)
Length	12.04 m	(39 ft 6 in)
Height	4.17 m	(13 ft 8 in)
Performance		
Max speed	845 km/h	(456 kt, 525 mph)
Cruising speed	772 km/h	(417 kt, 480 mph)
Initial climb	792 m/min	(2,600 fpm)
Range	2,480 km	(1,348 nm, 1,550 miles)
Weights		
Max takeoff	4,700 kg	(10,363 lbs)
Useful load	1,780 kg	(3,924 lbs)

Mitsubishi MU-2B-40 Solitaire (right) and MU-2B-60 Marquise (left)

Mitsubishi MH2000 — Japan

Initially designated Mitsubishi RP-1, the first of two prototypes of this 7/12 seat commercial helicopter made its maiden flight in July 1996. It is a streamlined general purpose helicopter with a tail fenestron stabilising rotor, a skid undercarriage and two 800 s.h.p. Mitsubishi MG5-110 turboshafts mounted above the fuselage driving a four-bladed composite main rotor. The cabin can accommodate two crew and up to ten passengers but can also be equipped for ambulance or SAR assignments with room for a full-length stretcher which is loaded through a port-side sliding door. The rear fuselage provides a large cargo bay and houses avionics and the fuel tanks. Japanese certification of the MH2000 was awarded in September 1999 and the first delivery was made to Excel Air Service of Tokyo in the following month.

Mitsubishi MH2000, JA001M

Specification	Mitsubishi MH2000	
Powerplant	Two 800 s.h.p (596.5 kW) Mitsubishi MG5-110 turboshafts	
Dimensions		
Rotor diameter	12.4 m	(40 ft 8 in)
Length	12.2 m	(40 ft 0 in)
Height	4.1 m	(13 ft 6 in)
Performance		
Max speed	280 km/h	(151 kt, 174 mph)
Cruising speed	250 km/h	(135 kt, 155 mph)
Range	780 km	(424 nm, 488 miles)
Weights		
Max takeoff	4500 kg	(9,922 lbs)
Useful Load	2000 kg	(4410 lbs)

Molniya I — Russia

Designed by the Molniya Research and Industrial Corporation, the Molniya I is a six-seat light transport aircraft for use in support of remote Russian communities. Its design is unconventional with a square-section fuselage containing the cabin and a pusher engine installation, twin booms carrying twin fins and a high-set tailplane. The Molniya I has a fixed tricycle undercarriage and is powered by the reliable M-14 radial engine although a Westernised version is planned with a 350 h.p. Continental TSIO-550-B piston engine. Molniya have also announced that the Molniya 3 would be fitted with an Allison 250 turboprop. The Molniya I prototype flew on 18th December 1992. Only two Molniya Is are believed to have flown to date.

Molniya I, RA-103

Specification	NPO Molniya Molniya I	
Powerplant	One 360 h.p. (268.5 kW) OKBM/ Voronezh M-14PM-1 piston engine	
Dimensions		
Span	8.51 m	(27 ft 11 in)
Length	7.87 m	(25 ft 10 in)
Height	2.31 m	(7 ft 7 in)
Performance		
Max speed	322 km/h	(174 kt, 200 mph)
Cruising speed	290 km/h	(157 kt, 180 mph)
Initial climb	229 m/min	(750 fpm)
Range	992 km	(539 nm, 620 miles)
Weights		
Max takeoff	1,740 kg	(3,837 lbs)
Useful load	500 kg	(1,102 lbs)

Monnett Sonerai — USA

The Sonerai has been one of the most popular amateur-built aircraft in the United States and is now marketed in single- and two-seat versions by Great Plains Aircraft. The prototype single-seat Sonerai I, designed by John Monnett, was first flown in 1971 since when many aircraft have been completed from plans and partial kits. Designed as a Formula V racer powered by a 1600 cc Volkswagen engine, it is of mixed construction with a tube and fabric fuselage and aluminium wings and has a fixed tailwheel undercarriage with spring steel main gear legs. The Sonerai II, which first flew in July 1973, is a tandem two-seat version which can be fitted with Volkswagen engines up to 2200 cc. The wings are mid-set on the Sonerai I and early versions of the Sonerai II but the later Sonerai IIL, and tricycle gear Sonerai IILT, have low-set wings. Great Plains have also marketed the Sonerai IILTS which is a stretched version with a longer cockpit and folding wings.

Monnett Sonerai IIL, G-BJLC

Specification	Monnett Sonerai IIL	
Powerplant	One 82 h.p. (61 kW) HAPI Volkswagen 2200 piston engine	
Dimensions		
Span	5.69 m	(18 ft 8 in)
Length	5.74 m	(18 ft 10 in)
Height	1.63 m	(5 ft 4 in)
Performance		
Max speed	257 km/h	(139 kt, 160 mph)
Cruising speed	209 km/h	(113 kt, 130 mph)
Initial climb	152 m/min	(500 fpm)
Range	560 km	(304 nm, 350 miles)
Weights		
Max takeoff	522 kg	(1,150 lbs)
Useful load	295 kg	(650 lbs)

Monnett Sonex — USA

John Monnett, designer of the popular Sonerai and Moni homebuilts, designed the Sonex two-seater to be a cheap and simply built all-metal sporting aircraft which would meet European ultralight rules. The prototype was first flown on 28th February 1998 powered by an 80 h.p. Jabiru 2200 engine but the aircraft can also be fitted with a 2180 cc Volkswagen or a 120 h.p. Jabiru 3300 six-cylinder engine. The Sonex has an enclosed side-by-side cabin and either a tailwheel or tricycle undercarriage. The aluminium structure is built from modular kits and covered by single-curvature aluminium panels and the wings are removable for transportation. By mid-1999 over 120 Sonex kits had been sold by Sonex Ltd. and six aircraft were flying.

Monnett Sonex, N12SX

Specification	Monnett Sonex	
Powerplant	One 80 h.p. (59.65 kW) Jabiru 2200 piston engine	
Dimensions		
Span	6.71 m	(22 ft 0 in)
Length	5.36 m	(17 ft 7 in)
Height	1.68 m	(5 ft 6 in)
Performance		
Max speed	241 km/h	(130 kt, 150 mph)
Cruising speed	225 km/h	(122 kt, 140 mph)
Range	512 km	(278 nm, 320 miles)
Weights		
Max takeoff	476 kg	(1,050 lbs)
Useful load	227 kg	(500 lbs)

Monocoupe 90 — USA

The designer of the Monocoupe line of high-wing light aircraft was Don Luscombe, who was to become well known in connection with the Luscombe Silvaire monoplanes. The original Monocoupe flew on 27th April 1927 and it was a strut-braced aircraft of tube, wood and fabric construction powered by a 60 h.p. Anzani or Detroit Air-Cat radial engine and with a cramped, fully enclosed side-by-side two-seat cockpit. Gradual improvements were introduced on the Model 70 and Model 113 Velie Monocoupe (powered by a 55 h.p. Velie engine) but the most popular version was the Model 90A which appeared in 1930 with a longer and distinctively waisted rear fuselage, a wider cabin, rounded wingtips and a redesigned undercarriage. It was powered by a fully cowled 90 h.p. Lambert R-266 engine and the company built a number of variants including the Model 90AF with a Franklin 4AC-199-E3 flat-four engine, the Monocoupe 110 with a 110 h.p. Warner Scarab, the D-145 with a 145 h.p. Warner and the clipped-wing Monocoupe 110 Special. Production ceased in 1942 but a small series of the Monocoupe 90AL-115, powered by the 115 h.p. Lycoming O-235-C1 engine, was built by Robert Sessler & Assoc. after the war. The Monocoupe 110 Special was revived in 1998 by Aviat Aircraft who flew the prototype of their new version, powered by a 200 h.p. Lycoming IO-360A-1B engine, on 25th July 1999. In total 324 of the two-seat Monocoupes were constructed.

Monocoupe 110, N2347

Specification	Monocoupe 90A	
Powerplant	One 90 h.p. (67.1 kW) Lambert R-266 piston engine	
Dimensions		
Span	9.75 m	(32 ft 0 in)
Length	6.25 m	(20 ft 6 in)
Height	2.08 m	(6 ft 10 in)
Performance		
Max speed	209 km/h	(113 kt, 130 mph)
Cruising speed	185 km/h	(100 kt, 115 mph)
Initial climb	238 m/min	(780 fpm)
Range	824 km	(448 nm, 515 miles)
Weights		
Max takeoff	730 kg	(1,610 lbs)
Useful load	289 kg	(637 lbs)

Mooney M-18 Mite — USA

The M-18 was designed by Al Mooney who had been chief designer for Culver Aircraft until it ceased business in 1946. Intended as a low-cost single-seater with superior performance, it had a fuselage of plywood and steel tube, wooden high-aspect-ratio laminar-flow wings, a retractable tricycle undercarriage and an all-flying tail with the distinctive apparently forward swept fin/rudder which was to become the Mooney trademark. The prototype, which flew on 18th May 1947, had a 25 h.p. Crossley Cobra motor car engine but production aircraft, built in Wichita, were built as the M-18L with a 65 h.p. Lycoming O-145-B2 or M-18C with a 65 h.p. Continental A-65-8. The M-18LA and M-18C-55 were versions with higher weights and later aircraft, known as the Wee Scotsman, had a larger fin and higher cockpit canopy. Several amateur-built Mites have been produced from plans and total factory production, which ceased in 1955, was 282 aircraft. More than half of these are still in existence.

Mooney M-18L, N4146

Specification	Mooney M-18L	
Powerplant	One 65 h.p. (48.5 kW) Textron Lycoming O-145-B2 piston engine	
Dimensions		
Span	8.2 m	(26 ft 11 in)
Length	5.36 m	(17 ft 7 in)
Height	1.9 m	(6 ft 3 in)
Performance		
Max speed	222 km/h	(120 kt, 138 mph)
Cruising speed	196 km/h	(106 kt, 122 mph)
Initial climb	332 m/min	(1,090 fpm)
Range	576 km	(313 nm, 360 miles)
Weights		
Max takeoff	354 kg	(780 lbs)
Useful load	127 kg	(280 lbs)

Mooney M.20 — USA

The four-seat Mooney M.20 private light aircraft shared many of the same design characteristics of the little Mite. It was designed by Al Mooney, first flying on 10th August 1953, and over the years it has been developed into a wide variety of models and remains in production with Mooney Aircraft at Kerrville, Texas. The original M.20 was an all-wooden high-performance aircraft with a low wing and retractable tricycle undercarriage and it had a fully enclosed cabin. Powered initially by a 150 h.p. Lycoming O-320 flat-four engine and then (as the M.20A) by a 180 h.p. IO-360-A1A, it entered production in 1955. After 700 had been built the M.20B 'Mark 21' was introduced and this was completely redesigned with a tubular frame and metal cladding. Among many subsequent variants were the M.20C Ranger with increased weights, M.20D Master economy model with a fixed undercarriage, M.20E Super 21 and Chapparal with a 200 h.p. IO-360-A1A engine and higher gross weight, M.20F Executive with a stretched fuselage and longer cabin and the M.20G Statesman with a 180 h.p. O-360-A1D engine and reduced payload. Mooneys built after 1969 by Butler Aviation were named Aerostars (e.g. the M.20E became the Aerostar 201) and some of these had bullet fairings on their fin tips. In 1974, the M.20 was substantially redesigned with numerous detailed aerodynamic improvements to enhance performance. As the M.20J (Mooney 201) it had a 200 h.p. Lycoming IO-360-A3B6D engine and was produced in several special editions (Lean Machine, Mooney 201SE etc.) and as the Mooney 205 with reshaped windows, Mooney ATS reduced specification trainer, Mooney MSE (later named Allegro) with upgraded IFR equipment, the M.20K Mooney 231 with a turbocharged 210 h.p. TSIO-360-GB-1 engine and the M.20K Mooney 252TSE (later named Encore) with reshaped windows and a TSIO-360-MB1 engine. The M.20L Mooney PFM was a version with a stretched fuselage and fitted with a 217 h.p. Porsche PFM.3200 engine, 41 of which were built. In 1989, the M.20M Mooney TLS was introduced and this had the stretched fuselage of the M.20L with a lengthened cabin and longer side windows combined with a 270 h.p. Lycoming TIO-540-AF1A engine. Current models include the M.20M Bravo, the M.20R Ovation, which is an M.20M with a 280 h.p. Continental IO-550G engine, and the M.20S Eagle, which is an economy version of the Ovation with a 245 h.p. IO-550 engine. In total, 10,000 Mooney M.20s had been built by the end of 1999.

Mooney M.20L-PFM, N1024Z

Specification	Mooney M.20R Ovation	
Powerplant	One 280 h.p. (208.77 kW) Teledyne Continental IO-550G piston engine	
Dimensions		
Span	11 m	(36 ft 1 in)
Length	8.15 m	(26 ft 9 in)
Height	2.54 m	(8 ft 4 in)
Performance		
Max speed	352 km/h	(190 kt, 219 mph)
Cruising speed	334 km/h	(180 kt, 207 mph)
Initial climb	366 m/min	(1,200 fpm)
Range	2,084 km	(1,130 nm, 1,301 miles)
Weights		
Max takeoff	1,527 kg	(3,368 lbs)
Useful load	518 kg	(1,143 lbs)

Mooney M.20B Mark 21, N5846Q

Mooney M.22 — USA

The M.22 was built as a top-of-the-line model to supplement Mooney's successful M.20C and M.20E high-performance light aircraft. It was a five-seat pressurised single-engined aircraft with a wider and longer fuselage than that of the M.20E Super 21 and a taller fin with a leading edge fillet. The cabin was entered via a single split door on the starboard side and the M.22 had a taller undercarriage than the other Mooneys. The prototype flew on 24th September 1964 powered by a 310 h.p. Lycoming TIO-540 turbocharged engine and the first customer delivery took place in 1965. The aircraft was initially named 'Mustang' but the name was dropped. Mooney made large losses on the aircraft and only produced 38 M.22s before the line was closed in 1970. Around 24 of these are still in existence.

Mooney M.22, N7727M

Specification	Mooney M.22	
Powerplant	One 310 h.p. (231.14 kW) Textron Lycoming TIO-541-A1A piston engine	
Dimensions		
Span	10.67 m	(35 ft 0 in)
Length	8.18 m	(26 ft 10 in)
Height	3.02 m	(9 ft 11 in)
Performance		
Max speed	402 km/h	(217 kt, 250 mph)
Cruising speed	370 km/h	(200 kt, 230 mph)
Initial climb	341 m/min	(1,120 fpm)
Range	1,760 km	(957 nm, 1,100 miles)
Weights		
Max takeoff	1,669 kg	(3,680 lbs)
Useful load	590 kg	(1,300 lbs)

Morane Saulnier MS.230 and MS.315 — France

During the 1930s, Morane Saulnier were a major producer of training aircraft, including DH.60 Moths built under licence, for civil flying schools but in 1930 they started to produce the MS.181 single-seat trainer. This was a tube and fabric aircraft, powered by an 80 h.p. Salmson 5Ac radial engine and having a strut-braced swept parasol wing, a fixed tailwheel undercarriage with bracing to the wing support struts and an open cockpit. Fewer than 20 were built but two still exist in France. The MS.230 which followed, based on the MS.130, was a tandem two-seater of similar appearance to the MS.181 but with a deeper and longer fuselage and with a 230 h.p. Salmson 9ABb radial engine in the nose. Morane built 1,080 MS.230s including approximately 40 completed in 1948/49. The MS.315 was a lighter version of the MS.230 which was designed for military training and flying club use and had a longer, slimmer fuselage and a 135 h.p. Salmson 9Nc radial or, as the MS.316, with a Regnier in-line engine. It was introduced in parallel with the MS.230, and 354 were built including approximately 100 completed by SNCAC after the war. Around 45 MS.315s were re-engined with a 220 h.p. Continental W-670-6A engine and redesignated MS.317, being primarily used as glider tugs. Twelve examples of the MS.315/317 remain active in France, Switzerland and Belgium.

Morane Saulnier MS.317, F-BCNL

Specification	Morane Saulnier MS.317	
Powerplant	One 220 h.p. (164 kW) Continental W-670-6A piston engine	
Dimensions		
Span	11.99 m	(39 ft 4 in)
Length	7.59 m	(24 ft 11 in)
Height	2.59 m	(8 ft 6 in)
Performance		
Max speed	180 km/h	(97 kt, 112 mph)
Cruising speed	161 km/h	(87 kt, 100 mph)
Initial climb	222 m/min	(730 fpm)
Range	800 km	(435 nm, 500 miles)
Weights		
Max takeoff	960 kg	(2,117 lbs)
Useful load	270 kg	(595 lbs)

Morane Saulnier MS.733 Alcyon — France

The Alcyon was devised by Morane Saulnier for military training and liaison. As the MS.730 it first flew on 8th August 1949 powered by a 220 h.p. Mathis 8G20 engine and later became the MS.731, with an Argus As.10. It was a low-wing all-metal aircraft with a fixed tailwheel undercarriage and a large cabin, enclosed by a large framed canopy and fitted with two front seats and a rear seat for an observer student or passenger. The definitive MS.733 followed with a first flight on 16th April 1951 and this had retractable gear and a 240 h.p. Potez 6D engine. A batch of 40 Alcyons was delivered to the French Aéronavale and further examples served with the French national training centre at St. Yan and the Air France training centre. The sole export order was for 27 for the Cambodian Air Force whose aircraft were equipped for ground attack with twin 7.5 mm machine guns and underwing pylons. Out of a total production of 150 aircraft, the 32 surviving Alcyons are now owned by private individuals in France, Belgium, Switzerland, the USA and the UK.

Morane Saulnier MS.733 Alcyon (Cont.)

Morane Saulnier MS.733 Alcyon, F-BKOD

Specification	Morane Saulnier MS.733 Alcyon	
Powerplant	One 240 h.p. (178.94 kW) Potez 6D.30 piston engine	
Dimensions		
Span	11.28 m	(37 ft 0 in)
Length	9.32 m	(30 ft 7 in)
Height	2.41 m	(7 ft 11 in)
Performance		
Max speed	262 km/h	(142 kt, 163 mph)
Cruising speed	225 km/h	(122 kt, 140 mph)
Initial climb	213 m/min	(700 fpm)
Range	912 km	(496 nm, 570 miles)
Weights		
Max takeoff	1,669 kg	(3,680 lbs)
Useful load	408 kg	(900 lbs)

Morane Saulnier MS.760 Paris — France

The MS.755 Fleuret was designed for military evaluation as a basic jet trainer for the French Armée de l'Air and first flew on 29th January 1953. It was an all-metal low-wing aircraft with side-by-side seating, a T-tail and a pair of Turboméca Marboré II turbojets buried in the wing roots. In the event, the Fleuret lost the military order to the Fouga Magister, but Morane Saulnier redesigned the aircraft as the MS.760 Paris (initially named the Fleuret II). Intended as a military liaison aircraft and light business jet, the Paris prototype flew on 29th July 1954 and it had a longer cabin with four seats and an enlarged sliding canopy. Some 27 civil examples of the Paris were sold to the USA where it was marketed by Beech, to Italy, Germany and in France, but the bulk of the 119 MS.760s built by Morane Saulnier were delivered to the French Armée de l'Air and Aéronavale. Military exports were made to Argentina (12) and Brazil (30) and a further 36 were built by FMA in Argentina. The majority were the MS.760A with 880 lb.s.t. Marboré II turbojets but later production aircraft were to Paris II standard with 1,058 lb.s.t. Marboré VI engines, increased fuel capacity and improved systems. The sole MS.760C Paris III, which flew in February 1964, had a redesigned five-seat cabin integrated into the fuselage structure and a port-side entry door instead of the sliding canopy. Several French and Argentine military MS.760s remain in service and 23 civil aircraft are active in the USA and France.

Morane Saulnier MS.760 Paris, N60GT

Specification	Morane Saulnier MS.760B Paris II	
Powerplant	Two 1,058 lb.s.t. (4.7 kN) Turboméca Marboré VI turbojets	
Dimensions		
Span	10.13 m	(33 ft 3 in)
Length	10.06 m	(33 ft 0 in)
Height	2.59 m	(8 ft 6 in)
Performance		
Max speed	708 km/h	(383 kt, 440 mph)
Cruising speed	676 km/h	(365 kt, 420 mph)
Initial climb	780 m/min	(2,560 fpm)
Range	1,728 km	(939 nm, 1,080 miles)
Weights		
Max takeoff	3,870 kg	(8,533 lbs)
Useful load	1,800 kg	(3,969 lbs)

Morane Saulnier MS.880 and MS.890 Rallye — France

The Morane Saulnier Rallye was the largest-volume European light aircraft built during the 1960s and it remains in production in Poland. Morane Saulnier designed the MS.880 as an entrant in a French light aircraft competition and flew the prototype, powered by a 90 h.p. Continental engine, on 10th June 1959. The production MS.880B was a low-wing aircraft with a sliding canopy covering the four-seat cabin and it had a fixed tricycle undercarriage and automatic leading edge slats which gave it excellent slow-speed performance. The MS.880B Rallye Club with a 100 h.p. Continental O-200-A engine and the MS.885 Super Rallye, powered by a 145 h.p. Continental O-300-A, were introduced in 1961 and other variants included the MS.881 (Potez 4E-20A engine), MS.883 (with a dorsal fin and 115 h.p. Lycoming O-235-C2A), MS.887 (with higher weights and a 125 h.p. Lycoming O-235-F2A), Rallye 100S and 100ST Galopin (two-seat Rallye Club cleared for spinning), Rallye 150T and 150ST (four-seater with enlarged tail and 150 h.p. Lycoming O-320-E2A) and Rallye 180T Galerien (a Rallye 150T with a 180 h.p. Lycoming O-360-A3A). Morane Saulnier (which became SOCATA in 1966) also developed the four-seat MS.890 Rallye Commodore with a heavier airframe. Again, this was built with various engines and models included the MS.890 (145 h.p. Continental O-300-B), MS.892 (150 h.p. Lycoming O-320), MS.893 (180 h.p. Lycoming O-360-A2A), MS.894 Minerva 220 (220 h.p. Franklin 6A-350-C1) and Rallye 235 Gabier (235 h.p. Lycoming O-540-B4B5). Various detailed changes were made over the life of the Rallye series. SOCATA also produced the Model 235CA Gaucho crop sprayer with a tailwheel undercarriage and rear cockpit hopper, and the Guerrier military close-support version. Between 1961 and 1992 some 1,857 standard Rallyes and 1,360 Commodores were completed. Licence production was started in Poland by PZL-Okecie in 1978 with the PZL-110 Koliber I, which is based on the Rallye 110ST and powered by a 126 h.p. Franklin 4A-235-B1 engine. The later Koliber 150A (Koliber II) has a 150 h.p. Lycoming O-320-E2A and the current Koliber 160A has a 160 h.p. Lycoming O-320-D2A and extra cabin windows. PZL has also developed the PZL-111 Koliber 235A (also known as Senior) with a stronger airframe, a baggage compartment, additional rear windows and a 235 h.p. Lycoming O-540-B4B5 engine. To date, PZL-Okecie has built over 80 Kolibers.

Morane Saulnier MS.880B Rallye Club, F-BPAI

PZL-110 Koliber 160A, SP-WGE

Specification	Morane Saulnier (SOCATA) MS.892 Rallye Commodore 150	
Powerplant	One 150 h.p. (111.8 kW) Textron Lycoming O-320-E2A piston engine	
Dimensions		
Span	9.6 m	(31 ft 6 in)
Length	7.14 m	(23 ft 5 in)
Height	2.79 m	(9 ft 2 in)
Performance		
Max speed	209 km/h	(113 kt, 130 mph)
Cruising speed	201 km/h	(109 kt, 125 mph)
Initial climb	192 m/min	(630 fpm)
Range	944 km	(513 nm, 590 miles)
Weights		
Max takeoff	980 kg	(2,161 lbs)
Useful load	445 kg	(981 lbs)

Mraz Sokol M-1C
— Czechoslovakia

The prewar Benes-Mraz company was actively involved in production of light private touring aircraft and during the war, while engaged on German military production, Ing. Zdenec Rublic designed a new side-by-side two-seat low-wing light aircraft: the M-1A Sokol. This was constructed from wood and fabric and had a fully enclosed cabin and a retractable tailwheel undercarriage. Mraz (later renamed Orlican) built a prototype of the Sokol, which flew on 9th March 1946, and it went into production at Chocen later that year with five versions being built. The basic M-1A had a 105 h.p. Walter Minor 4-III in-line engine, the single M-1B had a 105 h.p. Toma 4 engine, the M-1C was a three-seater with a higher gross weight, a longer cabin and modified wings with swept leading edges, the M-1D had a modified cockpit with a hinged clear-view canopy in place of the separate windshield and twin doors of earlier versions, and the M-1E was an M-1D on twin floats. During the period 1946 to 1950, 287 Sokols were completed and seven are currently registered in Europe.

Mraz Sokol M-1C, D-EEKW

Mraz Sokol M-1C (Cont.)

Specification	Mraz Sokol M-1C	
Powerplant	One 105 h.p. (78.29 kW) Walter Minor 4-III piston engine	
Dimensions		
Span	10.01 m	(32 ft 10 in)
Length	7.34 m	(24 ft 1 in)
Height	1.96 m	(6 ft 5 in)
Performance		
Max speed	241 km/h	(130 kt, 150 mph)
Cruising speed	212 km/h	(115 kt, 132 mph)
Initial climb	180 m/min	(590 fpm)
Range	992 km	(539 nm, 620 miles)
Weights		
Max takeoff	780 kg	(1,720 lbs)
Useful load	355 kg	(782 lbs)

Murphy Renegade Spirit — Canada

The Renegade was designed by Darryl Murphy as an ultra-light-category two-seat sport aircraft offering simple, inexpensive construction to amateur builders, and the first of over 600 kits was delivered in 1986. The definitive Renegade II was flown in May 1985 and it is sold in the form of plans or as a kit. It is a conventional light biplane of aluminium and fabric construction with tandem open cockpits. It has a swept upper wing and straight lower wings, fixed tailwheel landing gear and a radial cowling which hides the 53 h.p. Rotax 503 engine. The Renegade Spirit, which commenced testing in May 1987, is an alternative version which is stressed to accept a 65 h.p. Rotax 582 or 80 h.p. Rotax 912 and has improved performance and useful load, and is fitted with a distinctive helmeted cowling. The Renegade has dual controls and is capable of limited aerobatics. Examples of both the Renegade II and Renegade Spirit are flying in large numbers in the United States and Europe.

Murphy Renegade Spirit, G-MYRK

Specification	Murphy Renegade Spirit	
Powerplant	One 80 h.p. (59.65 kW) Rotax 912 piston engine	
Dimensions		
Span	6.48 m	(21 ft 3 in)
Length	5.61 m	(18 ft 5 in)
Height	2.08 m	(6 ft 10 in)
Performance		
Max speed	199 km/h	(107 kt, 124 mph)
Cruising speed	137 km/h	(74 kt, 85 mph)
Initial climb	274 m/min	(900 fpm)
Range	477 km	(259 nm, 298 miles)
Weights		
Max takeoff	431 kg	(950 lbs)
Useful load	222 kg	(490 lbs)

Murphy Rebel, Maverick and Elite — Canada

Following on from the success achieved by the Renegade biplane, Darryl Murphy designed the Rebel two-seat kit aircraft. The Rebel, which first flew in 1990, is a classic strut-braced high-wing aircraft with a spacious side-by-side two-seat cabin and spring-steel tailwheel gear, with optional floats or skis. It has good STOL performance and can be fitted with an 80 h.p. Rotax 912, 116 h.p. Lycoming O-235 or 160 h.p. Lycoming O-320. Construction is entirely metal semi-monocoque and over 250 Rebels are flying worldwide. Following on from the Rebel, Murphy designed the Maverick, a smaller and lighter version of the Rebel which complies with the 450 kg ultralight rules. It is powered by either a 53 h.p. Rotax 503DC or 65 h.p. Rotax 582 engine and can be fitted with long-span wings to improve low-speed performance. The Rebel has also been developed into the heavier Rebel Elite with a modified tailplane and square vertical tail, a strengthened structure, a tricycle undercarriage, improved useful load and a 180 h.p. Lycoming O-360 engine. This makes the Elite particularly suitable for bush operations on wheels or floats. The largest model is the Super Rebel SR2500 which is a four-seat version of the Elite with a 5 ft 6 in longer fuselage and increased wingspan and tail area. This can be used as a light freighter and is fitted with either the 180 h.p. or 200 h.p. Lycoming IO-360 or 250 h.p. Lycoming O-540 engine. Murphy Aircraft have sold over 1,600 kits and nearly 300 of the Rebel/Maverick series are flying.

Murphy Maverick, G-MYSS

Murphy Elite, C-FWSF

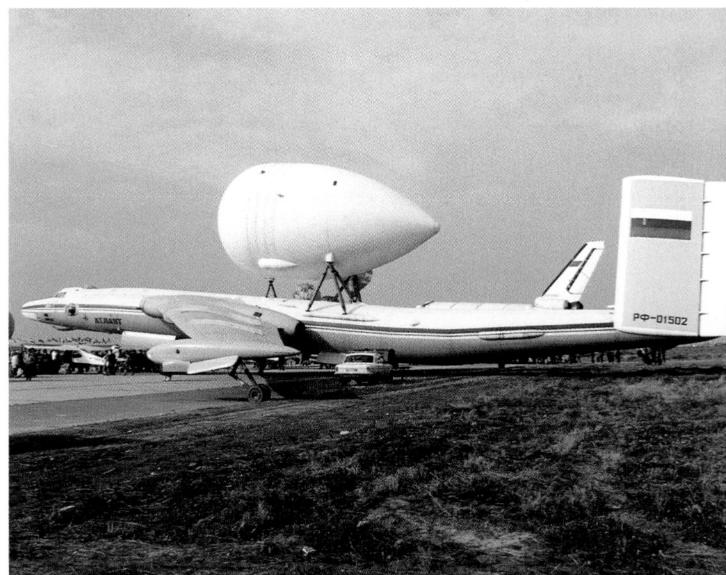

Myassichev VM-T Atlant, RA-01502

Specification	Murphy Rebel	
Powerplant	One 116 h.p. (86.49 kW) Textron Lycoming O-235 piston engine	
Dimensions		
Span	9.14 m	(30 ft 0 in)
Length	6.5 m	(21 ft 4 in)
Height	2.03 m	(6 ft 8 in)
Performance		
Max speed	201 km/h	(109 kt, 125 mph)
Cruising speed	177 km/h	(96 kt, 110 mph)
Initial climb	244 m/min	(800 fpm)
Range	1,274 km	(692 nm, 796 miles)
Weights		
Max takeoff	748 kg	(1,650 lbs)
Useful load	374 kg	(825 lbs)

Specification	Myassichev VM-T	
Powerplant	Four 20,944 lb.s.t. (93.2 kN) Mikulin RD-3M-500A turbojets	
Dimensions		
Span	40.69 m	(133 ft 6 in)
Length	21.21 m	(69 ft 7 in)
Height	5.26 m	(17 ft 3 in)
Performance		
Max speed	966 km/h	(522 kt, 600 mph)
Initial climb (est)	610 m/min	(2,000 fpm)
Range	12,320 km	(6,696 nm, 7,700 miles)
Weights		
Max takeoff	158,000 kg	(348,390 lbs)
Useful load	83,000 kg	(183,015 lbs)

Myassichev M-4 and VM-T — Russia

The M-4 (NATO name 'Bison') was developed in the 1950s as the Soviet Union's standard strategic bomber although its limited range and small bomb bay resulted in its being relegated to the medium-range bombing role and to reconnaissance and tanker duties. It was a very streamlined design with swept wings, a bicycle undercarriage and four RD-3M turbojets buried in the wing inner sections. The first flight took place on 20th January 1953 and around 200 aircraft were built. Latterly, the few surviving M-4s have been used for a range of test duties and two aircraft were converted as VM-T Atlants which are used for transportation of outsize loads such as the Buran space shuttle for the Russian space programme. The first of these conversions flew on 6th January 1982. The conversion involved fitting a new tail with large rectangular twin fins and cradle units on the forward and rear fuselage.

Myassichev M-17 and M-55 — Russia

Myassichev's M-17 Stratosfera (NATO name 'Mystic') was designed as a high-altitude atmospheric research aircraft although it may originally have been intended as a very-high-altitude military reconnaissance platform. It is a twin-boomed single-seat aircraft with a retractable tricycle undercarriage, high-set tailplane and high-aspect-ratio wings with marked anhedral. The initial M-17 first flew on 26th May 1982 and this and the second M-17 were powered by a single 15,430 lb.s.t. RKBM Rybinsk RD-36-51V turbofan. The two aircraft, both now retired, were tasked with research into the ozone layer and set several international records. The M-55 (M-17RM) Geofizika, which flew on 16th August 1988, is a developed version with two 9,920 lb.s.t. Aviadvigatel D-30 turbofans, shorter wings and larger equipment bays. Roles include atmospheric research, mapping, defence systems monitoring and cloud seeding. It is thought that five M-55s have been completed.

Myassichev M-17 and M-55 (Cont.)

Myassichev M-55 Geofizika, RA-55204

Specification	Myassichev M-55 Geofizika	
Powerplant	Two 9,920 lb.s.t. (44.13 kN) Aviadvigatel-Perm D-30-V12 turbofans	
Dimensions		
Span	37.46 m	(122 ft 11 in)
Length	22.86 m	(75 ft 0 in)
Height	4.83 m	(15 ft 10 in)
Performance		
Max speed	750 km/h	(405 kt, 466 mph)
Cruising speed	692 km/h	(374 kt, 430 mph)
Takeoff distance	900 m	(2,952 ft)
Range	4,472 km	(2,430 nm, 2,795 miles)
Weights		
Max takeoff	23,800 kg	(52,479 lbs)
Useful load	9,800 kg	(21,609 lbs)

Myassichev M-101T Gzhel
— Russia

The primary purpose of the M-101T is to provide local service to remote locations in the CIS although different versions will be marketed for freight operations and as a four-passenger executive aircraft equivalent to the Aérospatiale TBM.700. It is a pressurised low-wing aircraft of conventional layout with a retractable tricycle undercarriage. Standard accommodation is for seven passengers and one pilot. The M-101T is powered by a 760 s.h.p. Walter M601F turboprop but a westernised version, designated M-101PW, is planned with a Pratt & Whitney PT6A-64 engine. The prototype first flew on 31st March 1995 and by mid-1999 more than 15 development and production aircraft had been built at Myassichev's Zhukovsky factory.

Myassichev M-101T Gzhel, RA-15102

Specification	Myassichev M-101T Gzhel	
Powerplant	One 760 s.h.p. (567 kW) Walter M601F turboprop	
Dimensions		
Span	13 m	(42 ft 8 in)
Length	10.01 m	(32 ft 10 in)
Height	3.73 m	(12 ft 3 in)
Performance		
Max speed	539 km/h	(291 kt, 335 mph)
Cruising speed	515 km/h	(278 kt, 320 mph)
Initial climb	305 m/min	(1,000 fpm)
Range	1,400 km	(761 nm, 875 miles)
Weights		
Max takeoff	3,000 kg	(6,615 lbs)
Useful load	985 kg	(2,172 lbs)

Mylius My-102 and My-103
— Germany

Dipl.Ing. Hermann Mylius, former technical director for Bölkow, designed the MHK-101 light aircraft prototype which flew on 22nd December 1967 and this was developed into the Bö.209 Monsun which was built in quantity by MBB in the 1960s. In 1996, the design was revived by Mylius Flugzeugwerke as a production design as the My-102, My-103 and My-104. The initial My-102 Tornado is a development of the MHK-101, and two prototypes were flown in the 1970s. It is a single-seat all-metal aircraft with a low wing, fixed tricycle undercarriage incorporating a retractable nosewheel and a large sliding bubble canopy enclosing the cockpit, and it is intended for aerobatics and glider towing. It is powered by a 200 h.p. Lycoming AEIO-360 engine. The My-103, which flew in 1998, is a slightly larger side-by-side two-seat version which is available with either a 160 h.p. Lycoming O-320 or 200 h.p. Lycoming AEIO-360 engine. Mylius are also building a prototype of the My-104 which is a four-seater with a longer fuselage and cabin and has fully retractable gear and a 200 h.p. IO-360 engine.

Mylius My-103, D-ETMY

Specification	Mylius My-103/200	
Powerplant	One 200 h.p. (149.12 kW) Textron Lycoming AEIO-360 piston engine	
Dimensions		
Span	8.41 m	(27 ft 7 in)
Length	6.5 m	(21 ft 4 in)
Height	2.31 m	(7 ft 7 in)
Performance		
Max speed	297 km/h	(160 kt, 184 mph)
Cruising speed	274 km/h	(148 kt, 170 mph)
Initial climb	432 m/min	(1,417 fpm)
Range	1,224 km	(665 nm, 765 miles)
Weights		
Max takeoff	950 kg	(2,095 lbs)
Useful load	374 kg	(825 lbs)

N

NAMC YS-11 — Japan

The YS-11 was designed and built by the Nihon Aircraft Manufacturing Co. Ltd. (NAMC) which was formed by several Japanese companies including Fuji, Kawasaki, Mitsubishi and Shin Meiwa. It was intended as a short-haul airliner for Japanese domestic carriers and it is a conventional low-wing pressurised twin turboprop aircraft powered by two Rolls Royce Darts. The first prototype flew on 30th August 1962. In addition to the basic YS-11-100 60-passenger version, NAMC built the YS-11A-200 with higher weights, the YS-11A-300 combi for 46 passengers and freight, for which it was fitted with a cargo door, and the all-cargo YS-11A-400. First deliveries were made to Toa Airways (YS-11-101) in April 1965 and other customers included All Nippon (YS-11A-213), Japan Domestic Airlines (YS-11-109), the Japanese JCAB (YS-11-110) and the JASDF, who received four of a military variant (YS-11-103). Export orders included Piedmont Airlines, Hawaiian Airlines, Olympic Airways, Cruzeiro do Sul, VASP and Philippine Airlines, and among second user airlines were Reeve Aleutian, Mid-Pacific Airlines, the Philippine operator Aboitiz and Airborne Express which flew the YS-11 on small package services. Some 180 production YS-11s were built and half of these are still active including 23 used by the JASDF and JMSDF for transport and ASW and, as the YS-11E, for ECM training.

NAMC YS-11A, RP-C3202

Specification	NAMC YS-11-100	
Powerplant	Two 3,060 s.h.p. (2,281.5 kW) Rolls Royce Dart R.DA.10/1 Mk. 542-10 turboprops	
Dimensions		
Span	32 m	(105 ft 0 in)
Length	26.29 m	(86 ft 3 in)
Height	8.99 m	(29 ft 6 in)
Performance		
Max speed	478 km/h	(258 kt, 297 mph)
Cruising speed	470 km/h	(254 kt, 292 mph)
Initial climb	402 m/min	(1,320 fpm)
Range	1,376 km	(748 nm, 860 miles)
Weights		
Max takeoff	23,492 kg	(51,800 lbs)
Useful load	8,395 kg	(18,510 lbs)

Nanchang CJ-6 — People's Republic of China

The CJ-6A military basic trainer was derived from the CJ-5 which was itself a licence-built version of the Yakovlev Yak-18, 379 of which were built between 1954 and 1958. In reality, the CJ-6 was a new aircraft which mirrored Yakovlev's own Yak-18A and Yak-18P developments with all-metal monocoque construction and a low wing with dihedralled outer panels. It had a tandem two-seat cockpit with a multi-framed canopy and was equipped with a retractable tricycle undercarriage. The CJ-6 first flew on 27th August 1958 and the production version powered by a Chinese-built

Nanchang CJ-6 (Cont.)

Vedeneyev AI-14RF radial engine went into production as the CJ-6A in 1965. Ten examples of an armed version, the CJ-6B, were also built. Production of the CJ-6 totalled 1,796 by the end of 1986 and more than 1,900 are believed to have been delivered to date. A significant number have been sold in the West to private owners and the CJ-6A continues in service with the air forces of the PRC, Bangladesh, Albania, North Korea and Zambia.

Nanchang CJ-6A, ZK-OII

Specification	Nanchang CJ-6A	
Powerplant	One 285 h.p. (213 kW) Huosai 6A piston engine	
Dimensions		
Span	10.18 m	(33 ft 5 in)
Length	8.46 m	(27 ft 9 in)
Height	3.25 m	(10 ft 8 in)
Performance		
Max speed	298 km/h	(161 kt, 185 mph)
Cruising speed	257 km/h	(139 kt, 160 mph)
Initial climb	381 m/min	(1,250 fpm)
Range	1,024 km	(557 nm, 640 miles)
Weights		
Max takeoff	1,420 kg	(3,131 lbs)
Useful load	240 kg	(529 lbs)

Nanchang A-5 and Q-5
— People's Republic of China

The Nanchang J-6 (a licence-built version of the MiG-19) formed the basis for the Q-5 multi-role fighter which went into development at the Nanchang Aircraft Factory in 1958. The first Q-5 (NATO name 'Fantan') was flown on 4th June 1965 and full-scale production commenced in 1970. By comparison with the J-6, the Q-5 has twin air intakes close to the wing roots in place of the nose intake of the J-6 and area ruling of the centre fuselage, a pointed nose containing electronics, a redesigned wing of greater sweep, a larger tail unit and a new cockpit with an upward-opening canopy. The Fantan has three pylons under each wing and is fitted with two internally mounted 23 mm cannon. The Q-5I is a longer-range version with extra internal tankage, a WP6AIII engine and two fuselage pylons; the Q-5IA also has improved countermeasures equipment and a new bombsight system, and the Q-5III is an export version also designated A-5C which provides for use of various Western weapons systems. The A-5 has been sold to Pakistan, Bangladesh, Myanmar and North Korea and total production is believed to exceed 1,000.

Nanchang A-5, Bangladesh AF, 915

Specification	Nanchang Q-5 Fantan	
Powerplant	Two 8,267 lb.s.t. (36.8 kN) (wet) Shenyang Wopen-6 turbofans	
Dimensions		
Span	9.68 m	(31 ft 9 in)
Length	15.65 m	(51 ft 4 in)
Height	4.34 m	(14 ft 3 in)
Performance		
Max speed	1,191 km/h	(643 kt, 740 mph)
Initial climb	5,944 m/min	(19,500 fpm)
Range	800 km	(435 nm, 500 miles)
Weights		
Max takeoff	11,830 kg	(26,085 lbs)
Useful load	5,455 kg	(12,028 lbs)

Nanchang K-8 Karakorum 8
— PRC/Pakistan

The K-8 is a two-seat primary jet trainer jointly developed by the Nanchang Aircraft Factory and the Pakistan Military Aeronautical Complex. The K-8, which made its first flight on 21st November 1990, has a straight low-set wing, air intakes on the fuselage sides and a retractable tricycle undercarriage. The tandem cockpit is enclosed by a sideways-opening canopy and the aircraft has four underwing hardpoints for weapons training stores and a centreline strongpoint for a 23 mm cannon pod. An initial batch of six K-8s has been delivered to the Pakistan Air Force, powered by the Honeywell (Garrett) TFE731 turbofan, 12 went to Myanmar and 8 are on order for Sri Lanka. The K-8 as required by the Air Force of the People's Republic of China is to be powered by a Progress ZMKB AI-25-TL turbofan, but this variant of the K-8 had not been tested or ordered by the end of 1999.

Nanchang K-8 Karakorum 8

Specification	Nanchang K-8 Karakorum 8	
Powerplant	One 3,600 lb.s.t. (16.01 kN) Honeywell (Garrett) TFE731-2A turbofan	
Dimensions		
Span	9.63 m	(31 ft 7 in)
Length	11.58 m	(38 ft 0 in)
Height	4.22 m	(13 ft 10 in)
Performance		
Max speed	805 km/h	(435 kt, 500 mph)
Cruising speed	740 km/h	(400 kt, 460 mph)
Initial climb	1,622 m/min	(5,320 fpm)
Range	2,237 km	(1,216 nm, 1,398 miles)
Weights		
Max takeoff	4,330 kg	(9,548 lbs)
Useful load	1,640 kg	(3,616 lbs)

Naval Aircraft Factory N3N-1
— USA

The weighty N3N biplane was designed by the Naval Aircraft Factory in 1934 as a primary trainer for naval aviators. Provided with open tandem cockpits, it was powered by a 220 h.p. Wright J-5 radial engine and was constructed from steel tube and fabric with large removable fuselage panels to facilitate maintenance. The N3N prototype first flew in August 1935 and first deliveries of the N3N-1 took place in the following June. The N3N-3 was the second variant and it was powered by a 235 h.p. Wright J-6-7 (R-760) engine which was also retrospectively fitted to most of the earlier aircraft. While the N3N-1 had a tightly fitting engine cowling the N3N-3s were operated with the engines uncowled. A number of N3N-3s were operated as floatplanes with a single central float and stabilising floats at the wingtips. The Navy received 995 N3Ns and after the war many were civilianised and converted as crop sprayers and fitted with higher-powered engines such as the 600 h.p. Pratt & Whitney R1340 or 450 h.p. R-985 Wasp Junior. The N3N remains popular with private owners and nearly 200 are registered in the USA.

Navy N3N-3, N72792

Specification	Naval Aircraft Factory N3N-3	
Powerplant	One 235 h.p. (175.2 kW) Wright R-760-2 piston engine	
Dimensions		
Span	10.36 m	(34 ft 0 in)
Length	7.77 m	(25 ft 6 in)
Height	3.3 m	(10 ft 10 in)
Performance		
Max speed	203 km/h	(110 kt, 126 mph)
Cruising speed	145 km/h	(78 kt, 90 mph)
Initial climb	244 m/min	(800 fpm)
Range	752 km	(409 nm, 470 miles)
Weights		
Max takeoff	1,266 kg	(2,792 lbs)
Useful load	318 kg	(702 lbs)

Neiva Paulistinha — Brazil

The Paulistinha tandem two-seat light aircraft was originally built in 1935 as the EAY-201 Ypiranga by the Empresa Aeronautica Ypiranga and was externally almost identical to the Piper J.3 Cub with tube and fabric construction, a high braced wing and tailwheel undercarriage. In 1942, the Companhia Aeronáutica Paulista put an improved version into production as the CAP-4 Paulistinha with a 65 h.p. Franklin 4AC-176-B2 engine for civil and military use, and 782 had been completed by 1949. This was followed by the Paulistinha 56B which was built from 1953 onwards by the glider manufacturer Aeronautica Neiva Ltda. and this had a more streamlined appearance and a 100 h.p. Lycoming O-235-C1 engine. Other versions included the Paulistinha 56C with a 90 h.p. Continental C90-8F and the Paulistinha 56D for glider towing and agricultural use with a 150 h.p. Lycoming O-320-A1A. A total of 240 Neiva Paulistinhas was built and 20 CAP-4s and 65 Neiva 56s are currently active in Brazil.

Neiva Paulistinha 56, PP-TJR

Specification	Neiva 56C Paulistinha	
Powerplant	One 90 h.p. (67.1 kW) Teledyne Continental C90-8F piston engine	
Dimensions		
Span	10.74 m	(35 ft 3 in)
Length	6.76 m	(22 ft 2 in)
Height	2.18 m	(7 ft 2 in)
Performance		
Max speed	161 km/h	(87 kt, 100 mph)
Cruising speed	145 km/h	(78 kt, 90 mph)
Initial climb	239 m/min	(785 fpm)
Range	696 km	(378 nm, 435 miles)
Weights		
Max takeoff	587 kg	(1,294 lbs)
Useful load	197 kg	(435 lbs)

Neiva Regente — Brazil

Neiva's Regente 360C (initially designated IPD-5901) was designed as a civil four-seat light aircraft and military liaison and army cooperation type. It has a strut-braced high wing, a fully enclosed cabin and a fixed tricycle undercarriage and is of all-metal construction. It is powered by a 180 h.p. Lycoming O-360-A1D engine. The prototype made its first flight on 7th September 1961 and the Regente was ordered in quantity by the Brazilian Air Force as the U-42 (later C-42) for light transport and communications, 80 being delivered between 1965 and 1969. A modified version, the L-42 (Regente 420L), was developed with a cut-down rear fuselage and rear-view windows and 40 were supplied to the Brazilian Army for artillery spotting and liaison with a three-seat interior. Many of the C-42 and L-42 remain in military service. Neiva built two examples of a civil version of the L-42 as the N-593 Lanceiro. No further civil aircraft were produced although several military Regentes were sold to private users in which form they are designated Neiva N591-290.

Neiva Regente U-42, Brazilian AF, 2227

Specification	Neiva Regente 360C	
Powerplant	One 180 h.p. (134.2 kW) Textron Lycoming O-360-A1D piston engine	
Dimensions		
Span	9.12 m	(29 ft 11 in)
Length	7.04 m	(23 ft 1 in)
Height	2.92 m	(9 ft 7 in)
Performance		
Max speed	220 km/h	(119 kt, 137 mph)
Cruising speed	209 km/h	(113 kt, 130 mph)
Initial climb	210 m/min	(690 fpm)
Range	920 km	(500 nm, 575 miles)
Weights		
Max takeoff	1,040 kg	(2,293 lbs)
Useful load	400 kg	(882 lbs)

Neiva T-25 Universal — Brazil

The Neiva N-621 Universal was originally designed as a replacement for the North American T-6 trainers in service with the Brazilian Air Force. Unlike the T-6, the Universal had side-by-side seating and its large cabin was provided with a third rear seat for an observer pupil. It is a low-wing all-metal monoplane with retractable tricycle gear and a 300 h.p. Lycoming piston engine. The prototype Universal was flown on 29th April 1966 and 150 were delivered to the Brazilian Air Force as the T-25 between 1971 and 1975. Many of these were fitted with underwing hardpoints to carry 7.62 mm gun pods for armament training. A further development, the T-25B Universal II, was tested in 1978 but the Universal was largely replaced by the Tucano. A small number of Universals are thought still to be airworthy with the Brazilian Air Force but the Paraguay Air Force has withdrawn its small fleet.

Neiva YT-25 Universal, Brazilian AF, 1830

Specification	Neiva N-621 Universal T-25	
Powerplant	One 300 h.p. (224 kW) Textron Lycoming IO-540-K1D5 piston engine	
Dimensions		
Span	11 m	(36 ft 1 in)
Length	8.58 m	(28 ft 2 in)
Height	2.84 m	(9 ft 4 in)
Performance		
Max speed	298 km/h	(161 kt, 185 mph)
Cruising speed	285 km/h	(154 kt, 177 mph)
Initial climb	400 m/min	(1,313 fpm)
Range	1,000 km	(544 nm, 626 miles)
Weights		
Max takeoff	1,500 kg	(3,307 lbs)
Useful load	350 kg	(772 lbs)

Nesmith Cougar — USA

The Cougar is an amateur-built light aircraft designed by Robert E. Nesmith and first flown in March 1957. It is externally similar to the Wittman Tailwind and has a strut-braced high wing, a tailwheel undercarriage with spring-steel legs and a fully enclosed cabin with side-by-side seating for two. The Cougar can be powered by a variety of engines including the 85 h.p. Continental C85, 100 h.p. Continental O-200, 115 h.p. Lycoming O-235 or 125 h.p. Lycoming O-290 and the clean design of the aircraft gives it excellent performance with these engines. Construction is mixed with a steel tube and fabric fuselage and plywood-covered wooden wings. Several hundred Cougars have been completed from plans sold by Nesmith and at least 80 are currently active in the USA.

Nesmith Cougar, N3184G

Specification	Nesmith Cougar	
Powerplant	One 115 h.p. (85.7 kW) Textron Lycoming O-235 piston engine	
Dimensions		
Span	6.25 m	(20 ft 6 in)
Length	5.77 m	(18 ft 11 in)
Height	1.68 m	(5 ft 6 in)
Performance		
Max speed	314 km/h	(170 kt, 195 mph)
Cruising speed	267 km/h	(144 kt, 166 mph)
Initial climb	396 m/min	(1,300 fpm)
Range	1,200 km	(652 nm, 750 miles)
Weights		
Max takeoff	567 kg	(1,250 lbs)
Useful load	283 kg	(625 lbs)

New Standard D-25
— USA

The New Standard was an improved version of the Standard biplane which was designed by Charles Healy Day as a military trainer and built during the later years of World War I. The initial New Standard D-24 was a large tube and fabric biplane with tapered wings, an angular vertical tail and a stout strut-braced tailwheel undercarriage. It was designed for commercial barnstorming with a forward open cockpit seating four passengers and a separate pilot's cockpit behind. Built by the New Standard Aircraft Co., the D-24 had a 180 h.p. Hispano Suiza E ('Hisso') radial engine but later versions had a variety of radial engines. The 220 h.p. Wright J5 Whirlwind was used in the D-25, which was similar to the D-24, and in the D-26 and D-27, which were cargo-carrying models. Equivalent versions powered by the 225 h.p. Wright J6 were designated D-25A, D-26A and D-27A. Four New Standards remain active in the USA, two of which are still used for joyriding.

New Standard D-25, NC930V

Specification	New Standard D-25	
Powerplant	One 220 h.p. (164 kW) Wright J5 Whirlwind piston engine	
Dimensions		
Span	13.72 m	(45 ft 0 in)
Length	8.08 m	(26 ft 6 in)
Height	3.1 m	(10 ft 2 in)
Performance		
Max speed	177 km/h	(96 kt, 110 mph)
Cruising speed	158 km/h	(85 kt, 98 mph)
Initial climb	229 m/min	(750 fpm)
Range	784 km	(426 nm, 490 miles)
Weights		
Max takeoff	1,542 kg	(3,400 lbs)
Useful load	630 kg	(1,390 lbs)

NH Industries NH 90
— International

The NH 90 is a medium-lift transport helicopter developed by the NH Industries consortium set up in 1985 by Aérospatiale, MBB, Agusta and Fokker. It has capacity for up to 20 troops and has been designed to fulfil a wide variety of roles including tactical support and attack and naval ASW and SAR. The NH 90 is largely built from composites and is of conventional layout with four-blade main and tail rotors, an unobstructed full-length cabin and the twin RTM322 turboshafts positioned on top of the fuselage. The version proposed for the Italian Air Force is expected to have GE/Alfa Romeo T700/T6E engines. It has a retractable tricycle undercarriage which uses external sponsons. The two main versions are referred to as NFH 90 (naval frigate-based SAR and ASW) and TTH 90 (army tactical transport with provision for external tactical weapons). The first of five flying prototypes flew on 18th December 1995. Due to funding approval delays no deliveries had been made by the end of 2000 but expected sales, with first deliveries in 2003, include 95 for France, 243 for Germany, 20 for the Netherlands and 224 for Italy, of which 149 would be to the naval specification.

NH 90, MM-X-612

Specification	NH Industries NH 90 TTH	
Powerplant	Two 2,234 s.h.p. (1,666 kW) Rolls Turbo-méca MTU RTM322-01/9 turboshafts	
Dimensions		
Rotor diameter	16.3 m	(53 ft 6 in)
Length	15.98 m	(52 ft 5 in)
Height	5.44 m	(17 ft 10 in)
Performance		
Max speed	290 km/h	(157 kt, 180 mph)
Cruising speed	257 km/h	(139 kt, 160 mph)
Initial climb	690 m/min	(2,265 fpm)
Range	944 km	(513 nm, 590 miles)
Weights		
Max takeoff	8,698 kg	(19,180 lbs)
Useful load	2,268 kg	(5,000 lbs)

Nicollier Menestrel — France

Henri Nicollier has been responsible for a number of homebuilt designs based on his original HN.433 Menestrel which first flew on 25th November 1962. It is a very attractive single-seater built from wood and fabric and it has a low-set elliptical wing and a fixed tailwheel undercarriage. The cabin is fully enclosed with a moulded plexiglass canopy and the HN.433 is powered by a 30 h.p. Volkswagen 1300. A number of standard Menestrels were constructed from plans and partial kits and in 1985 the HN.434 Super Menestrel was announced. This featured a simplified structure for ease of fabrication, a larger cabin and increased fuel capacity. It can be powered by various engines in the 35 h.p. to 65 h.p. range but, typically, uses a 1,600 cc Volkswagen. Twenty Super Menestrels are flying with a number of others being built. The HN.700 Menestrel II is a side-by-side two-seat version of the Super Menestrel which first flew in 1989 and is powered by an 80 h.p. Limbach 2000 or (as the HN.701) by an 87 h.p. Limbach 2400. It is of similar construction but can be fitted with a tricycle or tailwheel undercarriage. Over 120 HN.700s are said to be under construction with over 60 flying.

Nicollier HN.700 Menestrel II, F-PMAR

Specification	Nicollier HN.700 Menestrel II	
Powerplant	One 80 h.p. (59.7 kW) Limbach 2000 piston engine	
Dimensions		
Span	7.8 m	(25 ft 7 in)
Length	5.31 m	(17 ft 5 in)
Height	1.47 m	(4 ft 10 in)
Performance		
Max speed	185 km/h	(100 kt, 115 mph)
Cruising speed	169 km/h	(91 kt, 105 mph)
Initial climb	421 m/min	(1,380 fpm)
Range	992 km	(539 nm, 620 miles)
Weights		
Max takeoff	500 kg	(1,102 lbs)
Useful load	218 kg	(481 lbs)

Noorduyn Norseman — Canada

The Noorduyn Norseman is one of the oldest and best-known bush aircraft. It was designed by Robert B. Noorduyn and first flew in November 1935, powered by a 420 h.p. Wright R-975-E3 radial. The Norseman was a classic high-wing tube and fabric monoplane with a fixed tailwheel undercarriage which included large heavily faired main legs and it had a capacious cabin able to transport eight passengers or large quantities of freight. It could also be operated on skis or floats. A small batch of aircraft was built before the war by Noorduyn Aviation Ltd. including three Mk.IIs and two Mk.IIIs, upgraded to a 450 h.p. Pratt & Whitney Wasp SC engine. However, the main production run was for the USAAF who received 762 aircraft for communications tasks in World War II including an initial batch of Norseman IVs (YC-64) with ten seats and a 600 h.p. R-1340-S3H1 engine, followed by 749 Norseman Vs powered by a 550 h.p. Pratt & Whitney Wasp R-1340-AN1. A further batch of float-equipped Norseman Vs (UC-64B) were used by the US Army Corps of Engineers and this model was also used by the RCAF. After the war, Canadian Car and Foundry built a further 53 civil Norseman Vs. Norseman production totalled 902 aircraft and military surplus aircraft were very popular after the war with bush operators and small airlines. The Norseman is still active in Canada, Sweden and the USA.

Noorduyn Norseman, N45TG

Specification	Noorduyn Norseman V	
Powerplant	One 550 h.p. (410 kW) Pratt & Whitney Wasp R-1340-AN1 piston engine	
Dimensions		
Span	15.75 m	(51 ft 8 in)
Length	9.85 m	(32 ft 4 in)
Height	3.07 m	(10 ft 1 in)
Performance		
Max speed	249 km/h	(135 kt, 155 mph)
Cruising speed	227 km/h	(123 kt, 141 mph)
Initial climb	218 m/min	(715 fpm)
Range	742 km	(403 nm, 464 miles)
Weights		
Max takeoff	3,419 kg	(7,540 lbs)
Useful load	1,288 kg	(2,840 lbs)

Nord N.2501 Noratlas — France

The Nord Noratlas was the standard military transport aircraft for the Armée de l'Air throughout the 1950s and 1960s until it was replaced in service by the Transall C.160. In general layout it followed the pattern of the Fairchild C-119 with a high wing, twin booms and a main fuselage pod with rear loading doors which could carry 45 equipped troops. It first flew on 10th September 1949 and Nord (SNCAN) built 231 Noratlases. These were mostly military N.2501s but the total also included a few N.2501A and N.2502B civil examples, and in addition 187 N.2501Ds were completed by Flugzeugbau Nord for the German Air Force. Once they were withdrawn from military service a number of aircraft were sold to civil operators, particularly in South America. Several examples of the Noratlas remain, including one which is flying in France.

Nord N.2501 Noratlas, F-AZVM

Specification	SNCAN N.2501 Noratlas	
Powerplant	Two 2,090 h.p. (1,558 kW) SNECMA Bristol Hercules 738 piston engines	
Dimensions		
Span	32.5 m	(106 ft 8 in)
Length	21.94 m	(72 ft 0 in)
Height	5.99 m	(19 ft 8 in)
Performance		
Max speed	439 km/h	(237 kt, 273 mph)
Cruising speed	323 km/h	(175 kt, 201 mph)
Initial climb	375 m/min	(1,230 fpm)
Range	2,584 km	(1,404 nm, 1,615 miles)
Weights		
Max takeoff	23,000 kg	(50,715 lbs)
Useful load	9,925 kg	(21,885 lbs)

Nord N.3202 — France

Nord (SNCAN) designed the N.3200 to meet a French ALAT (Aviation Légere de l'Armée de Terre) requirement for a new primary trainer to replace Nord-built Stampe SV.4 biplanes and the prototype made its first flight on 17th April 1957. The N.3202, which started to reach the ALAT in July 1959, is a low-wing monoplane constructed from steel tube with fabric and light alloy covering. It has a tandem two-seat cockpit with a framed two-part sliding canopy and the fixed tailwheel undercarriage has distinctive trailing-link suspension on the main units. Nord delivered 100 aircraft of which 50 were fitted with a 240 h.p. Potez 4D.32 in-line engine and the remainder with a 260 h.p. Potez 4D.34B. Production was completed in 1961 and many N.3202s were declared surplus in the 1980s with a significant number being acquired by private owners in Europe and the USA. In total 26 are registered in the USA and others are active in France and the UK.

Nord N.3202, NX2256B

Specification	Nord (SNCAN) N.3202	
Powerplant	One 260 h.p. (193.8 kW) Potez 4D.34B piston engine	
Dimensions		
Span	9.5 m	(31 ft 2 in)
Length	8.13 m	(26 ft 8 in)
Height	2.82 m	(9 ft 3 in)
Performance		
Max speed	257 km/h	(139 kt, 160 mph)
Cruising speed	249 km/h	(135 kt, 155 mph)
Initial climb	360 m/min	(1,180 fpm)
Range	992 km	(539 nm, 620 miles)
Weights		
Max takeoff	1,219 kg	(2,689 lbs)
Useful load	360 kg	(793 lbs)

Nord (Aérospatiale) N.262 — France

The Nord 262 turboprop transport was developed by Nord (SNCAN) from the MH-260 Super Broussard which had been designed and produced by Avions Max Holste and originally flew in July 1960. The Nord 262, which first flew on 24th December 1962, was a substantially redesigned version with a new circular-section pressurised 29-passenger fuselage, a taller tail unit and two 1,065 s.h.p. Turboméca Bastan VI turboprops. It had a high wing and a retractable tricycle undercarriage with the main units attached to external fuselage fairings. Early sales were made to Air Inter, Air Ceylon, Cimber Air and the American carrier Lake Central and 57 of the 110 total Nord 262 production went to the French Armée de l'Air and Aéronavale. Variants included the basic N.262A (some of which were later re-engined with Bastan VII engines as the N.262E), the N.262B for Air Inter, the N.262C Frégate upgraded civil model with 1,145 s.h.p. Bastan VII engines and the equivalent Armée de l'Air N.262D. The reliability of the Turboméca Bastan engines was a significant problem and Frakes Aviation carried out a programme of refitting the aircraft with a pair of Pratt & Whitney PT6A-45 engines as the Mohawk 298. At least nine aircraft were converted for use by Allegheny Commuter Airlines. Around 20 Frégates remain in French military service and 14 commercial aircraft still fly with small carriers in Africa and South America.

Nord N.262D Frégate, French AF, No.88

Specification	Nord (Aérospatiale) N.262C Frégate	
Powerplant	Two 1,145 s.h.p. (853.7 kW) Turboméca Bastan VII turboprops	
Dimensions		
Span	21.89 m	(71 ft 10 in)
Length	19.28 m	(63 ft 3 in)
Height	6.6 m	(21 ft 8 in)
Performance		
Max speed	418 km/h	(226 kt, 260 mph)
Cruising speed	410 km/h	(222 kt, 255 mph)
Initial climb	366 m/min	(1,200 fpm)
Range	2,384 km	(1,296 nm, 1,490 miles)
Weights		
Max takeoff	10,800 kg	(23,814 lbs)
Useful load	4,600 kg	(10,143 lbs)

Nord N.1101 Noralpha — France

During the middle of World War II, Messerschmitt designed an enlarged version of the Bf.108 light communications aircraft which was designated Me.208. This was intended to replace the Bf.108 (Nord 1000) in production at the Nord factory at Les Mureaux and two prototypes were built, powered by the 270 h.p. Argus As.10c engine. When the war ended Nord (SNCAN) went ahead with the aircraft as the Nord 1101 powered by a 233 h.p. Renault 6Q.10 engine. The civil version was named Noralpha and the military version was the Ramier I. A second military model, the N.1102 Ramier II, had a six-cylinder Renault 6Q.11 engine. The N.1101 was longer than the Nord 1000 with a full four-seat cabin, longer wings with pronounced dihedral and a tall, retractable tricycle undercarriage. The majority of the 200 aircraft built were Ramiers for the Armée de l'Air but civil Noralphas were also produced, largely as trainers and communications aircraft for the French government. Seven N.1101s remain active in France, Belgium and the UK.

Nord N.1101 Noralpha, G-ATDB

Specification	Nord (SNCAN) N.1101 Noralpha	
Powerplant	One 233 h.p. (173.7 kW) Renault 6Q.10 piston engine	
Dimensions		
Span	11.48 m	(37 ft 8 in)
Length	8.53 m	(28 ft 0 in)
Height	3.25 m	(10 ft 8 in)
Performance		
Max speed	306 km/h	(165 kt, 190 mph)
Cruising speed	282 km/h	(152 kt, 175 mph)
Initial climb	274 m/min	(900 fpm)
Range	1,192 km	(648 nm, 745 miles)
Weights		
Max takeoff	1,646 kg	(3,630 lbs)
Useful load	698 kg	(1,540 lbs)

Nord N.1203 Norecrin — France

Towards the end of the war, using the design basis established in their production of the N.1002 Pingouin and N.1101 Noralpha, Nord (SNCAN) drew up plans for a four-seat touring light aircraft for use by French flying clubs. The Nord 1200 prototype, which first flew on 15th December 1945, was a two-/three-seat cabin monoplane with pronounced dihedral to its wings, a tall, retractable tricycle undercarriage and a 100 h.p. Mathis engine. Production commenced in 1946, initially with the three-seat N.1201 Norecrin I powered by a 140 h.p. Renault 4P.O1 engine, but the main version was the N.1203 Norecrin II with a 135 h.p. Regnier 4L engine and a full four-seat cabin. The later Norecrin IV was fitted with a 170 h.p. Regnier 4L.02 and the Norecrin VI had a 145 h.p. Regnier 4L.14. A total of 378 Norecrins were built by Nord and they were sold to civil customers in Europe and South America. Approximately 20 Norecrins remain in flying condition, mainly in France.

Nord N.1203 Norecrin VI, F-BBEG

Specification	Nord (SNCAN) N.1203 Norecrin II	
Powerplant	One 135 h.p. (100.66 kW) Regnier 4L piston engine	
Dimensions		
Span	10.21 m	(33 ft 6 in)
Length	7.21 m	(23 ft 8 in)
Height	2.9 m	(9 ft 6 in)
Performance		
Max speed	280 km/h	(151 kt, 174 mph)
Cruising speed	220 km/h	(119 kt, 137 mph)
Initial climb	300 m/min	(985 fpm)
Range	896 km	(487 nm, 560 miles)
Weights		
Max takeoff	1,050 kg	(2,315 lbs)
Useful load	398 kg	(878 lbs)

Norman Aircraft Freelance — UK

Britten Norman's Desmond Norman designed the BN-3 Nymph as a new model to add to the successful Islander range. It was intended for production in kit form for completion under 'technology transfer' arrangements by overseas manufacturers. In layout, it was a conventional all-metal strut-braced high wing light aircraft with a four-seat cabin and a fixed tricycle undercarriage. The prototype was first flown on 17th May 1969 powered by a 115 h.p. Lycoming O-235-C1B piston engine. Following the 1971 collapse of Britten-Norman the Nymph was taken over by Desmond Norman's NDN Aircraft (Norman Aeroplane Company) and rebuilt as the prototype NAC1 Freelance. This has a modified wing section, a longer cabin, a 180 h.p. Lycoming O-360 engine and folding wings and it first flew on 29th September 1984 with production commencing in 1987. The prototype continues to be active and the initial five-aircraft production batch, which was substantially completed, remains unflown.

Norman NAC1 Freelance, G-NACI

Specification	Norman NAC1 Freelance	
Powerplant	One 180 h.p. (134 kW) Textron Lycoming O-360-A3A piston engine	
Dimensions		
Span	12.25 m	(40 ft 2 in)
Length	7.21 m	(23 ft 8 in)
Height	2.9 m	(9 ft 6 in)
Performance		
Max speed	230 km/h	(124 kt, 143 mph)
Cruising speed	220 km/h	(119 kt, 137 mph)
Initial Climb	203 m/min	(667 fpm)
Range	1,955 km	(1,062 nm, 1,222 miles)
Weights		
Max takeoff	1,225 kg	(2,700 lbs)
Useful Load	515 kg	(1,136 lbs)

Norman Aircraft Firecracker — UK

Desmond Norman, well-known as the co-designer of the Islander utility twin, conceived the NDN-1 Firecracker military trainer which was intended for licence production overseas. The Firecracker is an all-metal aircraft with a retractable tricycle undercarriage and a tandem two-seat cockpit with a side-hinged canopy. It has a low straight wing with slight dihedral on the outer panels and extended inboard leading edges. The prototype, which was flown on 26th May 1977, was powered by a 260 h.p. Lycoming AEIO-540-B4D5 piston engine and the NDN-1 received its type certificate two years later. No further piston-engined Firecrackers were built but subsequent airframes were completed, initially by Hunting and later by the Norman Aeroplane Company, as NDN-1T Turbo Firecrackers with a Pratt & Whitney PT6A-25A turboprop and various other changes including a taller vertical tail and enlarged cockpit canopy. Three Turbo Firecrackers were built for a UK customer but all are now flying in the USA as commercial advanced trainers.

NAC Turbo Firecracker, N50FK

Specification	NAC Turbo Firecracker	
Powerplant	One 715 s.h.p. (533 kW) Pratt & Whitney PT6A-25A turboprop	
Dimensions		
Span	7.92 m	(26 ft 0 in)
Length	8.33 m	(27 ft 4 in)
Height	3.25 m	(10 ft 8 in)
Performance		
Max speed	367 km/h	(198 kt, 228 mph)
Cruising speed	335 km/h	(181 kt, 208 mph)
Initial climb	762 m/min	(2,500 fpm)
Range	1,152 km	(626 nm, 720 miles)
Weights		
Max takeoff	1,633 kg	(3,600 lbs)
Useful load	567 kg	(1,250 lbs)

Norman Aircraft Fieldmaster — UK

The NDN.6 Fieldmaster agricultural aircraft was originally designed by Desmond Norman's NDN Aircraft Ltd. and the prototype was first flown on 17th December 1981. It was a large all-metal low-wing aircraft with a fixed tricycle undercarriage, powered by a 750 s.h.p. Pratt & Whitney PT6A-34AG turboprop. The fuselage was built round a titanium hopper which could carry 698 US gallons of liquid dressing or firefighting chemical retardant, and the cockpit was fully enclosed and positioned behind the wing trailing edge. The Fieldmaster, which had a second seat to allow for the transport of a ground crewman, was built at the Norman Aircraft Company's Cardiff factory and five production examples of the NAC.6 were built. Brooklands Aerospace then developed the more powerful Firemaster 65. The prototype, converted from a Fieldmaster, was fitted with a 1,230 s.h.p. PT6A-65 engine and five-blade Hartzell propeller. Following its first flight on 28th October 1989 two further Fieldmasters were converted. No further production has taken place but all six aircraft remain, two of which are active in Turkey.

NAC Fieldmaster, G-NACP (minus prop)

Specification	NAC Fieldmaster	
Powerplant	One 750 s.h.p. (559 kW) Pratt & Whitney PT6A-34AG turboprop	
Dimensions		
Span	16.33 m	(53 ft 7 in)
Length	10.97 m	(36 ft 0 in)
Height	4.11 m	(13 ft 6 in)
Performance		
Max speed	266 km/h	(143 kt, 165 mph)
Cruising speed	233 km/h	(126 kt, 145 mph)
Initial climb	291 m/min	(955 fpm)
Range	1,472 km	(800 nm, 920 miles)
Weights		
Max takeoff	4,535 kg	(10,000 lbs)
Useful load	2,381 kg	(5,250 lbs)

North American T-6 (Texan/Harvard) — USA

The famous T-6 has its origins in the NA-16 advanced trainer designed by North American in 1935 and developed into the BT-9 for the US Army Air Corps. The BT-9 was a tandem two-seat monoplane with an enclosed cockpit and a fixed, spatted tailwheel undercarriage. The fuselage was built from tube and fabric and it had a distinctive wing with a straight trailing edge and swept leading edge which was to become a hallmark of the North American trainers which were to follow. The BT-9 Yale (NA-19) was powered by a 400 h.p. Wright Whirlwind R-975-7 and the later BT-14 Yale had longer-span wings, a metal-covered fuselage, angular rudder and a 450 h.p. R-985-25 engine. In total, nearly 1,000 Yales were delivered to the USAAC and to France and Canada and several are still flying with private owners. The Yale was followed by the AT-6 (originally BC-1A) advanced combat trainer which differed in having a retractable undercarriage, semi-monocoque fuselage construction, provision for a forward-firing machine gun or rear cockpit-mounted gun position and a 600 h.p. Pratt & Whitney R-1340 radial engine. To meet wartime demands it was built in a number of versions, the USAAF aircraft being named Texan and the RCAF and RAF machines being the Harvard. Principal variants were the AT-6A (and USN SNJ-3) with additional fuel tanks, AT-6B with the rear gun position, AT-6C with a modified wood and light alloy structure and the AT-6D with a modified electrical system. Nearly 16,000 T-6s were built including aircraft built in Canada by Noorduyn for the RAF. Between 1949 and 1952 many AT-6s were upgraded to AT-6G standard with a stronger airframe which often allowed its conversion for counter-insurgency and ground attack tasks. The T-6 became the standard postwar basic trainer with many air forces. The majority of surviving T-6s are operating in the USA but several hundred are active with private owners worldwide.

North American SNJ-5B, VH-OVO

Specification	North American AT-6D	
Powerplant	One 600 h.p. (447 kW) Pratt & Whitney R-1340-AN1 piston engine	
Dimensions		
Span	12.8 m	(42 ft 0 in)
Length	8.84 m	(29 ft 0 in)
Height	3.56 m	(11 ft 8 in)
Performance		
Max speed	330 km/h	(178 kt, 205 mph)
Cruising speed	274 km/h	(148 kt, 170 mph)
Initial climb	500 m/min	(1,640 fpm)
Range	1,200 km	(652 nm, 750 miles)
Weights		
Max takeoff	2,404 kg	(5,300 lbs)
Useful load	518 kg	(1,142 lbs)

North American P-51 Mustang — USA

The Mustang (NA-73) fighter was originally built to meet the wartime needs of the RAF and was first flown on 25th October 1940. It was powered, initially, by a 1,100 h.p. Allison V-1710-F3R engine and had a straight laminar-flow wing, a retractable tailwheel undercarriage, a belly-mounted air scoop and a single-seat cabin integrated into the fuselage. First deliveries of RAF Mustang Is (P-51) took place in 1941 followed by the Mustang II (P-51A). Shortly afterwards the engine was changed, the P-51B and P-51C for the RAF and USAAC being powered by a 1,380 h.p. Packard-built Merlin V-1650-3. The P-51D was substantially improved with a cut-down rear fuselage and bubble cockpit canopy, a dorsal fin and a 1,490 h.p. Packard V-1650-7 engine. Many variants were built including the TP-51D two-seat trainer and the P-51H with a lighter airframe, longer fuselage and taller fin. The P-51D was built in Australia by Commonwealth Aircraft as the CA-17 and after the war Cavalier converted Mustangs as two-seaters and as ground attack aircraft, primarily for South American air forces. The Mustang also formed the basis for the Piper PA-48 Enforcer although this was not built in quantity. Production of the Mustang had reached 15,586 when the line closed in 1946 and approximately 145 are still flying with warbird owners.

North American P-51D, N51MX

Specification	North American P-51D Mustang	
Powerplant	One 1,490 h.p. (1,110.9 kW) Packard Merlin V-1650-7 piston engine	
Dimensions		
Span	11.28 m	(37 ft 0 in)
Length	9.83 m	(32 ft 3 in)
Height	4.17 m	(13 ft 8 in)
Performance		
Max speed	703 km/h	(380 kt, 437 mph)
Cruising speed	615 km/h	(332 kt, 382 mph)
Initial climb	701 m/min	(2,300 fpm)
Range	3680 km	(2,000 nm, 2,300 miles)
Weights		
Max takeoff	5,261 kg	(11,600 lbs)
Useful load	2,029 kg	(4,475 lbs)

North American B-25 Mitchell — USA

North American produced over 10,000 examples of the B-25 Mitchell medium bomber during the war years, many of which were delivered overseas to the UK, Russia, China etc. The B-25 was based on the NA-40 of 1939 and the first Mitchell flew on 19th August 1940. It was of all-metal construction with a twin-fin tail unit and retractable tricycle landing gear and the wing had a dihedralled centre section inboard of the 1,700 h.p. R-2600-9 Wright Cyclone radial engines. The B-25C had 1,700 h.p. R-2600-13 engines. Mitchell variants mainly differed in their armament configurations which included various combinations of a mid-upper or forward-upper gun turret, rear flank positions, a tail turret, nose-mounted cannon manually operated from a glasshouse nose, and cheek cannon pods in pairs at the wing roots. The B-25B had a retractable ventral turret and the B-25G and B-25H (US Navy PBJ-1H) had a solid nose for ground attack containing a fixed 75 mm M-4 cannon and two 0.5-inch guns. The main production version was the B-25J which was a B-25H with a glazed nose. After the war, the B-25 continued in service with many air forces including those of Canada, Indonesia, Peru and Venezuela and was used for various commercial tasks including passenger transport, cargo hauling, filming and running contraband. A number of B-25s have been preserved in flying condition and 42 examples are believed to be active.

North American B-25J, N9079Z

Specification	North American B-25J Mitchell	
Powerplant	Two 1,700 h.p. (1,267.5 kW) Wright R-2600-29 Cyclone piston engines	
Dimensions		
Span	20.6 m	(67 ft 7 in)
Length	16.13 m	(52 ft 11 in)
Height	4.83 m	(15 ft 10 in)
Performance		
Max speed	457 km/h	(247 kt, 284 mph)
Cruising speed	375 km/h	(203 kt, 233 mph)
Initial climb	366 m/min	(1,200 fpm)
Range	2,400 km	(1,304 nm, 1,500 miles)
Weights		
Max takeoff	15,419 kg	(34,000 lbs)
Useful load	4,490 kg	(9,900 lbs)

North American T-28 Trojan — USA

The T-28 was the successor to the very successful T-6 Harvard (Texan) basic trainer and it followed the same general layout with a low wing and a tandem two-seat cockpit which was enclosed by a large bubble canopy. It featured a tall, retractable tricycle undercarriage and was powered by a large 800 h.p. Wright R-1300-1A engine. The first T-28 flew on 26th September 1949 and the type was ordered for the USAF as the T-28A with production deliveries taking place between 1950 and 1953. The T-28B was a US Navy version with a 1,425 h.p. R-1820-86 engine and the Navy also received a batch of T-28Cs with a tail arrester hook in a cut-away rear fuselage recess. North American built 1,194 T-28As, 489 T-28Bs and 299 T-28Cs. Once released from US military service T-28s were sold to several overseas air arms for training and ground attack, conversions including the Fennec modification of the T-28A, 245 of which were produced by Sud Aviation and the Hamilton Nomair. North American's own ground attack T-28D was fitted with six underwing hardpoints and they also built the turboprop YAT-28E. Remaining T-28s are all civilian-owned and the type is a popular warbird with around 350 registered in the USA and 150 in operation.

North American T-28A Fennec, NX632NA

Specification	North American T-28A	
Powerplant	One 800 h.p. (596.48 kW) Wright R-1300-1A piston engine	
Dimensions		
Span	12.22 m	(40 ft 1 in)
Length	9.75 m	(32 ft 0 in)
Height	3.86 m	(12 ft 8 in)
Performance		
Max speed	455 km/h	(246 kt, 283 mph)
Cruising speed	306 km/h	(165 kt, 190 mph)
Initial climb	564 m/min	(1,850 fpm)
Range	1,680 km	(913 nm, 1,050 miles)
Weights		
Max takeoff	2,887 kg	(6,365 lbs)
Useful load	569 kg	(1,254 lbs)

North American F-86 Sabre — USA

Famous for its performance in the Korean War, the F-86 was the first United States swept-wing jet fighter. It was capable of supersonic flight in a dive and production started in early 1947 following the prototype's first flight on 1st October 1947. The F-86A was powered by a single 4,850 lb.s.t. General Electric J47-GE-1 turbojet. It was armed with six nose-mounted machine guns and had two underwing pylons for long-range tanks or ordnance. The F-86E (US Navy FJ-1 Fury) was similar but with an all-flying tailplane, and the F-86F was powered by a 5,910 lb.s.t. J47-GE-27 engine and did not have the original automatic leading edge slats. A further power increase came with the F-86H which was fitted with an 8,920 lb.s.t. J73-GE-3. Foreign production was carried out by Canadair as the CL-13 Sabre 1 (F-86A), Sabre 3 (with an Avro Orenda engine) and Sabre 4 and Sabre 6 for the RAF and Luftwaffe. The Government Aircraft Factory also built the CA-27 Sabre in Australia for the RAAF, powered by a Rolls Royce Avon RA.7 engine and Mitsubishi assembled the F-86F for the JASDF. In total 6,720 Sabres were built by North American including 2,506 F-86D and F-86L all-weather fighter versions. Sabres are no longer in military service but several are flown as jet warbirds by private owners.

North American F-86F, NX86F

Specification	North American F-86F-30 Sabre	
Powerplant	One 5,910 lb.s.t. (26.29 kN) General Electric J47-GE-27 turbojet	
Dimensions		
Span	11.3 m	(37 ft 1 in)
Length	11.43 m	(37 ft 6 in)
Height	4.5 m	(14 ft 9 in)
Performance		
Max speed	1,118 km/h	(604 kt, 695 mph)
Cruising speed	837 km/h	(452 kt, 520 mph)
Initial climb	2,835 m/min	(9,300 fpm)
Range	2,584 km	(1,404 nm, 1,615 miles)
Weights		
Max takeoff	9,232 kg	(20,357 lbs)
Useful load	4,293 kg	(9,467 lbs)

North American F-100 Super Sabre — USA

North American's F-100 was the replacement for the venerable F-86 Sabre and it followed the same general design layout although it was capable of speeds in excess of Mach 1.3 in level flight. The F-100A, which was powered by a reheated 9,700 lb.s.t. Pratt & Whitney J57 engine, first flew on 29th October 1953 and production aircraft entered service the following year. The F-100C was a fighter bomber variant with a strengthened wing with four hardpoints and the F-100D had increased power, a further increase in offensive load and a larger vertical tail. Production of single-seat F-100s totalled 1,955 and the Super Sabre was supplied to the French, Turkish, Danish and Taiwanese air forces. North American also built 339 F-100F conversion trainers with a lengthened forward fuselage and tandem two-seat cockpit. A few F-100s remain in service, primarily as target tugs and for commercial test and research work.

North American F-100F Super Sabre, N417FS

Specification	North American F-100D Super Sabre	
Powerplant	One 10,200 lb.s.t. (45.38 kN) Pratt & Whitney J57-P-21A turbojet	
Dimensions		
Span	11.81 m	(38 ft 9 in)
Length	14.45 m	(47 ft 5 in)
Height	4.93 m	(16 ft 2 in)
Performance		
Max speed	1,437 km/h	(776 kt, 893 mph)
Cruising speed	941 km/h	(509 kt, 585 mph)
Initial climb	5,517 m/min	(18,100 fpm)
Range	1,920 km	(1,043 nm, 1,200 miles)
Weights		
Max takeoff	17,255 kg	(38,048 lbs)
Useful load	7,896 kg	(17,410 lbs)

North American OV-10 Bronco — USA

The Bronco was devised to meet a combined USAF, US Marine Corps and US Army specification for an armed reconnaissance and close air support aircraft. North American's design had twin booms, a main fuselage pod with tandem seating for two and weapons hardpoints on the fuselage centre section. The Bronco (NA-300) was powered by a pair of Garrett AiResearch T76 turboprops and had a retractable tricycle undercarriage. The first flight took place on 16th July 1965 and the OV-10A was rapidly placed in production for service in Vietnam where it was used for forward air control and ground attack missions. Germany received 18 OV-10B target tugs with a supplementary 2,950 lb.s.t. J85-GE-4 turbojet mounted above the fuselage mid-section and Thailand had 32 OV-10Cs and Venezuela bought 16 OV-10Es. In total 323 Broncos were built. All have been retired from military service but a number remain operational as fire control spotters for the USFS, and one is preserved in flying condition in Germany.

North American (Rockwell) OV-10A, N97LM

Specification	North American OV-10A	
Powerplant	Two 715 s.h.p. (533 kW) Honeywell (Garrett) T76 turboprops	
Dimensions		
Span	12.19 m	(40 ft 0 in)
Length	12.67 m	(41 ft 7 in)
Height	4.62 m	(15 ft 2 in)
Performance		
Max speed	452 km/h	(244 kt, 281 mph)
Cruising speed	435 km/h	(235 kt, 270 mph)
Initial climb	610 m/min	(2,000 fpm)
Range	2,288 km	(1,243 nm, 1,430 miles)
Weights		
Max takeoff	4,493 kg	(9,908 lbs)
Useful load	1,333 kg	(2,939 lbs)

Northrop T-38 Talon — USA

Now in service for nearly 40 years, the T-38 advanced jet trainer continues to be used in large numbers by the USAF and by Turkey and South Korea, and in the USA by the German Air Force. It was also exported to the Portuguese Air Force which has now withdrawn the type from service. It was first flown as the YT-38 (N-156T) on 10th April 1959 and entered service in early 1961, progressively replacing the USAF's Lockheed T-33s and also flying with the US Navy and NASA. The Talon is a supersonic tandem two-seat aircraft with an elegant area-ruled fuselage incorporating twin General Electric J85 turbojets with air intakes just ahead of the wings. It has straight tapered wings of honeycomb construction and a conventional tail unit with a low-set all-moving tailplane. The T-38B is a lead-in fighter trainer version fitted with a fuselage centreline weapons hardpoint for practice bombs or a minigun pod. Some 1,145 T-38s were built, including prototypes, and around 550 remain operational.

Northrop T-38A, USAF 68-8172

Specification	Northrop T-38A Talon	
Powerplant	Two 2,500 lb.s.t. (11.12 kN) General Electric J85-GE-5 turbojets	
Dimensions		
Span	7.7 m	(25 ft 3 in)
Length	13.46 m	(44 ft 2 in)
Height	3.94 m	(12 ft 11 in)
Performance		
Max speed	1,350 km/h	(730 kt, 839 mph)
Initial climb	9,144 m/min	(30,000 fpm)
Range	2,024 km	(1,100 nm, 1,265 miles)
Weights		
Max takeoff	5,261 kg	(11,600 lbs)
Useful load	2,018 kg	(4,450 lbs)

Northrop F-5 — USA

The F-5 was originally known as the Freedom Fighter due to its intended role as a lightweight interceptor to be supplied under MAP to air forces of friendly nations. Externally, the F-5 closely resembled the T-38 Talon advanced trainer but it was a single-seater with a much stronger airframe and more powerful 4,080 lb.s.t (reheated) General Electric J85-GE-13 turbojets. The wing was redesigned incorporating leading edge extensions and a multi-spar design in place of the T-38's honeycomb structure so that four underwing hardpoints and wingtip Sidewinder rails could be accommodated. Northrop flew the prototype on 30th July 1959 and this was followed by the definitive F-5A and, on 24th February 1964, by the first F-5B tandem two-seat combat-capable conversion trainer. Some were built or converted as tactical reconnaissance RF-5As with an alternative nose. The F-5E Tiger II (and two-seat F-5F) is an improved dedicated interceptor version which first flew on 11th August 1972 and has uprated J85-GE-21B engines, increased weapons load and modified avionics and systems. Initial F-5 deliveries went to the USAF but the F-5A/F-5B and later F-5E were also supplied to 27 other countries including Brazil, Greece, the Philippines, Saudi Arabia, Turkey, Venezuela and Switzerland. Licence assembly took place in Switzerland, Taiwan, South Korea and by Canadair for the CAF (CF-5A/CF5D or CF-116) and by CASA for the Spanish Air Force (C.9/CE.9). Many upgrades have been carried out including the Chilean F-5 Plus Tigre III with an advanced cockpit system. In total 2,084 single-seat and 534 two-seat F-5s had been built when production ceased in 1987.

Northrop F-5E Tiger II, Swiss AF, J-3081

Specification	Northrop F-5E Tiger II	
Powerplant	Two 5,000 lb.s.t. (22.2 kN) (wet) General Electric J85-GE-21B turbojets	
Dimensions		
Span	8.13 m	(26 ft 8 in)
Length	14.45 m	(47 ft 5 in)
Height	4.09 m	(13 ft 5 in)
Performance		
Max speed	1,698 km/h	(917 kt, 1,055 mph)
Initial climb	10,363 m/min	(34,000 fpm)
Range	3,696 km	(2,009 nm, 2,310 miles)
Weights		
Max takeoff	11,185 kg	(24,664 lbs)
Useful load	6,848 kg	(15,100 lbs)

Northrop Grumman B-2A Spirit — USA

Drawing on its extensive experience of large flying wing aircraft gleaned during the postwar years, Northrop developed the B-2 as a fully stealthy strategic bomber to replace the increasingly aged B-52. The B-2 first flew on 17th July 1990. It has a highly swept wing with a unique jagged edge profile to the rear wing and fuselage, a blended body containing the three-crew flight deck and two large weapons bays in the central belly. The retractable tricycle undercarriage has two four-wheel main bogies and a twin nosewheel unit. The B-2 relies on a radar-absorbing structure of epoxy-graphite honeycomb for its stealth characteristics but, as in the F-117A, several straight surfaces are broken into jagged shapes to reduce the radar signature. The weapons load of the B-2 is normally up to 16 AGM-129A or AGM-69 cruise missiles but up to 75,000 lbs of conventional bomb load can be accommodated. In total 21 B-2As have been delivered to date but further procurement relies on funding approval.

Northrop Grumman B-2A Spirit, USAF, 89-0128

Specification	Northrop Grumman B-2A Spirit	
Powerplant	Four 19,000 lb.s.t. (84.52 kN) General Electric F118-GE-110 turbofans	
Dimensions		
Span	52.42 m	(172 ft 0 in)
Length	21.03 m	(69 ft 0 in)
Height	5.18 m	(17 ft 0 in)
Performance		
Max speed	982 km/h	(530 kt, 610 mph)
Cruising speed	954 km/h	(516 kt, 593 mph)
Initial climb	914 m/min	(3,000 fpm)
Range	18,400 km	(10,000 nm, 11,500 miles)
Weights		
Max takeoff	152,381 kg	(336,000 lbs)
Useful load	82,993 kg	(183,000 lbs)

Northrop Grumman Intruder and Prowler — USA

Grumman's A-6A Intruder first entered US Navy service in 1964 and replaced the Skyraider as the standard carrier-borne strike aircraft. The prototype first flew on 19th April 1960. The Intruder has a mildly swept wing with complex leading edge slats, full-span Fowler flaps and spoilers and airbrakes. It has a side-by-side two-seat cockpit and the two Pratt & Whitney J52 turbojets are fitted on the lower fuselage flanks with weapons hardpoints on the fuselage centreline. The Intruder has four wing hardpoints for fuel tanks and bombs or rockets. The A-6A distinguished itself in the Vietnam war with the US Navy and Marine Corps and was supported by a small number of EA-6As converted for ELINT and electronic countermeasures tasks with a large fin-tip antenna housing. Other variants included the KA-6D buddy tanker, the A-6B modified to carry the AGM-78 missile, the A-6C FLIR-equipped night attack model, the A-6E with substantially upgraded combat electronics and the A-6F with F404 turbofans. The EA-6B Prowler is a four-seat development of the EA-6A with a lengthened forward fuselage housing an additional two rear seats for ECM operators and equipped with new tactical jamming systems including up to three ALQ-99Fs carried in external pods. The Prowler can carry offensive loads including HARM missiles. Grumman built 708 Intruders and 170 Prowlers and production ceased in February 1992.

Northrop Grumman EA-6B Prowler, US Navy, Bu.160791

Specification	Grumman EA-6B Prowler	
Powerplant	Two 11,200 lb.s.t. (49.8 kN) Pratt & Whitney J52-P-408 turbojets	
Dimensions		
Span	16.15 m	(53 ft 0 in)
Length	18.24 m	(59 ft 10 in)
Height	4.95 m	(16 ft 3 in)
Performance		
Max speed	1,046 km/h	(565 kt, 650 mph)
Cruising speed	788 km/h	(426 kt, 490 mph)
Initial climb	3,932 m/min	(12,900 fpm)
Range	3,840 km	(2,087 nm, 2,400 miles)
Weights		
Max takeoff	29,478 kg	(65,000 lbs)
Useful load	15,156 kg	(33,420 lbs)

Northrop Grumman Hawkeye — USA

Grumman designed the Hawkeye to replace the smaller E-1B Tracer carrier-based airborne radar picket which was itself a development of the C-1A Trader. The Hawkeye first flew on 21st October 1960 and production is expected to continue until at least 2007. It is a high-wing aircraft with a triple-fin tail unit, retractable tricycle undercarriage and two wing-mounted Allison T56 turboprops. The circular-section fuselage houses two flight crew and five operators for the AN/APS96 long-range radar which is contained in a 24 ft diameter rotating radome on a strutted rear fuselage pylon. Deliveries of the E-2A (formerly W2F-1) started in January 1964 and most E-2As were subsequently upgraded to E-2B standard with an improved Litton L-304 computer and larger outer tail fins. The E-2C, which is now the standard service version, had a new AN/APS-111 radar and later upgrades were made to the APS-138 and APS-145. The E-2C has been exported to Egypt, France, Israel, Japan, Singapore and Taiwan and total Hawkeye production exceeds 250 aircraft. The latest Hawkeye 2000 has upgraded computers and workstations and improved satcom equipment including links to other airborne sensors and is being built for the US Navy and France.

Northrop Grumman E-2C Hawkeye, US Navy, Bu.161228

Specification	Northrop Grumman E-2C Hawkeye	
Powerplant	Two 5,100 s.h.p. (3,803 kW) Allison T56-A-427 turboprops	
Dimensions		
Span	24.56 m	(80 ft 7 in)
Length	17.6 m	(57 ft 9 in)
Height	5.59 m	(18 ft 4 in)
Performance		
Max speed	628 km/h	(339 kt, 390 mph)
Cruising speed	602 km/h	(325 kt, 374 mph)
Initial climb	884 m/min	(2,900 fpm)
Range	2,832 km	(1,539 nm, 1,770 miles)
Weights		
Max takeoff	24,683 kg	(54,426 lbs)
Useful load	6,323 kg	(13,942 lbs)

Northrop Grumman C-2A Greyhound — USA

The Greyhound is a COD (Carrier Onboard Delivery) transport for the US Navy which is derived from the E-2 Hawkeye. The C-2A, which first flew on 18th November 1964, has the wings, engines and undercarriage of the E-2C and a similar tail without the toed-in outer fins or tailplane dihedral. The pressurised fuselage, however, is an entirely new design which is wider and deeper and incorporates an upswept rear section with an integral loading ramp. It has wing folding for carrier deck storage. With high-density seating the Greyhound can carry 28 passengers or up to 12 medical stretchers. Grumman delivered an initial batch of 19 C-2A Greyhounds but these have now been replaced with 39 new-build aircraft delivered between 1985 and 1989. The majority of these remain in service.

Specification	Grumman C-2A Greyhound	
Powerplant	Two 4,910 s.h.p. (3,661 kW) Allison T56-A-425 turboprops	
Dimensions		
Span	24.56 m	(80 ft 7 in)
Length	17.32 m	(56 ft 10 in)
Height	4.83 m	(15 ft 10 in)
Performance		
Max speed	573 km/h	(309 kt, 356 mph)
Cruising speed	483 km/h	(261 kt, 300 mph)
Initial climb	796 m/min	(2,610 fpm)
Range	2,880 km	(1,565 nm, 1,800 miles)
Weights		
Max takeoff	26,077 kg	(57,500 lbs)
Useful load	9,594 kg	(21,155 lbs)

Northrop Grumman C-2A Greyhound, US Navy, Bu.162142

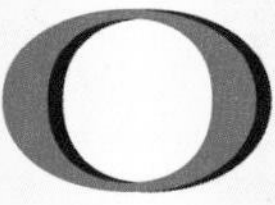

Oberlerchner JOB 15
— Austria

In 1957, the Josef Oberlerchner Holzindustrie, an established sailplane builder, built the prototype of the JOB 5 side-by-side two-seat light aircraft powered by a 95 h.p. Continental C90-12F piston engine. It had a low wing and fixed tailwheel undercarriage and was of mixed wood, tube, fabric and glass-fibre construction. The production JOB 15 was expanded to three seats with an enlarged streamlined blister canopy and larger vertical tail and Oberlerchner built the aircraft with either a 135 h.p. Lycoming O-290 engine or a 150 h.p. Lycoming O-320-A2B. The first JOB 15 was first flown in 1961 and 22 were subsequently built at the Spittal-Drau factory. Some were built or converted to JOB 15-150/2 standard with an enlarged rear seat to give total accommodation for four people. Three were re-engined with a 180 h.p. Lycoming O-360-A3A engine and redesignated JOB 15-180/2. The last JOB 15 was completed in 1966 and 16 remain active in Germany, Austria and Switzerland.

Oberlerchner JOB 15-150, D-ECFI

Specification	Oberlerchner JOB 15-150	
Powerplant	One 150 h.p. (111.8 kW) Textron Lycoming O-320-A2B piston engine	
Dimensions		
Span	10.08 m	(33 ft 1 in)
Length	7.67 m	(25 ft 2 in)
Height	1.98 m	(6 ft 6 in)
Performance		
Max speed	235 km/h	(127 kt, 146 mph)
Cruising speed	217 km/h	(117 kt, 135 mph)
Initial climb	264 m/min	(865 fpm)
Range	992 km	(539 nm, 620 miles)
Weights		
Max takeoff	965 kg	(2,127 lbs)
Useful load	364 kg	(803 lbs)

Oldfield Baby Lakes
— USA

The Baby Great Lakes was originally designed and built by Andrew Oldfield and was loosely modelled on the famous Great Lakes aerobatic biplane. The definitive Baby Lakes, which is powered by an 85 h.p. Continental flat-four engine, is a single-seat light biplane with an open cockpit and fixed undercarriage. It is intended for amateur construction from plans sold by Barney Oldfield Aircraft Company (formerly Great Lakes Airplanes) and has a wooden wing structure, welded tube fuselage and fabric covering. The Baby Lakes has been developed into the Super Baby Lakes, with a larger Lycoming engine in the 108 h.p. to 125 h.p. range, and the Buddy Baby Lakes, which is a side-by-side two-seat version with a wider fuselage and additional wing centre bay sections. Over 1,000 sets of plans for the Baby Lakes have been sold and approximately 150 are thought to have been flown.

Oldfield Baby Lakes, G-POND

Specification	Oldfield Baby Lakes	
Powerplant	One 85 h.p. (63.3 kW) Teledyne Continental C85 piston engine	
Dimensions		
Span	5.08 m	(16 ft 8 in)
Length	4.19 m	(13 ft 9 in)
Height	1.37 m	(4 ft 6 in)
Performance		
Max speed	217 km/h	(117 kt, 135 mph)
Cruising speed	190 km/h	(103 kt, 118 mph)
Initial climb	610 m/min	(2,000 fpm)
Range	402 km	(217 nm, 250 miles)
Weights		
Max takeoff	385 kg	(850 lbs)
Useful load	170 kg	(375 lbs)

Orlican L-40 Meta Sokol
— Czechoslovakia

The Czech company Orlican, which had built a postwar series of Mraz Sokol light aircraft, developed the Sokol design into the Mraz Bonzo and then into the all-metal XLD-40 Mir three-seater which went on to become the production L-40 Meta Sokol. The Meta Sokol was a low-wing monoplane with a wing based on that of the Sokol M-1D which incorporated a swept leading edge and straight trailing edge. It was a four-seater with a large rear-sliding bubble canopy and a 105 h.p. Walter Minor 4-III engine. Its 'reverse tricycle' undercarriage consisted of main legs retracting backwards as on the Sokol and a small retracting rear wheel placed under the fuselage at rear wing root level. The L-40 first flew on 29th March 1956 and most production aircraft used a 140 h.p. Walter M.332 engine although some were re-engined with a Lycoming O-290. Some also had long-range wingtip fuel tanks. A total of 107 Meta Sokols were produced, including the three prototypes. At least half were exported and around 15 are currently flying in Germany, Sweden, Slovakia and the UK.

Specification	Orlican L-40 Meta Sokol	
Powerplant	One 140 h.p. (104.4 kW) Walter M.332 piston engine	
Dimensions		
Span	10.06 m	(33 ft 0 in)
Length	7.54 m	(24 ft 9 in)
Height	2.51 m	(8 ft 3 in)
Performance		
Max speed	240 km/h	(130 kt, 149 mph)
Cruising speed	216 km/h	(117 kt, 134 mph)
Initial climb	270 m/min	(885 fpm)
Range	1,100 km	(598 nm, 688 miles)
Weights		
Max takeoff	935 kg	(2,062 lbs)
Useful load	400 kg	(882 lbs)

Orlican L-40 Meta Sokol, G-APUE

P

Pacific Aerospace FU-24 and Cresco — New Zealand

The FU-24 agricultural aircraft prototype was first flown on 14th June 1954 by the Sargent-Fletcher Company of El Monte, California. Designed by John Thorpe, the all-metal low-wing FU-24 was aimed at the New Zealand crop-spraying market as a Tiger Moth replacement and early-production FU-24s were built as kits in the USA and assembled by Cable-Price Corporation (later Air Parts Ltd. and then Pacific Aerospace) at Hamilton, New Zealand. It is a large aircraft with a straight wing with dihedralled outer panels and a fixed tricycle undercarriage. It has a hopper in the rear fuselage but some aircraft were converted to a six-seat passenger layout with oval portholes in the rear fuselage. The FU-24-950 as built by Air Parts had a 300 h.p. Continental IO-520-F engine and the FU-24A had dual controls. The later FU-24-954 has increased weights and a 400 h.p. Lycoming IO-720-A1A. Some 300 piston-engined FU-24s have been built. Several turboprop conversions of the FU-24 have been carried out and Pacific Aerospace builds the Cresco 600 which is similar to the FU-24-954 but with a longer nose housing a Lycoming LTP-101-700A-1A turboprop, a 470 USG hopper, a large dorsal fin and a port-side rear cargo door. The prototype first flew on 28th February 1979 and production now exceeds 18 aircraft with the later Cresco 750 being powered by a Pratt & Whitney PT6A-34AG.

Fletcher FU-24, ZK-BWD

Pacific Aerospace Cresco 600, ZK-FVV

Specification	Pacific Aerospace Cresco 750	
Powerplant	One 750 s.h.p. (559.2 kW) Pratt & Whitney PT6A-34AG turboprop	
Dimensions		
Span	12.8 m	(42 ft 0 in)
Length	11.07 m	(36 ft 4 in)
Height	3.63 m	(11 ft 11 in)
Performance		
Max speed	276 km/h	(149 kt, 172 mph)
Cruising speed	272 km/h	(147 kt, 169 mph)
Initial climb	475 m/min	(1,560 fpm)
Range	852 km	(460 nm, 530 miles)
Weights		
Max takeoff	3,741 kg	(8,250 lbs)
Useful load	2,449 kg	(5,400 lbs)

Pacific Aerospace Airtrainer — New Zealand

The Airtrainer has been developed from the Airtourer and four-seat Aircruiser designs of Dr. Henry Millicer (see entry on Victa Airtourer). Rights to the Aircruiser were acquired by Aero Engine Services (AESL, later Pacific Aerospace) in New Zealand and they redesigned it with a strengthened airframe and a rear-hinged clear-view canopy as a fully aerobatic military trainer, the prototype flying on 23rd February 1972. As the CT4A Airtrainer, powered by a 210 h.p. Continental IO-360-H engine, it was sold to the air forces of Australia, New Zealand and Thailand with 81 being com-

Pacific Aerospace Airtrainer (Cont.)

pleted between 1973 and 1977. Civil production of the similar CT4B followed with a further 32 aircraft for customers such as the British Aerospace Flying College and the Royal Thai Air Force. The latest version is the CT4E with the wing moved forward and a 300 h.p. Lycoming AEIO-540-L engine. Pacific Aerospace has also flown a prototype of the CT4C with an Allison 250-B17 turboprop engine.

Pacific Aerospace Airtrainer CT4A, A19-029

Specification	Pacific Aerospace CT4E Airtrainer	
Powerplant	One 300 h.p. (224 kW) Textron Lycoming AEIO-540-L1B5 piston engine	
Dimensions		
Span	7.92 m	(26 ft 0 in)
Length	7.16 m	(23 ft 6 in)
Height	2.59 m	(8 ft 6 in)
Performance		
Max speed	303 km/h	(163 kt, 188 mph)
Cruising speed	282 km/h	(152 kt, 175 mph)
Initial climb	558 m/min	(1,830 fpm)
Range	957 km	(520 nm, 598 miles)
Weights		
Max takeoff	1,179 kg	(2,600 lbs)
Useful load	419 kg	(925 lbs)

Panavia Tornado
— International

The Tornado multi-role strike aircraft is standard equipment with the air arms of Britain, Germany (air force and navy), Italy and Saudi Arabia and has distinguished itself in the Gulf War and other military engagements of the 1990s. Designed to meet a 1968 specification, the Tornado was flown in prototype form on 14th August 1974 and is built by the international Panavia consortium of DASA, Alenia and BAE Systems. It is a tandem two-seater with variable-sweep wings which can carry any current NATO air-launched weapons on four automatically aligning pylons. A further three fuselage hardpoints are available and the Tornado IDS has two fixed 27 mm IWKA-Mauser cannon in the nose. Initial aircraft had twin 14,840 lb.s.t. Turbo Union RB199 Mk.101 reheated turbofans but later batches were upgraded to the 16,000 lb.s.t. RB199 Mk.103. Variants include the standard Tornado IDV (RAF GR.Mk.1), the dual-control combat-capable GR.Mk.1(T) and the photo-reconnaissance Tornado ECR (RAF GR.Mk.1A) with a Honeywell infra-red imaging system and active countermeasures. The GR.Mk.4 (and GR.Mk.4A) are mid-life upgrades with much extra equipment including a TIALD target acquisition system, NVG night vision integration, a FLIR-linked HUD and improved weapons integration. The Tornado ADV is the dedicated long-range air defence variant, first flown on 27th October 1979. Delivered to the RAF as the Tornado F.Mk.2 it differs from the IDV in having a longer fuselage, a new long-range Marconi intercept radar, a retractable refuelling probe, single underwing pylons to carry 2,250-litre drop tanks and AIM-9L Sidewinders, a single 27 mm cannon and four belly-mounted Sky Flash AAMs. The later F.Mk.3 has a modified afterburner. Production is now nearing an end but 770 Tornado IDS and 221 Tornado ADVs have been built to date.

Panavia Tornado GR.1A, ZD996

Panavia Tornado F3, ZE292

Specification	Panavia Tornado IDS (GR.Mk.4)	
Powerplant	Two 16,000 lb.s.t. (71.2 kN) (wet) Turbo Union RB199 Mk.103 turbofans	
Dimensions		
Span (spread)	13.89 m	(45 ft 7 in)
Length	16.71 m	(54 ft 10 in)
Height	5.94 m	(19 ft 6 in)
Performance		
Max speed	1,480 km/h	(800 kt, 920 mph)
Initial climb (est)	13,716 m/min	(45,000 fpm)
Range	1,120 km	(609 nm, 700 miles)
Weights		
Max takeoff	27,982 kg	(61,700 lbs)
Useful load	13,483 kg	(29,730 lbs)

Specification	Papa-51 Thunder Mustang	
Powerplant	One 640 h.p. (477.2 kW) Falconar V-12 piston engine	
Dimensions		
Span	7.26 m	(23 ft 10 in)
Length	7.37 m	(24 ft 2 in)
Height	1.86 m	(6 ft 1 in)
Performance		
Max speed	603 km/h	(326 kt, 375 mph)
Cruising speed	555 km/h	(300 kt, 345 mph)
Initial climb	1,585 m/min	(5,200 fpm)
Range	2,395 km	(1,300 nm, 1,497 miles)
Weights		
Max takeoff	1,451 kg	(3,200 lbs)
Useful load	454 kg	(1,000 lbs)

Papa-51 Thunder Mustang — USA

The Thunder Mustang is one of the most recent replicas of the North American P-51D to be made available to amateur builders and apart from its size it is externally almost identical to the original aircraft. It is a 75% scale representation of the Mustang fighter, designed by Dan Denney, and the prototype first flew on 16th November 1996. The Thunder Mustang is a tandem two-seater built from composite materials with a retractable tailwheel undercarriage and it is powered by a 640 h.p. Falconar V-12 engine driving a four-blade propeller. The prototype was destroyed in a fatal crash on 30th May 1998 but two further examples have flown and more than 30 complete kits have been sold by Papa-51 Corporation of Nampa, Idaho.

Papa-51 Thunder Mustang, N151TM

Paramount Cabinaire — USA

The Cabinaire was a four-seat private aircraft of mixed construction designed by Walter J. Carr and built and tested in 1928. It was of unusual biplane layout with the upper wing braced separately from the fuselage rather than being directly attached to the fuselage upper longerons as might be expected. It had quite a capacious four-seat fully enclosed cabin and a fixed, strutted tailwheel undercarriage. Apparently, fewer than ten Cabinaires were built before Paramount Aircraft of Saginaw, Michigan went into liquidation in 1932. They had a variety of engines including the 100 h.p. or 110 h.p. Warner Scarab and 165 h.p. Continental A-70, but the sole surviving airworthy example has a 165 h.p. Wright R-540 (J6) radial engine, and several replicas of the type are under construction.

Paramount Cabinaire, NC17M

Paramount Cabinaire (Cont.)

Specification	Paramount Cabinaire 165	
Powerplant	One 165 h.p. (123 kW) Wright R-540 piston engine	
Dimensions		
Span	10.06 m	(33 ft 0 in)
Length	7.49 m	(24 ft 7 in)
Height	2.74 m	(9 ft 0 in)
Performance		
Max speed	193 km/h	(104 kt, 120 mph)
Cruising speed	164 m/min	(88 kt, 102 mph)
Initial climb	238 m/min	(780 fpm)
Range	800 km	(435 nm, 500 miles)
Weights		
Max takeoff	1,193 kg	(2,630 lbs)
Useful load	458 kg	(1,010 lbs)

Parker Teenie Too — USA

The Teenie Too was designed by Cal Parker as the smallest and simplest all-metal aircraft which could be built around a 40 h.p. Volkswagen converted car engine. It first flew in 1969 and in its simplest form it is a low-wing monoplane with an open cockpit and a fixed tricycle undercarriage. It is stressed for aerobatics and has a semi-monocoque structure using single-curvature aluminium panels making it suitable for construction by amateur builders with no previous metal-working experience. Plans and material kits for the Teenie Too are sold by the Teenie Company and over 100 examples have flown to date, many with detailed modifications including enclosed cockpits, detachable wings and engines of up to 65 horsepower.

Specification	Parker Teenie Too	
Powerplant	One 40 h.p. (29.8 kW) Volkswagen 1500 piston engine	
Dimensions		
Span	5.49 m	(18 ft 0 in)
Length	3.9 m	(12 ft 10 in)
Height	1.73 m	(5 ft 8 in)
Performance		
Max speed	193 km/h	(104 kt, 120 mph)
Cruising speed	177 km/h	(96 kt, 110 mph)
Initial climb	244 m/min	(800 fpm)
Range	640 km	(348 nm, 400 miles)
Weights		
Max takeoff	268 kg	(590 lbs)
Useful load	127 kg	(280 lbs)

Parks P-1 and P-2 — USA

The Parks P-1 was designed for its own use by the Parks Air College who built the first example in 1928. It was a very conventional tailwheel biplane with tandem open cockpits seating two in front and one person behind and was powered by a 90 h.p. Curtiss OX-5 eight-cylinder engine in a close cowling with the radiator positioned externally between the main undercarriage legs. Fuselage construction was of steel tube and fabric and the wings were built from wood and plywood with fabric covering. Around 45 P-1s were built and this was followed by the P-2 which had an almost identical airframe but was powered by a 115 h.p. Axelson radial engine and had a split-axle undercarriage in place of the earlier through-axle arrangement. The P-2A (later called the Ryan Speedster) was similar, but with a 165 h.p. Wright J6 radial. Fewer than 20 P-2s and P-2As were built and the aircraft were subsequently known as the Detroit-Parks P-1, P-2 and P-2A after Parks was sold to Detroit Aircraft Corp. Four Parks P-2As and one P-1 are currently owned by private individuals in the USA.

Parker Teenie Too, ZS-UHC

Parks P-2A, N499H

Specification	Parks P-2A	
Powerplant	One 165 h.p. (123 kW) Wright J6 piston engine	
Dimensions		
Span	9.14 m	(30 ft 0 in)
Length	7.01 m	(23 ft 0 in)
Height	2.82 m	(9 ft 3 in)
Performance		
Max speed	193 km/h	(104 kt, 120 mph)
Cruising speed	161 km/h	(87 kt, 100 mph)
Initial climb	244 m/min	(800 fpm)
Range	800 km	(435 nm, 500 miles)
Weights		
Max takeoff	1,079 kg	(2,380 lbs)
Useful load	407 kg	(897 lbs)

Parnall Elf — UK

The Elf was one of a wide range of aircraft built by George Parnall & Co. at Yate, Gloucestershire in the 1930s. Announced in 1929, the Elf was an open-cockpit tandem two-seat biplane and the prototype Mk.I was powered by a 105 h.p. Cirrus Hermes I in-line engine. It had a tailwheel undercarriage and the wings, which were unequal in span and fitted with full-span ailerons and Warren-truss interplane struts, were foldable for ground transportation or storage. Two further Elf IIs were built, both of which were fitted with the 120 h.p. ADC Cirrus Hermes II engine. One Parnall Elf survives, powered by a Hermes II and operated by the Shuttleworth Trust.

Parnall Elf, G-AAIN

Specification	Parnall Elf Mk.II	
Powerplant	One 120 h.p. (89.47 kW) ADC Cirrus Hermes II piston engine	
Dimensions		
Span	9.52 m	(31 ft 3 in)
Length	6.96 m	(22 ft 10 in)
Height	2.77 m	(9 ft 1 in)
Performance		
Max speed	185 km/h	(100 kt, 115 mph)
Cruising speed	169 km/h	(91 kt, 105 mph)
Initial climb	213 m/min	(700 fpm)
Range	640 km	(348 nm, 400 miles)
Weights		
Max takeoff	771 kg	(1,700 lbs)
Useful load	308 kg	(680 lbs)

Partenavia P.57 Fachiro and P.66 Oscar — Italy

Designed by Prof. Luigi Pascale, the P.57 Fachiro was built in series by Partenavia Costruzione Aeronautiche as a four-seat light aircraft for aero club use. The prototype first flew on 7th November 1958. The initial Fachiro II was of mixed steel tube and fabric construction with a 150 h.p. Lycoming O-320 or 160 h.p. O-360-B2A engine but the main production Fachiro IIf had a swept tail and a 180 h.p. O-360-A2A engine. In total, 36 Fachiros were built and the company followed on with the P.64 Fachiro III which had a metal-covered wing, a slimmer rear fuselage, a repositioned nosewheel, a taller fin and modified tailplane. This aircraft was further modified as the P.64B Oscar B (and higher-weight B-1155) with a cut-down metal fuselage and an all-round-vision cockpit. The P.64B Oscar 200 was a four-seat version with a 200 h.p. Lycoming IO-360-A1B engine, the P.66B Oscar 100 was a two-seat training version with a 100 h.p. O-235-C1B engine and the P.66B Oscar 150 had three seats and a 150 h.p. Lycoming O-320-E2A. The final model, of which 107 were built, was the P.66C Charlie four-seater with a 160 h.p. O-320-H2AD engine and a more streamlined rear cabin structure. In total 312 of the Oscar series were built, including 21 assembled in South Africa as the AFIC.200, and large numbers were delivered to the Italian state flying clubs.

Partenavia P.57 Fachiro IIf, I-FANA

Partenavia P.64B-1155 Oscar, Z-WCA

Partenavia P.57 Fachiro and P.66 Oscar (Cont.)

Specification	Partenavia P.66C Charlie	
Powerplant	One 160 h.p. (119 kW) Textron Lycoming O-320-H2AD piston engine	
Dimensions		
Span	9.98 m	(32 ft 9 in)
Length	7.24 m	(23 ft 9 in)
Height	2.77 m	(9 ft 1 in)
Performance		
Max speed	241 km/h	(130 kt, 150 mph)
Cruising speed	209 km/h	(113 kt, 130 mph)
Initial climb	290 m/min	(950 fpm)
Range	968 km	(526 nm, 605 miles)
Weights		
Max takeoff	990 kg	(2,183 lbs)
Useful load	390 kg	(860 lbs)

Partenavia AP.68TP-600 Viator, N901TP

Partenavia P.68 — Italy

Known initially as the 'Victor', the P.68 high-wing light piston twin was first flown by Partenavia on 25th May 1970 and production commenced at Casoria in 1972. The P.68, which was intended as an executive and general-utility aircraft, had a circular-section streamlined fuselage with seating for seven, including crew, and was unusual in having a fixed tricycle undercarriage. The initial P.68 had two 200 h.p. Lycoming IO-360-A1B engines but the P.68TC was fitted with 210 h.p. turbocharged TIO-360-C1A6Ds. Other variants included the P.68B which had a longer fuselage and higher weights, the P.68C with a longer nose and modified fuel system and the P.68R, one of which was built with a retractable undercarriage. Partenavia also built the P.68 Observer which was designed by Sportavia-Pützer and had a completely new transparent forward fuselage and cockpit making it ideal for surveillance and patrol work with police forces and maritime agencies. Having achieved success with the standard P.68, Partenavia moved on to the turboprop AP.68TP-300 Spartacus which was a P.68R with a deeper and longer fuselage, modified cockpit windows and a pair of 330 s.h.p. Allison 250-B17B engines. The P.68T prototype first flew on 11th September 1978 with retractable gear but production aircraft had a fixed undercarriage. The AP.68TP-600 Viator was a developed Spartacus with a further 25-inch fuselage stretch, an extra pair of cabin windows and retractable gear. Nearly 400 standard P.68s and 17 of the turboprop models have been built, including a small batch produced in India by Taneja Aerospace, and in April 1998 the line was bought by Vulcan Air who build the P.68C, the Observer 2 and the Viator at Casoria.

Partenavia P.68C-TC, N997JB

Specification	Partenavia (Vulcan Air) P.68C	
Powerplant	Two 200 h.p. (149.12 kW) Textron Lycoming IO-360-A1B6 piston engines	
Dimensions		
Span	12 m	(39 ft 5 in)
Length	9.55 m	(31 ft 4 in)
Height	3.4 m	(11 ft 2 in)
Performance		
Max speed	320 km/h	(172 kt, 199 mph)
Cruising speed	306 km/h	(165 kt, 190 mph)
Initial climb	378 m/min	(1,240 fpm)
Range	2,944 km	(1,598 nm, 1,842 miles)
Weights		
Max takeoff	2,084 kg	(4,592 lbs)
Useful load	764 kg	(1,685 lbs)

Pasped Skylark W-1 — USA

The Skylark was developed by the Pasped Aircraft Company of Glendale, California and first flew in 1936. It had a tubular steel fuselage with fabric and light alloy covering and fabric-covered wooden wings with the whole structure being extensively wire-braced. The wings mounted the substantial main undercarriage legs which were encased in large 'trouser' fairings. The Skylark was a side-by-side two-seater with a transparent cockpit enclosure and the initial Powerplant fitted was a 125 h.p. Warner Scarab radial but this was later upgraded to a 175 h.p. Warner Super Scarab. It is unclear how many Skylarks were built but at least one remains active in the USA.

Pasped Skylark, NC14919

Specification	Pasped Skylark W-1	
Powerplant	One 125 h.p. (93.2 kW) Warner Scarab piston engine	
Dimensions		
Span	10.92 m	(35 ft 10 in)
Length	7.62 m	(25 ft 0 in)
Height	2.41 m	(7 ft 11 in)
Performance		
Max speed	224 km/h	(121 kt, 139 mph)
Cruising speed	201 km/h	(109 kt, 125 mph)
Initial climb	259 m/min	(850 fpm)
Range	1,040 km	(565 nm, 650 miles)
Weights		
Max takeoff	855 kg	(1,885 lbs)
Useful load	271 kg	(597 lbs)

Specification	Payne Knight Twister KT-85	
Powerplant	One 90 h.p. (67.1 kW) Teledyne Continental C90 piston engine	
Dimensions		
Span	4.57 m	(15 ft 0 in)
Length	4.27 m	(14 ft 0 in)
Height	1.6 m	(5 ft 3 in)
Performance		
Max speed	257 km/h	(139 kt, 160 mph)
Cruising speed	209 km/h	(113 kt, 130 mph)
Initial climb	305 m/min	(1,000 fpm)
Range	624 km	(339 nm, 390 miles)
Weights		
Max takeoff	435 kg	(960 lbs)
Useful load	193 kg	(425 lbs)

Payne Knight Twister — USA

The Knight Twister sport aerobatic biplane dates back to 1928 when Vernon Payne designed it as an advanced light aircraft for construction by amateurs from plans. The original Knight Twister had a 50 h.p. radial engine but the majority of aircraft have a 70 h.p., 90 h.p. or 125 h.p. Lycoming or Continental although engines of up to 180 h.p. have been fitted. The Twister has an open single-seat cockpit and the straight tapered upper wings are attached by very short struts to sit close to the fuselage allowing the pilot a view under and over the wing. Three sizes of wing can be built for the Akro version (15.5 ft wing), the racing Twister (17.5 ft wing) or sport version (19.5 ft). Early Twisters had a divided rubber-damped undercarriage but later aircraft have spring-steel gear. Construction is mixed with fabric-covered wooden wings and a fuselage built from tube and wood with light alloy covering. Around 75 Twisters have been built from plans sold by Steen Aero Lab. although the aircraft can be demanding to fly and has suffered several accidents.

Pazmany PL-1 and PL-2 — USA

The PL-1 Laminar was designed by Ladislao Pazmany and first flown on 23rd March 1962. A low-wing single-seater with a fixed tricycle undercarriage it is distinguished by its straight metal wing and tip tanks. It has an enclosed cockpit with a canopy which either slides or opens via a scissor lever mechanism. In standard form, the PL-1 is powered by a 95 h.p. Continental engine, but the type has been built as the PL-1B for the Taiwanese Air Force with a 150 h.p. Lycoming O-320 and a wider cockpit. Fifty PL-1Bs were built and at least five were sold back to the USA in 1981 when their military service was over. More than 100 amateur-built PL-1s have been completed. The PL-2 is an improved two-seat version with a wider fuselage and larger cockpit. It was first flown on 4th April 1969 and is designed for Lycoming engines of 108 h.p. to 150 h.p. The PL-2, 200 of which have been built, was marketed in the Far East as a production design, but most examples completed to date are amateur-built.

ne Knight Twister, N3TL

Pazmany PL-1

Pazmany PL-1 and PL-2 (Cont.)

Specification	Pazmany PL-2	
Powerplant	One 135 h.p. (100.7 kW) Textron Lycoming O-290-D2B piston engine	
Dimensions		
Span	8.53 m	(28 ft 0 in)
Length	5.87 m	(19 ft 3 in)
Height	2.44 m	(8 ft 0 in)
Performance		
Max speed	238 km/h	(129 kt, 148 mph)
Cruising speed	209 km/h	(113 kt, 130 mph)
Initial climb	488 m/min	(1,600 fpm)
Range	789 km	(429 nm, 493 miles)
Weights		
Max takeoff	655 kg	(1,445 lbs)
Useful load	247 kg	(545 lbs)

Pazmany PL-4A
— USA

Ladislao Pazmany's second major design for amateur constructors is the Volkswagen-powered PL-4A. It is an all-metal single-seater built from plans sold by Pazmany Aircraft Corp. with simple construction involving single-curvature panels and standard riveted techniques. The cockpit is roomy with a rear baggage compartment and a side-opening canopy and the aircraft has a distinctive T-tail. The undercarriage is a fixed tailwheel type with spring-steel main legs and go-kart wheels and the constant-chord wings are foldable for ground transport. The prototype first flew on 12th July 1972 following which around 750 sets of plans have been sold with more than 50 aircraft now completed and flying in the USA, Australia, New Zealand and the UK.

Pazmany PL-4A, G-PAZY

Specification	Pazmany PL-4A	
Powerplant	One 50 h.p. (37.3 kW) Volkswagen 1600 piston engine	
Dimensions		
Span	8.13 m	(26 ft 8 in)
Length	5.03 m	(16 ft 6 in)
Height	1.73 m	(5 ft 8 in)
Performance		
Max speed	201 km/h	(109 kt, 125 mph)
Cruising speed	161 km/h	(87 kt, 100 mph)
Initial climb	198 m/min	(650 fpm)
Range	544 km	(296 nm, 340 miles)
Weights		
Max takeoff	385 kg	(850 lbs)
Useful load	122 kg	(270 lbs)

Péña Capéña and Bilouis
— France

Louis Péña, a noted French aerobatic pilot, has designed a group of low-wing light aircraft for amateur construction. The initial Capéña was a competition aerobatic monoplane built of wood and fabric and featuring a fixed tailwheel undercarriage and an enclosed single-seat cockpit. The first Capéña made its maiden flight at Dax on 24th July 1984 and distinguished itself at the World Aerobatic Championships in 1986 and in later international competitions. Various engines have been fitted to the six aircraft built including the 150 h.p. Lycoming IO-320-A1A and 200 h.p. IO-360-A1A. Louis Péña then went on to produce the Bilouis which flew in 1991. It is a larger tandem two-seat version of the Capéña with a 200 h.p. Lycoming IO-360-C1C6 engine and an optional retractable undercarriage. Over 30 examples of the Bilouis are under construction and five have flown to date. A one-off special version of the Bilouis is the Péña-Guilie CAPTR-04 which has a single-seat cockpit, retractable gear and a 160 h.p. IO-320 engine. The third Péña design is the Dahu which is very similar in layout to the Bilouis but is, again, larger and has a four-seat cabin and a Lycoming O-360-A3A engine. It flew in 1996 and six were under construction at the end of 1999 from plans supplied by Louis Péña.

Péña Bilouis, F-PENA

Specification	Péña Capéña	
Powerplant	One 150 h.p. (111.8 kW) Textron Lycoming IO-320-A1A piston engine	
Dimensions		
Span	6.81 m	(22 ft 4 in)
Length	5.38 m	(17 ft 8 in)
Height	1.78 m	(5 ft 10 in)
Performance		
Max speed	370 km/h	(200 kt, 230 mph)
Cruising speed	274 km/h	(148 kt, 170 mph)
Initial climb	604 m/min	(1,980 fpm)
Range	640 km	(348 nm, 400 miles)
Weights		
Max takeoff	550 kg	(1,213 lbs)
Useful load	110 kg	(243 lbs)

Percival Vega Gull and Proctor — UK

The Proctor four-seat light communications aircraft was derived from the prewar Gull Six and Vega Gull designed by Capt. Edgar W. Percival. The P.10 Vega Gull, of which one example remains flying and others are being restored, was an all-wood low-wing cabin monoplane with a fixed tailwheel undercarriage and a 200 h.p. de Havilland Gipsy Six in-line engine. It first flew in November 1935, 109 being produced by the Percival Aircraft Co. Ltd., and it was modified to become the Proctor which differed in being slightly longer, having a more streamlined cabin design and using a 205 h.p. Gipsy Queen II engine. The Proctor I was used initially as a three-seat radio trainer, but it was followed by the Proctor II and III with revised cabin layouts and the Proctor IV four-seat dual-control communications aircraft with a larger wing and longer fuselage. In total, 1,143 military Proctors were built. After the war many Proctors were declared surplus and Percival, which had become part of the Hunting Group in 1944, built 139 examples of the P.44 Proctor V postwar civil variant. Three Proctors remain airworthy in the UK and others are candidates for restoration.

Percival Proctor III, G-ALJF

Specification	Percival P.44 Proctor V	
Powerplant	One 205 h.p. (152.8 kW) de Havilland Gipsy Queen II piston engine	
Dimensions		
Span	12.04 m	(39 ft 6 in)
Length	8.58 m	(28 ft 2 in)
Height	2.21 m	(7 ft 3 in)
Performance		
Max speed	253 km/h	(137 kt, 157 mph)
Cruising speed	235 km/h	(127 kt, 146 mph)
Initial climb	207 m/min	(680 fpm)
Range	800 km	(435 nm, 500 miles)
Weights		
Max takeoff	1,587 kg	(3,500 lbs)
Useful load	476 kg	(1,050 lbs)

Percival P.40 Prentice — UK

The Prentice, designed by Percival Aircraft and manufactured by Hunting Percival for the RAF, was intended as an immediate postwar replacement for the de Havilland Tiger Moth. It was an all-metal low-wing monoplane and was much larger than the Tiger Moth with a three-seat cabin providing side-by-side seating for instructor and pupil and a rear seat for an observer pupil. Powered by a 250 h.p. Gipsy Queen 30 Mk.2 in-line engine, it first flew on 31st March 1946 and was built as the P.40 Prentice T.Mk.1, a total of 370 being delivered. In addition, Prentices were sold to the air forces of Argentina and the Lebanon. The Prentice T.Mk.3 was a version built by Hindustan Aircraft for the Indian Air Force with a 345 h.p. Gipsy Queen 70-2 engine. In 1956 most Prentices were declared surplus and 252 were acquired by Aviation Traders who converted 25 as five-/seven-seat civil aircraft. Four of these remain airworthy and two others are under long-term restoration.

Percival Prentice, VS610 (G-AOKL)

Percival P.40 Prentice (Cont.)

Specification	Percival P.40 Prentice	
Powerplant	One 250 h.p. (186.4 kW) de Havilland Gipsy Queen 30 Mk.2 piston engine	
Dimensions		
Span	14.02 m	(46 ft 0 in)
Length	9.6 m	(31 ft 6 in)
Height	3.78 m	(12 ft 5 in)
Performance		
Max speed	269 km/h	(145 kt, 167 mph)
Cruising speed	241 km/h	(130 kt, 150 mph)
Initial climb	168 m/min	(550 fpm)
Range	1,280 km	(696 nm, 800 miles)
Weights		
Max takeoff	1,973 kg	(4,350 lbs)
Useful load	544 kg	(1,200 lbs)

Pereira GP-4 — USA

Designed by George Pereira, the GP-4 originally flew in 1984 and over 360 sets of plans have been sold by Osprey Aircraft to amateur constructors. It is a high-performance side-by-side two-seater of wood and composite construction with a very-low-profile fuselage and a tapered laminar-flow wing. The GP.4, which has a retractable tricycle undercarriage, is a design aimed at advanced amateur builders and an estimated 4,000 hours of building time is involved. Various engines have been fitted to the GP.4 including a 250 h.p. Lycoming IO-540 used in one example but the standard powerplant is a 200 h.p. Lycoming IO-360 which gives high cross-country speed performance. Around ten GP.4s are currently flying in the USA.

Specification	Pereira GP.4	
Powerplant	One 200 h.p. (149.12 kW) Textron Lycoming IO-360 piston engine	
Dimensions		
Span	7.52 m	(24 ft 8 in)
Length	6.4 m	(21 ft 0 in)
Height	1.6 m	(5 ft 3 in)
Performance		
Max speed	402 km/h	(217 kt, 250 mph)
Cruising speed	386 km/h	(209 kt, 240 mph)
Initial climb	762 m/min	(2,500 fpm)
Range	2,240 km	(1,217 nm, 1,400 miles)
Weights		
Max takeoff	907 kg	(2,000 lbs)
Useful load	345 kg	(760 lbs)

Pereira Osprey — USA

George Pereira's Osprey has been one of the most popular amateur-built amphibian aircraft and was first flown as the Osprey I in August 1970. The original Osprey I was a small mid-wing flying boat without a land undercarriage. It had a wood and fibreglass fuselage, fabric-covered wings with outrigger floats and a T-tail. The pusher 90 h.p. Continental engine was mounted on a pylon on the mid-section with the open single-seat cockpit located just ahead. The Osprey I prototype was sold to the US Navy for testing as the X-28A Air Skimmer and a number of amateur-built Osprey Is were built. The Osprey II, which flew in April 1973, is the current version marketed by Osprey Aircraft and the main improvements are a fully enclosed side-by-side two-seat cabin with a large bubble canopy, a modified swept vertical tail, a redesigned strutted pylon to carry a 150 h.p. Lycoming O-320 engine and a retractable tricycle undercarriage. Over 500 Ospreys are flying including examples in Finland, France, Canada, New Zealand and the UK.

Pereira GP-4, N30C

Pereira Osprey II, N220DW

Specification	Pereira Osprey II	
Powerplant	One 150 h.p. (111.8 kW) Textron Lycoming O-320 piston engine	
Dimensions		
Span	7.92 m	(26 ft 0 in)
Length	6.26 m	(20 ft 6 in)
Height	1.83 m	(6 ft 0 in)
Performance		
Max speed	193 km/h	(104 kt, 120 mph)
Cruising speed	175 km/h	(95 kt, 109 mph)
Initial climb	290 m/min	(950 fpm)
Range	880 km	(478 nm, 550 miles)
Weights		
Max takeoff	707 kg	(1,560 lbs)
Useful load	254 kg	(560 lbs)

Specification	Performance Aircraft Legend	
Powerplant	One 660 s.h.p. (492 kW) Walter M-601 turboprop	
Dimensions		
Span	7.77 m	(25 ft 6 in)
Length	7.65 m	(25 ft 1 in)
Height	2.87 m	(9 ft 5 in)
Performance		
Max speed	649 km/h	(350 kt, 403 mph)
Cruising speed	555 km/h	(300 kt, 345 mph)
Initial climb	1,775 m/min	(5,825 fpm)
Range	2,400 km	(1,304 nm, 1,500 miles)
Weights		
Max takeoff	1,347 kg	(2,970 lbs)
Useful load	304 kg	(670 lbs)

Performance Aircraft Legend — USA

With an external design reminiscent of the North American Mustang, the Legend has been designed by Jeff Ackland of Olathe, Kansas as a very-high-performance unlimited-category racing and competition aircraft. It is constructed from composite materials and has a tandem two-seat cockpit enclosed by a large rear-hinged bubble canopy, a straight tapered wing, a retractable tricycle undercarriage and, like the P-51, a radiator air scoop under the centre section. In its original form as flown in mid-1996, the Legend was powered by a Donovan V-8 piston engine, but the prototype has been re-engined with a 660 s.h.p. Walter M-601 turboprop engine and three-blade Hamilton Standard propeller which increases the maximum speed from 370 mph to over 400 mph. At least a dozen Legends are being constructed from kits sold by Performance Aircraft.

Performance Aircraft Legend, N620L

Petrolini El Boyero — Argentina

The prototype El Boyero high-wing side-by-side two-seat light aircraft was built in 1940 by the Argentine state company Fabrica Militar de Aviones (FMA). Designed by Juan Peretti, this aircraft was externally very similar to a Taylorcraft with steel tube and fabric construction and was powered by a 50 h.p. Continental A50 engine. Production of the El Boyero was undertaken by Petrolini Hermanos S.A. who delivered the first eight out of an order for 100 aircraft in January 1949. These were for use by aero clubs and for the Argentine military forces as spotter aircraft. Two versions were built, using either a 65 h.p. Continental A65 engine or a 75 h.p. Continental C75. A total of 129 El Boyeros had been completed when Petrolini closed the production line in 1951. A number of El Boyeros remain active in Argentina with private owners.

Petrolini El Boyero, LV-YTF

Petrolini El Boyero (Cont.)

Specification	Petrolini El Boyero	
Powerplant	One 65 h.p. (48.5 kW) Teledyne Continental A65 piston engine	
Dimensions		
Span	11.53 m	(37 ft 10 in)
Length	7.14 m	(23 ft 5 in)
Height	1.8 m	(5 ft 11 in)
Performance		
Max speed	161 km/h	(87 kt, 100 mph)
Cruising speed	140 km/h	(76 kt, 87 mph)
Initial climb	183 m/min	(600 fpm)
Range	640 km	(348 nm, 400 miles)
Weights		
Max takeoff	550 kg	(1,213 lbs)
Useful load	225 kg	(496 lbs)

Piaggio P.136 and Royal Gull — Italy

In 1948, Piaggio S.p.A. designed the P.136 five-seat light amphibian. Generally conventional in appearance, it had a gull wing with two 215 h.p. Franklin 6AB-215-B9F engines mounted at the intersection of the inner and outer panels in a pusher installation. It had a retractable tailwheel undercarriage with the main wheels folding upwards into the fuselage sides. The prototype flew on 29th August 1948 and the initial production batch of 18 aircraft went mainly to the Italian Air Force for air-sea rescue duties. In 1954, the P.136L-1 was announced and it had 260 h.p. Lycoming GO-435-C2 engines, a deeper windshield and a taller squared-off fin. This was sold in the USA by Kearney and Trecker who marketed it as the 'Royal Gull'. The P.136L-2 was a further improved version with an enlarged dorsal fin and 320 h.p. GSO-480-B1C6 engines. Production finally ceased in 1967 after 63 examples had been completed. Several Royal Gulls remain airworthy in the USA.

Piaggio P.136L, N40029

Specification	Piaggio P.136L-2	
Powerplant	Two 320 h.p. (238.6 kW) Textron Lycoming GSO-480-B1C6 piston engines	
Dimensions		
Span	13.5 m	(44 ft 5 in)
Length	10.8 m	(35 ft 5 in)
Height	3.84 m	(12 ft 7 in)
Performance		
Max speed	335 km/h	(181 kt, 208 mph)
Cruising speed	306 km/h	(165 kt, 190 mph)
Initial climb	259 m/min	(850 fpm)
Range	1,440 km	(783 nm, 900 miles)
Weights		
Max takeoff	2,993 kg	(6,600 lbs)
Useful load	883 kg	(1,948 lbs)

Piaggio P.149 — Italy

In 1951, Piaggio built the first of a series of P.148 light training aircraft for the Italian Air Force. This all-metal low-wing machine, designed by Ing. C. Casiraghi, formed the design basis for the larger P.149. The P.149, which first flew on 19th June 1953, had a straight tapered wing, a retractable tricycle undercarriage and a large four-/five-seat cabin enclosed by a framed sliding canopy. As the P.149D, it became the standard trainer for the newly formed West German Luftwaffe. Piaggio built 88 examples of which 72 went to Germany with a further 190 being produced under licence by Focke Wulf. A few civil P.149s were also built including five P.149Es which had a larger dorsal fin and were acquired by Swissair for pilot training. Many of the German P.149Ds were released to the civil market in 1971 and over 100 are flying with private owners in Germany, Belgium, Denmark, the UK and the USA.

Piaggio P.149D, N5316W

Specification	Piaggio P.149D	
Powerplant	One 270 h.p. (201.3 kW) Textron Lycoming GO-480 piston engine	
Dimensions		
Span	11.12 m	(36 ft 6 in)
Length	8.76 m	(28 ft 9 in)
Height	2.9 m	(9 ft 6 in)
Performance		
Max speed	310 km/h	(167 kt, 192 mph)
Cruising speed	266 km/h	(143 kt, 165 mph)
Initial climb	299 m/min	(980 fpm)
Range	1,088 km	(591 nm, 680 miles)
Weights		
Max takeoff	1,680 kg	(3,704 lbs)
Useful load	520 kg	(1,147 lbs)

Piaggio P.166 — Italy

Following on from their successful P.136 amphibian, Piaggio used the same basic design to produce a larger ten-seat unpressurised twin-engined business aircraft. The P.166, which first flew on 26th November 1967, had a new circular-section fuselage without the planing sea hull and with a larger more swept tail unit. This was married to the P.136's gull wing and GSO-480 engines. P.166A production started in 1959 and in 1962 the higher-powered P.166BL2 Portofino with 380 h.p. IGSO-540-A1C engines was introduced. Piaggio also built the P.166C which was fitted with external main undercarriage nacelles and additional seats in the rear baggage area, and the P.166M for the Italian Air Force which had a strengthened cabin floor and larger doors. The P.166 was redesigned in 1975 as the P.166DL3, which first flew on 3rd July 1976 with two Lycoming LTP-101-700A-1A turboprop engines, large tip tanks, a ventral fin and double cabin entry doors. Customers included the Alitalia Flying School, Iraqi Airways and the Somali Air Force. Some 28 were delivered for Italian military use including seven for the Guardia di Finanza and a number of P.166DL3SEMs fitted with external search radar dishes for coastal patrol, most of which remain in service. A few P.166s remain airworthy with civil owners, particularly in Australia. In total, 147 P.166s were built.

Piaggio P.166DL3, MM25177

Specification	Piaggio P.166DL3	
Powerplant	Two 600 s.h.p. (448 kW) Textron Lycoming LTP-101-700 turboprops	
Dimensions		
Span	14.7 m	(48 ft 3 in)
Length	11.89 m	(39 ft 0 in)
Height	5 m	(16 ft 5 in)
Performance		
Max speed	400 km/h	(216 kt, 249 mph)
Cruising speed	300 km/h	(162 kt, 186 mph)
Initial climb	671 m/min	(2,200 fpm)
Range	2,074 km	(1,126 nm, 1,295 miles)
Weights		
Max takeoff	4,300 kg	(9,481 lbs)
Useful load	1,650 kg	(3,638 lbs)

Piaggio PD.808 — Italy

The PD.808 originated as a joint business jet project between Piaggio and Douglas Aircraft Company and it was known initially as the 'Vespa Jet'. It was a low-wing aircraft with a circular-section cabin containing up to eight seats and powered by a pair of Rolls Royce (Bristol Siddeley) Viper 525 jets fitted to the rear fuselage sides. The Piaggio-built prototype first flew on 29th August 1964 followed by two civil demonstrators, but no commercial sales were achieved and the only order was for a batch of 20 aircraft for the Italian Air Force powered by 3,350 lb.s.t. Piaggio-built Viper 526 engines. The majority of these remain in service and are configured either as PD.808TA six- or nine-seat communications aircraft for airport navaid checking or as PD.808GE ECM aircraft.

Piaggio PD.808TA, MM61955

Piaggio PD.808 (Cont.)

Specification	Piaggio PD.808TA	
Powerplant	Two 3,350 lb.s.t. (14.9 kN) Rolls Royce Viper Mk.526 turbojets	
Dimensions		
Span	11.43 m	(37 ft 6 in)
Length	12.85 m	(42 ft 2 in)
Height	4.8 m	(15 ft 9 in)
Performance		
Max speed	853 km/h	(461 kt, 530 mph)
Cruising speed	724 km/h	(391 kt, 450 mph)
Initial climb	1,649 m/min	(5,410 fpm)
Range	2,034 km	(1,104 nm, 1,270 miles)
Weights		
Max takeoff	8,165 kg	(18,000 lbs)
Useful load	3,333 kg	(7,350 lbs)

Piaggio P-180 Avanti — Italy

Piaggio's P-180 Avanti twin turboprop business aircraft started as a joint-venture project between Piaggio and Gates Learjet but Piaggio assumed sole control in January 1986. The P-180, which first flew on 23rd September 1986, is a seven- to ten-passenger aircraft of conventional metal construction with a highly streamlined circular-section fuselage and a tricycle undercarriage which retracts into fuselage wells. It has a straight high-aspect-ratio wing set well to the rear of the cabin section, mounting a pair of pusher 1,480 s.h.p. Pratt & Whitney PT6A-66A turboprops driving five-bladed Hartzell propellers. The Avanti is also fitted with a T-tail and has a canard foreplane in the extreme nose. Sales of the Avanti were slow but 38 had been built by the end of 2000 including prototypes and an Italian military batch of eight. The aircraft was relaunched by Piaggio Aero Industries in 1999 and production recommenced to meet outstanding orders for 14 aircraft.

Piaggio Avanti, MM62152

Specification	Piaggio P-180 Avanti	
Powerplant	Two 1,480 s.h.p. (1,103.5 kW) Pratt & Whitney PT6A-66A turboprops	
Dimensions		
Span	11.43 m	(37 ft 6 in)
Length	14.40 m	(47 ft 3 in)
Height	3.94 m	(12 ft 11 in)
Performance		
Max speed	732 km/h	(396 kt, 455 mph)
Cruising speed	708 km/h	(383 kt, 440 mph)
Initial climb	875 m/min	(2,870 fpm)
Range	3,168 km	(1,721 nm, 1,980 miles)
Weights		
Max takeoff	5,238 kg	(11,550 lbs)
Useful load	1,837 kg	(4,050 lbs)

Piel Emeraude and Super Emeraude — France

Claude Piel's CP.30 Emeraude is one of the best-known European amateur-built aircraft and it has been built with many variations by amateurs and produced in series by a number of commercial companies. The CP.30 was a larger version of the single-seat CP.20 of 1951 and it was of wood and fabric construction with a low-set elliptical wing, a tailwheel undercarriage and a side-by-side two-seat cabin. The CP.30 prototype flew on 19th June 1954, powered by a Continental A65 engine and was subsequently marketed as plans for home construction. The commercial CP.301A, powered by a 95 h.p. Continental C90-14F engine, was built in large numbers by Coopavia and also by Scanor, SOCA, Rouchaud and Renard during the 1950s. In England, five examples of the Linnet were constructed by Garland-Bianchi and, later, Fairtravel. Ets. Claude Rousseau of Dinard built the CP.301B which had a sliding bubble canopy and detailed performance improvements, Binder Aviatik in Germany marketed the CP.301S Smaragd, and the CP.301C, which was similar to the CP.301B, went into production with Scintex who built 84 examples. Scintex was also responsible for the CP.1310 Super Emeraude which had a strengthened airframe, some detailed refinements and a 100 h.p. Continental O-200-A engine or (as the CP.1315) a 105 h.p. Potez 4E-20. In total 43 Super Emeraudes were built and more than 550 CP.301s have been completed commercially and by amateurs.

Scintex CP.301C2 Emeraude

Specification	Piel (Scintex) CP.301C1 Emeraude	
Powerplant	One 95 h.p. (70.8 kW) Teledyne Continental C90-14F piston engine	
Dimensions		
Span	8.25 m	(27 ft 1 in)
Length	6.12 m	(20 ft 1 in)
Height	2.46 m	(8 ft 1 in)
Performance		
Max speed	216 km/h	(117 kt, 134 mph)
Cruising speed	201 km/h	(109 kt, 125 mph)
Initial climb	180 m/min	(590 fpm)
Range	992 km	(539 nm, 620 miles)
Weights		
Max takeoff	650 kg	(1,433 lbs)
Useful load	255 kg	(562 lbs)

Specification	Piel CP.601 Diamant	
Powerplant	One 100 h.p. (74.6 kW) Teledyne Continental O-200 piston engine	
Dimensions		
Span	9.6 m	(31 ft 6 in)
Length	6.63 m	(21 ft 9 in)
Height	1.85 m	(6 ft 1 in)
Performance		
Max speed	220 km/h	(119 kt, 137 mph)
Cruising speed	195 km/h	(105 kt, 121 mph)
Initial climb	180 m/min	(590 fpm)
Range	832 km	(452 nm, 520 miles)
Weights		
Max takeoff	770 kg	(1,698 lbs)
Useful load	321 kg	(708 lbs)

Piel CP.60 Diamant and CP.70 Beryl — France

Following the success of his CP.30 Emeraude, Claude Piel designed the larger CP.60 Diamant which provided an additional third seat in a lengthened cabin and had greater wing area and, as the CP.601, a 100 h.p. Continental O-200 engine. It first flew on 2nd December 1961 and 17 further examples were built from plans sold by Claude Piel. These included several with tricycle undercarriages and Super Diamants with alternative engines including the 145 h.p. Continental O-300 (CP.604), 150 h.p. Lycoming O-320-A (CP.605), 115 h.p. Lycoming O-235-A (CP.606) and 130 h.p. Continental O-240-A (CP.607). The later CP.1320 Saphir, of which three were built, was similar to the CP.60 but had a completely new straight tapered wing, a swept vertical tail unit and either retractable or fixed tailwheel or tricycle gear. The CP.70 Beryl was a further amateur-built derivative which retained the familiar elliptical wing but had a tandem two-seat cockpit and was also produced as the CP.750 with a tubular steel fuselage structure. At least seven of the CP.70 series were built with engines ranging from 100 h.p. to 180 h.p.

Piel CP.605B Diamant, F-PNUN

Piel CP.80 — France

Claude Piel, who was principally known for his two-seat Emeraude and Diamant light aircraft, designed the CP.80 single-seat Formula I racer to compete in European events during the 1970s. Designed as one of the earliest composite amateur light aircraft, the prototype was built by Jacques Calvel as the CP.80 Zeff and made its first flight in August 1973. The CP.80 was a tiny aircraft of classic layout with a low wing and tailwheel spring-steel undercarriage. The first CP.80 had a 90 h.p. Continental C90-8F engine but 18 further examples have been built with various engines including the 85 h.p. Continental A65-8F, 100 h.p. Continental O-200-A, 125 h.p. Lycoming O-235 and 150 h.p. Lycoming O-320. At least one of the 25 completed by amateur constructors has been built as a CP.80TR with a retractable undercarriage.

Piel CP.80TR, F-PYFY

Piel CP.80 (Cont.)

Specification	Piel CP.80	
Powerplant	One 90 h.p. (67.1 kW) Teledyne Continental C90-8F piston engine	
Dimensions		
Span	5.99 m	(19 ft 8 in)
Length	5.31 m	(17 ft 5 in)
Height	1.7 m	(5 ft 7 in)
Performance		
Max speed	311 km/h	(168 kt, 193 mph)
Cruising speed	282 km/h	(152 kt, 175 mph)
Initial climb	720 m/min	(2,362 fpm)
Range	450 km	(243 nm, 280 miles)
Weights		
Max takeoff	380 kg	(838 lbs)
Useful load	120 kg	(265 lbs)

Pietenpol Air Camper — USA

In 1934, B.H. Pietenpol designed the little parasol-wing Air Camper for amateur construction and supplied kits to many homebuilders during the prewar years. Initially, the Air Camper had a 40 h.p. converted Model A Ford car engine but later models used the 65 h.p. Continental A65, and various other engines of up to 100 h.p. have been fitted including a 45 h.p. Salmson 9Ad radial. The Pietenpol, which has a strut-braced constant-chord wing and tandem open cockpits, is of simple wood, tube and fabric construction and is now marketed in plans form by John W. Grega as the Air Camper GN-1. Many variations in the shape of the tail and fuselage have been incorporated by individual builders. Over 500 Air Campers have been built, mostly in the USA and Canada, but 29 are currently registered in the UK.

Pietenpol Air Camper, N3133

Specification	Pietenpol Air Camper GN-1	
Powerplant	One 65 h.p. (48.5 kW) Teledyne Continental A65 piston engine	
Dimensions		
Span	8.84 m	(29 ft 0 in)
Length	5.51 m	(18 ft 1 in)
Height	2.08 m	(6 ft 10 in)
Performance		
Max speed	185 km/h	(100 kt, 115 mph)
Cruising speed	153 km/h	(83 kt, 95 mph)
Initial climb	152 m/min	(500 fpm)
Range	640 km	(348 nm, 400 miles)
Weights		
Max takeoff	499 kg	(1,100 lbs)
Useful load	204 kg	(450 lbs)

Pilatus P-2 — Switzerland

Pilatus designed the P-2 as a primary trainer for the Swiss Air Force and the first prototype flew on 27th April 1945. It is an all-metal aircraft of very sturdy construction with a 465 h.p. Argus engine and it was produced in several versions including a dedicated weapons training model, 26 of which were built with underwing hardpoints to carry bombs or rockets and a 7.9 mm machine gun mounted in the forward fuselage. The P-2 has tandem dual-control cockpits enclosed by a large framed canopy and a retractable tailwheel undercarriage. Pilatus built 56 examples of the P-2 and in 1981, when they were retired from service, many of these were sold to private owners in Europe and the USA.

Pilatus P-2, HB-RAW

Specification	Pilatus P-2	
Powerplant	One 465 h.p. (346.7 kW) Argus As.410A-2 piston engine	
Dimensions		
Span	11 m	(36 ft 1 in)
Length	9.07 m	(29 ft 9 in)
Height	2.69 m	(8 ft 10 in)
Performance		
Max speed	338 km/h	(183 kt, 210 mph)
Cruising speed	322 km/h	(174 kt, 200 mph)
Initial climb	390 m/min	(1,280 fpm)
Range	848 km	(461 nm, 530 miles)
Weights		
Max takeoff	1,966 kg	(4,335 lbs)
Useful load	454 kg	(1,000 lbs)

Pilatus P-3 — Switzerland

The P-3 was built by Pilatus during the 1950s to supplement the existing fleet of Swiss Air Force P-2 two-seat basic trainers. While it was a new design with a retractable tricycle undercarriage, it followed the layout of the P-2 in having a tandem two-seat cockpit and a low wing and was powered by a 260 h.p. Lycoming GO-435-C2A flat-six engine. Two underwing hardpoints could carry a mixture of practice bombs and rockets or a gun pod mounting a 7.62 mm Oerlikon machine gun. The prototype first flew on 3rd September 1953 and the P-3 remained in Swiss Air Force service from 1954 until 1984 when the surviving examples were sold onto the civilian market. Pilatus built 72 examples of the P-3 for the Swiss Air Force, 14 of which were written off in service, and six for the Brazilian Navy.

Pilatus P-3, N826LT

Specification	Pilatus P-3	
Powerplant	One 260 h.p. (193.86 kW) Textron Lycoming GO-435-C2A piston engine	
Dimensions		
Span	10.39 m	(34 ft 1 in)
Length	8.74 m	(28 ft 8 in)
Height	3.05 m	(10 ft 0 in)
Performance		
Max speed	306 km/h	(165 kt, 190 mph)
Cruising speed	249 km/h	(135 kt, 155 mph)
Initial climb	427 m/min	(1,400 fpm)
Range	720 km	(391 nm, 450 miles)
Weights		
Max takeoff	1,497 kg	(3,300 lbs)
Useful load	385 kg	(850 lbs)

Pilatus PC-6 Porter — Switzerland

The Pilatus Porter utility aircraft has been in production at Stans since 1960 and has been sold widely for many roles including cargo hauling, light passenger transport, military STOL operations and parachute dropping. The Porter has a square-section fuselage accommodating up to ten passengers, straight strut-braced wings fitted with high-lift devices for short-field operation and a tailwheel undercarriage. The prototype, which flew on 4th May 1959, was powered by a 340 h.p. Lycoming GSO-480-B1A6 piston engine and some early-production aircraft had the 350 h.p. IGO-540-A1A, but a change was made to turboprop power with the PC6/A-H1 Turbo Porter, first flown in 1961 with a 523 s.h.p. Turboméca Astazou IIE. Relatively few PC-6As were built, the main versions being the PC-6/B1-H2 with a 550 s.h.p. Pratt & Whitney PT6A-20 turboprop, the PC-6/B2-H2 and PC-6/B2-H4 with a PT6A-27 and the PC-6/C1-H2 with a 575 s.h.p. Garrett AiResearch TPE331-1-100 which was built under licence by Fairchild Hiller as the Heli-Porter. Some of the 45 production piston Porters were also subsequently re-engined with turboprops. Many military users have purchased the Turbo Porter including the air forces of Australia, France, Myanmar, Peru, Switzerland and Argentina. The USAF, who received 20 AU-23As for close-support forward combat duties in Vietnam, and the US Army have two UV-20A Chiricahuas. Pilatus continues to build the Turbo Porter to order and production to date exceeds 520 aircraft.

Pilatus PC-6/B1-H2 Turbo Porter

Specification	Pilatus PC6/B2-H4 Turbo Porter	
Powerplant	One 680 s.h.p. (507 kW) Pratt & Whitney PT6A-27 turboprop	
Dimensions		
Span	15.87 m	(52 ft 1 in)
Length	10.9 m	(35 ft 9 in)
Height	3.2 m	(10 ft 6 in)
Performance		
Max speed	266 km/h	(143 kt, 165 mph)
Cruising speed	217 km/h	(117 kt, 135 mph)
Initial climb	287 m/min	(940 fpm)
Range	920 km	(500 nm, 575 miles)
Weights		
Max takeoff	2,800 kg	(6,174 lbs)
Useful load	1,530 kg	(3,374 lbs)

Pilatus PC-7 and PC-9 — Switzerland

The PC-7 military basic and advanced trainer is a much improved version of the Pilatus P-3 and the prototype, which was converted from a P-3 and initially designated P-3B, was first flown on 12th April 1966. The most significant changes were the 560 s.h.p. Pratt & Whitney PT6A-25 turboprop engine, the modified tandem-seat cockpit with a large blister canopy and the enlarged vertical and horizontal tail surfaces. The PC-7 Turbo Trainer has six underwing hardpoints including two wet stations for fuel tanks. Around 450 PC-7s have been built, mostly for military users such as Austria, Bolivia, Chile, France, Myanmar and Uruguay but also for some private purchasers such as the ECCO aerobatic team in France. The PC-7 Mk.II is the current version with a raised rear cockpit, glass cockpit, enlarged fin and 700 s.h.p. PT6A-25C engine. Also in current production is the PC-9, which is a substantially redesigned PC-7 with a raised rear cockpit and redesigned canopy, Martin Baker CH.11A ejection seats, a redesigned shorter-span wing and a 950 s.h.p. Pratt & Whitney PT6A-62 turboprop in a new cowling. Of the current production total of around 220 aircraft 59 have been built by Hawker de Havilland in Australia and others serve in Croatia, Iraq, Myanmar, Saudi Arabia and Slovenia. The PC-9B is a civil version adapted for target towing. A modified PC-9 is being built for the US Air Force by Beech/Raytheon as the T-6A Texan II (see separate entry).

Specification	Pilatus PC-7 Mk.II	
Powerplant	One 700 s.h.p. (522 kW) Pratt & Whitney PT6A-25C turboprop	
Dimensions		
Span	10.13 m	(33 ft 3 in)
Length	10.13 m	(33 ft 3 in)
Height	3.28 m	(10 ft 9 in)
Performance		
Max speed	555 km/h	(300 kt, 345 mph)
Cruising speed	467 km/h	(252 kt, 290 mph)
Initial climb	1,170 m/min	(2,840 fpm)
Range	1,408 km	(765 nm, 880 miles)
Weights		
Max takeoff	2,250 kg	(4,961 lbs)
Useful load	580 kg	(1,279 lbs)

Pilatus PC-7, Uruguay Navy, 214

Pilatus PC-9, RAAF, A23-006

Pilatus PC-12 — Switzerland

The Pilatus PC-12 (originally referred to as 'PC-XII') was launched in October 1989 and first flew on 31st May 1991. It is a single-engined multi-purpose utility aircraft with a low wing, retractable tricycle undercarriage and a T-tail and is powered by a Pratt & Whitney PT6A-67B turboprop. The pressurised fuselage can carry nine passengers and two crew for commuter operation and is fitted with a forward airstair door and a large cargo hatch behind the wing for freight or combi operations. Among PC-12 operators are the Royal Australian Flying Doctor Service who carry two stretcher cases on ambulance flights. Many PC-12s have also been delivered as executive or private-owner aircraft. A military variant, the PC-12M Eagle, is available and this is fitted with an under-fuselage pod containing surveillance equipment including the Northrop-Grumman WF-160DS dual sensor system. More than 240 PC-12s had been delivered by the end of 2000.

Pilatus PC-12, N133CZ

Specification	Pilatus PC-12	
Powerplant	One 1,200 s.h.p. (894.7 kW) Pratt & Whitney PT6A-67B turboprop	
Dimensions		
Span	16.23 m	(53 ft 3 in)
Length	14.4 m	(47 ft 3 in)
Height	4.27 m	(14 ft 0 in)
Performance		
Max speed	500 km/h	(270 kt, 311 mph)
Cruising speed	463 km/h	(250 kt, 288 mph)
Initial climb	512 m/min	(1,680 fpm)
Range	4,072 km	(2,210 nm, 2,545 miles)
Weights		
Max takeoff	4,500 kg	(9,922 lbs)
Useful load	1,733 kg	(3,821 lbs)

Piper E-2, J-2 and J-3 Cub and PA-11 Cub Special — USA

The E-2 Cub was designed by C.G. Taylor and first flew on 12th September 1930. This parasol-wing open two-seater was gradually developed with a cabin enclosure and a 37 h.p. Continental A40-2 flat-four engine and became a successful production model with 348 being completed for flying schools and private owners. With the company becoming Piper Aircraft Corporation, chief designer Walter Jamoneau developed a much improved machine designated J-2, 695 of which were built with a deeper rear fuselage and fully enclosed cabin, reshaped wings and tail and a chord-braced undercarriage. In 1937, the J-2 was developed into the J-3 which had a reshaped tail, modified wings, wheel brakes and a stronger frame and was powered by 40 h.p. or 50 h.p. Continental engines or equivalent Lycoming and Franklin powerplants. Output of the J-3-50 Cub started in 1938 and in 1940 the higher-powered J-3C-65 Cub Trainer was put into large-scale production for the Civil Air Training Program. Piper also built 5,677 of the O-59 and L-4 forward liaison spotter version for the US Army with a transparent roof and extensive rear cabin glazing, and 253 TG-8 training gliders. After the war, many L-4s were civilianised and some TG-8s were fitted with engines to become standard J-3s. Civil J-3C-65 production was reinstated and Piper also built 1,541 PA-11 Cub Specials with a fully enclosed engine cowling and wing tanks. In total 20,290 J-3s of all models were completed and several thousand, including a few E-2s and J-2s, are currently active worldwide.

Piper L-4H Cub, G-BBXS

Piper PA-11S Cub Special, NC4789M

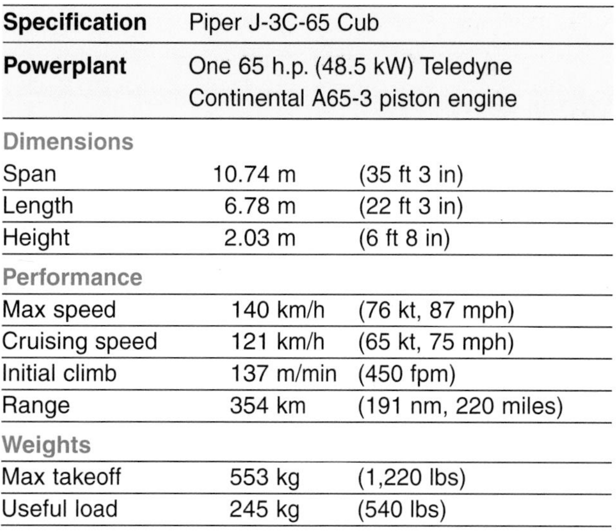

Specification	Piper J-3C-65 Cub	
Powerplant	One 65 h.p. (48.5 kW) Teledyne Continental A65-3 piston engine	
Dimensions		
Span	10.74 m	(35 ft 3 in)
Length	6.78 m	(22 ft 3 in)
Height	2.03 m	(6 ft 8 in)
Performance		
Max speed	140 km/h	(76 kt, 87 mph)
Cruising speed	121 km/h	(65 kt, 75 mph)
Initial climb	137 m/min	(450 fpm)
Range	354 km	(191 nm, 220 miles)
Weights		
Max takeoff	553 kg	(1,220 lbs)
Useful load	245 kg	(540 lbs)

Piper J-4 Cub Coupe — USA

With the success of the J-3 Cub well established, Piper produced an alternative version with side-by-side seating instead of the J-3's tandem configuration. The J-4 Cub Coupe, had the same strut-braced high-wing monoplane layout and tube and fabric structure as the J-3 but the fuselage was wider and the aircraft had a fully enclosed rear decking. The rudder was modified to a more rounded shape and the Coupe had rudimentary blind-flying instrumentation and a modified undercarriage with hydraulic brakes. It was also fitted with the more powerful Continental A75 engine although the J-4A had a 65 h.p. Continental A65-1 and the J-4B was fitted with a 60 h.p. Franklin 4AC-171. Later models had a fully enclosed engine cowling. The J-4 prototype first flew in May 1938 and 1,251 were built between 1938 and 1942.

Piper J-4 Cub Coupe (Cont.)

Piper J-4A Cub Coupe, NC26716

Specification	Piper J-4A Cub Coupe	
Powerplant	One 65 h.p. (48.5 kW) Teledyne Continental A65-1 piston engine	
Dimensions		
Span	11.02 m	(36 ft 2 in)
Length	6.86 m	(22 ft 6 in)
Height	2.08 m	(6 ft 10 in)
Performance		
Max speed	161 km/h	(87 kt, 100 mph)
Cruising speed	148 km/h	(80 kt, 92 mph)
Initial climb	183 m/min	(600 fpm)
Range	576 km	(313 nm, 360 miles)
Weights		
Max takeoff	590 kg	(1,300 lbs)
Useful load	254 kg	(560 lbs)

Piper J-5A Cruiser, PA-12 Super Cruiser and PA-14 Family Cruiser — USA

Having developed the side-by-side two-seat Cub Coupe, Piper produced an enlarged three-seat version, the J-5 Cub Cruiser, with a longer cabin and an extra rear seat. This was first flown in July 1939 and 1,506 examples were built. The J-5A was powered by the 75 h.p. Continental A75-8, the J-5B had a 75 h.p. Lycoming GO-145-C2 and the J-5C, also built as the HE-1 ambulance aircraft with a hinged rear decking for the US Navy, used a 100 h.p. Lycoming O-235-C. The J-5C, with modified fuel tanks and improved trim and instrumentation, was reintroduced after the war as the PA-12 Super Cruiser. Of the 3,759 built between 1946 and 1948 several hundred are currently active, some powered by the alternative 108 h.p. Lycoming O-235-C1 engine. The PA-14 Family Cruiser, 238 of which were built in 1948/49, provided further seating capacity. The prototype first flew on 21st March 1947 and it had four seats in a wider cabin and slotted flaps, and the powerplant was upgraded to a 115 h.p. Lycoming O-235-C1. Approximately half of the production Family Cruisers remain in the hands of American private owners.

Piper PA-12 Super Cruiser, N3562M

Specification	Piper PA-12 Super Cruiser	
Powerplant	One 100 h.p. (74.6 kW) Textron Lycoming O-235-C piston engine	
Dimensions		
Span	10.82 m	(35 ft 6 in)
Length	7.04 m	(23 ft 1 in)
Height	2.08 m	(6 ft 10 in)
Performance		
Max speed	185 km/h	(100 kt, 115 mph)
Cruising speed	169 km/h	(91 kt, 105 mph)
Initial climb	198 m/min	(650 fpm)
Range	480 km	(261 nm, 300 miles)
Weights		
Max takeoff	680 kg	(1,500 lbs)
Useful load	293 kg	(645 lbs)

Piper PA-15 and PA-17 Vagabond — USA

Faced with a slowdown in the postwar light aircraft market, Piper produced the PA-15 Vagabond side-by-side two-seat economy trainer. This was based on the P-2 prototype of 1941 and followed the Piper strut-braced high-wing layout having a fully enclosed cabin with a single entry door, redesigned short-span wings and basic instrumentation. The prototype PA-15 flew on 29th October 1947 and 387, powered by the 65 h.p. Lycoming O-145 engine, were built in 1948. The PA-15 was followed by the essentially similar PA-17 which had a higher level of trim, rubber-chord undercarriage suspension, dual controls and a 65 h.p. Continental A65-8 engine. This remained in production until 1949 with 214 being completed. The Vagabond is much sought after by private owners and over 300 are currently operating in the USA and 30 in the UK.

Piper PA-15 Vagabond, G-FKNH

Specification	Piper PA-15 Vagabond	
Powerplant	One 65 h.p. (48.5 kW) Textron Lycoming O-145-B2 piston engine	
Dimensions		
Span	8.91 m	(29 ft 3 in)
Length	5.69 m	(18 ft 8 in)
Height	1.83 m	(6 ft 0 in)
Performance		
Max speed	164 km/h	(89 kt, 102 mph)
Cruising speed	148 km/h	(80 kt, 92 mph)
Initial climb	155 m/min	(510 fpm)
Range	408 km	(222 nm, 255 miles)
Weights		
Max takeoff	499 kg	(1,100 lbs)
Useful load	218 kg	(480 lbs)

Piper PA-18 Super Cub and L-18 and L-21 — USA

The PA-18 was a logical development of the PA-11 Cub Special from which it differed primarily in having a stronger airframe, the rounded rudder used on the PA-12 and a substantial power increase. It was developed via the PA-19 military liaison aircraft which flew on 25th March 1949 and became the L-18B/C and L-21A/B. These military models had extensive cabin glazing and 1,493 were supplied to the US Army and US-friendly nations such as Italy, France and the Netherlands during the 1950s, many subsequently reaching the civil market. Early civil versions were the PA-18-95 which had the 90 h.p. Continental C90 and the PA-18-105 with a 108 h.p. Lycoming O-235, but later models were progressively fitted with the 105 h.p. Lycoming O-235-C1, 125 h.p. O-290-D, 135 h.p. O-290-D2 and 150 h.p. O-320. The PA-18A was an agricultural single-seat version with a hopper behind the pilot and the PA-18S was certificated for operation on twin floats. Super Cub production continued until 1994 by which time 10,326 had been built. Super Cubs are still built to order as the Top Cub by Aero Crafters in South Carolina.

Piper PA-18-150 Super Cub, G-HAHA

Specification	Piper PA-18-150 Super Cub	
Powerplant	One 150 h.p. (111.8 kW) Textron Lycoming O-320-A2A piston engine	
Dimensions		
Span	10.74 m	(35 ft 3 in)
Length	6.83 m	(22 ft 5 in)
Height	2.03 m	(6 ft 8 in)
Performance		
Max speed	209 km/h	(113 kt, 130 mph)
Cruising speed	185 km/h	(100 kt, 115 mph)
Initial climb	293 m/min	(960 fpm)
Range	736 km	(400 nm, 460 miles)
Weights		
Max takeoff	794 kg	(1,750 lbs)
Useful load	372 kg	(820 lbs)

Piper PA-16 Clipper, PA-20 Pacer and PA-22 Tri Pacer — USA

In early 1948, Piper flew the prototype PA-16 Clipper which became the replacement for the PA-14 Family Cruiser and was, essentially, a stretched four-seat version of the economy PA-15 Vagabond. Still built from tube and fabric, this differed from earlier Piper three-/four-seaters in having the new short wing produced for the Vagabond, dual controls, a modified fuel system and a stronger airframe which was fitted with a 115 h.p. Lycoming O-235-C1 engine. After building 736 Clippers, Piper produced the PA-20 Pacer with flaps, a modified trimmable tailplane, a wider undercarriage and increased fuel capacity. It flew in July 1949 and 1,120 Pacers were built with either a 115 h.p. Lycoming O-235-C1, 125 h.p. O-290-D or 135 h.p. O-290-D2 engine. To meet the challenge of the Cessna 172, Piper then introduced the PA-22 Tri Pacer which had a fixed tricycle undercarriage. Early aircraft had the 125 h.p. or 135 h.p. Lycomings but the PA-22-150 was upgraded to the 150 h.p. Lycoming O-320-A2B and this model became the Caribbean when Piper also introduced the PA-22-160 with a 160 h.p. O-320-B. Some Tri Pacers have been converted back to tailwheel Pacer standard. The final variant in the series was the PA-22-108 Colt, announced in 1961. This was a low-cost two-seat trainer introduced after the Tri Pacer had been replaced by the all-metal Cherokee and it was powered by a 108 h.p. Lycoming O-235-C1B. Piper built 1,120 Pacers, 7,629 Tri Pacers and 1,861 Colts between 1950 and 1964.

Piper PA-20 Pacer, N7369K

Piper PA-22-150 Caribbean, N8557D

Specification	Piper PA-22-160 Tri Pacer	
Powerplant	One 160 h.p. (119.3 kW) Textron Lycoming O-320-B piston engine	
Dimensions		
Span	8.94 m	(29 ft 4 in)
Length	6.25 m	(20 ft 6 in)
Height	2.54 m	(8 ft 4 in)
Performance		
Max speed	227 km/h	(123 kt, 141 mph)
Cruising speed	216 km/h	(117 kt, 134 mph)
Initial climb	244 m/min	(800 fpm)
Range	858 km	(466 nm, 536 miles)
Weights		
Max takeoff	907 kg	(2,000 lbs)
Useful load	404 kg	(890 lbs)

Piper PA-23 Apache and Aztec — USA

Derived from the Twin Stinson design acquired in 1948, the PA-23 Apache was Piper's first all-metal aircraft although its structure was based on an internal steel tube frame rather than stressed monocoque. The definitive PA-23 executive and air taxi aircraft, which first flew on 29th July 1953, had a four-seat cabin, a low-set broad-chord wing and a retractable tricycle undercarriage. The initial PA-23-150, which was launched in 1954, was powered by a pair of 150 h.p. Lycoming O-320-A engines but this was improved in 1958 as the PA-23-160 with 160 h.p. O-320-B powerplants and a fifth seat. The later Apache G had extra rear windows and the final Apache H had O-320-B2B engines. Many surviving Apaches have been modified with new engines, nose and tail changes, new windshields etc., the most popular conversions being the Vecto Geronimo and Miller Jet Profile. In total, 2,037 Apaches had been built when production ceased in 1963. The PA-23-250 (initially PA-27) Aztec was a higher-performance Apache H with a pair of 250 h.p. Lycoming O-540-A1D5s and a swept vertical tail. First flown on 13th June 1957, and marketed from 1960 onwards, it was ordered by the US Navy as the UO-1 and was also built as the budget PA-23-235 Apache 235 with 235 h.p. Lycoming O-540 engines. With the Aztec B, Piper lengthened the nose and increased seating to six and the Aztec C and D had new streamlined engine cowlings, full undercarriage doors and optional turbocharged TIO-540-C1A engines. The final Aztec E and F had longer pointed noses and, on the PA-23-250F, a modified elevator with tip mass balances. The last of 4,930 Aztecs and Apache 235s was built in 1981.

Piper PA-23-150 Apache, N2271P

Piper PA-23-250 Aztec E, ZK-PIX

Specification	Piper PA-23-250 Aztec F	
Powerplant	Two 250 h.p. (186.4 kW) Textron Lycoming IO-540-C4B5 piston engines	
Dimensions		
Span	11.38 m	(37 ft 4 in)
Length	9.52 m	(31 ft 3 in)
Height	3.07 m	(10 ft 1 in)
Performance		
Max speed	328 km/h	(177 kt, 204 mph)
Cruising speed	322 km/h	(174 kt, 200 mph)
Initial climb	427 m/min	(1,400 fpm)
Range	1,795 km	(976 nm, 1,122 miles)
Weights		
Max takeoff	2,358 kg	(5,200 lbs)
Useful load	976 kg	(2,151 lbs)

Piper PA-24 Comanche — USA

Widely regarded as one of Piper's most elegant aircraft, the Comanche first flew at Lock Haven on 19th May 1956 and was produced in quantity from 1958. It was a low-wing aircraft of all-metal monocoque construction with a streamlined fuselage, swept vertical tail and stabilator and a retractable tricycle undercarriage. The cabin had four seats accessed through a starboard-side door and from the outset it was available with either a 180 h.p. Lycoming O-360-A1A or 250 h.p. O-540-A1A5 engine and various levels of interior trim, equipment and external paint. From 1965, it became the Comanche B with a 260 h.p. O-540-E4A5 engine, extra side windows and optional fifth and sixth seats. The Comanche C was the final model, built from 1969 to 1972 with a modified nose cowling, optional wingtip tanks and either the injected IO-540-E4A5 or turbocharged IO-540-R1A5 engine. In total, 4,717 Comanches were completed. Piper also produced a small batch of high-performance Comanche 400s which had the early Comanche airframe fitted with a 400 h.p. Lycoming IO-720-A1A engine, but only 148 were built in 1964.

Piper PA-24-260, G-ATJL

Specification	Piper PA-24-260 Comanche C	
Powerplant	One 260 h.p. (193.9 kW) Textron Lycoming IO-540-E4A5 piston engine	
Dimensions		
Span	10.97 m	(36 ft 0 in)
Length	7.82 m	(25 ft 8 in)
Height	2.24 m	(7 ft 4 in)
Performance		
Max speed	314 km/h	(170 kt, 195 mph)
Cruising speed	298 km/h	(161 kt, 185 mph)
Initial climb	402 m/min	(1,320 fpm)
Range	1,960 km	(1,065 nm, 1,225 miles)
Weights		
Max takeoff	1,451 kg	(3,200 lbs)
Useful load	647 kg	(1,427 lbs)

Piper PA-25 Pawnee and PA-36 Pawnee Brave — USA

The Pawnee agricultural aircraft was the last steel tube, fabric and light alloy aircraft built by Piper Aircraft. Designed by Fred Weick based on his AG-1 prototype, its strut-braced low wing was similar to that of the Super Cub and the fuselage had a single-seat enclosed cockpit above the wing trailing edge and a 145 USG hopper between the cockpit and the engine firewall. It had a fixed tailwheel undercarriage and full-span wet spray bars or a belly-mounted dry disperser for chemicals. The prototype (AG-3) first flew in November 1954 and Pawnee production started in 1959, early aircraft having a 150 h.p. Lycoming O-320-A1A and later ones being the PA-25-235 with a 235 h.p. O-540-B2B5. The Pawnee B had a 150 USG hopper and the Pawnee C and Pawnee D had further minor improvements. Some 5,167 PA-25s had been built when the line closed in 1981. The PA-36 Pawnee Brave was a larger agricultural aircraft of similar general design to the PA-25 but with a modified wing, swept tail, spring-steel undercarriage and a 225 USG hopper. The prototype flew on 17th November 1969 and deliveries of the PA-36-285 with a 285 h.p. Continental Tiara engine commenced in 1973. The Tiara engine was later replaced by a 300 h.p. Lycoming IO-540-K1G5 on the PA-36-300 and the 375 h.p. IO-720-D1CD on the final production PA-36-375. Brave production was completed with the 923rd aircraft in 1983.

Piper PA-25-235 Pawnee C, G-AVXA

Piper PA-25 Pawnee and PA-36 Pawnee Brave (Cont.)

Piper PA-36-285 Pawnee Brave, YS-318-A

Specification	Piper PA-25-235 Pawnee C	
Powerplant	One 235 h.p. (175 kW) Textron Lycoming O-540-B2B5 piston engine	
Dimensions		
Span	11.05 m	(36 ft 3 in)
Length	7.52 m	(24 ft 8 in)
Height	2.21 m	(7 ft 3 in)
Performance		
Max speed	200 km/h	(108 kt, 124 mph)
Cruising speed	183 km/h	(99 kt, 114 mph)
Initial climb	213 m/min	(700 fpm)
Range	464 km	(252 nm, 290 miles)
Weights		
Max takeoff	1,315 kg	(2,900 lbs)
Useful load	671 kg	(1,480 lbs)

Piper PA-28 Cherokee, Warrior and Arrow — USA

The Cherokee was Piper's replacement for the tube and fabric PA-22 Tri Pacer and numerous variants have been built since its introduction in 1961. Designed by John Thorpe, it is a low-wing all-metal aircraft with a fixed tricycle undercarriage and a four-seat cabin. The prototype flew on 10th January 1960 and initial aircraft had optional 150 h.p. Lycoming O-320-A2B or 160 h.p. O-320-B2B engines, but the PA-28-180 with a 180 h.p. O-360-A2A was added in 1963. Minor changes were made during the 1960s and 1970s and the aircraft named Cherokee 160B, Cherokee 180E etc. Subsequently, the PA-28-180 was given a stretched fuselage as the 'Challenger' and 'Archer'. With the PA-28-151 and 161 Warrior, Piper modified the 150 h.p. and 160 h.p. Cherokees with a new semi-tapered wing and a stabilator and these changes were incorporated in the 180 h.p. PA-28-181 Archer II. For the training market they built the PA-28-140, initially as a two-seater and later with four seats, powered by a 140 h.p. O-320-A2A or 150 h.p. O-320-A2B, and later versions were named 'Cruiser' and 'Fliteliner'. The Cherokee 235, Charger, Pathfinder and Dakota were higher-powered variants with a 235 h.p. Lycoming O-540-B4B5 engine and Piper also built the PA-28-201T Turbo Dakota with a 200 h.p. turbocharged Continental TSIO-360-FB engine. Piper has built over 29,800 of the fixed-gear PA-28 series and production of the PA-28-161 Warrior III and PA-28-181 Archer III with reshaped windows and modified engine cowlings continues at Vero Beach. The Cherokee Arrow is a retractable-gear version of the PA-28-180 which first flew on 1st February 1966. Marketed from 1967 onwards, it progressively incorporated the improvements of other PA-28s, including the lengthened fuselage (Arrow II) and semi-tapered wing (Arrow III) and the 180 h.p. Lycoming IO-360 engine was replaced by a 200 h.p. IO-360-C1C in 1971 or the TSIO-360-F on the optional Turbo Arrow III. The Arrow IV had a slimmer rear fuselage and a T-tail with an all-moving tailplane but Piper has reverted to the PA-28R-201 Arrow III design with the standard tail for current production and had built over 6,800 Arrows by the end of 2000.

Piper PA-28-181 Archer III, OY-JAA

Piper PA-28RT-201 Arrow IV, F-GKPS

Specification	Piper PA-28-181 Archer III	
Powerplant	One 180 h.p. (134.2 kW) Textron Lycoming O-360-A4M piston engine	
Dimensions		
Span	10.82 m	(35 ft 6 in)
Length	7.31 m	(24 ft 0 in)
Height	2.24 m	(7 ft 4 in)
Performance		
Max speed	239 km/h	(129 kt, 149 mph)
Cruising speed	222 km/h	(120 kt, 138 mph)
Initial climb	203 m/min	(667 fpm)
Range	1,069 km	(580 nm, 668 miles)
Weights		
Max takeoff	1,169 kg	(2,550 lbs)
Useful load	417 kg	(919 lbs)

Piper PA-30 and PA-39 Twin Comanche — USA

The Twin Comanche was a development of the four-seat single-engined PA-24 and was engineered by Ed Swearingen and first flown on 12th April 1961. The PA-24 airframe was modified with a pointed nose in place of the existing engine and two 160 h.p. Lycoming IO-320-B engines mounted in streamlined nacelles on the wings. The Twin Comanche, which was very successful as a business aircraft and air taxi, was introduced in 1963. An optional turbocharged version with TIO-320-C1A engines was offered from 1966 and the Twin Comanche B had a lengthened cabin interior with two extra seats and extra rear windows. The PA-30 was replaced by the PA-39 Twin Comanche C/R in 1970. This differed in having counter-directional TIO-320 turbocharged engines giving improved handling characteristics. Piper built 2,001 PA-30s and 155 PA-39s and production ceased in 1972.

Piper PA-39 Twin Comanche C/R, N88WW

Specification	Piper PA-30-160B Twin Comanche B	
Powerplant	Two 160 h.p. (119.3 kW) Textron Lycoming IO-320-B piston engines	
Dimensions		
Span	10.97 m	(36 ft 0 in)
Length	7.67 m	(25 ft 2 in)
Height	2.49 m	(8 ft 2 in)
Performance		
Max speed	330 km/h	(178 kt, 205 mph)
Cruising speed	312 km/h	(169 kt, 194 mph)
Initial climb	445 m/min	(1,460 fpm)
Range	2,032 km	(1,104 nm, 1,270 miles)
Weights		
Max takeoff	1,633 kg	(3,600 lbs)
Useful load	630 kg	(1,390 lbs)

Piper PA-31 Navajo and Chieftain — USA

The Navajo was Piper's contender in the six-/eight-seat cabin-class executive and air taxi market, competing with the Beech Queen Air and Cessna 401, and was first marketed in 1967, the prototype having flown on 30th September 1964. It was of conventional low-wing layout with a main cabin seating six high-density or four executive passengers, a retractable tricycle undercarriage and two 300 h.p. Lycoming IO-540-M engines. The Navajo B was an improved model with 310 h.p. Lycoming TIO-540Es, and Piper also built the PA-31-325C/R with counter-directional L/TIO-540-F2BD engines. Some aircraft have been modified as Colemill Panther Navajos with 350 h.p. L/TIO-540 engines and winglets. The PA-31-350 Navajo Chieftain is a stretched eight-/ten-seat model intended for commuter airline operations which flew on 15th October 1970. This is powered by two 350 h.p. L/TIO-540-J2BD turbocharged engines and a small number of the higher capacity 11-seat T-1020 were also built between 1982 and 1985. A further commuter version was the T-1040 which combined the Chieftain fuselage with the wings and PT6A-28 turboprop engines of the Cheyenne II. The PA-31P Pressurized Navajo was based on the standard PA-31 but had a pressure cabin, revised smaller windows and 425 h.p. Lycoming TIGSO-540-E1A engines, and the Mojave was a later pressurised model with the fuselage of the PA-31T Cheyenne and 350 h.p. L/TIO-540-V2AD engines. Between 1967 and 1986 Piper built 3,944 examples of the Navajo series.

Piper PA-31-350 Navajo Chieftain, PT-EHL

Piper PA-31 Navajo and Chieftain (Cont.)

Specification	Piper PA-31-350 Navajo Chieftain	
Powerplant	Two 350 h.p. (261 kW) Textron Lycoming L/TIO-540-J2BD piston engines	
Dimensions		
Span	12.39 m	(40 ft 8 in)
Length	10.54 m	(34 ft 7 in)
Height	3.96 m	(13 ft 0 in)
Performance		
Max speed	437 km/h	(236 kt, 272 mph)
Cruising speed	423 km/h	(228 kt, 263 mph)
Initial climb	424 m/min	(1,390 fpm)
Range	1,751 km	(950 nm, 1,094 miles)
Weights		
Max takeoff	3,195 kg	(7,045 lbs)
Useful load	1,365 kg	(3,009 lbs)

Piper PA-42 Cheyenne III, N190AA

Piper PA-31T and PA-42 Cheyenne — USA

Several versions of the Cheyenne executive turboprop twin have been built, all based on the PA-31P Pressurized Navajo or PA-31-350 Chieftain airframe. The prototype PA-31T Cheyenne was a PA-31P with wingtip tanks and two 620 s.h.p. Pratt & Whitney PT6A-28 turboprops. It first flew on 20th August 1969 and went into production in 1974. This model became the Cheyenne II in 1978 when Piper added the lower-powered Cheyenne I (PA-31T1) with 500 s.h.p. PT6A-11s. A further model was the PA-31T2 Cheyenne IIXL which had a 2 ft fuselage stretch, extra cabin windows and 620 s.h.p. PT6A-135 engines. Between 1974 and 1985, Piper manufactured 823 of the standard Cheyenne twins. The PA-42 Cheyenne III was a larger business aircraft using a stretched, pressurised version of the longer Chieftain fuselage giving a nine-passenger main cabin. It had longer-span wings, a lengthened nose and a T-tail and was powered by two 720 s.h.p. PT6A-41 engines in large nacelles. The prototype flew on 20th August 1976 and first sales were made in 1980. The PA-42-1000 Cheyenne IV (Cheyenne 400LS) was a further version with 1,000 s.h.p. Garrett TPE331-14A engines. Only 192 of the stretched Cheyenne III/IV were built before production ceased in 1993.

Piper PA-31T1 Cheyenne I, PT-WMX

Specification	Piper PA-31T2 Cheyenne IIXL	
Powerplant	Two 620 s.h.p. (462 kW) Pratt & Whitney PT6A-135 turboprops	
Dimensions		
Span	13 m	(42 ft 8 in)
Length	11.18 m	(36 ft 8 in)
Height	3.89 m	(12 ft 9 in)
Performance		
Max speed	510 km/h	(275 kt, 317 mph)
Cruising speed	482 km/h	(260 kt, 299 mph)
Initial climb	533 m/min	(1,750 fpm)
Range	2,460 km	(1,336 nm, 1,538 miles)
Weights		
Max takeoff	4,327 kg	(9,540 lbs)
Useful load	1,838 kg	(4,053 lbs)

Piper PA-32 and PA-32R — USA

In 1964, Piper produced an enlarged six-seat version of the PA-28 Cherokee. This Cherokee Six, based on the PA-28-235, had a wider fuselage with additional sections added fore and aft of the wings, a port rear entry door and a 260 h.p. Lycoming O-540 engine. It first flew on 17th September 1964 and entered production as the PA-32-260 in 1965. It was joined by the PA-32-300 with a 300 h.p. IO-540-K the following year. The PA-32-301 Saratoga replaced the earlier models in 1980 and this had the semi-tapered wing introduced on other PA-28 models. Piper also built the PA-32-301T Turbo Saratoga with a 300 h.p. TIO-540-S1AD engine. Some 4,420 fixed-gear PA-32s were built and production ceased in 1991. The PA-32R Cherokee Lance was a Cherokee Six with a retractable tricycle undercarriage and it first flew on 30th August 1974. Two years later the Lance II and turbocharged Turbo Lance II were introduced with a T-tail, and the Lance III was similar but with the semi-tapered wing. The final version was the Saratoga SP and Turbo Saratoga SP which reverted to the standard tail used on the original Lance. These are now built as the Saratoga HP and Turbo Saratoga HP with smaller squared-off windows and high-speed engine cowls. Piper have built over 3,000 of the Lance and Saratoga SP.

Piper PA-32-260 Cherokee Six, N7SX

Piper PA-34 Seneca — USA

The Seneca six-seat light twin was designed as a larger-capacity companion for the Piper Twin Comanche and was based on the airframe of the PA-32 Cherokee Six. The resulting production-standard PA-34-200 Seneca, which had two 200 h.p. counter-turning Lycoming IO-360 engines mounted on the wings, a larger vertical tail, a longer-span wing and a pointed nose and retractable tricycle undercarriage, was flown on 20th October 1969. Production started in 1972 and in 1975 the aircraft was improved as the PA-34-200T Seneca II with turbocharged L/TSIO-360-E engines in new streamlined nacelles and various control changes. The Seneca III, which followed in 1981, had the increased power of 220 h.p. turbocharged L/TSIO-360-KB2A engines and higher weights. The Seneca IV, introduced in 1994, has the improved engine cowlings and squared-off windows of other current models, and the latest Seneca V has new interior trim with a standard five-seat layout. Piper had built 4,790 PA-34s by the end of 2000 and others have been built, mainly from kits, by Chincul in Argentina, Embraer in Brazil (EMB-810C), Pezetel in Poland (M-20 Mewa) and Aero Mercantil in Colombia.

Piper PA-32RT-300T Turbo Lance II, N39686

Piper PA-34-200 Seneca, G-BATR

Specification	Piper PA-32R-301 Saratoga II HP	
Powerplant	One 300 h.p. (223.7 kW) Textron Lycoming IO-540-K1G5D piston engine	
Dimensions		
Span	11.05 m	(36 ft 3 in)
Length	8.23 m	(27 ft 0 in)
Height	2.59 m	(8 ft 6 in)
Performance		
Max speed	308 km/h	(166 kt, 191 mph)
Cruising speed	302 km/h	(163 kt, 188 mph)
Initial climb	340 m/min	(1,116 fpm)
Range	1,473 km	(800 nm, 921 miles)
Weights		
Max takeoff	1,633 kg	(3,600 lbs)
Useful load	561 kg	(1,236 lbs)

Specification	Piper PA-34-220T Seneca V	
Powerplant	Two 220 h.p. (164 kW) Teledyne Continental L/TSIO-360-RB piston engines	
Dimensions		
Span	11.86 m	(38 ft 11 in)
Length	8.71 m	(28 ft 7 in)
Height	3.02 m	(9 ft 11 in)
Performance		
Max speed	365 km/h	(197 kt, 227 mph)
Cruising speed	352 km/h	(190 kt, 219 mph)
Initial climb	427 m/min	(1,400 fpm)
Range	1,521 km	(826 nm, 951 miles)
Weights		
Max takeoff	2,154 kg	(4,750 lbs)
Useful load	602 kg	(1,328 lbs)

Piper PA-38 Tomahawk
— USA

Piper's Tomahawk civil basic trainer was a completely new design with a low-set high-aspect-ratio wing, a T-tail and fixed tricycle undercarriage. It had a side-by-side two-seat cabin with all-round vision which was entered through forward hinged doors on either side. First flown on 17th July 1973, the PA-38-112 Tomahawk was powered by a 112 h.p. Lycoming O-235 engine and deliveries commenced in 1978. In 1981, the Tomahawk II was introduced with improved soundproofing and a modified undercarriage but production was terminated in 1982 after 2,519 aircraft had been built. A number of PA-38s were also assembled in Colombia and Argentina from Piper kits.

Piper PA-38-112 Tomahawk, G-BKAS

Specification	Piper PA-38-112 Tomahawk	
Powerplant	One 112 h.p. (83.5 kW) Textron Lycoming O-235-L2C piston engine	
Dimensions		
Span	10.36 m	(34 ft 0 in)
Length	7.04 m	(23 ft 1 in)
Height	2.64 m	(8 ft 8 in)
Performance		
Max speed	209 km/h	(113 kt, 130 mph)
Cruising speed	202 km/h	(109 kt, 126 mph)
Initial climb	213 m/min	(700 fpm)
Range	741 km	(402 nm, 463 miles)
Weights		
Max takeoff	757 kg	(1,670 lbs)
Useful load	275 kg	(606 lbs)

Piper PA-44 Seminole
— USA

Piper built the Seminole as a smaller four-seat companion to the six-seat Seneca and as a replacement for the Twin Comanche. It was based on the airframe of the PA-28R Arrow IV and had the same low wing, retractable tricycle gear and T-tail as the Arrow but with a new rounded nose and twin 180 h.p. counter-turning Lycoming L/O-360 engines. First flown in May 1976, the Seminole proved to be popular with flight schools for twin-engined training. Over 500 Seminoles had been delivered by the end of 2000, including 86 PA-44-180Ts with turbocharged L/TO-360-E1A6D engines and weather radar, and production is continuing at a low rate.

Piper PA-44-180 Seminole, N36699

Specification	Piper PA-44-180 Seminole	
Powerplant	Two 180 h.p. (134.2 kW) Textron Lycoming L/O-360-A1H6 piston engines	
Dimensions		
Span	11.76 m	(38 ft 7 in)
Length	8.41 m	(27 ft 7 in)
Height	2.59 m	(8 ft 6 in)
Performance		
Max speed	313 km/h	(169 kt, 195 mph)
Cruising speed	300 km/h	(162 kt, 187 mph)
Initial climb	408 m/min	(1,340 fpm)
Range	1,658 km	(900 nm, 1,036 miles)
Weights		
Max takeoff	1,723 kg	(3,800 lbs)
Useful load	580 kg	(1,280 lbs)

Piper PA-46 Malibu and Malibu Meridian — USA

The Malibu is unique in being the only successful pressurised high-performance single-piston-engined aircraft in production. It has a low-set high-aspect-ratio wing and a retractable tricycle undercarriage. The cabin is entered by a port-side rear split airstair door and it has standard club-four seating and a two-seat cockpit. The definitive prototype PA-46-310P was flown on 21st August 1982 and initial production aircraft, delivered from 1984, had a 310 h.p. Continental TSIO-520-BE turbocharged engine. In 1989 the power was increased to a 350 h.p. Lycoming TIO-540-AE2A and the aircraft renamed PA-46-350P Malibu Mirage. In total, over 900 PA-46s had been built by the end of 2000. Piper has used the Mirage airframe to develop the Malibu Meridian which is powered by a 400 s.h.p. Pratt & Whitney PT6A-42A turboprop. The first of four prototypes was first flown on 21st August 1998 and the first production Meridians were delivered in 2000.

Specification	Piper PA-46-350P Malibu Mirage	
Powerplant	One 350 h.p. (260.9 kW) Textron Lycoming TIO-540-AE2A piston engine	
Dimensions		
Span	13.11 m	(43 ft 0 in)
Length	8.71 m	(28 ft 7 in)
Height	3.51 m	(11 ft 6 in)
Performance		
Max speed	408 km/h	(220 kt, 253 mph)
Cruising speed	395 km/h	(213 kt, 245 mph)
Initial climb	371 m/min	(1,218 fpm)
Range	2,478 km	(1,345 nm, 1,549 miles)
Weights		
Max takeoff	1,968 kg	(4,340 lbs)
Useful load	553 kg	(1,219 lbs)

Piper PA-46-350P Malibu Mirage, N135MD

Pitcairn Mailwing — USA

The PA-5 Mailwing, which appeared in 1925, was a derivative of earlier Pitcairn biplanes designed by Agnew Larsen and built by Harold Pitcairn's Pitcairn Aircraft Inc. The PA-5 was produced as a high-speed air mail and light cargo carrier and it had an open pilot's cockpit to the rear and a cargo compartment in the centre fuselage capable of carrying a 500 lbs load. Structurally, the Mailwing was built of steel tube, wood and fabric and was powered by a 220 h.p. Wright J5 Whirlwind radial engine. The PA-6 Super Mailwing of 1928 was similar to the PA-5 but had a deeper and wider cargo compartment, and the PA-7M (and three-seat PA-7S Sport Mailwing) had a larger 225 h.p. Wright J6 engine which was often fully enclosed with a NACA cowling. The PA-8M was the final version, built for Eastern Air Transport and having up to 1,000 lbs of useful load and a 300 h.p. Wright J6-9 engine. Pitcairn built 117 Mailwings, half of which were the PA-6, and several have been restored with examples of the PA-6, PA-7M and PA-8 currently in flying condition.

Piper PA-46-400PT Meridian, N400PT

Pitcairn PA-7M Super Mailwing, NC95W

Pitcairn Mailwing (Cont.)

Specification	Pitcairn PA-6 Super Mailwing	
Powerplant	One 220 h.p. (164 kW) Wright J5 Whirlwind piston engine	
Dimensions		
Span	10.06 m	(33 ft 0 in)
Length	7.11 m	(23 ft 4 in)
Height	2.79 m	(9 ft 2 in)
Performance		
Max speed	206 km/h	(111 kt, 128 mph)
Cruising speed	175 km/h	(95 kt, 109 mph)
Initial climb	274 m/min	(900 fpm)
Range	960 km	(522 nm, 600 miles)
Weights		
Max takeoff	1,383 kg	(3,050 lbs)
Useful load	587 kg	(1,295 lbs)

Pitts Model S-12 Monster — USA

The success of the Pitts Special series (see details under Aviat) has led Curtis Pitts to develop the S-11-260 Super Stinker competition aircraft and subsequent S-12 Macho Stinker sport aerobatic biplane. This is marketed by Mid America Aircraft as the Model S-12 Monster in kit form for homebuilders. The Model S-12 was designed to be powered by the Vedeneyev M-14P radial engine and has a deeper fuselage than earlier Pitts Specials although the earlier swept upper wing and straight lower wing is retained. The modified aerofoil section and ailerons allow a roll rate of almost one revolution per second. The S-12 is a tandem two-seater with dual controls and a canopy-enclosed cockpit and has a tube frame fuselage and wooden wings with fabric and metal covering. It has a spring-steel cantilever tailwheel undercarriage. The first Pitts S-12 flew in the spring of 1996 and 30 kits had been sold by the end of 1999.

Pitts S-12, N80XP

Specification	Pitts S-12 Monster	
Powerplant	One 360 h.p. (268.4 kW) Vedeneyev M-14P piston engine	
Dimensions		
Span	7.01 m	(23 ft 0 in)
Length	6.6 m	(21 ft 8 in)
Height	2.36 m	(7 ft 9 in)
Performance		
Max speed	322 km/h	(174 kt, 200 mph)
Cruising speed	290 km/h	(157 kt, 180 mph)
Initial climb	762 m/min	(2,500 fpm)
Range	640 km	(348 nm, 400 miles)
Weights		
Max takeoff	1,020 kg	(2,250 lbs)
Useful load	329 kg	(725 lbs)

(Max) Plan MP.204 Busard — France

The original prototype Busard light competition racer was built by the aerodynamicist Max Plan and flown on 5th June 1952. It was a wooden aircraft with plywood covering and had a low wing and fixed tailwheel undercarriage. The prototype was powered by a 75 h.p. Minié 4-DC-32 engine but later became the MP.215 with a 90 h.p. Continental C.90. The Busard was redesigned for amateur construction by M. Robert Lefebvre with a lighter structure and spring-steel undercarriage and his MP.205 Busard can be fitted with Continental flat-four engines of 65 h.p. to 100 h.p, or a Volkswagen. More than 30 Busards are under construction in France and of the flying examples one is an MP.207 with a 100 h.p. Continental O-200-A engine.

Max Plan MP.205 Busard, F-PRJR

Specification	Max Plan MP.205 Busard	
Powerplant	One 90 h.p. (67.1 kW) Teledyne Continental C90 piston engine	
Dimensions		
Span	5.99 m	(19 ft 8 in)
Length	5.36 m	(17 ft 7 in)
Height	1.5 m	(4 ft 11 in)
Performance		
Max speed	290 km/h	(157 kt, 180 mph)
Cruising speed	266 km/h	(143 kt, 165 mph)
Initial climb	274 m/min	(900 fpm)
Range	448 km	(243 nm, 280 miles)
Weights		
Max takeoff	345 kg	(760 lbs)
Useful load	106 kg	(233 lbs)

Plätzer Kiebitz, D-MLAD

Plätzer P4 Motte and Kiebitz — Germany

The Motte is a single-seat parasol-wing design marketed in the form of plans by Michael Plätzer. It is an ultralight-category aircraft with a fixed tailwheel undercarriage, an open cockpit and a circular-section engine cowling which can enclose a variety of powerplants in the 50 h.p. category including the Rotax 462 or converted Nissan 12P or Citroen Visa car engines. Sixty Mottes are under construction with 15 flying in Germany. The Kiebitz is a larger two-seat biplane version of tube, wood and fabric construction with tandem open cockpits which is stressed for engines of up to 100 h.p. including the Midwest rotary, although most aircraft have a Volkswagen, Hirth or Limbach engine in the 75 h.p. range. Over 200 sets of plans for the Kiebitz have been sold and 140 are currently flying with another 30 under construction, mainly in Germany and Holland.

Specification	Plätzer Kiebitz	
Powerplant	One 80 h.p. (59.6 kW) Rotax 912 piston engine	
Dimensions		
Span	7.6 m	(24 ft 11 in)
Length	6.8 m	(22 ft 4 in)
Height	2.8 m	(9 ft 2 in)
Performance		
Max speed	150 km/h	(81 kt, 93 mph)
Cruising speed	135 km/h	(73 kt, 84 mph)
Initial climb	91 m/min	(300 fpm)
Range	547 km	(296 nm, 342 miles)
Weights		
Max takeoff	400 kg	(882 lbs)
Useful load	130 kg	(287 lbs)

Plätzer P4 Motte, D-MXAC

Polikarpov Po-2 — Russia

Originally known as the U-2, the Polikarpov Po-2 biplane was built in huge numbers before and during World War II. It was used for a wide variety of tasks in Soviet civil and military aviation including training, crop spraying, passenger transport, glider towing, observation, and even for light tactical bombing using underwing bomb racks. It first flew on 7th January 1928 powered by a 125 h.p. M-11D uncowled five-cylinder radial engine. After the war production continued until 1959 and it was built in Poland as the CSS-13. Many Po-2s (NATO name 'Mule') continued in public service in the Soviet Union and most Warsaw Pact countries well into the 1980s. The Po-2 was of steel tube, wood and fabric construction with a fixed tailwheel undercarriage, a distinctive overhung rudder and an unusually large tailplane and elevator. The ambulance versions (Po-2S and Po-2L) had an enclosed rear cabin capable of carrying two stretchers. Over 30,000 Po-2s were built and a number remain in private hands in Europe.

Polikarpov Po-2 (Cont.)

Polikarpov Po-2

Specification	Polikarpov Po-2	
Powerplant	One 125 h.p. (93.2 kW) M-11D piston engine	
Dimensions		
Span	11.4 m	(37 ft 5 in)
Length	8.15 m	(26 ft 9 in)
Height	3.02 m	(9 ft 11 in)
Performance		
Max speed	161 km/h	(87 kt, 100 mph)
Cruising speed	145 km/h	(78 kt, 90 mph)
Initial climb	213 m/min	(700 fpm)
Range	400 km	(217 nm, 250 miles)
Weights		
Max takeoff	1,120 kg	(2,470 lbs)
Useful load	351 kg	(775 lbs)

Polikarpov I-16 — Russia

The I-16 Rata single-seat monoplane fighter was designed by Nikolay Polikarpov and entered Russia military service in 1935. It had a short stubby fuselage and a broad-chord tapered wing which mounted the main units of a retractable tailwheel undercarriage. The cockpit was normally open with a large windshield but a sliding canopy was often fitted and the I-16 had a large 9-cylinder M-25 (licence-built Wright Cyclone) radial engine. Construction consisted of a wooden fuselage and metal wings with fabric covering. The I-153 Chaika was a similar biplane fighter with a gull-shaped upper wing and retractable gear. Around 3,500 Chaikas and 9,450 Ratas were built. In 1992 the New Zealander, Sir Tim Wallace, discovered the wrecks of six I-16s and three I-153s and these have all been restored to flying condition with ASh-621R engines by a Siberian aircraft factory, the first flying on 9th September 1995. Two I-16s and an I-153 now fly in the USA and the rest are airworthy in New Zealand.

Polikarpov I-16 Rata, ZK-JIO

Specification	Polikarpov I-16 Rata Type 24	
Powerplant	One 1,000 h.p. (745 kW) ASh-621R piston engine	
Dimensions		
Span	8.99 m	(29 ft 6 in)
Length	5.99 m	(19 ft 8 in)
Height	2.39 m	(7 ft 10 in)
Performance		
Max speed	439 km/h	(237 kt, 273 mph)
Initial climb	792 m/min	(2,600 fpm)
Range	800 km	(435 nm 500 miles)
Weights		
Max takeoff	1,834 kg	(4,043 lbs)
Useful load	309 kg	(681 lbs)

Porterfield 35 and Collegiate — USA

In 1935, Ed Porterfield launched the Porterfield 35 Flyabout light aircraft. It was a high-wing strut-braced monoplane of mixed construction with an enclosed tandem two-seat cockpit and a fixed tailwheel undercarriage. Due to its economical purchase price and running costs it was highly successful and 110 aircraft were built in several versions. The Model 35-70 had a 60 h.p. Le Blond 5D or 70 h.p. 5E radial engine, the Model 35V had a 75 h.p. Velie M-5 and the Model 35W (also known as the Model 90) was a higher-performance aircraft with better equipment and a 90 h.p. Warner Scarab Jr. The Porterfield Collegiate CP-50 was generally similar but with a slimmer fuselage and a taller tail unit. It was introduced in 1939 for use in the Civil Pilot Training Program and there were various engine options including the standard 50 h.p. Continental A50-4 (CP-50), the Lycoming O-145 (LP-50), the 55 h.p. Continental A50-8 (CP-55) or Lycoming O-145-A3 (LP-55), the 60 h.p. Franklin 4AC-171 (FP-60) and the 65 h.p. Continental A65-9 (CP-65). Collegiate production had reached 586 aircraft when the line was closed in 1942. Over 100 Porterfields (also known as the Northwestern or Columbia Porterfield) remain active worldwide.

Porterfield LP-65, N27281

Specification	Porterfield CP-65 Collegiate	
Powerplant	One 65 h.p. (48.5 kW) Teledyne Continental A65-9 piston engine	
Dimensions		
Span	10.59 m	(34 ft 9 in)
Length	6.91 m	(22 ft 8 in)
Height	2.11 m	(6 ft 11 in)
Performance		
Max speed	174 km/h	(94 kt, 108 mph)
Cruising speed	158 km/h	(85 kt, 98 mph)
Initial climb	183 m/min	(600 fpm)
Range	480 km	(261 nm, 300 miles)
Weights		
Max takeoff	544 kg	(1,200 lbs)
Useful load	227 kg	(500 lbs)

Potez 60 Sauterelle, F-PVQB

Specification	Potez 600 Sauterelle	
Powerplant	One 60 h.p. (44.74 kW) Potez 3B piston engine	
Dimensions		
Span	9.98 m	(32 ft 9 in)
Length	6.96 m	(22 ft 10 in)
Height	2.34 m	(7 ft 8 in)
Performance		
Max speed	145 km/h	(78 kt, 90 mph)
Cruising speed	121 km/h	(65 kt, 75 mph)
Initial climb	152 m/min	(500 fpm)
Range	640 km	(348 nm, 400 miles)
Weights		
Max takeoff	559 kg	(1,232 lbs)
Useful load	272 kg	(600 lbs)

Potez 600 Sauterelle
— France

In 1935, Ets. Henri Potez departed from its traditional transport aircraft business to design the tandem two-seat Potez 60 civil trainer. It had a strut-braced parasol wing with tapered outer panels and a fixed tailwheel undercarriage, the main units of which were attached to small stub supports. The cockpits were open with dual control and the aircraft was powered by an uncowled Potez 3B radial engine. Construction was wood and fabric with metal wing bracing struts. It first flew in August 1935 and 155 were built as the Potez 600 Sauterelle for French flying clubs. Two aircraft remain airworthy, one in France and one in Switzerland.

Pottier P.60 Minacro
— France

The prolific designer and Aérospatiale engineer, Jean Pottier has sold plans for the Minacro light biplane to a number of amateur builders. Eight are now flying in France and Austria with a further ten under construction. The P.60 is built from wood and fabric and has a spring-steel tailwheel undercarriage. The single-seat open cockpit is positioned just behind the wing and the aircraft, which first flew in 1974, is fully aerobatic. The airframe is stressed for engines in the 90 h.p. to 120 h.p. range and the examples flown to date have been fitted with either a Potez 4E-20A or Continental O-200-A.

Pottier P.60 Minacro (Cont.)

Pottier P.60 Minacro, F-PRIJ

Specification	Pottier P.60 Minacro	
Powerplant	One 100 h.p. (74.6 kW) Teledyne Continental O-200-A piston engine	
Dimensions		
Span	5 m	(16 ft 5 in)
Length	4.6 m	(15 ft 1 in)
Height	1.75 m	(5 ft 9 in)
Performance		
Max speed	225 km/h	(122 kt, 140 mph)
Cruising speed	206 km/h	(111 kt, 128 mph)
Initial climb	457 m/min	(1,500 fpm)
Range	560 km	(304 nm, 350 miles)
Weights		
Max takeoff	425 kg	(937 lbs)
Useful load	145 kg	(320 lbs)

Pottier P.70S, P.80S and P.180S — France

Jean Pottier drew up plans for the P.70 in 1970 and the first aircraft, built by Alain Besneux, was first flown on 19th July 1974. Pottier's design was for an all-metal single-seater which would be easy to build and would have good performance on low power. The P.70S, which is powered by Volkswagen engines of 1,200 cc to 1,700 cc, has a mid-set wing of constant chord, a fixed tailwheel or tricycle undercarriage and a vertical tail which is almost wholly a rudder with a small supportive fin fairing. The cockpit can be open or enclosed with a bubble canopy and the P.170S is a tandem two-seat version with a longer fuselage and a VW.1600 engine. Pottier then redesigned the aircraft as the P.80S which mainly differs in having a low-set wing and a redesigned cockpit affording improved vision. The P.180S is a side-by-side two-seat version with a wider fuselage and some aircraft have been modified with a larger fin and conventional rudder. The P.180S is generally powered by the Volkswagen VW.1700, VW.1835 or VW.2000 but some examples use the 90 h.p. Continental C90 or 100 h.p. Continental O-200-A engine. Over 100 of the series are flying in Europe with many more under construction.

Pottier P.180S, F-PYZY

Specification	Pottier P.180S	
Powerplant	One 90 h.p. (67.1 kW) Teledyne Continental C90 piston engine	
Dimensions		
Span	6.5 m	(21 ft 4 in)
Length	5.33 m	(17 ft 6 in)
Height	1.7 m	(5 ft 7 in)
Performance		
Max speed	209 km/h	(113 kt, 130 mph)
Cruising speed	193 km/h	(104 kt, 120 mph)
Initial climb	244 m/min	(800 fpm)
Range	560 km	(304 nm, 350 miles)
Weights		
Max takeoff	470 kg	(1,036 lbs)
Useful load	230 kg	(507 lbs)

Pottier P.130 Bleu Citron — France

The Bleu Citron is a recent amateur-built light aircraft sponsored by the French RSA amateur constructors' organisation and designed by their president, Jean Pottier. It is of fairly simple wood and fabric construction and has a high-set strut-braced wing and the distinctive vertical tail used on the Pottier P.80S. The tailwheel (or optional tricycle) undercarriage has cantilever steel main legs and the side-by-side two-seat cockpit is enclosed by a large clear-view canopy and is placed just ahead of the wing to give good all-round vision. Several engines can be fitted including the 80 h.p. JPX and Volkswagen engines of 65 to 100 h.p., and the Bleu Citron can be built as an ultralight or under the normal category. The prototype flew in 1998 and over 60 are reported to be under construction in France.

Pottier P.130L Bleu Citron, F-PBCJ

Specification	Pottier P.130 Bleu Citron	
Powerplant	One 65 h.p. (48.5 kW) Volkswagen VW1600 piston engine	
Dimensions		
Span	5.28 m	(17 ft 4 in)
Length	6.9 m	(22 ft 7 in)
Height	1.98 m	(6 ft 6 in)
Performance		
Max speed	195 km/h	(105 kt, 121 mph)
Cruising speed	181 km/h	(98 kt, 112 mph)
Initial climb	240 m/min	(790 fpm)
Range	480 km	(260 nm, 298 miles)
Weights		
Max takeoff	500 kg	(1,102 lbs)
Useful load	240 kg	(529 lbs)

Pottier P.220S Koala — France

The Pottier P.200 series of kit-built aircraft has been developed from the successful P.180 side-by-side two-seater. Among numerous detail differences are the separate fin and rudder of the P.220S compared with the all-rudder tail of the P.180, a cut-down rear fuselage and a revised nose undercarriage. Versions available are the P.220S Koala two-seater powered by a 75 h.p. Volkswagen, the P.230S Panda with a third rear seat and a 100 h.p. Continental O-200-A engine, and the four-seat P.240S Saiga with a two-place rear seat and a 150 h.p. Lycoming O-320-A. The P.200 series is commercially manufactured as a kit or factory-complete aircraft by SG Aviation in Italy. The P.220S is produced by them as the ultralight-category SG Storm 280.SI with a 79 h.p. Rotax 912 or as the standard Storm 320E with a 100 h.p. O-200-A or 105 h.p. Midwest engine, and the P.230S is the Storm 400.TI with three seats and a 116 h.p. Lycoming O-235-N2C engine. In Poland, Aero Co. builds the P.220S as the AT-3 with a Limbach L.2400 engine. The Evektor EV-97 Eurostar is a modified P.220S built in the Czech Republic and fitted with foldable wings, a fuselage fuel tank and an 80 h.p. Rotax 912 engine (see separate entry).

Pottier P.230S Panda, F-PRMD

Specification	SG Storm 320E	
Powerplant	One 100 h.p. (74.6 kW) Teledyne Continental O-200-A piston engine	
Dimensions		
Span	8.58 m	(28 ft 2 in)
Length	6.53 m	(21 ft 5 in)
Height	2.16 m	(7 ft 1 in)
Performance		
Max speed	238 km/h	(128 kt, 148 mph)
Cruising speed	220 km/h	(119 kt, 137 mph)
Initial climb	366 m/min	(1,200 fpm)
Range	1,150 km	(625 nm, 719 miles)
Weights		
Max takeoff	520 kg	(1,147 lbs)
Useful load	200 kg	(441 lbs)

Practavia Pilot Sprite — UK

The Sprite was designed by staff of the UK magazine *Pilot* and launched as an all-metal aerobatic aircraft for amateur construction. It has a low wing of constant chord with dihedralled outer panels and can be equipped with either a fixed or retractable tricycle undercarriage. It has a side-by-side two-seat cabin and can be fitted with optional wingtip tanks. The Sprite is stressed for engines in the 115 h.p. to 150 h.p. range but the first aircraft, which flew on 16th June 1976, had a 115 h.p. Lycoming O-235. Despite attempts to build the Sprite as a factory-supplied production aircraft Practavia only supplied plans and partial kits before it went out of business in 1982. Seven Sprites are currently registered in the UK of which four were active at the end of 1999.

Practavia Pilot Sprite (Cont.)

Practavia Pilot Sprite, G-BCWH

Specification	Practavia Pilot Sprite	
Powerplant	One 115 h.p. (86 kW) Textron Lycoming O-235 piston engine	
Dimensions		
Span	7.31 m	(24 ft 0 in)
Length	6.1 m	(20 ft 0 in)
Height	2.51 m	(8 ft 3 in)
Performance		
Max speed	225 km/h	(122 kt, 140 mph)
Cruising speed	209 km/h	(113 kt, 130 mph)
Initial climb	259 m/min	(850 fpm)
Range	800 km	(435 nm, 500 miles)
Weights		
Max takeoff	658 kg	(1,450 lbs)
Useful load	204 kg	(450 lbs)

Praga E-114
— Czechoslovakia

CKD-Praga designed the E-114 Praga Air Baby for the pre-war European sporting aircraft market, flying the prototype in September 1934. It was a side-by-side two-seater of wood and ply construction with a cantilever high wing, rearwards-hinged cockpit canopy and fixed tailwheel undercarriage. Some 63 examples of the E-114 powered by a 40 h.p. Praga B engine or 45 h.p. Praga B-2 were built together with 39 Hillson Pragas, built in England by F. Hills & Sons Ltd. The Air Baby was returned to production after the war as the E-114D which was powered by the 60 h.p. Praga D engine and had a larger tail, moulded windscreen, strengthened fuselage, increased wing dihedral and improved braking. The first E-114D flew on 14th September 1946 and ten were built followed by 95 of the E-114M powered by a 65 h.p. Walter Mikron III engine. The first E-114M (OK-AFM) made its first flight on 29th January 1947 and was followed by 95 production aircraft built by Praga and 26 by the Rudy Letov Company. Two E-114Ms are airworthy in Switzerland, one now powered by a 90 h.p. Continental C90-12F engine.

Praga E-114M, HB-UAD

Specification	Praga E-114M Air Baby	
Powerplant	One 65 h.p. (48.5 kW) Walter Mikron III piston engine	
Dimensions		
Span	11 m	(36 ft 1 in)
Length	6.6 m	(21 ft 8 in)
Height	2.6 m	(8 ft 6 in)
Performance		
Max speed	185 km/h	(100 kt, 115 mph)
Cruising speed	164 km/h	(88 kt, 102 mph)
Initial climb	143 m/min	(470 fpm)
Range	550 km	(296 nm, 342 miles)
Weights		
Max takeoff	550 kg	(1,213 lbs)
Useful load	210 kg	(463 lbs)

Preceptor N-3 Pup — USA

The little N-3 Pup (formerly Mosler Pup) has been one of the most popular of amateur-built very-light aircraft. Representing a 75% scale Piper Super Cub, the Pup is a strut-braced high-wing single-seater built from metal structural components provided by Preceptor Aircraft of Rutherfordton, North Carolina, and covered in Dacron fabric. In its basic form it is powered by a 40 h.p. TEC light piston engine and it has foldable wings and a fixed tailwheel undercarriage. The Super Pup is a higher-powered model with a 50 h.p. engine and the Ultra Pup is a slightly longer tandem two-seater with dual controls which can be fitted with engines in the 60 h.p. to 75 h.p. category, and typically uses a 65 h.p. Continental A65 flat-four. Over 800 plans sets and kits have been sold and more than 500 of the Pup series are flying. A single-seat open-cockpit parasol-wing version named 'Stinger' is also available.

Preceptor N-3 Ultra Pup

Specification	Preceptor Ultra Pup	
Powerplant	One 65 h.p. (48.5 kW) Teledyne Continental A65-8 piston engine	
Dimensions		
Span	9.3 m	(30 ft 6 in)
Length	5.28 m	(17 ft 4 in)
Height	1.68 m	(5 ft 6 in)
Performance		
Max speed	185 km/h	(100 kt, 115 mph)
Cruising speed	145 km/h	(78 kt, 90 mph)
Initial climb	396 m/min	(1,300 fpm)
Range	560 km	(304 nm, 350 miles)
Weights		
Max takeoff	454 kg	(1,000 lbs)
Useful load	249 kg	(550 lbs)

Procaer F.15 Picchio — Italy

The Italian engineer Stelio Frati produced many elegant light aircraft designs which were produced by a variety of Italian manufacturers and the F.15 Picchio was an improved version of the Aviamilano Nibbio (see separate entry). It was a low-wing cabin monoplane with a retractable tricycle undercarriage with basic wooden construction skinned with light alloy to give a very smooth finish. The prototype three-seat F.15 first flew on 7th May 1959 powered by a 160 h.p. Lycoming O-320-B1A engine. Variants built by Progetti Costruzione Aeronautiche (Procaer) included the F.15A four-seat model with a 180 h.p. O-360-A1A, the F.15B with larger wings containing the fuel tanks relocated from the fuselage, the F.15C with a 260 h.p. Continental IO-470-E engine and the F.15E which had an all-metal structure and a 300 h.p. Continental IO-520-K and was built as a prototype by Frati's General Avia company. General Avia also built a prototype of the F.15F Delfino which flew on 20th October 1977. This was fitted with a sliding bubble canopy in place of the integral cabin roof and a 200 h.p. IO-360-A1B engine. The F.15F was to be built as the Excalibur by Eurospace in association with the Russian company SOKOL. A military trainer version, the F.15F-300, was also planned but no production aircraft have been completed to date. Only 38 Picchios were built between 1960 and 1977 but 16 remain active in Italy, Germany, France, Belgium and Switzerland.

Procaer F.15A Picchio, F-BULT

Specification	Procaer F.15B Picchio	
Powerplant	One 180 h.p. (134.2 kW) Textron Lycoming O-360-A1A piston engine	
Dimensions		
Span	9.91 m	(32 ft 6 in)
Length	7.49 m	(24 ft 7 in)
Height	2.79 m	(9 ft 2 in)
Performance		
Max speed	311 km/h	(168 kt, 193 mph)
Cruising speed	275 km/h	(149 kt, 171 mph)
Initial climb	305 m/min	(1,000 fpm)
Range	1,584 km	(861 nm, 990 miles)
Weights		
Max takeoff	1,150 kg	(2,536 lbs)
Useful load	455 kg	(1,003 lbs)

Progressive Aerodyne SeaRey — USA

The SeaRey lightweight amphibian is produced in kit form by Florida-based Progressive Aerodyne and 190 are flying in the USA and Canada. It is a lightweight strut-braced high-wing aircraft with a glass-fibre boat hull fuselage and fabric-covered wings. The main units of the tailwheel undercarriage fold upwards and the SeaRey has fixed outrigger floats positioned at the outer-wing strut support points. The cockpit has side-by-side seating for two with dual controls and can be open or fully enclosed. Various Rotax piston engines can be fitted from the 64 h.p. Model 582 to the 115 h.p. Model 914, but the normal installation is an 80 h.p. Rotax 912 which is mounted as a pusher above the wing centre section. The first SeaRey flew in November 1992 and Progressive Aerodyne also market the Stingray which is a similar single-seat version with a 40 h.p. Rotax 447 engine.

Progressive Aerodyne SeaRey (Cont.)

Progressive Aerodyne SeaRey

Specification	Progressive Aerodyne SeaRey	
Powerplant	One 80 h.p. (59.6 kW) Rotax 912 piston engine	
Dimensions		
Span	9.4 m	(30 ft 10 in)
Length	6.83 m	(22 ft 5 in)
Height	1.88 m	(6 ft 2 in)
Performance		
Max speed	177 km/h	(96 kt, 110 mph)
Cruising speed	137 km/h	(74 kt, 85 mph)
Initial climb	229 m/min	(750 fpm)
Range	480 km	(261 nm, 300 miles)
Weights		
Max takeoff	567 kg	(1,250 lbs)
Useful load	227 kg	(500 lbs)

ProTech PT-2 — USA

Now marketed by ProStar Aircraft of Beeville, Texas, the PT-2 originally appeared as the strut-braced high-wing PT-2 Sassy, designed by Paul Seales and first flown in 1987. The PT-2, which has excellent short-field performance, is built from steel tube covered with light alloy and fabric and the wings, which are fitted with flaperons, are foldable for transport. It has a single-piece spring-steel tailwheel undercarriage and the roomy side-by-side cockpit has dual controls. The prototype was powered by a 75 h.p. Revmaster engine but most aircraft have a larger engine such as the 115 h.p. Lycoming O-235-C, and the P-2B ProStar is stressed for engines up to 160 h.p. The current PT-2C has more extensive cabin glazing and a larger tail. Over 50 are flying in the USA and one has been completed in the UK.

ProTech PT-2C, G-EWAN

Specification	ProTech PT-2C	
Powerplant	One 100 h.p. (74.6 kW) Teledyne Continental O-200-A piston engine	
Dimensions		
Span	9.91 m	(32 ft 6 in)
Length	5.33 m	(17 ft 6 in)
Height	1.93 m	(6 ft 4 in)
Performance		
Max speed	193 km/h	(104 kt, 120 mph)
Cruising speed	169 km/h	(91 kt, 105 mph)
Initial climb	213 m/min	(700 fpm)
Range	480 km	(261 nm, 300 miles)
Weights		
Max takeoff	703 kg	(1,550 lbs)
Useful load	340 kg	(750 lbs)

Pützer Elster — Germany

Alfons Pützer was one of the first companies to manufacture light aircraft in Germany following the lifting of postwar flying restrictions. The Elster, which first flew on 10th January 1959, was an all-wood aircraft with an enclosed side-by-side two-seat cabin and a fixed tricycle undercarriage. It had a strut-braced high wing and circular-section fuselage of wood and plywood construction, both of which drew on the design of the earlier Pützer Doppelraab glider. Some 25 Elsters were ordered by the German government for use by civil flying clubs and most of these flew in Luftwaffe insignia. In total, 45 production Elsters were constructed between 1957 and 1967, 32 being the standard Elster B with a 95 h.p. Continental C90-12F engine and the remaining 13 being Elster Cs equipped with a 150 h.p. Lycoming O-320-A2A and equipment for glider towing. Half of the Elsters are still flying in Germany, Denmark and the UK and one Elster B has been re-engined with a 100 h.p. Continental O-200-A engine.

Pützer Elster B, G-APVF

Specification	Pützer Elster B	
Powerplant	One 95 h.p. (70.8 kW) Teledyne Continental C90-12F piston engine	
Dimensions		
Span	13.2 m	(43 ft 4 in)
Length	7.09 m	(23 ft 3 in)
Height	2.49 m	(8 ft 2 in)
Performance		
Max speed	169 km/h	(91 kt, 105 mph)
Cruising speed	153 km/h	(83 kt, 95 mph)
Initial climb	213 m/min	(700 fpm)
Range	456 km	(248 nm, 285 miles)
Weights		
Max takeoff	700 kg	(1,543 lbs)
Useful load	240 kg	(530 lbs)

PZL Gawron — Poland

During the early 1950s, the Okecie factory of PZL (Panstwowe Zaklady Lotnicze) built a large series of the Yakovlev Yak-12 four-seat high-wing utility aircraft. This led to PZL redesigning it as the Gawron crop sprayer which was based on the Yak-12M but had a higher-powered 260 h.p. Ivchenko AI-14R radial engine and, consequently, completely new slightly swept wings with leading edge slats and large endplates, a modified horizontal tail and a large chemical hopper in the rear cabin. The prototype PZL-101G.1 first flew on 14th April 1958 and PZL completed 325 production PZL-101A aircraft with a further batch of around 25 being built in Indonesia by Nurtanio. Many of the Gawrons were four-seat PZL-101B light transports with extra windows and a rear two-/three passenger bench seat, and the PZL-101AF had a 300 h.p. AI-14RF engine and a higher useful load. A fair number of Gawrons remain with Polish flying clubs and as glider tugs and a few have been sold to American and European private owners.

PZL-101A Gawron, HA-SBO (N128GC)

Specification	PZL-101B Gawron	
Powerplant	One 260 h.p. (193.86 kW) Ivchenko AI-14R-VI piston engine	
Dimensions		
Span	12.67 m	(41 ft 7 in)
Length	8.99 m	(29 ft 6 in)
Height	3.12 m	(10 ft 3 in)
Performance		
Max speed	172 km/h	(93 kt, 107 mph)
Cruising speed	153 km/h	(83 kt, 95 mph)
Initial climb	146 m/min	(480 fpm)
Range	448 km	(243 nm, 280 miles)
Weights		
Max takeoff	1,660 kg	(3,660 lbs)
Useful load	660 kg	(1,455 lbs)

PZL Wilga — Poland

While they were successful with the PZL-101 Gawron, PZL-Okecie saw the need for a more modern replacement design and flew the prototype PZL-104 Wilga 1 on 21st July 1962. The production Wilga 2 was an angular all-metal cantilever high-wing monoplane with a heavily glazed four-seat cabin and a slim rear fuselage. It had a fixed tailwheel undercarriage with trailing-link suspension, and high-lift wing devices to give good STOL performance and was powered by a 195 h.p WN-6 radial engine. The Wilga has been used for a wide range of civil and military roles including crop spraying, glider towing, training, light passenger transport and armed border patrol. The first Wilga 2 flew on 11th October 1963 and the many variants included the Indonesian-built Lipnur Gelatik, the Wilga 2C with a 230 h.p. Continental O-470 engine, the Wilga 3 with a 260 h.p. PZL AI-14RA radial engine, the Wilga 32 and 35 which were the Wilga 2C and Wilga 3 with a new, shorter undercarriage, the Wilga 80 certificated for US sale, the Wilga 80-550 with a 300 h.p. Continental IO-550 and the PZL-104M Wilga 2000 which has a 300 h.p. Lycoming IO-540 engine, enlarged undercarriage and vertical tail fairings, modifications to the wings and a new three-piece windshield and reshaped side windows. Wilga manufacture for civil and military customers now exceeds 1,000 aircraft and production is continuing.

PZL Wilga (Cont.)

PZL-104 Wilga 35A, YR-VIS

Specification	PZL-104 Wilga 35	
Powerplant	One 260 h.p. (193.86 kW) PZL AI-14RA piston engine	
Dimensions		
Span	11.2 m	(36 ft 9 in)
Length	8.1 m	(26 ft 7 in)
Height	2.96 m	(9 ft 8 in)
Performance		
Max speed	192 km/h	(103 kt, 119 mph)
Cruising speed	165 km/h	(88 kt, 103 mph)
Initial climb	274 m/min	(900 fpm)
Range	557 km	(302 nm, 348 miles)
Weights		
Max takeoff	1,300 kg	(2,866 lbs)
Useful load	395 kg	(871 lbs)

PZL-106 Kruk — Poland

In 1972, PZL's Okecie factory designed a new agricultural aircraft intended as a replacement for the Gawron and the Wilga 35R. The first of four prototype Kruks was first flown in April 1973, powered by a 400 h.p. Lycoming IO-720 flat-eight engine, but this was replaced by the PZL-3S radial which was used on most production Kruks. The Kruk was an all-metal strut-braced low-wing aircraft with a classic structure incorporating a 1,400-litre hopper between the engine firewall and the cockpit and an enclosed cabin with a second rear-facing seat to transport a ground loader. A few PZL-106BRs have been fitted with an additional front cockpit with dual controls for training. Production started in 1975 with the PZL-106A Kruk being supplied in large numbers, particularly to East Germany. Variants included the PZL-106AR with a 600 h.p. PZL-3SR engine, the PZL-106B with longer-span wings and modified flaps and the PZL-106BS with a 1,000 h.p. Shvetsov ASz-621R. On 22nd June 1981 PZL flew the first PZL-106AT Turbo Kruk with a 760 s.h.p. Pratt & Whitney PT6A-34AG turboprop. This, and the PZL-106BT powered by the 730 s.h.p. Walter M-601D, are the current models, with a 1,600-litre hopper. They are in limited production but most of the 240 production Kruks are now out of service with a substantial number of early aircraft held in the USA for possible refurbishment.

PZL-106BT Turbo Kruk, SP-PAA

Specification	PZL-106BT Turbo Kruk	
Powerplant	One 730 s.h.p. (544.3 kW) Walter M-601D turboprop	
Dimensions		
Span	15 m	(49 ft 3 in)
Length	10.34 m	(33 ft 11 in)
Height	4.34 m	(14 ft 3 in)
Performance		
Max speed	240 km/h	(129 kt, 149 mph)
Cruising speed	180 km/h	(97 kt, 112 mph)
Initial climb	330 m/min	(1,080 fpm)
Range	480 km	(259 nm, 298 miles)
Weights		
Max takeoff	3,500 kg	(7,717 lbs)
Useful load	1,820 kg	(4,013 lbs)

PZL Dromader — Poland

Built by the Mielec factory of PZL, the Dromader is larger than its fellow Kruk agricultural aircraft and has been more commercially successful with over 550 aircraft completed to date. Designed in cooperation with Rockwell International it has long-span cantilever wings which use outer panels identical to those of the S-2R Thrush Commander. The standard-production M-18A, equipped with a second rear crew seat, is fitted with a 2,500-litre chemical tank ahead of the cockpit which allows it to take on tasks, including firefighting, which are too great for the smaller Kruk. It is powered by a 1,000 h.p. PZL-built Shvetsov ASz-621R radial engine but PZL has also built the scaled-up M-24 Dromader Super with a 1,200 h.p. engine and the M-24T Turbo Dromader with a PT6A-24AG turboprop. For agricultural training, the M-18ASz has also been built with a full tandem two-seat cockpit and limited hopper capacity. A smaller-capacity model is the M-21M Dromader Mini, flown as a prototype with a smaller hopper and a 600 h.p. PZL-3SR engine. Dromaders have been exported to most CIS countries and to many users in Africa, South America, Australia and the USA.

PZL M-18 Dromader, LZ-8014

Specification	PZL M-18A Dromader	
Powerplant	One 1,000 h.p. (745.6 kW) PZL-Kalisz ASz-621R piston engine	
Dimensions		
Span	17.7 m	(58 ft 1 in)
Length	9.47 m	(31 ft 1 in)
Height	3.71 m	(12 ft 2 in)
Performance		
Max speed	256 km/h	(138 kt, 159 mph)
Cruising speed	204 km/h	(110 kt, 127 mph)
Initial climb	347 m/min	(1,140 fpm)
Range	520 km	(280 nm, 323 miles)
Weights		
Max takeoff	5,300 kg	(11,687 lbs)
Useful load	2,830 kg	(6,240 lbs)

PZL TS-11 Iskra — Poland

PZL designed the Iskra as a standard Warsaw Pact through-jet trainer in the late 1950s and, although the Czech L-29 Delfin was preferred for general procurement, the Iskra was ordered by the Polish Air Force and was sold to the Indian Air Force. The prototype was first flown on 5th February 1960 and it went into Polish Air Force service, to equip the Deblin Air Force Academy, in 1964. The Iskra is a tandem two-seat aircraft with a straight wing and a retractable tricycle undercarriage. It has an unusual fuselage design with the Polish-built IL SO-3 turbojet engine positioned in the lower centre section, fed by wing root intakes, and a slim circular-section rear fuselage boom carrying the tail unit. Several variants were produced including the Iskra Bis trainer, the Iskra Bis-B ground attack trainer with two underwing armament hardpoints, the Iskra Bis-C photo-reconnaissance version, the improved Iskra Bis-D and the Iskra Bis-DF for mixed photo-reconnaissance and attack training fitted with a vertical camera operated from the rear cockpit. A total of 203 Iskras were delivered to the Polish Air Force and 50 to the Indian Air Force, and around 90 are believed to remain in military service. Several Iskras have been sold to warbird operators in the USA and Australia.

PZL TS-11 Iskra, VH-ISK

Specification	PZL TS-11 Iskra	
Powerplant	One 2,205 lb.s.t. (9.8 kN) Type IL SO-3 turbojet	
Dimensions		
Span	10.06 m	(33 ft 0 in)
Length	11.18 m	(36 ft 8 in)
Height	3.51 m	(11 ft 6 in)
Performance		
Max speed	766 km/h	(414 kt, 476 mph)
Cruising speed	603 km/h	(326 kt, 375 mph)
Initial climb	887 m/min	(2,910 fpm)
Range	1,243 km	(676 nm, 777 miles)
Weights		
Max takeoff	3,840 kg	(8,467 lbs)
Useful load	1,280 kg	(2,822 lbs)

PZL I-22 and M-93/96 Iryda — Poland

PZL-Mielec designed the Iryda as a replacement for the long-serving Iskra. The first of five prototype Irydas was flown on 5th March 1985. Externally similar to other jet trainers such as the Alpha Jet and Pampa, the Iryda has a shoulder wing, stepped tandem two-seat cockpit and retractable tricycle undercarriage with the two turbojet engines positioned in pods on the lower fuselage flanks. It is a multi-role aircraft capable of being used for light ground attack missions and is equipped with four underwing pylons capable of carrying up to 4,400 lbs of bombs, rockets, AAMs or 100 USG fuel tanks and a centreline hardpoint to carry a podded double-barrel 23 mm cannon. The initial I-22 was powered by two 2,425 lb.s.t. PZL-Rzeszow PZL-5-SO-3W22 turbojets and a batch of five was delivered to the Polish Air Force, but inadequate performance resulted in a redesign with new IL-K-15 engines, in which form the Iryda became the M-93K, flying on 6th June 1994. The M-93V export version has two 3,307 lb.s.t. Rolls Royce Viper 545s. The M-96 is an upgraded version with a new avionics fit, larger vertical tail, leading edge wing root extensions, leading edge slats and Fowler flaps. In total 13 M-93 prototypes and production aircraft have been delivered to the Polish Air Force but most of the fleet was grounded for modifications at the end of 1999.

PZL I-22 and M-93/96 Iryda (Cont.)

PZL I-22 Iryda, SP-PWB

Specification	PZL M-93K Iryda	
Powerplant	Two 3,307 lb.s.t. (14.7 kN) Instytut Lotnictwa K-15 turbojets	
Dimensions		
Span	9.6 m	(31 ft 6 in)
Length	13.21 m	(43 ft 4 in)
Height	4.29 m	(14 ft 1 in)
Performance		
Max speed	949 km/h	(513 kt, 590 mph)
Initial climb	2,520 m/min	(8,269 fpm)
Range	496 km	(270 nm, 310 miles)
Weights		
Max takeoff	8,700 kg	(19,183 lbs)
Useful load	4,050 kg	(8,930 lbs)

PZL-130TC Turbo Orlik, Polish AF, 034

PZL-130 Orlik — Poland

The Orlik has been built by PZL-Okecie as a basic to advanced military trainer for the Polish Air Force and it follows a similar layout to other turboprop trainers such as the Tucano and Pilatus PC-9. It is a fully aerobatic low-wing aircraft with a retractable tricycle undercarriage and a stepped tandem two-seat cockpit enclosed by a side-hinged clamshell canopy. PZL flew the prototype Orlik on 12th October 1984 powered by a Vedeneyev M-14Pm piston engine but only five PZL-130s were built before it was redesigned as the PZL-130T Turbo Orlik with a Pratt & Whitney PT6A-25A, first flying in this form on 13th July 1986. The production variants are the PZL-130TM with a 750 s.h.p. Motorlet M.601E turboprop, the PZL-130TB with an M.601T, the PZL-130TC with a 950 s.h.p. PT6A-62 and the PZL-130TD with a 750 s.h.p. PT6A-25C. The Polish Air Force has taken delivery of 30 Orliks including both the PZL-130TB and PZL-130TC for use by the training units, 58 LPSz at Deblin and 60 LPSz at Radom.

Specification	PZL-130TD Turbo Orlik	
Powerplant	One 750 s.h.p. (559.2 kW) Pratt & Whitney PT6A-25C turboprop	
Dimensions		
Span	9 m	(29 ft 6 in)
Length	9 m	(29 ft 6 in)
Height	3.53 m	(11 ft 7 in)
Performance		
Max speed	450 km/h	(243 kt, 280 mph)
Cruising speed	410 km/h	(221 kt, 255 mph)
Initial climb	714 m/min	(2,342 fpm)
Range	1,550 km	(842 nm, 968 miles)
Weights		
Max takeoff	2,700 kg	(5,953 lbs)
Useful load	1,100 kg	(2,425 lbs)

PZL M-26 Iskierka — Poland

PZL-Mielec developed the M-26 two-seat military and civil trainer using components and technology gained from their licence production of the Piper PA-34 Seneca (M-20 Mewa). The M-26 uses the tail unit and undercarriage of the Seneca together with a shortened version of its wing which are married to a new fuselage which is equipped with a tandem two-seat cockpit enclosed by a side-hinged clamshell canopy. The first M-26 was flown on 15th July 1986 powered by a 205 h.p. PZL-Franklin 6A-350CA piston engine, but the definitive M-26-01, named Air Wolf for export, has a 300 h.p. Lycoming AEIO-540-L1B5D engine and is fitted with additional fuel capacity. A small number have been delivered to Melex in the USA and at least two are believed to have been supplied to the Bolivian Air Force.

PZL M-26 Iskierka, N2601M

Specification	PZL M-26 Iskierka	
Powerplant	One 300 h.p. (224 kW) Textron Lycoming AEIO-540-L1B5D piston engine	
Dimensions		
Span	8.61 m	(28 ft 3 in)
Length	8.31 m	(27 ft 3 in)
Height	2.97 m	(9 ft 9 in)
Performance		
Max speed	330 km/h	(178 kt, 205 mph)
Cruising speed	314 km/h	(170 kt, 195 mph)
Initial climb	539 m/min	(1,770 fpm)
Range	1,400 km	(761 nm, 875 miles)
Weights		
Max takeoff	1,400 kg	(3,087 lbs)
Useful load	350 kg	(772 lbs)

PZL W-3 Sokól — Poland

With experience of building large numbers of Mi-2s and Kanias, PZL-Swidnik developed the medium-capacity W-3 Sokól for military and civil applications, flying the prototype on 16th November 1979. The Sokól has a conventional design layout with a main fuselage module containing a main cabin and two-crew cockpit, a tail boom carrying a three-bladed anti-torque rotor and a fixed tricycle undercarriage. The twin PZL-10W turboshafts are mounted side-by-side above the main 12-passenger cabin driving a four-blade composite main rotor. For military use, the Sokól is fitted with outrigger weapons hardpoints. Variants include the W-3A commercial export version, the armed military W-3W with externally mounted 23 mm guns or Mars-2 rocket launchers, the W-3RM Anakonda search & rescue helicopter and the S-1W Huzar anti-tank version. The Sokól has been delivered in quantity to the Polish military forces (40) and to Myanmar (12), the Czech Republic (11), Korea (7) and the German Border Police (6). Over 120 had been manufactured by the end of 1999.

PZL W-3A Sokól, Myanmar AF, 65-07

Specification	PZL W-3A Sokól	
Powerplant	Two 888 s.h.p. (662 kW) PZL Rzeszow PZL-10W turboshafts	
Dimensions		
Rotor diameter	15.7 m	(51 ft 6 in)
Length	14.22 m	(46 ft 8 in)
Height	6.02 m	(19 ft 9 in)
Performance		
Max speed	243 km/h	(131 kt, 151 mph)
Cruising speed	225 km/h	(122 kt, 140 mph)
Initial climb	610 m/min	(2,000 fpm)
Range	800 km	(435 nm, 500 miles)
Weights		
Max takeoff	6,400 kg	(14,112 lbs)
Useful load	2,550 kg	(5,623 lbs)

PZL SW-4 — Poland

PZL is developing the SW-4 light five-seat turbine-engined helicopter for sale to civil and military users. Falling in the same category as the Eurocopter AS.350, it is of conventional layout with a fixed skid undercarriage and a two-blade tail anti-torque rotor. Two versions are to be offered: the High Performance with a 615 s.h.p. Pratt & Whitney PW-200/9 turboshaft, and the Economy with a 450 s.h.p. Allison 250-C20R and lower gross weight. However, the SW-4 has been designed from the outset to be upgraded to twin engines in the future. The prototype made its first flight on 26th October 1996 and this and the second aircraft were continuing flight testing at the end of 2000.

PZL SW-4 (Cont.)

PZL SW-4

Specification	PZL SW-4	
Powerplant	One 615 s.h.p (459 kW) Pratt & Whitney PW-200/9 turboshaft	
Dimensions		
Rotor diameter	9.07 m	(29 ft 9 in)
Length	8.23 m	(27 ft 0 in)
Height	2.92 m	(9 ft 7 in)
Performance		
Max speed	240 km/h	(129 kt, 149 mph)
Cruising speed	230 km/h	(124 kt, 143 mph)
Initial climb	600 m/min	(1,968 fpm)
Range	900 km	(489 nm, 563 miles)
Weights		
Max takeoff	1,800 kg	(3,969 lbs)
Useful load	1,050 kg	(2,315 lbs)

Q

Quad City Challenger — USA

Several versions of the Challenger ultralight are available as kits for amateur builders. The original Challenger, first flown in November 1982, was a single-seat aircraft with a V-strut braced high wing mounted on a central fuselage pylon with a pusher Rotax engine of very low horsepower mounted on the wing centre section. It has an open cockpit which is positioned well forward of the wing, a fixed tricycle undercarriage and a conventional fin and tailplane at the end of a fuselage boom. There is a flying boat version with a planing lower fuselage. The basic Challenger has a 28 h.p. Rotax 277 but other Rotax engines including the 477 and 503 can be used and the Challenger Special is fitted with a 42 h.p. Rotax 447 and has shorter wings. Construction is of aluminium tube covered with fabric. The Challenger II, and short-wing Challenger II Special, is a longer tandem two-seat version with a Rotax 477 or 52 h.p. Rotax 503 engine and separate wing struts. It can be operated on floats. More than 700 Challengers have been built.

Specification	Quad City Challenger II	
Powerplant	One 52 h.p. (38.77 kW) Rotax 503 piston engine	
Dimensions		
Span	9.6 m	(31 ft 6 in)
Length	6.1 m	(20 ft 0 in)
Height	1.83 m	(6 ft 0 in)
Performance		
Max speed	145 km/h	(78 kt, 90 mph)
Cruising speed	121 km/h	(65 kt, 75 mph)
Initial climb	366 m/min	(1,200 fpm)
Range	240 km	(130 nm, 150 miles)
Weights		
Max takeoff	372 kg	(820 lbs)
Useful load	227 kg	(500 lbs)

Quad City Challenger II, N535PT

Questair Venture and Spirit — USA

The distinctive Questair Venture was designed by Jim Griswold, an engineer with Piper, and it embodies technology used on the Piper Malibu. The Venture was intended to combine a large side-by-side two seat cabin with rear baggage space and the smallest possible airframe in a highly streamlined design offering exceptional long-range performance. It is a low-wing all-metal aircraft built with preformed multi-curvature panels and provided as a kit to homebuilders. The Venture has a complex retractable tricycle undercarriage enclosed by several doors and the powerplant is a Continental IO-550-G designed for the aircraft. The Venture first flew on 1st July 1987 and in 1991 it was joined by the Questair Spirit which has a fixed undercarriage and optional third rear seat. More than 30 Ventures and Spirits are now flying in the USA.

Questair Venture, N71T

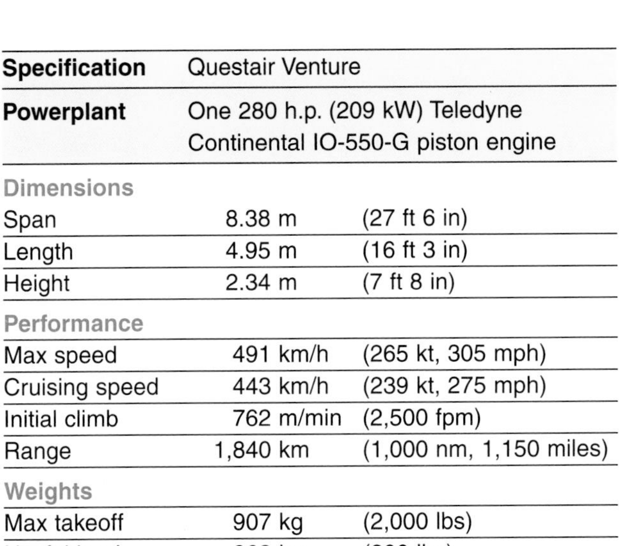

Specification	Questair Venture	
Powerplant	One 280 h.p. (209 kW) Teledyne Continental IO-550-G piston engine	
Dimensions		
Span	8.38 m	(27 ft 6 in)
Length	4.95 m	(16 ft 3 in)
Height	2.34 m	(7 ft 8 in)
Performance		
Max speed	491 km/h	(265 kt, 305 mph)
Cruising speed	443 km/h	(239 kt, 275 mph)
Initial climb	762 m/min	(2,500 fpm)
Range	1,840 km	(1,000 nm, 1,150 miles)
Weights		
Max takeoff	907 kg	(2,000 lbs)
Useful load	363 kg	(800 lbs)

Quickie Q-2 — USA

The Quickie was designed by Gene Sheehan and Tom Jewett with assistance from Burt Rutan and was first flown on 15th November 1977. It is a tandem-wing single-seater built largely from glass-fibre and it has an unusual curved fuselage with one wing mounted above and behind the cockpit and a forward wing below and behind the engine which carries the main wheels at its tips. Many Quickies have been built with a separate main undercarriage due to the vulnerability of the wing-mounted wheels. The original Quickie I was powered by a 22 h.p. Onan B48M engine but most use the Rotax 503. The Quickie Q-2, which flew on 1st July 1980, is a side-by-side two-seat version with a wider fuselage, increased wing area and engines in the 65 h.p. range. Most aircraft have used a 64 h.p. Revmaster 2100DQ engine but Quickie Aircraft also supplied kits for the Quickie Q-200 which has much improved performance and is stressed to use a 100 h.p. Continental O-200-A engine. Other, larger powerplants have also been fitted including the 115 h.p. Lycoming O-235C, and the Tri-Q-200 is a variant with a tricycle undercarriage. Over 1,000 Quickies have been completed in many countries and 23 are flying in the UK and more than 40 elsewhere in Europe.

Quickie Q-200, G-KWKI

Specification	Quickie Q-200	
Powerplant	One 100 h.p. (74.6 kW) Teledyne Continental O-200-A piston engine	
Dimensions		
Span	5.08 m	(16 ft 8 in)
Length	6.04 m	(19 ft 10 in)
Height	1.57 m	(5 ft 2 in)
Performance		
Max speed	354 km/h	(191 kt, 220 mph)
Cruising speed	330 km/h	(178 kt, 205 mph)
Initial climb	488 m/min	(1,600 fpm)
Range	1,632 km	(887 nm, 1,020 miles)
Weights		
Max takeoff	499 kg	(1,100 lbs)
Useful load	270 kg	(595 lbs)

Quikkit Glass Goose — USA

The Glass Goose is marketed as a homebuilt kit by Quikkit Corporation of Dallas, Texas. It is an improved version of the Aero Gare (later Aero Composites) SeaHawker which was designed by Garry LeGare and flown as a prototype in July 1982. The SeaHawker, a number of which have been completed, is an all-composite cantilever-wing biplane amphibian. It has a side-by-side two-seat cockpit and the prototype was fitted with a 100 h.p. Lycoming O-235-C engine fitted as a pusher on the centre section of the upper wing. In place of normal stabilising floats, the aircraft has small sponsons on the centre fuselage and the main units of the retractable tricycle undercarriage retract into fairings on the lower wing. The Glass Goose has many modifications to improve air and water handling including a modified planing hull, increased wing area and a revised engine housing to improve cooling to the 160 h.p. Lycoming O-320-D engine. Around 30 examples of the Glass Goose are under construction.

Quikkit Glass Goose (Cont.)

Glass Goose, N85TS

Specification	Quikkit Glass Goose	
Powerplant	One 160 h.p. (119.3 kW) Textron Lycoming O-320-D piston engine	
Dimensions		
Span	8.23 m	(27 ft 0 in)
Length	5.94 m	(19 ft 6 in)
Height	2.29 m	(7 ft 6 in)
Performance		
Max speed	257 km/h	(139 kt, 160 mph)
Cruising speed	233 km/h	(126 kt, 145 mph)
Initial climb	366 m/min	(1,200 fpm)
Range	1,760 km	(956 nm, 1,100 miles)
Weights		
Max takeoff	816 kg	(1,800 lbs)
Useful load	408 kg	(900 lbs)

R

Rand KR-2 — USA

Ken Rand designed the original KR-1 single-seat homebuilt in 1972 and over 700 have been built from Rand-Robinson kits using construction which consists of a wooden frame filled with hot-wired polyurethane foam and covered with glass-fibre cloth. The KR-1, which flew in February 1972, is a low-wing aircraft of conventional layout with a small cockpit covered with a transparent canopy, and it typically uses a Volkswagen engine in the 60 h.p. to 80 h.p. range. The KR-1's tailwheel undercarriage has main units mounted on the inner wing sections which retract backwards but many builders have opted for fuselage-mounted spring-steel gear which gives improved propeller clearance. The KR-2 is a larger side-by-side two-seater with a turtledeck rear fuselage and modified cockpit canopy which made its maiden flight in July 1974, and the KR-2S is a stretched KR-2 using moulded outer skinning and with a larger cockpit, a redesigned wing and optional tailwheel or tricycle undercarriage layouts. The KR-2T has tandem seating. It is thought that more than 1,250 of the KR-2 series are currently flying.

Specification	Rand-Robinson KR-2	
Powerplant	One 65 h.p. (48.46 kW) Volkswagen 1600 piston engine	
Dimensions		
Span	6.3 m	(20 ft 8 in)
Length	4.42 m	(14 ft 6 in)
Height	1.07 m	(3 ft 6 in)
Performance		
Max speed	322 km/h	(174 kt, 200 mph)
Cruising speed	298 km/h	(161 kt, 185 mph)
Initial climb	366 m/min	(1,200 fpm)
Range	2,560 km	(1,391 nm, 1,600 miles)
Weights		
Max takeoff	408 kg	(900 lbs)
Useful load	190 kg	(420 lbs)

Rand KR-2, OE-AHR

Rans S-4, S-5 and S-6 Coyote — USA

The Coyote ultralight was the first large production model produced by Randy Schlitter of Rans Inc. of Hayes, Kansas and over 1,000 kits have been sold for home construction. The Coyote I, which first flew in March 1983, is a single-seater with a tubular structure covered with pre-sewn fabric which allows a very short building time. The S-4 has a tailwheel undercarriage and the S-5 has tricycle gear. It has a strut-braced foldable high wing and is powered by a 42 h.p. Rotax 447 engine. The S-6ES Coyote II, introduced in April 1990, is a side-by-side two-seat development with a 47 h.p. Rotax 503 or 65 h.p. Rotax 582 engine and a broader tail. Two types of longer-span wings are available, one having trailing edge taper. With this wing the aircraft is designated S-6ES116. The S-6S has additional speed-enhancing features including a larger fin, standard fabric covering and an optional 80 h.p. Rotax 912 engine.

Rans S-4 Coyote Mk.I, G-MVXW

Rans S-6ES Coyote Mk.II, CS-UGR

Specification	Rans S-6ES Coyote II	
Powerplant	One 65 h.p. (48.46 kW) Rotax 582 piston engine	
Dimensions		
Span	10.52 m	(34 ft 6 in)
Length	6.1 m	(20 ft 0 in)
Height	1.8 m	(5 ft 11 in)
Performance		
Max speed	177 km/h	(96 kt, 110 mph)
Cruising speed	153 km/h	(82 kt, 95 mph)
Initial climb	305 m/min	(1,000 fpm)
Range	568 km	(309 nm, 355 miles)
Weights		
Max takeoff	442 kg	(975 lbs)
Useful load	243 kg	(535 lbs)

Rans S-7 Courier — USA

The Courier is a tandem two-seat homebuilt aircraft developed, initially as a trainer, from the side-by-side Rans Coyote II. It is more robust than the Coyote and has a lower stalling speed and can carry a greater useful load. It is of conventional tube and fabric construction with normal Ceconite covering and is fitted with a fixed tailwheel undercarriage. The S-7 prototype was first flown in November 1985. Like the Coyote, the S-7 has foldable wings for transportation and it is powered by either a 65 h.p. Rotax 582 or 80 h.p. Rotax 912 engine. The S-7C is a higher-performance factory-manufactured version with a longer fuselage and a 100 h.p. Continental engine. The Courier is popular for bush operations and can be equipped with twin floats or tundra tyres.

Rans S-7 Courier, 01-KG

Specification	Rans S-7 Courier	
Powerplant	One 80 h.p. (59.6 kW) Rotax 912 piston engine	
Dimensions		
Span	8.91 m	(29 ft 3 in)
Length	6.4 m	(21 ft 0 in)
Height	1.9 m	(6 ft 3 in)
Performance		
Max speed	185 km/h	(100 kt, 115 mph)
Cruising speed	169 km/h	(91 kt, 105 mph)
Initial climb	244 m/min	(800 fpm)
Range	640 km	(348 nm, 400 miles)
Weights		
Max takeoff	544 kg	(1,200 lbs)
Useful load	272 kg	(600 lbs)

Rans S-9 Chaos and S-10 Sakota — USA

Randy Schlitter designed the S-9 Chaos as a quickly constructed aerobatic single-seater for the amateur builder and introduced it in 1986. The kit consists of a fully factory-welded structure which is completed with fabric covering. It has a strut-braced mid-set wing and the cabin transparencies extend below the wing root to give all-round vision. The S-9, which has a fixed tailwheel undercarriage, is powered by a 47 h.p. Rotax 503 or 65 h.p. Rotax 582. The S-10 Sakota, which flew in March 1988, is externally similar but has a wider two-seat fuselage and is fitted with either a Rotax 582, a Hirth F.30 or the 80 h.p. Rotax 912. It is approved for single-seat aerobatics. Substantial numbers of the S-9 and S-10 have been completed, including 50 in Europe.

Rans S-9 Chaos and S-10 Sakota (Cont.)

Rans S-10 Sakota, G-BWIL

Specification	Rans S-10 Sakota	
Powerplant	One 80 h.p. (59.6 kW) Rotax 912 piston engine	
Dimensions		
Span	7.31 m	(24 ft 0 in)
Length	5.44 m	(17 ft 10 in)
Height	1.47 m	(4 ft 10 in)
Performance		
Max speed	209 km/h	(113 kt, 130 mph)
Cruising speed	193 km/h	(104 kt, 120 mph)
Initial climb	305 m/min	(1,000 fpm)
Range	416 km	(226 nm, 260 miles)
Weights		
Max takeoff	458 kg	(1,010 lbs)
Useful load	227 kg	(500 lbs)

Rans S-12 Airaile

Specification	Rans S-12XL Airaile	
Powerplant	One 65 h.p. (48.46 kW) Rotax 582 piston engine	
Dimensions		
Span	9.45 m	(31 ft 0 in)
Length	6.25 m	(20 ft 6 in)
Height	1.96 m	(6 ft 5 in)
Performance		
Max speed	185 km/h	(100 kt, 115 mph)
Cruising speed	121 km/h	(65 kt, 75 mph)
Initial climb	305 m/min	(1,000 fpm)
Range	240 km	(130 nm, 150 miles)
Weights		
Max takeoff	442 kg	(975 lbs)
Useful load	227 kg	(500 lbs)

Rans S-12 and S-14 Airaile — USA

Rans Inc. has designed the S-12 as a simple and economical two-seat ultralight which can be quickly constructed by the amateur builder at very low cost. It has an open cockpit pod section with a tubular aluminium tail boom and a strut-braced and supported high wing. The pusher 47 h.p. Rotax 503 engine is mounted on the rear wing centre section. The S-12 has a fixed tricycle undercarriage and the cabin and rear fuselage pylon area can be enclosed if necessary. The S-12XL is an improved higher-powered version with a more angled tail boom to give better takeoff clearance. The S-12S Super Airaile has a lower cabin and engine mounting position and new Dacron fabric covering. The S-14 Airaile is a single-seat development with a narrower fuselage pod, a larger Rotax 447, 503 or 582 engine and the two different high-performance wing options.

Rans S-16 Shekari — USA

The Shekari is a high-performance aerobatic light aircraft developed by Rans Inc. and sold as a quickly assembled kit. It departs from standard Rans tube and fabric construction in having an airframe based on a welded steel frame enclosed by pre-formed composite shells. The Shekari is a low-wing aircraft with a side-by-side two-seat cockpit which can be fitted with a tricycle or tailwheel undercarriage. Powerplants can range from the 80 h.p. Rotax 912 up to a 130 h.p. Continental IO-240. The prototype first flew in March 1997 and the first builder-completed S-16 was flown in late 1999.

Rans S-16 Shekari, N8072U

Specification	Rans S-16 Shekari	
Powerplant	One 129 h.p. (96.2 kW) Teledyne Continental IO-240 piston engine	
Dimensions		
Span	7.31 m	(24 ft 0 in)
Length	5.69 m	(18 ft 8 in)
Height	1.65 m	(5 ft 5 in)
Performance		
Max speed	386 km/h	(209 kt, 240 mph)
Cruising speed	274 km/h	(148 kt, 170 mph)
Initial climb	366 m/min	(1,200 fpm)
Range	1,360 km	(739 nm, 850 miles)
Weights		
Max takeoff	590 kg	(1,300 lbs)
Useful load	306 kg	(675 lbs)

Rawdon T-1 — USA

In 1951, Rawdon Brothers Aircraft launched the T-1 light aircraft which had been designed by Herb Rawdon for a variety of roles including crop spraying and light transport in remote conditions. It was based on the prewar Rawdon R-1 and 35 were built. The majority were T-1 trainers but Wichita-based Rawdon also built the T-1S and T-1CS crop sprayers and the T-1SD, which had a single seat and a larger chemical hopper in the centre fuselage. The T-1 was a strut-braced low-wing design with a tandem two-seat cockpit covered by a framed canopy. It was fitted with flaps and had a fixed tailwheel undercarriage and a tube and fabric airframe. Initial examples of the T-1 were powered by a 125 h.p. Lycoming O-290-C2 engine but later aircraft, including the crop sprayers, had a 150 h.p. Lycoming O-320. Four Rawdons are flying in the USA and one is believed to be active in El Salvador.

Rawdon T-1, N6810D

Specification	Rawdon T-1	
Powerplant	One 150 h.p. (111.8 kW) Textron Lycoming O-320 piston engine	
Dimensions		
Span	10.16 m	(33 ft 4 in)
Length	7.37 m	(24 ft 2 in)
Height	2.21 m	(7 ft 3 in)
Performance		
Max speed	225 km/h	(122 kt, 140 mph)
Cruising speed	201 km/h	(109 kt, 125 mph)
Initial climb	275 m/min	(900 fpm)
Range	800 km	(435 nm, 500 miles)
Weights		
Max takeoff	862 kg	(1,900 lbs)
Useful load	272 kg	(600 lbs)

Raytheon Hawker 800 — USA

In 1993, Raytheon Aircraft acquired all rights to the British Aerospace BAe.125 business jet and now builds the Hawker 800 in Wichita, Kansas. The BAe.125 was designed by de Havilland as the DH.125, which first flew on 13th August 1962. It went into production as the Hawker Siddeley HS.125 with first deliveries in October 1964 to civil customers, and 20 were delivered to the RAF as the HS.125 Srs.2 Dominie T.1 crew trainer. The low-wing HS.125 Series 1 had an eight-seat cabin and was powered by two rear-fuselage-mounted 3,000 lb.s.t. Bristol Siddeley Viper 520 turbojets. Further variants were the Series 1A for North American sale, the Srs.1A-522 with 3,360 lb.s.t. Viper 522s, the Srs.3, 3A (for USA) and 3B (other countries) with higher weights, and Srs.400A and 400B with an improved cockpit and higher weights. The Srs.600 had a stretched fuselage with a maximum 12-seat cabin, a faired-in cockpit roof, taller fin and 3,750 lb.s.t. Viper

Raytheon Hawker 800 (Cont.)

601 engines, and the Srs.700, which flew on 28th June 1976, was a Srs.600 with two 3,700 lb.s.t. Garrett TFE731-3 turbofans. In total 361 Viper-engined HS.125s and 215 of the Srs.700 were built. British Aerospace, which absorbed Hawker Siddeley in 1977, introduced the BAe.125-800, which was a Srs.700 with a longer wing, streamlined windshield, deeper rear fuselage and larger vertical tail. It was powered by two 4,300 lb.s.t. TFE731-5 turbofans and first flew on 26th May 1983. It is now built as the Raytheon Hawker 800XP which has 4,660 lb.s.t. TFE731-5BR engines and range, performance and systems improvements. A total of 475 of the –800 series had been built by the end of 1999 including a batch of U-125As for the Japanese MSDF and other specialised military special-missions versions. BAe also developed the BAe.1000 which was a BAe.125-800 with a stretched fuselage, increased fuel and 5,200 lb.s.t. Pratt & Whitney PW305 turbofans and flew on 16th June 1990. Some 52 were built but Raytheon has discontinued the model.

Specification	Raytheon Hawker 800XP	
Powerplant	Two 4,660 lb.s.t. (20.7 kN) Honeywell (Garrett) TFE731-5BR turbofans	
Dimensions		
Span	15.65 m	(51 ft 4 in)
Length	15.59 m	(51 ft 2 in)
Height	5.51 m	(18 ft 1 in)
Performance		
Max speed	861 km/h	(465 kt, 535 mph)
Cruising speed	853 km/h	(461 kt, 530 mph)
Takeoff distance	1,532 m	(5,025 ft)
Range	4,608 km	(2,504 nm, 2,880 miles)
Weights		
Max takeoff	12,698 kg	(28,000 lbs)
Useful load	5,376 kg	(11,855 lbs)

Hawker Siddeley HS.125-400B, 3D-AVL

Raytheon Hawker 800 (U-125A), JMSDF, 52-3003

Raytheon Premier I
— USA

The Premier I is the first of a new generation of business jets designed by Raytheon to give an entry-level aircraft slightly smaller than the Beechjet. The Premier I takes advantage of composite manufacturing technology pioneered on the Beech Starship and has a filament-wound carbon-fibre and resin honeycomb fuselage and metal wings. The two Williams Rolls FJ44 turbofans are mounted on the rear fuselage. The interior six-seat main cabin space is intended to be large enough to give passenger comfort on 1,500-mile sectors and the Premier I is designed to achieve a long-range cruise speed of Mach 0.8 and a maximum cruising altitude of 41,000 feet. The prototype was flown on 22nd December 1998 and five further development aircraft had flown by the end of 2000 with first deliveries to be made in 2001 and future production to run at 60 aircraft per annum.

Specification	Raytheon Premier I	
Powerplant	Two 2,300 lb.s.t. (10.23 kN) Williams Rolls FJ44-2A turbofans	
Dimensions		
Span	13.54 m	(44 ft 5 in)
Length	13.79 m	(45 ft 3 in)
Height	4.65 m	(15 ft 3 in)
Performance		
Max speed	855 km/h	(462 kt, 531 mph)
Cruising speed	821 km/h	(443 kt, 510 mph)
Takeoff distance	914 m	(3,000 ft)
Range	2,760 km	(1,500 nm, 1,727 miles)
Weights		
Max takeoff	5,669 kg	(12,500 lbs)
Useful load (est)	2,494 kg	(5,500 lbs)

Raytheon Premier I, N390TC

Rearwin 7000 and 8500 Sportster — USA

Rearwin Airplanes of Kansas City built a range of two- and three-seat light aircraft in the 1930s, the most successful being the Sportster series. The Model 7000 Sportster was a strut-braced high-wing monoplane with a tandem two-seat cabin and a 70 h.p. LeBlond radial engine, which was sometimes fully enclosed and sometimes left uncowled, and the first aircraft flew on 30th April 1935. It was produced for the flying school market and as a private sporting aircraft. The Model 8500, which appeared shortly after, had a strengthened airframe and an 85 h.p. LeBlond 5DF engine, and the Model 9000 had a 90 h.p. Warner Scarab Junior or LeBlond or Ken Royce engines of equivalent power. The Sportster could be flown on skis or floats and proved to be a very adaptable aircraft, used as a trainer by the Siamese Air Force and exported to countries such as Australia, Brazil, Peru, the Philippines and Rhodesia. A total of 261 were built by Rearwin and 12 were produced in Sweden as the Götaverken GV-38. The later Rearwin Cloudster and Skyranger are referred to under the entry for Commonwealth. Around 40 Sportsters remain in private ownership.

Rearwin 8500 Sportster, G-AEOF

Specification	Rearwin 8500 Sportster	
Powerplant	One 85 h.p. (63.3 kW) LeBlond 5DF piston engine	
Dimensions		
Span	10.67 m	(35 ft 0 in)
Length	6.78 m	(22 ft 3 in)
Height	2.06 m	(6 ft 9 in)
Performance		
Max speed	187 km/h	(101 kt, 116 mph)
Cruising speed	166 km/h	(90 kt, 103 mph)
Initial climb	213 m/min	(700 fpm)
Range	768 km	(417 nm, 480 miles)
Weights		
Max takeoff	639 kg	(1,410 lbs)
Useful load	263 kg	(580 lbs)

Refly Pelican — Russia

Developed from the Che-22 amateur-built aircraft of the early 1990s and the later Che-25, the Pelican is a light amphibian marketed as a standard or 'quick-build' kit for amateur construction. It has a strut-braced high wing which mounts two 66 h.p. Rotax 582 or, alternatively, 80 h.p. Rotax 912 piston engines. The three-seat cabin is fully enclosed and is entered via upward-opening transparent doors which can be removed if the aircraft is to be flown in open configuration. It can be fitted with full dual controls and the fuselage, which is formed from premoulded fibreglass shells, is equipped with a tail-wheel undercarriage with main units which retract forwards and upwards to allow water landings. The Pelican is promoted and manufactured by Refly Inc. of St. Petersburg and is being marketed in the USA.

Refly Pelican, RA-02777

Specification	Refly Pelican	
Powerplant	Two 66 h.p. (49.2 kW) Rotax 582 piston engines	
Dimensions		
Span	11.5 m	(37 ft 9 in)
Length	6.7 m	(22 ft 0 in)
Height	2.2 m	(7 ft 3 in)
Performance		
Max speed	160 km/h	(86 kt, 99 mph)
Cruising speed	140 km/h	(75 kt, 87 mph)
Initial climb	360 m/min	(1,181 fpm)
Range	540 km	(294 nm, 338 miles)
Weights		
Max takeoff	800 kg	(1,764 lbs)
Useful load	450 kg	(992 lbs)

Remos Gemini and Mirage — Germany

Originally developed in Poland in the mid-1980s, the G-2 Gemini Ultra is a side-by-side two-seat high-wing ultralight which has been marketed as a factory-complete aircraft by Remos Aircraft in Germany. It was powered, initially, by engines in the 65 h.p. range including the Rotax 582, Guzzi-4 and Wankel AE.50R, but later models have been fitted with the 80 h.p. Rotax 912 which improves performance substantially. The Gemini Ultra, of which around 35 are believed to have been built, is constructed from composite sandwich materials with fabric covering on the wings and is fitted with a fixed tricycle undercarriage and a ballistic emergency parachute system. The Remos G-3 Mirage, which replaced the Gemini and first flew on 20th September 1997, is a more elegant aircraft with a redesigned streamlined fuselage and modified fully composite wings which fold for transport and storage. More than 60 Mirages had been delivered by the end of 1999.

Remos G-3 Mirage, D-MSBG

Specification	Remos G-3 Mirage	
Powerplant	One 80 h.p. (59.6 kW) Rotax 912 piston engine	
Dimensions		
Span	9.8 m	(32 ft 2 in)
Length	6.47 m	(21 ft 3 in)
Height	1.7 m	(5 ft 7 in)
Performance		
Max speed	210 km/h	(113 kt, 130 mph)
Cruising speed	195 km/h	(105 kt, 121 mph)
Initial climb	348 m/min	(1,142 fpm)
Range	894 km	(485 nm, 559 miles)
Weights		
Max takeoff	450 kg	(992 lbs)
Useful load	166 kg	(366 lbs)

Republic P-47 Thunderbolt — USA

The Thunderbolt was one of the largest single-engined fighters to be deployed in World War II and the few remaining examples are much sought after by warbird owners in the USA. Dominated by its 2,000 h.p. Pratt & Whitney Wasp R-2800 radial engine, the P-47 was derived from earlier Seversky fighter designs and made its first flight on 6th May 1941. It was a low-wing aircraft with a retractable tailwheel undercarriage and it had six wing-mounted Browning machine guns. From the P-47C onwards, a belly hardpoint for a drop tank or 500 lbs bomb was also provided and later variants had additional underwing pylons. The initial P-47B and P-47C had a turtle-back fuselage with an integral cabin but from the middle of the P-47D production run (P-47D-25RE) the rear fuselage was cut down and a bubble canopy was fitted to provide much improved all-round vision. The P-47M had an improved turbocharger and the final P-47N variant was a long-range aircraft for Pacific operations. In total 15,676 Thunderbolts were built, the majority being the P-47D. At least 13 Thunderbolts remain airworthy.

Republic P-47D, 433240 (N4747P)

Specification	Republic P-47D-25RE	
Powerplant	One 2,300 h.p. (1,715 kW) Pratt & Whitney R-2800-59 piston engine	
Dimensions		
Span	12.42 m	(40 ft 9 in)
Length	11 m	(36 ft 1 in)
Height	4.32 m	(14 ft 2 in)
Performance		
Max speed	690 km/h	(373 kt, 429 mph)
Cruising speed	563 km/h	(304 kt, 350 mph)
Initial climb	847 m/min	(2,780 fpm)
Range	1,520 km	(826 nm, 950 miles)
Weights		
Max takeoff	7,937 kg	(17,500 lbs)
Useful load	3,084 kg	(6,800 lbs)

Republic RC-3 Seabee and Twin Bee — USA

In the postwar boom years for light aviation, the Republic Aviation Corporation produced the RC-3 Seabee and completed 1,060 examples, including prototypes, during 1946 and 1947. Based on the C-1 Thunderbolt Amphibian which first flew in November 1944, the Seabee was an all-metal high-wing amphibian with a four-seat fully enclosed cabin, a 215 h.p. Franklin 6A8-215-B8F pusher engine mounted on the wing centre section, a tailwheel undercarriage with the main wheels retracting upwards and backwards and a rear fuselage which was sharply cut away to provide propeller clearance. Production ceased in 1947 to make way for military programmes. The Seabee was underpowered and many have been fitted with larger engines of up to 350 h.p. A total of 24 aircraft have also been converted as five-seat Twin Bees by United Consultants Corp. (STOL Aircraft) with two 180 h.p. Lycoming IO-360-B1D engines mounted as tractor units on the upper wing surfaces. Around 500 Seabees remain registered around the world.

Specification	Republic RC-3 Seabee	
Powerplant	One 215 h.p. (160.3 kW) Franklin 6A8-215-B8F piston engine	
Dimensions		
Span	11.48 m	(37 ft 8 in)
Length	8.51 m	(27 ft 11 in)
Height	2.92 m	(9 ft 7 in)
Performance		
Max speed	193 km/h	(104 kt, 120 mph)
Cruising speed	167 km/h	(90 kt, 104 mph)
Initial climb	213 m/min	(700 fpm)
Range	880 km	(478 nm, 550 miles)
Weights		
Max takeoff	1,361 kg	(3,000 lbs)
Useful load	476 kg	(1,050 lbs)

Republic RC-3 Seabee, N565CB

Revolution Mini-500 — USA

The Revolution Mini-500 recreational light helicopter has been sold as a kit for home assembly by Revolution Helicopters of Excelsior Springs, Missouri and was first introduced in 1994. Externally, it is modelled on the Hughes 500D and has an egg-shaped fuselage pod containing the single-seat cockpit and engine installation, a fixed skid undercarriage, a slim tail boom and a T-tail. The standard Mini-500B is powered by a 67 h.p. Rotax 582 engine. It is constructed from pre-moulded composite shells and has a two-bladed main rotor made from Kevlar and aluminium. Basic construction time is claimed to be under 200 hours and over 450 kits have been sold with examples flying in Holland, South Africa and Brazil as well as substantial numbers in the United States. The prototype of a side-by-side two-seat version, the Voyager 500, has also been flown but Revolution suspended operations and sale of all its kits in October 1999.

United Consultants Twin Bee, N9508U

Revolution Mini-500, PH-RHC

Specification	Revolution Mini-500B	
Powerplant	One 67 h.p. (49.96 kW) Rotax 582 piston engine	
Dimensions		
Rotor diameter	5.84 m	(19 ft 2 in)
Length	6.86 m	(22 ft 6 in)
Height	2.46 m	(8 ft 1 in)
Performance		
Max speed	177 km/h	(96 kt, 110 mph)
Cruising speed	153 km/h	(83 kt, 95 mph)
Initial climb	396 m/min	(1,300 fpm)
Range	360 km	(196 nm, 225 miles)
Weights		
Max takeoff	381 kg	(840 lbs)
Useful load	161 kg	(355 lbs)

Rockwell-DASA Ranger 2000, N104NA

RFB Fantrainer — Germany

The Fantrainer was the outcome of experiments carried out by Rhein Flugzeugbau into aircraft driven by centre-mounted ducted fans. The experimental Fanliner used a pair of Wankel rotary piston engines but the AWI-2 Fantrainer, first flown on 27th October 1977, was designed for an Allison 250 turboprop. The Fantrainer was intended as a military trainer giving the characteristics of a jet trainer at lower cost. It has a tandem two-seat forward fuselage, a T-tail and retractable tricycle undercarriage, and a fuselage centre section containing the engine and ducted fan. The only customer was the Royal Thai Air Force who received 16 aircraft, some of which were locally assembled. The Fantrainer 400 has a 420 s.h.p. Allison 250-C20B and the Fantrainer 600 has a 650 s.h.p. Allison 250-C30 engine. A few of these remain in service. RFB (DASA) also built two prototypes of the Ranger 2000 in association with Rockwell. This was based on the Fantrainer airframe but had a conventional Pratt & Whitney JT15D-5C turbofan. It was entered in the USAF JPATS competition but was unsuccessful and has not been progressed further.

RFB Fantrainer 400, Luftwaffe 9876

Specification	RFB Fantrainer 400	
Powerplant	One 420 s.h.p. (313 kW) Allison 250-C20B turboprop	
Dimensions		
Span	9.73 m	(31 ft 11 in)
Length	9.47 m	(31 ft 1 in)
Height	3.17 m	(10 ft 5 in)
Performance		
Max speed	371 km/h	(200 kt, 230 mph)
Cruising speed	334 km/h	(180 kt, 207 mph)
Initial climb	472 m/min	(1,550 fpm)
Range	1,180 km	(640 nm, 737 miles)
Weights		
Max takeoff	1,800 kg	(3,969 lbs)
Useful load	685 kg	(1,510 lbs)

RLU Breezy — USA

The appropriately named Breezy was designed by Messrs. Roloff, Liposky and Unger of Chicago and first flown on 7th August 1964. It is a strut-braced high-wing machine with a completely open tubular-steel fuselage structure providing tandem seats for two people ahead of the wing. It has a fixed tricycle undercarriage and can be powered by a variety of engines in the 90 h.p. to 125 h.p. range. The engine is mounted as a pusher at the rear of the wing mounting structure. The Breezy was marketed in the form of plans for home construction. More than 500 sets of plans were sold and over 200 Breezys are believed to have been built.

RLU Breezy (Cont.)

RLU Breezy, N255Y

Specification	RLU Breezy	
Powerplant	One 90 h.p. (67.1 kW) Teledyne Continental C90-8F-P piston engine	
Dimensions		
Span	10.06 m	(33 ft 0 in)
Length	6.86 m	(22 ft 6 in)
Height	2.59 m	(8 ft 6 in)
Performance		
Max speed	161 km/h	(87 kt, 100 mph)
Cruising speed	129 km/h	(70 kt, 80 mph)
Initial climb	183 m/min	(600 fpm)
Range	400 km	(217 nm, 250 miles)
Weights		
Max takeoff	544 kg	(1,200 lbs)
Useful load	227 kg	(500 lbs)

Robin DR.253, DR.300 and DR.400 — France

Pierre Robin's company, Centre Est Aéronautique (renamed Avions Robin in 1969), established itself in the 1960s as a principal constructor of the wood and fabric Jodel DR.100 Ambassadeur/Sicile series and the improved DR.250 (see separate entry). On 30th March 1967, the prototype DR.253 Regent was flown and this was a redesigned DR.250 with a wider fuselage giving a larger four-seat cabin and a fixed tricycle undercarriage. It was powered by a 180 h.p. Lycoming O-360-D2A engine and 100 were built. The same airframe was developed into the DR.300 series of trainers and tourers which initially consisted of the DR.315 Petit Prince (115 h.p. Lycoming O-235-C2A), DR.340 Major (140 h.p. O-320-E2A) and DR.360 Chevalier (160 h.p. O-320-D2A). Several further versions with different engines followed, including the DR.300-180 with an O-360-A3A and the glider-towing DR.300-180R Remorqueur. In 1972, the DR.400 series was introduced to upgrade the DR.300 models. Among many changes, the DR.400 had a forward-sliding canopy in place of the earlier windshield and doors. The many variants, with designations suffixed with the engine power, included the DR.400-100 Cadet, DR.400-108 Dauphin 80, DR.400-125, DR.400-140B Major, DR.400-160 Chevalier/Knight/Major, DR.400-180 Regent and Remorqueur and DR.400-200R Remo-200. The higher-powered models were all modified with additional side windows in 1994. The most recent model, introduced in 1998, is the DR.500 President (DR.400-200i) which has a taller and wider cabin and a 200 h.p. Lycoming IO-360-A1B6 engine. Over 2,170 of the DR.300 and DR.400 series had been built by the end of 2000.

Robin DR.315 Petit Prince, F-BRFH

Robin DR.400-200i (DR.500) President, G-MOTI

Robin HR.100-250TR, F-BXGV

Specification	Robin DR.400-180 Regent	
Powerplant	One 180 h.p. (134.2 kW) Textron Lycoming O-360-A piston engine	
Dimensions		
Span	8.71 m	(28 ft 7 in)
Length	6.96 m	(22 ft 10 in)
Height	2.24 m	(7 ft 4 in)
Performance		
Max speed	278 km/h	(150 kt, 173 mph)
Cruising speed	259 km/h	(140 kt, 161 mph)
Initial climb	252 m/min	(826 fpm)
Range	1,450 km	(788 nm, 906 miles)
Weights		
Max takeoff	1,100 kg	(2,425 lbs)
Useful load	500 kg	(1,102 lbs)

Robin R.1180TD Aiglon, EI-BIS

Robin HR.100 and R.1180
— France

Avions Robin moved away from its traditional wood and fabric construction and cranked Jodel wing with the all-metal monocoque HR.100, designed by Chris Heintz. The HR.100 retained the general layout of other Robin designs with a low wing, fixed tricycle undercarriage and forward-sliding cockpit canopy and the prototype first flew on 3rd April 1969. The initial production HR.100-200B Royal had a 200 h.p. Lycoming IO-360-A1D engine but the later HR.100-210 Safari was fitted with a 210 h.p. IO-360-D. Robin further developed the airframe as the HR.100-250TR which had a 250 h.p. Continental Tiara IO-540-C4B5 engine, an enlarged vertical tail and a retractable tricycle undercarriage, and a batch of these aircraft was delivered to the French government. In total, 176 of the HR.100 series were built. The R.1180T Aiglon was an HR.100 with a lighter airframe, a swept fin and a 180 h.p. Lycoming IO-360-A3AD engine and this first flew on 25th March 1977. Robin built 66 Aiglons including 36 of the R.1180TD Aiglon II with new instrumentation and an external baggage-compartment door.

Specification	Robin HR.100-210 Safari	
Powerplant	One 210 h.p. (156.6 kW) Teledyne Continental IO-360-D piston engine	
Dimensions		
Span	8.86 m	(29 ft 1 in)
Length	7.31 m	(24 ft 0 in)
Height	2.26 m	(7 ft 5 in)
Performance		
Max speed	285 km/h	(154 kt, 177 mph)
Cruising speed	254 km/h	(137 kt, 158 mph)
Initial climb	285 m/min	(935 fpm)
Range	1,475 km	(802 nm, 922 miles)
Weights		
Max takeoff	1,260 kg	(2,780 lbs)
Useful load	544 kg	(1,200 lbs)

Robin HR.200 and R.2100 — France

Under the design leadership of Chris Heintz, Robin developed the HR.200 two-seat trainer, flying the first aircraft on 29th July 1971. It was, essentially, a scaled-down version of the HR.100 four-seat tourer and it had a fixed tricycle undercarriage, a low wing and all-metal construction. The cabin, which was enclosed by a split bubble canopy with a forward-sliding front section, had side-by-side seating and dual controls. It was built with various equipment options, the basic versions being the HR.200/100 Club with a 108 h.p. Lycoming O-235-H2C engine and the HR.200/120B with a 118 h.p. Lycoming O-235-L2A. Following a production lull, it was reintroduced in 1993 as the R.200/120B with a larger rudder and a new interior and instrumentation. A companion model was the 108 h.p. R.2100 Super Club which was stressed for aerobatics and had a modified vertical tail. The R.2160 Alpha Sport was the higher-powered version with a 160 h.p. Lycoming O-320-D2A. Total production of the two-seat Robins exceeds 240 aircraft to date.

Robin HR.200/100 Club, G-BDJN

Robin R.2160, VH-DXY

Specification	Robin R.2160	
Powerplant	One 160 h.p. (119 kW) Textron Lycoming O-320-D2A piston engine	
Dimensions		
Span	8.03 m	(26 ft 4 in)
Length	7.09 m	(23 ft 3 in)
Height	2.13 m	(7 ft 0 in)
Performance		
Max speed	256 km/h	(138 kt, 159 mph)
Cruising speed	241 km/h	(130 kt, 150 mph)
Initial climb	312 m/min	(1,025 fpm)
Range	792 km	(430 nm, 495 miles)
Weights		
Max takeoff	900 kg	(1,984 lbs)
Useful load	340 kg	(750 lbs)

Robin R.3000 — France

The R.3000 was a completely new all-metal design by Robin intended as a replacement for the HR.100 four-seat tourer. It had a low wing with tapered outer panels, a large four-seat cabin with a domed roof and forward-sliding section for entry, a T-tail and a fixed tricycle undercarriage. The company flew the prototype, powered by a 100 h.p. Lycoming engine, on 8th December 1980. Production aircraft were offered as the R.3120 (later R.3000/120) with a 116 h.p. Lycoming O-235-L2A, the R.3140 (R.3000/140) with a 140 h.p. O-320-D2A and the R.3160 (R.3000/160) with a 160 h.p. O-360-A3A engine. Current production is to customer order and more than 70 R.3000s have been built with examples flying in Germany, Switzerland, Holland, Luxembourg, the UK, Sweden and France.

Robin R.3140, PH-KAO

Specification	Robin R.3000/160	
Powerplant	One 160 h.p. (119.3 kW) Textron Lycoming O-360-A3A piston engine	
Dimensions		
Span	9.8 m	(32 ft 2 in)
Length	7.52 m	(24 ft 8 in)
Height	2.67 m	(8 ft 9 in)
Performance		
Max speed	270 km/h	(146 kt, 168 mph)
Cruising speed	254 km/h	(137 kt, 158 mph)
Initial climb	267 m/min	(875 fpm)
Range	1,600 km	(870 nm, 1,000 miles)
Weights		
Max takeoff	1,150 kg	(2,536 lbs)
Useful load	500 kg	(1,102 lbs)

Robin ATL — France

Robin developed the ATL (avion très léger) as a low-cost modern-technology trainer for French flying clubs, flying the prototype on 17th June 1983. For maximum economy it had a 47 h.p. JPX 4T-60A engine but the ATL-L version with a 70 h.p. Limbach L.2000-D2A was also available. The ATL was built with a GRP composite fuselage and wooden wings of fairly high aspect ratio. The side-by-side cabin was enclosed by a forward-hinged canopy and it had a slim rear fuselage with a V-tail and a fixed tricycle undercarriage. Two versions were sold: the ATL Club for training and the ATL Voyage for cross-country flying. Production of the ATL totalled 135 aircraft and due to certification problems most were sold in France with a few in Switzerland and Italy. The majority are currently operational.

Robin ATL, F-GFRF

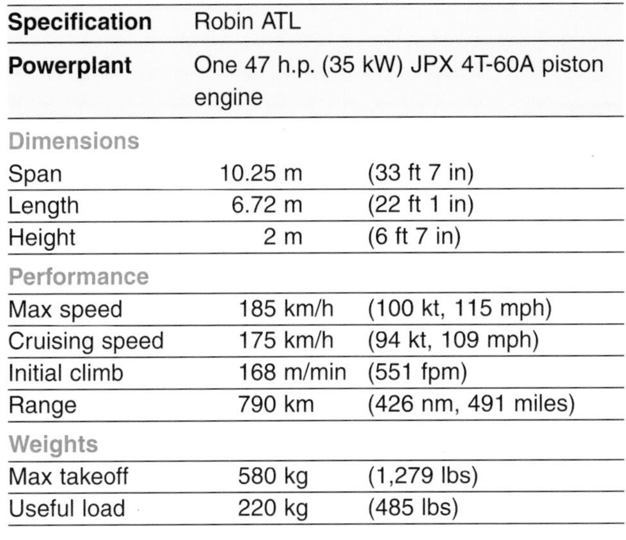

Specification	Robin ATL	
Powerplant	One 47 h.p. (35 kW) JPX 4T-60A piston engine	
Dimensions		
Span	10.25 m	(33 ft 7 in)
Length	6.72 m	(22 ft 1 in)
Height	2 m	(6 ft 7 in)
Performance		
Max speed	185 km/h	(100 kt, 115 mph)
Cruising speed	175 km/h	(94 kt, 109 mph)
Initial climb	168 m/min	(551 fpm)
Range	790 km	(426 nm, 491 miles)
Weights		
Max takeoff	580 kg	(1,279 lbs)
Useful load	220 kg	(485 lbs)

Robinson R.22 — USA

The R.22, designed by Frank Robinson, is the most successful light training and personal helicopter in current production. It has a basic pod and boom design with side-by-side seating for two and the engine is positioned in an open cowling below and behind the cabin driving a two-blade main rotor and a conventional tail anti-torque rotor. The prototype, which flew on 28th August 1975, had a 115 h.p. Lycoming O-235 engine, but production R.22s have a 124 h.p. O-320-A2B. The R.22HP is a modified version with a 131 h.p. O-320-B2C engine and a larger skid undercarriage, and the improved R.22 Alpha benefited from a higher gross weight and a repositioned tail boom. Robinson's current model is the R.22 Beta with a rotor brake and a larger instrument panel, and the Beta II has a 180 h.p. Lycoming O-360 engine and other refinements. The R.22 has been fitted with floats as the Mariner and is widely used by police authorities, wildlife control agencies and training organisations, and has been adopted by the Turkish Air Force for training. Production exceeds 3,000 aircraft to date from the Torrance, California factory.

Robinson R.22 Alpha, N84645

Specification	Robinson R.22 Beta II	
Powerplant	One 180 h.p. (97.7 kW) Textron Lycoming O-360-J2A piston engine	
Dimensions		
Rotor diameter	7.67 m	(25 ft 2 in)
Length	6.3 m	(20 ft 8 in)
Height	2.72 m	(8 ft 11 in)
Performance		
Max speed	190 km/h	(103 kt, 118 mph)
Cruising speed	177 km/h	(96 kt, 110 mph)
Initial climb	305 m/min	(1,000 fpm)
Range	336 km	(183 nm, 210 miles)
Weights		
Max takeoff	621 kg	(1,370 lbs)
Useful load	238 kg	(525 lbs)

Robinson R.44 Astro — USA

Following on from the success of the two-seat R.22 helicopter Frank Robinson designed the four-seat R.44 Astro. The prototype made its first flight at Torrance, California on 31st March 1990. The R.44 follows the same general layout as the R.22 but has a longer main fuselage pod containing a full four-seat cabin accessed by four separate doors. It retains the skid undercarriage and the single-stick dual-control system familiar to R.22 operators and is unique in being the only production four-seat non-turbine-engined helicopter. Specialised variants include the R.44 Clipper with large pontoon floats introduced in 1996 and the R.44 Newscopter equipped with gyro-stabilised cameras for electronic news gathering. The latest Robinson R.44 Raven has a new hydraulically actuated flight control system. Robinson had delivered over 900 R.44s by the end of 2000, more than half of which were exported.

Robinson R.44 Astro (Cont.)

Robinson R.44 Astro, G-OKES

Specification	Robinson R.44 Astro	
Powerplant	One 225 h.p. (168 kW) Textron Lycoming O-540 piston engine	
Dimensions		
Rotor diameter	10.06 m	(33 ft 0 in)
Length	9.07 m	(29 ft 9 in)
Height	3.28 m	(10 ft 9 in)
Performance		
Max speed	241 km/h	(130 kt, 150 mph)
Cruising speed	204 km/h	(110 kt, 127 mph)
Initial climb	304 m/min	(1,000 fpm)
Range	640 km	(348 nm, 400 miles)
Weights		
Max takeoff	1,088 kg	(2,400 lbs)
Useful load	444 kg	(980 lbs)

Rockwell Sabreliner — USA

North American Aviation Inc. (later acquired by Rockwell International) designed the Sabreliner light twin-jet transport to meet the US Air Force's UTX requirement for a fast general utility and training aircraft. The prototype NA.246 first flew on 16th September 1958 and 172 were built as the T-39A utility trainer (NA.265), T-39B NASARR radar trainer (NA.270) and US Navy T-39D (NA.277) with 3,000 lb.s.t. Pratt & Whitney J60-P-3 turbojets. These were followed by the commercial ten-passenger business jet Sabreliner 40 (NA.265-40) which differed in having three cabin windows each side and JT12A-6A engines. The Sabreliner 60 (NA.265-60) had a stretched fuselage with additional cabin windows and 3,300 lb.s.t. JT12A-8A engines, and the Sabreliner 65 was an improved Sabreliner 60 with a new supercritical wing and Garrett TFE731-3 turbofans. The US Navy received 13 Sabreliner 60s, designated CT-39G, as fleet tactical support aircraft and also acquired 17 civil Sabreliner 40s for use in the UNFO programme as T-39Ns. The Sabre 75 (NA.370) was a substantially redesigned version of the Sabreliner 60 with a deeper fuselage with square windows which first flew on 4th December 1969, and the Sabre 75A (NA.265-80) was the final model, flown in 1972, with General Electric CF700-202 turbofans. Rockwell (later Sabreliner Corp.) built 419 civil Sabreliners of which over 300 are in service.

Rockwell T-39N, US Navy Bu.165521 (N313NT)

Rockwell Sabreliner 60, LV-WOF

Specification	Rockwell Sabreliner 60	
Powerplant	Two 3,300 lb.s.t. (14.68 kN) Pratt & Whitney JT12A-8A turbojets	
Dimensions		
Span	13.54 m	(44 ft 5 in)
Length	14.73 m	(48 ft 4 in)
Height	4.88 m	(16 ft 0 in)
Performance		
Max speed	906 km/h	(490 kt, 563 mph)
Cruising speed	856 km/h	(463 kt, 532 mph)
Initial climb	1,433 m/min	(4,700 fpm)
Range	3,200 km	(1,739 nm, 2,000 miles)
Weights		
Max takeoff	9,070 kg	(20,000 lbs)
Useful load	4,252 kg	(9,376 lbs)

Rockwell T-2 Buckeye — USA

The Buckeye is an advanced jet trainer designed to the requirements of the U.S. Navy to fill a range of mission roles including carrier deck landing training and weapons instruction. It was designed by North American Aviation (later Rockwell) with a stepped tandem two-seat cockpit, a straight mid-set wing with wingtip tanks and a raised cruciform tail. The first YT2J-1 (NA.241), which was flown on 31st January 1958, was powered by a single 3,400 lb.s.t. Westinghouse J34-WE-36 turbojet positioned under the fuselage with a dual nose intake. As the T2J-1 Buckeye (later T-2A) it entered service in mid-1959 and 207 were delivered. The T-2B was a substantially modified and higher-powered version with two 3,000 lb.s.t Pratt & Whitney J60-P-6 turbojets mounted side by side, additional fuel and a taller undercarriage, and this model replaced the T-2A from 1965 onwards. A total of 328 were delivered, the majority being the T-2C with General Electric J85-GE-4 engines. Rockwell also built the T-2D export model, which was sold to Venezuela, and the T-2E, which was acquired by Greece. Some 64 export sales were made to these customers and the Buckeye continues in service with them and in large numbers with the US Navy.

Rockwell T-2E Buckeye, Greek AF, 160069

Specification	Rockwell T-2C Buckeye	
Powerplant	Two 2,950 lb.s.t. (13.1 kN) General Electric J85-GE-4 turbojets	
Dimensions		
Span	11.63 m	(38 ft 2 in)
Length	11.68 m	(38 ft 4 in)
Height	4.42 m	(14 ft 6 in)
Performance		
Max speed	869 km/h	(470 kt, 540 mph)
Cruising speed	772 km/h	(417 kt, 480 mph)
Initial climb	1,890 m/min	(6,200 fpm)
Range	1,680 km	(913 nm, 1,050 miles)
Weights		
Max takeoff	5,977 kg	(13,179 lbs)
Useful load	2,297 kg	(5,064 lbs)

Rockwell Lark Commander and Darter — USA

Rockwell Standard acquired Volaircraft Inc. in July 1965 and took over the Volair 10 light aircraft. It was a strut-braced all-metal high-wing machine with a three-seat 'omni-vision' cabin incorporating a rear-vision window and it had a vertical tail which appeared to be swept forward. The initial Volair 10 was powered by a 135 h.p. Lycoming O-290-D2C engine but the Volair 10A (also known as the Volaircraft 1050) which soon replaced it had a four-seat cabin and a 150 h.p. Lycoming O-320-A2B powerplant. Rockwell's Aero Commander subsidiary built this as the Aero Commander 100A Darter and total Rockwell and Volair production had reached 360 aircraft when manufacture ceased in 1969. The Rockwell Lark Commander 100-180 was a higher-powered version with increased weights. It had a swept fin in place of the angular tail of the Darter, the engine cowling was larger and more streamlined and it had new wheel fairings and a higher-quality interior finish. The Lark Commander was powered by a 180 h.p. Lycoming O-360-A2F engine and 213 were built by Aero Commander between 1968 and 1971.

Rockwell Commander 100A Darter, D-EHLP

Rockwell Lark Commander 100-180, N3706X

Rockwell Lark Commander and Darter (Cont.)

Specification	Rockwell Lark Commander 100-180	
Powerplant	One 180 h.p. (134.2 kW) Textron Lycoming O-360-A2F piston engine	
Dimensions		
Span	10.67 m	(35 ft 0 in)
Length	8.28 m	(27 ft 2 in)
Height	3.07 m	(10 ft 1 in)
Performance		
Max speed	222 km/h	(120 kt, 138 mph)
Cruising speed	212 km/h	(115 kt, 132 mph)
Initial climb	219 m/min	(718 fpm)
Range	896 km	(486 nm, 560 miles)
Weights		
Max takeoff	1,122 kg	(2,475 lbs)
Useful load	428 kg	(943 lbs)

Specification	Aero Commander 200D	
Powerplant	One 285 h.p. (212.5 kW) Teledyne Continental IO-520-A piston engine	
Dimensions		
Span	9.3 m	(30 ft 6 in)
Length	7.42 m	(24 ft 4 in)
Height	2.24 m	(7 ft 4 in)
Performance		
Max speed	370 km/h	(200 kt, 230 mph)
Cruising speed	349 km/h	(189 kt, 217 mph)
Initial climb	442 m/min	(1,450 fpm)
Range	1,968 km	(1,070 nm, 1,230 miles)
Weights		
Max takeoff	1,361 kg	(3,000 lbs)
Useful load	481 kg	(1,060 lbs)

Rockwell Commander 200 — USA

The Meyers Model 200 was a development of the MAC-145 two-seat light aircraft (see separate entry) with a lengthened fuselage providing a full four-seat cabin. It had a low wing and a retractable tricycle undercarriage, and the initial aircraft, which first flew on 8th September 1953, was powered by a 240 h.p. Continental O-470-M engine. The production Meyers 200A, built from 1958 onwards, had a 260 h.p. fuel-injected Continental IO-470-D and the 200C had a 285 h.p. Continental IO-520-A. Meyers built 41 examples of the Model 200 before they were acquired by Rockwell Standard in July 1965. Renamed Aero Commander 200D (later Rockwell Commander 200 and Spark Commander), the aircraft was given improved interior trim and some other minor changes, and production continued until 1967 by which time 88 Model 200Ds had been built.

Rockwell Commander 200D, N898LF

Rockwell Fuji Commander 700 — USA/Japan

The Model 700 (Fuji FA-300) piston-engined executive aircraft was developed as a joint venture by Fuji Heavy Industries and Rockwell's General Aviation Divisions. The 700 was a pressurised low-wing twin powered by a pair of 340 h.p. Lycoming TIO-540-R2AD turbocharged engines and it had accommodation for four passengers and two crew in a cabin entered through a rear airstair door. Fuji flew the first prototype on 13th November 1975, followed by the Rockwell prototype on 25th February 1976. First customer deliveries took place in August 1978. The basic Model 700 was underpowered and Rockwell built two prototypes of the Model 710 which had 450 h.p. Lycoming engines. However, the Model 700's poor sales record resulted in production terminating in December 1978, at which time 32 aircraft had been built. At least half of these are still flying.

Rockwell Commander 700, C-GBCM

Specification	Rockwell Commander 700	
Powerplant	Two 340 h.p. (253.5 kW) Textron Lycoming TIO-540-R2AD piston engines	
Dimensions		
Span	12.93 m	(42 ft 5 in)
Length	11.99 m	(39 ft 4 in)
Height	4.04 m	(13 ft 3 in)
Performance		
Max speed	428 km/h	(231 kt, 266 mph)
Cruising speed	406 km/h	(219 kt, 252 mph)
Initial climb	445 m/min	(1,460 fpm)
Range	1,296 km	(704 nm, 810 miles)
Weights		
Max takeoff	2,993 kg	(6,600 lbs)
Useful load	998 kg	(2,200 lbs)

Rockwell B-1B Lancer, USAF 85-0086

Rockwell B-1 Lancer
— USA

Rockwell (now Boeing) originally designed the supersonic B-1A nuclear bomber to meet the USAF Advanced Manned Strategic Aircraft Requirement. The B-1A, which first flew on 23rd December 1974, had a streamlined fuselage with a cruciform tail and a forward four-man crew compartment. It has swing wings to maximise its speed range and its four reheated General Electric F101 turbofans are housed in two paired nacelles beneath the wing roots. The definitive production B-1B Lancer, which commenced deliveries in 1985, has modified weapons capacity consisting of three separate bomb bays in the fuselage belly with a maximum load of 75,000 lbs. and it can carry either conventional free-fall nuclear weapons, up to 84 standard 500-lb Mk.82 HE bombs or a variety of guided weapons including the AGM-69A short-range attack missile and AGM-86B air-launched cruise missile. In addition it has six external fuselage hardpoints. Rockwell built four B-1A development aircraft and delivered the last of 100 B-1Bs in January 1988. The majority of these continue in USAF service despite a series of operational and political problems which have affected the aircraft.

Specification	Rockwell (Boeing) B-1B Lancer	
Powerplant	Four 30,780 lb.s.t (136.9 kN) (wet) General Electric F101-GE-102 turbofans	
Dimensions		
Span	41.65 m	(136 ft 8 in)
Length	44.8 m	(147 ft 0 in)
Height	10.62 m	(34 ft 10 in)
Performance		
Max speed	1,328 km/h	(717 kt, 825 mph)
Cruising speed	1,014 km/h	(548 kt, 630 mph)
Range	11,928 km	(6,483 nm, 7,455 miles)
Weights		
Max takeoff	216,327 kg	(477,000 lbs)
Useful load	129,252 kg	(285,000 lbs)

Rockwell B-1B Lancer, USAF 85-0064

Rockwell-MBB X-31A
— USA/Germany

The X-31A is a cooperative project between Rockwell International and MBB (DASA) under a DARPA and German Defence Ministry contract managed by the US Navy to develop new, agile fighter technologies. Two prototypes have been built, the first flying on 1st March 1990, and the enhanced fighter manoeuvrability (EFM) features incorporated on the aircraft include a controllable foreplane and thrust vectoring using deflector paddles attached to the engine jet exhaust. The X-31A is a single-seater with a low-set delta wing fitted with leading edge slats and combined flap/ailerons and a conventional vertical tail, but no horizontal tail surface. The initial test programme was completed in 1995 but the X-31A is being reactivated for the second phase of the VECTOR programme which is likely to include Sweden and, possibly, Spain and involve testing of thrust vectoring developed by General Electric and the Spanish manufacturer ITP.

Rockwell-MBB X-31A (Cont.)

Rockwell-MBB X-31A, Bu.164584

Specification	Rockwell-MBB X-31A	
Powerplant	One 16,000 lb.s.t. (71.18 kN) (wet) General Electric F404-GE-400 turbofan	
Dimensions		
Span	7.26 m	(23 ft 10 in)
Length	13.21 m	(43 ft 4 in)
Height	4.44 m	(14 ft 7 in)
Performance		
Max speed	2,736 km/h	(1478 kt, 1,700 mph)
Initial climb	13,106 m/min	(43,000 fpm)
Range	1,120 km	(609 nm, 700 miles)
Weights		
Max takeoff	7,227 kg	(15,935 lbs)
Useful load	2,052 kg	(4,525 lbs)

Rollason Beta — UK

The single-seat Beta ultralight racing aircraft was the winning design by the Luton Group in a competition run by Rollason Aircraft & Engines in 1965, and four examples were subsequently built by Rollasons, the first of these making its maiden flight on 21st April 1967. The Beta was a wood and fabric aircraft with a low wing and an enclosed cockpit and it was intended to be powered by a 55 h.p. Volkswagen engine. However, the prototype was a Beta B.1 with a 65 h.p. Continental A65 engine and the majority of Betas have been the B.2 with a 90 h.p. Continental C90-8F. The B.4 was intended to have a 100 h.p. Continental O-200-A. In addition to the Rollason-built aircraft, at least six further Betas have been built or are under construction by amateurs from plans, including one in Australia.

Rollason Beta, G-AWHV

Specification	Rollason Beta B.2	
Powerplant	One 90 h.p. (67.1 kW) Teledyne Continental C90-8F piston engine	
Dimensions		
Span	6.22 m	(20 ft 5 in)
Length	5.08 m	(16 ft 8 in)
Height	1.73 m	(5 ft 8 in)
Performance		
Max speed	322 km/h	(174 kt, 200 mph)
Cruising speed	274 km/h	(148 kt, 170 mph)
Initial climb	549 m/min	(1,800 fpm)
Range	480 km	(261 nm, 300 miles)
Weights		
Max takeoff	393 kg	(866 lbs)
Useful load	132 kg	(290 lbs)

Rose Parrakeet — USA

The little A-1 Parrakeet single-seat biplane was produced by the Rose Aeroplane and Motor Company in 1936. It was of mixed construction with wooden wings, a tubular steel fuselage and fabric covering. It had a triangulated shock-strut tailwheel undercarriage and an open cockpit. The standard aircraft used a semi-cowled 37 h.p. Continental A-40-3 engine but some Parrakeets were the A-2 model fitted with a 50 h.p. Menasco M-50. It is believed that seven were built and all have survived with three being airworthy. After the war, the design was revived as the Hannaford Bee (or Rose-Rhinehart A4C) and a further nine examples were built.

Rose Parrakeet, NC13676

Specification	Rose Parrakeet A-1	
Powerplant	One 37 h.p. (27.59 kW) Teledyne Continental A-40-3 piston engine	
Dimensions		
Span	6.1 m	(20 ft 0 in)
Length	4.88 m	(16 ft 0 in)
Height	1.73 m	(5 ft 8 in)
Performance		
Max speed	161 km/h	(87 kt, 100 mph)
Cruising speed	137 km/h	(74 kt, 85 mph)
Initial climb	229 m/min	(750 fpm)
Range	544 km	(296 nm, 340 miles)
Weights		
Max takeoff	330 kg	(728 lbs)
Useful load	117 kg	(258 lbs)

Rotary Air Force RAF.2000 — Canada

The RAF.2000 is one of the most popular kit-built autogyros and is manufactured by Rotary Air Force in Canada. The initial model was the single-seat RAF.1000 which was a conventional light gyroplane with a pusher 100 h.p. Subaru EA82 engine and a fully enclosed cabin module. Current production is exclusively the RAF.2000, which is similar to the earlier aircraft and uses the same engine but has a side-by-side two-seat cockpit. It is sold in standard form and also as the deluxe GTX-SE version with improved performance. Several hundred RAF.2000s are flying worldwide, including 17 in the UK.

RAF.2000, G-BWAD

Specification	Rotary Air Force RAF.2000	
Powerplant	One 100 h.p. (74.56 kW) Subaru EA82 piston engine	
Dimensions		
Rotor diameter	9.14 m	(30 ft 0 in)
Length	4.14 m	(13 ft 7 in)
Height	2.49 m	(8 ft 2 in)
Performance		
Max speed	161 km/h	(87 kt, 100 mph)
Cruising speed	121 km/h	(65 kt, 75 mph)
Initial climb	305 m/min	(1,000 fpm)
Range	672 km	(365 nm, 420 miles)
Weights		
Max takeoff	510 kg	(1,125 lbs)
Useful load	256 kg	(565 lbs)

RotorWay Scorpion and Exec — USA

RotorWay International is the leading manufacturer of kits for homebuilt helicopter enthusiasts. The original Scorpion, designed by B.J. Schramm, was based on the Schramm Javelin prototype which flew in August 1965. It was an open single-seater based on a tubular-steel structure with a formed aluminium body shell and was powered by a 100 h.p. Mercury powerboat engine. The Scorpion was sold in kit form and was followed by the Scorpion Too, which had an expanded fuselage structure with a two-seat fibreglass cabin enclosure and a 140 h.p. Evinrude marine engine. In 1980, RotorWay produced the sophisticated Exec which was based on the Scorpion Too's dynamic systems but had an all-metal monocoque and glass-fibre fuselage shell and a 152 h.p. RotorWay RW-152 water-cooled piston engine. The basic dual-control Exec was subsequently upgraded to Exec 90 standard with many detailed alterations including optional pontoon floats. The design was further changed in 1995 to become the Exec 162F with a FADEC electronic control system, changes to the kit structure and performance enhancements. Over 500 Exec kits have been sold and at least 300 are flying.

RotorWay Scorpion and Exec (Cont.)

RotorWay Scorpion Too

RotorWay Exec 162F, N21901

Specification	RotorWay Exec 162F	
Powerplant	One 152 h.p. (113.3 kW) RotorWay RI-162F piston engine	
Dimensions		
Rotor diameter	7.62 m	(25 ft 0 in)
Length	8.79 m	(28 ft 10 in)
Height	2.44 m	(8 ft 0 in)
Performance		
Max speed	185 km/h	(100 kt, 115 mph)
Cruising speed	153 km/h	(83 kt, 95 mph)
Initial climb	305 m/min	(1,000 fpm)
Range	288 km	(156 nm, 180 miles)
Weights		
Max takeoff	680 kg	(1,500 lbs)
Useful load	238 kg	(525 lbs)

Ruschmeyer R90
— Germany

In 1985, the Ruschmeyer Luftfahrttechnik GmbH designed the MF-85 tourer which first flew on 8th August 1988 powered by a 212 h.p. Porsche PFM3200N engine. It was a composite low-wing aircraft with a retractable tricycle undercarriage and a fully enclosed four-seat cabin. Discontinued production of the Porsche engine resulted in the production R90-230RG having a 230 h.p. Lycoming IO-540-C4D5 engine, and the production prototype flew on 25th September 1990 with first deliveries in 1992. Other versions flown or proposed included the R90-230FG and the R90-180FG, powered by a 180 h.p. IO-360 engine, both of which were fitted with fixed undercarriages, the turbocharged R90-300T-RG, the R90 Aerobat, the stretched R95 five-seater and the R90-420AT fitted with a 400 s.h.p. Allison 250-B20 turboprop. The R90-420AT prototype first flew on 2nd November 1993. Ruschmeyer became bankrupt in June 1996 before these plans could mature and had completed 28 aircraft, most of which are currently active.

Ruschmeyer R90-230RG, D-EFFA

Specification	Ruschmeyer R90-230RG	
Powerplant	One 230 h.p. (171.5 kW) Textron Lycoming IO-540-C4D5 piston engine	
Dimensions		
Span	9.5 m	(31 ft 2 in)
Length	7.92 m	(26 ft 0 in)
Height	2.46 m	(8 ft 1 in)
Performance		
Max speed	322 km/h	(174 kt, 200 mph)
Cruising speed	298 km/h	(161 kt, 185 mph)
Initial climb	347 m/min	(1,140 fpm)
Range	1,368 km	(743 nm, 855 miles)
Weights		
Max takeoff	1,350 kg	(2,977 lbs)
Useful load	452 kg	(997 lbs)

Rutan Varieze and LongEz — USA

The talented designer Burt Rutan experimented with canard aircraft in the early 1970s, flying his Model 27 VariViggen prototype on 27th February 1972. This was a wood and fabric aircraft with a delta wing mounting twin fins, a pusher Lycoming O-320 mounted behind the tandem two-seat cabin, a retractable tricycle undercarriage and a forward canard surface fitted with elevators ahead of the windshield. Rutan sold plans for the VariViggen and a number are flying in the USA. This concept was refined into the Model 33 Varieze, which had the same general pusher layout but was of modern composite construction with fibreglass covering over a urethane core. It had a completely redesigned high-aspect-ratio wing with leading-edge extensions and winglets, and the tricycle undercarriage had fixed main gear and a retractable nosewheel. The prototype had a 63 h.p. Volkswagen engine but the definitive powerplant was either a 100 h.p. Continental O-200-A or 115 h.p. Lycoming O-235. The prototype flew on 21st May 1975 and many Variezes were built worldwide before the design was withdrawn in the early 1980s. The Model 61 LongEz is an improved version, developed by Rutan Aircraft Factory Inc., with increased range, larger wings and rudders on the winglets. The LongEz first flew on 12th June 1979 and over 700 are believed to have flown.

Rutan LongEz, G-BMUG

Specification	Rutan LongEz	
Powerplant	One 115 h.p. (85.74 kW) Textron Lycoming O-235 piston engine	
Dimensions		
Span	7.95 m	(26 ft 1 in)
Length	5.11 m	(16 ft 9 in)
Height	2.39 m	(7 ft 10 in)
Performance		
Max speed	298 km/h	(161 kt, 185 mph)
Cruising speed	233 km/h	(126 kt, 145 mph)
Initial climb	533 m/min	(1,750 fpm)
Range	3,216 km	(1,748 nm, 2,010 miles)
Weights		
Max takeoff	601 kg	(1,325 lbs)
Useful load	279 kg	(615 lbs)

Rutan Defiant — USA

Following on from the canard Varieze and LongEz amateur aircraft, Burt Rutan produced a larger version, the Model 40 Defiant, which followed the same general layout with a two-stage swept wing fitted with winglets and a tricycle undercarriage with a retractable nosewheel. The Defiant, which made its first flight on 30th June 1978, is a complex aircraft powered by two 150 h.p. Lycoming engines mounted in push-pull fashion in the nose and tail. It has a four-seat cabin with a hinged windshield section for entry and is fitted with a fixed forward canard surface together with an additional rudder surface below the nose on the port side. Over 50 Defiants have been built from plans published by the Rutan Aircraft Factory, most of which are flying in the USA.

Rutan Defiant, N20FY

Specification	Rutan Defiant	
Powerplant	Two 150 h.p. (111.8 kW) Textron Lycoming O-320-E2A piston engines	
Dimensions		
Span	9.58 m	(31 ft 5 in)
Length	7.85 m	(25 ft 9 in)
Height	2.62 m	(8 ft 7 in)
Performance		
Max speed	338 km/h	(183 kt, 210 mph)
Cruising speed	314 km/h	(170 kt, 195 mph)
Initial climb	457 m/min	(1,500 fpm)
Range	2,208 km	(1,200 nm, 1,380 miles)
Weights		
Max takeoff	1,338 kg	(2,950 lbs)
Useful load	576 kg	(1,270 lbs)

Ryan PT-20 and PT-22 — USA

T. Claude Ryan designed the Model S-T (sport trainer) in 1933 for use by civilian flying schools and private owners, and the first aircraft flew on 8th June 1934. It was an attractive aircraft of metal construction with fabric wing covering, a wire and strut-braced low wing and tandem open cockpits. The fixed

Ryan PT-20 and PT-22 (Cont.)

tailwheel undercarriage had large speed fairings. The initial Model S-T was powered by a 95 h.p. Menasco Pirate in-line engine, but this was quickly altered in the Model S-T-A, which had the larger 125 h.p. Menasco C-4. The S-T-A Special, which was built as the S-T-M export military trainer (and was sometimes fitted with armament) had a supercharged 150 h.p. Menasco C4S engine and was supplied to various countries including Mexico, Guatemala and Honduras. To meet the build-up for war, Ryan delivered 56 examples of the S-T-M to the USAAC as the PT-16 and PT-20 with the 125 h.p. Menasco and 100 of the PT-21 with a 132 h.p. Kinner B.5 (R440-3) engine. They then developed the ST-3KR which had enlarged cockpits, a 160 h.p. Kinner R.56 radial engine in a partial cowling and a multi-strutted main undercarriage which either had cut-back speed fairings or was left completely open. This was built as the PT-21 and PT-22 Recruit for the USAAC. Over 1,500 of the S-T series were built, and many military ST-3KRs were civilianised after the war and currently fly with private owners.

Ryan ST-3KR, N46501

Specification	Ryan ST-3KR (PT-22)	
Powerplant	One 160 h.p. (119.3 kW) Kinner R.56 piston engine	
Dimensions		
Span	9.17 m	(30 ft 1 in)
Length	6.91 m	(22 ft 8 in)
Height	2.18 m	(7 ft 2 in)
Performance		
Max speed	187 km/h	(101 kt, 116 mph)
Cruising speed	177 km/h	(96 kt, 110 mph)
Initial climb	262 m/min	(860 fpm)
Range	464 km	(252 nm, 290 miles)
Weights		
Max takeoff	844 kg	(1,860 lbs)
Useful load	248 kg	(547 lbs)

Ryan SCW-145 — USA

In 1937, Ryan Aeronautical Co. introduced the SCW-145 private touring light aircraft. It was an all-metal machine with a slim monocoque fuselage and it had an enclosed cabin fitted with a sliding canopy. It was equipped with dual controls and had seating for two in front and one passenger behind. The tailwheel undercarriage was fixed and the main legs and wheels were enclosed in speed fairings. The SCW-145 had a sharply tapered wing fitted with a slotted speed brake which dropped down from its centre section. It was powered by a Warner Super Scarab radial engine in a helmeted cowling. Ryan built 12 examples of the SCW-145, eight of which are still in existence.

Ryan SCW-145, NC18915

Specification	Ryan SCW-145	
Powerplant	One 145 h.p. (108.1 kW) Warner Super Scarab piston engine	
Dimensions		
Span	11.43 m	(37 ft 6 in)
Length	7.75 m	(25 ft 5 in)
Height	2.13 m	(7 ft 0 in)
Performance		
Max speed	241 km/h	(130 kt, 150 mph)
Cruising speed	225 km/h	(122 kt, 140 mph)
Initial climb	271 m/min	(890 fpm)
Range	720 km	(391 nm, 450 miles)
Weights		
Max takeoff	975 kg	(2,150 lbs)
Useful load	365 kg	(805 lbs)

Ryan Navion and Navion Rangemaster — USA

In 1947, North American Aviation Inc. flew the prototype of their NA-143 private aircraft. It was an all-metal low-wing monoplane with a four-seat cabin enclosed by a sliding bubble canopy, a retractable tricycle undercarriage and 185 h.p. Continental engine. As the NA-145 Navion it went into production at Inglewood, California in mid-1947, and, in addition to the Continental E-185-3 engine, the aircraft was also offered with a 205 h.p. E-185-9 powerplant. After building 1,027 Navions, including 83 L-17As (NA-154) for the US Army, North American sold the design to Ryan Aeronautical

Corporation of San Diego who built 600 standard Navions and 602 of the 205 h.p. Navion A (including US Army L-17B). The Ryan Navion B, also known as the Super Navion 260, was a higher-powered version with a 260 h.p. Lycoming GO-435-C2 engine and Ryan built 222 examples before terminating production in 1951. Existing Navions were re-engined by Tusco in the 1950s as the Navion D, Navion E and Navion F with 240 h.p., 250 h.p. and 260 h.p. Continental IO-470 engines and tip tanks. The Navion Aircraft Company radically redesigned the aircraft in 1961 as the Navion G Rangemaster with a five-seat integral cabin structure replacing the sliding canopy and built 172 examples of the Rangemaster G and the Rangemaster H with a 285 h.p. Continental IO-520-B engine. A further eight Rangemaster Hs were built in 1975 and 1976 by Consolidated Holding. A large number of Navions of all models continue in service and many have been modified with new cockpit canopies and tip tanks.

Specification	Ryan Navion B Super 260	
Powerplant	One 260 h.p. (193.86 kW) Textron Lycoming GO-435-C2 piston engine	
Dimensions		
Span	10.18 m	(33 ft 5 in)
Length	8.38 m	(27 ft 6 in)
Height	2.64 m	(8 ft 8 in)
Performance		
Max speed	262 km/h	(142 kt, 163 mph)
Cruising speed	249 km/h	(135 kt, 155 mph)
Initial climb	274 m/min	(900 fpm)
Range	1,200 km	(652 nm, 750 miles)
Weights		
Max takeoff	1,293 kg	(2,850 lbs)
Useful load	417 kg	(920 lbs)

Ryan Navion B, N5191K

Navion G Rangemaster, N2447T

S

Saab 91 Safir — Sweden

The Model 91 Safir was created by the designer of the Bücker Bestmann, Anders J. Andersson, and was first flown on 20th November 1945. The initial S 91 was an all-metal low-wing monoplane with three seats and a retractable tricycle undercarriage produced as a civil and military trainer. The prototype and the initial batch of S 91As were powered by a 145 h.p. de Havilland Gipsy Major in-line engine but the S 91B, built in the largest numbers, had a 190 h.p. Lycoming O-435-A and the S 91D used a 180 h.p. Lycoming O-360-A1A. From the S 91C onwards, the Safir had a full four-seat cabin entered through a full-length side-hinged half canopy and a higher gross weight. Of the total of 323 Safirs, 120 S 91Bs were built in Holland by de Scheldt. Customers included the air forces of Sweden, Norway, Finland, Ethiopia, Tunisia and Austria, the Dutch Rijksluchtvaartschool and the Lufthansa and Air France training units. Around 90 Safirs, mostly released by military users, are active with private owners in Sweden, Norway, Austria and elsewhere in Europe.

Saab S 91D Safir, PH-RLA

Specification	Saab S91B Safir	
Powerplant	One 190 h.p. (141.66 kW) Textron Lycoming O-435-A piston engine	
Dimensions		
Span	10.59 m	(34 ft 9 in)
Length	7.8 m	(25 ft 7 in)
Height	2.21 m	(7 ft 3 in)
Performance		
Max speed	274 km/h	(148 kt, 170 mph)
Cruising speed	245 km/h	(132 kt, 152 mph)
Initial climb	321 m/min	(1,052 fpm)
Range	1,045 km	(568 nm, 653 miles)
Weights		
Max takeoff	1,241 kg	(2,736 lbs)
Useful load	511 kg	(1,126 lbs)

Saab 32 Lansen — Sweden

Together with the Saab J 29, the Saab Lansen formed the initial jet interception capability for the Swedish Air Force. The Lansen was a tandem two-seat night and all-weather fighter of fairly conventional layout, powered by a 7,490 lb.s.t. Rolls Royce Avon RA.7R turbojet. It flew on 3rd November 1952 and the initial A 32A, which was armed with four 20 mm cannon and hardpoints to carry a variety of missiles, bombs and fuel tanks, entered service in 1956. The J 32B, which could carry Sidewinder missiles, was a higher-powered variant with a 10,560 lb.s.t. reheated Avon 200 (RM6A) turbojet and the S 32C reconnaissance model was based on the A 32A but had a search radar and nose-mounted cameras in place of the standard armament. The J 32D was a target-towing conversion of the J 32B with underwing winch pods and the J 32E was used for ECCM training. Although the Lansen has largely been retired, a few target tugs remain and several Lansens have been sold to private owners.

Saab J 32E Lansen, Swedish AF 32512

Specification	Saab J 32B Lansen	
Powerplant	One 10,560 lb.s.t. (46.98 kN) Flygmotor RM6A turbojet	
Dimensions		
Span	13 m	(42 ft 8 in)
Length	14.91 m	(48 ft 11 in)
Height	4.65 m	(15 ft 3 in)
Performance		
Max speed	1,126 km/h	(609 kt, 700 mph)
Cruising speed	853 km/h	(461 kt, 530 mph)
Initial climb	6,000 m/min	(19,685 fpm)
Range	2,000 km	(1,087 nm, 1,249 miles)
Weights		
Max takeoff	11,194 kg	(24,683 lbs)
Useful load	3,117 kg	(6,873 lbs)

Saab 105 — Sweden

Conceived as a replacement for the Swedish Air Force's ageing de Havilland Vampire Trainers, the Saab 105 made its first flight on 1st July 1963 and, as the Sk 60A, deliveries to the air force commenced in early 1966. The Saab 105 has a shoulder-set wing with mild sweep and almost constant chord, a T-tail and a side-by-side two-seat dual-control cockpit. It is powered by two 1,638 lb.s.t. RM9 turbofans, developed from the Turboméca Aubisque, which are fitted beneath the wing roots. The Swedish Air Force received 150 aircraft, most of which are still operational for training and communications, and 60 were modified as the Sk 60B for attack training with two underwing hardpoints while others became Sk 60Cs with hardpoints and a photo-reconnaissance nose. The export Saab 105XT is a higher-powered multi-mission model with 2,850 lb.s.t. General Electric J-85-17B engines, increased fuel capacity and higher weights and, as the Saab 105OE, 40 were sold to the Austrian Air Force in 1970. More than half of these remain in service.

Saab 105 Sk 60A, Swedish AF, 60061

Specification	Saab 105OE	
Powerplant	Two 2,850 lb.s.t. (12.68 kN) General Electric J-85-17B turbojets	
Dimensions		
Span	9.5 m	(31 ft 2 in)
Length	10.49 m	(34 ft 5 in)
Height	2.69 m	(8 ft 10 in)
Performance		
Max speed	970 km/h	(524 kt, 603 mph)
Cruising speed	800 km/h	(432 kt, 497 mph)
Initial climb	4,572 m/min	(15,000 fpm)
Range	2,744 km	(1,491 nm, 1,715 miles)
Weights		
Max takeoff	6,500 kg	(14,332 lbs)
Useful load	3,985 kg	(8,787 lbs)

Saab MFI-15/17 and Mushshak — Sweden

The MFI-15 is a light army cooperation aircraft and trainer designed by Björn Andreasson and developed by Saab following its March 1968 takeover of Malmö Flygindustri (MFI). The shoulder-wing MFI-15 Safari, which first flew on 11th July 1969, has a side-by-side two-seat cockpit together with a small centre fuselage compartment to transport one passenger, and the design includes a fixed tricycle undercarriage and a cruciform tail. It is powered by a 160 h.p. Lycoming IO-320-B2 piston engine. The principal customer for the MFI-15 was the Norwegian Air Force which acquired 23. Saab then improved it as the MFI-17 Supporter which has a 200 h.p. Lycoming IO-360 engine and a modified wing with six underwing hardpoints capable of carrying a variety of rockets and other offensive stores. This version was acquired by Norway and Denmark, and by Pakistan, which also manufactured a number of Supporters under licence. The Pakistan Aeronautical Complex (AMF) has developed its own version, the Shahbaz, with a 210 h.p. Continental TSIO-360-MB engine, and also the higher-powered Super Mushshak which has a 260 h.p. Lycoming IO-540 and higher gross weight and first flew on 15th August 1995. Over 350 of the MFI-15/17 series have been built and around half are in current service, including three in Zambia and a small number of civil examples.

Saab MFI-17 Supporter, Danish Army, T-408

AMF Mushshak, Pakistan AF, 319AMF

Specification	Saab MFI-17 Supporter	
Powerplant	One 200 h.p. (149 kW) Textron Lycoming IO-360-A1B6 piston engine	
Dimensions		
Span	8.86 m	(29 ft 1 in)
Length	6.98 m	(22 ft 11 in)
Height	2.62 m	(8 ft 7 in)
Performance		
Max speed	235 km/h	(127 kt, 146 mph)
Cruising speed	209 km/h	(113 kt, 130 mph)
Initial climb	329 m/min	(1,080 fpm)
Range	1,050 km	(571 nm, 656 miles)
Weights		
Max takeoff	1,200 kg	(2,646 lbs)
Useful load	554 kg	(1,222 lbs)

Saab 35 Draken — Sweden

The Draken supersonic fighter was produced by Saab as a replacement for the J 29 Tunnen, which served the Swedish Air Force during the 1950s. Designated Saab 35, the single-seat Draken had an innovative double-delta wing which incorporated the air intakes for the afterburning 14,400 lb.s.t. RM6B (licence-built Rolls Royce Avon Srs.200) engine. Its offensive armament consisted of two 30 mm cannon together with four Sidewinder AAMs. The first Draken flew on 25th October 1955 and, as the J 35A, it went into production with first deliveries to the Swedish Air Force being made in 1959. The J 35B, which had a longer rear fuselage, was fitted with improved radar and had a larger weapons load, and the J 35D and J 35F were more powerful variants with a 17,200 lb.s.t. RM6C (Avon 300) engine and further improvements to radars and systems. Remaining J 35Fs have been upgraded to J 35J standard with additional centreline stores pylons, and later Drakens had a bulged cockpit canopy. The Sk 35C is a tandem two-seat trainer version, some of which were converted from the J 35A.

Saab 35 Draken (Cont.)

Export customers for the Draken included Denmark (designated F 35 and, in photo-reconnaissance configuration, RF 5), Finland (J 35F) and Austria (J 35D). In total 657 Drakens were built and 24 are still active with the Austrian Air Force and private operators, although the Swedish and Finnish air forces withdrew the type in 1999/2000.

Saab J 35F, Finnish AF, DK-201

Specification	Saab J 35F Draken	
Powerplant	One 17,200 lb.s.t. (76.52 kN) Volvo Flygmotor RM6C turbojet	
Dimensions		
Span	9.42 m	(30 ft 11 in)
Length	15.34 m	(50 ft 4 in)
Height	3.89 m	(12 ft 9 in)
Performance		
Max speed	2,130 km/h	(1,148 kt, 1,324 mph)
Initial climb	15,000 m/min	(49,212 fpm)
Range	2,750 km	(1,495 nm, 1,719 miles)
Weights		
Max takeoff	15,000 kg	(33,075 lbs)
Useful load	6,750 kg	(14,884 lbs)

Saab 37 Viggen — Sweden

The Viggen is the Swedish Air Force's second-generation supersonic interceptor, developed by Saab during the early 1960s. Its innovative design, aimed at achieving maximum agility and STOL performance, incorporated a complex delta wing positioned at the rear of the fuselage and a large forward fully-moving canard surface. It was powered by a reheated 26,000 lb.s.t. Volvo Flygmotor RM8 (Pratt & Whitney JT8D-22) engine equipped with a thrust reversal system. Saab flew the prototype on 8th February 1967 and the Swedish Air Force eventually acquired 329 aircraft. The initial AJ 37 attack variant has two underwing pylons and two fuselage stations to carry a mixture of ASMs, AAMs and anti-ship missiles. The JA 37 is an interceptor version with improved look down/shoot down radar, a higher-thrust engine, a slightly longer fuselage and an integral 30 mm cannon, and the SF 37 has photo-reconnaissance capability with a camera nose and the ability to carry external ECM and sensor pods. Most AJ 37 Viggens have been upgraded to AJS 37 standard with advanced datalinks and improved radar surveillance systems, and the JA 37 is now capable of carrying AMRAAM air-to-air missiles. No export sales of the Viggen were made but the majority of Swedish Air Force aircraft delivered remain in service.

Saab JA 37 Viggen, Swedish AF, 37432

Specification	Saab JA 37 Viggen	
Powerplant	One 28,110 lb.s.t. (125.05 kN) (wet) Volvo Flygmotor RM8B turbofan	
Dimensions		
Span	10.59 m	(34 ft 9 in)
Length	16.41 m	(53 ft 10 in)
Height	5.89 m	(19 ft 4 in)
Performance		
Max speed	2,125 km/h	(1,145 kt, 1,320 mph)
Initial climb	6,025 m/min	(19,767 fpm)
Range	2,000 km	(1,087 nm, 1,250 miles)
Weights		
Max takeoff	17,000 kg	(37,485 lbs)
Useful load (est)	7,500 kg	(16,537 lbs)

Saab 39 Gripen — Sweden

The eventual need to replace the Viggen resulted in Saab designing a completely new multi-role combat aircraft which would have enhanced capability but would be less costly to acquire and operate. The JAS 39 Gripen continues with Saab's delta wing layout and, like the Viggen, has a forward canard control surface, but it is less than half the weight of the Viggen and is built with a significant proportion of composite materials. With an internal 27 mm cannon, four underwing hardpoints and a centreline pylon, it can carry a similar offensive load to that of the Viggen and is fitted with the latest technology cockpit systems including a HUD and a three-screen MFD. The Gripen prototype, powered by a licence-built General Electric F404J turbofan, was flown on 9th December 1988 and variants include the JAS 39A single-seat interceptor and the stretched JAS 39B tandem two-seat combat-capable trainer. The JAS 39C, which is the basis for the export version being produced in cooperation with BAE Systems, is under development, powered by a Volvo Flygmotor RM12 Plus engine. First Swedish Air Force deliveries were made in June 1996 with over 70 being in service by mid-1999. At that time Swedish orders totalled 204 aircraft, including 28 two-seaters, and 28 are to be delivered to the South African Air Force from 2007.

Saab JAS 39 Gripen, Swedish AF, 39133

Specification	Saab JAS 39A Gripen	
Powerplant	One 18,105 lb.s.t. (80.54 kN) (wet) Volvo Flygmotor RM12 turbofan	
Dimensions		
Span	8.41 m	(27 ft 7 in)
Length	14.1 m	(46 ft 3 in)
Height	4.5 m	(14 ft 9 in)
Performance		
Max speed	1,223+ km/h	(660+ kt, 760+ mph)
Takeoff distance	800 m	(2,625 ft)
Range	1,600 km	(870 nm, 1,000 miles)
Weights		
Max takeoff	8,000 kg	(17,640 lbs)
Useful load	1,400 kg	(3,087 lbs)

Specification	Saab 340B	
Powerplant	Two 1,750 s.h.p. (1,304 kW) General Electric CT7-9B turboprops	
Dimensions		
Span	21.44 m	(70 ft 4 in)
Length	19.73 m	(64 ft 9 in)
Height	6.96 m	(22 ft 10 in)
Performance		
Max speed	523 km/h	(283 kt, 325 mph)
Cruising speed	512 km/h	(277 kt, 318 mph)
Initial climb	610 m/min	(2,000 fpm)
Range	1,676 km	(910 nm, 1,048 miles)
Weights		
Max takeoff	13,152 kg	(29,000 lbs)
Useful load	4,928 kg	(10,867 lbs)

Saab 340 and 2000
— Sweden

In 1979, Saab, in partnership with Fairchild Industries, designed the SF.340 pressurised local service airliner. This aircraft, which was larger than the competing Merlin and Twin Otter, had a conventional low-wing layout with a retractable tricycle undercarriage and a 35-passenger cabin. It was powered by a pair of 1,630 s.h.p. General Electric CT7-5A2 turboprops. The prototype flew on 25th January 1983 and mid-1984 saw first deliveries being made to Crossair and Comair followed by sales to commercial operators worldwide. There were also a number of military deliveries including aircraft for the Japanese Maritime Safety Agency and the Swedish Air Force, and Saab built the Saab 340 AEW&C military surveillance version with a roof-mounted Ericsson Erieye SLAR antenna. In 1987 Saab took over the whole SF.340 programme and introduced the higher-weight Saab 340B with 1,735 s.h.p. CT7-5A2 (later CT7-9B) engines which was first delivered in September 1989. The Saab 2000 is a stretched 58-seat model which flew on 26th March 1992 and is powered by two 4,125 s.h.p. Allison AE2100A turboprops with six-blade propellers. In 1997, Saab announced the end of the 340B/2000 production run after 457 340s and 63 2000s had been delivered.

Saab 340A, N322PX

Saab 2000, HB-IZD

Sadler Vampire and A.22 Piranha — USA

The Vampire ultralight aircraft was designed by William G. Sadler in 1982 and it has been manufactured for kit assembly by homebuilders and as a factory-complete aircraft at the Sadler factory in Scottsdale, Arizona. It is an all-metal twin-boomed aircraft with a large constant-chord wing and a fixed tricycle undercarriage. It has a single-seat cockpit which can be open or enclosed with a bubble canopy and is powered by a pusher 20 h.p. KFM 107ER engine. The Vampire is now manufactured in Australia by Skywise Ultraflight Pty. as the SV-2 with a 41 h.p. Rotax 447 engine, and at least 25 have been completed. Sadler has also developed the side-by-side two-seat SV-200 although this has not been sold to date. The Sadler A.22 Piranha is a substantially higher-powered and strengthened military version of the Vampire intended for use as an ultra-low-cost counter-insurgency aircraft for developing countries. It is fitted with four underwing hardpoints to carry up to 450 kg of ordnance and has a retractable undercarriage. Only one prototype has been flown to date.

Sadler A.22 Piranha, N22AB

Specification	Sadler Model A.22 Piranha	
Powerplant	One 450 h.p. (335.5 kW) Chevrolet V-8 piston engine	
Dimensions		
Span	6.71 m	(22 ft 0 in)
Length	5.13 m	(16 ft 10 in)
Height	2.13 m	(7 ft 0 in)
Performance		
Max speed	386 km/h	(209 kt, 240 mph)
Cruising speed	193 km/h	(104 kt, 120 mph)
Initial climb	1,372 m/min	(4,500 fpm)
Range	1,520 km	(826 nm, 950 miles)
Weights		
Max takeoff	1,200 kg	(2,646 lbs)
Useful load	700 kg	(1,543 lbs)

SAI KZ-II Kupe — Denmark

Just before the war, the Skandinavisk Aero Industri (SAI) was started by Viggo Kramme and Karl Zeuthen to build the KZ-IIK Kupe side-by-side two-seat light aircraft, which was flown on 11th December 1937. While 14 were built at that time, the main production model was the tandem open-cockpit KZ-IIS Sport with a 105 h.p. Hirth 504A engine, 14 of which were completed, including a small batch for the Danish Naval Air Service. The design was revived after the war with a further batch of 16 KZ-IIT Trainers, powered by a 145 h.p. de Havilland Gipsy Major engine, 15 of which were delivered to the Danish Air Force as primary trainers. The KZ-IITs were low-wing wood and fabric monoplanes with a strengthened airframe to accommodate the higher engine power, and some were fitted with a framed cockpit canopy. The KZ-IIT was phased out of military service in 1955 and four aircraft remain in Denmark with private owners.

SAI KZ-IIT, OY-FAK

Specification	SAI KZ-IIT Trainer	
Powerplant	One 145 h.p. (108.1 kW) de Havilland Gipsy Major 10 piston engine	
Dimensions		
Span	10.21 m	(33 ft 6 in)
Length	7.49 m	(24 ft 7 in)
Height	2.24 m	(7 ft 4 in)
Performance		
Max speed	233 km/h	(126 kt, 145 mph)
Cruising speed	209 km/h	(113 kt, 130 mph)
Initial climb	270 m/min	(885 fpm)
Range	896 km	(487 nm, 560 miles)
Weights		
Max takeoff	850 kg	(1,874 lbs)
Useful load	550 kg	(1,213 lbs)

SAI KZ-III and KZ-VII Laerk — Denmark

The KZ-III was developed by SAI (Skandinavisk Aero Industri) during the war as an ambulance aircraft. It was a tube, fabric and wooden high-wing aircraft with an enclosed side-by-side two-seat cabin. The first KZ-III made its maiden flight on 11th September 1944 from Kastrup airport, going into production in 1945 when hostilities had ceased. A total of 64 KZ-IIIs were built, powered by a 100 h.p. in-line Blackburn Cirrus Minor II engine, and SAI followed on with the four-seat KZ-VII Laerk which had a longer cabin with additional side windows. This was sold with either a 125 h.p. C-125-2 or 145 h.p. C-145-2 flat-four Continental engine. Despite a factory fire, SAI built 58 KZ-VIIs and they followed this with a batch of 13 KZ-X liaison aircraft for the Danish Army. The KZ series remains popular with private owners with 25 KZ-IIIs and 27 KZ-VIIs still flying in Europe with owners in Denmark, Sweden, Finland, Germany and Switzerland.

SAI KZ-VII, D-EKOF

Specification	SAI KZ-III	
Powerplant	One 100 h.p. (74.56 kW) Blackburn Cirrus Minor II piston engine	
Dimensions		
Span	9.6 m	(31 ft 6 in)
Length	6.55 m	(21 ft 6 in)
Height	2.06 m	(6 ft 9 in)
Performance		
Max speed	185 km/h	(100 kt, 115 mph)
Cruising speed	171 km/h	(92 kt, 106 mph)
Initial climb	213 m/min	(700 fpm)
Range	496 km	(270 nm, 310 miles)
Weights		
Max takeoff	659 kg	(1,453 lbs)
Useful load	273 kg	(603 lbs)

Saunders Roe Skeeter — UK

The Cierva Autogyro Company originally designed the Skeeter light helicopter, which made its first flight on 10th October 1948, but the design was refined by Saunders Roe with a view to sale to civil and military customers. The Skeeter had an enclosed side-by-side two-seat cabin, a slim tail boom with a small tail mast mounting the anti-torque propeller and a fixed tricycle undercarriage. The civil Skeeter 5, 6, 7 and 8 were built only as development aircraft; the principal version was the military Skeeter for the British Army. The initial Skeeter AOP.10 and T.11 were powered by a 200 h.p. Gipsy Major 200 piston engine, but the main production AOP.12, 64 of which were delivered between May 1958 and July 1960, had a 215 h.p. Gipsy Major. They served with the Army Air Corps as observation and training machines until they were withdrawn in 1968. Skeeters were also sold to the German Heeresflieger, which received six Mk.50 aircraft, and the Bundesmarine, which had four Mk.51s. Several military Skeeters were acquired by private owners and seven are registered in the UK.

Saunders Roe Skeeter AOP.12, XL809 (G-BLIX)

Specification	Saunders Roe Skeeter AOP.12	
Powerplant	One 215 h.p. (160.3 kW) Gipsy Major 215 piston engine	
Dimensions		
Rotor diameter	9.75 m	(32 ft 0 in)
Length	8.13 m	(26 ft 8 in)
Height	2.9 m	(9 ft 6 in)
Performance		
Max speed	175 km/h	(95 kt, 109 mph)
Cruising speed	171 km/h	(92 kt, 106 mph)
Initial climb	351 m/min	(1,150 fpm)
Range	416 km	(226 nm, 260 miles)
Weights		
Max takeoff	998 kg	(2,200 lbs)
Useful load	247 kg	(544 lbs)

Scaled Composites Proteus — USA

The Proteus was designed by Burt Rutan's Mojave-based Scaled Composites Inc. as a highly specialised high-altitude orbiting aircraft to carry communications relay equipment. A fleet of Proteuses will operate relay orbiting for the Angel Technologies HALO network, carrying podded equipment modules fitted under the centre fuselage. The Model 281 Proteus, which is made primarily from composites, is a tandem-wing aircraft with twin booms and two FJ44 turbofans mounted on the centre section of the rear wing. Its fuselage length can be varied by removal of a section and the wings can be extended asymmetrically if necessary. It will be flown by a crew of two in a pressurised cabin and will fly above 50,000 feet for 12-hour on-station orbits, but other missions could include military surveillance and a range of mapping and remote-sensing tasks. The prototype, which set a new class world record of 62,786 ft altitude in October 2000, first flew on 26th July 1998 and a fleet of up to 100 aircraft is planned.

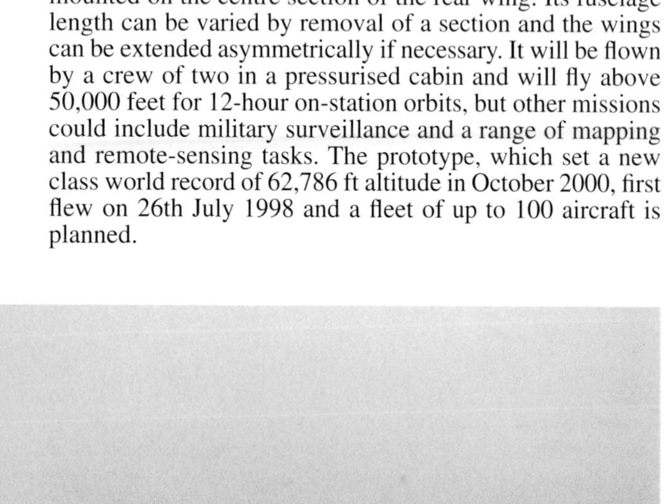

Scaled Composites Proteus, N281PR

Specification	Scaled Composites Proteus	
Powerplant	Two 2,293 lb.s.t. (10.2 kN) Williams/Rolls FJ44-2E turbofans	
Dimensions		
Span (standard)	23.65 m	(77 ft 7 in)
Length (standard)	17.14 m	(56 ft 3 in)
Height	5.36 m	(17 ft 7 in)
Performance		
Cruising speed	352 km/h	(190 kt, 219 mph)
Initial climb	1,829 m/min	(6,000 fpm)
Range	4,237 km	(2,300 nm, 2,648 miles)
Weights		
Max takeoff	5,669 kg	(12,500 lbs)
Useful load	3,011 kg	(6,640 lbs)

Scheibe SF-23 Sperling — Germany

The SF-23 Sperling is a two-seat light aircraft designed by Egon Scheibe and first flown on 8th August 1955 powered by a 65 h.p. Continental A.65 engine. It is a strut-braced high-wing aircraft with an enclosed side-by-side cabin and a tailwheel undercarriage. Construction is of steel tube and fabric with wood and fabric wings and the main production SF-23A was powered by a 95 h.p. Continental C90-12F flat-four piston engine. Between 1958 and 1961 Scheibe built 26 Sperlings for use by flying clubs and for glider towing. This batch included a few examples of the SF-23B with a 100 h.p. Continental O-200-B and the SF-23C with a 115 h.p. Lycoming O-235 engine. Three further Sperlings were constructed by amateur builders. Nine Sperlings remain operational with owners in Germany and the UK.

Scheibe SF-23C Sperling, D-ECYS

Specification	Scheibe SF-23A Sperling	
Powerplant	One 95 h.p. (70.83 kW) Teledyne Continental C90-12F piston engine	
Dimensions		
Span	9.85 m	(32 ft 4 in)
Length	6.2 m	(20 ft 4 in)
Height	2.18 m	(7 ft 2 in)
Performance		
Max speed	201 km/h	(109 kt, 125 mph)
Cruising speed	161 km/h	(87 kt, 100 mph)
Initial climb	210 m/min	(690 fpm)
Range	640 km	(348 nm, 400 miles)
Weights		
Max takeoff	730 kg	(1,609 lbs)
Useful load	270 kg	(595 lbs)

Scheibe SF-25 Motorfalke
— Germany

In the mid-1950s Scheibe Flugzeugbau developed the SF-24 Motor Spatz single-seat motor glider, based on the L-Spatz glider which the company manufactured, and 46 examples were converted. This was followed by the two-seat SF-25A Motorfalke, which was based on the tandem-seat Bergfalke glider, fitted with a high-mounted wing, a new forward fuselage incorporating an enclosed side-by-side cockpit, a monowheel undercarriage and a 30 h.p. Hirth F12A2C engine in the nose. The prototype Motorfalke (later just named Falke) flew in April 1963 and 56 production aircraft were built, followed by 335 of the SF-25B which was redesigned with a low-set wing, stabilising outriggers and a 45 h.p. Stark 1500 engine. Some SF-25Bs have become SF-25Ds with a Limbach SL1700A engine. The SF-25C was a higher-powered variant with a 60 h.p. Limbach SL1700EA engine which has appeared with many detailed modifications (as the C-Falke-76, C-Falke-78 etc.) including optional conventional tailwheel and tricycle undercarriages, and improvements to the cabin canopy enclosure. The Falke C-2000 was a version with an 80 h.p. Limbach L.2000EA engine, the Rotax Falke has a Rotax 912A engine and the SF-25E Super Falke has a larger wing and enlarged swept tail. Licence-manufacture of the Falke has been carried out by Loravia, Sportavia-Pützer and Aeronautica Umbra, and eight aircraft have been built by amateurs. Slingsby in the United Kingdom built 75 SF-25Bs as the civil T-61A and T-61C, and as the T-61E Venture for the RAF. Scheibe subsequently also built the SF-28A Tandem Falke which was structurally similar to the SF-25C but had tandem seating and a long clear-view canopy, and they have also produced prototypes and small series of several other motor gliders including the SF-29, SF-33, SF-36 and ultralight SF-40. Total Falke and Tandem Falke production by Scheibe to date exceeds 1,300 aircraft.

Slingsby T-61E Venture, G-BUXJ

Scheibe SF-28A Tandem Falke, F-CEYR

Specification	Scheibe SF-25 C-Falke	
Powerplant	One 60 h.p. (44.74 kW) Limbach SL1700EA piston engine	
Dimensions		
Span	15.3 m	(50 ft 2 in)
Length	7.5 m	(24 ft 7 in)
Height	1.85 m	(6 ft 1 in)
Performance		
Max speed	190 km/h	(102 kt, 118 mph)
Cruising speed	150 km/h	(81 kt, 93 mph)
Initial climb	138 m/min	(453 fpm)
Range	650 km	(350 nm, 404 miles)
Weights		
Max takeoff	610 kg	(1,345 lbs)
Useful load	210 kg	(463 lbs)

Schleicher AS-K16
— Germany

In common with other German sailplane manufacturers, Schleicher has expanded into motor gliders and built a small series of AS-K16 two-seaters in the 1970s. The AS-K16, designed by Rudolf Kaiser, is of welded tube, wood and fabric construction and has a low-set high-aspect-ratio wing and side-by-side seating for two under a fully transparent side-hinged canopy. The standard powerplant is a 72 h.p. Limbach Volkswagen 1700 driving a Hoffman variable-pitch propeller. It has a retractable tailwheel undercarriage with the main units mounted on the wings and retracting inwards and is fitted with dual controls for its primary training role. The prototype first flew on 2nd February 1971 and 44 were built, many of which are still operational in Germany.

Schleicher AS-K16, D-KAVT

Schleicher AS-K16 (Cont.)

Specification	Schleicher AS-K16	
Powerplant	One 72 h.p. (53.7 kW) Limbach SL.1700.EBI piston engine	
Dimensions		
Span	16 m	(52 ft 6 in)
Length	7.32 m	(24 ft 1 in)
Height	2.1 m	(6 ft 10 in)
Performance		
Max speed	200 km/h	(108 kt, 124 mph)
Cruising speed	170 km/h	(92 kt, 106 mph)
Initial climb	150 m/min	(492 fpm)
Range	330 km	(178 nm, 205 miles)
Weights		
Max takeoff	317 kg	(700 lbs)
Useful load	104 kg	(230 lbs)

Schweizer SGM 2-37 and RG-38A — USA

Schweizer, as the principal American manufacturer of gliders and sailplanes, developed a powered glider designated SGM 2-37 which first flew on 21st September 1982. The SGM 2-37, which has a two-seat cockpit with a sliding canopy and a fixed tailwheel undercarriage, combines the rear fuselage of the SGS 2-32 sailplane with wings from the SGS 1-36 and the 112 h.p. Lycoming O-235 engine unit of a Piper Tomahawk. The main customer was the USAF Air Academy at Colorado Springs which received 12 examples, designated TG-7A. The SA 2-37A is a specialised version for law enforcement and covert surveillance which first flew in 1986, and has a silenced 235 h.p. Lycoming IO-540-W3A5D engine, increased fuel capacity, a longer wing, a larger cockpit incorporating a belly FLIR turret and an equipment bay for cameras and sensors. Of the seven production aircraft three were delivered to the US Coast Guard as the RG-8A Condor for drug surveillance and at least two were supplied to Colombia. Schweizer has also re-engineered the RG-8A as the RU-38A Twin Condor with two push-pull 350 h.p. Continental GIO-550 engines mounted on the central pod fuselage, a fixed tricycle undercarriage and surveillance equipment fitted in the front section of each boom. The RU-38B has turbocharged 450 h.p. GTSIO-550 engines. The RU-38A first flew on 31st May 1995 and a second aircraft has also been delivered to the USCG.

Schweizer TG-7A, USAF, 82-0040 (N26AF)

Schweizer RG-8A, USCG, 8101

Specification	Schweizer SA 2-37A	
Powerplant	One 235 h.p. (175 kW) Textron Lycoming IO-540-W3A5D piston engine	
Dimensions		
Span	18.74 m	(61 ft 6 in)
Length	8.46 m	(27 ft 9 in)
Height	2.36 m	(7 ft 9 in)
Performance		
Max speed	257 km/h	(139 kt, 160 mph)
Cruising speed	238 km/h	(129 kt, 148 mph)
Initial climb	293 m/min	(960 fpm)
Range	560 km	(304 nm, 350 miles)
Weights		
Max takeoff	1,587 kg	(3,500 lbs)
Useful load	669 kg	(1,475 lbs)

Schweizer (Hughes) 269 — USA

The Model 269 light helicopter was designed by Hughes Helicopters as a training and general utility machine for civil and military use. The design was simple with a two-seat fully enclosed cabin module, a slim tubular tail boom carrying an anti-torque rotor, a skid undercarriage and a mounting for the Lycoming O-360 engine behind the cabin section. The prototype flew on 2nd October 1956 and, as the Hughes 269A, was sold with either a 160 h.p. Lycoming O-360-C2D or 180 h.p. O-360-B1A engine. In total 795 were delivered as the TH-55A Osage trainer to the US Army together with 354 commercial aircraft. The 269B had the 180 h.p. engine and a three-seat interior and the 269C (known as the 300C) was a higher-weight model with an injected 190 h.p. HIO-360-D1A engine. The Model 269 was also built in Italy by BredaNardi and 35 269As were completed by Kawasaki in Japan as the TH-55J for the JGSDF. Schweizer Aircraft took over manufacture in 1983 and acquired all rights in 1986. They have also built the TH-300C two-seat trainer version of the 269C, the 300C Sky Knight law enforcement version and the Model 300CB (269C-1) with a lower gross weight and 180 h.p. Lycoming GHO-360-C1A engine. Schweizer is also testing an unmanned UAV version of the 269. Over 2,550 examples of the Hughes and Schweizer 269 have been built.

Schweizer 300C (269C), G-BOVY

Specification	Schweizer 300C (269C)	
Powerplant	One 190 h.p. (141 kW) Textron Lycoming HIO-360-D1A piston engine	
Dimensions		
Rotor diameter	8.18 m	(26 ft 10 in)
Length	6.76 m	(22 ft 2 in)
Height	2.67 m	(8 ft 9 in)
Performance		
Max speed	176 km/h	(95 kt, 109 mph)
Cruising speed	159 km/h	(86 kt, 99 mph)
Initial climb	228 m/min	(750 fpm)
Range	360 km	(195 nm, 224 miles)
Weights		
Max takeoff	930 kg	(2,050 lbs)
Useful load	431 kg	(950 lbs)

Schweizer 330 — USA

The airframe of the Model 269 (Schweizer 300C) was developed by Schweizer for the US Army's 1990 NTH competition for a TH-55 replacement. The initial Model 330 (269D), which first flew in 1988, was a Model 269 with a wider three-/four-seat cabin, higher weights, broader chord rotor blades and a 420 s.h.p. (de-rated to 235 s.h.p.) Allison 250-C20W turboshaft engine. No US Army order was forthcoming, but the commercial Schweizer 330 was an improved model with a fully enclosed streamlined fuselage and tail boom, a modified skid undercarriage and a new vertical fin and horizontal tailplane with endplates. Seating is provided for four people in a staggered two-plus-two arrangement. The Model 330SP has a taller undercarriage, larger rotor blades and increased maximum speed and range, and the latest Schweizer 333 has increased useful load, longer rotor blades and higher speed performance. Nearly 60 Schweizer 330s had been built by the end of 1999, many being delivered for law enforcement.

Schweizer 330, N433CK

Specification	Schweizer 330SP	
Powerplant	One 235 s.h.p. (175 kW) Allison 250-C20W turboshaft	
Dimensions		
Rotor diameter	8.31 m	(27 ft 3 in)
Length	6.83 m	(22 ft 5 in)
Height	3.35 m	(11 ft 0 in)
Performance		
Max speed	200 km/h	(108 kt, 124 mph)
Cruising speed	185 km/h	(100 kt, 115 mph)
Initial climb	433 m/min	(1,420 fpm)
Range	590 km	(318 nm, 367 miles)
Weights		
Max takeoff	1,025 kg	(2,260 lbs)
Useful load	508 kg	(1,120 lbs)

Scintex ML.250 Rubis — France

The Rubis was first flown on 25th May 1961 as the ML.145, powered by a 145 h.p. Continental O-300-B engine. It was developed by Scintex who were builders of the Emeraude and Super Emeraude and, like those aircraft, the Rubis was of all-wooden construction and had a cantilever tapered low wing. It was a four-seat tourer with a swept tail and, unusually, a retractable tailwheel undercarriage. The production ML.250 Rubis, which first flew on 3rd June 1962 and had a five-seat interior and a larger tail, was upgraded to a 250 h.p. Lycoming O-540 engine. Only eight examples of the Rubis were built, including prototypes, but four remain in service in France.

Scintex ML.250 Rubis, F-BJMA

Scintex ML.250 Rubis (Cont.)

Specification	Scintex ML.250 Rubis	
Powerplant	One 250 h.p. (186.4 kW) Textron Lycoming O-540-A1D5 piston engine	
Dimensions		
Span	10.26 m	(33 ft 8 in)
Length	7.75 m	(25 ft 5 in)
Height	1.9 m	(6 ft 3 in)
Performance		
Max speed	315 km/h	(170 kt, 196 mph)
Cruising speed	299 km/h	(162 kt, 186 mph)
Initial climb	389 m/min	(1,275 fpm)
Range	1,192 km	(648 nm, 745 miles)
Weights		
Max takeoff	1,475 kg	(3,252 lbs)
Useful load	675 kg	(1,488 lbs)

Scottish Aviation Twin Pioneer — UK

Prestwick-based Scottish Aviation's first product was the military Pioneer utility aircraft and they followed this with the larger Twin Pioneer. It was a strut-braced high-wing light STOL transport fitted with high-lift wing devices and it had a large square-section fuselage with 16-passenger capacity and a fixed tailwheel undercarriage. It was fitted with a pair of 570 h.p. Alvis Leonides 503/8 radial piston engines. The prototype first flew on 25th June 1955 and first production deliveries took place in 1957. Variants included the Series 1 with 560 h.p. Leonides 514/8 engines, the Series 2 with 600 h.p. Pratt & Whitney Wasp R-1340-S1H1-Gs and the Series 3 with 640 h.p. Leonides 531s. The RAF received 39 Series 1 aircraft (later upgraded to Series 3 standard) as the Twin Pioneer CC.1 and CC.2 and other military users included the Malaysian Air Force, which received 15. In total, 86 production aircraft were completed and commercial users included Philippine Airlines and de Kroonduif in New Guinea. Several Twin Pioneers are still airworthy in the UK and Australia.

Scottish Aviation Twin Pioneer, G-APRS

Specification	Scottish Aviation Twin Pioneer Srs.3	
Powerplant	Two 640 h.p. (477.18 kW) Alvis Leonides 531 piston engines	
Dimensions		
Span	23.32 m	(76 ft 6 in)
Length	13.79 m	(45 ft 3 in)
Height	3.73 m	(12 ft 3 in)
Performance		
Max speed	301 km/h	(163 kt, 187 mph)
Cruising speed	212 km/h	(115 kt, 132 mph)
Initial climb	268 m/min	(880 fpm)
Range	1,120 km	(609 nm, 700 miles)
Weights		
Max takeoff	6,621 kg	(14,600 lbs)
Useful load	1,995 kg	(4,400 lbs)

Scottish Aviation B.125 Bulldog — UK

The B.125 Bulldog two-seat aerobatic military trainer was developed from the Beagle Pup (see separate entry) prior to the collapse of Beagle Aircraft in February 1970. The Bulldog differed from the Pup in having a larger sliding canopy, no seats in the rear cabin, a larger wing, higher weights and a 200 h.p. Lycoming IO-360 engine with a constant-speed propeller. The Beagle-built prototype flew on 19th May 1969 and after Scottish Aviation took over the project they flew a second aircraft on 14th February 1971. A total of 331 production aircraft were built including units for the air forces of Sweden (Srs.101), Nigeria (Srs.123), Botswana (Srs.1210), Hong Kong (Srs.128), Malaysia (Srs.102), Kenya (Srs.103), Ghana (Srs.122) and Jordan (Srs.125), and for the RAF to equip university air squadrons (Srs.121 Bulldog T.1). The Bulldog remains in service in Sweden but started to be withdrawn from RAF service during 2000. A number of ex-military Bulldogs which have been civilianised in Malaysia and the UK are flying with private owners and a batch of ex-RAF aircraft has been delivered to the Malta armed forces. Scottish Aviation also built a single prototype of the Bullfinch which was flown on 20th August 1976. It had a longer fuselage with four seats, increased wingspan and a retractable tricycle undercarriage, and it is privately owned in the UK.

Scottish Aviation Bulldog T.1, RAF, XX528

Specification	Scottish Aviation Srs.121 Bulldog T.1	
Powerplant	One 200 h.p. (149.12 kW) Textron Lycoming IO-360-A1B6 piston engine	
Dimensions		
Span	10.06 m	(33 ft 0 in)
Length	7.09 m	(23 ft 3 in)
Height	2.28 m	(7 ft 6 in)
Performance		
Max speed	241 km/h	(130 kt, 150 mph)
Cruising speed	222 km/h	(120 kt, 138 mph)
Initial climb	307 m/min	(1,006 fpm)
Range	992 km	(539 nm, 620 miles)
Weights		
Max takeoff	1,066 kg	(2,350 lbs)
Useful load	422 kg	(930 lbs)

Seabird Seeker — Australia

Seabird Aviation designed the Seeker as a dedicated surveillance aircraft for civil and military use to fulfil roles met by helicopters, but at a lower cost. The Seeker is a strut-braced high-wing aircraft with a low-set tubular boom rear fuselage, a tailwheel undercarriage and a pusher engine installation. The main fuselage module, fitted with side-by-side seating for two, is set well ahead of the wing with extensive cabin glazing to give maximum vision for search missions. The prototype SB5N Sentinel was first flown on 1st October 1989 powered by a Norton rotary engine, and the later SB5E had an Emdair engine. The definitive version intended for production, two of which have been built, is the SB7L Seeker, powered by a 160 h.p. Lycoming O-360, and the first example (initially with a 116 h.p. O-235 engine) flew on 6th June 1991. The Seeker has been certificated but only six development aircraft had been completed by the end of 2000, although proposals were in hand for production by Evektor in the Czech Republic.

Seabird Seeker SB7L, VH-ZIG

Specification	Seabird Seeker SB7L	
Powerplant	One 160 h.p. (119.3 kW) Textron Lycoming O-360-B2C	
Dimensions		
Span	10.59 m	(34 ft 9 in)
Length	6.76 m	(22 ft 2 in)
Height	2.39 m	(7 ft 10 in)
Performance		
Max speed	192 km/h	(103 kt, 119 mph)
Cruising speed	158 km/h	(85 kt, 98 mph)
Initial climb	229 m/min	(750 fpm)
Range	821 km	(446 nm, 513 miles)
Weights		
Max takeoff	800 kg	(1,764 lbs)
Useful load	250 kg	(551 lbs)

SEPECAT Jaguar — International

The highly capable Jaguar ground attack fighter, which has distinguished itself in recent European and Middle East conflicts and remains in front-line service, is the result of design and manufacturing cooperation between British Aerospace and Avions Breguet (later Dassault-Breguet) under the joint SEPECAT organisation (Société Européenne de Production de l'Avion de l'École de Combat et d'Appui Tactique). Distantly related to the Breguet Taon light fighter design, the Jaguar has a compound-sweep shoulder-set wing, ahead of which are intakes for the twin Rolls Royce Turboméca Adour reheated turbojets. It has four underwing hardpoints, two overwing pylons for Sidewinder AAMs and a centreline position for a fuel tank, reconnaissance pod or offensive ordnance. The prototype Jaguar first flew on 8th September 1968 and first deliveries were made to the RAF in early 1973, and to the Armée de l'Air in January 1972. Both single-seat and tandem two-seat combat-capable trainer versions were built as the Jaguar S (GR.Mk.1) and Jaguar B (T.Mk.2) for the RAF and Jaguar A and Jaguar E for the Armée de l'Air, although there is a different specification of equipment and avionics between the British and French aircraft including variations in the laser ranging and radar capability. A total of 325 single-seat and 75 two-seat aircraft were delivered to the UK and France between 1972 and 1978. The Jaguar International is the export version, 42 of which were sold in single- and two-seat forms and delivered to Oman (Jaguar OS and two-seat OB), Nigeria (Jaguar SN and two-seat BN) and Ecuador (Jaguar ES and two-seat EB). For the Indian Air Force, the Jaguar was manufactured by Hindustan Aircraft, which delivered 116 as the single-seat Jaguar IS and two-seat Jaguar IT.

SEPECAT Jaguar GR.1A, RAF 16 Sqn, XX745

SEPECAT Jaguar (Cont.)

SEPECAT Jaguar E, French AF, No. E9

Shenyang F-8IIM

Specification	SEPECAT Jaguar GR.Mk.1	
Powerplant	Two 8,040 lb.s.t. (35.75 kN) (wet) Rolls Royce-Turboméca Adour Mk.104 turbofans	
Dimensions		
Span	8.69 m	(28 ft 6 in)
Length	16.84 m	(55 ft 3 in)
Height	4.9 m	(16 ft 1 in)
Performance		
Max speed	1,698 km/h	(917 kt, 1,055 mph)
Initial climb	6,096 m/min	(20,000 fpm)
Range	1,696 km	(922 nm, 1,060 miles)
Weights		
Max takeoff	15,700 kg	(34,618 lbs)
Useful load	8,000 kg	(17,640 lbs)

Shenyang J-8II — People's Republic of China

Following a long period of manufacture of the MiG-21 (J-7), Chinese designers developed the J-8 high-altitude Mach 2.2 air superiority fighter in the mid-1960s. The prototype J-8 was completed and flown by the Shenyang factory on 5th July 1969. Broadly based on the J-7, the J-8 was a larger aircraft with two 13,450 lb.s.t. Guizhou WP-7B reheated turbojets positioned side by side in the rear fuselage. It retained the nose air intake layout of the J-7 and this contained a large centre-body radar cone on the J-8I (NATO name 'Finback-A') all-weather fighter variant. Production eventually commenced in 1985 and around 100 aircraft were completed. The J-8II (Finback-B) was a much improved air superiority and ground attack version with a new fire control system and avionics and increased carrying capacity for external armament. It was fitted with Guizhou WP-13A engines and the forward fuselage was redesigned with fuselage side air intakes allowing the aircraft to have a large radar nose. The J-8II was first flown on 12th June 1984 and Shenyang has also built prototypes of the F-8IIM, which is an improved export version with higher-thrust WP-13B engines and a modernised cockpit with a HUD and HOTAS controls.

Specification	Shenyang F-8IIM	
Powerplant	Two 15,432 lb.s.t. (68.7 kN) (wet) Guizhou WP-13B turbojets	
Dimensions		
Span	9.35 m	(30 ft 8 in)
Length	21.59 m	(70 ft 10 in)
Height	5.41 m	(17 ft 9 in)
Performance		
Max speed	2,695 km/h	(1,456 kt, 1,675 mph)
Initial climb	13,442 m/min	(44,100 fpm)
Range	1,600 km	(870 nm, 1,000 miles)
Weights		
Max takeoff	18,879 kg	(41,628 lbs)
Useful load	8,508 kg	(18,760 lbs)

Sherpa Aircraft Sherpa — USA

Intended as a rugged six-seat STOL utility aircraft for remote operations, the Sherpa prototype was built in 1994 and, together with two further aircraft, is under development for FAR Part 23 certification. It is of mixed construction with a tubular steel fuselage and tail covered in fabric and light alloy, and metal wings which are fitted with large flaps and additional spoilerons for roll control. The main cabin accommodates three rows of seats which can all be removed for cargo work, and loads of up to ten 55-gallon drums can be carried. A variety of landing gear configurations are available including amphibious floats, skis and oversize tundra tyres. After certification the definitive eight-seat Sherpa Turbo 8 is to be built by Byron Root's Sherpa Aircraft Manufacturing Co. at Scappoose, Oregon.

Sherpa Aircraft Sherpa, N1415B

Sherwood Ranger, G-MWND

Specification	Sherpa Aircraft Sherpa Turbo 8	
Powerplant	One 450 h.p. (298 kW) Textron Lycoming TIO-720-A1B piston engine	
Dimensions		
Span	13.69 m	(44 ft 11 in)
Length (prov)	13.51 m	(44 ft 4 in)
Height (prov)	2.29 m	(7 ft 6 in)
Performance		
Max speed	274 km/h	(148 kt, 170 mph)
Cruising speed	257 km/h	(139 kt, 160 mph)
Takeoff distance	31 m	(102 ft)
Range	640 km	(348 nm, 400 miles)
Weights		
Max takeoff	2,494 kg	(5,500 lbs)
Useful load	1,136 kg	(2,504 lbs)

Specification	Sherwood Ranger XP	
Powerplant	One 64 h.p. (47.72 kW) Rotax 582UL-2V piston engine	
Dimensions		
Span	7.01 m	(23 ft 0 in)
Length	6.1 m	(20 ft 0 in)
Height	2.59 m	(8 ft 6 in)
Performance		
Max speed	193 km/h	(104 kt, 120 mph)
Cruising speed	137 km/h	(74 kt, 85 mph)
Initial climb	366 m/min	(1,200 fpm)
Range	320 km	(174 nm, 200 miles)
Weights		
Max takeoff	450 kg	(992 lbs)
Useful load	227 kg	(500 lbs)

Sherwood Ranger — UK

The Ranger two-seat ultralight biplane was designed by Russell Light and developed by TCD Ltd. who flew a prototype in 1993. It is built primarily from light alloy tube with fabric covering and it has tandem open cockpits. The wings, which have ailerons on all surfaces, are quickly foldable for transport and storage and the Ranger has a fixed tailwheel undercarriage. The aircraft is available in plans or quickbuild kit form for amateur construction as the LW (lightweight) and ST (standard). It can be powered by a variety of lightweight engines in the 40 h.p. to 80 h.p. range including the Jabiru and Ultratech, or the 50 h.p. Rotax 503UL-2V (Ranger LW), the 64 h.p. Rotax 582 or the 74 h.p. Rotax 618UL-2V (Ranger ST). The Ranger XP is a short-wing aerobatic version with a greater roll rate which can be fitted with engines of up to 100 h.p. At least six Rangers are flying, including one Ranger XP in the USA.

ShinMaywa US-1A — Japan

Shin Meiwa (later ShinMaywa Industries) originally designed the SS-2 large flying boat in the mid-1960s to meet a requirement for a long-range patrol aircraft for the Japanese MSDF. The initial model, designated PS-1 for anti-submarine service with the JMSDF, was a pure flying boat and the prototype (designated PX-S) first flew on 6th October 1967. It was a high-wing aircraft with a T-tail and four 3,060 s.h.p. Ishikawajima-built General Electric T64-IHI-10 turboprops, and was designed to carry a crew of ten including radar and sonar operators. In addition to the two prototypes, Shin Meiwa delivered 23 production PS-1s. This was followed by the US-1 which is an amphibious search & rescue model flown on 16th October 1974 and fitted with a retractable tricycle undercarriage. In total 19 have been delivered to the JMSDF to replace the PS-1 fleet and all have now been upgraded to US-1A standard with higher-powered T64-IHI-10J engines. Some 16 continue in service with 71 Kokutai and it is intended that these will be upgraded to US-1Kai standard with Allison AE.2100 turboprops.

ShinMaywa US-1A (Cont.)

ShinMaywa US-1A, JMSDF, 9082

Specification	ShinMaywa US-1A	
Powerplant	Four 3,400 s.h.p. (2,535 kW) Ishikawajima T64-IHI-10J turboprops	
Dimensions		
Span	33.15 m	(108 ft 9 in)
Length	33.45 m	(109 ft 9 in)
Height	9.96 m	(32 ft 8 in)
Performance		
Max speed	512 km/h	(276 kt, 318 mph)
Cruising speed	426 km/h	(230 kt, 265 mph)
Initial climb	488 m/min	(1,600 fpm)
Range	3,792 km	(2,061 nm, 2,370 miles)
Weights		
Max takeoff	44,989 kg	(99,200 lbs)
Useful load	19,492 kg	(42,980 lbs)

Shorts Skyvan — UK

The SC.7 Skyvan is a high-wing utility aircraft developed by Short Bros. in the early 1960s incorporating design features of the Caravan project inherited from Miles Aircraft. The SC.7 was built around an unpressurised square-section fuselage with a rear loading ramp and had a fixed tricycle undercarriage and twin fins. The first of two prototypes, powered by a pair of 390 h.p. Continental GTSIO-520 piston engines, flew on 17th January 1963 but the initial production model was the Skyvan 2, fitted with two 637 s.h.p. Astazou X turboprops. Some 17 Skyvan 2s were built before the Skyvan 3 was introduced with 715 s.h.p. Garrett TPE331-201A engines. A total of 136 were completed and most of the Skyvan 2s were re-engined with the TPE331 powerplants. A number of SC.7s were built as 22-passenger Skyliner local service airliners which did not have the rear cargo ramp, and users included the Highlands and Islands service of British European Airways. Skyvan 3Ms with a nose radome and hardened interior were supplied to several military air arms including those of Argentina, Oman, Austria, Nepal, Yemen, Ghana, Mexico and the Thai Border Police, and the type was widely used by freight operators in Alaska and with Air America in Vietnam. Around half the production aircraft are still active including several used on passenger services in Malaysia.

Shorts Skyvan 3, C-GDRG

Specification	Shorts SC.7 Skyvan 3	
Powerplant	Two 715 s.h.p. (533.1 kW) Honeywell (Garrett) TPE331-201 turboprops	
Dimensions		
Span	19.79 m	(64 ft 11 in)
Length	12.22 m	(40 ft 1 in)
Height	4.60 m	(15 ft 1 in)
Performance		
Max speed	311 km/h	(168 kt, 193 mph)
Cruising speed	278 km/h	(150 kt, 173 mph)
Initial climb	472 m/min	(1,550 fpm)
Range	1,115 km	(606 nm, 697 miles)
Weights		
Max takeoff	5,669 kg	(12,500 lbs)
Useful load	2,363 kg	(5,210 lbs)

Shorts 360, G-BNFB

Shorts 330 and 360 — UK

Sales of the Shorts Skyliner version of the Skyvan resulted in a new commuter version being developed with a fuselage stretch to accommodate 33 passengers, and this was designated SD.330. Modifications to the SC.7 involved some alterations to the wings, a retractable undercarriage embodying external gear pods and installation of 1,198 s.h.p. Pratt & Whitney PT6A-45 turboprops. The SD.330 prototype first flew on 22nd August 1974. The SD.330 (later designated Shorts 330-200) was popular with American commuter operators due to its large cabin and Shorts sold aircraft to operators such as Allegheny Commuter, Golden West, Hawaiian Airlines and Mississippi Valley, and to European users including Olympic Airways and DLT. Some 34 Sherpa military freighters, fitted with a ventral rear loading ramp, were delivered to the USAF (C-23A) and US Army National Guard (C-23B), and the Model 330-UTT (utility tactical transport) was a dedicated military variant sold to the Royal Thai Army, Royal Thai Police and other military users. In total, 139 production Shorts 330s were built. Shorts also produced the Shorts 360 which was a 330 with a stretched 36-passenger fuselage and a single vertical tail unit. The prototype first flew on 1st June 1981 and production variants, powered by two 1,424 s.h.p. Pratt & Whitney PT6A-65AR engines, included the basic Srs.100 and 200 and the Srs.300 with six-blade propellers and modified wing support struts. Total production of the 360 was 164 aircraft and 17 commercial machines have been converted to C-23B Sherpa standard with twin tails and rear ramps for the US Army.

Shorts C-23B Sherpa, USAF, 88-1863

Specification	Shorts 330	
Powerplant	Two 1,198 s.h.p. (893 kW) Pratt & Whitney PT6A-45R turboprops	
Dimensions		
Span	22.76 m	(74 ft 8 in)
Length	17.69 m	(58 ft 0 in)
Height	4.95 m	(16 ft 3 in)
Performance		
Max speed	352 km/h	(190 kt, 218 mph)
Cruising speed	296 km/h	(160 kt, 184 mph)
Initial climb	360 m/min	(1,180 fpm)
Range	1,695 km	(921 nm, 1,059 miles)
Weights		
Max takeoff	10,385 kg	(22,900 lbs)
Useful load	3,707 kg	(8,173 lbs)

Shorts SC.5/10 Belfast — UK

The Belfast was designed specifically to meet a Royal Air Force requirement for a heavy freighter. It had a high wing in order to give an unobstructed internal cargo hold and the main undercarriage units were externally mounted in large fuselage side fairings. The fuselage had an upswept rear section to accommodate a ventral loading ramp and the Belfast C.Mk.1 was powered by four 5,730 s.h.p. Rolls Royce Tyne turboprops. For trooping work the aircraft could be fitted with 250 seats including 100 on the upper deck, and a standard crew of five was carried. The first of ten production aircraft, there being no prototype, was flown on 5th January 1964. Shorts sought further orders from civil or military customers but were unsuccessful and the final delivery was made in November 1971. They only served with the RAF until 1976, at which time they were declared surplus. Three remain in commercial ownership for heavy freight tasks.

Shorts SC.5/10 Belfast (Cont.)

Shorts SC.5 Belfast, G-BEPS

Specification	Shorts SC.5/10 Belfast	
Powerplant	Four 5,730 s.h.p. (4,272 kW) Rolls Royce Tyne RTy.12 turboprops	
Dimensions		
Span	48.38 m	(158 ft 9 in)
Length	41.58 m	(136 ft 5 in)
Height	14.32 m	(47 ft 0 in)
Performance		
Max speed	566 km/h	(306 kt, 352 mph)
Cruising speed	541 km/h	(292 kt, 336 mph)
Initial climb	323 m/min	(1,060 fpm)
Range	8,480 km	(4,609 nm, 5,300 miles)
Weights		
Max takeoff	102,040 kg	(225,000 lbs)
Useful load	45,351 kg	(100,000 lbs)

SIAI-Marchetti FN.333 Riviera — Italy

The FN.333, which was designed by Nardi S.A. per Costruzioni Aeronautiche and first flew on 4th December 1952, was a three-seat all-metal amphibian with a cantilever high wing, twin booms and a long tapered lower-fuselage planing hull. It also had a retractable tricycle undercarriage, and the first prototype's 145 h.p. Continental engine was mounted as a pusher on the wing centre section. The next four prototypes were the four-seat FN.333S, which had a 225 h.p. Continental C-125. The production aircraft, built by SIAI-Marchetti under licence as the FN.333 Riviera, had a larger vertical tail unit, outrigger floats which retracted into wingtip housings and enlarged side windows. This production version was fitted with a 250 h.p. Continental IO-470-P. SIAI built 23 commercial Rivieras, many of which were sold in the USA to private owners as the Lane Riviera, and at least eight remain airworthy.

SIAI-Marchetti FN.333 Riviera, N95DR

Specification	SIAI-Marchetti FN.333 Riviera	
Powerplant	One 250 h.p. (186.4 kW) Teledyne Continental IO-470-P piston engine	
Dimensions		
Span	10.39 m	(34 ft 1 in)
Length	7.39 m	(24 ft 3 in)
Height	3.23 m	(10 ft 7 in)
Performance		
Max speed	285 km/h	(154 kt, 177 mph)
Cruising speed	264 km/h	(143 kt, 164 mph)
Initial climb	372 m/min	(1,220 fpm)
Range	1,384 km	(752 nm, 865 miles)
Weights		
Max takeoff	1,483 kg	(3,270 lbs)
Useful load	440 kg	(970 lbs)

SIAI-Marchetti SM.1019E — Italy

The SM.1019 was a replacement for the fleet of Cessna O-1 Bird Dogs in service with the Italian Aviazione Leggera dell'Esercito (Army Aviation, now Air Cavalry). Two prototypes were built based on O-1 airframes which were refurbished and fitted with a 400 s.h.p. Allison 250 turboprop engine and an enlarged vertical tail, and the first of these flew on 24th May 1969. The production SM.1019E, which is equipped with tandem seating for two crew members, had many detail changes including a modified rearview cabin section, a rear entry door for the observer, who also had separate controls and an instrument panel, and a hardened wing to carry loads of up to 500 lbs. of rockets, bombs and podded guns. SIAI-Marchetti built 80 examples of the SM.1019E for use in forward air control, battlefield reconnaissance and army close support work. A few of these remain in service.

SIAI-Marchetti SM.1019E, Italian ALE, MM.57236

SIAI S.208M, Italian AF, MM.61975

Specification	SIAI-Marchetti SM.1019E	
Powerplant	One 400 s.h.p. (298 kW) Allison 250-B17 turboprop	
Dimensions		
Span	10.97 m	(36 ft 0 in)
Length	8.51 m	(27 ft 11 in)
Height	2.84 m	(9 ft 4 in)
Performance		
Max speed	298 km/h	(161 kt, 185 mph)
Cruising speed	282 km/h	(152 kt, 175 mph)
Initial climb	552 m/min	(1,810 fpm)
Range	1,120 km	(609 nm, 700 miles)
Weights		
Max takeoff	1,450 kg	(3,197 lbs)
Useful load	760 kg	(1,676 lbs)

Specification	SIAI-Marchetti S.205/20F	
Powerplant	One 200 h.p. (149.12 kW) Textron Lycoming IO-360-A1A piston engine	
Dimensions		
Span	10.85 m	(35 ft 7 in)
Length	8 m	(26 ft 3 in)
Height	2.9 m	(9 ft 6 in)
Performance		
Max speed	249 km/h	(135 kt, 155 mph)
Cruising speed	225 km/h	(122 kt, 140 mph)
Initial climb	235 m/min	(770 fpm)
Range	1,328 km	(722 nm, 830 miles)
Weights		
Max takeoff	1,300 kg	(2,866 lbs)
Useful load	575 kg	(1,268 lbs)

SIAI-Marchetti S.205 — Italy

On 4th May 1965, SIAI-Marchetti flew the prototype of their new S.205 four-seat civil and military light aircraft. The airframe was designed from the outset as the basis for a range of models with different powerplants and with fixed or retractable undercarriages. The S.205 was an all-metal low-wing aircraft and the standard S.205/18F had a 180 h.p. Lycoming O-360-A1A engine and a fixed tricycle undercarriage. Further variants, some of which were fitted with optional wingtip tanks, included the similar S.205/18R with retractable gear, the S.205/20F and S.205/20R with a 200 h.p. Lycoming IO-360-A1A engine and, respectively, fixed and retractable gear, and the S.205/22R for the American market with a 220 h.p. Franklin 6A-350.C1 engine, a fifth rear seat and a retractable undercarriage which was sold as the Waco Vela. The S.208 was a five-seat retractable gear version with additional rear side windows and a 260 h.p. Lycoming O-540-E4A engine. Some 45 military S.208Ms were acquired by the Italian Air Force for training and communications. In total, 313 of the S.205/208 series were built including a large batch for the Italian national flying clubs.

SIAI-Marchetti F.600 Canguro — Italy

Ing. Stelio Frati designed the F.600 as a 9-/11-seat twin-engined light utility aircraft and his company, General Avia, flew the prototype on 30th December 1978. In its original form, the F.600 was a cantilever high-wing aircraft powered by two 310 h.p. Lycoming TIO-540-A1B piston engines. It had a square-section fuselage, fitted with a large port-side freight door and a forward crew entry door, and a fixed tricycle undercarriage, the main units of which were attached to external stubs. The design was adopted by SIAI-Marchetti who decided also to build the SF.600TP version with 420 h.p. Allison 250-B17C engines. All production Canguros have been turboprop-powered and an alternative version with a retractable undercarriage has also been built. SIAI completed ten Canguros but it is now manufactured by Naples-based VulcanAir who are selling the SF.600A with 450 s.h.p. Allison 250-B17F1 engines.

SIAI-Marchetti F.600 Canguro (Cont.)

SIAI-VulcanAir SF.600A Canguro, I-VULA

MBB SIAT-223A-1 Flamingo, D-EHQI

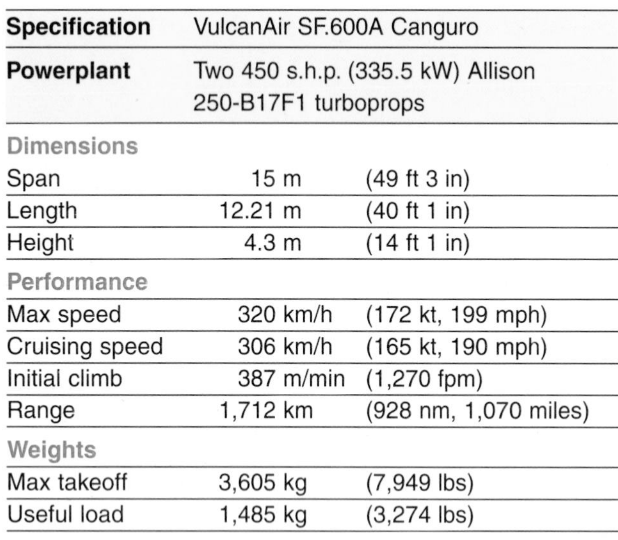

Specification	VulcanAir SF.600A Canguro	
Powerplant	Two 450 s.h.p. (335.5 kW) Allison 250-B17F1 turboprops	
Dimensions		
Span	15 m	(49 ft 3 in)
Length	12.21 m	(40 ft 1 in)
Height	4.3 m	(14 ft 1 in)
Performance		
Max speed	320 km/h	(172 kt, 199 mph)
Cruising speed	306 km/h	(165 kt, 190 mph)
Initial climb	387 m/min	(1,270 fpm)
Range	1,712 km	(928 nm, 1,070 miles)
Weights		
Max takeoff	3,605 kg	(7,949 lbs)
Useful load	1,485 kg	(3,274 lbs)

Specification	MBB SIAT-223A-1 Flamingo	
Powerplant	One 200 h.p. (149.12 kW) Textron Lycoming IO-360-C1B piston engine	
Dimensions		
Span	8.28 m	(27 ft 2 in)
Length	7.42 m	(24 ft 4 in)
Height	2.69 m	(8 ft 10 in)
Performance		
Max speed	243 km/h	(132 kt, 151 mph)
Cruising speed	216 km/h	(117 kt, 134 mph)
Initial climb	258 m/min	(846 fpm)
Range	875 km	(476 nm, 547 miles)
Weights		
Max takeoff	1,050 kg	(2,315 lbs)
Useful load	820 kg	(1,808 lbs)

SIAT (MBB) 223 Flamingo — Germany

The German company SIAT developed the low-wing SIAT-222 light aircraft during the late 1950s, flying the prototype on 15th May 1961. Powered by a 180 h.p. Lycoming engine, it was designed for both civil and military applications and had a fixed tricycle undercarriage and a four-seat cabin enclosed by a bubble canopy. The modified SIAT-223 with a shorter fuselage, modified canopy and larger tail went into production following its first flight on 1st March 1967. Named Flamingo by Messerschmitt-Bölkow-Blohm (MBB), which had absorbed SIAT, the aircraft was powered by a 200 h.p. Lycoming IO-360-C1B and was mainly sold to commercial flight training schools with examples going to the Swissair Training School, the Syrian Air Force and the Turkish Air League. In addition to the standard SIAT-223A-1 it was also built as the SIAT-223K-1 single-seat aerobatic aircraft. Some 29 were built by MBB followed by 17 completed by Farner. In Spain, CASA produced a further 50, most of which went to the Syrian Air Force which is believed still to have some in service. Twelve SIAT-223s are owned by private owners in Germany and Switzerland.

Sikorsky S-38 — USA

For its time, the Sikorsky S-38A Amphibion was one of the most unconventional aircraft built. It was designed by Igor Sikorsky, based on the earlier S-36, and flown in September 1924, intended as a small amphibious biplane flying boat for use by Pan American Airways for Caribbean services. The fuselage was devoted to a large eight-seat cabin and the large upper wing was supported on a central mast with secondary struts which carried the two 410 h.p. Pratt & Whitney Wasp radial engines and had twin booms attached at the rear to carry the tail unit. The fuselage was a wood structure with aluminium covering and the metal wing was fabric-covered. The S-38B had increased fuel capacity and 420 h.p. engines, and the S-38C had a larger cabin for up to ten passengers. None of the 101 original aircraft is now flying but a modern S-38C replica using a few original parts and built by Buzz Kaplan and Born Again Restorations for S.C. Johnson Wax flew on 13th August 1998, and a second replica was under construction at the end of 1999.

Sikorsky S-38C replica, NC-6V

Sikorsky S-43H, NC440

Specification	Sikorsky S-38C	
Powerplant	Two 420 h.p. (313.15 kW) Pratt & Whitney Wasp piston engines	
Dimensions		
Span	21.84 m	(71 ft 8 in)
Length	12.27 m	(40 ft 3 in)
Height	4.22 m	(13 ft 10 in)
Performance		
Max speed	201 km/h	(109 kt, 125 mph)
Cruising speed	177 km/h	(96 kt, 110 mph)
Initial climb	268 m/min	(880 fpm)
Range	960 km	(522 nm, 600 miles)
Weights		
Max takeoff	4,753 kg	(10,480 lbs)
Useful load	1,823 kg	(4,020 lbs)

Specification	Sikorsky S-43H	
Powerplant	Two 750 h.p. (559.2 kW) Pratt & Whitney Hornet S1EG piston engines	
Dimensions		
Span	26.21 m	(86 ft 0 in)
Length	15.93 m	(52 ft 3 in)
Height	5.38 m	(17 ft 8 in)
Performance		
Max speed	299 km/h	(162 kt, 186 mph)
Cruising speed	285 km/h	(154 kt, 177 mph)
Initial climb	335 m/min	(1,100 fpm)
Range	1,240 km	(674 nm, 775 miles)
Weights		
Max takeoff	9,070 kg	(20,000 lbs)
Useful load	3,338 kg	(7,360 lbs)

Sikorsky S-43 — USA

Igor Sikorsky was famous in the 1930s for his series of commercial flying boats which included the large 32-passenger S-42-A Clipper. A smaller version, the S-43, was flown in 1935 and this had a pylon-mounted high wing mounting two Pratt & Whitney Hornet radial engines and main wheels which retracted into large wells in the fuselage sides. The cabin could accommodate up to 25 passengers and there was a separate two-crew forward cockpit. It is thought that 53 S-43s were built, including examples of the twin-tailed S-43B and the S-43W with 760 h.p. Wright Cyclone GR-1820-F52 engines, and 17 were delivered to the US Navy as the JRS-1. The S-43H was a special version built for Howard Hughes for a round-the-world flight with 900 h.p. Wright Cyclone GR-1820-G102 engines. This is the sole survivor, having been recovered from Lake Mead and restored with Pratt & Whitney Hornet engines by Ron Van Kregten of Houston, Texas.

Sikorsky S-52 — USA

The S-52 was one of Sikorsky's early postwar production helicopters, intended primarily for use by the US Marines. The prototype S-52-1, which flew on 12th February 1947, was a side-by-side two-seater with a pod and boom fuselage and a fixed tricycle undercarriage, and was powered by a 178 h.p. Franklin engine. This was followed by the S-58-2 which had a longer forward fuselage giving a four-seat cabin, a four-wheel undercarriage and a 245 h.p. Franklin 6V6-245-B16F (O-425-1) engine. The main production version was the S-52-3, 87 of which were built as the HO5S-1 for the Marine Corps and HO5S-1G for the US Coast Guard with the 245 h.p. Franklin engine. A few civil S-52s were delivered and at least 12 remain active in the USA. Some have been updated using a modification engineered by Vertical Aviation Technologies, and first flown in February 1988, with a nose section similar to a Bell Jet Ranger and a 310 h.p. Ford V-6 engine.

Sikorsky S-52 (Cont.)

Vertical Aviation Technologies (Sikorsky) S-52-3, N9329R

Specification	Sikorsky S-52-3	
Powerplant	One 245 h.p. (182.67 kW) Franklin 6V6-245-B16F piston engine	
Dimensions		
Rotor diameter	10.06 m	(33 ft 0 in)
Length	8.38 m	(27 ft 6 in)
Height	2.64 m	(8 ft 8 in)
Performance		
Max speed	179 km/h	(97 kt, 111 mph)
Cruising speed	146 km/h	(79 kt, 91 mph)
Initial climb	320 m/min	(1,050 fpm)
Range	490 km	(266 nm, 306 miles)
Weights		
Max takeoff	1,224 kg	(2,700 lbs)
Useful load	401 kg	(885 lbs)

Sikorsky S-55 — USA

Sikorsky's S-55 was the standard NATO workhorse helicopter during the 1950s; it saw distinguished service in Korea and was widely used as a civil utility and agricultural machine. Its innovative design features included a nose-mounted 550 h.p. Pratt & Whitney R-1340-57 piston engine with a long drive shaft to the rotor head, a separate crew cockpit on top of the fuselage and a large main cabin capable of carrying up to ten passengers or bulky cargo loads. It had a four-leg undercarriage and a conventional tail boom with a tail anti-torque rotor. The many military versions included the H-19A (USAF), H-19C Chickasaw (US Army) and HO4S-1 (US Navy), and the 700 h.p. Wright R-1300-3-powered H-19B, H-19D, HO4S-3 and HRS-1. The S-55 was built under licence in the UK as the Alvis Leonides-powered Westland Whirlwind (and turbine Gnome Whirlwind), in France by SNCASE ('Elephant Joyeuse') and in Japan by Mitsubishi, and production of these together with Sikorsky units totalled 1,740. More than 100 S-55s remain active and many of these have been converted by Aviation Specialties Inc. to S-55-T standard with an 840 s.h.p. Garrett TSE331-3U-303N turboshaft engine.

Sikorsky S-55, N4549C

Specification	Sikorsky S-55-T	
Powerplant	One 840 s.h.p. (626.3 kW) Honeywell (Garrett) TSE331-3U-303N turboshaft	
Dimensions		
Rotor diameter	16.15 m	(53 ft 0 in)
Length	12.88 m	(42 ft 3 in)
Height	4.06 m	(13 ft 4 in)
Performance		
Max speed	183 km/h	(99 kt, 114 mph)
Cruising speed	158 km/h	(85 kt, 98 mph)
Initial climb	366 m/min	(1,200 fpm)
Range	592 km	(322 nm, 370 miles)
Weights		
Max takeoff	3,265 kg	(7,200 lbs)
Useful load	1,134 kg	(2,500 lbs)

Sikorsky S-58 — USA

The Sikorsky S-58 was developed, initially, as a US Navy anti-submarine helicopter with greater range and useful load than the HO4S (S-55), then in service. The prototype S-58 (XHSS-1), which first flew on 8th March 1954, had a forward fuselage similar to that of the S-55 but a tapered rear fuselage with an angled tailfin carrying the four-bladed anti-torque rotor and double the power of the S-55. The naval HSS-1 (later SH-34G) Seabat was operated in hunter-killer pairs and could carry either a full set of search equipment, including dipping sonar, or homing torpedoes and depth charges, and the US Army CH-34A Choctaw could carry 16 troops in the main cabin. Production commenced in 1955 with the H-34 becoming the standard utility helicopter for the American services and being supplied to a dozen other nations including Belgium, Brazil, the Netherlands and Thailand. Sud Aviation built 130 for the French Air Force and Navy, and Westland built 382 as the Wessex with a 1,450 s.h.p. Napier Gazelle or twin 1,350 s.h.p. Bristol-Siddeley Gnome NG.11 turboshafts. Some civil examples were built and used by city-centre shuttles and as utility aircraft, and many were re-engined as the S-58T with the Pratt & Whitney PT6T-6 TwinPac turboshaft. Total Sikorsky production was 1,821 units and over 200 S-58s remain in civil and military service.

Sikorsky S-58T, N15AH

Specification	Sikorsky S-58T Mk.II	
Powerplant	One 1,875 s.h.p. (1,398 kW) Pratt & Whitney PT6T-6 TwinPac twin turboshaft	
Dimensions		
Rotor diameter	17.07 m	(56 ft 0 in)
Length	20.07 m	(65 ft 10 in)
Height	4.34 m	(14 ft 3 in)
Performance		
Max speed	222 km/h	(120 kt, 138 mph)
Cruising speed	204 km/h	(110 kt, 127 mph)
Initial climb	564 m/min	(1,850 fpm)
Range	480 km	(261 nm, 300 miles)
Weights		
Max takeoff	5,896 kg	(13,000 lbs)
Useful load	2,107 kg	(4,646 lbs)

Sikorsky UH-3H Sea King, US Navy, Bu.148986

Sikorsky S-61 — USA

The S-61 was in production from 1960 to 1980 and has been built in a great number of variants, commencing with the US Navy's S-61B (HSS-2, later H-3) which was required as a larger capacity anti-submarine helicopter to replace the Seabat. The S-61B had a boat hull and outrigger floats and was fitted with two 1,175 s.h.p General Electric T58-GE-6 turboshafts driving a single large five-bladed carrier-foldable main rotor. The prototype YSH-3A first flew on 11th March 1959. Later versions were the SH-3D Sea King with 1,400 s.h.p. T58-GE-10 engines and enhanced SH-3G and SH-3H, the VH-3A Presidential Flight VIP aircraft, HH-3A search & rescue aircraft, RH-3A minesweeper and CH-124 for the Canadian armed forces. The S-61B airframe was stretched to form several civil transport variants including the 28-passenger amphibious S-61N powered by two 1,500 s.h.p. CT-58-140-1 turboshafts, which is used widely for offshore oil operations, and the S-61L, which was similar, but without the water-sealed hull. A number of S-61Ns have been rebuilt for heavy-lift work with a shortened fuselage by Helipro Corporation as the S-61 Short. The S-61R, acquired by the USAF as the CH-3C and CH-3E long-range tactical transports and the HH-3E 'Jolly Green Giant' rescue helicopter, is based on the S-61B but has a longer fuselage with external sponsons, a ventral loading ramp and a raised slim rear tail boom, and 1,500 s.h.p. T58-GE-5 engines. The similar HH-3F Pelican was delivered to the US Coast Guard with internal capacity for 15 stretchers, and Agusta has built this version for SAR missions for the Italian Navy. Exports were made to many countries including Malaysia, Brazil, Argentina and Iran, with Sikorsky building a total of 827 of all S-61 variants. Mitsubishi manufactured 185 S-61s including the SH-3A for the Japanese MSDF, and Westland has also built the Sea King (see separate entry).

Sikorsky S-61N, VH-BRI

Agusta-Sikorsky HH-3F Pelican, Italian AF, MM.80993

Specification	Sikorsky S-61N	
Powerplant	Two 1,500 s.h.p. (1,118 kW) General Electric CT58-140-1 turboshafts	
Dimensions		
Rotor diameter	18.9 m	(62 ft 0 in)
Length	22.2 m	(72 ft 10 in)
Height	5.63 m	(18 ft 5 in)
Performance		
Max speed	235 km/h	(127 kt, 146 mph)
Cruising speed	222 km/h	(120 kt, 138 mph)
Initial climb	395 m/min	(1,300 fpm)
Range	792 km	(430 nm, 495 miles)
Weights		
Max takeoff	9,297 kg	(20,500 lbs)
Useful load	3,624 kg	(7,990 lbs)

Sikorsky S-62 — USA

The S-62 was Sikorsky's first amphibious helicopter and established a basis of design which was carried on into the S-61 Sea King and other models. First flown on 14th May 1958, the S-62, which used various parts from the S-55, had a planing boat hull with outrigger floats attached to the forward fuselage and was powered by a single 1,050 s.h.p. General Electric T58 turboshaft positioned on top of the main cabin section driving a three-bladed main rotor. A batch of 99 S-62As was delivered to the US Coast Guard who operated them from 1963 to 1989 as the HH-52A Seaguard. The S-62B was an improved version with a 1,250 s.h.p. T58-GE-8 engine and a modified dynamic system. A total of 46 commercial aircraft were built as the S-62C for civil customers in the USA and in Argentina, South Africa, Canada and Thailand. A small batch of 25 was also completed under licence in Japan by Mitsubishi as the S-62J. Less than a dozen S-62s remain in operation.

Sikorsky S-62A HH-52A, US Coast Guard, 1378

Specification	Sikorsky S-62C	
Powerplant	One 1,250 s.h.p. (932 kW) General Electric T58-GE-8 turboshaft	
Dimensions		
Rotor diameter	16.15 m	(53 ft 0 in)
Length	13.84 m	(45 ft 5 in)
Height	4.32 m	(14 ft 2 in)
Performance		
Max speed	163 km/h	(88 kt, 101 mph)
Cruising speed	148 km/h	(80 kt, 92 mph)
Initial climb	347 m/min	(1,140 fpm)
Range	739 km	(402 nm, 462 miles)
Weights		
Max takeoff	3,583 kg	(7,900 lbs)
Useful load	1,379 kg	(3,040 lbs)

Specification	Sikorsky S-64E Skycrane	
Powerplant	Two 4,500 s.h.p. (3,355 kW) Pratt & Whitney JFTD-12-4A turboshafts	
Dimensions		
Rotor diameter	21.94 m	(72 ft 0 in)
Length	26.97 m	(88 ft 6 in)
Height	5.66 m	(18 ft 7 in)
Performance		
Max speed	204 km/h	(110 kt, 127 mph)
Cruising speed	175 km/h	(95 kt, 109 mph)
Initial climb	518 m/min	(1,700 fpm)
Range	405 km	(220 nm, 253 miles)
Weights		
Max takeoff	19,048 kg	(42,000 lbs)
Useful load	10,325 kg	(22,766 lbs)

Sikorsky S-64 Skycrane — USA

The unique S-64 Skycrane is a dedicated heavy-lift helicopter which was developed for the West German Army using the dynamic components of the S-56 Mojave heavy assault helicopter. The Skycrane is built around a central main girder with a forward crew pod, incorporating a rear-facing winch operator's station, a central power module with the two Pratt & Whitney turboshafts and the main six-blade rotor system, and a tail mast with a four-bladed stabilising rotor. A central winching unit is fitted to the centre section and a detachable 64-troop transport pod is also available, although this has seldom been used. The S-64A first flew on 9th May 1962, powered by two 4,050 s.h.p. Pratt & Whitney JFTD-12-A1 turboshafts, and 97 were delivered to the US Army as the CH-54A Tarhe with larger 4,500 s.h.p. JFTD-12-4A (T73-P-1) engines, or as the CH-54B with 4,800 s.h.p. T73-P-700 engines and improved rotor blades. Eight civil S-64Es were also built, and when the CH-54A was retired from US Army service a number were converted as S-64Fs for commercial use in logging operations, firefighting and other heavy-lift tasks. Around half the production Skycranes still exist, although not all are active.

Sikorsky S-64E Skycrane, N164AC

Sikorsky S-65 and S-80 — USA

The S-65 is Sikorsky's largest current production helicopter and was produced to a US Marines requirement for a 38-troop assault helicopter, making its first flight on 14th October 1964. It was larger than the S-61N/S-61R although it retained a similar layout to that of the HH-3E and used the dynamic components of the S-64. The two 2,850 s.h.p. General Electric T64-GE-6 turbines were mounted in pods either side of the main rotor pylon and the S-65 had external sponsons, containing fuel and the retracting main undercarriage units, which could also be used as mountings for long-range tanks or other stores. US Marine Corps aircraft were the CH-53A Sea Stallion, and other variants included the S-65A (RH-53A) with 3,925 s.h.p. T64-GE-413 engines for mine sweeping and countermeasures, CH-53C and HH-53C Super Jolly for USAF general transport, ASR and combat rescue missions, the Marines CH-53D 44-seater with 4,380 s.h.p. T64-GE-415 engines and the MH-53J equipped for special forces incursion. Some 110 examples of the CH-54G were built by VFW-Fokker for the German Army. The S-80 (CH-53E) Super Stallion is a further development which first flew on 1st March 1974 and is fitted with three 4,380 s.h.p. T64-GE-416 engines, a seven-bladed main rotor, much enlarged sponsons and a redesigned tailplane and foldable fin. As a mine countermeasures aircraft this is the MH-53E Sea Dragon for the US Navy and the Japanese MSDF (S-80M-1). Approximately 700 of the S-65/S-80 series have been built to date.

Sikorsky MH-53J, USAF, 69-5795

Sikorsky S-65 and S-80 (Cont.)

Sikorsky S-80M-1 Sea Dragon, JMSDF, 8623

Specification	Sikorsky CH-53E Super Stallion	
Powerplant	Three 4,380 s.h.p. (3,266 kW) General Electric T64-GE-416 turboshafts	
Dimensions		
Rotor diameter	24.08 m	(79 ft 0 in)
Length	22.35 m	(73 ft 4 in)
Height	5.31 m	(17 ft 5 in)
Performance		
Max speed	315 km/h	(170 kt, 196 mph)
Cruising speed	278 km/h	(150 kt, 173 mph)
Initial climb	762 m/min	(2,500 fpm)
Range	2,064 km	(1,122 nm, 1,290 miles)
Weights		
Max takeoff	31,633 kg	(69,750 lbs)
Useful load	16,563 kg	(36,522 lbs)

Sikorsky S-70 — USA

Sikorsky's S-70 was the winner of the 1972 US Army UTTAS (utility tactical transport aircraft system) competition and it has been built in various forms for the US military forces and overseas air arms. It has a conventional layout with a central cabin for up to 14 troops and a two-crew cockpit in the nose. The two General Electric T700 turboshafts are mounted externally on the rotor pylon and the S-70 has a four-bladed main rotor and a fixed tailwheel undercarriage. The prototype flew as the YUH-60A on 17th October 1974 with first UH-60A Black Hawk deliveries to the US Army in April 1979. The numerous variants have included the MH-60K special operations aircraft with external long-range tanks, a refuelling boom and special avionics (FLIR, jammers, terrain-following etc.), EH-60A tactical battlefield helicopter, MH-60G Pave Hawk for combat rescue, VH-60A VIP transport and UH-60Q medevac helicopter. Export deliveries have been made to 24 countries including Saudi Arabia, Spain, the Philippines, Thailand and Australia, and the S-70 has been built or assembled in Japan, Turkey, Korea and Australia. Some of these are the S-70B (SH-60B) Sea Hawk naval version designed to the US Navy's LAMPS-III specification with a modified undercarriage, folding tail, external torpedo hardpoints, IBM-fitted integrated ASW, anti-shipping electronics and two 1,690 s.h.p. T700-GE-401 (later 1,900 s.h.p. T700-GE-401C) turboshafts. This first flew on 12th December 1979 and several dedicated versions have been built, including the HH-60J Jayhawk for the US Coast Guard. Sikorsky have also flown the S-70C civil variant, but this has not been sold in any numbers although they are marketing the Firehawk for forest fire suppression. S-70 production continues and more than 1,850 had been built by the end of 2000.

Sikorsky UH-60L Black Hawk, US Army, 97-26783

Sikorsky HH-60J Jayhawk, US Coast Guard, 6009

Specification	Sikorsky UH-60L Black Hawk	
Powerplant	Two 1,800 s.h.p. (1,342 kW) General Electric T700-GE-701C turboshafts	
Dimensions		
Rotor diameter	16.36 m	(53 ft 8 in)
Length	15.26 m	(50 ft 1 in)
Height	3.76 m	(12 ft 4 in)
Performance		
Max speed	296 km/h	(160 kt, 184 mph)
Cruising speed	278 km/h	(150 kt, 173 mph)
Initial climb	239 m/min	(785 fpm)
Range	581 km	(316 nm, 363 miles)
Weights		
Max takeoff	9,977 kg	(22,000 lbs)
Useful load	4,762 kg	(10,500 lbs)

Sikorsky S-76 — USA

The S-76 is the principal civil helicopter in current production by Sikorsky and the prototype first flew on 13th March 1977. It is a 12-passenger high-performance executive and light transport helicopter with an integral fuselage and rear boom, a slim fin and tailplane, and a retractable tricycle undercarriage. The standard S-76 is powered by two 650 s.h.p. Allison 250-C30 turboshafts driving a four-bladed main rotor. The S-76 Mk.II and S-76A are improved versions with a modified dynamic system, and the S-76B has higher-powered 980 s.h.p. Pratt & Whitney PT6B-26B or 36A engines and higher weights. The S-76C is an alternative model with two Turboméca Arriel 1S1 engines, and the S-76C+ has 855 s.h.p. Arriel 2S1 engines and a FADEC system. Several earlier aircraft have been re-engined with Arriels and designated S-76A+. Sikorsky has also tested a dedicated military version named AUH-76 Eagle, but this has not been ordered by any customers to date although the S-76 is in use with several air forces including those of Chile, Spain and Honduras. Over 500 S-76s have been built.

Specification	Sikorsky S-76B	
Powerplant	Two 980 s.h.p. (731 kW) Pratt & Whitney PT6B-36A turboshafts	
Dimensions		
Rotor diameter	13.41 m	(44 ft 0 in)
Length	13.44 m	(44 ft 1 in)
Height	4.39 m	(14 ft 5 in)
Performance		
Max speed	286 km/h	(155 kt, 178 mph)
Cruising speed	267 km/h	(144 kt, 166 mph)
Initial climb	503 m/min	(1,650 fpm)
Range	656 km	(357 nm, 410 miles)
Weights		
Max takeoff	5,306 kg	(11,700 lbs)
Useful load	2,295 kg	(5,060 lbs)

Sikorsky S-76C+, N153AE

Sikorsky S-92 Helibus — USA

The Helibus medium-lift multi-role helicopter is aimed at both military and civil markets and is a smaller-capacity replacement for the S-61N with a 19-/22-passenger main cabin and the ability to handle transport, search & rescue, aeromedical and cargo operations. It has a main cabin with a ventral rear ramp for cargo loading, a two-crew cockpit and external sponsons which accommodate fuel, some baggage and the main undercarriage units. The S-92 has a dynamic system based on that of the S-70 and is powered by two 1,750 s.h.p. GE CT-7-8 turboshafts which are mounted either side of the main rotor pylon. Sikorsky flew the first S-92 on 23rd December 1998 and had flown three prototypes by the end of 1999. In production form the S-92 has an enlarged main door, a longer fuselage and a lowered tailplane. The S-92 is being developed under an international consortium which includes Embraer, Gamesa, Mitsubishi, CATIC and AIDC.

Specification	Sikorsky S-92A Helibus	
Powerplant	Two 1,750 s.h.p. (1,306 kW) General Electric CT-7-8 turboshafts	
Dimensions		
Rotor diameter	17.17 m	(56 ft 4 in)
Length	20.87 m	(68 ft 6 in)
Height	5.4 m	(17 ft 9 in)
Performance		
Max speed	290 km/h	(155 kt, 180 mph)
Range	736 km	(400 nm, 460 miles)
Weights		
Max takeoff	13,600 kg	(29,988 lbs)
Useful load	6,700 kg	(14,774 lbs)

Sikorsky S-92, N292SA

Silvercraft (SIAI) SH-4
— Italy

The SH-4 light three-seat helicopter was designed by Silvercraft Italiana and SIAI-Marchetti with the prototype making its first flight in March 1965. The layout was conventional with a fully enclosed cabin section behind which was attached the 235 h.p. Franklin 6A-350-D piston engine, a high-set tubular corrugated tail boom with a small fin, tailplane and two-bladed tail rotor, and a fixed skid undercarriage. The SH-4 was built by Silvercraft at Sesto Calende from 1968 onwards in standard form and as the SH-4/A for agricultural use. The SH-4/C was an optional model with a supercharged Franklin 6AS-350-D1 engine. In total 21 SH-4s were completed before Silvercraft ceased helicopter activities in 1979. Four SH-4s are believed to be active in Italy, South Africa and France.

Silvercraft SH-4, ZS-HDR

Specification	Silvercraft SH-4/C	
Powerplant	One 235 h.p. (175 kW) Franklin 6A-350-D1B piston engine	
Dimensions		
Rotor diameter	9.02 m	(29 ft 7 in)
Length	7.65 m	(25 ft 1 in)
Height	2.97 m	(9 ft 9 in)
Performance		
Max speed	161 km/h	(87 kt, 100 mph)
Cruising speed	130 km/h	(70 kt, 81 mph)
Initial climb	360 m/min	(1,180 fpm)
Range	320 km	(174 nm, 200 miles)
Weights		
Max takeoff	862 kg	(1,900 lbs)
Useful load	344 kg	(758 lbs)

Sindlinger HH-1 Hurricane
— USA

Designed by Fred G. Sindlinger, the HH-1 is a very convincing amateur-built scale replica of the Hawker Hurricane IIC fighter. It is to 63% scale and has been made available to homebuilders in the form of plans. The first aircraft, which flew in January 1972, was powered by a 150 h.p. Lycoming O-320 engine which required non-scale bulges on the outer cowlings, but subsequent examples have used other powerplants in the 100 h.p to 180 h.p. range which have allowed more authentic fully enclosed cowlings. The Sindlinger Hurricane has an all wood and fabric structure and a manually retracted tailwheel undercarriage. The single-seat cockpit is enclosed with a sliding canopy. As a result of its excellent performance, over 60 sets of plans were sold, and ten aircraft are known to have flown including examples in South Africa and Australia.

Sindlinger HH-1 Hurricane, N3941Q

Specification	Sindlinger HH-1 Hurricane	
Powerplant	One 150 h.p. (112 kW) Textron Lycoming O-320 piston engine	
Dimensions		
Span	7.65 m	(25 ft 1 in)
Length	5.99 m	(19 ft 8 in)
Height	1.78 m	(5 ft 10 in)
Performance		
Max speed	322 km/h	(174 kt, 200 mph)
Cruising speed	274 km/h	(148 kt, 170 mph)
Initial climb	564 m/min	(1,850 fpm)
Range	920 km	(500 nm, 575 miles)
Weights		
Max takeoff	624 kg	(1,375 lbs)
Useful load	177 kg	(391 lbs)

SIPA S.90 — France

Winner of the postwar French government light aircraft design competition, the S.90 was designed by Yves Gardan for SIPA (Société Industrielle pour l'Aéronautique) and was awarded a production order for 100 aircraft for French flying clubs. The S.90 was a low-wing monoplane built from wood and fabric and fitted with a fixed tailwheel undercarriage. The side-by-side two-seat cabin was enclosed by a sliding transparent canopy and the prototype, powered by a 75 h.p. Mathis G4F engine, first flew on 15th June 1947. The production version was the S.901 with a 75 h.p. Minié 4DC-32, but most aircraft were later converted with the Continental C90-12F (S.902) or C90-14F (S.903). A small number of S.91, S.92, S.93 and S.94 aircraft were built with plywood covering instead of fabric. SIPA completed 113 examples, including prototypes, and 15 remain active in France, Switzerland and the UK.

SIPA S.903, HB-SPP

Specification	SIPA S.902	
Powerplant	90 h.p. (67.1 kW) Teledyne Continental C90-12F piston engine	
Dimensions		
Span	8.74 m	(28 ft 8 in)
Length	5.74 m	(18 ft 10 in)
Height	1.75 m	(5 ft 9 in)
Performance		
Max speed	216 km/h	(117 kt, 134 mph)
Cruising speed	193 km/h	(104 kt, 120 mph)
Initial climb	213 m/min	(700 fpm)
Range	504 km	(274 nm, 315 miles)
Weights		
Max takeoff	600 kg	(1,323 lbs)
Useful load	234 kg	(516 lbs)

Sky Arrow (3i) 650 — Italy

Sky Arrow (formerly Meteor SpA, now Iniziative Industriali Italiane, shortened to '3i') devised the Sky Arrow as an affordable trainer and personal light aircraft which would use modern materials and be eligible for various certification categories, and could be powered by a range of engines. It is a high-wing all-composite aircraft with a centre-section-mounted pusher engine, fixed tricycle undercarriage, a T-tail and a tandem two-seat cockpit. The wings are foldable for transport. The prototype flew in July 1992 and first deliveries were made in 1995. Variants include the factory-complete Sky Arrow 450T, 480T and 500T (for the French market) with gross weights of 450, 480 and 500 kg respectively, and the 650TC, which is JAR-VLA certificated (and sometimes designated Model 1450L or 650TCN in the USA), all of which have an 81 h.p. Rotax 912 engine. The 1200LC is a Primary Category model for the USA. Homebuilt kit versions are the 650T, 650SP and the 650A/914 Exocet with twin amphibious floats. Models certificated as standard light aircraft with higher gross weights are the 1200LC and 1310SP (seaplane). Over 200 Sky Arrows have been completed to date and are flying worldwide.

Sky Arrow 650TC, I-TREO

Specification	Sky Arrow 650TC	
Powerplant	One 81 h.p. (60.39 kW) Rotax 912A piston engine	
Dimensions		
Span	9.7 m	(31 ft 10 in)
Length	7.59 m	(24 ft 11 in)
Height	2.57 m	(8 ft 5 in)
Performance		
Max speed	193 km/h	(104 kt, 120 mph)
Cruising speed	167 km/h	(90 kt, 104 mph)
Initial climb	229 m/min	(750 fpm)
Range	700 km	(380 nm, 438 miles)
Weights		
Max takeoff	649 kg	(1,430 lbs)
Useful load	299 kg	(660 lbs)

Skyfox Gazelle — Australia

The Denney (Skystar) Kitfox was adopted in Australia by the Calair Corporation of Caloundra, Queensland which produced a factory-complete model named the CA-21 Skyfox, the first of which flew on 15th September 1989 powered by a 78 h.p. Aeropower engine. It retains the tube and fabric construction of the Kitfox but has greater wing dihedral, the wing struts positioned further out on the wings, and a larger and taller rudder. The Calair (later Hedaro, trading as Skyfox Aviation) models were the CA-21 (later CA-22 and CA-22A Elan), approved under the Australian AUF ultralight category with a 450 kg gross weight, and the JAR-VLA certificated CA-25 Impala. These have been in production since 1992. The CA-25N Gazelle is a revised JAR-VLA certificated version of the CA-25 with a Rotax 912 engine and a tricycle undercarriage. To date over 100 of the various models have been completed.

Skyfox Gazelle, VH-SFK

Specification	Skyfox CA-22	
Powerplant	One 80 h.p. (59.6 kW) Rotax 912 piston engine	
Dimensions		
Span	9.52 m	(31 ft 3 in)
Length	5.61 m	(18 ft 5 in)
Height	1.75 m	(5 ft 9 in)
Performance		
Max speed	175 km/h	(95 kt, 109 mph)
Cruising speed	158 km/h	(85 kt, 98 mph)
Initial climb	287 m/min	(940 fpm)
Range	528 km	(287 nm, 330 miles)
Weights		
Max takeoff	450 kg	(992 lbs)
Useful load	160 kg	(353 lbs)

Skystar Aircraft Kitfox — USA

Designed by Don Denney, the Kitfox was first flown on 7th May 1984 and it has been produced in various forms for home kit construction and adapted and manufactured by companies in Brazil, the Philippines, Portugal, South Africa and Australia (see separate entry on Skyfox Gazelle). It has an enclosed side-by-side two-seat cockpit, a tailwheel undercarriage and a circular-section cowling enclosing the Rotax engine. The wings, which are foldable, are strut-braced and have large full-span flaperons which assist with its STOL performance. The structure is built from aluminium components, welded steel tube and fabric. The original Kitfox I had a 52 h.p. Rotax 503 or 64 h.p. Rotax 532 engine, but the Kitfox III, introduced in 1990, had a strengthened structure, larger tail and higher weights to allow it to use the 80 h.p. Rotax 912. This was followed by the Kitfox IV (and Kitfox Speedster), announced in 1991, which had shorter wings with a new aerofoil section and other speed-enhancing features, and this is currently sold by Skystar Aircraft Corp. as the Classic IV with optional Rotax 503, 618 or 912 engines, long or short wings and an optional float undercarriage. The Series 5 is a higher-performance touring aircraft with a strengthened structure and a wider cabin and rear baggage hold which can be fitted with the Rotax 912 or 914 or with a Continental O-200 or O-240. The Safari (also named Outback) is the Series 5 equipped with a 125 h.p. Continental IO-540B engine and spring-steel rough field gear, and the Vixen (later named Voyager) is the Series 5 with a tricycle undercarriage and swept vertical tail. Skystar has also launched the ultralight Kitfox Lite powered by a 35 h.p. 2SI-F35 engine. Over 3,500 kits have been sold to date and 2,500 are currently flying worldwide. The Eurofox is an aircraft produced by IkarusFlug in Germany which combines elements of the Kitfox and the Avid Flyer (which was also designed by Don Denney).

Skystar Kitfox IV, PH-RAY

Skystar Vixen, F-WSKJ

Skystar Aircraft Kitfox (Cont.)

Specification	Skystar Kitfox Classic IV	
Powerplant	One 80 h.p. (59.6 kW) Rotax 912 piston engine	
Dimensions		
Span	9.75 m	(32 ft 0 in)
Length	5.61 m	(18 ft 5 in)
Height	1.73 m	(5 ft 8 in)
Performance		
Max speed	180 km/h	(97 kt, 112 mph)
Cruising speed	177 km/h	(96 kt, 110 mph)
Initial climb	366 m/min	(1,200 fpm)
Range	368 km	(200 nm, 230 miles)
Weights		
Max takeoff	544 kg	(1,200 lbs)
Useful load	272 kg	(600 lbs)

Skystar Aircraft Pulsar
— USA

First introduced in 1988, the Pulsar was sold as a kit to amateur builders by Aero Designs of San Antonio, Texas and rights were later taken over by Skystar Aircraft. The design, which first flew as a prototype on 3rd April 1988, has its origins in the 'Star-Lite' single-seater created by Mark Brown and launched as a kit in 1983. Initially it was available in two different versions: the standard Pulsar with a 66 h.p. Rotax 582 engine and the Pulsar XP with an 80 h.p. Rotax 912. The current Pulsar III, modified for higher performance in 1998, has a turbocharged Rotax 914 which gives it a maximum speed of nearly 200 mph. Pulsars may be completed by the builder with a tricycle or tailwheel undercarriage. It is a side-by-side two-seater and the kit, over 600 of which have been sold, includes composite shells for the two fuselage halves and for the wing skins together with other systems and structural components, the standard building time being around 1,000 hours. The Pulsar was sold to Pulsar Aircraft Corporation in 1999 at which time a new Super Pulsar was launched with a larger cockpit and some aerodynamic modifications.

Skystar Pulsar, G-BSFA

Specification	Skystar Pulsar III	
Powerplant	One 115 h.p. (85.8 kW) Rotax 914 piston engine	
Dimensions		
Span	7.62 m	(25 ft 0 in)
Length	5.79 m	(19 ft 0 in)
Height	2.03 m	(6 ft 8 in)
Performance		
Max speed	306 km/h	(165 kt, 190 mph)
Cruising speed	290 km/h	(157 kt, 180 mph)
Initial climb	610 m/min	(2,000 fpm)
Range	960 km	(522 nm, 600 miles)
Weights		
Max takeoff	544 kg	(1,200 lbs)
Useful load	299 kg	(660 lbs)

Slepcev Storch Mk.4
— Australia

The Fieseler Storch wartime STOL liaison aircraft is the inspiration for the 75% scale version designed by Nestor Slepcev of Beechwood, New South Wales, Australia. Like the original aircraft, the Slepcev Storch has large wing flaps and leading edge slats and it has excellent slow flight characteristics with a stall speed of 16 mph and a takeoff distance of 30 feet. Constructed of steel tube and fabric, it has a strut-braced high wing and a heavily strutted undercarriage. The tandem two-seat cabin has roof and rear transparencies and the Storch, which falls into the Australian ultralight category, is powered by either a Rotax 912 or Rotax 914 engine. It is sold by Storch Aviation Australia either as a factory-complete aircraft or in kit form and 70 had been produced by the end of 1999 with examples being delivered to 19 countries including the USA, Italy and Taiwan, in addition to Australian customers.

Slepcev Storch, 55-954

Specification	Slepcev Storch Mk.4	
Powerplant	One 100 h.p. (74.56 kW) Rotax 912s piston engine	
Dimensions		
Span	10 m	(32 ft 10 in)
Length	6.8 m	(22 ft 4 in)
Height	2.49 m	(8 ft 2 in)
Performance		
Max speed	145 km/h	(78 kt, 90 mph)
Cruising speed	130 km/h	(70 kt, 81 mph)
Initial climb	213 m/min	(700 fpm)
Range	405 km	(220 nm, 253 miles)
Weights		
Max takeoff	550 kg	(1,213 lbs)
Useful load	210 kg	(463 lbs)

Slingsby T.67 and Firefly — UK

In 1981, the glider manufacturer Slingsby Aviation started to licence-build the Fournier RF-6B two-seat trainer/tourer and ten T.67As were built at Kirkbymoorside from Fournier-supplied components, the first aircraft flying on 15th May 1981. They were similar to the RF-6B with low-set high-aspect-ratio wings, all-wood construction, a single-piece canopy over the side-by-side two-seat cockpit, a fixed tricycle undercarriage and a 116 h.p. Lycoming O-235-L2A engine. Slingsby then re-engineered it in composite (GRP) materials with a wider fuselage and cockpit as the T.67B. Further variants included the T.67C with a 160 h.p. Lycoming AEIO-320-D1B engine and a separate windshield and canopy, and the T.67D with wing fuel tanks. The T.67M and T.67M Mk.II (with the separate windshield) are military versions with military equipment and a two-bladed constant-speed propeller, and are in service for flight screening of RAF officer trainees. The T.67M-200 Firefly is a higher-performance version with a 200 h.p. Lycoming AEIO-360-A1E and three-bladed constant-speed propeller. Slingsby developed the T.67M-260 with a strengthened structure and a 260 h.p. AEIO-540-D4A5 engine for the USAF enhanced flight screener (EFS) programme and delivered 113 as the T-3A, although these have now been withdrawn following poor accident history. Slingsby has built 120 of the T.67 series in addition to the USAF T-3A order.

Slingsby T.67M Firefly, G-BLDP

Specification	Slingsby T.67M Mk.II Firefly	
Powerplant	One 160 h.p. (119 kW) Textron Lycoming AEIO-320-D1B piston engine	
Dimensions		
Span	10.59 m	(34 ft 9 in)
Length	7.31 m	(24 ft 0 in)
Height	2.36 m	(7 ft 9 in)
Performance		
Max speed	241 km/h	(130 kt, 150 mph)
Cruising speed	224 km/h	(121 kt, 139 mph)
Initial climb	305 m/min	(1,000 fpm)
Range	1,008 km	(548 nm, 630 miles)
Weights		
Max takeoff	975 kg	(2,150 lbs)
Useful load	290 kg	(640 lbs)

Slingsby T.31M Motor Tutor — UK

Slingsby's Type 8 Tutor single-seat training glider dates back to 1937 and a large number of Tutors and Cadets were delivered both during and after the war. The Tutor had a strut-braced high wing mounted on a substantial pylon behind its open cockpit. It formed the basis, in 1947, for two examples of the Slingsby T.29B Motor Tutor which was a Tutor with a modified fuselage and an Aeronca JAP.99 engine fitted in the nose. Slingsby subsequently produced the T.31 Tandem Tutor glider which used the airframe of the T.29B with a second forward cockpit in place of the engine installation, and 131 were built for RAF cadet training as the Cadet TX.3. Many of these were sold subsequently to civil owners and at least 18 have been converted as single-seat T.31M Motor Tutors (or Motor Cadets) with a conventional tailwheel undercarriage and an engine installation in place of the front cockpit. A variety of powerplants have been fitted including a converted Triumph T.100, but most aircraft have a VW.1600, VW.1834 or Stark Stamo conversion of the Volkswagen car engine.

Slingsby T.31M Motor Tutor, G-BOOD

Specification	Slingsby T.31M Motor Tutor	
Powerplant	One 58 h.p. (43.24 kW) Volkswagen 1600 piston engine	
Dimensions		
Span	13.21 m	(43 ft 4 in)
Length	6.91 m	(22 ft 8 in)
Height	1.88 m	(6 ft 2 in)
Performance		
Max speed	129 km/h	(70 kt, 80 mph)
Cruising speed	113 km/h	(61 kt, 70 mph)
Initial climb	70 m/min	(230 fpm)
Range	288 km	(157 nm, 180 miles)
Weights		
Max takeoff	363 kg	(800 lbs)
Useful load	113 kg	(250 lbs)

SMAN Pétrel
— France

The Pétrel light sporting biplane was originally built in 1986 as the Hydroplum II amateur project by Claude Tisserand and was subsequently developed as a kit-built model for home construction, initially by SMAN (Soc. Morbihanaise d'Aéro Navigation) and later by Billie Marine. It is an all-composite amphibian with fabric-covered wings and falls into the 450 kg European ultralight airworthiness category. There is a central pylon mounted behind the cabin to support the upper wing and the pusher engine installation, and a short tail boom supports a cruciform tail unit. The side-by-side cabin can be left open but is normally enclosed with a bubble canopy. The Pétrel, which can be disassembled for ground transportation, has a retractable tricycle undercarriage with the main units folding upwards and the lower wing has tip-mounted outrigger floats. Around 60 Pétrel kits were sold before Billie Marine ceased production but the Pétrel is now built as the AAC Seastar in Canada (BC).

SMAN Pétrel, PH-2T2

Specification	SMAN Pétrel	
Powerplant	One 80 h.p. (59.6 kW) Rotax 912 piston engine	
Dimensions		
Span	13.21 m	(43 ft 4 in)
Length	6.91 m	(22 ft 8 in)
Height	1.88 m	(6 ft 2 in)
Performance		
Max speed	129 km/h	(70 kt, 80 mph)
Cruising speed	113 km/h	(61 kt, 70 mph)
Initial climb	70 m/min	(230 fpm)
Range	410 km	(223 nm, 256 miles)
Weights		
Max takeoff	363 kg	(800 lbs)
Useful load	113 kg	(250 lbs)

SME AeroTiga
— Malaysia

The Swiss manufacturer Max Dätwyler conceived the MD3-160 Swiss Trainer and flew the first of two prototypes on 12th August 1983. Its design was intended for simple modular construction with a single design for all control surfaces, common fin and tailplane units and prefabricated wing panels. The MD3 is a fully aerobatic mid-wing aircraft with a fixed tricycle undercarriage and an enclosed side-by-side two-seat cabin with a forward-sliding canopy. After flying five prototype and development aircraft and achieving Swiss certification, Dätwyler passed manufacturing rights to SME Aviation Sdn. Bhd. in Malaysia which commenced manufacture of the MD3-160 AeroTiga for civil and military customers with a batch of 20 aircraft for the Royal Malaysian Air Force and 20 for Malaysian flying schools. The first Malaysian aircraft flew in May 1995 and SME are marketing the aircraft in the USA and have sold aircraft to the Indonesian Air Force. The MD3-116 is also available with a 116 h.p. Lycoming O-235-N2A engine.

SME MD3 AeroTiga, N160MD

Specification	SME MD3-160 AeroTiga	
Powerplant	One 160 h.p. (119 kW) Textron Lycoming O-320-D2A piston engine	
Dimensions		
Span	9.98 m	(32 ft 9 in)
Length	7.11 m	(23 ft 4 in)
Height	2.92 m	(9 ft 7 in)
Performance		
Max speed	254 km/h	(137 kt, 158 mph)
Cruising speed	193 km/h	(104 kt, 120 mph)
Initial climb	297 m/min	(973 fpm)
Range	866 km	(470 nm, 541 miles)
Weights		
Max takeoff	920 kg	(2,028 lbs)
Useful load	280 kg	(617 lbs)

Smith Miniplane DSA-1
— USA

The late Frank W. Smith designed the DSA-1 (the initials stand for 'darned small airplane') and flew the prototype in October 1956. It was made available to homebuilders as plans and has been built in substantial numbers over the years. It is a classic open-cockpit single-seat biplane with limited aerobatic capability which is often altered in external shape to meet the whims of individual builders. It can be fitted with various engines from 65 h.p. to 125 h.p. and does not have flaps or upper wing ailerons. Construction is of steel tube and fabric for the fuselage and wood and fabric for the wings and it is fitted with a fixed tailwheel undercarriage which normally has triangulated main gear but may sometimes be constructed with spring-steel legs. Several hundred Miniplanes are flying in the USA.

Smith Miniplane DSA-1, N10WC

Specification	Smith Miniplane DSA-1	
Powerplant	One 108 h.p. (80.52 kW) Textron Lycoming piston engine	
Dimensions		
Span	5.18 m	(17 ft 0 in)
Length	4.65 m	(15 ft 3 in)
Height	1.52 m	(5 ft 0 in)
Performance		
Max speed	225 km/h	(122 kt, 140 mph)
Cruising speed	204 km/h	(110 kt, 127 mph)
Initial climb	427 m/min	(1,400 fpm)
Range	320 km	(174 nm, 200 miles)
Weights		
Max takeoff	454 kg	(1,000 lbs)
Useful load	175 kg	(385 lbs)

Smyth Sidewinder
— USA

The Sidewinder was one of the earliest all-metal plans-built amateur light aircraft and was designed by Jerry Smyth of Huntingdon, Indiana. The first Sidewinder flew on 21st February 1969 and the aircraft received the EAA's Outstanding Design award at the Rockford EAA Fly-In that year. The structure of the low-wing Sidewinder consists of a steel tube fuselage framework and built-up metal wing, all with aluminium sheet covering. It has a fixed tricycle undercarriage and carries two people in a side-by-side cockpit with a low-profile sliding canopy. For speed control it has a belly-mounted extendable airbrake and the horizontal tail is an all-moving surface with electric pitch trim. Various engines can be used, but the standard powerplant is the 125 h.p. Lycoming O-290. Over 200 Sidewinders have been built.

Smyth Sidewinder, G-BRVH

Specification	Smyth Sidewinder	
Powerplant	One 125 h.p. (93.2 kW) Textron Lycoming O-290-G piston engine	
Dimensions		
Span	7.57 m	(24 ft 10 in)
Length	5.89 m	(19 ft 4 in)
Height	1.65 m	(5 ft 5 in)
Performance		
Max speed	298 km/h	(161 kt, 185 mph)
Cruising speed	257 km/h	(139 kt, 160 mph)
Initial climb	274 m/min	(900 fpm)
Range	680 km	(370 nm, 425 miles)
Weights		
Max takeoff	658 kg	(1,450 lbs)
Useful load	263 kg	(580 lbs)

SNCAC (Aerocentre) NC.854 — France

The French company SNCAC (Aerocentre) built the NC.850 in 1947 for the postwar French government light aircraft competition and subsequently gained a contract for 100 aircraft for aero club use. The NC.850 had a strut-braced shoulder-mounted wing ahead of which was a side-by-side two-seat cabin with a clear-view bubble canopy. It was fitted with a fixed tailwheel undercarriage and in prototype form it had a 75 h.p. Mathis G4F engine and a single fin/rudder. The production version was the NC.853 with a twin-fin tail unit and an 80 h.p. Minié 4-DC.30 engine, and other variants included the NC.852 with a 90 h.p. Regnier 4EO and the NC.853S with a 75 h.p. Minié 4-DC.32. In total, 147 of the civil NC.850 series were built and all survivors were subsequently re-engined with the 65 h.p. Continental A65-8 or 90 h.p. C90-12F engine (NC.858S). Over 20 remain airworthy in France, Belgium and the UK. SNCAC also built the military NC.856 Norvigie army cooperation aircraft for the French Army (ALAT), flying the prototype on 12th March 1949. This was a tandem-seat NC.854 with a rearward extension to the cockpit, additional glazed area beneath the wing and a 135 h.p. Regnier 4LO-4 in-line engine. In total 112 Norvigies were built and two remain with private owners in France.

SNCAC NC.854, G-BIUP

Specification	Aerocentre NC.858S	
Powerplant	One 90 h.p. (67.1 kW) Teledyne Continental C90-12F piston engine	
Dimensions		
Span	11.25 m	(36 ft 11 in)
Length	6.83 m	(22 ft 5 in)
Height	2.08 m	(6 ft 10 in)
Performance		
Max speed	183 km/h	(99 kt, 114 mph)
Cruising speed	156 km/h	(84 kt, 97 mph)
Initial climb	259 m/min	(850 fpm)
Range	464 km	(252 nm, 290 miles)
Weights		
Max takeoff	671 kg	(1,480 lbs)
Useful load	281 kg	(620 lbs)

SNCAN (Nord) Stampe SV.4 — Belgium/France

The SV.4 two-seat training biplane was originally flown on 17th May 1933 by the Belgian firm Stampe & Vertongen. It was a classic design of mixed construction with a de Havilland Gipsy III engine and tandem open cockpits. A total of 33 prewar examples were built in Belgium including 24 SV.4Bs with 130 h.p. Gipsy Major engines for the Belgian Air Force. After the war, SNCAN started a production line at Sartrouville in France, building 700 SV.4As with Renault 4P-05 in-line engines between 1945 and 1948 for French aero clubs and the French Armée de l'Air. A further 150 Stampes were subsequently produced by the Algerian company Atelier Industriel de l'Aéronautique d'Alger, and in Belgium the reconstituted Stampe & Renard company also manufactured 65 SV.4Bs equipped with sliding framed canopies for the Belgian Air Force and one SV.4D with a 165 h.p. Continental IO-340-A engine before completing production in 1955. A number of aircraft were re-engined as SV.4Cs with 140 h.p. Renault 4P-01 engines, several Stampes have had their Renault engines replaced by the Gipsy Major 1C, and a few have converted to the SV.4L with a horizontally opposed Lycoming AEIO-320. More than 250 Stampes remain airworthy worldwide.

Stampe SV.4C, F-BCOT

Specification	Nord Stampe SV.4C	
Powerplant	One 140 h.p. (104.38 kW) Renault 4P-01 piston engine	
Dimensions		
Span	8.38 m	(27 ft 6 in)
Length	6.97 m	(22 ft 10 in)
Height	2.77 m	(9 ft 1 in)
Performance		
Max speed	205 km/h	(110 kt, 127 mph)
Cruising speed	175 km/h	(94 kt, 109 mph)
Initial climb	270 m/min	(886 fpm)
Range	420 km	(226 nm, 262 miles)
Weights		
Max takeoff	780 kg	(1,720 lbs)
Useful load	278 kg	(613 lbs)

Soko Type 522 — Yugoslavia

The Type 522, which first flew in February 1955, was designed by the Yugoslav Government Aircraft Factory (later Soko) as an advanced trainer to replace the earlier Type 213. The Type 213 was a low-wing monoplane of mixed construction with a tandem two-seat cockpit and a retractable tailwheel undercarriage. The Type 522 followed a very similar layout and was, essentially, an improved version with all-metal construction and powered by a large 600 h.p. Pratt & Whitney Wasp radial engine instead of the in-line Ranger used on the Type 213. More than 100 examples of the Type 522 were built between 1957 and 1960 and the type was finally phased out of JRV service in the mid-1960s at which time a number were released for use by the Yugoslav civil flying clubs. Some of the survivors have been sold to the USA where at least one has been restored and others still survive, mainly in non-airworthy condition, in Croatia and Serbia.

Soko 522, N1210Y

Specification	Soko 522	
Powerplant	One 600 h.p. (447.4 kW) Pratt & Whitney R-1340-AN1 piston engine	
Dimensions		
Span	11 m	(36 ft 0 in)
Length	9.2 m	(30 ft 2 in)
Height	3.58 m	(11 ft 9 in)
Performance		
Max speed	351 km/h	(189 kt, 218 mph)
Cruising speed	340 km/h	(183 kt, 211 mph)
Initial Climb	274 m/min	(900 fpm)
Range	978 km	(532 nm, 611 miles)
Weights		
Max takeoff	2,400 kg	(5,292 lbs)
Useful Load	570 kg	(1,257 lbs)

Soko Galeb and Jastreb — Yugoslavia

The Galeb was designed by the Mostar factory of Preduzece Soko to a Yugoslav Air Force (JRV) specification for a two-seat entry-level jet trainer and ground attack aircraft. The first Galeb was flown in 1962 and deliveries were started in 1965 with batches going to the JRV (approximately 120), Libyan Arab Air Force (120) and Zambian Air Force (6). The G-2A Galeb is a tandem two-seat aircraft with a single Soko-built Rolls Royce/Bristol Siddeley Viper Mk.11 turbojet fed by flank air intakes. The straight wing carries tip tanks as standard and is fitted with four weapons-hardpoints. Twin 12.7 mm machine guns are fitted in the nose. The J-1 Jastreb (JRV designation J-21) is a single-seat dedicated ground attack aircraft developed from the Viper 532-powered Galeb Mk.3 and equipped with an extra nose machine gun and eight underwing pylons. Around 200 Jastrebs are believed to have been built including 18 delivered to Zambia, 30 RJ-1 (JRV, IJ-21) and 15 two-seat trainers designated JT-1 (JRV, TJ-21). Export Galebs and Jastrebs are still in service but virtually all have been withdrawn in Serbia (former Yugoslavia) and 14 have been disposed of for private sale, of which six have been sold in the USA and four are operational in the UK.

Soko Galeb G-2A, YU-YAB

Soko J-1 Jastreb, JRV, 24409

Specification	Soko Galeb G-2A	
Powerplant	One 2,500 lb.s.t. (11.12 kN) Soko Rolls Royce Viper 11 Mk.22-6 turbojet	
Dimensions		
Span	10.46 m	(34 ft 4 in)
Length	11.61 m	(38 ft 1 in)
Height	3.28 m	(10 ft 9 in)
Performance		
Max speed	756 km/h	(409 kt, 470 mph)
Cruising speed	729 km/h	(394 kt, 453 mph)
Initial climb	1,372 m/min	(4,500 fpm)
Range	1,232 km	(670 nm, 770 miles)
Weights		
Max takeoff	3,987 kg	(8,792 lbs)
Useful load	1,368 kg	(3,017 lbs)

Soko G-4 Super Galeb — Yugoslavia

While it was given the Galeb name and is superficially similar, the Super Galeb military trainer is a completely new design. Flown as a prototype on 17th July 1978 the Super Galeb has a tandem two-seat cockpit and a mildly swept low wing. Like the Galeb it is armed, but the 23 mm GSh-23L twin-barrel cannon is carried in a pod mounted on the belly between the wheel wells. External weapons are also carried on four underwing hardpoints which allows the Super Galeb to be used in dual training and operational roles. The powerplant is a licence-built Viper 632-46 turbojet. Approximately 60 G-4s are thought to be in operation with the Serbian Air Force although many may have been destroyed during the 1999 Bosnian conflict. A batch of six has also been delivered to Myanmar.

Soko G-4 Super Galeb, JRV, 23686

Specification	Soko G-4 Super Galeb	
Powerplant	One 4,000 lb.s.t. (17.8 kN) Rolls Royce Viper Mk.632 turbojet	
Dimensions		
Span	9.88 m	(32 ft 5 in)
Length	11.86 m	(38 ft 11 in)
Height	4.27 m	(14 ft 0 in)
Performance		
Max speed	909 km/h	(491 kt, 565 mph)
Initial climb	1,798 m/min	(5,900 fpm)
Range	608 km	(330 nm, 380 miles)
Weights		
Max takeoff	6,329 kg	(13,955 lbs)
Useful load	3,079 kg	(6,790 lbs)

Soko P-2 Kraguj — Yugoslavia

The Kraguj is a single-seat COIN aircraft designed by the Yugoslav Central Research Establishment and first flown by Soko at Mostar in 1966. The Kraguj, which entered service in 1968, is a low-wing all-metal monoplane with a straight constant-chord wing and a fixed-tailwheel undercarriage. It has six underwing hardpoints of which the inner pair are fitted to carry heavier ordnance including pods containing 12 rockets, and is also fitted with two wing-mounted 7.7 mm machine guns. In service, the Kraguj, of which around 30 were produced as the J-20 for the JRV, was mainly used as a weapons trainer but also equipped police and National Guard units. All the Kragujs were retired in 1990 and seven have been exported for use by private owners in the UK and USA.

Soko P-2 Kraguj, G-RADA

Specification	Soko P-2 Kraguj	
Powerplant	One 340 h.p. (253.5 kW) Textron Lycoming GSO-480-B1A6 piston engine	
Dimensions		
Span	10.64 m	(34 ft 11 in)
Length	7.95 m	(26 ft 1 in)
Height	3 m	(9 ft 10 in)
Performance		
Max speed	295 km/h	(159 kt, 183 mph)
Cruising speed	280 km/h	(151 kt, 174 mph)
Initial climb	480 m/min	(1,575 fpm)
Range	800 km	(435 nm, 500 miles)
Weights		
Max takeoff	1,624 kg	(3,580 lbs)
Useful load	494 kg	(1,090 lbs)

Sorrell SNS-7 Hiperbipe — USA

In 1964 C. Hobart ('Hobie') Sorrell built his small SNS-1 single-seat light biplane which featured reverse-staggered wings, and in 1973 his company, Sorrell Aviation, followed this with the side-by-side two-seat Hiperbipe which had similar back-stagger. The SNS-7 Hiperbipe, which is fully aerobatic but also offers excellent cross-country performance and comfort, is a highly streamlined biplane with a cantilever tailwheel undercarriage and a swept fin and tailplane. It has a flat-sided fuselage which is profiled to give additional aerodynamic lift. Construction is of steel tube, wood and fabric. Various engines can be fitted from 150 h.p. to 260 h.p. but the prototype and most other examples have used the 180 h.p. Lycoming O-360. It won the Outstanding New Design award at Oshkosh in 1973 and has been sold by Sorrell as a kit for homebuilders with around 60 having been completed. An ultralight development by Hobie Sorrell is known as the SNS-9 Hiperlight, which can be built in single- and two-seat versions.

Sorrell SNS-7 Hiperbipe, G-HIPE

Specification	Sorrell SNS-7 Hiperbipe	
Powerplant	One 180 h.p. (134 kW) Textron Lycoming O-360-B1E piston engine	
Dimensions		
Span	6.96 m	(22 ft 10 in)
Length	6.35 m	(20 ft 10 in)
Height	1.8 m	(5 ft 11 in)
Performance		
Max speed	274 km/h	(148 kt, 170 mph)
Cruising speed	257 km/h	(139 kt, 160 mph)
Initial climb	457 m/min	(1,500 fpm)
Range	800 km	(435 nm, 500 miles)
Weights		
Max takeoff	867 kg	(1,911 lbs)
Useful load	306 kg	(675 lbs)

Spartan Arrow — UK

Originally designed as the Simmonds Spartan, the Spartan Arrow was an open tandem two-seat biplane aimed at flying schools and private owners. It was of conventional wood, ply and fabric construction with a fixed tailwheel undercarriage, and, apart from the distinctive shape of its tail unit and its folding wing mechanism, it was very typical of biplanes of the period. The first Spartan Arrow flew in May 1930 powered by a 105 h.p. Cirrus Hermes II, and fourteen further examples were built with a variety of powerplants including the 100 h.p. de Havilland Gipsy I, 120 h.p. Gipsy II, 95 h.p. Cirrus III and 160 h.p. Napier Javelin. Several survived the war but only one remains, powered by a Hermes II, and this was in airworthy condition at Redhill, UK in early 2000.

Spartan Arrow, G-ABWP

Specification	Spartan Arrow	
Powerplant	One 105 h.p. (78.29 kW) Cirrus Hermes II piston engine	
Dimensions		
Span	9.32 m	(30 ft 7 in)
Length	7.62 m	(25 ft 0 in)
Height	2.9 m	(9 ft 6 in)
Performance		
Max speed	171 km/h	(92 kt, 106 mph)
Cruising speed	148 km/h	(80 kt, 92 mph)
Initial climb	253 m/min	(830 fpm)
Range	692 km	(376 nm, 432 miles)
Weights		
Max takeoff	794 kg	(1,750 lbs)
Useful load	356 kg	(785 lbs)

Spartan C3 — USA

The Spartan C3 was typical of the many new biplanes which appeared in the USA in the early prewar years. Originating as the Mid-Continent Spartan of 1926 and built by the Spartan Aircraft Co. of Tulsa, the initial C3-1 gained type approval in September 1928. It seems that around 122 of the open-cockpit Spartans were built, the main variants being the C3-1 powered by a 125 h.p. Ryan-Siemens radial engine, the C3-120 (C3-2) with a 120 h.p. Walter engine, the C3-165 (C3-5) with a 165 h.p. Wright J6-5-165 and the C3-225 with a 225 h.p. Wright J6. A handful of the C3-4 (150 h.p. Axelson) and C3-166 (166 h.p. Comet 7E) were also completed. It was a tube, wood and fabric aircraft with two open cockpits accommodating three people, and the tail unit had a distinctive square shape. The Spartans were used by flying schools for instruction and by barnstorming companies. Only five Spartans are thought to have survived in the USA but at least two are currently airworthy.

Spartan C3 (Cont.)

Spartan C3-165, NC705N

Spartan 7W Executive, NC17667

Specification	Spartan C3-165	
Powerplant	One 165 h.p. (123 kW) Wright J6-5-165 piston engine	
Dimensions		
Span	9.75 m	(32 ft 0 in)
Length	7.26 m	(23 ft 10 in)
Height	2.69 m	(8 ft 10 in)
Performance		
Max speed	190 km/h	(103 kt, 118 mph)
Cruising speed	161 km/h	(87 kt, 100 mph)
Initial climb	244 m/min	(800 fpm)
Range	960 km	(522 nm, 600 miles)
Weights		
Max takeoff	1,187 kg	(2,618 lbs)
Useful load	439 kg	(968 lbs)

Specification	Spartan 7W Executive	
Powerplant	One 400 h.p. (298 kW) Pratt & Whitney Wasp Junior SB piston engine	
Dimensions		
Span	11.89 m	(39 ft 0 in)
Length	8.18 m	(26 ft 10 in)
Height	2.44 m	(8 ft 0 in)
Performance		
Max speed	341 km/h	(184 kt, 212 mph)
Cruising speed	335 km/h	(181 kt, 208 mph)
Initial climb	436 m/min	(1,430 fpm)
Range	1,360 km	(739 nm, 850 miles)
Weights		
Max takeoff	1,995 kg	(4,400 lbs)
Useful load	641 kg	(1,413 lbs)

Spartan 7W Executive
— USA

Designed by James B. Ford of Spartan Aircraft Co. the Executive was an expensive and substantially built private owner and light business-aircraft which first flew in January 1936. Including the prototype, 35 Executives were built between 1937 and 1939 and 21 are still registered in the USA although not all are active. The Executive was a low-wing all-metal monoplane with a retractable tailwheel undercarriage and a five-seat cabin entered through a port-side door. The prototype had a 285 h.p. Jacobs L-5 radial engine, but production aircraft used the 400 h.p. Wasp Junior SB. Several Executives were exported and others were impressed into the USAAF as UC-71s. One was also tested as a military fighter-bomber with an upper gun turret. After the war, Spartan tried to revive the design and built one Spartan 12, an Executive with a retractable tricycle undercarriage.

Spencer Air Car
— USA

The S-12-D Air Car amphibian was a development of the earlier two-seat Air Car designed by P.H. Spencer. He was also responsible for the Republic Seabee and the two aircraft share a very similar design layout. The Air Car, which is built from wood, steel tube and glass-fibre, has a strut-braced high wing and the four-seat fuselage and fuel-carrying wing floats are very similar to the Seabee's. The tail unit is more angular and a retractable tricycle undercarriage is fitted. The early Air Car S-12-C was powered by a 110 h.p. Lycoming but the S-12-D had a 180 h.p. Lycoming O-360 or 260 h.p. Lycoming O-540. The prototype, redesignated S-12-E, also flew with a 285 h.p. Continental Tiara. It has been sold in the form of plans for home construction and the first amateur-built example flew in September 1974. At least 50 have flown and P.H. Spencer also built one S-14 Air Car Junior, a two-seater with twin booms and a Lycoming O-320 engine.

Spencer S-12-D Air Car, N6PB

Specification	Spencer S-12-D Air Car	
Powerplant	One 260 h.p. (193.9 kW) Textron Lycoming O-540-E4B5 piston engine	
Dimensions		
Span	11.38 m	(37 ft 4 in)
Length	7.92 m	(26 ft 0 in)
Height	2.9 m	(9 ft 6 in)
Performance		
Max speed	237 km/h	(128 kt, 147 mph)
Cruising speed	217 km/h	(117 kt, 135 mph)
Initial climb	244 m/min	(800 fpm)
Range	1,120 km	(609 nm, 700 miles)
Weights		
Max takeoff	1,406 kg	(3,100 lbs)
Useful load	476 kg	(1,050 lbs)

Spezio Sport Tuholer
— USA

The Tuholer (so named because of its two tandem open cockpits) was designed and built by Tony and Dorothy Spezio and was first flown on 2nd May 1961. The structure is wood with fabric covering and the Tuholer has a strut-braced low wing and a chord-shock tailwheel undercarriage. The wing is foldable for home storage and transportation. The Tuholer has been made available as plans for amateur construction, latterly being marketed by W. Edwards, and various engines have been fitted in the 100 h.p. to 180 h.p. range.

Spezio Tuholer, G-NGRM

Specification	Spezio Sport Tuholer	
Powerplant	One 125 h.p. (93.2 kW) Textron Lycoming O-290-G4 piston engine	
Dimensions		
Span	7.54 m	(24 ft 9 in)
Length	5.56 m	(18 ft 3 in)
Height	1.52 m	(5 ft 0 in)
Performance		
Max speed	241 km/h	(130 kt, 150 mph)
Cruising speed	209 km/h	(113 kt, 130 mph)
Initial climb	610 m/min	(2,000 fpm)
Range	640 km	(348 nm, 400 miles)
Weights		
Max takeoff	635 kg	(1,400 lbs)
Useful load	268 kg	(590 lbs)

Sportavia RS-180 Sportsman
— Germany

A modified version of the low-wing RF-6 two-seat trainer, designed by René Fournier (see separate entry) was developed by the German company Sportavia with a longer four-seat cabin, and was first flown as the RF-6C on 28th April 1976. Due to severe stability problems, the RF-6C was further modified with a cruciform tail unit with increased side area and was fitted with a 180 h.p. Lycoming O-360-A3A engine. It had a large blister cockpit canopy of which the front section slid forwards for access, and several aircraft have been fitted with glider-towing equipment. Of wooden construction with glass-fibre cladding, the resulting RS.180 went into production in 1977 and 18 examples had been built when production ceased in 1979. Some 13 remain active in Germany with single examples in Switzerland and the UK.

Sportavia RS-180 Sportsman, G-VIZZ

Sportavia RS-180 Sportsman (Cont.)

Specification	Sportavia RS-180 Sportsman	
Powerplant	One 180 h.p. (134 kW) Textron Lycoming O-360-A3A piston engine	
Dimensions		
Span	10.49 m	(34 ft 5 in)
Length	7.14 m	(23 ft 5 in)
Height	2.57 m	(8 ft 5 in)
Performance		
Max speed	274 km/h	(148 kt, 170 mph)
Cruising speed	225 km/h	(122 kt, 140 mph)
Initial climb	324 m/min	(1,063 fpm)
Range	1,382 km	(751 nm, 864 miles)
Weights		
Max takeoff	1,100 kg	(2,425 lbs)
Useful load	460 kg	(1,014 lbs)

St. Just Super Cyclone — Canada

Cessation of production of Cessna's Model 185 Skywagon in 1985 meant that bush operators were denied one of the most effective aircraft for remote wheel- and float-equipped operations. In mid-1997, Montreal-based St. Just Aviation produced an almost exact copy, the four-seat Super Cyclone, which is sold as a kit and is normally powered by either a 230 h.p. or 300 h.p. Lycoming piston engine but may be fitted with other powerplants of a similar size. The Super Cyclone differs from the Cessna 185, primarily, in having a 24-inch longer inner wing structure which allows larger flaps and better STOL performance.

St. Just Super Cyclone, C-GCCQ

Specification	St. Just Super Cyclone	
Powerplant	One 300 h.p. (223.68 kW) Textron Lycoming IO-540-K piston engine	
Dimensions		
Span	11.53 m	(37 ft 10 in)
Length	7.85 m	(25 ft 9 in)
Height	2.36 m	(7 ft 9 in)
Performance		
Max speed	282 km/h	(152 kt, 175 mph)
Cruising speed	262 km/h	(142 kt, 163 mph)
Initial climb	488 m/min	(1,600 fpm)
Range	1,459 km	(793 nm, 912 miles)
Weights		
Max takeoff	1,587 kg	(3,500 lbs)
Useful load	703 kg	(1,550 lbs)

Starck AS.57 — France

The French designer André Starck established himself after the war by building a batch of 23 AS.70 low-wing single-seat light aircraft powered by various engines. A few of these survive, but none is believed to be airworthy. The later AS.57, which first flew on 4th April 1946, was a much developed and scaled-up AS.70. Like the AS.70 it was of wood and ply construction but it had a bubble canopy enclosing a side-by-side two-seat cockpit and a lengthened fuselage. Again, several engines were used, but the sole remaining airworthy AS.57 is powered by a Walter Minor 4-III. Ten AS.57s were completed during the late 1940s.

Starck AS.57, F-PCIM

Specification	Starck AS.57	
Powerplant	One 105 h.p. (78.29 kW) Walter Minor 4-III piston engine	
Dimensions		
Span	8.79 m	(28 ft 10 in)
Length	6.45 m	(21 ft 2 in)
Height	1.85 m	(6 ft 1 in)
Performance		
Max speed	201 km/h	(109 kt, 125 mph)
Cruising speed	185 km/h	(100 kt, 115 mph)
Initial climb	213 m/min	(700 fpm)
Range	792 km	(430 nm, 495 miles)
Weights		
Max takeoff	600 kg	(1,322 lbs)
Useful load	290 kg	(639 lbs)

Stearman C3 and Type 4 Speedmail — USA

Stearman Aircraft was established in Wichita in 1927 after a brief period in Venice, California where four Stearman C1 and C2 biplanes had been built. The new Wichita-built C3 was a rugged biplane with simple straight wings, a tough undercarriage with oleo shock absorbers and two open cockpits with the pilot in the rear and two passenger seats in front. The C3B was fitted with a 220 h.p. Wright J5 radial engine which was normally left uncowled, but there were also a few examples of the C2B (Wright J4), C3C (180 h.p. Hispano Suiza ('Hisso') E), C3K (128 h.p. Siemens Halske SH-12) and C3L (130 h.p. Comet). The C3R Business

Speedster was a high-performance version with a 225 h.p. Wright J6 and the C3MB was a special mail-carrying aircraft based on the C3B with the forward cockpit enclosed as a cargo compartment. The Stearman 4-E ('Bull Stearman') was slightly larger than the C3 with a deeper fuselage and was much more powerful with a 420 h.p. Pratt & Whitney Wasp radial in a fully enclosed circular-section cowling, and had a higher useful load. Other variants were the Model 4-C (300 h.p. Wright J6) and Model 4-D (300 h.p. Pratt & Whitney Wasp Junior). These were named Junior Speedmail, although they generally had two open cockpits, but the Senior Speedmail 4-EM, 4-CM and 4-DM were equivalent single-seat freight carriers with a forward hold for up to 600 lbs of cargo. Stearman built 179 Stearman C3s and 41 of the Model 4, and several of each are still in private ownership.

Stearman C3B, N6496

Stearman 4-D Junior Speedmail, NC774H

Specification	Stearman C3B	
Powerplant	One 220 h.p. (164 kW) Wright J5 Whirlwind piston engine	
Dimensions		
Span	10.67 m	(35 ft 0 in)
Length	7.31 m	(24 ft 0 in)
Height	2.74 m	(9 ft 0 in)
Performance		
Max speed	203 km/h	(110 kt, 126 mph)
Cruising speed	174 km/h	(94 kt, 108 mph)
Initial climb	305 m/min	(1,000 fpm)
Range	992 km	(539 nm, 620 miles)
Weights		
Max takeoff	1,202 kg	(2,650 lbs)
Useful load	465 kg	(1,025 lbs)

Steen Skybolt — USA

Designed by Lamar Steen as a high school student engineering project, the Skybolt was first flown in October 1970 and it has proved to be one of the most popular amateur-built types with over 400 completed to date. Plans have been sold by Steen Aero Lab Inc. to 29 countries, and ten are flying in the UK. The Skybolt has a classic structure consisting of a welded tube fuselage and wooden wings all of which are fabric-covered. It is a tandem open-cockpit two-seat biplane and is stressed for normal aerobatics. The cockpits are frequently constructed as a single tandem cabin with an enclosing bubble canopy, and some competition aircraft are built as single-seaters with the front cockpit closed off. The original Skybolt had a 180 h.p. Lycoming HO-360-B1B engine, but engines from 150 h.p. up to 260 h.p. can be used and several competition aircraft use the 250 h.p. Lycoming IO-540-C.

Steen Skybolt (Cont.)

Steen Skybolt, G-BRIS

Specification	Steen Skybolt	
Powerplant	One 180 h.p. (134.2 kW) Textron Lycoming HO-360-B1B piston engine	
Dimensions		
Span	7.31 m	(24 ft 0 in)
Length	5.79 m	(19 ft 0 in)
Height	2.13 m	(7 ft 0 in)
Performance		
Max speed	233 km/h	(126 kt, 145 mph)
Cruising speed	209 km/h	(113 kt, 130 mph)
Initial climb	762 m/min	(2,500 fpm)
Range	720 km	(391 nm, 450 miles)
Weights		
Max takeoff	748 kg	(1,650 lbs)
Useful load	259 kg	(570 lbs)

Stemme S-10 — Germany

Dr. Reiner Stemme designed the Stemme S-10 self-launching sailplane to take advantage of a revolutionary propeller system. The S-10 is a high-performance sailplane with a side-by-side two-seat cockpit and a retractable twin wheel undercarriage which folds into a fully enclosed under-fuselage well. The basic S-10 Chrysalis, which was first flown in 1986, is powered by a 93 h.p. Limbach L2400 engine which is buried in the centre fuselage and drives the propeller via a shaft running through the cockpit. For powered flight the nose slides forward ahead of the cockpit and the propeller unfolds within the slot. The S-10V is a version with a variable-pitch propeller and the S-10VT has a turbocharged 115 h.p. Rotax 914 engine. Special applications have included atmospheric research, pollution sensing and infra-red mapping for which Stemme sells the S-15 Utility, which can be fitted with underwing equipment pods. Over 130 S-10s had been delivered by the end of 1999.

Stemme S-10VT

Specification	Stemme S-10V	
Powerplant	One 93 h.p. (69.34 kW) Limbach L2400 piston engine	
Dimensions		
Span	23 m	(75 ft 6 in)
Length	8.42 m	(27 ft 7 in)
Height	1.7 m	(5 ft 7 in)
Performance		
Max speed	222 km/h	(120 kt, 138 mph)
Cruising speed	195 km/h	(105 kt, 121 mph)
Initial climb	192 m/min	(630 fpm)
Range	1,376 km	(748 nm, 860 miles)
Weights		
Max takeoff	850 kg	(1,874 lbs)
Useful load	206 kg	(454 lbs)

Stephens Akro — USA

For many years the Stephens Akro was a leader in competition aerobatics, although it has now been overtaken by more modern designs. Originally designed by Clayton L. Stephens of San Bernardino, California and first flown on 27th July 1967, it is a mid-wing aircraft with a single-seat cockpit enclosed by a sliding bubble canopy and it has a fixed spring-steel tailwheel undercarriage. It is stressed to +/– 11 g and the single piece wing is straight but with mild taper and an almost symmetrical aerofoil section. The aircraft, which is normally fitted with a 180 h.p. Lycoming AIO-360 engine but sometimes has powerplants of up to 230 h.p., is amateur-built from plans as the standard Akro A and the Akro B, which has a larger wing and reduced fuel tankage. Many developed versions such as Henry Haigh's Superstar have been constructed and the Extra series is based on the Akro. The Akro Laser 200 is a redesign by Leo Loudenschlager with a 200 h.p. IO-360 engine, a lighter fuselage with lower fuselage transparencies and a different aerofoil section. In this aircraft he became US aerobatic champion on seven occasions betwen 1975 and 1982, and world aerobatic champion in 1980. A number of Lasers have been constructed by amateurs.

Stephens Akro Laser 200, N10LL

Specification	Stephens Akro A	
Powerplant	One 180 h.p. (134.2 kW) Textron Lycoming AIO-360-A1A piston engine	
Dimensions		
Span	7.47 m	(24 ft 6 in)
Length	5.82 m	(19 ft 1 in)
Height	1.73 m	(5 ft 8 in)
Performance		
Max speed	274 km/h	(148 kt, 170 mph)
Cruising speed	201 km/h	(109 kt, 125 mph)
Initial climb	1,219 m/min	(4,000 fpm)
Range	560 km	(304 nm, 350 miles)
Weights		
Max takeoff	544 kg	(1,200 lbs)
Useful load	159 kg	(350 lbs)

Stewart S-51D Mustang — USA

Jim D. Stewart engineered a 70% scale amateur-built version of the North American P-51D Mustang and flew the prototype on 30th March 1994. The aircraft is fully aerobatic and has a tandem two-seat dual-control cockpit and all the other features of the original P-51D, including a fully retractable undercarriage. It is constructed from aluminium and is sold as a complete kit by Stewart 51 Inc. of Vero Beach, Florida. Various liquid-cooled engines have been fitted to the S-51D in the 300 h.p. to 600 h.p. range, mostly converted from motor car powerplants. By the end of 1999, 80 kits had been sold and six aircraft were flying.

Stewart S-51D, N51S

Specification	Stewart S-51D Mustang	
Powerplant	One 300 h.p. (224 kW) General Motors GMC V-350 piston engine	
Dimensions		
Span	8.15 m	(26 ft 9 in)
Length	6.81 m	(22 ft 4 in)
Height	2.84 m	(9 ft 4 in)
Performance		
Max speed	367 km/h	(198 kt, 228 mph)
Cruising speed	356 km/h	(192 kt, 221 mph)
Initial climb	610 m/min	(2,000 fpm)
Range	2,832 km	(1,539 nm, 1,770 miles)
Weights		
Max takeoff	1,410 kg	(3,110 lbs)
Useful load	345 kg	(760 lbs)

Stinson Junior SM — USA

In the mid-1920s Eddie Stinson's SM-1 Detroiter six-seat cabin monoplane had established a strong reputation as a small general purpose transport. This led to Stinson designing a very similar, but smaller, four-seat cabin aircraft which was known as the SM-2 Junior which first appeared in 1928. It was a strut-braced monoplane with a sturdy outrigger undercarriage which was braced against the wing support struts, and the 110 h.p. Warner Scarab radial engine was normally left uncowled. Later versions had significantly more power and included the SM-2AA (165 h.p. Wright J6), SM-2AB (220 h.p. Wright J5) and SM-2AC (225 h.p. Wright J6-7). With some minor modifications, the SM-2AC became the SM-8B and Stinson added the SM-8A (215 h.p. Lycoming R-680) and SM-8D (225 h.p. Packard diesel), and the higher-powered and more expensive versions, the SM-7A (300 h.p. Wright J6) and SM-7B (300 h.p. Wasp Junior). The Junior S, which was introduced in 1931, was an SM-8A with a fully cowled engine and other minor changes. The Junior R of 1932 had the same Lycoming R-680 engine but had a

Stinson Junior SM (Cont.)

deeper fuselage and a stub wing to mount the undercarriage and wing struts, and it was followed by the R-2 powered by a 240 h.p. Lycoming R-680-BA engine and the R-3 with a retractable undercarriage. A total of 321 Stinson Juniors were built of which 27 have survived, mainly of the SM-8A model, and several remain airworthy in private hands.

Stinson Junior SM-2AA, NC8471

Specification	Stinson SM-8A Junior	
Powerplant	One 215 h.p. (160.3 kW) Lycoming R-680 piston engine	
Dimensions		
Span	12.7 m	(41 ft 8 in)
Length	8.81 m	(28 ft 11 in)
Height	2.67 m	(8 ft 9 in)
Performance		
Max speed	201 km/h	(109 kt, 125 mph)
Cruising speed	169 km/h	(91 kt, 105 mph)
Initial climb	238 m/min	(780 fpm)
Range	720 km	(391 nm, 450 miles)
Weights		
Max takeoff	1,449 kg	(3,195 lbs)
Useful load	514 kg	(1,134 lbs)

Stinson SM-6000 Tri-Motor — USA

In 1930, Stinson announced its largest aircraft: the ten-passenger SM-6000 airliner (also known as the Model T). The SM-6000 monoplane bore a family resemblance to the earlier Junior R and Detroiter with its strut-braced high wing and outrigger-style undercarriage. It was a tri-motor with one uncowled 215 h.p. Lycoming R-680 engine in the nose and two engines with cowlings attached to the wing support struts. The SM-6000-A and SM-6000-B were versions with different interior passenger and cargo layouts. The structure was of steel tube and fabric with some aluminium cladding on wings and fuselage. Stinson built 57 SM-6000s between 1931 and 1933 and at least two are currently flying in the USA.

Stinson SM-6000-B, NC11170

Specification	Stinson SM-6000-B	
Powerplant	Three 215 h.p. (160.3 kW) Lycoming R-680 piston engines	
Dimensions		
Span	18.29 m	(60 ft 0 in)
Length	13.05 m	(42 ft 10 in)
Height	3.66 m	(12 ft 0 in)
Performance		
Max speed	222 km/h	(120 kt, 138 mph)
Cruising speed	185 km/h	(100 kt, 115 mph)
Initial climb	305 m/min	(1,000 fpm)
Range	560 km	(304 nm, 350 miles)
Weights		
Max takeoff	3,900 kg	(8,600 lbs)
Useful load	1,289 kg	(2,842 lbs)

Stinson Reliant SR — USA

The SR series followed on from Stinson's popular Junior R high-wing monoplane and had the Stinson R wide comfortable four-seat cabin and deeper fuselage and two wing struts each side. However, it was fitted with a revised undercarriage with large root fairings instead of the earlier sesquiplane winglets, and a less curved fin. Announced in 1933, the basic SR, powered by a 215 h.p. Lycoming R-680, was followed by the SR-2, SR-3, SR-4, SR-5 and SR-6 which were all very similar except for minor annual improvements to trim and equipment. There were many sub-variants with different engines of 215 h.p. to 285 h.p. most of which were Lycomings but also including the Wright R-760E (SR-4 and SR-5F). The SR-7 Reliant marked a major redesign. Known as the 'gullwing' Stinson it had a new wing with tapered outer sections and a markedly deep inner-wing aerofoil section, single wing support struts, a simpler cantilever undercarriage without the large root structure (which was introduced on the SR-6) and Lycoming R-680 radial engines of 225 h.p. (SR-7A), 245 h.p. (SR-7B) and 260 h.p. (SR-7C). The SR-8, SR-9 and SR-10 were all similar, but with Lycoming engines up to 290 h.p. and Wright R-760 engines of 285 h.p. to 420 h.p. From the SR-10C the ridged engine cowling was replaced by a straight cowl. The V-77 was the final version with a 300 h.p. Lycoming R-680-E3B and deep cabin windows for wartime Royal Navy use as the AT-19 five-seat navigation trainer and communications aircraft. In total 762 of the Reliant SR series were built together with 500 V-77s, and many remain in private ownership.

Stinson V-77 Reliant, G-BUCH

Stinson SR-5A, NC14572

Specification	Stinson SR-9C Reliant	
Powerplant	One 260 h.p. (193.86 kW) Lycoming R-680-B5 piston engine	
Dimensions		
Span	12.78 m	(41 ft 11 in)
Length	8.51 m	(27 ft 11 in)
Height	2.59 m	(8 ft 6 in)
Performance		
Max speed	238 km/h	(129 kt, 148 mph)
Cruising speed	225 km/h	(122 kt, 140 mph)
Initial climb	251 m/min	(825 fpm)
Range	1,104 km	(600 nm, 690 miles)
Weights		
Max takeoff	1,700 kg	(3,750 lbs)
Useful load	560 kg	(1,235 lbs)

Stinson HW-75 Voyager — USA

The Stinson HW-75 (also known as the Stinson 105) was designed as a lighter model to complement the large Stinson Reliant, and it first flew in February 1939 and went into production soon after. It was a classic strut-braced high-wing light aircraft with a fixed cantilever tailwheel undercarriage and a three-seat fully enclosed cabin. The initial HW-75 was powered by a 75 h.p. Continental A-75-3 flat-four engine and the HW-80, introduced in 1940, had an 80 h.p. A-80-6 engine. The Stinson 105 was built from steel tube, wood, aluminium and fabric, it had flaps and the undercarriage was normally fitted with wheel spats. The Stinson 10 was an improved model with a wider cabin, better-quality finish and an 80 h.p. Continental A-80 engine. The Model 10A had a 90 h.p. Franklin 4AC-199-E2 and in military service was designated L-9B. In total 277 Stinson 105s and 775 Model 10/10As were built by Vultee-Stinson before the war halted production in 1942.

Stinson 10 Voyager, NC26419

Stinson HW-75 Voyager (Cont.)

Specification	Stinson 10A Voyager 90	
Powerplant	One 90 h.p. (67.1 kW) Franklin 4AC-199-E2 piston engine	
Dimensions		
Span	10.36 m	(34 ft 0 in)
Length	6.6 m	(21 ft 8 in)
Height	1.98 m	(6 ft 6 in)
Performance		
Max speed	185 km/h	(100 kt, 115 mph)
Cruising speed	174 km/h	(94 kt, 108 mph)
Initial climb	183 m/min	(600 fpm)
Range	528 km	(287 nm, 330 miles)
Weights		
Max takeoff	762 kg	(1,680 lbs)
Useful load	297 kg	(655 lbs)

Stinson L-5A Sentinel — USA

Stinson designed the YO-54 (later L-5) Sentinel for wartime army cooperation duties, flying the prototype in 1941. It was, essentially, a tandem two-seat version of the Model 10 Voyager with a cut-down rear fuselage and rearview cabin transparencies, and a slightly larger fin. The steel tube undercarriage legs were generally left unfaired. The basic O-62 (L-5 and L-5A) had a 185 h.p. Lycoming O-435-1 flat-six engine but the final production L-5G was upgraded to a 190 h.p. O-435-11. The L-5B, to which standard over 700 L-5s were modified, had a deeper rear fuselage with an upward-hinged hatch to contain a casualty stretcher, and the L-5C (and L-5E) was a specialised version with a vertical camera installation. Vultee-Stinson's Wayne, Michigan plant built 3,902 Sentinels. Many are privately owned including a number used in Italy for glider towing.

Stinson L-5 Sentinel, N7971A

Specification	Stinson L-5 Sentinel	
Powerplant	One 185 h.p. (137.9 kW) Textron Lycoming O-435-1 piston engine	
Dimensions		
Span	10.36 m	(34 ft 0 in)
Length	7.34 m	(24 ft 1 in)
Height	2.16 m	(7 ft 1 in)
Performance		
Max speed	206 km/h	(111 kt, 128 mph)
Cruising speed	185 km/h	(100 kt, 115 mph)
Initial climb	297 m/min	(975 fpm)
Range	624 km	(339 nm, 390 miles)
Weights		
Max takeoff	979 kg	(2,158 lbs)
Useful load	311 kg	(686 lbs)

Stinson 108 Voyager — USA

The postwar Stinson 108 Voyager, announced in 1945, was a larger, full four-seat version of the prewar Model 10 with a 150 h.p. Franklin 6A4-150-B3 powerplant. The Stinson 108 was built of steel tube and fabric with an all-metal tail unit and sold in standard trim or as the Flying Station Wagon with a wood-clad utility interior. The initial version was the Model 108 Voyager 150 and higher-weight Model 108-1, and this was followed by the 108-2 with a 165 h.p. Franklin 6A4-165-B3 engine.The Model 108-3 had increased fuel capacity, higher weights and a larger vertical tail to improve stability with the higher powered 165 h.p. Franklin engine. Piper acquired Stinson in November 1948 and built the final batch of Voyagers. When production ceased in 1950 a total of 5,266 Stinson 108s had been built.

Stinson 108-2 Voyager, N9502K

Stinson 108-3 Flying Station Wagon, N6268M

Specification	Stinson 108-3 Voyager	
Powerplant	One 165 h.p. (123 kW) Franklin 6A4-165-B3 piston engine	
Dimensions		
Span	10.36 m	(34 ft 0 in)
Length	7.7 m	(25 ft 3 in)
Height	2.08 m	(6 ft 10 in)
Performance		
Max speed	214 km/h	(116 kt, 133 mph)
Cruising speed	201 km/h	(109 kt, 125 mph)
Initial climb	177 m/min	(580 fpm)
Range	960 km	(522 nm, 600 miles)
Weights		
Max takeoff	1,088 kg	(2,400 lbs)
Useful load	502 kg	(1,106 lbs)

Stits SA-11A Playmate, N77JA

Stits Playboy and Playmate — USA

Ray Stits designed a number of plans-built amateur aircraft during the 1950s including the Skybaby, claimed as the world's smallest biplane, the Skeeto and the SA-7 and SA-9 Skycoupe. The SA-3A Playboy is a single-seater with a strut-braced low wing and a conventional tailwheel undercarriage. The cockpit is normally enclosed with a sliding canopy. It is of mixed construction and can be powered by various engines in the 65 h.p. to 160 h.p. range. The SA-3B is a side-by-side two-seat version and the SA-6B Flut-R-Bug is a tandem two-seater based on the SA-3 with a strut-braced mid-set wing and tricycle undercarriage. The SA-11A Playmate is a three-seater development of the SA-3 with a low wing which can be folded for ground transport. It first flew in September 1963 and is powered by a 125 h.p. Lycoming O-290 engine. Stits ceased the sale of plans in 1970 but a fair number of Playboys and Playmates are still flying.

Specification	Stits SA-3A Playboy	
Powerplant	One 85 h.p. (63.38 kW) Teledyne Continental C85 piston engine	
Dimensions		
Span	6.76 m	(22 ft 2 in)
Length	5.28 m	(17 ft 4 in)
Height	1.73 m	(5 ft 8 in)
Performance		
Max speed	233 km/h	(126 kt, 145 mph)
Cruising speed	209 km/h	(113 kt, 130 mph)
Initial climb	305 m/min	(1,000 fpm)
Range	400 km	(217 nm, 250 miles)
Weights		
Max takeoff	409 kg	(902 lbs)
Useful load	136 kg	(300 lbs)

Stits SA-3A Playboy, G-BDRL

Stoddard-Hamilton Glasair — USA

The Glasair is one of the most popular kit-built light aircraft and Tom Hamilton made the first flight of the prototype in 1979. It was the first composite aircraft kit consisting of pre-moulded fuselage, wing and tail shells to be marketed, and offered much reduced building time compared with other types. The Glasair is a low-wing side-by-side two-seater, normally powered by a 150 h.p. or 160 h.p. Lycoming O-320, and many variants have been sold. These include the original tailwheel undercarriage Glasair TD, the Glasair RG with a retractable tricycle undercarriage and the Glasair FT with fixed tricycle gear. The redesigned Glasair II, introduced in 1986, had a wider and deeper cabin and simplified construction features, and the high-performance Glasair III had a stretched fuselage, a taller retractable undercarriage and a 300 h.p. Lycoming IO-540 engine. Other versions are the Glasair II-S with a longer fuselage and

Stoddard-Hamilton Glasair (Cont.)

the Super II with a further stretch and a larger tail, the Glasair III-LP with lightning protection, the turbocharged Glasair Turbo III and the Glasair Turbine 250/III with an Allison 250 turboprop. By mid-1999, 1,700 Glasair kits had been sold and 850 aircraft had been flown by amateur builders. Upon Stoddard-Hamilton's bankruptcy in early 2000 the designs were put up for sale.

Stoddard-Hamilton Glasair TD, N286YM

Stoddard-Hamilton Glasair III-LP, N540LP

Specification	Stoddard-Hamilton Glasair III	
Powerplant	One 300 h.p. (223.7 kW) Textron Lycoming IO-540-K1A5 piston engine	
Dimensions		
Span	7.11 m	(23 ft 4 in)
Length	6.5 m	(21 ft 4 in)
Height	2.29 m	(7 ft 6 in)
Performance		
Max speed	467 km/h	(252 kt, 290 mph)
Cruising speed	373 km/h	(202 kt, 232 mph)
Initial climb	911 m/min	(2,990 fpm)
Range	1,760 km	(957 nm, 1,100 miles)
Weights		
Max takeoff	1,088 kg	(2,400 lbs)
Useful load	351 kg	(775 lbs)

Stoddard-Hamilton GlaStar — USA

The GlaStar is the second kit aircraft produced by Stoddard-Hamilton. It first flew on 29th November 1994 and around 800 kits have been sold with 100 aircraft completed, including two in the UK. The GlaStar is a side-by-side two-seater with a large enclosed cabin, a high strut-braced wing with a folding mechanism and optional fixed tailwheel or tricycle gear. It has a wide performance range and is virtually unstallable. Construction consists of a welded tube fuselage frame covered by composite shells, and metal wings and tail unit. The standard powerplant is a 125 h.p. Continental IO-240 but it can also be built as the GlaStar 320 with a 160 h.p. Lycoming O-320. It is also approved for water operation, fitted with Aerocet 2200 floats. A factory-built version, the OMF-160 Symphony is being manufactured in Germany.

Stoddard-Hamilton GlaStar, N918V

Specification	Stoddard-Hamilton GlaStar 320	
Powerplant	One 160 h.p. (119.3 kW) Textron Lycoming O-320 piston engine	
Dimensions		
Span	10.67 m	(35 ft 0 in)
Length	6.81 m	(22 ft 4 in)
Height	2.77 m	(9 ft 1 in)
Performance		
Max speed	274 km/h	(148 kt, 170 mph)
Cruising speed	269 km/h	(145 kt, 167 mph)
Initial climb	632 m/min	(2,075 fpm)
Range	1,245 km	(677 nm, 778 miles)
Weights		
Max takeoff	862 kg	(1,900 lbs)
Useful load	363 kg	(800 lbs)

Stolp Starduster
— USA

Lou Stolp and George Adams designed and built the original SA-100 Starduster, flying their prototype, powered by a 125 h.p. Lycoming O-290, in November 1957. It was an open-cockpit single-seat non-aerobatic sport biplane and construction was traditional with a welded tube fuselage, wooden wings and overall fabric covering. Many Stardusters were built from plans sold by Stolp Starduster Corp. but it has been upgraded to the Super Starduster with improved performance, and Stolp has also introduced the similar aerobatic SA-900 V-Star which has a simplified structure. The SA-100 was followed by the SA-300 Starduster Too which had a lengthened fuselage to accommodate two tandem cockpits and is normally powered by a 180 h.p. Lycoming IO-360 but can accommodate engines up to a 375 h.p. IO-540. A fully aerobatic version of the SA-300, the SA-750 Acroduster Too with a 200 h.p. AEIO-360-A1A, is also available. In addition, Stolp has produced the SA-500 Starlet parasol single-seat monoplane, which is smaller but follows the same general lines as the biplanes and can be powered by engines in the 65 h.p. to 100 h.p. range, including the 65 h.p. Continental A65, Volkswagen 1500 or Continental O-200-A. Around 800 Stolp homebuilts are flying.

Stolp Starduster I, N40D

Stolp Acroduster Too, F-PYPF

Specification	Stolp SA-300 Starduster Too	
Powerplant	One 180 h.p. (134.2 kW) Textron Lycoming IO-360-A1A piston engine	
Dimensions		
Span	7.31 m	(24 ft 0 in)
Length	5.49 m	(18 ft 0 in)
Height	2.21 m	(7 ft 3 in)
Performance		
Max speed	322 km/h	(174 kt, 200 mph)
Cruising speed	185 km/h	(100 kt, 115 mph)
Initial climb	549 m/min	(1,800 fpm)
Range	960 km	(522 nm, 600 miles)
Weights		
Max takeoff	907 kg	(2,000 lbs)
Useful load	390 kg	(860 lbs)

Streamline Welding Ultimate 10-100 — Canada

The Ultimate 10-100 is a fully aerobatic single-seat competition biplane of mixed construction designed in Ontario, Canada by Streamline Welding Inc. (Ultimate Aircraft) and sold either as plans or as a kit for amateur assembly. The first aircraft flew on 6th October 1985 and the 10-100, powered by a 100 h.p. Continental O-200-A, has become popular in the USA, and one has been completed in France. Several versions can be built with different powerplants and aerobatic capability, including the 10-200 with an engine such as the 200 h.p. Lycoming IO-360 with a constant-speed propeller and the 10-300, which has a 300 h.p. TIO-540-S engine, longer-span wings and a longer fuselage. The Ultimate 20-300 is a further version with a tandem two-seat cockpit.

Ultimate 20-300, F-WSTC

Specification	Ultimate 10-200	
Powerplant	One 200 h.p. (149.1 kW) Textron Lycoming IO-360 piston engine	
Dimensions		
Span	4.83 m	(15 ft 0 in)
Length	5.33 m	(17 ft 6 in)
Height	1.68 m	(5 ft 6 in)
Performance		
Max speed	306 km/h	(165 kt, 190 mph)
Cruising speed	282 km/h	(152 kt, 175 mph)
Initial climb	594 m/min	(1,950 fpm)
Range	800 km	(435 nm, 500 miles)
Weights		
Max takeoff	612 kg	(1,350 lbs)
Useful load	193 kg	(425 lbs)

Sud Aviation SE-210 Caravelle — France

The SE-210 Caravelle 99-passenger short-/medium-haul jet airliner was designed by SNCASE (Sud-Est, later Sud Aviation) and first flown on 27th May 1955. It was a low-wing aircraft with twin rear-mounted turbojets and it had a highly streamlined fuselage with a nose section based on that of the de Havilland Comet. The Caravelle I had 10,500 lb.s.t. Rolls Royce Avon RA.29 Mk.522 engines. First deliveries to Air France were made in March 1959 followed by sales to SAS, VARIG, Finnair, Swissair, Alitalia and Sabena. Later variants were the Caravelle III with 11,400 lb.s.t. Mk.527s, Caravelle VI-N with 12,200 lb.s.t. Mk.531s and Caravelle VII, which was the Caravelle III re-engined with 16,100 lb.s.t. General Electric CJ805-23C engines. The Caravelle VI-R had larger cockpit windows and no dorsal fin with 12,600 lb.s.t. Mk.533R engines, and this became the Caravelle 10B (Super B) with 14,000 lb.s.t. Pratt & Whitney JT8D-1 turbofans and increased weights. The Caravelle 11R and Caravelle 12 both had stretched fuselages, in the latter case raising passenger capacity to 140. Sud Aviation built 280 Caravelles and a small number remain operational in Africa and South America.

Sud Caravelle III, 9U-BTA

Specification	Sud Caravelle VI-R	
Powerplant	Two 12,600 lb.s.t. (56.05 kN) Rolls Royce RA.29 Mk.533R turbojets	
Dimensions		
Span	34.29 m	(112 ft 6 in)
Length	32 m	(105 ft 0 in)
Height	8.71 m	(28 ft 7 in)
Performance		
Max speed	845 km/h	(456 kt, 525 mph)
Cruising speed	785 km/h	(424 kt, 488 mph)
Takeoff distance	2,073 m	(6,800 ft)
Range	2,288 km	(1,243 nm, 1,430 miles)
Weights		
Max takeoff	49,990 kg	(110,230 lbs)
Useful load	23,717 kg	(52,295 lbs)

Sukhoi Su-17, Su-20 and Su-22 — Russia

The Su-17 (Nato name 'Fitter') was a derivative of the earlier Su-7 ground attack aircraft which was built in large numbers for the VVS and Warsaw Pact countries in the 1960s. It was a single-seat aircraft with a highly swept low wing, tricycle undercarriage and a through-flow AL-7F-1 turbojet fed by a nose air intake. The Su-17 had a completely new wing with variable-sweep outer panels and detail changes including a deeper dorsal spine and a slightly longer forward fuselage. The prototype first flew on 2nd August 1966 and first deliveries of the Fitter-B took place in 1967, followed by the Su-20 Fitter-C, which had a higher-powered 24,800 lb.s.t. AL-21F-3 engine. The Fitter is normally equipped with four underwing pylons for bombs, rockets and ground attack weapons, and two fuselage hardpoints. Further variants included the Su-22M with improved attack electronics, the Su-17UM (and export Su-22UM) tandem two-seat attack-capable trainer and the final production Su-22M-4 Fitter-K, which has further avionics improvements and a ventral rear fin. At least 17 countries including Libya, Peru, the Czech Republic, Syria and Vietnam, still operate variants of the Fitter.

Sukhoi Su-22M-4, Czech AF, 4006

Specification	Sukhoi Su-22M-4 Fitter-K	
Powerplant	One 24,804 lb.s.t. (110.32 kN) (wet) Luyl'ka-Saturn AL-21F-3 turbojet	
Dimensions		
Span extended	13.79 m	(45 ft 3 in)
Length	18.74 m	(61 ft 6 in)
Height	5 m	(16 ft 5 in)
Performance		
Max speed	1,400 km/h	(756 kt, 870 mph)
Initial climb	13,716 m/min	(45,000 fpm)
Range	2,304 km	(1,252 nm, 1,440 miles)
Weights		
Max takeoff	19,500 kg	(42,997 lbs)
Useful load	6,500 kg	(14,332 lbs)

Sukhoi Su-24 — Russia

The Su-24 supersonic tactical medium bomber was developed by the Sukhoi OKB as the delta-winged T6-1 and was flown for the first time in June 1967. A major redesign resulted in the fitting of a variable-sweep wing with large fixed inboard leading edge cuffs, and the new version flew in May 1970 and subsequently entered production for the Soviet Air Force in 1974 as the Su-19 (NATO name Fencer-A) and the later Su-24 (Fencer-B). It is powered by a pair of AL-21F-3A afterburning turbojets positioned side by side in the rear fuselage and fed by flank intakes. Twin retractable speed brakes are fitted under the forward fuselage. The Su-24 has a crew of two and there is no internal bomb bay, all offensive weapons being carried on four underwing, two wing-root and three fuselage pylons. It also has a six-barrel 23 mm GSh-6-23M cannon in a starboard fuselage installation. The Fencer-C differs from the earlier models in having improved avionics, and the Su-24M Fencer-D has a retractable flight refuelling probe, a longer nose, overwing fences and new terrain-following radar. The Su-24MR Fencer-E is a maritime reconnaissance version. Approximately 1,200 Su-24s were built, including some export Su-24Mks delivered to Algeria, Libya, Iran and Syria, and many continue in service in Russia, Belarus and the Ukraine.

Sukhoi Su-24M, Russian AF, 15 white

Specification	Sukhoi Su-24M	
Powerplant	Two 24,800 lb.s.t. (110.32 kN) (wet) Luyl'ka-Saturn AL-21F-3A turbojets	
Dimensions		
Span extended	17.63 m	(57 ft 10 in)
Length	24.54 m	(80 ft 6 in)
Height	4.98 m	(16 ft 4 in)
Performance		
Max speed	1,835 km/h	(990 kt, 1,140 mph)
Initial climb (est)	3,962 m/min	(13,000 fpm)
Range	4,160 km	(2,260 nm, 2,600 miles)
Weights		
Max takeoff	39,700 kg	(87,538 lbs)
Useful load	20,700 kg	(45,643 lbs)

Sukhoi Su-25 — Russia

Sukhoi's Su-25 is a dedicated ground attack aircraft which began flight testing on 22nd February 1975. Carrying the NATO name 'Frogfoot', the Su-25 is a single-seater with a shoulder-mounted tapered wing and two Tumanski R-195 turbojets mounted on the fuselage sides. It has a retractable tricycle undercarriage and a conventional tail unit. Ten underwing pylons are fitted to carry all attack stores and long-range tanks can be carried on the inner points while the outer pylons are normally used for defensive AAMs such as the AA-8 Aphid. Over 300 Su-25s were built including export Su-25Ks delivered to the Czech Republic, Bulgaria, North Korea and Iraq. The Su-25UB (Frogfoot-B) is a tandem two-seat combat-capable trainer version with a longer forward fuselage and a framed cockpit canopy, 85 of which were built between 1988 and 1991, and the Su-25UT was an unarmed conversion trainer which was tested but not adopted. The Russian Navy has also received a small batch of Su-25UTG carrier-equipped two-seaters with folding wings, and an upgraded single-seat attack model, the Su-25T (Su-34), has been developed with the rear cockpit enclosed and used for extra fuel tanks and avionics. No production of this version appears to have taken place.

Sukhoi Su-25K, Slovak AF, 1006

Sukhoi Su-25UTG, Russian Naval Aviation, 11 red

Sukhoi Su-25 (Cont.)

Specification	Sukhoi Su-25K	
Powerplant	Two 9,920 lb.s.t. (44.13 kN) Tumanski (MNPK-Soyuz) R-195 turbojets	
Dimensions		
Span	14.35 m	(47 ft 1 in)
Length	15.52 m	(50 ft 11 in)
Height	4.8 m	(15 ft 9 in)
Performance		
Max speed	966 km/h	(522 kt, 600 mph)
Initial climb	5,090 m/min	(16,700 fpm)
Range	1,240 km	(674 nm, 775 miles)
Weights		
Max takeoff	17,530 kg	(38,654 lbs)
Useful load	8,100 kg	(17,860 lbs)

Sukhoi Su-26, Su-29 and Su-31 — Russia

The low-wing Su-26 is an advanced competition aerobatic aircraft which has been a leading contender in aerobatic competitions in the 1990s and has been exported widely. The production Su-26M is a sophisticated design built from steel tube and titanium with a composite wing and aluminium and composite cladding. It is a single-seater with a cockpit enclosed by an upward-hinged canopy, a spring-steel tailwheel landing gear and power provided by a Vedeneyev M-14P radial piston engine. The prototype flew in June 1984. The Su-26MX is a version stressed to higher limits with increased fuel capacity, and the Su-31, which replaced the Su-26, has a stretched fuselage and longer wings, a higher-powered M-14PF engine, a taller undercarriage, a cut-down rear fuselage and a modified side-hinged bubble canopy. The Su-29 is a stretched tandem two-seat version of the Su-31, and Sukhoi have also tested a special Su-29LL model with twin ejection seats. More than 150 of all the models have been built to date.

Sukhoi Su-26MX, RA-44519

Sukhoi Su-29, N929SU

Specification	Sukhoi Su-29	
Powerplant	One 360 h.p. (268.4 kW) Vedeneyev M-14P piston engine	
Dimensions		
Span	8.2 m	(26 ft 11 in)
Length	7.32 m	(24 ft 0 in)
Height	2.88 m	(9 ft 6 in)
Performance		
Max speed	325 km/h	(175 kt, 202 mph)
Cruising speed	314 km/h	(170 kt, 195 mph)
Initial climb	960 m/min	(3,150 fpm)
Range	1,200 km	(652 nm, 750 miles)
Weights		
Max takeoff	1,204 kg	(2,655 lbs)
Useful load	469 kg	(1,034 lbs)

Sukhoi Su-27 — Russia

The Su-27 (NATO name 'Flanker') air superiority fighter was developed in parallel with the MiG-29 tactical fighter. As the T-10-1 it first flew on 20th May 1977, but the production Su-27 was considerably modified with a new mildly swept wing with prominent leading edge extensions and changes to the tail unit and the twin afterburning AL-31F turbofans, which are positioned in the lower rear fuselage and fed by two large ventral air intakes. The Su-27 has a single-seat cockpit with a rear-hinged canopy and is fitted with a prominent retractable speed brake in the upper central fuselage. It is fitted with three underwing hardpoints, wingtip AAM stations and three belly weapons pylons. The definitive Su-27 flew on 20th April 1981 and first deliveries were made in 1984 in two versions which differed in weapons capability and electronic equipment. The VVS received the Su-27 dual-role interceptor/strike aircraft and the IA-PVO had the Su-27P long-range interceptor. Other variants included the Su-27PD aerobatic display aircraft and the export Su-27SK and Su-

27SMK. The Su-27UB (and export Su-27UBK) is a combat-capable tandem two-seat trainer with a raised rear cockpit, a common rear-hinged canopy and enlarged fins. This was also developed into the Su-30 two-seat interceptor and Su-30MK multi-role fighter, which are exported as the Su-30K and Su-30MK. The Su-27K is a navalised shipboard fighter version with folding wings and tailplane and modified leading edge extensions with additional canard control surfaces. Sukhoi has also flown the prototype of the Su-27KUB (Su-33UB), a naval trainer version of the Su-27K with a side-by-side two-seat cockpit. In addition, they have developed the high-agility Su-37 which is fitted with thrust-vectoring engine nozzles and forward canards similar to those of the Su-27K, and the Su-30MKI for India is to be fitted to this standard. Around 550 of the Su-27 series have been built and are in service in Russia, the Ukraine, Belorussia, China, India, Vietnam and Kazakhstan.

Sukhoi Su-30K

Sukhoi Su-30MK, 603

Specification	Sukhoi Su-27P	
Powerplant	Two 27,557 lb.s.t. (122.6 kN) (wet) Luyl'ka-Saturn AL-31F turbofans	
Dimensions		
Span	14.71 m	(48 ft 3 in)
Length	21.94 m	(72 ft 0 in)
Height	5.94 m	(19 ft 6 in)
Performance		
Max speed	2,500 km/h	(1,347 kt, 1,554 mph)
Initial climb	18,000 m/min	(59,054 fpm)
Range	1,400 km	(761 nm, 875 miles)
Weights		
Max takeoff	30,000 kg	(66,150 lbs)
Useful load	14,000 kg	(30,870 lbs)

Sukhoi Su-34
— Russia

The airframe of the Su-27 Flanker was used as the basis for the Su-27IB (later Su-34) all-weather interceptor. The complete forward fuselage was modified to create a side-by-side two-seat cabin accessed through a ventral hatch in the nosewheel well, and was large enough to contain a crew rest area. The forward fuselage also had the wing leading edge extensions running into ridged surfaces, extending to a flattened radar nose. The undercarriage has been redesigned with a rearward-retracting nosewheel and twin-wheel main bogies, and the tail sensor and countermeasures fairing have been substantially enlarged. The Su-34 has twelve external hardpoints and is fitted with a GSh-301 single-barrel 30 mm cannon. The prototype was first flown on 13th April 1990 and further development aircraft have flown, but the type has not yet been ordered into full-scale production. It is also known as the Su-32FN, probably for export variants.

Sukhoi Su-34 (Cont.)

Sukhoi Su-34, 45 white

Specification	Sukhoi Su-34	
Powerplant	Two 28,218 lb.s.t. (125.53 kN) (wet) Luyl'ka-Saturn AL-31FM turbofans	
Dimensions		
Span	14.71 m	(48 ft 3 in)
Length	23.29 m	(76 ft 5 in)
Height	5.99 m	(19 ft 8 in)
Performance		
Max speed	1,900 km/h	(1,024 kt, 1,181 mph)
Initial climb	16,800 m/min	(55,117 fpm)
Range	4,000 km	(2,174 nm, 2,500 miles)
Weights		
Max takeoff	44,360 kg	(97,814 lbs)
Useful load (est)	24,100 kg	(53,140 lbs)

Sukhoi Su-37 Berkut — Russia

The Sukhoi OKB has developed the Su-37 as a highly agile single-seat experimental fighter prototype to test a variety of aerodynamic concepts. The most notable feature is the forward swept wing of the Su-37 which is set well to the rear of the fuselage and blends into prominent wing leading edge fairings. The forward section of these fairings carries a canard surface with elevators, and the Su-37 is also fitted with rear tailplanes and twin fins. The two Aviadvigatel/Perm D-30F-6 afterburning turbofans do not have thrust vectoring, although this may be expected as a future change. The Su-37 first flew on 25th September 1997 and testing is continuing.

Sukhoi Su-37, 01 white

Specification	Sukhoi Su-37	
Powerplant	Two 34,170 lb.s.t. (152 kN) (wet) Aviadvigatel/Perm D-30F-6 turbofans	
Dimensions		
Span	16.71 m	(54 ft 10 in)
Length	22.55 m	(74 ft 0 in)
Height	6.4 m	(21 ft 0 in)
Performance		
Max speed	2,000 km/h	(1,078 kt, 1,243 mph)
Range	3,000 km	(1,630 nm, 1,875 miles)
Weights		
Max takeoff	25,000 kg	(55,125 lbs)
Useful load (est)	12,000 kg	(26,460 lbs)

Supermarine Spitfire — UK

Without doubt the most famous fighter of World War II, and probably of all time, the Spitfire was designed by R.J. Mitchell and was first flown on 5th March 1936. This low-wing monoplane with its elliptical wing and all-metal monocoque construction replaced the traditional tube and fabric biplane fighters of the 1930s. Some 20,351 Spitfires and 2,408 Seafires were built. It was produced in a large number of variants which initially had integral cockpit canopies but later moved to a bubble canopy on a cut-down fuselage. The pointed rudder was progressively introduced from the later Mk.VIIIs, and the wing, which was sometimes clipped, was constantly developed as new versions came in. The Merlin Spitfires were the Mk.I to Mk.IX (and Mk.XVI), of which the Mk.V and Mk.IX formed 70% of production, and in these marks engine power increased over the production life from the 1,030 h.p. Merlin II of the Spitfire Mk.I to the 1,760 h.p. Merlin 63 used in some Spitfire Mk.XIs. The Mk.XII to XVIII and the Mk.21, 22 and 24 were fitted with Rolls Royce Griffon engines, which ranged from the 1,730 h.p. Griffon IIB up to the 2,050 h.p. Griffon 65 on the Spitfire Mk.24, and the Seafire F.Mk.47 even had a 2,340 h.p. Griffon 88 with counter-rotating propellers. Specialised applications included high-altitude reconnaissance, ground attack and tropical operations, and some Spitfires were modified as Tr.8s with a second rear dual-control cockpit. A significant number of Spitfires survive and 50 were believed to be airworthy at the end of 2000.

Supermarine Spitfire IXB, MH434 (G-ASJV)

Supermarine Spitfire XVIE, TD248 (G-OXVI)

Swearingen SJ30-2, N30SJ

Specification	Supermarine Spitfire Mk.IX	
Powerplant	One 1,565 h.p. (1,166.8 kW) Rolls Royce Merlin 61 piston engine	
Dimensions		
Span	11.23 m	(36 ft 10 in)
Length	9.55 m	(31 ft 4 in)
Height	3.86 m	(12 ft 8 in)
Performance		
Max speed	657 km/h	(355 kt, 408 mph)
Initial climb	1,250 m/min	(4,100 fpm)
Range	694 km	(377 nm, 434 miles)
Weights		
Max takeoff	3,401 kg	(7,500 lbs)
Useful load	769 kg	(1,695 lbs)

Specification	Swearingen SJ30-2	
Powerplant	Two 2,300 lb.s.t. (10.23 kN) Williams Rolls FJ44-2A turbofans	
Dimensions		
Span	12.9 m	(42 ft 4 in)
Length	14.3 m	(46 ft 11 in)
Height	4.34 m	(14 ft 3 in)
Performance		
Max speed	980 km/h	(530 kt, 609 mph)
Cruising speed	956 km/h	(516 kt, 594 mph)
Takeoff distance	1,173 m	(3,850 ft)
Range	4,603 km	(2,502 nm, 2,877 miles)
Weights		
Max takeoff	5,986 kg	(13,200 lbs)
Useful load	2,494 kg	(5,500 lbs)

Swearingen SJ30
— USA

After selling the Merlin business aircraft line to Fairchild, Ed Swearingen's Swearingen Engineering & Technology Inc. designed the SA30 entry-level business jet as a cooperative project, initially with Gulfstream and later with Jaffe Group (as the SJ30). The prototype SJ30 made its first flight on 13th February 1991 and the company was reconstructed in 1995 as Sino-Swearingen to build a modified version. The SJ30 is a low-wing six-/seven-seat aircraft of primarily metal construction with twin Williams-Rolls FJ44 turbofans mounted on the rear fuselage. After initial testing, the prototype SJ30 was rebuilt as the SJ30-2 with a lengthened fuselage, longer wings and higher-rated engines, and it first flew in this form on 8th November 1996. Testing of a new conforming prototype is continuing towards FAR Part 23 certification and 164 orders were in hand by August 2000.

Swearingen SX300
— USA

The SX300 is an all-metal kit-built light aircraft designed by Ed Swearingen. It is highly streamlined to give good long-range cruise performance and has straight tapered wings which are low-set and have integral fuel tanks. Ths first SX300 was flown on 11th July 1984 and sales of kits commenced the following year. The SX300 has a fully enclosed side-by-side two-seat cockpit with a forward-hinged roof and windshield to give access. It has a retractable tricycle undercarriage with the main units folding backwards into fully enclosed fuselage wells. The standard engine is the 300 h.p. Lycoming IO-540 with a three-bladed Hartzell constant-speed propeller, and the engine cowling incorporates high-efficiency circular air intakes. Over 100 kits were sold and, though the aircraft is no longer available, more than 40 SX300s are flying in the USA.

Swearingen SX300 (Cont.)

Swearingen SX300, N377SX

Specification	Swearingen SX300	
Powerplant	One 300 h.p. (224 kW) Textron Lycoming IO-540-L1C5 piston engine	
Dimensions		
Span	7.42 m	(24 ft 4 in)
Length	6.43 m	(21 ft 1 in)
Height	2.39 m	(7 ft 10 in)
Performance		
Max speed	459 km/h	(248 kt, 285 mph)
Cruising speed	443 km/h	(239 kt, 275 mph)
Initial climb	732 m/min	(2,400 fpm)
Range	1,840 km	(1,000 nm, 1,150 miles)
Weights		
Max takeoff	1,088 kg	(2,400 lbs)
Useful load	363 kg	(800 lbs)

SZD-45 Ogar — Poland

The Polish glider experimental development establishment SZD (Szybowcowego Zakladu Doswiadczalnego) designed the SZD-45 Ogar motor glider, and the PZL factory at Bielsko-Biala flew a prototype on 29th May 1973. The Ogar is a side-by-side two-seater with a pod fuselage fitted with a monowheel undercarriage and a very narrow tail boom carrying a T-tail. It has a cantilever high wing fitted with tip-mounted supporting outrigger wheels. Of predominantly wooden construction, the Ogar is powered by a 68 h.p. Limbach SL-1700EC engine in a pusher installation mounted on the wing centre section. Approximately 230 SD-45A Ogars have been built and many are active in Poland and around Europe.

SZD-45 Ogar, G-OGAR

Specification	SZD-45 Ogar	
Powerplant	One 68 h.p. (50.7 kW) Limbach SL-1700EC piston engine	
Dimensions		
Span	17.53 m	(57 ft 6 in)
Length	7.95 m	(26 ft 1 in)
Height	1.73 m	(5 ft 8 in)
Performance		
Max speed	180 km/h	(97 kt, 112 mph)
Cruising speed	140 km/h	(76 kt, 87 mph)
Initial climb	159 m/min	(522 fpm)
Range	544 km	(296 nm, 340 miles)
Weights		
Max takeoff	700 kg	(1,544 lbs)
Useful load	225 kg	(496 lbs)

T

Taylor Monoplane and Titch — UK

The tiny JT.1 Taylor Monoplane was designed by John Taylor who aimed to produce a simple sporting aircraft for amateur construction with very low materials cost and a small and inexpensive powerplant. The design is a cantilever low-wing monoplane with an open single-seat cockpit, sometimes enclosed with a bubble canopy, and a fixed tailwheel undercarriage. The prototype, which first flew on 4th July 1959, was fitted with a 38 h.p. Aeronca J.A.P. two-cylinder engine, but later Monoplanes have generally used converted Volkswagen 1700s and, sometimes, the 65 h.p. Continental A65. The structure is all-wood with ply covering and fabric-covered control surfaces. The Taylor Monoplane, for which plans were sold, proved very popular and around 120 have been built, mostly in the UK, where 45 are currently registered, and in Australia and New Zealand. The Taylor JT.2 Titch was a midget racer development with a strengthened airframe, an 85 h.p. Continental C85 engine and a modified wing which flew as a prototype on 4th January 1967. The designer was killed in the Titch prototype shortly after but, again, plans were published and at least 40 have been built and flown.

Taylor JT.1 Monoplane, G-AYSH

Specification	Taylor Monoplane JT.1	
Powerplant	One 38 h.p. (28.33 kW) J.A.P. piston engine	
Dimensions		
Span	6.4 m	(21 ft 0 in)
Length	4.57 m	(15 ft 0 in)
Height	1.47 m	(4 ft 10 in)
Performance		
Max speed	167 km/h	(90 kt, 104 mph)
Cruising speed	148 km/h	(80 kt, 92 mph)
Initial climb	290 m/min	(950 fpm)
Range	368 km	(200 nm, 230 miles)
Weights		
Max takeoff	277 kg	(610 lbs)
Useful load	95 kg	(210 lbs)

Taylor Aerocar — USA

The innovative designer Molt Taylor developed the concept of a flying motor car and flew his prototype Aerocar I in October 1949. The all-metal Aerocar IA had a two-seat main body section with four wheels and a 143 h.p. Lycoming O-320 engine mounted in the rear, and it was fully functional as a normal automobile. For flight, strut-braced high wings could quickly be fitted and a tail cone was attached to the rear of the main body. This tail cone had a three-surface tail unit and a pusher propeller driven by a long driveshaft which automatically coupled to the engine when the tail cone was attached. The wings and tail cone could be fitted with wheels and trailed behind the car when in land-mode. The Aerocar was certificated in December 1956 and a further five were built, one of which (an Aerocar IC) has been restored by Ed Sweeney and is currently active, powered by a Lycoming O-360 engine. It was also intended to produce the Aerocar IB with a 154 h.p. O-340 engine, but this was not built. One of the five production Aerocars was converted to become the four-seat Aero-Plane, a non-roadable light aircraft with a fixed tricycle undercarriage and another was updated in the late 1960s as the Aerocar III with a more modern car body.

Taylor Aerocar IC, N102D

Specification	Taylor Aerocar IA	
Powerplant	One 143 h.p. (106.6 kW) Textron Lycoming O-320 piston engine	
Dimensions		
Span	10.36 m	(34 ft 0 in)
Length	6.55 m	(21 ft 6 in)
Height	2.29 m	(7 ft 6 in)
Performance		
Max speed	188 km/h	(102 kt, 117 mph)
Cruising speed	161 km/h	(87 kt, 100 mph)
Initial climb	186 m/min	(610 fpm)
Range	480 km	(261 nm, 300 miles)
Weights		
Max takeoff	930 kg	(2,050 lbs)
Useful load	249 kg	(550 lbs)

Taylor Coot — USA

Molt Taylor designed and built the prototype Coot light amphibian in 1967 using his 'floatwing' principle, which used the inner section of the dihedralled wing to rest on the water and assist stability and improve takeoff performance. The low-wing Coot has a retractable tricycle undercarriage, an enclosed side-by-side two-seat cabin and a cruciform tail. The prototype was followed by the improved Coot-A, which has been produced by a number of amateurs, and the Coot-B, which differs in having twin booms with twin fins and a bridge tailplane. The Coot-A was designed to fly with a 120 h.p. Franklin Sport 4R engine mounted as a pusher on a pylon behind the cabin but this was later changed to a 180 h.p. Franklin 335 Sport-6. The Coot is built with a glass-fibre hull but most of the structure is wood or tube with fabric covering. Molt Taylor's company, Aerocar, has marketed the aircraft as the Sooper Coot, powered by a 210 h.p. Continental IO-360 engine, although it is now only sold as Coot-A plans by the current owner, Richard Steeves. More than 400 Coot-A and Sooper Coot plans and kits have been sold and it is understood that at least 175 have flown.

Taylor Coot-A, N29LP

Specification	Taylor Coot-A	
Powerplant	One 180 h.p. (134.2 kW) Franklin 335 piston engine	
Dimensions		
Span	10.97 m	(36 ft 0 in)
Length	6.71 m	(22 ft 0 in)
Height	2.44 m	(8 ft 0 in)
Performance		
Max speed	225 km/h	(122 kt, 140 mph)
Cruising speed	209 km/h	(113 kt, 130 mph)
Initial climb	305 m/min	(1,000 fpm)
Range	960 km	(522 nm, 600 miles)
Weights		
Max takeoff	975 kg	(2,150 lbs)
Useful load	317 kg	(700 lbs)

Taylorcraft BC — USA

After leaving Piper in 1935, C.G. Taylor designed the high-wing side-by-side two-seat Taylorcraft 'A' light aircraft. It was built from steel tube, wood and fabric and had a chord-shock tailwheel undercarriage and a 40 h.p. Continental A40 flat-four engine. Taylorcraft built 606 Model As and licensed the design for production in the UK, where it became the first of the Auster range. The Taylorcraft B was an improved version with a modified wing. It was built as the BC-50 (Continental A50), BC-65 (Continental A65), BF-60 (Franklin 4AC-171), BF-65 (Franklin 4AC-176) and BL-65 (Lycoming O-145), the designation suffix indicating the engine horsepower in each case, and 2,401 prewar aircraft were completed. After the war, these types were reintroduced as the BC-12D Twosome (65 h.p. Continental A65) and the BC-12D-85 Sportsman (Continental A85), over 4,300 being manufactured. The Model 19 and F-19 (with a 100 h.p. Continental O-200-A engine) were later versions of the BC-12D-85, principally built by Taylorcraft Aviation Corp. in the 1970s. The final variants were the F-21, which had large rear side windows and a 118 h.p. Lycoming O-235-C engine, and the F-21A and F-21B, with higher weights and changes to the wing structure, together with the F-22 Classic which had new flaps and a wider interior, the F-22A Tracker with a tricycle undercarriage and the F-22B and F-22C with 180 h.p. Lycoming O-360-A4M engines and, respectively, tailwheel and tricycle gear. In total 217 of the F series were built before the Lock Haven-based Taylorcraft Aircraft Co. ceased business in 1992.

Taylorcraft F-21, G-BPJV

Specification	Taylorcraft BC-65	
Powerplant	One 65 h.p. (48.46 kW) Teledyne Continental A65 piston engine	
Dimensions		
Span	10.97 m	(36 ft 0 in)
Length	6.71 m	(22 ft 0 in)
Height	2.03 m	(6 ft 8 in)
Performance		
Max speed	169 km/h	(91 kt, 105 mph)
Cruising speed	153 km/h	(83 kt, 95 mph)
Initial climb	137 m/min	(450 fpm)
Range	400 km	(217 nm, 250 miles)
Weights		
Max takeoff	522 kg	(1,150 lbs)
Useful load	218 kg	(480 lbs)

Taylorcraft D — USA

Introduced in March 1941, the Taylorcraft DC-65 Tandem Trainer was a tandem two-seat version of the Model BC-65, which had been built in large numbers during the prewar period. It was particularly aimed at the needs of the Civilian Pilot Training Program and it had a narrower fuselage than that of the BC-65 but with extra side windows and a deeper centre section to accommodate the rear seat. As with the earlier model, it was powered by a 65 h.p. Continental engine, but Taylorcraft also built the DF-65 (65 h.p. Franklin 4AC-176) and DL-65 (65 h.p. Lycoming O-145-B2). Around 200 were built before production moved on to the military DCO-65. This was an army liaison and artillery observation version for the US Army, 1,040 of which were built as the O-57 (later L-2) with a cut-down rear fuselage and rear observation bubble window. Later versions were the L-2A with wing-root cutouts and L-2B, which had additional battle observation equipment. A number of civil Taylorcrafts were also impressed into war service with designations from L-2C to L-2L, and the L-2M, 900 of which were built, had a modified, fully enclosed engine cowling and spoilers to assist in short field landings. Taylorcraft also built 250 TG-6 (ST.100) three-seat training gliders based on the L-2 airframe with enlarged fins and spoilers, and some of these were rebuilt with standard A65 engines after the war. Many privately owned DC-65s and L-2s remain in private ownership.

Specification	Taylorcraft DCO-65	
Powerplant	One 65 h.p. (48.46 kW) Teledyne Continental A65-8 piston engine	
Dimensions		
Span	10.79 m	(35 ft 5 in)
Length	6.93 m	(22 ft 9 in)
Height	2.13 m	(7 ft 0 in)
Performance		
Max speed	164 km/h	(89 kt, 102 mph)
Cruising speed	148 km/h	(80 kt, 92 mph)
Initial climb	168 m/min	(550 fpm)
Range	432 km	(235 nm, 270 miles)
Weights		
Max takeoff	544 kg	(1,200 lbs)
Useful load	218 kg	(480 lbs)

Taylorcraft DCO-65, N36406

Taylorcraft 15 Tourist and 20 Topper — USA

For the postwar market, Taylorcraft designed the four-seat Model 15 Foursome, flying the prototype on 1st November 1944. It was a tube and fabric high-wing monoplane with a wide cabin which was provided with two front doors and one rear starboard door. Because the original Taylorcraft business went bankrupt in 1947 production did not commence with the reconstituted Taylorcraft Inc. until 1950, at which time 26 examples of the Model 15A Tourist were built, powered by the 145 h.p. Continental C145-2 engine. These were followed by 38 examples of the Model 20. This was a Model 15A with a glass-fibre shell in place of standard fabric covering for the fuselage and wings, and it was marketed as the Ranch Wagon, the float-equipped Seabird and the agricultural Topper with a chemical tank in the rear seat area. A later deluxe model was called the Zephyr 400. Several Model 15 and Model 20 Taylorcrafts continue to fly in private hands.

Taylorcraft DC-65, N49169

Taylorcraft 15A Tourist, N6653N

Taylorcraft 15 Tourist and 20 Topper (Cont.)

Taylorcraft 20 Ranch Wagon, C-GHKA

Specification	Taylorcraft 15A Tourist	
Powerplant	One 145 h.p. (108.1 kW) Teledyne Continental C145-2 piston engine	
Dimensions		
Span	10.97 m	(36 ft 0 in)
Length	7.31 m	(24 ft 0 in)
Height	2.16 m	(7 ft 1 in)
Performance		
Max speed	201 km/h	(109 kt, 125 mph)
Cruising speed	185 km/h	(100 kt, 115 mph)
Initial climb	213 m/min	(700 fpm)
Range	800 km	(435 nm, 500 miles)
Weights		
Max takeoff	998 kg	(2,200 lbs)
Useful load	420 kg	(925 lbs)

TEAM Mini-MAX — USA

The Mini-MAX was designed by TEAM (Tennessee Engineering & Manufacturing) as a simple, low-cost FAR Part 103 ultralight or amateur-category aircraft which could be built by homebuilders with minimum experience. The prototype Mini-MAX was first flown, powered by a 27 h.p. Rotax 277 engine, in February 1985 with kits being available to builders shortly after. The Mini-MAX is a wood and fabric aircraft with a fixed tailwheel undercarriage and an open single-seat cockpit. The wing is supported by V-struts which are braced off the undercarriage structure. Many versions have been produced with different powerplants, including the standard ultralight MAX-103UL/1030R and Mini-MAX 1100R with a Rotax 277, the standard category Mini-MAX 1500R (42 h.p. Rotax 447) and the Z-Max (45 h.p. Xenoah G-50). The Z-Max 1300Z is a modified version with a built-up rear fuselage and enclosed cabin, also powered by a Xenoah G-50. The Eros is a high-performance Mini-MAX which has a 50 h.p. Rotax 503 and optional flaps. TEAM has also produced the Hi-MAX 1400Z, a high-wing version with the Xenoah engine (or the Rotax 447 on the Model 1700R) using the same basic wings and fuselage as the Mini-MAX. Finally, there is the even more basic single-seat RX-40 Air Bike (and Tandem Air-Bike two-seater) which has an open-frame fuselage, Mini-MAX wings and a Rotax 447 engine. TEAM ceased business in 1999 at which time over 2,200 kits had been sold and nearly 1,600 aircraft had flown, including 1,200 examples of the Mini-MAX.

TEAM Mini-MAX, G-BUDD

TEAM Tandem Air-Bike

Specification	TEAM Mini-MAX 1500R	
Powerplant	One 42 h.p. (31.3 kW) Rotax 447 piston engine	
Dimensions		
Span	7.62 m	(25 ft 0 in)
Length	4.88 m	(16 ft 0 in)
Height	1.75 m	(5 ft 9 in)
Performance		
Max speed	161 km/h	(87 kt, 100 mph)
Cruising speed	105 km/h	(57 kt, 65 mph)
Initial climb	305 m/min	(1,000 fpm)
Range	240 km	(130 nm, 150 miles)
Weights		
Max takeoff	254 kg	(560 lbs)
Useful load	132 kg	(291 lbs)

Tech-Aero TR.200
— France

Also known as the Feugray TR.200, this two-seat competition aerobatic aircraft is available in plans or partial kit form from the French company Tech-Aero. It is derived from the low-wing single-seat Feugray ASA.200, which was built by Gérard Feugray, and the later TR.260, a mid-wing aircraft similar to the Stephens Akro, several of which were built for the 1986 World Aerobatic Championships. Tech-Aero has also built a prototype of the TR.300, which is also a single-seater developed from the TR.260 but with a larger engine. The TR.200 is a low-wing aircraft with a cantilever undercarriage and a tandem dual-control cockpit enclosed by a large bubble canopy. The normal powerplant is the 200 h.p. Lycoming IO-360-A1B6D or AEIO-360-A1B, but it can be fitted with other engines of up to 260 h.p. The structure is wood with ply and fabric covering. Ten TR.200s have been built and others are under construction.

Tech-Aero TR.200, F-PAUL

Tech-Aero TR.200 (Cont.)

Specification	Tech-Aero TR.200	
Powerplant	One 200 h.p. (149.1 kW) Textron Lycoming IO-360-A1B6D piston engine	
Dimensions		
Span	7.42 m	(24 ft 4 in)
Length	6.8 m	(22 ft 4 in)
Height	2.6 m	(8 ft 6 in)
Performance		
Max speed	325 km/h	(175 kt, 202 mph)
Cruising speed	270 km/h	(146 kt, 168 mph)
Initial climb	660 m/min	(2,165 fpm)
Range	1,070 km	(582 nm, 669 miles)
Weights		
Max takeoff	870 kg	(1,918 lbs)
Useful load	300 kg	(662 lbs)

Technoavia SM-92 Finist — Russia

First flown on 28th December 1993, the Finist is a general purpose utility aircraft developed by the Moscow-based Technoavia company. It is a classic all-metal strut-braced high-wing aircraft with a fixed tailwheel undercarriage and is powered by an M-14P radial piston engine. The Finist is intended for use in Russia's remote areas and it can carry a pilot and up to six passengers. There is a large sliding double door on the port side to load bulky freight, and the Finist can carry two stretchers and a medical attendant in ambulance configuration. Technoavia have also produced a prototype of the military SM-92P which has two rocket launchers and two machine guns fitted to the lower fuselage with a further machine gun mounted in the open door. Nine Finists have been built, but output is suspended following the closure of the Smolensk factory responsible for its manufacture.

Technoavia SM-92 Finist, RA-44485

Specification	Technoavia SM-92 Finist	
Powerplant	One 360 h.p. (268.5 kW) VOKBM Vedeneyev M-14P piston engine	
Dimensions		
Span	14.6 m	(47 ft 11 in)
Length	9.12 m	(29 ft 11 in)
Height	3.07 m	(10 ft 1 in)
Performance		
Max speed	217 km/h	(117 kt, 135 mph)
Cruising speed	200 km/h	(108 kt, 124 mph)
Initial climb	300 m/min	(984 fpm)
Range	1,088 km	(591 nm, 680 miles)
Weights		
Max takeoff	2,350 kg	(5,182 lbs)
Useful load	920 kg	(2,029 lbs)

Technoavia SP-91/95 — Russia

The SP-95 was designed by Vyacheslav Kondratyev, who also designed the Yakovlev Yak-55 and the Sukhoi Su-26 competition aerobatic aircraft. It has been built by Interavia as the I-3 and by Technoavia as the SP-91, and later the improved production SP-95 with longer wings and a deeper rudder. The SP-95 Slavia is a low-wing aircraft with a distinctive pointed tail, a fixed tailwheel undercarriage with tall-tapered tube legs and a closely cowled Vedeneyev radial engine. It has a tandem two-seat cockpit enclosed by a large bubble canopy, but for single-seat competition work the cockpit decking and canopy can be removed and replaced by a single rear canopy and a fairing covering the front cockpit. At least eight Slavias were built at the Smolensk production factory from 1995 onwards, most of which are in the United States. Technoavia is believed to have had an improved model, the SP-96, under development, although production of the Slavia has now been suspended for financial reasons. Interavia are thought to have completed around 10 examples of the I-3, which is a lower-cost variant.

Technoavia SP-95 Slavia, N195SF

Specification	Technoavia SP-95 Slavia	
Powerplant	One 360 h.p. (268.5 kW) VOKBM Vedeneyev M-14P piston engine	
Dimensions		
Span	9.02 m	(29 ft 7 in)
Length	7.04 m	(23 ft 1 in)
Height	2.21 m	(7 ft 3 in)
Performance		
Max speed	299 km/h	(162 kt, 186 mph)
Cruising speed	278 km/h	(150 kt, 173 mph)
Initial climb	1,020 m/min	(3,345 fpm)
Range	1,488 km	(809 nm, 930 miles)
Weights		
Max takeoff	1,080 kg	(2,381 lbs)
Useful load	280 kg	(617 lbs)

Technoflug Piccolo — Germany

Technoflug is a German producer of motor gliders which include the Piccolo and the new Carat motorised high-performance sailplane. The Piccolo, which originated as the Neukom AN-20B/AN-22, built in Switzerland in small series during the early 1980s, is a composite powered sailplane with a high strut-braced constant-chord wing, a fixed tricycle undercarriage and a T-tail. It has a 23 h.p. Solo engine providing sufficient power for normal takeoffs which is mounted as a pusher at the wing-fuselage intersection and is fitted with a foldable propeller to reduce drag when the engine is switched off for soaring flight. The cabin of the Piccolo accommodates a single pilot in a semi-prone position. Technoflug commenced production in 1986 and more than 100 Piccolos have been sold, mainly in Germany, Austria and Switzerland.

Technoflug Piccolo, HB-2179

Specification	Technoflug Piccolo b	
Powerplant	One 23 h.p. (17 kW) Solo 2350BS piston engine	
Dimensions		
Span	13.3 m	(43 ft 7 in)
Length	6.28 m	(20 ft 7 in)
Height	1.45 m	(4 ft 9 in)
Performance		
Max speed	170 km/h	(92 kt, 106 mph)
Cruising speed	155 km/h	(84 kt, 96 mph)
Initial climb	132 m/min	(433 fpm)
Range	420 km	(226 nm, 261 miles)
Weights		
Max takeoff	297 kg	(655 lbs)
Useful load	117 kg	(258 lbs)

Tecnam P92 Echo — Italy

Now built in significant numbers for the private and aero club market in Europe, the P92 is another product of Prof. Luigi Pascale, who was responsible for the range of Partenavia designs and formed Naples-based Tecnam in 1986. The Echo was designed to be powered by engines of various sizes and to fall within European ultralight rules. The P92, which first flew on 14th March 1993, is a strut-braced high-wing aircraft with an enclosed side-by-side two-seat cabin, a spring-steel tricycle undercarriage and mixed metal, composite and fabric construction. The initial P92 was powered by an 80 h.p. Rotax 912 engine, and this was later developed as the P92-J, which is certificated under JAR-VLA regulations. The P92-S is an improved model with a modified wing and nose cowling, a reshaped vertical tail, a more streamlined windshield and a rear cabin structure which joins into an upper fuselage spine and has extra rear-side windows. It is sold as the P92-S Echo 80 with an 81 h.p. Rotax 912U or as the P92-S Echo 100 with a 100 h.p. Rotax 912S, and a version on inflatable Lotus amphibious floats is known as the P22 Seasky. Over 400 P92s have been built to date.

Tecnam P92-J Echo, I-TECK

Tecnam P92 Echo (Cont.)

Specification	Tecnam P92-S Echo 100	
Powerplant	One 100 h.p. (74.56 kW) Rotax 912S piston engine	
Dimensions		
Span	9.3 m	(30 ft 6 in)
Length	6.3 m	(20 ft 8 in)
Height	2.49 m	(8 ft 2 in)
Performance		
Max speed	230 km/h	(124 kt, 143 mph)
Cruising speed	205 km/h	(111 kt, 127 mph)
Initial climb	384 m/min	(1,260 fpm)
Range	738 km	(400 nm, 461 miles)
Weights		
Max takeoff	450 kg	(992 lbs)
Useful load	169 kg	(373 lbs)

Tecnam P96 Golf — Italy

The Golf is a companion model to the high-wing Tecnam Echo with very similar performance but with a low wing. It is aimed at flying clubs and schools and has a side-by-side dual-control cabin with a sliding canopy which can be opened in flight and is constructed of light alloy and composites with a steel tube fuselage structure. The cantilever undercarriage, vertical tail and fuselage top decking are the same as those of the Echo but the Golf has an all-moving tailplane and a wet wing. Two engine options are available, the 81 h.p. Rotax 912U and the 100 h.p. Rotax 912S, but in each case the Golf is designed to meet the 450 kg European ultralight category regulations. Around 50 Golfs have been built and sold in Italy, Germany and France.

Tecnam P96 Golf

Specification	Tecnam P96 Golf 100	
Powerplant	One 100 h.p. (74.56 kW) Rotax 912S piston engine	
Dimensions		
Span	8.41 m	(27 ft 7 in)
Length	6.4 m	(21 ft 0 in)
Height	2.29 m	(7 ft 6 in)
Performance		
Max speed	240 km/h	(129 kt, 149 mph)
Cruising speed	215 km/h	(116 kt, 134 mph)
Initial climb	360 m/min	(1,180 fpm)
Range	746 km	(404 nm, 466 miles)
Weights		
Max takeoff	450 kg	(992 lbs)
Useful load	169 kg	(373 lbs)

Ted Smith Aerostar — USA

Ted R. Smith, designer of the Aero Commander twins, developed the Aerostar cabin business twin in the mid-1960s. The Aerostar 360 prototype first flew in November 1966 and was a mid-wing six-seat cabin monoplane with two wing-mounted piston engines, a swept fin and a circular-section fuselage, with a main cabin airstair door ahead of the wing. The first production Aerostar was the Model 600 powered by two 290 h.p. Lycoming IO-540 engines which flew in December 1967, and this was followed by the Aerostar 601 with turbocharged TIO-540-S1AS engines. Both models were built at Van Nuys, California by Ted Smith Aircraft, which was later owned by American Cement Co. and Butler Aviation. The new Ted Smith Aerostar Corp. of 1972 introduced the Model 601P, a pressurised version of the Model 601, and developed the Model 700 Superstar. Piper Aircraft acquired the designs in March 1978 and built the Models 600A, 601B and 601P until 1981 when the line was rationalised to one model: the PA-60-602P (known initially as the Sequoya), a Model 601P with 290 h.p. Lycoming TIO-540-AA1A5 engines. They also built the Aerostar 700P with 350 h.p. counter-rotating TIO-540-U2A engines. The last Aerostar was completed in 1984, by which time 1,010 aircraft had been built, the majority being the 601P, including 519 under Piper. Among conversions of the Aerostar are the Machen Superstar 700, an Aerostar 601 upgraded with 350 h.p. TIO-540 engines, and at least one Aerostar has been re-engined with Allison 250 turboprops.

Ted Smith Aerostar 600A, TG-EVL

Specification	Ted Smith Aerostar 601P	
Powerplant	Two 290 h.p. (216.22 kW) Textron Lycoming TIO-540-S1AS piston engines	
Dimensions		
Span	10.41 m	(34 ft 2 in)
Length	10.62 m	(34 ft 10 in)
Height	3.71 m	(12 ft 2 in)
Performance		
Max speed	476 km/h	(257 kt, 296 mph)
Cruising speed	436 km/h	(235 kt, 271 mph)
Initial climb	445 m/min	(1,460 fpm)
Range	2,155 km	(1,170 nm, 1,347 miles)
Weights		
Max takeoff	2,721 kg	(6,000 lbs)
Useful load	456 kg	(1,005 lbs)

Temco-Riley Twin Navion — USA

Several companies have carried out twin-engined conversions of the North American (Ryan) Navion light aircraft. The earliest was the X-16 Bi-Navion, engineered by the Dauby Equipment Company of Los Angeles in 1952, which involved the replacement of the existing engine installation with a solid nose and the mounting of two 130 h.p. Lycoming engines on the strengthened wings. Some 19 conversions were carried out by the Riley Aircraft Co., which used 150 h.p. Lycoming O-320 engines and fitted a larger vertical tail, and Temco then produced a further 46 of this D-16 model and 45 D-16As with 160 h.p. Lycoming O-340-A1A engines. The other Navion twin conversion was the Camair 480, produced by Cameron Aircraft Co. of Galveston, Texas. Their version, 35 of which were produced, had a variety of Continental engines ranging from 225 h.p. to 260 h.p. and a similar but slightly taller fin to that of the standard Twin Navion. A total of 50 Riley Twins and 14 Camair 480s remain registered in the USA.

Camair 480, N188V

Specification	Temco-Riley D-16 Twin Navion	
Powerplant	Two 150 h.p. (111.84 kW) Textron Lycoming O-320 piston engines	
Dimensions		
Span	10.16 m	(33 ft 4 in)
Length	8.28 m	(27 ft 2 in)
Height	2.9 m	(9 ft 6 in)
Performance		
Max speed	290 km/h	(157 kt, 180 mph)
Cruising speed	274 km/h	(148 kt, 170 mph)
Initial climb	427 m/min	(1,400 fpm)
Range	1,120 km	(609 nm, 700 miles)
Weights		
Max takeoff	1,519 kg	(3,350 lbs)
Useful load	476 kg	(1,050 lbs)

Temco T-35 Buckaroo — USA

In 1949, Temco, builders of the Globe Swift, produced the prototype TE-1A Buckaroo basic trainer. It was, essentially, a Globe Swift with a cut-down fuselage and a tandem two-seat cockpit enclosed by a framed canopy, and the production version had a larger squared-off rudder. The prototype had a 145 h.p. Continental C145-2H engine but the TE-1B, which represented the production version, was fitted with a 165 h.p. Franklin 6A4. The Buckaroo was an all-metal aircraft with a low wing and a retractable tailwheel undercarriage. It was ordered as the YT-35 for evaluation as the new standard USAF basic trainer but lost out to the competing Beech T-34 Mentor. However, ten were built for Saudi Arabia and, together with evaluation aircraft and prototypes, a total of 20 were finally completed. Four of these are still in existence with American private owners.

Temco T-35A Buckaroo, N904B

Specification	Temco T-35A Buckaroo	
Powerplant	One 165 h.p. (123 kW) Franklin 6A4-165-B3 piston engine	
Dimensions		
Span	8.94 m	(29 ft 4 in)
Length	6.6 m	(21 ft 8 in)
Height	1.85 m	(6 ft 1 in)
Performance		
Max speed	251 km/h	(136 kt, 156 mph)
Cruising speed	233 km/h	(126 kt, 145 mph)
Initial climb	304 m/min	(1,000 fpm)
Range	720 km	(391 nm, 450 miles)
Weights		
Max takeoff	896 kg	(1,975 lbs)
Useful load	283 kg	(625 lbs)

Thorp T-18 — USA

The well-respected designer John W. Thorp, who was responsible for the Piper Cherokee design, developed the T-18 Tiger as an all-metal aircraft for amateur construction. It first flew on 12th May 1964. The T-18 has a straight untapered wing with dihedralled outer panels set forward of the cockpit to provide good downward vision to the rear. The cockpit has side-by-side seating for two and is enclosed by a sliding canopy, and there is a large baggage compartment which makes the T-18 very suitable for cross-country flying. One

Thorp T-18 (Cont.)

T-18 was flown by its builder from Australia to Europe and back. The T-18 has a cantilever tubular steel tailwheel undercarriage and can be powered by various engines in the 125 h.p. to 200 h.p. range. Plans are sold by Eklund Engineering, and around 400 examples of the T-18 have flown, including at least 20 in Australia and New Zealand.

Thorp T-18 Tiger, N18Z

Specification	Thorp T-18 Tiger	
Powerplant	One 180 h.p. (134.2 kW) Textron Lycoming O-360 piston engine	
Dimensions		
Span	6.35 m	(20 ft 10 in)
Length	5.54 m	(18 ft 2 in)
Height	1.47 m	(4 ft 10 in)
Performance		
Max speed	232 km/h	(125 kt, 144 mph)
Cruising speed	209 km/h	(113 kt, 130 mph)
Initial climb	323 m/min	(1,060 fpm)
Range	656 km	(357 nm, 410 miles)
Weights		
Max takeoff	542 kg	(1,195 lbs)
Useful load	247 kg	(545 lbs)

Thorp T-211 and Sky Skooter — USA

One of John W. Thorp's earliest designs was the T-11 Sky Skooter, which flew on 15th August 1946 and was an all-metal side-by-side two-seat trainer with a low wing constructed with externally ribbed skins, a fixed tricycle undercarriage and a 65 h.p. Lycoming engine. Three prototypes were built, followed by the T-111 with a 90 h.p. Continental engine. The design was taken over by Tubular Aircraft, which built a new prototype, the T-211, with a 100 h.p. Continental O-200-A. Several attempts were made by other companies, including Adams Industries, Thorp Aero and Phoenix Aircraft, to build the T-211 Aerosport. In 1998, DM Aerospace Ltd. of Manchester, UK acquired the type certificate and production rights. The main current output, however, is a homebuilt kit for the T-211 produced by Venture Light Aircraft Resources of Tucson. At least 16 Thorps have been built including one completed by an amateur from spare parts.

Thorp T-211, G-BXPF

Specification	Thorp T-211	
Powerplant	One 100 h.p. (74.56 kW) Teledyne Continental O-200-A piston engine	
Dimensions		
Span	7.62 m	(25 ft 0 in)
Length	5.49 m	(18 ft 0 in)
Height	1.93 m	(6 ft 4 in)
Performance		
Max speed	209 km/h	(113 kt, 130 mph)
Cruising speed	193 km/h	(104 kt, 120 mph)
Initial climb	229 m/min	(750 fpm)
Range	760 km	(413 nm, 475 miles)
Weights		
Max takeoff	576 kg	(1,270 lbs)
Useful load	236 kg	(520 lbs)

Thruxton Jackaroo — UK

The Jackaroo was a conversion of the de Havilland DH.82A Tiger Moth biplane to a four-seat cabin configuration. It was engineered by the Wiltshire School of Flying with a 12-inch increase in fuselage width and an enclosed cabin structure. The upper wing was also lengthened at the roots and the undercarriage was adjusted. The first converted Jackaroo was flown on 2nd March 1957 and the second aircraft was built as the sole Jackaroo Srs.2 agricultural aircraft with the wider fuselage and a chemical hopper in place of the front cockpit. In total Jackaroo Aircraft Ltd. converted 18 Jackaroos between 1957 and 1959 and Rollason Aircraft & Engines also converted one. Some Jackaroos were subsequently converted back to normal Tiger Moths, but seven still exist with owners in the UK, Canada and Australia.

Thruxton Jackaroo, G-ANZT

Specification	Thruxton Jackaroo	
Powerplant	One 145 h.p. (108.1 kW) de Havilland Gipsy Major 1C piston engine	
Dimensions		
Span	9.25 m	(30 ft 4 in)
Length	7.62 m	(25 ft 0 in)
Height	2.67 m	(8 ft 9 in)
Performance		
Max speed	167 km/h	(90 kt, 104 mph)
Cruising speed	145 km/h	(78 kt, 90 mph)
Initial climb	194 m/min	(635 fpm)
Range	556 km	(300 nm, 345 miles)
Weights		
Max takeoff	989 kg	(2,180 lbs)
Useful load	372 kg	(820 lbs)

Thurston TSC-1A Teal — USA

Designed by David B. Thurston, who also designed the Colonial Skimmer amphibian (later Lake LA-4), the TSC-1 Teal was a small side-by-side two-seat amphibian which followed a similar general layout to the earlier types with a shoulder-mounted wing and pylon-mounted engine above the wing centre section. It had a T-tail and the main units of the tailwheel undercarriage retracted upwards to fit under the wingroots. The TSC-1 prototype made its first flight in June 1968 powered by a 150 h.p. Lycoming O-320-A3B engine. Thurston Aircraft, and, later, Schweizer Aircraft and Teal Aircraft, built 37 production TSC-1As, TSC-1A1s (with new fuel tanks and a retractable tailwheel) and TSC-1A2 Teal IIs (with slotted flaps and higher weights). The single Teal III was built by International Aeromarine with a tricycle undercarriage, longer wings and a 180 h.p. Lycoming engine. Other aircraft based on the general Teal design have included the Patchen Explorer 2000 observation prototype built in South Africa with a fixed tricycle undercarriage and a large omnivision cabin, and the Thurston Seafire, which is an amateur-built four-seater with tricycle gear powered by a 314 h.p. Continental IO-520 engine, two of which have been completed.

Thurston TSC-1A3 Teal III, N2022T

Thurston Seafire, N15BH

Specification	Thurston (Schweizer) TSC-1A2 Teal II	
Powerplant	One 150 h.p. (111.8 kW) Textron Lycoming O-320-A3B piston engine	
Dimensions		
Span	9.73 m	(31 ft 11 in)
Length	7.19 m	(23 ft 7 in)
Height	2.87 m	(9 ft 5 in)
Performance		
Max speed	193 km/h	(104 kt, 120 mph)
Cruising speed	187 km/h	(101 kt, 116 mph)
Initial climb	198 m/min	(650 fpm)
Range	752 km	(409 nm, 470 miles)
Weights		
Max takeoff	998 kg	(2,200 lbs)
Useful load	347 kg	(765 lbs)

Timm N2T-1 Tutor — USA

Timm Aircraft Corporation developed the Model S-160K military trainer and flew the prototype on 22nd May 1940. Although it was a conventional low-wing tandem open-cockpit two-seater with a fixed tailwheel undercarriage, it was unusual in its Aeromold construction. This was a plastic-bonded plywood structure which was moulded in major components and resulted in a very strong airframe which would not corrode and had a very smooth finish. Timm modified the higher-powered PT-175K version into the PT-220-C, which had a larger tail and a bigger Continental radial engine. It was built as the N2T-1 Tutor basic trainer for the US Navy, 262 examples being delivered, ten of which are currently registered with private owners in the USA.

Timm N2T-1 Tutor (Cont.)

Timm N2T-1, N61864

Specification	Timm N2T-1 Tutor	
Powerplant	One 220 h.p. (164 kW) Continental W-670-6 piston engine	
Dimensions		
Span	10.97 m	(36 ft 0 in)
Length	7.7 m	(25 ft 3 in)
Height	2.29 m	(7 ft 6 in)
Performance		
Max speed	220 km/h	(119 kt, 137 mph)
Cruising speed	185 km/h	(100 kt, 115 mph)
Initial climb	274 m/min	(900 fpm)
Range	560 km	(304 nm, 350 miles)
Weights		
Max takeoff	1,236 kg	(2,725 lbs)
Useful load	308 kg	(680 lbs)

Tipsy Belfair — Belgium

Ernest O. Tips designed the little S.1 and S.2 low-wing single-seat sporting aircraft in 1935, and 20 were built in Belgium and nine in Britain. Using the same basic design he developed the side-by-side two-seat Tipsy B with its distinctive elliptical wing and fixed tailwheel undercarriage. This was of mixed construction and the prototype made its first flight in Belgium, where 20 further examples were built together with additional production in the UK, where Tipsy Aircraft Ltd. completed 18 aircraft which were known as the Tipsy Trainer and had higher weights than the Belgian machines. After the war a further seven, known as Tipsy Belfairs, were built in Belgium with a built-up rear fuselage decking and an enclosed cockpit, and one Tipsy Trainer was converted in the UK to this configuration. Three Trainers and a Belfair are airworthy in the UK with a further four under restoration.

Tipsy Trainer, G-AFWT

Tipsy Belfair, G-APIE

Specification	Tipsy Belfair	
Powerplant	One 62 h.p. (46.23 kW) Walter Mikron piston engine	
Dimensions		
Span	9.5 m	(31 ft 2 in)
Length	6.6 m	(21 ft 8 in)
Height	1.73 m	(5 ft 8 in)
Performance		
Max speed	177 km/h	(96 kt, 110 mph)
Cruising speed	161 km/h	(87 kt, 100 mph)
Initial climb	152 m/min	(500 fpm)
Range	744 km	(404 nm, 465 miles)
Weights		
Max takeoff	499 kg	(1,100 lbs)
Useful load	254 kg	(560 lbs)

Tipsy Nipper — Belgium

After the war Ernest Tips continued to design simple, light aircraft, and two examples of his Tipsy Junior low-wing single-seater were built in 1946, one of which is still registered in the UK. However, his best-known design is the Nipper, which was just large enough to accommodate a pilot and a Volkswagen engine. Constructed of tube and fabric, the Nipper is a mid-wing machine with a fixed tricycle undercarriage, and the prototype, with an open cock-pit, was first flown on 2nd December 1957 powered by a 40 h.p. Pollman Hepu with production by Avions Fairey commencing at Gosselies in 1959. The production T.66 Nipper Mk.1 had a built-up rear fuselage faired into a large bubble canopy, and the Nipper Mk.2 was similar but powered by a 45 h.p. Stark Stamo 1400A. A total of 58 were manufactured by Tipsy followed by 18 built as the Cobelavia D-158 Nipper. In 1966, rights to the Nipper passed to Nipper Aircraft in England which had 31 Nipper Mk.III aircraft built by Slingsby Aircraft Ltd. and powered by a 1500cc Rollason Ardem (Volkswagen), and a further two were Nipper Mk.IIIAs with the 55 h.p. 1600cc Ardem. Some Nippers were fitted with wingtip fuel tanks. Out of the 110 Nippers built around 45 are active, the majority in the UK.

Cobelavia D-158 Nipper, OO-LEO

Specification	Tipsy T.66 Nipper Mk.2	
Powerplant	One 45 h.p. (33.55 kW) Stark Stamo 1400A piston engine	
Dimensions		
Span	5.99 m	(19 ft 8 in)
Length	4.5 m	(14 ft 9 in)
Height	1.88 m	(6 ft 2 in)
Performance		
Max speed	162 km/h	(88 kt, 101 mph)
Cruising speed	150 km/h	(81 kt, 93 mph)
Initial climb	192 m/min	(630 fpm)
Range	320 km	(174 nm, 200 miles)
Weights		
Max takeoff	299 kg	(660 lbs)
Useful load	112 kg	(248 lbs)

TL Ultralight TL232 Condor Plus — Czech Republic

Now sold in some numbers in the Czech Republic and in France, Holland, Sweden and Germany, the TL232 ultralight sporting aircraft is derived from the Rans S-6 Coyote. The initial version was the TL32 Typhoon, followed in 1993 by the TL132 Condor and in 1994 by the TL232 Condor Plus. The Condor Plus, which complies with the European 450 kg ultralight weight category, is a strut-braced high-wing aircraft with a tubular fuselage structure covered with light alloy and a metal wing with fabric covering. It has a fixed tricycle undercarriage and the all-round-vision cabin has side-by-side seating for two with dual controls and a rear baggage space. The wings and tailplane are foldable for storage and ground transport and the standard powerplant is an 80 h.p. Rotax 912, although the Rotax 582 can be installed as a lower-powered option and the 100 h.p. Rotax 912S can also be fitted. The aircraft is sold as a kit and more than 150 of the TL132 and TL232 were active at the end of 1999.

Specification	TL232 Condor Plus	
Powerplant	One 80 h.p. (59.65 kW) Rotax 912 piston engine	
Dimensions		
Span	10.6 m	(34 ft 9 in)
Length	6.08 m	(19 ft 11 in)
Height	2.03 m	(6 ft 8 in)
Performance		
Max speed	150 km/h	(81 kt, 93 mph)
Cruising speed	130 km/h	(70 kt, 81 mph)
Initial climb	276 m/min	(905 fpm)
Range	635 km	(342 nm, 395 miles)
Weights		
Max takeoff	450 kg	(992 lbs)
Useful load	185 kg	(408 lbs)

TL232 Condor Plus, D-MWTL

TL Ultralight TL96 Star — Czech Republic

The TL96 Star is a modern kit-built ultralight sporting aircraft manufactured by TL Ultralight of Hradec Kralove in the Czech Republic. It is currently sold as a factory-complete aircraft within the 450 kg ultralight category. The TL96 is built entirely with composite shells for fuselage, wings and tail and has side-by-side seating for two with dual controls. The cabin has a large clear-view canopy which hinges forward for entry. The Star is fitted with flaps and has a fixed tricycle undercarriage, and the standard powerplant is an 80 h.p. Rotax 912. It is thought that more than 40 have been completed since its introduction in 1998, and examples are flying in the Czech Republic, Holland and Germany.

TL96 Star, PH-3C9

Specification	TL96 Star	
Powerplant	One 80 h.p. (59.65 kW) Rotax 912 piston engine	
Dimensions		
Span	9 m	(29 ft 6 in)
Length	5.5 m	(18 ft 1 in)
Height	1.68 m	(5 ft 6 in)
Performance		
Max speed	260 km/h	(140 kt, 162 mph)
Cruising speed	235 km/h	(127 kt, 146 mph)
Initial climb	276 m/min	(905 fpm)
Range	1,068 km	(580 nm, 668 miles)
Weights		
Max takeoff	450 kg	(992 lbs)
Useful load	160 kg	(353 lbs)

Transall C-160
— International

The C-160 tactical transport was built by a consortium of Nord Aviation, Messerschmitt-Bölkow-Blohm and VFW-Fokker to meet the needs of the French and German air forces. It is a high-wing twin-turboprop aircraft with an upswept rear fuselage and inbuilt loading ramp, and is powered by two 6,100 s.h.p. Rolls Royce Tyne RTy.20 Mk.22 engines. While primarily used for carrying military freight, it can accommodate up to 93 troops. The first of three prototypes made its first flight at Melun Villaroche on 25th February 1963, and these were followed by series production of the C-160D (for the German Air Force) and C-160F (for the French Air Force). In total, 205 C-160s were built including prototypes, nine of which were sold as the C-160Z to the South African Air Force. The final batches, totalling 36 aircraft, were built in France as the C-160NG Nouvelle Generation with upgraded avionics, increased fuel capacity and aerial refuelling capability. Several ex-military Transalls were also acquired by civil operators and by the Turkish Air Force. The Transall remains in service with the French, Turkish and German air forces and some French aircraft have been modified to C-160G Gabriels with specialised ELINT and tactical jamming equipment. Other C-160s are equipped with the ASTARTE low-frequency communications system to allow independent emergency airborne command of the French strategic nuclear forces, although these are being withdrawn from use in 2000.

Transall C-160D, German AF, 5052

Specification	Transall C-160	
Powerplant	Two 6,100 s.h.p. (4,548 kW) Rolls Royce Tyne RTy.20 Mk.22 turboprops	
Dimensions		
Span	40 m	(131 ft 3 in)
Length	32.41 m	(106 ft 4 in)
Height	11.71 m	(38 ft 5 in)
Performance		
Max speed	539 km/h	(291 kt, 335 mph)
Cruising speed	515 km/h	(278 kt, 320 mph)
Initial climb	440 m/min	(1,445 fpm)
Range	4,500 km	(2,446 nm, 2,812 miles)
Weights		
Max takeoff	49,100 kg	(108,265 lbs)
Useful load	20,342 kg	(44,854 lbs)

Transavia Airtruk — Australia

The curious Airtruk agricultural aircraft was devised by Luigi Pellarini, initially as the PL-7 Tanker, which first flew on 21st September 1956, followed by two PL-11 Waitomo Airtrucks which were built in New Zealand. The definitive PL-12, which first flew in 1966, entered production with Transavia at Parramatta in Australia. The Airtruk has a sesquiplane layout with a straight mid-set wing to which are attached twin booms with individual fins and tailplanes. The smaller secondary wing is mounted on the lower fuselage and acts as a support structure for wing struts and the undercarriage. The fuselage of the Airtruk is built around a large 216 USG hopper which occupies the lower part of the body, and the single-seat cockpit is perched on top with a small cabin in the rear of the fuselage pod for transport of one or two ground support crewmen. Variants included the basic PL-12, initially fitted with a 285 h.p. Continental IO-520-A engine but later with a 300 h.p. IO-520-D, the PL-12U freighter, nine of which were built with a freight hold in place of the hopper/passenger compartment, the PL-12-T320 with a 320 h.p. Continental Tiara 6-320B engine and the PL-12-T300 with a 300 h.p. Lycoming IO-540-K1A5. The Skyfarmer was the renamed PL-12-T300A version introduced in 1981 with modifications to the undercarriage, cockpit and flaps, and the PL-12-T400 had a 400 h.p. Lycoming IO-720 engine, longer tail booms and larger sesquiplane wings. Transavia also modified one aircraft to PL-12-M300 military multi-role configuration, but this was not produced in quantity. A total of 118 Skytruks were built with examples going to South Africa, Kenya, Malaysia, China, Thailand and Denmark, in addition to the main deliveries to Australia and New Zealand.

Specification	Transavia Skyfarmer T-300A	
Powerplant	One 300 h.p. (224 kW) Textron Lycoming IO-540-K1B5 piston engine	
Dimensions		
Span	11.99 m	(39 ft 4 in)
Length	6.35 m	(20 ft 10 in)
Height	2.87 m	(9 ft 5 in)
Performance		
Max speed	200 km/h	(108 kt, 124 mph)
Cruising speed	191 km/h	(103 kt, 119 mph)
Initial climb	168 m/min	(550 fpm)
Range	394 km	(213 nm, 245 miles)
Weights		
Max takeoff	1,925 kg	(4,244 lbs)
Useful load	971 kg	(2,140 lbs)

Transavia Airtruk, VH-JFH

Travel Air 2000 and 4000
— USA

Formed in Wichita in January 1925, Travel Air became a major manufacturer of sporting and training biplanes. Designed by Lloyd Stearman, the Travel Air Model A was flown on 13th March 1925. It was a conventional tube and fabric biplane with an open rear pilot's cockpit and a forward cockpit for two passengers. Powered by a 90 h.p. Curtiss OX-5 engine, it had the distinctive overhung rounded rudder and projecting upper wing ailerons which were to become a Travel Air trademark. The production OX-5 powered Model B was soon joined by the Model BH (with a 150 h.p. or 180 h.p. Hispano Suiza A or E engine) and the Model BW (220 h.p. Wright J5 Whirlwind). In 1928 these became the Travel Air 2000, 3000 and 4000 respectively, and further models included the 8000 (120 h.p. Fairchild-Caminez) and the 9000 (125 h.p. Ryan-Siemens). The type number was later fixed as the Model 4000 for any new engine variations and subsequent models included the W-4000 (Warner 110), A-4000 (Axelson) and C-4000 (Curtiss Challenger 170). Several different wings were available on the Travel Airs including the speed wing, and most models were approved for operation on floats. Travel Air was taken over by Curtiss Wright in August 1929 just as the Depression was about to strike, and the big Travel Air biplanes were struck by a collapse in demand. It is thought that some 1,300 of the 2000, 3000 and 4000 series had been built when production ended, and over 200 remain in the USA, although many are inactive.

Travel Air 2000, NC8853

Specification	Travelair 4000	
Powerplant	One 220 h.p. (164 kW) Wright J5 Whirlwind piston engine	
Dimensions		
Span	10.57 m	(34 ft 8 in)
Length	7.16 m	(23 ft 6 in)
Height	2.77 m	(9 ft 1 in)
Performance		
Max speed	209 km/h	(113 kt, 130 mph)
Cruising speed	177 km/h	(96 kt, 110 mph)
Initial climb	366 m/min	(1,200 fpm)
Range	800 km	(435 nm, 500 miles)
Weights		
Max takeoff	1,094 kg	(2,412 lbs)
Useful load	346 kg	(762 lbs)

Tri-R KIS and KIS-Cruiser
— USA

Increasingly popular with homebuilders, the Tri-R KIS (which stands for 'Keep It Simple') has been built in large numbers from kits supplied by Tri-R Technologies. The TR-1 KIS was designed by Rich Trickel and was first flown in April 1991. The composite kit has been designed to have the smallest number of parts and is intended to use the smallest possible powerplant, with various engine options including the 125 h.p. Continental IO-240, 100 h.p. O-200-A, 108 h.p. O-235-C1B or 80 h.p. Limbach L.2000. Main airframe shells are provided in the kit and it has a side-by-side two-seat cockpit with gull-wing doors. The KIS can be fitted with either a fixed tricycle undercarriage or tailwheel gear (KIS-TD). Around 50 are thought to have been completed by amateurs and it is now marketed as the Sport 150 by Pulsar. The TR-4 KIS Cruiser (now Pulsar Super Cruiser) is a larger development which was flown on 1st July 1994 and is now being supplied as a kit with around ten believed to have flown to date. It is a cross-country touring aircraft and has a four-seat cabin with dual controls, a fixed tricycle undercarriage and a 180 h.p. Lycoming O-360 engine or alternative 210 h.p. O-360.

Tri-R KIS, G-TKIS

Tri-R KIS Cruiser, N98WG

Tri-R KIS and KIS-Cruiser (Cont.)

Specification	Tri-R KIS	
Powerplant	One 125 h.p. (93.2 kW) Teledyne Continental IO-240 piston engine	
Dimensions		
Span	7.01 m	(23 ft 0 in)
Length	6.71 m	(22 ft 0 in)
Height	1.88 m	(6 ft 2 in)
Performance		
Max speed	314 km/h	(170 kt, 195 mph)
Cruising speed	257 km/h	(139 kt, 160 mph)
Initial climb	305 m/min	(1,000 fpm)
Range	1,200 km	(652 nm, 750 miles)
Weights		
Max takeoff	544 kg	(1,200 lbs)
Useful load	236 kg	(520 lbs)

Tupolev Tu-16 — Russia

Now relegated to experimental testing and other limited roles, the Tu-16 (NATO name 'Badger') served with the Soviet forces as their standard twin-jet medium bomber from the mid-1950s onwards. The prototype flew on 27th April 1952 and over 1,500 had been built when production ceased in 1960. The Tu-16 has a slim circular-section fuselage with a large belly bomb-bay, although the main offensive armament, typically the K-16 and K-26 missiles, is normally carried on the two large underwing pylons which were fitted to the Tu-16K and later variants. The two AM-3M turbojets are closely fitted to the fuselage sides and the swept wing has pods on the inboard undersides to house the main undercarriage units. In standard form, the Tu-16 has a manned tail gun position. The Tu-16 was supplied to several foreign users including Egypt, Indonesia and Iraq, and it has been built in China as the Xian H-6, where it remained in production until at least 1990. The many variants included the Tu-16T naval ASW aircraft and the Tu-16K-10 (Badger-C) with a large flattened nose radome, the Tu-16K for air-sea rescue, the Tu-16Ye (Badger-D) ELINT aircraft with a large nose radome for the Puffball radar, and the Tu-16RM countermeasures version with a large belly fairing. It is estimated that no more than 30 Tu-16s are airworthy in Russia, but around 100 Xian H-6s continue in Chinese service.

Xian H-6, Chinese PLAAF, 10990

Specification	Tupolev Tu-16K	
Powerplant	Two 20,945 lb.s.t. (93.17 kN) Mikulin AM-3M-500 turbojets	
Dimensions		
Span	32.9 m	(108 ft 0 in)
Length	36.25 m	(118 ft 11 in)
Height	14 m	(46 ft 0 in)
Performance		
Max speed	1,050 km/h	(565 kt, 650 mph)
Cruising speed	850 km/h	(460 kt, 530 mph)
Range	7,200 km	(3,913 nm, 4,500 miles)
Weights		
Max takeoff	75,800 kg	(167,139 lbs)
Useful load	38,600 kg	(85,113 lbs)

Tupolev Tu-16, Russian AF, 57 red

Tupolev Tu-22M
— Russia

The Tu-22M (NATO name 'Backfire') was the replacement for the Tu-16 medium bomber in Soviet service and shared the Tu-22 designation with the earlier Tu-22 Blinder (now out of service), although the two designs are substantially different. The Tu-22M prototype, which first flew on 30th August 1969, had swing wings with a substantial highly swept inner section incorporating large flaps and slim, tapered variable-sweep outer sections. It is powered by two NK-144 reheated turbofans set side by side in the rear fuselage and fed by large, angled variable intakes. The tricycle undercarriage has six-wheel main bogies which retract inwards into the wingroots, and the nose section has a large radome for the attack radar and a cabin section with side-by-side seating for the two flight crew and a rear cabin for the navigator and communications specialist. Offensive stores are carried in a belly bomb-bay with a rotary dispenser for up to six AS-16 tactical missiles and on two pylons attached to the stub wing which can accommodate AS-4 Kitchen stand-off nuclear air-to-surface missiles. The initial Tu-22M1 Backfire-A went into production in 1969 but was quickly replaced by the Tu-22M2 Backfire-B, 211 of which were built before the Tu-22M3 Backfire C, with modernised systems and upgraded NK-25 engines with new air intake geometry, replaced it in 1976. It is thought that 280 Backfire-Cs were built. The Tu-22M is in front-line service with the Russian Air Force and Navy and 50 serve with the Ukrainian Air Force.

Specification	Tupolev Tu-22M3	
Powerplant	Two 55,115 lb.s.t. (245 kN) (wet) Kuznetsov NK-25 turbofans	
Dimensions		
Span (extended)	34.29 m	(112 ft 6 in)
Length	42.47 m	(139 ft 4 in)
Height	11.05 m	(36 ft 3 in)
Performance		
Max speed	2,301 km/h	(1,243 kt, 1,430 mph)
Initial climb (est)	5,486 m/min	(18,000 fpm)
Range	6,760 km	(3,674 nm, 4,225 miles)
Weights		
Max takeoff	53,550 kg	(118,078 lbs)
Useful load	24,005 kg	(52,931 lbs)

Tupolev Tu-22M, Ukraine AF, 57 red

Tupolev Tu-95 — Russia

The Tu-95 (NATO name 'Bear') is unique in being the world's only turboprop strategic intercontinental bomber, and, despite having first flown on 12th November 1952, it continues in front-line service with the Russian Air Force Bomber Aviation directorate. It has a slim circular-section fuselage with a large bomb bay capable of carrying a 26,000 lbs bomb load, a forward pressurised six-crew compartment and a manned tail turret. The wing is swept and mounts the four very large Kuznetsov NK-12M turboprops with counter-rotating propellers which give the Tu-95 both high subsonic speed and great efficiency for long-range reconnaissance and patrol missions. Many versions have been built including the basic Tu-95M Bear-A nuclear bomber, the Tu-95K Bear-B and Tu-95KM Bear-C, which were equipped to carry stand-off strategic missiles and had a prominent nose radome, the Tu-95K-22 Bear-G with external missile pylons on the inboard wings, and the Tu-95MS Bear-H, an upgraded Bear-A strategic bomber with a chin radome and a modified bomb bay to carry AS-15 Kent cruise missiles. The Tu-95RT Bear-D is a maritime patrol and ASW/ASR aircraft fitted with prominent belly and chin radomes, and this has been augmented with the Tu-142 Bear-F which has a lengthened forward fuselage, a strengthened wing, new radars and a prominent fin-tip tail stinger. A further Tu-142MR Bear-J version is also in service as a strategic airborne communications relay and command post.

Tupolev Tu-142M, Indian Navy, IN312

Specification	Tupolev Tu-95MS	
Powerplant	Four 14,795 s.h.p. (11,033 kW) Kuznetsov NK-12MV turboprops	
Dimensions		
Span	51.1 m	(167 ft 8 in)
Length	49.5 m	(162 ft 5 in)
Height	12.12 m	(39 ft 9 in)
Performance		
Max speed	925 km/h	(500 kt, 575 mph)
Cruising speed	716 km/h	(387 kt, 445 mph)
Initial climb	457 m/min	(1,500 fpm)
Range	3,500 km	(1,902 nm, 2,188 miles)
Weights		
Max takeoff	185,000 kg	(407,925 lbs)
Useful load	98,000 kg	(216,090 lbs)

Tupolev Tu-134 — Russia

Tupolev's modern series of jet airliners started with the twin-jet Tu-104, which was derived from the Tu-16 bomber, and this was followed by the similar but scaled-down 44-seat Tu-124. To improve operating economics, the Tu-124 was redesigned as the Tu-134 with a T-tail and new Soloviev D-30 turbofans, which were moved from the wingroot position used on the earlier aircraft to rear fuselage mountings. The fuselage was also stretched to accommodate 72 passengers. The prototype Tu-134 (NATO name 'Crusty') made its first flight on 29th July 1963 and started to operate with Aeroflot in September 1967. The Tu-134A was a later version with an 83-inch fuselage stretch allowing up to 84 passengers and a solid nose in place of the original glazed observer's position. The Tu-134B had further improvements including a modernised cockpit and new spoilers, and it could carry 90 passengers in a rearranged interior. In total 853 Tu-134s were built of which around 350 remain operational with the many CIS airlines.

Tupolev Tu-134A, UR-95782

Specification	Tupolev Tu-134A	
Powerplant	Two 14,990 lb.s.t. (66.7 kN) Soloviev D-30 Srs.II turbofans	
Dimensions		
Span	29.01 m	(95 ft 2 in)
Length	37.03 m	(121 ft 6 in)
Height	9.14 m	(30 ft 0 in)
Performance		
Max speed	885 km/h	(478 kt, 550 mph)
Cruising speed	853 km/h	(461 kt, 530 mph)
Takeoff distance	2,400 m	(7,874 ft)
Range	3,000 km	(1,630 nm, 1,875 miles)
Weights		
Max takeoff	47,000 kg	(103,635 lbs)
Useful load	17,950 kg	(39,580 lbs)

Tupolev Tu-144 — Russia

Tupolev's Tu-144 supersonic airliner (NATO name 'Charger') was conceived at about the same time as the BAC-Sud Concorde and its general layout was very similar with a slender delta wing and its four Kuznetsov NK-144 reheated turbofan engines clustered in a belly mounting. In addition it also had a drooping nose to resolve the problem of poor visibility in the landing configuration, but it also had retractable foreplanes behind the cockpit and was designed for a larger 140-passenger load. The prototype flew on 31st December 1968 but was substantially redesigned before it started proving flights with Aeroflot in late 1975, followed by passenger services at the end of 1977. The reported maximum speed achieved was Mach 2.4. Problems with range and high operating costs resulted in the Tu-144 only remaining in service for less than a year. A total of 16 Tu-144s were built and these were later used for various test assignments including ozone research. One aircraft has been refurbished as the Tu-144LL with NK-321 engines and modified fuel and control systems and used under contract to NASA in their High Speed Civil Transport programme, making its first flight for this purpose on 29th November 1996. Although it remains airworthy after the contract has been completed it seems doubtful if it will be operational in the long term.

Tupolev Tu-144, CCCP-77110

Specification	Tupolev Tu-144	
Powerplant	Four 44,090 lb.s.t. (196.1 kN) (wet) Kuznetsov NK-144 turbofans	
Dimensions		
Span	28.8 m	(94 ft 6 in)
Length	65.68 m	(215 ft 6 in)
Height	12.85 m	(42 ft 2 in)
Performance		
Max speed	2,494 km/h	(1,348 kt, 1,550 mph)
Cruising speed	2,301 km/h	(1,243 kt, 1,430 mph)
Takeoff distance	3,000 m	(9,842 ft)
Range	6,485 km	(3,524 nm, 4,035 miles)
Weights		
Max takeoff	180,000 kg	(396,900 lbs)
Useful load	95,000 kg	(209,475 lbs)

Tupolev Tu-154 — Russia

In recognition of Aeroflot's need for a medium-haul airliner with greater capacity than the Tu-134 could offer, the Tupolev OKB developed the three-engined Tu-154 (NATO name 'Careless') of which the first of six prototypes was flown on 4th October 1968. It has a similar general layout to that of the Tu-134 with a T-tail and a low wing with podded main undercarriage housings but it has the third NK-8-2 turbofan fitted in the base of the fin and capacity has risen to 167 passengers. There is a six-wheel bogie on each main undercarriage to allow it to operate from the poor surfaces of more remote Russian airfields. The initial version was the Tu-154, followed by the Tu-154A with increased fuel capacity and higher-powered NK-8-2U engines, the Tu-154B with a revised 180-passenger layout, and the all-freight Tu-154S. The Tu-154M is a new-generation version with 23,380 lb.s.t. Aviadvigatel D-30KU-154 turbofans fitted with thrust reversers, and the Tu-154M2, which has not yet entered quantity production, has 35,275 lb.s.t. Aviadvigatel PS-90A engines and commensurately improved performance. The Tu-154 is now the most widely used of all Tupolev's transport aircraft and remains in limited production. It is in service with many of the CIS airlines such as Tyumen, Vnukovo and Samara, and with foreign companies including Tarom, CSA, Cubana and several Chinese operators. More than 920 Tu-154s have been built to date.

Tupolev Tu-154B, RA-85106

Specification	Tupolev Tu-154M	
Powerplant	Three 23,380 lb.s.t. (104 kN) Aviadvigatel-Perm D-30KU-154-II turbofans	
Dimensions		
Span	37.54 m	(123 ft 2 in)
Length	47.9 m	(157 ft 2 in)
Height	11.4 m	(37 ft 5 in)
Performance		
Max speed	933 km/h	(504 kt, 580 mph)
Cruising speed	917 km/h	(496 kt, 570 mph)
Takeoff distance	2,500 m	(8,200 ft)
Range	6,560 km	(3,565 nm, 4,100 miles)
Weights		
Max takeoff	100,000 kg	(220,500 lbs)
Useful load	44,700 kg	(98,563 lbs)

Tupolev Tu-160 — Russia

Named 'Blackjack' by NATO, the Tu-160 is the Russian bomber force's principal supersonic strategic intercontinental bomber. Its design takes advantage of the swing-wing experience built up by the Tupolev OKB in the development of the Tu-22M and, like that aircraft, it has large inner wing sections of high sweep with long leading edge extensions. The moving outer wings are fitted with full-span leading edge slats and large flaps, and the Tu-160 has an all-moving upper vertical tail in place of a conventional rudder. The four Kuznetsov NK-321 reheated turbofans are mounted in boxed pairs beneath the inner wings. The Tu-160 is substantially larger than the equivalent Rockwell B-1 and an offensive weapons load is housed internally in two large belly weapons bays which can accommodate up to six AS-15 Kent cruise missiles. The Tu-160, which carries a normal crew of four, was first flown on 19th December 1981, but deliveries did not commence until 1987 and production ceased in 1992 after around 30 aircraft had been completed. No more than 20 of these are in active service with the Russian Air Force.

Tupolev Tu-160

Specification	Tupolev Tu-160	
Powerplant	Four 55,115 lb.s.t. (245.2 kN) (wet) Kuznetsov (SSPE Trud) NK-321 turbofans	
Dimensions		
Span (extended)	55.7 m	(182 ft 9 in)
Length	54.1 m	(177 ft 6 in)
Height	13.11 m	(43 ft 0 in)
Performance		
Max speed	2,012 km/h	(1,087 kt, 1,250 mph)
Cruising speed	901 km/h	(487 kt, 560 mph)
Takeoff distance	2,590 m	(8,500 ft)
Range	14,000 km	(7,609 nm, 8,750 miles)
Weights		
Max takeoff	275,000 kg	(606,375 lbs)
Useful load	157,000 kg	(346,185 lbs)

Tupolev Tu-204 — Russia

Tupolev's replacement for the medium-haul Tu-154 is the Tu-204, which was initiated in 1983. It is a wide-body twin-turbofan 200-passenger aircraft, competitive with the Boeing 757. The prototype made its maiden flight on 2nd January 1989 powered by two Aviadvigatel-Perm (Soloviev) PS-90A turbofans, but Russian type certification was not achieved until six years later, in January 1995. Sales of the Tu-204 have been hampered by lack of customer finance and only 28 aircraft have been built to date. Many of these remain undelivered, but the main operators are Vnukovo Airlines, Air Cairo Cargo, Perm Airlines and Transeuropean Airways. Other versions of the Tu-204 include the long-range Tu-204-100 and Tu-204-100C combi, the Tu-204-120 with Rolls Royce RB211-535E4 engines, and the Tu-204C freighter with a forward port cargo door. The Tu-204-200 (also known as the Tu-214) is a higher gross weight aircraft with increased fuel capacity which is also available in 200C combi and Rolls Royce RB211 Tu-204-220 versions. Tupolev has also built a prototype of the Tu-234 which was announced in 1995 and has a 19 ft shorter fuselage and 166 seats.

Tupolev Tu-204-100, RA-64017

Specification	Tupolev Tu-204-100	
Powerplant	Two 35,582 lb.s.t. (158.3 kN) Aviadvigatel-Perm PS-90A turbofans	
Dimensions		
Span	42.01 m	(137 ft 10 in)
Length	46 m	(150 ft 11 in)
Height	13.89 m	(45 ft 7 in)
Performance		
Max speed	853 km/h	(461 kt, 530 mph)
Cruising speed	806 km/h	(436 kt, 501 mph)
Takeoff distance	2,252 m	(7,390 ft)
Range	4,872 km	(2,648 nm, 3,045 miles)
Weights		
Max takeoff	103,000 kg	(227,115 lbs)
Useful load	44,200 kg	(97,461 lbs)

Tupolev Tu-334 — Russia

The Tupolev bureau has designed the Tu-334 short-haul airliner as a replacement for the Tu-134 to serve routes of up to 1,900 miles. With 102-passenger capacity the Tu-334 is a wide-body aircraft with six-abreast seating. It has a broad vertical tail, a deep fuselage with a short undercarriage allowing use of a built-in airstair for passenger loading, a low wing with winglets and twin Progress D-436T turbofans mounted on the rear fuselage. The Tu-334-100 prototype was rolled out in 1995 but not flown until 8th February 1999 as a result of insufficient funding. It is intended to complete certification in 2001, and a Westernised version, the Tu-334-120, is planned with BMW-Rolls Royce BR710-48 turbofans. Tupolev also intends to develop the Tu-334-100C combi, the extended-range Tu-334-100M and the stretched 126-seat Tu-334-200 (also known as the Tu-354).

Tupolev Tu-334, RA-94001

Specification	Tupolev Tu-334-100	
Powerplant	Two 16,535 lb.s.t. (73.55 kN) Progress D-436T turbofans	
Dimensions		
Span	29.77 m	(97 ft 8 in)
Length	17.83 m	(58 ft 6 in)
Height	5.21 m	(17 ft 1 in)
Performance		
Max speed	821 km/h	(443 kt, 510 mph)
Cruising speed	797 km/h	(430 kt, 495 mph)
Takeoff distance	2,300 m	(7,546 ft)
Range	1,800 km	(978 nm, 1,125 miles)
Weights		
Max takeoff	46,100 kg	(101,650 lbs)
Useful load	16,050 kg	(35,390 lbs)

Turkish Aerospace ZIU — Turkey

Turkish Aerospace (TAI) designed the ZIU agricultural aircraft in 1997 to meet a Turkish Government requirement for aircraft to service the Southeast Anatolian Project. The ZIU prototype was first flown on 26th June 2000 and development will continue as a cooperative project with Bangladesh, Egypt, Indonesia, Iran, Malaysia, Nigeria and Pakistan. It is a single-seat aircraft with an enclosed air-conditioned cockpit and a 400 USG hopper mounted between the cabin and the engine firewall. The tail unit and the wings, which have flaired tips, are of aluminium monocoque construction but the fuselage is of steel tube with quickly-removable composite panels. The ZIU is unusual in using a 600 h.p. water-cooled 8-cylinder turbocharged Orenda piston engine driving a three-blade propeller. It is expected that a turboprop version will be developed in future and that the ZIU will be exported after an initial Turkish requirement for around 100 aircraft has been met.

Turkish Aerospace ZIU

Specification	Turkish Aerospace ZIU	
Powerplant	One 600 h.p. (447.4 kW) Orenda OE600A piston engine	
Dimensions		
Span	15.95 m	(52 ft 4 in)
Length	10.43 m	(34 ft 3 in)
Height	4.01 m	(13 ft 2 in)
Performance		
Max speed	302 km/h	(163 kt, 188 mph)
Cruising speed	280 km/h	(151 kt, 174 mph)
Takeoff distance	250 m	(820 ft)
Range	900 km	(489 nm, 562 miles)
Weights		
Max takeoff	3,500 kg	(7,718 lbs)
Useful load (est.)	1,477 kg	(3,256 lbs)

U

Uetz U4M Pelikan
— Switzerland

The Walter Uetz Flugzeugbau was an established builder of the Minicab and of the Jodel D.119 and a straight-wing derivative, the Uetz U2V. In 1962, Uetz designed a larger four-seater based on the U2V. This U3M Pelikan had a four-seat cabin with a long transparent canopy, a swept vertical tail and fixed tailwheel undercarriage. The structure was wood, ply and fabric with some fibreglass components. It was powered by a 135 h.p. Lycoming O-290 engine and the prototype first flew on 21st May 1963, followed by one further U3M. The production U4M, of which two were built by Uetz and one by an amateur constructor, differed in having flaps and a 150 h.p. Lycoming O-320-A2B engine. Uetz, which ceased production in 1965, was also responsible for the initial construction of the prototype of the Marabu three-seater under contract from Albert Markwalder. All the Pelikans and the Marabu remain in Swiss ownership.

Uetz U3M Pelikan, HB-TBV

Specification	Uetz U4M Pelikan	
Powerplant	One 150 h.p. (111.84 kW) Textron Lycoming O-320-A2B piston engine	
Dimensions		
Span	9.6 m	(31 ft 6 in)
Length	7.49 m	(24 ft 7 in)
Height	2.03 m	(6 ft 8 in)
Performance		
Max speed	219 km/h	(118 kt, 136 mph)
Cruising speed	198 km/h	(107 kt, 123 mph)
Initial climb	213 m/min	(700 fpm)
Range	992 km	(539 nm, 620 miles)
Weights		
Max takeoff	1,000 kg	(2,205 lbs)
Useful load	434 kg	(957 lbs)

Ultrasport 331 and 496
— USA/Taiwan

The Ultrasport 254 was developed in 1990 by American Sportscopter. It is a single-seater light helicopter with a two-bladed main rotor and a semi-enclosed composite fuselage structure with a wide-track fixed skid undercarriage. The tubular tail boom carries a small tailplane with endplate fins and the tail stabilising rotor is enclosed in a large circular shroud. The Ultrasport is made available as a kit which is manufactured in Taiwan and the prototype first flew in July 1993. It is powered by a 55 h.p. Hirth 2703 engine mounted behind the cockpit rear bulkhead. The Ultrasport 331 is a larger experimental category version of the 254 with increased range and higher gross weight. This first flew in December 1993 and was followed by the Ultrasport 496 two-seater, which commenced flight testing in July 1995. The Ultrasport 496 has a wider cabin than the 331 and uses a 95 h.p. Hirth F.30 engine.

Ultrasport 331, N2137G

Specification	Ultrasport 496	
Powerplant	One 95 h.p. (71 kW) Hirth F.30 piston engine	
Dimensions		
Rotor diameter	7.01 m	(23 ft 0 in)
Length	5.84 m	(19 ft 2 in)
Height	2.39 m	(7 ft 10 in)
Performance		
Max speed	158 km/h	(85 kt, 98 mph)
Cruising speed	105 km/h	(56 kt, 65 mph)
Initial climb	305 m/min	(1,000 fpm)
Range	232 km	(126 nm, 145 miles)
Weights		
Max takeoff	492 kg	(1,085 lbs)
Useful load	268 kg	(590 lbs)

Ultravia Pelican Club
— Canada

Designed by Jean-René LePage, the original Le Pelican was a single-seat high-wing ultralight aircraft which first flew in May 1982 powered by a 21 h.p. Briggs & Stratton light piston engine. Of conventional metal and fabric construction, the Pelican was a strut-braced high-wing machine with a fixed tailwheel undercarriage and was sold either as a factory-complete aircraft, a kit or a set of plans. In early 1985, Ultravia flew the prototype Pelican Club which was a side-by-side two-seat version. The Pelican Club has a composite shell fuselage and a metal wing with fabric-covered control surfaces. The fixed undercarriage can be either tricycle or tailwheel depending on the builder's choice and the Pelican can operate on floats or skis. The later Pelican Club PL-912 has a wider fuselage giving a bigger cabin and larger doors and is powered by an 80 h.p. Rotax 912 engine or, as the PL-912S, by a 100 h.p. Rotax 912S. Ultravia also sell the Pelican Sport 450 and Pelican Sport 600 which are designed to meet 450 kg and 600 kg ultralight weight limits. The Pelican Turbo PL-914 is an alternative version with a 115 h.p. turbocharged Rotax 914 engine and improved performance. More than 450 Pelican kits have been sold and 350 have flown in North America and Europe.

Ultravia Pelican Turbo PL-914, PH-DAY

Specification	Ultravia Pelican Club PL-912S	
Powerplant	One 100 h.p. (74.56 kW) Rotax 912S piston engine	
Dimensions		
Span	8.99 m	(29 ft 6 in)
Length	6.02 m	(19 ft 9 in)
Height	2.54 m	(8 ft 4 in)
Performance		
Max speed	213 km/h	(115 kt, 132 mph)
Cruising speed	204 km/h	(110 kt, 127 mph)
Initial climb	366 m/min	(1,200 fpm)
Range	1,280 km	(696 nm, 800 miles)
Weights		
Max takeoff	635 kg	(1,400 lbs)
Useful load	295 kg	(650 lbs)

Urban Air UFM-13 Lambada
— Czech Republic

The Lambada is another of the rapidly growing European all-composite ultralight aircraft designed for low-cost operation using low-powered engines. It was designed by Pavel Urban and first flew in 1996, entering production the following year as either a kit for homebuilding or as a factory-complete aircraft. It is a side-by-side two-seater with a high-technology laminar-flow wing with slight forward sweep and high aspect ratio. The alternative high-performance UFM-11 has shorter-span wings which give improved cruise and rate of climb. The wings are quickly detachable for storage or transportation. The Lambada, which is powered by either a 39 h.p. Rotax 447 or a 50 h.p. BMW 800, has a slim rear fuselage with a T-tail and can be built with a fixed tailwheel or tricycle undercarriage.

Urban Lambada UFM-11, D-MPUE

Specification	Urban Air UFM-13 Lambada	
Powerplant	One 39 h.p. (29.08 kW) Rotax 447 piston engine	
Dimensions		
Span	13 m	(42 ft 8 in)
Length	6.6 m	(21 ft 7 in)
Height	1.85 m	(6 ft 1 in)
Performance		
Max speed	170 km/h	(91 kt, 106 mph)
Cruising speed	150 km/h	(81 kt, 93 mph)
Initial climb	120 m/min	(394 fpm)
Range	250 km	(135 nm, 155 miles)
Weights		
Max takeoff	450 kg	(992 lbs)
Useful load	180 kg	(397 lbs)

UTVA-66 — Yugoslavia

The UTVA-56 was developed by the UTVA Fabrika Aviona at Pancevo as a four-seat utility aircraft to meet the needs of flying clubs, for ambulance work, for crop spraying and for military liaison and artillery spotting. It was a strut-braced all-metal high-wing aircraft with a fixed tailwheel undercarriage and a 260 h.p. Lycoming GO-435-C2B2 flat-six engine. For ambulance duties the UTVA-60 had a hinged rear cabin window to allow loading of a stretcher. The prototype made its first flight on 22nd April 1959 and the production version, known as the UTVA-60, differed from the prototype in having modified flaps and a 270 h.p. Lycoming GO-430-B1A6 engine. Several versions were manufactured from 1962 onwards, including the agricultural UTVA-60AG and the UTVA-60H twin-float seaplane. The principal production model was the UTVA-66, a military model with wing slats, a larger tail, an improved undercarriage and a six-cylinder Lycoming GSO-480-B1J6 engine. In total 140 of the UTVA-60 and 66 are believed to have been built and a number have been exported to the UK, Canada and the USA.

UTVA-66, C-GDLZ

Specification	UTVA-66	
Powerplant	One 270 h.p. (201.3 kW) Lycoming GSO-480-B1J6 piston engine	
Dimensions		
Span	11.4 m	(37 ft 5 in)
Length	8.38 m	(27 ft 6 in)
Height	3.2 m	(10 ft 6 in)
Performance		
Max speed	230 km/h	(124 kt, 143 mph)
Cruising speed	215 km/h	(116 kt, 134 mph)
Initial climb	270 m/min	(885 fpm)
Range	750 km	(408 nm, 469 miles)
Weights		
Max takeoff	1,814 kg	(4,000 lbs)
Useful load	564 kg	(1,244 lbs)

UTVA-75 — Yugoslavia

During the mid-1970s, UTVA designed the UTVA-75 as a basic two-seat trainer for Yugoslav flying clubs and for JRV military use. It was a modern low-wing all-metal monocoque aircraft with side-by-side seating, a fixed tricycle undercarriage and upward-opening gull-wing cabin doors. The powerplant was a 180 h.p. Lycoming IO-360-B with a two-bladed Hartzell variable-pitch propeller. The wings were built with hardpoints to carry light armament or supplementary fuel tanks, and during the 1991/92 Slovenian and Croatian conflicts several UTVA-75s were fitted with rocket packs for ground attack missions. The first prototype UTVA-75 was flown at Pancevo on 19th May 1976 and the production model was later redesignated UTVA-75A21. UTVA built some 260 examples for the JRV and flying schools between 1978 and 1983 and several remain in service in Slovenia, Croatia and Serbia, despite large numbers being destroyed in the recent Balkan conflicts.

UTVA-75, SL-DCB

Specification	UTVA-75A21	
Powerplant	One 180 h.p. (134.21 kW) Textron Lycoming IO-360-B piston engine	
Dimensions		
Span	9.37 m	(30 ft 9 in)
Length	7.11 m	(23 ft 4 in)
Height	3.1 m	(10 ft 2 in)
Performance		
Max speed	215 km/h	(116 kt, 134 mph)
Cruising speed	185 km/h	(100 kt, 115 mph)
Initial climb	276 m/min	(906 fpm)
Range	800 km	(435 nm, 500 miles)
Weights		
Max takeoff	960 kg	(2,117 lbs)
Useful load	275 kg	(606 lbs)

Valentin Taifun — Germany

The Taifun is a sophisticated two-seat soaring and touring motor glider, designed and built by Valentin Flugzeugbau GmbH and built by them for commercial sale from 1982 onwards. It is a glass-fibre aircraft with a T-tail, side-by-side seating, wings which fold back alongside the fuselage for storage and transport, and a manually operated retractable tricycle undercarriage. Two main versions have been built: the Taifun 17E with a 17 metre sailplane wing and the Taifun 12E with a shorter 12-metre wing which is primarily intended for cross-country flying. The prototype Taifun was first flown on 28th February 1981 powered by an 80 h.p. Limbach L.2000EB (Volkswagen) engine. After building 102 of this version Valentin switched to an improved model with a 90 h.p. Limbach L.2400EB powerplant. In total 135 production examples were completed, and sales were made to Sweden, the USA and France in addition to those sold in Germany.

Valentin Taifun 17E, N10YY

Specification	Valentin Taifun 17E	
Powerplant	One 90 h.p. (67 kW) Limbach L.2400EB piston engine	
Dimensions		
Span	16.99 m	(55 ft 9 in)
Length	7.77 m	(25 ft 6 in)
Height	2.46 m	(8 ft 1 in)
Performance		
Max speed	249 km/h	(135 kt, 155 mph)
Cruising speed	220 km/h	(119 kt, 137 mph)
Initial climb	192 m/min	(630 fpm)
Range	1,243 km	(676 nm, 777 miles)
Weights		
Max takeoff	850 kg	(1,874 lbs)
Useful load	240 kg	(529 lbs)

Valmet Viima II — Finland

The Finnish State Aircraft Factory (Valtion Lentokonetehdas) designed the Viima training biplane in the 1930s for operation by the Finnish Air Force. First flown in 1935, the Viima was a tube and fabric biplane with tandem open cockpits and a strut-braced tailwheel undercarriage. Two prototypes were built followed by 20 military aircraft, which were designated Viima II and fitted with a 150 h.p. Siemens Sh.14A seven-cylinder radial engine. Most of the Viimas were released from military service in the late 1940s and 14 appeared on the Finnish civil register, many of these being fitted with enclosed framed cockpit canopies. At least one was converted as a Viima IIB with an in-line de Havilland Gipsy Major engine. Two Viimas are preserved in museums and one was operated in the UK for some years and is now active with a private owner in Belgium.

Valmet Viima II, G-BAAY

Specification	Valmet Viima II	
Powerplant	One 150 h.p. (111.84 kW) Siemens SH.14A piston engine	
Dimensions		
Span	10.49 m	(34 ft 5 in)
Length	7.87 m	(25 ft 10 in)
Height	3 m	(9 ft 10 in)
Performance		
Max speed	177 km/h	(96 kt, 110 mph)
Cruising speed	140 km/h	(76 kt, 87 mph)
Initial climb	158 m/min	(520 fpm)
Range	744 km	(404 nm, 465 miles)
Weights		
Max takeoff	930 kg	(2,050 lbs)
Useful load	340 kg	(750 lbs)

Valmet L-70 Vinka — Finland

Conceived as a replacement for the Finnish Air Force fleet of Saab Safirs in the primary training role, the Vinka was originally known as the Leko-70 and made its first flight on 1st July 1975. Of all-metal monocoque construction, the L-70 is fully aerobatic and is powered by a 200 h.p. Lycoming AEIO-360. It has a fixed tricycle undercarriage and the cockpit, which is covered by a large transparent canopy, is normally fitted with two seats and dual controls but can accommodate a further two passengers when a rear bench seat is installed. Some 30 Vinkas were delivered to the Finnish Air Force between 1980 and 1982, most of which are still in service, but despite Valmet marketing the type as the Miltrainer no further aircraft were built.

Valmet L-70 Vinka, Finnish AF, VN-4

Specification	Valmet L-70 Vinka	
Powerplant	One 200 h.p. (149 kW) Textron Lycoming AEIO-360-A1B6 piston engine	
Dimensions		
Span	9.63 m	(31 ft 7 in)
Length	7.49 m	(24 ft 7 in)
Height	3.3 m	(10 ft 10 in)
Performance		
Max speed	233 km/h	(126 kt, 145 mph)
Cruising speed	217 km/h	(117 kt, 135 mph)
Initial climb	341 m/min	(1,120 fpm)
Range	950 km	(516 nm, 594 miles)
Weights		
Max takeoff	1,250 kg	(2,756 lbs)
Useful load	483 kg	(1,065 lbs)

Vans RV-3, RV-4 and RV-6 — USA

Dick Van Grundsven has established a range of related low-wing kit homebuilt aircraft which offer tandem or side-by-side seating, various Lycoming O-320/O-360 powerplant options in the 150 h.p. to 180 h.p. range and fixed tricycle or tailwheel gear. His first model to achieve quantity production was the RV-3, which was first flown in August 1971 with a 125 h.p. Lycoming O-290-G engine and was made available as a kit in 1973. It had all-aluminium construction, a tailwheel undercarriage and a single-seat cockpit enclosed by a bubble canopy. The RV-4, introduced in 1981, was similar but had a longer fuselage and tandem seating for two. Several RV-4s have been built as the high-performance aerobatic Harmon Rocket with modifications developed by John Harmon including shorter-span wings, a wider cockpit, longer undercarriage legs and a 300 h.p. Lycoming IO-540-K engine. In 1995 the RV-4 was developed into the RV-8 (and tricycle-gear RV-8A) which has a larger cabin, a structure to accept engines up to 200 h.p. and increased baggage capacity. The RV-6 (and tricycle-gear RV-6A) has a side-by-side two-seat cockpit which is faired into a raised rear fuselage line, and the RV-9 is a lower-powered derivative of the RV-6A with a 118 h.p. Lycoming O-235 engine, a modified wing of larger area and a larger tail unit. The RV-6 was built in small numbers in Nigeria for military training as the Air Beetle. Around 10,000 RV kits have been sold and approximately 2,250 have been completed, including large numbers outside the USA.

Vans RV-6A, 9M-EPA

Vans RV-8, N801RV

Specification	Vans RV-6A	
Powerplant	One 160 h.p. (119.3 kW) Textron Lycoming O-320-D2A piston engine	
Dimensions		
Span	7.01 m	(23 ft 0 in)
Length	6.02 m	(19 ft 9 in)
Height	2.03 m	(6 ft 8 in)
Performance		
Max speed	320 km/h	(173 kt, 199 mph)
Cruising speed	303 km/h	(163 kt, 188 mph)
Initial climb	564 m/min	(1,850 fpm)
Range	1,400 km	(761 nm, 875 miles)
Weights		
Max takeoff	748 kg	(1,650 lbs)
Useful load	302 kg	(665 lbs)

Specification	Varga 2150A Kachina	
Powerplant	One 150 h.p. (112 kW) Textron Lycoming O-320-A2C piston engine	
Dimensions		
Span	9.14 m	(30 ft 0 in)
Length	6.45 m	(21 ft 2 in)
Height	2.13 m	(7 ft 0 in)
Performance		
Max speed	238 km/h	(129 kt, 148 mph)
Cruising speed	217 km/h	(117 kt, 135 mph)
Initial climb	442 m/min	(1,450 fpm)
Range	840 km	(457 nm, 525 miles)
Weights		
Max takeoff	824 kg	(1,817 lbs)
Useful load	314 kg	(692 lbs)

Varga Kachina 2160 — USA

The Varga Kachina is a low-wing tandem two-seat sporting and training monoplane with a fixed tricycle undercarriage. It originated as the wood and fabric Model 1000C Nifty, designed by William J. Morrisey, first flown in 1948 and powered by a 90 h.p. Continental C90 engine. It was re-engineered as the all-metal Morrisey 2150 with a 108 h.p. Lycoming O-235 engine and the Morrisey Aircraft Company built nine aircraft during 1958 and 1959. The rights were then sold to Shinn Engineering Inc. which built 35 improved Shinn 2150As with the 150 h.p. Lycoming O-320-A2C engine before ceasing production in 1962. The 2150A was sold to the Varga Aircraft Corporation in 1967 which manufactured the Varga 2150A Kachina at Chandler, Arizona from 1975 to 1982. They built 121 Kachinas together with 18 of the Varga 2180 with a 180 h.p. Lycoming O-360-A2D engine, and both models were available with an optional tailwheel undercarriage as the Varga 2150TG and 2180TG. Bill Morrisey later re-acquired the rights and launched a kit version of the original Morrisey 2000C. The Morrisey/Shinn/Varga 2150A remains in widespread use in the USA and several are owned in Europe.

VFW.614 — Germany

Designed in the early 1960s by VFW (Vereinigte Flugtechnische Werke), the VFW.614 was a low-wing short-haul 44-passenger airliner with a circular-section fuselage, a conventional tail and unique overwing pylon mountings for its two Rolls Royce SNECMA M45-501 turbofan engines. The prototype VFW.614 first flew on 14th July 1971 and the type certificate was awarded in August 1974. It was not a commercial success, receiving a handful of orders from Cimber Air, Air Alsace and Touraine Air Transport, all of whom operated the type for only a short time. VFW-Fokker, who saw more potential in the Fokker 100, ceased manufacture after completing three prototypes and 16 production airframes. The last three were delivered as VIP transports to the German Luftwaffe together with one which still flies for the DFVLR research organisation. The Luftwaffe has retired its aircraft, but at least two are still airworthy, although their future is uncertain.

Varga 2180, CC-KSB

VFW.614, German Luftwaffe, 1701

VFW.614 (Cont.)

Specification	VFW-Fokker VFW.614	
Powerplant	Two 7,280 lb.s.t. (32.4 kN) Rolls Royce SNECMA M45H Mk.501 turbofans	
Dimensions		
Span	21.5 m	(70 ft 6 in)
Length	20.6 m	(67 ft 7 in)
Height	7.84 m	(25 ft 8 in)
Performance		
Max speed	713 km/h	(384 kt, 443 mph)
Cruising speed	704 km/h	(379 kt, 437 mph)
Initial climb	945 m/min	(3,100 fpm)
Range	1,204 km	(654 nm, 753 miles)
Weights		
Max takeoff	19,950 kg	(43,990 lbs)
Useful load	7,770 kg	(17,133 lbs)

Vickers Viscount — UK

Vickers designed the Viscount to meet a British European Airways (BEA) requirement for a 43-seat pressurised turboprop short-haul airliner. Powered by four 1,380 s.h.p. Rolls Royce Dart R.Da.1 Mk.502 turboprops the prototype Viscount 630 flew on 16th July 1948, but the production Model 700 had a longer fuselage and 53-passenger seating. Because of the adaptability built into the airframe and the reliability of the Dart engines, the Viscount gained orders from airlines around the world including BEA, Capital Airlines, United Airlines, Continental Airlines, Air France, Lufthansa, South African Airways, Trans Australian and Trans Canada. It was very popular with passengers as a result of the excellent visibility through its large oval windows. A total of 443 Viscounts had been delivered when production ceased in 1963. Main variants included the 700 series with 1,400 s.h.p. Dart Mk.505/6 engines, the 800 series with a 46-inch fuselage stretch, up to 71 passenger seats and 1,600 s.h.p. Dart 510 engines in bulged cowlings, and the 810 series with a higher gross weight, strengthened structure and 1,850 s.h.p. Dart 541 engines. Most Viscounts have now been retired but a handful remain airworthy in South Africa.

Vickers Viscount 806, G-PFBT

Specification	Vickers Viscount 806	
Powerplant	Four 1,655 s.h.p. (1,234 kW) Rolls Royce Dart R.Da.1 Mk.520 turboprops	
Dimensions		
Span	28.55 m	(93 ft 8 in)
Length	25.91 m	(85 ft 0 in)
Height	8.46 m	(27 ft 9 in)
Performance		
Max speed	539 km/h	(291 kt, 335 mph)
Cruising speed	523 km/h	(283 kt, 325 mph)
Initial climb	427 m/min	(1,400 fpm)
Range	1,104 km	(600 nm, 690 miles)
Weights		
Max takeoff	29,252 kg	(64,500 lbs)
Useful load	10,567 kg	(23,300 lbs)

Vickers VC-10 — UK

Derived from the Vickers 1000 project, the VC-10 medium-/long-haul four-jet airliner was designed in 1957 to the requirements of British Overseas Airways Corporation (BOAC). It was a 135-passenger aircraft with two pairs of 20,370 lb.s.t. Rolls Royce Conway R.Co.42 engines mounted in tail pods, a low-set swept wing and a T-tail. The prototype VC-10 Srs.1100 made its first flight on 29th June 1962 and first deliveries of the Srs.1101 to BOAC took place in December 1964 with other aircraft being sold later to Ghana Airways (Srs.1102), Middle East Airlines (Srs.1109) and British United Airways, which received the Srs.1103 combi version with a forward freight door. In total 31 VC-10s were delivered, including 14 for the RAF as the 150-passenger high-density VC-10 Mk.1. On 7th May 1964, British Aircraft Corporation flew the first Super VC-10 with a stretched 163-passenger fuselage, additional fuel tanks in the vertical fin and 22,500 lb.s.t. Conway R. Co.43 engines. Some 22 Super VC-10s went to BOAC and East African Airways, the last being delivered in February 1970. After service with BOAC most VC-10s and Super VC-10s were sold to the RAF and were used initially for trooping duties, but were subsequently converted as flight refuelling tankers. A total of 26 remain in RAF service of which eleven are C.Mk.1(K) convertible transport/tankers and the remainder K.2, K.3 and K.4 dedicated tankers.

Vickers VC-10 Mk.K.2, RAF, ZA140

Specification	Vickers (BAC/BAe) VC-10 C. Mk.1(K)	
Powerplant	Four 20,370 lb.s.t. (90.62 kN) Rolls Royce Conway R. Co.42 Mk.540 turbojets	
Dimensions		
Span	44.55 m	(146 ft 2 in)
Length	40.54 m	(133 ft 0 in)
Height	12.04 m	(39 ft 6 in)
Performance		
Max speed	933 km/h	(504 kt, 580 mph)
Cruising speed	887 km/h	(479 kt, 551 mph)
Initial climb	808 m/min	(2,650 fpm)
Range	6,240 km	(3,391 nm, 3,900 miles)
Weights		
Max takeoff	146,485 kg	(323,000 lbs)
Useful load	80,272 kg	(177,000 lbs)

Victa Airtourer — Australia

The Airtourer was originally designed by Dr. Henry Millicer as the wooden Airtourer Mk.1 which first flew on 31st March 1959 powered by a 65 h.p. Continental A65 engine, and it was later redesigned for all-metal construction by Victa Ltd. The Airtourer, which was fully aerobatic and had a side-by-side two-seat cockpit with a bubble canopy and a central control stick between the seats, was a low-wing monoplane with a fixed tricycle undercarriage and was powered by a 100 h.p. Continental O-200-A (Airtourer 100) or the 115 h.p. Lycoming O-235-B (Airtourer 115). The metal prototype flew on 12th December 1961 and 169 aircraft were completed by Victa between 1962 and 1966. All rights to the Airtourer were then sold to AESL (Pacific Aerospace) of Hamilton, New Zealand who built 30 Airtourer T1s based on the Airtourer 115, together with 50 further aircraft including the Airtourer T3 with a 130 h.p. Continental engine, the T4 and T5 with a 150 h.p. Lycoming O-320-E1A and higher weights, and the T6 with a further gross weight increase. The Airtourer was later developed by Pacific Aerospace as the CT4 Airtrainer (see separate entry). The Airtourer was returned to production in 1997 by Millicer Aircraft Industries in Australia as the Millicer Airtourer 140 (140 h.p. Lycoming O-320-E2A) and Airtourer 160 (160 h.p. Lycoming IO-320-D1A).

Victa Airtourer, ZS-EBD

Specification	Millicer Airtourer 160	
Powerplant	One 160 h.p. (119.3 kW) Textron Lycoming IO-320-D1A piston engine	
Dimensions		
Span	7.92 m	(26 ft 0 in)
Length	6.55 m	(21 ft 6 in)
Height	2.24 m	(7 ft 4 in)
Performance		
Max speed	269 km/h	(145 kt, 167 mph)
Cruising speed	248 km/h	(134 kt, 154 mph)
Initial climb	320 m/min	(1,050 fpm)
Range	800 km	(435 nm, 500 miles)
Weights		
Max takeoff	862 kg	(1,900 lbs)
Useful load	372 kg	(820 lbs)

Vidor ASSO-V — Italy

This low-wing ultralight-category homebuilt was designed and built by Giuseppe Vidor and first flown on 10th June 1995. It is sold as a kit by Aerostyle and also marketed in North America by Gene Littner as the Champion V. The ASSO-V is a low-wing monoplane with a side-by-side two-seat cockpit enclosed by a sliding canopy, and it is equipped with a tricycle undercarriage which can be fixed or retractable according to the builder's wishes. The basic structure is wood with plywood and dacron covering for the tail and wings and a pre-moulded composite shell to clad the fuselage. Various engines, including Volkswagens, can be fitted in the 65 h.p. to 100 h.p. range, but the normal powerplant is a 95 h.p. Midwest Engines AE-100 rotary engine. Over 50 ASSO-Vs are believed to be under construction or flying in Europe.

Vidor ASSO-V

Specification	Vidor ASSO-V	
Powerplant	One 95 h.p. (70.83 kW) Midwest AE-100 piston engine	
Dimensions		
Span	7.5 m	(24 ft 7 in)
Length	6.1 m	(20 ft 0 in)
Height	1.75 m	(5 ft 9 in)
Performance		
Max speed	300 km/h	(162 kt, 186 mph)
Cruising speed	270 km/h	(145 kt, 168 mph)
Initial climb	244 m/min	(800 fpm)
Range	1,800 km	(978 nm, 1,125 miles)
Weights		
Max takeoff	450 kg	(992 lbs)
Useful load	165 kg	(364 lbs)

Viking Dragonfly — USA

Designed by Robert J. Walters, the Dragonfly is a high-performance two-seat amateur-built light aircraft of all-composite construction built from a kit sold by Viking Aircraft Ltd. It has an equal-span tandem-wing layout with the low front wing positioned at the engine firewall and the high rear wing behind the cabin section. The Dragonfly Mk.I, which first flew on 16th June 1980, has a tailwheel undercarriage with the main wheels fitted into the tips of the front wing. The Dragonfly Mk.II has a conventional undercarriage with the main legs attached to the inboard wings, and the Dragonfly Mk.III has tricycle gear. The cabin is fitted with a forward-hinged bubble canopy and side-by-side seating. The Dragonfly can be powered by various engines in the 55 h.p. to 65 h.p. range, but normally uses a 60 h.p. Volkswagen 1835 cc powerplant. Around 2,000 kits have been sold and it is estimated that 500 Dragonflys are flying, including a dozen in Europe.

Viking Dragonfly Mk.II, F-PCFD

Specification	Viking Dragonfly	
Powerplant	One 60 h.p. (44.74 kW) Volkswagen 1835 piston engine	
Dimensions		
Span	6.71 m	(22 ft 0 in)
Length	5.79 m	(19 ft 0 in)
Height	1.22 m	(4 ft 0 in)
Performance		
Max speed	270 km/h	(146 kt, 168 mph)
Cruising speed	266 km/h	(143 kt, 165 mph)
Initial climb	259 m/min	(850 fpm)
Range	800 km	(435 nm, 500 miles)
Weights		
Max takeoff	521 kg	(1,150 lbs)
Useful load	247 kg	(545 lbs)

Visionaire Vantage — USA

The Vantage single-engined business jet project was launched in 1988 and the proof-of-concept (POC) prototype, built by Scaled Composites Inc., first flew on 16th November 1996. The Vantage is a six-seat pressurised aircraft of all-composite construction with a mid-set forward-swept wing positioned behind the main cabin section of the fuselage. The cabin, which is entered by a forward port-side door, has a two-seat cockpit and a main four-seat cabin with a toilet. It has a retractable tricycle undercarriage, the main legs of which retract into fuselage recesses in the POC prototype but will be positioned under the wings in production aircraft. The Pratt & Whitney JT15D turbofan engine is fitted in the rear fuselage and is fed by twin air intakes fitted to the upper fuselage. In 1999, Visionaire undertook a major redesign which included a new wing with less forward sweep and a new aerofoil section, a higher-thrust engine, modified tail surfaces and repositioning of the undercarriage. The production-standard prototype is to fly in 2001 with certification planned for the end of the year.

Visionaire Vantage POC, N247VA

Specification	Visionaire Vantage (POC)	
Powerplant	One 2,900 lb.s.t. (12.9 kN) Pratt & Whitney JT15D-5 turbofan	
Dimensions		
Span	14.88 m	(48 ft 10 in)
Length	12.7 m	(41 ft 8 in)
Height	4.27 m	(14 ft 0 in)
Performance		
Max speed	649 km/h	(350 kt, 403 mph)
Cruising speed	463 km/h	(250 kt, 288 mph)
Initial climb	1,219 m/min	(4,000 fpm)
Range	1,769 km	(960 nm, 1,105 miles)
Weights		
Max takeoff	3,175 kg	(7,000 lbs)
Useful load	1,361 kg	(3,000 lbs)

Volmer VJ-22 Sportsman — USA

The little Volmer VJ-22 Sportsman, designed by Volmer Jensen of Burbank, California, has proved to be one of the most popular amateur-built light amphibians. Using standard strut-braced Aeronca Champion wings fitted with outrigger floats, the Sportsman has a wood and ply fuselage with fibreglass covering which has a side-by-side two-seat cabin enclosed by a full transparent framed canopy. The main undercarriage legs are fitted to the forward fuselage and rotate forwards and upwards for water landing. The prototype Sportsman, which first flew on 22nd December 1958, had an 85 h.p. Continental C85 engine mounted as a pusher on a pylon above the wing mid-section, but later aircraft have higher-powered engines including the 90 h.p. Continental C85, 100 h.p. O-200-B or even the 125 h.p. Lycoming O-290-D. Some builders have fitted these as tractor rather than pusher engines. Around 800 sets of plans have been sold and more than 100 examples of the Sportsman have flown.

Volmer Sportsman, CF-OZQ

Specification	Volmer VJ-22 Sportsman	
Powerplant	One 90 h.p. (67.1 kW) Teledyne Continental C85 piston engine	
Dimensions		
Span	11.12 m	(36 ft 6 in)
Length	7.31 m	(24 ft 0 in)
Height	2.44 m	(8 ft 0 in)
Performance		
Max speed	169 km/h	(91 kt, 105 mph)
Cruising speed	137 km/h	(74 kt, 85 mph)
Initial climb	152 m/min	(500 fpm)
Range	480 km	(261 nm, 300 miles)
Weights		
Max takeoff	680 kg	(1,500 lbs)
Useful load	227 kg	(500 lbs)

Vought F4U Corsair — USA

The Vought F4U remains a much-sought-after warbird and approximately 30 are in flying condition in the USA, Europe and New Zealand. Designed as a shipboard fighter for the US Navy, the Corsair had distinctive inverted gull wings with the main units of the tailwheel undercarriage attached at the join of the inner and outer sections and retracting backwards into wing wells. Early F4U-1 Corsairs, which were fitted with six wing-mounted guns, had an integral framed cockpit canopy faired into the rear fuselage, but later aircraft and those built as the FG-1 by Goodyear and F3A-1 by Brewster had a bulbous clear-view canopy. The F4U-1 (and FG-1) Corsair was powered by a 2,000 h.p. Pratt & Whitney Double Wasp R-2800-8 radial engine but later versions had the 2,100 h.p. R-2800-18W (F4U-4), 2,250 h.p. R-2800-8W (F4U-1D and FG-1D) and 2,300 h.p. R-2800-32W (F4U-5). Among later Corsair variants were the F4U-4N night fighter with an APS-6 radar, the F4U-4P photo-reconnaissance aircraft and the AU-1 ground attack version with underwing rocket rails and four 20 mm cannon. The prototype was first flown on 29th May 1940, and by the time production ceased in 1947 12,204 Corsairs had been built with a considerable number being supplied to the Royal Navy and French Aéronavale.

Vought F4U-4B Corsair, NX240CA

Specification	Vought F4U-4 Corsair	
Powerplant	One 2,100 h.p. (1,566 kW) Pratt & Whitney R-2800-18W Double Wasp piston engine	
Dimensions		
Span	12.5 m	(41 ft 0 in)
Length	10.26 m	(33 ft 8 in)
Height	4.5 m	(14 ft 9 in)
Performance		
Max speed	718 km/h	(388 kt, 446 mph)
Cruising speed	346 km/h	(187 kt, 215 mph)
Initial climb	1,180 m/min	(3,870 fpm)
Range	1,608 km	(874 nm, 1,005 miles)
Weights		
Max takeoff	6,653 kg	(14,670 lbs)
Useful load	2,478 kg	(5,465 lbs)

Vought (LTV) F-8 Crusader and A-7 Corsair II — USA

In 1953 Chance Vought initiated design work on a new carrier-borne air superiority fighter for the US Navy and flew the prototype XF8U-1 Crusader on 25th March 1955. The Crusader had a swept shoulder wing with an adjustable centre section to change incidence, a long forward fuselage containing the single-seat cockpit, a short radar nose and the engine air intake, and a 10,700 lb.s.t. afterburning Pratt & Whitney J57-P-14 turbojet. Some 286 were built by Ling-Temco-Vought (LTV) and the last user, the French Aéronavale, retired its aircraft at the end of 1999, although a few Crusaders continue in the USA as test aircraft. The Vought A-7 Corsair II carrier-based ground attack aircraft was derived from the F-8 but had a shortened forward fuselage, a new wing with less sweep and no incidence adjustment, and eight hardpoints of which two were belly-mounted. It was fitted with an 11,350 lb.s.t. Pratt & Whitney TF30-P-6 turbofan for US Navy service as the A-7A, and 395 were delivered, 81 of which were modified to TA-7C standard with a lengthened forward fuselage to accommodate a tandem two-seat dual-control cockpit for conversion training. The USAF A-7D (and two-seat TA-7H), of which 459 were built, was a battlefield close support version which differed from the A-7A in having an Allison TF41 (licence-built Rolls Royce Spey) turbofan, and the first aircraft flew on 26th September 1968. No A-7s remain in US service but the A-7H and TA-7H are still used by the Greek Air Force and the A-7P and TA-7P fly with the Portuguese Air Force.

Vought F-8E Crusader, French Navy, No.7

Specification	Vought A-7H Corsair II	
Powerplant	One 14,500 lb.s.t. (64.5 kN) Allison TF41A-1 turbofan	
Dimensions		
Span	11.81 m	(38 ft 9 in)
Length	14.07 m	(46 ft 2 in)
Height	4.9 m	(16 ft 1 in)
Performance		
Max speed	1,123 km/h	(607 kt, 698 mph)
Initial climb	4,572 m/min	(15,000 fpm)
Range	3,648 km	(1,983 nm, 2,280 miles)
Weights		
Max takeoff	19,048 kg	(42,000 lbs)
Useful load	10,363 kg	(22,850 lbs)

Vought TA-4H Corsair II, Greek AF, 156747

Vultee BT-13 Valiant — USA

Vultee's BT-13 (Model 54) Valiant was the main World War II basic trainer for the US Army Air Corps and was used to take pilots from the initial stage of Stearman PT-17 tuition to advanced training on derivatives of operational aircraft. It was a low-wing all-metal aircraft with a fixed tailwheel undercarriage, a tandem two-seat cockpit enclosed by a large framed canopy and a large 540 h.p. Pratt & Whitney R-985 radial piston engine. First flown in 1939 and built by the Consolidated Vultee Aircraft Corporation, the Valiant was built in a series of variants with different engines including the BT-13 (450 h.p. R-985-25), BT-13A (R-985-AN1) and the BT-15 (450 h.p. R-975-11). A large number of BT-13As were used by the US Navy as the SNV. In total Consolidated Vultee completed 7,832 Valiants, and many of these were civilianised after the war with a reasonable number surviving into the 1990s with private owners. Several BT-13s have been used as the basis for creating film replicas of Japanese aircraft, such as the Aichi D3A 'Val' torpedo bomber.

Specification	Vultee BT-13 Valiant	
Powerplant	One 450 h.p. (335.5 kW) Pratt & Whitney R-985-25 Wasp Junior piston engine	
Dimensions		
Span	12.8 m	(42 ft 0 in)
Length	8.79 m	(28 ft 10 in)
Height	3.51 m	(11 ft 6 in)
Performance		
Max speed	293 km/h	(158 kt, 182 mph)
Cruising speed	274 km/h	(148 kt, 170 mph)
Initial climb	472 m/min	(1,550 fpm)
Range	1,160 km	(630 nm, 725 miles)
Weights		
Max takeoff	2,039 kg	(4,495 lbs)
Useful load	508 kg	(1,120 lbs)

Vultee BT-13

Vultee BT-13 – Aichi D3A-1 film replica

Vultee Stinson L-1 Vigilant — USA

The Vultee-designed Vigilant was one of the earliest World War II army cooperation aircraft. It was a fairly large and heavy strut-braced monoplane with a 'glasshouse' cabin seating the two crew in tandem, and had a complex main undercarriage with external absorbing shock struts. Initially designated O-49 and, later, L-1, it was of mixed construction and had large automatic wing leading edge slats and trailing edge flaps to gain maximum short takeoff and landing performance, and a large 295 h.p. Lycoming R-680-9 radial engine in the nose. Vultee built 324 Vigilants, some of which were handed over to the RAF. Later examples were built as the L-1A with a lengthened fuselage and higher gross weight, and a number of these were modified to L-1B and L-1E standard as ambulance aircraft. The Vigilant was soon replaced by the cheaper and more agile Piper L-4, Stinson L-5 and Taylorcraft L-2, but a few still survive in private hands.

Specification	Vultee L-1A Vigilant	
Powerplant	One 295 h.p. (220 kW) Lycoming R-680-9 piston engine	
Dimensions		
Span	15.52 m	(50 ft 11 in)
Length	10.44 m	(34 ft 3 in)
Height	3.1 m	(10 ft 2 in)
Performance		
Max speed	196 km/h	(106 kt, 122 mph)
Cruising speed	185 km/h	(100 kt, 115 mph)
Initial climb	213 m/min	(700 fpm)
Range	448 km	(243 nm, 280 miles)
Weights		
Max takeoff	1,542 kg	(3,400 lbs)
Useful load	331 kg	(730 lbs)

Vultee L-1 Vigilant, NL12S

Waco 10 (Model O) — USA

Waco was the largest light aircraft manufacturing company in the United States during the 1930s. Originally named Advance Aircraft Company, it developed a series of three- and four-seat biplanes which culminated in the Model 10, introduced in 1927. The Waco 10 was a conventional tailwheel biplane with straight wings and an open rear single cockpit and forward two-seat passenger cockpit. It had a steel tube fuselage structure with wooden formers and stringers and wooden wings all covered in fabric. Over 300 were built with the in-line 90 h.p. Curtiss OX-5 engine, and the company also built the sporting Waco 10-T Taperwing with tapered unequal-span upper and lower wings. The Waco 10 (later called the GXE) was developed with a series of engines. These models were initially known as the Model 10H, 10W etc. to indicate the different engines, but in 1929 were given letter designations ending in 'O' with the middle letter 'S' or 'T' indicating straight or tapered wings. These included the ASO (220 h.p. Wright J5 Whirlwind radial), CSO (225 h.p. Wright J6), CTO (a Taperwing CSO) and DSO (180 h.p. Hispano Suiza Model E). The 'O' series was discontinued in 1933 in favour of the 'F' series. More than 150 of the Waco 9, 10, GXE and O series are still registered in the USA.

Waco DSO, NC8558

Specification	Waco CSO	
Powerplant	One 225 h.p. (167.7 kW) Wright J6 Whirlwind piston engine	
Dimensions		
Span	9.32 m	(30 ft 7 in)
Length	6.86 m	(22 ft 6 in)
Height	2.79 m	(9 ft 2 in)
Performance		
Max speed	206 km/h	(111 kt, 128 mph)
Cruising speed	174 km/h	(94 kt, 108 mph)
Initial climb	335 m/min	(1,100 fpm)
Range	864 km	(470 nm, 540 miles)
Weights		
Max takeoff	1,179 kg	(2,600 lbs)
Useful load	441 kg	(972 lbs)

Waco Model F — USA

Introduced in 1930, the Waco 'F' series of biplanes replaced the original Waco 10 ('O' series). The F series had an airframe which was smaller and around 450 lbs lighter than that of the O series while still providing seating for three in tandem open cockpits. Similar performance was available on the power of smaller and more economical engines. The initial models were the INF (125 h.p. Kinner B5), KNF (100 h.p. Kinner K5) and RNF (110 h.p. Warner Scarab), all of which had externally braced undercarriages. The PCF (and PBF with modified 'B' wings), the QCF and the UBF were improved versions with cross-braced undercarriages, powered by 170 h.p. Jacobs LA-1, 165 h.p. Continental A70 and 210 h.p. Continental R-670 radial engines respectively. The UMF and YMF, introduced in 1934, had a modified wider and longer fuselage and a larger vertical tail and were powered by a 210 h.p. Continental R-670-A and 225 h.p. Jacobs L-4 engine respectively. The YMF-5 was returned to production in the 1980s by Classic Aircraft of Lansing, Michigan, the first new example flying on 20th November 1985, and over 90 have been built to date. The UPF-7 was a tandem two-seat training version with a wider-track undercarriage, taller pointed tail and a 220 h.p. Continental radial engine and was produced in considerable numbers for the wartime US Civil Pilot Training Program, and designated PT-14 by the USAAF. Over 250 UPF-7s and 100 of the other F series models are still operational worldwide.

Waco UPF-7, N32132

Classic Waco YMF-5, N21WF

Waco Model F (Cont.)

Specification	Classic Aircraft Waco YMF-5	
Powerplant	One 275 h.p. (205 kW) Jacobs R-755B-2 piston engine	
Dimensions		
Span	9.14 m	(30 ft 0 in)
Length	7.26 m	(23 ft 10 in)
Height	2.59 m	(8 ft 6 in)
Performance		
Max speed	233 km/h	(126 kt, 145 mph)
Cruising speed	193 km/h	(104 kt, 120 mph)
Initial climb	427 m/min	(1,400 fpm)
Range	640 km	(348 nm, 400 miles)
Weights		
Max takeoff	1,338 kg	(2,950 lbs)
Useful load	438 kg	(965 lbs)

Waco Model C — USA

Waco's first cabin biplane was introduced to the market in 1931 as the Model QDC. Based on the Series F airframe, the Model C had a raised centre and rear fuselage forming a four-seat cabin which was entered through a door over the lower wing and had a rather ugly framed rear-view window. The QDC was powered by a 165 h.p. Continental A70 cowled radial engine and was fitted with a triangulated shock-chord undercarriage. It was followed in 1932 by the UEC and OEC (powered by the 210 h.p. Continental R-670 and 210 h.p. Kinner C5-210 respectively) with many detailed improvements including a new rear window which was flush with the upper fuselage. The UIC was a UEC with a longer fuselage and cabin, and the UKC, UKC-S and Jacobs L-4-powered YKC had further cabin enlargement. With the UOC of 1935, Waco changed the wings to a more pointed shape with shorter span for the lower wing, modified the cabin for up to five people, changed the rear fuselage eliminating the rear-view window and altered the undercarriage to a semi-cantilever structure similar to that of the UPF. The UOC had a Continental R-670-A engine and other versions were the YOC (285 h.p. Jacobs L-5MB), the CUC (250 h.p. Wright R-760-E), DQC-6 (285 h.p. Wright R-760-E1) and YQC-6 (225 h.p. Jacobs L-4). The final models in the 'C' series were the Custom Cabin EGC-7 and EGC-8 of 1937/38 with a large 320 h.p. Wright R-760-E2 radial. Around 100 of the Waco C models are still flying in the USA.

Waco YOC, NC15244

Waco UIC, NC13562

Specification	Waco YOC	
Powerplant	One 285 h.p. (212.5 kW) Jacobs L-5MB piston engine	
Dimensions		
Span	10.67 m	(35 ft 0 in)
Length	7.72 m	(25 ft 4 in)
Height	2.51 m	(8 ft 3 in)
Performance		
Max speed	261 km/h	(141 kt, 162 mph)
Cruising speed	212 km/h	(115 kt, 132 mph)
Initial climb	280 m/min	(920 fpm)
Range	720 km	(391 nm, 450 miles)
Weights		
Max takeoff	1,519 kg	(3,350 lbs)
Useful load	494 kg	(1,090 lbs)

Waco Model A — USA

Waco's KBA biplane was announced in 1932 as an affordable private-owner aircraft with cross-country range and baggage capacity, a more sporting image than the larger Model 'F' Wacos and a number of engine options. It had equal-span wings and, for its time, a very streamlined fuselage with a side-by-side two-seat cockpit enclosed by a framed bubble canopy. The KBA was powered by a 100 h.p. Kinner K5 and other engine combinations were offered on the IBA (125 h.p. Kinner B5), the PBA (170 h.p. Jacobs LA-1), RBA (125 h.p. Warner Scarab), the TBA (160 h.p. Kinner R5) and UBA (210 h.p. Continental R-670). The Model PLA Sportsman was a later version announced in 1933 with a longer and wider fuselage and a higher useful load. It had a 170 h.p. Jacobs LA-1 radial engine, and ULA was the last 'A' model with a 210 h.p. Continental R-670 engine. The Series A is now fairly rare with only around six remaining in private ownership.

Waco RBA, N12444

Specification	Waco PLA Sportsman	
Powerplant	One 170 h.p. (126.75 kW) Jacobs LA-1 piston engine	
Dimensions		
Span	8.99 m	(29 ft 6 in)
Length	7.16 m	(23 ft 6 in)
Height	2.67 m	(8 ft 9 in)
Performance		
Max speed	196 km/h	(106 kt, 122 mph)
Cruising speed	169 km/h	(91 kt, 105 mph)
Initial climb	259 m/min	(850 fpm)
Range	800 km	(435 nm, 500 miles)
Weights		
Max takeoff	1,043 kg	(2,300 lbs)
Useful load	403 kg	(889 lbs)

Waco Model S — USA

The Waco S series were cabin biplanes very similar in structure and appearance to the C series, except for having a more rounded vertical tail, but were intended as lower-cost aircraft for commercial operators. They were referred to as the 'Standard Cabin' Waco as compared to the more luxurious C series 'Custom Cabin' Waco. The YKS-7 was announced in 1937 and it was fitted with the straight non-tapered wings of the earlier C series aircraft. Internally it had seating for up to five people and was available as the YKS-7 (225 h.p. Jacobs L-4), ZKS-7 (285 h.p. Jacobs L-5), UKS-7 (225 h.p. Continental W-670K) and VKS-7 (240 h.p. Continental W-670M). It was of standard Waco tube, wood and fabric construction with the semi-cantilever undercarriage used on the later models, and production continued until 1941. A few were used by the USAAF as the UC-72K. Around 55 examples of the Waco S series are currently operational.

Waco YKS-7, G-BWAC

Specification	Waco YKS-7	
Powerplant	One 225 h.p. (167.7 kW) Jacobs L-4 piston engine	
Dimensions		
Span	10.13 m	(33 ft 3 in)
Length	7.7 m	(25 ft 3 in)
Height	2.59 m	(8 ft 6 in)
Performance		
Max speed	241 km/h	(130 kt, 150 mph)
Cruising speed	225 km/h	(122 kt, 140 mph)
Initial climb	244 m/min	(800 fpm)
Range	944 km	(513 nm, 590 miles)
Weights		
Max takeoff	1,474 kg	(3,250 lbs)
Useful load	620 kg	(1,368 lbs)

Waco Model N — USA

Waco introduced the luxury N series biplane in 1938. It was based on the Waco C five-seat Custom Cabin Waco with the curved pointed wings but had an unusual tricycle undercarriage with prominent spats and a modified tail with a lower rudder extension to give increased side area. The Waco N was also fitted with flaps on all four wings to improve its landing characteristics. The prototype, designated ZVN-7, was flown in 1937, and only around 20 examples were built with a few being impressed during the war as the UC-72J and UC-72L. They were powered by either the 285 h.p. Jacobs L-5 (ZVN-8) or 300 h.p. Jacobs L-6 (AVN-8). Six of the N series are registered in the USA.

Waco ZVN-8, N1937S

Specification	Waco AVN-8	
Powerplant	One 300 h.p. (223.68 kW) Jacobs L-6 piston engine	
Dimensions		
Span	10.59 m	(34 ft 9 in)
Length	8.41 m	(27 ft 7 in)
Height	2.59 m	(8 ft 6 in)
Performance		
Max speed	259 km/h	(140 kt, 161 mph)
Cruising speed	224 km/h	(121 kt, 139 mph)
Initial climb	274 m/min	(900 fpm)
Range	880 km	(478 nm, 550 miles)
Weights		
Max takeoff	1,723 kg	(3,800 lbs)
Useful load	560 kg	(1,236 lbs)

Waco Model E — USA

The Waco E series, which marked the end of the prewar Waco biplane line, was first flown in 1939. It was a four-seat cabin biplane with the best performance of any of the Wacos. It had a much slimmer and more streamlined fuselage than earlier Waco C and S models and heavily staggered unequal-span parallel-chord wings with rounded tips. It also had wire cross bracing between the wings in place of the solid strut used on previous models. Several engine options were available on the ARE (300 h.p. Jacobs L-6MB), HRE (285 h.p. Lycoming R-680-E3), SRE (400 h.p. Pratt & Whitney Wasp Jr. SB-2) and WRE (420 h.p. Wright R-975-E3), and all these radial engines were enclosed in a tightly fitting streamlined cowling. Waco built 29 of the E series, the most popular being the SRE, and five are currently registered in the USA.

Waco SRE, N1252W

Specification	Waco SRE	
Powerplant	One 400 h.p. (298.2 kW) Pratt & Whitney Wasp Jr. SB-2 piston engine	
Dimensions		
Span	10.59 m	(34 ft 9 in)
Length	8.48 m	(27 ft 10 in)
Height	2.64 m	(8 ft 8 in)
Performance		
Max speed	325 km/h	(176 kt, 202 mph)
Cruising speed	314 km/h	(170 kt, 195 mph)
Initial climb	472 m/min	(1,550 fpm)
Range	1,712 km	(930 nm, 1,070 miles)
Weights		
Max takeoff	1,905 kg	(4,200 lbs)
Useful load	665 kg	(1,466 lbs)

Wallace Touroplane — USA

Designed by Stanley Wallace, the Touroplane B was typical of a number of high-wing cabin monoplanes produced during the 1930s. It first flew in 1928, powered by an 80 h.p. Anzani engine, and 13 production aircraft were produced by American Eagle Aircraft Corp., which acquired Wallace Aircraft in 1929. The Touroplane, which was also known as the American Eagle 330, was a strut-braced monoplane with a fixed tailwheel undercarriage and production aircraft were mostly powered by the 100 h.p. Kinner K5 five-cylinder radial engine, although two were fitted with the Curtiss OX-5. The structure was fabric-covered with wooden wings and a welded tube fuselage, and the cabin had a front seat for the pilot and one passenger with a rear side-facing seat for a third occupant. One Touroplane is maintained in airworthy condition in the USA

Wallace Touroplane, N276K

Specification	Wallace Touroplane B	
Powerplant	One 100 h.p. (74.56 kW) Kinner K5 piston engine	
Dimensions		
Span	11.28 m	(37 ft 0 in)
Length	7.26 m	(23 ft 10 in)
Height	2.29 m	(7 ft 6 in)
Performance		
Max speed	169 km/h	(91 kt, 105 mph)
Cruising speed	145 km/h	(78 kt, 90 mph)
Initial climb	192 m/min	(630 fpm)
Range	800 km	(435 nm, 500 miles)
Weights		
Max takeoff	952 kg	(2,100 lbs)
Useful load	354 kg	(780 lbs)

WAR P-47 and FW.190
— USA

War Aircraft Replicas, now based in Tampa, Florida, has designed a range of approximately half-scale replicas of World War II fighters for amateur construction. Each type is based on a common wood and plywood frame structure for the fuselage, wings and tail with blocks of polyurethane foam as filling. The foam can be formed to give the external shape of different aircraft types including the P-47 Thunderbolt, Focke Wulf 190, P-51 Mustang, Vought Corsair, Mitsubishi Zero and Hawker Sea Fury. The WAR aircraft which are aerobatic, normally have retractable undercarriages and can be powered by various engines in the 70 h.p. to 100 h.p. range, although the standard powerplant is the 100 h.p. Continental O-200 flat-four. WAR flew the prototype, constructed as an FW.190, on 21st August 1974, and more than 600 sets of plans have been sold with many examples of all the optional models flying in the USA and Europe.

Specification	WAR FW.190	
Powerplant	One 100 h.p. (74.56 kW) Teledyne Continental O-200-A piston engine	
Dimensions		
Span	6.1 m	(20 ft 0 in)
Length	5.05 m	(16 ft 7 in)
Height	1.73 m	(5 ft 8 in)
Performance		
Max speed	314 km/h	(170 kt, 195 mph)
Cruising speed	233 km/h	(126 kt, 145 mph)
Initial climb	305 m/min	(1,000 fpm)
Range	640 km	(348 nm, 400 miles)
Weights		
Max takeoff	408 kg	(900 lbs)
Useful load	122 kg	(270 lbs)

WAR P-47, F-PYQQ

Wassmer Wa-40 Super IV
— France

Wassmer, an established manufacturer of the Jodel 112 and 120, designed the Wa-40 Super IV private-owner touring aircraft, which first flew on 8th June 1959. It was a low-wing machine built from tube and fabric with a four-seat cabin enclosed by a sliding canopy. It had a retractable tricycle undercarriage and was powered by a 180 h.p. Lycoming O-360-A1A engine. Several versions were offered with different trim and equipment levels, including the 'Sancy', 'President', 'Pariou' and 'Commandant de Bord'. The initial production Wa-40 was followed by the Wa-40A Sancy, with a swept tail in place of the earlier square fin, and by the similar Wa-41 Baladou, which had a fixed undercarriage. In total 167 standard Super IVs were built, many of which are still operational. Wassmer then produced a higher-powered version named the Super 4/21 Prestige (also named Wa.41-250) which was fitted with a 250 h.p. Lycoming IO-540-C4B5 engine and featured a revised engine cowling, a modified undercarriage and a streamlined cockpit canopy. It first flew in March 1967 and 30 were completed between 1968 and 1970.

WAR Corsair, N883DL

Wassmer Super IV, F-BKJE

Wassmer Wa-40 Super IV (Cont.)

Wassmer Super 4/21, F-BPZP

Specification	Wassmer Wa-40A Super IV	
Powerplant	One 180 h.p. (134.2 kW) Textron Lycoming O-360-A1A piston engine	
Dimensions		
Span	9.98 m	(32 ft 9 in)
Length	8.08 m	(26 ft 6 in)
Height	2.87 m	(9 ft 5 in)
Performance		
Max speed	270 km/h	(146 kt, 168 mph)
Cruising speed	266 km/h	(143 kt, 165 mph)
Initial climb	276 m/min	(905 fpm)
Range	1,688 km	(917 nm, 1,055 miles)
Weights		
Max takeoff	1,200 kg	(2,646 lbs)
Useful load	460 kg	(1,014 lbs)

Wassmer Wa-50 Pacific, Atlantic and Europa — France

Experience in the design and manufacture of glass-fibre sailplanes led Wassmer Aviation to design the GRP (glass-reinforced plastic) Wa-50 four-seat light aircraft, which first flew on 18th March 1966. It was a streamlined four-seat low-wing touring machine with a retractable tricycle undercarriage and a 150 h.p. Lycoming O-320 engine. It was certificated in 1970, but the production models had many detailed design changes and all were equipped with fixed undercarriages. The production versions were the Wa-51 Pacific with a 150 h.p. Lycoming O-320-E2C engine, the Wa-52 Europa with a 160 h.p. O-320-D1F and the Wa-54 Atlantic with a 180 h.p. O-360-A1LD engine and higher weights. Wassmer built 153 of the Wa-50 series and 80 are still active, mainly in France and Germany, but also in Belgium, Finland and the UK.

Wassmer Wa-52 Europa, D-EMGM

Specification	Wassmer Wa-52 Europa	
Powerplant	One 160 h.p. (119.3 kW) Textron Lycoming O-320-D1F piston engine	
Dimensions		
Span	9.4 m	(30 ft 10 in)
Length	7.29 m	(23 ft 11 in)
Height	2.26 m	(7 ft 5 in)
Performance		
Max speed	274 km/h	(148 kt, 170 mph)
Cruising speed	259 km/h	(140 kt, 161 mph)
Initial climb	240 m/min	(787 fpm)
Range	1,392 km	(757 nm, 870 miles)
Weights		
Max takeoff	1,079 kg	(2,380 lbs)
Useful load	470 kg	(1,036 lbs)

Wassmer Wa-80 Piranha — France

Wassmer Aviation added the Wa-80 Piranha two-seat trainer to their range of light aircraft in 1976. This used the same GRP construction as the Wa-50 series of four-seaters and was, in effect, a lower-powered version of the Europa. The main external difference, apart from its narrower vertical tail, was the unusual cantilever main undercarriage. This had composite legs with the wheels attached to the inside surface and it was not fitted with the spats which were common on the larger model. The powerplant was a 100 h.p. Rolls Royce Continental O-200-A. The Wa-81 Piranha, which was the main production version, had an additional third rear seat. Wassmer built 24 Piranhas before the company went out of business in 1977.

Wassmer Wa-81 Piranha, F-GAIL

Specification	Wassmer Wa-81 Piranha	
Powerplant	One 100 h.p. (74.56 kW) Rolls Royce Continental O-200-A piston engine	
Dimensions		
Span	9.4 m	(30 ft 10 in)
Length	7.5 m	(24 ft 7 in)
Height	2.1 m	(6 ft 10 in)
Performance		
Max speed	241 km/h	(130 kt, 150 mph)
Cruising speed	190 km/h	(103 kt, 118 mph)
Initial climb	210 m/min	(690 fpm)
Range	696 km	(378 nm, 435 miles)
Weights		
Max takeoff	800 kg	(1,764 lbs)
Useful load	300 kg	(661 lbs)

Weatherly 620 — USA

Weatherly Aviation of Hollister, California, who had built a small series of WM-62C crop-spraying conversions of the Fairchild Cornell during the 1960s, designed the Weatherly 201 agricultural aircraft, which first flew in 1965. The Model 201 was a low-wing design of tube and light alloy semi-monocoque construction with a 240-USG hopper, a fixed tail-wheel undercarriage and an enclosed cockpit. The wing design was complex with slight dihedral on the outer panels and various aerodynamic devices including vortex generators and a wing booster fairing. Production of the Model 201A, powered by a 450 h.p. Pratt & Whitney R-985 radial engine, started in 1968, followed by the 201B and 201C, which had minor improvements. The 201C and subsequent versions were fitted with small wingtip vanes to improve the swath width of chemical spray. A total of 88 of the Model 201 were built. The current Model 620, which first flew in 1979, was externally similar to the 201 but with the gross weight increased to 5,800 lbs and a hopper capacity of 335 USG. The 620A has increased fuel capacity and the 620B has a longer fuselage. Weatherly also builds the Model 620A-TP and 620B-TP powered by a 500 s.h.p. Pratt & Whitney PT6A-11AG turboprop. To date, Weatherly has built 153 of the Model 620.

Weatherly 620A, N4627G

Specification	Weatherly 620A-TP	
Powerplant	One 500 s.h.p. (372.8 kW) Pratt & Whitney PT6A-11AG turboprop	
Dimensions		
Span	12.5 m	(41 ft 0 in)
Length	9.3 m	(30 ft 6 in)
Height	2.46 m	(8 ft 1 in)
Performance		
Max speed	225 km/h	(122 kt, 140 mph)
Cruising speed	185 km/h	(100 kt, 115 mph)
Initial climb	244 m/min	(800 fpm)
Range	1,120 km	(609 nm, 700 miles)
Weights		
Max takeoff	1,814 kg	(4,000 lbs)
Useful load	590 kg	(1,300 lbs)

Westland Lysander — UK

The Lysander played an important wartime role as an army cooperation aircraft and was particularly famed for carrying out clandestine missions to insert and extract British agents. Westland designed the Lysander to have excellent slow-speed handling, a good field of vision and a rugged airframe which could cope with unprepared fields. Constructed of tube and fabric, it had a strut-braced high wing which tapered from its mid-point into the root and tapered out to the wingtip, and was fitted with leading edge slats and interconnected flaps. The tall cantilever undercarriage with its large fairings was another distinctive feature. The Lysander prototype flew on 15th June 1936 and 1,427 examples were built by Westland with another 225 being built in Canada by NSCC. Apart from several museum examples at least three Lysanders are airworthy, including one in Belgium, and others are under restoration to flying condition.

Westland Lysander IIIA, V9545 (G-BCWL)

Specification	Westland Lysander Mk.III	
Powerplant	One 870 h.p. (649 kW) Bristol Mercury XX piston engine	
Dimensions		
Span	15.24 m	(50 ft 0 in)
Length	9.3 m	(30 ft 6 in)
Height	4.42 m	(14 ft 6 in)
Performance		
Max speed	339 km/h	(183 kt, 211 mph)
Cruising speed	298 km/h	(161 kt, 185 mph)
Initial climb	381 m/min	(1,250 fpm)
Range	2,240 km	(1,217 nm, 1,400 miles)
Weights		
Max takeoff	2,871 kg	(6,330 lbs)
Useful load	891 kg	(1,965 lbs)

Westland Sea King — UK

In 1959, Westland took a licence to build the Sikorsky S-61 to meet a Royal Navy requirement for an anti-submarine helicopter to replace the Westland Wessex. While the Westland-built Sea King was based on the US Navy's Sikorsky SH-3D, it was powered by two 1,400 s.h.p. Rolls Royce Gnome (licence-built General Electric T58) H.1400 turboshafts with an HSD FADEC engine management system, and had numerous other systems and equipment changes. Westland flew the first Sea King HAS.1 on 7th May 1969 and later variants were the HAS.2 with a six-bladed tail rotor and uprated 1,535 s.h.p. H.1400-1 engines, the RAF's search & rescue HAR.3, the HC.4 commando assault helicopter and the HAS.5 and HAS.6 improved anti-submarine aircraft with a large Sea Searcher radome on the upper fuselage. The Commando Mk.1 is an assault version with a fixed undercarriage, and the Sea King AEW.2A has a Searchwater radar in a large extendable radome. Export customers for the Sea King have included Egypt (Commando Mk.70, Sea King 47), Qatar (Commando), Germany (Mk.41), India (Mk.42), Norway (Mk.43), Pakistan (Mk.45), Belgium (Mk.48) and the Royal Australian Navy (Mk.50). Westland had completed 328 Sea Kings by the time the last RAF HAR.3A was delivered in 1996.

Westland Sea King AEW.2A, XV704

Westland Sea King HAS.50A, Royal Australian Navy, N16-238

Westland Sea King HAR.3

Specification	Westland Sea King HAS Mk.6	
Powerplant	Two 1,660 s.h.p. (1,238 kW) Rolls Royce Gnome H.1400-1T turboshafts	
Dimensions		
Rotor diameter	18.9 m	(62 ft 0 in)
Length	17.42 m	(57 ft 2 in)
Height	5.13 m	(16 ft 10 in)
Performance		
Max speed	217 km/h	(117 kt, 135 mph)
Cruising speed	203 km/h	(110 kt, 126 mph)
Initial climb	564 m/min	(1,850 fpm)
Range	1,473 km	(800 nm, 921 miles)
Weights		
Max takeoff	9,750 kg	(21,500 lbs)
Useful load	2,420 kg	(5,337 lbs)

Westland Scout and Wasp — UK

Having inherited the P.531 light helicopter from Saunders-Roe, Westland developed it for the British Army into the Scout AH.1 battlefield support and army liaison helicopter. The Scout prototype flew on 9th August 1959 and entered service with the Army Air Corps (AAC) in March 1963. In total 149 Scouts were built, mainly for the AAC, but a few were also sold to Jordan and Uganda. It was a fairly conventional all-metal aircraft with an extensively glazed cabin accommodating two crew in front and up to four passengers on a rear bench seat, and powered by a Bristol Siddeley Nimbus turboshaft positioned behind the cabin. The Scout was withdrawn in 1994 but a number are still flying in private ownership in the UK and New Zealand. The Westland Wasp was a frigate-based naval derivative of the Scout, but the main fuselage pod was longer and the undercarriage had four swivelling legs in place of the Scout's skids. The Wasp also had a smaller fin and a small single tailplane and could carry a pair of Mk.44 torpedoes under the belly. A total of 125 Wasps were built for the Royal Navy, and other users have included the Netherlands, South Africa, New Zealand and Brazil, who have now withdrawn them, and Malaysia and Indonesia, who still have the type in service.

Specification	Westland Scout AH Mk.1	
Powerplant	One 685 s.h.p. (510.7 kW) Rolls Royce Nimbus 101 turboshaft	
Dimensions		
Rotor diameter	9.83 m	(32 ft 3 in)
Length	9.25 m	(30 ft 4 in)
Height	2.69 m	(8 ft 10 in)
Performance		
Max speed	211 km/h	(114 kt, 131 mph)
Cruising speed	196 km/h	(106 kt, 122 mph)
Initial climb	509 m/min	(1,670 fpm)
Range	506 km	(275 nm, 316 miles)
Weights		
Max takeoff	2,426 kg	(5,350 lbs)
Useful load	1,028 kg	(2,266 lbs)

Westland Scout, XV130

Westland Lynx — UK

The Lynx medium-capacity military helicopter was designed by Westland for co-production with Aérospatiale to meet British needs for an army utility helicopter, an RAF trainer, and ASW versions for the Royal Navy and French Aéronavale. The first of 13 development aircraft flew at Yeovil on 21st March 1971. The Lynx has a two-crew cockpit and a main cabin which can carry up to 12 troops. The Army Lynx AH.1, which has a skid undercarriage, is able to carry external armament including up to eight TOW missiles. It is powered by twin 900 s.h.p. Rolls Royce Gem 2 engines, but the Lynx AH.7 has higher-powered Gem 41 engines and the AH.9 has a higher gross weight, a fixed tricycle undercarriage and redesigned rotor blades with BERP tip extensions. The Navy Lynx HAS.2, which is primarily used as a frigate-based anti-submarine helicopter, has a tricycle undercarriage and operates with a normal crew of three, the main cabin being used for ASW electronics. It is fitted with a deck-landing harpoon-system and can carry four Sea Skua anti-shipping missiles on external hardpoints, and the French naval version has an Alcatel dipping sonar operated through a floor hatch. Variants include the HAS.3 with upgraded Gem 41-1 turboshafts and the HAS.8 with the modified BERP rotor blades. Foreign deliveries of the Navy Lynx have been made to Brazil (Mk.21), the Netherlands (Mk.25, Mk.27 and Mk.81), Qatar (Mk.28), Denmark (Mk.80), Norway (Mk.86), Germany (Mk.88 and 88A), Nigeria (Mk.89), Portugal (Mk.95) and Korea (Mk.99). The Super Lynx 200 is an advanced version with LHTEC CTS800-4N, and the Super Lynx 300 has new weapons electronics, a glass cockpit and a new navigation suite. More than 400 examples of the Lynx/Navy Lynx have been built to date.

Westland Lynx AH.9, Army Air Corps, ZE380

Specification	Westland Lynx AH Mk.9	
Powerplant	Two 900 s.h.p (671 kW) Rolls Royce Gem 2 turboshafts	
Dimensions		
Rotor diameter	12.8 m	(42 ft 0 in)
Length	12.17 m	(39 ft 11 in)
Height	3.53 m	(11 ft 7 in)
Performance		
Max speed	259 km/h	(140 kt, 161 mph)
Cruising speed	242 km/h	(130 kt, 150 mph)
Initial climb	536 m/min	(1,760 fpm)
Range	540 km	(292 nm, 336 miles)
Weights		
Max takeoff	4,535 kg	(10,000 lbs)
Useful load	1,749 kg	(3,856 lbs)

Westland Lynx HMA.8, Royal Navy, ZD265

Wilson Private Explorer — USA

Now available to amateur builders in kit form, the Private Explorer is an 'airborne recreational vehicle' designed by Dean Wilson as a flying camper van with enough space to provide sleeping accommodation. It is a smaller version of the enormous twin-engined Explorer amphibian, two of which were built for Hubert de Chevigny, the first flying in April 1991. The Private Explorer is a strut-braced high-wing aircraft with a tubular steel frame covered in fabric, and the interior has four seats in the front section and a rear accommodation compartment which has a double bed and two armchairs. The undercarriage is fixed but the aircraft can be fitted with floats and various engines from 235 h.p. to 300 h.p. to give the Private Explorer excellent short-field performance and up to eight hours' endurance. One Private Explorer has been completed to date, and it first flew in January 1998.

Specification	Wilson Private Explorer	
Powerplant	One 235 h.p. (175.2 kW) Textron Lycoming O-540 piston engine	
Dimensions		
Span	14.4 m	(47 ft 3 in)
Length	9.07 m	(29 ft 9 in)
Height	3.4 m	(11 ft 2 in)
Performance		
Max speed	180 km/h	(97 kt, 112 mph)
Cruising speed	161 km/h	(87 kt, 100 mph)
Initial climb	361 m/min	(1,184 fpm)
Range	1,280 km	(696 nm, 800 miles)
Weights		
Max takeoff	1,860 kg	(4,102 lbs)
Useful load	888 kg	(1,957 lbs)

Wilson Private Explorer, N7065H

Windecker Eagle — USA

The Eagle was one of the earliest types designed for construction from glass reinforced plastic (GRP). Designed by Dr. Leo Windecker, the prototype X-7 first flew on 7th October 1967. It was a low-wing four-seat light aircraft with a fixed tricycle undercarriage and a 290 h.p. Lycoming IO-540 engine. The production Eagle I, which appeared in early 1969, differed from the X-7 in having a retractable undercarriage, a redesigned wing and a 285 h.p. Lycoming IO-520-C engine. The Eagle went into production in 1969 and eight were built, including one YE-5 for U.S. Air Force evaluation, before Windecker went out of business. All rights to the Eagle were acquired by the Canadian Aerospace Group, which plans to build the Windeagle E-285 and a new version, the E-750T, powered by a 750 s.h.p. Pratt & Whitney PT6A-25C turboprop. One existing Eagle has been re-engined with an Allison 250 turboprop.

Wilson Explorer, N376LC

Windecker Eagle, N4196G

Windecker Eagle (Cont.)

Specification	Windecker Eagle E-285	
Powerplant	One 285 h.p. (212.5 kW) Teledyne Continental IO-520-C piston engine	
Dimensions		
Span	9.14 m	(30 ft 0 in)
Length	9.75 m	(32 ft 0 in)
Height	3.05 m	(10 ft 0 in)
Performance		
Max speed	338 km/h	(183 kt, 210 mph)
Cruising speed	328 km/h	(177 kt, 204 mph)
Initial climb	372 m/min	(1,220 fpm)
Range	1,968 km	(1,070 nm, 1,230 miles)
Weights		
Max takeoff	1,542 kg	(3,400 lbs)
Useful load	658 kg	(1,450 lbs)

Wing Derringer — USA

Wing Aircraft developed the D-1 Derringer light twin based on a design created by John Thorp. The Derringer was intended as a high-performance personal aircraft with a secondary application as an affordable twin-engined trainer. It is a streamlined all-metal monocoque design, the prototype of which was powered by two 115 h.p. Continental O-200 engines, with a low wing, a retractable tricycle undercarriage and a side-by-side cabin for two people with an upward-opening transparent canopy. The first prototype Derringer made its maiden flight at Torrance, California on 1st May 1962. Due to continuing problems with company ownership only 11 development and production Derringers with 160 h.p. engines were built before Wing Aircraft collapsed in July 1982. Several Derringers remain in flying condition and the type was relaunched under new ownership in 1999.

Wing Derringer, N8602J

Specification	Wing Derringer D-1	
Powerplant	Two 160 h.p. (119 kW) Textron Lycoming IO-320-B1C piston engines	
Dimensions		
Span	8.89 m	(29 ft 2 in)
Length	7.01 m	(23 ft 0 in)
Height	2.44 m	(8 ft 0 in)
Performance		
Max speed	373 km/h	(202 kt, 232 mph)
Cruising speed	352 km/h	(190 kt, 219 mph)
Initial climb	518 m/min	(1,700 fpm)
Range	1,856 km	(1,009 nm, 1,160 miles)
Weights		
Max takeoff	1,383 kg	(3,050 lbs)
Useful load	444 kg	(980 lbs)

Winter LF-1 Zaunkönig — Germany

The Zaunkönig single-seat light aircraft was built by the students of Braunschweig Technical College during World War II under the instruction of Prof. Hermann Winter and flown in April 1945. It was intended to be capable of safe flight in the hands of novice pilots and the parasol wing had full-span leading edge slots, drooped ailerons and large trailing edge flaps. The Zaunkönig, which was powered by a 51 h.p. Zundapp engine, had an open cockpit, a T-tail and a fixed tailwheel undercarriage. Two LF-1 Zaunkönig aircraft were built at Braunschweig followed, in 1957, by a further two completed by amateur constructors. Two aircraft remain in existence, of which one is currently airworthy in Germany.

Winter Zaunkönig, D-EBCQ

Specification	Winter Zaunkönig LF-1	
Powerplant	One 51 h.p. (38.03 kW) Zundapp Z.9-092 piston engine	
Dimensions		
Span	8.05 m	(26 ft 5 in)
Length	6.07 m	(19 ft 11 in)
Height	2.39 m	(7 ft 10 in)
Performance		
Max speed	140 km/h	(76 kt, 87 mph)
Cruising speed	85 km/h	(46 kt, 53 mph)
Initial climb	171 m/min	(560 fpm)
Range	368 km	(200 nm, 230 miles)
Weights		
Max takeoff	352 kg	(776 lbs)
Useful load	101 kg	(223 lbs)

Wittman W-8 Tailwind — USA

Designed by Steve Wittman, the Tailwind has been built in large numbers from plans by amateur constructors and more than 400 are believed to be flying. First flown in 1953, it benefited from Wittman's experience with lightweight racers and it offers high performance on relatively low-powered engines. The Tailwind is constructed from steel tube and fabric and the fuselage is designed to give some lift which results in a relatively short-span strut-braced wing with root cut-outs, which allows it to be positioned forward of the windshield, and sharply tapered tip sections. The fully enclosed cabin has side-by-side seating for two and the tailwheel undercarriage has raked-back tubular legs, patented by the designer. Individual Tailwinds have detailed modifications according to the builder, including various shapes for the vertical tail, tricycle and retractable undercarriages and a range of engines from the 90 h.p. Continental C90-12F to the 160 h.p. Lycoming O-320. The W-9L Tailwind was a development with a larger engine and a tricycle undercarriage, and the W-10 has a modified longer-span wing, a new undercarriage with faired legs and various powerplants including a 125 h.p. converted Oldsmobile F85 car engine.

Wittman Tailwind, F-PLBT

Specification	Wittman W-8 Tailwind	
Powerplant	One 90 h.p. (67 kW) Teledyne Continental C90-12F piston engine	
Dimensions		
Span	6.86 m	(22 ft 6 in)
Length	5.87 m	(19 ft 3 in)
Height	1.73 m	(5 ft 8 in)
Performance		
Max speed	266 km/h	(143 kt, 165 mph)
Cruising speed	209 km/h	(113 kt, 130 mph)
Initial climb	274 m/min	(900 fpm)
Range	960 km	(522 nm, 600 miles)
Weights		
Max takeoff	590 kg	(1,300 lbs)
Useful load	272 kg	(600 lbs)

Wolf W-11 Boredom Fighter — USA

The Boredom Fighter was designed by Don Wolf of New York as a simply fabricated recreational aircraft and made its maiden flight on 30th August 1979, since when over 200 sets of plans have been sold. It is built from wood and fabric and is intended to represent a World War I fighter, possibly a Spad XIII, but actually not any specific type. It is very light and agile with a single-seat open cockpit and is designed around the 65 h.p. Continental A65 flat-four engine, although some examples have been fitted with larger Continental engines. It is thought that around 40 Boredom Fighters are flying, including two completed by British homebuilders.

Wolf W-11 Boredom Fighter, 146-11083 (G-BNAI)

Specification	Wolf W-11 Boredom Fighter	
Powerplant	One 65 h.p. (48.5 kW) Teledyne Continental A65 piston engine	
Dimensions		
Span	6.1 m	(20 ft 0 in)
Length	4.77 m	(15 ft 8 in)
Height	1.83 m	(6 ft 0 in)
Performance		
Max speed	190 km/h	(103 kt, 118 mph)
Cruising speed	161 km/h	(87 kt, 100 mph)
Initial climb	366 m/min	(1,200 fpm)
Range	746 km	(405 nm, 466 miles)
Weights		
Max takeoff	349 kg	(770 lbs)
Useful load	135 kg	(297 lbs)

Wolfsburg-Evektor Raven — Czech Republic

Designed by Alec Clark of Wolfsburg Aircraft, the Raven is a twin piston-engined utility aircraft aimed at the market served by the Britten-Norman Islander but offering greater internal capacity and ease of loading for palletised cargo and 'D' Type containers. It is of all-metal construction and has a twin boomed layout, a fixed tricycle undercarriage and a square section fuselage with large rear loading and side loading doors. It can be fitted with eight main-cabin passenger seats or can be used as a freighter, for parachuting or in aeromedical configuration. The prototype first flew on 28th July 2000 and it is being developed,and will be built in quantity, by Evektor-Aerotechnik of Kunovice in the Czech Republic.

Wolfsburg-Evektor Raven (Cont.)

Wolfsburg-Evektor Raven, OK-RAV

Specification	Wolfsburg-Evektor Raven 257	
Powerplant	Two 300 h.p. (223.7 kW) Teledyne Continental IO-550-N piston engines	
Dimensions		
Span	14 m	(45 ft 11 in)
Length	12.29 m	(40 ft 4 in)
Height	3.99 m	(13 ft 1 in)
Performance		
Max speed	268 km/h	(144 kt, 167 mph)
Cruising speed	240 km/h	(129 kt, 149 mph)
Initial climb	450 m/min	(1,476 fpm)
Range	1,325 km	(720 nm, 828 miles)
Weights		
Max takeoff	2,700 kg	(5,954 lbs)
Useful load (est.)	860 kg	(1,895 lbs)

Yakovlev Yak-3 and Yak-9U — Russia

The Yak-9 and the later Yak-3 were the backbone of the Soviet fighter strength in World War II. Derived from the earlier Yak-1 and Yak-7, the Yak-9 was a low-wing monoplane with an inward-retracting tailwheel undercarriage and a cockpit enclosed by a sliding bubble canopy. It was of mixed construction with a light alloy and tube forward fuselage, a wood and fabric rear fuselage and wings with a metal mainspar and wood and ply structure and covering, although the final Yak-9P had an all-metal wing. The first Yak-9s (later given the NATO name 'Frank') appeared at the end of 1942 and 16,769 had been built when production ended in December 1948. Several engines were fitted from the 1,210 h.p. M-105PF on the first Yak-9 to the 1,620 h.p. VK-107A used on the Yak-9U. The Yak-3, which joined the Yak-9 in production in 1943, had better performance and was fitted with a smaller redesigned wing and the higher-powered VK-105PF2 engine. A total of 4,848 Yak-3s were built. At least 21 Yak-3U/As and Yak-9UMs are flying in the USA together with one in New Zealand, following the 1991 opening of a limited production line in Russia. The Yak-9UMs have a second rear seat and all new production Yak-3s and Yak-9s are powered by an Allison V-1710 engine. At least one original Klimov-engined Yak-9U has also been restored to flying condition.

Yakovlev Yak-9UM, N900EA

Yakovlev Yak-3, ZK-YAK

Specification	Yakovlev Yak-3U/A	
Powerplant	One 1,240 h.p. (925 kW) Allison V-1710 piston engine	
Dimensions		
Span	9.2 m	(30 ft 2 in)
Length	8.75 m	(28 ft 8 in)
Height	2.43 m	(7 ft 11 in)
Performance		
Max speed	647 km/h	(350 kt, 402 mph)
Cruising speed	563 km/h	(304 kt, 350 mph)
Initial climb	1,036 m/min	(3,400 fpm)
Range	875 km	(476 nm, 547 miles)
Weights		
Max takeoff	2,697 kg	(5,947 lbs)
Useful load	835 kg	(1,841 lbs)

Yakovlev Yak-11 — Russia

The Yak-11 military trainer was derived from the Yak-3 fighter, having a very similar tapered low wing and retractable tailwheel undercarriage. It was first flown in 1946 and entered service with the Soviet Air Force the following year. The fuselage of the Yak-11 was wider than that of the Yak-3 with a long tandem two-seat cockpit enclosed by a framed transparent sliding canopy, and its structure was steel tube with wooden formers and stringers and fabric covering. The forward end mounted the large, closely cowled ASh-21 radial engine and a 7.7 mm machine gun could be mounted in the upper port coaming. A total of 3,859 Yak-11s (NATO name 'Moose') were built in Russia with a further 707 being built in Czechoslovakia as the C-11 by LET, together with a few C-11Us with a tricycle undercarriage. Several dozen Yak-11s are currently airworthy, many of them former Egyptian Air Force C-11s, including seven in the UK, eight in France, at least 15 in the USA and one in Belgium.

Yakovlev Yak-11 (LET C-11), G-BTUB

Specification	Yakovlev Yak-11	
Powerplant	One 730 h.p. (544.3 kW) Shvetsov ASh-21 piston engine	
Dimensions		
Span	9.4 m	(30 ft 10 in)
Length	8.51 m	(27 ft 11 in)
Height	1.98 m	(6 ft 6 in)
Performance		
Max speed	475 km/h	(257 kt, 295 mph)
Cruising speed	330 km/h	(178 kt, 205 mph)
Initial climb	540 m/min	(1,772 fpm)
Range	1,152 km	(626 nm, 720 miles)
Weights		
Max takeoff	2,439 kg	(5,379 lbs)
Useful load	540 kg	(1,190 lbs)

Yakovlev Yak-12 — Russia

First flown in 1947, the Yak-12 (NATO name 'Creek') was for many years the standard light liaison and general utility aircraft for the Soviet forces, and several thousand were built. It was a classic strut-braced high-wing monoplane with a fixed tailwheel undercarriage and a large enclosed four-seat cabin. The wings were of parallel chord with full-length fixed leading edge slats and large flaps. Construction was tube and fabric for the fuselage and wood, ply and fabric for the wings, and the basic Yak-12 was powered, initially, by a fully cowled 145 h.p. M-11D or M-11FR radial engine, but was later upgraded as the Yak-12R with the 260 h.p. AI-14R. Variants included the Yak-12S ambulance version with a rear hatch for loading stretchers, the Yak-12SKh crop sprayer with a chemical tank in place of the rear seats, and the Yak-12M, which was a development of the Yak-12R with a lengthened fuselage and an all-metal airframe structure. All Yak-12M production was taken over by PZL-Okecie in Poland from 1955 and they built 1,054 of them and 137 of the Yak-12A, which had a new wing without leading edge slats and with tapered outer panels, extra cabin windows and a modified tail. PZL later replaced the Yak-12 with the PZL-101 Gawron (see separate entry).

Yakovlev Yak-12, RA02116

Specification	Yakovlev Yak-12M	
Powerplant	One 260 h.p. (193.86 kW) AI-14R piston engine	
Dimensions		
Span	12.6 m	(41 ft 4 in)
Length	8.99 m	(29 ft 6 in)
Height	2.44 m	(8 ft 0 in)
Performance		
Max speed	182 km/h	(98 kt, 113 mph)
Cruising speed	153 km/h	(83 kt, 95 mph)
Initial climb	300 m/min	(984 fpm)
Range	760 km	(412 nm, 475 miles)
Weights		
Max takeoff	1,450 kg	(3,197 lbs)
Useful load	424 kg	(935 lbs)

Yakovlev Yak-18 and Yak-18T — Russia

The Yak-18 trainer (NATO name 'Max'), which went into production in 1947, was a much developed version of the Yakovlev UT-2. It was a low-wing monoplane with a metal structure with light alloy and fabric covering and tandem seating enclosed by a long multi-section canopy. The 160 h.p. M-11FR radial engine was enclosed in a helmeted cowling and it was fitted with a rearward-retracting main undercarriage. The Yak-18 rapidly became the standard Soviet bloc basic trainer, and further variants included the Yak-18U with a tricycle undercarriage and the considerably modified Yak-18A with a 260 h.p. Ivchenko AI-14R engine. Specialised aerobatic variants were the Yak-18P with a single cockpit, a larger tail and a modified wing, the Yak-18PM with the cockpit moved backwards, a new wing with reduced dihedral and a 300 h.p. Ivchenko AI-14RF engine, and the Yak-18PS, which was a Yak-18PM with a tailwheel undercarriage. The Yak-18T is a much modified four-seat cabin version with a new fuselage, a retractable tricycle undercarriage with inward-retracting main legs and a 360 h.p. Vedeneyev M-14P radial engine. This has been built in recent years as the Technoavia SM-94 with a six-seat cabin. It is believed that production of the basic Yak-18 exceeded 8,700 aircraft and that over 500 Yak-18Ts have been built to date. Many Yak-18Ts are in service in the CIS, Europe and the USA, but relatively few Yak-18s remain.

Yakovlev Yak-18, D-EYAK

Yakovlev Yak-18T, LY-AMJ

Specification	Yakovlev Yak-18T	
Powerplant	One 360 h.p. (268.5 kW) VOKBM Vedeneyev M-14P piston engine	
Dimensions		
Span	11.15 m	(36 ft 7 in)
Length	8.38 m	(27 ft 6 in)
Height	3.4 m	(11 ft 2 in)
Performance		
Max speed	294 km/h	(159 kt, 183 mph)
Cruising speed	249 km/h	(135 kt, 155 mph)
Initial climb	300 m/min	(984 fpm)
Range	600 km	(323 nm, 373 miles)
Weights		
Max takeoff	1,650 kg	(3,638 lbs)
Useful load	433 kg	(955 lbs)

Yakovlev Yak-38 — Russia

Russia's first vertical takeoff fighter, the Yak-38 (NATO name 'Forger'), was developed using vectored thrust technology established with the earlier Yak-36 research aircraft. The Yak-38 prototype was first flown as the Yak-36M on 28th May 1970 and production followed with 100 being built for operation from Soviet carriers such as the *Kiev*, *Minsk*, *Baku* and *Novorossiysk*. The Yak-38 is powered by a Tumanski R27V-300 turbojet engine positioned in the rear fuselage with twin thrust-vectoring exhausts giving forward thrust and some lift and a pair of Koliesov/Rybinsk RD-36 lifting jets fitted in the forward fuselage just aft of the cockpit giving direct vertical takeoff thrust. The aircraft has a small delta wing with folding outer panels and four underwing hardpoints to carry rocket pods or AA-8 Aphid missiles. The tail unit is conventional and the Yak-38 has a retractable tricycle undercarriage with the main units retracting into fuselage recesses. A two-seat trainer version, the Yak-38U, has also been produced with an extended forward fuselage to accommodate the extra cockpit. The remaining Yak-38s are operated by the Ukraine, but in small numbers. Yakovlev OKB also developed the Yak-41 (NATO name 'Freestyle'), a supersonic second-generation VTOL aircraft which flew in March 1989 as the Yak-141, but development has been abandoned.

Yakovlev Yak-38, 38 yellow

Yakovlev Yak-141, 141 white

Specification	Yakovlev Yak-38	
Powerplant	One 14,990 lb.s.t. (66.7 kN) Tumanski R27V-300 turbojet and two 7,175 lb.s.t. (31.9 kN) Koliesov/Rybinsk RD-36-35FVR turbine lift jets	
Dimensions		
Span	7.31 m	(24 ft 0 in)
Length	15.49 m	(50 ft 10 in)
Height	4.37 m	(14 ft 4 in)
Performance		
Max speed	1,014 km/h	(548 kt, 630 mph)
Initial climb	4,500 m/min	(14,763 fpm)
Range	720 km	(391 nm, 450 miles)
Weights		
Max takeoff	13,000 kg	(28,665 lbs)
Useful load	5,510 kg	(12,150 lbs)

Yakovlev Yak-40 — Russia

In 1964, the Yakovlev OKB started work on a new small 32-passenger airliner to serve remote short-haul routes in the Soviet Union. The Yak-40 (NATO name 'Codling'), which was powered by three rear-mounted 3,300 lb.s.t. Ivchenko AI-25 turbofans, had a straight unswept low wing set well to the rear of the fuselage, a ventral rear airstair door and a T-tail. The first Yak-40 was flown on 21st October 1966, with first deliveries to Aeroflot in 1968. The Yak-40K was a cargo version with a forward port-side cargo door. A total of 1,136 Yak-40s went to Soviet military and civil users and military and airline operators, mostly in the Warsaw Pact countries. Air forces using the type included those of Poland, Bulgaria, Slovakia, Laos and Czechoslovakia. The Yak-40 was built at the Saratov Aviation Plant, the final aircraft being completed in 1980. Some examples were sold in Western Europe to General Air (five aircraft) and Aertirrena (three) but they had poor economics and were withdrawn after a short time. However, the Yak-40 continues to operate in large numbers in the CIS on regional airline operations and as a business and air taxi aircraft.

Yakovlev Yak-40, RA-87244

Specification	Yakovlev Yak-40	
Powerplant	Three 3,300 lb.s.t. (14.7 kN) Ivchenko AI-25 turbofans	
Dimensions		
Span	25 m	(82 ft 0 in)
Length	20.36 m	(66 ft 10 in)
Height	6.5 m	(21 ft 4 in)
Performance		
Max speed	550 km/h	(296 kt, 342 mph)
Cruising speed	470 km/h	(253 kt, 292 mph)
Initial climb	480 m/min	(1,575 fpm)
Range	1,800 km	(978 nm, 1,125 miles)
Weights		
Max takeoff	16,000 kg	(35,280 lbs)
Useful load	6,600 kg	(14,553 lbs)

Yakovlev Yak-42 — Russia

The Yak-42 (NATO name 'Clobber') was developed by the Yakovlev OKB as a replacement for the Il-18 and Tu-134 in regional service in the Soviet Union. It is a wide-body aircraft with six-abreast seating for 120 passengers, and Yakovlev followed the example of the successful Yak-40 in using the same T-tail, three-turbofan layout with a ventral rear airstair passenger entrance. The wing of the Yak-42 is swept and it has a conventional retractable tricycle undercarriage with four-wheel main bogies for landing on the poorer remote airfields. The prototype Yak-42 flew on 7th March 1975, the first production aircraft being delivered from the Smolensk factory to Aeroflot in 1980. The current Yak-42D has additional fuel and range, the Yak-42A is a combi passenger/freight aircraft and the Yak-42F is a version for geophysical survey with underwing sampling pods. A new version is the Yak-42D-90 which has an increased fuel load and range but reduced 90-passenger seating. Production of the Yak-42 at Saratov is believed to be around 200 aircraft to date, and the type is widely used by airlines serving the former Aeroflot domestic network. Foreign users include Kazair, Lithuanian Airlines, Cubana, Turkmenistan Airlines and China General Airlines.

Yakovlev Yak-42 (Cont.)

Yakovlev Yak-42D, RA-42427

Yakovlev Yak-50, RA-01386

Specification	Yakovlev Yak-42D	
Powerplant	Three 14,330 lb.s.t. (63.7 kN) Lotarev (ZMKB-Progress) D-36 turbofans	
Dimensions		
Span	34.88 m	(114 ft 5 in)
Length	36.38 m	(119 ft 5 in)
Height	9.83 m	(32 ft 4 in)
Performance		
Max speed	810 km/h	(436 kt, 503 mph)
Cruising speed	750 km/h	(404 kt, 466 mph)
Takeoff distance	2,200 m	(7,218 ft)
Range	2,200 km	(1,196 nm, 1,375 miles)
Weights		
Max takeoff	57,500 kg	(126,787 lbs)
Useful load	22,985 kg	(50,682 lbs)

Yakovlev Yak-52, LY-ALS

Yak-50 and Yak-52 — Russia

The Yak-50 single-seat competition aerobatic aircraft was designed as a successor to the Yak-18PS for entry in the 1976 World Aerobatic Championships. The Yak-50 was an all-metal monocoque design with a very similar fuselage to that of the Yak-18PS but using a new shorter wing with straight taper and without the separate centre section of the earlier type. It had a retractable tailwheel undercarriage and the power was increased to the 360 h.p. Vedeneyev M-14P radial. The Yak-50 led the field in the 1976 and subsequent championships and a large number were built for use by DOSAAF and for sale to export customers. Around a dozen are used in the USA, and more than 25 are flown in Europe by private owners. The Yak-52 was developed from the Yak-50 as a basic trainer for Warsaw Pact countries with a tandem two-seat cockpit enclosed by a three-piece sliding canopy, a retractable tricycle undercarriage and a modified fuel system. The first Yak-52 flew in 1979 and production was taken over by the Romanian IAv. Bacau (later Aerostar), which continues production with more than 1,600 examples having been produced, largely for civil and military export. The Yak-52 is very popular with civil owners in the USA, Australia, New Zealand and throughout Europe, and many examples are flying in Russia and with the air forces of Hungary, Romania and Lithuania.

Specification	Yakovlev (Aerostar) Yak-52	
Powerplant	One 360 h.p. (268 kW) Vedeneyev M-14P piston engine	
Dimensions		
Span	9.3 m	(30 ft 6 in)
Length	7.75 m	(25 ft 5 in)
Height	2.7 m	(8 ft 10 in)
Performance		
Max speed	285 km/h	(154 kt, 177 mph)
Cruising speed	266 km/h	(143 kt, 165 mph)
Initial climb	600 m/min	(1,968 fpm)
Range	500 km	(270 nm, 311 miles)
Weights		
Max takeoff	1,305 kg	(2,878 lbs)
Useful load	290 kg	(639 lbs)

Yakovlev Yak-54 and Yak-55 — Russia

Designed by Vacheslav Kondratyev, who was later responsible for the Su-26 and Technoavia SP-91, the Yak-55 is a light competition aerobatic aircraft produced for the 1982 World Aerobatic Championships at Spitzerberg in Austria, where it allowed the Soviet team to win six gold medals. First flown on 28th May 1981, it has a slim fuselage, spring-steel tailwheel landing gear and a short mid-set straight tapered wing with relatively thick section and no dihedral. The single-seat cockpit is enclosed by a sliding bubble canopy and the Yak-55 is powered by the ubiquitous 360 h.p. Vedeneyev M-14P nine-cylinder radial in a streamlined cowling. The Yak-55M is a later version with a thinner symmetrical-section wing introduced in 1989. The Yak-54, which first flew on 24th December 1993, is derived from the Yak-55 and uses the same M-14P engine but has a tandem two-seat cockpit faired into the rear fuselage, new tubular undercarriage legs and an enlarged rudder. Some 214 examples of the Yak-55 and around 15 Yak-54s have been built at Saratov and significant numbers are flying in the USA and Europe.

Yakovlev Yak-54, RA-02001

Yakovlev Yak-55M, DOSAAF 23

Specification	Yakovlev Yak-55M	
Powerplant	One 360 h.p. (268 kW) Vedeneyev M-14P piston engine	
Dimensions		
Span	8.1 m	(26 ft 7 in)
Length	6.98 m	(22 ft 11 in)
Height	2.79 m	(9 ft 2 in)
Performance		
Max speed	360 km/h	(195 kt, 224 mph)
Cruising speed	338 km/h	(183 kt, 210 mph)
Initial climb	930 m/min	(3,050 fpm)
Range	720 km	(391 nm, 450 miles)
Weights		
Max takeoff	840 kg	(1,852 lbs)
Useful load	135 kg	(298 lbs)

Yakovlev Yak-58 — Russia

Intended for use as a light general purpose six-seat transport with good short-field performance for support of remote Russian communities, the Yak-58 was first flown on 17th April 1994. It has an unconventional twin-boomed layout with the main fuselage pod positioned ahead of a high-aspect-ratio wing and is fitted with a retractable tricycle undercarriage. A small canard surface is fitted at the fuselage mid-point and the large fins have a bridging tailplane at the top. The M-14PT radial engine is fitted behind the cabin as a pusher with a circular shroud to provide pressure airflow for cooling. Four prototypes are believed to have been completed but at least one has been destroyed in an accident. One aircraft has been equipped with a Thomson-CSF radio-communications surveillance system. Full-scale production of the Yak-58 by the Tbilisi Aviation State Association appears to have been delayed owing to lack of funding.

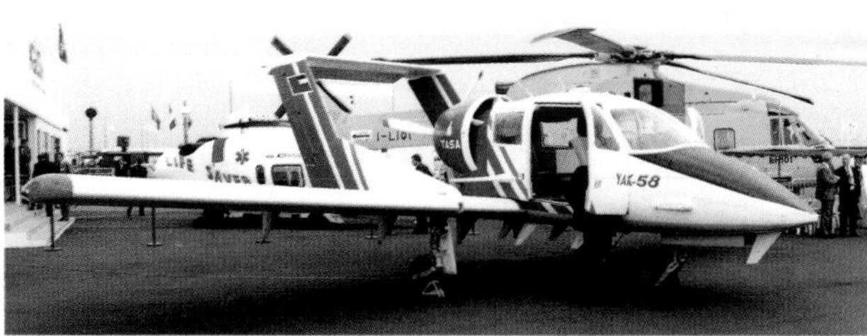

Yakovlev Yak-58, 4L-02010

Specification	Yakovlev Yak-58	
Powerplant	One 360 h.p. (268 kW) Vedeneyev M-14PT piston engine	
Dimensions		
Span	12.7 m	(41 ft 8 in)
Length	8.53 m	(28 ft 0 in)
Height	3.15 m	(10 ft 4 in)
Performance		
Max speed	300 km/h	(162 kt, 186 mph)
Cruising speed	285 km/h	(154 kt, 177 mph)
Initial climb	274 m/min	(900 fpm)
Range	1,000 km	(543 nm, 625 miles)
Weights		
Max takeoff	2,080 kg	(4,586 lbs)
Useful load	810 kg	(1,786 lbs)

Yakovlev Yak-112 — Russia

The Yak-112 is a four-seat light aircraft of somewhat unusual appearance with a large main cabin section giving a high level of all-round vision and a slim tailboom mounting a conventional fin and tailplane. The strut-braced high wing has slight anhedral and is fitted with prominent drooped wingtips. The prototype first flew on 20th October 1992 and the aircraft is being built at the Irkutsk Aviation Plant, although it is thought that fewer than 10 prototypes and production aircraft have been completed. Several powerplants have been tested on the aircraft including the 210 h.p. Continental IO-360-ES, 260 h.p. Teledyne Continental IO-540E and the 260 h.p. Continental IO-550-M, which is used on the production version.

Yakovlev Yak-112 (Cont.)

Yakovlev Yak-112, RA-00012

Specification	Yakovlev Yak-112	
Powerplant	One 260 h.p. (194 kW) Teledyne Continental IO-550-M piston engine	
Dimensions		
Span	10.26 m	(33 ft 8 in)
Length	6.96 m	(22 ft 10 in)
Height	2.9 m	(9 ft 6 in)
Performance		
Max speed	230 km/h	(124 kt, 143 mph)
Cruising speed	209 km/h	(113 kt, 130 mph)
Initial climb	244 m/min	(800 fpm)
Range	970 km	(527 nm, 606 miles)
Weights		
Max takeoff	1,385 kg	(3,054 lbs)
Useful load	445 kg	(981 lbs)

Yakovlev-Aermacchi AEM-130, RA-43130

Yakovlev-Aermacchi AEM-130 — Russia

Initiated in 1992, the Yak-130D was designed by the Yakovlev OKB to meet a Russian Air Force requirement for a replacement for the L-29 and L-39 jet trainer fleet, and is in competition with the MiG-AT for an order of around 300 aircraft. First flown on 25th April 1996 it is a high subsonic advanced lead-in fighter trainer with complex thin near-delta variable camber wings with large leading edge extensions. It is equipped with fly-by-wire systems and FADEC engine control and has a large tandem two-seat cockpit which is sharply stepped and enclosed with a two-piece clamshell canopy. The two DV-2S twin-shaft turbofans are fitted in nacelles beneath the lower fuselage flanks which also incorporate the main undercarriage wells. It has six underwing hardpoints and wingtip and centreline stores stations to allow carriage of weapons such as the AIM-9 Sidewinder, AA-11 Archer SRAAM and AGM-65 Maverick. The Yak-130 has been developed by Sokol at Nizhny-Novgorod and Aermacchi for western sale as the AEM-130 and the definitive version will be the M-346 with Honeywell F124 engines, a modified cockpit and lighter structure.

Specification	Yakovlev-Aermacchi AEM-130	
Powerplant	Two 4,850 lb.s.t. (21.58 kN) Povazské Strojárne DV-2S turbofans	
Dimensions		
Span	9.72 m	(31 ft 10 in)
Length	11.49 m	(37 ft 8 in)
Height	4.76 m	(15 ft 7 in)
Performance		
Max speed	1,038 km/h	(560 kt, 645 mph)
Initial climb	3,353 m/min	(11,000 fpm)
Range	3,317 km	(1,800 nm, 2,073 miles)
Weights		
Max takeoff	9,500 kg	(20,947 lbs)
Useful load	4,900 kg	(10,804 lbs)

Z

Zenair Zenith and CH-601 Zodiac — Canada

The Zenith all-metal two-seat amateur-built light aircraft was designed by Chris Heintz in France and first flown on 22nd March 1970. It was a low-wing all-metal aircraft similar to the Robin HR.200, which Heintz had also designed, with side-by-side seating, a 100 h.p. Continental O-200-A engine and a fixed tricycle undercarriage. The Zenith CH-200 was developed by Heintz's Canadian-based company, Zenair, and more than 100 have been flown. The Mono-Z CH-100, and aerobatic CH-150, is a single-seat variant with dihedralled outer wing panels and a 55 h.p. Volkswagen engine, and the Tri-Z CH-300, which first flew on 9th July 1977, is a three-seat model powered by a 150 h.p. Lycoming O-320 engine with a longer fuselage, increased span and an extra rear seat. The Zodiac CH-601 two-seater was introduced in 1984 and it has a similar fuselage to that of the CH-200 but with a three-bay wing with dihedralled outer panels, a cut-down rear fuselage with a bubble-canopied cockpit and either fixed tailwheel or tricycle gear. It is sold in kit form from Zenair's factory at Mexico, Missouri and by Czech Aircraft Works as the standard Super Zodiac CH.601HD, the CH.601HDS with short-span tapered wings and the CH.601UL ultralight category model. Various engines can be fitted in the 65 h.p. to 90 h.p. category including a Volkswagen, Rotax 912 and the Continental C65 or C85. Zenair is also developing the CH.620 Gemini, which is a twin-engined version of the CH.601 with two Jabiru 2200 engines and a retractable tailwheel (or optional tricycle) undercarriage.

Zenair CH.620 Gemini, N6265N

Specification	Zenair Super Zodiac CH.601HD	
Powerplant	One 80 h.p. (59.65 kW) Rotax 912 piston engine	
Dimensions		
Span	8.23 m	(27 ft 0 in)
Length	5.79 m	(19 ft 0 in)
Height	1.57 m	(5 ft 2 in)
Performance		
Max speed	217 km/h	(117 kt, 135 mph)
Cruising speed	193 km/h	(104 kt, 120 mph)
Initial climb	351 m/min	(1,150 fpm)
Range	608 km	(330 nm, 380 miles)
Weights		
Max takeoff	544 kg	(1,200 lbs)
Useful load	254 kg	(560 lbs)

Zenair Zenith CH-125, F-PYEG

Zenair Zodiac CH.601UL, PH-3C7

Zenair STOL CH.701 and CH.801 — Canada

Sold as an amateur-built kit, the Zenair CH.701 first flew in 1986. It was intended to be a simply constructed two-seater with excellent STOL performance made possible by the fixed leading edge slats and full-span flaperons on its strut-braced high wing. The CH.701 is built from aluminium with a slab-sided fuselage, a fixed tricycle undercarriage and a 80 h.p. Rotax 912 piston engine. An ultralight-category version is available and the CH.701 can be operated on Zenair-designed amphibious floats. The CH.801 is an enlarged version with a four-seat longer cabin and a 180 h.p. Lycoming O-360 engine. Over 400 CH.701s are flying in 36 countries.

Zenair STOL CH.701 and CH.801 (Cont.)

Zenair CH.701, 26-IL

Specification	Zenair STOL CH.701	
Powerplant	One 80 h.p. (59.65 kW) Rotax 912 piston engine	
Dimensions		
Span	8.23 m	(27 ft 0 in)
Length	6.1 m	(20 ft 0 in)
Height	2.29 m	(7 ft 6 in)
Performance		
Max speed	153 km/h	(83 kt, 95 mph)
Cruising speed	129 km/h	(70 kt, 80 mph)
Initial climb	488 m/min	(1,600 fpm)
Range	720 km	(391 nm, 450 miles)
Weights		
Max takeoff	435 kg	(960 lbs)
Useful load	227 kg	(500 lbs)

Zenair Zenith CH.2000
— USA

Zenair's CH.2000 is a certificated two-seat civil club trainer. It is of all-metal monocoque construction and is derived from the Zodiac homebuilt but has a different wing with parallel chord and no separate centre section and a wider fuselage for the side-by-side cabin, which is faired into the rear decking. The CH.2000 is equipped with a fixed tricycle undercarriage with cantilever spring-steel legs and is powered by a 116 h.p. Lycoming O-235-N2C engine. The prototype flew in June 1993 and first deliveries were made in August 1995, with over 40 completed by the end of 1999. In mid-2000 production was taken over by Aircraft Manufacturing & Development of Eastman, Georgia, who build the type as the Alarus CH2000.

Zenair Zenith CH.2000, N36ZA

Specification	Zenair Zenith CH.2000	
Powerplant	One 116 h.p. (86.49 kW) Textron Lycoming O-235-N2C piston engine	
Dimensions		
Span	8.79 m	(28 ft 10 in)
Length	7.01 m	(23 ft 0 in)
Height	2.08 m	(6 ft 10 in)
Performance		
Max speed	209 km/h	(113 kt, 130 mph)
Cruising speed	193 km/h	(104 kt, 120 mph)
Initial climb	250 m/min	(820 fpm)
Range	800 km	(435 nm, 500 miles)
Weights		
Max takeoff	728 kg	(1,606 lbs)
Useful load	252 kg	(556 lbs)

Zlin Trener Z-26 to Z-726
— Czech Republic

The Zlinska Letecka A.S. (which became Moravan in 1950) used its successful side-by-side Zlin 22 light aircraft design as the basis for the Z-26 aerobatic basic trainer developed for the Czech Air Force. The Z-26 Trener used a refined version of the Z-22 wooden wing but had a new steel tube and fabric fuselage with two seats in tandem under a framed sliding canopy, and was first flown on 20th October 1947. In total 162 Z-26s were built as the C.5 for military and civil training, powered by a 105 h.p. Walter Minor 4-III engine and fitted with a fixed tailwheel undercarriage. The Zlin Trener, which became the leading competition aerobatic aircraft in the 1950s and 1960s, was developed with increasingly powerful engines. The main variants were the Z-126 with metal wings and a 160 h.p. Walter Minor 6-III, the Z-226T Trener 6 with a strengthened structure and higher weights, the Z-326 and Z-526 Trener Master with longer wings, a retractable tailwheel undercarriage and modified cockpit, the Z-526L with a 200 h.p. Lycoming AIO-360-B1B engine and the Z-726 Universal, which had an Avia M-137Z engine, shorter wings and higher weights. The Akrobat versions (Z-226A, Z-226AS,

Z-326A, Z-526A and Z-526AFS) were all single-seat dedicated aerobatic variants of the standard trainers with sophisticated wings and control surfaces to enhance aerobatic performance. Production of the Z-126 to Z-726, which ceased in 1973, totalled 1,331 aircraft, and many Zlin Treners are still active with private owners worldwide.

Zlin Z-126 Trener, N247D

Zlin Z-526F Trener Master, OO-YUG

Specification	Zlin Z-526 Trener Master	
Powerplant	One 160 h.p. (119.3 kW) Walter Minor 6-III piston engine	
Dimensions		
Span	10.59 m	(34 ft 9 in)
Length	7.8 m	(25 ft 7 in)
Height	2.06 m	(6 ft 9 in)
Performance		
Max speed	238 km/h	(129 kt, 148 mph)
Cruising speed	204 km/h	(110 kt, 127 mph)
Initial climb	300 m/min	(985 fpm)
Range	576 km	(313 nm, 360 miles)
Weights		
Max takeoff	975 kg	(2,150 lbs)
Useful load	295 kg	(651 lbs)

Zlin Z50L — Czech Republic

Moravan's Zlin Z50L was produced as the first new-generation contender in the aerobatic championship field, which had been dominated by the Zlin Trener series in the 1960s. First flown on 18th July 1975, it was an all-metal aircraft with a spacious single-seat cockpit enclosed by a bubble canopy and a spring-steel tailwheel undercarriage. The straight wing, which was low-set and had a relatively large area, could be fitted with optional tip tanks to extend ferry range. The initial Z50L was powered by a 260 h.p. Lycoming AEIO-540-D4B5 flat-six engine, and the later Z50LA was similar but had a variable-pitch propeller with a speed governor. The Z50LS was a higher-weight model with a 300 h.p. Lycoming AEIO-540-L1B5D engine, and the Z50M, which flew in April 1988, had a 210 h.p. Avia M-137AZ. Moravan also sold the Z50LE with a lighter airframe and a new wing with pointed tips. The Z50 won the World Aerobatic Championships in 1984 and 1986. Between 1980 and 1992 Moravan built 80 Z50s before the Su-26 and Yak-55 appeared, offering superior performance. Most of the Z50s went to Eastern European countries, but several were sold to the USA, the UK, Italy, South Africa and Germany, and many are still flying.

Zlin Z50LA, N50ZL

Specification	Zlin Z50LS	
Powerplant	One 300 h.p. (224 kW) Textron Lycoming AEIO-540-L1B5D piston engine	
Dimensions		
Span	8.58 m	(28 ft 2 in)
Length	9.02 m	(29 ft 7 in)
Height	2.08 m	(6 ft 10 in)
Performance		
Max speed	307 km/h	(166 kt, 191 mph)
Cruising speed	275 km/h	(149 kt, 171 mph)
Initial climb	840 m/min	(2,755 fpm)
Range	480 km	(261 nm, 300 miles)
Weights		
Max takeoff	840 kg	(1,852 lbs)
Useful load	230 kg	(507 lbs)

Zlin Z42 to Z242
— Czech Republic

In 1966, Moravan designed a modern replacement for the Zlin Trener for operation by Czech flying clubs and the Czech Air Force. The Z 41 was an all-metal aircraft stressed for aerobatics with a low wing with slight forward sweep, a side-by-side two-seat cabin and a fixed tricycle undercarriage. The production model was the Z 42, which first flew on 17th October 1967 powered by a 180 h.p. Avia M-137A in-line engine, and the later Z 42M had a V-503A constant-speed propeller. The Z 142 was a later version with a forward-sliding bubble canopy and a 210 h.p. M-337AK engine, and the Z 242L is a developed Z 142 with a 200 h.p. Lycoming AEIO-360-A1B6 engine and modified wings without the forward sweep. The Z 43 is a four-seat version with a lengthened fuselage and 210 h.p. M-337A engine which first flew on 10th December 1968, and the Z 143L is also a four-seater, developed from the Z 142 with an enlarged fuselage and a clear-view canopy with the forward-sliding front section. It is powered by a 235 h.p. Lycoming O-540-J3A5 engine. Over 800 of the models in this series had been built by the end of 1999, and the Z 142 and Z 242L are in current production with many aircraft being sold to the USA and Canada.

Zlin Z 143L, OK-AOA

Zlin Z 142, HA-SFJ

Specification	Zlin Z 242L	
Powerplant	One 200 h.p. (149 kW) Textron Lycoming AEIO-360-A1B6 piston engine	
Dimensions		
Span	9.35 m	(30 ft 8 in)
Length	6.93 m	(22 ft 9 in)
Height	2.95 m	(9 ft 8 in)
Performance		
Max speed	230 km/h	(124 kt, 143 mph)
Cruising speed	212 km/h	(115 kt, 132 mph)
Initial climb	270 m/min	(886 fpm)
Range	1,050 km	(570 nm, 656 miles)
Weights		
Max takeoff	1,090 kg	(2,403 lbs)
Useful load	360 kg	(794 lbs)

Zlin Z 43, Hungarian AF, 076

GLOSSARY OF TERMS AND ABBREVIATIONS

3-i	Iniziative Industriali Italiane
AAC	Army Air Corps (UK)
AAM	Air-to-Air Missile
AAMSA	Aeronautica Agricola Mexicana SA
AESL	Aero Engine Services Ltd.
AEW	Airborne Early Warning
AEW&C	Airborne Early Warning and Control
AFRes	Air Force Reserve (USA)
AIA	Aircraft Industries of Australia
AIDC	Aero Industry Development Center (Taiwan)
AISA	Aeronautica Industrial SA (Spain)
ALAT	Aviation Légère de l'Armée de Terre (French Army Aviation)
AMC	The Aircraft Manufacturing Company (USA)
AMI	Aeronautica Militare Italiana (Italian AF)
AMRAAM	Advanced Medium Range Air-to-Air Missile
ANG	Air National Guard (USA)
AOP	Air Observation Post
APU	Auxiliary Power Unit
ASM	Air-Surface Missile
ASR	Anti Submarine Reconnaissance
ASW	Anti-Submarine Warfare
AWACS	Airborne Warning and Control System
BA	British Aircraft Manufacturing Co.
BAC	British Aircraft Corporation
BAe	British Aerospace
BDLI	Bundesverband der Deutschen Luft-und-Raumfahrtindustrie
BOAC	British Overseas Airways Corporation
CAARP	Cooperatives des Ateliers Aéronautiques de la Région Parisienne
CAB	Constructions Aéronautique de Béarn
CAC	Commonwealth Aircraft Corp. (Australia)
CASA	Construcciones Aeronauticas SA (Spain)
CEA	Centre Est Aéronautique
CERVA	Consortium Européen de Réalisation et de Ventes d'Avions
CFT	Conformal Fuel Tank
CIA	Central Intelligence Agency (USA)
CIS	Commonwealth of Independent States
COD	Carrier-Onboard-Delivery
COIN	Counter Insurgency
Comint	Communications Intelligence
CPTP	Civil Pilot Training Program (USA)
CTA	Centro Tecnico Aerospacial (Brazil)
Cruising Speed	Level speed at 75% power at optimum altitude
DARPA	Defense Advanced Research Projects Agency (USA)
DASA	Daimler-Benz Aerospace AG (Deutsche Aerospace)
DFVLR	Deutsche Forschungs-und-Versuchsanstalt für Luft-und-Raumfahrt
DHA	de Havilland Aircraft Pty. Ltd. (Australia)
DHC	The de Havilland Aircraft of Canada Ltd.
DINFIA	Dirección Nacional de Fabricaciones e Investigaciones Aeronauticas
DOSAAF	Soviet Military Voluntary Support Organisation
EAA	Experimental Aircraft Association
ECCM	Electronic Counter-Countermeasures
ECM	Electronic Countermeasures
EFIS	Electronic Flight Instrumentation System
EFM	Enhanced Fighter Manoeuvrability
EFS	Enhanced Flight Screener (USAF programme)
EKW	Eidg. Konstruktions Werkstatte (Switzerland)
ELINT	Electronic Intelligence
EMS	Emergency Medical Service
Empty Weight	Standard airframe weight including standard avionics and equipment but excluding fuel, crew and payload.
ENAER	Empresa Nacional de Aeronautica de Chile
ESM	Electronic Signal Monitoring
ETOPS	Extended-range Twin-engined Operations
Ets.	Etablissement
FAA	Fleet Air Arm (Royal Navy)
FAA	Federal Aviation Administration
FAB	Forca Aérea Brasileira (Brazilian AF)
FAC	Forward Air Control
FADEC	Full Authority Digital Electronic Control (engine management system)
FAI	Féderation Aéronautique Internationale
FAR	Federal Aviation Regulations
FBW	Fly-by-Wire
FFA	Flug und Fahrzeugwerke AG (Switzerland)
FLIR	Forward-Looking Infra-red
FMA	Fabrica Militar de Aviones (Argentina)
fpm	Feet per Minute
GAF	Government Aircraft Factory (Australia)
GRP	Glass-Reinforced Plastic
HALO	High Altitude Long Operation (Proteus project)
HARM	High Speed Anti-Radiation Missile
HE	High explosive
HOTAS	Hands-on Throttle and Stick
hp	Horsepower
HUD	Head-Up Display
IAE	International Aero Engines
IAI	Israeli Aircraft Industries
IA-PVO	Russian Air Defence Fighter Forces
IAR	Industria Aeronautica Romana
IGN	Institut Géographique Nationale (France)
IMCO	Intermountain Manufacturing Company
imp.	Imperial (measures)
IPTN	Industri Pesawat Terbang Nusantara (Indonesia)
Initial Climb	Maximum rate of climb at full rated power at sea level
JAR	Joint Airworthiness Requirements
JAR-VLA	Joint Airworthiness Requirements – Very Light Aircraft
JASDF	Japanese Air Self Defence Force
JCAB	Japanese Civil Aviation Board
JGSDF	Japanese Ground Self Defence Force
JMSDF	Japanese Maritime Self Defence Force
JPATS	Joint Primary Aircraft Training System
JRV	Jugoslovensko Ratno Vazduhoplovstvo (Yugoslav AF)
JSF	Joint Strike Fighter
km	Kilometres
km/h	Kilometres per hour
kN	Kilo-Newtons
kt	Knots
kW	Kilowatts

LAMPS	Light Airborne Multi-Purpose System (US Navy)
LANTIRN	Low-Altitude Navigational Targeting Infra-Red
lbs	Pounds (weight)
lb.s.t.	Pounds Static Thrust (turbine engine rating)
LD/SD	Look-down, Shoot-down (radar)
LOH	Light Observation Helicopter
LTV	Ling-Temco-Vought
m	Metres
MAD	Magnetic Anomaly Detector
MAP	Military Assistance Program (USA)
MAPO	Moscow Aircraft Production Organisation
MBB	Messerschmitt Bölkow Blohm
Max Speed	Maximum level speed at optimum altitude
MFD	Multi-Functional Display
Max Takeoff weight	Maximum loaded weight allowed in the approved type certificate
MFI	Malmö FlygIndustri
mph	Miles per hour
m/min	Metres per minute
NACA	National Advisory Committee for Aeronautics (USA – later NASA)
NAMC	The Nihon Aircraft Manufacturing Co. Ltd.
NASA	National Aeronautics and Space Administration (USA)
NATO	North Atlantic Treaty Organisation
nm	Nautical miles
NOAA	National Oceanic and Atmospheric Administration (USA)
NOTAR	No Tail Rotor
NTH	New Technology Helicopter
NVG	Night Vision Goggles
OGMA	Oficina Gerais de Material Aeronautico (Portugal)
OKB	Opytno Konstrooktorskoye Byuro (Russian Design Bureau)
OTH	Over The Hill (targeting)
PADC	Philippine Aerospace Development Corporation
POC	Proof of Concept
PRC	People's Republic of China
PVC	Polyvinyl Chloride
PZL	Panstwowe Zaklady Lotnicze (Poland)
RAF	Royal Air Force
RAAF	Royal Australian Air Force
RAuxAF	Royal Auxiliary Air Force (UK)
RCAF	Royal Canadian Air Force
Range	Maximum distance which can be travelled with full standard fuel at optimum speed and minimum payload with no reserves.
RFB	Rhein Flugzeugbau
RFDS	Royal Flying Doctor Service
RJ	Regional Jet
RMAF	Royal Malaysian Air Force
RNZAF	Royal New Zealand Air Force
R.Neth.AF	Royal Netherlands Air Force
Saab	Svenska Aeroplan AB
SAAF	South African Air Force
SAI	Skandinavisk Aero Industri
SAN	Société Aéronautique Normande
SAR	Search and Rescue
SCAN	Société des Constructions Aéronavales
SEPECAT	Société Européenne de Production de l'Avion de l'Ecole de Combat et d'Appui Tactique
SFERMA	Société Francaise d'Entretien et de Réparation de Matériel Aéronautique
s.h.p.	Shaft Horsepower (Helicopter turbine engines)
Sigint	Signal Intelligence
SIPA	Société Industrielle pour l'Aéronautique
SLAR	Sideways-Looking Airborne Radar
SMAN	Société Morbihanaise d'Aéro Navigation
SNCAC	Société Nationale de Constructions Aéronautiques du Centre
SNCAN	Société Nationale de Constructions Aéronautiques du Nord
SNCASE	Société Nationale de Constructions Aéronautiques Sud Est
SOCATA	Société de Construction d'Avions de Tourisme et d'Affaires
SRAAM	Short Range Air-to-Air Missile
STOL	Short Takeoff and Landing
SZD	Szybowcowego Zaklady Doswiadczalnego
TACAMO	Take Command and Move Out (U.S. Navy programme)
TARPS	Tactical Air Reconnaissance Pod System
TC	Type Certificate
TC	Turbocharged
TEAM	Tennessee Engineering & Manufacturing
TIALD	Thermal Imaging and Laser Designation (module)
TNT	Trägsflugels Neuer Technologie
TOW	Tube-launched Optically-tracked Wire-guided (missile)
TWA	Trans World Airlines
UACL	United Aircraft of Canada Ltd. (Pratt & Whitney)
UAV	Unmanned Air Vehicle
ULM	Ultra-Légère Motorisé (Powered ultra-light)
Useful Load	The difference between Maximum Gross Weight and Empty Weight
USAAC	United States Army Air Corps
USAAF	United States Army Air Force
USAF	United States Air Force
USCG	United States Coast Guard
USG	U.S. Gallons
USMC	United States Marine Corps
USN	United States Navy
USSR	Union of Soviet Socialist Republics
UTA	Union de Transport Maritime
UTTAS	Utility Tactical Transport Aircraft System
VFR	Visual Flight Rules
VFW	Vereinigte Flugtechnische Werke
VIP	Very Important Person
VLA	Very Light Aircraft (certification standard)
VLR	Very Light Rotorcraft (certification standard)
VVS	Russian Air Force
VW	Volkswagen
V/STOL	Vertical and Short Takeoff and Landing
WAR	War Aircraft Replicas

INDEX